1994

Tests

THIRD EDITION

Richard C. Sweetland, Ph.D.
Daniel J. Keyser, Ph.D.
General Editors

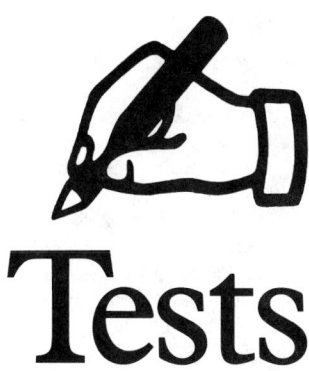

Tests

A Comprehensive Reference
for Assessments in Psychology,
Education, and Business

THIRD EDITION

pro·ed

8700 Shoal Creek Boulevard
Austin, Texas 78758
512/451-3246

Library of Congress Cataloging-in-Publication Data

Tests : a comprehensive reference for assessments in psychology,
   education, and business / Richard C. Sweetland, Daniel J. Keyser,
   general editors.—3rd ed.
       p.   cm.
   ISBN 0–89079–255–0 (hardcover)
   ISBN 0–89079–256–9 (softcover)
   1. Psychological tests.   2. Educational tests and measurements.
  3. Occupational aptitude tests.   I. Sweetland, Richard C., 1931– .
  II. Keyser, Daniel J., 1935– .
  BF176.T43   1990
  150′.28′7—dc20   89–78495
                                                 CIP

Printed in the United States of America

1 2 3 4 5 6 7 8 9 10   95 94 93 92 91

8700 Shoal Creek Boulevard
Austin, Texas 78758

Table of Contents

152, 257

Preface

As this third edition of *Tests* is published, it seems appropriate to say a few words about the project's development and background and to recognize the contributions of the people who made the task possible.

Tests: First Edition was published in response to the need for a resource containing consistent codified information describing and cataloging tests available for use by psychologists, educators, and human resource personnel. The professional community received *Tests* enthusiastically. Within one year of publication, the first edition was in its third printing, indicating to us that thousands of professionals and libraries had come to rely on its quick-scanning, easy-to-read format. Committed to providing our readers with the most current information possible on assessment instruments, we launched a "search and find" effort that resulted in the 1984 publication of *Tests: Supplement,* a complement to the first edition containing information on more than 500 new tests. The *Supplement* was followed by *Tests: 2nd Edition* in 1986.

Our ongoing "search and find" efforts, which have upturned information on hundreds of new tests; rapid developments in areas such as substance abuse, eating disorders, and chronic illness; the increasing role of technology in assessment; and our continued firm commitment to providing users with quick access to current test information convinced us of the necessity of developing this third edition. We thank our readers for the numerous suggestions they have offered, particularly for contacting us with the names of assessment instruments not referenced in the previous edition. We especially are grateful to the many test publishers and authors who generously and graciously contributed their staff time, information, and support for this book.

Particular recognition must be given to Cari Dunn, Tammy Agnew, Jeanne Doyle, Dr. Jim Patton, and Kelly Scanlon who coordinated this project. Their persistence and dedication to quality proved to be a major factor in the fruition of this project.

Throughout the research and production of *Tests,* Eugene Strauss and Leonard Strauss have given encouragement, suggestions, and invaluable advice in all aspects of the business of publishing. Our thanks go to them for their continued support. In addition, we wish to acknowledge Sam Pirnazar for his contributions as a consultant to the first edition.

Richard C. Sweetland, Ph.D
Daniel J. Keyser, Ph.D.
Editors

Introduction

Tests, a reference guide containing information on thousands of assessment instruments, is designed especially for psychologists, educators, and human resource personnel who search for tests to satisfy assessment needs. In addition, students, librarians, and other nonspecialists who need to familiarize themselves with the broad range of available tests will find the contents and format helpful. *Tests* does not attempt to review or evaluate tests; its purpose is to present concise descriptions in a quick-scanning, easy-to-read-format. This third edition, which presents the tests of 467 publishers, not only revises the information contained in the second edition but also presents descriptions of over 700 new or revised tests.

Regarding matters of style, the editors have chosen to use the commonly acceptable masculine pronoun and, in most cases the word "subject" for the individual being assessed. In so doing, the editors do not intend to show any sexual bias or disregard for those being evaluated. British spelling has been retained in proper titles.

How *Tests* Is Organized

The assessments described herein are organized according to a system of primary classification and cross-referencing intended to make information as accessible to the reader as possible. Each of the book's three main sections—Psychology, Education, and Business—is divided into subsections. For example, Psychology contains 20 subsections; Education, 54 subsections; and Business, 13 subsections. Each test has been given a primary classification in one of the Psychology, Education, or Business subsections and is described in detail in that subsection. Each test may also be cross-referenced in other subsections, (e.g., the Wechsler Adult Intelligence Scale, described within Psychology: Intelligence and Related is cross-referenced under Education: Intelligence and Related). Because of the expanded subsections, some tests are cross-referenced in three or more places. The tests and cross-references within each subsection are listed alphabetically according to title.

In order to establish subsections that would be practical and functional for the reader, considerable consultation was sought from professionals who use tests on a daily basis. Based on feedback from these sources, the subsections in this third edition have been expanded from 73 to 87 and some have been renamed, both to facilitate the reader's search for assessments and to reflect contemporary terminology.

Format and Content of Descriptions

The format and content of each test entry are designed to provide the basic information necessary to decide whether a particular test is appropriate to consider for a given assessment need. Each test entry is structured as follows: test title and author, a scan line with coded visual keys indicating the population for which the test is intended and whether the test is examiner- or self-administered, a purpose statement, a brief description highlighting the test's major features, timing information, scoring method, relevant cost and availability information, and primary publisher. Each of these components will be explained in greater detail.

The TITLE of each test is presented exactly as it appears in the test publisher's materials. For example, one would find the description of the REEL Scale under The

Bzoch-League Receptive-Expressive Emergent Language Scale. Readers who are familiar with a test's common or popular name rather than its published title may find the Author Index useful if difficulty is encountered in finding the test.

The test AUTHOR(S) appear(s) in italics below the test title.

The SCAN LINE, which is set off by bars between the author(s) and the purpose statement, identifies the population for which the test is intended (child/adolescent/ adult and age or grade range) and indicates whether a test is examiner- or self-administered.

✍ : symbolizes that a test is self-administered.

☞ ✍ : symbolizes that an examiner is required.

The PURPOSE statement offers a succinct overview of the test's intended application and what it purports to measure, assess, diagnose, evaluate, or identify.

The DESCRIPTION presents the number of test items, test format (paper-pencil, true-false, projective, oral, observational, etc.), factors or variables measured, materials used, manner in which the test is administered, foreign language availability, and special features.

The terms TIMED and UNTIMED indicate whether a test is administered with time limitations. For timed tests, the exact amount of time allotted for the subject to complete the test is indicated; for untimed tests, the amount of time usually required to complete the test is provided.

The SCORING line specifies the method used to score the test: *hand key, examiner evaluated, machine scored, or computer scored.* Hand key indicates that the test is scored using an answer key or template provided by the test publisher. An examiner-evaluated test is scored using an examiner's opinion, skills, and knowledge. A computer- or machine-scored test uses answer sheets that are scored by machine or computer. When a combination of these terms appears in the scoring line, the first listed is the primary method employed.

The COST line contains price information that is as accurate as the editors could establish at the time of the book's publication. Because the pricing structure for some tests (covering the various forms, kits, options, etc.) is so extensive, only representative costs are included here. The editors encourage readers to contact the publisher for complete cost information.

The PUBLISHER line identifies the test's primary publisher. When a publisher has indicated that a test is distributed by a firm other than itself, the name of the distributor follows that of the publisher. (The Publisher/Distributor Index contains complete address and telephone information.)

The editors attempted to confirm the acccuracy of every test entry through direct correspondence with the test publisher. But despite repeated attempts to contact them, some publishers did not respond to queries. However, in order to provide read-ers with a comprehensive listing of available assessment instruments, an editorial decision was made to include descriptions that were not verified due to lack of publisher response. These entries contain a disclaimer to that effect following the name of the test publisher. The year the test information was last verified is also provided.

Indexes

Tests: Third Edition contains eight indexes and an out-of-print listing. The indexes were compiled based on information provided by the test publishers in response to specific questions regarding special populations, in-print status, and other aspects of test development.

The TEST TITLE INDEX lists, according to the published test title, each of the tests described in this book.

The OUT-OF-PRINT listing contains the titles and authors of tests that publishers have indicated are out-of-print.

The HEARING-IMPAIRED INDEX identifies tests that are suitable for or that may be adapted for use with hearing-impaired populations, as well as tests that assess the sense of hearing.

The PHYSICALLY IMPAIRED INDEX lists tests that are suitable for or adaptable for use with physically impaired populations, as well as tests designed to assess motor and/or orthopedic handicaps.

The VISUALLY IMPAIRED INDEX contains tests that are suitable for or may be adapted for use with visually impaired populations, as well as tests designed to assess vision.

The FOREIGN LANGUAGE AVAILABILITY INDEX contains tests that are available in language versions other than English.

The COMPUTER-SCORED INDEX lists tests that may be scored by computer, either on-site or via mail-in or teleprocessing services.

The AUTHOR INDEX lists all test authors except for corporate and institutional staffs.

In addition to page numbers, the PUBLISHER/DISTRIBUTOR INDEX provides addresses and telephone numbers.

The purpose of *Tests* from the outset has been to provide a quick reference for tests available in the English language. When the first edition of this volume was published, a decision was made to omit reliability, validity, and normative data—aspects considered too complex to reduce to the quick-scanning desk-reference format. The editors were aware, however, that a fuller treatment of each test was needed and were encouraged by librarians, educators, psychologists, and forensic specialists to create the *Tests*

Critiques series, which serves as a complement to *Tests* and as a vital componet within the array of test review resources currently available. The editors strongly urge readers interested in reliability and validity or other in-depth technical information about a particular test to consult the appropriate volume of *Test Critiques* or contact the test author(s) or publisher.

How to Use This Book

The system of classification and cross-referencing used in *Tests* and the inclusion of the indexes just described are designed to accommodate readers who need information about a particular test as well as those conducting a general search for appropriate assessment instruments. The following suggestions for using *Tests* are intended to minimize the reader's efforts to locate information.

1. The editors encourage readers to scan the sections of the book relevant to particular assessment needs. This "scanning-by-section" approach may be most helpful to readers who know how the particular tests for which they are searching are likely to be classified or for readers whose search is focused on an assessment area rather than on a particular test.
2. By following up on cross-references, readers may discover additional tests relevant to their particular assessment situations.
3. Readers who are unable to locate tests using the Test Title Index should consult the Author Index and /or the Publisher/Distributor Index if these elements are known.
4. Readers interested in assessment instruments for testing impaired populations or in the broad range of tests available for assesing specific handicaps can consult the appropriate indexes.
5. Tests that cannot be located by perusing the indexes may be found in the Out-of-Print listing.

PRO-ED fully supports the ethical and professional standards established by national and state professional organizations. The inclusion of specific restrictions on test accessibility noted in some descriptions in *Tests* usually has been requested by the publisher or author; the fact that a test description does not list restrictions does not imply that such restrictions do not exist. When ordering tests, the reader should ask each publisher for the standards or requirements for purchasing.

Order forms, catalogs and further information regarding tests may be obtained from each publisher. Anyone interested in ordering a specific test should contact the publisher using the Publisher/Distributor Index, which provides mailing addreses and telephone numbers.

Although the information in this book was obtained from primary sources, the editors are aware of possibilities for error. Each test entry has been researched, screened, written, edited, and read by professional test administrators; however, the editors ask that the reader understand that the job of checking and ensuring the accuracy of a book such as this is a process that will continue throughout the publication of subsequent editions. The editors welcome on an ongoing basis the submission of information about new tests and encourage test publishers and authors to apprise the PRO-ED staff of changes due to revisions of tests or errors in the test descriptions.

Psychology

The tests presented and described in the Psychology section have been selected on the basis of their appropriate usage in a clinical or counseling setting. In general, tests found in this section are those that might be used by a mental health professional, rather than by an educator or human resources specialist.

The classification of tests on the basis of typical usage or function is, of course, arbitrary, and the reader is encouraged to review the Education and Business sections for additional assessment instruments.

Psychology Section

Behavioral Medicine: Chronic and Terminal Illness

DIABETES OPINION SURVEY (DOS)
Suzanne Bennett Johnson

Child

Purpose: Measures attitudes toward diabetes in children. Used for clinical assessment and research in medical settings.

Description: 78–item paper-pencil Likert-scale test of five aspects of attitudes regarding diabetes: stigma, rule orientation, divine intervention, family interruption, and sick role. The Lie scale from the Children's Manifest Anxiety Scale also is included in the DOS. The child expresses degree of agreement or disagreement with the attitude expressed in each item. A sixth-grade reading level is required. The examiner may read items aloud to individuals reading below that level. A measure of parent attitudes may be obtained by using the Parent Diabetes Opinion Survey (PDOS). Examiner/self-administered. Suitable for group use.

Untimed: Varies

Scoring: Hand key

Cost: Sample $30.00

Publisher: Suzanne Bennett Johnson, Ph.D.

Information and availability unconfirmed; last verified in 1988.

ILLNESS BEHAVIOUR QUESTIONNAIRE (IBQ)
Refer to page 181.

NATIONAL ADULT READING TEST
Refer to page 58.

PARENT DIABETES OPINION SURVEY (PDOS)
Suzanne Bennett Johnson

Adult

Purpose: Measures attitudes toward diabetes of parents with diabetic children. Used for clinical assessment and research in medical settings.

Description: 68–item paper-pencil Likert-scale test of eight aspects of attitudes regarding diabetes: attitudes toward medical staff, stigma, rule orientation/high supervision, divine intervention, family interruption, manipulativeness, reactions (observation/detection) and sweet consumption. The Lie scale from the Personality Inventory for Children also is included in the PDOS. The parent expresses degree of agreement or disagreement with the attitude expressed in each item. A fifth-grade reading level is required. The examiner may read items aloud to individuals reading below that level. A measure of child attitude may be obtained by using the Diabetes Opinion Survey (DOS). Examiner/self-administered. Suitable for group use.

Untimed: Varies

Scoring: Hand key

Cost: Sample $30.00

Publisher: Suzanne Bennett Johnson, Ph.D.

Information and availability unconfirmed; last verified in 1988.

PSYCHOSOCIAL ADJUSTMENT TO ILLNESS SCALE (PAIS)
Leonard R. Derogatis

Adult

Purpose: Assesses the psychological and social adjustment of medical patients or their immediate families to a serious illness.

Description: 46–item paper-pencil self-report instrument or structured interview guide assessing the psychosocial adjustment of medical patients and their immediate families in terms of seven principal domains: health care orientation, vocational environment, domestic environment, sexual relationships, extended family relationships, social environment, and psychological distress. A total score summarizes overall adjustment to illness. The self-report form (PAIS-SR) and the interview guide (PAIS) measure equivalent items. Norms and profile/score sheets are available for lung cancer patients and renal dialysis patients for the self-report form. SCORPAIS Version 2.1 is a microcomputer scoring program for both the interview and the self-report versions. It generates seven primary domain scores and an overall adjustment to illness score, which may be converted to standardized score formats for any of the available norm groups (renal dialysis, cardiac bypass, lung cancer, acute burn, and essential hypertension). Examiner required. The self-report form is suitable for group use; the interview guide is individually administered.

Untimed: 20–30 minutes

Scoring: Examiner evaluated; may be computer scored

Cost: Interview booklet $3.00; self-report form $0.75; score/profile sheets $0.25; manual $18.00; SCORPAISPC Version 2.1 $160.00

Publisher: Clinical Psychometric Research, Inc.

QUESTIONNAIRE ON RESOURCES AND STRESS FOR FAMILIES WITH CHRONICALLY ILL OR HANDICAPPED MEMBERS
Jean Holroyd

Adult

Purpose: Measures stress in families of ill or disabled persons. Used with families of individuals with developmental disabilities, psychiatric problems, renal disease, cystic fibrosis, neuromuscular disease, and cerebral palsy.

Description: 285–item true-false paper-pencil test with 15 subtests assessing the impact of an individual's illness or handicap on other family members. The subtests are Poor Health/Mood, Excess Time Demands, Negative Attitude, Overprotection/Dependency, Lack of Social Support, Overcommitment/Martyrdom, Pessimism, Lack of Family Integration, Limits on Family Opportunity, Financial Problems, Physical Incapacitation, Lack of Activities, Occupational Limitations, Social Obtrusiveness, and Difficult Personality Characteristics. The test yields information including problem areas about the examinee, the family, and the disabled individual. Raw scores are converted to standard scores. A long form and a short form are available. A sixth-grade reading level is required. Self-administered. Not suitable for group use.

Untimed: 1 hour or less

Scoring: Hand key; may be examiner evaluated

Cost: Specimen kit (manual, 5 test booklets, 25 answer and profile sheets, scoring templates) $70.00; sample kit (manual, test booklet, answer and profile sheet, short form booklet, short form answer sheet) $30.00

Publisher: Clinical Psychology Publishing Co., Inc.

TEST OF DIABETES KNOWLEDGE—CHEMSTRIP SKILLS DEMONSTRATION TEST
Suzanne Bennett Johnson

Ages 5–adult

Purpose: Assesses diabetics' skill at home monitoring of blood glucose using Chemstrips. Used in diabetes education.

Description: 15–item task-performance test in which the examiner observes the patient demonstrating the behavioral skills necessary for using Chemstrips to assess blood glucose. The patient is scored on a pass/fail basis. Results yield the percent of total items correct and the number of serious errors committed. Materials used include a Chemstrip bottle, a cotton or synthetic fiber ball, a watch with a sweep second hand, an alcohol swab, a monolet, autolet, or similar device. The examiner must be familiar with the correct use of Chemstrips for blood glucose testing. Examiner required. Not suitable for group use.

Untimed: 10 minutes

Scoring: Examiner evaluated

Cost: $15.00

Publisher: Suzanne Bennett Johnson, Ph.D.

Information and availability unconfirmed; last verified in 1988.

TEST OF DIABETES KNOWLEDGE—GENERAL INFORMATION AND PROBLEM SOLVING (TDK)—R2
Suzanne Bennett Johnson

All ages

Purpose: Examines an individual's knowledge of diabetes. Used with insulin-dependent diabetes patients and their families.

Description: 75–item multiple-choice paper-pencil test measuring an individual's factual knowledge of diabetes and ability to apply that knowledge. A seventh-grade reading level is required for the general information portion of the test, and a fourth-grade reading level is required for the problem-solving portion. Individuals with reading abilities below these levels may take the test by having an examiner read the items aloud. Examiner/self-administered. Suitable for group use.

Untimed: 20 minutes–1 hour

Scoring: Hand key

Cost: Test, scoring key, normative data $15.00

Publisher: Suzanne Bennett Johnson, Ph.D.

Information and availability unconfirmed; last verified in 1988.

TEST OF DIABETES KNOWLEDGE—INSULIN INJECTION DEMONSTRATION TEST
Suzanne Bennett Johnson

Ages 5–adult

Purpose: Assesses diabetics' skill at self-injection of insulin. Used in diabetes education.

Description: 24–item task-performance test in which the examiner observes the patient's skill in self-administering insulin. The patient is scored on a pass/fail basis. Results yield percent of total items correct and number of serious errors committed. Materials used include vials of insulin, insulin syringes, and alcohol pads. The examiner must be familiar with the correct method of insulin injection. Examiner required. Not suitable for group use.

Untimed: Varies

Scoring: Examiner evaluated

Cost: $15.00

Publisher: Suzanne Bennett Johnson, Ph.D.

Information and availability unconfirmed; last verified in 1988.

TEST OF DIABETES KNOWLEDGE—URINE GLUCOSE TESTING SKILLS DEMONSTRATION TEST
Suzanne Bennett Johnson

Ages 5–adult

Purpose: Assesses diabetics' skill at conducting urine glucose and ketone test. Used in diabetes education.

Description: 34–item task-performance test in which diabetic patients demonstrate their skill at conducting the urine glucose and ketone test. Patients are scored on a pass/fail basis. Results provide the percent of total items correct and the number of serious errors committed. Materials used include a standard "urine" sample consisting of 7% glucose in an acetone solution, Ames Clinitest 2–drop method test kit, a bottle of Acetest tablets, two color charts (one for the 2–drop method, one for Acetest), paper toweling, and a clock or a watch with a sweep second hand. The examiner must be familiar with the correct method of urine glucose testing. Examiner required. Not suitable for group use.

Untimed: Varies

Scoring: Examiner evaluated

Cost: $15.00

Publisher: Suzanne Bennett Johnson, Ph.D.

Information and availability unconfirmed; last verified in 1988.

Behavioral Medicine: Eating Disorders

BULIMIA TEST (BULIT)
*Marcia C. Smith and
Mark H. Thelen*

Adolescent, adult

Purpose: Assesses bulimia symptoms in adolescents and adults. Used as a screening device to identify individuals suffering from or at risk for bulimia, in clinical settings to aid in prevention and treatment, and in research.

Description: 36–item self-report forced-choice test consisting of five factors related to binges, feelings, vomiting, food, and weight and two factors related to laxative/diuretic abuse and regularity of menstrual cycles. Items are scored on a 5–point scale (5 = extreme bulimic direction; 1 = extreme normal direction). Examiner required. Suitable for group use.

Untimed: Varies

Scoring: Examiner evaluated

Cost: Contact publisher

Publisher: Mark H. Thelen, Ph.D.

Information and availability unconfirmed; last verified in 1987.

COMPUTERIZED DIAGNOSTIC INTERVIEW SCHEDULE (C-DIS)
Refer to page 165.

EATING DISORDER INVENTORY (EDI)
*David M. Garner,
Marion P. Olmsted, and Janet Polivy*

Adolescent, adult

Purpose: Assesses the psychological and behavioral traits common in eating disorders. Distinguishes individuals with serious psychopathology from normal dieters. Used in the treatment of individuals with eating disorders.

Description: 64–item paper-pencil or computer-administered self-report inventory consisting of eight subscales (Drive for Thinness, Bulimia, Body Dissatisfaction, Ineffectiveness, Perfectionism, Interpersonal Distrust, Interoceptive Awareness, and Maturity Fears) measuring specific cognitive and behavioral dimensions related to eating disorders. The inventory identifies individuals with serious eating disorders and differentiates between subgroups of eating disorders. The computer version operates on Apple systems with 64K, an 80–column card, and two floppy disk drives and on IBM PC systems with 256K and two disk drives. Examiner required. Suitable for group use.

Untimed: 20 minutes

Scoring: Hand key

Cost: Kit (manual, manual supplement, scoring keys, 25 test booklets, 25 profile forms) $30.00

Publisher: Psychological Assessment Resources, Inc.

THE EATING INVENTORY
*Albert J. Stunkard and
Samuel Messick*

Adult—Ages 17 and older

Purpose: Measures behavior important to the understanding and treatment of eating-related disorders such as anorexia and bulimia. Also used to predict response to weight-loss programs, weight gain after quitting smoking, and weight change during depression.

Description: 51–item paper-pencil questionnaire measuring three dimensions of eating behavior: cognitive restraint of eating, disinhibition, and hunger. This test is for use only by persons with at least a master's degree in psychology or a related discipline. Registration is required. Self-administered. Suitable for group use.

Untimed: 15 minutes

Scoring: Hand key

Cost: Complete kit (manual, 25 questionnaires, 25 Ready-Score answer sheets) $59.00; manual $25.00

Publisher: The Psychological Corporation

Information and availability unconfirmed; last verified in 1988.

KIDDIE LIFE
Refer to page 246.

LIFE EAT II
Martin B. Keller and Eileen Nielsen

Adolescent, adult—Ages 12 and older

Purpose: Collects longitudinal data on the course of Anorexia Nervosa and/or Bulimia Nervosa. Used with research subjects participating in studies on eating disorders.

Description: Interview providing information about the individual's a) psychiatric status for the three months preceding the interview, b) suicidal gestures, c) use of psychotropic medication, d) longitudinal course of treatment, e) psychosocial functioning, and f) global functioning. Must be administered by a trained interviewer. Suitable for use with individuals with physical or mental impairments. Examiner required. Not suitable for group use.

Untimed: 45 minutes

Scoring: Examiner evaluated

Cost: Contact publisher

Publisher: Martin B. Keller

MULTIDIMENSIONAL SELF-ESTEEM INVENTORY (MSEI)
Refer to page 197.

MULTISCORE DEPRESSION INVENTORY FOR ADOLESCENTS AND ADULTS (MDI)
Refer to page 199.

PSYCHIATRIC DIAGNOSTIC INTERVIEW—REVISED
Refer to page 210.

Behavioral Medicine: Health and Wellness: Stress, Anxiety, and Biofeedback

ADOLESCENT SEPARATION ANXIETY TEST
Refer to page 231.

COMPUTERIZED STRESS INVENTORY (CSI)
Allan N. Press and Lynn Osterkamp

Adult

Purpose: Assesses the level of stress in various areas of a person's life. Used in stress management, wellness, fitness, and illness-prevention programs of normal, healthy adults.

Description: Paper-pencil or computer-administered multiple-choice test of stress in such areas of life as work, life-style, marriage, sexuality, friends and social life, self-esteem, and physical symptoms. Two versions are available. The Comprehensive CSI assesses over 30 areas of a person's life. Each respondent answers approximately 325 of a possible 450 questions that are then analyzed individually to compile a 12- to 16–page stress profile. The Brief CSI assesses 16 areas, asks each respondent 115 questions, and creates an individualized five- to seven-page stress profile.

The computer program operates on IBM, Apple II, Macintosh, and CP/M

---

computers. An accompanying book that teaches 14 different stress management techniques is available, as well as an 8–week workbook and audio tape. Group or corporate reports are available at no additional cost. The publisher processes the paper-pencil questionnaires. The test may be used with visually (items may be read aloud), physically, and hearing-impaired individuals. Self-administered. Suitable for group use.

Untimed: Comprehensive 45–60 minutes; Brief 20 minutes

Scoring: Computer scored

Cost: Complete program (disks for both forms, instruction manual, 1 copy of *Stress? Find Your Balance*) $490.00; paper-pencil additions (one-time cost of two reproducible copies of either form and the Batch-Input program) $100.00

Publisher: Preventive Measures, Inc.

COPING INVENTORY FOR STRESSFUL SITUATIONS (CISS)
Norman Endler and James Parker

Adolescent, adult

Purpose: Measures coping styles in individuals.

Description: 48–item paper-pencil or computer-administered instrument measuring three major types of coping styles: Task Oriented, Emotion Oriented, and Avoidance Coping. The CISS also identifies two types of Avoidance Coping patterns: Distraction and Social Support. Scores provide a profile of an individual's coping strategy. Adult and adolescent forms available. Self-administered. Suitable for group use.

Untimed: 10 minutes

Scoring: Carbonized scoring forms; may be computer scored

Cost: Kit (test manual, 25 Quik Score forms) $29.00; IBM PC compatible version (50 administrations and scorings) contact publisher for cost

Publisher: Multi-Health Systems Inc.

COPING OPERATIONS PREFERENCE ENQUIRY (COPE)
Refer to page 166.

COPING STRATEGIES SCALES (COSTS)
Refer to page 166.

DEATH ANXIETY SCALE
Refer to page 237.

DEFENSE MECHANISMS INVENTORY
Refer to page 168.

DEROGATIS STRESS PROFILE (DSP)
Leonard R. Derogatis

Adult

Purpose: Measures the amount of stress an individual experiences in terms of interactional stress theory.

Description: 77–item paper-pencil test assessing 11 dimensions of stress grouped in the following three domains: environmental stress, personality mediators, and emotional response. In addition to 11 dimension scores and 3 domain scores, 2 global stress indices are also derived. An optical scanning version, SCANTRON, is available for use with computer scoring and interpretation services. Examiner required. Suitable for group use.

Untimed: 12–15 minutes

Scoring: Examiner evaluated; may be computer scored

Cost: 100 self-scoring forms $40.00; 100 score/profile forms $25.00; 100 optical scan forms $45.00; SCORDSP Version 2.1 $160.00

Publisher: Clinical Psychometric Research, Inc.

THE HOME ENVIRONMENT QUESTIONNAIRE
Refer to page 74.

IPAT ANXIETY SCALE (OR SELF-ANALYSIS FORM)
Raymond B. Cattell,
Ivan H. Scheier, and IPAT Staff

Adolescent, adult
Grades 10 and above

Purpose: Measures anxiety in senior high-school students and adults of most educational levels. Used for both clinical diagnosis and psychological research on anxiety.

Description: 40–item paper-pencil questionnaire measuring the five principal 16 PF factors of anxiety: emotional instability (C–), suspiciousness (L+), guilt-proneness (O+), low integration (Q3–), and tension (Q4+). Norms are provided for adult, college, and high-school populations, with both separate and combined sex tables. A sixth-grade reading level is required. Examiner required. Suitable for group use. Available in Spanish.

Untimed: 10 minutes

Scoring: Hand key

Cost: Anxiety Scale testing kit (handbook, nonreusable test booklet, scoring key) $12.25; Anxiety Scale Handbook $8.60; scoring key $3.25; 25 nonreusable test booklets $8.35

Publisher: Institute for Personality and Ability Testing, Inc.

JENKINS ACTIVITY SURVEY (JAS)
C. David Jenkins,
Stephen J. Zyzanski, and
Ray H. Rosenman

Adult

Purpose: Identifies persons with the Type A behavior pattern associated with coronary heart disease. Used for research and clinical screening.

Description: 52–item paper-pencil test of several aspects of Type A behavior, including speed and impatience, job involvement, and hard driving and competitive. Items include questions about behavior found useful in medical diag-

nosis. Scores are associated with the individual's future risk of heart disease. Self-administered. Suitable for group use.

Untimed: Not available

Scoring: Scoring service available

Cost: 25 questionnaires $28.00; 10 questionnaires with prepared scoring certificates $135.00; manual $15.00; examination kit (manual, questionnaire, scoring service fact sheet) $16.00

Publisher: The Psychological Corporation

Information and availability unconfirmed; last verified in 1988.

JOB STRESS INDEX (JSI)
Bonnie A. Sandman and
Patricia C. Smith

Adult

Purpose: Assesses various aspects of job stress of employed adults.

Description: Paper-pencil attitude questionnaire divided into 11 subtests. Subtests include Lack of Feedback, Lack of Participation, Lack of Achievement, Time Pressure, Lack of Interpersonal Skills of Supervisor, Lack of Competence of Supervisor, Lack of Interpersonal Skills of Others, Lack of Competence of Others, Red Tape, Job Insecurity, and Physical Demands and Danger. Items are answered in a "yes-no-sometimes" format. Scores are obtained for each subtest, yielding a profile of employee attitudes. A 6th-grade reading level is required. Self-administered. Suitable for group use.

Untimed: 10 minutes

Scoring: May be hand scored; computer scoring available from publisher

Cost: 100 booklets $92.00

Publisher: Smith, Sandman & McCreery

MILLON BEHAVIORAL HEALTH INVENTORY (MBHI)
Refer to page 194.

MULTIPLE AFFECT ADJECTIVE CHECK LIST (MAACL)
Refer to page 198.

NEO-FIVE FACTOR INVENTORY (NEO-FFI)
Refer to page 200.

NEO PERSONALITY INVENTORY (NEO-PI)
Refer to page 201.

OCCUPATIONAL STRESS INDICATOR (OSI)
Refer to page 1015.

OCCUPATIONAL STRESS INVENTORY (OSI), RESEARCH VERSION
Refer to page 1015.

PARENTING STRESS INDEX (PSI)
Refer to page 79.

PIKUNAS ADULT STRESS INVENTORY (PASI)
Justin Pikunas

Adolescent, adult—Ages 16 and older

Purpose: Measures the intensity of stress present in adults and adolescents. Used to identify individuals needing counseling in order to deal more efficiently with stress.

Description: 3–page paper-pencil inventory examining the effects of stress on the subject's personal efficiency, adjustment, and physical health. A sixth-grade reading level is required. Test results are compared to a college student sample. Self-administered. Suitable for group use.
Untimed: 15 minutes
Scoring: Hand key
Cost: Testing form $2.00; 25 forms and manual $10.00
Publisher: Justin Pikunas, Ph.D.

PSYCHOLOGICAL DISTRESS INVENTORY (PDI)
Refer to page 771.

QUESTIONNAIRE ON RESOURCES AND STRESS FOR FAMILIES WITH CHRONICALLY ILL OR HANDICAPPED MEMBERS
Refer to page 4.

REVISED CHILDREN'S MANIFEST ANXIETY SCALE
Cecil R. Reynolds and Bert O. Richmond

Ages 6–19

Purpose: Measures level of anxiety in children and adolescents.

Description: 37–item paper-pencil true-false test of a range of anxiety-related dimensions. Scores are obtained for Total Anxiety, Physiological Anxiety, Worry/Oversensitivity, Social Concerns/Concentration. There is also a Lie Scale. Separate norms are available in one-year intervals for males and females ages 6–17; combined norms are available for ages 18–19. Examiner/self-administered. Suitable for group use.
Untimed: 10–15 minutes
Scoring: Hand key
Cost: Complete kit (manual, 100 test sheets, scoring key) $40.00
Publisher: Western Psychological Services

ROSENZWEIG PICTURE-FRUSTRATION STUDY (P-F)
Refer to page 251.

SCHEDULE OF RECENT EXPERIENCE (SRE)
Thomas H. Holmes

Adolescent, adult

Purpose: Measures how often various stress-producing events have occurred in an individual's life during the recent past. Used for counseling and discussion purposes and as an aid to general health maintenance programs.

Description: 42–item paper-pencil inventory assessing the amount of psychological change (adaptive behavior) an individual has undergone in the recent past. Each test item is an event that causes change in a person's life that has been observed in a large number of patients preceding the onset of their medical illness or clinical symptoms. Test items include stress-related socially undesirable events and socially desirable events (birth of a baby or a promotion at work). The individual indicates for each item how often the event has occurred during a specific time period (ranging from less than 1 year up to 10 years). The inventory also may be used as a framework for a structured interview. The manual includes instructions for administering the test to individuals of all ages, sample test forms (both one-year and three-year versions), templates for scoring both versions, a report of the studies on which the test is based, and a list of suggested preventive measures for maintenance of health and prevention of illness based on test results. Examiner/self-administered. Suitable for group use.

Untimed: Varies

Scoring: Hand key

Cost: Complete package (manual, 50 one-year test forms, templates, vinyl folder) $35.00; kit with 50 three-year test forms $50.00

Publisher: University of Washington Press

SCHOOL CHILD STRESS SCALE (SCSS)
Refer to page 150.

SCL–90-R®
Refer to page 218.

SCL–90-R ANALOGUE
Refer to page 218.

STATE-TRAIT ANGER EXPRESSION INVENTORY (STAXI)
Charles D. Spielberger

Adolescent, adult—Ages 13–65

Purpose: Measures type and expression of anger. Used as a screening and outcome measure in psychotherapy and stress management programs, with particular application in behavioral medicine. May be used with individuals at risk for heart disease, chronic pain sufferers, and individuals suffering from other psychosomatic and behavioral disorders.

Description: 44–item paper-pencil Likert-type test assessing anger along six scales: State Anger, Trait Anger, Anger Expression, Anger Control, and Subtypes of Trait Anger (Angry Temperament and Angry Reaction). A scoring service is available from PAR. Self-adminstered. Suitable for group use.

Untimed: 10 minutes

Scoring: Hand key; may be machine scored

Cost: Kit (manual, 50 item booklets, 50 rating sheets) $39.00

Publisher: Psychological Assessment Resources, Inc.

STRESS ANALYSIS SYSTEM
P.B. Nelson, K.M. Schmidt, and Noel Nelson

Adult

Purpose: Used by adults to assess, understand, and deal with their own stress.

Description: Multiple-item paper-pencil test used by adults for developing a personal stress profile, pinpointing symptoms of stress, and managing stress. The test examines the amount of stress experienced from each of six sources: the Type A, controller personality; the anger-in personality; situational stress and life readjustments; corollary health habits; low accountability/victim syndrome; and interpersonal stress. Self-administered. Suitable for group use.

Untimed: 30 minutes

Scoring: Self-scored

Cost: SAS Kit (test, stress profile, and stress category information) $6.50

Publisher: Interdatum

Information and availability unconfirmed; last verified in 1987.

STRESS AUDIT
Lyle H. Miller and Alma Dell Smith

Adult—Ages 18 and older

Purpose: Measures sources, symptoms, and vulnerability to stress. May be used to facilitate treatment planning in clinical settings and to identify high stress groups in corporate settings.

Description: 238–item paper-pencil or computer-administered multiple-choice test assessing the types and degree of stress an individual experiences, as well as the individual's vulnerability to stress. Six subtests containing 148 total items examine the sources of stress: Family, Individual Roles, Social Being, Environment, Financial, and Work/School. Symptoms of stress are measured by seven subscales containing 10 items each: Muscular, Parasympathetic, Sympathetic, Emotional, Cognitive, Endocrine, and Immune. Items assessing vulnerability cover life-style, health behaviors, and coping resources. Scores are yielded for each of the sources of stress subtests, symptoms of stress subtests, and vulnerability. The Stress Profile Sheet is optional. A scoring service is available from the publisher. The computer version operates on IBM PC, Apple II, and MacIntosh systems. A sixth-grade reading level is required. Examiner/self-administered. Suitable for group use.

Untimed: 30 minutes

Scoring: Computer scored; examiner evaluated; may be machine scored; self-scored

Cost: Specimen set (test booklet, profile sheet, manual) $20.00

Publisher: Biobehavioral Associates

STRESS IMPACT SCALE (SIS)
Refer to page 775.

STRESS IN GENERAL (SIG)
G.H. Ironson and Patricia C. Smith

Adult

Purpose: Assesses overall, long-term job stress.

Description: 18–item employee attitude survey assessing global feelings of job stress. Items are answered in a "yes-no-occasionally" format. A scoring service is available by special arrangement with the publisher. A second-grade reading level is required. May be adminstered in conjunction with the Job Stress Index. May be used with individuals with hearing impairments and physical impairments. Self-administered. Suitable for group use.

Untimed: 1 minute

Scoring: May be computer scored; hand key

Cost: 100 booklets $25.00

Publisher: Smith, Sandman & McCreery

SUBSTANCE ABUSE QUESTIONNAIRE (SAQ)
Refer to page 24.

TEACHER STRESS INVENTORY (TSI)
Refer to page 860.

TEENAGE STRESS PROFILE (TSP)
Lyle H. Miller, Bruce L. Mehler, and Alma Dell Smith

Ages 14–20

Purpose: Assesses sources, symptoms, and vulnerability to stress.

Description: 263–item paper-pencil or computer-administered Likert scale assessing the types and degrees of stress an individual experiences, as well as an individual's vulnerability to stress. Six subtests examine sources of stress: Family (40 items), Individual (28 items), Social (24), Environment (15), Financial (14), and School (52). Symptoms of stress are measured by seven subtests containing 10 items each: Muscular, Parasympathetic Nervous System, Sympathetic Nervous System, Emotional, Cognitive, Endocrine, and Immune. Items assessing vulnerability address life-style, health behaviors, and coping resources. Scores are yielded for each of the sources of stress subtests, symptoms of stress subtests, and vulnerability to stress subtests. A scoring service is available from the publisher. The computer version operates on IBM PC and compatible systems. An 8th-grade reading level is required. Self-administered. Suitable for group use. Available in Spanish.

Timed: 20 minutes

Scoring: Computer scored; self-scored

Cost: Booklet $3.00

Publisher: Biobehavioral Associates

TEST OF WORK COMPETENCY AND STABILITY
Refer to page 1033.

WAHLER PHYSICAL SYMPTOMS STABILITY
Refer to page 229.

Behavioral Medicine: Health and Wellness: Wellness

CLINICAL CHECKLIST SERIES
Refer to page 164.

COMPUTERIZED STRESS INVENTORY (CSI)
Refer to page 7.

FEELING GREAT! A HEALTH AWARENESS SIMULATION
Refer to page 389.

HEALTH PROBLEMS CHECKLIST
John A. Schinka

Adult

Purpose: Assesses the health problems of adults. Used as a survey instrument in clinical and counseling settings to initiate the consultation process and introduce the client to formal diagnostic testing.

Description: 200–item paper-pencil test identifying health problems that may

affect overall psychological well-being. The test, which can be used as a screening tool for medical referrals, covers 13 areas: general health, cardiovascular/pulmonary, endocrine/hematology, gastrointestinal, dermatological, visual, auditory/olfactory, mouth/throat/nose, orthopedic, neurological, genitourinary, habits, and history. The test is a component of the Clinical Checklist Series. Self-administered. Suitable for group use.

Untimed: 10–20 minutes

Scoring: Examiner evaluated

Cost: 50 checklists $17.95

Publisher: Psychological Assessment Resources, Inc.

HEALTH-RISK APPRAISAL PROGRAM

Adult

Purpose: Identifies behaviors and habits that may adversely affect health. Used to educate and motivate individuals to make life-style changes that will improve their health.

Description: 62–item paper-pencil or computer-administered multiple-choice questionnaire determining the areas of an individual's life-style that place his health at risk. Written reports are generated that show the individual's health risks due to his life-style. The latest statistics and algorithms from the Emory University/Carter Center Update are used as well as the National Cholesterol Education Program recommendations. The test administrator may use either the 1959 or the 1983 Metropolitan Weight Tables.

The client may choose to receive either the Standard Individual Report or the Brief Individual Report. The Standard Report (8–9 pages) includes a bar graph showing "Your Top Ten Killers Within the Next Ten Years." A second bar graph details the changes needed to improve life expectancy. The report also contains individualized paragraphs on diet, exercise, cholesterol/HDL levels, stress, and weight as well as a two-page summary of the client's assets and liabilities and suggested remedies. The Brief report (4–5 pages) is a condensed version of the Standard report.

Other reports and results available for administrator of test include 1) a detailed epidemiological report for those wishing more information on the 42 diseases for which the computer actually calculates the person's risks, 2) a printout of the client's responses to the questionnaire, 3) 22 group summary reports that summarize information about the group as a whole, including risk factor distribution and cholesterol/HDL information, and 4) customized mailing list files. An ASCII file containing all the questionnaire information and calculations may be produced. These ASCII files may then be used in other database management or statistical programs.

The program operates on an IBM or compatible computer with 512K of free memory. A hard disk is suggested, although the program can be run on a system with dual floppy drives, one of which must be high density. The printer must have a graphics mode. Examiner required. Suitable for group use.

Untimed: Varies

Scoring: Computer scored

Cost: Contact publisher

Publisher: Planetree Medical Systems, Inc.

Information and availability unconfirmed; last verified in 1988.

PROFILE OF ADAPTATION TO LIFE—HOLISTIC (PAL-H)
Refer to page 209.

QUALITY OF LIFE QUESTIONNAIRE (QLQ-D)
David Evans and Wendy Cope

Adult

Purpose: Measures an individual's quality of life.

Description: 192–item paper-pencil or computer-administered self-report measure consisting of 15 content scales and a social desirability scale. The five major domains are General Well-Being, Inter-

personal Relations, Organizational Activity, Occupational Activity, and Leisure and Recreational Activity. An overall Quality of Life score is obtained from the questionnaire. Computer version generates a narrative report summarizing the findings. Self-administered. Suitable for group use.

Untimed: 30 minutes

Scoring: Carbonized scoring forms; may be computer scored

Cost: Kit (manual, booklet, 25 forms) $32.00; IBM PC compatible computer version (50 administrations and scorings) contact publisher for cost

Publisher: Multi-Health Systems Inc.

THE SOCIAL BEHAVIOR ASSESSMENT SCHEDULE
Refer to page 222.

Behavioral Medicine: Pain

CHRONIC PAIN BATTERY (CPB)
Stephen R. Levitt

Adult—Ages 18 and older

Purpose: Collects medical, psychological, behavioral, and social data and assesses correlates of chronic pain. Used by physicians, dentists, oral surgeons, psychologists, nurses, and other health professionals to suggest treatment and management approaches of individuals suffering from chronic malignant or non-malignant pain.

Description: 204–item paper-pencil and computer-administered multiple-choice and true-false instrument consisting of the Pain Assessment Questionnaire—Revised (PAQ-R) and SCL–90-R. The results are presented in a computer-generated report with a two-fold purpose: to coordinate therapeutic strategies in multidisciplinary health care settings and to aid the private practitioner's specific evaluation. The report topics include demographic and social history, past and current pain history, pain intensity ratings, medication and treatment history, medical history, personality and pain coping style, psycho-social factors (stress, psychological dysfunction, and support system), behavioral-learning factors (prior models, illness-behavior reinforcement, litigation-compensation, activity assessment), patient expectations and goals, and patient problem ratings.

Two scoring options are available: mail-in and computer-scoring software. The mail-in service has a same-day turn-around. The computer-scoring software operates on IBM PC, XT, AT, PS2, or compatible systems. The computer-administered version operates on IBM PC, XT, AT, PS, and compatible systems. An eighth-grade reading level is required. The test administrator must meet APA guidelines. Examiner/self-administered. Suitable for group use. Available in Spanish.

Untimed: 30–60 minutes

Scoring: Computer scored; may be machine scored

Cost: Contact publisher

Publisher: Pain Resource Center

Information and availability unconfirmed; last verified in 1988.

MCGILL PAIN QUESTIONNAIRE (MPQ)
Ronald Melzack

Adult

Purpose: Assesses and diagnoses pain states. Used in clinical research to provide quantitative information that can be treated statistically, detect differences among the different methods used to treat pain, and provide information about the effects of a particular method on the sensory, affective, and evaluative dimensions of pain.

Description: 21–item paper-pencil or computer-administered test consisting primarily of three classes of word descriptors used by examinees to describe subjective pain experience: sensory (temporal, spatial, pressure, thermal, etc.), affective (tension, fear, etc.), and evaluative (overall intensity of total pain experience). The examiner reads the word descriptors aloud to the examinee, who indicates the word that describes the pain

as it is being experienced at the time the test is administered. Only one descriptor from each of the 21 sets may be chosen. The examiner should explain the meaning of any descriptors the examinee does not understand. The questionnaire yields a pain rating index based on the examinee's mean scale values [PRI (S)], a pain rating index based on the rank values of the words [PRI (R)], the number of words chosen (NWC), and present pain intensity (PPI). The software program is designed for use on Apple computer systems. Examiner required. Suitable for group use. Available in French, Italian, German, Spanish, Finnish, and Japanese. CANADIAN PUBLISHER

Untimed: 15 minutes

Scoring: Examiner evaluated

Cost: Contact publisher

Publisher: International Association for the Study of Pain

MULTISCORE DEPRESSION INVENTORY FOR ADOLESCENTS AND ADULTS (MDI)
Refer to page 199.

PAIN AND DISTRESS SCALE
William W.K. Zung

Adult

Purpose: Measures degree of pain and evaluates the characteristics of associated dysfunctions. Used in research and clinical settings to establish pain treatment programs and to monitor the effectiveness of such programs.

Description: 20–item paper-pencil self-report rating scale assessing the presence of somato-sensory pain and associated changes in mood and behavior. Scale items describe the 20 characteristics most commonly described by individuals when pain and associated distress are present. Individuals use a 4–point scale ranging from "none or little of the time" to "most of the time" to rate each item on the degree to which each statement describes their own feelings or behaviors. Items include both symptomatically positive and symptomatically negative statements. Standardized analysis provides an index of the pain and distress present. The manual includes directions for administering, scoring, and interpreting the scale; information concerning development, reliability, and validity; normative data; suggested applications; and a list of references for further research. Examiner required. Suitable for group use.

Untimed: Varies

Scoring: Examiner evaluated

Cost: Contact publisher

Publisher: William W. K. Zung, M.D.

PAIN APPERCEPTION TEST
Donald V. Petrovich

Adult

Purpose: Examines the emotional aspects of pain. Used in settings in which pain might be experienced or anticipated.

Description: 25–item oral-response projective test assessing pain's emotional aspects within a psychological context by measuring an individual's perception of intensity and duration of pain and by focusing on total reactions and not just thresholds. Items consist of 25 picture cards dealing with three major groups of pain situations: felt pain sensations, anticipation versus felt-sensation of pain, and self-inflicted versus other-inflicted pain. Responses are recorded on the protocol sheet. Adult normative data are provided. Examiner required. Suitable for group use.

Untimed: 15–20 minutes

Scoring: Examiner evaluated

Cost: Complete kit (100 protocol sheets, set of plates, manual) $60.00

Publisher: Western Psychological Services

PERSONALITY ASSESSMENT QUESTIONNAIRE (PAQ)
Refer to page 248.

PSYCHOSOCIAL PAIN INVENTORY (PSPI)
Robert K. Heaton,
Ralph A. W. Lehman, and
Carl J. Getto

Adult

Purpose: Evaluates psychosocial factors related to chronic pain problems. Used in the treatment of chronic pain patients.

Description: 8–page multiple-item paper-pencil inventory assessing the following psychosocial factors considered important in maintaining and exacerbating chronic pain problems: several forms of secondary gain, the effects of pain behavior on interpersonal relationships, the existence of stressful life events that may contribute to subjective distress or promote avoidance learning, and components of past history that familiarize the patient with the chronic invalid role and with its personal and social consequences. Ratings take into account that patients differ in the degree to which they are likely to be influenced by potential sources of secondary gain. The inventory yields a total score. High scores predict poor response to medical treatment for pain. Examiner required. Not suitable for group use.

Untimed: Varies

Scoring: Examiner evaluated

Cost: Test kit (25 PSPI forms, manual) $18.00

Publisher: Psychological Assessment Resources, Inc.

QUICK TEST (QT)
Refer to page 59.

THE SEEKING OF NOETIC GOALS TEST (SONG)
Refer to page 219.

STATE-TRAIT ANGER EXPRESSION INVENTORY (STAXI)
Refer to page 11.

can be written to a text file for later modification is available. The computer version runs on IBM PC or compatible systems. Self-administered. Not suitable for group use.

Untimed: Not available

Scoring: Computer scored

Cost: 20 paper-pencil versions $20.00; IBM PC version $295.00

Publisher: Psychologistics, Inc.

Information and availability unconfirmed; last verified in 1988.

COLLATERAL INTERVIEW FORM (CIF)
William R. Miller and G. Allan Marlatt

Adult

Purpose: Assesses the problem drinker from the perspective of the drinker's significant other.

Description: Multiple-item paper-pencil structured interview designed to verify the accuracy of the information supplied by the drinker, obtain information and perspectives not available from the drinker, increase the accuracy of information offered by the drinker through awareness that his or her information will be checked, and involve persons close to the drinker in the change process. The test is adapted from the Comprehensive Drinker Profile (CDP). The CDP manual is used for scoring and interpretation. A CDP manual supplement provides administration instructions. Examiner required. Not suitable for group use.

Untimed: Not available

Scoring: Examiner evaluated

Cost: 15 CIF forms $16.50; CDP manual supplement $9.00; CDP manual $12.00

Publisher: Psychological Assessment Resources, Inc.

COMPREHENSIVE DRINKER PROFILE (CDP)
G. Alan Marlatt and William R. Miller

Adult

Purpose: Assesses alcoholism in men and women. Used for intake-screening in alcohol abuse treatment programs. Provides a basis for selecting, planning, and implementing individualized treatment programs.

Description: Multiple-item paper-pencil structured interview guide assessing an individual's history and current status regarding the use and abuse of alcohol. The profile measures items in the following areas: basic demographics, family and employment status, history of problem development, current drinking pattern and problem status, severity of dependence, social aspects of alcohol use, associated behaviors, relevant medical history, motivations for drinking and seeking treatment, and problem areas other than drinking. The Michigan Alcoholism Screening Test, which provides a survey of current drinking problems and a summary score of problem severity, is part of the profile. The profile also yields scores on problem duration, family history of alcoholism, alcohol consumption, alcohol dependence, range of drinking situations, quantity and frequency of other drug use, emotional factors related to drinking, and life problems other than drinking. The profile is used by professionals and paraprofessionals, including physicians, psychologists, psychiatrists, social workers, nurses, and alcohol abuse counselors. Examiner required. Not suitable for group use.

Untimed: 1–2 hours

Scoring: Examiner evaluated

Cost: Interview kit (manual, 25 interview forms, 8 reusable card sets) $49.95

Publisher: Psychological Assessment Resources, Inc.

COMPUTERIZED DIAGNOSTIC INTERVIEW SCHEDULE (C-DIS)
Refer to page 165.

DISCOVERY DRUG AND ALCOHOL ASSESSMENT PROFILE
E.R. Oetting, Fred Beauvais, and Ruth Edwards

Adolescent, adult—Ages 12 and older   Grades 7 and above

THE TMJ SCALE
Stephen R. Levitt, Tom F. Lundeen, and Michael W. McKinney

Adolescent, adult—Ages 13 and older

Purpose: Screens for and assesses temporomandibular disorders and craniofacial pain and dysfunction. Used by dental practitioners in general practice, orthodontics, prosthodontics, periodontics, oral and maxillofacial surgery, and specialists in TM disorder assessment and treatment. Also used by physicians, EEN&T specialists, and psychologists involved in screening and assessing patients with TM disorders and craniofacial pain and dysfunction. Applications include disability and workers' compensation evaluations and insurance claims and TMJ injury litigation.

Description: Multiple-item paper-pencil self-report tool measuring physical and psychosocial factors contributing to craniomuscular dysfunction. The TMJ Scale Report™ yields 10 scored scales in three domains: Physical (Pain Report, Palpation Pain, Perceived Malocclusion, Joint Dysfunction, Range of Motion Limitation, Non-TM Disorder), Psychosocial (Psychological Factors, Stress, Chronicity), and Global (Global scale—predicts TM disorders). Patients may complete the report at home or in the office. A narrative report and a printout of the patient's scores and responses is generated. The TMJ Scale Profile™ presents patient's scale scores graphically. Tests may be scored using TMJ/Score™ software or via publisher mail-in service. The program operates on IBM PC, XT, AT, or PS/2 systems and is available on 3½" and 5¼" disks. Self-administered. Suitable for group use. Available in Spanish.

Untimed: 15 minutes

Scoring: Computer scored

Cost: Contact publisher

Publisher: Pain Resource Center

Information and availability unconfirmed; last verified in 1988.

Behavioral Medicine: Substance Abuse

ADOLESCENT CHEMICAL DEPENDENCY INVENTORY (ACDI)
Behavior Data Systems, Ltd.

Adolescent—Ages 12–18

Purpose: Screens for and evaluates adolescent substance abuse. Used in intake/referral settings, adolescent chemical dependency treatment programs, and juvenile court/probation systems.

Description: 104–item paper-pencil or computer-administered multiple-choice and true-false inventory containing five scales: Truthfulness, Alcohol, Drugs, Adjustment, and Distress. The Truthfulness scale measures how truthfully the examinee responded to ACDI items. The Alcohol scale measures alcohol-related problems. The Drugs scale measures drug use or abuse-related problems. The Adjustment scale measures overall level of adjustment (personal, home, school, authority, relationship). The Distress scale measures anxiety and depression levels. Results are reported as percentiles, corrected raw scores, and risk-level classifications (low, low-medium, high-medium, high). Narrative explanations and recommendations are presented in automated reports. The computer version operates on IBM PC or compatible systems. Floppy diskettes containing 50, 100, or 150 ACDS test applications are provided. A scoring service is available from the publisher. A sixth-grade reading level is required. Self-administered. Suitable for group use. Available in large print.

Untimed: 20 minutes

Scoring: Computer scored

Cost: Contact publisher; volume discounts available

Publisher: Behavior Data Systems, Ltd.

ALCADD TEST-REVISED
Morse P. Manson, Lisa A. Melchior, and G. J. Huba

Adult—Ages 18 and older

Purpose: Assesses the extent of alcohol addiction. Used for diagnosis, treatment, and alcoholism research.

Description: 65–item paper-pencil multiple-choice test consisting of five subscales measuring regularity of drinking, preference for drinking over other activities, lack of controlled drinking, rationalization of drinking, and excessive emotionality. Materials include WPS Autoscore Form or Alcadd Microcomputer Disk. Computer versions available for IBM PC, XT, or AT (or compatible). Fourth-grade reading level required. This test is suitable for individuals with visual, hearing, and physical impairments. Test can be read to individuals with visual impairments. This is a revision of the 1978 Alcadd Test. Self-administered. Suitable for group use.

Untimed: 5–15 minutes

Scoring: Hand key; computer scored

Cost: Kit $35.00; disk (25 uses) $185.00

Publisher: Western Psychological Services

ALCOHOL ASSESSMENT AND TREATMENT PROFILE (AATP)

Adult

Purpose: Provides information about individuals with drinking problems. Used to evaluate level of motivation for treatment and to make treatment recommendations.

Description: Multiple-item paper-pencil or computer-administered structured interview evaluating an individual's drinking history, patterns of drinking, reinforcement decisions, drinking attitudes, self-concept, and interpersonal relations. A 3- to 4–page computer-generated report, which may be written to a text file for later modification, is provided. The computer-administered

version requires an IBM PC or compatible system. Self-administered. Suitable for group use.

Untimed: Not available

Scoring: Computer scored

Cost: 20 paper-pencil versions $20.00; IBM PC version $200.00

Publisher: Psychologistics, Inc.

Information and availability unconfirmed; last verified in 1988.

ALCOHOL USE INVENTORY (AUI)
J.L. Horn, K.W. Wanberg, and F.M. Foster

Adult

Purpose: Identifies patterns of behavior, attitudes, and symptoms associated with the use and abuse of alcohol. Used for planning treatments.

Description: 228–item self-report inventory measuring the alcohol-related problems of addicted, dependent, binge, and violent drinkers along four domains: benefits, styles, consequences, and concerns associated with alcohol use. The test contains 24 scales (17 primary, 6 second-order, and 1 general) covering drinking for social or mental improvement, drinking to manage moods, gregarious vs. solo drinking, compulsive obsession about drinking, sustained vs. periodic drinking, social role maladaptation, loss of control over behavior when drinking, perceptual and somatic withdrawal symptoms, relationship of marital problems and drinking, quantity of alcohol consumed when drinking, guilt and worry associated with drinking, prior attempts to deal with drinking, and awareness of drinking problems and readiness for help. A profile report is included. Items are written at a 6th-grade reading level. Although the test is designed to be self-administered, it may be orally administered by the examiner. Suitable for group use.

Untimed: 35–60 minutes

Scoring: Computer scored; hand scored

Cost: Specimen set (manual, test booklet, profile report answer sheet) $14.95

Publisher: National Computer Systems/ PAS Division

AMERICAN DRUG AND ALCOHOL SURVEY (ADAS)
Refer to page 734.

AMERICAN DRUG AND ALCOHOL SURVEY (ADAS)— CHILDREN'S FORM
Refer to page 735.

ASSESSMENT OF CHEMICAL HEALTH INVENTORY (ACHI)
Renovex

Adolescent, adult—Ages 12 and older

Purpose: Assesses chemical use and associated problems.

Description: 128–item computer-administered instrument assessing chemical misuse and associated problems including family estrangement, personal consequences, use involvement, alienation, social impact, depression, family support, family chemical use, and self-regard/ abuse. Fourth-grade reading level required. Self-administered by client on computer. Also available in paper form. Examiner must be a counselor. This is one test in the Case Management System series. Self-administered. Not suitable for group use.

Untimed: 15–25 minutes

Scoring: Examiner evaluated; computer scored

Cost: $5.75

Publisher: Renovex

BEXLEY-MAUDSLEY AUTOMATED PSYCHOLOGICAL SCREENING (BMAPS)
Refer to page 97.

BRIEF DRINKER PROFILE (BDP)
William R. Miller and G. Allan Marlatt

Adult

Purpose: Evaluates problem drinking. Used as a component of a screening battery in mental health facilities, forensic

centers, medical and hospital settin[g]s and alcohol treatment centers.

Description: Multiple-item paper-intake interview covering an indivi[dual's] family and employment status, dem[o-]graphics, history of problem develo[p-]ment, current drinking pattern, alc[ohol-]related problems, severity of depen[dence,] other drug use, additional life probl[ems,] and motivation for treatment. The i[nstru-]ment, which is a shortened version [of the] Comprehensive Drinker Profile (CD[P),] incorporates the Michigan Alcoholis[m] Screening Test (MAST). The BDP i[s] used in situations not requiring the [depth] of information elicited by the CDP. [Cards] from the CDP card deck are require[d,] and the CDP manual is used for sco[ring] and interpretation. A new CDP man[-] supplement provides administration instructions. Examiner required. No[t] suitable for group use.

Untimed: 50 minutes

Scoring: Examiner evaluated

Cost: 25 BDP forms $32.00; CDP m[an-] ual supplement $9.00; CDP manual $12.00; CDP card sets $9.00

Publisher: Psychological Assessment Resources, Inc.

CARLSON PSYCHOLOGICAL SURVEY (CPS)
Refer to page 162.

CHEMICAL DEPENDENCY ASSESSMENT PROFILE (CDAP)

Adult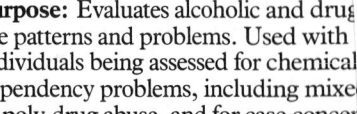

Purpose: Evaluates alcoholic and drug use patterns and problems. Used with individuals being assessed for chemical dependency problems, including mixe[d] or poly-drug abuse, and for case concep[-] tualization and treatment planning.

Description: Multiple-item paper-pen[cil] or computer-administered structured interview covering history of dependen[-] cies, patterns and reinforcement dimensions of use, belief about use and dependency, self-concept, and interpersonal relations. A 5- to 8–page report th[at]

Purpose: Assesses drug and alcohol use and psycho-social correlates of drug and alcohol use.

Description: 233–item paper-pencil multiple-choice and short answer test yielding a profile of drug use, rationales for use, when and where the drugs were used, as well as over 30 additional scales of psycho-social correlates of drug and alcohol use. A scoring service is provided by the publisher. A fourth-grade reading level is required. Self-administered. Suitable for group use.

Untimed: 40 minutes

Scoring: Computer scored

Cost: Profile $20.00

Publisher: Rocky Mountain Behavioral Science Institute, Inc.

DRIVER RISK INVENTORY (DRI)
Behavior Data Systems, Ltd.

**Adult—Ages 16 and older
Grades 8 and above**

Purpose: Measures the driving risk of DWI (driving while intoxicated) or DUI (driving under the influence) offenders. Used to identify problem drinkers, substance abusers, and high-risk drivers.

Description: 130–item paper-pencil or computer-administered multiple-choice and true-false screening inventory containing five scales. The Validity, or Truthfulness, scale measures how truthfully the examinee responded to DRI items. The Alcohol Proneness scale measures the examinee's alcohol proneness and related problems. The Drug Abuse Proneness scale measures the examinee's drug use or abuse proneness and related problems and distinguishes between alcohol and drug abuse. The Driver Risk scale measures driver risk potential, identifying the problem-prone driver independent of the respondent's substance abuse history. The Stress Quotient is a measure of the examinee's ability to cope with stress.

Results are presented in the DRI Profile and as percentiles. In addition, the risk range (low, low-medium, high-medium, high) for each scale as well as scores for all five scales are reported. Intervention and treatment recommenda-

tions are based on the examinee's risk levels for the five scales. The DRI Report summarizes test data and includes a brief structured interview. The examinee must have a sixth-grade reading level. The examiner must complete an orientation offered by the test publisher. An IBM PC or compatible system is required for operation of the computer version. Floppy diskettes containing 50, 100, or 150 test applications are provided. Self-administered. Suitable for group use. Available in Spanish and large print.

Untimed: 20 minutes

Scoring: Computer scored

Cost: Contact publisher; volume discounts available

Publisher: Behavior Data Systems, Ltd.

DRUG USE INDEX (DUI)
*Frazier M. Douglass and
Khalil A. Khavari*

Ages 14–adult

Purpose: Measures polydrug use. Used by researchers, counselors, physicians, and therapists for diagnosis and planning treatment.

Description: Multiple-item paper-pencil questionnaire assessing and predicting drug use. Individuals indicate their use of 19 different drugs and categories of drugs (including alcohol, tobacco, and over-the-counter drugs) on a scale of 0 (never) to 7 (several times a day). An overall drug use pattern is computed by summing across all drugs. The test is a predictive measure for use of 18 drugs or drug classes (except over-the-counter drugs). The questionnaire can be used for determining social and cultural variables that foster drug use and the kinds of drugs used. It also can be used for diagnosing and planning treatment for possible underlying psychiatric problems. Examiner required. Suitable for group use.

Untimed: Varies

Scoring: Examiner evaluated

Cost: One questionnaire provided free to each user; users may reproduce copies for their own use

Publisher: Khalil A. Khavari, Ph.D.

FOLLOW-UP DRINKER PROFILE (FDP)
William K. Miller and
G. Allan Marlatt

Adult

Purpose: Evaluates the progress of diagnosed alcoholics.

Description: Multiple-item paper-pencil structured interview designed for evaluating, at regular intervals, the progress of alcoholics after treatment. The content of the FDP parallels that of the Comprehensive Drinker Profile and the Brief Drinker Profile (see individual descriptions). The CDP manual is used for scoring and interpretation, and cards from the CDP card deck are required for administration. A new CDP manual supplement provides administration instructions. Examiner required. Not suitable for group use.

Untimed: 30–50 minutes

Scoring: Examiner evaluated

Cost: 15 FDP forms $18.75; CDP manual supplement $9.00; CDP manual $12.00; CDP card sets $9.00

Publisher: Psychological Assessment Resources, Inc.

INTEGRATED CHEMICAL DEPENDENCY CASE MANAGEMENT SYSTEM

Adolescent, adult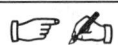

Purpose: Evaluates and assesses chemical use history. Used by chemical dependency professionals working in alcohol and drug abuse facilities for various stages of treatment planning.

Description: Computer-administered chemical dependency system comprised of three modules. The Evaluation and Assessment Module collects social and chemical use history. The Treatment Planning and Aftercare module, which contains more than 1,200 intervention and strategy statements covering 19 problem areas, is used for initial, preliminary, master, and aftercare planning as well as for teaching. The Utilization Review module generates dated schedules that report due dates for required documentation, assessment, and utilization review tasks. Information from the schedules can be used to meet admission and extended stay criteria for insurance companies. The program operates on IBM PC systems and Novelle networks. Examiner required. Not suitable for group use.

Untimed: Not available

Scoring: Computer scored

Cost: Contact publisher

Publisher: Renovex

IPS SOCIAL HISTORY (SOCH)
Refer to page 184.

KIDDIE LIFE
Refer to page 246.

MALADAPTED BEHAVIOR RECORD (MBR)
Refer to page 247.

MANSON EVALUATION-REVISED
Morse P. Manson and George J. Huba

Adult

Purpose: Assesses alcohol abuse proneness and eight related personality characteristics. Used for personnel screening, diagnosis, therapy, research, and alcohol abuse programs.

Description: 72–item paper-pencil or computer-administered true-false test with seven subscales measuring anxiety, depressive fluctuations, emotional sensitivity, resentfulness, incompleteness, aloneness, and interpersonal relations. Raw scores, T-scores, and percentiles are yielded. This revised version provides 1985 norms as well as a new test form featuring the WPS AutoScore system, which makes it possible for the administrator to score, profile, and interpret the test in just a few minutes. A computer version for IBM PC, XT, AT, or compatible with 128K is available. Examiner required. Suitable for group use.

Untimed: 5–10 minutes

Scoring: Hand key; computer scored; scoring service available from the publisher

Cost: Kit (25 tests/profiles, manual) $35.00; WPS Test Report: Manson Evaluation Microcomputer Disk (IBM) $185.00

Publisher: Western Psychological Services

NATIONAL ADULT READING TEST
Refer to page 58.

PERSONAL EXPERIENCE INVENTORY (PEI)
Ken C. Winters and George H. Henly

Adolescent—Ages 12-18

Purpose: Assesses chemical dependency of adolescents.

Description: 300–item paper-pencil multiple-choice computer-administered two-part test. Part I contains 129 items relating to personal involvement with chemicals, effects of drug use, social benefits of drug use, consequences of drug use, polydrug use, social-recreational use, psychological benefits of drug use, trans-situational use, preoccupation with drugs, and loss of control. In addition to documenting the degree, duration, and onset of drug use, this section also provides several clinical scales, validity indexes, and a problem severity section.

Part II consists of 147 items that measure aspects of psychosocial functioning related to patterns of drug use and treatment responsiveness. Eight personal risk factor scales and four environmental risk factor scales are included in this section.

Scores are used to generate a PEI computer report and PEI chromagraph. This is one test in the Minnesota Chemical Dependency Adolescent Assessment Package. A sixth-grade reading level is required. A computer version for IBM PC, XT, AT, or PS/2 and compatibles is available. This test is suitable for individuals with visual, hearing, and physical impairments. It can be read to those with visual impairments. Self-administered. Suitable for group use.

Untimed: 40–50 minutes

Scoring: Computer scored; scoring service available from publisher

Cost: Kit (10 WPS test reports, PEI answer booklets, manual)$170.00; computer disk (25 uses) $270.00

Publisher: Western Psychological Services

PHASE II PROFILE INTEGRITY STATUS INVENTORY
Refer to page 1020.

PSYCHIATRIC DIAGNOSTIC INTERVIEW—REVISED
Refer to page 210.

PSYCHIATRIC STATUS SCHEDULE (PSS)
Refer to page 211.

QUIT SMOKING NOW PROGRAM
Robert Gordon

Adolescent, adult

Purpose: Evaluates a person's addiction to smoking cigarettes. Used by therapists to assist patients who wish to quit smoking.

Description: 40–item paper-pencil survey assessing the causes and nature of an individual's addiction to smoking and commitment to change during the attempt to quit. After the initial survey is completed, the therapist graphs on the Progress Chart the number of cigarettes smoked versus days of treatment. Monitoring cards are placed in front of patients' cigarette packages and are used for recording frequency and time of smoking. The test may be used in conjunction with hypnosis, behavioral techniques, and/or counseling. Self-administered. Suitable for group use.

Untimed: Not available

Scoring: Examiner evaluated

Cost: Kit (25 smoking surveys, 25 progress charts, 25 monitors, instructions) $18.00

Publisher: The Wilmington Press

Information and availability unconfirmed; last verified in 1987.

REYNOLDS ADOLESCENT DEPRESSION SCALE (RADS)
Refer to page 214.

SEARCH INSTITUTE PROFILES OF STUDENT LIFE: ALCOHOL AND OTHER DRUGS
Search Institute

Adolescent—Ages 11–18 Grades 6–12

Purpose: Assesses student attitudes, behaviors, and perceptions concerning alcohol and other drugs. Used as baseline information for programming in public and private schools and youth-serving agencies.

Description: 117–item paper-pencil survey that provides a portrait of alcohol and drug use patterns for establishing program needs and priorities. May be used to evaluate the impact of prevention programs. The information is analyzed and presented in a 40–page student report containing graphics and explanatory text. This is one survey in the Search Institute Profiles of Student Life Series. It is a revision of the 1983 MN Survey on Drug Use and Drug-Related Attitudes. Examiner required. Suitable for group use.

Untimed: 30 minutes

Scoring: Machine scored; scoring service available from publisher

Cost: System $2,500.00; charge per student $1.25

Publisher: Search Institute

SECURITY, APTITUDE, FITNESS EVALUATION—RESISTANCE (SAFE-R)
Refer to page 1025.

THE SEEKING OF NOETIC GOALS TEST (SONG)
Refer to page 219.

SUBSTANCE ABUSE PROBLEM CHECKLIST (SAPC)
Jerome F.X. Carroll

Adult

Purpose: Identifies client problems associated with substance abuse. Used for diagnosis, referral, and development of treatment plans for substance abusers and for research on treatment needs and outcomes.

Description: 377–item paper-pencil test of client problems in the following areas: motivations for treatment, general health, personal problems, social problems, job problems, problems relating to leisure time, religious problems, and legal problems. Each item lists a problem related to substance abuse; the examinee underlines those items that apply to self. The client indicates problems that are especially troublesome by circling the number next to the problem statement. Specific items/problems are later discussed individually by the client and counselor. A fourth-grade reading level is required. Examiner/self-administered. Suitable for group use.

Untimed: 40–45 minutes

Scoring: Examiner evaluated

Cost: 100 test booklets, clinical manual $50.00

Publisher: Eagleville Hospital

SUBSTANCE ABUSE QUESTIONNAIRE (SAQ)
Behavior Data Systems, Ltd.

Adult—Ages 18 and older Grades 8 and above

Purpose: Screens and evaluates adult chemical dependency. Used as an intake/referral device in chemical dependency treatment settings and in the criminal justice system.

Description: 151–item paper-pencil or computer-administered multiple-choice and true-false test designed to screen for and evaluate chemical dependency. The Truthfulness scale measures how truthfully the examinee responded to the SAQ items. The Alcohol scale measures the examinee's alcohol-related problems and proneness. The Drug scale measures drug use or abuse-related problems and proneness. The Aggressivity scale measures the examinee's risk-taking behavior and aggressiveness. The Resistance scale measures uncooperativeness and resistance to assistance or treatment. The Stress Coping scale measures the examinee's ability to cope with stress, tension, and anxiety. The SAQ Profile reports scores, percentiles, and risk levels (low, low-medium, high-medium, high) for all six scales. The computer version operates on IBM PC and compatible systems. Floppy diskettes containing 50, 100, or 150 test applications are provided. A seventh-grade reading level is required. Self-administered. Suitable for group use. Available in Spanish and large print.

Untimed: 25 minutes

Scoring: Computer scored

Cost: Contact publisher; volume discounts available

Publisher: Behavior Data Systems, Ltd.

TAYLOR-JOHNSON TEMPERAMENT ANALYSIS
Refer to page 226.

WESTERN PERSONALITY INVENTORY (WPI)
Morse P. Manson

Adult

Purpose: Diagnoses the presence and degree of alcoholism. Useful in alcohol rehabilitation programs.

Description: Paper-pencil or computer-administered test that combines the "Manson Evaluation," which identifies the potential alcoholic personality, and the "Alcadd Test," which measures the extent of alcohol addiction, into one booklet. The computer version is available on IBM PC or compatible systems. Computer scoring is available via mail-in services or on-site. Examiner required. Suitable for group use.

Untimed: 15–20 minutes

Scoring: Hand key; may be computer scored

Cost: Paper-pencil version complete kit (10 booklets, Manson Evaluation manual, Alcadd Test manual, 2 mail-in computer-scored answer sheets) $60.00; IBM version (25 uses) $250.00

Publisher: Western Psychological Services

Child and Child Development

ASSESSING PRELINGUISTIC AND EARLY LINGUISTIC BEHAVIORS
Lesley Olswang, Carol Stoel-Gammon, Truman Coggins, and Robert Carpenter

---

Child—Ages 9–24 months

Purpose: Identifies early emerging speech and language behaviors for children ages 9–24 months and older children whose functional age is below 24 months. Used for developing assessment procedures and generating normative data documenting language development.

Description: Program containing five scales assessing prelinguistic and early linguistic development: Cognitive Antecedents to Word Meaning, Play, Communicative Intention, Language Comprehension, and Language Production. This assessment protocol is described in a 165–page manual *Assessing Prelinguistic and Early Linguistic Behaviors in Developmentally Young Children*. For each scale, the manual discusses the scale's theoretical foundation; describes the administration procedures, behaviors, and normative data; and provides a training supplement. The manual is accompanied by a videotape (optional) that demonstrates the methods used in assessing the behaviors outlined in the manual. Examiner required. Not suitable for group use.

Timed: Not available

Scoring: Examiner evaluated

Cost: Manual (binder format) $40.00; ½" VHS video $225.00

Publisher: University of Washington Press

ASSESSMENT IN INFANCY: ORDINAL SCALES OF PSYCHOLOGICAL DEVELOPMENT
Ina C. Uzgiris and J. McV. Hunt

Child—Ages 3 weeks–2 years

Purpose: Assesses the psychological and cognitive development of infants in the first two years of life. Used with severely retarded and handicapped individuals and to compare different populations of children.

Description: Six paper-pencil observational scales assessing an infant's psychological and cognitive development: The Development of Visual Pursuit and the Performance of Objects, The Development of Means for Obtaining Desired Environmental Events, The Development of Imitation, The Development of Operational Causality, The Construction of Object Relations in Space, and The Development of Schemes for Relating to Objects. The book *Assessment in Infancy* describes the six scales and provides the methodology for testing severely mentally retarded individuals and handicapped infants, analyzing language development, and comparing different populations of children. The record forms are designed for use with the book. Supplementary instructional films (16 mm. or videocassette) are available for each of the six scales. Examiner required. Not suitable for group use.

Untimed: Varies

Scoring: Examiner evaluated

Cost: *Assessment in Infancy* (274 pp.) $24.95; 5 record forms $15.75

Publisher: University of Illinois Press

Information and availability unconfirmed; last verified in 1988.

THE BARBER SCALES OF SELF-REGARD FOR PRESCHOOL CHILDREN
Lucie W. Barber

Preschoolers

Purpose: Assesses young children's level of development. Used to help parents recognize and develop a child's self-regard.

Description: Multiple-item paper-pencil assessment profile of seven developmental factors, each measured on a 5–point scale. The factors are purposeful learning skills, completing tasks, coping with fears, cooperating with parental requests, dealing with frustrations, social adjustment, and developing imagination in play. The scales were designed for parents with aid of professional educators. Worksheets direct parents to the next level of their child's development. Examiner required. Suitable for group use.

Untimed: Varies

Scoring: Examiner evaluated

Cost: Contact publisher

Publisher: Personality Research Services, Limited

BATTELLE DEVELOPMENTAL INVENTORY (BDI)
Refer to page 533.

BATTELLE DEVELOPMENTAL INVENTORY (BDI) SCREENING TEST
Refer to page 533.

BAYLEY SCALES OF INFANT DEVELOPMENT
Nancy Bayley

Child—Ages 2–30 months

Purpose: Assesses mental, motor, and behavioral development. Used for assessing developmental progress, comparison with peers, and providing an objective basis for determining eligibility for special services.

Description: Two-scale test of infant mental and motor development. The Mental Scale assesses sensory-perceptual behavior, learning ability, and early communication attempts. The Motor Scale measures general body control, coordination of large muscles, and skills in fine-muscle control of hands. The materials include a kit containing stimulus items and the Infant Behavior Record for noting qualitative aspects of behavior. Examiner required. Not suitable for group use.

Untimed: 45 minutes

Scoring: Examiner evaluated

Cost: Complete set (all necessary equipment, manual, 25 each of 3 record forms, carrying case) $449.00; manual supplement $10.00

Publisher: The Psychological Corporation

Information and availability unconfirmed; last verified in 1988.

BEHAVIOR RATING INSTRUMENT FOR AUTISTIC AND OTHER ATYPICAL CHILDREN (BRIAAC)
Bertram Ruttenberg, Beth Kalish, Charles Wenar, and Enid Wolf

Child

Purpose: Evaluates the status of low functioning, atypical, and autistic children of all ages. Used to evaluate children who will not or cannot cooperate with formal testing procedures.

Description: Paper-pencil inventory of observations taken over a two-day period assessing a child's present level of functioning and measuring behavioral change in eight areas: relationship to an adult, communication, drive for mastery, vocalization and expressive speech, sound and speech reception, social responsiveness, body movement (passive and active), and psychobiological development. Each of the eight scales begins with the most severe autistic behavior and progresses to behavior roughly comparable to that of a normally developing 3½- to 4½-year-old. The complete BRIAAC includes a manual, report forms, individual scale score sheet, total score sheet, intrascale and interscale profile forms, descriptive

guides, and suggested individual plans. Examiner required. Not suitable for group use.

Untimed: Two days

Scoring: Examiner evaluated

Cost: Complete kit (manual, all required forms) $175.00

Publisher: Stoelting Co.

BEHAVIOUR STUDY TECHNIQUE
Isla Stamp

Child
Grades PreK–1

Purpose: Measures behavioral development and adjustment of preschool children. Identifies children in need of further testing and assistance. Used by kindergarten teachers.

Description: Multiple-item observational instrument for systematic evaluation of behavior in preschool children. Although intended for use by kindergarten teachers, a psychologist's manual that is available with the test presents a coding system enabling psychologists to classify children as apparently mentally healthy, in need of some help in adjusting, or urgently in need of referral for diagnosis and therapy. Australian norms are provided for preschool and first-grade children. The manual and score keys are restricted to use by psychologists. Materials include a questionnaire, teacher's guide (revised 1979), psychologist's manual, and score keys. Examiner required. AUSTRALIAN PUBLISHER

Untimed: Varies

Scoring: Hand key; examiner evaluated

Cost: Contact publisher

Publisher: The Australian Council for Educational Research Limited

THE BINGHAM BUTTON TEST
William Bingham

Child—Ages 3–6

Purpose: Measures a child's ability to discern color, shape, size, and spatial relationships as an indication of preschool readiness.

Description: One jar and 10 buttons of different colors and sizes are presented by the examiner to the child, who is asked to maneuver the buttons to reveal the ability to determine how colors, objects, and space relate to each other. The test also is used in the diagnosis of problems with visual perception or motor skills. Examiner required. Not suitable for group use.

Untimed: 25–30 minutes

Scoring: Hand key

Cost: Complete set $4.00

Publisher: Bingham Button Test

Information and availability unconfirmed; last verified in 1987.

BIRTH TO THREE ASSESSMENT AND INTERVENTION SYSTEM: A PARENT-TEACHER INTERACTION PROGRAM
Tina E. Bangs and Susan Dodson

Child—Ages 0–3

Purpose: Assesses developmental skills. Used in the selection of intervention activities.

Description: Multiple-item test consisting of two instruments assessing language comprehension, language expression, problem solving, social/personal skills, and motor skills. The Screening Test of Language and Learning Development assesses developmental domains and provides age norms at 6-month intervals. The criterion-referenced Checklist of Language and Learning Behavior lists developmental behaviors. The Intervention Manual provides activities and lesson plans for developing programs. Examiner required. Not suitable for group use.

Untimed: Varies

Scoring: Examiner evaluated

Cost: Complete program (screening test examiner's manual, 25 record forms; checklist examiner's manual, 25 record forms; intervention manual) $130.00

Publisher: DLM Teaching Resources

BIRTH TO THREE DEVELOPMENTAL SCALE— SCREENING TEST
Refer to page 533.

BOEHM TEST OF BASIC CONCEPTS—PRESCHOOL VERSION
Refer to page 534.

THE BRIGANCE® DIAGNOSTIC INVENTORY OF EARLY DEVELOPMENT
Refer to page 535.

BURKS' BEHAVIOR RATING SCALES, PRESCHOOL AND KINDERGARTEN EDITION
Refer to page 136.

THE BZOCH-LEAGUE RECEPTIVE-EXPRESSIVE EMERGENT LANGUAGE SCALE (REEL)
Kenneth R. Bzoch and Richard League

Child—Ages 0–36 months

Purpose: Assesses emerging factors of expressive and receptive language in children. Identifies children needing further evaluation.

Description: 132–item paper-pencil inventory measuring the development of language in infants. The child's overt speech and response behaviors are rated by a parent or individual who has daily contact with the child and has the opportunity to observe the child's language behavior. Test items consist of statements of language behavior typical of children ages 0–36 months. The evaluator rates each item as being present or absent. Three expressive and three receptive factors are measured for each of 22 age levels. Three scores are derived: expressive language quotient, receptive language quotient, and overall language quotient. Results also yield receptive, expressive, and combined expressive and receptive language ages. Examiner required. Not suitable for group use.

Untimed: Varies

Scoring: Examiner evaluated

Cost: Complete kit $39.00; manual $22.00; 25 test forms $19.00

Publisher: PRO-ED

CALLIER-AZUSA SCALE: G-EDITION
Robert Stillman (Editor)

Handicapped children

Purpose: Assesses the development of deaf-blind and severely and profoundly handicapped children. Used to plan developmentally appropriate activities and to evaluate a child's developmental progress, particularly at the lower developmental levels.

Description: Multiple-item paper-pencil observational inventory measuring 18 developmental subscales in five developmental areas: motor development (postural control, locomotion, fine motor, and visual motor); perceptual abilities (visual, auditory, and tactile development); daily living skills (undressing and dressing, personal hygiene, development of feeding skills, and toileting); cognition, communication, and language (cognitive development, receptive communication, expressive communication, and development of speech); and social development (interactions with adults, peers, and the environment).

Each subscale is made up of sequential steps describing developmental milestones. Some steps are divided into two or more items describing behaviors appearing at approximately the same time in development. The developmental steps described in the scale take into account the specific sensory, motor, language, and social deficits of deaf-blind and severely and profoundly impaired children (scale items differ from behaviors typically observed among normal children at the same developmental level).

Administration of the scale is based on at least two weeks of observation of spontaneously occurring behaviors typically appearing in conjunction with classroom activities. The scale must be administered by someone thoroughly familiar with the child's behavior. No specific testing expertise is required other than good observational skills and a knowledge of the child's repertoire of behaviors. The most accurate results are obtained if several individuals with close contact with the child (teachers, aides, parents, specialists) evaluate the child on a consensus basis.

Scale items are rated according to the presence or absence of the specific behaviors listed. Age equivalencies are included only to provide a rough means of comparing functioning levels in different areas of behavior. Interpretation of scale results is based on the sequence in which the behaviors occur, not on the age norms for normal children. A profile sheet is provided for summarizing scale results. Examiner required. Not suitable for group use.

Untimed: Varies

Scoring: Examiner evaluated

Cost: Contact publisher

Publisher: Callier Center for Communication Disorders

CATTELL INFANT INTELLIGENCE SCALE
Psyche Cattell

Child—Ages 3–30 months

Purpose: Assesses the mental development of infants.

Description: Test of early development rating infant verbalizations and motor control, such as the manipulation of cubes, pencils, pegboards, and other stimulus items. The test has been modified with items from the Gesell, Minnesota Preschool, and Merrill-Palmer scales and is applicable to a younger age range than the Stanford-Binet Intelligence Scale. Materials include a kit containing stimulus items. Examiner required. Not suitable for group use.

Untimed: 20–30 minutes

Scoring: Examiner evaluated

Cost: Complete set (all necessary equipment, 25 record forms, carrying case, no manual) $350.00; manual $55.00

Publisher: The Psychological Corporation

Information and availability unconfirmed; last verified in 1988.

CHILDPACE—CHILD DEVELOPMENT PROGRAM

Child—Ages 3 months to 5 years

Purpose: Evaluates and monitors developmental behavior. Used to help develop specific skills. May be used in day-care centers and classrooms.

Description: Multiple-item computer-administered program evaluating a child's gross-motor control, fine-motor control, language, and personal and social skills from the parent's point of view. The parent enters developmental information about the child, and the program evaluates the child's developmental level. Results may be used to help develop specific skills and to detect developmental delays necessitating professional intervention. The test is adapted from the Denver Developmental Screening Test. The software program runs on Apple and IBM PC systems. Examiner required. Suitable for group use.

Untimed: Not available

Scoring: Computer scored

Cost: Contact publisher

Publisher: Computerose

Information and availability unconfirmed; last verified in 1988.

COMMUNICATIVE EVALUATION CHART
Ruth M. Anderson, Madeline Miles, and Patricia A. Matheny

Child—Ages 0–5

Purpose: Assesses children's development of overall abilities in language and visual-motor-perceptual skills. Identifies children needing referral for clinical evaluation.

Description: Task-assessment and oral-response test measuring the development of skills required for speech development. The tasks are designed to cover the coordination of the speech musculature; development of hearing acuity and auditory perception; acquisition of consonants, grammar, and vocabulary; and growth of receptive and expressive language. The test also evaluates a child's well-being, growth and development, motor coordination, and beginning visual-motor-perceptual skills. The examiner elicits responses from the child and evaluates the responses as present, not present, or fluctuating. It is occasionally necessary to consult with the parent, guardian, or pediatrician for pertinent information. The test is subdivided into nine levels of 13–30 items for each of the following age groups: 3, 6, or 9 months; 1, 1½, 2, 3, 4, or 5 years. Examiner required. Not suitable for group use.

Untimed: 5–10 minutes

Scoring: Examiner evaluated

Cost: Test $1.00; 50 tests $37.50

Publisher: Educators Publishing Service, Inc.

COMPREHENSIVE DEVELOPMENTAL EVALUATION CHART (CDEC)
Shirley Cliff, Diane Carr, Jennifer Gray, Carol Nymann, and Sandra Redding

Child—Ages 0–3

Purpose: Measures a child's developmental abilities. Used for evaluation by either transdisciplinary or conventional team approaches.

Description: Multiple-item observational instrument used to collect comprehensive data and follow a child's development. The chart includes evaluations of gross-motor skills, fine-motor skills, muscle tone, reflexes, parental attitudes, height and weight, receptive language, head circumference, expressive language, cognitive/social development, feeding, vision, hearing, and others. Examiner required. Not suitable for group use.

Untimed: 30 minutes

Scoring: Examiner evaluated

Cost: CDE packet (2 charts, manual) $12.00

Publisher: El Paso Rehabilitation Center

COMPREHENSIVE DEVELOPMENTAL EVALUATION MANUAL WITH CHARTS
Shirley Cliff, Diane Carr, Jennifer Gray, Carol Nymann, and Sandra Redding

Child—Ages 0–3

Purpose: Assesses and screens for developmental delays.

Description: Criterion-referenced test with six subtests (Gross Motor, Manipulation, Feeding, Receptive Language, Expressive Language, and Cognitive/Social) that measure abnormal/normal development in children. Scores yield developmental age. Materials include the Serial Screening Recording Form, the Comprehensive Developmental Evaluation Chart, and common toys. Examiner must have a knowledge of normal development. This test is suitable for use with individuals with visual, hearing, physical, and mental impairments. Examiner required. Not suitable for group use.

Untimed: Varies

Scoring: Examiner evaluated

Cost: $12.00

Publisher: El Paso Rehabilitation Center

COMPREHENSIVE IDENTIFICATION PROCESS (CIP)
Refer to page 539.

DENVER DEVELOPMENTAL SCREENING TEST (DDST)
William K. Frankenburg

Child—Ages 0–6

Purpose: Evaluates a child's personal, social, fine- and gross-motor, language, and adaptive abilities as a means of identifying possible problems and screening for further evaluation.

Description: 105–item "pick and choose" test in which the items are blocks, a bell, a ball, a bottle, raisins, a rattle, yarn, and a pencil. Items are presented to the child in chronological stepwise order to permit a more dynamic profile (i.e., a growth curve) of the child's development. The examiner observes what the child does with the items and makes recommendations based on perceived abnormalities. Examiner required. Not suitable for group use. Available in Spanish.

Untimed: 10–20 minutes

Scoring: Examiner evaluated

Cost: Kit $24.00; 100 English test forms $13.00; 100 Spanish test forms $14.00; manual $17.00

Publisher: Denver Developmental Materials, Inc.

DEVELOPMENTAL ACTIVITIES SCREENING INVENTORY-II (DASI-II)
Refer to page 540.

DEVELOPMENTAL ASSESSMENT FOR THE SEVERELY HANDICAPPED (DASH)
Refer to page 662.

THE DEVELOPMENTAL PROFILE II (DP-II)
Refer to page 541.

EARLY CHILD DEVELOPMENT INVENTORY (ECDI)
Harold Ireton

Child—Ages 15 months to 3 years

Purpose: Measures developmental level, symptoms, and behavioral problems. Used as a screening instrument to identify children with problems that may interfere with the ability to learn.

Description: 88–item paper-pencil questionnaire for obtaining a parent's report of the child's current functioning. The ECDI is divided into six sections.

The General Development section is a 60–item assessment of the child's overall development. Items cover seven developmental areas: language comprehension, expressive language, fine motor, self-help, personal-social, situation-comprehension, and gross motor. The Possible Problems section is a 24–item list of symptoms and behavior problems. The 15 symptoms describe sensory, speech and language, comprehension, physical, and quasi-physical symptoms. The nine behavioral problem items relate to immaturity, behavioral problems, hyperactivity, and emotional problems. The Child Description section is the parents' brief description of the child. The Problems or Disabilities section is the parents' report of problems that may be major handicaps or obstacles to learning. The Questions or Concerns section is the parents' report of their concerns or questions about the child. The Parents' Functioning section asks parents how they are doing, as parents or otherwise.

The ECDI is especially suited for use with a developmental screening test; however, when used as a pretest questionnaire itself, only children whose parents report some concern should be tested. The parent may complete the inventory at home and bring it to the screening where it can be scored and interpreted. The results for each section of the inventory are interpreted as a) showing no evidence of any problems, b) raising concern about a possible problem, or c) suggesting a possible major problem. These results indicate the need for follow-up evaluation. The manual includes instructions for administering, scoring, and interpreting the questionnaire. Examiner required. Suitable for group use.

Untimed: Varies

Scoring: Examiner evaluated

Cost: Manual $5.00; 25 answer sheets $7.00

Publisher: Behavior Science Systems, Inc.

THE EARLY COPING INVENTORY
Shirley Zeitlin,
G. Gordon Williamson, and
Margery Szezepanski

Child—Ages 4–36 months

Purpose: Assesses the coping-related behaviors used by infants and toddlers in everyday living.

Description: 48–item behavioral observation inventory designed to assess the coping-related behaviors of toddlers and

older disabled children who function in the 4– to 36–month age range. Items are divided into three categories: sensorimotor organization, reactive behavior, and self-initiated behavior. The manual contains instructions for rating, scoring, and implementing results. Examiner required. Not suitable for group use.

Timed: Varies

Scoring: Hand key

Cost: Starter set (manual, 20 forms) $25.00; specimen set $14.00

Publisher: Scholastic Testing Services, Inc.

EGAN BUS PUZZLE TEST
Dorothy Egan

Child—Ages 20 months–4 years

Purpose: Assesses developmental deficit, delay, and handicap in children. Used by community health professionals.

Description: Multiple-item response screening test consisting of a display board with a printed street scene and nine lift-out pieces for assessing comprehension of verbal labels, expressive verbal labels, comprehension of illustrated situations related to experience, expressive language response, and the beginnings of intuitive verbal thinking. Examiner required. Not suitable for group use. BRITISH PUBLISHER

Untimed: 7–8 minutes

Scoring: Hand key

Cost: Specimen set (Bus Puzzle board, manual, 25 answer sheets) $75.00

Publisher: The Test Agency Ltd.

EXTENDED MERRILL-PALMER SCALE
Rachel Stutsman Ball,
Philip R. Merrifield, and
Leland H. Stott

Child—Ages 3–5

Purpose: Measures intelligence in children.

Description: 16–item task-assessment and oral-response test measuring the mental processes of evaluation and production with both semantic and figural units. The 16 tasks include tower building, ambiguous forms, food naming, dot joining, word meaning, pie completion, action agents, copying, round things, block sorting, following directions, 3–cube pyramid, 6–cube pyramid, action agents, stick manipulation, and design productions. Scores and percentile ranges are provided in six intervals from ages 3–5 for four specific abilities, each of which are tested by four of the tasks. The abilities are semantic production, figural production, semantic evaluation, and semantic production. The manual includes information on the development of the test items, instructions for administering and scoring, and case studies for 16 separate patterns of the four abilities at two age levels. Examiner required. Not suitable for group use.

Timed: 4–5 minutes

Scoring: Examiner evaluated

Cost: Complete kit (test materials, record forms, scoring forms, manual, carrying case) $425.00

Publisher: Stoelting Co.

THE FIVE P'S: PARENT/ PROFESSIONAL PRESCHOOL PERFORMANCE PROFILE
Refer to page 544.

===

THE FLINT INFANT SECURITY SCALE: FOR INFANTS AGED 3–24 MONTHS
Betty M. Flint

Child—Ages 3–24 months

Purpose: Assesses an infant's mental health and the behavior of the mother (or other parent) as she interacts with the child.

Description: 74–item paper-pencil behavior scale assessing a child's sense of security and feeling of self-worth and parental behavior. When the "psychological parent" is other than the natural mother or father, the scale is of special value to physicians, social workers, and child care agencies responsible for adop-

tion placements and foster care. Examiner required. Not suitable for group use.
CANADIAN PUBLISHER

Untimed: Not available

Scoring: Examiner evaluated

Cost: Specimen set (manual, scoring booklet) $5.50

Publisher: Guidance Centre

Information and availability unconfirmed; last verified in 1987.

GRIFFITHS MENTAL DEVELOPMENT SCALES
Refer to page 52.

===

HAWAII EARLY LEARNING PROFILE (HELP)
S. Furuno, K. O'Reilly, C. Hosaka, T. Inatsuka, P. Allman, and B. Zeisloft

---

Child—Ages 0–3

Purpose: Assesses self-help, language, motor, social, and cognitive skills of children. Used for early intervention, preschool placement, individual education prescriptions, and home plans.

Description: 650–item criterion-referenced inventory assessing the skills and behaviors of children. This visual assessment tool is used for planning, setting objectives, and recording progress. Two forms are available: chart and checklist. HELP Charts are a set of three charts displaying skills and behaviors formatted for visual tracking of progress and needs. The HELP Checklist presents each developmental area in column format for interdisciplinary team assessment and recording. The Activity Guide offers thousands of activities for each of the 650 skills. Cards and blocks are used as stimuli. Examiner required. Not suitable for group use.

Untimed: 8 hours

Scoring: Not available

Cost: Charts, checklists $2.95 each; activity guide $17.95

Publisher: VORT Corporation

Information and availability unconfirmed; last verified in 1988.

HOME OBSERVATION FOR MEASUREMENT OF THE ENVIRONMENT (HOME)
Refer to page 74.

HOME SCREENING QUESTIONNAIRE (HSQ)
Refer to page 74.

HOUSTON TEST FOR LANGUAGE DEVELOPMENT
Margaret Crabtree

Child—Ages 0–6

Purpose: Assesses verbal and nonverbal communication abilities in children. Diagnoses problems resulting from emotional deprivation, neurological disabilities, retardation, auditory or visual-motor deficits, or environmental linguistic influence. Used to plan specific intervention procedures and to monitor the child's progress.

Description: Multiple-item verbal and nonverbal checklist of communication abilities at two age levels. The Infant Scale consists of an observational checklist of linguistic and prelinguistic skills characteristic of normal infants up to 18 months of age. The 2–6 Year Test consists of 18 subtests that include both verbal and nonverbal tasks. The 18 subtests are Self-Identity, Vocabulary, Body Orientation, Gesture, Auditory Judgments, Oral Monitoring with Toys, Sentence Length, Temporal Content, Syntax, Prepositions, Serial Counting, Counting Objects, Imitates Linguistic Structure, Imitates Prosodic Patterns, Imitates Designs, Drawing, and Oral Monitoring While Drawing and Telling About Drawing. The manual provides normative data and information on reliability and validity. Individual child record forms serve as a work sheet, score sheet, and permanent record of the test performance. Examiner required. Not suitable for group use.

Untimed: 30 minutes

Scoring: Examiner evaluated

Cost: Complete kit (25 record forms, vocabulary cards, necessary manipulatives, manual) $82.75

Publisher: Stoelting Co.

HUMAN FIGURES DRAWING TEST
Eloy Gonzales

Child—Ages 5–10

Purpose: Measures the cognitive maturation of children. Used by teachers, diagnosticians, psychologists, speech therapists, and other professionals.

Description: Paper-pencil test assessing the nonverbal conceptual ability of children through analysis of drawings of human figures. Because the test does not require speech, it is useful with children who have verbal problems or do not speak English. Examiner required. Suitable for group use.

Untimed: 10–15 minutes

Scoring: Hand key; examiner evaluated

Cost: Complete kit (examiner's manual, 100 scoring forms, storage box) $49.00

Publisher: PRO-ED

HUMANICS NATIONAL CHILD ASSESSMENT FORMS: AGES 0–3 YEARS
Refer to page 548.

HUMANICS NATIONAL CHILD ASSESSMENT FORMS: AGES 3–6 YEARS
Refer to page 548.

KAUFMAN INFANT AND PRESCHOOL SCALE (KIPS)
Harvey Kaufman

Child

Purpose: Measures early high-level cognitive process and indicates possible need for intervention in normal children ages one month to four years and in retarded children and adults with mental ages of four years or less. Used by special education and early childhood teachers, psychologists, and physicians for a variety of screening purposes.

Description: Multiple-item task-assessment and observation measure of high-level cognitive thinking. The child is observed and asked to perform a number of tasks indicative of his level. All test items are "maturational prototypes" that can be taught to enhance maturation. The test covers general reasoning, storage, and verbal communication. The test yields the following scores: Overall Functioning Age (Mental Age) and Overall Functioning Quotient. Based on a child's performance on the scale, the manual suggests types of activities and general experience the child needs for effective general adaptive behavior. Examiner required. Not suitable for group use.

Untimed: 30 minutes

Scoring: Examiner evaluated

Cost: Complete kit (manipulatives, stimulus cards, 10 evaluation booklets) $225.00

Publisher: Stoelting Co.

KAUFMAN TEST OF EDUCATIONAL ACHIEVEMENT (K-TEA)
Refer to page 465.

KENT INFANT DEVELOPMENT SCALE (KID SCALE)
Jeanette M. Reuter, Lewis Katoff, and Kent Developmental Metrics, Inc. Staff

Child—Ages 0–8 years

Purpose: Screens and assesses the developmental strengths and weaknesses of infants and young handicapped children chronologically or developmentally under one year of age. Used by teachers, pediatricians, psychologists, nurses, therapists, and social workers for developmental evaluation, prescriptive programming, and as a basis for caregiver/professional conferences and counseling.

Description: 252–item paper-pencil or computer-administered inventory in which each item is a sentence stem that describes behaviors characteristic of an infant in its first year of life. Test items

cover five behavioral domains: Cognitive (52 items), Motor (78 items), Language (38 items), Self-Help (39 items), and Social (51 items). The child's parents or other caregivers mark the answer sheet to indicate which behaviors of the child have been observed.

A computer-scored printout lists items in order of developmental age by domain, compares the results for each domain and for the full scale with a normative sample of healthy infants, and furnishes developmental ages, a profile of strengths and weaknesses, and a timetable showing which developmental milestones will be achieved next.

Specifically, the test can be used with healthy infants (ages 0–12 months), infants at risk (ages 0–20 months), developmentally disabled infants (0–36 months), and severely handicapped young children (ages 2–8 years). The scale has been used for evaluating early intervention projects; monitoring the developmental progress of NICU graduates; teaching teenage mothers about their child's development and caregivers about techniques for observing infant behavior; designing Individual Habilitation Programs for severely brain-damaged children; and testing developmental hypotheses about at-risk infants and developmentally delayed children.

The computer version runs on Apple II systems. The publisher provides a computer scoring service. The English version requires a fourth-grade reading level. Examiner required. Suitable for group use. Available in Spanish (Castillian and Hispanic) and Dutch.

Untimed: 30–40 minutes

Scoring: Computer scored; hand key

Cost: Contact publisher

Publisher: Kent Developmental Metrics

LEXINGTON DEVELOPMENTAL SCALES (LDS)
Refer to page 552.

LINCOLN-OSERETSKY MOTOR DEVELOPMENT SCALE
Refer to page 613.

MAXFIELD-BUCHOLZ SOCIAL MATURITY SCALE FOR BLIND PRE-SCHOOL CHILDREN
Refer to page 665.

MCCARTHY SCALES OF CHILDREN'S ABILITIES
Dorothea McCarthy

Child—Ages 2.5–8.5

Purpose: Assesses intellectual and motor development of children.

Description: Measure of five aspects of children's thinking, motor, and mental abilities. The subtests are Verbal Ability, Short-Term Memory, Numerical Ability, Perceptual Performance, and Motor Coordination. The verbal, numerical, and perceptual performance scales are combined to yield the General Cognitive Index. Items involve puzzles, toy-like materials, and game-like tasks. Six of the 18 task components that predict the child's ability to cope with school work in the early grades form the McCarthy Screening Test. Examiner required. Not suitable for group use.

Untimed: 45–60 minutes

Scoring: Examiner evaluated

Cost: Complete set (all necessary equipment, manual, 25 record forms, 25 drawing booklets, carrying case) $295.00

Publisher: The Psychological Corporation

Information and availability unconfirmed; last verified in 1988.

MERRILL-PALMER SCALE
Refer to page 57.

MINNESOTA CHILD DEVELOPMENT INVENTORY (MCDI)
Harold Ireton and Edward Thwing

Child—Ages 1–6½

Purpose: Measures development of young child based on mother's observations. Used for clinical evaluation.

Description: 320–item paper-pencil or computer-administered yes-no format inventory completed by the mother to assess her child's current level of development. The inventory measures the child's general development, gross-motor, fine-motor, expressive language, comprehension-conceptual, situation-comprehension, self-help, and personal-social skills. For use with mothers with a high-school education. A computerized version of the MCDI is now available for use with Apple computers. The computerized version contains a complete system for self-administration, scoring, and interpretation. It also includes diskettes and a manual and produces a computerized MCDI Report. Examiner required. Suitable for group use.

Untimed: 20–30 minutes

Scoring: Hand key; may be computer scored

Cost: 10 reusable booklets $10.00; 25 answer sheets $7.00; 25 profile forms (specify male or female) $7.00; scoring templates $15.00; manual $14.00

Publisher: Behavior Science Systems, Inc.

MINNESOTA INFANT DEVELOPMENT INVENTORY (MIDI)
Harold Ireton and Edward Thwing

Child—Birth–15 months

Purpose: Assesses infant development in the first 15 months. Used for pediatric review, infant screening, and educating parents about their child's development.

Description: 75–item paper-pencil inventory completed by the child's mother in order to measure the child's development in five areas: gross motor, fine motor, language, comprehension, and personal-social. The test does not yield scores. Instead, it provides a framework for making sound professional judgments and serves as a guide for interviewing the mother. For use with mothers who have a high-school education. Examiner required. Suitable for group use.

Untimed: 10 minutes

Scoring: Examiner evaluated

Cost: 10 reusable booklets $7.00

Publisher: Behavior Science Systems, Inc.

MULLEN SCALES OF EARLY LEARNING (MSEL)
Eileen M. Mullen

Child—Ages 15–69 months

Purpose: Assesses the learning abilities and learning patterns of children. Identifies learning disabilities, mental retardation, the manner in which a child learns, and the manner in which a child should be taught.

Description: Multiple-item oral-response task-performance test consisting of four separate scales of visual and language ability. The scales can be used together for comprehensive evaluation or separately to assess problems in visual discrimination and memory, fine-motor development, language comprehension and memory, and verbal ability. The Visual Receptive Organization Scale assesses visual discrimination, organization, sequencing, visual concepts, and short-term visual memory. The Visual Expressive Organization Scale assesses unilateral and bilateral fine-motor development and writing. The Language Receptive Organization Scale assesses listening, listening/looking, sequencing, verbal concepts, general knowledge, and short- and long-term auditory memory. The Language Expressive Organization Scale assesses verbal ability, visual and oral vocabulary, abstract and practical reasoning, and short and long-term auditory memory. Examiner required. Not suitable for group use.

Untimed: Individual scales 12 minutes; complete test 45 minutes

Scoring: Examiner evaluated

Cost: Complete kit (carrying case, 25 record forms, 25 Paths worksheets, child safe materials) $279.00

Publisher: T.O.T.A.L. Child, Inc.

THE NEONATAL BEHAVIORAL ASSESSMENT SCALE
T. Berry Brazelton

Ages 0–1 month

Purpose: Evaluates selected reflexes, motor responses, and interactive behavioral responses of newborn infants. Predicts cognitive and emotional patterns in the infant. Used by medical professionals and paraprofessionals to teach parents about their newborn's state changes, temperament, and individual behavior patterns and to improve early health and developmental care.

Description: 47–item paper-pencil assessment procedure measuring neonatal reflex responses in a behavioral context. Twenty-seven behavioral items measure the infant's inherent neurological capacities, as well as responses to certain sets of stimuli. The behavioral section includes items that assess how soon the infant diminishes responses to stimuli of light, sound, and pinprick to the heel; auditory and visual items that determine how much and when the infant attends to, focuses on, and gives feedback in response to animate or inanimate stimuli; items assessing the degree and organization of the infant's motor coordination and control of motor activities throughout the examination; items assessing the infant's rate and amount of change during periods of alertness and state changes, color, activity, and peaks of excitement throughout the examination; items assessing how much, how soon, and how effectively the infant uses his own resources to quiet and console himself when upset or distressed (this category includes the graduated efforts of the caregiver to intervene and quiet the infant); and items assessing the infant's smiling and amount of cuddling behaviors. A second section of the scale includes 20 items assessing specific elicited reflexes and movements on a 3–point scale (hypoactive, normal, and hyperactive).

All scale items are scored in a manner which takes into account the infant's state (ranging from deep sleep to intense crying) at the time of testing. Some of the 27 behavioral items are scored during a specific interaction with the infant (such as head turning in response to a voice), but more are scored according to total continuous observations that are made throughout the entire assessment examination. For example, state changes, color changes, periods of alertness, and peaks of excitement are observed throughout the examination and scored at the conclusion. Repeated assessments (up to one month of age) are of considerably more value than just one assessment completed in the usual 20–30 minutes.

All persons using the scale must be trained in the proper administration of test items, order of examination procedures, optimal conditions of treating, and method of scoring. A list of trained examiners who can provide training may be obtained by writing directly to the principal investigator, Brazelton, at Children's Hospital Medical Center, 333 Longwood Avenue, Boston, MA 02115. It is essential that each examiner have a wide range of experience in assessing normal infants as a basis for scoring and interpreting the results of this scale. Examiner required. Not suitable for group use.

Untimed: 20–30 minutes per assessment

Scoring: Examiner evaluated

Cost: Contact publisher

Publisher: MacKeith Press; distributed in U.S.A. by Lippincott/Harper Publishers, Inc.

PEDIATRIC EARLY ELEMENTARY EXAMINATION (PEEX)
Refer to page 116.

PIP DEVELOPMENTAL CHARTS
Dorothy M. Jeffree and
Roy McConkey

Child—Ages 0–5

Purpose: Assesses the behavioral development of children. Identifies weaknesses in particular developmental areas. Provides a structured framework for recording a child's developmental progress. Used for screening and survey purposes.

Description: Paper-pencil inventory providing a behavioral checklist and profile of the most important stages of development in the first five years of a child's life. Development is measured in five main areas: physical, social, eye-hand coordination, play, and language skills. Each of these areas is subdivided into developmental sections, each beginning with a target behavior representing a "milestone" of development. Each section then lists the behavioral skills that lead up to that milestone and the approximate ages at which the skills are "normally" acquired. The purpose of the charts is the evaluation and furthering of individual children's development, not normative comparisons. Use of the charts secures the active participation of the parents and is particularly useful when developmental delay or handicap is suspected. Examiner required. Suitable for group use.
BRITISH PUBLISHER

Untimed: Not available

Scoring: Examiner evaluated

Cost: 10 charts £5.00 plus VAT

Publisher: Hodder & Stoughton

PRE-SCHOOL BEHAVIOUR CHECKLIST
Refer to page 745.

PRESCHOOL DEVELOPMENT INVENTORY (PDI)
Harold Ireton

Child—Ages 3–6

Purpose: Measures developmental level, symptoms, and behavioral problems. Identifies children with problems that may interfere with the ability to learn.

Description: 87–item paper-pencil questionnaire for obtaining a parent's report of the child's current functioning. The PDI is divided into five sections. The General Development section is a 60–item assessment of the child's overall development. It covers seven developmental areas: language comprehension (19 items), expressive language (14 items), fine motor (9 items), self-help (9 items), personal-social (5 items), situation-comprehension (2 items), and gross motor (2 items). The Possible Problems section is a 24–item list of symptoms and behavior problems. The 14 symptom items describe sensory, speech and language, comprehension, physical, and quasiphysical symptoms. The 10 behavioral problem items relate to immaturity, behavioral problems, hyperactivity, and emotional problems. The Child Description section is the parent's brief description of the child. The Special Problems or Handicaps section is the parent's report of problems that may be major handicaps or obstacles to learning. The Questions or Concerns section is the parent's report of their concerns or questions about the child.

The PDI is especially suited for use with a developmental screening test; however, when used as a pretesting questionnaire itself, only children whose parents report some concern should be tested. The parent may complete the inventory at home and bring it to the screening where it can be scored and interpreted. The results for each section of the inventory can be interpreted as showing no evidence of any problems, raising concern about a possible problem, or suggesting a possible major problem. These results indicate the need for follow-up evaluation. The manual includes instructions for administering, scoring, and interpreting the questionnaire. Examiner required. Suitable for group use.

Untimed: Varies

Scoring: Examiner evaluated

Cost: Manual $5.00; 25 answer sheets $7.00

Publisher: Behavior Science Systems, Inc.

PRESCREENING DEVELOPMENTAL QUESTIONNAIRE (PDQ)
Refer to page 557.

PRIMARY ACADEMIC SENTIMENT SCALE (PASS)
Refer to page 558.

PSYCHOLOGICAL STIMULUS RESPONSE
Eileen M. Mullen

Child—Ages 0–5

Purpose: Assesses the underlying intelligence and functional age of severely cerebral-palsied multihandicapped infants and young children and helps provide them with alternate ways of responding to questions and statements.

Description: Card-response test measuring language, visual processing, and general intelligence. Materials include a manual, vocabulary card booklet, response card booklet, and a protocol-score sheet book. The examiner shows the appropriate cards to the child. The child chooses one of three cards presented and, if mute, can respond with eye movements or by pointing. Examiner required. Not suitable for group use.

Untimed: 15 minutes

Scoring: Hand key

Cost: Complete set $35.00

Publisher: Meeting Street School, Rhode Island Easter Seal Society

Information and availability unconfirmed; last verified in 1987.

A QUICK SCREENING SCALE OF MENTAL DEVELOPMENT
Katherine M. Banham

Child—Ages 6 months–10 years

Purpose: Assesses a child's mental development. Identifies children in need of clinical evaluation. Used in clinics, hospitals, and special schools.

Description: Task-assessment and observational instrument arranged in five behavioral categories to measure a child's mental development. The test booklet consists of brief descriptions of behavior occurring in certain situations. The situations are to be checked and scored directly on the booklet. Instructions for administering are provided in the manual. Professional persons skilled in clinical interviewing procedures may administer the test, but persons trained in clinical psychology should interpret the results. The test provides a profile of scores in the five behavior categories for diagnostic purposes and educational guidance. Tentative norms for 50 children, along with the children's scores on the Cattell Infant

Scale and the Stanford-Binet Scale, are provided. Examiner required. Not suitable for group use.

Untimed: 30 minutes

Scoring: Hand key

Cost: Specimen set $5.00; 25 tests $5.00

Publisher: Psychometric Affiliates

THE REVISED DEVELOPMENTAL SCREENING INVENTORY
Hilda Knobloch, Frances Stevens, and Anthony F. Malone

Child—Ages 4 weeks–36 months

Purpose: Determines whether a child is functioning at age level. Screens for abnormalities requiring more detailed examination.

Description: Multiple-item yes-no assessment covering 20 age levels. Five areas are assessed: adaptive, gross motor, fine motor, language, and personal-social. Preliminary questions answered by the child's parent or caregiver are followed by observation of the child's behavior. The evaluation begins at the child's chronologic age and proceeds to lower or higher age levels as needed. The maturity level is assigned by determining how well a child's behavior fits one age level constellation. Nine videotapes are available in addition to the questionnaire. Examiner required. Not suitable for group use.

Untimed: 10–30 minutes

Scoring: Examiner evaluated

Cost: 100 copies $40.00

Publisher: Developmental Evaluation Materials, Inc.

Information and availability unconfirmed; last verified in 1987.

REVISED PRESCREENING DEVELOPMENTAL QUESTIONNAIRE (R-PDQ)
Refer to page 560.

REYNELL DEVELOPMENTAL LANGUAGE SCALES—SECOND REVISION
Joan Reynell and M. Huntley

Child—Ages 1½–6

Purpose: Assesses expressive language and verbal comprehension. Used for evaluation of language development.

Description: Multiple-item performance tests of expressive and receptive language development: Verbal Comprehension Scale and Expressive Language Scale. Materials include the necessary toys and pictures. The test is suitable for use with hearing-impaired children. The test is a revision of the Experimental Edition of the scales. Examiner required. Not suitable for group use.
BRITISH PUBLISHER

Untimed: 1 hour

Scoring: Examiner evaluated

Cost: Contact publisher

Publisher: NFER-NELSON Publishing Company Ltd.

REYNELL-ZINKIN DEVELOPMENT SCALES FOR YOUNG VISUALLY HANDICAPPED CHILDREN
Refer to page 561.

RING AND PEG TESTS OF BEHAVIOR DEVELOPMENT FOR INFANTS AND PRESCHOOL CHILDREN
Katherine M. Banham

Child—Ages 0–6

Purpose: Measures the development of infants and preschool children and helps identify the social and motivational factors influential in a child's development. Used for clinical assessment of infant and child development.

Description: Task-assessment test measuring five categories of behavioral performance and ability: ambulative, manipulative, communicative, social-adaptive, and emotive. The test covers a wider range of items than standard intelligence tests in order to provide the clinical psychologist with diagnostic information. The scale yields a point score and a behavior age for the whole test, as well as for each of the five categories. A developmental quotient (D Q) may be derived from the full-scale behavior age. The test kit includes minimally culture-bound manipulation objects, manual, test booklet, and scoring sheet. Examiner required. Not suitable for group use.

Untimed: 45 minutes

Scoring: Hand key

Cost: Professional examination kit (25 tests, handbook) $20.00; 25 score sheets $5.00

Publisher: Psychometric Affiliates

ROCKFORD INFANT DEVELOPMENTAL SCALES (RIDES)
Refer to page 561.

SCALE OF SOCIAL DEVELOPMENT (SSD)
John J. Venn, Thomas S. Serwatka, and Robert A. Anthony

Child—Ages birth–6 years

Purpose: Screens for deficits, diagnoses social skills, measures progress, assists in writing program objectives, guides instruction and remediation, and assesses strengths and weaknesses. Used with deaf, multihandicapped, visually impaired, hearing impaired, orthopedically impaired, mentally retarded, and language-disordered children.

Description: Multiple-item nonverbal observation of the examinee engaged in various activities. The Screening form contains 40 items. The Comprehensive Assessment (120 items) covers the following skill clusters: Identifies/Investigates (38 items), Complies/Prefers (41 items), and Participates/Socializes (41 items). Results are presented as subtest raw scores, percent accuracy, and age equivalents. Examiner required. Not suitable for group use.

Untimed: Varies

Scoring: Examiner evaluated

Cost: Complete kit $39.00

Publisher: PRO-ED

THE SCHEDULE OF GROWING SKILLS (DEVELOPMENTAL SCREENING PROCEDURE 0–5)
M. Bellman and J. Cash

Child—Ages 0–5

Purpose: Assesses the developmental progress of children. Used by health visitors, doctors, clinical medical officers, pediatricians, and psychologists as a screening and record system.

Description: Multiple-item task-performance screening test measuring child development in nine areas: passive posture, active posture, locomotor skills, manipulative skills, visual skills, hearing and language skills, speech and language skills, interactive social skills, and self-care social skills. Items are listed in developmental sequence within the nine fields. Results can be expressed numerically or as a profile. Up to four screenings of one child may be recorded on the main record form. The test is based on Mary Sheridan's STYCAR developmental sequences. Examiner required. Not suitable for group use.

BRITISH PUBLISHER

Untimed: 10–15 minutes

Scoring: Examiner evaluated

Cost: Contact publisher

Publisher: NFER-NELSON Publishing Company Ltd.

THE SCHOOL READINESS CHECKLIST
Refer to page 562.

SCHOOL READINESS EVALUATION BY TRAINED TESTERS (SETT)—1984
Refer to page 563.

SCHOOL READINESS SCREENING TEST
Refer to page 563.

SCHOOL READINESS SURVEY
Refer to page 563.

S.E.E.D. DEVELOPMENTAL PROFILES

Child

Purpose: Assesses the functioning level of children between the developmental ages of 4 weeks–6 years.

Description: Multiple-item paper-pencil criterion-referenced inventories for assessing gross-motor, fine-motor, adaptive reasoning, social and emotional, self-help, and speech and language skills. The test provides a functional appraisal of a handicapped child's abilities, monitors individual progress, and helps plan individual education programs. Items below the one-year level are presented in four-week intervals; between the one- and two-year level, in three-month intervals; and between the two- and six-year level, in six-month intervals. The test contains a graph for each development area and a master graph for a composite picture of the child's levels and progress. The profiles are compiled from various standardized assessment tools. Examiner required. Not suitable for group use.

Untimed: 1 hour

Scoring: Examiner evaluated

Cost: Complete kit (record forms, instructions, material list) $6.00

Publisher: Sewall Rehabilitation Center

Information and availability unconfirmed; last verified in 1987.

SMITH-JOHNSON NONVERBAL PERFORMANCE SCALE
Alathena J. Smith and Ruth E. Johnson

Child—Ages 2–4

Purpose: Provides a nonverbal assessment of the developmental level of children. Used to evaluate hearing-impaired, language-delayed, culturally deprived, and handicapped children.

Description: 14–category examination using nonverbal tasks to measure the developmental level of a broad range of skills in young children. Each category consists of a series of subtasks presented in order of increasing difficulty. With the exception of two tasks, the examiner proceeds to the first task in the next category as soon as the child has failed two consecutive tasks. All but one of the tasks are untimed. The test measures strengths and weaknesses across a broad range of skills without constricting the evaluation by labeling the child with a single quantitative score. Norms are provided for both hearing-impaired children and normals. Examiner required. Not suitable for group use.

Untimed: 30–45 minutes

Scoring: Hand key; examiner evaluated

Cost: Complete kit (test materials, record sheets, manual) $120.00

Publisher: Western Psychological Services

SONKSEN-SILVER ACUITY SYSTEM
Refer to page 730.

STEPS UP DEVELOPMENTAL SCREENING PROGRAM (SUDS)
Shirley Cliff, Diane Carr, Jennifer Gray, Carol Nymann, and Sandra Redding

Child—Ages 0–3

Purpose: Assesses/screens developmental delays.

Description: Criterion-referenced test with nine subtests: Gross Motor, Fine Motor, Language, Cognitive/Social, Vision, Hearing, Head Circumference, Congenitally Dislocated Hips, and Convulsive Disorders. The program consists of a series of 32 test cards designed to be used by trained volunteers to screen children aged 0–3 years. Tests measure abnormal/normal development. Scores yield developmental age. Other materials include common toys. This test is suitable for use with individuals with visual, hearing, physical, and mental impairments. Examiner must have a knowledge of normal development. Examiner required. Not suitable for group use.

Untimed: 5 minutes

Scoring: Examiner evaluated

Cost: Manual $7.00; kit alone $28.00; combined $35.00

Publisher: El Paso Rehabilitation Center

STYCAR CHART OF DEVELOPMENTAL SEQUENCES (REVISED 1975 EDITION)
Mary D. Sheridan

Child—Ages 1 month–5 years

Purpose: Assesses normal development of children. Used for clinical screening.

Description: Multiple-item chart indicating the steps in normal child development. The package includes testing procedures designed to supplement a general pediatric examination. The instrument is available as a wall chart and as a pocket-size pamphlet. It is not for public display in clinic waiting rooms. Available to medical doctors, speech therapists, and teachers of the deaf, blind, and physically handicapped. Examiner required. Not suitable for group use.
BRITISH PUBLISHER

Untimed: Not available

Scoring: Examiner evaluated

Cost: Contact publisher

Publisher: NFER-NELSON Publishing Company Ltd.

STYCAR VISION TESTS
Refer to page 731.

SYMBOLIC PLAY TEST—SECOND EDITION (SPT: 2 ED)
Refer to page 715.

TEST OF RELATIONAL CONCEPTS (TRC)
Refer to page 568.

VULPÉ ASSESSMENT BATTERY
Shirley German Vulpé

Handicapped children— Ages 0–6

Purpose: Evaluates the developmental status of atypically developing children.

Description: 1,127–item performance analysis/developmental assessment of functioning in eight developmental skill areas (basic senses and functions, gross-motor behaviors, fine-motor behaviors, language behaviors, cognitive processes and specific concepts, the organization of behavior, activities of daily living) and one environmental domain (environment). Information about an individual child is obtained through direct observation or from a knowledgeable informant. Examiner required. Not suitable for group use.

Untimed: Not available

Scoring: Examiner evaluated

Cost: Complete battery $20.00; 75 scoring pads $2.50

Publisher: National Institute on Mental Retardation

Information and availability unconfirmed; last verified in 1987.

THE WISCONSIN BEHAVIOR RATING SCALE (WBRS)
Refer to page 669.

Geropsychology

AMSLER CHART
Refer to page 723.

ANOMALOUS SENTENCES REPETITION TEST
Refer to page 95.

CALIFORNIA LIFE GOALS EVALUATION SCHEDULES
Refer to page 161.

CALIFORNIA VERBAL LEARNING TEST, RESEARCH EDITION
Refer to page 98.

CLIFTON ASSESSMENT PROCEDURES FOR THE ELDERLY (CAPE)
A.H. Pattie and C.J. Gilleard

Elderly adults

Purpose: Assesses level of dependency in the elderly. Used by general practitioners, community nurses, health visitors, occupational therapists, social workers, and hospital personnel.

Description: Two multiple-item paper-pencil rating scales assessing cognitive and behavioral competence in the elderly. The Cognitive Assessment Scale is a short psychological test comprised of three sections: information/orientation, mental ability, and psychomotor. The psychomotor section utilizes the Gibson Spiral Maze. The Behavioral Rating Scale consists of 18 items measuring physical disability, apathy, communication difficulties, and social disturbance. The scoring procedure relates the level of cognitive and behavioral dependency to likely need for community or hospital care. The test is restricted to senior staff members of any recognized medical or educational institution, medical doctors, and BPS and APA members. Examiner required. Not suitable for group use.

Untimed: Varies

Scoring: Examiner evaluated

Cost: Contact publisher

Publisher: Hodder and Stoughton Educational; distributed in U.S.A. by The Psychological Corporation

CONTINUOUS VISUAL MEMORY TEST (CVMT)
Refer to page 100.

DEMENTIA RATING SCALE (DRS)
Steven Mattis

Adult—Ages 65–81

Purpose: Provides a brief, comprehensive measure of cognitive status in individuals with cortical impairment, particularly of the degenerative type.

Description: 36–task oral-response short-answer verbal and copying test comprised of five subscales that measure Attention, Initiation/Perseveration, Construction, Conceptualization, and Memory. It provides a measure of cognitive function at lower levels of ability. Test-retest reliability for the DRS total score, subscale correlations, split-half reliability, and validity is detailed in the manual. The manual also includes further studies describing the development and validation of the DRS. Materials include manual, scoring/recording forms, and stimulus cards. Examiner must meet APA guidelines. Examiner required. Not suitable for group use.

Untimed: 15–45 minutes

Scoring: Examiner evaluated

Cost: DRS Kit (manual, 25 scoring/recording forms, stimulus cards) $39.00

Publisher: Psychological Assessment Resources, Inc.

ENVIRONMENTAL RESPONSE INVENTORY (ERI)
Refer to page 262.

FRENCHAY APHASIA SCREENING TEST (FAST)
Refer to page 104.

FULD OBJECT-MEMORY EVALUATION
Paula Altman Fuld

Adult—Ages 70–90

Purpose: Measures memory and learning in adults regardless of vision, hearing, or language handicaps; cultural differences; or inattention problems.

Description: 10 common objects in a bag are presented to the patient to determine whether he can identify them by touch. The patient names the item and then pulls it out of the bag to see if he was right. After being distracted, the patient is asked to recall the items from the bag. The patient is given four additional chances to learn and recall the objects.

The test provides separate scores for long-term storage, retrieval, consistency of retrieval, and failure to recall items even after being reminded. The test also provides a chance to observe naming ability, left-right orientation, stereognosis, and verbal fluency. Separate norms are provided for total recall, storage, consistency of retrieval, ability to benefit from reminding, and ability to say words in categories. Examiner required. Not suitable for group use.

Timed: 60 seconds for each first trial, 30 seconds for each second trial

Scoring: Examiner evaluated

Cost: Complete kit (testing materials, manual, record forms) $22.25; 30 record forms $6.25

Publisher: Stoelting Co.

FUNCTIONAL PERFORMANCE RECORD
Refer to page 651.

GERIATRIC DEPRESSION SCALE
T.L. Brink, Jerome Yesavage,
P. Heersema, O. Lum, M. Adey,
T.L. Rose, V.O. Leirer, and V. Huang

Elderly adults

Purpose: Diagnoses depression in the elderly.

Description: 30–item oral-response test assessing the level of depression in older adults. Questions seek "yes" or "no" responses. The test can be administered in oral or written format. The test can be used with other age groups, including adolescents, but loses validity as dementia increases. Examiner required. Not suitable for group use. Available in Spanish and French.

Untimed: 5–15 minutes

Scoring: Examiner evaluated

Cost: Free

Publisher: T.L. Brink

GERIATRIC PARANOIA SCALE
T.L. Brink and Javaid Sheikh

Elderly adults

Purpose: Measures paronoid behavior in older adults.

Description: Paper-pencil rating scale completed by examiner to measure paranoid behavior in elderly adults. Examiner required. Not suitable for group use.

Untimed: Not available

Scoring: Examiner evaluated

Cost: Free

Publisher: T.L. Brink

GERIATRIC SENTENCE COMPLETION FORM (GSCF)
Peter LeBray

Elderly adults

Purpose: Assesses the personal and social adjustment of elderly adults. Used by clinicians working with the elderly in hospitals, long-term care facilities, outpatient settings, community care programs, and private offices.

Description: 30–item oral-response or paper-pencil projective test assessing elderly individuals' adjustment in four domains: physical, psychological, social, and temporal. The individual is asked to complete fragmentary sentence stems by using either written or verbal responses. The manual includes information on the development, structure, administration, and interpretation of the test and a number of clinical case illustrations. Examiner required. Suitable for group use.

Untimed: Varies

Scoring: Examiner evaluated

Cost: Manual, 50 forms $8.95

Publisher: Psychological Assessment Resources, Inc.

THE GRADED NAMING TEST
Refer to page 105.

GROOVED PEGBOARD
Refer to page 106.

HILL INTERACTION MATRIX-A (HIM-A)
Refer to page 242.

HILL INTERACTION MATRIX-B (HIM-B)
Refer to page 243.

HILL INTERACTION MATRIX-G (HIM-G)
Refer to page 243.

HOUSE-TREE-PERSON (H-T-P) PROJECTIVE TECHNIQUE
Refer to page 244.

HUMAN ACTIVITY PROFILE (HAP)
Refer to page 180.

HYPOCHONDRIASIS SCALE: INSTITUTIONAL GERIATRIC
*T.L. Brink, James Bryant,
Judy Belanger, Diane Capri,
Suzanne Jascula, Connie Janakes,
and Charmaine Oliveira*

Elderly adults

Purpose: Assesses hypochondriacal attitudes of institutionalized elderly.

Description: 6–item oral-response test measuring hypochondriacal attitudes, rather than behaviors, of the institutionalized elderly. The test can be administered in an oral or written format and used with noninstitutionalized elderly, young adults, and adolescents, although no precise validity studies have been performed with the latter two groups. Examiner required. Not suitable for group use. Available in Spanish.

Untimed: 1–3 minutes

Scoring: Examiner evaluated

Cost: Free

Publisher: T.L. Brink

INTERNATIONAL VERSION OF MENTAL STATUS QUESTIONNAIRE
Refer to page 108.

INVENTORY FOR CLIENT AND AGENCY PLANNING (ICAP)
Refer to page 665.

KENDRICK COGNITIVE TESTS FOR THE ELDERLY
D. Kendrick

Adult—Ages 55 and older

Purpose: Identifies early dementia and depressive psychosis of adults.

Description: Multiple-item paper-pencil oral-response test made up of two subtests detecting early dementia and depressive psychosis by assessing short-term memory and speed of responding. The two subtests, Object Learning and Digit Copying, are designed for longitudinal use in hospitals or clinics. The test is a major revision of the Kendrick Battery for detecting dementia in the elderly. Examiner required. Not suitable for group use. BRITISH PUBLISHER

Untimed: 15 minutes

Scoring: Examiner evaluated

Cost: Contact publisher

Publisher: NFER-NELSON Publishing Company Ltd.

OARS MULTIDIMENSIONAL FUNCTIONAL ASSESSMENT QUESTIONNAIRE
Refer to page 114.

ORGANIC INTEGRITY TEST (OIT)
Refer to page 115.

THE PROJECTIVE ASSESSMENT OF AGING METHOD (PAAM)
*Bernard D. Starr,
Marcella Bakur Weiner, and
Marilyn Rabetz*

Adult

Purpose: Assesses the adaptations, potential crisis situations, and areas of conflict unique to the phenomenology of aging. Used for clinical evaluation.

Description: 28–item oral-response projective test consisting of 31 drawings for use in clinical administration: 14 standard pictures with male/female alternatives and 14 alternates. The scenes are related to aging and elicit feelings, attitudes, and perceptions of the subjects that give clues to their emotional and cognitive frame of mind. Examiner required. Not suitable for group use.

Untimed: Not available

Scoring: Examiner evaluated

Cost: Complete kit (28 cards, manual) $35.00

Publisher: Springer Publishing Company

Information and availability unconfirmed; last verified in 1987.

RANDT MEMORY TEST
Refer to page 120.

RECOGNITION MEMORY TEST
Refer to page 121.

RETIREMENT DESCRIPTIVE INDEX (RDI)
Refer to page 214.

REVISED TOKEN TEST
Refer to page 123.

SALAMON-CONTE LIFE SATISFACTION IN THE ELDERLY SCALE (LSES)
Michael J. Salamon and Vincent A. Conte

Elderly adults

Purpose: Assesses the quality of life of the elderly. Used with the elderly for screening, counseling, and treatment evaluation.

Description: 40–item paper-pencil multiple-choice sentence-completion inventory assessing elderly adults' reactions to their ecological, emotional, and social environ-

ments. The inventory evaluates the following areas, which are particularly important to the elderly: taking pleasure in daily activities, regarding life as meaningful, the relationship between desired and achieved goals, positive mood, positive self-concept, perceived health and financial security, and satisfaction with number and quality of social contacts. The inventory yields a total score and eight subscale scores. Examiner required. Suitable for group use.

Untimed: 20 minutes

Scoring: Hand key

Cost: Test kit (manual, 50 test booklets, 50 scoring sheets) $21.95

Publisher: Psychological Assessment Resources, Inc.

THE SEEKING OF NOETIC GOALS TEST (SONG)
Refer to page 219.

THE SENIOR APPERCEPTION TECHNIQUE (SAT)
Refer to page 220.

SERIAL DIGIT LEARNING TEST
Refer to page 127.

STIMULUS RECOGNITION TEST
Refer to page 129.

STROOP NEUROPSYCHOLOGICAL SCREENING TEST (SNST)
Refer to page 130.

THE TEST OF NONVERBAL INTELLIGENCE-2 (TONI-2)
Refer to page 63.

TESTS OF MENTAL FUNCTION IN THE ELDERLY

Adult

Purpose: Screens for impairment of mental functions in the elderly.

Description: 20–item paper-pencil and verbal test assessing 10 areas of mental function in the elderly: orientation, sentence learning, counting backwards, mental control, digit retention, 5–minute memory, digit copying, associated memory, simple arithmetic, and general knowledge. Items are contained on a series of paper sheets and are presented orally by the examiner. Responses are recorded by the examiner on the provided score pad. Comments regarding age norms and interpretation of test results are presented on the flip side of each test question sheet. Examiner required. Not suitable for group use.

Untimed: 15 minutes

Scoring: Examiner evaluated

Cost: Contact publisher

Publisher: Wyeth Laboratories, Inc.

Information and availability unconfirmed; last verified in 1987.

WECHSLER MEMORY SCALE (WMS)
Refer to page 134.

WECHSLER MEMORY SCALE—REVISED (WMS-R)
Refer to page 134.

Intelligence and Related

ACER ADVANCED TEST AL-AQ (SECOND EDITION) AND BL-BQ
Refer to page 582.

ACER ADVANCED TEST B40 (REVISED)
Refer to page 583.

ACER HIGHER TESTS: WL-WQ, ML-MQ (SECOND EDITION) AND PL-PQ
Refer to page 584.

ACER INTERMEDIATE TEST F
Refer to page 584.

ACER INTERMEDIATE TEST G
Refer to page 584.

ACER JUNIOR A TEST
Refer to page 585.

AN ADAPTATION OF THE WECHSLER INTELLIGENCE SCALE FOR CHILDREN—REVISED FOR THE DEAF
Steven Ray

Child, adolescent—Ages 6–16

Purpose: Assesses the intellectual ability of deaf children. Used by psychologists with or without signing skills.

Description: Multiple-item test providing alternate and supplemental items for the Performance Scale of the Wechsler Intelligence Scale for Children—Revised. The subscales of this adaptation are the same as those of the WISC-R: Picture Completion, Picture Arrangement, Block Design, Object Assembly, Coding, and Mazes. The adaptation is designed to minimize communication variables between the child and the examiner, resulting in a nonbiased assessment. Instructions for using an interpreter are included. Examiner required. Not suitable for group use. Available in American Sign Language.

Untimed: Varies

Scoring: Examiner evaluated

Cost: Manual with supplemental and alternate instructions $37.00; postage and handling $2.50

Publisher: Steven Ray Publishing

Information and availability unconfirmed; last verified in 1988.

AN ADAPTATION OF THE WECHSLER PRESCHOOL AND PRIMARY SCALE OF INTELLIGENCE FOR DEAF CHILDREN
Steven Ray and Stephen M. Ulissi

Child

Purpose: Assesses intelligence in deaf children.

Description: Multiple-item test providing alternate and supplemental items for the Performance Scale of the Wechsler Preschool and Primary Scale of Intelligence for Deaf Children. The subscales for this adaptation are the same as those of the WPPSI: Animal House, Picture Completion, Mazes, Geometric Design, and Block Design. The adaptation is designed to minimize communication variables between the child and the examiner, resulting in a nonbiased assessment. Examiner required. Not suitable for group use. Available in American Sign Language.

Untimed: Not available

Scoring: Examiner evaluated

Cost: Manual with supplemental and alternate instructions $37.00; postage and handling $2.50

Publisher: Steven Ray Publishing

Information and availability unconfirmed; last verified in 1988.

ADVANCED PROGRESSIVE MATRICES (APM)
J.C. Raven

Adolescent, adult

Purpose: Assesses the mental ability of people with above-average intellectual ability by means of nonverbal abstract reasoning tasks. Used for school and vocational counseling and placement and for research.

Description: 48–item paper-pencil nonverbal test in two sets. Set I contains 12 problems and is used as a practice test for Set II, which consists of 36 problems. In each problem, the subject is presented with a pattern or figure design with a missing part. The subject selects one of six possible parts as the correct one. Answer sheets are provided. Examiner required. Suitable for group use. BRITISH PUBLISHER

Timed: 40 minutes

Untimed: 60 minutes

Scoring: Hand key

Cost: 25 Set I tests £30.00; 25 Set II tests £70.00; 50 hand-scorable Set I and Set II record forms £4.50; plastic marking key £6.70 plus V.A.T.

Publisher: H.K. Lewis & Co. Ltd.; distributed in U.S.A. by The Psychological Corporation

Information and availability unconfirmed; last verified in 1987.

AH4 GROUP TEST OF GENERAL INTELLIGENCE (REGULAR EDITION)
Refer to page 585.

AH5 GROUP TEST OF HIGH GRADE INTELLIGENCE
Refer to page 586.

ARTHUR POINT SCALE OF PERFORMANCE, FORM I
Grace Arthur

Ages 4–adult

Purpose: Measures intelligence of children and adults. Used as a nonverbal supplement to the highly verbalized Binet tests, especially with people with language, speech, emotional, or cultural problems.

Description: 10 nonverbal task-assessment subtests measuring intelligence: Mare-Foal Formboard, Sequin-Goddard Formboard, Pintner-Paterson 2–Figure Formboard, Casuist Formboard, Pintner-Manikin Test, Knox-Kempf Feature Profile Test, Knox Cube Imitation Test, Healy Pictorial Completion Test 1, Kohs Block Design Test, and Porteus Mazes. The test is particularly useful as a supplement to the Binet scale in cases in which a child's environmental conditions vary widely from those of the average child. The comparison is of value whether it confirms the Binet ratings or reveals a disparity in verbal and nonverbal development. Examiner required. Not suitable for group use.

Untimed: Not available

Scoring: Examiner evaluated

Cost: Complete kit (tests, 50 record cards, manual) $495.00; 50 record cards $14.00

Publisher: Stoelting Co.

BLOOM ANALOGIES TEST (BAT)
Philip Bloom

Adult

Purpose: Assesses high-level verbal reasoning ability in adults.

Description: 50–item paper-pencil multiple-choice test providing rapid assessment of general intelligence level to a 5 sigma ceiling (top 3 million) without testing for factual knowledge or perseverance traits. Examinee chooses best response to a verbal analogy. Used to select members for high I Q societies, including Triple Nine Society, International Society for Philosophical Enquiry, Prometheus, and Mega. May require a general high-school education within the United States for representative scoring by examinees. Separate norms are provided for individuals who take the test while being timed and for those who take the test untimed. Self-administered. Suitable for group use.

Timed: 15 minutes

Untimed: Varies

Scoring: Hand key; scoring completed only by publisher

Cost: Test copies are free; scoring report from publisher $5.00

Publisher: Philip Bloom

Information and availability unconfirmed; last verified in 1987.

THE BRITISH ABILITY SCALES, REVISED EDITION
Refer to page 587.

CATTELL INFANT INTELLIGENCE SCALE
Refer to page 29.

COGNITIVE DIAGNOSTIC BATTERY (CDB)
Refer to page 649.

COLOURED PROGRESSIVE MATRICES
J.C. Raven

Child, adult—Ages 5–11 and adult

Purpose: Assesses the mental ability of young children and older adults who are mentally subnormal or impaired. Used for school and clinical counseling and research.

Description: 36–item paper-pencil nonverbal test consisting of design and pattern problems printed in several colors, including the two easiest sets from SPM, and a dozen additional items of similar difficulty. In each problem, the subject is presented with a pattern or figure design with a missing part. The subject selects one of six possible parts as the correct one. Examiner required. Suitable for group use above age eight. Standard norms were developed in Great Britain; U.S. norms are available. BRITISH PUBLISHER

Untimed: 15–30 minutes

Scoring: Hand key

Cost: Specimen set (book of tests, 12 combined Coloured Matrices, Sections 1, 2, and 6 of manual, Crichton Vocabulary Scale Forms) £13.90 plus V.A.T.; 25 tests £86.00

Publisher: H.K. Lewis & Co. Ltd.; distributed in U.S.A. by The Psychological Corporation

Information and availability unconfirmed; last verified in 1987.

COLUMBIA MENTAL MATURITY SCALE (CMMS)
Bessie B. Burgemeister,
Lucille Hollander Blum, and
Irving Lorge

Child—Ages 3¹⁄₂–10

Purpose: Assesses mental ability. Used with preschoolers, kindergartners, or children with physical or verbal impairments.

Description: 92–item test of general reasoning abilities. Items are arranged in a series of eight overlapping levels. The level administered is determined by the child's chronological age. Items are printed on 95 (6″ x 19″) cards. The child responds by selecting from each series of drawings the one that does not belong. Materials include item cards and a Guide for Administration and Interpretation, which includes directions in Spanish. Examiner required. Not suitable for group use.

Untimed: 15–20 minutes

Scoring: Examiner evaluated

Cost: Examiner's kit (95 item cards, guide) $249.00; 35 individual record forms $29.00

Publisher: The Psychological Corporation

Information and availability unconfirmed; last verified in 1988.

THE CULTURE FAIR SERIES: SCALES 1, 2, 3
Raymond B. Cattell and A.K.S. Cattell

Ages 4 and older

Purpose: Measures individual intelligence for a wide range of ages without, as much as possible, the influence of verbal fluency, cultural climate, and educational level. Identifies learning and emotional problems. Used in employee selection and placement, special education decisions, and college, career, and vocational counseling.

Description: Nonverbal paper-pencil (except for part of Scale 1) tests arranged in three scales to cover the age range of four years to adult. Test items require only that the subject be able to perceive relationships in shapes and figures. Scale 1 (ages 4–8 and older retardates) differs from Scales 2 and 3 in that it is not wholly nonverbal or wholly group administered. It consists of eight subtests, four of which must be individually administered. A set of cards and some common objects are required for two of the subtests. Scales 2 and 3 contain four paper-pencil subtests

of perceptual tasks: Completing Series, Classifying, Solving Incomplete Designs, and Evaluating Conditions. Scale 2 can be used with children as young as eight years old and with older children and adults. Scale 3 is more difficult than Scale 2 and obtains a greater refinement in the higher intelligence ranges. It is used with high school and college students and adults of superior intelligence. The choice of scales to be administered is based on the examiner's evaluation of the potential ability level to be tested. Scale 1 provides mental age and IQ scores; Scales 2 and 3 provide percentiles (by age), IQs, and special norms for untimed administration of Scale 2. Examiner required. Suitable for group use (except as noted for Scale 1). Available in Spanish.

Timed: Scale 1 22 minutes; Scales 2 and 3 12½ minutes per form

Scoring: Hand key

Cost: Scale 1: reusable classification test cards $18.25; 25 nonreusable test booklets $13.00; scoring key $3.25; handbook $3.75; Scales 2 and 3: 25 reusable test booklets $11.95–12.50; 50 answer sheets (all scales) $8.75; scoring keys (answer sheets) $3.75; scoring keys (test booklets) $3.25; tape recording (Scale 2) $29.95; manual $6.95; technical supplement $7.75

Publisher: Institute for Personality and Ability Testing, Inc.

EXTENDED MERRILL-PALMER SCALE
Refer to page 32.

===

FOUR SIGMA QUALIFYING TEST (FSQT)
Kevin Langdon et al.

Adult

Purpose: Assesses general intelligence and attention in reasoning. Used by individuals seeking information on their intelligence quotients or admission to societies such as Minerva, Triple 9, Four Sigma, and Prometheus. May also be used with gifted children.

Description: 54–item paper-pencil or computer-administered multiple-choice test assessing general intelligence and

---

attention in reasoning. The items are divided into two categories, each containing 27 items: Symbolic and Spatial. The Symbolic category includes nine number series items, six letter series items, and 12 miscellaneous symbolic items. The Spatial category contains nine figure series and 18 miscellaneous spatial items. Symbolic, Spatial, and Total scores are reported. This test first appeared in *NET* in 1985. A good command of the English language is required. Computer version operates on IBM PC, XT, and AT systems. Self-administered. Not suitable for group use.

Untimed: 10–20 hours

Scoring: Computer scored by publisher

Cost: Test booklet, answer sheet, score report, and statistical report $19.85

Publisher: Polymath Systems

FULL-RANGE PICTURE VOCABULARY TEST (FRPV)
R.B. Ammons and H.S. Ammons

Ages 2–adult

Purpose: Assesses individual intelligence. May be used for testing special populations, such as physically handicapped, uncooperative, aphasic, or very young subjects.

Description: 16–item test of verbal comprehension. The subject matches each item (a word) to one of four drawings on 16 cards. The subject may respond either by pointing or by indicating "yes" or "no" as the examiner points to each drawing. No reading or writing is required of the subject. Two parallel forms, A and B, which use the same set of stimulus plates, are available. Examiner required. Not suitable for group use.

Untimed: 5–10 minutes

Scoring: Hand key; examiner evaluated

Cost: Set of plates, with instructions, norms, and sample answer sheets $15.00; 25 answer sheets (specify Form A or B) $2.50

Publisher: Psychological Test Specialists

GOODENOUGH-HARRIS DRAWING TEST
Florence L. Goodenough and Dale B. Harris

Child, adolescent—Ages 3–15

Purpose: Assesses mental ability without requiring verbal skills.

Description: Measures intelligence through three drawing tasks in three tests: Goodenough Draw-a-Man Test, Draw-a-Woman Test, and the experimental Self-Drawing Scale. The man and woman drawings may be scored for the presence of up to 73 characteristics. Materials include Quality Scale Cards, which are required for the short-scoring method. Separate norms are available for males and females. Examiner required. Suitable for group use.

Untimed: 10–15 minutes

Scoring: Hand key

Cost: Examiner's kit (test booklet, manual, Quality Scale Cards) $39.00; 35 tests $29.00; manual $20.00; Quality Scale Cards $25.00; text $49.00

Publisher: The Psychological Corporation

Information and availability unconfirmed; last verified in 1988.

GRADED ANAGRAM TASK (GAT)
Refer to page 263.

GRIFFITHS MENTAL DEVELOPMENT SCALES
Ruth Griffiths

Child—Ages 0–8

Purpose: Measures cognitive/intellectual development in infants and children. Used to assess need for remedial treatment and to assess progress.

Description: Multiple-item test of intellectual development meauring social development, fine- and gross-motor skills, hearing, eye-hand coordination, and speech. The test is available on two levels. Scale 1 (27 items) is for children from birth to age two. Scale 2 (22 items) is for children from ages two to eight. Some items appear on both scales.

Materials include toys, form boards, pictures, and models packed in a carrying case. There are different materials for each age group. Two books by the author, *The Abilities of Babies* and *The Abilities of Young Children,* are available separately. They describe the methods employed in the development and standardization of the scales. Examiner required. Not suitable for group use. Available in Swedish and Italian.
BRITISH PUBLISHER

Untimed: Varies

Scoring: Examiner evaluated

Cost: Kit Scale 1.0-2 yrs. $200.00, Scale 2.2-8 yrs. $200.00; 25 record forms $17.50; 25 record books $35.00; manual *The Abilities of Babies* $22.00; manual *The Abilities of Young Children* $22.00

Publisher: The Test Agency Ltd.

GROUP TESTS—1974

Child

Purpose: Assesses developmental intelligence. Used for psychological-educational evaluation.

Description: 6–subtest measure of general intelligence. Three subtests are verbal; three are nonverbal. The test provides three scores: verbal, nonverbal, and total. Materials include three series: Junior Series for Standards 4 to 6, Intermediate Series for Standards 6 to 8, and Senior Series for Standards 8 to 10. Examiner required. Suitable for group use.
SOUTH AFRICAN PUBLISHER

Timed: 2½ hours

Scoring: Hand key; examiner evaluated

Cost: Contact publisher; orders from outside the RSA will be dealt with on merit

Publisher: Human Sciences Research Council

HAPTIC INTELLIGENCE SCALE
Harriet C. Shurrager and Phil S. Shurrager

Adult blind

Purpose: Measures the intelligence of blind and partially sighted adults. Used as a substitute for or supplement to the Wechsler Adult Intelligence Scale.

Description: Seven nonverbal (except for instructions) task assessments measuring the intelligence of blind and partially sighted adults. The subtests are Digit Symbol, Object Assembly, Block Design, Plan-of-Search, Object Completion, Pattern Board, and Bead Arithmetic. Wechsler's procedures were followed in establishing age categories and statistical treatment of the data. Examiner required. Not suitable for group use.

Timed: 1 hour, 30 minutes

Scoring: Examiner evaluated

Cost: Complete kit (25 record blanks, testing materials, manual) $525.00

Publisher: Stoelting Co.

HEALY PICTORIAL COMPLETION TEST II
William Healy

All ages

Purpose: Measures mental ability and intelligence based on an individual's apperceptive ability. Used with all age groups and the mentally defective.

Description: 10–item task-assessment test of problems that are visual, non-language, and ideational measures of important apperceptive abilities. The test consists of two boards containing a total of eleven 5″ x 3½″ pictures representing the sequence of events occurring during the day in the life of a school boy. A square piece of each picture is missing. The child must complete each test picture by selecting the proper square from the accompanying 60 choices. There is only one correct choice for each picture, and the concepts embodied in the test items vary greatly according to difficulty. The 60 answer pieces are numbered on the back for scoring purposes. Examiner required. Not suitable for group use.

Timed: 20 minutes

Scoring: Examiner evaluated

Cost: Complete set (test, manual, carrying case) $160.00

Publisher: Stoelting Co.

INDIVIDUAL SCALE FOR INDIAN SOUTH AFRICANS (ISISA)—1971
Refer to page 592.

JUNIOR SOUTH AFRICAN INDIVIDUAL SCALES (JSAIS)—1979

Child—Ages 3–7

Purpose: Assesses cognitive functioning of children. Used for psychological-educational diagnosis.

Description: 22–scale measure of various aspects of a child's cognitive abilities. Twelve empirically selected scales yield the following IQ measures: General Intellectual Ability (GIQ), Verbal Ability (VIQ), and Perceptual-Performance Ability (PIQ), as well as estimates of memory and quantitative ability. Any scale or group of scales may be administered. Examiner required. Not suitable for group use.
SOUTH AFRICAN PUBLISHER

Untimed: Not available

Scoring: Hand key; examiner evaluated

Cost: (In Rands) manual-part 1, 15,00; part II 15,00; part III 10,00; 10 answer booklets 10,00; profile sheet (specify 3–5 years or 6–7 years) 0,20; vocabulary set 16,50; picture puzzles 12,00; number and quantity concepts 14,40; picture series 12,00; visual memory 4,50 per set; picture riddles 13,00; orders from outside the RSA will be dealt with on merit

Publisher: Human Sciences Research Council

KAHN INTELLIGENCE TEST (KIT:EXP): A CULTURE-MINIMIZED EXPERIENCE
T.C. Kahn

All ages

Purpose: Assesses individual intelligence. May be used for special groups, such as the blind and deaf, or individuals from different educational and cultural backgrounds.

Description: Performance measure of several aspects of intelligence, including concept formation, recall, and motor coordination. A special scale for assessment of blind subjects' intelligence is included. The test requires no reading, writing, or verbal knowledge. It uses the same materials as the Kahn Test of Symbol Arrangement (KTSA): 16 plastic objects and a cloth strip containing 15 equal segments. The manual contains instructions for obtaining mental age, IQ, or developmental level. The test may be used only by psychologists, psychiatrists, counselors, and others with comparable training. Examiner required. Not suitable for group use.

Untimed: 15 minutes

Scoring: Hand key; examiner evaluated

Cost: Complete set $52.00; 50 record sheets $16.00; manual $5.00

Publisher: Psychological Test Specialists

KASANIN-HANFMANN CONCEPT FORMATION TEST (VYGOTSKY TEST) AND MODIFIED VYGOTSKY CONCEPT FORMATION TEST
Paul L. Wang

All ages

Purpose: Measures an individual's ability to think in abstract concepts. Used with uneducated adults, children, and special groups such as psychotic patients.

Description: Task-assessment test consisting of 22 blocks that the subject analyzes and sorts. The blocks are of different colors, shapes, and sizes but are alike in some way. The subject must determine the common factor and sort the blocks according to that factor. The Modified Vygotsky Concept Formation Test provides a new method of administering and scoring. The modification standardizes and simplifies the observation of the subject and adds a divergent thinking test. The modification is particularly useful in the study of mental retardation, schizophrenia, and cerebral organicity (e.g., frontal lobe pathology). Examiner required. Not suitable for group use.

Untimed: Not available

Scoring: Examiner evaluated

Cost: Test materials $125.00; Modified Vygotsky Concept Formation manual $7.50; 30 record forms $13.50

Publisher: Stoelting Co.

KAUFMAN ASSESSMENT BATTERY FOR CHILDREN (K-ABC)
Alan S. Kaufman and Nadeen L. Kaufman

Child—Ages 2¹/₂–12¹/₂

Purpose: Measures intelligence and achievement. Defines intelligence as ability of children to process information and solve problems. Used for psychological and clinical assessment of children, especially the learning disabled, mentally retarded, gifted, preschoolers, and minority groups and for neuropsychological research.

Description: 16 subtests of mental processing skills and achievement. There are three subtests of sequential processing, seven subtests of simultaneous processing, and six subtests of achievement (acquired knowledge, reading, and arithmetic). The examiner presents to the child a test plate containing a stimulus item and gives a verbal direction, and the child responds. Directions may be given in the child's native language or with gestures for the hearing impaired. The test yields four major scores: Sequential Processing, Simultaneous Processing, Mental Processing Composite, and Achievement. For children with language problems, a universal scale score also can be obtained. Each score has a mean of 100 and a standard deviation of 15. National percentile ranks, age and grade equivalents (only for the Arithmetic, Reading/Decoding, and

Reading/Understanding subtests), and sociocultural percentile ranks are also available. Standardization is based on 1980 census data. Separate scales for mental processing and achievement were normed on the same sample. Materials include test plates bound into three easel kits, interpretive manual, 118 photo series cards, a magic window wheel, seven matrix chips, nine triangles, 25 individual test records, and a container. Examiners must have necessary qualifications to use the test. Not suitable for group use.

Untimed: Varies

Scoring: Examiner evaluated; may be computer scored

Cost: Complete test kit, regular edition $175.00; special edition $228.00

Publisher: American Guidance Service

LANGDON ADULT INTELLIGENCE TEST (LAIT)
Kevin Langdon

Adult

Purpose: Measures reasoning of highly gifted adults. Used by individuals seeking information on their intelligence quotients or admission to societies such as Minerva, Four Sigma, Triple 9, and Prometheus.

Description: 56–item paper-pencil or computer-administered multiple-choice test assessing abstract reasoning, common sense or judgment, spatial ability, inductive reasoning, verbal ability, intellectual sophistication, perseverance and, to a limited extent, creativity. The 1979 revision first appeared in *Omni*. A good command of English is recommended. Computer version operates on IBM PC, XT, and AT systems and includes the Polymath Intellectual Ability Scale (see separate entry), LAIT scoring, and a statistical report. Self-administered. Not suitable for group use.

Untimed: 10–20 hours

Scoring: Computer scored by publisher

Cost: Test booklet, answer sheet, computer-generated score report, statistical report $10.00

Publisher: Polymath Systems

LEITER ADULT INTELLIGENCE SCALE (LAIS)

Adult

Purpose: Measures general intelligence in adults. Used with individuals from the upper and lower levels of the socio-economic hierarchy and with the psychologically disabled.

Description: Six oral-response and task-performance tests assessing verbal and nonverbal intelligence. The verbal tests are Similarities-Differences, Digits Forward and Backward, and Free Recall-Controlled Recall. The nonverbal tests are Pathways (following a prescribed sequence), Stencil Designs (reproduction of designs), and Painted Cube Test (duplication of designs). Test results identify deficits in cognitive, psychophysical, or social areas and provide a measure of functional efficiency for psychologically disabled and superior individuals. Examiner required. Not suitable for group use.

Untimed: 40 minutes

Scoring: Examiner evaluated

Cost: Test kit (all test materials, manual, 100 record blanks) $132.00

Publisher: Stoelting Co.

LEITER INTERNATIONAL PERFORMANCE SCALE (ARTHUR ADAPTATION)

Child—Ages 2–12

Purpose: Assesses general intelligence of nonverbal or non-English-speaking individuals.

Description: Multiple-item nonverbal intelligence test consisting of 54 subtests contained in two trays for measuring intelligence of individuals ages 2–7 (Tray 1) and 8–12 (Tray 2). The test requires no verbal instructions or responses. Individuals match blocks with corresponding characters in a wooden frame. Categories of matching are concretistics (matching of specific relationships), symbolic transformation (judging relationships between two events), quantitative discriminations,

spatial imagery, genus matching, progression discriminations, and immediate recall.

There are significant positive correlations between this test and the Stanford-Binet, Wechsler, Peabody Picture Vocabulary, and others. The test can be used with individuals who are deaf, cerebral palsied, non-English-speaking, culturally disadvantaged, mentally retarded, and mentally superior. Examiner required. Not suitable for group use.

Untimed: Varies

Scoring: Examiner evaluated

Cost: Complete set (test materials, manual, carrying case, 100 record forms) $500.00

Publisher: Stoelting Co.

LEITER INTERNATIONAL PERFORMANCE SCALE (LIPS)
Russell G. Leiter

Child, adolescent—Ages 2–18

Purpose: Measures intelligence and mental age for all individuals ages 2–18, including the deaf, cerebral palsied, non-English-speaking, and culturally disadvantaged.

Description: Multiple-item nonverbal task assessment of intelligence in which the subject matches blocks with corresponding characteristic strips positioned in a sturdy wooden frame. The difficulty of the task increases at each level. The categories measured are concretistics (matching of specific relationships), symbolic transformation (judging relationships between two events), quantitative discriminations, spatial imagery, genus matching, progression discriminations, and immediate recall.

Test materials include three trays of blocks and strips that make up the 54 subtests. Tray 1 covers ages 2–7, Tray 2 covers ages 8–12, and Tray 3 covers ages 13–17. Instructions for all age levels are delivered by easily learned pantomime. The LIPS yields Mental Age and I Q The Binet-type year scale has four tests at each year level from Year II through Year XVI and six tests at year XVII. The test kit includes all materials, wooden frame, carrying case, 100 record cards, and manual. Examiner required. Not suitable for group use.

Untimed: 45 minutes

Scoring: Examiner evaluated

Cost: Complete kit $610.00; 100 record forms $19.00

Publisher: Stoelting Co.

THE MEGA TEST
Ronald K. Hoeflin

Ages 16 and older

Purpose: Assesses very high levels of intelligence in adults. Used as an admission test for those high-IQ societies for which ordinary intelligence tests lack sufficient ceilings.

Description: 48–item paper-pencil test of intelligence. The Mega Test contains 24 verbal analogies, 12 spatial problems, and 12 numerical problems. The numerical problems include six descriptive problems and six number series. Subjects work on the test at their own pace at home or in a library. Participants may use any books they wish; pocket calculators are permitted. Computers are prohibited because not everyone has equal access to them. The test is administered to individuals by mail and scored only by the publisher. Self-administered. Not suitable for group use.

Untimed: 2–120 hours

Scoring: Hand key

Cost: Test booklet $1.00; score report $25.00

Publisher: Ronald K. Hoeflin

MERRILL-PALMER SCALE
Rachel Stutsman

Child—Ages 18 months–4 years

Purpose: Measures intelligence in children. Used as a substitute for or a supplement to the Binet Scale.

Description: 19 task-assessment and oral-response tests measuring language skills, motor skills, dexterity, and matching. The 19 subtests are Stutsman Color Matching Test; Wallin Pegboards A & B;

Stutsman Buttoning Test; Stutsman Stick and String; Scissors; Stutsman Language Test; Stutsman Picture Formboards 1, 2, and 3; Mare-Foal Formboard; Seguin-Goddard Formboard; Pintner-Manikin Test; Decroly Matching Game; Stutsman Nested Cubes; Woodworth-Wells Association Test; Stutsman Copying Test; Stutsman Pyramid Test; Stutsman Little Pink Tower Test; and Kohs Blocks. The test deals directly with the problem of resistance in the testing situation and provides a comprehensive listing of the many factors influencing a child's willingness to cooperate. Refused and omitted items are considered when arriving at a total score, which may then be converted into mental age, sigma value, or percentile rank. The test is significant in its complete independence from The Stanford-Binet Scale. All subtests may be ordered separately. Examiner required. Not suitable for group use.

Untimed: Not available

Scoring: Examiner evaluated

Cost: Complete kit (tests, 50 record blanks, carrying case) $525.00

Publisher: Stoelting Co.

MULTIDIMENSIONAL APTITUDE BATTERY—FORM L
Douglas N. Jackson

Adolescent, adult

Purpose: Assesses aptitudes and intelligence for adolescents and adults. Used for clinical and research purposes with normal and deviant populations, including prison inmates, neurotic, psychotic, and neurologically impaired psychiatric patients, persons in business and industry, and high-school and college students.

Description: Multiple-item paper-pencil multiple-choice test consisting of two batteries of five subtests each. The Verbal Battery includes the following subtests: Information, Comprehension, Arithmetic, Similarities, and Vocabulary. The Performance Battery subtests include Digit Symbol, Picture Completion, Spatial, Picture Arrangement, and Object Assembly.

Verbal, Performance, and Full Scale IQs and standard scores for the 10 sub-

---

tests have been calibrated to those of another popular IQ test and permit appraisal of intellectual functioning at nine different age levels, ranging from ages 16–74. Separate test booklets and answer sheets are provided for the two batteries. One battery of five subtests (seven minutes per test) can be administered in one sitting. An optional tape recording of instructions and timing may be used to administer all subtests. Scoring templates are available for hand scoring. Profiles and scoring sheets may be used for recording raw scores, converting scores to standard form, and recording IQs. The scoring service provides a five-page computerized report for each individual tested, including a one-page summary for the counselor (tests may be submitted for scoring in any quantity). The manual contains instructions for administering the tests, interpretive and technical information, and norms tables and profiles. On-line software is available. Examiner required. Suitable for group use.

Timed/Untimed: 70 minutes (7 minutes per subtest)

Scoring: Hand key; machine-scoring and computer analysis available

Cost: Machine scoring examination kit $18.00; hand scoring examination kit $25.00

Publisher: SIGMA Assessment Systems, Inc., Research Psychologists Press Division

---

NATIONAL ADULT READING TEST
Hazel E. Nelson

Adult—Ages 20–70

Purpose: Measures the effects of dementia, alcohol, drugs, or illness on the intellectual functioning of adults.

Description: 50–item oral-response test measuring premorbid intelligence in the assessment of dementia. Test items comprise a list of 50 words whose pronunciation cannot be guessed by phonemic decoding but must be recognized in order to be read correctly. The individual reads the words aloud. The raw score predicts

IQs that approximate closely to the premorbid IQ level. Examiner required. Not suitable for group use.
BRITISH PUBLISHER
Untimed: Varies
Scoring: Examiner evaluated
Cost: Contact publisher
Publisher: NFER-NELSON Publishing Company Ltd.

NON-LANGUAGE LEARNING TEST
Mary K. Bauman

Visually handicapped individuals

Purpose: Measures nonverbal intelligence and learning abilities of blind and visually handicapped individuals.

Description: Multiple-item task-performance test assessing shape discrimination, flexibility of thinking, and ability to profit from instruction and experience when using concrete materials. The test kit includes instructions and diagrams for constructing testing materials, instructions for administering the test, and rough norms. Examiner required. Not suitable for group use.

Timed: Varies
Scoring: Examiner evaluated
Cost: Instructions to produce test $10.00
Publisher: Associated Services for the Blind

NON-VERBAL ABILITY TESTS (NAT)
Refer to page 595.

OHIO CLASSIFICATION TEST
DeWitt E. Sell, Robert W. Scollay, and Leroy N. Vernon

Adult

Purpose: Assesses general mental ability. Used for evaluation of penal populations, factory workers, general populations, management, and student populations.

Description: Four-subtest performance measure of general intellectual ability. The subtests include Block-Counting,

---

Digit-Symbol, Number Series, and Memory Span for Objects. The directions are given by the examiner. Some number reading is required. The test may be used in any situation where a culture-fair measure of intelligence is needed. Examiner required. Not suitable for group use.

Timed: 20 minutes

Scoring: Hand key

Cost: Specimen set $5.00; 25 tests $8.75; 25 answer sheets $7.00

Publisher: Psychometric Affiliates

PEABODY PICTURE VOCABULARY TEST-REVISED (PPVT-R)
Refer to page 596.

PICTORIAL TEST OF INTELLIGENCE
Refer to page 596.

POLYMATH INTELLECTUAL ABILITY SCALE (PIAS)
Kevin Langdon

Adult

Purpose: Assesses general intelligence and attention in reasoning. Used by individuals seeking information on their intelligence quotients or admission to societies such as Minerva, Triple 9, Four Sigma, and Prometheus.

Description: 30–item paper-pencil or computer-administered multiple-choice test assessing general intelligence and attention in reasoning. The test includes 10 miscellaneous symbolic items, 10 figure series items, and 10 miscellaneous spatial items. A Total score, but no subscores, are reported. This test first appeared in *Games* in 1987. The computer version operates on IBM PC, XT, AT and compatible systems and includes the Langdon Adult Intelligence Test (see separate entry), a PIAS score report, and a PIAS statistical report. A good command of the English language is required. Self-administered. Not suitable for group use.

Untimed: 5–10 hours

Scoring: Computer scored by publisher

Cost: Complete kit $10.00; diskette $10.00

Publisher: Polymath Systems

PORTEUS MAZES
S.D. Porteus

All ages

Purpose: Assesses mental ability of verbally handicapped subjects. Used in anthropological studies and in research on the effects of drugs and neurosurgery.

Description: Nonlanguage test of mental ability in which the items are mazes. Materials include the Vineland Revision, Porteus Maze Extension, and Porteus Maze Supplement. The Vineland Revision, consisting of twelve mazes, is the basic test. The Porteus Maze Extension is a series of eight mazes designed for retesting and is not intended for use as an initial test. The Porteus Maze Supplement is designed for a third testing in clinical and research settings. Examiner required. Not suitable for group use.

Untimed: 25 minutes per scale

Scoring: Examiner evaluated

Cost: Basic sets (mazes and 100 score sheets), Vineland Revision $98.00; Porteus Maze Extension $72.00; Porteus Maze Supplement (no score sheets) $67.00; manual $45.00

Publisher: The Psychological Corporation

Information and availability unconfirmed; last verified in 1988.

QUICK TEST (QT)
R.B. Ammons and C.H. Ammons

Ages 2–adult

Purpose: Assesses individual intelligence. May be used for evaluation of the severely physically handicapped, individuals with short attention spans, or uncooperative subjects.

Description: 50–item test of general intelligence. The subject looks at plates with four line drawings and indicates which picture best illustrates the meaning of a given word. The subject usually responds by pointing. The test requires no reading, writing, or speaking. Usual

---

administration involves the presentation of 15 to 20 of the items. Items are administered until the subject scores six consecutive passes and six consecutive failures. Materials include plates with stimulus pictures and three alternate forms. Examiner required. Suitable for group use.

Untimed: 3–10 minutes

Scoring: Hand key; examiner evaluated

Cost: Complete kit (3 plates, 100 record sheets, instruction cardboard, item cardboard) $16.00; 100 record sheets $10.00; 3 plates $4.00; instruction cardboard $0.80; item cardboard $0.70; manual $5.00

Publisher: Psychological Test Specialists

SCHAIE-THURSTONE ADULT MENTAL ABILITIES TEST (STAMAT)
K. Warner Schaie

Adult—Ages 22–84

Purpose: Measures five separate factors of intelligence.

Description: Multiple-item paper-pencil test in two forms measuring verbal, spatial, reasoning, number, and word fluency abilities of adults. Form A (adult) is the original Thurstone Primary Mental Abilities Test, Form 11–17, with new adult norms. Form OA (older adult) is a large-type version of the original test plus two additional scales relevant for adults ages 55 and older. The test was used by Schaie for assessing the development of adult intelligence longitudinally and cross-sectionally. New normative data are based on 4,500 people ages 22–84. Instructions have been written to enhance performance by older adults. Examiner required. Suitable for group use.

Timed: Form A 26 minutes; Form B 37 minutes

Scoring: Hand key

Cost: Specimen set $27.00; manual $18.00; 25 Form OA test booklets (includes scoring instructions) $55.00; 25 Form A booklets $39.00; Form A score key $6.00; 25 profiles $7.00; 50 Form A answer sheets $12.00

Publisher: Consulting Psychologists Press, Inc.

SENIOR SOUTH AFRICAN INDIVIDUAL SCALE (SSAIS)—1964

Child, adolescent—Ages 6–17

Purpose: Assesses general intelligence in children. Used for psychological-educational evaluation.

Description: 9–subtest measure of general intellectual ability consisting of five verbal subtests and four nonverbal subtests. Verbal, Nonverbal, and Total IQ scores may be obtained. Examiner required. Not suitable for group use. SOUTH AFRICAN PUBLISHER

Untimed: 50 minutes

Scoring: Hand key; examiner evaluated

Cost: (In Rands) complete kit (manual, tests 1–9, globite holder, 2 examples of the answer sheets, practice samples) 153,00; orders from outside the RSA will be dealt with on merit

Publisher: Human Sciences Research Council

SHIPLEY INSTITUTE OF LIVING SCALE (SILS)
Walter C. Shipley (Test) and Robert A. Zachary (Manual)

Adolescent, adult—Ages 14 and older

Purpose: Assesses general intellectual functioning.

Description: 60–item paper-pencil multiple-choice and fill-in-the-blanks scale composed of two subtests: a 40–item vocabulary test, requiring the respondent to choose which of four listed words "means the same or nearly the same" as a specified target word, and a 20–item thinking test, requiring the respondent to fill in numbers or letters that logically complete a given sequence. The scale produces six summary scores: Vocabulary Score, Total Score, Abstract Quotient, Abstraction Score, Conceptual Quotient, and Estimated Full Scale WAIS or WAIS-R IQ scores. The manual provides standard scores, updated norms, an impairment index with empirically derived corrections for age and education, and age-adjusted norms for estimating WAIS and WAIS-R IQs. A computer version for IBM personal computers and compatibles is available. Self-administered. Suitable for group use.

Timed: 20 minutes

Scoring: Hand key; computer scored; test scoring service available from publisher

Cost: Kit (100 tests, manual, hand scoring key) $70.00; micro disk (25 uses) $119.50

Publisher: Western Psychological Services

SLOSSON SCREENING INTELLIGENCE TEST-REVISED (SSIT-R)
Richard L. Slosson

All ages

Purpose: Measures the mental age, IQ, and reading level of children and adults. Used by psychologists, guidance counselors, special educators, and learning disability and remedial reading teachers to provide a quick assessment of a person's mental abilities.

Description: 195–item oral screening instrument consisting of questions arranged on a scale of chronological age from one-half month to 27 years. A basal age is established at the point before which the subject gives an incorrect answer after giving at least 10 correct answers in a row. Additional credit is given for correct answers above the basal age. The basal age and added months credit are used to determine mental age and IQ. Norms are not provided for infants below the chronological age of 2. The norms tables include alternate scoring systems, such as percentiles, normal curve equivalents, stanines, and T-scores. The results can be used to predict reading achievement, plan educational programs, predict success and acceptance in college, screen students for reading disabilities, and determine the IQs of blind individuals. The SIT includes the Slosson Oral Reading Test (SORT), which yields a reading grade level ranging from primary to high school based on the ability to pronounce words at different levels of

difficulty. The SORT also is used to identify reading handicaps. Item analysis is available to identify strengths and weaknesses in eight learning areas. Examiner required. Not suitable for group use.

Untimed: 10–20 minutes

Scoring: Examiner evaluated

Cost: Complete kit (manual, directions, 50 SIT score sheets, norms tables) $48.00

Publisher: Slosson Educational Publications, Inc.

SOUTH AFRICAN WECHSLER ADULT INDIVIDUAL INTELLIGENCE SCALE

Adult—Ages 18–59

Purpose: Assesses intelligence of Afrikaans and English-speaking South Africans.

Description: Multiple-item paper-pencil and performance test consisting of five verbal tests covering information, comprehension, arithmetic, digit span, and similarities and five performance tests covering picture completion, object assembly, block design, digit symbols, and picture arrangement. An IQ score can be obtained by adding the standard scores of the tests. Examiner required. Not suitable for group use. SOUTH AFRICAN PUBLISHER

Timed: Not available

Scoring: Not available

Cost: Contact publisher

Publisher: National Institute for Personnel Research

THE STANDARD PROGRESSIVE MATRICES (SPM-1956)
J.C. Raven

Ages 8–65

Purpose: Measures an individual's mental ability through assessment of nonverbal abstract reasoning tasks. Used for school and vocational counseling and placement.

Description: 60–item paper-pencil nonverbal test in five sets of 12 problems each. In each problem, the subject is presented with a pattern or figure design

with a missing part. The subject selects one of six possible parts as the correct one. The patterns are arrayed from simple to complex. The test often is used with the Mill Hill Vocabulary Scale. U.S. norms are available. Examiner required. Suitable for group use.
BRITISH PUBLISHER

Untimed: 45 minutes

Scoring: Hand key; may be machine scored

Cost: Specimen set (book of tests, 5 each of combined matrices and Mill Hill Vocabulary record forms, Sections 1, 3, and 5a of manual, sample machine-scorable record form) £15.20 plus V.A.T.; 25 tests £65.00; 50 record forms £4.50; plastic marking key £6.70 plus V.A.T.

Publisher: H.K. Lewis & Co., Ltd.; distributed in U.S.A. by The Psychological Corporation

Information and availability unconfirmed; last verified in 1987.

STANDARD PROGRESSIVE MATRICES—NEW ZEALAND STANDARDIZATION

Child, adolescent—Ages 8–15

Purpose: Measures nonverbal reasoning skills.

Description: 60–item paper-pencil nonverbal test in five sets of 12 problems each. Each item presents a design, or matrix, from which a part has been removed. The student must select from a number of alternatives the pattern that correctly completes the design. The problems in each set become progressively more difficult. Examiner required. Suitable for group use.
NEW ZEALAND PUBLISHER

Untimed: 30 minutes

Scoring: Hand key

Cost: Contact publisher

Publisher: New Zealand Council for Educational Research

STANFORD-BINET INTELLIGENCE SCALE, FORM L-M
Robert L. Thorndike, Lewis M. Terman, and Maud A. Merrill

Ages 2–adult

Purpose: Measures an individual's mental abilities. Used to substantiate questionable scores from group tests and when the subject has physical, language, or personality disorders which rule out group testing.

Description: 142–item verbal and nonverbal IQ test assessing language, memory, conceptual thinking, reasoning, numerical reasoning, visual motor, and social reasoning. In most cases, only 18–24 test items need to be administered to a subject. First, the basal age is established (year level at which all items are passed). Testing continues until the ceiling age is reached (year level at which all items are failed). Responses then are scored according to established procedures to yield mental age and IQ. The results identify children and adults who would benefit from specialized learning environments. Administered only by professionally trained, certified examiners. Examiner required. Not suitable for group use.

Untimed: 45–90 minutes

Scoring: Examiner evaluated

Cost: Examiner's kit (manual, large and small printed card material, miniaturized objects) $378.00; 35 record booklets $39.00; 35 record forms $27.00

Publisher: The Riverside Publishing Company

THE STANFORD-BINET INTELLIGENCE SCALE, FOURTH EDITION
Robert L. Thorndike, Elizabeth P. Hagen, and Jerome M. Sattler

Ages 2–adult

Purpose: Measures an individual's mental abilities. Used to substantiate questionable scores from group tests, to provide more comprehensive assessment, and when the subject has physical, language, or personality disorders that prevent group testing.

Description: Verbal and nonverbal performance test assessing mental abilities in four areas: verbal reasoning (vocabulary, comprehension, verbal relations, absurdities), abstract/visual reasoning (pattern analysis, matrices, paper folding and cutting, copying), quantitative comprehension (quantitative, number series, equation building), and short-term memory (memory for sentences, memory for digits, memory for objects, and bead memory). Items are arranged according to item type and order of difficulty. The following scores can be obtained: raw and scaled scores for each of the 15 subtests, four content area scores, a composite of the four area scores, a composite of any combination of the four area scores, and a profile on all 15 subtests. Results identify children and adults who would benefit from specialized learning environments. Administered only by professionally trained, certified examiners. Examiner required. Not suitable for group use.

Untimed: 45–90 minutes

Scoring: Examiner evaluated

Cost: Examiner's kit $420.00; 35 record booklets $37.50; guide for administering and scoring $33.00; expanded guide for interpreting $21.00; technical manual $12.00; videotape $99.00

Publisher: The Riverside Publishing Company

THE TEST OF NONVERBAL INTELLIGENCE–2 (TONI–2)
Linda Brown, Rita J. Sherbenou, and Susan K. Johnsen

Ages 5–85.11　　　

Purpose: Provides a language-free measure of intelligence and reasoning. Used with subjects suspected of having difficulty in reading, writing, listening, or speaking, including the mentally retarded, stroke patients, bilingual and non-English-speaking individuals, the speech or language handicapped, learning dis-

abled persons, the deaf, and brain-injured persons.

Description: Multiple-item response test assessing intellectual capacities in a format completely free of reading, writing, and verbalizing. The examiner pantomimes the instructions, and the subject responds by pointing to the selected answer. Test items use abstract symbols to present a variety of reasoning tasks, arranged in increasing order of complexity and difficulty. The test yields a TONI quotient and percentile ranks, accurately discriminating between retarded and normal subjects. Available in two equivalent forms, A and B. The examiner must be formally trained in assessment. Examiner required. May be administered to small groups of up to five subjects.

Untimed: 10–15 minutes

Scoring: Examiner evaluated

Cost: Complete kit (manual, picture book, 50 Forms A and B answer sheets, storage box) $109.00

Publisher: PRO-ED

THE TITAN TEST
Ronald K. Hoeflin

Adult—Ages 16 and older　　

Purpose: Assesses general intelligence. Used for admission to high-IQ societies.

Description: 48–item paper-pencil test measuring general intelligence. Items include 24 verbal analogies, 12 spatial reasoning problems, and 12 numerical problems. Self-administered. Not suitable for group use.

Untimed: Varies

Scoring: Hand key; examiner evaluated

Cost: Scoring fee $25.00

Publisher: Ronald K. Hoeflin

WECHSLER MEMORY SCALE (WMS)
Refer to page 134.

WECHSLER SCALES: WECHSLER ADULT INTELLIGENCE SCALE (WAIS)
David Wechsler

Adolescent, adult—Ages 16–adult

Purpose: Measures intelligence in adolescents and adults.

Description: 11 subtests divided into two major divisions yielding a verbal IQ, a performance IQ, and a full scale IQ for individuals ages 16 and older. The verbal section of the test consists of the following subtests: Information, Comprehension, Arithmetic, Similarities, Digit Span, and Vocabulary. The performance or nonverbal section of the test consists of the following subtests: Digit Symbol, Picture Completion, Block Design, Picture Arrangement, and Object Assembly. Some units of the test require verbal responses from the subject, and others require the subject to manipulate test materials to demonstrate performance ability. Raw scores are converted into scale scores after the examiner records and scores the subject's performance. Examiner required. Not suitable for group use. Available in Spanish as Escala de Inteligencia Wechsler para Adultos (EIWA).

Untimed: 1 hour

Scoring: Examiner evaluated

Cost: Complete set (all necessary equipment, manual, 25 record forms, without attache case) $275.00; attache case $55.00

Publisher: The Psychological Corporation

Information and availability unconfirmed; last verified in 1988.

WECHSLER SCALES: WECHSLER ADULT INTELLIGENCE SCALE— REVISED (WAIS-R)
David Wechsler

Adolescent, adult

Purpose: Assesses intelligence in adolescents and adults.

Description: 11 subtests divided into two major divisions yielding a verbal IQ, a performance IQ, and a full-scale IQ for individuals ages 16 and older. The verbal section of the test consists of the following subtests: Information, Comprehension, Arithmetic, Similarities, Digit Span, and Vocabulary. The performance or nonverbal section of the test consists of the following subtests: Digit Symbol, Picture Completion, Block Design, Picture Arrangement, and Object Assembly. Some units of the test require verbal responses from the subject, and others require the subject to manipulate test materials to demonstrate performance ability. Raw scores are converted into scale scores after the examiner records and scores the subject's performance. The WAIS-R is a revision of the 1955 edition of the WAIS. Examiner required. Not suitable for group use. Available in Spanish.

Untimed: 75 minutes

Scoring: Examiner evaluated

Cost: Complete set (all necessary equipment, manual, 25 record forms with attache case) $298.00; complete without attache case $275.00; manual $39.00

Publisher: The Psychological Corporation

Information and availability unconfirmed; last verified in 1988.

WECHSLER SCALES: WECHSLER INTELLIGENCE SCALE FOR CHILDREN—1949 EDITION (WISC)
David Wechsler

Adolescent—Ages 5–15

Purpose: Measures intelligence for children ages 5–15.

Description: 12 subtests divided into two major divisions yielding a verbal IQ, a performance IQ, and a full-scale IQ for children tested individually. The verbal section of the test consists of the following subtests: General Information, General Comprehension, Arithmetic, Similarities, Vocabulary, and Digit Span. The performance section consists of the following subtests: Picture Completion, Picture Arrangement, Block Design, Object Assembly, Coding, and Mazes. Some units of the test require verbal responses from the subjects, and others require the subject to manipulate test materials to demonstrate performance ability. Raw scores are converted into scale scores after the subject's performance has been recorded and scored on the provided answer form by the examiner. Examiner required. Not suitable for group use. Available in Spanish.

Untimed: 1 hour

Scoring: Examiner evaluated

Cost: Complete set (all equipment, manual, 5 record forms and test blanks, without carrying case) $275.00; manual $39.00

Publisher: The Psychological Corporation

Information and availability unconfirmed; last verified in 1988.

WECHSLER SCALES: WECHSLER INTELLIGENCE SCALE FOR CHILDREN—REVISED (WISC-R)
David Wechsler

Child, adolescent—Ages 6–16

Purpose: Assesses intellectual ability in children.

Description: 12 subtests divided into two major divisions yielding a verbal IQ, a performance IQ, and a full-scale IQ for children tested individually. The verbal section of the test consists of the following subtests: General Information, General Comprehension, Arithmetic, Similarities, Vocabulary, and Digit Span. The performance section consists of the following subtests: Picture Completion, Picture Arrangement, Block Design, Object Assembly, Coding, and Mazes. Some units of the test require verbal responses from the subject, and others require the subject to manipulate test materials to demonstrate performance ability. Raw scores are converted into scale scores after the examiner records and scores the subject's performance. The WISC-R is a revised form of the 1949 edition of the WISC. Examiner required. Not suitable for group use. Available in Spanish as Escala de la Inteligencia Weschler para Ninos (EIWN).

Untimed: 1 hour

Scoring: Examiner evaluated

Cost: Complete set (all necessary equipment, manual, 25 record forms, mazes, coding booklet, carrying case) $298.00; complete set without carrying case $175.00; manual $39.00; 25 record forms $29.00

Publisher: The Psychological Corporation

Information and availability unconfirmed; last verified in 1988.

WECHSLER SCALES: WECHSLER INTELLIGENCE SCALE FOR CHILDREN—REVISED (WISC-R) SPLIT-HALF SHORT FORM
Kenneth L. Hobby

Child—Ages 6–16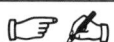

Purpose: Assesses cognitive abilities using the short form of the WISC-R.

Description: Oral-response test consisting of 12 subtests yielding scores: Information (general information), Similarities (verbal concept information), Arithmetic (numerical reasoning), Vocabulary (language development), Comprehension (social judgment), Digit Span (short-term memory), Picture Completion (ability to judge essential details), Picture Arrangement (planning ability), Block Design (visual-motor coordination), Object Assembly (perceptual organization), Coding Ability (matching codes with shapes), and Mazes (ability to trace within mazes). The Coding, Digit Span, and Mazes subtests are given in their entirety. On the remaining nine subtests, only selected items are used in order to reduce administration time by up to 45% without sacrificing diagnostic information.

This short form facilitates compliance with PL 94–142. The manual documents the concurrent and predictive validity of this technique and provides modified administration, scoring, and scaling procedures for all the subtests. The Record Form is used to facilitate the calculation of IQ scores when using standard WISC-R record forms. (NOTE: The WISC-R test materials are needed to administer the WISC-R Split-Half Short Form. They are *not* provided.) Materials include WISC-R kit, stopwatch, and pencil. Examiner required. Not suitable for group use.

Untimed: Varies

Scoring: Examiner evaluated

Cost: Kit (record form, manual, scoring booklet) $62.00

Publisher: Western Psychological Services

WECHSLER SCALES: WECHSLER PRESCHOOL AND PRIMARY SCALE OF INTELLIGENCE (WPPSI)
David Wechsler

Child—Ages 4–6½

Purpose: Assesses intelligence in children.

Description: 10 subtests divided into two major divisions yielding a verbal IQ, a performance IQ, and a full-scale IQ for children tested individually. The verbal section of the test consists of the following subtests: Information, Vocabulary, Arithmetic, Similarities, and Comprehension. A supplementary Sentences Test is available within the verbal section of the test. The performance section consists of the following subtests: Animal House, Picture Completion, Mazes, Geometric Design, and Block Design. An Animal House Retest unit is available within the performance section. Selected subtests require verbal response, and other subtests require the subject to manipulate test materials to demonstrate performance ability. Raw scores are converted to scale scores after the examiner records and scores the subject's responses. Examiner required. Not suitable for group use.

Untimed: 1 hour

Scoring: Examiner evaluated

Cost: Complete set (all necessary equipment, manual, 25 record forms, maze test, 50 geometric design sheets, carrying case) $249.00; complete set without carrying case $225.00; 25 record forms $30.00

Publisher: The Psychological Corporation

Information and availability unconfirmed; last verified in 1988.

WIDE RANGE ASSESSMENT OF MEMORY AND LEARNING (WRAML)
Wayne Adams and David Sheslow

Child, adolescent— Ages 5–17

Purpose: Measures an individual's verbal and visual memory ability. Aids in measuring memory-related learning ability and problems within the psychological, educational, and medical communities.

Description: Multiple-item assessment consisting of nine subtests, some with repetitive trials and recall administrations. Subtests include Picture Memory, Design Memory, Verbal Learning, Story Memory, Finger Windows, Sound Symbol Learning, Sentence Memory, Visual Learning, and Number/Letter Memory. Examiner required. Not suitable for group use.

Untimed: 1 hour

Scoring: Examiner evaluated

Cost: Contact publisher

Publisher: Jastak Associates, Inc.

WIDE RANGE INTELLIGENCE-PERSONALITY TEST (WRIPT)
Refer to page 258.

Marriage and Family: Family

ACTUALIZING ASSESSMENT BATTERY (AAB)
Refer to page 151.

ADAPTIVE BEHAVIOR INVENTORY OF CHILDREN (ABIC)
Jane R. Mercer and June F. Lewis

Child—Ages 5–11

Purpose: Measures a child's social role performance in his family, peer group, and community.

Description: 242–item inventory in an interview format measuring six aspects of adaptive behavior, including family, community, peer relations, nonacademic school rules, earner/consumer, and self-maintenance. Items are divided into two sections. The first section is applicable to all children, and the second section consists of age-graded questions. The ABIC is one component of the System of Multicultural Pluralistic Assessment (SOMPA). Examiner required. Not suitable for group use. The manual includes the ABIC questions in both Spanish and English.

Untimed: 45 minutes

Scoring: Hand key; examiner evaluated

Cost: Basic kit (manual, 6 keys, 25 record forms) $50.00; English-Spanish Reference Handbook for Educators $30.00

Publisher: The Psychological Corporation

Information and availability unconfirmed; last verified in 1988.

ADOLESCENT FAMILY INVENTORY OF LIFE EVENTS AND CHANGES (A-FILE)
Hamilton I. McCubbin, Joan Patterson, and Lance Wilson

Adolescent

Purpose: Measures level of stress in families of adolescents. Used for research and clinical work with families.

Description: 50–item paper-pencil self-report instrument recording the life events and changes an adolescent perceives his family has experienced during the last 12 months. Changes are grouped in six dimensions: transitions, sexuality, losses, responsibilities and strains, substance use, and legal conflict. Examiner/self-administered. Suitable for group use.

Untimed: Varies

Scoring: Hand key

Cost: Manual, unlimited copying $10.00

Publisher: Family Social Science

THE AMERICAN HOME SCALE
W.A. Kerr and H.H. Remmers

Adolescent, adult
Grades 8 and above

Purpose: Evaluates the cultural, aesthetic, and economic factors of an individual's home environment. Used for counseling students and other individuals who may be experiencing problems due to their home environment.

Description: Multiple-item paper-pencil inventory assessing an individual's home environment. Construction of the test is based on profile and factor analyses. The test discriminates between sociological areas. The norms are based on over 16,000 eighth-grade students in over 42 American cities. Examiner required. Suitable for group use.

Timed: 40 minutes

Scoring: Examiner evaluated

Cost: Specimen set $4.00; 25 surveys $5.00

Publisher: Psychometric Affiliates

BORROMEAN FAMILY INDEX: FOR MARRIED PERSONS
Panos D. Bardis

Adolescent, adult

Purpose: Measures a married person's attitudes and feelings toward his immediate family. Used for clinical assessment, family and marriage counseling, family attitude research, and discussions in family education.

Description: 18–item paper-pencil test in which the subject rates nine statements about "forces that attract you to your family" on a scale from 0 (absent) to 4 (very strong) and nine statements about "forces that pull you away from your family" on a scale from 0 (does not pull you away at all) to 4 (very strong). Examiner/self-administered. Suitable for group use.

Untimed: 10 minutes

Scoring: Examiner evaluated

Cost: Free

Publisher: Panos D. Bardis

BORROMEAN FAMILY INDEX: FOR SINGLE PERSONS
Panos D. Bardis

Adolescent, adult

Purpose: Measures an individual's attitudes and feelings toward his family. Used for clinical assessment, family counseling, family attitude research, and discussion in family education.

Description: 18–item paper-pencil test in which the subject rates nine statements about "forces that attract you to your family" from 0 (absent) to 4 (very strong) and nine statements about "forces that pull you away from your family" from 0 (does not pull you away at all) to 4 (very strong). Examiner/self-administered. Suitable for group use.

Untimed: 10 minutes

Scoring: Examiner evaluated

Cost: Free

Publisher: Panos D. Bardis

THE BRICKLIN PERCEPTUAL SCALES: CHILD-PERCEPTION-OF-PARENTS-SERIES
Barry Bricklin

Ages 4–adult

Purpose: Measures a child's perceptions of each parent. Used with children from age four for family therapy and custody arrangements.

Description: 64–item response test assessing a child's verbal and nonverbal perception of parents in four areas: competence, supportiveness, follow-up consistency, and possession of admirable personality traits. An overall score based on nonverbal responses indicates which parent more frequently acts in the child's best interest. Each of the items is presented to the child on a separate card by means of a special card holder. Administration directions are printed on each card, as well as on an "invisible grid" that scores the card automatically as the child responds. The test, which elicits nonverbal responses by means of a continuum stimulus, has been used with children as young as age 4 who understand the instructions. Examiner required. Not suitable for group use.

Untimed: 25–45 minutes

Scoring: Hand key

Cost: Complete kit (4 sets of cards—64 cards per set, 4 scoring sheets, BPS stylus, foam insert and test box, instruction manual) $69.00

Publisher: Village Publishing

Information and availability unconfirmed; last verified in 1987.

CHILDREN'S VERSION/FAMILY ENVIRONMENT SCALE (CV/FES)
C. J. Pino, Nancy Simons, and Mary Jane Slawinowski

Child—Ages 5–12

Purpose: Evaluates the home environment of children. Used by guidance counselors, psychologists, clinicians, family therapists, and family educators.

Description: 30–item paper-pencil or oral-response test assessing 10 areas of family functioning along three dimensions: Relationship Dimensions (cohesion, expressiveness, and conflict), Personal Growth Dimensions (independence, achievement orientation, intellectual-cultural orientation, active-recreational orientation, and moral-religious orientation), and System Maintenance Dimensions (organization and control). Questions are presented to the child in a pictorial nonprojective format. The manual describes clinical use, research, and test administration and scoring. Examiner required. Not suitable for group use.

Untimed: Varies

Scoring: Examiner evaluated

Cost: Test kit (manual, 10 reusable test booklets, 50 profiles, 50 examiner's worksheets, 50 answer sheets) $48.00

Publisher: Slosson Educational Publications, Inc.

CLINICAL RATING SCALE (CRS)
David H. Olson and Elinor Killorin

All ages

Purpose: Assesses family and family coalitions structure. Used in counseling and research.

Description: 11–item paper-pencil rating form measuring cohesion and adaptability. Items are rated by an observer or clinician. Scores are provided for each of the two subscales as well as the location on the Circumplex Model. Examiner required. Not suitable for group use.

Untimed: Varies

Scoring: Examiner evaluated

Cost: Manual, unlimited copying $5.00

Publisher: Family Social Science

DYADIC PARENT-CHILD INTERACTION CODING SYSTEM (DPICS)
Sheila M. Eyberg and Elizabeth A. Robinson

Child, adult

Purpose: Assesses the quality of interaction between parents and young children in the laboratory or clinical setting. Used to aid in evaluation of family functioning, monitor progress of treatment, and evaluate treatment outcome.

Description: Multiple-item paper-pencil coding system comprising a direct observation procedure for monitoring interactions between parents and young children. Data are collected by observing a parent-child dyad in three 5-minute semistructured situations that vary in the amount of parental control elicited: child-directed play, parent-directed play, and clean-up. Parents are observed for the following behaviors: descriptive statement, reflective statement, descriptive/reflective question, acknowledgment, physical positive, physical negative, labeled praise, unlabeled praise, critical statement, direct command, and indirect command. Each command is coded as to whether the child complies, noncomplies, or is given no opportunity to comply. Additional child behaviors observed include whine, cry, yell, smart talk, physical negative, destructive, and changes activity. Whether the parent responds to or ignores each deviant behavior also is recorded. In the manual, the behaviors listed above are operationally defined, examples are given, decision rules are delineated, normative data are provided, and research is summarized. Examiner required. Not suitable for group use.

Untimed: 15 minutes

Scoring: Examiner evaluated

Cost: Manual $19.50; microfiche $6.00

Publisher: Social and Behavioral Sciences Documents, Ms. No. 2582

A FAMILISM SCALE
Panos D. Bardis

Adolescent, adult

Purpose: Assesses individual attitudes toward both nuclear and extended families. Used for clinical evaluation, marriage and family counseling, research on the family, and discussion in family life education.

Description: 16–item paper-pencil test in which the subject reads 10 statements about nuclear family relationships and 6 statements about extended family relationships and rates them according to personal beliefs on a scale from 0 (strongly disagree) to 4 (strongly agree). The "familism" score equals the sum of the 16 numerical responses. The theoretical range of scores extends from 0 (least familistic) to 64 (most familistic). Separate scores may be obtained for "nuclear family integration" and "extended family integration." Examiner/self-administered. Suitable for group use.

Untimed: 10 minutes

Scoring: Examiner evaluated

Cost: Free

Publisher: Panos D. Bardis

A FAMILISM SCALE: EXTENDED FAMILY INTEGRATION
Panos D. Bardis

Adolescent, adult

Purpose: Measures attitudes toward the extended family (beyond the nuclear family, but within the kinship group). Used for clinical assessment, marriage and family counseling, family attitude research, and discussions in family education.

Description: 6–item paper-pencil test in which the subject reads a list of statements concerning extended family relationships and rates them according to personal beliefs on a scale from 0 (strongly disagree) to 4 (strongly agree). The "familism" score is the sum of the six numerical responses. The theoretical range of scores extends from 0 (least familistic) to 24 (most familistic). Examiner/self-administered. Suitable for group use.

Untimed: 5 minutes
Scoring: Examiner evaluated
Cost: Free
Publisher: Panos D. Bardis

A FAMILISM SCALE: NUCLEAR FAMILY INTEGRATION
Panos D. Bardis

Adolescent, adult

Purpose: Measures attitudes toward the solidarity of the nuclear family. Used for clinical assessment, marriage and family counseling, family attitude research, and discussion in family education.

Description: 10–item paper-pencil test in which the subject rates 10 statements about family relationships from 0 (strongly disagree) to 4 (strongly agree). The "familism" score equals the sum of the 10 numerical responses. The theoretical range of scores extends from 0 (least familistic) to 40 (most familistic). Examiner/self-administered. Suitable for group use.

Untimed: 5 minutes
Scoring: Examiner evaluated
Cost: Free
Publisher: Panos D. Bardis

FAMILY ADAPTABILITY AND COHESION EVALUATION SCALES (FACES III)
David H. Olson, Joyce Portner, and Yoav Lavee

Families or couples

Purpose: Assesses family and/or couple functioning. Used for research and clinical work with couples and families.

Description: 20–item paper-pencil test of adaptability and cohesion. Examinees respond by rating each item on a 5–point Likert scale. The authors recommend that FACES III be administered to all family members so that family member reports can be compared and couple and family scores can be used. With FACES

III it is possible to obtain a measure of a family's ideal structure in addition to the family's perceived structure. A couple version is also available for couples without children in the home. A seventh-grade reading level is required. Examiner/self-administered. Suitable for group use. Available in Spanish, German, and Chinese.

Untimed: Varies
Scoring: Hand key
Cost: Manual, copying privileges $30.00
Publisher: Family Social Science

THE FAMILY ADJUSTMENT TEST (ELIAS FAMILY OPINION SURVEY)
Gabriel Elias and edited by H.H. Remmers

Adolescent, adult

Purpose: Measures intrafamily homeyness-homelessness (acceptance-rejection) while appearing to be concerned only with attitudes toward general community life. Used for clinical evaluations and research.

Description: Paper-pencil or oral-response projective test measuring adult and adolescent feelings of family acceptance. The test yields 10 subscores: attitudes toward mother, father, relatives preference, oedipal, independence struggle, parent-child friction, interparental friction, family status feeling, child rejection, and parental quality. Subtest scores and clinical indicators of a number of adjustment trends, as well as an overall index of feelings of intrafamily homeyness-homelessness, are provided. Percentile norms are provided by sex for the following age groups: ages 12–13, 14–15, 16–18, and 19 and older. Interpretation is provided in terms of subtest profiles. Norms for specific parent-child relationships are provided also. No third party should be present if the test is administered orally. Examiner required. The paper-pencil format is suitable for group use.

Timed: 45 minutes
Scoring: Hand key; scoring service available

Cost: Specimen set (test, manual, key) $5.00; 25 tests $8.50

Publisher: Psychometric Affiliates

FAMILY COPING STRATEGIES (F-COPE)
Hamilton I. McCubbin,
Andrea Larsen, and David H. Olson

Families

Purpose: Identifies effective problem-solving and behavioral strategies utilized by families in difficult or problematic situations. Used for research and clinical work with families.

Description: 29–item paper-pencil scale measuring coping skills via five subscales: acquiring social support, reframing, seeking spiritual support, mobilizing family to acquire and accept help, and passive appraisal. Examiner/self-administered. Suitable for group use.

Untimed: Varies

Scoring: Hand key

Cost: Manual, unlimited copying $10.00

Publisher: Family Social Science

FAMILY ENVIRONMENT SCALE
Rudolf H. Moos and Bernice S. Moos

Adolescent, adult

Purpose: Assesses characteristics of family environments. Used for family therapy.

Description: 90–item paper-pencil test measuring 10 dimensions of family environments: cohesion, expressiveness, conflict, independence, achievement orientation, intellectual-cultural orientation, active-recreational orientation, moral-religious emphasis, organization, and control. These dimensions are further grouped into three categories: relationship, personal growth, and system maintenance. Materials include the Real Form (Form R), which measures perceptions of current family environments; the Ideal Form (Form I), which measures conceptions of ideal family environments; and the Expectancies Form (Form E), which measures expectations about family settings. Forms I and E are not published; however, reworded instructions and items

may be requested from the publisher. Examiner required. Suitable for group use.

Untimed: Not available

Scoring: Examiner evaluated

Cost: Manual $7.00; key $1.75; 25 reusable tests $8.50; 50 answer sheets $5.50; 50 profiles $3.75

Publisher: Consulting Psychologists Press, Inc.

FAMILY INVENTORIES
David H. Olson,
Hamilton I. McCubbin,
Howard Barnes, Andrea Larsen,
Marla Muxen, and Marc Wilson

Families, couples

Purpose: Measures various aspects of family functioning. Used for research and clinical work with couples and families.

Description: Series of 11 paper-pencil measures of family functioning. Inventories available are FACES III: Family Adaptability and Cohesion Evaluation Scales; Family Satisfaction; Parent-Adolescent Communication; ENRICH: Marital Satisfaction Scale; ENRICH: Marital Communication Scale; Clinical Rating Scale; FILE: Family Inventory of Life Events and Changes; A-FILE: Adolescent Family Inventory of Life Events and Changes; F-COPES: Family Coping Strategies; Family Strengths; and Quality of Life. The following information is provided for each inventory: conceptual development, construct validity, internal consistency (alpha) reliability, test-retest reliability, scoring procedures, cutting points, and national norms. A copy of each inventory is provided so it can be reproduced for research projects and clinical work. Permission to use and duplicate these inventories will be granted by the publisher upon receipt of an abstract form. Examiner/self-administered. Suitable for group use.

Untimed: Varies

Scoring: Hand key

Cost: Manual, unlimited copying $45.00

Publisher: Family Social Science

FAMILY INVENTORY OF LIFE EVENTS AND CHANGES (FILE)
*Hamilton I. McCubbin,
Joan Patterson, and Lance Wilson*

Families

Purpose: Assesses level of stress on family. Used for research and clinical work with couples and families.

Description: 72–item paper-pencil measure of family stress in nine areas: intrafamily strains, marital strains, pregnancy and childbearing strains, finance and business strains, work-family transitions and strains, illness and family care strains, losses, transition in and out, and family legal violations. Family members indicate whether particular stressful events have occurred in their family. Examiner/self-administered. Suitable for group use.

Untimed: Varies

Scoring: Hand key

Cost: Manual, unlimited copying $10.00

Publisher: Family Social Science

FAMILY RELATIONS TEST— ADULT AND MARRIED COUPLES VERSION
Eva Bene

Adolescent, adult

Purpose: Explores family interactions, particularly between spouses and among parents and children. Used for marital and family counseling and as a research tool.

Description: Multiple-item test measuring perception of family interactions. The subject chooses family figures representing the spouse and/or other family members. Item cards reflecting emotions, attitudes, or sentiments are assigned to each family figure. The test may be used with the children's version to provide a more complete picture of present and past family relationships. Examiner required. Not suitable for group use.
BRITISH PUBLISHER

Untimed: 20–25 minutes

Scoring: Hand key; examiner evaluated

Cost: Contact publisher

Publisher: NFER-NELSON Publishing Company Ltd.

FAMILY RELATIONS TEST— CHILDREN'S VERSION
Eva Bene and James Anthony

Child, adolescent—Ages 3–15

Purpose: Assesses a child's subjective perception of the interpersonal relationships in the family. Used for individual and family counseling and as a research tool.

Description: Multiple-item test of a child's perception of family relationships. The child is presented a set of family figures and a pack of cards with a single emotion, attitude, or sentiment printed on each card. The child selects a family figure to represent every member of the family. An additional figure is called "nobody." The child then assigns each family member the cards printed with an emotion, attitude, or sentiment. Scoring consists of counting the number of items in each attitude area for each figure. The results indicate the relative psychological importance of each family member; whether feelings are positive, ambivalent, or negative; and whether feelings are reciprocal. Materials include two item sets: one for children ages 3–7 and one for children ages 7–15. Examiner required. Not suitable for group use.
BRITISH PUBLISHER

Untimed: 20–25 minutes

Scoring: Examiner required

Cost: Contact publisher

Publisher: NFER-NELSON Publishing Company Ltd.

FAMILY RELATIONSHIP INVENTORY (FRI)
*Ruth B. Michaelson and
Harry L. Bascom*

Ages 5–adult

Purpose: Evaluates family relationships along positive and negative lines. Used as an aid in individual and child-adult counseling, family therapy, youth groups, high-school instruction, and marriage and family enrichment programs.

Description: 50–item paper-pencil test measuring self-esteem, positive or negative perception of self and significant others, most and least esteemed family members, and closest and most distant relationships within the family. One numbered item is printed on each of 50 cards. Items 1–25 have positive valence, and items 26–50 have negative valence. The subject lists "self" and "family members" across the top of a tabulating form and assigns each item to self, significant other, or the wastebasket column and tallies the data on scoring forms with the help of a counselor. Materials include item cards, tabulating forms, scoring forms, a relationship wheel to graphically portray the responses, a Familygram to show family interrelationships, and a test manual. Examiner required. Suitable for group use.

Untimed: 30–45 minutes

Scoring: Examiner evaluated

Cost: Complete FRI kit (manual, 50 reusable item cards, 50 tabulating forms, 25 scoring forms, 50 individual relationship sheets, 25 Familygrams) $50.00

Publisher: Psychological Publications, Inc.

FAMILY SATISFACTION SCALE
David H. Olson

Families

Purpose: Assesses family functioning. Used for research and clinical work with couples and families.

Description: 14–item paper-pencil Likert scale measure of satisfaction with one's family. Scores for satisfaction with family levels of adaptability and cohesion may be obtained in addition to the total score. Examiner/self-administered. Suitable for group use.

Untimed: Varies

Scoring: Hand key

Cost: Manual, unlimited copying $10.00

Publisher: Family Social Science

FAMILY STRENGTHS
David H. Olson, Andrea Larsen, and Hamilton I. McCubbin

Families

Purpose: Measures family members' perceptions of their family's strengths. Used for research and clinical work with families.

Description: 12–item paper-pencil measure of two aspects of perceived family strength: pride and accord. Family members use a 5–point Likert scale format to indicate degree of agreement with items relating to respect, trust, loyalty, pride, and sense of competency. Examiner/self-administered. Suitable for group use.

Untimed: Varies

Scoring: Hand key

Cost: Manual, unlimited copying $10.00

Publisher: Family Social Science

FAMILY VIOLENCE SCALE
Panos D. Bardis

Adolescent, adult

Purpose: Measures the degree of verbal and physical violence in an individual's family during childhood. Used for clinical assessment, marriage and family counseling, research on attitudes toward family and violence, and classroom discussion.

Description: 25–item paper-pencil test in which the subject rates 25 statements about family violence on a scale from 0 (never) to 4 (very often). The "family violence" score equals the sum of the 25 numerical responses. The theoretical range of scores extends from 0 (least violent) to 100 (most violent). Self-administered. Suitable for group use.

Untimed: 10 minutes

Scoring: Examiner evaluated

Cost: Free

Publisher: Panos D. Bardis

THE FLINT INFANT SECURITY SCALE: FOR INFANTS AGED 3–24 MONTHS
Refer to page 33.

THE HOME ENVIRONMENT QUESTIONNAIRE
Jacob O. Sines

Child, adolescent—Ages 5–16

Purpose: Assesses behaviorally relevant dimensions of children's psychosocial environments. Used to investigate sources of environmental stress.

Description: True-false paper-pencil test completed by the mother of the child being studied. The HEQ can be scored for 10 dimensions of the child's psychosocial environment that exert pressure on the child: p(ress) achievement, p aggression-external, p aggression-home, p aggression-total, p supervision, p change, p affiliation, p separation, p sociability, and p socioeconomic status. Two forms are available: HEQ–2R (123 items) for use with two-parent families and HEQ–1R (91 items) for use with one-parent families. Examiner/self-administered. Suitable for group use.

Untimed: 15–20 minutes

Scoring: Hand key

Cost: Specimen set (manual and norms, scoring keys, 25 each HEQ–2R and HEQ–1R) contact publisher

Publisher: Psychological Assessment and Services, Inc.

HOME INDEX
Refer to page 741.

HOME OBSERVATION FOR MEASUREMENT OF THE ENVIRONMENT (HOME)
Bettye M. Caldwell and Robert H. Bradley

Child—Ages birth–10

Purpose: Assesses the quality and quantity of support for cognitive, social, and emotional development available to a child in the home environment.

Description: Observation and semistructured interview conducted in the home with the parent and child. There are three versions of the HOME Inventory: Infant and Toddler (45 items with 6 subscales); Early Childhood (55 items with 8 subscales), and Middle Childhood (59 items with 8 subscores). The inventory has three primary intended uses: identification of home environments that pose a "risk" for children's development, evaluation of programs designed to improve "parenting" skills, and basic research on the relationship between home environments and children's health and development. Each of the HOME inventories is available in versions for use with children with learning, visual, orthopedic, and mental impairments. This is a revised edition of the 1984 HOME Inventory. Examiner required. Not suitable for group use.

Untimed: 1 hour

Scoring: Examiner evaluated

Cost: Contact publisher

Publisher: Center for Research on Teaching and Learning

HOME SCREENING QUESTIONNAIRE (HSQ)
C. Cooms, E. Gay, A. Vandal, C. Ker, and William F. Frankenberg

Child—Ages 0–6

Purpose: Evaluates the quality of a child's home environment; used to indicate need for further evaluation.

Description: 64–item paper-pencil questionnaire filled out by the parents and scored by an examiner. Suspect results must be followed by an evaluation of the home by a trained professional to see if intervention is needed. A 30–item blue form is available for children up to age 3, and a 34–item white form is available for ages 3–6. Both forms have toy checklists. The questionnaires are written at third- and fourth-grade reading levels. Self-administered. Not suitable for group use.

Untimed: 15–20 minutes

Scoring: Hand key

Cost: 25 test forms $7.75; manual $7.75

Publisher: Denver Developmental Materials, Inc.

INTRA AND INTERPERSONAL RELATIONS (IIRS)—1973
Refer to page 183.

IRRATIONAL BELIEFS TEST
Refer to page 185.

THE JONES-MOHR LISTENING TEST
Refer to page 1045.

LIFE INTERPERSONAL HISTORY ENQUIRY (LIPHE)
Will Schutz

Adult

Purpose: Evaluates an individual's retrospective account of relationship to parents before age six. Used for counseling and therapy.

Description: Paper-pencil report of an individual's early relationship with parents in areas of inclusion, control, and affection at both the behavioral and the feeling levels. Separate scores are obtained for the father, the mother, and the respondent's perception of the relationship between the parents. Examiner/self-administered. Suitable for group use.

Untimed: Not available

Scoring: Hand key

Cost: Sample set (test booklet, scoring key) $4.25; 25 tests $10.50

Publisher: Consulting Psychologists Press, Inc.

MARYLAND PARENT ATTITUDE SURVEY (MPAS)
Donald Pumroy

Adult

Purpose: Assesses parents' attitudes toward the way they rear their children; particularly useful as a research instrument.

Description: 95–item paper-pencil test in which the subject chooses one of each pair of A or B forced-choice statements that best represents the parents' attitudes towards child rearing: indulgent, disciplinarian, protective, and rejecting. The survey indicates child-rearing "type" or approach. Materials consist of a cover letter, a copy of the research article, and scoring keys. Self-administered. Suitable for group use.

Untimed: 45 minutes

Scoring: Hand key

Cost: Complete set $2.00

Publisher: Donald K. Pumroy, Ph.D.

MCMASTER FAMILY ASSESSMENT DEVICE (FAD)
Nathan B. Epstein,
Lawrence M. Baldwin, and
Duane S. Bishop

Adolescent, adult—Ages 12 and older

Purpose: Measures dimensions of family functioning. Used by therapists and researchers with individuals ages 12 and older for screening, identifying problems, and collecting clinically relevant information on the family system.

Description: 60–item self-report questionnaire assessing an individual's perceptions of family roles and functions. The questionnaire contains seven intercorrelated scales: Problem Solving (family's ability to resolve issues threatening its integrity and functioning), Communication (exchange of information among members), Roles (whether family has established behavior patterns for handling repetitive family functions), Affective Responsiveness (extent to which members experience appropriate affect over a range of stimuli), Affective Involvement (extent to which members are interested in and value others' activities and concerns), Behavior Control (way in which family expresses and maintains members' behavior standards), and General Functioning (overall health/pathology of family).

Individuals rate items on a 4–point scale (strongly agree-strongly disagree) according to how well the item describes their family. The test has cut-off scores for identifying healthy and unhealthy families that have adequate sensitivity and specificity. A microcomputer scoring program allows interactive administration on a MacIntosh computer. The program, used with MicroSoft Basic, provides individual scores, a family mean score, and item analysis. Self-administered. Suitable for group use. Available in French, Spanish, Portuguese, Hungarian, and Afrikaans.

Untimed: 15–20 minutes

Scoring: Hand key; computer scored; examiner evaluated

Cost: Kit (test, reprints, scoring key, biannual updates) $20.00

Publisher: Brown University Family Research Program

Information and availability unconfirmed; last verified in 1988.

MEASURE OF CHILD STIMULUS SCREENING (CONVERSE OF AROUSABILITY)
Albert Mehrabian and Carol Falender

Child—Ages 3 months–7 years

Purpose: Measures major components of a child's arousability and stimulus screening. Used for research, counseling, and education program selection purposes.

Description: Multiple-item paper-pencil observational inventory measuring parents' descriptions of their children's arousability (responses of one parent are sufficient). Test results indicate the child's characteristic arousal response to complex, unexpected, or unfamiliar situations. Stimulus screening/arousability has been shown to be a major component of many important personality dimensions, such as anxiety, neuroticism, extroversion, or hostility. This test is based on the same conceptual framework used to develop the corresponding adult measure. Examiner required. Suitable for group use.

Untimed: 20 minutes

Scoring: Examiner evaluated

Cost: Test kit (scale, scoring directions, norms, descriptive material) $20.00

Publisher: Albert Mehrabian

MEASURES OF PLEASURE-, AROUSAL-, AND DOMINANCE-INDUCING QUALITIES IN PARENTAL ATTITUDES
Albert Mehrabian

Child—Ages 3 months–7 years

Purpose: Evaluates the emotional climate parents create for their children. Used for research and counseling purposes.

Description: Multiple-item paper-pencil self-report questionnaire consisting of three orthogonal measures of parental child-rearing attitudes. The test measures the levels of pleasure, arousal, and dominance experienced by the child. Three scores concerning parental attitudes are provided: pleasure-inducing, arousal-inducing, and dominance-inducing. Examiner required. Suitable for group use.

Untimed: 20 minutes

Scoring: Examiner evaluated

Cost: Test kit (scales, scoring directions, norms, descriptive material) $20.00

Publisher: Albert Mehrabian

MICHIGAN SCREENING PROFILE OF PARENTING (MSPP)
Ray E. Helfer, James K. Hoffmeister, and Carol J. Schneider

Adult

Purpose: Evaluates an individual's perceptions in areas that are critically important for positive parent-child interactions. Profiles segments of the individual's early childhood experiences and current relationships that seem to affect the individual's ability to interact with others. Used to identify those in need of further assessment.

Description: Multiple-item paper-pencil self-report questionnaire for parents and prospective parents. The questionnaire consists of four sections. Section A provides information about family characteristics, the respondent's health history, and relationships with employers, social agencies, and spouse. Section B provides information regarding respondent perceptions of childhood experiences and current interactions with family and friends. Section C (answered only by individuals having one or more children) provides information about the respondent's child (or children) and current parent-child interactions. Section D (answered only by individuals who do not have children) provides information with regard to the respondent's expectations for future interactions with prospective children. Section A requires various types of answers depending on the type of biographical information being requested. Sections B, C, and D use 7-point Likert scales to rate responses to individual test items.

Computerized scoring generates four scores based on the responses in Section B: emotional needs met, relationship with parents, expectations of children, and coping. High scores indicate a potential for parent-child interaction problems and may be used to identify individuals in need of further assessment or counseling. Scores are not intended to diagnose specific problems, nor do they predict the future behavior of parents. The manual includes a discussion of the scale's background, development, and content; administration and scoring procedures; item measure characteristics; uses of the scale; and a list of available consulting services. Self-administered. Suitable for group use.

Untimed: Varies

Scoring: Computer scored

Cost: 25 questionnaires (including scoring service) $50.00

Publisher: Test Analysis and Development Corporation

MOTHER-CHILD RELATIONSHIP EVALUATION
Robert M. Roth

Adult

Purpose: Measures a mother's attitudes and how they relate to her children. Used for counseling and treatment programs.

Description: 48-item paper-pencil test measuring four areas of mother-child relationships: acceptance, overprotection, overindulgence, and rejection. The mother responds to each item on a

5-point scale ranging from "strongly agree" to "strongly disagree." Raw scores are converted to percentiles and T-scores for developing the profile. Examiner required. Suitable for group use.

Untimed: 30 minutes

Scoring: Hand key

Cost: Kit (25 forms, manual) $18.00

Publisher: Western Psychological Services

MOTIVATION AND POTENTIAL FOR ADOPTIVE PARENTHOOD SCALE (MPAPS)
B. W. Lindholm and J. Touliatos

Adult

Purpose: Measures individual motivation and potential for adoptive parenthood. Used by caseworkers evaluating persons seeking to adopt children.

Description: 72-item paper-pencil test based on the traits formalized by the Child Welfare League of America as standards for adoption services. The Motivation Scale is composed of items covering both positive reasons for wanting to adopt and lack of negative reasons for wanting to adopt. The Potential Scale covers attitude toward adoption and the natural parents of adopted children, acceptance and flexibility regarding the children that the applicants are willing to adopt, ability to use help relationships with one's family, relationships with one's spouse, relationships with one's friends, positive experiences with children, being able to enjoy and have a relationship with a child, being able to assume responsibility for others, and dealings with previous life situations. Self-administered. Suitable for group use.

Untimed: 20 minutes

Scoring: Hand key

Cost: Specimen set $8.00; 35 scales $14.00; manual $4.00

Publisher: Monitor

MULTIMODAL LIFE HISTORY QUESTIONNAIRE
Refer to page 197.

PARENT AS A TEACHER INVENTORY (PAAT)
Robert D. Strom

Adult

Purpose: Assesses parents' attitudes toward their parent-child relationship. Used with parents of children ages 3–9.

Description: Multiple-item pencil-paper inventory measuring parental attitudes in the following areas: feelings toward the parent-child interactive system, standards for assessing the importance of certain aspects of child behavior, and value preferences and frustrations concerning child behavior. Examiner required. Suitable for group use. Available in Spanish.

Untimed: 30–45 minutes

Scoring: Examiner evaluated

Cost: Starter set (manual, 20 inventory booklets, 20 identification questionnaires, 20 profiles) $30.00; specimen set $10.00

Publisher: Scholastic Testing Service, Inc.

PARENT-ADOLESCENT COMMUNICATION
Howard Barnes and David H. Olsen

Adolescent, adult
Families

Purpose: Assesses family communication. Used for research and clinical work with couples and families.

Description: 20–item paper-pencil measure of two aspects of communication between parents and adolescents: open family communication and problems in family communication. The inventory may be used with families with younger children. Examiner/self-administered. Suitable for group use.

Untimed: Varies

Scoring: Hand key

Cost: Manual, unlimited copying $15.00

Publisher: Family Social Science

Information and availability unconfirmed; last verified in 1988.

PARENT ATTACHMENT STRUCTURED INTERVIEW
Samuel Roll, Julianne Lockwood, and Elizabeth Jaffe Roll

Child—Ages 4–12

Purpose: Assesses a child's attachment to significant adults. Used in child custody cases.

Description: 50–item oral-response and short-answer inventory measuring the strength of a child's attachment to significant adults and identifying the attachment figures. The test covers four aspects of attachment: responsiveness (who is engaged with the child in pleasant or neutral activities); confidence (who deals with the child in difficult situations); security (who provides a supportive, permanent, affective relationship); and hostility (who is involved in hurtful, frustrating situations). The examiner presents each question, which can be modified according to the child's age or comprehension level, and records the child's answers on an answer sheet. Distractor questions are included to overcome boredom or anxiety.

The inventory is recommended for use by a psychologist trained in assessing children and as part of a complete assessment battery. Presentation of only half the questions at any one session is recommended. Scores are provided for each factor as well as for Total Positive Attachment, Negative Attachment, and Total Positive and Negative Attachment. Examiner required. Not suitable for group use.

Untimed: 5–20 minutes

Scoring: Hand key

Cost: 25 intermediate forms, 25 scoring sheets, manual $32.95; postage and handling not included

Publisher: Samuel Roll, Ph.D.

Information and availability unconfirmed; last verified in 1987.

PARENTAL ACCEPTANCE-REJECTION QUESTIONNAIRE (PARQ)
Ronald P. Rohner

Ages 7–adult

Purpose: Assesses perceived parental acceptance and rejection in individuals ages 7–adult. Used for screening with clinical populations, in research studies with student and community populations, as a tool for parental education programs, in evaluating family problems, and in detecting potential child abuse.

Description: 60–item paper-pencil questionnaire measuring perceived parental acceptance and rejection in four scales: Warmth/Affection (20 items), Hostility/Aggression (15 items), Indifference/Neglect (15 items), and Undifferentiated Rejection (10 items). The test, designed to cut across social classes, can be combined with the formal interview (Parental-Acceptance Rejection Interview Schedule) and behavior observations. It is scored on a 4–point scale (almost always to almost never), with some items reversed scoring to reduce response bias. Scores range from 60 (maximum acceptance, minimum rejection) to 240 (maximum rejection, minimum acceptance).

Three versions are available: mother (includes father; reflects on what they do to child), adult (adult reflects back on own childhood), and child (reflects on present actions in family). The *Handbook for the Study of Parental Acceptance and Rejection* (Rohner, 1984) provides scoring instructions, descriptions of validity and reliability, and other information needed for administration, scoring, and interpretation. A computer scoring program is available for IBM PC and compatible systems. Examiner/self-administered. Suitable for group use. Available in Arabic, Bengali, Czech, French, Hindi, Korean, Mexican Spanish, Puerto Rican Spanish, Swedish, Tamil, Telugu, Tiv, Urdu, and Japanese.

Untimed: 10 minutes

Scoring: Hand key; may be computer scored

Cost: Free

Publisher: Center for the Study of Parental Acceptance and Rejection, University of Connecticut

PARENTING STRESS INDEX (PSI)
Richard R. Abidin

Adult

Purpose: Identifies emotional pathology in children ages 1 month to 11 years and parent-child systems under stress and at risk for dysfunctional parenting.

Description: 101–item paper-pencil screening and diagnostic instrument yielding a total index of stress and scores related to stressors associated with child characteristics (adaptability, acceptability, demandingness, mood, hyperactive/distractibility, reinforces parent), parent characteristics (depression, attachment, restriction of role, sense of competence, social isolation, relationship with spouse, parental health), and life stress events. The test is used clinically in medical centers, mental health centers, universities, and family programs for intervention, education, treatment planning, research, child-abuse risk assessment, and forensic evaluations for child custody.

The test yields a Total score, a Child Domain score, a Parent Domain score, and 13 subtest scores. The test may be computer scored using an Apple II, IIe, IIc, or IBM PC or compatible with two disk drives. The examinee's responses are transferred from the answer sheet to the program, where they are scored and profiled. A four- to seven-page interpretive report may be generated. The publisher also provides a scoring service.

A sixth-grade reading level is required. The test is suitable for use with visually, physically, mentally, and hearing-impaired individuals. Items may be read aloud to individuals with vision problems. Examiner required. Suitable for group use.

Untimed: 20 minutes

Scoring: Hand key; may be computer scored

Cost: Specimen set (manual, 2 test booklets, 10 answer sheets, 10 profile sheets) $30.00

Publisher: Pediatric Psychology Press

Information and availability unconfirmed; last verified in 1988.

PERCEPTIONS OF PARENTAL ROLE SCALES
Lucia A. Gilbert and Gary R. Hansen

Adult

Purpose: Measures perceived parental role responsibilities. Used with male and female adults for education, counseling, and research.

Description: 78–item paper-pencil instrument assessing parental perceptions in three domains yielding 13 scales: teaching a child (cognitive development, social skills, handling of emotions, physical health, norms and social values, personal hygiene, and survival skills), meeting a child's basic needs (health care, child care, child's emotional needs, and food, clothing, and shelter), and serving as the interface between the child and the family and other social institutions (social institutions and family unit). The test takes into account current societal views about men's and women's roles. An eighth-grade reading level is required. Self-administered. Suitable for group use.

Untimed: 15 minutes

Scoring: Hand key

Cost: Kit (manual, 25 questionnaires) $25.00; 50 questionnaires $25.00

Publisher: Marathon Consulting and Press

PSYCHOSOCIAL ADJUSTMENT TO ILLNESS SCALE (PAIS)
Refer to page 4.

QUALITY OF LIFE
David H. Olson and Howard Barnes

Adolescent, adult Families

Purpose: Measures family members' perceptions of the quality of their lives. Used for research and clinical work with families.

Description: 40–item paper-pencil measure of satisfaction with quality of life in 12 areas: marriage and family life, friends, extended family, health, home, education, time, religion, employment, mass media, financial well-being, and neighborhood and community. A 25–item form for adolescents is also available. Family members indicate their degree of satisfaction by rating items using a 5–point Likert scale. Examiner/self-administered. Suitable for group use.

Untimed: Varies

Scoring: Hand key

Cost: Manual, unlimited copying $10.00

Publisher: Family Social Science

QUESTIONNAIRE ON RESOURCES AND STRESS FOR FAMILIES WITH CHRONICALLY ILL OR HANDICAPPED MEMBERS
Refer to page 4.

RELATIONSHIP PROFILE (EGOGRAM®)
N. Robert Heyer

Adult—Ages 18 and older

Purpose: Compares the personality traits of individuals in diadic relationships (couples, family members, work groups). Used in family and couples therapy for diagnosis and treatment and in business for training and counseling in work relationships.

Description: 50–item paper-pencil multiple-choice questionnaire for each member of a relationship diad. For each person, it measures the relative strength of six basic personality traits identified by Eric Berne, M.D., and widely used in transactional analysis. Graphic matching of profiles highlights areas of complementary ego state strength, as well as areas of dependency and unfilled needs in the relationship. A computer printout shows diagnostic guidelines and a measure of relationship stress. The test is normed for individuals ages 18 and older but may also be used for individuals ages 14–18. Self-administered. Suitable for group use. Available in Spanish.

Untimed: 10–16 minutes

Scoring: Computer scored

Cost: 10 sets $190.00; manual $24.00

Publisher: Psychological Measurement Systems

A RELIGION SCALE
Panos D. Bardis

Adolescent, adult

Purpose: Measures attitudes toward religion. Used for clinical assessment, family and marriage counseling, research on attitudes toward religion, and discussion in religion and social science classes.

Description: 25–item paper-pencil test in which the subject reads 25 statements about religious issues and rates them according to beliefs on a scale from 0 (strongly disagree) to 4 (strongly agree). The score is the sum of the 25 numerical responses. The theoretical range of scores extends from 0 (least religious) to 100 (most religious). Examiner/self-administered. Suitable for group use.

Untimed: 10 minutes

Scoring: Examiner evaluated

Cost: Free

Publisher: Panos D. Bardis

THERAPY ATTITUDE INVENTORY (TAI)
Sheila M. Eyberg

Adult

Purpose: Assesses the amount of satisfaction parents feel in response to parent training programs or individual parent-child interaction training. Used to evaluate therapy programs.

Description: 10–item paper-pencil inventory asking parents to rate their feelings from one (indicating dissatisfaction or deterioration of condition) to five (indicating maximum satisfaction or improvement) regarding the following areas: acquisition of new disciplinary techniques, techniques for teaching their child new skills, relationship with their child, confidence in ability to discipline, intensity of current behavior problems, level of child's compliance, progress of child, general benefits of treatment program, satisfaction with type of program, and general feeling about the program. Space is provided for personal comments

concerning the child and the treatment program. Self-administered. Suitable for group use.

Untimed: 5–10 minutes

Scoring: Examiner evaluated

Cost: Free

Publisher: Distributed by Sheila M. Eyberg, Ph.D.

A VIOLENCE SCALE
Refer to page 229.

Marriage and Family: Premarital and Marital Relations

ABORTION SCALE
Panos D. Bardis

Adolescent, adult

Purpose: Measures attitudes toward many aspects of abortion. Used in clinical assessment, marriage and family counseling, research on attitudes toward abortion, and discussion in family education.

Description: 25–item paper-pencil test in which the subject reads statements about issues concerning abortion and rates them according to personal beliefs on a scale from 0 (strongly disagree) to 4 (strongly agree). The score equals the sum of the 25 numerical responses. Theoretical range of scores extends from 0 (lowest approval of abortion) to 100 (highest approval). Examiner/self-administered. Suitable for group use.

Untimed: 10 minutes

Scoring: Examiner evaluated

Cost: Free

Publisher: Panos D. Bardis

BACKGROUND SCHEDULE
Marriage Council of Philadelphia

Adolescent, adult

Purpose: Aids counselors of couples by obtaining a wide range of relevant background material without using interview time to secure information.

Description: 39–item paper-pencil questionnaire used to obtain from couples in a relationship independent answers to questions about vital statistics, religion, activities shared with partner, occupation, siblings, parental data, interaction between self and parent before teens, during teens, and at the present time. The questionnaire is completed independently by the couple prior to their first interview. Not a psychological test. Self-administered. Not suitable for group use.

Untimed: 30 minutes

Scoring: Examiner evaluated

Cost: Schedule $0.20; 100 schedules $15.00

Publisher: Marriage Council of Philadelphia, Inc.

Information and availability unconfirmed; last verified in 1988.

BI/POLAR INVENTORIES OF CORE STRENGTHS
J. W. Thomas and T. J. Thomas

Adult—Ages 15–100

Purpose: Determines lead personality strengths. Used in marital counseling, management development, and professional development.

Description: 45–item paper-pencil test in which the examinee uses a Likert-type scale to rate personality statements. A scoring service is available from the publisher. Training required for certification to administer. Self-administered. Suitable for group use. Available in Spanish and Finnish.

Untimed: Not available

Scoring: Computer scored

Cost: Individuals $30.00; schools and churches $20.00

Publisher: Bi/Polar, Inc.; distributed in Finland by Oy Integro Finland Ab; in Mexico by Grupo Anastasis; and in Canada by Rick Matishak and Jerry Mings and Associates

CALIFORNIA MARRIAGE READINESS EVALUATION
Morse P. Manson

Adult

Purpose: Measures a couple's readiness for marriage and indicates areas where potential difficulties are most likely to occur. Used for premarital counseling.

Description: 115–item paper-pencil inventory consisting of 110 true-false items and 5 projective completion items. The inventory measures strengths and weaknesses in eight areas of marriage readiness within three general categories: personality (character structure, emotional maturity, marriage readiness), preparation for marriage (family experiences, dealing with money, planning ability), and interpersonal compatibility (marriage motivation and compatibility). In addition to providing scores for each of the eight areas measured, a total score indicating overall readiness for marriage is provided. Self-administered. Suitable for group use.

Untimed: 15–30 minutes

Scoring: Hand key

Cost: Kit (25 forms, manual) $18.00

Publisher: Western Psychological Services

CARING RELATIONSHIP INVENTORY (CRI)
Everett L. Shostrom

Adult

Purpose: Measures the essential elements of caring (or love) in the relationship between a man and a woman. Used for evaluation and discussion in marriage and family counseling.

Description: 83–item paper-pencil true-false test consisting of a series of statements that the subject applies first to the other member of the couple (spouse, fiance, etc.) and second to his or her "ideal" mate. Responses are scored on seven scales: Affection, Friendship, Eros, Empathy, Self-Love, Being Love, and Deficiency Love. Separate forms are available for adult males and females.

Items were developed based on the responses of criterion groups of successfully married couples, troubled couples in counseling, and divorced individuals. Percentile norms for successfully married couples are presented separately for men and women. Means and standard deviations are presented for troubled couples and divorced individuals. The CRI is a component of the Actualizing Assessment Battery (AAB). Examiner required. Suitable for group use.

Untimed: 40 minutes

Scoring: Hand key

Cost: Speciman set (manual, all forms) $5.50; 25 booklets (specify male or female) $13.25; 50 expendable profile sheets $8.50; 7 hand-scoring keys $14.75; manual $2.75

Publisher: EdITS/Educational and Industrial Testing Service

CLINICAL CHECKLIST SERIES
Refer to page 164.

COITOMETER
Panos D. Bardis

Adolescent, adult

Purpose: Measures knowledge of the anatomical and physiological aspects of coitus. Used for clinical assessment, marriage and family counseling, research on human sexuality, and discussion in family and human sexuality classes.

Description: 50–item paper-pencil true-false four-page instrument consisting of the questionnaire and a measure key. Examiner/self-administered. Suitable for group use.

Untimed: 12 minutes

Scoring: Hand key

Cost: Free

Publisher: Panos D. Bardis

COUPLE'S PRE-COUNSELING INVENTORY, REVISED EDITION, 1987
Richard B. Stuart and Barbara Jacobson

Adult

Purpose: Provides couples with information regarding expected roles in the treatment process and collects data concerning the feelings and behaviors that may be relevant to marriage, relationship, and family counseling. Used prior to counseling and for periodic evaluation of progress in treatment.

Description: Multiple-item paper-pencil inventory covering the following areas of marital/family life: general and specific happiness with your relationship; caring behaviors; conflict management; communication assessment; sexual interaction; moods and management of personal life; decision making; division of home, child care, and work responsibilities; child management; goals of counseling; previous marriages and/or relationships; and additional information. The inventory emphasizes discovering the strengths of the relationship, as well as the problem areas. Average reading skill is required. This revised edition supersedes earlier versions. Self-administered. Suitable for group use.

Untimed: 1 hour

Scoring: Examiner evaluated

Cost: Complete set (25 booklets, guide) $19.95

Publisher: Research Press

Information and availability unconfirmed; last verified in 1988.

A DATING SCALE
Panos D. Bardis

Adolescent, adult

Purpose: Measures attitudes toward various aspects of dating. Used for clinical assessment, marriage and family counseling, research on attitudes toward dating, and discussion in family education.

Description: 25–item paper-pencil test in which the subject notes 25 statements about dating from 0 (strongly disagree) to 4 (strongly agree). The score equals the sum of the 25 numerical responses. The-oretical range of scores extends from 0 (least liberal) to 100 (most liberal). Examiner/self-administered. Suitable for group use.

Untimed: 10 minutes

Scoring: Examiner evaluated

Cost: Free

Publisher: Panos D. Bardis

DEROGATIS SEXUAL FUNCTIONING INVENTORY (DSFI)
Leonard R. Derogatis

Adult

Purpose: Measures and describes the quality of an individual's sexual functioning.

Description: 255–item paper-pencil or computer-administered inventory consisting of 10 subtests assessing the following factors related to an individual's sexual functioning: information, experience, drive, attitude, psychological symptoms, affects, gender role definition, fantasy, body image, and sexual satisfaction. Scaled scores from each subtest are combined to derive an overall sexual functioning score. Norms are available separately for men and women.

The computer version, SCORDSFI Version 2.1, is available for IBM PC, XT, and AT systems. Items are introduced via 10 input screens corresponding to the 10 subtests. The program generates the 255 raw item scores by subtest, Dimension and Global Raw and Area T-scores, and the DSFI Graphic Profile plotted against standard norms. Results may be saved on disk. Examiner required. Suitable for group use. Available in over 20 languages.

Untimed: 30–40 minutes

Scoring: Examiner evaluated; may be computer scored

Cost: 10 reusable test booklets $30.00; 30 expendable test booklets $33.00; 50 answer sheets $10.00; 50 score/profile forms $12.50; manual $8.00; SCORDSFI Version 2.1 $175.00

Publisher: Clinical Psychometric Research, Inc.

DYADIC ADJUSTMENT SCALE (DAS)
Graham Spanier

Adult

Purpose: Measures relationship dissatisfaction. Used in marital counseling.

Description: 32–item paper-pencil or computer-administered self-report measure consisting of four factored subscales: Dyadic Satisfaction, Dyadic Cohesion, Dyadic Consensus, and Affectional Expression. Total score below 100 points indicates relationship distress. Computer version generates interpretive statements. Self-administered. Suitable for group use.

Untimed: Varies

Scoring: Carbonized Quik Score forms; may be computer scored

Cost: Kit (manual, 20 Quik Score Forms) $32.00; IBM PC compatible or Apple computer versions (50 administrations and scorings) $100.00

Publisher: Multi-Health Systems Inc.

ENGAGEMENT SCHEDULE
Marriage Council of Philadelphia

Engaged couples

Purpose: Aids counselors of couples engaged to be married by obtaining information about the couple's feelings and plans.

Description: 41–item paper-pencil questionnaire that secures independent responses from couples regarding their engagement, feelings about future in-laws, feelings about their own parents, confiding, affection, need for more information about sex, number of children planned, and sharing interests and activities. The questionnaire is not a measuring instrument for predicting future marriage possibilities or a psychological test. The schedule is to be completed independently in the waiting room prior to the clients' first interview. Self-administered. Not suitable for group use.

Untimed: 30 minutes

Scoring: Examiner evaluated

Cost: Schedule $0.20; 100 schedules $15.00

Publisher: Marriage Council of Philadelphia, Inc.

Information and availability unconfirmed; last verified in 1988.

EROTOMETER: A TECHNIQUE FOR THE MEASUREMENT OF HETEROSEXUAL LOVE
Panos D. Bardis

Adolescent, adult

Purpose: Measures the intensity of an individual's love for a member of the opposite sex. Used for clinical assessment, marriage and family counseling, research on love, and discussions in family and sex education.

Description: 50–item paper-pencil test in which the subject reads statements concerning actual feelings, attitudes, desires, and wishes regarding one specific member of the opposite sex and rates them on the following scale: 0 (absent), 1 (weak), 2 (strong). The score equals the sum of the 50 numerical responses. The theoretical range of scores extends from 0 (no love) to 100 (strongest love). Self-administered. Suitable for group use.

Untimed: 12 minutes

Scoring: Examiner evaluated

Cost: Free

Publisher: Panos D. Bardis

FEELINGS AND BEHAVIOR OF LOVE (LOVE SCALE)
Clifford H. Swensen

Adolescent, adult—Ages 14 and older

Purpose: Assesses various aspects of intimate relationships, including the expression of love.

Description: 120–item paper-pencil multiple-choice and oral-response test comprised of six subscales measuring various areas of a couple's relationship: Expression of Affection (24 items), Self-Disclosure (20 items), Tolerance (16 items), Moral Support (20 items), Instrumental and Material Support (20 items), and Unexpressed Feelings (20 items). The test yields a total score and scores for each subscale. Items may be read aloud to visually, physically, and hearing-impaired individuals. Examiner/self-administered. Suitable for group use. Available in Norwegian.

Untimed: Varies

Scoring: Hand key

Cost: $5.00

Publisher: Clifford H. Swensen, Ph.D.

GOLOMBOK RUST INVENTORY OF MARITAL STATE (GRIMS)
J. Rust, I. Bennun, M. Crowe, and S. Golombok

Adult

Purpose: Assesses the quality of a relationship and identifies areas of conflict between partners. Used by clinical psychologists; marriage guidance counselors; sex, marital, and family therapists; and psychotherapists.

Description: 28–item paper-pencil rating scale identifying problems within a marriage or heterosexual relationship. Each partner rates each item on a 4–point scale ranging from "strongly agree" to "strongly disagree." Responses then can be compared in order to identify the severity of the problem and which of the partners perceives the problem. The total raw score is converted onto a pseudo-stanine scale with problematic relationships indicated by a score of 5 or above. When used in conjunction with the Golombok Rust Inventory of Sexual Satisfaction, GRIMS will discriminate between sexual problems and more general marital problems. The test also may be used with multiple relationships or homosexual relationships, although no standardization data is available for these groups. Examiner required. Suitable for group use.
BRITISH PUBLISHER

Untimed: 10–15 minutes

Scoring: Self-scored

Cost: Contact publisher

Publisher: NFER-NELSON Publishing Company Ltd.

GOLOMBOK RUST INVENTORY OF SEXUAL SATISFACTION (GRISS)
Susan Golombok and John Rust

Adult

Purpose: Assesses sexual functioning of adults.

Description: 28–item paper-pencil questionnaire used for developing a diagnostic profile of sexual satisfaction. The test provides a main scale of dysfunction and 12 diagnostic subscales: impotence, premature ejaculation, anorgasmia, vaginismus, noncommunication, infrequency, male and female avoidance, male and female nonsensuality, and male and female dissatisfaction. Separate forms for males and females are provided. Self-administered. Suitable for group use. BRITISH PUBLISHER

Timed: 10 minutes

Scoring: Examiner evaluated

Cost: Contact publisher

Publisher: NFER-NELSON Publishing Company Ltd.

GRAVIDOMETER
Panos D. Bardis

Adolescent, adult

Purpose: Measures knowledge of the anatomical and physiological aspects of pregnancy. Used in clinical assessments, marriage and family counseling, and research on human sexuality and family classes.

Description: 50–item paper-pencil true-false test measuring knowledge of human pregnancy. Self-administered. Suitable for group use.

Untimed: 12 minutes

Scoring: Hand key

Cost: Free

Publisher: Panos D. Bardis

GROW
Thomas J. Henry, Virginia M. Henry, and Samuel E. Krug

Adult

Purpose: Assesses and assists in the development of marital counseling and marriage enrichment programs.

Description: Program of assessment, learning activities, and personal development. The 189–item paper-pencil

multiple-choice inventory is divided into four sections assessing various areas of personality. Results of the inventory are used to develop four individualized lessons covering bonding, communication, decision making, and clarification of roles. Each lesson contains a self-evaluation exercise designed to increase individual awareness of the topic area. Combined, the assessment and lessons are designed to provide a program of marital growth and communication. The inventory is based on the Adult Personality Inventory (see separate entry). Self-administered. Suitable for group use.

Untimed: Inventory 45 minutes; lessons vary

Scoring: Computer scored

Cost: $20.00–$45.00 per couple depending on quantities and options

Publisher: MetriTech, Inc.

GROWING LOVE IN CHRISTIAN MARRIAGE
Richard A. Hunt and Joan A. Hunt

Adolescent, adult

Purpose: Enables a couple to explore and discuss perceptions and issues in their relationship. Used to elicit comparisons and similarities between partners as part of a counselor's sessions.

Description: Interactive computer presentation of four major components of a couple's relationship: clarifying goals and values, views of personality, conflict resolution, and expectations about wants and needs. The instrument requires an IBM compatible computer for administration, with the option for printing results, as well as seeing results, on the computer screen. The program is related to the authors' book for couples, *Preparing for Christian Marriage* (also titled *Growing Love in Christian Marriage*.) Each partner enters own data directly into the computer. Examiner required. Suitable for group use.

Untimed: 20–30 minutes

Scoring: Computer scored

Cost: Computer program, couple's book $69.00

Publisher: Datascan

Information and availability unconfirmed; last verified in 1987.

HALL-TONNA INVENTORY OF VALUES
Refer to page 177.

HARDING STRESS-FAIR COMPATIBILITY TEST
Christopher P. Harding

Adult

Purpose: Measures an individual's intellectual, social, emotional, and philosophical orientation. Identifies and matches compatible pairs of individuals. Used for research and personal matching services.

Description: 46–item paper-pencil multiple-choice inventory assessing 10 factors related to the degree of compatibility between two individuals: intellective (tendency to think things through to a final conclusion), extroversion, sensitivity, idealism, goal setting, awareness (aware beyond immediate concerns), group detachment, advocacy (cooperative maturity), complexity (degree of inner defensiveness), and dominance-aggression.
Tables printed on the back of the test identify 12 levels of compatibility: optimum compatibility, beginnings of identity fusion, complete mutual reciprocation, equivalent evaluations, "best friend" status, deep friendship possible, reciprocation with reservations in certain areas, awareness of others' viewpoint, indifferent relationship, mild antagonism, antagonism, and complete alienation. The scoring sheet contains data on norm distribution, formulae for matching, and explanation. Not available to residents of the United States and Canada. Examiner required. Suitable for group use.
AUSTRALIAN PUBLISHER

Untimed: Varies

Scoring: Computer scored

Cost: Inventory with computer scoring and matching service $100.00; inventory with scoring sheet available for research purposes free of charge

Publisher: Harding Tests

INTERPERSONAL BEHAVIOR SURVEY (IBS)
Refer to page 245.

MARITAL EVALUATION CHECKLIST
Leslie Navran

Adult

Purpose: Assesses common characteristics and problem areas in a marital relationship. Used as a survey instrument in clinical and counseling settings to initiate the consultation process and introduce the client to formal diagnostic testing.

Description: 140–item paper-pencil test organized in three sections: reasons for marrying, current problems, and motivation for counseling. Areas surveyed include interpersonal/emotional, material/economic, social, personal, money and work, sex, personal characteristics, and marital relationship. The test is a component of the Clinical Checklist Series. Self-administered. Suitable for group use.

Untimed: 10–20 minutes

Scoring: Examiner evaluated

Cost: 50 checklists $17.95

Publisher: Psychological Assessment Resources, Inc.

MARITAL SATISFACTION INVENTORY (MSI)
Douglas K. Snyder

Adult

Purpose: Identifies the nature and extent of marital distress. Used in marital and family counseling.

Description: Multiple-item paper-pencil or computer-administered true-false test providing information concerning nine basic measured dimensions of marriage: affective communication, problem-solving communication, time together, disagreement about finances, sexual dissatisfaction, role orientation, family history of distress, dissatisfaction with children, and conflict over childrearing. In addition, a validity scale and a global distress scale measure each spouse's overall dissatisfaction with the marriage. The test is available in two forms: a 280–item version for couples with children and a 239–item version for childless couples. The results for both spouses are recorded on the same profile form, graphically identifying the areas of marital distress. Each spouse's scores can be individually evaluated as well as directly compared, thereby facilitating diagnostic and intervention procedures. Group mean profiles for each sex are provided for couples seeking general marital therapy, couples seeking divorce, couples with specific sexual dysfunctions, physically abused wives, and couples with specific distress about childrearing. The manual presents a number of case illustrations. The microcomputer version is available on IBM PC or compatible systems. Examiner required. Not suitable for group use.

Untimed: 30–40 minutes

Scoring: Hand key; may be computer scored

Cost: Complete kit (booklets, answer sheets, profile forms, key, manual) $75.00; IBM version (25 uses) $110.00

Publisher: Western Psychological Services

MARITAL SATISFACTION SCALE (MSS) AND MARITAL COMMUNICATION SCALE (MCS) IN FAMILY INVENTORIES
David H. Olson, David G. Fournier, and Joan Druckman

Couples

Purpose: Assesses marital functioning. Used for research and clinical work with couples and families.

Description: Two 10–item paper-pencil subscales from the ENRICH inventory. Examinees rate items on a 5–point Likert scale. Examiner/self-administered. Suitable for group use.

Untimed: Varies

Scoring: Hand key

Cost: Manual, unlimited copying $10.00

Publisher: Family Social Science

MARRIAGE ADJUSTMENT INVENTORY
Morse P. Manson and Arthur Lerner

Adult

Purpose: Identifies causes of marital tension and distress. Used for marital and family counseling.

Description: 157–item paper-pencil multiple-choice test measuring 12 common marital problem areas: family relations, dominance, immaturity, neurotic traits, sociopathic traits, money management, children, interests, physical, abilities, sexual, and incompatibility. Clients indicate which of the problem statements apply to themselves, their spouses, or both. The test yields four evaluative scores indicating the severity of marital maladjustment. Self-administered. Suitable for group use.

Untimed: 10–15 minutes

Scoring: Hand key

Cost: Kit (25 forms, manual) $18.00

Publisher: Western Psychological Services

MARRIAGE ADJUSTMENT SCHEDULE 1A
Marriage Council of Philadelphia

Married couples

Purpose: Aids counselors of married couples by obtaining a wide range of relevant information.

Description: 34–item paper-pencil test that secures independent responses about the couple's shared activities, feelings about those activities, problem areas in the marriage, and the sharing of responsibilities. The test provides data on attitudes, feelings, and problem areas for the counselor to review as he continues to work with the couple. The schedule is completed independently by couples prior to the first interview. Not to be considered a psychological test. Self-administered. Not suitable for group use.

Untimed: 30 minutes

Scoring: Examiner evaluated

Cost: Schedule $0.20; 100 schedules $15.00

Publisher: Marriage Council of Philadelphia, Inc.

Information and availability unconfirmed; last verified in 1988.

MARRIAGE ADJUSTMENT SCHEDULE 1B
Marriage Council of Philadelphia

Married couples

Purpose: Provides the counselor with information concerning a couple's feelings, attitudes, and behavior regarding sex.

Description: 36–item paper-pencil schedule. The counselor completes the inventory during the counseling hour by using an interview format to survey the couple's feelings, attitudes, and behavior. The schedule does not attempt to assess the couple's factual knowledge of human sexuality, nor does it provide a psychological basis for counseling. Examiner required. Not suitable for group use.

Untimed: Varies

Scoring: Examiner evaluated

Cost: Schedule $0.20; 100 schedules $15.00

Publisher: Marriage Council of Philadelphia, Inc.

Information and availability unconfirmed; last verified in 1988.

MARRIAGE AND FAMILY ATTITUDE SURVEY
Donald V. Martin and Maggie Martin

Adolescent, adult

Purpose: Assesses attitudes towards a variety of marital issues. Used as an aid in premarriage and marriage counseling.

Description: 60–item paper-pencil multiple-choice test assessing attitudes toward finances, health, children, and in-laws. A fifth-grade reading level is required. Examiner/self-administered. Suitable for group use.

Untimed: 10 minutes

Scoring: Hand key

Cost: Specimen set (includes manual) $5.00; replacement manual $4.50; 25 test forms $15.00

Publisher: Psychologists and Educators, Inc.

MARRIAGE PROBLEMS SCALE
Clifford H. Swenson and Anthony Fiore

Adult—Ages 16 and older

Purpose: Assesses various aspects of marital relationships.

Description: 43–item paper-pencil multiple-choice test consisting of six subscales measuring various areas of a married couple's relationship: Goals of Marriage, Childrearing, Money, Physical Care and Housekeeping, Relatives and In-laws, and Expression of Affection. The test yields a total score and scores for each subscale. Items may be read to visually, physically, or hearing-impaired individuals. Examiner/self-administered. Suitable for group use. Available in Norwegian.

Untimed: Not available

Scoring: Hand key

Cost: $5.00

Publisher: Professional Resource Exchange

MARRIAGE SCALE
J. Gustav White

Adult

Purpose: Compares the opinions, attitudes, and beliefs of premarital or marital partners. Used for premarital, marital, and family counseling.

Description: 21–item paper-pencil inventory measuring factors related to marital life and compatibility. Each partner is asked to rate on a 10–point scale statements pertaining to the following topics: mutual understanding, outlook on life, religion, love, intercommunication, objectional habits, pleasures, relatives, children, sex, occupation, interests, aesthetic tastes, finances, major plans, and so forth. After each subject completes his or her scale, each partner's profile is copied onto the profile of the other partner for a direct comparison of their responses.

A four-page folder serves as a permanent file record. Not suitable for persons with below average reading ability. Self-administered. Suitable for group use.

Untimed: 10–15 minutes

Scoring: Hand key; examiner evaluated

Cost: Specimen set $5.00; 25 rating folders $15.00

Publisher: Psychologists and Educators, Inc.

MATE (MARITAL ATTITUDE EVALUATION)
Will Schutz

Adult

Purpose: Assesses the relationship between husband and wife or other closely related persons. Used for stimulating discussion and for analysis of relationships.

Description: Multiple-item paper-pencil inventories used for exploring the relationship between husband and wife or other closely related persons. Respondents indicate the kinds of inclusion, control, and affection they desire from their partner and their understanding of their partners' desires. The three dimensions tested are described in *The Interpersonal Underworld* by Will Schutz. Examiner required. Suitable for group use.

Untimed: Not available

Scoring: Hand key

Cost: 25 test booklets $8.00; score key $3.25

Publisher: Consulting Psychologists Press, Inc.

MENOMETER
Panos D. Bardis

Adolescent, adult

Purpose: Measures knowledge of the anatomical and physiological aspects of menstruation. Used for clinical assessment, marriage and family counseling, research on human sexuality, and discussion in family and human sexuality classes.

Description: 50–item paper-pencil true-false test in which the subject marks the appropriate answers. Examiner/self-administered. Suitable for group use.

Untimed: 12 minutes

Scoring: Hand key

Cost: Free

Publisher: Panos D. Bardis

MIRROR-COUPLE RELATIONSHIP INVENTORY
Joan A. Hunt and Richard A. Hunt

Adolescent, adult

Purpose: Measures a couple's perceptions of self and each other. Used for counseling, premarital, and enrichment work with couples.

Description: 336–item paper-pencil test measuring content and process dimensions of marriage. The content areas are life-style, parents, career, money, sex, leisure, religion, friends, children, and future. The process areas are personality, self-awareness, security, freedom, problem solving, fight/flight, valuing self, valuing partner, stress, positive communication, negative communication, and satisfaction. One attitude scale measures bias of answers. A couple uses a guidebook to discuss the computer-generated profile of scale scores and item answers. Self-administered. Suitable for group use.

Untimed: 30–45 minutes

Scoring: Computer scored; interactive computer-scoring disk available

Cost: Specimen set (includes scoring for one couple) $10.00; interactive computer scoring disk with booklets $69.00

Publisher: Datascan

Information and availability unconfirmed; last verified in 1987.

MYERS-BRIGGS TYPE INDICATOR (MBTI)
Refer to page 199.

PAIR ATTRACTION INVENTORY (PAI)
Everett L. Shostrom

Adult

Purpose: Measures aspects contributing to adults' selection of a mate or friend. Used for premarital, marital, and family counseling.

Description: 224–item paper-pencil test assessing the feelings and attitudes of one member of a male-female pair about the nature of the relationship. Percentile norms are provided based on adult samples. The inventory may be used as a component of the Actualizing Assessment Battery (AAB). Examiner required. Suitable for group use.

Untimed: 30 minutes

Scoring: Hand key

Cost: Kit (3 male, 3 female booklets, 50 answer sheets, 50 profiles, manual) $15.00

Publisher: EdITS/Educational and Industrial Testing Service

PARTNER RELATIONSHIP INVENTORY, RESEARCH EDITION (PRI)
Carol Noll Hoskins

Adult

Purpose: Evaluates the level of conflict within a relationship through each partner's perceived feelings about the other partner. Used for research and counseling, especially in conflict resolution in a test-retest situation.

Description: Paper-pencil test evaluating how successfully emotional and interaction needs are being met by an existing relationship. Three forms, each with separate male and female inventories, are available. The Long Form contains 80 items describing the dynamics of the relationship. Individuals rate their agreement or disagreement with the items according to their own perceptions. Form I (40 items) has two alternate forms, IA and IB. Each form contains two scales: Interactional Needs and Emotional Needs. Examiner required. Suitable for group use.

Untimed: 10–30 minutes

Scoring: Hand key; examiner evaluated

Cost: Manual $18.00; 25 Long Forms (specify male or female) $9.00; 25 Long scoring forms $9.00; 25 Form IA or IB test booklets (specify) $9.50; 25 Form IA or IB scoring forms (specify) $9.00

Publisher: Consulting Psychologists Press, Inc.

A PILL SCALE
Panos D. Bardis

Adolescent, adult
Grades 10 and above

Purpose: Measures attitudes towards oral contraceptives. Used for clinical assessment, marriage and family counseling, family attitude research, and discussions in family and sex education.

Description: 25–item paper-pencil test in which the subject reads statements concerning moral, sexual, psychological, and physical aspects of "the pill" and rates them on a scale from 0 (strongly disagree) to 4 (strongly agree). The score equals the sum of the 25 numerical responses. The theoretical range of scores extends from 0 (least liberal) to 100 (most liberal). Examiner/self-administered. Suitable for group use.

Untimed: 10 minutes

Scoring: Examiner evaluated

Cost: Free

Publisher: Panos D. Bardis

PRE-MARITAL COUNSELING INVENTORY
Richard B. Stuart and Freida Stuart

Adult

Purpose: Assesses a couple's relationship before marriage. Identifies basic discrepancies in attitudes and expectations, measures each partner's understanding of the other and provides information that is used to help the couple negotiate a relationship contract before they marry to reduce the intensity of conflict after marriage.

Description: 16–page paper-pencil inventory administered separately to each member of a couple preparing for marriage. The factors covered include religious background, family background, relationships with others, past marital history, history of relationship with prospective marital partner, marital role expectations, division of duties within marriage, and confidence in ability to handle various aspects of marriage. An average reading skill is required. The manual describes use of the instrument in a three-session premarital counseling program. Self-administered. Suitable for group use.

Untimed: 1 hour

Scoring: Computer scored; examiner evaluated

Cost: 20 booklets, guide $19.95; guide $1.95

Publisher: Compuscore

Information and availability unconfirmed; last verified in 1987.

RELATIONSHIP SATISFACTION SURVEY
Rose Lucas

Adolescent, adult—Ages 16 and older

Purpose: Assesses marital conflicts and issues. Used in couple, family, and marital counseling.

Description: 120–item paper-pencil survey assessing the following factors of a relationship: communication patterns, emotional factors, child-rearing practices, habits, affection, career, finances, social-recreational activities, and values. The survey is most helpful when both partners cooperate in completing it. Self-administered. Suitable for group use.

Untimed: 25 minutes

Scoring: Examiner evaluated

Cost: 50 survey forms $15.00

Publisher: The Wilmington Press

Information and availability unconfirmed; last verified in 1987.

SEARCH INSTITUTE PROFILES OF STUDENT LIFE: SEXUALITY
Refer to page 757.

SEX KNOWLEDGE AND ATTITUDE TEST (SKAT)
Harold I. Lief and David Reed

Ages 18 and older

Purpose: Assesses an individual's sexual knowledge and attitudes. Used as a research and educational tool.

Description: 106–item paper-pencil test assessing sexual knowledge (71 items) and attitudes (35 items). The sexual attitudes section contains four subsections: heterosexual relationships, sexual myths, abortion, and autoeroticism. Using medical students for the norm, attitudes are measured for conservatism vs. liberalism. The test should not be administered to individuals with less than a college education. Self-administered. Suitable for group use. Available in Spanish.

Untimed: 20–30 minutes

Scoring: Hand key; may be computer scored

Cost: Test booklet $1.00; answer sheet $0.25; manual $2.50; norms booklet $0.50; set of scoring keys $3.00; Sexual Performance Evaluation $2.00; SKAT-related articles $3.00

Publisher: Marriage Council of Philadelphia, Inc.

Information and availability unconfirmed; last verified in 1988.

SEXOMETER
Panos D. Bardis

Adolescent, adult

Purpose: Assesses knowledge of human reproductive anatomy and physiology. Used for clinical assessment, marriage and family counseling, research on sex knowledge, and discussion in family and sex education.

Description: 50–item paper-pencil test consisting of short-answer and identification questions concerning human reproduction, anatomy, function, physiology, disease, birth control, and sexual behavior. Materials include the test form and answer key. Examiner/self-administered. Suitable for group use.

Untimed: 15 minutes

Scoring: Hand key
Cost: Free
Publisher: Panos D. Bardis

THE SEXUAL COMPATABILITY TEST
Arthur L. Foster

Adult

Purpose: Assesses a couple's sexual relationship. Used to plan sex therapy programs and to predict success of sexual treatment.

Description: 101-item paper-pencil multiple-choice and short-answer test assessing the following factors: sexual satisfaction, sexual dysfunction, variety, communication, interests or desires, and a broad range of sexual activities. The test contains 14 subtests yielding 75 scores. Couples must have an ongoing sexual relationship of at least one year. Materials include test form, answer sheet, and manual. A computer scoring service is available from the publisher. A high-school reading level is required. The test may be administered to physically, visually, and hearing-impaired individuals. Self-administered. Suitable for group use. Available in large print.

Untimed: 1 hour
Scoring: Hand key; may be computer scored
Cost: Complete test $50.00
Publisher: The Phoenix Institute of California

Information and availability unconfirmed; last verified in 1988.

SEXUALITY EXPERIENCE SCALES
J. Frenken and P. Vennix

Adult—Ages 18–55

Purpose: Assesses characteristics of heterosexual behavior. Used in counseling, therapy, and social and medical research.

Description: 83-item paper-pencil instruments measuring four dimensions of sexual experience. SES–1 (21 items) measures restrictive sexual morality (rejection versus acceptance); SES–2 (15

items) measures psychosexual stimulation (seeking, allowing versus avoiding of symbolic sexual stimuli); SES–3 (29 items) measures sexual motivation (approach tendency versus avoidance tendency in sexual interaction with partner); and SES–4 (18 items) measures attraction to own marriage (low versus high). SES–1 and SES–2 are administered to persons who have no sexual partners. The latter two are administered to persons who have durable heterosexual relationships. The tests, derived from item analysis and factor analysis, have 14 relatively independent subscales. Norms are available for married men and women ages 18–55 and for women complaining of sexual dysfunction and their male partners. Examiner/self-administered. Not suitable for group use.
DUTCH PUBLISHER
Untimed: Not available
Scoring: Computer scored
Cost: Manual $46.35; questionnaire for men (scoring form included) $1.50; questionnaire for women (scoring form included) $1.50
Publisher: SWETS and Zeitlinger B.V.

Information and availability unconfirmed; last verified in 1988.

SOCIO-SEXUAL KNOWLEDGE AND ATTITUDES TEST (SSKAT)
Joel Wish, Katherine F. McCombs, and Barbara Edmonson

Developmentally disabled—Ages 18–42

Purpose: Measures sexual knowledge and attitudes of the developmentally disabled of all ages. Used for educational and clinical counseling, planning, and placement.

Description: 227-page stimulus picture book presents realistic pictures illustrating "yes or no" and point-to response questions relevant to 14 socio-sexual topic areas: anatomy terminology, menstruation, dating, marriage, intimacy, intercourse, pregnancy and childbirth, birth control, masturbation and homosexuality, venereal disease, alcohol and drugs, community risks and hazards, and a terminology check. Subjects to be tested must have visual and verbal comprehension; expressive language requirements are minimal. This is a criterion test to determine what the subject knows, believes, and does not know about human sexuality. It does not establish standards. Normative data are based on developmentally disabled individuals ages 14–42, although the test also is used in determining the sexual knowledge and attitudes of nonretarded persons of all ages. The manual presents data on reliability and item-total correlations for each subtest. Examiner required. Not suitable for group use.

Untimed: Open ended

Scoring: Examiner evaluated

Cost: Complete kit (record forms, stimulus picture book, manual) $100.00

Publisher: Stoelting Co.

TEMPERAMENT INVENTORY TESTS
Refer to page 227.

VASECTOMY SCALE: ATTITUDES
Panos D. Bardis

Adolescent, adult
Grades 10 and above

Purpose: Measures attitudes toward the social and psychological aspects of vasectomy. Used for clinical assessment, marriage and family counseling, research on human sexuality, and discussions in family and sex education.

Description: 25–item paper-pencil test in which the subject rates 25 statements concerning vasectomy on a scale from 0 (strongly disagree) to 4 (strongly agree). The score equals the sum of the 25 numerical responses. The theoretical range of scores extends from 0 (lowest approval of vasectomy) to 100 (highest approval). Examiner/self-administered. Suitable for group use.

Untimed: 10 minutes

Scoring: Examiner evaluated

Cost: Free

Publisher: Panos D. Bardis

Neuropsychology and Related

ADULT GROWTH EXAMINATION (AGE)
Robert F. Morgan

Adult

Purpose: Measures an individual's body age. Identifies individuals needing further diagnostic screening. Used in employment and health settings for initial screening purposes.

Description: Three blood pressure tests, a hearing test, and a vision test measuring body age (versus calendar age). Tests are administered in the following order: blood pressure, hearing, blood pressure, vision, and blood pressure. Administration requires a portable electronic blood pressure monitor allowing rapid accurate measurement without a stethoscope, a portable audiometric monitor with a variable volume dial up to 59 db for two frequencies—1000 cps and 6000 cps, and a portable visual near-point indicator (visual targets with pica type sentence—near point of clear focus tested). Raw scores for each of the subtests are converted to equivalent age scores. These scores are arranged in rank order with the median score being the tested body age of the individual being examined. The examination may be administered by trained paraprofessionals. The 1986 manual includes complete instructions for administration and scoring, conversion tables, and discussions of validity, reliability, and uses. Examiner required. Not suitable for group use.

Untimed: 10–15 minutes

Scoring: Examiner evaluated

Cost: $14.00

Publisher: Robert F. Morgan

ADULT NEUROPSYCHOLOGICAL QUESTIONNAIRE
Fernando Melendez

Adolescent, adult—Ages 16 and older

Purpose: Evaluates conditions that may suggest underlying brain dysfunctions or other organic conditions. Used as a symptom checklist for making appropriate referrals to other doctors and for further neuropsychological testing.

Description: 59-item paper-pencil questionnaire evaluating complaints, symptoms, and signs that may suggest brain dysfunction. The questionnaire also monitors the course of a person's recovery or decline over a period of time. The examiner asks questions and instructs the subject to elaborate when appropriate. Examiner required. Not suitable for group use. Available in Spanish.

Untimed: 10–15 minutes

Scoring: Examiner evaluated

Cost: Complete kit (50 forms, manual) $13.00

Publisher: Psychological Assessment Resources, Inc.

ANOMALOUS SENTENCES REPETITION TEST
D. Weeks

Adult—Ages 55–90

Purpose: Differentiates between dementia and depression in the elderly or in younger patients with brain damage. Used by psychologists, geriatricians, speech therapists, occupational therapists, doctors, nurses and psychiatrists.

Description: 6-item orally administered test designed to distinguish between dementia and depression in older adults. The test is also used to assess cognitive function in patients with suspected organic impairment of the central nervous system. The examinee repeats anomalous sentences after the examiner has read them aloud. Two practice sentences are provided in addition to the six scored items. To facilitate retesting, four parallel versions of the test are provided. Medica-

tion levels, ECT, and minor neurotic symptoms should not affect performance. No visual or motor skills are required. Raw error scores are converted to age adjusted scores and compared with cutoff scores for individuals ages 55 and older. Separate cutoff scores are provided for younger patients. Examiner required. Not suitable for group use.

Untimed: 5 minutes for each parallel version

Scoring: Hand key

Cost: Contact publisher

Publisher: NFER-NELSON Publishing Company Ltd.

APRAXIA BATTERY FOR ADULTS (ABA)
Barbara L. Dabul

Adult

Purpose: Assesses presence of apraxia in adult patients and determines severity of disorder. Also used to document progress.

Description: Multiple-item test assessing the presence of apraxia. The test contains seven subtests: Diadochokinetic Rate, Increasing Word Length, Limb and Oral Apraxia, Latency and Utterance Time for Polysyllabic Words, Repeated Trials Test, and Inventory of Articulation Characteristics. Stimuli are used to elicit a physical response. A Profile for Severity of Apraxia is generated. Materials required are an examiner's manual, picture plates, response forms, summary/profile sheets, a stopwatch, and a tape recorder. The examiner must be a speech-language clinician. Examiner required. Not suitable for group use.

Untimed: Varies

Scoring: Examiner evaluated

Cost: Complete kit $54.00

Publisher: PRO-ED

ASSESSMENT OF APHASIA AND RELATED DISORDERS, SECOND EDITION
Harold Goodglass and Edith Kaplan

Adult

Purpose: Assesses the functioning of aphasic patients. Used for clinical evaluations.

Description: Multiple-item oral-response paper-pencil and task-performance test yielding 43 scores relating to recognized aphasic syndromes, including severity rating, fluency, auditory comprehension, naming, oral reading, repetition, paraphasia, automatized speech, reading comprehension, writing, and music. The test also provides the following seven ratings: melodic line, phrase length, articulatory agility, grammatical form, paraphasia in running speech, word finding, and auditory comprehension. The test manual, *The Assessment of Aphasia and Related Disorders*, includes information on the nature of aphasic deficits, common clusters of defects, statistical information, administration and scoring procedures, and illustrations of test profiles that correspond to major aphasic syndromes. Examiner required. Not suitable for group use.

Untimed: Varies

Scoring: Examiner evaluated

Cost: Complete set (manual, examination booklets, and Boston Naming Test) $36.50; 25 examination booklets $15.00

Publisher: Lea and Febiger

AUTISM SCREENING INSTRUMENT FOR EDUCATIONAL PLANNING (ASIEP)
Refer to page 231.

BAY AREA FUNCTIONAL PERFORMANCE EVALUATION, 2ND EDITION (BAFPE)
Refer to page 158.

BEHAVIOR RATING INSTRUMENT FOR AUTISTIC AND OTHER ATYPICAL CHILDREN (BRIAAC)
Refer to page 27.

BENDER VISUAL MOTOR GESTALT TEST
Lauretta Bender

Ages 3–adult

Purpose: Assesses visual-motor functions. Also used to evaluate developmental problems in children, learning disabilities, retardation, psychosis, and organic brain disorders.

Description: Test consists of nine Gestalt cards. The examiner presents the cards to the subject one at a time and in order, and the subject reproduces on blank paper the configuration or design shown on each card. Responses are scored according to the development of the concepts of form, shape, and pattern and orientation in space. Analysis of performance may indicate the presence of psychosis and maturational lags. Scoring service is provided by Koppitz and Grune & Stratton. Examiner required. Slides may be used for group administration.

Untimed: 15–20 minutes

Scoring: Examiner evaluated; scoring service available

Cost: Test cards with manual of instruction $5.00; monograph and its clinical uses $12.00; slides with manual of instruction $15.00

Publisher: American Orthopsychiatric Association, Inc.

Information and availability unconfirmed; last verified in 1987.

BENTON REVISED VISUAL RETENTION TEST
Arthur Benton

Ages 8–adult

Purpose: Measures visual memory, visual perception, and visuoconstructive abilities. Used as a supplement to mental examinations. Also useful in experimental research.

Description: 10–item test of visual perception, visual memory, and visuoconstructive abilities. Items are designs that are shown to the subject one by one. The subject studies each design and reproduces it as exactly as possible by drawing it on plain paper. Materials include Design Cards and three alternate and equivalent forms, C, D, and E. Examiner required. Not suitable for group use.

Untimed: 5 minutes

Scoring: Examiner evaluated

Cost: Complete set (manual, 3 forms of design cards, 50 record forms) $59.00; manual $25.00; 50 record forms $15.00

Publisher: The Psychological Corporation

Information and availability unconfirmed; last verified in 1988.

BEXLEY-MAUDSLEY AUTOMATED PSYCHOLOGICAL SCREENING (BMAPS)
William Acker and Clare Acker

Adult

Purpose: Assesses psychological defects resulting from organic brain damage. Used to evaluate chronic alcoholics and to screen new patients before referring them for further evaluation.

Description: Six computer-administered tests assessing psychological functioning: Visual Spatial Ability Test—Little Men, Symbol Digit Coding, Visual Perceptual Analysis, Verbal Recognition Memory, Visual Spatial Recognition Memory, and the Bexley-Maudsley Category Sorting Test (abstract problem solving). Versions are available for use with the Commodore 64 and Apple II microcomputer systems. A specially designed patient keyboard, which clips over the computer keyboard, contains nine response keys and three masks for those tests that require fewer keys. Raw and standardized scores are available immediately upon completion of the test. The manual provides details of administration, scoring, and theoretical background. The test may be administered by psychologists, psychiatrists, and nurses. Examiner required. Not suitable for group use.
BRITISH PUBLISHER

Untimed: Varies

Scoring: Computer scored

Cost: Contact publisher

Publisher: NFER-NELSON Publishing Company Ltd.

THE BODER TEST OF READING-SPELLING PATTERNS
Refer to page 631.

THE BOOKLET CATEGORY TEST (BCT)
Nick A. DeFilippis and Elizabeth McCampbell

Adolescent, adult—Ages 15 and older

Purpose: Diagnoses brain dysfunction. Used for clinical assessment of brain damage.

Description: 208–item test of concept formation and abstract reasoning. Figures are presented one at a time to the subject, who responds with a number between one and four. This is the booklet version of the Halstead Category Test. The first four subtests may be used to predict total error scores if time limitations do not allow administration of the entire BCT. Cutoff scores are used. Examiner required. Not suitable for group use.

Untimed: 30–60 minutes

Scoring: Examiner evaluated

Cost: Complete set (BCT in 2 volumes, manual, 50 scoring forms) $165.00

Publisher: Psychological Assessment Resources, Inc.

BOSTON NAMING TEST
Edith Kaplan, Harold Goodglass, and Sandra Weintraub

All ages

Purpose: Used with learning disabled, brain-damaged, dementing, and aphasic populations.

Description: 60–item wide-range picture naming test used as part of language assessment in populations at risk for brain damage. The 60 pictures are contained in a single test booklet. Examiner required. Not suitable for group use. Available in Spanish.

Untimed: 30 minutes

Scoring: Examiner evaluated

Cost: 25 answer booklets $6.00

Publisher: Lea and Febiger

CALIFORNIA VERBAL LEARNING TEST, RESEARCH EDITION
Dean C. Delis, Joel H. Kramer, Edith Kaplan, and Beth A. Ober

Adolescent, adult—Ages 13 and older

Purpose: Assesses verbal learning and memory deficits and aids in designing and monitoring rehabilitation. Used with the elderly and the neurologically impaired.

Description: Multitrial verbal-learning task consisting of 16 categorized words used in immediate and delayed free-recall, cued-recall, and recognition trials. A second word list also is presented to obtain interference measures. Indices of learning strategies, error types, primacy/recency effects, and other process data are provided. Optional software provides a scoring and administration system that produces graphic representations of test data and automatically calculates over 25 critical parameters of learning and memory. Examiner required. Not suitable for group use.

Untimed: 35 minutes, including a 20–minute delay period

Scoring: Examiner evaluated; may be computer scored

Cost: 25 record booklets $20.00; 25 scorings and administrative software $79.00; manual $40.00

Publisher: The Psychological Corporation

Information and availability unconfirmed; last verified in 1988.

CANTER BACKGROUND INTERFERENCE PROCEDURE (BIP) FOR THE BENDER GESTALT TEST
Arthur Canter

Adolescent, adult—Ages 15 and older

Purpose: Assesses the probability of organic brain damage among individuals ages 15 and older. Used for diagnosis and to plan rehabilitation programs.

Description: 10–item paper-pencil test comparing the subject's results on the standard Bender Gestalt Test (in which the subject is presented with stimulus cards and asked to copy the designs on a blank sheet of paper) with the results of a Bender Gestalt Test in which the subject reproduces the designs on a special sheet with intersecting sinusoidal lines that provide a background "noise" or interference during the copying task. The difference between the standard and the BIP results provides the basis for defining the subject's level of impairment. Specific ranges of adequacy and inadequacy of performance are defined to permit a measure of impairment having a high probability of association with organic brain damage or disease. Scoring is a modification of the standard Pascal-Suttell system. Examiner required. Not suitable for group use.

Untimed: 20–30 minutes

Scoring: Examiner evaluated

Cost: Complete kit (25 tests, manual) $27.50

Publisher: Western Psychological Services

CAPTAIN'S LOG
Joseph A. Sandford and Richard J. Browne

Child, adolescent, adult— Ages 6 and older

Purpose: Assesses brain dysfunction and used in diagnosing learning disabilities. Used with individuals whose full cognitive potential was not developed or whose cognitive functioning was lost through disease or injury, including learning disabled, mentally retarded, special vocational, and stroke and head injury populations. Designed primarily for cognitive training and rehabilitation.

Description: Series of 28 computer-administered tasks covering attention, visual/motor, numeric concepts, and conceptual skills. The Attention Skills module contains eight programs: Auditory Discrimination/Rhythm, Auditory Discrimination/Tones, Color Discrimination/Inhibition, Scanning Reaction/Inhibition, Scanning Reaction Time, Stimulus Reaction/Fields, Stimulus Reaction/Inhibition, and Stimulus Reaction Time. Seven programs comprise the Visual/Motor Skills module: Finger Tapping, Maze Learning, Spatial Orientation, Visual Tracking/Discrimination, Visual Tracking/Inhibition, Visual Tracking/Response, and Visuospatial Memory. The Conceptual Skills module consists of six programs: Pattern Display Match, Numeric Skills, Size Discrimination, Symbolic Display Match, Trail Sequence A, and Trail Sequence B. The Numeric Concepts/Memory Skills module consists of seven programs: Numeric Discrimination, Numeric Combination, Number Line Logic, Numeric Distinctions, Ordinal Numbers, Numeric Sequences, and Numeric Classification. Responses are input using the Apple mouse, a trackball, or a sip-and-puff headset. Each program offers three levels of skill—beginner, intermediate, and advanced. The programs operate on Apple IIe, Apple II+, or IBM PC systems. Examiner required. Not suitable for group use.

Untimed: 3 minutes per program

Scoring: Computer scored

Cost: Contact publisher

Publisher: Brain Train, Inc.

CARD SORTING BOX

Refer to page 1064.

THE CHILD NEUROPSYCHOLOGICAL QUESTIONNAIRE
Fernando Melendez

Child, adolescent—Ages 6–16

Purpose: Evaluates children suspected of having brain dysfunction. Used as part of a comprehensive evaluation that should include a neuropsychological and pediatric neurological examination.

Description: 41–item paper-pencil questionnaire reviewing possible complaints, symptoms, and signs that suggest underlying brain dysfunction. The test encourages the examiner to consider alternative problems and make appropriate referrals for further studies. The questionnaire can be used as a basis for dis-

cussion with the child's parents. Examiner required. Not suitable for group use. Available in Spanish.

Untimed: 10–15 minutes

Scoring: Examiner evaluated

Cost: Complete kit (50 forms, manual) $13.00

Publisher: Psychological Assessment Resources, Inc.

COGNITIVE BEHAVIOR RATING SCALES (CBRS), RESEARCH EDITION
J. Michael Williams

Adult

Purpose: Determines the presence and assesses the severity of cognitive impairment, behavioral deficits, and observable neurological signs in individuals with possible brain impairment. Also used to assess dementia.

Description: 116–item paper-pencil instrument consisting of nine scales intended to elicit information about the examinee's daily behaviors: Language Deficit, Agitation, Need for Routine, Depression, Higher Cognitive Deficits, Memory Disorder, Dementia, Apraxia, and Disorientation. The items on the scales are rated by the examinee's significant other. T-scores and percentiles are reported for each of the nine scale scores. Examiner required. Not suitable for group use.

Untimed: 15–20 minutes

Scoring: Examiner evaluated

Cost: Kit (manual, 25 reusable item booklets, 50 rating booklets) $32.00

Publisher: Psychological Assessment Resources, Inc.

THE COGNITIVE PARTICIPATION RATING SCALE (CPRS)
Rosamond Gianutsos

Adolescent, adult

Purpose: Assesses progress following head injury or CVA.

Description: 23–item computer-administered index of the cognitive status of individuals undergoing rehabilitation for brain injury. The behavioral domains covered are Awareness of Therapy, Planning, Memory (Recent), Orientation, Quality of Participation, and Social/Metacognition. The scale focuses on how well the individual meets the challenges presented in therapy situations.

The computer program, which operates on Apple II series (80–column display) and IBM PC systems (and compatibles, CGA display), displays items, individual scale points, and normal ranges. For each item and scale, the program also provides definitions, illustrations, and suggestions for unusual situations. Full and subscale scores are compiled, results are displayed and printed, and scores may be saved to disk for analysis. Examiner required. Not suitable for group use.

Untimed: Varies

Scoring: Computer scored

Cost: $75.00

Publisher: Life Science Associates

COMMUNICATIVE ABILITIES IN DAILY LIVING (CADL)
Refer to page 691.

COMPLEX-ATTENTION REHABILITATION PROGRAM
Robert J. Sbordone and Steven Hall

Adolescent, adult

Purpose: Trains cognitively impaired and brain-injured adolescents and adults to improve their attentional skills.

Description: Computer-administered program that presents the patient with visual tracking tasks that increase in complexity according to the patient's performance. The patient uses a hand-held joystick to keep a small circle within a constantly moving square. At the intermediate level, the task involves simultaneously tracking two squares of different sizes and speeds. At more advanced levels, the program trains the patient to utilize language and problem-solving strategies to perform the task. The program makes decisions such as whether to interpose a rest period, increase or decrease the complexity of the task, provide

external cues, or terminate the session. It also contains a speech synthesizer option for vocal presentation to patients with reading problems. The program operates on an Apple (II+, IIe, IIc) computer system using only one disk drive. Examiner/self-administered. Not suitable for group use.

Untimed: Not available

Scoring: Computer scored

Cost: Complete program, including instructional manual $195.00; shipping fee $3.00

Publisher: Robert J. Sbordone

Information and availability unconfirmed; last verified in 1988.

CONTINUOUS VISUAL MEMORY TEST (CVMT)
Donald E. Trahan and Glenn J. Larrabee

Adult—Ages 18–70

Purpose: Assesses the visual memory of neurologically impaired individuals.

Description: Multiple-item verbally administered oral-response visual memory test in three parts. The Acquisition Task (recognition memory) requires the individual to discriminate between new and old repeated stimuli from among 112 designs presented at 2–second intervals. The Delayed Recognition Task measures retrieval from long-term storage and is administered after a 30–minute delay. The Visual Discrimination Task assesses the individual's ability to perceive and discriminate stimuli, thus distinguishing visual discrimination deficits from visual memory problems. Examiner required. Not suitable for group use.

Untimed: 45–50 minutes (includes 30–minute delay)

Scoring: Examiner evaluated

Cost: Kit (manual, stimulus cards, 50 scoring forms) $59.95

Publisher: Psychological Assessment Resources, Inc.

DEMENTIA RATING SCALE (DRS)
Refer to page 44.

DEVELOPMENTAL TEST OF VISUAL-MOTOR INTEGRATION (VMI)
*Keith E. Beery and
Norman A. Buktenica*

Ages 3–18

Purpose: Identifies children with visual perception, hand control, and eye-hand coordination problems. Used with children ages 3–18 and developmentally delayed adults.

Description: Multiple-item paper-pencil test measuring the integration of visual perception and motor behavior. Test items, arranged in order of increasing difficulty, consist of geometric figures that the children are asked to copy. The Short Test Form (15 figures) is used with children ages 3–8. The Long Test Form (24 figures) is used with children ages 3–18 and adults with developmental delays. The manual includes directions for administration, scoring criteria, developmental comments, age norms, suggestions for teaching, percentiles, and standard score equivalents. Examiner required. Suitable for group use.

Untimed: Varies

Scoring: Examiner evaluated

Cost: 25 short forms $30.20; 100 short forms $115.50; 25 long forms $41.95; 100 long forms $162.75; manual for both forms $15.00; monograph $17.00

Publisher: Modern Curriculum Press, Inc.

THE DIGIT-DIGIT TEST
*Robert J. Sbordone, Steven Hall, and
Mark Seecof*

Child, adolescent, adult

Purpose: Assesses and trains complex attentional skills in normal, brain-injured, and cognitively impaired patients.

Description: Computer-administered test of complex attentional skills sensitive to the effects of traumatic brain injury and a variety of subtle neurological disorders in children. It is a numerical coding task in which the patient selects an appropriate stimulus (digit) within a horizontal array, identifies a second stimulus (digit) in a vertical array, and rapidly enters the latter digit on the keyboard. The program permits assessment and training of complex attentional skills that are typically impaired following brain injury. The program includes a training paradigm to teach the patient how to take the test. The patient's motor and cognitive processing speeds can be separated and compared. The program is designed for use with Apple (II+, IIe, IIc, III) and IBM PC computer systems. Examiner required. Not suitable for group use.

Untimed: Not available

Scoring: Computer scored

Cost: Complete program, including instructional manual $250.00; shipping fee $3.00

Publisher: Robert J. Sbordone

Information and availability unconfirmed; last verified in 1988.

DIGITAL FINGER TAPPING TEST (DFTT)
*Allen D. Brandon and
Thomas L. Bennett*

All ages

Purpose: Assesses psychomotor performance as an element of neuropsychological functioning. Used in neuropsychological assessments.

Description: Electronic tapping test consisting of five 10–second finger tapping trials. This test is suitable for individuals with visual and hearing impairments. Individuals with physical impairments who have intact hand function can be tested. Examiner required. Not suitable for group use.

Timed: 1 minute, 40 seconds

Scoring: Machine scored

Cost: Test kit and digital tapper $207.00

Publisher: Western Psychological Services

DRIVING ADVISEMENT SYSTEM (DAS)
Rosamond Gianutsos

Adult

Purpose: Assesses an individual's readiness to drive after experiencing head injury or stroke.

Description: 5–task computer-administered program assessing the cognitive abilities required to operate a motor vehicle, including a) choice and execution of components of reaction time, b) response to complex processing demands, c) impulse control, d) ability to sustain performance, e) flexibility (ability to adjust readily to changed circumstances), f) eye-hand coordination (tracking), and g) judgment (based on self-appraisal). Also included is a report generation program that displays the individual's scores in comparison to the scores of over 70 safe drivers representing a variety of age groups. The system, which operates on an Apple II series or IBM PC (or compatible, CGA display) computer system, is sold as a package that includes the software, steering and foot pedal modules, a computer interface, and a 1-day application seminar. User qualifications and a description of the professional setting in which the program is to be used must accompany all orders. Examiner required. Not suitable for group use.

Untimed: 1 hour
Scoring: Computer scored
Cost: Complete system $1,200.00
Publisher: Life Science Associates

THE DYSINTEGRAL LEARNING CHECKLIST FOR DYSLEXIA
Mary Meeker and Valerie Maxwell

Child, adolescent, adult

Purpose: Identifies students with potential learning problems. Used by pediatricians, neurologists, special education diagnosticians, and teachers.

Description: Multiple-item paper-pencil inventory of symptoms that are predictive of each of the four systems integrated into the cerebellum. The inventory, which identifies dysintegrated functions for learning, covers the following areas: vision, speech and auding, motoric, proprioceptor, and behavioral. Test results are coded to training materials for each system involved. Examiner required. Suitable for group use.

Untimed: Varies
Scoring: Examiner evaluated
Cost: 10 checklists $25.00
Publisher: M & M Systems

DYSLEXIA SCHEDULE
Refer to page 634.

THE DYSLEXIA SCREENING SURVEY (DSS)
Robert E. Valett

Child
Grades 1–6

Purpose: Evaluates basic neuropsychological skills. Used for screening elementary pupils who may be dyslexic and to plan remedial strategies.

Description: 90–item paper-pencil test covering seven factors: functional reading level, reading potential, significant reading discrepancy, specific processing skill deficiencies, neuropsychological dysfunctions, associated factors, and development-remedial strategies. The test is administered individually in several steps, including a compilation of available information and subsequent testing of paper-pencil and body-movement tasks. The survey is recommended for use by special educators, remedial reading specialists, psychologists, and speech therapists. Use is not restricted. Remedial methods are presented in the test author's book, *Dyslexia.* Examiner required. Not suitable for group use.

Untimed: 30 minutes
Scoring: Examiner evaluated
Cost: 10 forms $7.95
Publisher: David S. Lake Publishers
Information and availability unconfirmed; last verified in 1987.

ELIZUR TEST OF PSYCHO-ORGANICITY: CHILDREN & ADULTS
Abraham Elizur

Ages 6–adult

Purpose: Differentiates between organic and non-organic brain disorders. Used by neurologists, psychologists, educators, counselors, and researchers.

Description: Multiple-item task assessment test using drawings, digits, and blocks to provide "uni-dimensional" measurements. Test tasks are easily performed by subjects so that results are not biased by intelligence factors. Separate instructions are provided for administering to adults and to children. The test yields quantitative and qualitative results with cutoff points provided for classifying examinees as organic. Examiner required. Not suitable for group use.

Untimed: 10 minutes

Scoring: Hand key; examiner evaluated

Cost: Kit (25 protocol booklets, 1 set of test materials, manual) $49.50

Publisher: Western Psychological Services

ERROR DETECTION IN TEXTS (DETECT)
Rosamond Gianutsos, Georgine Vroman, and Pauline Matheson

Ages 10–adult

Purpose: Measures foveal imperception in patients with reading deficiencies and head injury and stroke victims.

Description: Paper-pencil or computer-administered test of ability to locate errors in a text. The patient reads 10 typewritten paragraphs and locates errors systematically placed in the left or right half of the page. Some errors are at the beginning of the word, others at the end. The test is available in two forms: A and B. The subject must be able to read simple English words. Operates on Apple II series computers or IBM PC computers with CGA display and compatibles. Examiner required. Not suitable for group use.

Untimed: 20–30 minutes

Scoring: Hand key

Cost: $10.00

Publisher: Life Science Associates

FACIAL RECOGNITION TEST
Arthur L. Benton

Adolescent, adult

Purpose: Assesses a subject's capacity to identify and discriminate photographs of unfamiliar human faces.

Description: Multiple-item multiple-choice test consisting of three parts: matching identical front-view photographs, matching front-view with three-quarter-view photographs, and matching front-view photographs taken under different lighting conditions. The test is available in a 27–item short form and a 54–item long form. The test is arranged so that the first 13 stimulus and response pictures presented comprise the short form. The test is administered orally by the examiner. Each correct response is assigned a score of 1; scores are corrected for age and education. Materials required include a spiral-bound booklet containing stimulus photographs and corresponding response choices, a record sheet, and a manual. Examiner required. Not suitable for group use.

Untimed: Varies

Scoring: Examiner evaluated

Cost: Contact publisher

Publisher: Oxford University Press

FINGER LOCALIZATION TEST
Arthur L. Benton

All ages

Purpose: Assesses subject's finger localization abilities.

Description: 60–item nonverbal test in three parts requiring the subject to indicate which of his fingers is touched by the examiner when a) the subject's hand is visible, b) the subject's hand is hidden from the subject's view, and c) the subject's hand is hidden from the subject's view and the examiner touches a pair of the subject's fingers rather than a single finger. For each of the three phases of the test, the subject places his hand on the table, palm-side up with fingers extended and slightly separated. In the last two phases, the subject's hand is concealed by a curtain. For each of the three phases, the examiner firmly touches the subject's fingertip (two fingertips simultaneously in the third phase) for 2–4 seconds using the pointed end of a pencil. The patient responds by naming the touched fingers, pointing to them on an outline drawing of the stimulated hand, or calling out their numbers. Testing of spastic hemiplegic patients is restricted to the unaffected hand. Examiner required. Not suitable for group use.

Untimed: Varies
Scoring: Hand key
Cost: Contact publisher
Publisher: Oxford University Press

FREE RECALL (FREEREC)
*Rosamond Gianutsos and
Carol Klitzner*

Ages 10–adult

Purpose: Measures short- and long-term memory. Used to assess head injury or stroke as it affects verbal memory.

Description: Computer-administered test measuring short- and long-term retention. Subjects are required to memorize word lists and recall them either after a short delay or after an intervening task. Words are commonly used, monosyllabic nouns from the 1944 Thorndike-Lorge list. Operates on Apple II series computers or IBM PC computers with CGA display and compatibles. Examiner required. Not suitable for group use.

Untimed: 10–12 minutes
Scoring: Computer scored
Cost: $35.00
Publisher: Life Science Associates

FRENCHAY APHASIA SCREENING TEST (FAST)
P. Enderby, V. Wood, and D. Wade

Adult

Purpose: Screens for aphasia. Used by doctors, speech therapists, and nurses on neurological and geriatric hospital wards and in the community as an aid in diagnosis and in making referral and treatment decisions.

Description: Stimulus-response test assessing language comprehension, expression, reading, and writing. The patient is asked a series of questions about a composite picture and also is required to respond to five sentences, which are of graded difficulty, about the picture. The patient also must identify a set of shapes. Examiner required. Not suitable for group use.

BRITISH PUBLISHER
Untimed: 3–10 minutes
Scoring: Examiner evaluated
Cost: Contact publisher
Publisher: NFER-NELSON Publishing Company Ltd.

FRENCHAY DYSARTHRIA ASSESSMENT
Refer to page 697.

FULD OBJECT-MEMORY EVALUATION
Refer to page 44.

FULLERTON LANGUAGE TEST FOR ADOLESCENTS (EXPERIMENTAL EDITION)
Refer to page 697.

GIBSON SPIRAL MAZE
H.B. Gibson

All ages

Purpose: Measures psychomotor performance in both children and adults. Used for screening and clinical diagnosis.

Description: Paper-pencil test measuring psychomotor performance. The test consists of a printed design on a large card that provides a "maze" for the subject to run under timed conditions. Scores of quickness and accuracy are obtained through a standard marking procedure defined in the manual. The test is restricted to senior staff members of any recognized medical or educational institution, medical doctors, and BPS and APA members. Examiner required. Not suitable for group use.

BRITISH PUBLISHER

Untimed: Not available

Scoring: Hand key

Cost: Specimen set £2.95; 20 test cards £4.95 plus VAT; manual £2.00

Publisher: Hodder & Stoughton

GOLDSTEIN-SCHEERER TESTS OF ABSTRACT AND CONCRETE THINKING
Kurt Goldstein and Martin Scheerer

Brain-injured adults

Purpose: Measures impairment of the brain's abstract and concrete reasoning functions. Used for assessment of patients with brain injuries.

Description: Battery of performance tests assessing abstract and concrete reasoning. The Goldstein-Scheerer Cube Test requires the subject to copy colored designs with blocks. The Gelb-Goldstein Color Sorting Test measures the ability to sort a variety of colors according to definite color concepts. The Goldstein-Scheerer Object Sorting Test requires the subject to sort a variety of simultaneously presented objects according to general concepts. The Weigl-Goldstein-Scheerer Color Form Sorting Test involves sorting different colored figures according to categories of color and form. The Goldstein-Scheerer Stick Test measures the subject's ability to copy figures composed of sticks and reproduce them from memory. Materials include all necessary equipment for the five tests. Examiner required. Not suitable for group use.

Untimed: 20–30 minutes

Scoring: Examiner evaluated

Cost: Complete set (all necessary equipment for all 5 tests, monograph, 50 each of 6 record forms) $350.00; component parts for separate tests available

Publisher: The Psychological Corporation

Information and availability unconfirmed; last verified in 1988.

THE GRADED NAMING TEST
Pat McKenna and Elizabeth K. Warrington

Adult

Purpose: Identifies naming deficits. Indicates impaired language functioning in brain-damaged patients. Used with psychiatric, neurological, and geriatric patients.

Description: Multiple-item oral-response test assessing naming deficits in individuals, regardless of range of intellectual ability. Test items consist of picture stimuli that the patient is asked to name. Object pictures have been selected to prevent ambiguous answers. Items of sufficient difficulty are included to adequately assess patients with above-average premorbid intelligence. Equivalent scores on the Wechsler Adult Intelligence Scale Vocabulary, the National Adult Reading Test, and the Schonell Graded Word Reading Test can be derived from a conversion table. Examiner required. Not suitable for group use.

BRITISH PUBLISHER

Untimed: Varies

Scoring: Examiner evaluated

Cost: Contact publisher

Publisher: NFER-NELSON Publishing Company Ltd.

GRASSI BASIC COGNITIVE EVALUATION
Joseph R. Grassi

Child—Ages 4–8

Purpose: Identifies cognitive deficits in children with brain dysfunction. Used by psychologists and educators for clinical assessment.

Description: Measures 27 traits in visual, auditory, and kinesthetic areas. The test is designed for children who are brain damaged, mentally retarded, cognitively disadvantaged, or learning disabled. Examiner required. Not suitable for group use.

Untimed: 30 minutes

Scoring: Examiner evaluated

Cost: Complete kit (25 record forms, manual) $35.00

Publisher: SWETS and Zeitlinger B.V.

Information and availability unconfirmed; last verified in 1988.

GRASSI BLOCK SUBSTITUTION TEST
Joseph R. Grassi

Adolescent, adult

Purpose: Detects the early symptoms of organic brain pathology in adolescents and adults. Used for clinical screening procedures.

Description: Task-assessment test measuring abstract behavior as an indicator of organic brain pathology. Test materials consist of five specially designed semicubes and a manual. The manual is available from Charles C. Thomas Publisher. The examiner must be a clinical psychologist with training and experience in the concepts of abstract versus concrete behavior. Examiner required. Not suitable for group use.

Untimed: Not available

Scoring: Examiner evaluated

Cost: Test materials $30.00; manual $15.00

Publisher: SWETS and Zeitlinger B.V.

Information and availability unconfirmed; last verified in 1988.

GROOVED PEGBOARD

Ages 5–adult

Purpose: Measures hand-eye coordination and fine-finger dexterity. Used as part of a clinical neuropsychological evaluation battery in cases involving brain damage, alcoholism, aging, and epilepsy.

Description: Multiple-operation manual test using a 8″ x 4″ board with a shallow well in the lid and a hole plate containing 25 keyed slots oriented in random directions and a set of 25 keyed pegs. The subject inserts all 25 pegs into the slots with first one hand and then the other. Separate times are recorded for the dominant hand and the nondominant hand. The test is used with the Trites Neuropsychological and the Halstead-Reitan Test Batteries. It is also used to discriminate multiple sclerosis patients from those with other neurological diseases. Examiner required. Suitable for group use.

Untimed: 5 minutes

Scoring: Hand key

Cost: Model 32025 $80.00; 30 replacement pegs (Model 32104) $26.40

Publisher: Lafayette Instrument Company, Inc.

HALSTEAD CATEGORY TEST
Michael Hill

Adult

Purpose: Assesses individuals' perceptual ability to categorize graphic items.

Description: Multiple-item computer-administered test measuring an individual's ability to categorize along a number of different dimensions. The client observes a series of graphic items on the screen and chooses whether an object belongs to or differs from a set of objects. The series gradually increases in difficulty. Fifty sets of client scores may be saved on disk for later examination. Available for use with the Apple II Plus, IIe, and IIc computers and the IBM PC and compatible computers. Examiner required. Not suitable for group use.

Untimed: Not available

Scoring: Computer scored

Cost: $199.00

Publisher: Precision People, Inc.

Information and availability unconfirmed; last verified in 1987.

HALSTEAD-REITAN NEUROPSYCHOLOGICAL TEST BATTERY FOR ADULTS
Reitan Neuropsychology Laboratory and others

Adult

Purpose: Evaluates brain function and dysfunction in adults. Used for clinical evaluation.

Description: Battery of tests assessing adult neuropsychological functioning, including the Halstead Neuropsychological Test Battery, the Wechsler Adult Intelligence Scale, the Trail Making Test, the Reitan-Indiana Aphasia Screening Test, various tests of sensory-perceptual functions, and the Minnesota Multiphasic Personality Inventory. Materials include a category test projection box with electric control mechanism and projector; 208 adult category slides in carousels; tactual performance test (10–hole board, stand, 10 blocks); manual finger tapper; tape cassette for speech-sounds perception test; tactile form recognition test; and a manual for administration and scoring. The components may be ordered separately. Examiner required. Not suitable for group use.

Timed/Untimed: Varies

Scoring: Examiner evaluated

Cost: Adult battery $1,648.95

Publisher: Reitan Neuropsychology Laboratory

HALSTEAD-REITAN NEUROPSYCHOLOGICAL TEST BATTERY FOR CHILDREN
Reitan Neuropsychology Laboratory and others

Child, adolescent—Ages 9–14

Purpose: Evaluates brain function and dysfunction in children. Used for clinical evaluations.

Description: Battery of tests assessing the neuropsychological functioning of children, including the Halstead Neuropsychological Test Battery, the Wechsler Intelligence Scale for Children, the Trail Making Test, the Reitan-Indiana Aphasia Screening Test, various tests of sensory-perceptual functions, and measures of academic achievement. The tests in this battery have been adapted from the Halstead-Reitan Neuropsychological Test Battery for Adults. Much of the equipment used for testing adults also can be used with the children's battery. Adaptations for use with this age group include new slides (stimulus material) for the category test, a new answer form for the speech-sounds perception test, a 6–hole board instead of a 10–hole board for the tactual performance test, and a shortened form of the Trail Making Test. Materials include all necessary equipment, test stimuli, slide carousels, recording forms, and manual for administration, scoring, and evaluation of all tests. The compo-

nents may be purchased separately. Examiner required. Not suitable for group use.

Timed/Untimed: Varies

Scoring: Examiner evaluated

Cost: Older children's battery $1,552.00

Publisher: Reitan Neuropsychology Laboratory

THE HEARING MEASUREMENT SCALE
Refer to page 678.

HOOPER VISUAL ORGANIZATION TEST (HVOT)
H. Elston Hooper

Adolescent, adult

Purpose: Assesses organic brain pathology of both hemispheres. Used for clinical diagnosis.

Description: 30–item pictorial test differentiating between functional and motivational disorders. After being presented with drawings of simple objects cut into several parts and rearranged, the subject is asked to name the objects. Examiner required. Suitable for group use.

Untimed: 15 minutes

Scoring: Hand key

Cost: Complete kit (4 test booklets, manual, 25 administration booklets, 100 answer sheets, scoring key) $120.00

Publisher: Western Psychological Services

HOUSTON TEST FOR LANGUAGE DEVELOPMENT
Refer to page 34.

ILLINOIS TEST OF PSYCHOLINGUISTIC ABILITIES (ITPA)
Refer to page 548.

THE INTERMEDIATE BOOKLET CATEGORY TEST (IBCT)
Paul A. Byrd

Child, adolescent—Ages 9–14

Purpose: Assesses concept formation and abstract reasoning. Used by clinicians to detect brain dysfunction.

Description: 168–item test replicating in booklet format the slides used in the Halstead Category Test. Figures are presented one at a time to the subject, who responds with a number between one and four. The test consists of six subtests. A cutoff score is derived. Examiner required. Not suitable for group use.

Untimed: 30–60 minutes

Scoring: Examiner evaluated

Cost: Complete kit (IBCT in 2 volumes, manual, 50 scoring forms) $195.00

Publisher: Psychological Assessment Resources, Inc.

INTERNATIONAL VERSION OF MENTAL STATUS QUESTION-NAIRE
T.L. Brink

Elderly adults

Purpose: Assesses confusion due to senile dementia in adults.

Description: 10–item oral-response test measuring short-term memory of elderly individuals, primarily in institutional and community environments. A Spanish translation is available. Examiner required. Not suitable for group use.

Untimed: 2–5 minutes

Scoring: Examiner evaluated

Cost: Free

Publisher: T.L. Brink

IS THIS AUTISM?
Refer to page 144.

JORDAN LEFT-RIGHT REVERSAL TEST (JLRRT)–1990 REVISION
Refer to page 636.

JUDGMENT OF LINE ORIENTATION TEST
Arthur L. Benton

Adolescent, adult

Purpose: Measures subject's ability to judge line orientation (direction), one aspect of "spatial thinking."

Description: 30–item test available in two forms, H and V. Both forms present the same items, though in a somewhat different order (each form maintains an ascending order of difficulty). The subject is presented with pairs of partial lines, each of which represents (with respect to origin) a distal, middle, or proximal segment of a response-choice line. There are four types of test stimuli (line-segment pairs): HH (distal), LL (proximal), MM (middle), and mixed. The subject is scored on the number of completely correct responses. Materials required are a record sheet, manual, and spiral-bound booklet containing stimuli and multiple-choice response cards (includes five practice items). Examiner required. Not suitable for group use.

Untimed: Varies

Scoring: Examiner evaluated

Cost: Contact publisher

Publisher: Oxford University Press

JUMP: EYE MOVEMENT EXERCISE
Rosamond Gianutsos, Georgine Vroman, and Pauline Matheson

Ages 8–adult

Purpose: Assesses rapidity of eye movements. Used to assess head injury, stroke, or visual system damage.

Description: Computer-administered test of visual and oculomotor systems. Symbols flash at the left or right edge of the screen, and the subject judges whether they are the same or different. Rapid lateral saccadic movements are required, both left-to-right and right-to-left. The program finds and adjusts to the patient's ability level. Operates on Apple

II series computers or IBM PC computers with CGA display and compatibles. Self-administered. Not suitable for group use.

Untimed: 8–12 minutes

Scoring: Computer scored

Cost: $35.00

Publisher: Life Science Associates

KAHN TEST OF SYMBOL ARRANGEMENT (KTSA)
Theodore C. Kahn

All ages

Purpose: Assesses personality dynamics and the extent of cerebral competence. Used for individual diagnosis and therapy, as well as vocational counseling.

Description: Multiple-task performance test of a subject's cultural/symbolic thinking. The subject is required to sort plastic objects of varying size, color, thickness, and translucence in several ways. The examiner evaluates the subject's symbol pattern and compares it to patterns of normal and clinical groups. For use only by clinical psychologists, psychiatrists, counseling psychologists, school psychologists, and others with professional competence in clinical assessment. Examiner required. Not suitable for group use.

Untimed: 15 minutes

Scoring: Hand key; examiner evaluated

Cost: Complete kit (plastic objects, felt strip, 10 individual record sheets, manual, clinical manual) $50.00; 50 record sheets $15.00; manual $4.00; clinical manual $6.00

Publisher: Psychological Test Specialists

KASANIN-HANFMANN CONCEPT FORMATION TEST (VYGOTSKY TEST) AND MODIFIED VYGOTSKY CONCEPT FORMATION TEST
Refer to page 54.

KENDRICK COGNITIVE TESTS FOR THE ELDERLY
Refer to page 46.

LATERAL PREFERENCE SCHEDULE (LPS)
Raymond S. Dean

Child, adolescent, adult—
Ages 7–adult

Purpose: Measures lateral preference and screens for neurological and cognitive disorders.

Description: 59–item multiple-choice paper-pencil test consisting of six clinical scales (General Laterality, Visually Guided Activities, Visual Activities, Auditory Activities, Strength, and Foot Use) that assess lateral preference for 49 common activities. Two 5–item research scales (Maternal and Paternal) query parental lateral preference. Individuals respond to each item using a 5–point scale ranging from "Left Always" to "Right Always." Materials include manual, test booklets, and profile forms. Examiner must meet APA guidelines. Examiner required. Suitable for group use.

Untimed: 15 minutes

Scoring: Hand key

Cost: Kit (manual, 50 test booklets, 50 profile forms) $32.00

Publisher: Psychological Assessment Resources, Inc.

LEARNING DISABILITY RATING PROCEDURE (LDRP)
Refer to page 638.

LINE BISECTION (BISECT)
*Rosamond Gianutsos,
Georgine Vroman, and
Pauline Matheson*

Ages 8–adult

Purpose: Measures visual hemi-imperception. Used to assess head injury, stroke, or visual system damage.

Description: Computer-administered test measuring the presence of an intact visual system. The computer presents horizontal or vertical lines that have a visible gap somewhere near the center. The subject attempts to center the gap using the arrow keys. Operates on Apple II

---

series computers or IBM PC computers with CGA display and compatibles. Examiner required. Not suitable for group use.

Untimed: 6–8 minutes

Scoring: Computer scored

Cost: $35.00

Publisher: Life Science Associates

LURIA-NEBRASKA NEUROPSYCHOLOGICAL BATTERY
Charles J. Golden, Arnold D. Purisch, and Thomas A. Hammeke

Adolescent, adult—Ages 15 and older

Purpose: Assesses a broad range of neuropsychological functions for individuals ages 15 and older. Used to diagnose specific cerebral dysfunction and to select and assess rehabilitation programs.

Description: Multiple-item verbal, observational test available in two forms: Form I (269 items) and Form II (279 items). The discrete, scored items produce a profile for the following scales: Motor, Rhythm, Tactile, Visual, Receptive Speech, Expressive Speech, Writing, Reading, Arithmetic, Memory, Intellectual, Pathognomonic, Left Hemisphere, Right Hemisphere, Impairment, and Profile Evaluation. Form II also assesses intermediate memory. The battery diagnoses the presence of cerebral dysfunction and determines lateralization and localization.

Test materials include six stimulus cards, a tape cassette, comb, quarter, and stopwatch. A manual provides instructions for administering the test, evidence of reliability and validity, interpretive guides, and copies of the Administration and Scoring Booklet and the Patient Response Booklet. The Administration and Scoring Booklet includes the Profile Form and Computation of Critical Level Tables. It is used to record all scores during administration and provides verbal instructions to be read to the patient. The Patient Response Booklet is provided for items requiring written answers. Microcomputer software is available for computer scoring and interpretation of both forms. Examiner required. Not suitable for group use.

Untimed: 1½–2½ hours

Scoring: Hand key; may be computer scored

Cost: Complete kit Form I (manual, stimulus cards including Christensen cards, tape cassette, 10 scoring booklets, 10 response booklets, 2 answer sheets including publisher scoring and reports) $310.00; complete kit Form II (stimulus cards, tape cassette, manual, 10 patient response booklets, 10 scoring booklets, 2 answer sheets including publisher scoring and reports) $275.00

Publisher: Western Psychological Services

LURIA-NEBRASKA NEUROPSYCHOLOGICAL BATTERY: CHILDREN'S REVISION (LNNB-C)
Charles J. Golden

Child—Ages 8–12

Purpose: Measures cognitive strengths and weaknesses. Used to diagnose cerebral dysfunction and to select and assess rehabilitation programs.

Description: 149–item verbal observational adaptation of the Luria-Nebraska Neuropsychological Battery assessing cognitive functioning. The clinical scales are Motor Functions, Tactile Functions, Receptive Speech, Writing, Arithmetic, Intellectual Processes, Rhythm, Visual Functions, Expressive Speech, Reading, and Memory. The summary scales are Pathognomonic, Left Sensorimotor, and Right Sensorimotor. Two optional scales, Spelling and Motor Writing, are available. Microcomputer software for use with IBM PC or Apple II computers is available for computer scoring and interpretation. Examiner required. Not suitable for group use.

Untimed: 2 hours, 30 minutes

Scoring: Hand key; computer scored

Cost: $310.00

Publisher: Western Psychological Services

LURIA'S NEUROPSYCHOLOGICAL INVESTIGATION
Anne-Lise Christensen

Adult

Purpose: Diagnoses type and severity of brain injury. Used as a basis for planning rehabilitational measures for brain-damaged adults.

Description: Oral-response and task-assessment test begins with a structure for preliminary conversation with the patient and continues with an assessment of the following neurological areas: motor functions, acoustico-motor organization, higher cutaneous and kinesthetic functions, higher visual functions, impressive speech, expressive speech, writing and reading, arithmetical skill, mnestic processes, and intellectual processes. Materials include a set of cards, manual, and text. Examiner required. Not suitable for group use.

Untimed: Not available
Scoring: Examiner evaluated
Cost: Contact publisher
Publisher: Munksgaard; distributed in U.S.A. by Western Psychological Services

MEMORY SPAN (SPAN)
Rosamond Gianutsos and Carol Klitzner

Ages 10–adult

Purpose: Measures concentration and short-term memory. May also be used as a retraining exercise with head injury or stroke patients.

Description: Computer-administered test providing assessment and remediation of memory deficits. A list of words appears on the screen one at a time. After the entire list has appeared, the patient tries to recall a certain number of words from the end of the list. On the first five trials, the patient is asked to recall the last two words; the number to be recalled increases by one for each set of five lists up to a maximum of seven. The patient must be able to read simple English

words. Operates on Apple II series computers or IBM PC computers with CGA display and compatibles. Examiner required. Not suitable for group use.

Untimed: 8–12 minutes
Scoring: Computer scored
Cost: $35.00
Publisher: Life Science Associates

MEMORY-FOR-DESIGNS TEST (MFD)
Frances K. Graham and Barbara S. Kendall

Ages 8.5–60

Purpose: Assesses perceptual-motor coordination. Used to differentiate between functional behavior disorders and those associated with brain injury.

Description: 15–item performance measure of perceptual-motor coordination. Items consist of designs on cardboard cards. The subject is shown a design for five seconds and then attempts to draw it from memory. This procedure is repeated for each of the 15 items. Diagnostic testing and evaluation should be closely supervised by a clinical or school psychologist, psychiatrist, neurologist, or pediatrician. Examiner required. Not suitable for group use.

Untimed: 10 minutes
Scoring: Hand key; examiner evaluated
Cost: Complete kit (revised general manual, 15 design cards, utility set of scoring examples and norms) $17.00; 15 design cards $15.00; scoring examples and norms $2.50; revised manual $5.00
Publisher: Psychological Test Specialists

MINI INVENTORY OF RIGHT BRAIN INJURY (MIRBI)
Patricia A. Pimental and Nancy A. Kingsbury

Adult—Ages 18 and older

Purpose: Identifies severity of right brain injury. Used by psychologists, speech pathologists, neurologists, psychiatrists, physiatrists, occupational therapists, physical therapists, nurses, and other health care professionals.

Description: Multiple-item screening test of right brain injury. Items require visual scanning, finger gnosis, stereognosis, 2–point discrimination, unilateral neglect, reading, writing, attention, visuo-symbolic processing and calculating, praxis, visuo-motor skills, affective language, understanding of humor, explanations of incongruities and absurdities, explanations of figurative language, explanations of similarities, general expressive language ability, emotion and affect processing, general behavior, and psychic integrity. The test provides a severity index and a deficit profile based on underlying process disorders. Cutoff scores are provided for normal vs. brain-injured individuals. Results are printed as percentiles in the various deficit areas. A narrative triplicate report form that can be used to answer consultations is generated. Examiner required. Not suitable for group use.

Untimed: Not available

Scoring: Examiner evaluated

Cost: Complete kit (examiner's manual, 25 test booklets, 25 report forms, storage box) $59.00

Publisher: PRO-ED

MINNESOTA PERCEPTO-DIAGNOSTIC TEST (MPD), 1982 REVISION
Gerald B. Fuller

Ages 5 and older

Purpose: Assesses visual perception and visual motor abilities. Used to classify reading and learning disabilities, identify individuals with emotionally disturbed or schizophrenic perception, and differentiate between brain-damaged and non-brain-damaged individuals.

Description: 6–item paper-pencil test consisting of Gestalt designs on separate cards that the examiner presents individually to the subject. The subject draws each design on a separate sheet of paper. The drawings are scored for degrees of rotation, separation, and distortion, indicating whether perception is normal, emotionally disturbed, or brain damaged. The results also are used to classify reading and learning disabilities as visual,

auditory, or mixed and to measure the maturational level of normal and retarded children. All scores are adjusted for both age and IQ. The test is available in separate scales for children (ages 5–12) and adults (ages 13 and older). Examiner required. Not suitable for group use.

Untimed: 6–8 minutes

Scoring: Hand key; examiner evaluated

Cost: Manual $12.50; cards $6.00; 50 record blanks $5.00; sample kit $18.00

Publisher: Clinical Psychology Publishing Co., Inc.

MINNESOTA SPATIAL RELATIONS TEST
Refer to page 614.

MINNESOTA TEST FOR DIFFERENTIAL DIAGNOSIS OF APHASIA
Refer to page 702.

MOTOR IMPERSISTENCE BATTERY
Arthur L. Benton

All ages

Purpose: Assesses motor impersistence.

Description: Battery of eight tests requiring the maintenance of a movement or posture: keeping eyes closed, protruding tongue (blindfolded), protruding tongue (eyes open), fixation of gaze in lateral visual fields, keeping mouth open, central fixation during confrontation testing of visual fields, head turning during sensory testing, and saying "ah." The procedure for each test is explained in the manual. Examiner required. Not suitable for group use.

Timed: Varies depending on test

Scoring: Examiner evaluated

Cost: Contact publisher

Publisher: Oxford University Press

MULTILINGUAL APHASIA EXAMINATION (MAE)
*Arthur L. Benton and
K. deS. Hamsher*

Adult

Purpose: Assesses various aspects of aphasia.

Description: Multiple-item battery of 11 tests and rating scales assessing visual naming, repetition, fluency, articulation, spelling, aural comprehension, reading, and writing. The battery complements other neuropsychological tests developed at the Benton Laboratory of Neuropsychology. Examiner required. Not suitable for group use.

Untimed: Not available

Scoring: Not available

Cost: Kit (manual, two picture books, set of tokens and letters, 50 each of all record forms) $110.00

Publisher: Distributed by Psychological Assessment Resources, Inc.

NEUROPSYCHOLOGICAL DEFICIT SCALE (NDS) FOR ADULTS
Ralph M. Reitan

Adult

Purpose: Identifies the nature and severity of neuropsychological deficit. Used as a general indicator in clinical situations and in classifying the degree of deficit in circumstances involving litigation.

Description: 42 variables measuring the severity of neuropsychological deficit. Each variable is organized into four sections reflecting the methodological approaches of the Halstead-Reitan Neuropsychological Test Battery for Adults: level of performance, pathognomonic signs, patterns and relationships, and right/left comparisons. Individuals are rated on a 4–point scale ranging from 0 (normal) to 3 (severely impaired). A computer program that converts raw scores from the Halstead-Reitan Neuropsychological Battery for Adults into scores representing clinical competence or degree of deficit is available. The program

yields a four-page report that lists raw scores and converted scores for all 42 variables as well as the individual's overall neuropsychological status. The program is designed for use with IBM PC or Apple II computer systems. Examiner required. Not suitable for group use.

Untimed: Not available

Scoring: Examiner evaluated

Cost: Contact publisher

Publisher: Reitan Neuropsychological Laboratory

NEUROPSYCHOLOGICAL SCREENING EXAM
John Preston

Adolescent, adult—Ages 16 and older

Purpose: Assesses probable learning disabilities and neurological impairment. Used in clinical settings by mental health professionals with some neuropsychological background.

Description: Multiple-item paper-pencil test measuring the following neurological factors: level of consciousness, brain and behavioral abnormalities, handedness, verbal and language functioning, emotional problems, memory and cognitive functioning, and psychomotor development. The battery includes a screening exam (background information), examination record form, patient response record, stimulus cards, instructional audiotape for examiner, and three subtests from the Halstead-Reitan battery, which are purchased separately. Examiner required. Not suitable for group use.

Untimed: 50 minutes

Scoring: Examiner evaluated

Cost: Complete kit $38.00

Publisher: The Wilmington Press

Information and availability unconfirmed; last verified in 1987.

NEUROPSYCHOLOGICAL STATUS EXAMINATION (NSE)
Psychological Assessment Resources, Inc.

Adult

Purpose: Evaluates, organizes, and collates data pertaining to an individual's neuropsychological functioning. Used for a variety of neuropsychological assessments ranging from screening procedures to extensive work-ups and preparation for expert-witness testimony.

Description: 10–page multiple-item paper-pencil assessment evaluating neuropsychological information, such as patient data, observational findings, test administration parameters, neuroanatomical correlates, reports of test findings, clinical impressions, and recommendations for treatment. The instrument consists of 13 sections, including patient and referral data; neuropsychological symptom checklist (NSC); premorbid status; physical, emotional, and cognitive status; results of neuropsychological testing; diagnostic comments; and follow-up and treatment recommendations. The NSC is a two-page screening instrument used to assess the status of potential neurological/neuropsychological signs and symptoms. Each section was designed with consideration of base rate data for common findings in neuropsychological evaluations. The manual includes a discussion of the rationale of the logic underlying the structure of the instrument and provides suggestions for its most efficient use. Examiner required. Not suitable for group use.

Untimed: Varies

Scoring: Examiner evaluated

Cost: Examination kit (manual, 25 NSE and NSC forms) $13.50

Publisher: Psychological Assessment Resources, Inc.

NUMBER SERIES PROBLEMS (NSERIES)
Linda Laatsch

Ages 10–adult

Purpose: Measures simple problem-solving ability. Used to assess head injury, stroke, or visual system damage.

Description: Computer-administered test of problem-solving ability in which the subject solves addition (10, 12, 14, ?), subtraction (75, 70, 65, ?), and pattern (9, 8, 8, 9, ?) series. Two levels of difficulty

are provided. The user receives feedback and can choose to receive a prompt. Scoring is separate for each type of series. Operates on Apple II series computers or IBM PC computers with CGA display and compatibles. Examiner required. Not suitable for group use.

Untimed: 5–12 minutes

Scoring: Computer scored

Cost: $35.00

Publisher: Life Science Associates

OARS MULTIDIMENSIONAL FUNCTIONAL ASSESSMENT QUESTIONNAIRE
Center for the Study of Aging and Human Development, Duke University

Adult

Purpose: Assesses the functional status of adults, particularly the elderly. Suitable for use with visually, physically, mentally, and hearing-impaired populations.

Description: 101–item criterion-referenced paper-pencil and oral-response test assessing five areas of functioning: social (13 items), economic (20 items), mental health (15 items), physical health (22 items), and ADL (14 items). The test also contains a 24–item services section, demographic information, and interviewer sections. The test yields both subscore ratings and summary ratings on 6–point scales for social, economic, mental health, physical health, and ADL. A scoring service is available from the publisher. A videocassette is available for training purposes. Norms for the elderly (age 60+) are available. Examiner/self-administered. Not suitable for group use. Available in Spanish, Portuguese, and French.

Untimed: 45 minutes

Scoring: Examiner evaluated; may be computer scored

Cost: $29.95; shipping and handling $2.00

Publisher: Center for the Study of Aging and Human Development, Duke University

ORGANIC INTEGRITY TEST (OIT)
H.C. Tien

Grades K-adult

Purpose: Detects and helps diagnose organic brain dysfunctions, organic brain disorders, psychoses, mental retardation, and organicity. Used in clinical psychiatry, neurology, and psychometrics, for routine or mass screening of dementias in nursing homes, and for school assessment of perceptual lag, learning disabilities, and mental retardation.

Description: Nonverbal form-color matching test using 10 sets of three pictures, with one single-picture card and one two-picture card (20 cards total). The examiner shows the patient a set of two cards with pictures of objects. The patient is asked which one of the two pictures on the second card (blue suitcase or red shirt) is most like the picture on the first card (blue shirt). Based on Tien's Theory of Chromphilia, a brain-disordered or cortically damaged individual tends to match pictures by similar colors rather than by similar forms, revealing brain dysfunction or damage as a loss of form perception. Low scores indicate decreased brain functioning. In the school setting, low performances point to perceptual lag, mental retardation, and reading disabilities. Clinically, low scores help diagnose dementias (e.g., Alzheimer's disease), organic brain disorders, psychoses, schizophrenias, and atypical or latent thought disorders. Examiner required. Suitable for group use.

Untimed: 3–5 minutes

Scoring: Hand key

Cost: Complete set (20 cards, manual) $47.50; postage and handling $2.50

Publisher: Psychodiagnostic Test Company

PAIN AND DISTRESS SCALE
Refer to page 15.

PAIRED WORD MEMORY TASK (PAIRMEM)
Rosamond Gianutsos

Ages 8–adult

Purpose: Measures associative verbal learning skills. Used with head injury and stroke victims.

Description: Computer-administered test of verbal associative memory. Pairs of unrelated words are presented for study. Later, the subject attempts to type the second word upon presentation of the first. Both the number of pairs and the study time can be adjusted to increase the difficulty of the task. Interference may be given between trials to prevent reliance on rote, short-term memory skills. The subject must have some visual function, the ability to read simple English words, rudimentary keyboarding skills, and the ability to follow simple instructions. Operates on Apple II series computers or IBM PC computers with CGA display and compatibles. Self-administered. Not suitable for group use.

Untimed: 8–12 minutes

Scoring: Computer scored

Cost: $50.00

Publisher: Life Science Associates

PANTOMIME RECOGNITION TEST
Arthur L. Benton

Adult

Purpose: Assesses a patient's ability to understand nonlinguistic pantomimed actions.

Description: 30–item test in which pantomimes, which are presented on a television monitor via a ¾–inch videotape cassette, depict a man pretending to use various common objects (spoon, pen, saw) followed by seven seconds of blank tape. Four types of response choices, which are presented as line drawings, are available for each item: correct choice (the object whose action is pantomimed), semantic foil (an object belonging to the same class of objects as the stimulus), neutral foil (an object whose use is pantomimed elsewhere on the test), and odd foil (an object whose use is not suitable for pantomime). The person points to one of the four line drawings after viewing the pantomime on the television monitor. Four practice items are provided in addition to the 30 test items. If a patient responds incorrectly to two or more practice items, the test should be terminated. Examiner required. Not suitable for group use.

Untimed: Varies

Scoring: Hand key

Cost: Contact publisher

Publisher: Oxford University Press

PEDIATRIC EARLY ELEMENTARY EXAMINATION (PEEX)
Melvin D. Levine

Child—Ages 7–9

Purpose: Assesses neurological development, behaviors, and health of children. Used by clinicians in health care and other settings for educational planning, counseling, use of medication, and general programming.

Description: Multiple-item response test providing standardized observation procedures for characterizing children's functional health and its relationship to neurodevelopmental and physical status. The test enables clinicians to integrate medical, developmental, and neurological findings while making observations of behavioral adjustment and style. Examiner required. Not suitable for group use.

Untimed: 45–60 minutes

Scoring: Examiner evaluated

Cost: Record forms and response booklets $36.00; complete set $74.50; contact publisher for other prices

Publisher: Educators Publishing Service, Inc.

PEDIATRIC EXAMINATION OF EDUCATIONAL READINESS (PEER)
Refer to page 555.

PEDIATRIC EXAMINATION OF EDUCATIONAL READINESS AT MIDDLE CHILDHOOD (PEERAMID)
Melvin D. Levine

Child, adolescent—Ages 9–15

Purpose: Assesses children's and adolescents' neurological development, behaviors, and health. Used by clinicians in health care and other settings.

Description: Multiple-item response test providing standardized observation procedures for characterizing children's and adolescents' functional health and its relationship to neurodevelopmental and physical status. The test assesses a wide range of functions, including neuromaturation, attention, many aspects of memory, motor efficiency, language, and other areas critical to the academic and social adjustment of older children. It is designed to be particularly sensitive to the often subtle developmental dysfunctions of junior high-school students. Examiner required. Not suitable for group use.

Untimed: 45–60 minutes

Scoring: Examiner evaluated

Cost: Complete set $80.50; specimen set (manual, form) $9.50; contact publisher for other prices

Publisher: Educators Publishing Service, Inc.

PEDIATRIC EXTENDED EXAMINATION AT THREE (PEET)
Melvin D. Levine

Child—Ages 3–4

Purpose: Enables clinicians to integrate medical, developmental, and neurological findings and make observations of behavioral adjustment and style. Assists in identifying specific interventions. Used for diagnosis, screening, research, and professional training.

Description: Verbal paper-pencil show-tell performance measure of five developmental areas: gross motor, language, visual-fine motor, memory, and intersensory integration. The child is asked to perform gross-motor tasks (jumping, throwing, kicking a small ball), identify pictures, name objects, follow directions, and copy figures with a pencil. Tasks are presented using numerous miscellaneous items (sticks, crayon, doll) contained in the kit. Words and sentences are provided for language assessment. The examination produces an empirically derived profile of the child in the developmental areas, based on performance of age-appropriate tasks, which can be used to clarify concerns, determine need for further evaluation in specific areas, and initiate services or continued surveillance. Examiner administered. Not suitable for group use.

Untimed: 1 hour

Scoring: Examiner evaluated

Cost: Record forms $16.00; examiner's manual $8.00; stimulus book $10.50; kit $28.00; complete set $62.50; specimen set (manual, record form) $8.50

Publisher: Educators Publishing Service, Inc.

PERCEPTUAL MAZE TEST (PMT)
Janice Smith, David Jones, and Alick Elithorn

Ages 7–adult

Purpose: Assesses perceptual and intellectual skills. Used for diagnosis and localization of cerebral damage, particularly right hemisphere damage.

Description: Multiple-item paper-pencil or computer-administered test of spatial abilities. Items are mazes consisting of a number of target dots superimposed upon the intersection of a lattice background. The subject's task is to find a path along the lattice that passes through the greatest number of target dots. Several forms are available: two parallel forms of the neuropsychiatric sets, NP1 and NP2, each with 12 test items; mirrored versions, NP1M and NP2M, also are available; the VC Series, VC1 and VC2, each consist of 18 items; mirror image sets, VC1M and VC2M, also are available. An automated version of the test is available for use on the Apple II and IBM PC and compatibles. A special children's version of the PMT, with 16 items, is available for use

with younger children. Examiner required. Suitable for group use.
BRITISH PUBLISHER
Untimed: 15–20 minutes
Scoring: Hand key
Cost: 100 neuropsychiatric sets $120.00; 100 VC Series $105.00; 100 children's version $105.00
Publisher: Elithorn and Levander

PHONEME DISCRIMINATION TEST
Arthur L. Benton

Adult

Purpose: Assesses a subject's phoneme discrimination abilities.

Description: Brief screening instrument consisting of 30 tape-recorded pairs of nonsense words spoken by an adult male. Of the 30 word pairs, 10 pairs are one-syllable words and 20 pairs are two-syllable words. In 15 of the items, the word pairs differ in only one phonemic feature. After each word pair is spoken, the subject vocally responds either "same" or "different," points to a card printed with either "same" or "different," nods, or gestures. One point is awarded for each correct response. Examiner required. Not suitable for group use.
Untimed: Varies
Scoring: Hand key
Cost: Contact publisher
Publisher: Oxford University Press

THE PICTURE STORY LANGUAGE TEST (PSLT)
Refer to page 292.
===

THE PIN TEST
Paul Satz and Lou D'Elia

Adolescent, adult—Ages 16–69

Purpose: Assesses manual dexterity. Used in neuropsychological evaluation.

Description: 4–trial (30 seconds each) test measuring manual dexterity. The examinee is required to push a pin through a pattern of circles. Scores yield percentiles and standard scores for total hits for each hand. Advantage Index provided. Materials include manual, record forms, trial sheets, and test components. Examiner must meet APA guidelines. Examiner required. Not suitable for group use.

Timed: 2 minutes

Scoring: Hand scored without key

Cost: PIN Test Kit (test, manual, 50 record forms, 200 trial sheets, 5 resistance cardboard pieces, 10 pins) $79.00

Publisher: Psychological Assessment Resources, Inc.

THE POLLACK-BRANDEN BATTERY: FOR IDENTIFICATION OF LEARNING DISABILITIES, DYSLEXIA, AND CLASSROOM DYSFUNCTION
Refer to page 639.

PORCH INDEX OF COMMUNICATIVE ABILITY (PICA)
Bruce E. Porch

Adolescent, adult—Ages 13 and older

Purpose: Evaluates the ability of aphasic individuals to communicate with other people. Useful for diagnosis and therapy.

Description: 180–item paper-pencil verbal test covering nine modalities of communication: writing, copying, reading, pantomime, verbal, auditory, visual, gestural, and graphic. The test measures changes in functioning due to time, treatment, and surgery. Items are scored for accuracy, responsiveness, completeness, promptness, and efficiency. Software for computing means and percentiles is available from Sunset Software (11750 Sunset Boulevard, Suite 414, Los Angeles, CA 90049; 213/476-0245).

Materials include 10 pairs of test objects, plastic stimulus cards, and graphic test sheets. A fiber-tip pen is required for the graphic items. The test is not recommended for children under age 12. Users must undergo extensive practice administrations to achieve maximum results.

Training workshops are recommended. Examiner required. Not suitable for group use.

Untimed: 30–60 minutes

Scoring: Examiner evaluated

Cost: Complete kit for 25 subjects (carrying case, two each of test items, 1 set stimulus cards, 2–volume manual, test format booklet, 25 sets of basic profiles and test sheets) $135.00

Publisher: Consulting Psychologists Press, Inc.

PORCH INDEX OF COMMUNICATIVE ABILITY IN CHILDREN (PICAC)
Bruce E. Porch

Child—Ages 3–12

Purpose: Assesses a child's communicative behavior. Used for diagnosis, prognosis, and treatment planning.

Description: Battery of paper-pencil verbal tests measuring three modalities of communication: gestural, verbal, and graphic. Visual and auditory level scores are obtained also. The test documents changes in a child's processing ability over time. Items are scored for accuracy, responsiveness, completeness, promptness, and efficiency. The Basic Battery tests preschool children ages 3–6. The Advanced Battery is administered to children ages 6–12. Materials include 10 pairs of test objects, plastic stimulus cards, and graphic test sheets. A black-tip pen is required for graphic items. Software for computing means and percentiles is available from Sunset Software (11750 Sunset Boulevard, Suite 414, Los Angeles, CA 90049; 213/476-0245). Users must undergo extensive practice administrations to achieve maximum results. Training workshops are recommended. Examiner required. Not suitable for group use.

Untimed: 30–60 minutes

Scoring: Examiner evaluated

Cost: Deluxe test kit for 25 subjects (complete manual, test format booklet, set of stimulus cards, spirit masters, scoring templates, profiles and test sheets for 25 subjects, two each of test items, leather briefcase) $142.00
Publisher: Consulting Psychologists Press, Inc.

PORTABLE TACTUAL PERFORMANCE TEST (P-TPT)
Psychological Assessment Resources, Inc.

Child, adolescent—Ages 5-14

Purpose: Measures spatial perception in children.

Description: Multiple-task examination measuring spatial perception, discrimination of forms, manual or construction ability, motor coordination, and the ability to meet new situations. This portable version features a wooden carrying case, which can be set up for standardized administration. Examiner required. Not suitable for group use.
Untimed: Not available
Scoring: Examiner evaluated
Cost: Kit (manual, 50 record forms) $265.00
Publisher: Psychological Assessment Resources, Inc.

PROBLEM SOLVING I REHABILITATION PROGRAM
Robert J. Sbordone and Steven Hall

Adolescent, adult

Purpose: Trains cognitively impaired patients to improve their problem-solving skills and ability to tolerate frustration.

Description: Computer-administered rehabilitation and training program in which the patient is visually presented with a series of tasks of increasing complexity requiring the use of a joystick. The first series of tasks involves moving a small square to a goal box. Initially, the patient is able to see both the goal box and the location of the square. At higher levels, visual cues are eliminated progressively, requiring the patient to develop effec-

tive problem-solving strategies to solve the task. At the intermediate levels, patients must improve their frustration tolerance and persistence to solve each task because the program creates invisible barriers and obstacles that obscure the goal box. The program has been designed to monitor the patient's progress and level of fatigue over many training sessions. The program also makes decisions, based on the patient's performance, to increase or decrease the complexity of the task, provide a variety of different cues, allow short rest periods, or terminate the session. It also remembers the patient's performance on previous training sessions, as well as the length of time since the last training session. A speech synthesizer option permits vocal presentation of cues and instructions to patients with reading difficulties. An analysis of the patient's problem-solving strategies at each of 10 levels of difficulty is provided. The program is designed for use with the Apple (II+, IIe, IIc) computer system. Examiner/self-administered. Not suitable for group use.
Untimed: Not available
Scoring: Computer scored
Cost: Complete program, including instructional manual $195.00; shipping fee $3.00
Publisher: Robert J. Sbordone
Information and availability unconfirmed; last verified in 1988.

PROBLEM SOLVING II REHABILITATION PROGRAM
Robert J. Sbordone and Steven Hall

Adolescent, adult

Purpose: Trains high-functioning brain-injured patients to improve their sequential thinking, problem-solving, and cognitive flexibility skills. Designed for use with high-functioning brain-injured patients with residual frontal lobe dysfunction (problem-solving skills, poor sequential thinking, impaired self-critical attitude, and cognitive inflexibility).

Description: Computer-administered rehabilitation and training program that trains the patient to anticipate the consequences of his actions. It presents the patient with a series of problems (carrying passengers across a river in a boat) of increasing difficulty and complexity requiring the patient to consider as many as 10 different variables simultaneously. The program critically analyzes the problem-solving approaches utilized by the patient and determines their effectiveness. It also monitors the patient's level of cognitive fatigue. A speech synthesizer option allows vocal presentation to patients with reading difficulties. The program is designed for use with an Apple IIc or IIe with at least 64K of internal memory. Examiner/self-administered. Not suitable for group use.

Untimed: Not available

Scoring: Computer scored

Cost: Complete program, including instructional manual $195.00; shipping fee $3.00

Publisher: Robert J. Sbordone

Information and availability unconfirmed; last verified in 1988.

PURDUE PERCEPTUAL-MOTOR SURVEY (PPMS)
Refer to page 616.

PYRAMID PUZZLE
Refer to page 1071.

QUICK NEUROLOGICAL SCREENING TEST (QNST)
Harold M. Sterling, Margaret Mutti, and Norma V. Spalding

Grades K–12

Purpose: Assesses neurological integration as it relates to the learning abilities of children and teenagers.

Description: Multiple-task nonverbal test of 15 functions, each involving a motor task similar to those observed in neurological pediatric examinations. The areas measured include maturity of motor development, skill in controlling large and small muscles, motor planning and sequencing, sense of rate and rhythm, spatial organization, visual and auditory perceptual skills, balance and cerebellar-vestibular function, and disorders of

attention. Materials include geometric form reproduction sheets and flipcards printed with directions for administration and scoring. Scoring occurs simultaneously and neurodevelopmental difficulties result in an increasingly larger numerical score. Examiner required. Not suitable for group use.

Untimed: 20 minutes

Scoring: Examiner evaluated

Cost: Manual $15.00; 25 scoring forms $10.00; 25 geometric form reproduction sheets $6.00; 25 remedial guideline form reproduction sheets $6.00

Publisher: Academic Therapy Publications

THE RAIL-WALKING TEST
S. Roy Heath

Ages 6–adult

Purpose: Measures locomotor coordination. Screens for central nervous system disorder or injury.

Description: Task-performance test assessing balance and motor coordination. The subject, shoes removed, is asked to walk "heel-to-toe" three times along each of three rails specifically constructed for the task. The first rail is four inches wide and nine feet long, the second rail is two inches wide and nine feet long, and the third rail is one inch wide and six feet long. Scores are based on the distance the subject walks without falling off. Special weight is given to each rail according to width. Directions are provided for local construction of the test rails. Examiner required. Not suitable for group use.

Untimed: 10 minutes

Scoring: Examiner evaluated

Cost: Instructions and norms $5.00

Publisher: S. Roy Heath, Ph.D.

Information and availability unconfirmed; last verified in 1987.

RANDT MEMORY TEST
C. T. Randt and E. R. Brown

Adult—Ages 20–80

Purpose: Measures memory processes in neurologically impaired populations, including the elderly.

Description: Computer-administered test of memory changes, including process of association, primary memory deficits, recall vs. recognition memory, and transfer to and retrieval from secondary store memory. Test materials include picture recognition cards; documentation; a program for test administration control; response recording; and computation of scaled scores, standard scores, and summary of test scores. Norms are included for age decades from 20 to 80. Operates on Apple II series computers or IBM PC computers with CGA display and compatibles. Examiner/self-administered. Not suitable for group use.

Untimed: Varies

Scoring: Hand key; may be computer scored

Cost: Test, manual scoring $85.00; Apple computer scoring program $40.00

Publisher: Life Science Associates

REACTION TIME MEASURE OF VISUAL FIELD (REACT)
Rosamond Gianutsos and Carol Klitzner

Ages 8–adult

Purpose: Diagnoses and trains visual field deficits and blind spots. Used to assess head injury, stroke, or visual system damage.

Description: Computer-administered test detecting slowed response to visual stimuli. The patient presses any key on the keyboard to stop the "runaway numbers" on the screen. The numbers are presented in different locations in the visual field while the subject fixates on a point. Possible modifications include a hand-held or other specially arranged switch for responding. Operates on Apple II series computers or IBM PC computers with CGA display and compatibles. Examiner required. Not suitable for group use.

Timed: 8 minutes

Scoring: Computer scored

Cost: $35.00

Publisher: Life Science Associates

READING COMPREHENSION BATTERY FOR APHASIA (RCBA)
Leonard L. LaPointe and Jennifer Horner

Adult

Purpose: Evaluates the nature and degree of reading impairment in aphasic adults and provides a focus for therapy.

Description: Multiple-item stimulus-response test utilizing pictures to assess the reading comprehension of aphasic adults. The 10 subtests included are Single Word Comprehension (Visual Confusions, Auditory Confusions, and Semantic Confusions), Functional Reading, Synonyms, Sentence Comprehension (Picture), Short Paragraph Comprehension (Picture), Paragraphs (Factual and Inferential Comprehension—2 subtests), and Morpho-Syntactic Reading with Lexical Controls. Examiner required. Not suitable for group use.

Untimed: Not available

Scoring: Examiner evaluated

Cost: Complete kit (manual, stimulus items, picture plates, 50 response record forms, storage box) $64.00

Publisher: PRO-ED

RECEPTIVE-EXPRESSIVE OBSERVATION (REO)
Refer to page 617.

RECOGNITION MEMORY TEST
Elizabeth Warrington

Adults—Ages 18–70

Purpose: Identifies minor visual and verbal memory deficits indicative of organic neurological disease. Used by clinicians with adults ages 18–70.

Description: Multiple-item response tests made up of two subtests based on pictures of words and faces and assessing verbal and visual recognition memory. The test enables clinicians to distinguish between right and left hemisphere damage and measures memory of verbally handicapped individuals. Examiner required. Not suitable for group use. BRITISH PUBLISHER

Untimed: 12–15 minutes

Scoring: Hand key

Cost: Contact publisher

Publisher: NFER-NELSON Publishing Company Ltd.

REITAN EVALUATION OF HEMISPHERIC ABILITIES AND BRAIN IMPROVEMENT TRAINING (REHABIT)
Ralph M. Reitan

All ages

Purpose: Provides training of neuropsychological functions that may be impaired or deficient in both adults and children who may be suffering from brain damage or neurological dysfunction. Specific neurocortical training sequences are included.

Description: Task-assessment and oral-response test measuring three fundamental areas of brain function: verbal and language functions (left hemisphere); visual-spatial, manipulatory, and sequential abilities (right hemisphere); and abstraction, reasoning, logical analysis, and ability to understand the essential nature of problem situations (general cerebral functioning). Based on the results of the testing, five tracks of remedial training have been developed. Track A contains equipment and procedures that are specifically designed for developing expressive and receptive language and verbal skills. Track B also specializes in language and verbal materials, but includes elements of abstraction, reasoning, logical analysis, and organization. Track C includes various tasks that do not depend upon particular content as much as they do on reasoning, organization, and abstraction. Track D also emphasizes abstraction but uses material that requires the subject to deal with visual-spatial, sequential, and manipulatory skills. Track E specializes in tasks and materials that require the subject to exercise fundamental aspects of visual-spatial and manipulatory abilities. The training mate-

rials in each track are organized roughly from simple to complex; the subject is started at a level that allows satisfactory performance to be achieved easily. Examiner required. Not suitable for group use.

Untimed: Not available

Scoring: Examiner evaluated

Cost: Contact publisher

Publisher: Reitan Neuropsychology Laboratory

REITAN-INDIANA NEUROPSYCHOLOGICAL TEST BATTERY FOR CHILDREN
Ralph M. Reitan and others

Child—Ages 5–8

Purpose: Assesses brain-behavior functioning in children. Used for clinical evaluation.

Description: Battery of tests assessing the neurological functioning of young children, including the Wechsler Intelligence Scale for Children, sensory-perceptual tests, modifications of the Reitan-Indiana Aphasia Screening Test and A Neuropsychological Test Battery, which includes a number of tests (Color Form Test, Target Test, Matching Pictures Test, Progressive Figures Test, Marching Test, and Individual Performance Tests).

This battery is related to the Halstead-Reitan neuropsychological test batteries for adults and older children, but a number of adaptations have been made for use with this age 5–8 group. The Category Test uses a different set of slides for stimuli, and colored instead of numbered caps as the guide to lever choice on the answer panel. The Tactual Performance Test uses a 6–hole board in a horizontal instead of a vertical position. The Aphasia Screening Test deletes a number of items from the adult version, adds a number of simple procedures, and uses a different recording form. An electric finger tapping was devised because young children had trouble manipulating the manual apparatus.

Materials include all necessary equipment, test stimuli, slide carousels, recording forms, and a manual for administration, scoring, and evaluation of all tests. The components may be purchased separately. Examiner required. Not suitable for group use.

Untimed: Varies

Scoring: Examiner evaluated

Cost: Young children's battery $1,661.00

Publisher: Reitan Neuropsychology Laboratory

THE REVERSALS FREQUENCY TEST

Refer to page 640.

REVISED TOKEN TEST
Malcolm M. McNeil and Thomas E. Prescott

Brain-damaged adults—
Ages 20–80

Purpose: Assesses auditory disorders associated with brain damage and aphasia in adults. Used for designing rehabilitation programs and for research.

Description: Quantitative and descriptive test consisting of 10 subtests assessing auditory disorders associated with brain damage and aphasia. Percentile ranks are available for normal, right, and left hemisphere brain-damaged adults for each subtest and for overall performance. Examiner required. Not suitable for group use.

Timed: Not available

Scoring: Examiner evaluated

Cost: Complete kit (examiner's manual, administration manual, scoring forms, profile forms, 24 tokens, storage box) $84.00

Publisher: PRO-ED

RIGHT-LEFT ORIENTATION TEST
Arthur L. Benton

All ages

Purpose: Measures subject's ability to discriminate between the right and left sides of the body.

Description: Test in which the subject is asked to point to lateral body parts on verbal command in order to assess three components of right-left orientation: orientation toward one's own body, orientation toward a confronting person, and combined orientation toward one's own body and a confronting person. Items range in difficulty from Level A (requiring identification of single lateral parts of one's own body) to Level E (requiring the combined operation of both the "own body" and "other person" systems of orientation). One point is credited for each correct response, including any corrections of an initially incorrect response. Two forms, A and B, are available; Form B is a mirror image of Form A (i.e., commands are reversed—right hand instead of left, etc.). Demands on the subject's motor skill are minimal, and no naming ability is required. Modified versions (Form R and Form L) have been developed for use with hemiplegics. Materials required are a record form and manual. Examiner required. Not suitable for group use.

Untimed: 5 minutes

Scoring: Examiner evaluated

Cost: Contact publisher

Publisher: Oxford University Press

RILEY MOTOR PROBLEMS INVENTORY
Glyndon D. Riley

Child—Ages 4–9

Purpose: Measures a child's oral, fine-, and gross-motor skills. Used to determine whether further clinical evaluation is needed.

Description: Multiple-task verbal screening test providing a quantified system of observing neurological signs that may indicate a need for referral. The test measures the motor component as a factor in any related syndrome and is useful for differentiating neurogenic disorders from psychogenic disorders. Norms are provided for children ages 4–9. Cutoff scores are provided to indicate children who need further evaluation. Examiner required. Not suitable for group use.

Untimed: 5–10 minutes

Scoring: Hand key

Cost: Complete kit (100 record forms, manual) $23.00

Publisher: Western Psychological Services

RIVERMEAD PERCEPTUAL ASSESSMENT BATTERY
S. Whiting, N.B. Lincoln, G. Bhavnani, and J. Cockburn

Adolescent, adult—Ages 16–69

Purpose: Assesses a wide range of perceptual abilities of adults. Used by occupational therapists for determining the degree of visual perceptual dysfunction and planning treatment.

Description: Multiple-item paper-pencil response test consisting of 16 subtests yielding information on different aspects of visual perceptual ability. The subtests are Picture Matching, Object Matching, Color Matching, Size Recognition, Series, Animal Halves, Missing Article, Figure-Ground Discrimination, Sequencing-Pictures, Body Image, Right/Left Copying Shapes, Right/Left Copying Words, Three-Dimensional Copying, Cube Copying, Cancellation, and Body-Image Self-Identification. Items used during testing include illustrated sheets, picture cards, blocks, wooden figures, and a 3–D model. Assessment may be carried out in two sittings if preferred. Examiner required. Not suitable for group use. BRITISH PUBLISHER

Untimed: 45–60 minutes

Scoring: Examiner evaluated

Cost: Contact publisher

Publisher: NFER-NELSON Publishing Company Ltd.

ROSS INFORMATION PROCESSING ASSESSMENT (RIPA)
Deborah G. Ross

Adolescent, adult

Purpose: Diagnoses disorders following closed head injury. Used to quantify information processing deficits and establish severity ratings.

Description: Multiple-item paper-pencil instrument for establishing the severity of head injury in 10 areas: immediate memory, recent memory, temporal orientation (recent memory), temporal orientation (remote memory), spatial orientation, orientation to environment, recall of general information, problem solving and abstract reasoning, organization, and auditory retention and processing. Results may be used for developing treatment objectives. Periodic retesting provides an evaluation of the treatment program. Examiner required. Not suitable for group use.

Untimed: 30–45 minutes

Scoring: Examiner evaluated

Cost: Complete kit (manual, 25 response record sheets, 25 test record sheets, storage box) $54.00

Publisher: PRO-ED

SBORDONE-HALL MEMORY BATTERY
Robert J. Sbordone and Steven Hall

Adult

Purpose: Measures memory functions in normal, brain-injured, and cognitively impaired adults. Used for clinical assessment, cognitive rehabilitation, or research.

Description: Computer-administered test providing a fully automatic assessment of 18 discrete memory functions, including free recall of alphanumeric stimuli over trials, delayed recall of alphanumeric stimuli, memory loss due to proactive and retroactive interference, recognition memory of alpha-numeric stimuli, verbal memory errors, serial position learning, immediate word recognition memory, delayed word recognition memory, picture recognition memory, intentional word recognition memory, incidental word recognition memory, word origin memory, memory loss due to temporal delay or interference, immediate visual recognition memory for single and multiple geometric figures, types of visual memory errors, and storage versus retrieval memory deficits. The program either generates random stimuli or randomly selects test stimuli from a large pool and provides automatic cueing of the subject during testing.

A 12–page statistical and clinical analysis of the patient's performance, including a comparison of the patient's performance (in terms of Z scores) to age-matched organic, psychiatric, and normal controls is provided. In addition, the program utilizes powerful statistical techniques, such as signal detection and discriminant function analyses, to evaluate such factors as freedom from distraction, response bias, and test-taking efficiency. The battery is designed for use with Apple (II +, IIe, IIc, III) and IBM PC computer systems. Examiner/self-administered. Not suitable for group use.

Untimed: 45–50 minutes

Scoring: Computer scored

Cost: Complete program, including instructional manual $375.00; shipping fee $3.00

Publisher: Robert J. Sbordone

Information and availability unconfirmed; last verified in 1988.

SCREENING TEST FOR THE LURIA-NEBRASKA NEUROPSYCHOLOGICAL BATTERY

Ages 8–adult

Purpose: Assesses cognitive functioning. Used to identify individuals who will show a significant degree of impairment when administered the complete battery. Also used for neuropsychological screening in schools and alcohol abuse programs.

Description: 15–item screening test predicting overall performance on the Luria-Nebraska Neuropsychological Battery. Testing is discontinued when the client reaches the critical score. Materials include an administration and scoring booklet, spiral-bound stimulus cards, and easel. Forms are available for children 8–12 and adults 13 and older. Examiner required. Suitable for group use.

Untimed: 20 minutes or less

Scoring: Examiner evaluated

Cost: $80.00

Publisher: Western Psychological Services

SEARCH FOR THE ODD SHAPE (SOSH)
Rosamond Gianutsos, Georgine Vroman, and Pauline Matheson

Ages 6–adult

Purpose: Assesses foveal imperception and differentiates scanning skill from shape examination and matching hemi-imperception. Used to assess head injury, stroke, or visual system damage.

Description: Computer-administered nonverbal shape comparison task. The subject scans an array of identical patterns for the "odd" one. Operates on Apple II series computers or IBM PC computers with CGA display and compatibles. Examiner required. Not suitable for group use.

Untimed: 8–10 minutes

Scoring: Computer scored

Cost: $35.00

Publisher: Life Science Associates

SEARCH-A-WORD (SAW)
Rosamond Gianutsos and Carol Klitzner

Ages 6–adult

Purpose: Diagnoses hemi-imperception and visual attentional deficits. Used to assess head injury, stroke, or visual system damage.

Description: 30–task paper-pencil test of intact visual systems and central visual processing. The subject scans a 13″x 13″ character array and stops when a target three-character word is found. Materials include the SAW test booklet, stopwatch, and a pencil. The subject must be able to read simple English words. Operates on Apple II series computers or IBM PC computers with CGA display and compatibles. Examiner required. Not suitable for group use.

Untimed: 8–20 seconds per task

Scoring: Hand key

Cost: $10.00
Publisher: Life Science Associates

SEARCHING FOR SHAPES (SEARCH)
*Rosamond Gianutsos and
Carol Klitzner*

Ages 8–adult

Purpose: Detects and treats differences in attention and responsiveness on the two sides of the visual field. Used to assess head injury, stroke, or visual system damage.

Description: Computer-administered test of visual systems and central visual processing. The subject looks at a shape in the center of the screen and searches for a match elsewhere on the screen as quickly as possible. Examiner then indicates whether or not the response is correct. The computer stores the search times for correct responses and the number of incorrect responses for later display. Operates on Apple II series computers or IBM PC computers with CGA display and compatibles. Examiner required. Not suitable for group use.

Untimed: 10 minutes
Scoring: Computer scored
Cost: $35.00
Publisher: Life Science Associates

SEGUIN-GODDARD FORMBOARDS (TACTUAL PERFORMANCE TEST)

Child, adolescent—Ages 5–14

Purpose: Measures spatial perception in children. Used in a variety of neuropsychological applications.

Description: Multiple-task examination of spatial perception, discrimination of forms, manual or construction ability, motor coordination, and the ability to meet new situations. The test materials consist of 10 sturdy blocks cut in the geometric forms of semicircle, triangle, cross, elongated hexagon, oblong, circle, square, flatted oval, star and lozenge, and a base with corresponding shapes cut into it. The child must place the blocks in the

appropriate spaces on the formboard base. Two types of bases are available: one with raised geometric figures and one with flush geometric figures. Examiner required. Not suitable for group use.

Untimed: Not available
Scoring: Examiner evaluated
Cost: Raised formboard (used in Halstead-Reitan Battery) $175.00; flush formboard (used in Merrill-Palmer Scale) $125.00
Publisher: Stoelting Co.

SELF-ADMINISTERED FREE RECALL (FRSELF)
Rosamond Gianutsos

Ages 10–adult

Purpose: Measures short- and long-term verbal memory in head injury and stroke victims.

Description: Computer-administered test of verbal memory in which the subject memorizes word lists and recalls them after either a short delay or an intervening task. This test is similar to FREEREC but is designed to be self-administered. The subject must be able to read simple English words. Operates on Apple II series computers or IBM PC computers with CGA display and compatibles. Self-administered. Not suitable for group use.

Untimed: 8–12 minutes
Scoring: Computer scored
Cost: $50.00 (minimum of 3 orders in Cat. #965 series)
Publisher: Life Science Associates

SENSORY INTEGRATION AND PRAXIS TESTS (SIPT)
Refer to page 618.

SEQUENCE RECALL (SEQREC)
*Rosamond Gianutsos and
Carol Klitzner*

Ages 10–adult

Purpose: Assesses wide-range, nonverbal memory. Used to diagnose severe memory deficits.

Description: Computer-administered test of nonverbal memory. Shapes, short words, or pictures are presented one at a time and are followed by a "menu" of items that may or may not have appeared. The subject is asked to indicate which ones appeared. Because it does not require reading aloud, this program can be used for diagnosis and treatment with patients unable to process verbal material, including non-English speakers, aphasics, and others. It can be set to a wide range of difficulty. Operates on Apple II series computers or IBM PC computers with CGA display and compatibles. Examiner required. Not suitable for group use.

Untimed: 10–15 minutes

Scoring: Computer scored

Cost: $35.00

Publisher: Life Science Associates

SERIAL DIGIT LEARNING TEST
Arthur L. Benton

Adolescent, adult

Purpose: Measures short-term memory in a clinical assessment of mental status.

Description: Test in which the examiner presents either eight (Form SD8) or nine (Form SD9) randomly selected single digits for a varying number of trials up to a maximum of 12 trials. Three alternate versions are provided for each form, the selection of which is based primarily on the subject's age and educational level. Generally, Form SD9 is given to patients under age 65 who have 12 or more years of education and Form SD8 to those age 65 or older and those under age 65 with less than 12 years of education. The manual provides exceptions to these criteria. Testing is discontinued after two consecutive correct repetitions. One point is scored for each "near-correct" response; correct repetitions are credited two points. Examiner required. Not suitable for group use.

Untimed: 5–10 minutes

Scoring: Examiner evaluated

Cost: Contact publisher

Publisher: Oxford University Press

SHAPE MATCHING (MATCH)
Rosamond Gianutsos,
Georgine Vroman, and
Pauline Matheson

Ages 6–adult

Purpose: Assesses foveal imperception associated with head injury, stroke, or visual system damage.

Description: Computer-administered nonverbal shape comparison task. Two detailed shapes are displayed one above the other. The subject has to decide whether they are the same or different in some small but distinct way. Operates on Apple II series computers or IBM PC computers with CGA display and compatibles. Examiner required. Not suitable for group use.

Untimed: 8–10 minutes

Scoring: Computer scored

Cost: $35.00

Publisher: Life Science Associates

SHORT CATEGORY TEST, BOOKLET FORMAT
Linda C. Wetzel and Thomas J. Boll

Adolescent, adult—
Ages 15 and older

Purpose: Assesses brain dysfunction. Used for clinical diagnosis of brain damage.

Description: Multiple-item paper-pencil test assessing adaptibility, abstract concept formation, capacity to learn from experience, and cognitive flexiblity. This booklet format reduces the length and complexity of the Category Test of the Halstead-Reitan Neuropsychological Battery by using only half the items of the original and eliminating the equipment necessary for administering it. The test may be administered at bedside. Examiner required. Not suitable for group use.

Untimed: 15–30 minutes

Scoring: Examiner evaluated

Cost: $105.00

Publisher: Western Psychological Services

SINGLE AND DOUBLE SIMULTANEOUS STIMULATION (SDSS)

Rosamond Gianutsos, Georgine Vroman, and Pauline Matheson

Ages 6–adult

Purpose: Assesses imperception due to unilateral visual field loss. Used to assess head injury, stroke, or visual system damage.

Description: Computer-administered test for intact visual systems and central visual processing. The subject indicates whether symbols appear on either the left, right, both, or neither side of the screen. Operates on Apple II series computers or IBM PC computers with CGA display and compatibles. Examiner required. Not suitable for group use.

Untimed: 8–10 minutes
Scoring: Computer scored
Cost: $35.00
Publisher: Life Science Associates

SINGLE AND DOUBLE SIMULTANEOUS STIMULATION (SDSS)

Carmen C. Centofanti and Aaron Smith

Adult

Purpose: Diagnoses brain and central nervous system damage.

Description: A simple point-to test of specific somatosensory functions consisting of 20 stimuli items. These items measure the accuracy with which subjects can identify single- and double-simultaneous tactile stimulation applied to the cheek and/or hand. Error scores yield norms in percentiles for age-specific 10–year categories. Materials include score sheet and manual. Examiner required. Not suitable for group use.

Untimed: Varies
Scoring: Examiner evaluated
Cost: Kit (100 score sheets; manual) $23.00
Publisher: Western Psychological Services

SKLAR APHASIA SCALE— REVISED 1983

Maurice Sklar

Adult

Purpose: Assesses auditory decoding, visual decoding, oral encoding, and graphic encoding. Used for adults with suspected speech/language disturbances.

Description: 100–item oral-response criterion-referenced short-answer verbal point-to true-false test providing objective measurements and evaluations of speech and language disorders resulting from brain damage. Provides a reliable determination of the kind and extent of disturbance and potential for benefiting from therapy. Yields raw scores and impairment profile for five scales plus total. Examiner required. Not suitable for group use.

Untimed: Varies
Scoring: Examiner evaluated
Cost: Kit (protocol booklets, manual, stimulus cards) $52.50
Publisher: Western Psychological Services

SLOSSON DRAWING COORDINATION TEST (SDCT)

Richard L. Slosson

All ages

Purpose: Screens for serious forms of brain dysfunction or damage and aids in the diagnosis of visual-perceptual or visual-motor coordination problems. Also indicates the possibility of severe emotional disturbances.

Description: Multiple-item paper-pencil screening test identifying individuals suffering from serious forms of brain dysfunction or damage in which eye-hand coordination is involved. The subject is given 12 figures and asked to make three free-hand copies of each figure. The subject's copies are scored for degree of distortion indicative of brain damage or dysfunction, visual-motor coordination problems, emotional disturbances, or poor motivational attitude. Suggested cutoff scores are provided. The test is not intended as a definitive diagnostic instrument; therefore, it should be used in conjunction with the Slosson Intelligence Test (or other intelligence test) to cover problems in which eye-hand coordination is not a factor. Examiner required. Suitable for group use.

Untimed: 10–15 minutes

Scoring: Hand key

Cost: Complete kit (manual, scoring procedures, two score sheets, vinyl binder) $38.00

Publisher: Slosson Educational Publications, Inc.

SOFTWARE FOR THE INDIVIDUAL EMERGING FROM COMA INTO CONSCIOUSNESS
Rosamond Gianutsos

All ages

Purpose: Assists in evaluating and treating the cognitive aspects of response capability in patients emerging from comas.

Description: 10 computer-administered programs assessing the responsivity of the emerging coma patient. The therapist is guided by a hierarchy of "milestones" that begin with a single discrete response to multiswitch response differentiation. Using an input interface, responses can be recorded from any switches (microswitches, pedals, finger-extension, etc.). The programs, which operate on Apple II series and IBM PC computers (or compatible CGA display), use sound and bold displays when possible and can be customized by user. Scores are automatically stored on computer for analysis of performance across sessions. Examiner required (special training with programs required). Not suitable for group use.

Untimed: Varies

Scoring: Computer scored

Cost: Program (specify computer model) $200.00; input interface $109.00; pedal switch $19.95; finger extension switch $29.95

Publisher: Life Science Associates

SPATIAL ORIENTATION MEMORY TEST
Refer to page 642.

SPEEDED READING OF WORD LISTS (SRWL)
Rosamond Gianutsos and Carol Klitzner

Ages 8–adult

Purpose: Diagnoses and trains visual scanning. Used to assess head injury, stroke, or visual system damage.

Description: Computer-administered test of four basic functions of visual information processing: anchoring at the margin, scanning horizontally, identification of words within the perceptual span, and monitoring the periphery. Words are presented by the computer in different positions on the screen. The user can vary word displacement from the center and display time. Once an individual's problems have been diagnosed, SRWL can be used for rehabilitation. Operates on Apple II series computers or IBM-PC computers with CGA display and compatibles. Examiner required. Not suitable for group use.

Untimed: 10–15 minutes

Scoring: Computer scored

Cost: $35.00

Publisher: Life Science Associates

STEADINESS TESTER—GROOVE TYPE
Refer to page 1072.

STEADINESS TESTER—HOLE TYPE
Refer to page 1073.

STIMULUS RECOGNITION TEST
T.L. Brink, James Bryant, Mary Lou Catalono, Connie Janakes, and Charmaine Oliveira

---

Adult

Purpose: Assesses confusion due to senile dementia in adults.

Description: 10–item response test measuring short-term memory via recognition. The examiner presents oral and visual stimuli during the test. Examiner required. Not suitable for group use.
Untimed: 5–10 minutes
Scoring: Examiner evaluated
Cost: Free
Publisher: T.L. Brink

STROOP NEUROPSYCHOLOGICAL SCREENING TEST (SNST)
Max R. Trenerry

Adult—Ages 18–79　　

Purpose: Screens neuropsychological functioning.

Description: A 2–part (Color Task, Color Word Task) oral-response short-answer test measuring neuropsychological functioning. Scores yield percentile and probability values for Color Score and Color-Word Score. Materials include Form C Stimulus Sheets, Form C-W Stimulus Sheets, record form, and manual. Examiner must meet APA guidelines. Examiner required. Not suitable for group use.
Timed: 4 minutes
Scoring: Hand key
Cost: SNST Kit (manual, 25 Form C stimulus sheets, 25 Form C-W stimulus sheets, 25 record forms) $39.95
Publisher: Psychological Assessment Resources, Inc.

SYMBOL DIGIT MODALITIES TEST
Aaron Smith

Ages 8–75　　

Purpose: Measures brain damage. Used to screen and predict learning disorders and to identify children with potential reading problems.

Description: Multiple-item test in which the subject is given 90 seconds to convert as many meaningless geometric designs as possible into their appropriate numbers according to the key provided. When group-administered, the test may be used as a screening device. The test may be administered orally to individuals who cannot take written tests. Since numbers are nearly universal, the test is virtually culture-free. Examiner required. Suitable for group use.
Timed: 90 seconds
Scoring: Hand key
Cost: Complete kit (100 tests, key, manual) $40.00
Publisher: Western Psychological Services

TACHISTOSCOPIC READING (FASTREAD)
Rosamond Gianutsos

Ages 10–adult　　

Purpose: Assesses areas of attention deficits, foveal imperception, and difficulty in planning and articulating words. Used with head injury and stroke victims.

Description: Computer-administered reading test in which the computer flashes a word and the subject types what he saw. The task speed adjusts to the subject's performance. The program may be used for retraining and has diagnostic capabilities. Operates on Apple II series computers or IBM PC computers with CGA display and compatibles. Self-administered. Not suitable for group use.
Untimed: 8–12 minutes
Scoring: Computer scored
Cost: $50.00
Publisher: Life Science Associates

TACTILE FORM PERCEPTION TEST
Arthur L. Benton

All ages　　

Purpose: Assesses subject's ability to process nonverbal tactile information.

Description: Tactile form perception test using two parallel sets of 10 cards each to assess the subject's ability to process nonverbal tactile information. The cards, each of which presents a geometric figure made of fine-grade sandpaper, are placed face up in a covered box. The patient inserts either his right or his left hand into the box and examines the card for no more than 30 seconds. The patient then is allowed an additional 15 seconds to visually examine a multiple-choice card containing line drawings of the sandpaper figures. The patient uses the opposite hand to point to the line drawing which represents the sandpaper figure. When the patient has examined the first set of 10 cards, testing should continue with the second set of cards, using the opposite hand. If motor or sensory disability prohibits testing with the opposite hand, testing should be terminated. Each response is scored for correctness. Specific incorrect responses should be identified. Scores may be obtained for each hand separately and for both hands together. Examiner required. Not suitable for group use.

Timed: 45 seconds per card

Scoring: Hand key

Cost: Contact publisher

Publisher: Oxford University Press

TAPPING BOARD
Refer to page 1073.

TEST OF PERCEPTUAL ORGANIZATION (TPO)
William T. Martin

Adult

Purpose: Measures abstract reasoning abilities, psychomotor functioning, and the ability to follow specific, exacting instructions in an accurate manner. Identifies persons with emotional disturbance or perceptual-motor disabilities. Used for clinical research and screening purposes.

Description: 10–item paper-pencil test consisting of abstract reasoning and visual-motor tasks. Test items consist of written statements (instructions for plotting points on a map) presented in order of increasing difficulty. The subjects read the instructions and mark an "X" at each of the 10 coordinate points on a street map containing 54 one-inch square blocks confined within a 6″ x 9″ area. Objective scoring discriminates between persons with emotional disturbance and/or perceptual-motor disabilities and those with one or few of these problems. Subjective analysis of the test protocol identifies persons with emotional disturbances or intellect-abstraction problems. Clinical analysis must be done in terms of personality dynamics and visual-motor theory. A fourth-grade reading level is required. Examiner required. Suitable for group use.

Timed: 10 minutes

Scoring: Hand key; examiner evaluated

Cost: Examiner's set $40.00; 25 test forms $15.00; keys $2.75; 25 profile sheets $8.25; manual $6.75

Publisher: Psychologists and Educators, Inc.

TEST OF TEMPORAL ORIENTATION
Arthur L. Benton

Adult

Purpose: Assesses the accuracy of a patient's temporal orientation. Used as a component of a mental status examination.

Description: 5–item oral-response test in which the examiner asks temporal orientation questions (day of week, day of month, month, year, and time of day) and assigns points based on criteria provided in the manual. The test is used to disclose and interpret minor as well as gross temporal disorientation within a prescribed range of normal variation. The total number of error points constitutes the patient's obtained score, resulting in classifications ranging from normal to severely defective. Examiner required. Not suitable for group use.

Untimed: Varies

Scoring: Examiner evaluated

Cost: Contact publisher

Publisher: Oxford University Press

TEST OF VISUAL-MOTOR SKILLS (TVMS)
Refer to page 620.

TESTS OF MENTAL FUNCTION IN THE ELDERLY

Refer to page 47.

THREE-DIMENSIONAL BLOCK CONSTRUCTION

All ages

Purpose: Assesses constructional apraxia.

Description: 3–item manual test in which three block models are presented one at a time to the patient, who is re-quired to construct an exact replica of the model by using the appropriate blocks from a set of loose blocks on a tray. The set of loose blocks is placed to the pa-tient's side, and the model to be copied is placed in front of the patient. The patient is instructed to arrange the loose blocks so that they look like the model. The max-imum time allowed for the construction of each model is 5 minutes. If construction is not completed within that time, the model is removed and the next model is pre-sented. Four types of errors are recorded: omissions, additions, substitutions, and displacements. The test is available in two forms, A and B. In Form A, Model 1 consists of a pyramid made from six 1–inch cubes; Model 2 is an 8–block four-level construction; and Model 3 is a 15–block four-level construction. In Form B, Model 1 is a pyramidal structure of six blocks; Model 2 is an 8–block four-level construction; and Model 3 is a 15–block four-level construction. One point is awarded for each block that is placed cor-rectly. Examiner required. Not suitable for group use.

Timed: 5 minutes per model

Scoring: Examiner evaluated

Cost: Contact publisher

Publisher: Oxford University Press

TRIPLET RECALL (TRIPREC)
Rosamond Gianutsos and Carol Klitzner

Ages 10–adult

Purpose: Measures short- and long-term memory. Used to assess head injury or stroke as it affects verbal memory.

Description: Computer-administered test measuring short- and long-term retention. The task is easier than that in Free Recall and can be used for practice and remediation with patients for whom Free Recall is too difficult. Three words are presented one at a time and followed by 0, 3, or 9 words to be read, but not recalled, after a constant time interval. Operates on Apple II series computers or IBM PC computers with CGA display and compatibles. Examiner required. Not suitable for group use.

Untimed: 10–15 minutes

Scoring: Computer scored

Cost: $35.00

Publisher: Life Science Associates

TWO ARM COORDINATION TEST
Refer to page 1073.

VISCO CHILD DEVELOPMENT SCREENING TEST (THE CHILDS TEST)
Refer to page 643.

VISUAL ATTENTION TASKS (ATTEND)
Linda Laatsch

Ages 10–adult

Purpose: Diagnoses attention and vig-ilance deficits. Used to assess head injury, stroke, or visual system damage.

Description: Computer-administered test of attentional skills in which the examiner selects targets to which the sub-ject responds and non-targets to which the subject inhibits response. The stimuli appear at selectable intervals, randomly or nonrandomly. The task can be con-structed to suit the level of the deficit. Operates on Apple II series computers or IBM PC computers with CGA display and compatibles. Examiner required. Not suitable for group use.

Untimed: 2–15 minutes

Scoring: Computer scored

Cost: $35.00

Publisher: Life Science Associates

VISUAL FORM DISCRIMINATION TEST

Arthur L. Benton

Adult

Purpose: Assesses a subject's capacity for discriminating complex visual forms.

Description: 16–item multiple-choice test in which each item consists of a stimulus design comprised of major and peripheral figures and four response choices: the correct foil (C), an incorrect foil involving displacement or rotation of the peripheral figure (PE), an incorrect foil involving rotation of a major figure (MR), and an incorrect foil involving distortion of the other major figure (MD). The subject's task is to discriminate among the response choices and identify the one design that matches the stimulus design. Items are scored 0, 1, or 2 points. Examiner required. Not suitable for group use.

Untimed: Varies

Scoring: Examiner evaluated

Cost: Contact publisher

Publisher: Oxford University Press

VISUAL MEMORY TASK (VISMEM)

Rosamond Gianutsos

Ages 8–adult

Purpose: Measures visual, nonverbal memory in head injury and stroke victims.

Description: Computer-administered test of visual memory. Irregular shapes are presented for study. The subject then "paints" the shape as recalled. Operates on Apple II series computers or IBM PC computers with CGA display and compatibles. Self-administered. Not suitable for group use.

Untimed: 8–12 minutes

Scoring: Computer scored

Cost: $25.00

Publisher: Life Science Associates

VISUAL SCANNING (SCAN)

Linda Laatsch

Ages 10–adult

Purpose: Diagnoses visual scanning deficits. Used to assess head injury, stroke, or visual system damage.

Description: Computer-administered test of visual scanning deficits. Two formats are provided: TEXTSCAN and LINESCAN. In TEXTSCAN, letters move across the screen. The subject must respond when the target letter is briefly bracketed. In LINESCAN, a letter or number appears briefly at the right or left edge of the screen, and the same or a different letter or number appears at the opposite edge. The subject must indicate whether they are the same. The required scanning speed is adjustable over a wide range in both formats. May be used in retraining and for diagnosis. Operates on Apple II series computers or IBM PC computers with CGA display and compatibles. Examiner required. Not suitable for group use.

Untimed: 5–12 minutes

Scoring: Computer scored

Cost: $35.00

Publisher: Life Science Associates

WECHSLER MEMORY SCALE (WMS)

David Wechsler and C. P. Stone

Adult

Purpose: Assesses memory functions. Used for adult subjects with special problems, such as aphasics, the elderly, and organically brain-injured individuals.

Description: A short, standardized scale featuring seven subtests assessing memory functions and yielding a memory quotient. Two alternate forms, I and II, are available. Examiner required. Not suitable for group use.

Untimed: Not available

Scoring: Examiner evaluated

Cost: Specimen set (manual, design cards, both record forms) $20.00; 50 record forms $35.00 (specify Form I or II); manual $15.00

Publisher: The Psychological Corporation

Information and availability unconfirmed; last verified in 1988.

WECHSLER MEMORY SCALE— REVISED (WMS-R)
David Wechsler and C.P. Stone

Adult—Ages 16–74

Purpose: Assesses memory functioning. Used with aphasic and organically brain-injured individuals and with the elderly.

Description: 10–subtest verbal and nonverbal scale assessing memory functioning. Three new subtests have been added: Figural Memory, Visual Paired Associates, and Visual Memory Span. The Logical Memory, Verbal Paired Associates, Visual Paired Associates, and Visual Reproduction subtests are administered twice to provide separate estimates of immediate and delayed recall. The revised edition also features more explicit scoring guidelines for the Logical Memory and Visual Reproduction subtests. This test is for use only by persons with at least a master's degree in psychology or a related discipline. Examiner required. Not suitable for group use.

Untimed: 50 minutes, including 30–minute delayed recall procedure

Scoring: Examiner evaluated

Cost: Complete set (35 record forms, carrying case) $189.00; manual $40.00; 25 record forms $19.00

Publisher: The Psychological Corporation

Information and availability unconfirmed; last verified in 1988.

THE WESTERN APHASIA BATTERY (WAB)
Andrew Kertesz

All ages

Purpose: Evaluates an individual's ability to read, write, and calculate. Measures the language functions of content, fluency, auditory comprehension, repetition, and naming. Used to evaluate the severity of language impairment (aphasia) and the nonverbal skills of drawing, block design, and praxis.

Description: Three-part test covering oral language; reading, writing, calculation, and praxis; and nonverbal skills (apraxia, drawing, block design, calculation, Raven's matrices). The nonverbal part is optional. The oral part requires a stopwatch, four Kohs blocks, and a Raven's Colored Progressive Matrices test to measure spontaneous speech, comprehension, naming, repetition, and, thus, aphasia. The subtests require conversational speech in response to questions and a picture interview. The reading and writing tests measure functional communication, spontaneous speech and fluency, and comprehension. Examiner required. Not suitable for group use.

Timed: 1 hour

Scoring: Examiner evaluated

Cost: Complete set $56.50

Publisher: The Psychological Corporation

Information and availability unconfirmed; last verified in 1988.

WISCONSIN CARD SORTING TEST (WCST)
David A. Grant and Esta A. Berg

Adolescent, adult—Ages 16 and older

Purpose: Assesses perseveration and abstract thinking. Used for neuropsychological assessment of individuals suspected of having brain lesions involving the frontal lobes. When used in conjunction with more comprehensive ability testing, the test can help discriminate frontal from nonfrontal lesions.

Description: Multiple-task nonverbal test in which the subject matches cards in two response decks to one of four stimulus cards for color, form, or number. Responses are recorded on a form for later scoring. The test provides measures of overall success and particular sources of difficulty. A computerized version operates on Apple II systems with a color monitor, two floppy disk drives, and a paddle. The scoring program operates on IBM PC systems with 256K and two disk drives. Examiner required. Not suitable for group use.

Untimed: Not available

Scoring: Examiner evaluated; may be computer scored

Cost: Complete kit (2 card decks, 50 response and scoring forms, manual) $85.00; manual $10.00

Publisher: Psychological Assessment Resources, Inc.

WISCONSIN CARD SORTING TEST: COMPUTER VERSION, RESEARCH EDITION
Refer to page 267.

WORD MEMORY TASK (WORDMEM)
Rosamond Gianutsos

Ages 8–adult

Purpose: Assesses immediate memory in head injury and stroke victims.

Description: Computer-administered test of verbal memory. The computer displays a random list of words one by one. The subject then types the list in order. Both number of words in the list and duration of exposure are adjustable. The subject must have some visual function, the ability to read simple English words, rudimentary keyboarding skills, and the ability to follow simple instructions. Self-administered. Not suitable for group use.

Untimed: 8–12 minutes

Scoring: Computer scored

Cost: $50.00

Publisher: Life Science Associates

Personality: Normal and Abnormal, Assessment and Treatment: Child

---

ASSESSMENT AND THERAPY PROGRAMME FOR DYSFLUENT CHILDREN
Refer to page 685.

AUTISTIC BEHAVIOR COMPOSITE CHECKLIST AND PROFILE
Anita Marcott Riley

Autistic and emotionally handicapped children

Purpose: Assesses behaviors associated with autism. Used with autistic, emotionally handicapped, and severely learning disabled students.

Description: 148–item inventory assessing a subject's interfering behaviors in eight categories: prerequisite learning behaviors; sensory perceptual skills; motor development; prelanguage skills; speech, language, and communication skills; developmental rates and sequences; learning behaviors; and relating skills. The checklist and profile help establish and support a diagnosis of autism, prioritize problem areas for intervention, and follow a student's behavior over time. Examiner required. Not suitable for group use.

Untimed: Not available

Scoring: Hand key

Cost: 20 test booklets $19.95

Publisher: Communication Skill Builders, Inc.

AUTOMATED CHILD/ ADOLESCENT SOCIAL HISTORY (ACASH)
Mark Rhode

Child, adolescent—Ages 5–19

Purpose: Assists in obtaining child/adolescent psychosocial history information.

Description: Series of computer-administered questions yielding a narrative summary of a child or adolescent seeking counseling treatment. Questions address the following areas: reason for referral-identifying information; developmental history, prenatal to infancy; developmental history, childhood to present; educational history; current family members and background; religious affiliation; problem identification; and subject and strengths. Ninth-grade reading level required. Self-administered. Not suitable for group use.

Untimed: 45–90 minutes

Scoring: PC-based MICROTEST™ system required; computer scored by publisher

Cost: MICROTEST™ system (10 administrations) $80.00; 50 administrations $337.50; 100 administrations $600.00

Publisher: National Computer Systems/PAS Division

BAR-ILAN PICTURE TEST FOR CHILDREN
Rivkah Itskowitz and Helen Strauss

Child—Ages 4–10

Purpose: Assesses child's perceptions of home, school, peers, and family. Used for diagnosis, screening, and research.

Description: Multiple-item semiprojective interview instrument used for assessing emotional status, motivation and locus of control, interpersonal behavior and conflicts, attitudes towards significant others, feelings of mastery and competence, thought processes, and general level of activity. The test consists of nine basic drawings, six of which have separate versions for boys and for girls, depicting realistic situations from a day in the life of a child. The test was designed for use with children ages 4–10 but has been used successfully with children up to age 16. Examiner required. Not suitable for group use.

Untimed: 20 minutes

Scoring: Examiner evaluated

Cost: Folder with 15 test drawings $34.00; manual $11.00

Publisher: Dansk Psykologisk Forlag

THE BEHAVIOR OBSERVATION SCALE FOR AUTISM
Betty Jo Freeman

Child—Ages 2–5

Purpose: Assesses the presence of clusters of symptoms characteristic of the syndrome of autism.

Description: 24–item observational measure of behavior in four areas: solitary, relation to objects, relation to people, and language. Within each group, repetitive and nonrepetitive behaviors are coded separately. The scale is divided into three elements: recording, recognition, and measurement of behavior. Examiner required. Not suitable for group use.

Untimed: 30 minutes

Scoring: Examiner evaluated

Cost: Contact publisher

Publisher: Betty Jo Freeman, Ph.D.

Information and availability unconfirmed; last verified in 1987.

BURKS' BEHAVIOR RATING SCALES, PRESCHOOL AND KINDERGARTEN EDITION
Harold F. Burks

Child
Grades PreK-K

Purpose: Identifies patterns of behavior problems in children ages 3–6. Used to aid differential diagnosis.

Description: 105–item paper-pencil inventory used by parents and teachers to rate a child on the basis of descriptive statements of observed behavior. The inventory contains 18 subscales: excessive self-blame, anxiety, withdrawal, dependency, suffering, sense of persecution, aggressiveness, resistance, poor ego strength, physical strength, coordination, intellectuality, attention, impulse control, reality contact, sense of identity, anger control, and social conformity. This inventory is a downward extension of Burk's Behavior Rating Scale. Examiner required. Not suitable for group use.

Untimed: 15–20 minutes

Scoring: Hand key

Cost: Complete kit (25 profile sheets and booklets, manual) $19.50

Publisher: Western Psychological Services

CALIFORNIA CHILD Q-SORT SET
Jeanne H. Block and Jack Block

Child

Purpose: Describes individual behavior and personality in contemporary psychodynamic terms. Used for research in child development.

Description: 100–item formulation of personality descriptions. Items are descriptive personality statements sorted from most to least applicable to the subject. Materials include individual 2¼" x 3½" cards. Examiner required. Not suitable for group use.
Untimed: Not available
Scoring: Examiner evaluated
Cost: Q-Sort Deck $8.50
Publisher: Consulting Psychologists Press, Inc.

CHILD & ADOLESCENT ADJUSTMENT PROFILE (CAAP)
Robert E. Ellsworth

Child, adolescent

Purpose: Measures the adjustment of children and adolescents to life and the community. Used for evaluation of treatment programs.

Description: 20–item paper-pencil rating scale assessing a child's or adolescent's adjustment through five factored dimensions: peer relations, dependency, hostility, productivity, and withdrawal. The child may be rated every three months by a parent, teacher, or probation officer to evaluate the success of the child's mental-health program. The manual explains the rationale and validity of the scales and provides detailed norms for the general and clinical population with respect to adjustment to life and the community. Examiner required. Suitable for group use.
Untimed: 20–30 minutes
Scoring: Examiner evaluated
Cost: Manual $6.50; 25 scales and profile sheets $6.50
Publisher: Consulting Psychologists Press, Inc.

CHILD ANXIETY SCALE (CAS)
John S. Gillis

Child—Ages 6–8

Purpose: Diagnoses adjustment problems in children. Helps to prevent emotional and behavioral disorders in later life by identifying children who would benefit from therapeutic intervention at an early age. Used for clinical evaluations and educational and personal counseling.

Description: Paper-pencil test measuring anxiety-based disturbances in young children. Test items are based on extensive research of the form anxiety takes in the self-report of 6–8–year-olds. An audiocassette tape is used to present the questionnaire items, and brightly colored, easy-to-read answer sheets are specially designed for use with children of this age group. The CAS manual contains reliability and validity information, scoring instructions, and percentiles and standard scores for both sexes separately and combined. Examiner required. Suitable for group use.
Untimed: 15 minutes
Scoring: Hand key
Cost: CAS introductory kit $36.45; CAS manual $10.00; 50 hand-scoring answer sheets $8.25; scoring key $5.25; cassette tape $12.95
Publisher: Institute for Personality and Ability Testing, Inc.

CHILD ASSESSMENT SCHEDULE
Kay Hodges

Child

Purpose: Assesses the present episode of psychiatric illness.

Description: Diagnostic interview in three parts. In the first part, the interviewer asks the child approximately 75 questions about school, friends, activities and hobbies, family, fears, worries, self-image, mood, somatic concerns, expression of anger, and thought disorder symptomatology and then records the child's answers. In the second section, the interviewer obtains from the child information about the onset and duration of symptoms. In the third section, the examiner's observations about the child are recorded. This section consists of 53 items about insight, grooming, motor coordination, activity level, spontaneous physical behavior, estimate of cognitive ability, quality of verbal communication and emotional expression, and impressions about quality of interpersonal interactions. These items are scored by the examiner after the interview is completed. A parent form, which is similar in content to the CAS, is available for administration to parents. When both forms are used, they are administered to the parent and to the child individually. The clinician can make DSM-III diagnoses based on information from each form and can generate quantitative scores for various diagnostic clusters for use in making group comparisons. Examiner required. Not suitable for group use.

Untimed: 45–60 minutes

Scoring: Examiner evaluated

Cost: Manual, interview $7.50

Publisher: Kay Hodges, Ph.D.

Information and availability unconfirmed; last verified in 1988.

CHILD BEHAVIOR CHECKLIST AND REVISED CHILD BEHAVIOR PROFILE

Thomas H. Achenbach and Craig Edelbrock

Child, adolescent—Ages 2–16

Purpose: Assesses the behavioral problems and competencies of children and adolescents.

Description: Five multiple-item paper-pencil multiple-choice and free-response inventories evaluating child behavioral problems from four perspectives. The Child Behavior Checklist assesses behavior from the parents' point of view; the Teacher's Report Form assesses the child's classroom behavior; the Direct Observation Form employs an experienced observer to rate the child on the basis of a series of 10–minute observation periods; and the Youth Self-Report (ages 11–18) gathers information directly from the child.

The four-page Child Behavior Checklist (available in two forms, one for ages 2–3 and one for ages 4–16) contains two pages of questions regarding the child's social history, interests, and school per-

formance. Most items combine free-response questions about the child with multiple-choice rating scales for comparing the child with his peers. The last two pages of the checklist present 118 items (item 56 includes a-g) describing a variety of problem behaviors. Parents rate each item from 0 (not true) to 2 (very true) according to their child's behavior over the past six months (time period may be changed to suit user's aims). Responses are scored according to the Revised Child Behavior Profile, which yields scores for social competence scales and behavior problem scales as well as internalizing, externalizing, and total problem scores. Norms are provided in terms of T-scores.

The Teacher's Report Form, presented in a four-page format, gathers background information and assesses 118 items related to classroom behavior. The scoring profile includes standard scores, four general adaptive characteristics, eight behavior problem scales, internalizing and externalizing problems, and total problem scores.

The Direct Observation Form rates 96 problem behaviors from 0 (not observed) to 3 (severe intensity) for a 10–minute period and provides for scoring on-task behavior at 1–minute intervals. The observer writes a narrative description of the child's behavior during the observation period and then rates the behavioral items accordingly. Stable scores are obtained by averaging the ratings obtained on different occasions. Individual item scores, total behavior problem scores, and on-task scores serve as direct indices of behavior problems and change over time and provide a basis for group comparison.

The Youth Self-Report form, presented in a four-page format, gathers first-hand information related to the items on the Child Behavior Checklist. The scoring profile includes standard scores, three competence scales, behavior problem scales, internalizing and externalizing problems, and total problem scores.

Separate manuals are available for the Child Behavior Checklist, Teacher's Report Form, and Youth Self-Report. They discuss development and construction of the scales; the internalizing-externalizing dichotomy, factor loadings; standardization and norms; reliability and validity; effects of clinical status, socioeconomic status, and race; clinical cutoff scores, cluster analyses, profile patterns, and taxonomy; classification of children according to their profile patterns; distribution and correlates of profile types; clinical and research applications; and scoring procedures by hand and computer. The *Practical Guide for the Child Behavior Checklist and Related Materials* describes all the instruments, their applications, and their relationships. Self-administered (except for the Direct Observation Form). All self-administered forms suitable for group use. Available in Chinese, Dutch, French (Canadian and Parisian), German, Greek, Hebrew, Hindi, Italian, Korean, Spanish, Swedish, Norwegian, Finnish, Japanese, Thai, Afrikaans, Icelandic, Russian, Hungarian, Vietnamese, Cambodian, Portuguese, and Turkish.

Untimed: Varies

Scoring: Examiner evaluated; computer scoring programs available

Cost: Sample packet (Child Behavior Checklist, Revised Child Behavior Profile scoring forms, Teacher Report Form and scoring profile, Direct Observation Form, and Youth Self-Report Form, scoring profile, instructions) $12.10

Publisher: Department of Psychiatry, University of Vermont

Information and availability unconfirmed; last verified in 1988.

CHILD BEHAVIOR RATING SCALE
Russell N. Cassel

**Child
Grades PreK–3**

Purpose: Measures the behavior and personality adjustment of children. Used for research and to counsel both normal and emotionally handicapped children.

Description: 78–item paper-pencil inventory consisting of brief statements about behavior and personality that an evaluator (someone familiar with the child) applies to the child and answers on a 6–point scale ranging from "yes" to "no." The inventory yields a total personality adjustment score and a profile of the child's adjustment in five areas: self, home, social, school, and physical. Examiner required. Suitable for group use.

Untimed: 30–40 minutes

Scoring: Hand key

Cost: Complete kit (25 scales, manual) $14.75

Publisher: Western Psychological Services

CHILDHOOD AUTISM RATING SCALE (CARS)
Eric Schopler, Robert J. Reichler, and Barbara Rochen Renner

Child, adolescent

Purpose: Diagnoses children with autism syndrome and distinguishes them from developmentally handicapped children who are not autistic. Used for psychological, medical, or educational evaluations.

Description: 15–item behavior rating scale. Items include relating to people; imitation; emotional response; body use; object use; adaptation to change; visual response; listening response; taste, smell, and touch response and use; fear or nervousness; verbal communication; nonverbal communication; activity level; level and consistency of intellectual response; and general impression. The child is rated on each of the 15 items using a 7–point scale that indicates the degree to which the child's behavior deviates from that of a normal child of the same age. A total score is then computed by summing the individual ratings. Children who score above a given point are categorized as autistic. Scores within the autistic range can then be divided into two categories: mild-to-moderate autism and severe autism. Examiner required. Not suitable for group use.

Untimed: Varies

Scoring: Examiner evaluated

Cost: Kit $25.00

Publisher: Western Psychological Services

THE CHILDREN'S ADAPTIVE BEHAVIOR REPORT (CABR)
Richard H. Kicklighter and Bert O. Richmond

Child—Ages 5–11

Purpose: Assesses adaptive behavior of children as reported by parents or guardians.

Description: Multiple-item interview tool used for soliciting perceptions of adults related to a child's adaptability in language development, independent functioning, family role performance, economic and vocational activity, and socialization. Since the five domains assessed match those in the Children's Adaptive Behavior Scale (CABS), the clinician can contrast adult perceptions with the child's performance on the CABS. Examiner required. Not suitable for group use.
Untimed: 20–30 minutes
Scoring: Examiner evaluated
Cost: 25 test booklets $24.95
Publisher: Humanics Psychological Test Corporation, A Division of Humanics Limited
Information and availability unconfirmed; last verified in 1988.

THE CHILDREN'S APPERCEPTION TEST (CAT-A)
Leopold Bellak and Sonya Sorel Bellak

Child—Ages 3–10

Purpose: Assesses children's personality. Used in clinical evaluation and diagnosis.

Description: 10–item oral-response projective personality test measuring the traits, attitudes, and psychodynamics involved in the personalities of children ages 3–10. Each test item consists of a picture of animals in a human social context through which the child becomes involved in conflicts, identities, roles, and family structures. Examinees are required to tell a story about each picture. The test also includes informational material on the history, nature, and purpose of CAT, Ego Function Graph, test interpretation, use

of the Short Form, research possibilities, and bibliography. Examiner required. Not suitable for group use. Available in Spanish, Indian, French, German, Japanese, Flemish, Portuguese, and Italian.
Untimed: 20–30 minutes
Scoring: Examiner evaluated
Cost: Complete kit (pictures, manual) $19.00
Publisher: C.P.S., Inc.

THE CHILDREN'S APPERCEPTION TEST—HUMAN FIGURES (CAT-H)
Leopold Bellak and Sonya Sorel Bellak

Child—Ages 3–10

Purpose: Assesses children's personality. Used for clinical evaluation and diagnosis.

Description: 10–item oral-response projective personality test measuring the traits, attitudes, and psychodynamics involved in the personalities of children. The test consists of 10 pictures of human figures in situations of concern to children: conflicts, identities, roles, and family structure. The test also includes a review of the literature concerning the use of animal vs. human figures in projective techniques, a discussion of the process of transposing animal figures to human forms, a copy of Haworth's Schedule of Adaptive Mechanisms in CAT Responses, and a bibliography. Examiner required. Not suitable for group use. Available in Spanish, Portuguese, Flemish, and Japanese.
Untimed: 20–30 minutes
Scoring: Examiner evaluated
Cost: Complete kit (10 pictures and manual) $19.00
Publisher: C.P.S., Inc.

THE CHILDREN'S APPERCEPTION TEST— SUPPLEMENT (CAT-S)
Leopold Bellak and Sonya Sorel Bellak

Child—Ages 3–10

Purpose: Assesses children's personality. Used for clinical evaluation and diagnosis.

Description: 10–item oral-response projective personality test measuring the traits, attitudes, and psychodynamics at work in the personalities of children ages 3–10. The test items consist of 10 pictures of animal figures in family situations that are common, but not as universal as those of the Children's Apperception Test. Among the situations depicted are prolonged illness, physical disability, mother's pregnancy, and separation of parents. The picture plates are constructed like pieces of a large jigsaw puzzle, with irregularly shaped outlines. Children who do not relate stories readily can manipulate these forms in play techniques. The test also includes informational material on test techniques and a bibliography. Examiner required. Not suitable for group use. Available in Spanish, French, Flemish, and Italian.

Untimed: 20–30 minutes

Scoring: Examiner evaluated

Cost: Complete kit (10 pictures, manual) $19.00

Publisher: C.P.S., Inc.

CHILDREN'S APPERCEPTIVE STORY-TELLING TEST (CAST)
Mary F. Schneider

Child—Ages 6–13

Purpose: Evaluates the emotional functioning of school-age children.

Description: Multiple-item apperceptive test employing colored picture stimuli to evoke stories from students. The test yields a T-score profile for four major factors (adaptive, nonadaptive, immature, and uninvested) and 15 adaptive, nonadaptive, and problem-solving scales. Profiles are available for attention deficit disordered, conduct disordered, anxiety disordered, oppositional disordered, and childhood depression. Examiner required. Not suitable for group use.

Untimed: Varies

Scoring: Examiner evaluated

Cost: Complete kit (examiner's manual, 31 picture cards, 50 record scoring forms, storage box) $89.00

Publisher: PRO-ED

CHILDREN'S EMBEDDED FIGURES TEST (CEFT)
Stephen A. Karp and Norma Konstadt

Child—Ages 5–12

Purpose: Assesses cognitive style in perceptual tasks. Used for measuring field dependence in studies of psychological differentiation.

Description: 25–item verbal/manual test of perceptual processes including field dependence/independence. The child's performance is related to analytic ability, social behavior, and body concept. Materials include cut-out models of two forms, 38 plates for the 25 items and 13 practice items, clear plastic envelopes to protect the plates, and a star rubber stamp. A washable ink stamp pad is required. The subject finds simple forms in complex figures and stamps the correct choice. Examiner required. Not suitable for group use.

Untimed: Open ended

Scoring: Examiner evaluated

Cost: Test kit (50 recording sheets, cardboard forms, 38 color plates, clear plastic envelopes, rubber stamp) $25.50

Publisher: Consulting Psychologists Press, Inc.

THE CHILDREN'S HYPNOTIC SUSCEPTIBILITY SCALE
Perry London

Child, adolescent—Ages 5–17

Purpose: Measures susceptibility to hypnosis in children and adolescents. Used for teaching, research, and experimentation.

Description: 22–item test containing instructions for inducing and testing the hypnotic state of children on two age levels. The instructions use permissive, nonauthoritarian language and gentle challenges. Items are of increasing difficulty, and testing may be ended after Item 12 if the child is not experiencing hypnosis. The test was adapted from the Stanford Hypnotic Susceptibility Scale Forms A, B, and C. Examiner required. Not suitable for group use.

Untimed: 50 minutes

Scoring: Hand key

Cost: Kit (25 scales and scoring and observation forms) $31.50

Publisher: Consulting Psychologists Press, Inc.

CHILDREN'S PERSONALITY QUESTIONNAIRE (CPQ)
Rutherford B. Porter and Raymond B. Cattell

Child, adolescent—Ages 8–12

Purpose: Assesses personality development in children. Used for clinical evaluations and educational and personal counseling.

Description: 140–item paper-pencil test measuring 14 primary personality traits useful in predicting and evaluating the course of personal, social, and academic development. The traits measured include emotional stability, self-concept level, excitability, and self-assurance. Scores for extraversion, anxiety, and other broad trait patterns are obtained as combinations of the primary scales. Percentiles and standard scores are presented for both sexes together and separately. The test is available in four forms: A, B, C, and D. Each form is divided into two parts for scheduling convenience in school settings. A third-grade reading level is required. Examiner required. Suitable for group use. Available in Spanish and German.

Untimed: 30–60 minutes per form

Scoring: Hand key; interpretation services available

Cost: CPQ introductory kit $24.95; handbook with norms $12.75; 25 reusable test booklets (forms A & B) $15.60; 25 reusable test booklets (forms C & D) $20.80; 50 answer sheets $8.25; 50 profile sheets $8.25; 50 answer-profile sheets (forms A & B) $10.75; scoring key $11.50

Publisher: Institute for Personality and Ability Testing, Inc.

CHILDREN'S PROBLEMS CHECKLIST
John A. Schinka

Parents of children ages 5–12

Purpose: Assesses children's problems as reported by parent or guardian. Used as a survey instrument in clinical and counseling settings to initiate the consultation process and introduce the client to formal diagnostic testing.

Description: 190–item paper-pencil test completed by a parent or guardian identifying problems in 11 areas: emotions, self-concept, peers/play, school, language/thinking, concentration/organization, activity level/motor control, behavior, values, habits, and health. The test is a component of the Clinical Checklist Series. Self-administered. Suitable for group use.

Untimed: 10–20 minutes

Scoring: Examiner evaluated

Cost: 50 checklists $17.95

Publisher: Psychological Assessment Resources, Inc.

CHILDREN'S STATE-TRAIT ANXIETY INVENTORY
Charles D. Spielberger, C.D. Edwards, J. Montuori, and R. Lushene

Child, adolescent Grades 4–8

Purpose: Assesses anxiety in children. Used for research screening and treatment evaluation.

Description: Two 20–item scales measuring two types of anxiety: state anxiety (current level of anxiety, or S-Anxiety) and trait anxiety (anxiety-proneness, or T-Anxiety). The S-Anxiety scales ask how the child feels at a particular moment in time, and the T-Anxiety scales ask how he generally feels. The inventory is based on the same concept as the State-Trait Anxiety Inventory and is used in conjunction with the adult form manual. Self-administered. Suitable for group use.

Untimed: 10–20 minutes

Scoring: Hand key; examiner evaluated

Cost: Manual $4.75; key $1.25; 25 expendable tests $4.25

Publisher: Consulting Psychologists Press, Inc.

DEVEREUX CHILD BEHAVIOR RATING SCALE (DCB)
Refer to page 651.

DIABETES OPINION SURVEY (DOS)
Refer to page 3.

DIAGNOSTIC CHECKLIST FOR BEHAVIOR-DISTURBED CHILDREN: FORM E-2
Bernard Rimland

Child—Ages 3½-5

Purpose: Diagnoses infantile autism. Differentiates truly autistic children from autistic-type children.

Description: 80–item paper-pencil inventory assessing speech and behavior symptoms related to autism in young children. The checklist consists of questions (intended for the child's parents) covering social interaction and affect; speech, motor, and manipulative ability; intelligence and reaction to sensory stimuli; family characteristics; illness development; and physiological and other biological data. A total score is derived, as well as separate scores for speech and behavior. Cutoff scores and interpretive guidelines are provided to assist in diagnosing autism and other forms of childhood psychoses. Examiner required. Not suitable for group use.

Untimed: Not available

Scoring: Scored by publisher

Cost: Contact publisher

Publisher: Institute for Child Behavior Research

Information and availability unconfirmed; last verified in 1987.

EARLY SCHOOL PERSONALITY QUESTIONNAIRE (ESPQ)
*Raymond B. Cattell,
Richard W. Coan, and IPAT Staff*

Child—Ages 6-8

Purpose: Measures personality in children in the early school years. Used for clinical evaluation and educational and personal counseling.

Description: 160–item paper-pencil test measuring personality in children. Questions are read aloud by the teacher (an optional tape recording may be used instead), and the students mark their answers on the answer sheet. To use the answer sheet, children need only to be able to discriminate the letter A from the letter B and to recognize pictures of a bird, cat, tree, flower, and other common objects. Percentiles and standard scores are provided for both sexes separately and together. The test is divided into two equal parts of 80 items each for scheduling convenience. Examiner required. Suitable for group use. Available in Spanish.

Untimed: 1 hour

Scoring: Hand key

Cost: ESPQ introductory kit $16.95; manual $5.75; 25 answer booklets $7.80; 50 profile sheets $7.80; 2 scoring keys $10.50; tape recording $12.95

Publisher: Institute for Personality and Ability Testing, Inc.

EYBERG CHILD BEHAVIOR INVENTORY
Sheila Eyberg

Child, adolescent—Ages 2-17

Purpose: Assesses conduct problem behaviors.

Description: 36–item paper-pencil multiple-choice inventory divided into two scales. On the Intensity Scale, parents rate the frequency of their child's behavioral problems from 1 (never) to 7 (always). The Problem Scale contains a "yes-no" scale, which parents use to identify the number of problem behaviors the

---

personality: child

child currently exhibits. This test is suitable for individuals with visual, hearing, physical, and mental impairments. Parents with visual impairments can have the items read aloud and their answers recorded for them. Examiner required. Suitable for group use. Available in Spanish.

Untimed: 5 minutes

Scoring: Self-scored

Cost: Contact publisher

Publisher: Sheila Eyberg

EYSENCK PERSONALITY QUESTIONNAIRE (EPQ)
Refer to page 172.

FROST SELF-DESCRIPTION QUESTIONNAIRE
Barry P. Frost

Child, adolescent—Ages 8–14

Purpose: Diagnoses various aspects of a child's feelings of anxiety, aggression, and separation.

Description: 107–item paper-pencil true-false test covering 14 scales of anxiety: test, social, worry and tension, concentration, separation from family, spatial separation, body damage, free-floating, externalized aggression, internalized aggression, projective aggression, denial, affiliation, and submission. Materials consist of a booklet, answer sheet, and answer keys. Use is restricted to psychologists. Examiner required. Suitable for group use. Available in Spanish and Japanese.
AUSTRALIAN PUBLISHER

Untimed: 15 minutes

Scoring: Hand key

Cost: Manual $5.00; 25 questionnaire booklets $25.00; 25 answer sheets $10.00; 4 keys $8.00

Publisher: Barry P. Frost, Ph.D.

Information and availability unconfirmed; last verified in 1988.

FROST SELF-DESCRIPTION QUESTIONNAIRE: EXTENDED SCALE (FSDQ: EXTENDED)
Barry P. Frost

Child, adolescent—Ages 9–14

Purpose: Assesses personality variables, specifically anxiety, aggression, affiliation, and denial in children.

Description: 310–item paper-pencil test in three forms measuring externalized, internalized, and projective aggression; free-floating, body-damage, separation, test, concentration, and social anxiety; worry and tension; and denial and affiliation. The scales can be used separately or to follow-up on indications from the original Frost Self-Description Questionnaire. Form I (aggression) contains 85 items; Form II (four anxiety scales), 105 items; and Form III (three anxiety scales, denial, and affiliation), 120 items. Children are asked to read each question, decide if a description is true of how the child acts or feels, and mark an answer. The scales are appropriate for most children, except those with low intellectual skills. Examiner required. Suitable for group use.
AUSTRALIAN PUBLISHER

Untimed: 20–30 minutes per form

Scoring: Examiner evaluated

Cost: Specimen set $50.00

Publisher: Barry P. Frost, Ph.D.

Information and availability unconfirmed; last verified in 1988.

INTERMEDIATE PERSONALITY QUESTIONNAIRE FOR INDIAN PUPILS (IPQI)—1974
Refer to page 766.

IS THIS AUTISM?
M. Aarons and T. Gittens

Child—Ages 2–8

Purpose: Identifies autistic features. Used as a basis for planning treatment.

Description: Multiple-item paper-pencil checklist designed to help childcare professionals identify and treat autistic children. The checklist covers attention control, sensory function, nonverbal symbolic function, concept formation, sequencing and rhythmic abilities, speech and language, educational attainments, and intelligence. The accompanying handbook helps the examiner to decide which features to look for, how to interpret the information obtained, and how to use it to form appropriate treatment programs. It also discusses the wider implications of specific behaviors. Examiner required. Not suitable for group use.

Untimed: Varies

Scoring: Examiner evaluated

Cost: Contact publisher

Publisher: NFER-NELSON Publishing Company Ltd.

JUNIOR EYSENCK PERSONALITY INVENTORY (JEPI)
Sybil B.G. Eysenck

Child, adolescent—Ages 7–16

Purpose: Measures the major personality dimensions of children. Used as a research instrument.

Description: 60–item paper-pencil yes-no inventory measuring extraversion-introversion (24 items) and neuroticism-stability (24 items). A falsification scale (12 items) detects response distortion. Scores are provided for E-Extraversion, N-Neuroticism, and L-Lie. American norms are available for selected samples of majority and minority children. Examiner required. Suitable for group use. Available in Spanish.

Untimed: 10 minutes

Scoring: Hand key

Cost: Specimen set (manual, one copy of all forms) $5.25; 25 inventories $8.00; key $6.25; manual $2.75

Publisher: EdITS/Educational and Industrial Testing Service

KOHN PROBLEM CHECKLIST (KPC), RESEARCH EDITION
Refer to page 742.

KOHN SOCIAL COMPETENCE SCALE (KSC), RESEARCH EDITION
Refer to page 742.

MARTINEK-ZAICHKOWSKY SELF-CONCEPT SCALE FOR CHILDREN (MZSCS)
Refer to page 768.

MICHIGAN PICTURE TEST, REVISED
Max L. Hutt

Child, adolescent Grades 3–12

Purpose: Differentiates between emotionally maladjusted children and emotionally well-adjusted children. Diagnoses type and severity of conflicts and identifies children in need of rehabilitative/psychotherapeutic procedures.

Description: Oral-response projective test measuring degree of emotional adjustment or maladjustment, areas of emotional conflict, and types of emotional conflict. Four "core" pictures presented to both sexes yield scores on several emotional areas. Eight additional pictures for boys and eight for girls yield information about areas and types of conflict. Students are presented with picture cards one at a time and asked to create stories about them. Scoring employs simple objective methods along with characteristics of partially structured projective tests. Examiner required. Suitable for group use.

Untimed: Short form 15 minutes; long form 1 hour

Scoring: Hand key; examiner evaluated

Cost: Contact publisher

Publisher: The Psychological Corporation

Information and availability unconfirmed; last verified in 1988.

MISSOURI CHILDREN'S PICTURE SERIES (MCPS)
J.O. Sines, J.D. Pauker, and L.K. Sines

Child, adolescent—Ages 5–16

Purpose: Measures child personality characteristics. Used to screen school-age children for personality difficulties and to evaluate in terms of clinical diagnosis.

Description: 238–item test consisting of picture diagrams of everyday situations printed on 3 x 5 cards, which the examiner presents to the children, asking them to select those which look like fun and those which do not. The examiner separates the cards by color dividers to score the answers on the following scales: Conformity, Masculinity/Femininity, Maturity, Aggression, Introversion, Hyperactivity, Sleep Disturbance, and Systematic Complaint. The results yield information regarding the possibility of personality difficulties. The test is available only to psychologists, trained teachers, and counselors. Examiner required. Suitable for group use.

Untimed: 25 minutes

Scoring: Hand key

Cost: Specimen set $40.00

Publisher: Psychological Assessment and Services, Inc.

PEER NOMINATION INVENTORY OF DEPRESSION (PNID)
*Monroe M. Lefkowitz and
Edward P. Tesiny*

Child—Ages 8–11
Grades 3–5

Purpose: Assesses symptoms of depression in normal children. Used by researchers to collect epidemiological data regarding depressive symptoms in the general child population.

Description: 23–item paper-pencil inventory measuring depression, happiness, and popularity. For each item, the child is rated on a 2–point scale (0 = not selected; 1 = selected) by his peers. Each rated child receives two scores: an item score and a total score (sum of item scores). A third-grade reading level is required. Examiner required. Suitable for group use only.

Untimed: 30 minutes

Scoring: Hand key

Cost: One-time fee of $25.00 per administrator or institution

Publisher: Monroe M. Lefkowitz, Ph.D.

Information and availability unconfirmed; last verified in 1988.

PERSONALITY INVENTORY FOR CHILDREN (PIC), REVISED FORMAT
*Robert D. Wirt, David Lachar,
James E. Klinedinst, Philip D. Seat,
and William E. Broen, Jr.*

Child, adolescent—Ages
3–16

Purpose: Evaluates the personality attributes of children and adolescents. Used by professionals for counseling and identification of psychopathology, developmental problems, and social disabilities.

Description: 280–item paper-pencil true-false inventory completed by one of the child's parents producing a profile of 16 scales: Intellectual Screening, Family Relations, Hyperactivity, Somatic Concern, Social Skills, Achievement, Development, Depression, Delinquency, Withdrawal, Psychosis, Anxiety, Lie, Frequency, Defensiveness, and Adjustment. A 420–item version is available for higher scale reliabilities, and a 131–item version is available for screening. Examiner required. Not suitable for group use.

Untimed: Not available

Scoring: Hand key; may be computer scored

Cost: Complete kit $150.00; 10 booklets $17.50; 100 profile forms $13.50 (specify ages 3–5 or 6–16); 100 answer sheets $13.50; scoring templates $31.50

Publisher: Western Psychological Services

PERSONALITY RATING SCALE
Sister Mary Amatora

Child, adolescent
Grades K–12

Purpose: Assesses personality strengths and weaknesses of children. Identifies children needing further psychological evaluation.

Description: 22–item paper-pencil test of personality functioning. The items are characteristics of good and poor habits of interaction acquired in childhood and strengthened in early adolescence that affect personality development and the process of maturation. The rating scale may be completed by the child, teacher, or peers. The test may be used with students in Grades K–3 with the special instructions provided in the manual. Self-administered. Suitable for group use.

Untimed: 30–40 minutes

Scoring: Hand key; examiner and student evaluated

Cost: Specimen set $5.00; complete kit (35 scales, 35 pupil rating sheets, 3 class record sheets, key, manual) $15.00; additional manuals $2.00 each

Publisher: Educators/Employers' Tests & Services Associates

PIERS-HARRIS CHILDREN'S SELF-CONCEPT SCALE (PHCSCS)
Ellen V. Piers and Dale B. Harris

Child, adolescent
Grades 4–12

Purpose: Measures a child's self-concept. Identifies problem areas in a child's self-concept. Used for research.

Description: 80–item paper-pencil test assessing six aspects of a child's self-esteem: behavior, intellectual and school status, physical appearance and attributes, anxiety, popularity, and happiness and satisfaction. Items are written at a third-grade reading level and require a simple "yes-no" answer. Percentile and standard scores are provided for the total score and for each of the six subscales. Scores can be used for research purposes or to identify extreme problem areas. The manual provides the information necessary for administering and interpreting the scale, as well as the information included in Research Monograph #1 concerning use of the scale with minority and special education groups. Examiner/self-administered. Suitable for group use.

Untimed: 15–20 minutes

Scoring: Hand key; may be computer scored

Cost: Kit (25 test booklets, 25 profile forms, scoring key, 2 computer answer sheets, manual) $55.00

Publisher: Western Psychological Services

PLAY AND TELL CARDS: A THERAPEUTIC GAME
Robert Gordon

Child—Ages 6–12

Purpose: Allows children to verbalize thoughts and fears in a nonthreatening environment. Aids in building a therapeutic relationship by stimulating dialogue and establishing rapport between child and therapist.

Description: 80–item interview guide consisting of cards presenting topics to be discussed during a game of checkers. After each move in the game, the child selects a card and discusses it with the therapist. The cards ask questions about home, family, emotions, relationships, school, values, safety, health, discipline, thought processes, conflicts, and fears. The checkers and board are not provided. Examiner required. Suitable for group use.

Untimed: Not available

Scoring: Examiner evaluated

Cost: Complete set (cards, instructions) $13.00

Publisher: The Wilmington Press
Information and availability unconfirmed; last verified in 1987.

THE PRESCHOOL BEHAVIOR QUESTIONNAIRE
*Lenore B. Behar and
Samuel Stringfield*

Child—Ages 3–6

Purpose: Screens preschool children for symptoms indicating behavior problems. Used by teachers and/or child psychologists to screen for further assessment.

Description: 30–item paper-pencil observational scale consisting of behavioral statements, which a teacher or parent rates "doesn't apply," "applies sometimes," or "certainly applies" for the child in question. Measures hostile-aggressive, anxious, and distractible behaviors. Materials include score sheet, answer sheet, and manual. Examiner/self-administered. Suitable for group use.

Untimed: 10 minutes

Scoring: Examiner evaluated

Cost: Complete kit (50 score sheets and answer sheets, manual) $15.00

Publisher: Lenore Behar

PRESCHOOL SELF-CONCEPT PICTURE TEST (PS-CPT)
Refer to page 771.

PSYCHOLOGICAL EVALUATION OF CHILDREN'S HUMAN FIGURE DRAWINGS (HFD)
Elizabeth M. Koppitz

Child—Ages 5–12

Purpose: Assesses a child's mental maturity, personality characteristics, and family relationships. Used to screen school beginners, as part of a psychological test battery, and to measure progress.

Description: Multiple-item paper-pencil test in which the child draws "one whole person" and answers three questions. The drawing is scored and analyzed for developmental items, emotional indicators, and content. The factors measured include mental maturity, self-concept, attitudes (concerns, anxiety, conflict), and interpersonal relationships. Examiner required. Suitable for group use. Available in German, Spanish, and Japanese.

Untimed: 5–12 minutes

Scoring: Examiner evaluated

Cost: Manual $35.95

Publisher: The Psychological Corporation

Information and availability unconfirmed; last verified in 1988.

REYNOLDS CHILD DEPRESSION SCALE (RCDS)
William M. Reynolds

Child
Grades 3–6

Purpose: Assesses and screens for depressive symptomatology.

Description: 30–item paper-pencil multiple-choice test. Percentiles by grade and sex are provided for the total score. A second-grade reading level is required. This is one test in the Reynolds Depression Scale series. May be used with individuals with visual, hearing, physical, and mental impairments. Examiner must meet APA guidelines. Examiner required. Suitable for group use.

Untimed: 10 minutes

Scoring: Hand key; scoring service available from publisher

Cost: RCDS Kit (manual, 25 hand scorable answer sheets, scoring key) $29.00; contact publisher for scoring service cost

Publisher: Psychological Assessment Resources, Inc.

ROBERTS APPERCEPTION TEST FOR CHILDREN
Glen E. Roberts and
Dorothea S. McArthur

Child, adolescent—Ages 6–15

Purpose: Identifies emotionally disturbed children. Used for clinical diagnosis, particularly with children just entering counseling or therapy.

Description: 16–item oral-response test in which the child is shown cards containing realistic line illustrations and is asked to make up stories about each. The illustrations depict adults and children in up-to-date clothing and emphasize the everyday, interpersonal events of contemporary life, including (in addition to the standard situations of the TAT and CAT) such situations as parental disagreement, parental affection, observation of nudity, and school and peer interpersonal events. Stimuli are chosen to elicit psychologically meaningful responses. The clinical areas measured and reported on the Interpersonal Chart are conflict, anxiety, aggression, depression, rejection, punishment, dependency, support, closure, resolution, unresolved indicator, maladaptive outcome, and deviation response. Other measures include the Ego Functioning Index, the Aggression Index, and the Levels of Projection Scale. The manual includes a number of case studies and examples. Examiner required. Not suitable for group use.

Untimed: 20–30 minutes

Scoring: Examiner evaluated

Cost: Complete kit (set of test pictures, 25 record booklets, manual) $75.00

Publisher: Western Psychological Services

ROBERTS APPERCEPTION TEST FOR CHILDREN: TEST PICTURES FOR BLACK CHILDREN
Glen E. Roberts and Dorothea S. McArthur

Child, adolescent—Ages 6–15

Purpose: Identifies emotionally disturbed children. Used for clinical diagnosis.

Description: 16–item oral-response projective test measuring conflict, anxiety, aggression, depression, rejection, punishment, dependency, support, closure, resolution, unresolved problems, maladaptive outcome, and deviation response. An Ego Functioning Index, Aggression Index, and Levels of Projection Scale are included also. The child is asked to make up stories about the situations depicted on cards containing realistic line illustrations of children and adults engaged in everyday, interpersonal events. Among the situations presented are parental disagreement, parental affection, observation of nudity, and school and peer interpersonal events. The stimulus cards parallel those used in the original test but feature black rather than white individuals. Examiner required. Not suitable for group use.

Untimed: 20–30 minutes

Scoring: Examiner evaluated

Cost: Set of test pictures $42.50

Publisher: Western Psychological Services

ROGERS PERSONAL ADJUSTMENT INVENTORY—UK REVISION
Patricia M. Jeffrey, based on original test by Carl Rogers

Child—Ages 9–13

Purpose: Assesses the personal adjustment of problem children. Used to initiate treatment programs and personality assessment.

Description: Multiple-item paper-pencil inventory assessing significant aspects of a child's personality, including attitude toward the environment; adjustment to peers, family, and self; and the manner in which the child approaches problems. Many test items have been completely rewritten, anglicized, and updated. Separate test forms have been developed for boys and girls. Examiner required. Suitable for group use.
BRITISH PUBLISHER

Untimed: Varies

Scoring: Examiner evaluated

Cost: Contact publisher

Publisher: NFER-NELSON Publishing Company Ltd.

SCHOOL APPERCEPTION METHOD (SAM)
Irving L. Solomon and Bernard D. Starr

Child, adolescent Grades K–9

Purpose: Assesses the emotional and cognitive frame of mind of children and adolescents. Used for clinical evaluations.

Description: 12–item oral-response projective test consisting of 12 drawings and 12 alternates focused on school situations. The scenes are designed to elicit school-oriented fantasies, feelings, attitudes, and perceptions. The manual is included. Examiner required. Suitable for group use.

Untimed: Not available

Scoring: Examiner evaluated

Cost: Complete kit (24 pictures plus manual) $22.50

Publisher: Springer Publishing Company

Information and availability unconfirmed; last verified in 1987.

SCHOOL CHILD STRESS SCALE (SCSS)
Justin Pikunas

Child, adolescent
Grades 1–8

Purpose: Measures the intensity of stress present in normal to mildly retarded children. Used to identify children who need special adjustment counseling.

Description: Multiple-item oral-response questionnaire examining a child's levels of efficiency and adjustment in dealing with the stress often encountered by the normal and mildly retarded. The examiner reads through the one-page instrument, questions the child, and records the answers. Examiner required. Not suitable for group use.

Untimed: 20 minutes

Scoring: Examiner evaluated

Cost: Testing form (includes guidelines for interpretation) $2.00; 25 forms $6.00

Publisher: Justin Pikunas, Ph.D.

SELF-CONCEPT ADJECTIVE CHECKLIST
Alan J. Politte

Child
Grades K–8

Purpose: Measures personality and self-concept. Used for diagnosis, screening, and measuring changes due to therapy.

Description: 114–item paper-pencil test of self-concept in which the items are traits categorized as physical traits, social values, intellectual abilities, and miscellaneous. Children in Grades K–3 check "I Am" or "I Am Not" for each item. Children in Grades 4–8 have the additional choice of an "I Would Like To Be" column. The items may be rated by the student or an observer. Examiner required. Suitable for group use.

Untimed: 10 minutes

Scoring: Hand key; examiner evaluated

Cost: Specimen set $5.00; 25 rating checklists $15.00

Publisher: Psychologists and Educators, Inc.

STRESS RESPONSE SCALE
Refer to page 748.

TEMPERAMENT ASSESSMENT BATTERY FOR CHILDREN (TABC)
Roy P. Martin

Child—Ages 3–7

Purpose: Measures the basic personality-behavioral dimensions or temperaments of children.

Description: Multiple-item paper-pencil test assessing six temperamental variables: Activity, Adaptability, Approach/Withdrawal, Intensity, Distractibility, and Persistence. Items are rated on a 7–point scale ranging from "hardly ever" to "almost always." Three forms are used. The 48–item Parent Form describes the child's behavior at home. The 48–item Teacher Form reflects the child's classroom behavior. The Clinician Form is a questionnaire used by professionals involved in the child's psychoeducational evaluation. The test produces a description of the child and a comparison of other children in the same age range. Three factor scores are yielded: Emotionality, Persistence, and Sociability. Raw scores are converted to percentile equivalents for each temperament and factor scale. Examiner required. Not suitable for group use.

Untimed: 12 minutes

Scoring: Hand key; examiner evaluated

Cost: Sample kit (manual, 1 copy of each component test form) $30.00

Publisher: Clinical Psychology Publishing Co., Inc.

TEST BEHAVIOR CHECKLIST
Glen P. Aylward and Robert W. MacGruder

Child

Purpose: Assesses and provides a means of recording behaviors observed during psychological testing.

Description: 18–item paper-pencil checklist in which the examiner uses a 5–point scale to rate the examinee's behavior during testing. The checklist consists of three sections. The first section collects general information, demographic data, and physical appearance and assesses motor skill development, articulation and language, activity level, and test-taking anxiety. The second section assesses test-taking approach (attention span, following directions, response latency, variability). The third section covers social-emotional style, cooperativeness, and social skills. Examiner required. Not suitable for group use.

Untimed: 5–10 minutes

Scoring: Examiner evaluated

Cost: Specimen set $17.00; manual $9.00; record sheets $10.00

Publisher: Clinical Psychology Publishing Co., Inc.

Personality: Normal and Abnormal, Assessment and Treatment: Adolescent and Adult

ACTIVITY COMPLETION TECHNIQUE (ACT)
Joseph Sacks

Adult

Purpose: Assesses personality characteristics of adults. Used by clinicians for planning treatment, monitoring progress, and conducting research.

Description: 60–item paper-pencil sentence completion test covering four areas: family, interpersonal, affect, and self-concept. This revised form of the Sacks Sentence Completion Test yields 15 categories of information, including relationship with mother, relationship with father, heterosexual relationships, relationships with authority figures, hostility, anxiety, adequacy, future, and fantasy. The test provides an adjustment rating scale and is used to evaluate general personality characteristics and positive personality tendencies, such as self-actualization and activity-passivity. Examiner/self-administered. Suitable for group use.

Untimed: 30–40 minutes

Scoring: Examiner evaluated

Cost: Kit (manual, 25 test forms, 25 rating sheets) $24.95

Publisher: Psychological Assessment Resources, Inc.

ACTUALIZING ASSESSMENT BATTERY (AAB)
Everett L. Shostrom

Adult

Purpose: Measures an individual's sense of actualization with himself and within his relationships with others. Used by therapists, marriage and family counselors, personnel administrators, and school psychologists for a wide variety of counseling situations.

Description: Four paper-pencil tests measuring 13 dimensions of a person's sense of actualization: being, weakness, synergistic integration, time orientation, core centeredness, love, trust in humanity, creative living, mission, strength, manipulation awareness, anger, and potentiation. The Personal Orientations Dimensions (POD) and the Personal Orientation Inventory (POI) primarily measure intrapersonal actualizing, and the Caring Relationship Inventory (CRI) and the Pair Attraction Inventory (PAI) primarily measure interpersonal actualizing. The AAB may be scored locally by using the POI, CRI, and PAI or may be sent to EdITS for scoring. Results are reported through the AAB Interpretation Brochure, a 6–page booklet containing descriptions and profiles for each of the four tests. Examiner required. Suitable for group use.

Untimed: 3 hours

Scoring: Computer scored

Cost: Contact publisher

Publisher: EdITS/Educational and Industrial Testing Service

THE ADJECTIVE CHECK LIST (ACL)
Harrison G. Gough and Alfred B. Heilbrun, Jr.

Adolescent, adult Grades 9 and above

Purpose: Describes self and relations with others; used for personality assessment and research.

Description: 300–item paper-pencil test of up to 37 dimensions of personality, including four Method of Response scales, 15 Need scales, nine Topical scales, five Transactional scales, and four Origence-Intellectence scales. Items are adjectives that are checked if they apply to self, but they may be answered with reference to others. Scores need not be obtained on all 37 scales. Hand scoring requires users to prepare their own stencils. Self-administered. Suitable for group use. Available in Spanish.

Untimed: 15–20 minutes

Scoring: Hand key; computer scoring available from publisher

Cost: Manual $19.00; 25 checklists (hand scored) $8.00; 50 profiles $7.50; Spanish test booklet $1.50

Publisher: Consulting Psychologists Press, Inc.

THE ADJUSTMENT INVENTORY: ADULT FORM
Hugh M. Bell

Adult

Purpose: Measures the personal and social adjustment of adults.

Description: Multiple-item paper-pencil self-report inventory assessing five areas of personal adjustment: home, health, social, emotional, and occupational. Items may be answered on the test booklet or on a separate answer sheet. Examiners must

prepare their own scoring stencils for the answer sheets. Self-administered. Suitable for group use.

Untimed: 25 minutes

Scoring: Hand key

Cost: Specimen kit (manual, scoring stencil, answer sheet) $2.50

Publisher: Consulting Psychologists Press, Inc.

THE ADJUSTMENT INVENTORY: STUDENT FORM
Refer to page 762.

ADOLESCENT ALIENATION INDEX (AAI)
F.K. Heussenstamm

Adolescent—Ages 12–19

Purpose: Identifies emergent or developing alienation in adolescents. Provides a measure of incipient estrangement that may give clues to personality disjunctures long before behavioral symptoms are evident.

Description: 41–item paper-pencil test in which students choose between two self-descriptive statements for each test item. The test covers facets of youthful alienation such as normlessness, meaninglessness, powerlessness, self-estrangement, and social isolation. Form A offers separate answer sheets for ease of test-taking and scoring. Form C offers consumable test forms designed for students with less sophisticated test-taking skills. Norms are based on suburban white, urban black, and rural Mexican-American high-school students and on black Job Corps enrollees. Self-administered. Suitable for group use.

Timed: 20 minutes

Scoring: Hand key

Cost: 35 forms (specify form) $10.00; 35 answer sheets (Form A) $4.00; scoring stencil (Form A) $3.00; scoring guide (Form C) $3.00; manual $4.00

Publisher: Monitor

ADOLESCENT-COPING ORIENTATION FOR PROBLEM EXPERIENCES (A-COPE)
Joan M. Patterson and Hamilton I. McCubbin

Adolescent—Ages 12–18
Grades 6–12

Purpose: Identifies behaviors adolescents find helpful in managing problems or difficult situations that happen to them or members of their families. Used in counseling, clinical, and research settings.

Description: 54–item paper-pencil self-report instrument covering behaviors for coping with problems. Items, which are presented in yes-no format, are grouped conceptually into seven behavioral patterns: developing and maintaining a sense of competence and self-esteem, investing in family relationships and fitting into the family life-style, investing in extra-familial relationships and seeking social support, developing positive perceptions about life situations, relieving tension through diversions, relieving tension through substance use and/or expression of anger, and avoiding confrontation and withdrawing. A scoring service is available from the publisher. Examiner required. Suitable for group use.

Untimed: Varies

Scoring: Examiner evaluated

Cost: Manual $37.50 ($30.50 for students); assessment form $0.10

Publisher: Family Stress, Coping and Health Project, University of Wisconsin-Madison

Information and availability unconfirmed; last verified in 1988.

ADOLESCENT DIAGNOSTIC SCREENING BATTERY
James J. Smith and Joseph M. Eisenberg

Adolescent—Ages 13–17

Purpose: Identifies diagnostic possibilities among those listed in DSM-III-R. Used with adolescents in clinical settings.

Description: Paper-pencil or computer-administered screening battery assessing symptoms important for diagnostic considerations. The system consists of a questionnaire for the adolescent and a questionnaire for the clinician. The adolescent's parent or guardian may provide independent information through the use of the Child Diagnostic Screening Battery. The system is structured so that once data is entered in the computer, it is compared with all possible DSM-III-R diagnoses. A manual describing the use and application of the program and the use of printouts generated by the program is provided. Self-administered. Suitable for group use.

Untimed: 15 minutes

Scoring: Computer scored

Cost: Total system $195.00

Publisher: Reason House

ADOLESCENT EMOTIONAL FACTORS INVENTORY
Mary K. Bauman

Adolescent

Purpose: Measures emotional and personality factors of visually handicapped adolescents.

Description: 150–item paper-pencil or oral-response questionnaire assessing the personal and emotional adjustment of visually handicapped adolescents. The inventory yields scores on the following nine scales: sensitivity, somatic symptoms, social competency, attitudes of distrust, family adjustment, boy-girl adjustment, school adjustment, morale, and attitudes concerning blindness. A validation score is also provided. The questionnaire is presented in large-print format. Instructions for tape recording the questions are included. Supplementary materials provided in the test kit include a discussion of the inventory and a discussion of personality assessment for blind adolescents. This test is an adolescent form of the Emotional Factors Inventory. Examiner required. The paper-pencil version is suitable for group use.

Untimed: Varies

Scoring: Examiner evaluated

Cost: Test kit (test booklet, scoring overlays, 10 IBM answer sheets, supplementary materials, and norms) $25.00
Publisher: Associated Services for the Blind

ADOLESCENT MULTIPHASIC PERSONALITY INVENTORY (AMPI)
Bruce Duthie

Adolescent—Ages 10–19

Purpose: Assesses personality characteristics in adolescents. Used for clinical evaluation in applied settings.

Description: 133–item paper-pencil true-false test of adolescent personality functioning. The AMPI has three validity scales (Lie, Fake, and Defensiveness) and 10 clinical scales (Hypochondriasis, Depression, Hysteria, Psychopathic Deviance, Feminism, Paranoia, Psychasthenia, Schizophrenia, Mania, and Social Introversion). With the exception of the Feminism scale, AMPI scales generally parallel their MMPI counterparts. A fourth-grade reading level is required. Examiner/self-administered. Suitable for group use.
Untimed: Varies
Scoring: Hand key; may be computer scored with IBM-PC compatible software
Cost: Start-up kit (manual, answer keys, 50 test booklets, 50 profile sheets, 2 computer interpretation coupons) $65.00
Publisher: Pacific Psychological

ADULT DIAGNOSTIC SCREENING BATTERY
James J. Smith and Joseph M. Eisenberg

Adult—Ages 18 and older

Purpose: Identifies diagnostic possibilities among those listed in DSM-III-R. Used with adults in clinical settings.

Description: Paper-pencil or computer-administered screening battery assessing symptoms important for diagnostic considerations. The system consists of two parts: a questionnaire for the patient and a questionnaire for the clinician. The structured interview is completed by the patient directly or by someone who has direct and sufficient knowledge of the individual referred for services. The system is structured so that once data is entered in the computer, it is compared with all possible diagnosis. A manual describing the use and application of the program and the use of the printouts generated by the program is provided. Self-administered. Suitable for group use.
Untimed: 15 minutes
Scoring: Computer scored
Cost: Total system $195.00
Publisher: Reason House

ADULT PERSONAL ADJUSTMENT AND ROLE SKILLS (PARS)
Robert E. Ellsworth

Adult

Purpose: Measures adults' adjustment to life and to the community. Used for evaluation of treatment programs.

Description: 31–item paper-pencil observational rating scale assessing eight dimensions of adult personal adjustment and role skills: close relations, alienation-depression, anxiety, confusion, alcohol/drug use, house activity, child relations, and employment. The scale is completed by a spouse, parent, or person close to the patient. The manual explains the rationale and validity of the scale and provides detailed norms for the general and clinical population with respect to adjustment to life and the community. Examiner required. Suitable for group use.
Untimed: 20–30 minutes
Scoring: Examiner evaluated
Cost: Manual $7.50; 25 scales and profile sheets $6.50
Publisher: Consulting Psychologists Press, Inc.

ADULT PERSONALITY INVENTORY
Samuel E. Krug

Adult

Purpose: Evaluates individual personality characteristics, interpersonal relations, and life-style. Used by professionals in industry, public service, health care, and education.

Description: Multiple-item paper-pencil inventory assessing personality characteristics. While it maintains continuity with Cattell's theory of behavior first introduced more than 40 years ago, the Adult Personality Inventory offers several contemporary features. Items have been shortened to increase the number of items on the inventory (for increased reliability), and the required reading level has been lowered to the fourth-grade level. The computer scoring service provides a nine-page verbal and graphic report examining significant individual characteristics, interpersonal relations, and life-style. Examiner required. Suitable for group use.

Untimed: 1 hour

Scoring: Computer scored

Cost: 10 test booklets $13.45; 25 answer sheets $8.25; 10 decision-making worksheets $10.40

Publisher: Institute for Personality and Ability Testing, Inc.

AFFECTS BALANCE SCALE (ABS)
Leonard R. Derogatis

Adult

Purpose: Evaluates psychological adjustment and well-being in terms of mood and affect balance.

Description: 40–item paper-pencil self-report adjective mood scale assessing four positive affect dimensions (joy, contentment, vigor, and affection) and four negative affect dimensions (anxiety, depression, guilt, and hostility). Scoring and interpretation procedures are structured on the concept that healthy psychological adjustment is based on the presence of active positive emotions and the relative absence of negative emotions. The overall score of the test is expressed as the Affect Balance Index, reflecting the balance between positive and negative affects in terms of standardized scores. SCORABS Version 2.1 is a computer-scoring program designed for IBM XT and AT systems. It generates eight positive and negative primary affect dimension scores,

positive and negative Affect Total scores, and an Affect Balance Index. Examiner required. Suitable for group use.

Untimed: 3–5 minutes

Scoring: Examiner evaluated; may be computer scored

Cost: 100 test forms $28.00; 100 profile sheets $20.00

Publisher: Clinical Psychometric Research, Inc.

ALCOHOL ASSESSMENT AND TREATMENT PROFILE (AATP)
Refer to page 18.

ALCOHOL USE INVENTORY (AUI)
Refer to page 18.

ANIMA INKBLOT SERIES
Wilfred A. Cassell

Adolescent, adult

Purpose: Assesses feminine consciousness in females and feminine characteristics in males. Used with adolescents and adults.

Description: 40–card test created by female artists for evaluating conscious-unconscious aspects of feminine psychology. The cards range from those with little structure regarding external visual reality to those with specific, interpersonal connotations. Wilfred Cassell's book *Body Symbolism* is included with the series. Examiner required. Not suitable for group use.

Untimed: 90 minutes

Scoring: Examiner evaluated; scoring service available

Cost: Cards, scoring sheets, *Body Symbolism* $95.00

Publisher: Aurora Publishing

Information and availability unconfirmed; last verified in 1987.

ANIMA VIDEO SERIES
Wilfred A. Cassell

Adolescent, adult

Purpose: Assesses feminine consciousness in females and feminine mental characteristics in males.

Description: 40–item inkblot test presented in a video format entitled "Living Images" for evaluating conscious-unconscious aspects of feminine psychology. The test incorporates the Anima Inkblot Series, adding movement and a soundtrack developed by a female musician. A semihypnotic state of consciousness is created in which the viewer can respond without the potential contaminating effect of an examiner's presence. Scoring should be done by examiners experienced in projective techniques, hypnotherapy, and dream analysis. The tape includes two examples of how to respond and standard instructions. The tapes are available in a VHS and Beta videocassette format. A 16mm film version is available for teaching purposes. Examiner/self-administered. Not suitable for group use.

Untimed: 1 hour

Scoring: Examiner evaluated

Cost: Tape (state ½″ or ¾″ tape size) $95.00

Publisher: Aurora Publishing

Information and availability unconfirmed; last verified in 1987.

ASSESSMENT OF SUICIDE POTENTIAL (RESEARCH EDITION)
Robert Yufit and Bonnie Benzies

Adolescent, adult—Ages 16–81

Purpose: Evaluates an individual's feelings about the past, present, and future. Used for the exploration and quantitative assessment of suicide potential.

Description: Multiple-item four-page paper-pencil or oral semiprojective measure of feelings about the present, future, and past. Usually called the *Time Questionnaire*, it is composed of three types of items: multiple-choice, open-ended, and rating scales. The questionnaire provides an index of time perspective found to be related to suicide potential. Examiner required. Not suitable for group use.

Untimed: 15 minutes

Scoring: Examiner evaluated

Cost: Specimen set (manual, test booklet) $4.75; manual $4.25; 25 expendable questionnaires $8.50

Publisher: Consulting Psychologists Press, Inc.

ASSOCIATION ADJUSTMENT INVENTORY (AAI)
Martin M. Bruce

Adult

Purpose: Evaluates the extent to which the subject is maladjusted, immature, and deviant in ideation; used as an aid to predicting potential deviant behavior and job tenure.

Description: 100–item test in which the subject matches one of four words with a stimulus word, allowing the examiner to score for ideational deviation, general psychosis, depression, hysteria, withdrawal, paranoia, rigidity, schizophrenia, impulsiveness, sociopathy, psychosomapathia, and anxiety. The scores are compared to "norms" to measure deviation. Examiner/self-administered. Suitable for group use. Available in Spanish and German.

Untimed: 10 minutes

Scoring: Hand key

Cost: Package of reusable tests for use with IBM answer sheets $42.50; package of tests with fan key $42.50; manual $14.75; manual's supplement (1984) $15.50; package of profile sheets $18.00

Publisher: Martin M. Bruce, Ph.D., Publishers

AT RISK EVALUATION SURVEYS (ARES)
Renovex

Adolescent, adult—Ages 12 and older

Purpose: Assesses psychosocial functioning. Used to facilitate and focus clinical interviews.

Description: Computer-administered or paper-pencil instrument consisting of 20 individual surveys (containing more than 700 items) addressing clients' issues, problems, and concerns. Areas examined include personal perceptions, personal concerns, emotional/psychological adjustment, nutrition, physical health, vocational adjustment, financial status, living environment, education, family/marital status, recreation/social, and drug and alcohol use. Acuity scores, problem severity, and items of a critical or significant nature are reported. Computer version available for IBM PC and compatibles. This is one test in the Case Management System series. Self-administered. Suitable for group use.

Untimed: Varies

Scoring: Examiner evaluated; computer scored

Cost: $5.75

Publisher: Renovex

ATHLETIC MOTIVATION INVENTORY (AMI)
Thomas A. Tutko, Bruce C. Ogilvie, and Leland P. Lyon

Adolescent, adult—Ages 12 and older—Grades 7 and above

Purpose: Measures the mental attitudes of male and female athletes competing in all sports at the junior high, high school, college, recreational, and professional levels.

Description: 190–item paper-pencil or computer-administered multiple-choice inventory measuring 11 traits and containing two control scales (accuracy and objectivity). Traits measured are Drive, Aggressiveness, Determination, Responsibility, Leadership, Self-confidence, Emotional Control, Mental Toughness, Coachability, Conscientiousness, and Trust. Scores in each of these areas are interpreted in three reports: a) Coach's Report, b) Athlete's Report, and c) Team Profile and Sub-Group Profiles. Although one form is used for both sexes and all sports, answers are compared with those of other athletes of the same sex, sport, and level of competition. The computer version operates on IBM PC systems. A seventh-grade reading level is required. Contact publisher for information on licensing the software program. Self-administered. Suitable for group use. Available in French and Spanish.

Untimed: 30–45 minutes

Scoring: Computer scored; scoring service available from publisher and licensed representatives

Cost: AMI booklet, scoring service, and reports $25.00 per athlete for nonprofit teams; $75.00 per athlete for professional and recreational athletes

Publisher: Institute of Athletic Motivation

AUTOMATED CHILD/ADOLESCENT SOCIAL HISTORY (ACASH)
Refer to page 135.

THE BASIC PERSONALITY INVENTORY (BPI)
Douglas N. Jackson

Adolescent, adult

Purpose: Identifies personality dimensions indicating personal strengths as well as psychopathological dimensions. Used in psychological, psychiatric, and counseling practices; psychiatric hospitals, community mental health centers, juvenile and adult correctional facilities; general hospitals with psychological and psychiatric services; college counseling centers; personnel departments and consulting firms; and for court referrals.

Description: 240–item paper-pencil or computer-administered true-false multiphasic personality inventory used with both normal and clinical populations to identify personal strengths or sources of maladjustment. The test contains 11 substantive clinical scales and 1 critical item scale: Hypochondriasis, Anxiety, Depression, Thinking Disorder, Denial, Impulse Expression, Interpersonal Problems, Social Introversion, Alienation, Self-Deprecation, Persecutory Ideas, and Deviation (critical item scale). The computer version, which operates on IBM PC, AT, XT and compatible systems, yields scores, profiles, and reports. Examiner required. Suitable for group use.

Untimed: 20–45 minutes

Scoring: Hand key; may be machine scored; may be computer scored

Cost: Examination kit (test manual, 10 test booklets, 25 answer sheets, 25 profile sheets, scoring template) $32.00; software (licensed for 25 scorings, includes manual and key overlays) $150.00

Publisher: SIGMA Assessment Systems, Inc., Research Psychologists Press Division

BAY AREA FUNCTIONAL PERFORMANCE EVALUATION, 2ND EDITION (BAFPE)
Susan Lang Williams and Judith S. Bloomer

Adult

Purpose: Evaluates ability to perform intellectual functions necessary for daily living and relating to others. Used with psychiatric and neurologically impaired patients and mentally retarded adults for treatment planning and programming in occupational therapy, special education, or counseling and psychotherapy.

Description: Task-performance test consisting of two instruments designed to evaluate functional performance, the Task-Oriented Assessment (TOA) and the Social Interaction Scale (SIS). The TOA utilizes five goal-directed tasks scored on 12 functional parameters divided into three components: cognitive, performance, and affective. A Qualitative Signs and Referral Indicators section on the TOA rating sheets is intended to indicate the possibility of organic problems. The SIS assesses social behavior in five specific settings scored on seven functional parameters. An optional self-report includes information about the examinee's current social interaction skills and problems. The two instruments are scored separately. The TOA requires a stopwatch. Examiner required. Not suitable for group use.

Timed: TOA 27 minutes

Untimed: SIS 50–60 minutes

Scoring: Examiner evaluated

Cost: Kit (manual, specialized reusable items, expendable forms for testing 25 subjects) $135.00

Publisher: Consulting Psychologists Press, Inc.

BECK DEPRESSION AND HOPELESSNESS SCALE
Aaron T. Beck

Adult

Purpose: Assesses level of depression and the possibility of suicide. Used for clinical assessment and diagnosis.

Description: Multiple-item computer-administered instrument consisting of two scales: the Beck Depression Scale and the Beck Hopelessness Scale. The Beck Depression Scale measures the level of severity of dysphoric mood and assesses the current state of the individual's mood. The Beck Hopelessness Scale, when used in conjunction with the depression scale, indicates the level of depression and the possibility of suicide. The Beck Hopelessness Scale was developed on a large sample of patients who had attempted suicide. The program administers and scores the two scales and provides an interpretive printout of the test. The program may be used only on PsychSystems-supplied hardware, available in various configurations starting with single-users systems at approximately $25,000. A per-test fee (based on hardware configuration) also applies. Examiner required. Suitable for group use.

Untimed: Varies

Scoring: Computer scored

Cost: Contact publisher

Publisher: Center for Cognitive Therapy

BECK DEPRESSION INVENTORY
Aaron T. Beck

Adult

Purpose: Measures an individual's level of depression. Used for treatment planning and evaluation in mental health settings.

Description: 21–item inventory assessing the severity of an individual's complaints, symptoms, and concerns related to his current level of depression. The symptoms assessed are sadness, pessimism, sense of failure, dissatisfaction, feelings of guilt, expectation of punishment, self-dislike, self-accusations, suicidal ideas, crying, irritability, social withdrawal, indecisiveness, change in body image, work difficulty, insomnia, loss of appetite, weight loss, somatic preoccupation, fatigability, and loss of libido. A microcomputer printout indicates the severity of the depressed mood, lists major symptom complaints, and shows a table of responses. Questions are presented on an eighth-grade reading level. The test may be administered only on a psychometer. Examiner required. Not suitable for group use.

Untimed: 15–20 minutes

Scoring: Microcomputer scored

Cost: Contact publisher

Publisher: Center for Cognitive Therapy

BEHAVIOR STATUS INVENTORY (BSI)
William T. Martin

Adolescent, adult

Purpose: Measures behavioral traits of adults and adolescents in mental health settings. Used to evaluate emotionally disturbed, brain-damaged, and mentally retarded patients. Used to monitor patient progress in response to therapy.

Description: 91–item observational inventory assessing seven behavioral areas: personal appearance, manifest (obvious) behavior, attitude, verbal behavior, social behavior, work behavior, and cognitive behavior. An aide or staff member familiar with the individual can complete the questionnaire, rating each of the behavioral statements from 1 to 4 based upon observed patient behavior during the past week. Scores for each of the seven subscales and a Total Patient Asset Score are derived. Item analysis and subscale scores can be machine scored for onetime or for ongoing patient or program analysis. Examiner required. Suitable for group use.

Untimed: No time limit

Scoring: Examiner evaluated

Cost: Specimen set $5.00; 25 forms $15.00; 25 profile sheets $6.75

Publisher: Psychologists and Educators, Inc.

BEM SEX-ROLE INVENTORY (BSRI)
Refer to page 259.

THE BIPOLAR PSYCHOLOGICAL INVENTORY (BPI)

Adult

Purpose: Measures psychological adjustment. Used for clinical evaluation and diagnosis, personnel screening, and police officer selection.

Description: Multiple-item paper-pencil or computer-administered self-report inventory assessing affect and behavior along 15 bipolar dimensions: honest/lie, open/defensive, psychic comfort/psychic pain, optimism/depression, self-esteem/self-degradation, self-sufficiency/dependence, achieving/unmotivated, gregariousness/social withdrawal, family harmony/family discord, sexual maturity/sexual immaturity, social conformity/social deviancy, self-control/impulsiveness, kindness/hostility, empathy/insensitivity, and valid/invalid.

A narrative computer printout includes separate male/female formats, raw scores and percentile scores, a personal adjustment profile, a printout of answers to all questions, and a printout of significant (problem) items. The computer program is sold on disk (with backup disk and instructions) for use with Apple II computers with 48K, one disk drive, and printer (optical reader optional). Normative data are available for normal populations. Examiner required. Paper-pencil version suitable for group use.

Untimed: Varies

Scoring: Examiner evaluated; may be computer scored

Cost: Clinical sample kit (manual, test booklet, 5 answer sheets, set of scoring keys, profiles, scale items booklet, reliability-validity booklet) $20.00; computer program $250.00

Publisher: Diagnostic Specialists, Inc.

Information and availability unconfirmed; last verified in 1987.

THE BLACK INTELLIGENCE TEST OF CULTURAL HOMOGENEITY (BITCH)
Robert L. Williams

Adolescent, adult—Ages 16 and older

Purpose: Measures white Americans' sensitivity to the black experience and black Americans' identification with the black experience. Used in racial relations seminars or interracial workshops.

Description: 41–item paper-pencil multiple-choice test providing a culture-specific measure of racial attitudes. Two forms are available. Self-administered. Suitable for group use.

Untimed: 20 minutes

Scoring: Hand key

Cost: Complete set (20 tests, directions, key) $22.00; manual $3.75

Publisher: Robert L. Williams & Associates, Inc.

Information and availability unconfirmed; last verified in 1987.

BLOOM SENTENCE COMPLETION ATTITUDE SURVEY
Wallace Bloom

Adolescent, adult

Purpose: Assesses adult and student attitudes toward self and important factors in everyday living. Used to identify change in an individual over time and to compare individuals and groups.

Description: 40–item paper-pencil free-response test consisting of sentence stems which the subject completes in his own words. The responses measure attitudes toward age mates or people, physical self, family, psychological self, self-directedness, education or work (depending on

which version is used), accomplishment, and irritants. Two versions are available: one for adults and one for unmarried students. The scoring system facilitates use of the test as both an objective and a projective instrument. Examiner required. Suitable for group use.

Untimed: 25 minutes

Scoring: Examiner evaluated

Cost: Complete kit, specify version (30 test forms, 30 analysis record forms, manual) $25.50

Publisher: Stoelting Co.

BODY ELIMINATION ATTITUDE SCALE
Donald I. Templer, Frank L. King, Robert K. Brooner, and Mark Corgiat

Adult

Purpose: Assesses attitudes related to body elimination.

Description: 26–item paper-pencil Likert-format scale measuring seven factors: fecal smell, personal hygiene, sight, dirty hair, animal feces, mucous-like discharge, and sound. Future research may indicate applications to Freudian and other personality theory and practical applications, including selection of persons for health-care occupations and indications of psychosomatic disorders such as colitis and medical procedures such as ostomies. Self-administered. Suitable for group use.

Untimed: Varies

Scoring: Contact publisher

Cost: Free

Publisher: Donald I. Templer, Ph.D.

BRIEF SYMPTOM INVENTORY (BSI)
Leonard R. Derogatis

Adolescent, adult

Purpose: Evaluates psychological symptomatic distress. Used with medical and psychiatric patients and adult and adolescent nonpatients.

Description: 53–item paper-pencil self-report inventory assessing symptomatic distress in terms of nine symptom dimensions (somatization, obsessive-compulsive, interpersonal sensitivity, depression, anxiety, hostility, phobic anxiety, paranoid ideation, and psychoticism) and three global indices of distress (global severity index, positive symptom index, and positive symptom total). Score/profile forms and published norms are available by sex for four populations: nonpatient adult, nonpatient adolescent, outpatient psychiatric, and inpatient psychiatric. This inventory is a brief form of the SCL–90–R and may be used in conjunction with the matching observer's scales in the Psychopathology Rating Scales Series (the SCL–90–R Analogue and the Hopkins Psychiatric Rating Scale). SCORBSI Version 2.1 is the computer scoring program for use with IBM PC and XT systems. Examiner required. Suitable for group use. Available in over 20 languages.

Untimed: 10–12 minutes

Scoring: Examiner evaluated; may be computer scored

Cost: Manual $18.00; 100 test forms $35.00; 100 score/profile forms $25.00; SCORBSI Version 2.1 $160.00

Publisher: Clinical Psychometric Research, Inc.

BULIMIA TEST (BULIT)
Refer to page 6.

CALIFORNIA BRIEF LIFE HISTORY INVENTORY (CBLHI)
*Donald I. Templer and
David M. Veleber*

Ages 12–adult

Purpose: Summarizes the life history of individuals ages 12 and older. Used for diagnosis and treatment planning.

Description: Multiple-item paper-pencil inventory in student and adult forms summarizing a client's background and present circumstances, medical/psychological history, family life, work or school, and substance abuse. Clients complete the inventory prior to the initial interview. Clinicians use the information for identifying problem areas and developing treatment plans. Self-administered. Suitable for group use.

Untimed: Varies

Scoring: Examiner evaluated

Cost: 25 student forms $8.00; 25 adult forms $8.00

Publisher: United Educational Services, Inc.

CALIFORNIA LIFE GOALS EVALUATION SCHEDULES
Milton E. Hahn

Adult—Ages 15 and older

Purpose: Differentiates "life goals" from "interests" by identifying significant motivational forces in normal individuals. Used for career planning, adjusting to aging or retirement, evoking insights in areas of psychological normality, and college counseling.

Description: 150–item paper-pencil test measuring 10 life goals: esteem, profit, fame, leadership, power, security, social service, interesting experiences, self-expression, and independence. Using a 5–point acceptance or rejection scale, the subject responds to "debatable" statements. Norms are presented based on age, sex, occupation, familial relationships, and projected academic studies. Self-administered. Suitable for group use.

Untimed: 20–30 minutes

Scoring: Hand key

Cost: Complete kit (100 profile forms, manual, 25 reusable test booklets, key, 100 answer sheets) $79.50

Publisher: Western Psychological Services

CALIFORNIA PSYCHOLOGICAL INVENTORY, 1987 REVISED EDITION
Harrison G. Gough

Adolescent, adult—Ages 14–adult

Purpose: Assesses personality characteristics important for daily living. Used in business for personnel selection, identifying creativity, and vocational and personal counseling; in schools and colleges for academic counseling, identifying leaders, and predicting success in various public service occupations; in clinics and counseling agencies for evaluating substance abuse, susceptibility to physical illness, marital discord, juvenile delinquency and criminality, and social immaturity; and for cross-cultural and other research.

Description: 468–item paper-pencil true-false test measuring behavioral tendencies along 20 scales: Dominance, Capacity for Status, Sociability, Social Presence, Self-acceptance, Independence, Empathy, Responsibility, Socialization, Self-control, Good Impression, Communality, Well-being, Tolerance, Achievement via Independence, Intellectual Efficiency, Psychological-mindedness, Flexibility, and Femininity/Masculinity. The revised edition contains semantic changes in 29 items and two additional scales (Empathy and Independence). In addition, three new independent themes representing the CPI's conceptual foundations have been introduced to organize results and aid interpretation. The first two themes, interpersonal orientation and normative orientation, interact to form four types (alphas, betas, gammas, deltas). The third theme, realization, describes the level of integration or effectiveness within the type. Three scoring reports are available: the Profile Report, Gough Interpretive Report, and McAllister Interpretive Report. Self-administered. Suitable for group use. Available in French, Spanish, Italian, and German.

Untimed: 45–60 minutes

Scoring: Hand key; may be computer scored

Cost: 1987 Administrator's Guide $15.00; handscoring stencils $40.00; 25 test booklets $20.00; 100 profiles (specify male or female) $15.00; 50 non-prepaid answer sheets $7.50

Publisher: Consulting Psychologists Press, Inc.

CALIFORNIA Q-SORT DECK
Jack Block; adapted by Daryl Bem

Adult

Purpose: Describes individual personality in contemporary psychodynamic terms. Used for research.

Description: 100–item test used to formulate personality descriptions. Items are descriptive personality statements on cards sorted from most to least applicable to the subject's experience. Materials include individual $2\frac{1}{4}''$ x $3\frac{1}{2}''$ cards and a sorting guide. May be sorted by professionals or laymen. Examiner required. Not suitable for group use.

Untimed: Not available

Scoring: Examiner evaluated

Cost: Q-Sort Deck $9.00; guide and 50 recording pads $8.00

Publisher: Consulting Psychologists Press, Inc.

CARLSON PSYCHOLOGICAL SURVEY (CPS)
Kenneth A. Carlson

Adolescent, adult

Purpose: Assesses and classifies criminal offenders. Used to evaluate persons presenting behavioral or substance-abuse problems and analyze the effects of intervention programs.

Description: 50–item paper-pencil questionnaire in a five-category response format with space for the respondent's comments. The scales measured are Chemical Abuse, Thought Disturbance, Antisocial Tendencies, Self-Deprecation, and Validity. The test is designed for offenders, those charged with crimes, and others who have come to the attention of the criminal justice or social welfare systems. The results are classified into 18 offender types. A companion edition, the Psicologico Texto (PT), is designed for use with Spanish-literate offenders. A fourth-grade reading level is required. Use is restricted to APA-registered psychologists. Examiner required. Suitable for group use. Available in French.

Untimed: 15 minutes

Scoring: Hand key

Cost: Complete set $22.00

Publisher: SIGMA Assessment Systems, Inc., Research Psychologists Press Division

CENTER FOR EPIDEMIOLOGIC STUDIES—DEPRESSION SCALE (CES-D)

Adult

Purpose: Measures symptoms associated with depression in adults. Used to identify high-risk groups for research and screening.

Description: 20–item paper-pencil test in which the subject is asked to rank his experiences and feelings for the past week on a 3–point scale ranging from "less than once a day" (0) to "most or all of the time" (3). Questions deal with symptoms of depressed mood, lack of energy, insomnia, and appetite loss. The scale may be read to a subject by an examiner or completed in privacy by the client. Scales are weighted for scoring and interpretation. Self-administered. Suitable for group use. Available in Spanish.

Untimed: 5 minutes

Scoring: Hand key

Cost: Contact publisher

Publisher: Epidemiology and Psychopathology Branch, NIMH

Information and availability unconfirmed; last verified in 1988.

CHARACTER ASSESSMENT SCALE (CAS)
Paul F. Schmidt

Adolescent, adult—Ages 15 and older

Purpose: Assesses a person's moral strengths and weaknesses. Allows individuals to explore their moral character. Used in pastoral counseling, clinical psychology, and religious research.

Description: 225–item paper-pencil true-false test measuring moral character strengths and weaknesses. The eight basic scales are Respect, Concern, Anger, Money, Time and Energy, Sexuality, Body and Health, and Truthfulness. The basic scales are divided further between eight subscales assessing moral strengths and eight assessing moral weaknesses. The moral character strengths examined are humility, compassion, peacemaking,

resourcefulness, enthusiasm, sexual integrity, physical fitness, and honesty. Weaknesses include vanity, envy, resentment, greed, laziness, lust, gluttony, and denial. Software to generate a profile and narrative is available on PC-DOS systems. A ninth-grade reading level is required. Self-administered. Suitable for group use.

Untimed: 45 minutes

Scoring: Hand key; computer scored

Cost: 10 test booklets $8.00; 25 answer sheets $5.00; 25 feedback booklets $10.00; scoring service $5.00; manual $20.00

Publisher: Institute for Character Development

CHEMICAL DEPENDENCY ASSESSMENT PROFILE (CDAP)
Refer to page 19.

CHILD ABUSE POTENTIAL INVENTORY
Joel Milner

Adult

Purpose: Screens for physical child abuse potential in adults. Designed for use in social service, mental health, and research settings.

Description: 160–item paper-pencil forced-choice test of child abuse potential. In addition to the full CAP abuse scale, six descriptive factors are scored: distress, rigidity, unhappiness, problems with child and self, problems with family, and problems from others. Three validity scales are available and combine to make three response distortion indexes: faking good, faking bad, and random response. A third-grade reading level is required. Examiner/self-administered. Suitable for group use.

Untimed: 12–20 minutes

Scoring: Hand key; may be computer scored

Cost: Contact publisher

Publisher: Psytec, Inc.

CHRONIC PAIN BATTERY (CPB)
Refer to page 14.

CLINICAL ANALYSIS QUESTIONNAIRE
Raymond B. Cattell and IPAT Staff

Adolescent, adult—Ages 16 and older

Purpose: Evaluates personality and psychiatric/psychological difficulties. Used as a measure of primary behavioral dimensions in adults and adolescents. Used for clinical diagnosis, evaluation of therapeutic progress, and vocational and rehabilitation guidance.

Description: 272–item paper-pencil multiple-choice test measuring 16 personality factors (the 16PF factors) as well as hypochondriasis, agitated depression, suicidal depression, anxious depression, guilt, energy level, boredom, and five other dimensions in the pathology domain. Norms are provided for adults and college men and women. Special adolescent norms are provided for Part II. The manual contains profiles for a number of special groups, including alcoholics, narcotic addicts, various types of neurotic and psychotic disorders, criminals, and others. The test has been organized in two parts so that the entire test need not be given in a single sitting. A sixth-grade reading level is required. Examiner required. Suitable for group use. Available in Spanish.

Untimed: 2 hours

Scoring: Hand key; may be computer scored

Cost: 25 hand-scorable answer sheets $8.25; manual $13.75; scoring keys 19.95; computer profile and interpretation $14.50–$23.00; 25 reusable test booklets $26.25; for teleprocessing and computer software contact publisher

Publisher: Institute for Personality and Ability Testing, Inc.

CLINICAL CHECKLIST SERIES

Adolescent, adult

Purpose: Assesses personal, marital, and health problems. Used for initiating the consultation process and introducing the client to formal diagnostic testing.

Description: Multiple-item paper-pencil series of five checklists used, as appropriate, with adolescents and adults to identify relevant problems, establish rapport, and provide written documentation of presenting problems consistent with community standards of care. Checklists include Personal Problems Checklist—Adult, Personal Problems Checklist—Adolescent, Children's Problems Checklist, Marital Evaluation Checklist, and Health Problems Checklist. Items are presented in terms understood by adolescents and adults from most educational and occupational levels. Self-administered. Suitable for group use.

Untimed: 10–20 minutes

Scoring: Examiner evaluated

Cost: 50 checklists $17.95–$26.95

Publisher: Psychological Assessment Resources, Inc.

COGNITIVE TRIAD INVENTORY
E. Edward Beckham,
William R. Leber, John T. Watkins,
Jenny L. Boyer, and J. Cook

Adult—Ages 18 and older

Purpose: Measures an individual's view of self, world, and future.

Description: 36–item paper-pencil test in which the examinee rates on a 7–point Likert-type scale statements pertaining to Aaron T. Beck's cognitive triad: view of self (10 items), view of world (10 items), and view of future (10 items). The test yields four scores—an overall score and scores for each of the three subtests. An SAS computer-scoring program is available free of charge. Self-administered. Suitable for group use.

Untimed: Varies

Scoring: Hand key; may be computer scored

Cost: Free

Publisher: E. Edward Beckham, Ph.D.

COLLATERAL INTERVIEW FORM (CIF)
Refer to page 20.

COMPREHENSIVE DRINKER PROFILE (CDP)
Refer to page 20.

COMPUTERIZED DIAGNOSTIC INTERVIEW SCHEDULE (C-DIS)
Arthur G. Blouin

Adolescent, adult

Purpose: Screens patients for DSM-III-R disorders. Used in psychiatric research centers, outpatient clinics, emergency rooms, specialized clinics, and private clinical practice for patient referral and treatment planning.

Description: Multiple-item computer-administered version of the NIMH Diagnostic Interview Schedule (DIS) containing 19 sections: Demographics, Tobacco Use Disorder, Somatization, Panic Disorder, Phobic Disorder, Post Traumatic Stress Disorder, Depression, Manic Disorders, Schizophrenia, Anorexia Nervosa, Bulimia, Alcohol Abuse, Obsessive Compulsive Disorder, Drug Abuse, Youth Antisocial Personality, Psychosexual Dysfunction, Adult Antisocial Personality, Pathological Gambling, and Organic Brain Syndrome. The clinician can choose to administer all or a combination of the sections. Questions are presented on the computer screen. The patient responds by pressing a number corresponding to the chosen answer. The program interacts with the patient to conduct an "intelligent" interview based on his or her previous responses. The computer-generated report provides a list of the DSM-III-R diagnoses for which the patient tests positive. It also provides other information designed to aid the clinician in confirming the diagnosis: recency, duration, and age of onset of symptoms; other diagnoses that must be ruled out before the diagnosis can be assigned; and physical explanations and symptoms caused by drugs or medication. The program operates on IBM PC systems. Self-administered. Not suitable for group use. CANADIAN PUBLISHER

Untimed: 1–2 hours

Scoring: Computer scored

Cost: Contact publisher

Publisher: Ottawa Civic Hospital, Department of Psychiatry

COMREY PERSONALITY SCALES (CPS)
Andrew L. Comrey

Adolescent, adult
Grades 10 and above

Purpose: Measures major personality characteristics of adults and high-school and college students. Used in educational, clinical, and business settings where personality structure and stability are important.

Description: 180–item paper-pencil test consisting of eight personality dimension scales (20 items each), a validity scale (8 items), and a response bias scale (12 items). The eight personality scales are Trust vs. Defensiveness, Orderliness vs. Lack of Orderliness, Social Conformity vs. Rebelliousness, Activity vs. Lack of Energy, Emotional Stability vs. Neuroticism, Extraversion vs. Introversion, Masculinity vs. Femininity, and Empathy vs. Egocentrism. Subjects respond to items according to 7–point scales ranging from "never" or "definitely not," to "always" or "definitely." The profile presents a description of the personality structure of "normal" socially functioning individuals. Extreme scores on any of the scales may provide a clue to the source of current difficulties, predict future problems, aid in selection of therapy programs, and screen job applicants. Norms are presented as T-scores for male and female college students. Examiner required. Suitable for group use.

Untimed: 30–50 minutes

Scoring: Hand key; may be computer scored

Cost: Specimen set (manual, all forms) $5.50; 25 reusable test booklets $15.00; 50 answer sheets $10.25; 50 computer answer sheets $11.25; 50 profile sheets $8.50; handbook $8.75; manual $3.25

Publisher: EdITS/Educational and Industrial Testing Service

COPING OPERATIONS PREFERENCE ENQUIRY (COPE)
Will Schutz

Adult

Purpose: Measures individual preference for certain types of coping or defense mechanisms; used for counseling and therapy.

Description: 6–item paper-pencil test measuring the characteristic use of five defense mechanisms: denial, isolation, projection, regression-dependency, and turning-against-the-self. Each item describes a person and his behavior in a particular situation. The respondent rank orders five alternative ways a person might feel; the alternatives represent the inventory's five coping mechanisms. Materials include separate forms for men and women. May be self-administered; however, an examiner is recommended. Suitable for group use.

Untimed: Not available

Scoring: Examiner evaluated

Cost: 25 tests (specify male or female) $15.75

Publisher: Consulting Psychologists Press, Inc.

COPING RESOURCES INVENTORY (CRI)
*Allen L. Hammer and
M. Susan Marting*

Adult

Purpose: Measures an individual's resources for coping with stress. Used in individual counseling, workshops, and health settings.

Description: 60–item paper-pencil inventory consisting of five scales measuring an individual's cognitive, social, physical, emotional, and values resources. The results identify the resources a person has developed for coping with stress and those that still must be developed. The manual includes scale descriptions, reliability and validity information, separate norms for males and females, and case

illustrations for interpreting the profiles. Examiner required. Suitable for group use.

Untimed: 10 minutes

Scoring: Hand key; may be computer scored

Cost: Manual $9.00; score keys $10.00; 25 test booklets $8.00; 10 prepaid answer sheets $36.00; 50 non-prepaid answer sheets $22.00; 50 profiles $12.50

Publisher: Consulting Psychologists Press, Inc.

COPING STRATEGIES SCALES (COSTS)
*E. Edward Beckham and
Russell Adams*

Adult—Ages 18 and older

Purpose: Assesses the coping strategies used by individuals who are depressed or under stress. Used by researchers and clinicians.

Description: 142–item paper-pencil multiple-choice questionnaire assessing coping strategies along 10 dimensions. An SAS computer-scoring program is available free of charge. Self-administered. Suitable for group use. Available in French.

Untimed: Varies

Scoring: Hand key; may be computer scored

Cost: Free

Publisher: E. Edward Beckham, Ph.D.

CORNELL INDEX
Arthur Weider

Adult

Purpose: Evaluates an individual's psychiatric history. Identifies individuals with serious personal and psychosomatic disturbances. Used for clinical evaluations and research purposes.

Description: 101–item paper-pencil questionnaire measuring neuropsychiatric and psychosomatic symptoms. Administered in the form of a structured interview. Analysis of responses provides a standardized evaluation of an individual's psychiatric history and differentiates statistically individuals with serious personal and psychiatric disturbances. Self-administered. Suitable for group use.

Untimed: 5 minutes

Scoring: Examiner evaluated

Cost: 25 questionnaires $8.00; 100 copies $30.00; specimen set $20.00

Publisher: Arthur Weider, Ph.D.

CORNELL WORD FORM
Arthur Weider

Adult

Purpose: Assesses an individual's adaptive mechanisms. Used in a variety of clinical and research settings.

Description: Multiple-item paper-pencil test employing a modification of the word association technique. For each test item, the subject selects one word of a pair of printed responses that he associates with a given stimulus word. Analysis of the responses contributes to a descriptive sketch of the subject's adaptive mechanisms in a manner not easily apparent. Self-administered. Suitable for group use.

Untimed: 5 minutes

Scoring: Examiner evaluated

Cost: Specimen set $20.00; 25 copies $8.00; 100 copies $30.00

Publisher: Arthur Weider, Ph.D.

CORRECTIONAL INSTITUTIONS ENVIRONMENT SCALE (CIES)
Rudolf H. Moos

Adult

Purpose: Assesses the social environment of juvenile and adult correctional programs.

Description: 90–item paper-pencil true-false test of nine aspects of social environment: involvement, support, expressiveness, autonomy, practical orientation, personal problem orientation, order and organization, clarity, and staff control. Materials include four forms: the Real Form (Form R), which measures perceptions of the current correctional program; the 36–item Short Form (Form S); the Ideal Form (Form I), which measures

conceptions of an ideal program; and the Expectations Form (Form E), which measures expectations of a new program. Forms I and E are not published, but items and instructions appear in the Appendix of the CIES manual. Items and subscales are similar to those used in the Ward Atmosphere Scale. One of a series of nine Social Climate Scales. Examiner required. Suitable for group use.

Untimed: Not available

Scoring: Hand key; examiner evaluated

Cost: 25 reusable tests $8.50; 50 answer sheets $5.50; 50 profiles $3.75; key $1.75; manual $15.00

Publisher: Consulting Psychologists Press, Inc.

CROWN-CRISP EXPERIMENTAL INDEX (CCEI)
Sidney Crown and A.H. Crisp

Adolescent, adult

Purpose: Diagnoses psychoneurotic illness and personality disorder. Used for clinical screening and research, measuring change before and after defined intervention, and comparing defined groups. Used with a wide range of intelligence levels.

Description: 48–item paper-pencil questionnaire consisting of six subtests designed to facilitate the rapid quantification of common symptoms and traits relevant to the conventional categories of psychoneurotic illness and personality disorder. The index provides a profile that can be related to the scores of defined groups. The manual includes reliability and validity data and statistics relating CCEI scores to age, sex, and social class. The questionnaire is restricted to senior staff members of any recognized medical or educational institution, medical doctors, and BPS and APA members. Not for sale in the United States. Examiner required. Not suitable for group use.
BRITISH PUBLISHER

Untimed: 5–10 minutes

Scoring: Examiner evaluated

Cost: Specimen set £4.95; 20 question-naires £3.95 plus VAT; scoring template £4.25 plus VAT; manual £4.00
Publisher: Hodder & Stoughton

CURTIS COMPLETION FORM
James W. Curtis

Adolescent, adult

Purpose: Evaluates the emotional adjust-ment of older adolescents and adults. Used in employment situations to screen individuals whose emotional adjustment makes them poor employment risks. Also used in educational and industrial coun-seling to identify individuals who would benefit from clinical treatment.

Description: Multiple-item paper-pencil free-response sentence-completion test measuring emotional adjustment. It is similar to a projective test, but is scored using relatively objective, standardized criteria. Examiner required. Suitable for group use.
Untimed: 30 minutes
Scoring: Examiner evaluated
Cost: Kit (50 forms, manual) $19.50
Publisher: Western Psychological Services

DEFENSE MECHANISMS INVENTORY
Goldine C. Gleser and David Ihilevich

Adolescent, adult—Ages 10 and older

Purpose: Assesses an individual's use of such defense mechanisms as projection and reversal.

Description: 10 vignettes (male and fe-male forms) with five defensive responses to a variety of situations are presented to the subject. Each vignette is followed by four questions: "What would you do?", "What would you like to do?", "What do you think?", and "How do you feel?" There are five possible responses to each question corresponding to the following five defense mechanisms: turning against an object, projection, principalization, turning against self, and reversal. Mate-rials include adolescent, adult, and elder-

ly male and female forms, answer sheets, a manual, and male and female profiles. The adult version may be used in clinical settings; the adolescent and elderly ver-sions are restricted to research applica-tions. Self-administered. Suitable for group use. Available in German, French, and Portuguese.
Untimed: 40 minutes
Scoring: Hand key
Cost: 10 test booklets (specify form and sex) $10.00; 25 answer sheets $6.00; 25 profiles $6.00; specimen set $6.00; scor-ing templates $10.00; manual $22.00; comprehensive kit $45.00
Publisher: DMI Associates

THE DELUSIONS-SYMPTOMS-STATES INVENTORY
A. Bedford and G. Foulds

Adult

Purpose: Measures acute psychiatric symptoms. Used by psychologists and psychiatrists with normal adults and psy-chiatric referrals.

Description: 84–item paper-pencil inven-tory assessing states of anxiety, states of depression, states of elation, conversion symptoms, dissociative symptoms, phobic symptoms, compulsive symptoms, rumi-native symptoms, delusions of persecu-tion, delusions of grandeur, delusions of contrition, and delusions of disintegra-tion. In addition, two subscales, State of Anxiety and Depression and Neurotic Symptoms, are included for use with indi-viduals in nonpsychotic admission wards and in therapeutic groups where the delu-sional items would not be relevant. Each of the 12 symptom groups yields a total raw score. The symptom groups also are divided into four hierarchical classes (per-sonal illness, dysthymic states, neurotic symptoms, and integrated delusions and delusions of disintegration) to obtain the individual's DSSI pattern. Examiner/self-administered. Not suitable for group use.
BRITISH PUBLISHER
Untimed: 30 minutes
Scoring: Not available
Cost: Contact publisher
Publisher: NFER-NELSON Publishing Company Ltd.

DEMENTIA RATING SCALE (DRS)
Refer to page 44.

DEPRESSION ADJECTIVE CHECK LIST (DACL)
Bernard Lubin

Adolescent, adult
Grades 10 and above

Purpose: Differentiates between depressed and nondepressed high-school and college students and adults. Used for counseling, group screening, and large-scale depression studies.

Description: Multiple-item paper-pencil checklist measuring transient depressive moods, feelings, or emotions. Seven parallel forms allow repeated measurement of these factors. The subject responds by checking the adjectives on the checklist that describe how he feels at the time of testing. Seven parallel forms, A, B, C, D (32 items each) and E, F, G (34 items each), allow repeated measurement. None of the adjectives appear on more than one of Forms A, B, C, or D or on more than one of Forms E, F, or G. Norms are presented for male and female normals and for depressed patients. Exmainer/self-administered. Suitable for group use.

Untimed: 5 minutes per form

Scoring: Hand key

Cost: Specimen set $8.00; 25 checklists $5.25; key $3.50; manual $4.50

Publisher: Consulting Psychologists Press, Inc.

DEROGATIS STRESS PROFILE (DSP)
Refer to page 8.

DESCRIPTION OF BODY SCALE (DOBS)
R.E. Carney

Adolescent, adult—Ages 12 and older
Grades 7 and above

Purpose: Measures perceived masculinity/femininity of body.

Description: 14–item paper-pencil test utilizing a 6–point scale ranging from male to female. Items are divided evenly between the Present Body scale and the Ideal Body scale. The test yields a Total Masculinity (S) score, Ideal Masculinity (I) score, Inconsistency (K) score, and a Present-Ideal Incongruence (C) score. The test form integrates items, scoring, and a profile. A scoring service is available from the publisher. Examinees must have a seventh-grade reading level. Test forms must be ordered in quantities of 50 or more. Examiner/self-administered. Suitable for group use.

Untimed: Varies

Scoring: Hand key; may be computer scored

Cost: 50 forms $7.50; specimen set (manual, form) $7.00

Publisher: Carney, Weedman and Associates

DIAGNOSTIC INVENTORY OF PERSONALITY AND SYMPTOMS (DIPS)
Ken R. Vincent

Adult

Purpose: Measures psychopathology in adults. Used for personality assessment in applied and research settings.

Description: 171–item paper-pencil true-false measure of symptoms characteristic of DSM-III-R diagnosis from both Axis I and Axis II. Scales corresponding to Axis I diagnoses are Alcohol Abuse, Drug Abuse, Schizophrenic Psychosis, Paranoid Psychosis, Affective Depressed, Affective Excited, Anxiety Disorders, Somatoform Disorders, Dissociative Disorders, Stress-Adjustment Disorders, and Psychological Factors Affecting Physical Condition. Axis II disorders are collapsed into three major categories: Withdrawn Character, Immature Character, and Neurotic Character. Scores on two validity scales are also provided. Examiner/self-administered. Suitable for group use.

Untimed: Varies

Scoring: Hand key; may be computer scored with IBM PC compatible software

Cost: Start-up kit (manual, answer keys, 50 test booklets, 50 profile sheets, 2 computer interpretation coupons) $55.00

Publisher: Pacific Psychological

DRUG USE INDEX (DUI)
Refer to page 21.

EATING DISORDER INVENTORY (EDI)
Refer to page 6.

THE EATING INVENTORY
Refer to page 6.

EDWARDS PERSONAL PREFERENCE SCHEDULE (EPPS)
A.L. Edwards

Adult—Ages 18 and older

Purpose: Assesses an individual's personality. Used for both personal counseling and personality research.

Description: Paper-pencil forced-choice test designed to show the relative importance of 15 needs and motives: achievement, deference, order, exhibition, autonomy, affiliation, intraception, succorance, dominance, abasement, nurturance, change, endurance, heterosexuality, and aggression. Self-administered. Suitable for group use.

Untimed: 45 minutes

Scoring: Hand key

Cost: Specimen set (schedule booklet, hand-scorable answer document and template; IBM 805 and NCS answer documents; manual) $19.00

Publisher: The Psychological Corporation

Information and availability unconfirmed; last verified in 1988.

EGO FUNCTION ASSESSMENT (EFA)
Leopold Bellak

Adolescent, adult—Ages 13 and older

Purpose: Assesses ego functions. Used for a variety of purposes including personnel assessment, drug effects, and evaluation.

Description: Oral-response criterion-referenced test measuring 12 ego functions: Reality Testing, Judgment, Sense of Reality, Regulation and Control of Drives, Object Relations, Thought Processes, Adaptive Regression in the Service of the Ego, Defensive Functions, Stimulus Barrier, Autonomous Functions, Synthetic Functions, and Mastery-Competence. Examiner required. Not suitable for group use.

Untimed: Varies

Scoring: Examiner evaluated

Cost: $12.00

Publisher: C.P.S., Inc.

EGO-IDEAL AND CONSCIENCE DEVELOPMENT TEST (EICDT)
R.N. Cassel

Adolescent—Ages 12-18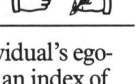

Purpose: Evaluates an individual's ego-ideal or conscience. Used as an index of parole or probation readiness for delinquents and to assess a person's knowledge of social expectations when confronted with problems.

Description: 80–item paper-pencil multiple-choice test measuring the extent to which the examinee agrees with the mainstream of U.S. society regarding solutions to social problems. The test consists of eight sections of 10 items each: home and family, inner development, community relations, rules and law, school and education, romance and psychosexual, economic sufficiency, and self-actualization. It yields a total score reflecting general agreement with society and eight section scores representing ego-ideal and conscience development. Two parallel forms are available. Interpretation forms, which describe the scale scores in detail and provide a normed profile for each examinee, are available. The manual describes the test rationale, gives directions for administering, scoring, and interpreting the test, and provides a complete description of the psychometric analyses of the instrument. Examiner/self-administered. Suitable for group use.

Untimed: 1 hour

Scoring: Hand key

Cost: 35 tests $30.00; 35 answer sheets $4.00; 35 interpretation forms $5.00; scoring stencil $3.00; manual $4.00 (specify form A or B for each item)

Publisher: Monitor

EGO STATE PERSONALITY PROFILE (EGOGRAM®)
N. Robert Heyer

Adult—Ages 18 and older

Purpose: Assesses the personality traits of individuals ages 18 and older in terms of enduring characteristics called "ego states." Used in psychology for diagnosis, treatment planning, counseling, and therapy; in business for placement, career counseling, training, and team building; and as a social research measure.

Description: 50–item paper-pencil multiple-choice questionnaire measuring the relative strength of six basic personality traits identified by Eric Berne, M.D., and widely used in transactional analysis: critical/judgmental, nurturing/caring, objective/logical, playful/impulsive, demonstrative/emotive, and conforming/compliant. The test yields a graphic profile. Differential ego state dominance indicates direction of subject's psychological aptitudes and typical behavior pattern in life and work situations; pronounced imbalance in a profile indicates the types of psychological problems and relationship difficulties to be found. The test is normed for individuals ages 18 and older, but it may be used also for individuals ages 14–18. Self-administered. Suitable for group use. Available in Spanish.

Untimed: 10–16 minutes

Scoring: Computer scored

Cost: 10 profiles (includes computer output and client guide) $70.00; manual $16.00

Publisher: Psychological Measurement Systems

EIGHT STATE QUESTIONNAIRE: FORMS A & B (8SQ)
James P. Curran and Raymond B. Cattell

Adolescent, adult—Ages 17 and older

Purpose: Assesses the state of mind of adults and adolescents. Measures experimental manipulations of a person's moods and progress of related therapeutic intervention. Used for clinical evaluation and personal counseling.

Description: Multiple-item paper-pencil questionnaire measuring eight important mood states: anxiety, stress, depression, regression, fatigue, guilt, extraversion, and arousal. The questionnaire is available in two equivalent forms to allow for accurate retesting. Standard scores and percentiles are presented for men and women together, men alone, women alone, and male prisoners. A sixth-grade reading level is required. Examiner required. Suitable for group use.

Untimed: 30 minutes

Scoring: Hand key

Cost: Specimen set $9.95; manual $7.25; 10 reusable test booklets (for both Forms A & B) $11.50; 25 answer sheets $8.95; 25 profile sheets $8.95; and scoring key $10.40

Publisher: Institute for Personality and Ability Testing, Inc.

EMOTIONS PROFILE INDEX
Robert Plutchik and Henry Kellerman

Adolescent, adult

Purpose: Measures personality traits and conflicts in adults and adolescents. Used for counseling and guidance, therapy, and diagnostic evaluations.

Description: 62–item paper-pencil forced-choice test in which the subject chooses which of the two words presented in each item best describes himself. Four bipolar scales measure eight dimensions of emotions: Timid vs. Aggressive, Trustful vs. Distrustful, Controlled vs. Dyscontrolled, and Gregarious vs. Depressed. A unique circular profile displays percen-

---

tile scores and compares the basic personality dimensions. Norms are provided on 1,000 normal adult men and women. Data also are given for certain special groups. Examiner required. Suitable for group use.

Untimed: 10–15 minutes

Scoring: Hand key

Cost: Complete kit (25 tests and profile sheets, manual) $23.00

Publisher: Western Psychological Services

ENVIRONMENTAL RESPONSE INVENTORY (ERI)
Refer to page 262.

EYSENCK PERSONALITY INVENTORY (EPI)
H. J. Eysenck and
Sybil B. G. Eysenck

Adolescent, adult
Grades 10 and above

Purpose: Measures extraversion and neuroticism, the two dimensions of personality that account for most personality variance. Used for counseling, clinical evaluation, and research.

Description: 57–item paper-pencil yes-no inventory measuring two independent dimensions of personality: extraversion-introversion and neuroticism-stability. A falsification scale detects response distortion. Scores are provided for three scales: E-Extraversion, N-Neuroticism, and L-Lie. The inventory is available in two equivalent forms, A and B, for pre- and posttesting. The instrument also is available in Industrial Form A-I for industrial workers. College norms are presented in percentile form for Forms A and B both separately and combined. Adult norms are presented for Form A-I. Self-administered. Suitable for group use. Available in Spanish.

Untimed: 10–15 minutes

Scoring: Hand key; may be computer scored

Cost: Specimen set (manual, one copy of all forms) $5.75; 25 inventories (specify form) $7.00; keys $6.60; manual $2.75

Publisher: EdITS/Educational and Industrial Testing Service

EYSENCK PERSONALITY QUESTIONNAIRE (EPQ)
H. J. Eysenck and
Sybil B. G. Eysenck

Adolescent, adult—Ages
7–adult

Purpose: Measures the personality dimensions of extraversion, emotionality, and toughmindedness (psychoticism in extreme cases). Used for clinical diagnosis, educational guidance, occupational counseling, personnel selection and placement, and market research.

Description: 90–item paper-pencil yes-no inventory measuring three important dimensions of personality: extraversion-introversion (21 items), neuroticism-stability (23 items), and psychoticism (25 items). The falsification scale consists of 21 items. The questionnaire deals with normal behaviors that become pathological only in extreme cases; hence, use of the term "toughmindedness" is suggested for nonpathological cases. Scores are provided for E-Extraversion, N-Neuroticism or emotionality, P-Psychoticism or toughmindedness, and L-Lie. College norms are presented in percentile form for Forms A and B both separately and combined. Adult norms are provided for an industrially employed sample. An 81–item junior form is available for testing young children. Self-administered. Suitable for group use.

Untimed: 10–15 minutes

Scoring: Hand key

Cost: Specimen set (manual, one copy of each form) $5.75; 25 forms (specify form) $7.25; keys $8.50; manual $2.75

Publisher: EdITS/Educational and Industrial Testing Service

FAMILY HISTORY—RESEARCH DIAGNOSTIC CRITERIA (FH-RDC)
Jean Endicott and
The Department of Research
Assessment and Training

Adolescent, adult

Purpose: Provides criteria for diagnosing mental disorders in family background. Used for psychiatric evaluation.

Description: 26–item checklist measuring the existence of mental disorders in family history. The clinician rates the items based on an interview of a family member about other family members. Examiner required. Not suitable for group use.

Untimed: 30–120 minutes, depending on the size of the family

Scoring: Examiner evaluated

Cost: Booklet with score sheet $1.50; parent work and data sheet $0.20; sibling work and data sheet $0.20; child work and data sheet $0.20; mate work and data sheet $0.20; summary data sheet 1 or 2 $0.20 each; sample set of all score sheets $1.10; case vignettes and keys $1.50 plus postage and handling

Publisher: Department of Research Assessment and Training—N.Y. State Psychiatric Institute

Information and availability unconfirmed; last verified in 1987.

FEAR SURVEY SCHEDULE (FSS)
Joseph Wolpe and Peter J. Land

Adult

Purpose: Evaluates the manner in which an individual deals with fear-related situations. Particularly useful in behavior therapy.

Description: Multiple-item paper-pencil survey of a patient's reactions to a variety of possible sources of maladaptive emotional reactions. The reactions are unpleasant and often fearful, fear-tinged, or fear-related. The schedule reveals reactions to many stimulus classes in a short time. Examiner required. Suitable for group use.

Untimed: 3 minutes

Scoring: Examiner evaluated

Cost: 25 response forms, manual $9.00

Publisher: EdITS/Educational and Industrial Testing Service

FORER STRUCTURED SENTENCE COMPLETION TEST
Bertram R. Forer

Adolescent, adult—Ages 10–adult

Purpose: Evaluates personality dynamics and interrelationships of individuals ages 10 and older. Used for clinical evaluation.

Description: 100–item paper-pencil sentence-completion test available in separate forms for men, women, adolescent boys, and adolescent girls. The items are highly structured for wide coverage of attitude-value systems and to point out evasiveness, individual differences, and defense mechanisms. Objective interpretation is assisted by a checklist. Examiner required. Suitable for group use.

Untimed: 40–60 minutes

Scoring: Examiner evaluated

Cost: 25 tests $8.70; 25 checklists $8.70; manual $11.50 (specify adolescent or adult; male or female)

Publisher: Western Psychological Services

THE FORTY-EIGHT ITEM COUNSELING EVALUATION TEST: REVISED
Frank B. McMahon, Jr.

Adolescent, adult

Purpose: Assesses the personal and emotional problems of adolescents and adults. Used by high-school and college counselors.

Description: 48–item paper-pencil true-false personality questionnaire employing a "double-question" technique in which each item actually consists of two questions: (a) an introductory question probing a specific aspect of behavior or personality and (b) a contingency question that qualifies and amplifies the introductory question. Responses are evaluated in six problem areas: anxiety, compulsion, depression, socialization, goals, and inadequacy. The total score indicates severity of maladjustment, and subscores provide insights into each of the six problem areas. Examiner required. Suitable for group use.

Untimed: 10–20 minutes

Scoring: Hand key

Cost: Complete kit (25 tests, manual) $15.50

Publisher: Western Psychological Services

FUNDAMENTAL INTERPERSONAL RELATIONS ORIENTATION—FEELINGS (FIRO-F)
Will Schutz

Adult

Purpose: Evaluates an individual's characteristic feelings toward others. Used to assess both individual and interactional traits as an aid to counseling and therapy.

Description: 54–item paper-pencil test measuring six dimensions of an individual's feelings toward others: expressed significance, expressed competence, expressed lovability, wanted significance, wanted competence, and wanted lovability. Dimensions parallel the three dimensions of the FIRO-B. Examiner/self-administered. Suitable for group use.

Untimed: 15–20 minutes

Scoring: Hand key

Cost: Specimen set (tests, key) $7.50; 25 tests $7.50

Publisher: Consulting Psychologists Press, Inc.

GENERAL HEALTH QUESTIONNAIRE (GHQ)
D. Goldberg

Adolescent, adult

Purpose: Screens for psychiatric disorders among respondents in community settings, such as primary care, or among general medical outpatients.

Description: Multiple-item paper-pencil self-report measure of psychiatric prob-

lems. The test requires a minimum of subjective responses by the examinee. The items are aimed at detecting disorders that may be relevant to the subject's presence in a medical clinic. Three forms—GHQ–60, GHQ–30 (a short form) and GHQ–28—are available. GHQ 28 provides separate scale scores for somatic symptoms, anxiety and insomnia, social dysfunction, severe depression for research studies requiring more than one severity score. A new user's guide is available as well, providing additional data and improved instructions for administration' and interpretation of the materials. The test is available to psychiatrists, qualified medical doctors, and clinically experienced psychologists. Self-administered. Suitable for group use.
BRITISH PUBLISHER

Untimed: Not available

Scoring: Examiner evaluated

Cost: Contact publisher

Publisher: NFER-NELSON Publishing Company Ltd.

GERIATRIC DEPRESSION SCALE
Refer to page 45.

GERIATRIC PARANOIA SCALE
Refer to page 45.

GERIATRIC SENTENCE COMPLETION FORM (GSCF)
Refer to page 45.

GIANNETTI ON-LINE PSYCHOSOCIAL HISTORY (GOLPH)
Ronald A. Giannetti

Adult

Purpose: Gathers information on an individual's background and current life circumstances. Used to obtain psychosocial history for general or psychiatric patients, evaluate job applicants' work history, criminal offenders' history of legal difficulties, or training applicants' educational history.

Description: Multiple-item multiple-choice and completion-item questionnaire presented on microcomputer. Questions and their order of appearance are determined by answers to the preceding items. The examiner selects from the following areas to gather appropriate information: current living situation, family of origin, client development, educational history, marital history/present family, occupational history/current finances, legal history, symptom screening (physical), symptom screening (psychological), and military history. Questions are presented at a sixth-grade reading level. The length of the examination depends on the areas chosen for exploration and the extent of the individual's problems. A 3–12–page report presents the individual's responses in narrative fashion. Self-administered. Not suitable for group use.

Untimed: 30 minutes–2 hours

Scoring: PC-based MICROTEST™ system required

Cost: MICROTEST system (10 administrations) $80.00; 50 administrations $337.50; 100 administrations $600.00

Publisher: National Computer Systems/PAS Division

GLOBAL ASSESSMENT SCALE (GAS)
Jean Endicott and The Department of Research Assessment and Training

Adolescent, adult

Purpose: Assesses general level of psychopathology. Used for diagnosis.

Description: Multiple-item paper-pencil measure of overall individual functioning. Information from family, case records, and clinical workup are used to rate the client's overall health or sickness on a 100–point scale. Examiner required. Not suitable for group use.

Untimed: After evaluation, 2 minutes

Scoring: Examiner evaluated

Cost: Scale $0.25; case vignettes and keys $1.50; instructions/examples $0.50 plus postage and handling

Publisher: Department of Research Assessment and Training—N.Y. State Psychiatric Institute

Information and availability unconfirmed; last verified in 1987.

GORDON PERSONAL PROFILE AND INVENTORY (GPP-I)
Leonard V. Gordon

Adolescent, adult

Purpose: Assesses aspects of an individual's personality that are significant in the functioning of the normal person.

Description: Paper-pencil measure of eight aspects of personality. The Personal Profile measures ascendancy, responsibility, emotional stability, and sociability. Four traits combine to yield the Self-Esteem score. The Personal Inventory measures cautiousness, original thinking, personal relations, and vigor. Respondents mark one item in each group of three as being most like them and one item as being least like them. Self-administered. Suitable for group use.

Untimed: 15 minutes per instrument

Scoring: Hand key; may be machine scored locally

Cost: Specimen set (booklet, manual for both profile and inventory) $30.00; 35 booklets, manual, profile and inventory combined, keys $79.00; 35 booklets, manual, keys for either profile or inventory $43.00; 35 answer documents $31.00; hand-scoring keys $17.00 (specify profile or inventory for each item ordered)

Publisher: The Psychological Corporation

Information and availability unconfirmed; last verified in 1988.

GROUP ENVIRONMENT SCALE (GES)
Rudolf H. Moos

Adolescent, adult

Purpose: Assesses the social climate of therapeutic, social, or task-oriented groups.

Description: 90–item paper-pencil true-false test of 10 aspects of group social environments: cohesion, leader support, expressiveness, independence, task orientation, self-discovery, anger and aggression, order and organization, leader control, and innovation. These scales are grouped into three dimensions: relationship, personal growth, and system maintenance and system change. Materials include the Real Form (Form R), which measures perceptions of a current group; the Ideal Form (Form I), which measures conceptions of an ideal group; and the Expectations Form (Form E), which measures expectations of a new group. Forms I and E are not published, but reworded items and instructions may be requested from the publisher. One in a series of nine Social Climate scales. Examiner required. Suitable for group use.

Untimed: 20–30 minutes

Scoring: Examiner evaluated; hand key

Cost: Manual $7.00; key $1.75; 25 reusable tests $8.50; 50 answer sheets $5.50; 50 profiles $3.75

Publisher: Consulting Psychologists Press, Inc.

GROUP PSYCHOTHERAPY EVALUATION SCALE
Clifton E. Kew

Adult

Purpose: Evaluates behavior and ego strength as a measure of a person's suitability for group therapy techniques. Discriminates between patients who can function in a group setting and those who would be overwhelmed with anxiety in the group experience.

Description: Paper-pencil inventory measuring the cognitive, emotional, and behavioral aspects of a patient in terms of his group functioning ability. The therapist rates the patient from 0–4 in four areas: amount of communication, amount of relatedness, capacity for change, and capacity for involvement. The therapist rates himself on amount of verbal activity and direction of therapist verbal activity. Suggested cutoff scores are provided for

patients most and least suited for group therapy. Examiner required. Not suitable for group use.

Untimed: 5 minutes

Scoring: Examiner evaluated

Cost: Contact publisher

Publisher: Clifton E. Kew; distributed by Educational Testing Service

---

GROUP SHORR IMAGERY TEST (GSIT)
Joseph E. Shorr

Adult

Purpose: Evaluates a person's use of imagery and assesses self-image, areas of conflict, and strategies for coping with the world. Used for in-depth personality analysis.

Description: 15–item paper-pencil projective personality test in which the subjects (listening to a tape cassette) are asked to imagine a particular situation and then to expand (in writing) in a direct way upon the image evoked. These imaginary situations are used to reveal a wide range of personality variables, including the individual's personal world, relationships between self and others, self-image, sexual attitudes, and internal and external forces acting upon the individual. The responses are quantitatively scored according to degree of conflict within the subject's personality. The test is not limited by intelligence and is minimally culture bound. The manual includes instructions for scoring, a sample of the theoretical basis for in-depth personality analysis, and normative data. Examiner required. Suitable for group use.

Untimed: 1 hour

Scoring: Examiner evaluated

Cost: Complete set $44.50

Publisher: Institute for Psycho-Imagination Therapy

Information and availability unconfirmed; last verified in 1988.

GUILFORD-ZIMMERMAN TEMPERAMENT SURVEY (GZTS)
J.P. Guilford and
Wayne S. Zimmerman

Adolescent, adult
Grades 10 and above

Purpose: Measures personality traits. Used for personnel selection, vocational guidance, and clinical practice.

Description: 300–item paper-pencil measure of 10 factor-analytically derived traits: general activity, restraint, ascendance, sociability, emotional stability, objectivity, friendliness, thoughtfulness, personal relations, and masculinity/femininity. C-scale, centile, and T-scale norms are provided for high-school and college students and adults. The test is restricted to APA members. Examiner required. Suitable for group use.

Untimed: 45 minutes

Scoring: Hand key; may be computer scored

Cost: Contact distributer

Publisher: Distributed by Consulting Psychologists Press

HALL-TONNA INVENTORY OF VALUES
Brian P. Hall and Benjamin Tonna

Adult—Ages 16 and older

Purpose: Identifies and prioritizes an individual's values. Used for values clarification in vocational and career, premarital, and pastoral counseling; clinical assessment; group, marital, and family process; corporate human resource development; and self-help.

Description: 77–item paper-pencil multiple-choice inventory assessing an individual's values. An 18– to 32–page report relating the examinee's prior and current values to future personal and psychological growth is provided. A workbook containing interactive exercises has been designed to help the examinee understand the information in the report and how his daily life is affected by his value system. Three specialized optional supplements apply the results to three specific areas:

leadership; skills, time, and vocation; and faith and ethics. A group report may also be requested. The inventory is available in both religious and secular versions. Examiner/self-administered. Suitable for group use.

Untimed: 30 minutes

Scoring: Computer scored by publisher

Cost: Report $25.00–$40.00 each; specimen set (manual, group workbook, individual workbook, questionnaire, response sheet, coupon for free computerized report) $24.95

Publisher: Behaviordyne, Inc.

Information and availability unconfirmed; last verified in 1988.

THE HAND TEST, REVISED 1983
Edwin E. Wagner

Adolescent, adult—Ages
16–adult

Purpose: Measures an individual's attitudes and action tendencies that are likely to be expressed in overt behavior, particularly aggression. Used for diagnosis and screening.

Description: 10–item oral-response projective test using picture cards that present line drawings of hands in various positions. For each card, the subject explains what the hand is doing. The tenth card, which is blank, requires the subject to imagine a hand and describe what it is doing. Responses are scored on a variety of qualitative and quantitative indices to measure potential behavior toward persons and objects in the environment, pathological inefficiency, and social withdrawal. Reading skill is not required. Scoring takes a few minutes. Examiner required. Not suitable for group use.

Untimed: 10 minutes

Scoring: Examiner evaluated

Cost: Kit (25 scoring booklets, 1 set of picture cards, manual) $39.50

Publisher: Western Psychological Services

HARVARD GROUP SCALE OF HYPNOTIC SUSCEPTIBILITY
Ronald E. Shor and Emily C. Orne

College students, adult

Purpose: Screens large numbers of individuals for hypnotic susceptibility. Used for classroom demonstration and research.

Description: Multiple-item scale with instructions for inducing hypnosis. Subjects record their own responses. The test was adapted for group administration from the Stanford Hypnotic Susceptibility Scale Form A. Examiner required. Suitable for group use.

Untimed: 50 minutes

Scoring: Examiner evaluated

Cost: 25 response booklets $26.00; manual $6.50

Publisher: Consulting Psychologists Press, Inc.

HEALTH PROBLEMS CHECKLIST
Refer to page 13.

HIGH SCHOOL PERSONALITY QUESTIONNAIRE (HSPQ)
Raymond B. Cattell and Mary D. Cattell

Adolescent—Ages 12–18

Purpose: Identifies adolescents with high potentials for dropping out of school, drug abuse, and low achievement. Used in correctional situations to facilitate parent-teacher, parent-officer, and parent-clinic cooperation.

Description: 142–item paper-pencil questionnaire measuring 14 primary personality dimensions, such as stability, tension, warmth, and enthusiasm. Scores for anxiety, extraversion, creativity, leadership, and other broad trait patterns are also obtained. The test is available in four equivalent forms, A, B, C, and D. Percentiles and standard scores are provided for boys, girls, and combined. A sixth-grade reading level is required. Examiner required. Suitable for group use. Available in Spanish.

Untimed: 45–60 minutes per form

Scoring: Hand key; scoring and interpretation services available

Cost: Computer interpretation kit $21.95; manual $10.95; 25 reusable test booklets $15.60–$23.75; 25 machine-scorable answer sheets $8.25; 50 hand-scorable answer sheets $8.25; 50 hand-scorable answer-profile sheets $10.75; and 2 scoring keys $11.50

Publisher: Institute for Personality and Ability Testing, Inc.

HILSON ADOLESCENT PROFILE (HAP)
Robin E. Inwald

Adolescent—Ages 10–18

Purpose: Identifies and predicts troubled and/or delinquent behavior in adolescents.

Description: 310–item behaviorally oriented paper-pencil true-false test consisting of a validity measure and 15 scales assessing specific external behaviors, attitudes and temperament, interpersonal adjustment measures, and internalized conflict measures: Guardedness (GR; 21 items), Alcohol (AL; 13 items), Drugs (DG; 15 items), Educational Adjustment Difficulties (ED; 19 items), Law/Society Violations (LV; 21 items), Frustration Tolerance (FT; 23 items), Antisocial/Risk-Taking Attitudes (AR; 19 items), Rigidity/Obsessiveness (RI; 21 items), Interpersonal/Assertiveness Difficulties (IA; 26 items), Homelife Conflicts (HL; 33 items), Social/Sexual Adjustment (SS; 22 items), Health Concerns (HC; 14 items), Anxiety/Phobic Avoidance (PP; 25 items), Depression/Suicide Potential (DP; 25 items), Suspicious Temperament (ST; 17 items), and Unusual Responses (UR; 10 items).

Raw scores and three sets of T-scores are provided for each scale. T-scores are based on juvenile offender norms, clinical inpatient norms, and student norms. A fifth- to sixth-grade reading level is required. A computer scoring service available from the publisher provides mail-in and teleprocessing services. The mail-in service has a turnaround time of 24 hours. Teleprocessing software operates on IBM PC or compatible systems and allows examinees to input test responses either manually or through optical scanning. Results for each test are provided within 6 seconds. Self-administered. Suitable for group use.

Untimed: 30–45 minutes

Scoring: Computer scored

Cost: Starter kit (technical manual, test booklet, answer sheets for 3 computer-scored reports) $45.00; reusable test booklets $1.50; processing fees $3.00–$20.00

Publisher: Hilson Research, Inc.

HOFFER-OSMOND DIAGNOSTIC TEST (HOD)
Abram Hoffer, Humphrey Osmond, and Harold Kelm

Adolescent, adult—Ages 13–adult

Purpose: Diagnoses the degree and nature of psychiatric illness. Monitors treatment and establishes prognosis. Used by mental health practitioners to screen for mental illness.

Description: 145–item true-false test measuring the amount of paranoia, depression, and perceptual distortion in patients. Each item consists of a statement printed on a card. The subject reads each card and either answers on a separate answer sheet or places the card in a true box or a false box. If the patient is illiterate, the items may be read aloud. The test helps determine when a patient requires hospitalization or is ready to be discharged from the hospital. Materials include 145 test cards, a manual, score sheet, and test booklet. Self-administered under clinical supervision. Suitable for group use.

Untimed: 30 minutes

Scoring: Hand key

Cost: Complete test $55.00; HOD text $22.00

Publisher: Behavior Science Press

HOGAN PERSONALITY INVENTORY
Robert Hogan

College student, adult

Purpose: Assesses normal personality characteristics. Used for counseling, employment decisions, research, and self-development.

Description: 310–item paper-pencil true-false inventory assessing six primary traits: intellectance, adjustment, prudence, ambition, sociability, and likeability. The test contains one validity scale and six occupational scales (service orientation, clerical performance, sales performance, management performance, stress tolerance, and reliability). Test items are presented at a fourth-grade reading level. A three-page computerized report presents raw and T-scores for six primary traits, one validity scale, and six occupational scales, as well as a narrative based on the six primary scales. Examiner required. Suitable for group use.

Untimed: 30–40 minutes

Scoring: Computer scored

Cost: Specimen set $12.00

Publisher: National Computer Systems/ PAS Division

HOPKINS PSYCHIATRIC RATING SCALE (HPRS)
Leonard R. Derogatis

Adolescent, adult

Purpose: Evaluates the psychological symptomatic distress of medical and psychiatric patients in terms of the observer's judgment. Used in mental health settings for psychological screening and in treatment planning and evaluation.

Description: 17–item paper-pencil observational inventory assessing symptomatic distress in terms of nine primary symptom dimensions (somatization, obsessive-compulsive, interpersonal sensitivity, depression, anxiety, hostility, phobic anxiety, paranoid ideation, and psychoticism) and eight additional dimensions. Each dimension is defined by a brief descriptive paragraph coupled with verbal descriptive anchors at seven discrete scale points. This HPRS is a part of the Psychopathology Rating Scale Series, which includes the SCL–90-R, the SCL–90 Analogue, and the Brief Symptom Inventory (BSI). The nine primary symptoms assessed are common to all four scales. A brief version

(B-HPRS) that rates only the nine primary symptoms is available. A microcomputer program (COMPAR–90) is available to calculate and assess differences in terms of standardized scores between HPRS or B-HPRS ratings of patients and self-ratings by the patients on the SCL-90-R or BSI. Examiner required. Not suitable for group use.

Untimed: 2–5 minutes

Scoring: Examiner evaluated; may be computer scored

Cost: 100 HPRS forms $32.00; 100 B-HPRS forms $28.00

Publisher: Clinical Psychometric Research, Inc.

HOW WELL DO YOU KNOW YOURSELF
Thomas N. Jenkins

**Adolescent, adult
Grades 10 and above**

Purpose: Assesses normal personality. Used for educational guidance.

Description: Multiple-item paper-pencil test measuring 17 personality traits: irritability, practicality, punctuality, novelty-loving, vocational assurance, cooperativeness, ambitiousness, hypercriticalness, dejection, general morale, persistence, nervousness, seriousness, submissiveness, impulsiveness, dynamism, and emotional control. Two additional measures of response style, consistency and test objectivity, are included. Examiner required. Suitable for group use.

Untimed: 20 minutes

Scoring: Hand key

Cost: Complete kit (3 test booklets of each edition and manual) $10.00; 25 tests (specify secondary, college, or personnel) $20.00; keys $6.75; manual $6.75

Publisher: Psychologists and Educators, Inc.

HOWARTH PERSONALITY QUESTIONNAIRE (HPQ)
Edgar Howarth

Adult—Ages 18 and older

Purpose: Assesses personality factors of adults.

Description: 120–item paper-pencil binary-type yes-no and true-false test measuring general personality factors and dimensions along 10 scales. Each scale yields a separate score. Examiner required. Suitable for group use. Available in French.

Untimed: 20–30 minutes

Scoring: Hand key

Cost: Test, score sheet $1.00; scoring key $2.00

Publisher: Edgar Howarth, Ph.D.

Information and availability unconfirmed; last verified in 1988.

HUMAN ACTIVITY PROFILE (HAP)
*A. James Fix and
David M. Daughton*

Adult—Ages 20–79

Purpose: Assesses activity levels. Used in rehabilitation settings, quality-of-life programs, and drug side-effects studies.

Description: 94–item paper-pencil multiple-choice test based on estimated metabolic equivalents (METS). Scores provide various measures of energy expenditure, age equivalents, and estimates of potential and current oxygen consumption. Suitable for use with the physically impaired. Materials include the manual and test booklets. This is a revision of the Additive Activities Profile Test. Examiner required. Suitable for group use.

Untimed: 15 minutes

Scoring: Hand key

Cost: Kit (manual, 50 test booklets) $36.95

Publisher: Psychological Assessment Resources, Inc.

HUMAN RELATIONS INVENTORY
Raymond S. Bernberg

**Adolescent, adult
Grades 10 and above**

Purpose: Measures a person's tendency toward social or lawful conformity. Differentiates between conformist and nonconformist individuals.

Description: Multiple-item paper-pencil test measuring an individual's sense of social conformity. Social conformity is defined and tested in terms of moral values, positive goals, reality testing, ability to give affection, tension level, and impulsivity. The test is constructed using the "direction of perception" technique, and the purpose of the test is disguised from subjects to produce more valid results. The test discriminates between samples of law violators and ordinary conformists. Norms are provided for senior high-school boys, college students, regular churchgoers, Los Angeles police officers, male inmates of a California youth prison, adult male inmates of the Los Angeles County Jail, and adult female inmates of the Los Angeles County Jail. Examiner required. Suitable for group use.

Untimed: Not available

Scoring: Examiner evaluated

Cost: Specimen set $5.00; 25 inventories $5.00

Publisher: Psychometric Affiliates

HYPOCHONDRIASIS SCALE: INSTITUTIONAL GERIATRIC
Refer to page 46.

ILLNESS BEHAVIOUR QUESTIONNAIRE (IBQ)
Issy Pilowsky

Adult

Purpose: Assesses attitudes toward illness, affective disturbance, and hypochondriasis.

Description: 62–item paper-pencil yes-no test with seven scales yielding separate scores: General Hypochondriasis, Disease Conviction, Psychological vs. Somatic Perception of Illness, Affective Inhibition, Affective Disturbance, Denial, and Irritability. In addition to the scale scores, the test yields the Whiteley Index of Hypochondriasis. A version for administration in nonclinical settings (i.e., where the respondent cannot be assumed to suffer from an illness or to be in a patient role) is

available. Self-administered. Suitable for group use. Available in Italian, Greek, Serbo-Croatian, French, Spanish, Portuguese, German, Hindi, Chinese, Swedish, and Polish.

AUSTRALIAN PUBLISHER

Untimed: 15 minutes

Scoring: Hand key; may be computer scored

Cost: Manual $25.00

Publisher: I. Pilowsky, M.D.

IMPACT MESSAGE INVENTORY
Donald J. Kiesler, Jack C. Anchin, Michael J. Perkins, Bernie M. Chirico, Edgar M. Kyle, and Edward J. Federman

Adolescent, adult

Purpose: Measures the affective, behavioral, and cognitive reactions of one individual to another. Assesses the personality and interpersonal style of an individual by measuring the attitudes and feelings the individual arouses in the respondent. Helpful in clarifying interpersonal transactions in any dyad, including teacher-student, friends, employer-employee, and therapist-client.

Description: 90–item paper-pencil inventory assessing one individual's reactions to the interpersonal or personality style of another person. Items describe ways in which people are emotionally engaged or affected when interacting with another person. Individuals respond on a 4–point scale ranging from "not at all" to "very much so" to indicate the extent to which each item describes the feeling aroused by the other person, behaviors they want to direct toward the other person, or descriptions of the other person that come to mind when in the other person's presence. Each test item describes a reaction characteristically elicited by a person high on one of the following 15 interpersonal dimensions: dominant, competitive, hostile, mistrusting, detached, inhibited, submissive, succorant, abrasive, deferent, agreeable, nurturant, affiliative, sociable, and exhibitionistic. Scores are derived for each of the 15 subscales as well as for four cluster scores: dominant, submissive, friendly, and hostile. Kiesler has completed a revised manual, *Research Manual for the Impact Message Inventory*, which includes descriptions of the subscales and tables for converting raw scores to T-scores. Examiner required. Suitable for group use.

Untimed: 15 minutes

Scoring: Examiner evaluated

Cost: 25 question booklets (specify male or female) $11.00; 50 answer sheets $8.50

Publisher: Consulting Psychologists Press, Inc.

INCOMPLETE SENTENCES TASK
Barbara Lanyon and Richard Lanyon

**Adolescent, adult
Grades 7 and above**

Purpose: Identifies potential emotional problems in students from junior high-school through college to begin intervention before problems become too severe.

Description: 39–item paper-pencil test consisting of incomplete sentence stems that the subject completes in his own words. The test is both projective and psychometric and measures hostility, anxiety, and dependency. Scoring is based on examples for each item found in the manual. Two forms are available: a School Form (Grades 7–12) and a College Form (college-age adolescents). Norms are provided for three groups: Grades 7–9, Grades 10–12, and college-age adolescents. Self-administered. Suitable for group use.

Untimed: 15–20 minutes

Scoring: Examiner evaluated

Cost: Complete kit, specify form (30 test forms, manual) $17.00

Publisher: Stoelting Co.

INTERPERSONAL CHECK LIST (ICL)
Rolfe LaForge and R. Suczek

Adult

Purpose: Describes an individual's perception of another individual's personality. Used for clinical and social research.

Description: 134–item paper-pencil checklist for describing self or another person. Each item is categorized according to one of 16 interpersonal categories and one of four intensity levels. Summary variables are dominance, love, number of items endorsed, and average intensity of endorsed items. The subject is required to describe one or more persons, possibly self or a hypothetical person, by checking the items. The test may be duplicated. Examiner required. Suitable for group use.

Untimed: 15 minutes

Scoring: Computer scored

Cost: Test is free; technical report $15.00

Publisher: Rolfe LaForge

INTERPERSONAL COMMUNICATION INVENTORY (ICI)
Millard J. Bienvenu

Adolescent, adult—Ages 15 and older

Purpose: Evaluates interpersonal communication skills. Used in counseling and teaching communication skills.

Description: 40–item paper-pencil multiple-choice test measuring the following communication skills: self-disclosure, expression of feelings, listening skills, nonverbal communication, acceptance of feelings, and confrontation. Materials include a questionnaire, answer sheet, and manual. Self-administered. Suitable for group use.

Untimed: 15 minutes

Scoring: Hand key; examiner evaluated

Cost: Test $0.35 each; guide $2.50

Publisher: Counseling and Self-Improvement Programs/Millard Bienvenu, Ph.D.

Information and availability unconfirmed; last verified in 1988.

INTERPERSONAL RELATIONS QUESTIONNAIRE (IRQ)—1981

Adolescent—Ages 12–15

Purpose: Assesses personal adjustment in adolescence. Used for counseling and guidance.

Description: 260– or 100–item paper-pencil test measuring 12 components of adjustment: self-confidence, self-esteem, self-control, nervousness, health, family influences, personal freedom, general sociability, sociability with the opposite sex, sociability with the same sex, moral sense, and formal relations. Items are answered on a 4–point scale. A 100–item abridged questionnaire provides a more general indication of adjustment involving five components. Examiner required. Suitable for group use.
SOUTH AFRICAN PUBLISHER
Untimed: 2 hours; abridged questionnaire 1 hour
Scoring: Hand key; examiner evaluated
Cost: (In Rands) questionnaire 1,70; 10 answer sheets 1,20; scoring stencil (positive items) 5,00; scoring stencil (negative items) 5,00; test profiles 3,00; manual 9,30; supplement to manual (norms and statistics for Indian pupils) 5,50; orders from outside The RSA will be dealt with on merit
Publisher: Human Sciences Research Council

INTERPERSONAL STYLE INVENTORY (ISI)
Maurice Lorr and Richard P. Youniss

Adolescent, adult—Ages 14 and older

Purpose: Assesses an individual's manner of interacting with other people and style of impulse control. Used for self-understanding, counseling and therapy, personnel guidance, and research.

Description: 300–item paper-pencil true-false inventory assessing an individual's style of interpersonal interactions along 15 primary scales: Directive, Sociable, Help-Seeking, Nurturant, Conscientious, Trusting, Tolerant, Sensitive, Deliberate, Independent, Rule Free, Orderly, Persistent, Stable, and Approval Seeking. Each item is a statement describing ways in which people relate and respond to each other. The individual reads each statement and decides whether it is

mostly true or not true for himself. High-school and college norms are provided by sex. The computer report includes a full-color WPS ChromaGraph profile of major scores. Self-administered. Suitable for group use.
Untimed: 30 minutes
Scoring: Computer scored
Cost: Test kit (5 reusable administration booklets; 5 computer scorable answer sheets; manual) $60.00
Publisher: Western Psychological Services

INTRA AND INTERPERSONAL RELATIONS (IIRS)—1973

Child, adolescent

Purpose: Measures the relationship with self and parental figures. Used for counseling and assessment.

Description: Paper-pencil test of relationships with self and others. The scale also measures the relationship between the real and ideal selves and indicates self-acceptance. Examiner required. Suitable for group use.
SOUTH AFRICAN PUBLISHER
Untimed: 30 minutes
Scoring: Hand key; examiner evaluated
Cost: (In Rands) test booklet 3,50; manual 15,00; 10 answer sheets 1,00; scoring stencil 1,50; orders from outside The RSA will be dealt with on merit
Publisher: Human Sciences Research Council

INTREX
Lorna Smith Benjamin

Adolescent, adult—Ages 14 and older

Purpose: Assesses interpersonal relationships and their impact on the self.

Description: 32–item paper-pencil rating instrument on which the examinee rates his spouse, child, boss, or other familiar person (18 items) and then himself in relation to that person (18 items). The standard series (160 total items) includes spouse at best and worst, mother, father, and parents' relationship during examinee's childhood. A profile based on structural analysis of social behavior (SASB) compares and contrasts relationships and their effect on the examinee. A high-school reading level is required. The test, which must be administered by a licensed psychotherapist, may be used with mentally impaired individuals. Self-administered. Suitable for group use. Available in Italian, Swedish, and German.

Untimed: Not available

Scoring: Computer scored; examiner evaluated

Cost: $20.00 prepaid

Publisher: INTREX Interpersonal Institute, Inc.

INVENTORY OF ANGER COMMUNICATION (IAC)
Millard J. Bienvenu

Adolescent, adult—Ages 15 and older

Purpose: Helps individuals learn about their style of handling anger. Used as a counseling and teaching tool.

Description: 30–item paper-pencil multiple-choice questionnaire covers areas such as handling anger, confrontation, expression of feelings, and measurement of anger. Materials include a questionnaire, manual, and scoring key. Examiner/self-administered. Suitable for group use.

Untimed: 15 minutes

Scoring: Hand key; examiner evaluated

Cost: IAC $0.35; guide $1.50

Publisher: Counseling and Self-Improvement Programs/Millard Bienvenu, Ph.D.

Information and availability unconfirmed; last verified in 1988.

INVENTORY OF SELF-HYPNOSIS
Ronald E. Shor

Adult

Purpose: Assesses an individual's hypnotizability. Also used for inducing or demonstrating self-hypnosis.

Description: Multiple-item inventory in which subjects read instructions for inducing hypnosis, give themselves 12 suggestions, and rate their own performances. The inventory, adapted from the Harvard Group Scale, allows the subject to control the induction, which reduces anxiety. Self-administered. Not suitable for group use.

Untimed: 1½ hours

Scoring: Examiner evaluated

Cost: 25 reusable instruction booklets $42.00; 50 response sheets $10.50

Publisher: Consulting Psychologists Press, Inc.

IPAT DEPRESSION SCALE
Samuel E. Krug and James E. Laughlin

Adult

Purpose: Diagnoses depression in adults of most educational levels. Used for both clinical diagnosis and psychological research on depression.

Description: 40–item paper-pencil questionnaire diagnosing and measuring depression in adults. Norms are provided for adult, college, prison, and certain clinical populations. A fifth-grade reading level is required. Self-administered. Suitable for group use. Available in Spanish.

Untimed: 10 minutes

Scoring: Hand key

Cost: Complete kit $12.95; manual $9.25; 25 nonreusable test booklets $8.35; scoring key $3.25

Publisher: Institute for Personality and Ability Testing, Inc.

IPS SOCIAL HISTORY (SOCH)

Adult

Purpose: Gathers information necessary to assess an individual's social, medical, and psychological history.

Description: Multiple-item computer-administered or paper-pencil test gathering personal information in the following areas: current status, childhood, education, military, criminal, substance abuse, personal relations with friends and family members, and self-descriptive adjectives. As a microcomputer program, a series of questions are presented on the answer screen, and the individual responds by pressing numbers on the keyboard. For paper-pencil administration, item responses are entered directly into the computer by clerical staff. A narrative report is produced describing major problem areas and psychological/medical history. This report then can be used as a guide during subsequent personal interviews or to identify topics needing further exploration. The test is available for use with OSI and Apple computers. A national scoring service also is available. Examiner required. Paper-pencil version suitable for group use.

Untimed: Varies

Scoring: Computer scored

Cost: Contact publisher for information concerning software requirements and administration costs

Publisher: Integrated Professional Systems, Inc.

Information and availability unconfirmed; last verified in 1987.

IRRATIONAL BELIEFS TEST
Richard G. Jones

Adult

Purpose: Assesses an individual's irrational beliefs. Used for clinical assessment and diagnosis; personnel selection and evaluation; personal, marital, and family counseling; vocational guidance counseling; and educational evaluation and planning.

Description: Multiple-item paper-pencil test assessing an individual's irrational belief system along 10 dimensions derived from Ellis' Rational Emotive Therapy. Computer analysis provides scores and a narrative report based upon the 10 dimensions and a factor-analytic model. The report incorporates empirical relationships between the scales and other conditions such as stress, pathology, personality, motivation, organization roles, and decision styles. Examiner required. Suitable for group use.

Untimed: Varies

Scoring: Hand key; may be computer scored

Cost: Mail-in scoring service $12.00

Publisher: Test Systems International

Information and availability unconfirmed; last verified in 1987.

JACKSON PERSONALITY INVENTORY (JPI)
Douglas N. Jackson

Adolescent, adult

Purpose: Assesses personality characteristics of normal people who have average and above-average intelligence. Used to evaluate behavior in a wide range of settings, including those involving work, education, organizations, interpersonal, and high-level performance.

Description: 320–item paper-pencil true-false test covering 15 substantive scales and one validity scale. The scales measured are Anxiety, Breadth of Interest, Complexity, Conformity, Energy Level, Innovation, Interpersonal Affect, Organization, Responsibility, Risk Taking, Self Esteem, Social Adroitness, Social Participation, Tolerance, Value Orthodoxy, and Infrequency. Materials include a manual, reusable test booklets, answer sheet, and template and profiles. Norms are based on random college sampling. High-school norms are available. This test differs from the Personality Research Form (PRF) in terms of the nature of the variables measured and is a further refinement of substantive psychometric and computer-based strategies for scale development. Machine-readable answer sheets and a mail-in batch scoring service to produce a two-page Basic Report are available. Examiner required. Suitable for group use. Available in French.

Untimed: 1 hour

Scoring: Hand key; may be machine scored

Cost: Complete set $28.50

Publisher: SIGMA Assessment Systems, Inc., Research Psychologists Press Division

JENKINS ACTIVITY SURVEY (JAS)
Refer to page 9.

JESNESS BEHAVIOR CHECK LIST
Carl F. Jesness

Adolescent

Purpose: Assesses the social behavior of adolescents. Used to evaluate behavioral change in school or institutional settings and for comparisons between self and observer ratings for use in counseling or research.

Description: 80–item paper-pencil rating scale measuring 14 bipolar behavioral tendencies: unobtrusiveness vs. obtrusiveness, friendliness vs. hostility, responsibility vs. irresponsibility, considerateness vs. inconsiderateness, independence vs. dependence, rapport vs. alienation, enthusiasm vs. depression, sociability vs. poor peer relations, conformity vs. nonconformity, calmness vs. anxiousness, effective communication vs. inarticulateness, insight vs. unawareness and indecisiveness, social control vs. attention-seeking, and anger control vs. hypersensitivity. Materials include an Observer Form for ratings by teachers and therapists and a Self-Appraisal Form for self-evaluation.

Computer scoring, which is available from the publisher, yields a profile of the 14 Factor Scores, percentiles for the 14 Self- or Observer-Rating Factors, and items indicating that the subject or observer was significantly critical. When both the Observer and the Self-Appraisal forms are used for the same individual, scoring provides Self-Observer Distance, Correlation, and Relative Position; Overall Observer Rating; and Overall Self-Rating. Self-administered. Suitable for group use.

Untimed: 10–20 minutes

Scoring: Hand key; computer scoring service available

Cost: Specimen set (manual, profile, copy of each test form) $12.00; manual $9.00; key $26.00

Publisher: Consulting Psychologists Press, Inc.

KATZ ADJUSTMENT SCALES (KAS)
Martin M. Katz

Adult

Purpose: Describes and measures an individual's social behavior, symptoms, and performance. Evaluates personal and social adjustment. Used for both normal and mentally disordered persons.

Description: 225–item paper-pencil test consisting of five scales and a self-report form. The test measures the following factors: emotional stability, general psychopathology, belligerence, expansiveness, negativism, anxiety, helplessness, suspiciousness, withdrawal and retardation, nervousness, confusion, hyperactivity, bizarreness, level of performance, and satisfaction with level of socially expected activities. The test is administered to a relative or "significant other" in a position to observe the subject for at least several weeks. It is used in the experimental study of various mental disorders as perceived in the United States and other cultures and in the evaluation of treatments. The test may be administered by interview if the observer is illiterate. Materials include the scale, a list of references, and a brief manual. Self-administered. Not suitable for group use. Translated into 12 European and Asian languages.

Untimed: 20–40 minutes

Scoring: Hand key; may be computer scored

Cost: Complete kit (scale, references list, manual) $15.00

Publisher: Martin M. Katz, Ph.D.

Information and availability unconfirmed; last verified in 1988.

KEEGAN TYPE INDICATOR (KTI), FORM B
Refer to page 1045.

KIRTON ADAPTION-INNOVATION INVENTORY (KAI)
Michael J. Kirton

Adolescent, adult

Purpose: Evaluates an individual's cognitive style preference in creativity, problem solving, and decision making. Used in personality and occupational psychology and in business management for training and team building.

Description: 33–item paper-pencil test containing three subtests: Sufficiency (Proliferation of Originality), Efficiency Preference, and Rule/Group Conformity Preference. Scores are yielded for each subtest. The preferred cognitive style measured (adaption-innovation) is unrelated to an individual's capacity; however, it is strongly related to a critical cluster of personality traits. Examiner required. Suitable for group use. Available in Italian, Dutch, Slavic, German, French, Spanish, Russian, and Czech.
BRITISH PUBLISHER

Untimed: 10–15 minutes

Scoring: Hand key

Cost: 25 response sheets (including report back forms) $32.00; manual $40.00

Publisher: Occupational Research Centre

KUNDU INTROVERSION-EXTRAVERSION INVENTORY (K.I.E.I.)
Ramanath Kundu

Adolescent, adult

Purpose: Assesses the introversion-extroversion dimension of adolescent and adult personalities. Used for clinical diagnosis, research, guidance, and placement.

Description: Multiple-item paper-pencil test measuring introversion and extroversion. A minimum English reading level is required. Self-administered. Suitable for group use.
PUBLISHED IN INDIA

Untimed: 15 minutes

Scoring: Hand key

Cost: (In Rupees) Specimen set 50–00Rs.; 25 reusable booklets 160–00Rs.; 10 manuals with scoring 100–00Rs.; 100 answer sheets 180–00Rs

Publisher: Ramanath Kundu

KUNDU NEUROTIC PERSONALITY INVENTORY (K.N.P.I.)
Ramanath Kundu

Adolescent, adult

Purpose: Assesses degrees of neuroticism. Used for clinical diagnosis, research, guidance, and employee selection.

Description: 66–item paper-pencil test measuring neuroticism. A minimum English reading level is required. The author plans to publish a new manual containing detailed information about the test. Self-administered. Suitable for group use.
PUBLISHED IN INDIA

Untimed: 15 minutes

Scoring: Hand key

Cost: (In Rupees) Specimen set 50–00Rs.; 25 reusable booklets 160–00Rs.; 10 manuals with scoring 75–00Rs.; 100 answer sheets 180–00Rs

Publisher: Ramanath Kundu

THE LAWRENCE PSYCHOLOGICAL FORENSIC EXAMINATION AND MENTAL COMPETENCY TEST (LAW-COMP)
Stephen B. Lawrence

Adolescent, adult

Purpose: Determines an individual's present legal competency to stand trial.

Description: 250–item paper-pencil test consisting of a worksheet and scaling procedures designed to aid clinicians in making decisions regarding an individual's ability to stand trial. The test is published in a 142–page portable handbook, *LAW-PSI: The Lawrence Psychological Forensic Examination.* Examiner required. Not suitable for group use.

Untimed: Not available

Scoring: Not available

Cost: *LAW-PSI: The Lawrence Psychological Forensic Examination* $29.50

Publisher: Distributed by Psychological Assessment Resources, Inc.

THE LEEDS SCALES FOR THE SELF-ASSESSMENT OF ANXIETY AND DEPRESSION
R.P. Snaith, C.W.K. Bridge, and Max Hamilton

Adult

Purpose: Measures severity of depression and anxiety. Used for individual counseling and therapy.

Description: 15–item paper-pencil test measuring patient's self-report of depression and anxiety. Four scale scores are obtained: Depression Specific Scale, Anxiety Specific Scale, Depression General Scale, and Anxiety General Scale. Specific scales provide a measure of the severity of diagnosed affective illness. Self-administered. Suitable for group use. BRITISH PUBLISHER

Untimed: Varies

Scoring: Hand key

Cost: Specimen set (answer sheet, specific and general scale stencils manual) $13.50; keys $6.90; 50 answer sheets $10.75; manual $5.55

Publisher: Psychological Test Publications; distributed by The Test Agency Ltd.

LEITER RECIDIVISM SCALE

Adult

Purpose: Measures the potential for recidivism. Used by judges in criminal courts and at each stage of the correctional process to determine in a given case whether society would be best served by probation or incarceration.

Description: Multiple-item paper-pencil inventory assessing nine variables related to recidivism: instability, age-time ratio, social immaturity, social control (lack of control), vocational adjustment (lack of adjustment), personality dynamics, abnormal authority reaction, institutional adjustment, and offense level. An individual's recidivism score is the sum of his scores on the nine variables, each of which is a predictor of recidivism in its

own right. Self-administered by a judge, probation officer, or correctional personnel. Not suitable for group use.

Untimed: Varies

Scoring: Examiner evaluated

Cost: Test kit (manual, 25 profile sheets, 25 record blanks) $24.00

Publisher: Stoelting Co.

LEVINE-PILOWSKY DEPRESSION QUESTIONNAIRE (L.P.D.)
I. Pilowsky, S. Levine, and D. Boulton

Adult

Purpose: Measures severity of depression and probability of endogenous or non-endogenous depression.

Description: 57–item paper-pencil yes-no instrument measuring an individual's probability of membership in non-endogenous, endogenous, or nondepressive categories. The test also yields a Depression score. Version for nonpatients available. Self-administered. Suitable for group use. Available in Italian, Greek, and Serbo-Croatian. AUSTRALIAN PUBLISHER

Untimed: 10–15 minutes

Scoring: Hand key; may be computer scored

Cost: 20 questionnaires, score sheets with bibliography $20.00

Publisher: I. Pilowsky, M.D.

LEWIS COUNSELING INVENTORY
D.G. Lewis and P.D. Pumfrey

Adolescent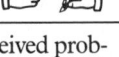

Purpose: Measures self-perceived problems of adolescents. Used for individual counseling and screening for pupils most in need of guidance.

Description: 46–item paper-pencil test measuring the need for professional help. Six Lie scale items are included, as well as a series of direct statements scored in six areas: relationship with teachers, relationship with family, irritability, social confidence, relationship with peers, and health. The pupil indicates whether he agrees or disagrees with each item. The inventory may be followed by Part 2, a short questionnaire allowing the pupil to expand on specifics about his perceived problems. Response patterns may indicate the type of help needed. Examiner required. Suitable for group use. BRITISH PUBLISHER

Untimed: Part I 10–15 minutes; Part II 15 minutes

Scoring: Hand key

Cost: Contact publisher

Publisher: NFER-NELSON Publishing Company Ltd.

LIFE ORIENTATION INVENTORY (LOI)
Brian Kowalchuk and John D. King

Adolescent, adult—Ages 13 and older

Purpose: Assesses suicide risk.

Description: 113–item paper-pencil test assessing suicidal orientation along six factors: a) self-esteem vulnerability, b) overinvestment, c) overdetermined misery, d) affective domination, e) alienation, and f) suicide tenability. The items are presented as statements, half of which are life affirming and half of which are pessimistic. The examinee indicates agreement or disagreement with each statement. A screening form consisting of 30 items is available. Examiner required. Suitable for group use.

Untimed: 30 minutes; screening form 10 minutes

Scoring: Examiner evaluated

Cost: Complete kit (examiner's manual, 25 profile and response forms, 50 screen response forms, storage box) $59.00

Publisher: PRO-ED

LONGITUDINAL INTERVAL FOLLOW-UP EVALUATION (LIFE)
Robert W. Shapiro, Martin B. Keller, and Philip W. Lavori

Adolescent, adult—Ages 18 and older

Purpose: Collects an individual's psychosocial, psychopathologic, and psychiatric

treatment information. Used for 6–month follow-up.

Description: Multiple-item paper-pencil rating interview using Research Diagnostic Criteria to assess 24 psychiatric disorders and psychosocial ratings, including episodic affective disorders, chronic depressive disorders, and other nonaffective disorders. Weekly psychiatric status ratings (PSRs), overall severity of illness rating, and treatment ratings are provided. The instrument may be adapted for use with special populations (children and visually, mentally, and physically impaired). Examiner required. Not suitable for group use.

Untimed: 30–60 minutes

Scoring: Examiner evaluated

Cost: Contact publisher

Publisher: Martin B. Keller, M.D.

LONGITUDINAL INTERVAL FOLLOW-UP EVALUATION-UPJOHN (LIFE-UP)
Martin B. Keller and Eileen Nielsen

Adult—Ages 18 and older

Purpose: Evaluates DSM-III-R, anxiety, and depressive disorders. Used primarily in psychiatric research.

Description: Oral-response assessment examining the individual's a) psychiatric status for the four months preceding the interview, b) use of psychotropic drugs, c) suicidal gestures, d) mental health contacts, e) psychosocial functioning, and f) global functioning. Must be completed by a trained clinical interviewer. Suitable for use with individuals with physical or mental impairments. Examiner required. Not suitable for group use.

Untimed: 60 minutes

Scoring: Examiner evaluated

Cost: Contact publisher

Publisher: Martin B. Keller

M'NAUGHTEN COMPETENCE TEST
Linda L. Appenfeldt

Adult—Ages 18 and older

Purpose: Assesses an individual's competency to stand trial. Used by clinicians. May be used with mentally impaired individuals.

Description: Multiple-item paper-pencil short-answer and oral-response criterion-referenced test assessing an individual's competency to stand trial based on 11 statutory criteria: appreciation of charge, range of penalty, understanding of legal process, capacity to disclose facts, ability to relate to attorney, assist with defense, challenge witnesses, manifest appropriate courtroom behavior, testify relevantly, help self in legal process, and cope with stress of incarceration. The examiner must be a forensic psychiatrist, psychologist, or attorney. A third-grade reading level is required. Examiner required. Not suitable for group use.

Untimed: 1 hour

Scoring: Examiner evaluated

Cost: Kit (manual, 10 record forms) $236.25

Publisher: Linda Appenfeldt, Ph.D.

Information and availability unconfirmed; last verified in 1988.

MAKE A PICTURE STORY (MAPS)
Edwin S. Shneidman

Adolescent, adult

Purpose: Measures fantasies, defenses, and impulses.

Description: Projective oral-response test consisting of 22 stimulus cards and a set of 67 "cut-out" figures. Stimulus cards range from structured situations (bedroom, bathroom, schoolroom, baby's room) to more ambiguous presentations (a blank doorway, a cave, and a totally blank card). Figures include men, women, boys, girls, policemen, mythical characters, animals, cripples, nudes, and a variety of frequently encountered individuals. The examiner asks the patient to select a stimulus card, place figures on the background stimulus card, and tell a story explaining those choices. The examiner may also be asked to act out a story about the figures and their environment. The Location Sheet is used to record the placement of the figures on the stimulus card. Examiner required. Not suitable for group use.

Untimed: Varies

Scoring: Examiner evaluated

Cost: Kit (manual, 25 Location Sheets) $50.00

Publisher: Western Psychological Services

MANSON EVALUATION-REVISED
Refer to page 22.

MARTIN S-D INVENTORY
William T. Martin

Adolescent, adult

Purpose: Identifies persons with depressive and suicidal tendencies. Serves as a screening instrument for suicide prevention centers and mental health facilities. Also used for research on suicide and depression.

Description: 50–item paper-pencil inventory measuring behavioral and cognitive aspects related to depression and suicide. Subjects rate statements (both negative and positive) on a scale from 1 to 4 as they apply to their own beliefs and behavior. A total Adjusted Score is derived, with norms provided for normals, depressed persons, and psychiatric patients. Suggested cutoff scores are provided for persons considered depressed, moderately depressed, and significantly depressed. The inventory may be used in conjunction with the S-D Proneness Checklist. A pamphlet on suicide/depression also is available. Examiner required. Suitable for group use.

Untimed: 15 minutes

Scoring: Hand key; examiner evaluated

Cost: Specimen set $9.00; 25 tests $8.25; scoring templates $2.75; manual $6.75

Publisher: Psychologists and Educators, Inc.

MATHEMATICS ANXIETY RATING SCALE
Richard M. Suinn

Adolescent, adult

Purpose: Measures college students' anxieties regarding situations involving the use of mathematics. Used for screening and diagnostic purposes, research on mathematics anxiety, and as a means for developing anxiety hierarchies for desensitization therapy.

Description: 98–item paper-pencil test assessing the level of a student's mathematics anxiety. Test items refer to situations involving the use of mathematics. The student is asked to rate on a 5–point scale ranging from "not at all" to "very much" how anxious he is made by each situation. Norms are available for college students. Use is restricted to APA membership guidelines. Self-administered. Suitable for group use.

Untimed: 45 minutes

Scoring: Hand key

Cost: 100 scales $60.00

Publisher: Rocky Mountain Behavioral Science Institute, Inc.

MATHEMATICS ANXIETY RATING SCALE-A (MARS-A)
Refer to page 768.

MAUDSLEY PERSONALITY INVENTORY (MPI)
H. J. Eysenck

Adolescent, adult
Grades 10 and above

Purpose: Measures the personality dimensions of extraversion-introversion and neuroticism-stability in high-school and college students and adults. Used for industrial and educational prediction and screening, clinical evaluation, and research.

Description: 48–item paper-pencil checklist measuring two pervasive and independent dimensions of personality: extraversion-introversion (24 items) and neuroticism-stability (24 items). Test items are selected on the basis of item and factor analyses. Scores are provided for E-Extraversion and N-Neuroticism. College norms are presented in percentiles and stanines. Norms for many clinical and

occupational subgroups are included. Examiner required. Suitable for group use.

Untimed: 10–15 minutes

Scoring: Hand key

Cost: Specimen set (manual, all forms) $5.50; 25 inventories $7.00; keys $4.25; manual $2.75

Publisher: EdITS/Educational and Industrial Testing Service

MEASURE OF ACHIEVING TENDENCY
Albert Mehrabian

Adult

Purpose: Assesses an individual's motivation to achieve. Used for research, counseling, and employee selection and placement purposes.

Description: Multiple-item verbal questionnaire assessing all major components of achievement. Test items are based on extensive factor-analytic investigation of most experimentally identified components of achievement. Examiner required. Suitable for group use.

Untimed: 15 minutes

Scoring: Examiner evaluated

Cost: Test kit (scales, scoring directions, norms, test manual) $28.00

Publisher: Albert Mehrabian

MEASURE OF AROUSAL SEEKING TENDENCY
Albert Mehrabian

Adult

Purpose: Assesses an individual's desire for change, stimulation, and arousal. Used for research, job placement, and counseling purposes.

Description: Multiple-item verbal questionnaire measuring an individual's arousal-seeking tendencies. Test items are based on extensive factor-analytic and experimental studies of all aspects of change-seeking, sensation-seeking, and variety-seeking and, generally, on desire to master high-uncertainty situations. Examiner required. Suitable for group use.

Untimed: 15 minutes

Scoring: Examiner evaluated

Cost: Test kit (scale, scoring directions, norms, descriptive material) $20.00

Publisher: Albert Mehrabian

MEASURE OF DOMINANCE-SUBMISSIVENESS
Albert Mehrabian and Melissa Hines

Adult

Purpose: Measures aspects of dominance and submissiveness in an individual's personality. Used for research, counseling, job placement purposes, and matching of co-workers.

Description: Multiple-item verbal questionnaire assessing personality characteristics related to dominance and submissiveness. Test items are based on extensive factor-analytic and experimental studies on aspects of dominance (controlling, taking charge) versus submissiveness characteristics. This measure has been shown to be a basic component of many important personality attributes such as extroversion, dependency, anxiety, or depression. Examiner required. Suitable for group use.

Untimed: 15 minutes

Scoring: Examiner evaluated

Cost: Test kit (scale, scoring directions, norms, descriptive material) $20.00

Publisher: Albert Mehrabian

MEASURE OF STIMULUS SCREENING (CONVERSE OF AROUSABILITY)
Albert Mehrabian

Adult

Purpose: Measures major components of arousability and stimulus screening. Used for research, counseling, and job placement purposes.

Description: Multiple-item verbal questionnaire assessing the extent of an individual's arousal response to complex, unexpected, or unfamiliar situations. The test items are based on extensive factor-analytic and experimental investigations of all major components of arousability

and stimulus screening. Stimulus screening/arousability has been shown to be a major component of many important emotional characteristics, such as anxiety, neuroticism, extroversion, or hostility. Examiner required. Suitable for group use.

Untimed: 15 minutes

Scoring: Examiner evaluated

Cost: Test kit (scales, scoring directions, norms, descriptive material) $20.00

Publisher: Albert Mehrabian

MEASURES OF AFFILIATIVE TENDENCY AND SENSITIVITY TO REJECTION
Albert Mehrabian

Adult

Purpose: Assesses an individual's interpersonal and social approach-avoidance characteristics. Used for research and counseling purposes.

Description: Multiple-item verbal questionnaire consisting of two subscales: affiliative tendency and sensitivity to rejection. The standardized sum of the scores on both subscales also provides a measure of dependency. Examiner required. Suitable for group use.

Untimed: 10 minutes per scale

Scoring: Examiner evaluated

Cost: Test kit (scales, scoring directions, norms, descriptive material) $20.00

Publisher: Albert Mehrabian

MEASURES OF PSYCHOSOCIAL DEVELOPMENT (MPD)
Gwen A. Hawley

Adolescent, adult—Ages 13 and older

Purpose: Provides an index of overall psychosocial health and personality development through the eight stages of the life span based on Erik Erikson's criteria.

Description: 112–item paper-pencil multiple-choice test measuring the positive and negative attitudes or attributes of personality associated with each developmental stage, the status of conflict resolution at each stage, and overall psychosocial health. The items are rated on a 5–point scale ranging from "very much like me" to "not at all like me." Results are reported as T-scores or percentiles and can be plotted on profile forms that are available separately for males and females by age groups from 13 to over 50. Rather than a pathology-oriented focus, interpretation of the MPD is consistent with Erikson's focus on healthy personality development and growth. A sixth-grade reading level is required. Examiner must meet APA guidelines. Examiner required. Suitable for group use.

Untimed: 15–20 minutes

Scoring: Hand key

Cost: Kit (manual, 25 reusable item booklets, 50 answer sheets, 25 male and 25 female profile forms) $49.95

Publisher: Psychological Assessment Resources, Inc.

MENSTRUAL DISTRESS QUESTIONNAIRE (MDQ)
Rudolf H. Moos

Adolescent, adult—Ages 13 and older

Purpose: Assesses the characteristics of a woman's menstrual cycle in order to diagnose and treat premenstrual symptoms.

Description: Multiple-item paper-pencil or computer-administered questionnaire assessing the examinee on eight characteristics (pain, concentration, behavior change, autonomic reactions, water retention, negative affect, arousal, and control) during each of three phases of the menstrual cycle: premenstrual, menstrual, and intermenstrual. A diskette for administration, scoring, and interpretation on IBM PC and compatible systems is available. The paper-pencil version provides mail-in answer sheets. Self-administered. Suitable for group use.

Untimed: Not available

Scoring: Computer scored

Cost: $80.00

Publisher: Western Psychological Services

MENTAL STATUS CHECKLIST— ADULT
John A. Schinka

Adult

Purpose: Surveys the mental status of adults. Used to identify problems and establish rapport in order to prepare individuals for further diagnostic testing. Also provides written documentation of presenting problems.

Description: 120–item paper-pencil or computer-administered checklist covering presenting problems, referral data, demographics, mental status, personality function and symptoms, diagnosis, and disposition. The computer version operates on IBM PC systems with 256K and two floppy disk drives. The checklist is a component of the Clinical Checklist Series. Self-administered. Suitable for group use.

Untimed: 10–20 minutes

Scoring: Examiner evaluated

Cost: 25 checklists $23.95; computer version (unlimited use, 25 booklets) $295.00

Publisher: Psychological Assessment Resources, Inc.

MILLON ADOLESCENT PERSONALITY INVENTORY (MAPI)
Theodore Millon, Catherine J. Green, and Robert B. Meagher, Jr.

Adolescent— Ages 13–18

Purpose: Evaluates adolescent personality. Used as an aid to clinical assessment and academic and vocational guidance. Identifies student behavioral and emotional problems.

Description: 150–item paper-pencil true-false test covering eight personality style scales, eight expressed concern scales (such as peer security), and four behavioral correlates scales (such as impulse control). The clinical version is coordinated with DSM-III-R and is available to those with experience in the use of self-administered clinical tests. The test may be computer scored in three ways: via mail-in services, Arion II teleprocessing,

---

personality: adolescent and adult

psychology **193**

or PC-based MICROTEST™ Assessment system. Self-administered. Suitable for group use.

Untimed: 20–30 minutes

Scoring: Computer scored

Cost: Manual $17.50; clinical interpretive report $14.55–$19.90 depending on quantity and scoring method; guidance interpretive report $6.10–$9.95 depending on quantity and scoring method

Publisher: National Computer Systems/PAS Division

MILLON BEHAVIORAL HEALTH INVENTORY (MBHI)
Theodore Millon, Catherine J. Green, and Robert B. Meagher, Jr.

Adult—Ages 18 and older

Purpose: Assesses attitudes of physically ill adults toward daily stress factors and health care personnel. Used for clinical evaluation of possible psychosomatic complications.

Description: 150–item paper-pencil true-false inventory covering eight basic coping styles (e.g., cooperation), six psychogenic attitudes (e.g., chronic tension), three psychosomatic correlatives (e.g., allergic inclinations), and three prognostic indexes (e.g., pain treatment responsivity). The test is designed for use with medical patients by examiners experienced in the use of clinical instruments. May be computer-scored in one of three ways: via mail-in services, Arion II teleprocessing, or PC-based MICROTEST™ Assessment system. Self-administered. Suitable for group use.

Untimed: 20 minutes

Scoring: Computer scored by NCS

Cost: Manual $16.50; interpretive report $12.95–$18.15 depending on quantity and scoring method

Publisher: National Computer Systems/PAS Division

MILLON CLINICAL MULTIAXIAL INVENTORY (MCMI)
Theodore Millon

Adult—Ages 18 and older

Purpose: Diagnoses emotionally disturbed adults. Used to screen individuals who may require more intensive clinical evaluation and treatment.

Description: 175–item paper-pencil true-false test evaluating adults who have psychological or psychiatric difficulties. The test covers three categories that include eight basic personality patterns (DSM-III, Axis II) reflecting a patient's lifelong traits existing prior to the behavioral dysfunctions; three pathological personality disorders (DSM-III, Axis II) reflecting chronic or severe abnormalities, and nine clinical symptom syndromes (DSM-III, Axis I) describing episodes or states in which active pathological processes are clearly evidenced. This instrument is intended for use only with psychiatric-emotionally disturbed populations. The examiner must be experienced in the use of clinical tests. Interpretation is available exclusively from NCS, and test results are available immediately via Arion II teleprocessing or PC-based MICROTEST™ Assessment system. Mail-in computer scoring services also are provided. Self-administered. Suitable for group use.

Untimed: 25 minutes

Scoring: Computer scored; may be hand scored

Cost: Manual $21.00; interpretive report $21.25–$28.35 depending on quantity and scoring method; profile report $5.75–$8.00 depending on quantity and scoring method

Publisher: National Computer Systems/PAS Division

MILLON CLINICAL MULTIAXIAL INVENTORY-II (MCMI-II)
Theodore Millon

Adult—Ages 18 and older

Purpose: Diagnoses adults with personality disorders. Used in private or group practice, mental health centers, outpatient clinics, and general and psychiatric hospitals and clinics with individuals in assessment or treatment programs.

Description: 175–item paper-pencil true-false test evaluating adults with emotional or interpersonal problems. The revised version of the MCMI contains 25 scales measuring both the state and the trait features of personality. The Clinical Personality Pattern scales are Schizoid, Avoidant, Dependent, Histrionic, Narcissistic, Antisocial, Aggressive/Sadistic, Compulsive, Passive/Aggressive, and Self-defeating. There are three Modifier Indices—Disclosure, Desirability, and Debasement—and three Severe Pathology scales—Schizotypal, Borderline, and Paranoid. The Clinical Syndrome scales are Anxiety Disorder, Somatoform Disorder, Hypomanic Disorder, Dysthymic Disorder, Alcohol Dependence, and Drug Dependence. There are three Severe Syndrome Scales: Thought Disorder, Major Depression, and Delusional Disorder. A validity index is included also. The new edition is intended to reflect proposed DSM-III-R diagnoses changes. Of the 175 items in the revised edition, 45 are new or reworded. In addition, the MCMI-II features a new scoring method and a revised interpretive report. Computer scored in one of three ways: via mail-in services, Arion II teleprocessing, or PC-based MICROTEST™ assessment system. Self-administered. Suitable for group use.

Untimed: 20–30 minutes

Scoring: Computer scored

Cost: Manual $21.00; interpretive report $21.25–$28.35 depending on quantity and scoring method; profile report $5.75–$8.00 depending on quantity and scoring method

Publisher: National Computer Systems/PAS Division

THE MINER SENTENCE COMPLETION SCALE: FORM H
Refer to page 1011.

THE MINER SENTENCE COMPLETION SCALE: FORM P
Refer to page 1012.

THE MINER SENTENCE COMPLETION SCALE: FORM T
Refer to page 1012.

THE MINNESOTA MULTIPHASIC PERSONALITY INVENTORY: NEW GROUP FORM (FORM R)
Starke R. Hathaway and Charnley McKinley

Adolescent, adult—Ages 16 and older

Purpose: Assesses individual personality. Used for clinical diagnosis and research on psychopathology.

Description: 566–item true-false test of 10 clinical variables or factors of personality: hypochondriasis, depression, hysteria, psychopathic-deviate, masculinity-femininity, paranoia, psychasthenia, schizophrenia, hypomania, and social introversion. Scores are also obtained on four validity scales: Question, Lie (L), Validity (F), and Defensiveness (K). Items required for these 14 basic scores are grouped as items 1–399. Items used only in research are presented as items 400–566. Materials include a hardcover question booklet with step-down pages. Individual and Old Group Forms also are available. Personality scores are plotted on a profile sheet reflecting standard deviations from the mean. Self-administered. Suitable for group use. Available in 45 languages.

Untimed: 45–90 minutes

Scoring: Hand key; examiner evaluated; may be computer scored

Cost: Test booklet $7.75; 25 answer sheets $5.00; 25 answer keys (includes manual) $12.50

Publisher: University of Minnesota Press; distributed exclusively by National Computer Systems/PAS Division

---

THE MINNESOTA MULTIPHASIC PERSONALITY INVENTORY: OLD GROUP FORM
Starke R. Hathaway and Charnley McKinley

Adolescent, adult—Ages 16 and older

Purpose: Assesses individual personality. Used for clinical diagnosis and research on psychopathology and mental health.

Description: 556–item true-false test of 10 clinical variables or factors of personality: hypochondriasis, depression, hysteria, psychopathic-deviate, masculinity-femininity, paranoia, psychasthenia, schizophrenia, hypomania, and social introversion. Scores also are obtained on four validity scales: Question, Lie (L), Validity (F), and Defensiveness (K). Subjects respond to items on a separate answer sheet. Individual and New Group Forms also are available. Personality scores are plotted on a profile sheet reflecting standard deviations from the mean. Self-administered. Suitable for group use. Available in 45 languages.

Untimed: 45–90 minutes

Scoring: Hand key; examiner evaluated; may be computer scored

Cost: 10 test booklets $6.00; 25 machine-scored answer sheets $5.00; 25 hand-scored answer sheets $3.40; hand-scored answer keys $3.40; 25 case summary and profile forms $3.20; tape recorded version of MMPI $38.00

Publisher: University of Minnesota Press; distributed exclusively by National Computer Systems/PAS Division

THE MINNESOTA MULTIPHASIC PERSONALITY INVENTORY: THE INDIVIDUAL FORM (MMPI)
Starke R. Hathaway and Charnley McKinley

Adolescent, adult—Ages 16 and older

Purpose: Assesses individual personality. Used for clinical diagnosis and research on psychopathology.

Description: 550–item true-false test of 10 clinical variables or factors of personality: hypochondriasis, depression, hysteria, psychopathic-deviate, masculinity-femininity, paranoia, psychasthenia, schizophrenia, hypomania, and social introversion. Scores also are obtained on four validity scales: Question, Lie (L), Validity (F), and Defensiveness (K). Materials include 550 cards to which the individual responds. Personality scores are plotted on a profile sheet reflecting standard deviations from

the mean. Old and New Group Forms are also available. Examiner required. Not suitable for group use. Available in 45 languages.

Untimed: 1 hour, 30 minutes

Scoring: Hand key; examiner evaluated; may be computer scored

Cost: 25 recording sheets $5.00; item cards $54.00; answer keys (includes manual) $18.00

Publisher: University of Minnesota Press; distributed exclusively by National Computer Systems/PAS Division

MISKIMINS SELF-GOAL-OTHER DISCREPANCY SCALE (MSGO-I & MSGO-II)
R. W. Miskimins

Adolescent, adult

Purpose: Measures a person's self-concept in terms of self-perception, self-goals, and others' perception of self. Used for clinical diagnosis and research.

Description: Paper-pencil test assessing social, emotional, and general aspects of a person's self-concept. The test is available in two forms. MSGO—I contains 15 items and five blank items in which the subject or examiner can insert his or her own dimensions. MSGO—II contains 12 items and four blank items presented in a simplified format and worded for use with younger people, seriously debilitated individuals, or the educationally handicapped. The two forms differ slightly in item content and administration but use the same rating procedure and yield nearly identical results. For each test item, the subject rates himself or herself three times on a scale consisting of bipolar adjectives separated by a 9–point Likert scale. When scores for all items have been combined, it is possible to determine discrepancies between "Self" and "Goal" and between "Self" and "Others." A greater discrepancy indicates a lower self-concept. A profile of each subject's responses can be drawn, and interpretative data are available for the most common types of profiles. In addition, the MSGO-I yields 28 subscores (19 of which significantly distinguish between normal and psychiatric populations), and the MSGO-

II yields seven subscores. Use is restricted to APA membership guidelines. Examiner required. Suitable for group use.

Untimed: 15–20 minutes

Scoring: Hand key; may be computer scored

Cost: 100 scales and profiles (specify form) $50.00; manual $15.00

Publisher: Rocky Mountain Behavioral Science Institute, Inc.

MOONEY PROBLEM CHECKLIST
R.L. Mooney and L. V. Gordon

Adolescent, adult
Grades 7 and above

Purpose: Identifies individuals who want or need help with personal problems. Used for individual counseling, increasing teacher understanding of students, and preparing students for counseling interviews.

Description: Multiple-item paper-pencil self-assessment of personal problems. The subjects read examples of problems, underline those of "some concern," circle those of "most concern," and write a summary in their own words. The areas covered vary from form to form but include health and physical development, home and family, boy and girl relations, morals and religion, courtship and marriage, economic security, school or occupation, and social and recreational. Materials include separate checklists for junior-high students, high-school students, college students, and adults. Self-administered. Suitable for group use.

Untimed: 30 minutes

Scoring: Hand key; may be machine scored

Cost: Examiner's kit (materials without separate answer documents, junior high, high school, college, adult) $5.00; examiner kit (separate answer documents, junior high, high school, college) $9.00; both kits include checklist and manual

Publisher: The Psychological Corporation

Information and availability unconfirmed; last verified in 1988.

MULTIDIMENSIONAL SELF-ESTEEM INVENTORY (MSEI)
Edward J. O'Brien and Seymour Epstein

College age students

Purpose: Assesses global self-esteem and its components. Used to evaluate job dissatisfaction, eating disorders, anxiety/depression, and treatment intake/outcome.

Description: 116–item paper-pencil multiple-choice test that measures global self-esteem and eight components of self-esteem: Competence, Lovability, Likability, Personal Power, Self-Control, Moral Self-Approval, Body Appearance, and Body Functioning. The MSEI uses a 5–point response format, reporting results as T-scores and percentiles. A tenth-grade reading level is required. Examiner must meet APA guidelines. Examiner required. Suitable for group use.

Untimed: 15–30 minutes

Scoring: Hand key

Cost: Kit (manual, 25 test booklets, 25 rating forms, 25 profile forms) $38.00

Publisher: Psychological Assessment Resources, Inc.

MULTIMODAL LIFE HISTORY QUESTIONNAIRE
Arnold A. Lazarus

Adult

Purpose: Provides information on personal and social history of adults for clinical assessment, marriage and family counseling, and psychotherapy.

Description: 12–page paper-pencil questionnaire assessing client's behavior, feelings, physical sensations, images, thoughts, interpersonal relationships, and biological factors. The client completes the questionnaire during his own time rather than during the counseling session. The therapist assesses information to design a treatment program. Self-administered. Suitable for group use.

Untimed: 2 hours

Scoring: Examiner evaluated

Cost: 20 questionnaires $16.00

Publisher: Multimodal Publications, Inc.

MULTIPHASIC SEX INVENTORY
H.R. Nichols and Ilene Molinder

Adolescent, adult

Purpose: Measures the sexual characteristics of adolescent and adult male sexual offenders. Used to evaluate sexual deviance and assess progress in the treatment of sexual deviance.

Description: 300–item paper-pencil true-false test of psychosexual characteristics from which 20 scales and a 50–item sexual history are derived. Six of the 20 scales are validity scales. The inventory also contains a Treatment Attitudes Scale. The sex deviance scales include the Child Molest Scale, Rape Scale, and Exhibitionism Scale. There are five atypical sexual outlet scales: Fetish, Voyeurism, Obscene Call, Bondage and Discipline, and Sado-Masochism. The four sexual dysfunction scales include the Sexual Inadequacy Scale, Premature Ejaculation Scale, Impotence Scale, and Physical Disabilities Scale. There is also a Sexual Knowledge and Beliefs Scale. The 50–item Sexual History Scale includes a sex deviance development section, marriage development section, gender identity section, gender orientation development section, and a sexual assault behavior section. Scores are yielded for all 20 scales and are recorded on the profile form. Two forms are available: Adult Male (Form A) and Juvenile Male (Form J). An eighth-grade reading level is required; however, a taped version of the test is available for use by reading-impaired persons. Examiner/self-administered. Suitable for group use. Available in Spanish.

Untimed: 45 minutes

Scoring: Hand key

Cost: Complete kit (manual, 5 test booklets, 25 answer sheets, 25 profile forms, set of 14 scoring templates) $35.00; shipping and handling $3.50

Publisher: Nichols and Molinder

MULTIPLE AFFECT ADJECTIVE CHECK LIST (MAACL)
Marvin Zuckerman and Bernard Lubin

Adolescent, adult
Grades 10 and above

Purpose: Measures anxiety, depression, and hostility in high-school and college students and adults. Used for clinical evaluation and research application.

Description: 132–item paper-pencil inventory measuring affects of Anxiety (A), Depression (D), and Hostility (H). The inventory may be administered under two different test sets, In General and Today Now. The Today form measures current affect states and requires examinees to check the adjectives that describe how they feel at the time of testing. The In General form instructs subjects to check those adjectives which describe a more general state of their feelings. The Today form is sensitive to changes in affect resulting from examination anxiety among college students, perceptual isolation, therapy sessions, combat training, and intake of alcohol. College student and adult job applicant norms are presented in the form of T-score equivalents. Means and standard deviations are presented for a variety of clinical groups and experimental situations. The new MAACL-R contains trait and state forms that have been shown to differentiate patients with affective disorders from other types of patients and normals. The MAACL-R may be used in studies of stress and stress reduction, diagnosis and treatment of psychological disorders, and in basic research on personality and emotions. Scales on the MAACL-R are Anxiety (A), Depression (D), Hostility (H), Positive Affect (PA), and Sensation Seeking (SS). The two summary scores are Dysphoria (A + D + H) and Positive Affect and Sensation Seeking (PA + SS). Examiner/self-administered. Suitable for group use.

Untimed: 5 minutes per form

Scoring: Hand key; may be computer scored

Cost: Specimen Set $5.75
Publisher: EdITS/Educational and Industrial Testing Service

THE MULTIPLE AFFECT ADJECTIVE CHECK LIST— REVISED (MAACL-R)
Marvin Zuckerman and Bernard Lubin

Adolescent, adult
Grades 10 and above

Purpose: Measures positive and negative affects as both traits and states. Used in studies of stress and stress reduction, diagnosis and treatment of psychological disorders, and in basic research on personality and emotions.

Description: Multiple-item paper-pencil inventory measuring the affects of Anxiety (A), Depression (D), Hostility (H), Positive Affect (PA), and Sensation Seeking (SS). This revised edition contains trait and state forms that have been shown to differentiate patients with affective disorders from other types of patients and normals. The test yields two summary scores: Dysphoria $(A+D+H)$ and Positive Affect and Sensation Seeking $(PA+SS)$. Examiner/self-administered. Suitable for group use.

Untimed: 5 minutes per form
Scoring: Hand key; may be computer scored
Cost: Specimen set $5.50
Publisher: EdITS/Educational and Industrial Testing Service

MULTISCORE DEPRESSION INVENTORY FOR ADOLESCENTS AND ADULTS (MDI)
David J. Berndt

Adolescent, adult—Ages 13 and older

Purpose: Measures the severity and specific aspects of depression and detects subtle variations in mild forms of depression. Used with normal individuals.

Description: 118–item paper-pencil or computer-administered true-false questionnaire containing 10 subscales: Low Energy Level, Cognitive Difficulty, Guilt,

Low Self-Esteem, Social Introversion, Pessimism, Irritability, Sad Mood, Instrumental Helplessness, and Learned Helplessness. An interpretive report that provides a general score as well as scores for each subscale is available. In addition, one section of the report indicates the probability that the examinee is a depressed, conduct disordered, psychotic, suicidal, bulimic, anorexic, or nondepressed individual; an individual with a mixed diagnoses; an individual with endogenous depression; or a chronic pain sufferer. The computer version, which is designed for use on IBM PC, XT, or AT systems with 128K, offers on-line scoring that generates the interpretive report; a mail-in scoring service that yields the report is available for the paper-pencil version. A short form consisting of the first 47 items of the full-length inventory and nine of the subscales is available. Self-administered. Suitable for group use.

Untimed: 20 minutes
Scoring: Paper-pencil version, hand key or scoring service; computer version, computer scored
Cost: Paper-pencil version (manual, 100 profile forms, 100 hand-scored answer sheets, 1 set of scoring keys, 2 prepaid WPS TEST REPORT: MDI answer sheets) $80.00; diskette for administration, scoring, and interpretation (25 uses) $185.00; MDI answer sheet $9.25
Publisher: Western Psychological Services

MYERS-BRIGGS TYPE INDICATOR (MBTI)
Isabel Briggs Myers and Katharine C. Briggs

Adolescent, adult—
Ages 12–adult

Purpose: Measures personality dispositions and interests based on Jung's theory of types. Used in personal, vocational, and marital counseling, executive development programs, educational settings, and personality research.

Description: 126–item (Form G) to 166–item (Form F) paper-pencil or computer-administered test of four bipolar aspects of personality: Introversion-Extraversion, Sensing-Intuition, Thinking-Feeling, and Judging-Perceptive. The subjects are classified as one of two "types" on each scale. Results for the four scales may be expressed as continuous scores or reduced to a 4–letter code or "type." Report forms containing a profile sheet with a brief interpretation of the scores and a chart explanation of each of the 16 MBTI types are available.

The test has applications in four major settings: organizations (identification of leadership style, improvement of teamwork, improvement of communication, promotion of management development, career development, and conflict resolution), counseling (parent, child, and couple), education (development of teaching methods, understanding motivation for learning and individual learning styles, curriculum analysis), career guidance (choosing of school major, profession, occupation, work setting).

The test is heavily influenced by Jungian theories of personality types and the ways in which these types express their personality traits through perceptions, judgments, interests, values, and motivations. A theoretical background in dynamic psychology is helpful in maximizing the benefits of research compiled for this test. Materials include Form F (166 items) and Form G (126 items), which eliminates 40 items not scored on the Form F preference scales and changes a few item weights on the Thinking-Feeling dimension. A software package containing a diskette, user's guide, and carrying case is available for use with the IBM PC and IBM-compatible personal computers. Self-administered. Suitable for group use.

Untimed: 20–30 minutes

Scoring: Hand key; scoring service available; may be computer scored

Cost: Manual $24.00; 50 individual report forms $6.00; *Introduction to Type* $2.00; 25 question booklets (specify Form F or G) $12.00; 50 answer sheets (specify form) $8.50; 10 Spanish Form G test booklets $20.00; 25 Spanish Individual Report Forms $12.00

Publisher: Consulting Psychologists Press, Inc.

MYERS-BRIGGS TYPE INDICATOR FORM G, SELF-SCORABLE EDITION
Katharine C. Briggs and Isabel Briggs Myers

Adult

Purpose: Measures personality dispositions and interests based on Jung's theory of types. Used for personal, marital, and vocational counseling, especially in workshops, seminars, or other settings, where immediate feedback is needed or time restraints are important.

Description: 94–item paper-pencil self-report inventory assessing personality type along four bipolar scales: introversion-extroversion, sensing-intuition, thinking-feeling, and judging-perceptive. The test booklet presents instructions for administration and the test items. Answers are marked in a separate answer booklet. As examinees mark answers on the first page of the booklet, their responses automatically transfer to the second page, which contains item weights and scoring directions. After the responses are scored, respondents transfer their type code to the Report booklet, which contains a brief introduction to type, definitions of the eight preferences, effects of the preferences in work settings, brief descriptions of the 16 types, a section on type verification, and a checklist of things to remember about type. This self-scorable edition replaces the original MBTI Abbreviated Version. Self-administered. Suitable for group use.

Untimed: 20 minutes

Scoring: Self-scored

Cost: 25 test booklets $10.50; 50 answer sheets $22.50; 25 report booklets $16.00; sampler (test booklet, answer sheet, report booklet) $2.00

Publisher: Consulting Psychologists Press, Inc.

NEO-FIVE FACTOR INVENTORY (NEO-FFI)
Paul T. Costa, Jr. and Robert R. McCrae

Adult—Ages 19–93

Purpose: Assesses the five major personality domains. Used in clinical psychology, psychiatry, behavioral medicine, vocational counseling, and industrial psychology.

Description: 60–item paper-pencil multiple-choice test providing a general description of an adult's personality. The NEO-FFI is a shortened version of the NEO Personality Inventory. Domains assessed are Neuroticism (N), Extraversion (E), Openness to Experience (O), Agreeableness (A), and Conscientiousness (C). The NEO-FFI is based on NEO-PI normative data and is interpreted in the same manner. Examiner must meet APA guidelines. Examiner required. Suitable for group use.

Untimed: Varies

Scoring: Hand key

Cost: NEO-FFI Kit (manual, manual supplement, 25 Form S test booklets, 25 summary feedback sheets) $49.00

Publisher: Psychological Assessment Resources, Inc.

NEO PERSONALITY INVENTORY (NEO-PI)
Paul T. Costa, Jr. and Robert R. McCrae

Adult

Purpose: Measures five major personality domains of adults. Used in clinical psychology, psychiatry, behavioral medicine, vocational counseling, and industrial psychology.

Description: 181–item paper-pencil test providing a general description of an adult's personality. Domains assessed are Neuroticism (N), Extraversion (E), Openness to Experience (O), Agreeableness (A), and Conscientiousness (C). Facet scales for the N, E, and O domains yield a more detailed analysis of personality structure. Domain N scales are Anxiety, Hostility, Depression, Self-Consciousness, Impulsiveness, and Vulnerability. Domain E scales are Warmth, Gregariousness, Assertiveness, Activity, Excitement-Seeking, and Positive Emotions. Domain O scales are Fantasy, Aesthetics, Feelings, Actions, Ideas, and Values. Two versions of the inventory are available. Form S,

appropriate for men and women, is self-administered. Answers are provided on a 5–point scale. Form R is written for observer ratings by a peer, spouse, or professional. A computer version is available. A scoring service is available from the publisher. Examiner/self-administered. Suitable for group use.

Untimed: 30 minutes

Scoring: Hand key; may be computer scored

Cost: Professional kit (manual, scoring keys, 10 reusable test booklets-Form S, 25 profile forms-Form S, 25 answer sheets) $42.00; computer version (50 uses) $195.00

Publisher: Psychological Assessment Resources, Inc.

NEUROTICISM SCALE QUESTIONNAIRE (NSQ)
Raymond B. Cattell and Ivan H. Scheier

Adolescent, adult
Grades 10 and above

Purpose: Measures neuroticism in senior high-school students and adults of most educational levels. Used for clinical evaluation, personal counseling, and research on neuroticism.

Description: 40–item paper-pencil questionnaire measuring degree of "neurotic trend" in adults and adolescents. Standard scores are provided for men, women, and men and women together. A sixth-grade reading level is required. Self-administered. Suitable for group use.

Untimed: 10 minutes

Scoring: Hand key

Cost: Testing kit $11.25; handbook $7.50; 25 test booklets $8.50; scoring key $3.25

Publisher: Institute for Personality and Ability Testing, Inc.

NURSES' OBSERVATION SCALE FOR INPATIENT EVALUATION (NOSIE-30)
Gilbert Honigfeld, Roderic D. Gillis, and C. James Klett

Adult

Purpose: Assesses the ward behavior of psychiatric inpatients. Used by nursing personnel to evaluate patient status and change.

Description: 30–item paper-pencil observational inventory assessing inpatient psychiatric behavior. Measures six factors: social competence (refuses to do the ordinary things expected of him; has trouble remembering), social interest (shows interest in the activities around him; tries to be friendly to others), personal neatness (keeps his clothes neat; is messy in his eating habits), irritability (gets angry or annoyed easily; is irritable and grouchy), manifests psychosis (hears things that are not there; talks, mutters, or mumbles to himself), and retardation (sits, unless directed into activity; is slow and sluggish). A global score, Total Patient Assets, is also calculated as a composite of the six factor scores. Scale items consist of statements about the patient's ward behavior and are rated on a 5–point scale from 0 (never) to 4 (always). Factor scores are based on two raters' combined scores in which each item receives unit weight. Profile forms convert raw scores to T-scores or centile ranks for normative comparison. Examiner required. Not suitable for group use.

Untimed: Varies

Scoring: Examiner evaluated

Cost: Contact publisher

Publisher: Behavior Arts Center

OBJECT RELATIONS TECHNIQUE
H. Phillipson

Adolescent, adult

Purpose: Assesses interpersonal relations. Used for individual therapy and counseling.

Description: 12–item projective test of interpersonal relations. Items are cards presenting important interpersonal situations in varying environmental and emotional contexts. The subject creates a story about each picture. Evaluation of the responses is based on object relations theory in psychoanalysis. Examiner required. Not suitable for group use.
BRITISH PUBLISHER

Untimed: 1 hour

Scoring: Examiner evaluated

Cost: Contact publisher

Publisher: NFER-NELSON Publishing Company Ltd.

OBJECTIVE ANALYTIC BATTERIES (O-A)
Raymond B. Cattell and James M. Schueiger

Adolescent, adult—Ages 14 and older

Purpose: Evaluates personality in adults and adolescents. Used for clinical evaluations, research on personality source traits, and personal counseling.

Description: 10 paper-pencil tests providing an objective measure of 10 personality source traits: ego strength, anxiety, independence, extraversion, regression, control, cortertia, depression, and others. The batteries are arranged in a kit, from which tests for half an hour, an hour, two hours, and so forth, may be scheduled, according to purpose and testing time. The handbook for the O-A Kit combines practical tests with broad developments in psychometry (defining validity, reliability, function fluctuation, state-trait differences) and in personality theory concerning the source-trait structures and their mode of interaction. The handbook is designed explicitly as supportive reading and realistic illustration for courses on personality theory. Norms are calculated directly for each of the 10 factors; the norm base covers ages 14–30 years; age trends are included for other situations. Examiner required. Suitable for group use.

Untimed: 30 minutes

Scoring: Hand key

Cost: Professional testing kit $139.25; handbook $53.50; test kit $40.50; 10 expendable booklets (OA359) $10.40; (OA360) $8.25; (OA361) $10.40; 25 answer sheets (OA362) $8.25; score summary sheets for handscoring available from IPAT

Publisher: Institute for Personality and Ability Testing, Inc.

OETTING'S COMPUTER ANXIETY SCALE (COMPAS)
Refer to page 770.

THE OFFER PARENT-ADOLESCENT QUESTIONNAIRE (OPAQ)
Daniel Offer, Eric Ostrov, and Kenneth I. Howard

Parents

Purpose: Measures parents' perceptions of their adolescent's self-image and provides a measure of communication among members of an adolescent's family.

Description: 50–item paper-pencil test of 11 areas of self-image: impulse control, emotional tone, body and self-image, social relationships, sexual attitudes, family attitudes, mastery of the external world, vocational and educational goals, emotional health, superior adjustment, and idealism. The test items require the parent to choose among six choices presented in a Likert-scale format and mark the appropriate space in the test booklet or on the answer sheet. The OPAQ usually is used in conjunction with the Offer Self-Image Questionnaire (OSIQ) for Adolescents. Alternate forms are available for sons and daughters. Self-administered. Suitable for group use.

Untimed: 10–15 minutes

Scoring: Computer scored

Cost: Questionnaire $2.00; answer sheet $0.25; computer analysis $10.00 base fee and $2.00 per subject

Publisher: Center for the Study of Adolescence, Michael Reese Hospital

THE OFFER SELF-IMAGE QUESTIONNAIRE (OSIQ) FOR ADOLESCENTS
Daniel Offer

Adolescent—Ages 13–19

Purpose: Assesses teenagers' self-image and personality adjustment. Used as an aid to clinical counseling and research.

Description: 130–item paper-pencil or computer-administered test evaluating 11 categories of adolescent self-image: psychological self, social self, sexual self, familial self, and coping self. Items are responded to on a 6–point scale ranging from "describes me very well" to "does not describe me at all." The test is standard scored. A low standard score indicates that the taker is poorly adjusted in the corresponding area of adjustment. A high score indicates good adjustment. Subjects read the front page of the booklet and provide the requested personal information, asking questions of the examiner if necessary. Software is available for computer administration and scoring. Reliability and validity data are available. Examiner required. Suitable for group use.

Untimed: 40 minutes

Scoring: Examiner evaluated; may be computer scored

Cost: Manual $25.00; M/F questionnaire $2.00 each; answer sheet $0.25; sample kit (includes reprints, etc.) $35.00; scoring service per questionnaire $2.00, plus $10.00 base fee

Publisher: Center for the Study of Adolescence, Michael Reese Hospital

THE OFFER TEACHER-STUDENT QUESTIONNAIRE (OTSQ)
Daniel Offer

Teachers

Purpose: Measures teacher perceptions of an adolescent student's self-image and provides a measure of communication between teacher and adolescent.

Description: 50–item paper-pencil test of the following areas of self-image as rated by a teacher: impulse control, emotional tone, body and self-image, social relationships, sexual attitudes, family attitudes, mastery of the external world, vocational and educational goals, emotional health, superior adjustment, and idealism. The test items require the teacher to choose from among six choices presented in a Likert-scale format and mark the appropriate space in the test booklet or on an answer sheet. The OTSQ usually is used in conjunction with the Offer Self-Image Questionnaire (OSIQ) for Adolescents. Self-administered. Suitable for group use.

Untimed: 10–15 minutes

Scoring: Computer scored

Cost: Questionnaire $2.00; answer sheet $0.25; computer analysis $10.00 base fee and $2.00 per subject

Publisher: Center for the Study of Adolescence, Michael Reese Hospital

---

THE OFFER THERAPIST-ADOLESCENT QUESTIONNAIRE (OTAQ)
Daniel Offer, Eric Ostrov, and Kenneth I. Howard

Therapists

Purpose: Measures therapist perceptions of an adolescent client's self-image and provides a measure of communication between therapist and adolescent.

Description: 50–item paper-pencil test of the following areas of self-image as rated by a therapist: impulse control, emotional tone, body and self-image, social relationships, sexual attitudes, family attitudes, mastery of the external world, vocational and educational goals, emotional health, superior adjustment, and idealism. The test items require the therapist to choose from among six choices presented in a Likert-scale format and mark the appropriate space in the test booklet or on the answer sheet. The OTAQ usually is used in conjunction with the Offer Self-Image Questionnaire (OSIQ) for Adolescents. Self-administered. Suitable for group use.

Untimed: 10–15 minutes

Scoring: Computer scored

Cost: Questionnaire $2.00; answer sheet $0.25; computer analysis $10.00 base fee and $2.00 per subject

Publisher: Center for the Study of Adolescence, Michael Reese Hospital

---

OMNIBUS PERSONALITY INVENTORY (OPI)
Refer to page 770.

THE PERSONAL AUDIT
Refer to page 1017.

PERSONAL ORIENTATION DIMENSIONS (POD)
Everett L. Shostrom

Adult

Purpose: Measures attitudes and values in terms of concepts of the actualizing person, one who is more fully functioning and lives a more enriched life. Used to introduce humanistic value concepts, indicate a person's level of positive mental health, and measure the effects of various treatment and training techniques.

Description: 260–item paper-pencil two-choice test consisting of bipolar pairs of statements of comparative values and behavior judgments. The subject must choose from each pair the statement that is closest to his beliefs. Items are stated both negatively and positively; opposites are dictated not by word choice but by context. Test items are nonthreatening in order to facilitate communication of the results and provide a positive approach for measuring the following personality dimensions: orientation (time orientation and core centeredness), polarities (strength/weakness and love/anger), integration (synergistic integration and potentiation), and awareness (being, trust in humanity, creative living, mission, and manipulation awareness). Test results indicate whether (and to what degree) an individual is actualizing or non-actualizing. The inventory may be used as a component of the Actualizing Assessment Battery (AAB). Examiner required. Suitable for group use.

Untimed: 30–40 minutes

Scoring: Computer scored

Cost: Specimen set (manual, all forms) $5.75; 25 reusable test booklets $15.00; 50 NCS answer sheets $10.00; EdITS scoring $1.10

Publisher: EdITS/Educational and Industrial Testing Service

PERSONAL ORIENTATION INVENTORY (POI)
Everett L. Shostrom

**Adolescent, adult
Grades 10 and above**

Purpose: Measures values and behaviors important in the development of the actualizing person, one who is more fully functioning and lives a more enriched life. Used in counseling and group training sessions and as a pre- and posttherapy measure to indicate a person's level of positive mental health.

Description: 150–item paper-pencil two-choice test containing bipolar pairs of statements of comparative values and behavioral judgments. The subject must choose from each pair the statement that is closest to his beliefs. The inventory is scored for two major scales and 10 subscales: Time Ratio, Support Ratio, Self-Actualizing Value, Existentiality, Feeling Reactivity, Spontaneity, Self-Regard, Self-Acceptance, Nature of Man, Synergy, Acceptance of Aggression, and Capacity for Intimate Contact. College norms are presented in percentile scores. Adult mean scores and profiles are provided. Means, standard deviations, and plotted profiles are provided for clinically nominated self-actualized and non-self-actualized groups, as well as for many other clinical and industrial samples. The inventory may be used as a component of the Actualizing Assessment Battery (AAB). Examiner required. Suitable for group use.

Untimed: 30 minutes

Scoring: Hand key; may be computer scored

Cost: Specimen set (manual, all forms) $6.00; 25 reusable test booklets $15.00; 50 profile sheets $8.50; set of 14 hand-scoring stencils $29.50; handbook $15.75; manual $3.50

Publisher: EdITS/Educational and Industrial Testing Service

PERSONAL PREFERENCE SCALE
Maurice H. Krout and Johanna Krout

Adult

Purpose: Assesses aspects of personality that are usually available only through projective tests. Used for clinical evaluations, vocational guidance, and industrial placement. Provides drawing analysis and specific material on basic issues.

Description: 100–item paper-pencil multiple-choice test consisting of 10 subtests of 10 items each. The test items are drawn from everyday activities relating to a variety of early experiences. The subject rates each item on a 3–point scale according to personal likes and dislikes. The responses indicate important attitudes and personality traits derived from those early experiences. The factors measured include adventuresomeness vs. security-seeking, communicativeness vs. taciturnity, optimism vs. pessimism, altruism vs. punitivism, emotional lability vs. emotional rigidity, aspiration level, assertiveness level, sentimentality, and impersonal affiliativeness.

A guide for interpretation is available, but more sophisticated approaches in terms of personality development and structure will yield more valuable insights from the scores. In industrial applications, specific subtests have proven most valuable in discriminating between workers who were well-motivated and successful with certain operations and those who were poorly suited for such work. Self-administered. Suitable for group use.

Untimed: 20 minutes

Scoring: Hand key

Cost: Test $0.35 (free guide with each set of 50 purchased)

Publisher: Johanna Krout Tabin, Ph.D.

Information and availability unconfirmed; last verified in 1988.

PERSONAL PROBLEMS CHECKLIST—ADOLESCENT
John A. Schinka

Adolescent—Ages 13–17

Purpose: Assesses personal problems of adolescents. Used as a survey instrument in clinical and counseling settings to initiate the consultation process and introduce the client to formal diagnostic testing.

Description: 240–item paper-pencil or computer-administered test identifying common problems cited by adolescents in 13 areas: social, appearance, job, family, home, school, money, religion, emotions, dating, health, attitude, and crises. The test is a component of the Clinical Checklist Series. Self-administered. Suitable for group use.

Untimed: 10–20 minutes

Scoring: Examiner evaluated

Cost: 50 checklists $17.95

Publisher: Psychological Assessment Resources, Inc.

PERSONAL PROBLEMS CHECKLIST—ADULT
John A. Schinka

Adult

Purpose: Assesses the personal problems of adults. Used as a survey instrument in clinical and counseling settings to initiate the consultation process and introduce the client to formal diagnostic testing.

Description: 211–item paper-pencil or computer-administered test identifying problems in 13 areas: social, appearance, vocational, family and home, school, finances, religion, emotions, sex, legal, health and habits, attitude, and crises. The test is a component of the Clinical Checklist Series. Self-administered. Suitable for group use.

Untimed: 10–20 minutes

Scoring: Examiner evaluated

Cost: 50 checklists $17.95

Publisher: Psychological Assessment Resources, Inc.

PERSONAL QUESTIONNAIRE RAPID SCALING TECHNIQUE (PQRST)
David Mulhall

Adolescent, adult

Purpose: Measures changes in feelings, beliefs, and symptoms. Used for clinical and educational counseling.

Description: Multiple-item paper-pencil test of issues important to an individual. In cooperation with a consultant, the respondent defines a set of constructs to be measured. The constructs may include feelings or attitudes on behavior. The technique provides a framework through which the intensity of each construct can be measured. Two forms, PQ10 and PQ14, are available. Form PQ10 contains slightly fewer constructs. Availability is limited to experienced psychologists or persons with equivalent qualifications. Examiner required. Not suitable for group use.
BRITISH PUBLISHER

Untimed: Not available

Scoring: Hand key

Cost: Contact publisher

Publisher: NFER-NELSON Publishing Company Ltd.

PERSONAL RELATIONSHIPS QUESTIONNAIRE
Ronald R. McCormick

Adult—Ages 16 and older
Grades 11 and above

Purpose: Assesses personal relationships. Used in counseling.

Description: 3–item paper-pencil short-answer projective technique based on the assumption that a person's relationships with others influence who he or she is. Within a 5–minute time period, the client lists as many names of people he or she can remember. The client then chooses six people from the list and ranks them in order of the impact they have had on his or her life. Next, the client states how each of the six people has affected his life. The client then analyzes his responses for an overall factor that might increase self-understanding. The technique also may be used with an examiner for extended analysis of personal relationships and for therapeutic use. Examiner/self-administered. Suitable for group use.

Untimed: 10–15 minutes

Scoring: Self-scored; examiner evaluated

Cost: 25 questionnaires $25.00

Publisher: Dr. R.R. McCormick and Associates

Information and availability unconfirmed; last verified in 1988.

PERSONALITY DEVIANCE SCALE
A. Bedford and G. Foulds

Adult

Purpose: Assesses intro-punitiveness, extra-punitiveness, and dominance. Used by psychologists to identify individuals who are overly critical of themselves or others and to formulate therapy programs.

Description: Multiple-item paper-pencil Likert-type test in which examinees respond to items on a 4–point scale. Subscales include Lack of Self-Confidence, Over-Dependence on Others, Hostile Thoughts, Denigratory Attitudes towards Other People, Domineering Social Attitudes, and Overt or Inhibited Acts. Raw scores can be converted to percentiles for the three personality traits and six subscales. Examiner/self-administered. Suitable for group use. BRITISH PUBLISHER

Untimed: 15 minutes

Scoring: Hand key

Cost: Contact publisher

Publisher: NFER-NELSON Publishing Company Ltd.

PET ATTITUDE SCALE
Donald I. Templer, Charles A. Salter, Sarah Dickey, and Roy Baldwin

Adult

Purpose: Measures an individual's attitudes toward pets.

Description: 18–item Likert-format scale indicating whether an individual has a favorable attitude toward pets. The test measures three factors: love and interaction, pets in the home, and joy of pet ownership. Self-administered. Suitable for group use.

Untimed: Varies

Scoring: Contact publisher

Cost: Free

Publisher: Donald I. Templer, Ph.D.

PHSF RELATIONS QUESTIONNAIRE—1970
Refer to page 744.

THE PICTORIAL STUDY OF VALUES
Charles Shooster

Adult

Purpose: Examines personal values. Used for self-awareness programs, discussion groups, and research on values and mores. Suitable for illiterates and non-English-speaking persons.

Description: Multiple-item paper-pencil test measuring reactions to six basic value areas: social, political, economic, religious, aesthetic, and theoretical. Test items are composed of photographs. College norms are provided. Examiner required. Suitable for group use.

Untimed: 20 minutes

Scoring: Examiner evaluated

Cost: Specimen set $5.00; 25 tests $5.00

Publisher: Psychometric Affiliates

THE PICTURE IDENTIFICATION TEST
Jay L. Chambers

Adolescent, adult

Purpose: Assesses a person's effectiveness in dealing with combative, personal, and competitive motivational dimensions. Used for personality analysis and research in psychotherapy.

Description: Multiple-item two-part paper-pencil test in which the subject is presented a card with 12 photographs representing a variety of facial expressions (6 male, 6 female, ages 21–23). In Part I, the subject rates each facial expression on a scale ranging from "very positive" to "very negative." In Part II, the subject is given a list of 22 needs (based on Murray's Need System). The subject uses a scale ranging from "very definite expression of the motive" to "definitely does not express the motive." The ratings are computer analyzed by the author and yield two types of scores. A multidimensional scale analysis yields three dimension scales: Combative, Personal, and Competitive. Specific attitude, judgment, and association scores are computed for each need. The attitude scores are correlated with target dimension need locations to provide an attitude score for each dimension. Examiner/self-administered. Suitable for group use.

Untimed: 45–60 minutes

Scoring: Computer scored

Cost: Manual $13.00; scoring and interpretation $3.00

Publisher: Jay L. Chambers, Ph.D.

PICTURE PERSONALITY TEST FOR INDIAN SOUTH AFRICANS (PPT-ISA)—1982

Adult—Ages 16 and older

Purpose: Measures attitudes of Indian South Africans.

Description: Multiple-item paper-pencil projective test predicting job success in industry and business and indicating relations with significant others for clinical purposes. A picture album (one for males and one for females) is used for determining attitude towards demands, family relationships, father-son or mother-daughter relationship, mother-son or father-daughter relationship, attitude towards Indian authority, self-concept, sexual relationship, attitude towards white authority, social adjustment, and aggression. The test has 11 picture cards (constructs) that can be selected according to the purpose of the evaluation. Distinction can be made for Hindus, Mohammedans, and Christians. The test can be analyzed for positive (favorable), negative (hostile), and ambivalent (unsure) reactions. An item analysis also can be performed. Individual testing is recommended for individuals who have only a primary school qualification. Examiner required. Suitable for group use. SOUTH AFRICAN PUBLISHER

Untimed: 2 hours

Scoring: Hand key

Cost: (In Rands) Manual 8,00; test album (specify male or female) 45,00; 10 answer booklets 12,00

Publisher: Human Sciences Research Council

POLYFACTORIAL STUDY OF PERSONALITY
Martin M. Bruce

Adult

Purpose: Aids in the clinical evaluation of an individual's personality.

Description: 300-item paper-pencil true-false test measuring 11 aspects of psychopathology: hypochondriasis, sexual identification, anxiety, social distance, sociopathy, depression, compulsivity, repression, paranoia, schizophrenia, and hyperaffectivity. Self-administered. Suitable for group use.

Untimed: 45 minutes

Scoring: Hand key

Cost: Manual $13.00; IBM scoring stencil $26.00; package of profile sheets $19.00; package of IBM answer sheets $19.00; specimen set $53.50

Publisher: Martin M. Bruce, Ph.D., Publishers

PORTEOUS PROBLEM CHECKLIST
Refer to page 744.

PRESENT STATE EXAMINATION (PSE)
J.K. Wing, J.E. Cooper, and N. Sartorius

Adult

Purpose: Assesses psychiatric symptoms experienced during preceding month. Used with psychiatric patients.

Description: Multiple-item paper-pencil clinical interview for rating psychiatric symptoms the examinee has experienced during the preceding month. The instrument yields 38 syndrome scores and several derived scores. A computer-scoring program is available. Examiner required. Not suitable for group use.

Untimed: Not available

Scoring: Computer scored

Cost: Contact publisher

Publisher: Cambridge University Press

PROBLEM APPRAISAL SCALES (PAS)
Jean Endicott and
The Department of Research
Assessment and Training

Adolescent, adult

Purpose: Assesses psychiatric functioning. Used for diagnosis of psychopathology.

Description: Multiple-item paper-pencil measure of a broad range of psychiatric signs and symptoms consisting of 40 scales and one checklist item. The PAS covers the same areas as the Psychiatric Evaluation Form (PEF) and also includes items covering physical functioning and intellectual development. The PAS is completed by the examiner after a clinical workup. Examiner required. Not suitable for group use.

Untimed: After clinical workup, 3–5 minutes

Scoring: Examiner evaluated; computer scored for primary scales

Cost: Scale $0.50; interview guide $0.50; suggested procedures and instruction $0.40; summary scale scores/tables $0.50 plus postage and handling

Publisher: Department of Research Assessment and Training—N.Y. State Psychiatric Institute

Information and availability unconfirmed; last verified in 1987.

PROFILE OF ADAPTATION TO LIFE—CLINICAL (PAL-C)
Robert E. Ellsworth

Adult

Purpose: Measures the personal and social adaptation of adults. Used as an intake screening instrument in clinical settings.

Description: 41-item paper-pencil self-report inventory providing scores on seven factorial scales: negative emotions, psychological well-being, income management, physical symptoms, alcohol/drugs, close relations, and child relations. The manual explains the rationale and validity of the scale and provides detailed

norms for the general and clinical populations with respect to adjustment to life and the community. Self-administered. Suitable for group use.

Untimed: 20–30 minutes

Scoring: Self-scored or examiner evaluated

Cost: Manual $8.00; 25 scales and profile sheets $7.50; specimen set (manual, scale, profile sheet) $9.00

Publisher: Consulting Psychologists Press, Inc.

PROFILE OF ADAPTATION TO LIFE—HOLISTIC (PAL-H)
Robert E. Ellsworth

Adult

Purpose: Measures an individual's adaptation to life in terms of the individual's life-style and spiritual awareness. Used by ministers and counselors working with people who are interested in health-related activities and spiritual awareness as part of their remedial program.

Description: Multiple-item paper-pencil self-report inventory assessing seven clinical scales (negative emotions, psychological well-being, income management, physical symptoms, alcohol/drugs, close relations, and child relations) and five scales relating to life-style and spiritual awareness (social activity, self-activity, nutrition and exercise, personal growth, and spiritual awareness). The seven clinical scales are the same as those contained in the Profile of Adaptation to Life—Clinical (PAL-C). The manual explains the rationale and validity of the scale and provides detailed norms for the general and clinical populations in terms of adjustment to life and the community. Self-administered. Suitable for group use.

Untimed: 20–30 minutes

Scoring: Examiner evaluated

Cost: Manual $8.00; 25 scales and profile sheets $7.50

Publisher: Consulting Psychologists Press, Inc.

PROFILE OF MOOD STATES (POMS)
Douglas M. McNair, Maurice Lorr, and Leo Droppleman

Adolescent, adult—Ages 18 and older

Purpose: Assesses dimensions of affect or mood in individuals ages 18 and older. Used to measure outpatients' response to various therapeutic approaches, including drug evaluation studies.

Description: 65-item paper-pencil test measuring six dimensions of affect or mood: tension-anxiety, depression-dejection, anger-hostility, vigor-activity, fatigue-inertia, and confusion-bewilderment. An alternative POMS-Bipolar Form measures the following mood dimensions in terms of six bipolar affective states identified in recent research: composed-anxious, elated-depressed, agreeable-hostile, energetic-tired, clear-headed-confused, and confident-unsure. Norms are provided for POMS for college and outpatient populations. Norms are provided for POMS-Bipolar for high school, college, and outpatient populations. POMS is available in a shortend form and large print. Examiner required. Suitable for group use. Available in French and Japanese.

Untimed: 3–5 minutes

Scoring: Hand key; may be computer scored

Cost: Specimen set (manual, all forms) $5.50; 25 inventories (specify POMS or Bipolar) $7.00; 25 profile sheets (specify college or outpatient) $5.25; keys $12.50; manual $3.00

Publisher: EdITS/Educational and Industrial Testing Service

THE PROJECTIVE ASSESSMENT OF AGING METHOD (PAAM)
Refer to page 46.

PROJECTIVE PERSONALITY TEST (ANALAGOUS TO THE TAT)

Adult

Purpose: Evaluates basic personality characteristics. Intended for use exclusively with Black African subjects.

Description: 16–18 picture cards provide the stimuli for a projective personality test analagous to the TAT. Each picture presents some degree of ambiguity to facilitate a variety of interpretations. Where humans are depicted, black characters are used except where the situation, according to the test publisher, "requires a Caucasian." There is one set of cards for each of the following groups: urban men, urban women, rural men, and rural women. Use is restricted to competent persons properly registered with the South African Medical and Dental Council. Examiner required. Not suitable for group use.
SOUTH AFRICAN PUBLISHER

Untimed: Open ended

Scoring: Examiner evaluated

Cost: Contact publisher

Publisher: National Institute for Personnel Research

PSYCHIATRIC DIAGNOSTIC INTERVIEW—REVISED
Ekkehard Othmer, Elizabeth C. Penick, Barbara J. Powell, Marsha Read, and Sigliende Othmer

Adult

Purpose: Identifies frequently encountered psychiatric disorders. Used in all phases of diagnostic screening, intake, and follow-up.

Description: Multiple-item verbally administered oral-response or computer-administered test consisting of questions usually requiring a "yes" or "no" answer. The test offers diagnostic summaries evaluating the following basic syndromes: organic brain syndrome, alcoholism, drug abuse, mania, depression, schizophrenia, antisocial personality, somatization disorder, anorexia nervosa, obsessive-compulsive neurosis, phobic neurosis, anxiety neurosis, mental retardation, bulimia, post traumatic stress disorder, generalized anxiety, and adjustment disorder. In addition, four derived syndromes are evaluated: polydrug abuse, schizoaffective disorder, manic-depressive disorder, and bulimarexia. The questions for each of the basic syndromes are divided into four sections. If simple response criteria are not met, the interviewer omits the remainder of the questions for that syndrome and proceeds to the next syndrome. All positive syndromes are recorded on the Time Profile, which graphically displays which syndromes were positive, the patient's age when they were positive, and how long they were positive. This revised edition, which contains several new items, eliminates two syndromes—homosexuality and transsexualism—but adds four: bulimia, post traumatic stress disorder, generalized anxiety, and adjustment disorder. In addition, criteria used to define the syndromes have been modified for greater consistency with DSM-III and DSM-III-R diagnostic categories. The test may be computer scored using the microcomputer diskette. Examiner required. Not suitable for group use.

Untimed: 15–60 minutes

Scoring: Examiner evaluated; may be computer scored

Cost: $70.00

Publisher: Western Psychological Services

PSYCHIATRIC EVALUATION FORM (PEF)
*Jean Endicott and
The Department of Research
Assessment and Training*

Adolescent, adult

Purpose: Assesses current psychiatric functioning. Used for the diagnosis of psychopathology.

Description: Multiple-item paper-pencil measure of a broad range of psychiatric symptoms consisting of 27 scales and two checklist items. The PEF measures the same areas as the Psychiatric Status Schedule and also includes characteristics of present illness and the major reason for admission. The PEF is completed by the examiner based on a clinical workup or client interview. Examiner required. Not suitable for group use.

Untimed: 25–50 minutes total interview

Scoring: Examiner evaluated; computer scored for summary scales

Cost: Booklet with score sheet $3.00; score sheet $0.30; manual of instructions $1.00; teaching tape and key $4.00; summary scale scores $0.55; editing/coding instructions $0.20; Fortran program $125.00 plus postage and handling

Publisher: Department of Research Assessment and Training—N.Y. State Psychiatric Institute

Information and availability unconfirmed; last verified in 1987.

PSYCHIATRIC STATUS SCHEDULE (PSS)
*Jean Endicott and
The Department of Research
Assessment and Training*

Adolescent, adult

Purpose: Assesses current psychiatric functioning. Used for the diagnosis of psychopathology.

Description: 321–item paper-pencil measure of psychopathology, organicity, and alcoholism or drug abuse. The subject's role as a wage earner, housekeeper, student, mate, and parent are also covered. Items are in true-false and checklist form. The interviewer answers the items based on a meeting with the subject. Materials include a 21–page stepdown booklet. The instrument covers many of the same areas as the Psychiatric Evaluation Form (PEF). Examiner required. Not suitable for group use.

Untimed: 30–50 minutes

Scoring: Hand key; examiner evaluated; may be computer scored

Cost: Booklet with score sheet $3.50; score sheet $0.30; suggested training procedures $0.20; manual $1.00; teaching tape and key $4.00; summary scale scores $1.50; editing/coding instructions $0.20; hand stencils $5.00; Fortran program $125.00 plus postage and handling

Publisher: Department of Research Assessment and Training—N.Y. State Psychiatric Institute

Information and availability unconfirmed; last verified in 1987.

PSYCHOEPISTEMOLOGICAL PROFILE (PEP)
J.R. Royce and L.P. Mos

Adolescent, adult

Purpose: Evaluates an individual's epistemological hierarchy (approach to reality). Used with high-school students and adults.

Description: 90–item paper-pencil test assessing the psychological processes and criterion for truth that determine an individual's particular world view. The test identifies and quantifies three basic epistemic styles (a major personality integrator or higher order personality factor that determines an individual's basic approach to reality): rationalism (30 items), empiricism (30 items), and metaphorism (30 items). Test items consist of value statements, which the individual rates on a 5–point scale ranging from "complete agreement" to "complete disagreement." The test yields independent scores for each of the three epistemic styles. The highest of the three scores indicates the individual's dominant epistemology. Norms are provided by sex for a junior-college population. Self-administered. Suitable for group use. Available in French (with separate norms). CANADIAN PUBLISHER

Untimed: 20–30 minutes

Scoring: Examiner evaluated; may be machine scored

Cost: Manual, test $10.00

Publisher: Center for Advanced Study in Theoretical Psychology/University of Alberta

Information and availability unconfirmed; last verified in 1987.

PSYCHOLOGICAL SCREENING INVENTORY (PSI)
Richard I. Lanyon

Adolescent, adult
Grades 10 and above

Purpose: Identifies adults and adolescents who may need a more extensive mental health examination or professional attention. Used in clinics, hospitals, schools, courts, and reformatories.

Description: 130–item true-false test covering five scales: Alienation, Social Nonconformity, Discomfort, Expression, and Defensiveness. Materials include a manual, question and answer sheet, scoring template, and profile. Use is restricted to certified psychologists. Examiner required. Suitable for group use. Available in Spanish.

Untimed: 15 minutes

Scoring: Hand key

Cost: Complete kit $36.00

Publisher: SIGMA Assessment Systems, Inc., Research Psychologists Press Division

PSYCHOLOGICAL/PSYCHIATRIC STATUS INTERVIEW (PPSI)

Adult

Purpose: Evaluates an individual's present psychological/psychiatric status. Used by clinicians to identify areas requiring further evaluation.

Description: Multiple-item computer-administered intake interview covering presenting problems, current living situation, mental status, biological/medical status, interpersonal relations, and socialization. The completed interview serves as a client database that can be used to prepare for a personal interview. A 3– to 5–page report is generated. The program runs on IBM PC or compatible systems. Self-administered. Not suitable for group use.

Untimed: Not available

Scoring: Computer scored

Cost: $250.00

Publisher: Psychologistics, Inc.

Information and availability unconfirmed; last verified in 1988.

PSYCHOLOGICAL/SOCIAL HISTORY REPORT

Adult

Purpose: Gathers basic information relevant to a psychological intake interview. Used for iniating discussion between the clinician and patient.

Description: Multiple-item paper-pencil or computer-administered psychological intake interview covering presenting problem, family/developmental history, education, financial history/status, employment history, military service, alcohol/drug history, medical history, marital/family life, diet/exercise, and psychological/social stressors. The program generates an Important Responses section of patient responses that may be clinically significant. This section allows the clinician to see areas requiring further evaluation. The program operates on IBM PC and Apple II+, IIe, or IIc systems. Examiner required. Not suitable for group use.

Untimed: 30–45 minutes

Scoring: Examiner evaluated; may be computer scored

Cost: Computer version $295.95

Publisher: Psychometric Software, Inc.

PSYCHOTIC INPATIENT PROFILE
Maurice Lorr and Norris D. Vestre

Adult

Purpose: Measures the behavior patterns of adult psychiatric patients. Used with difficult patients and to evaluate treatment progress.

Description: 96–item paper-pencil inventory consisting of questions about the subject's behavior, which a nurse or psychiatric aide answers by indicating frequency of observation. Analysis of the responses provides objective and quantitative measures of 12 syndromes of observable psychotic behavior: excitement, hostile belligerence, paranoid projection, anxious depression, retardation, seclusiveness, care needed, psychotic disorganization, grandiosity, perceptual distortion, depressive mood, and disorientation. The 6–page test booklet is a revised and expanded version of the Psychotic Reaction Profile. Norms are provided for men and women, both drug free and drug treated. Examiner required. Not suitable for group use.

Untimed: 20–30 minutes

Scoring: Hand key

Cost: Complete kit (25 forms, manual) $26.50

Publisher: Western Psychological Services

PURPOSE IN LIFE (PIL)
James C. Crumbaugh and Leonard T. Maholick

Adult

Purpose: Measures degree to which an individual has found meaning in life. Used with addicted, retired, handicapped, and philosophically confused individuals for purposes of clinical assessment, student counseling, vocational guidance, and rehabilitation.

Description: 34–item paper-pencil test assessing an individual's major motivations in life. Subjects must rate 20 statements according to their own beliefs, complete 13 sentence stems, and write an original paragraph describing their aims, ambitions, and goals in life. Based on Viktor Frankl's "Will to Meaning," the test embraces his logotherapeutic orientation in recognition of threat of the existential vacuum. Norms are provided for mental patients and normals. A fourth-grade reading level is required. Self-administered. Suitable for group use. Available in Spanish and Portuguese.

Untimed: 10–15 minutes

Scoring: Scoring service available

Cost: Specimen set (test, manual, bibliography) $4.00; 25 tests $5.00

Publisher: Psychometric Affiliates

RATING OF BEHAVIOR SCALES (ROBS)
Robert C. Newman II and Richard E. Carney

Adolescent, adult—Ages 12 and older—Grades 6 and above

Purpose: Assesses an individual's adoption of stereotypic sex-role behaviors, androgyny, and degree and type of motivation to change role behaviors. May be used with the visually, physically, or hearing-impaired.

Description: 40–item paper-pencil multiple-choice test measuring sex-role adoption and androgyny. The items are presented in two sections: present behavior (20 items) and ideal behavior (20 items). The test yields several scores, including Total Behavior (S), Male Behavior (M), Female Behavior (F), Total Inconsistency (K), Inconsistency Between Sex Roles (K1), Inconsistency Within Sex Roles (K2), F Ratio for Androgyny (K3), Total Incongruence (C; present vs. ideal), Difference Between Male Items (M1), Difference Between Female Items (F1), Difference Between Male and Female Difference (C1), Inconsistency Within Male and Female Items (C2), and F Ratio Between C1 and C2 (C3). A computer scoring service is available from the publisher. A sixth-grade reading level is required. The test may be read to those with vision problems. Self-administered. Suitable for group use.

Untimed: Varies

Scoring: Hand key; may be computer scored

Cost: 50 forms $12.50; specimen set (manual, form) $7.00

Publisher: Carney, Weedman and Associates

RESEARCH DIAGNOSTIC CRITERIA (RDC)
Jean Endicott and
The Department of Research
Assessment and Training

Adolescent, adult

Purpose: Provides criteria for the diagnosis of mental disorders and subtypes of disorders. Used for the diagnosis of affective and schizophrenic disorders.

Description: 25–item paper-pencil measure of present or previous illnesses. Items are a list of 25 diagnoses: present, past, and lifetime. The clinician checks the applicable diagnosis based on a clinical workup or Schedule for Affective Disorders and Schizophrenia (SADS) interview. Examiner required. Suitable for group use.

Untimed: After clinical workup, 10–15 minutes

Scoring: Examiner evaluated

Cost: Booklet $1.50; score sheet $0.25; checklist $0.50; suggested training procedures $0.25; case vignettes/training exercise #1 $7.50; case vignettes/training exercise #2 for testing $7.50; editing/coding instructions $0.25 plus postage and handling

Publisher: Department of Research Assessment and Training—N.Y. State Psychiatric Institute

Information and availability unconfirmed; last verified in 1987.

RETIREMENT DESCRIPTIVE INDEX (RDI)
Patricia C. Smith, Lorne M. Kendall, and Charles L. Hulin

Adult

Purpose: Assesses satisfaction with activities, finances, people, and health. Used with retired persons and other non-working adults. Suitable for use with hearing or physically impaired individuals.

Description: 63–item paper-pencil test consisting of four scales measuring satisfaction: Activities (18 items), Income (9 items), Persons (18 items), and Health (18 items). The items follow a "yes-?-no" format. The test yields scores for each of the four scales. A scoring service is available by special arrangement with the publisher. A second-grade reading level is required. Self-administered. Suitable for group use.

Untimed: 10 minutes

Scoring: Hand key; may be computer scored; may be machine scored

Cost: 100 booklets $34.00

Publisher: Bowling Green State University, Department of Psychology

---

REYNOLDS ADOLESCENT DEPRESSION SCALE (RADS)
William M. Reynolds

Adolescent—Ages 13–18

Purpose: Measures depression in adolescents. Used to identify depression in school and clinical groups, for research on depression and its constructs, and for clinical assessment and evaluation of treatment programs. Also used for routine screening of behavior and conduct disorder referrals and of academic or substance abuse problems.

Description: 30–item paper-pencil test to which students respond on a 4–point Likert-type scale. The test is available in three forms: HS, I, and G. Form HS is the hand-scorable version. Form I, for use with individuals and small groups, includes a four- to five-page report that includes a validity check, score comparisons against cutoff and normative data, critical item responses, and total item responses. Form G, designed for large groups and mail-in scoring, is used in research and for program evaluation. The survey report includes group summary data, a list of protocols above the cutoff, protocols above the 95th percentile, invalid protocols, scores for all protocols, and means and ranges for all scores. A scoring service is available from the publisher. Self-administered. Suitable for group use.

Untimed: 5–10 minutes

Scoring: Form HS hand key; Forms I and G computer scored

Cost: Professional kit (manual, 25 Form HS answer sheets, scoring key) $29.00; 50 Form G prepaid mail-in answer sheets (scoring and report) $100.00; 10 Form I prepaid mail-in answer sheets (scoring and report) $47.50

Publisher: Psychological Assessment Resources, Inc.

ROGERS CRIMINAL RESPONSIBILITY ASSESSMENT SCALES (R-CRAS)
Richard Rogers

Adult

Purpose: Evaluates the criminal responsibility of individuals who may or may not, depending on their sanity or insanity at the time they committed a crime, be held legally accountable for their actions.

Description: Multiple-item paper-pencil inventory evaluating criminal responsibility. The instrument quantifies essential

psychological and situational variables at the time of the crime that are to be used in a criterion-based decision model. This allows the clinician to quantify the impairment at the time of the crime, conceptualize the impairment with respect to the appropriate legal standards, and render an expert opinion with respect to those standards. Descriptive criteria are provided on scales measuring the individual's reliability, organicity, psychopathology, cognitive control, and behavioral control at the time of the alleged crime. Part I establishes the degree of impairment on psychological variables significant to the determination of insanity. Part II articulates the decision process towards rendering an accurate opinion on criminal responsibility with the ALI standard and includes experimental criteria and decision models for guilty-but-mentally-ill (GBMI) and M'Naughten standards. Results classify sane and insane individuals across age, sex and race, and all important legal variables. Examiner required. Not suitable for group use.

Untimed: Varies

Scoring: Examiner evaluated

Cost: Test kit (manual and 15 examination booklets) $22.00

Publisher: Psychological Assessment Resources, Inc.

ROTTER INCOMPLETE SENTENCES BLANK
Julian B. Rotter

Adolescent, adult

Purpose: Studies personality by using sentence completion.

Description: 40–item paper-pencil test of personality. Items are stems of sentences to be completed by the subject. Responses may be classified into three categories: conflict or unhealthy responses, neutral responses, and positive or healthy responses. The test is available in high-school, college, and adult forms. Self-administered. Suitable for group use.

Untimed: 20–40 minutes

Scoring: Hand key; examiner evaluated

Cost: 25 blanks (specify form) $13.00;
manual $20.00
Publisher: The Psychological
Corporation
*Information and availability unconfirmed; last
verified in 1988.*

RUST INVENTORY OF SCHIZOTYPAL COGNITIONS (RISC)
John Rust

Adult

Purpose: Identifies and evaluates eccentric or bizarre thought patterns. Provides an estimate of client risk for schizotypal symptoms phenomenologically related to acute schizophrenia. Used in clinical assessment, occupational counseling, and academic and psychiatric research.

Description: 26–item paper-pencil inventory assessing the cognitions associated with schizotypal personality disorder and acute schizophrenia. Self-administered. Suitable for group use. Available in Spanish.
BRITISH PUBLISHER
Untimed: 10 minutes
Scoring: Self-scored
Cost: Contact publisher
Publisher: NFER-NELSON Publishing
Company Ltd.

S-D PRONENESS CHECKLIST
William T. Martin

Adolescent, adult

Purpose: Identifies persons with depressive and suicidal tendencies. Used by persons and agencies involved in suicide prevention. May be administered via telephone.

Description: 30–item paper-pencil inventory assessing a person's level of depression and suicide tendencies. Any trained counselor can complete the questionnaire, based on information gained through interviews and observation. The evaluator rates each of the statements on a 5–point scale ranging from "does not apply" to "most significant." Three scores are derived: Suicidal Score, Depression Score, and Total Suicide-

Depression Proneness Score. Interpretative guidelines are provided with each form, including suicide correction factors. A pamphlet on suicide/depression also is available. Examiner required. Not suitable for group use.
Untimed: Open ended
Scoring: Examiner evaluated
Cost: Specimen set $5.00; 25 rating forms $8.25
Publisher: Psychologists and Educators, Inc.

SCHEDULE FOR AFFECTIVE DISORDERS AND SCHIZOPHRENIA (SADS)
*Jean Endicott and
The Department of Research
Assessment and Training*

**Adolescent, adult—Ages
12 and older**

Purpose: Describes the psychopathology of the past week and the current episode of illness. Used as an aid in diagnosing and estimating prognosis and severity.

Description: Paper-pencil measure of recent psychopathology consisting of over 200 scales and many checklist items. The examiner rates the items based on a subject interview, case records, and a clinical workup. The instrument is similar in concept to the Schedule for Affective Disorders and Schizophrenia—Lifetime Version (SADS-L) and the Schedule for Affective Disorders and Schizophrenia—Change Version (SADS-C). The instrument must be used in conjunction with the Research Diagnostic Criteria (RDC). Examiner required. Not suitable for group use.
Untimed: 90–120 minutes
Scoring: Examiner evaluated; computer scored for summary scale
Cost: SADS booklet $2.00; SADS score sheet $0.30; SADS, SAD-L, RDC suggested procedures $0.50; SADS, SADS-L instructions $0.50; SADS, SADS-L, RDC Clars $1.00; summary scale booklet $1.50; editing/coding instructions $0.40; Fortran program $125.00 plus postage and handling
Publisher: Department of Research Assessment and Training—N.Y. State Psychiatric Institute
Information and availability unconfirmed; last verified in 1987.

SCHEDULE FOR AFFECTIVE DISORDERS AND SCHIZOPHRENIA—CHANGE VERSION (SADS-C)
Jean Endicott and
The Department of Research
Assessment and Training

Adolescent, adult

Purpose: Assesses change in psychopathological symptoms for the previous week. Used in diagnosis and treatment planning.

Description: Paper-pencil measure of symptom changes over the last week consisting of 29 scaled items and several checklist items. Examiner rates the items based on a subject interview and clinical records. The instrument is one of a series of measures that includes the Schedule for Affective Disorders and Schizophrenia (SADS) and the Schedule for Affective Disorders and Schizophrenia—Lifetime Version (SADS-L). Examiner required. Not suitable for group use.

Untimed: 20–30 minutes

Scoring: Examiner evaluated; computer scored for summary scale

Cost: Booklet $1.00; score sheet $0.20; summary scale booklet $1.00; editing/coding instructions $0.20; Fortran program $125.00 plus postage and handling

Publisher: Department of Research Assessment and Training—N.Y. State Psychiatric Institute

Information and availability unconfirmed; last verified in 1987.

SCHEDULE FOR AFFECTIVE DISORDERS AND SCHIZOPHRENIA—LIFETIME VERSION (SADS-L)
Jean Endicott and
The Department of Research
Assessment and Training

Adolescent, adult

Purpose: Assesses clinical history of psychopathology. Used for differential diagnosis of mental disorders.

Description: Measure of history relevant to diagnosis, prognosis, and severity of ill-

ness consisting of several scales and numerous checklist items. The examiner rates the items based on a subject interview, case records, and a clinical workup. Items are similar to those on the Schedule for Affective Disorders and Schizophrenia (SADS) and Schedule for Affective Disorders and Schizophrenia—Change Version (SADS-C). The instrument must be used in conjunction with the Research Diagnostic Criteria (RDC). Examiner required. Not suitable for group use.

Untimed: If not ill, 45 minutes; in an episode, 45–90 minutes

Scoring: Examiner evaluated; may be computer scored

Cost: SADS-L booklet $1.00; score sheet $0.25; editing/coding instructions $0.20; summary data program $125.00; editing program $125.00 plus postage and handling

Publisher: Department of Research Assessment and Training—N.Y. State Psychiatric Institute

Information and availability unconfirmed; last verified in 1987.

SCHOOL MOTIVATION ANALYSIS TEST (SMAT)
Samuel E. Krug,
Raymond B. Cattell, and
Arthur B. Sweney

Adolescent—Ages 12–18

Purpose: Assesses the psychological motivations of adolescents. Used for clinical evaluation, educational and personal counseling, and psychological research on adolescent motivations.

Description: 190–item paper-pencil multiple-choice test measuring 10 important achievement, social, and comfort needs of 12- to 18–year-olds. Six of the needs are basic drives: protectiveness, caution, self-assertion, sexual identity, aggressiveness, and self-indulgence. Four are interests that develop and mature through learning experiences: interest in school, dependency, responsibility, and self-fulfillment. Test items consist of objective devices, which are less susceptible to deliberate faking or distortion than standard questionnaires or checklists. For each of the 10 interest areas, scores measure drive or need level, satisfaction level, degree of conflict, and total motivational strength. Norms are provided for males and females separately. A fourth-grade reading level is required. Examiner required. Suitable for group use.

Untimed: 45–60 minutes

Scoring: Hand key

Cost: Specimen set $15.05; handbook $13.00; 10 reusable test booklets $13.00; 25 answer sheets $8.35; 3 scoring keys $15.60

Publisher: Institute for Personality and Ability Testing, Inc.

SCL-90-R®
Leonard R. Derogatis

Adolescent, adult

Purpose: Evaluates the psychological symptomatic distress of medical and psychiatric patients. Used for psychological screening and in treatment planning and evaluation in mental health settings.

Description: 90–item paper-pencil self-report symptom inventory assessing psychological symptomatic distress in terms of nine symptom dimensions (somatization, obsessive-compulsive, interpersonal sensitivity, depression, anxiety, hostility, phobic anxiety, paranoid ideation, and psychoticism) and three global indices of distress (global severity index, positive symptom index, and positive symptom total). Score/profile forms and published norms are available by sex for four populations: nonpatient adult, nonpatient adolescent, outpatient psychiatric, and inpatient psychiatric. The SCL-90-R is the pivotal instrument in the Psychopathology Rating Scale Series, which includes the Brief Symptom Inventory, the SCL-90-R Analogue, and the Hopkins Psychiatric Rating Scale. The inventory is available in an optical scanning version. A microcomputer scoring program is available for the IBM PC and Apple computers. A psychometer diskette version is available from National Computer Systems/PAS Division. Examiner required. Suitable for group use. Available in over 20 languages.

Untimed: 12–15 minutes

Scoring: Examiner evaluated; may be machine or computer scored

Cost: Manual $18.00; 100 test forms $35.00; 100 optical scan forms $40.00; 100 score/profile forms $25.00; microcomputer scoring program (SCOR90-1) $160.00

Publisher: Clinical Psychometric Research, Inc.

SCL-90-R ANALOGUE
Leonard R. Derogatis

Adolescent, adult

Purpose: Evaluates the psychological symptomatic distress of medical and psychiatric patients in terms of observer's ratings. Used in mental health settings for psychological screening and in treatment planning and evaluation.

Description: 10–item paper-pencil observational inventory assessing symptomatic distress in nine primary symptom dimensions (somatization, obsessive-compulsive, interpersonal sensitivity, depression, anxiety, hostility, phobic anxiety, paranoid ideation, and psychoticism) and one global psychopathology scale. Each primary symptom is represented as a continuum along 100mm lines. The observer marks each continuum line proportionally. This inventory is a part of the Psychopathology Rating Scale Series and is intended to be used in conjunction with either the SCL-90-R or the Brief Symptom Inventory (BSI). The nine primary dimensions are the same as those measured on the other tests in the series. The test may be used by observers, such as physicians, nurses, or technicians, without extensive training in psychiatric disorders. Examiner required. Not suitable for group use.

Untimed: 1–2 minutes

Scoring: Examiner evaluated

Cost: 100 inventory forms $28.00

Publisher: Clinical Psychometric Research, Inc.

THE SEEKING OF NOETIC GOALS TEST (SONG)
James C. Crumbaugh

Adolescent, adult

Purpose: Measures the strength of a person's motivation to find meaning in life. Used for pre- and posttesting of logotherapy programs with addicted, retired, handicapped, and philosophically confused individuals.

Description: 20–item paper-pencil test consisting of statements that the subject rates on a 7–point scale according to his or her own beliefs. The test is used in conjunction with the Purpose in Life Test to predict therapeutic success. The manual includes a discussion of the test's rationale, validity, reliability, administration, scoring, norms, and other technical data. A fourth-grade reading level is required. Self-administered. Suitable for group use. Available in Portuguese.

Untimed: 10 minutes

Scoring: Scoring service available

Cost: Specimen set (test, manual) $4.00; 25 tests $5.00

Publisher: Psychometric Affiliates

SELF-INTERVIEW INVENTORY
H. Birnet Hovey

Adult

Purpose: Measures an individual's level of emotional adjustment and identifies individuals with neurotic tendencies. Used for self-awareness and counseling programs with both psychiatric and normal patients.

Description: 185–item paper-pencil inventory containing a high loading level of unique content. A Composite Neurotic score is derived from subscores on current complaints, emotional insecurity, and guilt feelings. A Composite Maladjustment score is derived from subscores on pre-psychotic and psychotic behavior and childhood illness. Two validating scores are also provided: one on carefulness and one on truthfulness of response. Norms

are provided for control groups. Examiner/self-administered. Suitable for group use.

Untimed: 30 minutes

Scoring: Hand key

Cost: Specimen set $4.00; 25 inventories $5.00; 25 answer sheets $5.00; 25 profiles $5.00

Publisher: Psychometric Affiliates

SELF-PERCEPTION INVENTORY
William T. Martin

Adolescent, adult—Ages 12 and older

Purpose: Evaluates an individual's personality and general level of adjustment. Used for screening procedures, clinical research on personality, and evaluation of therapeutic progress.

Description: 200–item paper-pencil true-false test of personality. Test items consist of symptomatic and descriptive statements grouped according to the following syndromes: consistency, self-actualization, supervision, rigidity-dogmatism, authoritarianism, anxiety, depression, and paranoia. Subscale scores are provided for each syndrome. General Adjustment and General Maladjustment scores are derived from these subscales to provide an index of personality patterning. A fifth-grade reading level is required. Examiner required. Suitable for group use.

Untimed: 20–35 minutes

Scoring: Hand key

Cost: Examiner's manual (10 tests, 25 answer sheets, 25 profile sheets, keys, manual) $40.00; 25 tests $27.50; 25 answer and 25 profile sheets $6.75 each; keys $9.00; manual $6.75

Publisher: Psychologists and Educators, Inc.

SELF-RATING PSYCHIATRIC INVENTORY LIST (SPIL)
William W.K. Zung

Clinical patients

Purpose: Assesses psychiatric symptomatology. Used for diagnosis, evaluation of treatment outcome, and research.

Description: 88–item paper-pencil self-report measure of psychiatric symptoms for which subject checks one of the following: "none or a little of the time," "some of the time," "good part of the time," or "most or all of the time." Scores are obtained in seven areas: psychoticism, elation, depression, anxiety, neuroticism, emotional status, and drug abuse. Self-administered. Suitable for group use.

Untimed: Varies

Scoring: Hand key; examiner evaluated; may be computer scored

Cost: Contact publisher

Publisher: William W. K. Zung, M.D.

THE SENIOR APPERCEPTION TECHNIQUE (SAT)
Leopold Bellak and Sonya Sorel Bellak

Adult

Purpose: Assesses personality in individuals age 60 and older. Used by psychiatrists, psychologists, physicians, nurses, and social workers for clinical evaluation and diagnosis.

Description: 16–item oral-response projective personality test measuring the traits, attitudes, and psychodynamics involved in the personalities of individuals age 60 and older. Each test item consists of a picture of human figures in situations of concern to the elderly. The examinee is asked to tell a story about each picture. The test also includes informational material on technique, administration, research possibilities, and a bibliography. Examiner required. Not suitable for group use. Available in Spanish and Japanese.

Untimed: 20–30 minutes

Scoring: Examiner evaluated

Cost: Complete kit (pictures, manual) $16.00

Publisher: C.P.S., Inc.

SENTENCE COMPLETION TEST
Floyd S. Irvin

Adolescent, adult
Grades 10 and above

Purpose: Assesses personality functioning. Used for clinical counseling and academic guidance.

Description: 90–item paper-pencil test measuring six aspects of personality: self-concept, parental attitude, peer attitude, need for achievement, learning attitude, and body image. Items are sentence stems, which the subject completes. They are scored on a 5–point scale ranging from outright positive to outright negative. Examiner required. Not suitable for group use.

Untimed: 15 minutes

Scoring: Hand key; examiner evaluated

Cost: Specimen set $6.75; 25 forms $8.25

Publisher: Psychologists and Educators, Inc.

SHORR IMAGERY TEST (SIT)
Joseph E. Shorr

Adolescent, adult

Purpose: Evaluates a person's use of imagery and assesses self-image, areas of conflict, and strategies for coping with the world. Used for in-depth personality analysis.

Description: 15–item orally administered and oral-response projective personality test in which the respondent is asked to imagine a particular situation and then to expand in a directed way upon the image evoked. These imaginary situations are used to reveal a wide range of personality variables: the individual's personal world, relationships between self and others, self-image, sexual attitudes, and internal and external forces acting upon the person. Answers are recorded by the examiner and quantitatively scored according to the degree of conflict within the subject's personality. The test, which is not limited by intelligence, is suitable for use with the blind, illiterate, and physically handicapped. It is minimally culture bound. Examiner required. Not suitable for group use.

Untimed: 1 hour

Scoring: Examiner evaluated

Cost: Complete set $37.50
Publisher: Institute for Psycho-Imagination Therapy
Information and availability unconfirmed; last verified in 1988.

SHORT IMAGINAL PROCESS INVENTORY (SIPI)
G.J. Huba, J.L. Singer, C.S. Aneshensel, and J.S. Antrobus

Adolescent, adult

Purpose: Evaluates the content and style of an individual's daydreams and general inner experience. Used for personal assessment, to study the relation of inner experience to other psychological functions, and to investigate group differences in imaginal processes.

Description: 45–item paper-pencil test consisting of five alternative responses covering three scales: Positive-Constructive Daydreaming, Guilt and Fear of Failure Daydreaming, and Poor Attentional Control. Responses are recorded in the question-and-answer booklet. Materials include profiles and scoring templates. Examiner required. Suitable for group use.
Untimed: 10 minutes
Scoring: Hand key
Cost: Complete kit $18.00
Publisher: SIGMA Assessment Systems, Inc., Research Psychologists Press Division

SINGER-LOOMIS INVENTORY OF PERSONALITY, EXPERIMENTAL EDITION (SLIP)
June Singer and Mary Loomis

Adult

Purpose: Assesses cognitive style or personality dispositions. Used in research.

Description: 120–item paper-pencil test measuring eight cognitive modes independently. The eight modes are Introverted Thinking (IT), Introverted Feeling (IF), Introverted Sensation (IS), Introverted Intuition (IN), Extraverted Thinking (ET), Extraverted Feeling (EF), Extraverted Sensation (ES), Extraverted Intuition (EN). Each of the 15 situations

that make up the test contain possible behavioral responses representing the eight cognitive modes. Items are answered on a 5–point scale. A manual provides technical information, and an interpretive guide describes the eight Jungian modes that the test measures, as well as some combinations of different modes. Examiner required. Suitable for group use.
Untimed: 30-40 minutes
Scoring: Hand key
Cost: 25 booklets $12.50; 50 answer sheets/scoring forms $29.00; manual and interpretive guide $11.50
Publisher: Consulting Psychologists Press, Inc.

SITUATIONAL PREFERENCE INVENTORY
Carl N. Edwards

Adult

Purpose: Assesses an individual's preferred styles of social interaction. Used for counseling and research purposes.

Description: 28–item paper-pencil rating scale assessing preferred styles of social interaction. Each test item consists of a set of three statements, each representing a different style of interaction: cooperational, instrumental, or analytic. Individuals are asked to indicate which of the three statements they agree with most and which they agree with least, leaving the third statement unmarked (neutral). Independent scores are derived for each of the three interactional styles. Norms are available by sex for 14 populations. Self-administered. Suitable for group use.
Untimed: Varies
Scoring: Examiner evaluated
Cost: Contact publisher
Publisher: Carl N. Edwards

SIXTEEN PERSONALITY FACTOR QUESTIONNAIRE
Raymond B. Cattell and IPAT Staff

Adolescent, adult—Ages 16 and older

Purpose: Evaluates the normal, adult personality. Used for personnel selection and placement, vocational and educational guidance, marriage counseling, clinical evaluations, and psychological research on personality.

Description: Multiple-item paper-pencil test measuring 16 primary personality traits, including levels of assertiveness, emotional maturity, shrewdness, self-sufficiency, tension, anxiety, neuroticism, and rigidity. Test results have specific applications for business, psychotherapy, and education.

For business and industry, the 16PF predicts important job-related criteria, such as length of time an employee is likely to remain with the company, sales effectiveness, work efficiency, tolerance for routine, and other specific measures. In diagnostic and therapeutic settings, measures are provided for anxiety, neuroticism, rigidity, and other behavior trends. Educators and school psychologists can use the 16PF to counsel college-bound and university students and to identify potential drop-outs, drug users, low achievers, and so forth. Occupational profile data (based on more than 11,000 cases) are summarized in the handbook for use in vocational and rehabilitation counseling.

Five forms of the test are available. Forms A and B (187 items each) require a seventh-grade reading level. Forms C and D (105 items each) require a sixth-grade reading level. Form E (128 items) requires a third-grade reading level and presents shorter, more concrete items in a forced-choice format with large type.

Six types of computer-analyzed reports are available: the Personal Career Development Profile provides information about individual strengths, behavioral attitudes, and gratifications to accomplish personal career development objectives; the Karson Clinical Report provides an in-depth analysis of underlying personality dynamics in clinical terms for use in psychiatric and psychological applications; and the Marriage Counseling Report examines individual and joint strengths and weaknesses in the personality organization of two individuals; the 16PF Narrative Scoring Report provides a complete report for each individual, including descriptions of all significant personality characteristics and relevant

vocational and occupational comparisons. A Human Resources Development Report and a Law Enforcement and Development Report are available.

The manual is a nontechnical guide for administration, scoring, and basic interpretation of Forms A, B, C, and D. The handbook, which must be ordered separately, is the primary source of technical information on the 16PF. A videotape recording of the Form A test booklet in American Sign Language is available. The Form E test booklet also is available on cassette tape. Examiner/self-administered. Suitable for group use. Available in Spanish and 40 other languages.

Untimed: 45–60 minutes

Scoring: Hand key; may be computer scored

Cost: 25 reusable test booklets (specify form) $20.80–$24.25; 25 machine-scorable answer sheets (specify form) $8.25–$10.95; 50 hand-scorable answer sheets (specify form) $9.25; 50 profile sheets $9.25; 50 hand-scorable answer-profile sheets (specify form) $13.00; scoring keys $12.95–$14.30; contact publisher for information on computer reports

Publisher: Institute for Personality and Ability Testing, Inc.

THE SOCIAL BEHAVIOR ASSESSMENT SCHEDULE
Stephen Platt, Steven Hirsch, and Anne Weyman

Adult

Purpose: Assesses an individual's social functioning, changes in performance arising from psychiatric or physical illness, and the effects of the individual's behavior on other members of the household. Used by health visitors, medical doctors, occupational therapists, social workers, psychologists, and psychiatrists.

Description: Multiple-item semistructured interview guide assessing an individual's behavioral disturbance and altered social performance. The test also evaluates the related difficulties suffered by the individual's household and close friends. Based on an interview with a relative or close friend (the informant), the

schedule describes as fully as possible the patient activities and the extent to which his or her performance falls short of the main role requirements in the household or community. The effect of the individual's behavior on others (objective burden) is assessed in a section of the schedule that takes into account the changes that have occurred in the household and the lives of the informant and relatives. Distress caused to the informant (subjective distress) is rated on an item-by-item basis. Examiner required. Not suitable for group use.
BRITISH PUBLISHER

Untimed: Varies

Scoring: Examiner evaluated

Cost: Contact publisher

Publisher: NFER-NELSON Publishing Company Ltd.

SOCIAL RETICENCE SCALE (SRS)
Warren H. Jones

Adolescent, adult

Purpose: Assesses shyness and interpersonal problems in high school and college students and adults. Used to provide client feedback and to assess the effectiveness of therapeutic interventions. Also used in research of interpersonal relationships.

Description: 20–item paper-pencil measure of shyness. Items are answered using a 5–point Likert-type scale. Examiner required. Suitable for group use.

Untimed: 5–10 minutes

Scoring: Not available

Cost: Manual $10.50; scoring key $1.70; 25 test booklets $4.25

Publisher: Consulting Psychologists Press, Inc.

SOMATIC INKBLOT SERIES (SIS)
Wilfred A. Cassell

Adolescent, adult

Purpose: Assesses an individual's body perception and general personality dynamics. Used to evaluate the psychopathological significance of somatic

symptoms, conversion reactions, and sexual dysfunction.

Description: 20–item verbal examination consisting of 20 cards, each containing a carefully designed inkblot. The cards are presented individually to the subject, who describes his perceptions and associations to the examiner. The inkblots are oriented towards body perceptions. The subject's awareness of somatic similarities in the inkblots is used to provide clinical data of a projective nature regarding conscious-unconscious somatic attitudes, as well as general psychodynamics. The test is accompanied by Dr. Cassell's book, *Body Symbolism*, which describes scoring techniques. An examiner qualified in projective techniques is required. Not suitable for group use.

Untimed: 45 minutes

Scoring: Examiner evaluated; scoring service available

Cost: Cards, scoring sheets $45.00

Publisher: Aurora Publishing

Information and availability unconfirmed; last verified in 1987.

SOMATIC INKBLOT SERIES II
Wilfred A. Cassell

Adolescent, adult

Purpose: Assesses body perception and general personality characteristics of adolescents and adults. Used for determining conscious-unconscious health-related perceptions.

Description: 56–item verbal examination consisting of inkblot cards for assessing perceptions and associations related to anatomical structures. The anatomical structure is minimal for some cards to minimize the subject's tendency to develop a perceptual structure for seeing body parts. The cards are presented individually to the subject, who reports perceptions and associations to the examiner. Data provide information on psychopathology regarding how people experience conscious-unconscious health-related issues. The underlying principles of the test are outlined in Wilfred Cassell's book, *Body Symbolism*. An examiner qualified in projective techniques is required. Not suitable for group use.

Untimed: 90 minutes

Scoring: Examiner evaluated

Cost: Cards, scoring sheets $95.00

Publisher: Aurora Publishing

Information and availability unconfirmed; last verified in 1987.

SOMATIC VIDEO SERIES II
Wilfred A. Cassell

Adolescent, adult

Purpose: Assesses body perception and related personality characteristics of adolescents and adults. Used for determining conscious-unconscious health-related perceptions.

Description: 56–item test presented in two videotapes ("Images I" and "Images II") of 28 items each for evaluating body perceptions. The test incorporates the Somatic Inkblot Series II inkblots along with dreamlike video techniques making "lungs" breathe, "hearts" beat, and phallic symbols penetrate. The tapes include nature scenes and ambient music producing a hypnotic-like state in which viewers' written responses are not contaminated by the presence of an examiner. The test can be administered in the standard or shortened version, which eliminates the nature scenes. Diagnostic and therapeutic use of the procedure are outlined in Wilfred Cassell's book, *Body Symbolism*. The tapes are available in VHS and beta videocassette. A 16mm film version is available for teaching purposes. An examiner qualified in projective techniques, hypnotherapy, and dream analogies is required. Not suitable for group use.

Untimed: Standard version 2 hours; abbreviated version 1 hour

Scoring: Examiner evaluated; scoring service available

Cost: Images I $95.00; Images II $95.00 (state ½" or ¾" film size)

Publisher: Aurora Publishing

Information and availability unconfirmed; last verified in 1987.

SOUTH AFRICAN PERSONALITY QUESTIONNAIRE

Adolescent, adult
Grades 10 and above

Purpose: Measures general personality traits in the context of South African society. Used for employee screening and selection. Suitable for matriculants and higher.

Description: 150–item paper-pencil test consisting of bipolar forced-choice items measuring the following personality traits: social responsiveness, dominance, hostility, flexibility, and anxiety. Use is restricted to competent persons properly registered with the South African Medical and Dental Council. Examiner required. Suitable for group use.

SOUTH AFRICAN PUBLISHER

Untimed: Open ended

Scoring: Hand key; examiner evaluated

Cost: Contact publisher

Publisher: National Institute For Personnel Research

STATE-TRAIT ANGER EXPRESSION INVENTORY (STAXI)
Refer to page 11.

STATE-TRAIT ANXIETY INVENTORY, FORM Y (STAI)
Charles D. Spielberger

Adolescent, adult
Grades 7 and above

Purpose: Evaluates individual anxiety levels as an aid to clinical screening for anxiety-prone students, as an indicator of current anxiety level of therapy and counseling clients, and as a research tool.

Description: 20–item paper-pencil test of two aspects of anxiety: state (current level of anxiety, or S-Anxiety) and trait (anxiety-proneness, or T-Anxiety). The T-Anxiety scale asks the subject to indicate how he "generally" feels; the S-Anxiety scale asks how he feels "at a particular moment in time." Form Y is a revision of the original Form X in which six items on each scale have been changed. Self-administered. Suitable for group use. Form X is no longer available in English; a Spanish version is available.

Untimed: 15 minutes

Scoring: Hand key

Cost: Specimen set (tests, manual, key) $8.00; 25 tests $5.00; key $1.25; manual $7.00; 25 tests in Spanish $5.25; Spanish manual $14.75

Publisher: Consulting Psychologists Press, Inc.

STREAMLINED LONGITUDINAL INTERVAL CONTINUATION EVALUATION (SLICE)
Martin B. Keller and
Philip W. Lavori

Adult—Ages 18 and older

Purpose: Collects an individual's psychosocial, psychopathologic, and psychiatric treatment information. Used for one-year follow-up.

Description: Multiple-item paper-pencil and oral-response rating interview using Research Diagnostic Criteria to assess 24 psychiatric disorders and psychosocial ratings, including episodic affective disorders, chronic depressive disorders, and other nonaffective disorders. Weekly psychiatric status ratings (PSRs), overall severity of illness rating, and treatment ratings are provided. The instrument may be adapted for use with special populations (children and visually, mentally, and physically impaired). Examiners must have diagnostic experience and be familiar with RDC. This instrument is a brief version of the Longitudinal Interval Follow-up Evaluation (see separate entry). Examiner required. Not suitable for group use.

Untimed: 30–45 minutes

Scoring: Examiner evaluated

Cost: Contact publisher

Publisher: Martin B. Keller, M.D.

STRUCTURED AND SCALED INTERVIEW TO ASSESS MALADJUSTMENT (SSIAM)
Barry J. Gurland

Adult

Purpose: Identifies problems in social adjustment and rates them quantitatively. Used for clinical evaluations of mental patients.

Description: 32–page interview booklet including scales, profile chart, and instructions for administering and rating the interview. Eleven ratings are provided (five for deviant behavior, one for friction with others, three for distress, and two inferential) for five areas (work, social-leisure, family, marriage, and sex). An additional 11 overall ratings are provided. Examiner required. Not suitable for group use.

Untimed: Not available

Scoring: Examiner evaluated

Cost: 10 copies (scales, profile chart, instructions) $24.00

Publisher: Springer Publishing Company

Information and availability unconfirmed; last verified in 1987.

STUDENT ADAPTATION TO COLLEGE QUESTIONNAIRE (SACQ)
Refer to page 775.

SUICIDAL IDEATION QUESTIONNAIRE (SIQ)
William M. Reynolds

Adolescent—Ages 13–18

Purpose: Assesses suicidal ideation in adolescents.

Description: 30–item paper-pencil test utilizing a 7–point Likert-type response format designed as a companion instrument to the Reynolds Adolescent Depression Scale. The 15–item SIQ-JR version is available for students in Grades 7-9. Both the full version and the JR version are available in Form G, which is designed for use with large groups and with mail-in answer sheets. Self-administered. Suitable for group use.

Untimed: Not available

Scoring: Hand key; Form G computer scored

Cost: Professional kit (manual, 25 each of SIQ and SIQ-JR Form HS answer sheets, scoring keys) $42.00; manual $15.00; 25 SIQ answer sheets (specify SIQ or SIQ-JR) $12.00; scoring key (specify version) $4.00; 50 Form G prepaid mail-in answer sheets (specify version) $100.00

Publisher: Psychological Assessment Resources, Inc.

SUICIDE INTERVENTION RESPONSE INVENTORY (SIRI)
Refer to page 918.

SUICIDE PROBABILITY SCALE (SPS)
John G. Cull and Wayne S. Gill

Ages 14–65

Purpose: Predicts the probability of suicidal behavior. Used by clinicians to assess the probability that an individual may harm himself. May be used for screening, monitoring changes in suicide potential over time, clinical exploration, and research.

Description: 36–item paper-pencil or computer-administered test in which the subject uses a 4–point scale ranging from "none or little of the time" to "most or all of the time" to indicate how often the behavior described in the statements would be descriptive of his behavior or feelings. The test itself does not mention suicide. Items are broken down into four subscales: Hopelessness, Suicide Ideation, Negative Self-Evaluation, and Hostility. Scoring yields a total weighted score, a normalized T-score, and a Suicide Probability Score. The manual presents cutoff scores indicating the level of probable suicide behavior, interpretive guidelines, and clinical strategies for each level. The computer version is available for IMB PC or compatible systems. Examiner required. Suitable for group use.

Untimed: 5–10 minutes

Scoring: Hand key; may be computer scored

Cost: Paper-pencil version complete kit (25 tests, manual, 25 profile sheets) $44.00; IBM diskette (25 uses) $185.00

Publisher: Western Psychological Services

SUINN TEST ANXIETY BEHAVIOR SCALE (STABS)
Refer to page 776.

SURVEY OF INTERPERSONAL VALUES
Leonard V. Gordon

Adolescent, adult
Grades 10 and above

Purpose: Measures individuals' values by assessing what they consider important in relationships with others. Used to measure values associated with adjustment and performance for selection, placement, employment counseling, and research purposes.

Description: 30–item paper-pencil inventory assessing interpersonal values. Each item consists of a triad of value statements. For each triad, examinees must indicate most and least important values. Six values are measured: support, conformity, recognition, independence, benevolence, and leadership. Self-administered. Suitable for group use.

Untimed: 15 minutes

Scoring: Hand key

Cost: 25 test booklets $35.00; scoring stencil $5.50; examiner's manual $10.00

Publisher: SRA/London House

TASKS OF EMOTIONAL DEVELOPMENT TEST (TED)
Refer to page 748.

TAYLOR-JOHNSON TEMPERAMENT ANALYSIS
Robert M. Taylor and Lucille P. Morrison

Adolescent, adult—Ages
13–adult

Purpose: Provides a clinical assessment of personality. Used for individual, premarital, marital, and family counseling; educational and vocational guidance; and substance abuse counseling.

Description: 180–item paper-pencil test measuring common personality traits to assist in assessing individual adjustment and formulation of an overall counseling plan. The regular edition, for ages 18–adult, has a special feature allowing "criss-cross" testing in which questions are answered as applied to self and again as applied to significant other (e.g., husband's perception of both self and spouse and vice versa), thereby adding the dimension of interpersonal perception to counseling perspective. An eighth-grade reading level is required.

The secondary edition, for ages 13–18 and adults who are poor readers, is presented in direct-question format with simplified vocabulary for lower-level readers. A fifth-grade reading level is required.

Evaluation is presented as bipolar graphs of trait pairs: nervous/composed, depressive/light-hearted, active-social/quiet, expressive-responsive/inhibited, sympathetic/indifferent, subjective/objective, dominant/submissive, hostile/tolerant, and self-disciplined/impulsive. The following additional scales are available when the publisher's computer scoring service is utilized: Consistency, Emotional Pressure (Stress), Adequacy of Self-Image (Self-Esteem), Alienating, Interpersonal Relationship Skills (Potential for Success in Marriage), Family Relationship Skills (Parenting Effectiveness Potential), Leadership (Preference/Potential), and Persuasive/Influential. Self-administered. Suitable for group use. Available in Spanish, French, German, and Portuguese.

Untimed: 20–30 minutes

Scoring: Hand key; may be computer scored

Cost: Basic package (manual, handscoring stencils, pens, ruler, 5 test booklets—regular or secondary, 50 handscorable answer sheets, 50 profiles) $85.00; practice scoring training packet $10.00; manual $50.00; 10 test booklets $8.00; 100 handscorable answer sheets $12.50; 100 computer scorable answer sheets $12.50

Publisher: Psychological Publications, Inc.

TEMPERAMENT INVENTORY TESTS
Robert J. Cruise and W. Peter Blitchington

Adult

Purpose: Assesses an individual's basic temperament traits according to the four-temperament theory. Used by professionals and laymen in marital, vocational, social, moral, and spiritual counseling settings.

Description: 80–item paper-pencil test determining an individual's basic temperament traits. The test is available in a self-report form and a group form. The self-report form consists of a 42–page booklet, *Understanding Your Temperament*, containing the test and instructions for self-administration, self-scoring, and interpreting the scores from a Christian viewpoint. The group form, called the Temperament Inventory, is administered and scored with temperament templates by the examiner or group leader. Interpretive material is not included with the group form. Self-administered. Available in French, German, and Spanish.

Untimed: Varies

Scoring: Self-scored; examiner evaluated

Cost: *Understanding Your Temperament* $3.95; Temperament Inventory $0.80; set of temperament templates $3.95

Publisher: Andrews University Press

Information and availability unconfirmed; last verified in 1988.

TENNESSEE SELF CONCEPT SCALE
William H. Fitts

Adolescent, adult—Ages 12–adult

Purpose: Measures an individual's self-concept in terms of identity, feelings, and behavior. Used for a wide range of clinical applications.

Description: 100–item paper-pencil test consisting of self-descriptive statements that subjects rate on a scale ranging from 1 (completely false) to 5 (completely true). The test is available in two forms: Counseling (Form C) and Clinical and Research (Form C & R). Form C is appropriate if the results are to be used directly with the subject. It provides a number of measures, including response defensiveness, a total score, and self-concept scales that reflect "What I Am," "How I Feel," and "What I Do." The scales include Identity, Self Satisfaction, Behavior, Physical Self, Moral-Ethical Self, Personal Self, Family Self, and Social Self. It does not require scoring keys. Form C & R yields the same scores as Form C as well as the following six empirical scales, which require special scoring keys: Defensive Positive, General Maladjustment, Psychosis, Personality Disorder, Neurosis, and Personality Integration. Both forms use the same test booklet but require different answer-profile sheets. The test may be administered to individuals regardless of whether they are psychologically disturbed or healthy. A sixth-grade reading level is required. Self-administered. Suitable for group use.

Untimed: 10–20 minutes

Scoring: Computer scored; hand key (only Form C & R)

Cost: Complete kit (10 reusable test booklets, 5 Form C answer-profile sheets, 5 Form C & R answer-profile sheets, scoring key, 2 computerized answer sheets, manual) $75.00

Publisher: Western Psychological Services

TEST ANXIETY PROFILE (TAP)
Refer to page 776.

THEMATIC APPERCEPTION TEST (TAT)
Henry Alexander Murray

Adolescent, adult—Ages 14–40

Purpose: Assesses personality through projective technique focusing on dominant drives, emotions, sentiments, complexes, attitudes, and conflicts.

Description: 20–item projective-type test in which a subject is shown pictures one at a time and asked to make up a story about each picture. The examiner records the subject's stories for later analysis. The projective test seeks to measure, among other things, the subject's temperament, level of emotional maturity, observational ability, intellectuality, imagination, psychological insight, creativity, sense of reality, and factors of family and psychic dynamics. Generally the subject is asked to make up stories based on 10 cards in each of two sessions. A trained examiner is required. Not suitable for group use.

Untimed: 1 hour per series

Scoring: Examiner evaluated

Cost: Complete set $18.50; manual $2.50

Publisher: Harvard University Press

TRAINING PROFICIENCY SCALE
James M. Gardner

Adult

Purpose: Assesses an individual's ability to apply behavior modification techniques. Useful for in-service training and as a dependent variable in research.

Description: 30–item role-play test measuring an individual's ability to train another person using behavior modification techniques, including reinforcement, shaping, and stimulus control. Examiner/self-administered. Not suitable for group use.

Untimed: 15 minutes

Scoring: Hand key

Cost: Scale $5.00

Publisher: Planet Press

TRANSACTIONAL ANALYSIS LIFE POSITION SURVEY (TALPS)
F.D. Kramer and B. Strade

Adult

Purpose: Measures an individual's life position as defined in transactional analysis "I'm OK" and "You're OK" dimensions. Used for personnel screening, personal assessment, and counseling aid and as a before-and-after measure for teachers presenting transactional analysis to large groups.

Description: 40–item paper-pencil test measuring attitudes toward self and others. Both "I'm OK" and "You're OK" scores are normed in percentiles for various age groups. The normed scores can be charted on a life position graph. The test is used as both a discussion-starter and as a tool for in-depth analysis. Self-administered. Suitable for group use.

Untimed: 10–15 minutes

Scoring: Hand key

Cost: Specimen set $8.00; 35 surveys $12.00; 2 scoring stencils $4.00; 35 report forms $6.00; manual $4.00

Publisher: Monitor

TRIADAL EQUATED PERSONALITY INVENTORY
United Consultants Research Staff

Adult

Purpose: Assesses personality. Used to predict job success and to measure personal adjustment.

Description: 633–item paper-pencil test of personality. Items are simple adjectives equated for response popularity. The test yields 21 self-image scores: dominance, self-confidence, decisiveness, independence, toughness, suspicion, introversion, activity, depression, foresight, industriousness, warmth, enthusiasm, conformity, inventiveness, persistence, sex drive, recognition, drive, cooperativeness, humility-tolerance, and self-control. Examiner required. Suitable for group use.

Untimed: 50–120 minutes

Scoring: Examiner evaluated

Cost: Professional examination kit for 24 $50.00

Publisher: Psychometric Affiliates

TYPE DIFFERENTIATION INDICATOR (RESEARCH EDITION)
Refer to page 266.

A VIOLENCE SCALE
Panos D. Bardis

Adolescent, adult

Purpose: Measures attitudes toward violence (words and actions aimed at property damage and personal injury).

Used for clinical assessment, marriage and family counseling, research on violence, and discussions in social science classes.

Description: 25–item paper-pencil test in which the subjects rate 25 statements concerning various aspects of violence on a scale from 0 (strongly disagree) to 4 (strongly agree). The "violence" score equals the sum of the 25 numerical responses. The theoretical range of scores extends from 0 (lowest approval of violence) to 100 (highest approval). Examiner/self-administered. Suitable for group use.

Untimed: 10 minutes

Scoring: Examiner evaluated

Cost: Free

Publisher: Panos D. Bardis

WAHLER PHYSICAL SYMPTOMS INVENTORY
H. J. Wahler

Adult

Purpose: Discriminates between patients with medical ailments and those with psychogenic complaints. Used to screen new patients.

Description: 42–item paper-pencil test consisting of physical problems on which the subjects must rate themselves using a 6–point frequency scale ranging from "almost never" to "nearly every day." The test helps identify conversion hysteria, hypochondriasis, and psychophysiological reactions, as well as physically determined disorders. Self-administered. Suitable for group use.

Untimed: 15–20 minutes

Scoring: Hand key

Cost: Complete kit (100 inventory pads, manual) $24.00

Publisher: Western Psychological Services

WAHLER SELF-DESCRIPTION INVENTORY
H. J. Wahler

Adult

Purpose: Measures the extent to which individuals emphasize their favorable and unfavorable characteristics in self-evaluations. Used to identify individuals who may be overcompensating for real or imagined inadequacies or who have poor self-images.

Description: 66–item paper-pencil test consisting of descriptive statements that the subject rates on a 9–point scale from "not at all like me" to "beyond question very much like me." Scoring provides information about defensiveness, maladjustment, potential for change, and actual change during treatment. A sixth-grade reading level is required. Self-administered. Suitable for group use.

Untimed: 10–15 minutes

Scoring: Hand key

Cost: Complete kit (100 inventory sheets, manual, key) $29.00

Publisher: Western Psychological Services

WHITAKER INDEX OF SCHIZOPHRENIC THINKING (WIST)
Leighton C. Whitaker

**Adolescent, adult
Grades 8 and above**

Purpose: Provides an index of schizophrenic thinking. Used for intake screening.

Description: 25–item paper-pencil multiple-choice test discriminating between schizophrenic and nonschizophrenic thinking. The test can be completed by anyone with an eighth-grade education. The test is available in two equivalent forms. A revised (1980) manual provides a discussion of relevant diagnostic issues and the development of the test, directions for administration and scoring, standardization and validity data, a discussion of diagnostic and clinical uses, case illustrations, references, and specimen copies of the test forms. Self-administered. Suitable for group use.

Untimed: 15 minutes

Scoring: Hand key

Cost: Kit (25 each form, key, manual) $38.00

Publisher: Western Psychological Services

WILLIAMS AWARENESS SENTENCE COMPLETION (WASC)
Robert L. Williams

Adolescent, adult

Purpose: Measures ethnic awareness and consciousness of black Americans.

Description: 40–item paper-pencil sentence-completion test pertaining to black awareness as manifested in four factors: prowhite, antiblack, problack, and antiwhite sentiments. Self-administered. Suitable for group use.

Untimed: 20 minutes

Scoring: Examiner evaluated

Cost: Complete (tests, manual) $12.00

Publisher: Robert L. Williams & Associates, Inc.

Information and availability unconfirmed; last verified in 1987.

Personality: Normal and Abnormal, Assessment and Treatment: Multilevels

ABERRANT BEHAVIOR CHECKLIST (ABC)
Michael G. Aman and Nirbhay N. Singh

Mentally retarded individuals

Purpose: Assesses the problem behaviors of mentally retarded individuals living in hospital and residential facilities. Used by psychologists, nurses, direct caregivers, and others to measure treatment effectiveness.

Description: 58–item paper-pencil symptom checklist assessing the problem behaviors of mentally retarded individuals and measuring treatment effectiveness. The instrument contains five subscales: irritability; lethargy, social withdrawal; stereotypic behavior; hyperactivity, noncompliance; and inappropriate speech. Examiner required. Not suitable for group use.

Untimed: Varies

Scoring: Examiner evaluated

Cost: Complete kit (manual, 50 checklist/score sheets) $35.00

Publisher: Slosson Educational Publications, Inc.

ADOLESCENT SEPARATION ANXIETY TEST
Henry G. Hansburg

Ages 10–adult

Purpose: Evaluates the emotional and personality patterns with which individuals react to separation experiences. Used by clinical psychologists as a counseling tool when separation anxieties are suspected.

Description: 12–item verbal-response test consisting of illustrations of severe and mild separation experiences ranging from a picture of a child being transferred to a new class to a picture of a child and father standing at the mother's coffin. Each picture contains a set of 17 statements describing a range of possible feelings associated with the situation depicted. The subjects look at each picture and then tell the examiner which statements best describe their reactions. The test measures interaction of attachment, individuation, hostility, fear-anxiety-pain syndrome, defensiveness, and self-evaluation (self-esteem, self-love identity). The diagnostic categories most frequently used with the instrument consist of mild, strong, severe anxious attachment; hostile anxious attachment; hostile detachment; and excessive self-sufficiency or dependence. The test has been used experimentally with whole families. A 3–volume series on separation problems

based on the use of the Separation Anxiety Test is available. Examiner required. Not suitable for group use.

Untimed: 20 minutes

Scoring: Examiner evaluated

Cost: Complete kit (Volumes I and II, boy test, girl test, evaluation pads) $22.50; Volume I *ST of Adolescent Separation Problems* $6.95; Volume II *Separation Disorders* $8.96; tests $3.00 (specify boy or girl); 30 evaluation sheets $6.00; Volume III *Researches in Separation Anxiety*

Publisher: Robert E. Kreiger Publishing Company, Inc.

Information and availability unconfirmed; last verified in 1988.

AUTISM SCREENING INSTRUMENT FOR EDUCATIONAL PLANNING (ASIEP)
David A. Krug, Joel R. Arick, and Patricia J. Almond

Ages 18 months–adult

Purpose: Assesses the behavioral, social, and educational development of autistic, mentally retarded, deaf/blind, and emotionally disturbed students. Used to establish IEPs, evaluate program effectiveness, and monitor student progress.

Description: Multiple-item paper-pencil observational inventory consisting of five subtests: Autism Behavior Checklist (ABC), Sample of Vocal Behavior, Interaction Assessment, Educational Assessment, and Prognosis of Learning Rate.

The Autism Behavior Checklist contains 57 observable behaviors discriminating autism from other severely handicapping conditions, such as deaf/blind, severely emotionally disturbed, and mentally retarded.

The Sample of Vocal Behavior assesses spontaneous verbal behavior in low-language developmentally delayed students. The examiner records 50 representative vocalizations in an unstructured setting. The sample is then analyzed for repetitive level, communicative value, vocal complexity, and syntactic complexity. The results yield a standardized language-age equivalency score.

The Interaction Assessment provides a data-based assessment of social interaction between an adult and a child, recording observable behaviors such as self-stimulation, crying, laughing, gestures, toy manipulation, conversation, and tantrums. During a 12–minute period, the examiner observes the child for 10 seconds, then in the next 5 seconds codes the interval according to the student's behavior on a matrix coding sheet yielding a general social interaction profile.

The Educational Assessment measures language performance and communicative ability. The student uses either sign language or verbal speech to answer the examiner's questions. The responses are interpreted quantitatively in the following areas: in-seat behavior, receptive language, expressive language, body concept, and speech imitation.

The Prognosis of Learning Rate involves teaching each student a standardized task within a specific framework of responses. The student's learning acquisition rate is assessed in terms of responses to learn a black/white sequencing task.

The observational methods involved in all five subtests allow all students to be "testable." Examiner required. Not suitable for group use. The Autism Behavior Checklist with instructions and profile is available in Spanish.

Untimed: Varies

Scoring: Examiner evaluated

Cost: Kit (administration manual, 10 record form booklets, all materials needed for administration) $194.00; Spanish Edition of the Autism Behavior Checklist with 20 administration and scoring booklets $29.00

Publisher: PRO-ED

BEHAVIOR DIMENSIONS RATING SCALE (BDRS)
Lyndal M. Bullock and Michael J. Wilson

Ages 5–adult

Purpose: Measures behavior patterns in individuals ages 5 to adult.

Description: 43–item rating-scale used by psychologists, teachers, counselors, or parents to rate subjects' behavior on a 7–point scale. Scores provide a profile of four behavior subscales: Aggressive/Acting Out, Irresponsible/Inattentive, Socially Withdrawn, and Fearful/Anxious. Record forms are on carbonless NCR paper. Results are automatically transferred to the scoring sheet. Self-administered. Suitable for group use.

Untimed: 5–10 minutes

Scoring: Carbonless automatic scoring/record forms

Cost: Kit (examiners manual, 25 record forms) $65.00

Publisher: DLM Teaching Resources

BEHAVIORAL DEVIANCY PROFILE
Betty Ball and Rita Weinberg

Ages 3–21

Purpose: Diagnoses deviancy and disturbance in children and adolescents with moderate to severe social and emotional problems. Used to compare deviance of physical, psychological, and social factors in a child before and after intervention and to improve the observations of staff in mental health and educational programs.

Description: Multiple-item paper-pencil questionnaire in which the examiner records the child's observed behavior in four major developmental areas: physical and motor development, cognitive development, speech and language development, and social and emotional development. The profile looks at the total functioning of the child via a developmental and dynamic method. Severity of behavior, duration, and age appropriateness of the behavior are considered. Examiner required. Not suitable for group use.

Untimed: Observation time

Scoring: Examiner evaluated

Cost: Complete kit (manual, 15 record booklets) $15.25

Publisher: Stoelting Co.

BEHAVIORAL INTERVENTION PLAN
James M. Gardner

All ages

Purpose: Produces multimodal behavior intervention strategies for individuals of all ages. Used by professional mental health and education personnel for psychotherapy and behavior modification and management. May be used with handicapped and nonhandicapped individuals.

Description: 2000–item paper-pencil multiple-choice and fill-in-the-blank test assessing the severity of an individual's behavior problems, including aggression, destructiveness, and self-abuse. Test items focus on the person, the setting, and the behavior. Results are used for reducing the incidence and severity of the behavior problem. Examiner required. Suitable for group use.

Untimed: 30 minutes

Scoring: Computer scored

Cost: $150.00 per evaluation

Publisher: Planet Press

THE BLACKY PICTURES
Gerald S. Blum

Ages 5–adult

Purpose: Clinical assessment of personality dynamics. Used for psychodynamically oriented research.

Description: 68–item paper-pencil picture test of personality using a set of 12 pictures. The subject views the pictures, makes up a story and answers six or seven multiple-choice or short-answer questions for each picture, and then sorts pictures according to preference. The instrument helps determine conflicts and defenses in the area of psychosexual development. The test also is suitable as a semistructured projective test of psychosexual stages of development. Materials include the pictures, inquiry booklets, record blanks, and a manual. The test may be administered individually or to groups using slides of pictures. The slides are not yet available commercially. Examiner required. Suitable for group use. Available in Italian.

Untimed: 45 minutes

Scoring: Examiner evaluated

Cost: Complete set (12 pictures, inquiry booklets, manual, 25 record blanks) $50.00

Publisher: Psychodynamic Instruments

BRIEF LIFE HISTORY INVENTORY
Donald I. Templer and
David M. Veleber

All ages

Purpose: Assesses history of psychological adjustment. Used in psychodiagnostic counseling.

Description: Multiple-item paper-pencil short-answer checklist that summarizes general information, present problems, medical/psychological history, family life, work or school, and substance abuse of clients. Separate forms are available for students and adults. Examiner required. Not suitable for group use.

Untimed: Varies

Scoring: Examiner evaluated

Cost: 25 inventories $12.00

Publisher: United Educational Services, Inc.

BRISTOL SOCIAL ADJUSTMENT GUIDES
Refer to page 737.

BRISTOL SOCIAL ADJUSTMENT GUIDES, AMERICAN EDITION (BSAG)
Refer to page 737.

BURKS' BEHAVIOR RATING SCALES
Harold F. Burks

Child, adolescent
Grades 1–9

Purpose: Identifies patterns of behavior problems in children. Used as an aid to differential diagnosis.

Description: 110–item paper-pencil inventory used by parents and teachers to rate a child on the basis of descriptive statements of observed behavior. Nineteen subscales measure excessive self-blame, anxiety, withdrawal, dependency,

---

suffering, sense of persecution, aggressiveness, resistance, poor ego strength, physical strength, coordination, intellectuality, academics, attention, impulse control, reality contact, sense of identity, anger control, and social conformity. The Parents' Guide and the Teacher's Guide define each of the scales, present possible causes for the problem behavior, and offer suggestions on how to deal with the undesirable behavior from the point of view of the parent or teacher. The manual discusses causes and manifestations and possible intervention approaches for each of the subscales as well as use with special groups, such as the educable mentally retarded, educationally and orthopedically handicapped, and speech and hearing handicapped. Examiner required. Not suitable for group use.

Untimed: 15–20 minutes

Scoring: Hand key

Cost: Complete kit (25 booklets and profile sheets, manual, 2 parents' guides, 2 teacher's guides) $23.50

Publisher: Western Psychological Services

THE C.P.H. (COLORADO PSYCHOPATHIC HOSPITAL) PATIENT ATTITUDE SCALE
Marvin W. Kahn and Nelson F. Jones

Adult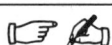

Purpose: Assesses a mental patient's attitudes toward hospital treatment. Used as a research tool and for examining ward programs and comparing occurrences in the hospital with the patient's social station in life.

Description: 45–item paper-pencil short-answer test assessing five attitude dimensions: authoritarian control and nonpsychological orientation; negative hospital orientation; external control, cause and treatment; mental illness and treatment as the hospital supplies regressive dependence; and let-down of control for therapeutic gain-arbitrary restriction. Items are scored on a 5–point Likert scale ranging from strongly agree to strongly disagree. Scores are provided for each dimension. Materials include scales and manual. A

fifth-grade reading level is required. Examiner/self-administered. Suitable for group use.

Untimed: 10–30 minutes

Scoring: Hand key

Cost: Specimen set $3.50

Publisher: Marvin W. Kahn, Ph.D.

Information and availability unconfirmed; last verified in 1988.

CALIFORNIA ADAPTIVE BEHAVIOR SCALE
James M. Gardner

Child, adolescent—
Ages 0–18

Purpose: Measures an individual's overall adaptive behavior. Used for assessment and placement.

Description: 353–item paper-pencil or computer-administered multiple-choice test assessing adaptive behavior and school and/or vocational readiness. An individual familiar with the person being rated uses a booklet or computer to assess self-help, socialization, language, gross-motor, perceptual motor, vocational, independent living, and academic skills. Can be purchased for Apple II, CP/M, or MS-DOS computers. Examiner/self-administered. Suitable for group use.

Untimed: 15 minutes

Scoring: Computer scored

Cost: Disk $350.00; mail-in service $10.00 per evaluation

Publisher: Planet Press

THE CHILD DIAGNOSTIC SCREENING BATTERY
James J. Smith and Joseph M. Eisenberg

Child, adolescent—
Ages 2–17

Purpose: Identifies diagnostic possibilities among those listed in DSM III-R. Used with children in clinical settings.

Description: Paper-pencil or computer-administered screening battery assessing symptoms important for diagnostic considerations. The system consists of two parts: a questionnaire for the child's parent or guardian and a questionnaire for the clinician. The clinician gathers information through a structured interview with the child's parent or guardian. The system is structured so that once data is entered in the computer, it is compared with all possible DSM-III-R diagnoses related to children. A manual describing the use and application of the program and the use of printouts generated by the program is provided. Self-administered. Suitable for group use.

Untimed: 15 minutes

Scoring: Computer scored

Cost: Total system $195.00

Publisher: Reason House

THE CHILDREN'S DEPRESSION INVENTORY (CDI)
Maria Kovacs

Child, adolescent—Ages 8-17

Purpose: Assesses severity of depression in children and adolescents. Also used for measuring progress during treatment and for classifying for research purposes.

Description: 27–item paper-pencil inventory measuring an array of overt symptoms of child depression, such as sadness, anhedonia, suicidal ideation, and sleep and appetite disturbances. The examiner reads aloud three related statements, such as "I am sad once in a while," "I am sad many times," and "I am sad all the time." The child reads along silently and selects the statement that best reflects his feelings and ideas during the previous two weeks. The three choices for each item are assigned numerical values from 0–2, graded in order of increasing psychopathology. A total score (ranging from 0–54) is obtained by adding the numerical scores of the individual items. A first-grade reading level is required. Examiner required. Suitable for group use. Available in Arabic, Hebrew, Hungarian, Italian, Spanish, French, German, Bulgarian, Japanese, and Portuguese.

Untimed: Varies

Scoring: Hand key

Cost: Inventory and supplementary materials $2.75

Publisher: Maria Kovacs, Ph.D.

CHILDREN'S DEPRESSION SCALE—SECOND RESEARCH EDITION
Moshe Lange and Miriam Tisher

Child, adolescent—Ages 9-16

Purpose: Measures depression in children. Identifies depressed children in need of further evaluation.

Description: 66–item (48 "depressive" and 18 "positive") scale measuring six aspects of childhood depression: affective response, social problems, self-esteem, preoccupation with own sickness or death, guilt, and pleasure. Items are presented on cards that the child sorts into five boxes ranging from "very right" to "very wrong" according to how he or she feels the item applies to himself. A paper-pencil questionnaire identical in content to the cards but appropriately reworded, is available for use with parents, teachers, or other adults familiar with the child. The complete set of materials includes 66 cards, five boxes, 25 record forms, and a manual. Examiner required. Not suitable for group use.

AUSTRALIAN PUBLISHER

Untimed: Varies

Scoring: Examiner evaluated

Cost: Contact publisher

Publisher: The Australian Council for Educational Research Limited

---

CHILDREN'S INTERACTION MATRIX (CIM)
William Fawcett Hill

Child
Grades 1-6

Purpose: Assesses grade-school children's suitability for assignment to counseling groups or other small groups. Used to determine group composition.

Description: 64–item paper-pencil test determining the child's overall acceptance of small groups, what the children talk about in the group, and their manner and degree of participation. The child reads statements describing a group situation and marks his reaction on the answer sheet scale. Examiner/self-administered. Suitable for group use.

Untimed: 20 minutes

Scoring: Hand key; may be computer scored

Cost: Monograph $4.00; manual $3.00; computer programs $2.00 each

Publisher: William Fawcett Hill

CONNERS' PARENT AND TEACHER RATING SCALES
C. Keith Conners

Child, adolescent—Ages 3–17

Purpose: Measures hyperactivity and other patterns of child behavior.

Description: Paper-pencil or computer-administered instrument used to evaluate problem behaviors of children as reported by the child's teacher, parents, or alternate caregiver. The Teacher Version is available in a 28–item (CTRS–28) or 39–item (CTRS–39) form and includes the following scales: Hyperactivity, Conduct Problem, Emotional Overindulgent, Anxious-Passive, Asocial, and Daydream Attendance Problem. The Parent Version is available in a 48–item (CPRS–48) or 93–item (CPRS–93) form and includes the following scales: Conduct Disorder, Psychosomatic, Learning Problem-Immature, Restless-Disorganized, Fearful-Anxious, Obsessional, Hyperactive-Immature, Impulsive-Hyperactive, and Antisocial. Derived T-scores can be obtained for the Teacher and Parent versions. Self-administered. Not suitable for group use.

Untimed: Varies

Scoring: Carbonized Quik Score forms; may be computer scored

Cost: Complete kit (test manual, 25 Quik Score forms for each of 4 versions) $80.00; IBM PC comaptible version (50 administrations and scorings for each of 4 versions) $145.00

Publisher: Multi-Health Systems Inc.

COOPERSMITH SELF-ESTEEM INVENTORIES (CSEI)
Stanley Coopersmith

Ages 8–adult

Purpose: Measures attitudes toward the self in social, academic, and personal contexts. Used for individual diagnosis, classroom screening, pre-post evaluations, and clinical and research studies.

Description: 58– or 25–item paper-pencil test of self-attitudes in four areas: social-self-peers, home-parents, school-academic, and general-self. Materials include the 58–item School Form, 25–item School Short Form, and 25–item Adult Form. The School Form is suitable for use with individuals ages 8–15; the Adult Form is administered to individuals ages 15 and older. The School Form may be used with Behavioral Academic Self-Esteem (BASE) for individual diagnosis, classroom screening, and pre- and post-evaluations, as well as in clinical and research studies. Self-administered. Suitable for group use.

Untimed: 15 minutes

Scoring: Hand key

Cost: 25 School Form test booklets $5.25; 25 Adult Form test booklets $3.75; scoring key (specify student or adult) $2.25; manual $6.50

Publisher: Consulting Psychologists Press, Inc.

CULTURE-FREE SELF-ESTEEM INVENTORIES
James Battle

Grades 3 and above

Purpose: Assesses the self-esteem of children and adults. Identifies individuals needing psychological assistance.

Description: Multiple-item paper-pencil test assessing five areas of self-esteem: general, school-related, peer-related, parent-related, and defensiveness. Raw scores for each subscale and a total score are obtained with acetate scoring templates. Percentile ranks and standard scores are provided for children in Grades 3–9 and adults. Separate forms are available for children and adults; parallel forms are available for children for pre- and posttesting. The test may be administered orally or with a cassette tape to low-level readers. Suitable for group use.

Untimed: 10–15 minutes

Scoring: Hand key; may be computer scored

Cost: Test kit (25 each of forms A and B for children, 25 of form AD for adults, manual quick-scoring acetates, 25 computer-scorable answer sheets, oral administration on cassette tape) $51.00

Publisher: PRO-ED

CURRENT AND PAST PSYCHOPATHOLOGY SCALES (CAPPS)
Jean Endicott and The Department of Research Assessment and Training

All ages

Purpose: Assesses past and present psychiatric functioning. Used for diagnosis of psychopathology.

Description: 171 scales and checklist items measuring psychiatric signs and symptoms and covering a broad range of material similar to the Psychiatric Evaluation Form. Additional items cover history relevant to severity, prognosis, and diagnosis. The CAPPS is completed by the examiner after a clinical workup or thorough client interview. Examiner required. Not suitable for group use.

Untimed: 1–2 hours with interview

Scoring: Examiner evaluated; computer diagnosis available

Cost: Booklet with score sheets $1.00; score sheet $0.20; suggested procedure/ training $0.20; instructions $0.40; Fortran program (scoring) $125.00; Family Evaluation Form (FEF) booklets $1.00; scoring system $1.50 plus postage and handling

Publisher: Department of Research Assessment and Training—N.Y. State Psychiatric Institute

Information and availability unconfirmed; last verified in 1987.

DEATH ANXIETY SCALE
Donald I. Templer

Adult

Purpose: Assesses anxiety related to death.

Description: 15–item paper-pencil scale in both true-false and Likert format measuring death anxiety as it permeates a wide range of life experiences. Self-administered. Suitable for group use. Available in German, Spanish, Hindi, Arabic, Chinese, Japanese, Korean, and Afrikaans.

Untimed: Varies

Scoring: Contact publisher

Cost: Free

Publisher: Donald I. Templer, Ph.D.

DYSPHORIMETER
Leopold Bellak

All ages

Purpose: Assesses degree of dysphoria. Used in therapy.

Description: Criterion-referenced instrumental analogue to subjective dysphoria states, such as depression, anxiety, depersonalization, and pain. The subject matches his or her subjective way of feeling to the sound on some point of the scale from 1 to 10. Examiner required. Not suitable for group use.

Untimed: Varies

Scoring: Examiner evaluated

Cost: $85.00

Publisher: C.P.S., Inc.

ELEMENTS OF AWARENESS (CLINICAL & RESEARCH EDITION)—ELEMENT B (BEHAVIOR)
Will Schutz

All ages

Purpose: Measures an individual's behavior toward others. Used in experimentation and research.

Description: 54–item paper-pencil test containing six Guttman-type scales assessing behavior in three areas: inclusion (amount of interpersonal contact), control (amount of control over others), and openness (closeness and candor in relationships). Examinees are instructed to answer each item twice—first describing how things are (perceived) and then describing how they would like things to be (wanted). Forms for Element F (Feelings) and Element R (Relationship) are also available. Examiner/self-administered. Suitable for group use.

Untimed: Not available

Scoring: Hand key

Cost: 25 reusable question booklets $8.25; 50 each of response sheets and interpretive guides $18.00

Publisher: Consulting Psychologists Press, Inc.

ELEMENTS OF AWARENESS (CLINICAL & RESEARCH EDITION)—ELEMENT F (FEELINGS)
Will Schutz

All ages

Purpose: Evaluates an individual's feelings toward others. Used in experimentation and research.

Description: 54–item paper-pencil test containing six Guttman-type scales measuring significance, likeability, and competence. The scales attempt to combine examinees' feelings toward others and their perceptions of how others feel about them. Forms for Element B (Behavior) and Element R (Relationship) are available. Examiner/self-administered. Suitable for group use.

Untimed: Not available

Scoring: Hand key

Cost: 25 reusable question booklets $8.25; 50 each response sheets and interpretive guides $18.00

Publisher: Consulting Psychologists Press, Inc.

ELEMENTS OF AWARENESS (CLINICAL & RESEARCH EDITION)—ELEMENT R (RELATIONSHIP)
Will Schutz

All ages

Purpose: Assesses the perceptions two people in a relationship have of their behavior toward each other. Used in experimentation and research.

Description: 108–item paper-pencil test consisting of 12 Guttman-type scales assessing how two people in a relationship perceive their behavior toward each other. Respondents first answer the questions based on how things are (perceived) and then on how they would like things to be (wanted). Forms are also available for Element B (Behavior) and Element F (Feelings). Examiner/self-administered. Suitable for group use.

Untimed: Not available

Scoring: Hand key

Cost: 50 question booklets $20.00; 50 each response sheets and interpretive guides $18.00

Publisher: Consulting Psychologists Press, Inc.

EMBEDDED FIGURES TEST (EFT)
Herman A. Witkin

Ages 10–adult

Purpose: Assesses cognitive style in perceptual tasks. Used in counseling.

Description: 12–item verbal-manual test of perceptual processes including field dependence-independence. The task requires the subject to locate and trace a previously seen simple figure within a larger complex figure. Performance is related to analytic ability, social behavior, body concept, and preferred defense mechanisms. Materials include cards with complex figures, cards with simple figures, and a stylus for tracing. A stopwatch with a second hand is needed also. Two alternate forms are available. Examiner required. Not suitable for group use.

Untimed: 10–45 minutes

Scoring: Examiner evaluated

Cost: Test kit (card sets, stylus, 50 recording sheets) $18.00

Publisher: Consulting Psychologists Press, Inc.

EMOTIONAL FACTORS INVENTORY
Mary K. Bauman

Visually handicapped individuals

Purpose: Measures emotional and personality factors of individuals with visual handicaps.

Description: 170–item paper-pencil or oral-response questionnaire assessing the personal and emotional adjustment of individuals with visual impairments. The questionnaire yields scores on the following seven scales: sensitivity, somatic symptoms, social competency, attitudes of distrust, feelings of inadequacy, depression, and attitudes concerning blindness. A validation score is also obtained. The questionnaire is presented in large-print format. Instructions for tape recording the questions are included. Supplementary materials provided in the test kit include a discussion of the inventory, instructions for administering and scoring the inventory, and a comparative study of personality factors in blind, other handicapped, and nonhandicapped individuals. Examiner required. The paper-pencil version is suitable for group use.

Untimed: Varies

Scoring: Examiner evaluated

Cost: Test kit (test booklet, scoring overlays, 10 IBM answer sheets, supplementary materials, and norms) $15.00

Publisher: Associated Services for the Blind

ENVIRONMENTAL DEPRIVATION SCALE
Gerald R. Pascal and William O. Jenkins

Ages 10–adult

Purpose: Clinical measurement of an individual's environmental deprivation. Predicts recidivism of offenders, mental hospital patients, and others who exhibit maladaption. Useful to pinpoint areas requiring intervention.

Description: 16–item paper-pencil test measuring environmental support/deprivation. Items include employment, income, debts, parental relationship, education, and fear. Behavioral interviewing techniques are used in face-to-face contact with subjects. Scoring is a forced-choice technique: "0" for no deprivation and "1" for deprivation. Materials include manual and answer sheets. A juvenile version is available. Examiner required. Not suitable for group use.

Untimed: 30 minutes

Scoring: Hand key

Cost: Complete kit (25 test forms, manual) $35.00

Publisher: Behavior Science Press

FACIAL INTERPERSONAL PERCEPTION INVENTORY (FIPI)
J. Luciani and R.E. Carney

Ages 3 and older

Purpose: Assesses an individual's self-perception. Suitable for use with normal subjects as well as with illiterate non-English-speaking individuals or the physically, mentally, or hearing-impaired.

Description: 26–item paper-pencil nonverbal projective point-to instrument using cartoon faces to assess present and ideal self-perception or perception of others, as well as incongruence between present and ideal perception. The items are divided into two categories, Present Perception (13 items) and Ideal Perception (13 items). The test yields 15 scores: Total Positive Perception (S), Pleasant-Unpleasant (PU), Attention-Rejection (AR), Sleep-Tension (ST), Total Inconsistency (K), Systematic Inconsistency (K1), Unsystematic Inconsistency (K2), Inconsistency F ratio (K3), Total Incongruence (C), PU Incongruence (PU1), AR Incongruence (AR1), ST Incongruence (ST1), Systematic Incongruence (C1), Unsystematic Incongruence (C2), and Incongruence F ratio (C3). The test form integrates items, scoring, and a profile. A scoring service is available from the publisher. The test requires no reading skills; however, if the subject is illiterate, the examiner must speak the subject's native language. Materials must be ordered in quantities of 50 or more. Examiner/self-administered. Not suitable for group use unless examinee is literate. Available in Spanish.

Untimed: Not available

Scoring: Hand key; may be computer scored

Cost: 50 test forms $12.50; specimen set $7.00

Publisher: Carney, Weedman and Associates

FOUR PICTURE TEST
D. J. VanLennep and R. Houwink

Ages 10 and older

Purpose: Assesses personality. Used for diagnosis and individual counseling.

Description: 4–item projective test of personality in which the subject looks at four pictures for one minute. The pictures are removed, and the subject is asked to write a single story based on memory in which all four pictures are used. Materials include four picture cards and manual. Examiner required. Suitable for group use.
DUTCH PUBLISHER
Untimed: 30–45 minutes
Scoring: Examiner evaluated
Cost: Contact publisher
Publisher: SWETS and Zeitlinger B.V.
Information and availability unconfirmed; last verified in 1988.

FUNCTIONAL ANALYSIS OF BEHAVIOR
James M. Gardner

Child, adolescent, adult

Purpose: Provides a detailed and comprehensive description and analysis of individuals exhibiting severe behavior problems. Used with handicapped and nonhandicapped individuals for assessment and intervention.

Description: 90–item paper-pencil multiple-choice and fill-in-the-blank test. Computer analysis produces a functional analysis of behavior, including topogra-

phy, course of the behavior, analysis of antecedents, severity of behavior, history of behavior, analysis of consequences, independent learning style, and suggested techniques. Completed by informant. Suitable for group use.

Untimed: 15 minutes

Scoring: Computer scored

Cost: $50.00 per evaluation

Publisher: Planet Press

FUNCTIONAL PERFORMANCE RECORD
Refer to page 651.

FUNDAMENTAL INTERPERSONAL RELATIONS ORIENTATION—BEHAVIOR (FIRO-B)
Will Schutz

All ages

Purpose: Measures an individual's characteristic behavior toward others. Used in individual and group psychotherapy, in executive development programs, and as a measure of compatibility in relationships.

Description: 54–item paper-pencil or computer-administered test measuring six dimensions of an individual's behavior toward others: expressed inclusion, expressed control, expressed affection, wanted inclusion, wanted control, and wanted affection. Optional materials include the FIRO-BC, a form developed for use with children. Software for administration and scoring is available for IBM PC or compatible systems with 256K, one disk drive, and DOS 2.0 or greater. Examiner/self-administered. Suitable for group use.

Untimed: Paper-pencil version 20 minutes; computer version 10 minutes

Scoring: Hand key; may be computer scored

Cost: Specimen set, paper-pencil version (tests, key, self-scoring test with profile, and *Understanding Your FIRO-B Results*) $5.50; IBM version (100 client administrations, 1 counselor practice administration) $150.00

Publisher: Consulting Psychologists Press, Inc.

FUNDAMENTAL INTERPERSONAL RELATIONS ORIENTATION—BEHAVIOR CHARACTERISTICS (FIRO-BC)
Will Schutz and Marilyn Wood

Child, adolescent

Purpose: Measures characteristic behavior of children toward other people. Used with upper elementary and junior high school children for counseling and therapy.

Description: 54–item paper-pencil test containing six Guttman-type scales measuring the characteristic behavior of children in the areas of inclusion, control, and affection—the three dimensions of interpersonal behavior described by the author in his book, *The Interpersonal Underworld.* The test measures the relative strength of the needs within the individual. Because it does not compare a person with a population, norms are not provided. Examiner/self-administered. Suitable for group use.

Untimed: Not available

Scoring: Hand key

Cost: 25 test booklets $8.75; scoring key $7.50

Publisher: Consulting Psychologists Press, Inc.

GRID TEST OF SCHIZOPHRENIC THOUGHT DISORDER
D. Bannister and Fay Fransella

All ages

Purpose: Identifies schizophrenic thought disorder. Used for diagnosis of schizophrenia.

Description: Multiple-item test of thought disorder based on ranking photographs of people on various dimensions. Eight photographs are presented to the

subject, and the subject ranks the pictures from most to least likely to be kind. The subject then ranks the pictures for stupid, selfish, sincere, mean, and honest. Responses are scored on the basis of consistency and intensity. The relationship between the sorting categories, rather than the "correctness" of the sorts, is the most important evaluative factor. Materials include eight photographs. Examiner required. Not suitable for group use.

BRITISH PUBLISHER

Untimed: 20 minutes

Scoring: Examiner evaluated

Cost: Specimen set (pictures, manual, record sheet, analysis sheet) $17.25; set of pictures $7.50; 50 analysis sheets $18.45; manual $7.80

Publisher: Psychological Test Publishers; distributed by The Test Agency Ltd.

GRIM
Martin B. Keller

Ages 6 and older
Grades K and above

Purpose: Evaluates suicidal gestures, attempts, and deaths. Used with psychiatric populations.

Description: 21–item oral-response test examining a) the events that took place the week prior to a suicide attempt, b) the type of report (i.e., gesture/attempt, completed suicide), c) the suicidal behavior, d) the circumstances surrounding the attempt, and e) a narrative description of the event. A new report is completed for each suicide gesture or attempt. Completed by a cohort rater. Suitable for use with individuals with physical and mental impairments. Examiner required. Not suitable for group use.

Timed: 5 minutes

Scoring: Examiner evaluated

Cost: Contact publisher

Publisher: Martin B. Keller

GROUP EMBEDDED FIGURES TEST (GEFT)
Philip K. Oltman, Evelyn Raskin, and Herman A. Witkin

Ages 10–adult

Purpose: Assesses cognitive style in perceptual tasks. Used in counseling.

Description: 25–item paper-pencil test of perceptual processes, including field dependence-independence. Performance is related to analytic ability, social behavior, body concept, and preferred defense mechanisms. Subjects find one of eight simple figures in the 18 complex designs. Examiner required. Suitable for group use.

Untimed: 20 minutes

Scoring: Hand key

Cost: Sample set (test booklet, scoring key) $2.00; manual $3.75; 25 tests $18.50; scoring key $1.25

Publisher: Consulting Psychologists Press, Inc.

GROUP PERSONALITY PROJECTIVE TEST (GPPT)
R. N. Cassel and T.C. Kahn

Ages 11 and older

Purpose: Measures major personality characteristics. Used to screen potentially pathological personalities.

Description: 90–item paper-pencil test measuring seven aspects of personality, including tension, nurturance, withdrawal, neuroticism, affiliation, succorance, and total. Items are stick drawings accompanied by five descriptive or interpretative statements. The subject chooses the statement he believes is most accurate. Self-administered. Suitable for group use.

Untimed: 40 minutes

Scoring: Hand key; examiner evaluated

Cost: Examiner's set (manual, 7 scoring keys, 12 test booklets, 100 answer and profile sheets) $27.00; 25 test booklets $25.00; 100 answer and profile sheets $13.00; scoring keys $4.00; manual $4.00

Publisher: Psychological Test Specialists

HARTMAN VALUE PROFILE (HVP)
Robert S. Hartman

Ages 5–adult

Purpose: Assesses a person's capacity to value and indicates presence of emotional or existential problems. Used for mental health screening, personnel evaluation, research, educational program evaluation, assessment of special education class needs, and development of individual goals.

Description: Multiple-item paper-pencil or oral-response inventory measuring a person's capacity to value in terms of both intellectual and emotional capacities. Scores are provided on the following scales: World Concept-Self Concept Potentials, Cognitive-Affective Domain Relationships, Social-Emotional Handicaps, and Interpersonal Compatibility. Computer processing makes large-scale screening possible, while in-depth analysis provides significant psychiatric and psychological insight. The profile is available in three forms (regular, card, and pictorial), making testing possible with subjects from ages five to adult. Examiner/self-administered. Suitable for group use. Available in Spanish.

Untimed: 20–30 minutes

Scoring: Hand key; examiner evaluated; may be computer scored

Cost: 35 profile forms $8.75; profile card form $12.00; profile pictorial form $15.00; 35 keys $5.00; manual $18.00; text $9.50

Publisher: Research Concepts

Information and availability unconfirmed; last verified in 1987.

HILL INTERACTION MATRIX-A (HIM-A)
William Fawcett Hill

Ages 8–80

Purpose: Assesses adolescents' and adults' suitability for assignment to counseling groups or other small groups. Used to determine group composition and diagnose problem members. May be used with the elderly.

Description: 64–item paper-pencil multiple-choice test measuring an individual's overall acceptance of small groups, discussion topic preferences, and participation tendencies. The subject reads statements describing a group situation and marks reactions on the 6–position answer sheet scale for each item. Hill Interaction Matrix-B is available with more sophisticated language. A computer scoring service that operates on IBM PC systems is available from the publisher. Examiner/self-administered. Suitable for group use. Available in German.

Untimed: 20 minutes

Scoring: Hand key; may be computer scored

Cost: Monograph $4.00; manual $3.00; computer programs $2.00 each

Publisher: William Fawcett Hill

HILL INTERACTION MATRIX-B (HIM-B)
William Fawcett Hill

Ages 8–80

Purpose: Assesses suitability of adolescents and adults for assignment to counseling groups or other small groups. Used to determine group composition. May be used with the elderly.

Description: 64–item paper-pencil test measuring an individual's overall acceptance of small groups, discussion topic preferences, and style of participation. The subject reads statements describing a group situation and marks reactions on the 6–position answer sheet scale for each item. Hill Interaction Matrix-A is available with simpler language. A computer scoring service that operates on IBM PC systems is available from the publisher. Examiner/self-administered. Suitable for group use. Available in German.

Untimed: 20 minutes

Scoring: Hand key; may be computer scored

Cost: Monograph $4.00; manual $3.00; computer programs $2.00 each

Publisher: William Fawcett Hill

HILL INTERACTION MATRIX-G (HIM-G)
William Fawcett Hill

Ages 8–80

Purpose: Assesses verbal interaction in counseling and encounter groups. May be used to estimate current functioning of a group and to determine group development through repeated evaluation. May be used with the elderly.

Description: 74–item paper-pencil test measuring the work mode, topic preference, risk-taking ratio, and therapist-member interaction ratio of a group. The subject observes, listens to, or views a tape recording, or reads a transcript of a group session and marks the amount of interaction for each item on a 7–point scale. A computer scoring service that operates on IBM PC and compatible systems is available from the publisher. Examiner/self-administered. Suitable for group use.

Untimed: 20 minutes

Scoring: Hand key; may be computer scored

Cost: Monograph $4.00; manual $3.00; computer programs $2.00 each

Publisher: William Fawcett Hill

HOLTZMAN INKBLOT TECHNIQUE (HIT)
W. H. Holtzman

Ages 5–adult

Purpose: Assesses an individual's personality characteristics. Used for diagnosis and therapy planning.

Description: 45–item projective measure of personality in which the examinee responds to 45 inkblots. Some inkblots are asymmetric, and some are in a color other than black. An objective scoring system has been developed. Materials include two alternate and equivalent forms, A and B, for a total of 90 stimulus cards. Examiner required. Not suitable for group use.

Untimed: Not available

Scoring: Examiner evaluated

Cost: Complete set (45 inkblots, 25 record forms with summary sheets, scoring guide) Form A or B $160.00; Forms A and B combined $298.00; monograph $50.00

Publisher: The Psychological Corporation

Information and availability unconfirmed; last verified in 1988.

HOUSE-TREE-PERSON (H-T-P) PROJECTIVE TECHNIQUE
John N. Buck

Ages 3 and older

Purpose: Assesses personality disturbances in individuals ages 3 and older in psychotherapy, school, and research settings. May be used with the culturally disadvantaged, educationally deprived, mentally retarded, and aged.

Description: Multiple-item paper-pencil and oral-response test providing a projective study of personality. The test consists of two steps. The first, which is nonverbal, creative, and almost completely unstructured, requires the subject to make a freehand drawing of a house, a tree, and a person. The second step, which is verbal, apperceptive, and more formally structured, gives the subject an opportunity to describe, define, and interpret the drawings and their respective environments. Examiner required. Not suitable for group use.

Untimed: 15–20 minutes

Scoring: Hand key; examiner evaluated

Cost: Complete set (manual for administering and scoring; interpretive catalogs and manuals, 25 drawing forms, 25 interrogation folders, 25 scoring folders, 25 post-drawing interrogation folders, 25 two-copy drawing forms) $140.00

Publisher: Western Psychological Services

THE IES TEST
Lawrence A. Dombrose and Morton S. Slobin

Ages 10 and older

Purpose: Assesses the relative strengths of various personality forces. Used for individual diagnosis, clinical evaluation, and research.

Description: 57–item four-subtest projective measure of personality. Picture Title is a 12–item test in which the subject creates titles for pictures. Picture Story Completion requires the subject to select a cartoon to end each of 13 incomplete cartoon stories. Photo-Analysis consists of nine men's photographs with two objectively scored questions about each. Arrow-Dot is a set of 23 graphic problems requiring the subject to draw a line from an arrow to a dot goal without creating or crossing barriers. All responses are scored Impulse (I), Ego (E), or Superego (S). Use is limited to psychologists, psychiatrists, and other professionals in the areas of clinical and research psychology. Examiner required. Not suitable for group use.

Untimed: 30 minutes

Scoring: Examiner evaluated

Cost: Complete kit (Picture Title cards, Picture Story Completion cards, Photo-Analysis cards, 25 Arrow-Dot test forms, 25 record forms, separate instruction cards, general manual, heavy storage boxes) $43.50; 100 record forms $10.00; 25 Arrow-Dot forms $9.00; manual $6.00

Publisher: Psychological Test Specialists

INFORMATION TEST ON DRUGS AND DRUG ABUSE
Refer to page 389.

INTER-PERSON PERCEPTION TEST (IPPT)
F.K. Heussenstamm and R. Hoepfner

All ages

Purpose: Assesses interpersonal perception or social cognition. Used to assess changes accompanying sensitivity training, counseling, and psychotherapy; to select personnel who must deal with people; and for cross-cultural, sociological, and psychological research.

Description: 40–item multiple-choice paper-pencil test assessing interpersonal perception. Examinees select from four alternative facial photographs the one that expresses the same thoughts, feelings, and intentions as the given example. Test items are divided equally by sex (20 each for males and females) and by ethnicity (10 each for Caucasians, blacks, Mexican-Americans, and Oriental-Americans). The test is available in Form AC with faces of children and youths and Form AA with faces of adults. Examiner required. Suitable for group use.

Untimed: 20 minutes

Scoring: Hand key

Cost: Specimen set (test booklet, answer sheet, scoring stencil, manual) $8.00

Publisher: Monitor

INTERPERSONAL BEHAVIOR SURVEY (IBS)
Paul A. Mauger, David R. Adkinson, Suzanne K. Zoss, Gregory Firestone, and J. David Hook

Adolescent, adult
Grades 9 and above

Purpose: Measures and distinguishes assertive and aggressive behaviors among adolescents and adults. Used for assertiveness training, marriage counseling, and in a variety of clinical settings.

Description: 272–item paper-pencil test in which the subject responds to statements written in the present tense to provide sensitivity to ongoing changes. The test yields eight aggressiveness scales (including one that measures general aggressiveness over a broad range of item content, including aggressive behaviors, feelings, and attitudes), nine assertiveness scales (including one that measures general assertiveness over a broad range of behaviors), three validity scales, and three relationship scales (Conflict Avoidance, Dependency, and Shyness). Two shorter forms are available: a 38–item form providing a general sampling of behaviors and a 133–item form providing information on all scales. The Profile Form provides a display of raw scores, T-scores, and percentiles. Norms are provided for adult males, adult females, high-school students, college students, and blacks. The manual presents validity and reliability data, interpretive guidelines, and a

number of illustrated cases. A sixth-grade reading level is required. Self-administered. Suitable for group use.

Untimed: 10–45 minutes depending on form

Scoring: Hand key

Cost: Complete kit (5 booklets, 25 profile forms, 25 answer sheets, key, manual) $65.00

Publisher: Western Psychological Services

AN INVENTORY OF ATTITUDES TOWARD BLACK/WHITE RELATIONS IN UNITED STATES
James H. Morrison

Adolescent, adult

Purpose: Initiates discussions of black-white relations in training sessions. Used as a self-examination to sensitize a person to his attitudes towards race relations and for research.

Description: 28–item paper-pencil inventory measuring attitudes toward black-white relations in the United States on an integrationist-separationist continuum. Instructions are read to the subjects, who are allowed as much time as necessary to complete the test. The test requires a 10th-grade reading level. Norms are provided for supervisors. Self-administered. Suitable for group use.

Timed: 25 minutes

Scoring: Hand key

Cost: Specimen set (inventory, manual) $2.00; 20 tests (with manual) $4.00

Publisher: James H. Morrison
Information and availability unconfirmed; last verified in 1988.

THE JESNESS INVENTORY OF ADOLESCENT PERSONALITY
Carl F. Jesness

Child, adolescent—Ages
8–18

Purpose: Evaluates personality disorders predictive of asocial tendencies. Used to classify disturbed children and adolescents for treatment.

Description: 155–item paper-pencil true-false test of 11 personality characteristics: social maladjustment, value orientation, immaturity, autism, alienation, manifest aggression, withdrawal, social anxiety, repression, denial, and asocial. The test distinguishes delinquents from nondelinquents. Administration requires either test booklets or a tape recorder and tape. Examiner/self-administered. Suitable for group use.

Untimed: 20–30 minutes

Scoring: Hand key; computer scoring service available

Cost: Specimen set (manual, test booklet, answer sheet, profile) $9.00; manual $6.50; key $14.50

Publisher: Consulting Psychologists Press, Inc.

JUNG PERSONALITY QUESTIONNAIRE (JPQ)—1983

All ages

Purpose: Assesses personality based on the theory of Carl Gustav Jung.

Description: Multiple-item paper-pencil test measuring the following personality factors: extraversion, introversion, thought, feeling, sensation, intuition, judgment, and perception. The JPQ may also assist in vocational guidance. Examiner required. Suitable for group use.
SOUTH AFRICAN PUBLISHER

Untimed: 25 minutes

Scoring: Hand key; examiner evaluated; may be machine scored

Cost: (In Rands) test booklet 1,70; 10 answer sheets (machine–3881) 2,00; scoring stencil 6,00; manual 10,00; orders from outside The RSA will be dealt with on merit

Publisher: Human Sciences Research Council

KIDDIE LIFE
Martin B. Keller and Eileen Nielsen

Child, adolescent—Ages 6–19—Grades 1–12

Purpose: Diagnoses DSM-III-R childhood disorders, RDC Affective/Anxiety

disorders, substance abuse, and eating disorders. Used primarily for research.

Description: Follow-up oral-response interview providing information in five categories: psychiatric status for diagnostic categories listed in DSM-III-R childhood disorders, RDC affective/anxiety disorders, substance abuse, and eating disorders for the six months preceding the interview; medical history; use of psychotropic medication; mental health contacts; and global assessment scale. Must be administered by a trained interviewer. May be used with individuals with physical or mental impairments. Examiner required. Not suitable for group use.

Untimed: 45 minutes

Scoring: Examiner evaluated

Cost: Contact publisher

Publisher: Martin B. Keller

KINETIC DRAWING SYSTEM FOR FAMILY AND SCHOOLS (KFD AND KSD)
Refer to page 767.

LAW ENCOUNTER SEVERITY SCALE (LESS)
A.D. Witherspoon, E.K. de Valera, and W.O. Jenkins

Ages 10–adult

Purpose: Assesses the severity of an individual's law encounter. Used for counseling purposes and follow-up studies with parolees and probationers.

Description: 38–item oral-response test measuring the frequency, variety, severity, and consequences of any criminal offense. Items are classified in five groups, ranging from no encounter to felony offenses for which the offender is sentenced to prison for more than one year. Data are obtained through face-to-face interviews in which the examiner uses behavioral interviewing techniques. Can be used as a criterion for criminal acts. Examiner required. Not suitable for group use.

Untimed: 30 minutes

Scoring: Hand key

Cost: Complete kit (includes 25 test forms and manual) $25.00

Publisher: Behavior Science Press

LOUISVILLE BEHAVIOR CHECKLIST
Lovick C. Miller

Child, adolescent—Ages 4–17

Purpose: Measures the entire range of social and emotional behaviors indicative of psychopathological disorders in children and adolescents. Used as an intake screening device.

Description: 164–item paper-pencil or computer-administered true-false inventory in which parents record their child's behavior by answering questions that provide relevant information on a number of interpretive scales. The inventory is available in three forms for three different age groups: Form E1 (ages 4–6), Form E2 (ages 7–12), and Form E3 (ages 13–17).

The scales measured in Form E1 are Infantile Aggression, Hyperactivity, Antisocial Behavior, Aggression, Social Withdrawal, Sensitivity, Fear, Inhibition, Intellectual Deficit, Immaturity, Cognitive Disability, Normal Irritability, Prosocial Deficit, Rare Deviance, Neurotic Behavior, Psychotic Behavior, Somatic Behavior, Sexual Behavior, School Disturbance Predictor, and Severity Level.

The scales measured in Form E2 are Infantile Aggression, Hyperactivity, Antisocial Behavior, Aggression, Social Withdrawal, Sensitivity, Fear, Inhibition, Academic Disability, Immaturity, Learning Disability, Normal Irritability, Prosocial Deficit, Rare Deviance, Neurotic Behavior, Psychotic Behavior, Somatic Behavior, Sexual Behavior, and Severity Level.

The scales measured in Form E3 are Egocentric-Exploitive, Destructive-Assaultive, Social Delinquency, Adolescent Turmoil, Apathetic Isolation, Neuroticism, Dependent-Inhibited, Academic Disability, Neurological or Psychotic Abnormality, General Pathology, Longitudinal, Severity Level, and Total Pathology.

General and clinical norms are provided for forms E1 and E2; Form E3 has only clinical norms. Norms are provided by sex and age for Form E1 and by sex only for forms E2 and E3. The manual provides a number of case studies. The computer version, which includes administration, scoring, and interpretation, is available for IBM PC and compatible systems. The paper-and-pencil version can be scored using a mail-in answer sheet that provides scoring and an interpretive report. Examiner required. Not suitable for group use.

Untimed: 20–30 minutes

Scoring: Hand key; may be computer scored

Cost: Paper-pencil complete kit for all ages $195.00; individual kit (specify Form E1, E2, or E3) $70.00; IBM version (25 uses) $149.50

Publisher: Western Psychological Services

MALADAPTED BEHAVIOR RECORD (MBR)
W.O. Jenkins, A.D. Witherspoon, E.K. de Valera, and John M. McKee

Ages 10–adult

Purpose: Assesses behavioral maladaption and predicts the likelihood of habitual relapse of maladaptive individuals and groups. Used for counseling purposes with offender groups and drug and alcohol abuse cases and for predicting parole success.

Description: 16–item oral-response test measuring the following response categories: working conditions, amount of income, employer interactions, work attendance, alcohol use, gambling, money management, fighting, psychological adjustment, and others. Data are obtained through face-to-face interviews in which the examiner uses behavioral interviewing techniques. Each item is scored as "maladaption" or "no maladaption." A juvenile version is available. Examiner required. Not suitable for group use.

Untimed: 30 minutes

Scoring: Hand key

Cost: Complete kit (includes 25 test forms and manual) $35.00

Publisher: Behavior Science Press

MODES OF EXISTENCE TEST
S. Roy Heath

Adolescent, adult—Ages 12 and older

Purpose: Assesses personality in terms of temperament and emotional and intellectual maturity. Used for student and employee counseling when temperament and maturity are important factors.

Description: 11-item paper-pencil test measuring a person's self-concept of his personality. The test items consist of personality descriptions from which the subject is asked to select the three that most closely approximate the way he sees himself. The subject then ranks each of the three selected descriptions on a ladder chart according to how closely each represents his sense of self. The subject then selects and records which of the 11 personality descriptions are least like his sense of self. The examiner scores the responses according to three dimensions of temperament related to Heath's model of ego-functioning (group cooperative, group competitive, or group independent) and three levels of intellectual and emotional maturity (high, medium, and low). The test should not be administered to children under age 12. A sixth-grade reading level is required. Self-administered. Suitable for group use.

Untimed: 20 minutes

Scoring: Examiner evaluated

Cost: $2.00 per copy

Publisher: S. Roy Heath, Ph.D.

Information and availability unconfirmed; last verified in 1987.

NON-VERBAL SCALE OF SUFFERING (N-V SOS)
Theodore C. Kent

Ages 5–80

Purpose: Assesses the level of subjective feelings of emotional distress in children and adults. Used as a pictorial screening instrument in a variety of settings to iden-

tify level of distress and provide clues of its origin.

Description: 24–item paper-pencil oral-response and point-to test of experienced suffering. Each item presents five nonverbal figures reflecting different degrees of distress, and subjects are asked to circle the drawing that best reflects their current feelings. The test measures degree of subjective suffering, self-image, denial of feelings, and inconsistency of feelings. Six scoring categories are used: No Suffering, No Significant Suffering, Mild Suffering, Significant Suffering, Severe Suffering, and Profound Suffering. Instructions may be given in any language; English and Spanish instructions are provided on the test blank. The test may be used with mentally, physically, and hearing-impaired individuals. Examiner/self-administered. Suitable for group use.

Untimed: 10 minutes

Scoring: Hand key

Cost: 1 test booklet, manual $4.00; 10 booklets, manual $28.00; 25 booklets, manual and duplication rights $75.00

Publisher: Human Sciences Center

PAIN APPERCEPTION TEST
Refer to page 16.

PERSONALITY ASSESSMENT QUESTIONNAIRE (PAQ)
Ronald P. Rohner

Ages 7–adult

Purpose: Predicts personality and mental health outcome of variations in perceived parental acceptance-rejection.

Description: Multiple-item paper-pencil instrument measuring seven personality dimensions: Hostility/Aggression, Dependence/Independence, Self-Esteem, Self-Adequacy; Emotional (Un)Responsiveness, Emotional (In)Stability, and World View. Theoretically, these dispositions are linked to the acceptance-rejection process. (See entry for the Parental Acceptance Rejection Questionnaire.) The test is available in child version (42 items on which the child assesses his or her own behavioral disposition), an adult version (63 items on which the individual assesses his or her own personality and behavioral disposition), and a mother version (63 items on which the mother assesses child's behavioral dispositions). The questionnaire yields seven scale scores in addition to the Total Test score, which is often used as a measure of overall mental health. A computer scoring program is available for IBM PC systems. The examiner may read the items to visually impaired individuals and explain the meanings of words to very young or mentally impaired individuals. The *Handbook for the Study of Parental Acceptance and Rejection* (Rohner, 1984) contains all versions of the PAQ and provides scoring instructions, descriptions of validity and reliability, and other information needed for administration, scoring, and interpretation. Examiner/self-administered. Suitable for group use. Available in Arabic, Bengali, Czech, French, Greek, Hindi, Korean, Mexican Spanish, Puerto Rican Spanish, Telugu, and Tiv.

Untimed: 10 minutes

Scoring: Self-scored; may be computer scored

Cost: Handbook $15.00

Publisher: Center for the Study of Parental Acceptance and Rejection, University of Connecticut

---

PERSONALITY RESEARCH FORM (PRF)
Douglas N. Jackson

Adolescent, adult
Grades 6 and above

Purpose: Assesses personality traits relevant to the functioning of an individual in a variety of situations. Used in self-improvement courses and guidance centers and for personnel selection.

Description: Multiple-item paper-pencil or computer-administered true-false test in five forms. Forms AA and BB contain 440 items covering 22 areas of normal functioning. Form E has 352 items in 22 scales. Forms A and B have 300 items in 15 scales. The 22 scales measured are Abasement, Achievement, Affiliation, Aggression, Autonomy, Change, Cognitive Structure, Defendance, Dominance, Endurance, Exhibition, Harm-

Avoidance, Impulsivity, Nurturance, Order, Play, Sentience, Social Recognition, Succorance, Understanding, Infrequency, and Desirability. A 90-minute cassette tape with simplified wording is available for use with those who have limited verbal skills or sight or reading problems. Materials include a manual, reusable test booklet, answer sheets, profiles, scoring template, cassette tape, and tape manual. The computer version operates on IBM PC and compatible systems. The test must be administered by a certified psychologist. Suitable for group use. Form E available in French and Spanish.

Timed: Form E 1 hour; Forms A and B 45 minutes; Forms AA and BB 1 hour, 15 minutes; cassette tape 90 minutes

Scoring: Hand key; computer scoring available for Form E

Cost: Specimen set $28.50; computer version (licensing agreement and 25 uses) $150.00

Publisher: SIGMA Assessment Systems, Inc., Research Psychologists Press Division

---

PIKUNAS GRAPHOSCOPIC SCALE (PGS)
Justin Pikunas

All ages

Purpose: Assesses an individual's cognitive development, emotionality, and adjustment. Used by clinical and school psychologists to build rapport, test deficits, and evaluate various forms of psychopathology.

Description: Nonverbal test using a single sheet containing 10 framed, partial drawings containing perceptual cues in various colors. The subject is asked to add to the drawings. The results provide an indication of self-expressive balance, intelligence, creativity, emotional disturbance, and some forms of psychopathology. Materials include the test, graphic scale, and manual. Two forms are available: PGSI (Grades K–8) and PGSII (Grades 9–adult). Examiner required. Suitable for group use.

Untimed: PGSI 20 minutes; PGSII 30 minutes

Scoring: Examiner evaluated

Cost: Specimen set (specify form) $6.75
Publisher: University Press of America
Information and availability unconfirmed; last verified in 1988.

POLITTE SENTENCE COMPLETION TEST (PSCT)
Refer to page 770.

THE Q-TAGS TEST OF PERSONALITY
Arthur G. Storey and Louis I. Masson

Ages 6 and older

Purpose: Measures individual personality traits. Used for counseling, self-examination, and research.

Description: 54–card test measuring five factors of personality: assertive, effective, hostile, reverie, and social. By sorting cards, subjects are able to describe themselves both as they are and as they wish to be. The test was developed with norms for age, grade, occupation, and sex based on a wide range of subjects. Self-administered. Suitable for group use. CANADIAN PUBLISHER

Untimed: 30 minutes
Scoring: Examiner evaluated
Cost: Contact publisher
Publisher: Institute of Psychological Research, Inc.

THE REVISED BEHAVIOR PROBLEM CHECKLIST (RBPC)
Refer to page 746.

RISK-TAKING ATTITUDE-VALUES INVENTORY (RTAVI)
R.E. Carney

All ages—Ages 3 and older

Purpose: Measures basic values and needs, behavior potentials for risks, credibility of sources of help (ways of changing behavior).

Description: 71– to 101–item (depending on form) paper-pencil, multiple-choice test based on the subjective utility model of risk-taking. It measures values and needs (16 items), utilities and expectations of behavior (30–50 items), frequencies of behavior (15–25 items), and ways of changing behavior (10 items). The test yields several scores, including Total Need, Need for Affection, Respect, Skill, Knowledge, Power, Wealth, Need for Well-Being, 15–25 behavior potential scores (depending on form used), Socially Disapproved Behavior Style (SDB), Masculine-Aggressive Behavior Style (MAB), Socially Approved Behavior Style (SAB), Institutional Ways of Change (IST), and Interpersonal Ways of Change (INT). The test form integrates items, scoring, and a profile. Several forms are available: Preschool-Primary, Elementary, Secondary, Post-Secondary, and Adult. Materials must be ordered in quantities of 50 or more. Examiner/self-administered. Suitable for group use.

Untimed: Not available
Scoring: Hand key; may be computer scored
Cost: 50 forms (specify form) $15.00; specimen set (includes all forms) $9.00
Publisher: Carney, Weedman and Associates

ROKEACH VALUE SURVEY
Milton Rokeach

Ages 11–adult

Purpose: Measures personal values and provides objective feedback about them in comparison with reference group. Used for value therapy, values clarification, and changing socially undesirable values.

Description: 36–item ranking test requiring minimum literacy. The respondent arranges values, which are printed on gummed labels, in rank order. The test assesses values divided into terminal ("comfortable life" and "world peace") and behavioral ("loving" and "ambition"). Self-administered. Suitable for group use. Available in Spanish, French, German, Czech, Japanese, Vietnamese, Russian, Hungarian, Swedish, Chinese, Lithuanian, and Hebrew.

Untimed: 15 minutes
Scoring: Examiner evaluated; may be computer scored

Cost: Test $0.50–$1.00 (depending on quantity)

Publisher: Halgren Tests

Information and availability unconfirmed; last verified in 1988.

ROKEACH VALUE SURVEY: FORM G
Milton Rokeach

All ages

Purpose: Measures human values concerning possible end-states of existence and modes of behavior. Used for value therapy, values clarification, and to identify socially undesirable value structures.

Description: 36–item label-ranking test consisting of two sets of 18 values (one set of terminal values and one set of behavioral values), printed on gummed labels, which the individual must arrange in order of personal importance. Terminal values include comfortable life, exciting life, sense of accomplishment, world at peace, world of beauty, equality, family security, freedom, health, inner harmony, mature love, national security, pleasure, salvation, self-respect, social recognition, true friendship, and wisdom. Behavior values include ambitious, broadminded, capable, clean, courageous, forgiving, helpful, honest, imaginative, independent, intellectual, logical, loving, loyal, obedient, polite, responsible, and self-controlled. Form G is a revision of Form D; the values "health" and "loyal" replace "happiness" and "cheerful." An extensive list of reference materials is provided. Normative data are available for many populations within American society. Self-administered. Suitable for group use.

Untimed: Adults 15–20 minutes; children 20–25 minutes

Scoring: Self-scored

Cost: Test kit (2 sets of 18 gummed labels with printed array for final rankings) $0.75–$1.00 each depending on quantity

Publisher: Halgren Tests

Information and availability unconfirmed; last verified in 1988.

RORSCHACH PSYCHODIAGNOSTIC TEST
Hermann Rorschach

Ages 3 and older

Purpose: Evaluates personality through projective technique. Used in clinical evaluation.

Description: 10–card oral-response projective personality test in which the subject is asked to interpret what he sees in 10 inkblots, based on the assumption that the individual's perceptions and associations are selected and organized in terms of his motivations, impulses, and other underlying aspects of personality. Extensive scoring systems have been developed. Although many variations are in use, this entry refers only to the Psychodiagnostic Plates first published in 1921. Materials include inquiry charts, tabulation sheets, and a set of 10 inkblots. A set of 10 Kodaslides of the inkblots may be imported on request. Trained examiner required. Not suitable for group use.

Untimed: Not available

Scoring: Examiner evaluated

Cost: Contact publisher

Publisher: Hans Huber

ROSENZWEIG PICTURE-FRUSTRATION STUDY (P-F)
Saul Rosenzweig

Ages 4–adult

Purpose: Measures aggression in personality. Used in clinical counseling.

Description: Paper-pencil semiprojective technique assessing an individual's patterns of response to everyday frustration or stress. It consists of 24 cartoon pictures, each depicting two persons in a frustrating situation. One person is acting as the frustrator. The subject provides a reply for the anonymous frustrated person in the second picture. The instrument measures three types of aggression (obstacle-dominance, ego-defense, and need-persistence) and three directions of aggression (extraggression, imaggression, and intraggression). Nine factors, derived by combining the types and directions of aggression, constitute the score. The scoring guide is provided in the manual. Three versions are available: adult, adolescent, and child. Examiner required. Suitable for group use.

Timed: 15–20 minutes

Scoring: Hand key

Cost: Study kit (manual, manual supplement, 25 test booklets and scoring sheets) $28.00; specify version

Publisher: Psychological Assessment Resources, Inc.

SELF-CONCEPT EVALUATION OF LOCATION FORM (SELF)
R.E. Carney, C.W. Weedman, and G. Spielberger

Ages 12 and older

Purpose: Assesses self-concept.

Description: 32–item paper-pencil self-rating or observer-rating instrument assessing present self (16 items) and ideal self (16 items). The test yields 15 scores: Total Positive Self-Concept (S), Evaluation Self-Concept (E), Potency Self-Concept (P), Activity Self-Concept (A), Total Inconsistency (K), Systematic Inconsistency (K1), Unsystematic Inconsistency (K2), Inconsistency F ratio (K3), Total Incongruence (C), Evaluation Incongruence (E1), Potency Incongruence (P1), Activity Incongruence (A1), Systematic Incongruence (C1), Unsystematic Incongruence (C2), and Incongruence F ratio (C3). The test form integrates items, scoring, and a profile. A scoring service is available from the publisher. When used as a self-rating instrument, examinees must be at least 12 years old. Examinees must have a seventh-to eighth-grade reading level. The test is suitable for use with hearing-impaired individuals. Test booklets must be purchased in quantities of 50 or more. Examiner/self-administered. Suitable for group use.

Untimed: Varies

Scoring: Hand key; may be computer scored

Cost: 50 test forms $12.50; specimen set $7.00

Publisher: Carney, Weedman and Associates

SELF-ESTEEM INDEX (SEI)
Linda Brown and Jacquelyn Alexander

Ages 7–18

Purpose: Measures the way individuals perceive and value themselves.

Description: 120–item paper-pencil survey assessing self-esteem. Items are divided into four scales: Perception of Familial Acceptance, Perception of Academic Competence, Perception of Peer Popularity, and Perception of Personal Security. Results are reported as standard scores and percentiles. Self-administered. Suitable for group use.

Untimed: 30 minutes

Scoring: Hand key

Cost: Contact publisher

Publisher: PRO-ED

SELF-ESTEEM QUESTIONNAIRE (SEQ–3)
James K. Hoffmeister

Grades 4 and above

Purpose: Evaluates how individuals feel about various aspects of themselves, including their capabilities, worth, and acceptance by others.

Description: 21–item paper-pencil self-report rating scale consisting of two subscales: Self-Esteem (12 items) and Self-Other Satisfaction (9 items). Items on the Self-Esteem subscale consist of statements, such as "Most of my friends accept me as much as they accept other people," that the individual rates on a 5–point scale from 1 ("not at all") to 5 ("yes, very much"). Items on the Self-Other Satisfaction subscale immediately follow items on the Self-Esteem subscale and take the form "Does the situation described in [the previous question] upset you?" These items are rated on a 5–point scale also. Scores are provided for both subscales according to the computerized convergence analysis process (a score is computed only if the individual has responded in a reasonably consistent fashion to the items used to measure that factor). The manual includes a description of the test's variables and content, directions for administering and scoring the questionnaire, information concerning development, validity, and reliability, and normative data. Examiner required. Suitable for group use.

Untimed: Varies

Scoring: Computer scored

Cost: 50 questionnaires (includes computer scoring service) $50.00

Publisher: Test Analysis and Development Corporation

SELF-OTHER LOCATION CHART
Theodore C. Kent

Ages 4 and older

Purpose: Measures self-esteem. Used in counseling settings to identify feelings of superiority and inferiority.

Description: A projective test measuring feelings of inferiority and superiority. Examinees respond to an illustration of a group of figures walking. They indicate a) where they think they are in the illustration, b) where they would like to be, c) who they think the "leader" is, and d) who they think the "loser" is. May be used with individuals with hearing, physical, or mental impairments. Examiner required. Suitable for group use.

Untimed: Varies

Scoring: Examiner evaluated

Cost: 40 copies $25.00; 10 copies with duplication rights $50.00

Publisher: Human Science Center

STANFORD HYPNOTIC SUSCEPTIBILITY SCALE
Andre M. Weitzenhoffer and Ernest R. Hilgard

Adolescent, adult

Purpose: Measures hypnotic susceptibility. Used for teaching, research, and experimentation in hypnosis.

Description: Multiple-item test of subject's responsiveness to hypnotic suggestions. Includes verbatim instructions for inducing and testing hypnotic states. The subject's scores are based on a 12–point scale. The test is available in three forms.

Forms A and B are equivalent; Form C contains more difficult items and a wider variety of hypnotic experiences. Restricted to APA guidelines. Examiner required. Not suitable for group use.

Untimed: 40 minutes

Scoring: Examiner evaluated

Cost: Manual and scales for Forms A, B, and C $12.50; complete kit, Forms A and B (manuals, scales, scoring sheets, interrogatory blanks for 50 subjects) $17.25; complete kit, Form C $12.50

Publisher: Consulting Psychologists Press, Inc.

STANFORD PROFILE SCALES OF HYPNOTIC SUSCEPTIBILITY
Andre M. Weitzenhoffer and Ernest R. Hilgard

Adolescent, adult

Purpose: Assesses differential susceptibility to a variety of hypnotic state suggestions. Used for teaching, research, and experimentation in hypnosis.

Description: Multiple-item test of hypnotic susceptibility yielding 25 scores in six areas: agnosia and cognitive distortion, positive hallucinations, negative hallucinations, dreams and regressions, amnesia and post-hypnotic compulsions, and total susceptibility. The test is available in two roughly equivalent forms: I and II. Both must be administered to yield the profile. Profile scales may be used with subjects chosen by the Stanford Hypnotic Susceptibility Scale. Examiner required. Not suitable for group use.

Untimed: Not available

Scoring: Examiner evaluated

Cost: 25 scoring booklets of each form $16.50; 100 profile sheets $10.50; manual (includes scoring booklet and profile sheet) $7.75

Publisher: Consulting Psychologists Press, Inc.

THE STERN ACTIVITIES INDEX (AI)
George Stern and Associates

All ages

Purpose: Measures personality in terms of the need-press paradigm of human behavior as conceptualized by Henry Murray. Used for counseling and research purposes.

Description: 300–item (long form) or 91–item (either of two short forms) paper-pencil inventory assessing personality along 30 basic need scales. The test items are descriptions of routine activities and feelings to which the individual indicates a personal "like" or "dislike." The long form provides scores on each of the 30 need scales (10 items per scale), 12 first-order scores (self-assertion, audacity-timidity, intellectual interests, motivation, applied interests, orderliness, submissiveness, closeness, sensuousness, friendliness, expressive-constraint, and egoism-diffidence), and four second-order scores (achievement orientation, dependency needs, emotional expression, and educability). The two short forms provide scores for the 12 first-order dimensions and four second-order dimensions. Short forms are used when administration time is a problem or when scores on the 30 basic need scales are not required. Short form SAI–1158SF is primarily for adults, but it can be used with individuals as young as age 12 who have a minimum seventh-grade reading level. Short form SAI–1173SF is used with younger children who have a minimum fourth-grade reading level. The long form requires a seventh-grade reading level. Self-administered. Suitable for group use.

Untimed: Long form 40 minutes; short forms 20 minutes

Scoring: Examiner evaluated; may be computer scored

Cost: Test booklet $0.50; answer sheet $0.10; profile form $0.10; technical manual $7.50; prices for computer and analysis scoring available on request

Publisher: FAAX Corporation

STROOP COLOR AND WORD TEST
Charles Golden

Grades 2 and above

Purpose: Evaluates personality, cognition, stress response, psychiatric disorders, and other psychological phenomena. Used to differentiate normal, non-brain-damaged psychiatric from brain-damaged subjects.

Description: Multiple-item response test of an individual's ability to separate word and color stimuli and react to them independently. The test consists of three pages: a Word Page containing color words printed in black ink; a Color Page with a series of X's printed in colored inks; and a Word-Color page on which the words on the first page are printed in the colors of the second page except that the word and color do not match. The subject is given all three pages and asked to read the Word Page. He then names the colors of the X's on the Color Page. Next he must name the color of the ink in which the words on the Word-Color Page are printed, ignoring the semantic meaning of the words. The test requires a second-grade reading level. Examiner required. Not suitable for group use.

Timed: 5 minutes

Scoring: Examiner evaluated

Cost: Complete kit (manual, 25 sets of 3 sheets) $45.00

Publisher: Stoelting Co.

STRUCTURED-OBJECTIVE RORSCHACH TEST (SORT)—1975

Ages 11–54

Purpose: Evaluates personality tendencies of white South Africans. Used in guidance, selection, and placement.

Description: Multiple-item paper-pencil test of mental functioning (8 components), interests (2 components), responsiveness (2 components), and temperament (13 components). The test was adapted from J.B. Stone's SORT and standardized for white South Africans of both sexes and both official languages (Afrikaans and English). There is a training course for interpreting the test. Examiner required. Suitable for group use.
SOUTH AFRICAN PUBLISHER

Untimed: 30 minutes

Scoring: Hand key

Cost: Test booklet 2,50; manual 15,70; 15 scoring stencils 25,00; 10 answer sheets 1,20; slides of the Rorschach inkblots 70,00; literature survey 7,10
Publisher: Human Sciences Research Council

SYMBOL ELABORATION TEST (S.E.T.)
Johanna Krout Tabin

All ages

Purpose: Assesses personality. Used for individual evaluation and cross-cultural research.

Description: 11-item projective measure of personality. Items are simple line figures. The subjects use each line figure as a beginning stimulus for their own drawings and answer seven brief questions aimed at eliciting feelings and associations. The factors measured include concepts of maleness and femaleness; views of interactions between same-sex, opposite sex, and mixed-groups; handling of aggression; diffuse and sexual anxiety; and self-concept. Examiner required. Suitable for group use.
Untimed: 30 minutes
Scoring: Examiner evaluated
Cost: Test booklet $0.75; guide $3.50
Publisher: Johanna Krout Tabin, Ph.D.
Information and availability unconfirmed; last verified in 1988.

TEMAS (TELL-ME-A-STORY)
Giuseppe Costantino,
Robert G. Malgady, and Lloyd Rogler

Child, adolescent

Purpose: Measures strengths and deficits in cognitive, affective, interpersonal, and intrapersonal functioning in children and adolescents.

Description: Multicultural thematic apperception test designed for use with minority and nonminority children and adolescents ages 5–18. The test, which features 35 scales, uses 23 full color stimulus cards to elicit stories from the examinee. Two parallel forms, minority and nonminority, are available. Separate norms are available for blacks, Hispanics, and whites. Examiner required. Not suitable for group use.
Untimed: Short form 1 hour; long form 3 hours
Scoring: Examiner evaluated
Cost: Complete kit (set of stimulus cards, set of minority stimulus cards, 25 record booklets, administration instruction card, manual) $175.00
Publisher: Western Psychological Services

THE TEST OF SOCIAL INSIGHT: YOUTH AND ADULT EDITIONS
Russel N. Cassel

Ages 10–adult

Purpose: Measures the subject's understanding of and adaptation to acceptable patterns of culture in the United States.

Description: 60-item paper-pencil multiple-choice test involving five ways of responding to interpersonal problems: withdrawal, passivity, cooperation, competition, and aggression. The potential conflict areas covered include home and family, authority figures, avocational contacts, and work situations. The Youth Edition is appropriate for individuals ages 10–18; the Adult Edition is designed for individuals ages 18 and older. A fifth-grade reading level is required. Self-administered. Suitable for group use.
Untimed: 30–40 minutes
Scoring: Hand key
Cost: Manual $16.50; manual's supplement (1984) $15.50; package of reusable tests $42.50; package of profile sheets $18.00; IBM scoring stencils $19.00; IBM answer sheets pkg $18.00; specimen set $42.50
Publisher: Martin M. Bruce, Ph.D., Publishers

TEST PLUS
Refer to page 1033.

THEMATIC APPERCEPTION TEST (TAT-Z)—1976

Ages 10 and older

Purpose: Measures personality characteristics. Used for assessment and diagnosis of abnormal personality.

Description: 10-card projective measure of personality using the method of choosing cards that reveal, ter alia, the level of Westernization and adjustment to Western demands. The subject chooses pictures that relate to the following 10 areas: degree and direction of acculturation, family relationships, father-son relationship, mother-son relationship, attitude toward black authority, attitude toward white authority, self-concept, heterosexual relationships, social relationships, and handling of aggression. Examiner required. Not suitable for group use. SOUTH AFRICAN PUBLISHER

Untimed: 2 hours

Scoring: Hand key; examiner evaluated

Cost: (In Rands) test album 20,00; answer book 1,00; manual 15,00; interpretation form 0,50; 10 shortened answer books 5,00; orders from outside the RSA will be dealt with on merit

Publisher: Human Sciences Research Council

THEMES CONCERNING BLACKS (TCB)
Robert L. Williams

Grades PreK and above

Purpose: Assesses culturally specific attitudes of black people. Used as a personality or diagnostic test.

Description: 20-item oral-response projective test assessing black Americans' feelings and attitudes toward their ethnic experience in American society. Each test item consists of a picture card depicting some facet of the black experience. The subject is asked to elaborate on each card. When used as a diagnostic instrument, the test must be administered by a trained psychologist. May be administered to groups with slides and projector.

Untimed: 30 minutes

Scoring: Examiner evaluated

Cost: Complete (20 cards, manual) $30.00

Publisher: Robert L. Williams & Associates, Inc.

Information and availability unconfirmed; last verified in 1987.

TWITCHELL-ALLEN THREE-DIMENSIONAL PERSONALITY TEST (T-A 3-DPT)
Doris Twitchell-Allen

Ages 3-adult

Purpose: Evaluates the general personality structure of children and adults. Used for clinical diagnosis and research on personality.

Description: Four task-assessment and oral-response tests providing a projective evaluation of an individual's personality. Test materials consist of 28 small objects, all of an abstract nature (some are suggestive of human forms). The four subtests are Pre-Naming Story, in which the subject is asked to choose one or more of the objects and make up a story; Naming Test, in which the subject is asked to name all of the objects; Post-Naming Story, which allows the subject to tell a second story; and the Fein Testing of Limits, in which the examiner arranges a few of the objects in a vaguely suggestive pattern (according to test directions) and asks the subject to tell a story explaining the arrangement. The following types of responses are recorded by the examiner: gestures, general behavior, construction with the test forms, vocalizations (everything the subject says, not just the stories and names), sequence, and time. The test may be administered to individuals with visual impairments with only minor procedural adaptations. Examiner required. Not suitable for group use.

Untimed: 1 hour

Scoring: Examiner evaluated

Cost: Complete set (instructions, recording forms) $115.00

Publisher: Doris Twitchell-Allen, Ph.D.

TWITCHELL-ALLEN THREE-DIMENSIONAL PERSONALITY TEST, 1985 REVISION (3DPT)
Doris Twitchell-Allen

Ages 3–adult

Purpose: Diagnoses critical areas of personality in children and adults. Helps teachers and human service personnel provide guidance in terms of an individual's current functional status and more permanent characteristics of personality.

Description: Four action and oral-response tests providing a projective evaluation of an individual's personality. Test materials consist of 28 small objects, all of an ambiguous or abstract nature (some are suggestive of human forms). The four subtests are Naming Test, in which the subject is asked to name 14 designated objects; Story Production, in which the subject chooses as many forms as he likes and makes up one story about them; Fein Testing Limits 1 (for intrafamilial relations), in which the examiner arranges three designated objects in a designated pattern (according to test directions) and asks the subject to tell a story about the examiner's chosen pieces; and Fein Testing Limits 2, in which the examiner begins a story using the three pieces from the previous test and asks the subject to complete it. The following types of responses are recorded by the examiner: gestures, general behavior, constructions with test forms, vocalizations (everything the subject says, not just the stories and names), sequence, and time. May be administered to individuals with visual impairments with only minor procedural adaptations. Examiner required. Not suitable for group use.

Untimed: 1 hour

Scoring: Examiner evaluated

Cost: Complete set (carrying case, instructions, 5 sets of recording forms) $115.00

Publisher: Doris Twitchell-Allen, Ph.D.

VINELAND ADAPTIVE BEHAVIOR SCALES
Sara S. Sparrow, David A. Balla, and Dominic V. Cicchetti

Child, adolescent

Purpose: Measures the personal and social sufficiency of individuals from birth to adulthood. Used with individuals with mental retardation or handicaps.

Description: Multiple-item inventory in three forms assessing adaptive behavior in the following four domains: communication (receptive, expressive, and written), daily living skills (personal, domestic, and community), socialization (interpersonal relationships, play and leisure time, and coping skills), and motor skills (gross and fine). These four domains are combined to form the Adaptive Behavior Composite. An optional Maladaptive Behavior domain is included in the Interview Edition, Survey Form and Interview Edition, Expanded Form.

In the Interview Edition, Survey Form (297 items), a trained interviewer administers the inventory to a parent or caregiver in a semistructured interview. The record booklet is used to record item scores and informal observations and contains a score summary page for recording and profiling derived scores. The Survey Form may be administered to individuals from birth to 18 years, 11 months of age and to low-functioning adults.

The Interview Edition, Expanded Form (577 items) offers a more comprehensive assessment of adaptive behavior and provides a basis for preparing individual educational, habilitative, or treatment programs. The Expanded Form, like the Survey Form, assesses individuals from birth to 18 years, 11 months of age, as well as low-functioning adults. Administration is similar to that of the Survey Form. Scores are recorded in the item booklet. The score summary and profile booklet includes a page for summarizing derived scores and four program planning profiles, each of which identifies clusters of items describing activities that should be included in the individual programs.

The Classroom Edition (244 items) assesses adaptive behavior of students ages 3–12 years, 11 months. It is administered as a questionnaire that is completed independently by teachers. A qualified professional is required to determine and interpret derived scores.

Each form has a manual with guidelines for administration, scoring, and interpreting results. Supplementary materials include an audiocassette presenting sample Survey and Expanded Form interviews; ASSIST microcomputer software programs for score conversion, profiling, and record management; the Technical and Interpretive Manual; and reports to parents explaining an individual's derived scores in relation to strengths and weaknesses. This instrument is the 1984 revision of The Vineland Social Maturity Scale. Examiner required. Not suitable for group use. The Survey Form, record booklet, and reports to parents for all three versions are available in Spanish.

Untimed: Survey form 20–60 minutes; expanded form 60–90 minutes; classroom edition 20 minutes

Scoring: Examiner evaluated

Cost: Survey Form Starter Set (10 record booklets, manual, 1 report to parents) $32.00; Expanded Form Starter Set (10 item booklets, 10 score summary and profile reports, manual, 1 program planning report, 1 report to parents) $55.00; Classroom Edition Starter Set (10 questionnaire booklets, manual, 1 report to parents) $25.00

Publisher: American Guidance Service

VISUAL-VERBAL TEST, 1981 EDITION
*Marvin J. Feldman and
James Drasgow*

Schizophrenic patients

Purpose: Measures conceptual thinking and abstraction in schizophrenics. Used for diagnosis and assessment related to therapy.

Description: 42–item oral-response test measuring conceptual deviancy in schizophrenic patients. Each test item consists of a stimulus card depicting four items. Using three of the four items, the examinee formulates two different concepts for each card. The test items are based upon

simple concepts such as color, form, size, structural similarities, naming, and position. Normative data are provided for normals, neurotics, schizophrenics, and special groups. Examiner required. Not suitable for group use.

Untimed: 30–40 minutes

Scoring: Hand key

Cost: Complete kit (set of test cards, 25 protocol booklets, manual) $41.00

Publisher: Western Psychological Services

WELSH FIGURE PREFERENCE TEST (WFPT)
George S. Welsh

Ages 6–adult

Purpose: Evaluates individual personality traits through figure identification. Used for counseling and research.

Description: 400–item paper-pencil nonverbal test measuring an individual's personality traits by evaluating his preference for types of black-and-white figures. The subject responds by indicating "likes" or "dislikes" for each figure. Scales include Conformity, Male-Female, Neuropsychiatric, Consensus, Origence, Intellectence, Barron-Welsh Original Art Scale, Revised Art Scale, Repression, Anxiety, Children, Movement, Figure-Ground Reversal, Sex Symbol, and several measuring preferences for specific kinds of geometric figures. All scales need not be scored. The Barron-Welsh Art Scale (86 items) is available separately. Examiner required. Suitable for group use.

Untimed: 50 minutes

Scoring: Hand key

Cost: Specimen set (manual, test booklet, answer sheet) $19.00; manual $18.00; 10 reusable test booklets $25.00; 50 hand-scored answer sheets $6.00

Publisher: Consulting Psychologists Press, Inc.

WIDE RANGE INTELLIGENCE-PERSONALITY TEST (WRIPT)
Joseph F. Jastak

Ages 9½–adult

Purpose: Measures general mental ability and personality structure. Used for clinical diagnosis and research relating personality to intelligence, academic achievement, and vocational aptitudes and performances.

Description: 10 paper-pencil subtests measuring verbal, numerical, pictorial, spatial, social competency, and other abilities. The test provides a "g" (global) or intelligence score and identifies the extent to which this general factor influences behavior. The test also provides cluster (lobal) scores for language, reality set, motivation, and psychomotor skills. In addition, the test offers several areas of special effectiveness: measuring mental abilities through a wide range of abilities; studying personality makeup; measuring changes in specific personality traits due to age, health, education, or other factors; demonstrating the role of group (lobal) factors in schooling, job selection, and social adjustment; studying variances contributing to the diagnosis of mental retardation, mental illness, learning disabilities, and antisocial and asocial behavior; showing how cultural neglect or environmental limits influence a person's overall functioning; and many research applications. Use is limited to educational and psychological professionals. Examiner required. Suitable for group use.

Timed: 50 minutes

Scoring: Hand key

Cost: Manual $20.50; 25 test forms $17.50; scoring stencil $12.50

Publisher: Jastak Assessment Systems

Research

ALTERNATE USES (AU)
Paul R. Christensen, J.P. Guilford, Philip R. Merrifield, and Robert C. Wilson

Adolescent, adult
Grades 7 and above

Purpose: Measures ability to produce spontaneously ideas in response to objects or other ideas. Used for research and experiment.

Description: Multiple-item paper-pencil test measuring spontaneous flexibility, defined as the ability to produce a variety of class ideas in connection with an object or other unit of thought. This ability is also known as the "divergent production of semantic classes." Forms B and C are equivalent. Norms are provided for sixth-grade, ninth-grade, and college students. The test is restricted to APA members. Examiner required. Suitable for group use.

Timed: 12 minutes

Scoring: Examiner evaluated

Cost: Contact distributer

Publisher: Distributed by Consulting Psychologists Press, Inc.

ASSOCIATIONAL FLUENCY (AF)
Paul R. Christensen and J.P. Guilford

Adolescent, adult
Grades 7 and above

Purpose: Measures the ability to produce spontaneously meaningful words. Used in research and experimental applications.

Description: Multiple-item paper-pencil test measuring the factor of "divergent production of semantic relations," which is defined as the ability to produce efficiently ideas bearing prescribed relations to other ideas or to produce alternate relations. Form A employs adjectives; Form B employs verbs (the forms are equivalent). In each case, the task is to list as many words as possible that bear a specified meaningful relation to the stimulus words. Instructions are included in the manual. Norms are provided for ninth-grade and college students. The test is restricted to APA members. Examiner required. Suitable for group use.

Timed: 4 minutes

Scoring: Examiner evaluated

Cost: Contact distributer

Publisher: Distributed by Cousulting Psychologists Press, Inc.

BEM SEX-ROLE INVENTORY (BSRI)
Sandra L. Bem

Adult

Purpose: Measures masculinity and femininity. Used for research on psychological androgyny.

Description: 60–item paper-pencil measure of integration of masculinity and femininity. Items are three sets of 20 personality characteristics: masculine, feminine, and neutral. The subject indicates on a 7–point scale how well each characteristic describes him- or herself. Materials include a 30–item short form. Self-administered. Suitable for group use.

Untimed: 10 minutes

Scoring: Hand key

Cost: Manual $10.00; handscoring key $2.00; 25 expendable inventories $5.00; specimen set $11.00

Publisher: Consulting Psychologists Press, Inc.

CALIFORNIA CHILD Q-SORT SET
Refer to page 136.

CALIFORNIA Q-SORT DECK
Refer to page 162.

CENTER FOR EPIDEMIOLOGIC STUDIES—DEPRESSION SCALE (CES-D)
Refer to page 163.

CHILDREN'S STATE-TRAIT ANXIETY INVENTORY
Refer to page 142.

THE CLASSROOM ENVIRONMENT INDEX (CEI)
Refer to page 601.

COGNITIVE TRIAD INVENTORY
Refer to page 164.

COMMUNITY ORIENTED PROGRAMS ENVIRONMENT SCALE (COPES)
Rudolf H. Moos

Adult

Purpose: Assesses the social environments of community-based psychiatric treatment programs.

Description: 100–item paper-pencil true-false test of 10 aspects of social environment: involvement, support, spontaneity, autonomy, practical orientation, personal problem orientation, anger and aggression, order and organization, program clarity, and staff control. Materials include the Real Form (Form R), which measures perceptions of a current program; the 40–item Short Form (Form S); the Ideal Form (Form I), which measures conceptions of an ideal program; and the Expectations Form (Form E), which measures expectations of a new program. Forms I and E are not published, but items and instructions are printed in the Appendix of the COPES manual. Items are modified from the Ward Atmosphere Scale. One in a series of nine Social Climate Scales. Examiner required.

Untimed: 20 minutes

Scoring: Hand key

Cost: Manual $5.00; key $1.75; 25 reusable tests $8.50; 50 answer sheets $5.50; 50 profiles $3.75

Publisher: Consulting Psychologists Press, Inc.

CONSEQUENCES (CQ)
Paul R. Christensen,
Philip R. Merrifield, and
J.P. Guilford

Adolescent, adult
Grades 7 and above

Purpose: Measures ability to produce spontaneously original ideas in response to associated ideas. Used for research and experiment.

Description: Multiple-item paper-pencil test measuring two factors: ideational fluency (divergent production of semantic units), and originality (divergent production of semantic transformations). Originality in this test is shown by giving remotely associated ideas that are likely to require revisions of other ideas. Ideational fluency is scored by count of obvious responses. Originality is scored by count of remote responses. The test is available in two equivalent forms, AI and AII. One manual covers both forms. The review set includes the manual and a portion of CQAI. Norms are provided for ninth-grade and engineering students. The test is restricted to APA members. Examiner required. Suitable for group use.

Timed: 10 minutes

Scoring: Examiner evaluated

Cost: Contact publisher

Publisher: Distributed by Consulting Psychologists Press, Inc.

COPING STRATEGIES SCALES (COSTS)
Refer to page 166.

CORNELL CONDITIONAL REASONING TEST, FORM X
Refer to page 451.

CORNELL CRITICAL THINKING TEST, LEVEL X
Refer to page 451.

CORNELL CRITICAL THINKING TEST, LEVEL Z
Refer to page 452.

DECORATIONS (DEC)
Sheldon Gardner, Arthur Gershon, Philip R. Merrifield, and J.P. Guilford

Adolescent, adult
Grades 10 and above

Purpose: Measures ability to add meaningful decorations to simple drawings. Used for research and experimentation.

Description: Paper-pencil test measuring the "divergent production of figural implications," which is the ability to add meaningful details to what is given. The subjects are presented with outlines of well-known articles of furnishings and asked to add decorative lines. Figural ideas, rather then artistic quality, is stressed. The test is scored by a simple count of acceptable responses. The test is restricted to APA members. Examiner required. Suitable for group use.

Timed: 12 minutes

Scoring: Examiner evaluated

Cost: Contact publisher

Publisher: Sheridan Psychological Services, Inc.

THE DEFINING ISSUES TEST OF MORAL JUDGMENT
James R. Rest

Adolescent, adult—Ages 13–adult

Purpose: Measures moral judgment concerning social issues. Used for research purposes only.

Description: 72–item paper-pencil test consisting of six short stories, each followed by 12 related statements. The stories present social problems or moral dilemmas, and the statements present a range of considerations to be taken into account as one tries to determine what a proper (morally "right") course of action would be in a given situation. Individuals indicate each consideration's importance by rating each statement on a 5–point scale ranging from "none" to "great." Individuals then rank in order of importance the four statements they consider the most important of the 12 statements provided for each story. The test provides scores for Stages (of moral development) 2, 3, 4, 4½, 5A, 5B, and 6; the most used index is a combination of Stages 5 and 6, a "principled" morality score ("P" score). An internal consistency check identifies individuals who are randomly checking responses or who do not understand the directions. The test is inappropriate for use with individuals who are not fluent in English or do not have an eighth-grade reading level. The manual (available from Minnesota Moral Research Projects) contains information on administering and scoring the test, interpretation and sample analyses of test scores, reliability and validity, and norms for various groups. A detailed discussion of the rationale of test development, theoretical issues, and empirical findings is provided in *Development in Judging Moral Issues* (University of Minnesota Press). Self-administered. Suitable for group use.

Untimed: 40 minutes

---

research

Scoring: Examiner evaluated; computer scored

Cost: Manual $25.00; prepaid answer sheets and test booklets $0.95–$1.90; volume discount

Publisher: Center for the Study of Ethical Development

ELEMENTS OF AWARENESS (CLINICAL & RESEARCH EDITION)—ELEMENT B (BEHAVIOR)
Refer to page 237.

ELEMENTS OF AWARENESS (CLINICAL & RESEARCH EDITION)—ELEMENT F (FEELINGS)
Refer to page 238.

ELEMENTS OF AWARENESS (CLINICAL & RESEARCH EDITION)—ELEMENT R (RELATIONSHIP)
Refer to page 238.

ENVIRONMENTAL RESPONSE INVENTORY (ERI)
George E. McKechnie

Adult

Purpose: Measures individuals' dispositions toward different physical/psychological environments. Used for research in retirement counseling, environmental planning, architecture, and urban design.

Description: 184–item paper-pencil inventory measuring people's attitudes toward the physical environment. Scores may be obtained for eight scales: Pastoralism, Urbanism, Environmental Adaptation, Stimulus Seeking, Environmental Trust, Antiquarianism, Need Privacy, and Mechanical Orientation. The subjects indicate their degree of agreement or disagreement on a 5–point scale. Currently intended for research use only. Self-administered. Suitable for group use.

Untimed: 30 minutes

Scoring: Hand key

Cost: Specimen set (manual, test booklet, answer sheet, profile) $8.50; manual $7.50; key $12.50

Publisher: Consulting Psychologists Press, Inc.

EXPRESSIONAL FLUENCY (EF)
Paul R. Christensen and J. P. Guilford

Adolescent, adult
Grades 7 and above

Purpose: Measures the ability to produce spontaneously statements of organized thought. Used in research and experimental applications.

Description: Multiple-item paper-pencil test measuring the factor of "divergent production of semantic systems," which is defined as the ability to produce efficiently appropriate verbal expressions of organized thought. Instructions are included in the manual. Norms are provided for ninth-grade students. The test is restricted to APA members. Examiner required. Suitable for group use.

Timed: 8 minutes

Scoring: Examiner evaluated

Cost: 25 tests $10.00

Publisher: Sheridan Psychological Services, Inc.; distributed by Consulting Psychologists Press, Inc.

FAMILY RELATIONS TEST— ADULT AND MARRIED COUPLES VERSION
Refer to page 72.

FAMILY RELATIONS TEST— CHILDREN'S VERSION
Refer to page 72.

FAMOUS SAYINGS (FS)
Refer to page 1003.

GRADED ANAGRAM TASK (GAT)
Lawrence Scrima

Adolescent, adult—Ages 13–100
Grades 8 and above

Purpose: Assesses memory following exposure to a complex associative information task. Used in research for investigating various aspects of information processing, including relationship to developmental cognition, problem solving, creative thinking, learning, memory, and psychophysiological aspects of information processing.

Description: Oral-response test consisting of 10 lists of 10 five-letter anagrams each. The letters in each anagram can be unscrambled to form two words. Two of the lists are used for practice, and one of the remaining eight lists then is administered. As the examinee solves each anagram, he or she first must say and spell aloud the word that it forms and then associate the word with something. The examinee then searches for the second possible word that can be formed from the anagram. This process is repeated for all 10 anagrams. After completing the task, the examinee is instructed to do whatever the examiner deems appropriate, (e.g. card game to prevent rehearsal, simply allow time to elaspe, etc.). Following a controlled interval, the examinee is asked to recall and spell the words that he or she formed earlier (free recall test). Finally, the examinee is given another trial using the same list of anagrams (cued recall test). The anagrams are printed in lowercase letters on 3″ x 5″ cards, one per card. Each card containing an anagram is separated by a blank card. Within each list, anagrams are presented in ascending order of difficulty. All 10 lists are of comparable difficulty. An eighth-grade reading level is required. Examiner required. Not suitable for group use.

Timed: 10 minutes (1 minute per anagram)

Scoring: Examiner evaluated

Cost: 10 card lists, instructions $30.00

Publisher: Lawrence Scrima, Ph.D.

GRIEF EXPERIENCE INVENTORY (RESEARCH EDITION)
Catherine M. Sanders,
Paul A. Mauger, and
Paschal N. Strong, Jr.

Adult

Purpose: Assesses attitudes and experiences related to grief. Used for research on grief and for training bereavement counselors.

Description: 135–item paper-pencil true-false inventory covering somatic and emotional content associated with the process of bereavement. The test yields three validity scales and nine symptom scales (Despair, Guilt, Somatization, Death Anxiety, Anger/Hostility, Social Isolation, Loss of Control, Depersonalization, and Rumination). Scale reliabilities and normative data are provided. Examiner required. Suitable for group use.

Untimed: 20–30 minutes

Scoring: Hand key

Cost: Manual $10.00; 25 reusable tests $15.00; 50 answer sheets $8.50; 50 profiles $18.00; scoring key $12.50

Publisher: Consulting Psychologists Press, Inc.

GRIM
Refer to page 241.

THE HIGH SCHOOL CHARACTERISTICS INDEX (HSCI) AND THE ELEMENTARY AND SECONDARY SCHOOL INDEX (ESI)
Refer to page 604.

HUMAN INFORMATION PROCESSING SURVEY: HIP SURVEY
Refer to page 975.

INTER-PERSON PERCEPTION TEST (IPPT)
Refer to page 244.

INTERPERSONAL CHECK LIST (ICL)
Refer to page 182.

JUNIOR EYSENCK PERSONALITY INVENTORY (JEPI)
Refer to page 145.

KATZ-ZALK OPINION QUESTIONNAIRE
Refer to page 754.

KIDDIE LIFE
Refer to page 246.

LEISURE ACTIVITIES BLANK (LAB)
Refer to page 829.

LIFE EAT II
Refer to page 7.

LONGITUDINAL INTERVAL FOLLOW-UP EVALUATION-UPJOHN (LIFE-UP)
Refer to page 189.

MARYLAND PARENT ATTITUDE SURVEY (MPAS)
Refer to page 75.

MCGILL PAIN QUESTIONNAIRE (MPQ)
Refer to page 15.

NEW USES (NU)
Ralph Hoepfner and J.P. Guilford

**Adolescent, adult
Grades 10 and above**

Purpose: Measures the ability to redefine and find new ways of looking at things. Used in research and experimental applications.

Description: Multiple-item paper-pencil test measuring the Structure-of-Intellect ability of "convergent production of semantic transformations," which involves the capacity to redefine. A low score on this test probably indicates "functional fixedness," which serves as an inhibitor in problem solving by preventing insights. Norms are provided for entering college students. The test is restricted to APA members. Examiner required. Suitable for group use.

Timed: 9 minutes
Scoring: Examiner evaluated
Cost: Contact publisher
Publisher: Sheridan Psychological Services, Inc.

PARTNER RELATIONSHIP INVENTORY, RESEARCH EDITION (PRI)
Refer to page 91.

PEER NOMINATION INVENTORY OF DEPRESSION (PNID)
Refer to page 146.

PERTINENT QUESTIONS
Raymond M. Berger and J.P. Guilford

**Adolescent, adult
Grades 10 and above**

Purpose: Measures conceptual foresight. Used in experimental and research applications.

Description: Multiple-item paper-pencil test measuring the cognition of semantic implications, the ability to see implications of a meaningful kind (e.g., anticipating, being aware of consequences, and making predictions). Norms are provided for college groups. The test is restricted to APA members. Examiner required. Suitable for group use.

Timed: 12 minutes
Scoring: Examiner evaluated
Cost: Contact publisher
Publisher: Sheridan Psychological Services, Inc.

PICTURE SITUATION TEST
Refer to page 1020.

PIERS-HARRIS CHILDREN'S SELF-CONCEPT SCALE (PHCSCS)
Refer to page 147.

PLOT TITLES (PT)
Raymond M. Berger and
J.P. Guilford

Adolescent, adult
Grades 10 and above

Purpose: Measures ability to spontaneously produce original ideas. Used in research and experimental applications.

Description: Multiple-item paper-pencil test measuring two factors: ideational fluency (divergent production of semantic units) and originality (divergent production of semantic transformations). Originality in this test is seen in the production of ideas of high quality with respect to the criterion of "cleverness." Ideational fluency is scored by a count of nonclever responses; originality is scored by a count of clever responses. The test is available in two equivalent forms AI and B. Norms are provided for ninth-grade and architecture students. The test is restricted to APA members. Examiner required. Suitable for group use.

Timed: 6 minutes
Scoring: Examiner evaluated
Cost: Contact publisher
Publisher: Sheridan Psychological Services, Inc.

POSSIBLE JOBS (PJ)
Arthur Gershon and J.P. Guilford

Adolescent, adult
Grades 7 and above

Purpose: Measures the ability to elaborate upon given information. Used in research and experimental applications.

Description: Multiple-item paper-pencil test measuring "divergent production of semantic implications," which is defined as the ability to elaborate upon given information or to suggest alternative deductions or extensions. The test is scored by a simple count of acceptable responses. Norms are provided for ninth-

and tenth-grade students. The test is restricted to APA members. Examiner required. Suitable for group use.

Timed: 10 minutes
Scoring: Examiner evaluated
Cost: Contact publisher
Publisher: Sheridan Psychological Services, Inc.

PROVERBS TEST
Refer to page 597.

REACTION TIME TESTING
Refer to page 617.

REACTION TO EVERYDAY SITUATIONS TEST
Refer to page 1024.

ROKEACH VALUE SURVEY
Refer to page 250.

RUST INVENTORY OF SCHIZOTYPAL COGNITIONS (RISC)
Refer to page 216.

THE SCALE OF BELIEFS IN EXTRAORDINARY PHENOMENA (SOBEP)
George Windholz and Louis Diamant

Adolescent, adult

Purpose: Measures belief in extraordinary phenomena and possible natural phenomena that evoke an aura of mystery and sensationalism. Used in research on personality traits.

Description: 35–item paper-pencil Likert-scale test measuring beliefs in extraordinary phenomena on the periphery of Western thought, such as astrology, ghosts, magic, and witchcraft and in possible natural phenomena such as ESP; UFOs; and some aspects of hypnosis, dreams, and death. Subject indicates level of agreement or disagreement with each item. Examiner/self-administered. Suitable for group use.

Untimed: 20 minutes
Scoring: Examiner evaluated
Cost: Free
Publisher: George Windholz, Ph.D.

SEXUALITY EXPERIENCE SCALES
Refer to page 93.

SITUATIONAL PREFERENCE INVENTORY
Refer to page 221.

SLOAN ACHROMATOPSIA TEST
Munsell Color

Ages 6–adult

Purpose: Screens the congenital achromat in populations that are completely colorblind and measures how such persons see color. Used in research.

Description: Visual-verbal test consisting of seven neutral gray scales each displaying 17 steps between black and white. The scales are mounted on red, orange, yellow, green, blue, and magenta color references. The subject is asked to select the gray on the scale that appears to match the color reference mounted behind it. Examiner required. Not suitable for group use.
Untimed: 3–4 minutes
Scoring: Examiner evaluated
Cost: Complete $100.00
Publisher: Munsell Color

SMOKING AND HEALTH
Refer to page 391.

SPORTS EMOTION TEST (SET)
E.R. Oetting and C.W. Cole

Athletes

Purpose: Evaluates emotional responses of athletes prior to and during competition. Used as a research instrument.

Description: 132–item paper-pencil rating scale measuring feelings of anxiety, concentration, intensity, and physical

readiness. Subjects rate each response area on a 7–point scale according to how they feel at different times: 24 hours before, at breakfast, just before, and just after the start of the event and just after "something goes wrong." Self-administered. Suitable for group use.
Timed: 20 minutes
Scoring: Examiner evaluated
Cost: 100 scales and profiles $60.00; manual $12.00
Publisher: Rocky Mountain Behavioral Science Institute, Inc.

SYMBOL ELABORATION TEST (S.E.T.)
Refer to page 255.

TEST OF BASIC ASSUMPTIONS
James H. Morrison and Martin Levit

Adolescent, adult

Purpose: Diagnoses philosophical preferences. Used to examine assumptions about reality or philosophy and for research and group discussion.

Description: 20–item paper-pencil measure of realism, idealism, and pragmaticism. Instructions are read to the subjects, who are allowed as much time as they need to complete the test. A minimum 12th-grade reading level is necessary. The test should not be used for prediction purposes. Self-administered. Suitable for group use.
Untimed: 40 minutes
Scoring: Hand key
Cost: Specimen set (manual, score sheet, test) $2.00; 25 tests (score sheets, manual) $4.30
Publisher: James H. Morrison
Information and availability unconfirmed; last verified in 1988.

TYPE DIFFERENTIATION INDICATOR (RESEARCH EDITION)
*Katharine C. Briggs,
Isabel Briggs Myers, and
David Saunders*

Adolescent, adult

Purpose: Measures personality dispositions and interests based on Jung's theory of types. Used in personality research.

Description: 290–item paper-pencil instrument containing 27 subscales measuring four bipolar aspects of personality: introversion-extraversion, sensing-intuition, thinking-feeling, and judging-perceptive. Each subscale yields a weighted raw score. Overall MBTI type, preference scores, and raw scores based on Form G weights also are provided. Results may be useful for differentiating among individuals with the same type and understanding type development. Test items consist of Form F and 124 items used in earlier forms. The basic preferences may be obtained using the Form F scoring stencils, but the remaining indices are available only through the CPP Palo Alto Scoring Center. Only psychologists who are thoroughly familiar with type theory and the MBTI should use this test. Self-administered. Suitable for group use.

Untimed: 40–50 minutes

Scoring: Hand key; computer scored

Cost: 25 reusable question booklets $27.00; 10 prepaid answer sheets $38.00.

Publisher: Consulting Psychologists Press, Inc.

WISCONSIN CARD SORTING TEST: COMPUTER VERSION, RESEARCH EDITION
Milton E. Harris, Robert Adler, and Albert Kastl

Adolescent, adult—Ages 16 and older

Purpose: Assesses perseveration and abstract thinking. Used for neuropsychological assessment of individuals suspected of having brain lesions involving the frontal lobes. This edition is designed for research purposes only.

Description: Nonverbal computer-administered test in which the subject, using a paddle, matches color reproductions of the print version's two decks of response cards to one of four reproduced stimulus cards for color, form, or number. The test produces a scored protocol. Results may be saved on disk. The program is designed for use on Apple II+,

IIe, and IIc computer systems with a color monitor, two floppy disk drives, and a paddle. Examiner required. Not suitable for group use.

Untimed: Not available

Scoring: Computer scored

Cost: Unlimited use $195.00

Publisher: Psychological Assessment Resources, Inc.

Education

Tests classified in the Education section generally are used in an educational or school setting to assess the cognitive and emotional growth and development of persons of all ages. Typically, professionals who use the tests listed in this section are school psychologists, school counselors, and classroom teachers.

As the classification of tests by function or usage is somewhat arbitrary, the reader is encouraged to check the Psychology and Business sections for additional tests that may be helpful in meeting assessment needs.

Education Section

Academic Subjects: Business Education

CLERICAL SKILLS SERIES
Refer to page 930.

COMPLETE STANDARDIZED TEST OF COMPUTER LITERACY (VERSION AZ) REVISED (STCL)
Mary Montag and Michael R. Simonson

Adolescent, adult

Purpose: Assesses computer literacy and computer anxiety. Used to determine the progress of students enrolled in introductory computer literacy courses. Assists program planners in evaluating various computer literacy experiences.

Description: 80–item criterion-referenced paper-pencil multiple-choice achievement test assessing computer literacy and 26–item computer anxiety rating scale. Three subtests form the achievement test: Computer Systems (29 items measuring 25 competencies), Computer Applications (23 items measuring 25 competencies), and Computer Programming (19 items measuring 20 competencies). A separate 26–item instrument, the Computer Anxiety Index (CAIN), measures any computer-related anxieties the examinee may have (see separate test description). The three subtests of the STCL Achievement Test as well as the CAIN may be administered separately or in any combination. STCL Achievement Test scores may be reported in one or in any combination of the following ways: a) total STCL score for each student, b) STCL subtest scores for each student, or c) user-identified group scores for the total STCL or for subtests of the STCL. A mail-in scoring service is available from the publisher. Examiner required. Suitable for group use.

Timed: Achievement test 30 minutes per subtest
Untimed: CAIN 10 minutes
Scoring: Computer scored; hand key
Cost: 1 each STCL and CAIN test booklets $2.10; manual $5.00
Publisher: ISU Research Foundation, Iowa State University

COMPUTER ANXIETY INDEX (VERSION AZ) REVISED (CAIN)
Matthew Maurer and Michael R. Simonson

Adolescent, adult—Ages 15 and older Grades 8–adult

Purpose: Identifies students with computer-related anxieties. Used at the beginning of computer literacy courses to identify anxious students and provide them with remedial assistance designed to reduce their fears. Also used at the end of courses to identify changes in student attitudes as a consequence of learning about computers.

Description: 26–item paper-pencil instrument. Items are rated on a 6–point scale ranging from "strongly agree" to "strongly disagree." The actual instrument is labeled the Computer Opinion Survey to minimize the possibility of response bias. The CAIN may be used separately or in conjunction with the Standardized Achievement Test of Computer Literacy (Version AZ) Revised (see separate description), which measures computer literacy. Research has shown that students with anxieties about computers have difficulty acquiring cognitive computer literacy competencies. A mail-in scoring service is provided by the publisher. Examiner required. Suitable for group use.

Untimed: 10 minutes

Scoring: Computer scored; hand key

Cost: CAIN $0.50 per test; STCL $1.75 per test; CAIN and STCL $2.10

Publisher: ISU Research Foundation, Iowa State University

COMPUTER COMPETENCE TESTS (CCT)

Grades 4–adult

Purpose: Assesses an individual's knowledge of computers. Points out areas of instructional need.

Description: Multiple-item paper-pencil criterion-referenced test consisting of five modules: Development and Impact, Computer Operations I, Computer Operations II, Applications I, and Applications II. Teachers can select any or all modules that best match the content of their particular course. Although primarily designed for junior and senior high school students, the CCT can be used as early as Grade 4. National norms are not available. Examiner required. Suitable for group use.

Untimed: 20–25 minutes per module

Scoring: Hand key

Cost: Examination kit for each module (test booklet, ready-score answer document, directions for administration, manual, class record folder) $10.00

Publisher: The Psychological Corporation

Information and availability unconfirmed; last verified in 1988.

KEYBOARD SKILLS TEST (KST)
Refer to page 938.

NATIONAL BUSINESS COMPETENCY TESTS: ACCOUNTING PROCEDURES TEST (TRIAL EDITION)

Adolescent, adult

Purpose: Measures knowledge and skills related to accounting positions. Used for employee screening and educational evaluation.

Description: Multiple-item paper-pencil task-performance test in two parts assessing a variety of accounting knowledge and skills. Part 1 measures knowledge of basic accounting procedures and requires individuals to compute payroll earnings, prepare payroll reports, reconcile a bank statement, and complete a worksheet. In Part 2, individuals use source documents to make journal entries, post to a general ledger, prepare a trial balance, and make out a deposit slip. The test has optional questions on microcomputers in accounting. Examiner/self-administered. Suitable for group use.

Timed: Not available

Scoring: Hand key

Cost: Test booklet $0.75; manual/key $0.75

Publisher: National Business Education Association

NATIONAL BUSINESS COMPETENCY TESTS: SECRETARIAL PROCEDURES TEST

Adolescent, adult

Purpose: Measures knowledge and skills related to secretarial positions. Used for employee screening and educational evaluation.

Description: Multiple-item paper-pencil and task-performance test in two parts assessing a variety of secretarial skills and abilities. Part 1 measures knowledge of basic secretarial procedures and editing skills, including punctuation, grammar, spelling, and word usage. In Part 2, individuals prioritize and complete five typing assignments and a calendar updating task. Examiner/self-administered. Suitable for group use.

Timed: Not available

Scoring: Hand key

Cost: Test booklet $0.75; manual $0.75

Publisher: National Business Education Association

NATIONAL BUSINESS COMPETENCY TESTS: WORD PROCESSING TEST

Adolescent, adult

Purpose: Measures knowledge and skills related to word processing. Used for employee screening and educational evaluation.

Description: Multiple-item paper-pencil multiple-choice test in two parts. Part 1 assesses knowledge of word processing terminology, concepts, and principles. Part 2 assesses advanced word processing applications, including producing a business letter, invoice, and manuscript with revisions. Examiner/self-administered. Suitable for group use.

Untimed: 50 minutes

Timed: 50 minutes

Scoring: Hand key

Cost: Test $0.75; manual and key $0.75

Publisher: National Business Education Association

OETTING'S COMPUTER ANXIETY SCALE (COMPAS)
Refer to page 770.

THE OHIO VOCATIONAL ACHIEVEMENT TESTS IN BUSINESS EDUCATION: ACCOUNTING/COMPUTING CLERK
Refer to page 792.

THE OHIO VOCATIONAL ACHIEVEMENT TESTS IN BUSINESS EDUCATION: CLERK-STENOGRAPHER
Refer to page 793.

THE OHIO VOCATIONAL ACHIEVEMENT TESTS IN BUSINESS EDUCATION: DATA PROCESSING
Refer to page 793.

THE OHIO VOCATIONAL ACHIEVEMENT TESTS IN BUSINESS EDUCATION: GENERAL OFFICE CLERK
Refer to page 794.

THE OHIO VOCATIONAL ACHIEVEMENT TESTS IN MARKETING EDUCATION: GENERAL MERCHANDISE RETAILING
Refer to page 797.

SRA TYPING 5
Refer to page 948.

SRA TYPING SKILLS TEST
Refer to page 948.

STANDARDIZED ACHIEVEMENT TEST OF COMPUTER LITERACY (VERSION AZ) REVISED (STCL)
*Mary Montag and
Michael R. Simonson*

Adolescent, adult

Purpose: Assesses computer literacy. Used to determine the progress of students enrolled in introductory computer literacy courses. Assists program planners in evaluating various computer literacy experiences.

Description: 80–item criterion-referenced paper-pencil multiple-choice achievement test assessing computer literacy. Three subtests form the achievement test: Computer Systems (29 items measuring 25 competencies), Computer Applications (23 items measuring 25 competencies), and Computer Programming (19 items measuring 20 competencies). The STCL may be used in conjunction with the Computer Anxiety Index (CAIN), which measures any computer-related anxieties the examinee may have (see separate test description). The three subtests of the STCL Achievement Test may be administered separately or in any combination. STCL Achievement Test scores may be reported in one or in any combination of the following ways: a) total

STCL score for each student, b) STCL subtest scores for each student, or c) user-identified group scores for the total STCL or for subtests of the STCL. A mail-in scoring service is available from the publisher. Examiner required. Suitable for group use.

Timed: 30 minutes per subtest

Scoring: Computer scored; hand key

Cost: STCL $1.75 per test; CAIN $0.50 per test; STCL and CAIN $2.10

Publisher: ISU Research Foundation, Iowa State University

STUDENT OCCUPATIONAL COMPETENCY ACHIEVEMENT TESTING: ACCOUNTING/BOOKKEEPING

Adolescent

Purpose: Measures students' achievement in vocational accounting/bookkeeping programs. Used for grade assignment, identifying curriculum strengths and weaknesses, and evaluating job applicants.

Description: Two-part test measuring accounting and bookkeeping skills and knowledge. The multiple-choice written test covers processing purchases and payables, sales and receivables, cash receipts and cash payments, processing payroll and related records, inventory, operating mechanical and electronic accounting devices, and completing the accounting cycle. The optional advanced accounting practices portion covers general accounting adjustments, departmental accounting, partnerships, terminology, petty cash, inventory methods, and accounting concepts. The performance test measures abilities in journalizing, payroll procedures, banking, worksheet and statement preparation, and locating source data. The optional advanced accounting portion covers journalizing business transactions, aging accounts receivable, and determination of net income or loss. Examiner required. Suitable for group use.

Timed: Written test 3 hours; performance test 3 hours; optional section 80 minutes

Scoring: Scoring service provided

Cost: Contact publisher

Publisher: National Occupational Competency Testing Institute

STUDENT OCCUPATIONAL COMPETENCY ACHIEVEMENT TESTING: COMPUTER PROGRAMMING

Adolescent

Purpose: Measures competencies related to computer programming. Used for educational evaluation and employee screening.

Description: Multiple-item paper-pencil and task-performance test in two parts assessing knowledge and skills related to computer programming. The multiple-choice written test (150 items) measures general information, design, flowcharting, operations, BASIC, COBOL, RPG, related mathematics, and problem solving. The performance test requires candidates to design a program and code, test, and output it. Examiner required. Suitable for group use.

Timed: Written test 3 hours; performance test 4 hours

Scoring: Scoring service provided

Cost: Contact publisher

Publisher: National Occupational Competency Testing Institute

STUDENT OCCUPATIONAL COMPETENCY ACHIEVEMENT TESTING: GENERAL OFFICE

Adolescent

Purpose: Measures students' achievement in vocational general office programs. Used for grade assignment, identifying curriculum strengths and weaknesses, and evaluating job applicants.

Description: Two-part test of skills and knowledge in general office work. The multiple-choice written test covers keyboarding and word processing, office procedures, communications, filing and records management, mail, computational skills, and interpersonal and employability skills. The performance test measures abilities in filing and records management, computational skills, tabulation, business correspondence, forms preparation, envelope preparation, and communication. Examiner required. Suitable for group use.

Timed: Written test 3 hours; performance test 3 hours

Scoring: Scoring service provided

Cost: Contact publisher

Publisher: National Occupational Competency Testing Institute

---

WORD PROCESSOR ASSESSMENT BATTERY (WPAB)
Refer to page 963.

Academic Subjects: English and Related: Preschool, Elementary, and Junior High School

CARROW ELICITED LANGUAGES INVENTORY (CELI)
Refer to page 689.

DENVER HANDWRITING ANALYSIS (DHA)
Refer to page 611.

DIAGNOSTIC SPELLING TEST
Denis Vincent and Jenny Claydon

Child

Purpose: Assesses spelling skills. Used for diagnosing individual student weaknesses.

Description: Multiple-item paper-pencil test of spelling skills. Items include editing and correcting a passage of text and recognizing common letter groups in non-

sense words. The test also contains a questionnaire measuring attitudes toward spelling, a short dictation passage, and a short section measuring understanding of alphabetical order. Two parallel and equivalent forms, A and B, are available. Examiner required. Suitable for group use.

BRITISH PUBLISHER

Untimed: Complete test 45 minutes

Scoring: Hand key; examiner evaluated

Cost: Contact publisher

Publisher: NFER-NELSON Publishing Company Ltd.

DOS AMIGOS VERBAL LANGUAGE SCALES
Refer to page 573.

ENGLISH PROGRESS TESTS
The National Foundation for Educational Research

Child, adolescent—Ages 7.25–13.5

Purpose: Assesses the range of children's English attainment. Used by teachers to identify students needing help with basic skills and to compare achievement within a class or a group or with a nationally standardized sample.

Description: 8 multiple-item paper-pencil tests covering various English skills. Test A2 (7 years, 3 months–8 years, 11 months; 50 minutes) covers rhymes, plurals, spelling, vocabulary, pronouns, tenses, and reading comprehension. Test B2 (8 years, 6 months–10 years; 40 minutes) tests the ability to provide rhymes and opposites, pluralize nouns, change verbs to the past tense, spell and punctuate, write sentences, and read a passage and then answer comprehension questions. Test C2 (9 years, 6 months–11 years; 40–45 minutes) covers spelling, punctuation, vocabulary, and comprehension. Test C3 (9 years, 7 months–10 years, 10 months; 45 minutes) includes basic punctuation questions and items that assess the ability to arrange phrases in a meaningful order. Test D2 (10 years, 6 months–12 years; 40–45 minutes) assesses

spelling, punctuation, and comprehension. Test D3 (10 years–11 years, 8 months; 45 minutes) assesses the ability to use contextually correct words and includes punctuation and comprehension exercises. Test E2 (11 years–12 years, 9 months; 40 minutes) tests grammatical usage, written expression, vocabulary, comprehension, and punctuation. Test F2 (12 years–13 years, 6 months; 40 minutes) requires the use of expressive language. Questions cover grammatical usage, written expression, vocabulary, comprehension, and punctuation. Although the tests at each level follow a similar format, the style and size of print of the test booklets vary according to the age of the children being tested. Examiner required. Suitable for group use.
BRITISH PUBLISHER

Untimed: 40–50 minutes, depending on test

Scoring: Hand key

Cost: Contact publisher

Publisher: NFER-NELSON Publishing Company Ltd.

GATES-MCKILLOP-HOROWITZ READING DIAGNOSTIC TESTS
Refer to page 342.

GILLINGHAM-CHILDS PHONICS PROFICIENCY SCALES: SERIES I, BASIC READING AND SPELLING; SERIES II, ADVANCED READING
Refer to page 343.

GROUP LITERACY ASSESSMENT
Frank A. Spooncer

Child—Ages 10.6–12.6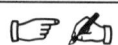

Purpose: Measures overall ability of children at the stage of transfer from primary to secondary education to deal effectively with written material. Identifies students needing help, indicates standards within a school district, and suggests appropriate follow-up procedures for both class groups and individual students.

Description: Multiple-item paper-pencil test in two sections measuring written ver-

bal abilities. In the first section, the student identifies and corrects mistakes in a simple story. In the second section, the story is continued as a modified cloze text. Children are required to use and combine pictorial, contextual, and grammatical cues offered by continuous prose. The test measures the students' ability to note significant details, carry information in short-term memory, and make inferential judgments. It also provides information about the student's spelling skills. Norms are presented as deviation quotients for ages 10.6–12.6 and reading age equivalents for ages 7–14. Scoring averages two minutes per paper. Examiner required. Suitable for group use.
BRITISH PUBLISHER

Untimed: 30 minutes

Scoring: Hand key

Cost: Specimen set £3.75; 20 test forms £2.05; manual £3.65

Publisher: Hodder & Stoughton

THE HUNTER-GRUNDIN LITERACY PROFILES LEVELS 1, 2, 3, 4 AND 5
Elizabeth Hunter-Grundin and Hans U. Grundin

Child, adolescent—Ages 6¹⁄₂–13¹⁄₂

Purpose: Assesses child's progress in reading and language development. Used for directing teaching towards a wider range of language and literacy skills.

Description: Battery of brief paper-pencil and oral tests measuring five components of literacy skills, including reading for meaning, attitude toward reading, spelling, free writing, and spoken language. The test is available on five levels: Level 1 (ages 6¹⁄₂–8), Level 2 (ages 8–9), Level 3 (ages 9–10), Level 4 (ages 10–11+), and Level 5 (ages 11–12+). The Reading for Meaning passage is different at each level. The score correlates with the Schonell Reading Test, Holborn Reading Scale, and the Neale Analysis of Reading Ability. Examiner required. Suitable for group use with the exception of the Spoken Language subtest, which must be administered individually.
BRITISH PUBLISHER

Timed: Levels 1 and 2 40 minutes; Levels 3, 4, 5 35 minutes

Scoring: Hand key; examiner evaluated

Cost: Complete kit (30 Reading for Meaning, 30 Spelling, 1 each of other tests in that level, 1 manual, 1 key, 1 Spoken Language Picture) Level 1 $55.00, Level 2–5 each $35.50

Publisher: The Test Agency Ltd.

LANGUAGE INVENTORY FOR TEACHERS (LIT)
Refer to page 637.

LISTENING COMPREHENSION TESTS IN ENGLISH FOR STANDARDS 5 AND 8

Child, adolescent

Purpose: Measures ability to understand spoken English. Used for educational evaluation.

Description: Multiple-item paper-pencil tests of listening comprehension for students in Standards 5 and 8. Pupils listen to recorded questions and mark answers on answer sheets. Materials include a cassette tape with questions for two alternate forms, A and B. Examiner required. Suitable for group use.
SOUTH AFRICAN PUBLISHER

Untimed: 50 minutes

Scoring: Hand key; examiner evaluated

Cost: (In Rands) Standard 5 manual 5,00; cassette 9,00; 10 answer sheets A 0,60; 10 answer sheets B 0,60; scoring stencils (specify A or B) 2,50; Standard 8 manual 5,00; cassette 9,00; 10 answer sheets A 1,80; 10 answer sheets B 1,80; scoring stencil A or B 2,50 each; orders outside the RSA will be dealt with on merit

Publisher: Human Sciences Research Council

MICROCOMPUTER MANAGED INFORMATION FOR CRITERION REFERENCED OBJECTIVES-LANGUAGE ARTS (MMICRO-LANGUAGE ARTS)
Educational Development Corporation

Child
Grades K–8

Purpose: Assesses students' language arts abilities. Provides information on skills mastered, skills requiring review, and skills to learn.

Description: Multiple-item (96 per grade) criterion-referenced paper-pencil test measuring spelling, grammar, and writing/reference skills. With the computerized system, diagnostic and objective tests are automatically scored in the school with a card or sheet reader recording information onto the software. Available for Apple and IBM microcomputers. Examiner required. Suitable for group use.

Untimed: Varies

Scoring: Computer scored

Cost: Not available

Publisher: Educational Development Corporation

MONITORING BASIC SKILLS PROGRESS—SPELLING
Lynn S. Fuchs, Carol Hamlett, and Douglass Fuchs

Child

Purpose: Monitors progress in basic spelling.

Description: Computer-assisted measurement program that tests and monitors progress in basic spelling. Students sitting at a computer type in words from a year-long curriculum. The computer generates and administers the tests, automatically scores the students' performance, shows the student the results of the testing, and provides a graph of scores over time. The computer also generates a detailed skills analysis, which provides the teacher with specific ideas for program development. The complete program includes one master disk for student measurement and

---

feedback; one teacher disk to view student assessment profiles, including graphed analysis and skills analysis; and a manual with a case study describing the use of the procedures and instructions. Available for use with an Apple II family computer with 64K. Self-administered. Not suitable for group use.

Untimed: Varies

Scoring: Computer scored

Cost: Complete kit $89.00

Publisher: PRO-ED

NATIONAL ACHIEVEMENT TESTS: ENGLISH, READING, LITERATURE, AND VOCABULARY TESTS—VOCABULARY (GRADES 3–8)
Refer to page 473.

PARALLEL SPELLING TESTS
Dennis Young

Child—Ages 6.5–13

Purpose: Measures spelling skills at all levels of ability. Used for program planning and evaluation.

Description: Multiple-item paper-pencil test of spelling ability. Test items are selected from banks of sentences presented in the test booklet according to the level of ability of the students being tested. Twelve matched tests without overlap (a much larger number with partial overlap) can be formed. The test booklet also includes sections on examining and extending the results, an introduction to children's spelling errors and the assessment of spelling in children's writing, fundamental guidance on the teaching of spelling, and a method for systematically charting the progress of children at all levels of ability over a period of six years (ages 6.5–13). Examiner required. Suitable for group use.
BRITISH PUBLISHER

Untimed: 20 minutes per test

Scoring: Examiner evaluated

Cost: Tests booklet £3.95

Publisher: Hodder & Stoughton

PHONOVISUAL DIAGNOSTIC TESTS
Edna B. Smith and Mazie Lloyd

Child
Grades 1–3

Purpose: Assesses students' knowledge of the sounds of letters. Used to determine strengths and weaknesses in the use of phonics.

Description: 24–item paper-pencil test measuring initial and final consonant sounds, short and long vowels, vowel spelling, 22 initial blends, and 14 final blends. The student writes 24 words as the examiner dictates them. Examiner required. Suitable for group use.

Untimed: 5–10 minutes

Scoring: Examiner evaluated

Cost: Complete set $4.50

Publisher: Phonovisual Products, Inc.

Information and availability unconfirmed; last verified in 1987.

PROOFREADING TESTS OF SPELLING (PRETOS)
Cedric Croft, Alison Gilmore, Neil Reid, and Peter Jackson

Child—Ages 8–13

Purpose: Measures ability to discriminate between misspelled and correctly spelled words. Used for providing diagnostic information about individual spelling accomplishments.

Description: Multiple-item paper-pencil tests of spelling achievement. The items are reading passages containing misspelled words. The child is required to detect spelling mistakes, correct words identified as misspelled, and indicate lines of text without mistakes. Five non-overlapping tests for use with different grade levels are available. Each test consists of three or four paragraphs consisting of 12–14 lines of text; two lines contain no misspelled words. Percentile rank norms are provided for recognition of spelling errors and production of correct spellings. Examiner required. Suitable for group use.
NEW ZEALAND PUBLISHER

Timed: 30 minutes

Scoring: Hand key; examiner evaluated

Cost: Contact publisher

Publisher: New Zealand Council for Educational Research

SOUTH AFRICAN WRITTEN LANGUAGE TEST (SAWLT)—1981

Grades II-Standard 5

Purpose: Measures written language ability of English-speaking primary-school students. Used for educational guidance.

Description: Test of written language requiring the subject to write a passage in response to a stimulus photo. Materials include the stimulus photo, which should be provided to each subject in group administrations. Examiner required. Suitable for group use.

SOUTH AFRICAN PUBLISHER

Untimed: 30 minutes

Scoring: Hand key; examiner evaluated

Cost: (In Rands) manual 8,00; stimulus photo 1,50; writing pad 1,00; scoring pad 1,50; orders from outside the RSA will be dealt with on merit

Publisher: Human Sciences Research Council

THE SPELLMASTER ASSESSMENT AND TEACHING SYSTEM
Claire R. Greenbaum

All ages

Purpose: Measures spelling abilities and diagnoses individual and group spelling difficulties. Used to plan instructional and remedial spelling programs and provide direct teaching for classroom teachers, reading specialists, LD specialists, ESL teachers, special education teachers, teachers of gifted and talented, and adult education teachers.

Description: Multiple-item paper-pencil tests measuring eight levels of spelling abilities corresponding to grade levels 1-8. Regular word tests, irregular word tests, and homophone tests are provided for all levels. Entry level tests are provided

to determine the appropriate level of regular word, irregular word, and homophone tests to administer to each student.

The Regular Word tests (Levels 1-2, 20 words each; levels 3-8, 40 words each) are criterion-referenced diagnostic tests, each featuring a unique scoring form that identifies specific erroneous elements within words. On the basis of this diagnosis, students are placed for individual or group instruction. Class data charts are provided to assist in grouping according to needs. Students may correct their own tests to gain insight into their strengths and weaknesses.

The Irregular Words tests (Level 1, 20 words; levels 2-8, 40 words) measure mastery of frequently used words that violate phonic rules.

The Homophone Tests (Level 1, 20 words; levels 2-8, 40 words) measure mastery of words whose spelling must be learned in conjunction with meaning; the words may be regular or irregular.

The examiner's manual provides instructions for the administration and scoring of all tests and contains detailed teaching aids and techniques, analysis of errors, specific teaching suggestions for each regular phonic and structural element and for irregular words and homophones. Approximately 5,000 supplementary words are included for individual study. Also included are individual progress records that are organized to record scores and dates for each regular word, irregular word, and homophone test and that allow space for two retests. Also included are information on classroom management of the program; visual, auditory, and kinesthetic memory techniques; and learning activities for both reinforcement and challenge. This test is a revision of the Spellmaster Diagnostic Spelling System. Examiner required. Suitable for group use.

Untimed: Varies

Scoring: Hand key; examiner evaluated; self-scored

Cost: Complete kit (Examiner's manual, 50 student answer sheets, 8 pads of 25 scoring forms for diagnostic levels 1-8, storage box) $69.00

Publisher: PRO-ED

TEST OF WRITTEN ENGLISH (TWE)
Velma R. Andersen and Sheryl K. Thompson

Child, adolescent Grades 1-6 and older remedial students

Purpose: Measures written language skills of elementary school children and older remedial students. Used to screen for mastery in areas of capitalization, punctuation, written expression, and paragraph writing.

Description: Multiple-item paper-pencil test in which the student corrects various errors of capitalization, punctuation, and usage and writes a brief paragraph. Items in each skill area are grouped according to difficulty from Grades 1-6. Remedial activities are provided for each of the areas tested. Items may be read by the students themselves or by the examiner so that poor readers can be accurately evaluated. A conversion table is provided for translating scores to approximate grade-level placement. Examiner required. Suitable for small group use if all students are capable readers.

Untimed: 30 minutes

Scoring: Hand key

Cost: Manual $15.00; 50 test forms $18.00

Publisher: Academic Therapy Publications

TEST OF WRITTEN SPELLING-2 (TWS-2)
Stephen C. Larsen and Donald D. Hammill

Child, adolescent—Ages 6.6-18.5—Grades 1-12

Purpose: Measures students' spelling abilities by using both words that are easily predictable by their sound and words that are more irregular. Identifies the spelling strengths and weaknesses of students, identifies words to be studied, guides instructional practices, and measures progress.

Description: 100-item paper-pencil test assessing student spelling performance with three groups of words: words readily predictable in sound-spelling pattern, words less predictable, and both types of words presented together. Standard scores and percentiles are provided for each of the three groups. In addition, a Written Spelling Quotient, a Predictable Words Quotient, and an Unpredictable Words Quotient are calculated. Test items were developed after review of 2,000 spelling rules, with words drawn from 10 basal spelling programs. Braille typing is available for visually impaired individuals. Examiner required. Suitable for group use.

Untimed: 20 minutes

Scoring: Examiner evaluated

Cost: Complete kit (examiner's manual, 50 answer sheets, class profile sheet, storage box) $39.00

Publisher: PRO-ED

VISUAL MEMORY SCALE (VMS)
Refer to page 360.

VOCABULARY COMPREHENSION SCALE (VCS)
Tina E. Bangs

Child—Ages 2-6

Purpose: Evaluates a young child's comprehension of pronouns and words of position, quality, quantity, and size. Used for instructional programming and remediation work.

Description: 61-item test in which the subject responds to the examiner's spoken directions by manipulating the appropriate item (card, doll, cube, cylinder, buttons in a box, garage, fence, ladder, tea set) included among the test materials. The data collected can be used to plan activities for developing vocabulary needed to enter kindergarten or first grade. Suggestions for teaching unfamiliar words and concepts are included in the test manual. Examiner required. Not suitable for group use.

Untimed: 20 minutes

Scoring: Examiner evaluated

Cost: Complete $70.00
Publisher: DLM Teaching Resources

Academic Subjects: English and Related: High School and College

AMERICAN LITERATURE TESTS—ESSAY

Adolescent
Grades 6–12

Purpose: Measures literal and interpretive comprehension of specific American novels commonly taught in secondary schools. Evaluates writing skills through paragraph organization and content.

Description: Series of tests covering students' literal and interpretive comprehension of 157 American novels, including *To Kill a Mockingbird, The Scarlet Letter, A Separate Peace, The Call of the Wild, Of Mice and Men,* and *The Outsiders.* Each test contains 6–10 reproducible essay questions with answer key. Questions are leveled according to thinking skills. The reading level of each test corresponds to the reading level of the book it covers. Examiner required. Suitable for group use.

Untimed: Varies
Scoring: Examiner evaluated
Cost: Test and key $2.75
Publisher: The Perfection Form Company

AMERICAN LITERATURE TESTS—50-QUESTION AND 100-QUESTION

Adolescent
Grades 6–12

Purpose: Measures literal comprehension of specific American novels commonly taught in secondary schools. Used as a posttest.

Description: 100–item and 50–item paper-pencil multiple-choice matching and true-false tests covering students' literal comprehension of various novels. Tests are available for 157 novels, including *To Kill a Mockingbird, The Scarlet Letter, A Separate Peace, Of Mice and Men, Death of a Salesman,* and *When the Legends Die.* The reading level of each test corresponds to the reading level of the book it covers. Examiner required. Suitable for group use.

Untimed: Varies
Scoring: Hand key
Cost: 50–Q test and key $1.95; 100–Q test and key $2.75
Publisher: The Perfection Form Company

BOOKLET OF GRAMMAR TESTS
Kenneth Stratton and
George Christian

Adolescent
Grades 7–12

Purpose: Assesses skills in grammar. Used for identifying student strengths and weaknesses as part of an educational evaluation.

Description: 10 paper-pencil tests of grammar skills. Both diagnostic and achievement tests are available in four areas: parts of speech, parts of the sentence, joining parts of the sentence, and punctuation and capitalization. Six other areas are covered by shorter tests designed to be used as measures of student knowledge: nouns, pronouns, verbs, adjectives and adverbs, prepositions, conjunctions and interjections, correct usage, and variety in sentence arrangement. Examiner required. Suitable for group use.

Untimed: Not available
Scoring: Hand key
Cost: Set of tests $3.95 each
Publisher: Stratton-Christian Press, Inc.
Information and availability unconfirmed; last verified in 1988.

CLARKE READING SELF-ASSESSMENT SURVEY (SAS)
Refer to page 363.

COLLEGE ENGLISH PLACEMENT TEST
Oscar M. Haugh and James I. Brown

College freshmen

Purpose: Measures English composition skills of incoming college freshmen. Used to place college freshmen in English composition classes.

Description: Multiple-item paper-pencil test consisting of two parts. Part 1 is an objective test measuring English composition skills. Part 2, which is optional, consists of two essays. The test items reflect the results of a survey of college English professors concerning the relative importance of elements of composition in the assignment of freshmen to composition classes. The elements found to be vital in English composition and placement and their weight on the test are organization and paragraph structure (36%); syntax and grammar (17%); and conventions, usage, and capitalization (22%). The sections of the test are arranged to follow the actual steps in writing a composition. Examiner required. Suitable for group use.

Timed: Part 1 45 minutes; Part 2 55 minutes

Scoring: Examiner evaluated

Cost: 50 test booklets $49.50; 50 self-marking answer sheets $37.50; manual for administrators and examiners $4.80

Publisher: The Riverside Publishing Company

COOPERATIVE ENGLISH TESTS
Educational Testing Service

Adolescent
Grades 9–14

Purpose: Measures high-school and college students' achievement in reading comprehension and written expression. Used to screen students who are advanced or lacking in basic English abilities and for placement in the appropriate level of instruction.

Description: 210–item paper-pencil test designed to assess a student's mastery of basic English skills. Four subtests are independently available: Reading Comprehension Part I, measuring vocabulary; Reading Comprehension Part II, measuring level and speed of comprehension in varied style and content; English Expression Part I, measuring effectiveness in conveying exact meaning; and English Expression Part II, measuring mechanics (usage, spelling, punctuation, capitalization). Two levels are available for each subtest: Level 1 for Grades 12–14 and Level 2 for Grades 9–12. Examiner required. Suitable for group use.

Timed: 40 minutes per section

Scoring: Hand key; may be computer scored

Cost: 20 reusable test books $18.40 (specify level); 100 answer sheets $18.00

Publisher: CTB/Macmillan/McGraw-Hill

THE ENGLISH LANGUAGE SKILLS PROFILE (TELS)
The Godfrey Thomson Unit, Edinburgh University

Adolescent—Ages 14–16

Purpose: Assesses language skills. Used for diagnosing teaching needs.

Description: Multiple-item paper-pencil multiple-choice true-false oral-response and essay test assessing language skills. The criterion-referenced test is composed of four categories: reading, writing, listening, and communications. Each area yields a scaled score. The test is available in two forms, each emphasizing a different theme: community or relationships. Examiner/self-administered. Suitable for group use.
BRITISH PUBLISHER

Timed: Not available

Untimed: Varies

Scoring: Hand key; examiner evaluated; self-scored

Cost: Evaluation pack £18.99; starter pack (specify form) £160.00

Publisher: Macmillan Education Ltd.

ENGLISH/WORLD LITERATURE TESTS—ESSAY

Adolescent
Grades 7-12

Purpose: Measures literal and interpretive comprehension of specific English and world literature novels commonly taught in secondary schools. Evaluates writing skills through paragraph organization and content.

Description: Multiple-item paper-pencil essay tests measuring students' literal and interpretive comprehension of specific novels. Tests are available for 106 novels, including *Animal Farm, Romeo and Juliet, Hamlet, A Tale of Two Cities, Brave New World,* and *The Hobbit.* Each test contains 6–10 essays. The reading level of each test corresponds to the reading level of the novel it covers. Examiner required. Suitable for group use.

Untimed: Varies

Scoring: Examiner evaluated

Cost: Test and key $2.75

Publisher: The Perfection Form Company

ENGLISH/WORLD LITERATURE TESTS—50-QUESTION AND 100-QUESTION

Adolescent
Grades 7-12

Purpose: Measures literal comprehension of specific English or world literature novels commonly taught in secondary schools.

Description: 100–item and 50–item paper-pencil multiple-choice matching and true-false tests covering 106 titles, including *Hamlet, A Tale of Two Cities, Macbeth, Siddhartha, Animal Farm,* and *The Hobbit.* The reading level of the test corresponds to that of the book the test covers. Examiner required. Suitable for group use.

Untimed: Varies

Scoring: Hand key

Cost: 50–Q test and key $1.95; 100–Q test and key $2.75

Publisher: The Perfection Form Company

JOURNALISM TEST
Francis Miller and Kenneth Stratton

Adolescent
Grades 10-12

Purpose: Assesses journalism skills. Used for diagnosing strengths and weaknesses and measuring student achievement.

Description: Multiple-item paper-pencil test of major journalism areas: judgment of news values, paragraphing, sentence variety, news sources, sports, judgment of feature values, speech-interview stories, editorials, make-up, headlines, terminology, copyreading, style, columns, and advertising. Item types include true-false and identifying errors. Examiner required. Suitable for group use.

Untimed: Not available

Scoring: Hand key

Cost: Test $0.39 each (minimum order of 10)

Publisher: Stratton-Christian Press, Inc.

Information and availability unconfirmed; last verified in 1988.

MYTHOLOGY TESTS

Adolescent
Grades 7-12

Purpose: Measures literal comprehension of specific mythology novels and texts.

Description: 100–item and 50–item paper-pencil multiple-choice matching and true-false reproducible tests assessing students' literal level of comprehension. Tests are available for 14 titles, including *Gods, Heroes, and Men of Ancient Greece; The Once and Future King; The Iliad; Le Morte D'Arthur; Words from the Myths;* and *The Adventures of Ulysses.* The reading level of each test corresponds to the reading level of the book that it covers. Examiner required. Suitable for group use.

Untimed: Varies

Scoring: Hand key

Cost: 50–Q test and key $1.95; 100–Q test and key $2.75

Publisher: The Perfection Form Company

MYTHOLOGY TESTS—ESSAY

Adolescent
Grades 7-12

Purpose: Measures literal and interpretive comprehension of specific mythology novels and texts. Evaluates writing skills through paragraph organization and content.

Description: Multiple-item paper-pencil essay tests measuring literal and interpretive comprehension and evaluating writing skills. Revised tests are available for 14 titles, including *Gods, Heroes, and Men of Ancient Greece; The Once and Future King; The Iliad; Le Morte D'Arthur; Words from the Myths;* and *The Adventures of Ulysses.* Each test contains 6–10 essay questions. The reading level of each test corresponds to the reading level of the book it covers. Examiner required. Suitable for group use.

Untimed: Varies

Scoring: Examiner evaluated

Cost: Test, key $2.75

Publisher: The Perfection Form Company

NATIONAL ACHIEVEMENT TESTS: ENGLISH, READING, LITERATURE, AND VOCABULARY TESTS—COLLEGE ENGLISH FOR HIGH SCHOOL AND COLLEGE
Refer to page 472.

NATIONAL ACHIEVEMENT TESTS: ENGLISH, READING, LITERATURE, AND VOCABULARY TESTS—ENGLISH
Refer to page 472.

NATIONAL ACHIEVEMENT TESTS: ENGLISH, READING, LITERATURE, AND VOCABULARY TESTS—VOCABULARY (GRADES 7-COLLEGE)
Refer to page 473.

PURDUE HIGH SCHOOL ENGLISH TEST
R.D. Franklin, J.H. McKee, H.H. Remmers, and G.S. Wykoff

Adolescent
Grades 9-13

Purpose: Measures the English language skills of high-school students and college freshmen.

Description: Multiple-item paper-pencil test measuring a student's knowledge and ability in five areas of English: grammar, punctuation, effective expression, vocabulary, and spelling. Fall and spring norms in terms of percentiles and standard scores are provided by grade and sex for high-school students. Norms for college freshmen and other interpretive data are included also. The test is available in two alternate forms, 1 and 2. Examiner required. Suitable for group use.

Timed: 36 minutes

Scoring: Hand key; may be computer scored

Cost: 35 test booklets $28.83; 100 self-marking answer sheets $60.09; manual $5.85; 35 class record sheets $8.10

Publisher: The Riverside Publishing Company

READING, COMPREHENSION, GRAMMAR USAGE AND STRUCTURE, AND VOCABULARY TESTS
William A. McCartney

Adolescent
Grades 10-13

Purpose: Assesses English knowledge or potential of students seeking to enter four-year colleges. Used to predict degree of success in freshman composition or other English classes and for admission and placement.

Description: 198-item paper-pencil battery of three tests designed to be used together but which may be taken separately to measure performance in the following areas: reading comprehension (48 multiple-choice items based on 16 short selections); grammar, usage, and structure (100 two-choice items based on logic of expression, idiom, and good taste); and vocabulary (50 five-choice items calling for recognition of synonyms). Examiner required. Suitable for group use.

Timed: Complete battery 2 hours

Scoring: Hand key; may be computer scored

Cost: Contact publisher

Publisher: William A. McCartney

Information and availability unconfirmed; last verified in 1987.

STRUCTURE TESTS, ENGLISH LANGUAGE (STEL)
Jeanette Best and Donna Ilyin

Adolescent, adult
Grades 10 and above

Purpose: Determines student knowledge of English-language structure. Used as an aid to assessing skill levels, diagnosing problems, and student placement.

Description: 50-item paper-pencil multiple-choice test available in beginning, intermediate, and advanced levels. There are two categories of difficulty for each level. The student selects which of three statements is written in correct English. The test can be used with an oral interview such as the Ilyin Oral Interview Test. Examiner required. Suitable for group use.

Untimed: 30 minutes per test

Scoring: Hand key

Cost: Contact publisher

Publisher: Newbury House Publishers, Inc.

Information and availability unconfirmed; last verified in 1987.

WESTERN MICHIGAN UNIVERSITY ENGLISH QUALIFYING EXAM (EQE)
Bernadine P. Carlson

Adolescent, adult
Grades 15 and above

Purpose: Assesses level of English usage skills for graduate students and college juniors and seniors. Used for academic placement and as a criterion for graduation and an evaluation of skills for graduate work.

Description: 195-item paper-pencil multiple-choice test consisting of six parts: grammatical errors (30 items); punctuation for meaning (45 items); sentence structure (30 items); spelling (30 items); word usage, diction (30 items); and reading comprehension and rhetorical style (30 items). Test items consist of sentences taken from papers written by students in Grades 15 and above. The test yields a mean score for the overall test and for each part. A scoring service is available from the publisher. The test, which is available in both forms A and B, may be used for pre- and posttesting in writing classes and with any type of skills handbook. A specimen booklet, which includes sample questions from each of the six parts, is available. The test may be read aloud to visually impaired individuals and is not timed in such cases. Examiner required. Suitable for group use.

Timed: 1 hour, 40 minutes

Scoring: Hand key; may be computer scored

Cost: Contact publisher

Publisher: Bernadine P. Carlson

WESTERN MICHIGAN UNIVERSITY ENGLISH USAGE-ORIENTATION FORM (EUO)
Refer to page 926.

WORD UNDERSTANDING (WU)
R. Hoepfner, M. Hendricks, and R.H. Silverman

Adolescent
Grades 7–12

Purpose: Measures verbal comprehension and vocabulary. Used for personal and program evaluation.

Description: 32–item paper-pencil multiple-choice test consisting of two parts of 16 items each arranged in order of difficulty. Scores reflect the breadth and depth of vocabulary. Two forms are available: Form A is reusable, and answers are recorded on answer sheets. A lay-over stencil is available for scoring. Form C is consumable and used with subjects who may be expected to perform poorly on answer-sheet tests. A response guide is available for scoring. The test has been normed on over 1,300 junior high-school students. Examiner required. Suitable for group use.

Timed: 4 minutes per part

Scoring: Hand key

Cost: Specimen set (specify form) $4.00; 35 tests (specify form) $8.00; 35 answer sheets (Form A) $4.00; scoring stencil (Form A) $3.00; scoring guide (Form C) $2.00; manual $2.00

Publisher: Monitor

Academic Subjects: English and Related: Multilevel

BENCH MARK MEASURES
Aylett Cox

Child, adolescent

Purpose: Assesses a student's general phonic knowledge, including reading, alphabet and dictionary skills, handwriting, and spelling, as a means of diagnosing particular deficiencies and to gauge progress during remediation.

Description: Three paper-pencil verbal tests arranged in sequence to cover four areas of remedial language: alphabet and dictionary skills, reading, handwriting, and spelling. The alphabet and reading sections must be administered individually, but the handwriting and spelling schedules may be administered to groups.

The kit contains step-by-step directions for administration, along with reading passages and spelling lists. The Guide to Bench Mark Measures contains a description of testing, scoring, and evaluation. The Graphs of Concepts and Multisensory Introductions shows the graphemes and concepts in the order taught in the Alphabetic Phonics curriculum. Summary sheets are used to record responses and mark errors. Also included in the complete kit is the skeleton dictionary, sheet of letters, spirit duplicating master for specially-lined paper, 26 three-dimensional letters, and 56 cards. The examination was designed primarily for use with the Alphabetic Phonics curriculum, the three levels of which correspond to the Bench Mark's alphabet, reading, and writing schedules. The test can, however, be used with any student as a diagnostic tool and should be administered by a trained examiner in a quiet setting. The last two sections may be administered to small groups.

Untimed: 30 minutes–1 hour for each of the four levels

Scoring: Examiner evaluated

Cost: Complete kit $55.00; 24 summary sheets $10.00; graph $1.25; skeleton dictionary $4.50

Publisher: Educators Publishing Service, Inc.

BILINGUAL SYNTAX MEASURE I AND II (BSM)
Refer to page 571.

CAT WRITING ASSESSMENT SYSTEM

Child, adolescent
Grades 3–12

Purpose: Measures students' ability to write compositions. Provides survey information for determining the effectiveness of instructional programs and diagnostic information for individual remediation.

Description: Paper-pencil essay test evaluating writing programs by assessing the writing skills of students enrolled in those programs. Writing booklets with assignments designed to prompt one of four types of writing are available on various levels: Descriptive (Grades 2.6–7.2); Narrative (Grades 2.6–11.2); Expository (Grades 4.6–12.9); and Persuasive (Grades 6.6–12.9). Scoring may be performed locally using training materials developed by CTB or by the CTB Composition Evaluation Center. An administration and scoring guide for each prompt provides holistic and analytic scoring guidelines. Examiner required. Suitable for group use.

Timed: 25–40 minutes

Scoring: Examiner evaluated

Cost: Examination kit (1 booklet for each type of writing, sample manual, test coordinator's directions, CTB answer sheet supplement) $24.10

Publisher: CTB/Macmillan/McGraw-Hill

COMPREHENSIVE ASSESSMENT PROGRAM (CAP): ASSESSMENT OF WRITING
Louis A. Gatta and Thomas Valentin

Adolescent, adult

Purpose: Assesses writing ability of students at the elementary, junior high, and high school level.

Description: Paper-pencil essay test comprised of three levels: Secondary 1 (Grades 7 and 8), Secondary 2 (Grades 9 and 10), and Secondary 3 (Grades 11 and 12). An elementary level is also available. Each level offers three writing prompts that typically require a student to draw upon personal experience and/or opinion without requiring the recall of any specific factual knowledge. Prompts generally imply a particular mode of writing—descriptive, narrative, persuasive, or expository—but do not mandate that students write in the most apparent mode. Essays are evaluated using a holistic six-point rating scale. Each essay is scored independently by two raters, and the scores are averaged for the overall holistic score. However, if the scores differ by more than one point, the essay is evaluated by a "head" rater whose score overrides the first two. Essays may also be

evaluated using diagnostic scoring, providing an optional set of scores. Examiner required. Suitable for group use.

Timed: 40 minutes

Scoring: Hand scored by AT Scoring Service

Cost: Kit (25 test booklets, directions) $37.10

Publisher: American Testronics

DIAGNOSTIC SCREENING TEST: LANGUAGE, SECOND EDITION (DSTL)
Thomas D. Gnagey and Patricia A. Gnagey

Child, adolescent
Grades K–13

Purpose: Determines a student's ability to write English and diagnoses common problems in the use of the language.

Description: 110–item multiple-choice paper-pencil test yielding six scores: total, sentence structure, grammar, punctuation, capitalization, and formal spelling rules. All subtests yield applied versus formal knowledge for a total of 12 scores in all. The examiner explains the procedure to individuals or groups and reads the test if the students have poor reading skills. Examiner required. Suitable for group use.

Untimed: 5–10 minutes

Scoring: Hand key

Cost: Manual, 50 test forms $35.00

Publisher: Slosson Educational Publications, Inc.

DIAGNOSTIC SCREENING TEST: SPELLING, THIRD EDITION (DSTS)
Thomas D. Gnagey

Child, adolescent
Grades 1–12

Purpose: Measures a student's ability to spell words and diagnoses common spelling problems.

Description: 78–item pencil-paper test measuring sight or phonics orientation for spelling instruction, relative efficiency of verbal and written testing procedures, analysis of sequential and gross auditory memory, and spelling potential. A pretest is available to determine the appropriate level of entry. The examiner, using the test form, pronounces 78 developmentally arranged words and the student spells them orally; the examiner then repronounces difficult words and the student writes them. When administered to groups, the test yields a grade equivalent score. The test is available in Forms A and B. Examiner required. Suitable for group use.

Untimed: 5–10 minutes

Scoring: Hand key

Cost: Manual, 25 Form A, 25 Form B $32.00

Publisher: Slosson Educational Publications, Inc.

DIAGNOSTIC SPELLING POTENTIAL TEST (DSPT)
John Arena

Ages 7–adult

Purpose: Assesses the spelling skills of students.

Description: Multiple-item paper-pencil test consisting of four subtests: Spelling, Word Recognition, Visual Recognition, and Auditory-Visual Recognition. Tables are provided for converting raw scores to standard scores, percentile ranks, and grade ratings. Standard scores and percentiles may be plotted on a profile chart that compares spelling efficiency with requisite skills such as decoding, utilization of phonetic generalizations, visual recall, and matching auditory with visual representations. Two parallel forms are available for pre- and posttesting. The manual includes provisions for group administration of three of the subtests and presents a wide range of remedial activities. Examiner required. Suitable for group use.

Untimed: 25–40 minutes

Scoring: Examiner evaluated

Cost: Test kit (manual, Form A–1: 25 Spelling/Word Recognition Record Forms, Form A–2: 25 Visual/Auditory-Visual Recognition Record Forms, 25 Profile Sheets, in vinyl folder) $39.50

Publisher: Academic Therapy Publications

ENGLISH PROGRESS TESTS SERIES

Child, adolescent—Ages 7–14

Purpose: Assesses the English skills of children. Used for measuring individual pupil progress.

Description: Series of eight paper-pencil tests providing continuous assessment of reading skills. The English Progress Test A2 (ages 7–9) covers rhymes, plurals, spelling, vocabulary, pronouns, tenses, and reading comprehension. Test B2 (ages 8–10) requires the child to provide rhymes and opposites, spell and punctuate, and write sentences. Test C2 (ages 9–11) requires written answers covering spelling, punctuation, vocabulary, and comprehension. Test C3 (ages 9–10) tests basic punctuation, vocabulary, and comprehension. Children also are required to join pairs of sentences into longer sentences and to construct acceptable sentences. Test D3 (ages 10–11) consists of 50 questions assessing the ability to use words correctly, elementary punctuation, and comprehension of both a poetry and a prose passage. Test E2 (ages 11–12) contains 12 different types of questions testing grammatical usage, written expression, vocabulary comprehension, and punctuation. Test F2 (ages 12–13) consists of "creative response" questions covering grammatical usage, written expression, vocabulary, comprehension, and punctuation. English Progress Tests A, B3, E, F3, and G are out of print. Examiner required. Suitable for group use.
BRITISH PUBLISHER

Untimed: 40–45 minutes per test

Scoring: Hand key

Cost: Contact publisher

Publisher: NFER-NELSON Publishing Company Ltd.

THE ENNIS-WEIR CRITICAL THINKING ESSAY TEST
Robert H. Ennis and Eric Weir

**Adolescent, adult
Grades 7 and above**

Purpose: Measures the ability to think critically. Used for teaching and in research.

Description: Paper-pencil essay test incorporating the following aspects of critical thinking: getting the point, seeing the reasons and assumptions, stating one's point, offering good reasons, seeing other possibilities, responding appropriately to/ avoiding equivocation, irrelevance, circularity, reversal of an if-then relationship, overgeneralization, credibility questions, and the use of emotive language to persuade. Self-administered. Suitable for group use.

Untimed: 40 minutes

Scoring: Examiner evaluated

Cost: Manual (includes scoring directions, 1 test, 1 scoring sheet) $9.95

Publisher: Midwest Publications Critical Thinking Press

GRADED WORD SPELLING TEST
P.E. Vernon

Ages 6 and older

Purpose: Measures spelling ability. Used with students ages six and older, extending to the level of spelling reached by well-educated adults.

Description: 80–item paper-pencil test measuring students' ability to correctly spell words that are presented orally. Each word is placed in the context of a short sentence, and the test items are graded in order of difficulty. The particular items to be used on any one occasion are selected from the 80–word list according to the age and ability of the pupils to be tested; no pupil takes the whole test. The test is contained in a single reusable booklet and is designed to be administered orally. Full instructions for administration, scoring, and interpretation are provided. Examiner required. Suitable for group use.
BRITISH PUBLISHER

Untimed: 30 minutes

Scoring: Hand key

Cost: Test booklet £3.50

Publisher: Hodder & Stoughton

HUDSON EDUCATION SKILLS INVENTORY-WRITING (HESI-W)
Refer to page 461.

THE INFORMAL WRITING INVENTORY
Refer to page 636.

INTERNATIONAL SOCIETY FOR PHILOSOPHICAL ENQUIRY VOCABULARY FORM A

Adult

Purpose: Measures knowledge of vocabulary at a high level of achievement (ceiling circa 170+ A Q). Used as preparation for the supervised vocabulary test, Form B.

Description: 70–item paper-pencil multiple-choice test provides a high-level measure of linguistic aptitude. Subjects are asked to select from four choices the one word most closely "related" to the given test-item word. Norms are available for the top 6% to top 00.002% of the population. Answers and norms are printed on the back of the test form. Self-administered. Suitable for group use.
AUSTRALIAN PUBLISHER

Untimed: Varies

Scoring: Self-scored

Cost: Test $25.00

Publisher: Harding Tests

INTERNATIONAL SOCIETY FOR PHILOSOPHICAL ENQUIRY VOCABULARY FORM B

Adult

Purpose: Measures knowledge of vocabulary at a high level of achievement. Provides best accuracy with the top 6% to top 00.13% of the population.

Description: 136–item paper-pencil multiple-choice test providing a high level

measure of linguistic ability. Subjects are asked to select from three choices the one word most closely "related" to the given test-item word. Answers and norms are printed on the back of the test form. Examiner required. Suitable for group use.
AUSTRALIAN PUBLISHER

Untimed: Varies

Scoring: Self-scored

Cost: Test $25.00

Publisher: Harding Tests

LANGUAGE PROFICIENCY TEST (LPT)
Refer to page 578.

LAURITA-TREMBLEY DIAGNOSTIC WORD PROCESSING TEST
Raymond E. Laurita and Phillip W. Trembley

Child, adolescent, adult
Grades 1 and above

Purpose: Identifies the level of categorical word processing that a student is able to utilize in spelling. Used for program planning, establishing IEPs, monitoring progress, and evaluating instructional programs in spelling.

Description: 64–item paper-pencil test using a dictation spelling format to assess the ability to discriminate among 15 vowel forms at five sequentially organized levels of difficulty. Criterion-referenced test items are based on an orthographic model that holds that spelling relies on a given set of word-processing generalizations. The results are profiled on the Individual Progress Chart, which details the student's level of word processing ability, identifies categories of words that the student is ready to learn, and provides an estimate of the number of words in the student's spelling vocabulary. Examiner required. Suitable for group use.

Untimed: 20–30 minutes

Scoring: Examiner evaluated

Cost: Test kit (manual, 10 Individual Progress Charts, 20 record forms for pre- and posttesting) $25.00

Publisher: Leonardo Press
Information and availability unconfirmed; last verified in 1988.

THE LISTENING FOR MEANING TEST
M.A. Brimer

Child—Ages 3–18

Purpose: Measures the level of intelligent verbal functions of which an individual is capable. Used by teachers, psychologists, or speech therapists.

Description: Multiple-item picture-response test using an individual's understanding of spoken English words as a means of measuring the individual's level of verbal functioning. The individual indicates which picture represents the meaning of a word spoken by the examiner. A focusing scale is used to determine at which point testing should begin within 10 hierarchically ordered scales of 12 items each. Examiner required. Not suitable for group use.
BRITISH PUBLISHER

Untimed: Varies

Scoring: Not available

Cost: Contact publisher

Publisher: Educational Evaluation Enterprises
Information and availability unconfirmed; last verified in 1987.

LISTENING TEST

Child, adolescent
Grades 3.5–12.9

Purpose: Measures the ability of students to follow directions and understand connected discourse.

Description: Multiple-item orally administered paper-pencil multiple-choice test. The teacher reads short passages and dictates problems designed to measure students' listening skills. Questions and answer choices for the short passages are printed in the test booklets so that students can follow along as the teacher reads aloud. Students mark their answers in the booklets. The teacher then dictates a problem that students must solve on a worksheet. The test, which is adapted from the Sequential Test of Educational Progress III, is available on six levels. Examiner required. Suitable for group use.

Untimed: 40 minutes

Scoring: Hand key; may be machine scored

Cost: 35 test booklets, manual $21.00; (levels 1–4) $15.40; (levels 5–6) 50 answer sheets $11.50, examiner's manual $7.15, hand-scoring stencils $9.08

Publisher: CTB/Macmillan/McGraw-Hill

METROPOLITAN LANGUAGE INSTRUCTIONAL TESTS
Irving H. Balow, Roger Farr, Thomas P. Hogan, and George A. Prescott

Child, adolescent
Grades K.5–9.9

Purpose: Assesses basic skill areas in language arts. Used for providing prescriptive information on educational performance of individual pupils.

Description: Multiple-item series of paper-pencil tests measuring major components of language arts skills, including listening comprehension, punctuation and capitalization, usage, grammar and syntax, spelling, and study skills. The test is divided into six levels: Primer (Grades K.5–1.4), Primary 1 (Grades 1.5–2.4), Primary 2 (Grades 2.5–3.4), Elementary (Grades 3.5–4.9), Intermediate (Grades 5.0–6.9), and Advanced 1 (Grades 7.0–9.9). Each level assesses three to six of the above language skills components. This test is one in a series of instructional tests related to the Metropolitan Achievement Test Survey Battery. The test is available only while supplies last. Examiner required. Suitable for group use.

Timed: Varies

Scoring: Scoring service available

Cost: Specimen sets, specify level (test, manual) $17.00; the Intermediate and Advanced 1 set includes hand-scorable answer document

Publisher: The Psychological Corporation

Information and availability unconfirmed; last verified in 1988.

MICHIGAN PRESCRIPTIVE PROGRAM IN ENGLISH (GRAMMAR)
William E. Lockhart

Adolescent, adult
Grades 6 and above

Purpose: Measures English grammar abilities and identifies skill deficits. Used to help students obtain a 10th-grade equivalency and pass the GED test in English grammar.

Description: Multiple-item paper-pencil test assessing the following high-school-level English grammar skills: capitalization, subjects, verbs, verb tense, moods, prepositions, case, possessive and indefinite pronouns, adjectives, adverbs, punctuation, synonyms, homonyms, plurals, and spelling. English study materials have allowed students to gain 0.8–3.0 years in English achievement for 24 clock hours of study. Examiner required. Suitable for group use.

Untimed: Varies

Scoring: Examiner evaluated

Cost: Test book $1.50; 7 response and prescription sheet booklets $2.00; answer key $1.00; English study materials $4.00

Publisher: Academic Therapy Publications

NATIONAL ACHIEVEMENT TESTS: ENGLISH, READING, LITERATURE, AND VOCABULARY TESTS—AMERICAN LITERACY TEST
Refer to page 472.

NATIONAL PROFICIENCY SURVEY SERIES (NPSS): ENGLISH IV
Dale P. Scannell

Adolescent—Ages 12–18 Grades 8–12

Purpose: Measures end-of-course achievement in English courses.

Description: 42–item paper-pencil multiple-choice test for evaluating student proficiency in English. The test, which may be administered as a survey test or as an end-of-course test, is designed to assess 14 objectives. Each objective is tested by three questions. Normative and criterion-referenced data are available. One in a series of 13 NPSS tests. Examiner required. Suitable for group use.

Timed: 40 minutes

Scoring: Self-scored; hand key

Cost: Contact publisher for price and availability

Publisher: The Riverside Publishing Company

NATIONAL PROFICIENCY SURVEY SERIES (NPSS): LITERATURE
Dale P. Scannell

Adolescent—Ages 12–18 Grades 8–12

Purpose: Measures end-of-course achievement in literature courses.

Description: 39–item paper-pencil multiple-choice test used for evaluating student proficiency in literature. The test, which may be administered as a survey test or as an end-of-course test, is designed to assess 14 objectives. Each objective is tested by three questions. Normative and criterion-referenced data are available. One in a series of 13 NPSS tests. Examiner required. Suitable for group use.

Timed: 40 minutes

Scoring: Self-scored; hand key

Cost: Contact publisher for price and availability

Publisher: The Riverside Publishing Company

NATIONAL PROFICIENCY SURVEY SERIES (NPSS): WRITING FUNDAMENTALS
Dale P. Scannell

Adolescent—Ages 12–18 Grades 8–12

Purpose: Measures end-of-course achievement in writing courses.

Description: 66–item paper-pencil multiple-choice test used for evaluating the writing fundamentals of students. The test, which may be administered as a survey test or as an end-of-course test, is designed to assess 14 objectives. Each objective is tested by three questions. Normative and criterion-referenced data are available. One in a series of 13 NPSS tests. Examiner required. Suitable for group use.

Timed: 40 minutes

Scoring: Self-scored; hand key

Cost: Contact publisher for price and availability

Publisher: Riverside Publishing Company

THE PICTURE STORY LANGUAGE TEST (PSLT)
Helmer R. Myklebust

Child, adolescent—Ages 7–17

Purpose: Determines a child's ability to express ideas through writing. Used to evaluate differences between learning disabled, mentally retarded, emotionally disturbed, reading disabled, and speech-handicapped individuals and to diagnose childhood dyslexia.

Description: Multiple-item paper-pencil test in which the examiner asks the subject to write the best story he can about a picture on an easel. Factors measured include number of words written, number of sentences, number of words per sentence, syntax accuracy, and success in expression of meaning. Administration suitable for groups of less than 10 children. Examiner required.

Untimed: 15–20 minutes

Scoring: Hand key; examiner evaluated

Cost: Test $20.50; 50 record forms $20.50; *Development and Disorders of Written Language,* Volume 1 and Volume 2 $38.00 per volume

Publisher: The Psychological Corporation

PRI READING SYSTEMS (PRI/RS)
Refer to page 374.

SPAR (SPELLING AND READING) TESTS, 2ND EDITION
Dennis Young

Child, adolescent—Ages 7–8.11

Purpose: Measures children's ability to read and write. Identifies students needing remedial attention (designed to discriminate particularly among lower ability levels).

Description: Multiple-item paper-pencil test consisting of two sections (spelling and reading) that provide a complementary approach to testing literacy at a simple level. The spelling items are presented in the manual as "banks," allowing the user to select 10 matched tests without overlap and many more with partial overlap. The reading items follow the same format as Dennis Young's Group Reading Test and can be scored using the same templates. Two parallel forms, A and B, are available. The age range may be extended for older, less able students. Examiner required. Suitable for group use.
BRITISH PUBLISHER

Untimed: Not available

Scoring: Hand key

Cost: Contact publisher

Publisher: Hodder & Stoughton

TEST OF LEGIBLE HANDWRITING (TOLH)
Refer to page 619.

TEST OF WRITTEN LANGUAGE–2 (TOWL–2)
Donald D. Hammill and Stephen C. Larsen

Child, adolescent—Ages 7–17—Grades 2–12

Purpose: Identifies students who have problems in written expression and pinpoints specific areas of deficit. Also useful for documenting progress and conducting research. May be used with language-disordered, communicatively disordered, and special education students.

Description: Paper-pencil free-response test in which students write a story about a given theme. The test yields information in 10 areas of writing competence: a) Vocabulary (30 items), b) Spelling (25 items), c) Style (same 25 items as Spelling subtest), d) Logical Sentences (25 items), e) Sentence Combining (25 items), f) Thematic Maturity (30 items), g) Contextual Vocabulary, h) Syntactic Maturity, i) Contextual Spelling, and j) Contextual Style. The information is derived from an analysis of a sample of continuous writing, as well as from an analysis of subtest performance. Subtest raw scores, standard scores, percentiles, a Contrived Writing Quotient, Spontaneous Writing Quotient, and Overall Written Language Quotient are generated. The test is available in Forms A and B. The examiner must have formal training in assessment. Examiner required. Suitable for group use. Available in Spanish.

Untimed: 15 minutes

Scoring: Examiner evaluated; computer scored

Cost: Complete kit (examiner's manual, 50 student response sheets, 50 profile sheets) $97.00; IBM and Apple PRO-SCORE systems each $69.00

Publisher: PRO-ED

THE VOCABULARY GRADIENT TEST
Edgar M. VanVleck

Adolescent, adult

Purpose: Measures the size of an individual's vocabulary. Used with high-school students and adults for placement or for personal information.

Description: 50-item paper-pencil multiple-choice test assessing the number of words known by an individual. Using an answer key provided, individuals can score their own tests and determine their percentile scores. Self-administered. Suitable for group use.

Untimed: 30 minutes

Scoring: Self-scored

Cost: Complete kit $6.00

Publisher: Polymath Systems

WRITTEN LANGUAGE ASSESSMENT (WLA)
J. Jeffrey Grill and Margaret M. Kirwin

Child, adolescent, adult—Ages 8–18 and older

Purpose: Assesses written language.

Description: Essay test offering direct assessment of written language through an evaluation of writing samples that reflect three modes of discourse: expressive, instructive, and creative writing. Analytic scoring techniques are used to yield scores in General Writing Ability, Productivity, Word Complexity, and Readability. A Written Language Quotient that is a composite of the four subscores is also reported. Raw scores for the four subskill areas and the Written Language Quotient can be converted to scaled scores and percentile ranks and plotted on the scoring/profile form. Examiner required. Suitable for group use.

Untimed: 1 hour

Scoring: Examiner evaluated

Cost: Test kit (manual, writing record forms, scoring/profile forms, hand counter) $58.00

Publisher: Academic Therapy Publications

WRITTEN LANGUAGE SYNTAX TEST
Sharon R. Berry

Hearing-impaired students—Grades K–12

Purpose: Measures hearing-impaired students' command of the English language. Used for academic placement and evaluation of hearing-impaired students.

Description: Multiple-item paper-pencil test assessing hearing-impaired student's command of written syntax. The test includes three levels (1, 2, and 3) of assessment, as well as a preliminary exercise to determine which levels of the test are appropriate for a given student. The task that students perform entails viewing a picture, scanning a short list of randomly ordered English words, and using those words to form a sentence based on the picture. The manual includes information for administering and scoring the tests and interpreting the results. Picture stimuli are included on the test forms. Examiner required. Suitable for group use.

Untimed: Varies

Scoring: Examiner evaluated

Cost: Test kit (manual, one each of four levels of tests, one folder) $10.00; 10 screening tests $4.00; 10 tests (specify level) $6.00; 10 folders $4.00

Publisher: Gallaudet University Press

Academic Subjects: Fine Arts

APTITUDE FOR AND SENSITIVITY TO MUSIC—JUNIOR FORM (ASM J)—1982

Child Standards 3–5

Purpose: Measures aptitude and sensitivity to music.

Description: Multiple-item paper-pencil test in which students listen to taped music and answer questions designed to assess their musical aptitude and sensitivity. The five subtests are Fantasy, Various Endings, Interval, Rhythm, and Mood. A record player is required for playing the three albums on which the test is recorded. Examiner required. Suitable for group use.

SOUTH AFRICAN PUBLISHER

Untimed: 1 hour, 30 minutes

Scoring: Hand key

Cost: Contact publisher

Publisher: Human Sciences Research Council

APTITUDE FOR AND SENSITIVITY TO MUSIC—SENIOR FORM—1982 (ASM S)

Adolescent, adult
Standards 6–10 and
college

Purpose: Measures aptitude and sensitivity to music.

Description: Multiple-item paper-pencil test in which students listen to taped music and answer questions designed to assess their musical aptitude and sensitivity. The test consists of eight subtests: Selective Listening, Performance, Accompaniment, Interval, Harmony, Rhythm, Mood, and Degrees of Musical Enjoyment. A record player is required for playing the three albums of music. Examiner required. Suitable for group use.

SOUTH AFRICAN PUBLISHER

Untimed: 2 hours, 15 minutes

Scoring: Hand key

Cost: Contact publisher

Publisher: Human Sciences Research Council

ART VOCABULARY (AV)
R.H. Silverman, R. Hoepfner, and M. Hendricks

Grades 7–12

Purpose: Measures verbal-conceptual achievement in art.

Description: 96–item paper-pencil pictorial test measuring art vocabulary. Examinees choose the picture depicting the presented word. Items range from simple names of tools and basic figural shapes to more sophisticated concepts involving balance, perspective, and surface qualities and artistic styles and periods. Items are arranged in order of difficulty. Two forms, A and C, are available. Examinees using Form A, which is reusable, respond on separate answer sheets. Form C is a consumable form on which examinees circle their answers. Examiner required. Suitable for group use.

Untimed: 20 minutes

Scoring: Hand key

Cost: Specimen kit, specify form (test booklet, answer sheet, scoring stencil, manual) $5.00

Publisher: Monitor

FARNUM MUSIC TEST
Stephen Farnum

Child, adolescent—Ages 10–16

Purpose: Measures student musical achievement and ability as a way of helping teachers distinguish individuals with aptitude from those with less ability.

Description: 165–item paper-pencil instrument utilizing four subtests to assess musical achievement and ability: Music Notation Test (40 items), Symbol Digit Test (65 items), Tonal Patterns (30 items), and Cadence (30 items). The symbol section measures eye-focus speed and reaction speed to stimuli. The notation section measures the ability to differentiate between written notes and different notes played on the piano. With tonal patterns, the student identifies which of four tones has been changed. In the cadence section, the student indicates whether a tone should rise or fall to complete a musical phrase. Materials include a 16–page manual for testing, scoring, and selecting beginning band members; a 12–inch LP phonograph record; answer sheets; and correction keys. The test is suitable for use with visually impaired individuals. Examiner required. Suitable for group use.

Untimed: 40–45 minutes
Scoring: Hand key
Cost: Test kit $14.75; 100 answer sheets $15.00
Publisher: Bond Publishing Company

FARNUM STRING SCALE
Stephen Farnum

Child, adolescent
Grades 4–12

Purpose: Measures student performance and progress playing stringed instruments. Used to place individuals in orchestras.

Description: Performance test in which the student is presented with a series of musical exercises of increasing difficulty to sight-read. The performance level is recorded by noting the number of errors in the execution. Examiner required. Not suitable for group use.

Untimed: 10–15 minutes
Scoring: Examiner evaluated
Cost: Testing book $6.00; 100 score sheets $12.95
Publisher: Hal Leonard Publishing Corporation

INDIANA-OREGON MUSIC DISCRIMINATION TEST
Newell H. Long and Kate Hevner Mueller

Adolescent, adult—Ages
11 and older
Grades 5 and above

Purpose: Assesses musical judgment with regard to rhythm, melody, and harmony. Used in music appreciation classes.

Description: 43–item paper-pencil multiple-choice and short-answer test in which the examiner plays a 12–inch LP record (classical music from baroque to contemporary). Students listen and record their responses on an answer sheet. A shortened version with 37 items is available for junior high school students. This test is a revision of the Oregon Music Discrimina-

tion Test. The test may be used with visually, physically, and mentally impaired individuals, but is unsuitable for use with those with hearing impairments. Examiner required. Suitable for group use.

Timed: 40 minutes
Scoring: Hand key
Cost: Complete (12–inch LP, manual, 3 answer sheets, 2 scoring keys) $12.50; outside U.S. $17.50
Publisher: Midwest Music Tests

INSTRUMENT TIMBRE PREFERENCE TEST
Edwin E. Gordon

Ages 9 and older

Purpose: Assesses the timbre preference of students ages 9 and older. Used to help students select appropriate brass or woodwind instruments.

Description: Multiple-item paper-pencil test identifying the timbre preferences of students. Students listen to different melodic synthesized sounds on a cassette recording and indicate their preferences on an answer sheet. Results help students choose instruments that match their timbre preferences, which improves the performance of beginning band students and reduces dropout rates. Examiner required. Suitable for group use.

Untimed: 30 minutes
Scoring: Hand key; may be machine scored
Cost: Complete kit (cassette, 100 test sheets, scoring masks, manual) $39.00
Publisher: G.I.A. Publications

Information and availability unconfirmed; last verified in 1988.

INTERMEDIATE MEASURES OF MUSIC AUDIATION
Edwin E. Gordon

Child
Grades 1–4

Purpose: Measures the music aptitude of children.

Description: Multiple-item paper-pencil test measuring and discriminating among the music aptitudes of children who obtained exceptionally high scores on the Primary Measures of Music Audiation or who are slightly older than the students targeted for the primary test. The test requires no language or music skills. Children listen to tonal and rhythm tape recordings, decide if pairs of patterns are the same or different, and circle an appropriate picture on the answer sheet. The manual contains information on converting raw scores to percentile ranks, interpreting results, and formal and informal music instruction suggestions. Examiner required. Suitable for group use.

Untimed: 24 minutes

Scoring: Hand key

Cost: Complete kit $62.00

Publisher: G.I.A. Publications

Information and availability unconfirmed; last verified in 1988.

MEASURES OF MUSICAL ABILITIES
Arnold Bentley

Child, adolescent—Ages 7–14

Purpose: Measures pitch discrimination, tonal memory, chord analysis, and rhythmic memory. Used to select children for musical activities and to assess readiness for various types of musical instruction.

Description: Battery of four multiple-item tests presented via a recording. Children respond to each item by marking either a single letter or number on an answer sheet. Tests may be administered separately in order to assess a specific ability. Examiner/self-administered. Suitable for group use.
BRITISH PUBLISHER

Untimed: 30 minutes

Scoring: Hand key

Cost: Contact publisher

Publisher: NFER-NELSON Publishing Company Ltd.

MODERN PHOTOGRAPHY COMPREHENSION
Martin M. Bruce

Adolescent, adult

Purpose: Assesses knowledge of photography. Used for vocational guidance and as a measure of classroom progress.

Description: 40–item paper-pencil multiple-choice test measuring photographic understanding. Individuals are rated on a scale of superior, high average, average, and low average. Materials include a manual and grading keys. Self-administered. Suitable for group use.

Untimed: 20–25 minutes

Scoring: Hand key

Cost: 20 tests $39.50; manual $1.90; keys $1.95; specimen set $7.50

Publisher: Martin M. Bruce, Ph.D., Publishers

MUSICAL APTITUDE PROFILE
Edwin E. Gordon

Child, adolescent Grades 4–12

Purpose: Assesses the basic musical needs, abilities, and aptitudes of elementary and high-school students.

Description: 250–item paper-pencil test consisting of seven subtests arranged in three musical categories: tonal imagery (melody, harmony), rhythm imagery (tempo, meter), and musical sensitivity (phrasing, balance, style). Test items consist of short musical selections (played by professional artists) administered via audiotape. Scores are provided for each of the seven subtests. Examiner required. Suitable for group use.

Untimed: 110 minutes

Scoring: Examiner evaluated

Cost: Complete Musical Aptitude Profile (three cassette tapes, manual, 100 MRC answer sheets, scoring masks, 100 record file folders, 100 musical talent profiles, two class record sheets) $204.48

Publisher: The Riverside Publishing Company

MUSICAL APTITUDE TESTS— MUSAT J AND MUSAT S

Child, adolescent

Purpose: Assesses musical aptitude. Used for educational evaluation.

Description: Two tests of musical ability. MUSAT J (Standards 1 to 5) measures ability to perceive seven aspects of music: interval, harmony, timbre, rhythm, duration, speed, and counting units. MUSAT S (Standards 6 to 10) measures 10 aptitudes: interval, harmony, timbre, rhythm, duration, speed, counting, loudness of tone, intonation, and selective listening. Materials include records containing music especially composed for this test. A record player is required for test administration. Groups should not contain more than 20 students. Examiner required. Suitable for group use. SOUTH AFRICAN PUBLISHER

Untimed: Junior 1½ hours; Senior 2½ hours

Scoring: Hand key; examiner evaluated

Cost: (In Rands) Junior complete kit (container and 2 records) 8,10; 10 answer sheets 1 1,10; 10 answer sheets 2 1,10; scoring stencils 1,80; manual 3,90; Senior complete kit (container and 3 records) 11,20; 10 answer sheets I or II 0,70 each; scoring stencils 2,20; manual 3,90; orders from outside the RSA will be dealt with on merit

Publisher: Human Sciences Research Council

THE OHIO VOCATIONAL ACHIEVEMENT TESTS IN TRADE AND INDUSTRIAL EDUCATION: COMMERICAL ART
Refer to page 799.

PRIMARY MEASURES OF MUSIC AUDIATION (K–3)
Edwin E. Gordon

Child
Grades K–3

Purpose: Measures the music aptitude of students.

Description: Multiple-item paper-pencil test diagnosing the musical potential of students with average to low musical aptitudes. The test requires no language or music skills. Children listen to tonal and rhythm tape recordings, decide if pairs of tonal or rhythm patterns sound the same or different, and circle an appropriate picture on the answer sheet. The manual contains information on converting raw scores to percentile ranks, interpreting results, and formal and informal music instruction. Examiner required. Suitable for group use.

Untimed: 24 minutes

Scoring: Hand key

Cost: Complete kit $62.00

Publisher: G.I.A. Publications

Information and availability unconfirmed; last verified in 1988.

SEASHORE MEASURES OF MUSICAL TALENTS
C.E. Seashore

Grades 4–adult

Purpose: Assesses abilities fundamental to the development of musical proficiency.

Description: Six auditorily presented tests measuring aspects of auditory discrimination: Pitch, Loudness, Time, Timbre, Rhythm, and Tonal Memory. Materials include audio test stimulus on a record or reel-to-reel tape. Examiner required. Suitable for group use.

Untimed: 1 hour

Scoring: Hand key

Cost: Complete set (audio stimulus, 50 IBM 805 answer documents, key, manual), record version $75.00; tape version reel-to-reel $85.00

Publisher: The Psychological Corporation

Information and availability unconfirmed; last verified in 1988.

STUDENT OCCUPATIONAL COMPETENCY ACHIEVEMENT TESTING: GRAPHIC ARTS

Adolescent

Purpose: Measures students' achievement in vocational printing programs.

Used for grade assignment, identifying curriculum strengths and weaknesses, and evaluating job applicants.

Description: Two-part test of skills and knowledge in printing. The multiple-choice written test covers layout and design, composition, copy preparation, darkroom, stripping and platemaking, presswork, and finishing/paper. Three performance tests, which may be taken singly or in combination, are offered. The first test measures thumbnail sketches, rough and comprehensive layouts, type-setting, and paste-up. The second test measures line and half-tone negatives, stripping, proofing, and platemaking. The third test measures press preparation and cleanup, printing, finishing operations, and packaging. Examiner required. Suitable for group use.

Timed: Written test 3 hours; performance tests 3 hours each

Scoring: Scoring service provided

Cost: Contact publisher

Publisher: National Occupational Competency Testing Institute

---

WATKINS-FARNUM PERFORMANCE SCALE
Stephen Farnum and John Watkins

Child, adolescent
Grades 4–12

Purpose: Measures student performance and progress in playing musical instruments. Used to place individuals in musical groups.

Description: Multiple-item performance test in which the student is required to sight-read a series of increasingly difficult musical exercises. The performance level is recorded by noting the number of errors in the execution. A second version, Form B, provides a different set of exercises. Examiner required. Not suitable for group use.

Untimed: 10–15 minutes

Scoring: Examiner evaluated

Cost: Testing book $9.00; 100 score sheets $7.00

Publisher: Hal Leonard Publishing Corporation

Academic Subjects: Foreign Language

AATG FIRST LEVEL TEST

High-school and college students

Purpose: Measures knowledge of basic German. Used with secondary and college-level students.

Description: 70–item paper-pencil test assessing understanding of the German language by secondary-school students completing one year of study and by college or university students completing one semester of study. Examiner required. Suitable for group use.

Untimed: 1 hour

Scoring: Hand key

Cost: $2.00

Publisher: AATG (American Association of Teachers of German)

AATG NATIONAL GERMAN EXAMINATION FOR HIGH SCHOOL STUDENTS

Adolescent
Grades 9–12

Purpose: Measures German language achievement of high-school students in their second, third, and fourth year of study. Used to place transfer students, assess the progress of students and entire classes, and compare the results of various teaching methods.

Description: Multiple-item paper-pencil test assessing the German language competency of high-school students. Test sections include listening comprehension (via tape cassette), grammar, situational questions (testing reading as well as conversational skills), and comprehension of connected passages of approximately 200 words each. The questions in each section are of graded difficulty. The tests are administered once a year in January and may be administered in school or at an

---

AATG chapter test center. In-school testing is accomplished under the direct supervision of the school's testing or guidance personnel. Teachers who are unable or who prefer not to have their students tested in school may have their students tested at a chaper test center. AATG will send Regional Chairpersons (list available) a copy of all test orders submitted from their chapter area. Regional Chairpersons will establish chapter test centers and inform teachers who have requested this service when and where testing is to occur. Students are eligible to take the test designed for the level on which they are studying at the time of test administration. Students who take a test below their current level of work, or take more than one test, will be excluded from any awards program. The test company returns scores to test administrators and regional chairpersons in February. A total score, as well as scores for each section of the test, are provided. Practice tests are available. Examiner required. Suitable for group use.

Timed: 1 hour

Scoring: All tests scored by Software Design, Inc.

Cost: $3.00 per student

Publisher: AATG (American Association of Teachers of German)

ADVANCED RUSSIAN PROFICIENCY TEST (ARPT)

Adult
College students

Purpose: Measures the listening comprehension and reading proficiency of native English-speaking students studying the Russian language. The test is appropriate for use with students who have completed the equivalent of three to five years or more of college-level Russian study.

Description: Multiple-item orally administered and paper-pencil test in two major sections: Listening Comprehension and Reading Proficiency. The Listening Comprehension section is administered via a tape recording that presents the student with a variety of material spoken in Russian. Questions about this material are printed in a test booklet, and students respond on machine-scorable answer sheets. In the Reading Proficiency section, the student reads passages printed in Russian and selects responses that complete or answer the questions. Examiner required. Suitable for group use.

Timed: 2 hours

Scoring: Computer scored

Cost: $15.00 per test booklet

Publisher: Educational Testing Service

Information and availability unconfirmed; last verified in 1988.

AUSTRALIAN SECOND LANGUAGE PROFICIENCY RATINGS (ASLPR)
D.E. Ingram and E. Wylie

Adult

Purpose: Assesses English as a second language proficiency of adult non-English-speaking migrants.

Description: Multiple-item criterion-referenced oral-response and paper-pencil test in which the examinee's reading, writing, listening, and speaking skills are rated on a 9–point scale (0, 0+, 1, 1–, 1+, 2, 3, 4, 5) ranging from no proficiency to nativelike. Examiner required. Not suitable for group use. AUSTRALIAN PUBLISHER

Untimed: Not available

Scoring: Examiner evaluated

Cost: Contact publisher

Publisher: Australian Government Publishing Service

THE BER-SIL SPANISH TESTS: ELEMENTARY TEST 1987 REVISION
Marjorie L. Beringer

Child—Ages 5–12

Purpose: Assesses the functioning level of children ages 5–12 in Spanish. Used to assist in placing Spanish-speaking and speech-impaired students for efficient instruction.

Description: Multiple-item paper-pencil criterion-referenced test consisting of five sections: Vocabulary (Spanish; 100

words), Action Responses to Directions (13 items), Visual-Motor Activity (3 parts), Mathematics (70 items), and Vocabulary (English; 100 words). Writing samples, geometric figures, and figure drawing are included in the test. Spanish Vocabulary, Comprehension of Spanish, Visual-Motor Abilities, Math Skills, and English Vocabulary scores are yielded. The revision includes the math and English vocabulary tests. Directions are on cassette tape. Available in Spanish, Mandarin, Cantonese, Tagalog, Ilocano, Korean, and Persian translations. Examiner required. Not suitable for group use.

Untimed: 30–60 minutes

Scoring: Hand key; examiner evaluated

Cost: Complete kit $50.00; combination kit (elementary and secondary) $85.00; translation tapes $15.00

Publisher: The Ber-Sil Company

THE BER-SIL SPANISH TESTS: SECONDARY TEST
Marjorie L. Beringer

Adolescent—Ages 13–17

Purpose: Assesses Spanish-language and mathematics abilities of junior and senior high-school students. Used to assist in placing secondary Spanish-speaking or speech-impaired students for efficient instruction.

Description: Multiple-item paper-pencil multiple-choice and point-to criterion-referenced test in four sections: Spanish Vocabulary (100 words), Dictation in Spanish (4 sentences), Draw a Boy or Girl (maturity level), and Mathematics (70 items). Scores indicating the level of the examinee's ability in Spanish vocabulary, Spanish grammar and spelling, maturity level, and mathematical processes are generated. The test is administered with cassette tape instructions by psychologists, psychometricians, counselors, and speech specialists. It is useful for curriculum planning and academic counseling. Available in Ilocano and Tagalog translations. Examiner required. Not suitable for group use.

Untimed: 20–30 minutes

Scoring: Hand key; examiner evaluated

Cost: Complete kit $50.00; combination kit (elementary and secondary) $85.00; translation tapes $15.00

Publisher: The Ber-Sil Company

CHINESE SPEAKING TEST (CST)
Center for Applied Linguistics

Adolescent, adult
College and above

Purpose: Assesses the ability to speak Chinese in contemporary, real-life language-use situations.

Description: 28–item oral-response test measuring oral language proficiency in Chinese. Via a question tape and test booklet, examinees are asked questions in six areas: Personal Conversation, Giving Directions, Detailed Descriptions, Picture Sequences, Topical Discourse, and Situations. The examinee's oral responses to the six item types are recorded and then sent to the publisher for scoring. Ratings are based on the speaking proficiency scale of the American Council on the Teaching of Foreign Language (ACTFL). Four forms (A,B,C,D) are available. May be used with individuals with physical impairments. Examiner required. Suitable for group use.

Timed: 45 minutes

Scoring: Publisher scored

Cost: $60.00

Publisher: Center for Applied Linguistics

FRENCH COMPREHENSION TESTS
H.C. Barik

Child
Grades 1–8

Purpose: Measures French listening comprehension. Used with students involved in French immersion programs or intensive French programs at early grade levels.

Description: 45–item paper-pencil multiple-choice test assessing listening comprehension in French. The answer choices are presented in picture form. The test consists of three sections: words and sentences, questions, and stories. Separate

---

test manuals for the Primer (K) level and Level 1 are available. An optional reel-to-reel tape is available for test administration. Examiner required. Suitable for group use. CANADIAN PUBLISHER

Untimed: 40 minutes

Scoring: Hand key

Cost: 35 Primer level tests $23.25; tape $16.00 (specify test); 35 Level 1 tests $25.85; manual (specify test) $6.00 (Canadian exchange)

Publisher: The Ontario Institute for Studies in Education

Information and availability unconfirmed; last verified in 1988.

HAUSA SPEAKING TEST (HAST)
Center for Applied Linguistics

Adolescent, adult
College and above

Purpose: Assesses the ability to speak Hausa in contemporary, real-life language-use contexts.

Description: 30–item oral-response test measuring oral language proficiency in Hausa. Via a question tape and test booklet, examinees are asked questions in five areas: Personal Conversation, Giving Directions, Picture Sequences, Topical Discourse, and Situations. Their oral responses to the five item types are recorded and then sent to the publisher for scoring. Ratings are based on the speaking proficiency scale of the American Council on the Teaching of Foreign Languages (ACTFL). A,B, male, and female forms are available. May be used with individuals with physical impairments. Examiner required. Suitable for group use.

Timed: 40 minutes

Scoring: Publisher scored

Cost: $60.00

Publisher: Center for Applied Linguistics

HEBREW SPEAKING TEST (HEST)
Center for Applied Linguistics

Adolescent, adult
College and above

Purpose: Assesses the ability to speak Hebrew in contemporary, real-life language-use contexts.

Description: 27–item oral-reponse test measuring oral language proficiency in Hebrew. Via a question tape and test booklet, examinees are asked questions in six areas: Personal Conversation, Giving Directions, Detailed Descriptions, Picture Sequences, Topical Discourse, and Situations. The examinee's oral responses to the six item types are recorded and then sent to the publisher for scoring. Ratings are based on the speaking proficiency scale of the American Council on the Teaching of Foreign Language (ACTFL). U.S. and Israeli versions are available in A, B, male, and female forms. May be used with individuals with physical impairments. Examiner required. Suitable for group use.

Timed: 45 minutes

Scoring: Publisher scored

Cost: $60.00

Publisher: Center for Applied Linguistics

INDONESIAN SPEAKING TEST (IST)
Center for Applied Linguistics

Adolescent, adult
College and above

Purpose: Assesses the ability to speak Indonesian in contemporary, real-life language-use contexts.

Description: 27–item oral-response test measuring oral language proficiency in Indonesian. Via a question tape and test booklet, examinees are asked questions in five areas: Personal Conversation, Giving Directions, Picture Sequences, Topical Discourse, and Situations. The examinee's oral responses to the five item types are recorded and then sent to the publisher for scoring. Ratings are based on the proficiency scale on the American Council on the Teaching of Foreign Language (ACTFL). Two forms (A, B) are available. May be used with individuals with physical impairments. Examiner required. Suitable for group use.

Timed: 40 minutes

Scoring: Publisher scored

Cost: $60.00

Publisher: Center for Applied Linguistics

JAPANESE PROFICIENCY TEST (JPT)

Students, adult

Purpose: Evaluates American or other English-speaking students' level of proficiency in Japanese. Used for measuring achievement in language programs.

Description: 130–item paper-pencil multiple-choice test measuring two aspects of proficiency in Japanese. The test consists of two major sections: Listening Comprehension and Reading Comprehension. The items in these sections are based on realistic language-use situations and contemporary tests and do not presuppose a particular course of study. The stimulus material for the Listening Comprehension section is recorded in standard modern Japanese. Audio equipment is required for the listening comprehension stimulus material.

Separate Listening Comprehension, Reading Comprehension, and Japanese Character Recognition scores are reported. Norming information based on data obtained from test administrations at 38 colleges and universities in the United States is provided for beginning, intermediate, and advanced levels of Japanese study. The test is available in two equivalent versions to allow pre- and posttesting. Examiner required. Suitable for group use.

Timed: 2 hours

Scoring: Computer scored

Cost: $15.00 per examinee (includes scoring)

Publisher: Educational Testing Service

Information and availability unconfirmed; last verified in 1988.

MODERN LANGUAGE APTITUDE TEST (MLAT)
J.B. Carroll and S.M. Sapon

Adolescent, adult
Grades 9 and above

Purpose: Assesses the ease with which students will learn a foreign language in a typical foreign language program.

Description: Five-part series of exercises in learning various aspects of language: number learning (aural), phonetic script (audio-visual), spelling clues, words in sentences, and paired associates. The number learning and phonetic script exercises require the use of a reel-to-reel or cassette tape recorder. The spelling clues, words in sentences, and paired associates exercises may be used together as a Short Form. Materials include test tapes with instructions and auditory stimuli. Examiner required. Suitable for group use.

Untimed: Short form 30 minutes; complete test 1 hour

Scoring: Hand key; may be machine scored

Cost: Examination kit (test, IBM 805 answer document and key, practice exercise sheet, manual) $9.00; reel-to-reel tape $35.00; cassette tape $35.00; 25 test booklets $17.00; 50 IBM 805 answer documents $19.00

Publisher: The Psychological Corporation

Information and availability unconfirmed; last verified in 1988.

PIMSLEUR LANGUAGE APTITUDE BATTERY
Paul Pimsleur

Child, adolescent
Grades 6–12

Purpose: Assesses aptitude for learning languages. Used for screening potential foreign language students and grouping for instruction.

Description: Battery of tests assessing aptitude for learning modern languages. The six parts include information on the student's grade point average, interest in studying a foreign language, verbal ability, and auditory ability. Materials include a test tape providing auditory stimuli for Parts 5 and 6. Examiner required. Suitable for group use.

Untimed: 50–60 minutes

Scoring: Hand key; computer scoring service available

Cost: Specimen set (manual, test, class record, IBM 805 answer documents) $11.00; basic scoring services $0.98 per student

Publisher: The Psychological Corporation

Information and availability unconfirmed; last verified in 1988.

PORTUGUESE SPEAKING TEST (PST)
Center for Applied Linguistics

Adolescent, adult
College and above

Purpose: Assesses the ability to speak Portuguese in contemporary, real-life language-use contexts.

Description: 28–item oral-response test measuring oral language proficiency in Portuguese. Via a question tape and test booklet, examinees are asked questions in six areas: Personal Conversation, Giving Directions, Detailed Descriptions, Picture Sequences, Topical Discourse, and Situations. Their oral-responses are recorded and then sent to the publisher for scoring. Ratings are based on the speaking proficiency scale of the American Council on the Teaching of Foreign Languages (ACTFL). A,B, and C forms are available. Examiner required. Available in Brazilian and Lusitanian. Suitable for group use.

Timed: 45 minutes

Scoring: Scored by publisher

Cost: $60.00

Publisher: Center for Applied Linguistics

SENTENCE COMPREHENSION TEST: REVISED EDITION AND PANJABI VERSION
Refer to page 712.

TEST OF BASIC LITERACY IN THE SOTHO LANGUAGES

Adult

Purpose: Assesses the literacy skill of adults in the South Sotho, North Sotho, and Tswana languages. Also used to assess Higher Primary level students.

Description: Series of three multiple-item paper-pencil tests assessing proficiency in the South Sotho, North Sotho, and Tswana languages. Each language is covered in a separate test, and each test is available in two forms, I and II. All forms contain three subtests: Reading Comprehension (items relate to practical knowledge or coping skills), Reading Comprehension (items cover a continuous prose passage and a letter written in cursive script), and Writing Skill (dictation items and form completion). Subtests may be administered separately. Questions are answered directly in the test booklets. Examiner required. Suitable for group use.

SOUTH AFRICAN PUBLISHER

Untimed: 1 hour, 30 minutes

Scoring: Examiner evaluated

Cost: Contact publisher

Publisher: Human Sciences Research Council

TEST OF ENGLISH FOR INTERNATIONAL COMMUNICATION (TOEIC)
Refer to page 922.

Academic Subjects: Home Economics

MASTERY TEST IN CONSUMER ECONOMICS
Les Dlabay

Adolescent
Grades 8–12

Purpose: Measures knowledge of major consumer economics topics as set forth in various state education agencies and professional organization curriculum guides.

Description: Multiple-item paper-pencil test measuring achievement in consumer economics. The topics covered include the individual consumer in the market place; the consumer in the economy; personal money management; consumer credit; wise use of credit; food buying; housing; transportation; furniture, appliances, and clothing; personal and health services; banking services; saving and investments; insurance; taxes and government; and the consumer in society. Each test item is keyed to one of these 15 topics. The results identify the concepts students have mastered and those on which they perform poorly. The manual includes a scoring key. The scoring service provides three alphabetical lists, class analysis data, and one set of pressure-sensitive labels. Examiner required. Suitable for group use.

Timed: 40 minutes

Scoring: Hand scored; may be computer scored

Cost: Starter set (manual, 20 test booklets, 20 answer sheets) $26.50; scoring service $1.00 per pupil; specimen set $9.00

Publisher: Scholastic Testing Service, Inc.

STUDENT OCCUPATIONAL COMPETENCY ACHIEVEMENT TESTING: COMMERCIAL FOODS

Adolescent

Purpose: Assesses competencies related to commercial food service occupations. Used for educational evaluation and employee screening.

Description: Multiple-item paper-pencil and task-performance test in two parts measuring skills and knowledge related to food service and preparation. The multiple-choice written test (184 items) covers information on food preparation, food service occupations, sanitation, safety, equipment, service, purchasing, management skills, and specialty service. The performance test covers preparation of a cold

salad, entree, quick bread, and table service. Examiner required. Suitable for group use.

Timed: Written test 3 hours; performance test 3 hours

Scoring: Scoring service provided

Cost: Contact publisher

Publisher: National Occupational Competency Testing Institute

---

STUDENT OCCUPATIONAL COMPETENCY ACHIEVEMENT TESTING: GENERAL MERCHANDISING

Adolescent

Purpose: Measures students' achievement in vocational general merchandising programs. Used for grade assignment, identifying curriculum strengths and weaknesses, and evaluating job applicants.

Description: Two-part test of skills and knowledge in general merchandising. The multiple-choice written test covers operations, merchandising, economics, communication, human relations, sales, advertising, display, and computational skills. The performance test assesses product knowledge and selling, human relations and communications, mechanics of completing a sale and handling money, and computational skills. Examiner required. Suitable for group use.

Untimed: Written test 3 hours; performance test 2 hours, 40 minutes

Scoring: Scoring service provided

Cost: Contact publisher

Publisher: National Occupational Competency Testing Institute

---

STUDENT OCCUPATIONAL COMPETENCY ACHIEVEMENT TESTING: SEWN PRODUCTS

Adolescent

Purpose: Measures students' achievement in vocational sewn product programs. Used for grade assignment, identifying curriculum strengths and weaknesses, and evaluating job applicants.

Description: Two-part test of skills and knowledge in sewn products occupations. The multiple-choice written test covers textiles, pressing, industrial sewing methods, operation of equipment, fitting garments, altering finished garments, and construction. The performance test measures abilities in machine usage, industrial sewing machine maintenance, industrial sewing methods, garment construction methods, taking body measurements, pattern alterations, and alteration of finished garments. Examiner required. Suitable for group use.

Timed: Written test 3 hours; performance test 3 hours

Scoring: Scoring service provided

Cost: Contact publisher

Publisher: National Occupational Competency Testing Institute

Academic Subjects: Industrial Arts

NM CONSUMER RIGHTS AND RESPONSIBILITIES TEST (NMCRRT)
S.P. Klein

Adolescent
Grades 9–12

Purpose: Measures understanding of consumer rights and responsibilities. Used for program evaluation and needs assessment.

Description: 20–item paper-pencil multiple-choice test measuring a student's understanding of consumer protection laws, economic conditions and terms, insurance, purchase payment plans, personal finance, and product information. The test booklets are reusable, and a layover stencil is used for scoring. Reliability and norms have been determined from samples of 9th- and 12th-grade secondary students. Examiner required. Suitable for group use.

Timed: 20 minutes

Scoring: Hand key

Cost: Specimen set $5.00; 35 tests $10.00; 35 answer sheets $3.00; scoring stencil $2.00; manual $2.00

Publisher: Monitor

STUDENT OCCUPATIONAL COMPETENCY ACHIEVEMENT TESTING (SOCAT)

Adolescent

Purpose: Measures students' achievement in vocational education programs. Used for grade assignment, identification of curriculum strengths and weaknesses, and evaluation of job applicants.

Description: Multiple-item tests of skills and knowledge in 69 vocational fields, including accounting/bookkeeping, agricultural mechanics, auto body, auto mechanics, carpentry, commercial foods, computer programming, construction electricity, construction masonry, drafting, electronics, general merchandising, general office, graphic arts, heating and air conditioning, home entertainment equipment repairs, horticulture, industrial electricity, industrial electronics, machine trades, plumbing, practical nursing, refrigeration, sewn products, small engine repair, and welding. Each test consists of a written section and a performance section. The multiple-choice written section covers factual knowledge, technical information, understanding of principles, and problem-solving abilities related to the occupation. The performance section is administered in a laboratory, school shop, or clinical setting and enables students to demonstrate knowledge and skills of competent craft persons. Mental aptitude tests are available for administration at the same time as the competency test. Examiner required. Suitable for group use.

Timed: Varies

Scoring: Scoring service provided

Cost: Contact publisher

Publisher: National Occupational Competency Testing Institute

STUDENT OCCUPATIONAL COMPETENCY ACHIEVEMENT TESTING: AGRICULTURE MECHANICS

Adolescent

Purpose: Measures students' achievement in vocational agriculture mechanics programs. Used for grade assignment, identifying curriculum strengths and weaknesses, and evaluating job applicants.

Description: Two-part test of skills and knowledge in agriculture mechanics. The multiple-choice written test covers orientation and safety, agricultural mechanic skills, agricultural power and machinery, agricultural electrical power and processing, agricultural structures, and soil and water management. The performance test measures abilities in shielded metal arc welding, oxyacetylene cutting, wheel bearings, electrical installation, agricultural structures, and farm level. Examiner required. Suitable for group use.

Untimed: Written test 3 hours; performance test 3 hours

Scoring: Scoring service provided

Cost: Contact publisher

Publisher: National Occupational Competency Testing Institute

STUDENT OCCUPATIONAL COMPETENCY ACHIEVEMENT TESTING: AUTO BODY

Adolescent

Purpose: Measures students' achievement in vocational auto body programs. Used for grade assignment, identifying curriculum strengths and weaknesses, and evaluating job applicants.

Description: Two-part test of skills and knowledge in auto body. The multiple-choice written test covers body construction, body/panel alignment, welding, sheet metal repair, plastic/fiberglass repair, glass/trim/hardware, estimating, refinishing, and electrical. The performance test measures abilities in welding,

sheet metal repair, panel construction, and painting. Examiner required. Suitable for group use.

Timed: Written test 3 hours; performance test 2 hours, 40 minutes

Scoring: Scoring service provided

Cost: Contact publisher

Publisher: National Occupational Competency Testing Institute

STUDENT OCCUPATIONAL COMPETENCY ACHIEVEMENT TESTING: AUTO MECHANICS

Adolescent

Purpose: Measures students' achievement in vocational auto mechanics programs. Used for assigning grades, identifying curriculum strengths and weaknesses, and evaluating job applicants.

Description: Two-part test of skills and knowledge in auto mechanics. The multiple-choice written test covers brakes, front end, engine repair, engine tune-up, automatic transmission, manual transmission/rear axle, electrical systems, and heating/air conditioning. The performance test measures abilities in brakes, inspection/lubrication, tune-up, and electrical systems. Examiner required. Suitable for group use.

Timed: Written test 3 hours; performance test 3 hours

Scoring: Scoring service provided

Cost: Contact publisher

Publisher: National Occupational Competency Testing Institute

STUDENT OCCUPATIONAL COMPETENCY ACHIEVEMENT TESTING: CARPENTRY

Adolescent

Purpose: Assesses knowledge and ability related to carpentry. Used for educational evaluation and employee screening.

Description: Multiple-item paper-pencil and task-performance test in two parts measuring competencies related to carpentry. The multiple-choice section (171 items) measures blueprint reading, preparation of specifications, building materials, hand and power tools, foundations, forms, rough framing, roof components, interior and exterior finish, and stair construction. The performance test measures layout of rafters, installation of door frames, engineer's transit, batter board elevation, stairway stringer, and sole plates. Examiner required. Suitable for group use.

Timed: Written test 3 hours; performance test 3 hours

Scoring: Scoring service provided

Cost: Contact publisher

Publisher: National Occupational Competency Testing Institute

STUDENT OCCUPATIONAL COMPETENCY ACHIEVEMENT TESTING: CONSTRUCTION ELECTRICITY

Adolescent

Purpose: Measures students' achievement in vocational construction electricity programs. Used for grade assignment, identifying curriculum strengths and weaknesses, and evaluating job applicants.

Description: Two-part test of skills and knowledge in construction electricity. The multiple-choice written test covers safety; tools and equipment; blueprints; planning and layout; electronics; AC electricity; transformers; AC motors and starters; branch circuits; wiring methods; lighting, heating, and air conditioning; and low voltage. The performance test measures abilities in planning and layout, wiring methods, and service installation. Examiner required. Suitable for group use.

Timed: Written test 3 hours; performance test 3 hours

Scoring: Scoring service provided

Cost: Contact publisher

Publisher: National Occupational Competency Testing Institute

STUDENT OCCUPATIONAL COMPETENCY ACHIEVEMENT TESTING: CONSTRUCTION MASONRY

Adolescent

Purpose: Measures knowledge and skills related to construction masonry. Used for educational evaluation and employee screening.

Description: Multiple-item paper-pencil and task-performance test in two parts assessing competencies related to masonry. The multiple-choice written test (145 items) covers safety, tools and equipment, masonry materials, fastening devices, blueprint reading, interpretation of measurements, building site layout, construction methods, fireplace construction, maintenance of masonry structures, specialty construction areas of bricklaying, blocklaying, or stone masonry. The performance tests measure layout techniques, tools and equipment, building materials, construction techniques, and safety in choice of bricklaying, blocklaying, or stone masonry. Examiner required. Suitable for group use.

Timed: Written test 3 hours; performance test 3 hours, 15 minutes

Scoring: Scoring service provided

Cost: Contact publisher

Publisher: National Occupational Competency Testing Institute

STUDENT OCCUPATIONAL COMPETENCY ACHIEVEMENT TESTING: DRAFTING

Adolescent

Purpose: Measures students' achievement in vocational drafting programs. Used for grade assignment, identifying curriculum strengths and weaknesses, and evaluating job applicants.

Description: Two-part test of skills and knowledge in drafting. The multiple-choice written test covers interpretation of drawings, machine drawing, architectural drawing, mathematical calculations, electrical/electronic drawing, sheet metal drawing, mapping and cartography, and computer-assisted drawing. The performance test measures abilities in orthographic projection, auxiliary, threads, production/detail, and specialty areas. Examiner required. Suitable for group use.

Timed: Written test 3 hours; performance test 3 hours

Scoring: Scoring service provided

Cost: Contact publisher

Publisher: National Occupational Competency Testing Institute

STUDENT OCCUPATIONAL COMPETENCY ACHIEVEMENT TESTING: ELECTRONICS

Adolescent

Purpose: Measures students' achievement in vocational electronic programs. Used for grade assignment, identifying curriculum strengths and weaknesses, and evaluating job applicants.

Description: Multiple-item paper-pencil and task-performance test in two parts assessing knowledge and skills related to electronics. The 150–item multiple-choice test covers AC and DC circuits, solid-state circuits, digital circuits, and use of equipment. The performance test covers skills, including circuit construction, selection of components, tests and measurements, desoldering/soldering, economy of time, and safety. Examiner required. Suitable for group use.

Timed: Written test 3 hours; performance test 3 hours

Scoring: Scoring service provided

Cost: Contact publisher

Publisher: National Occupational Competency Testing Institute

STUDENT OCCUPATIONAL COMPETENCY ACHIEVEMENT TESTING: HEATING AND AIR CONDITIONING

Adolescent

Purpose: Measures students' achievement in vocational heating and air conditioning programs. Used for grade assignment, identifying curriculum

strengths and weaknesses, and evaluating job applicants.

Description: Two-part test of skills and knowledge in heating and air conditioning. The multiple-choice written test covers theory and fundamentals of air conditioning, oil heating, and gas heating; installation and service of air conditioning, oil heating, and gas heating equipment; electricity; solar heating; heat pumps; hydronic heating; humidity; and air movement. The performance test measures the ability to troubleshoot and repair a cooling and/or heating system and fabricate a heat exchanger. Examiner required. Suitable for group use.

Timed: Written test 3 hours; performance test 3 hours

Scoring: Scoring service provided

Cost: Contact publisher

Publisher: National Occupational Competency Testing Institute

STUDENT OCCUPATIONAL COMPETENCY ACHIEVEMENT TESTING: HOME ENTERTAINMENT EQUIPMENT REPAIR

Adolescent

Purpose: Measures students' achievement in vocational home entertainment equipment programs. Used for grade assignment, identifying curriculum strengths and weaknesses, and evaluating job applicants.

Description: Two-part test of skills and knowledge in home entertainment equipment. The multiple-choice written test covers basic skills, television receiver circuits, audio systems, radio receivers, tape players/recorders, television antennas, digital and logic circuits, safety, and customer services. The performance test measures the ability to perform color television setup procedures, diagnose and repair AM/FM receivers, and repair black-and-white televisions. Examiner required. Suitable for group use.

Timed: Written test 3 hours; performance test 2 hours, 45 minutes

Scoring: Scoring service provided

Cost: Contact publisher
Publisher: National Occupational Competency Testing Institute

STUDENT OCCUPATIONAL COMPETENCY ACHIEVEMENT TESTING: HORTICULTURE

Adolescent

Purpose: Measures achievement of students in vocational horticulture programs. Used for grade assignment, identifying curriculum strengths and weaknesses, and evaluating job applicants.

Description: Multiple-item paper-pencil and task-performance test of skills and knowledge related to horticulture. The multiple-choice written test (158 items) covers arboriculture, landscaping, nursery, turf, floriculture, floristry, greenhouse management, vegetables, small fruit, and tree fruits. The performance test measures abilities in the same areas. Examiner required. Suitable for group use.
Timed: Written test 3 hours; performance test 3 hours
Scoring: Scoring service provided
Cost: Contact publisher
Publisher: National Occupational Competency Testing Institute

STUDENT OCCUPATIONAL COMPETENCY ACHIEVEMENT TESTING: INDUSTRIAL ELECTRICITY

Adolescent

Purpose: Measures abilities related to industrial electricity. Used for educational evaluation and employee screening.

Description: Multiple-item paper-pencil and task-performance test in two parts assessing knowledge and skills related to industrial electricity. The multiple-choice written test (156 items) covers AC and DC current theory, test equipment, electrical drawings, general wiring, controls, generators, alternators, motors, and transformers. The performance test covers skills, including identification of tools and equipment, care and use of tools and equipment, diagrams, installation techniques, conduit, motor circuit, safety, and testing. Examiner required. Suitable for group use.
Timed: Written test 3 hours; performance test 3 hours
Scoring: Scoring service provided
Cost: Contact publisher
Publisher: National Occupational Competency Testing Institute

STUDENT OCCUPATIONAL COMPETENCY ACHIEVEMENT TESTING: INDUSTRIAL ELECTRONICS

Adolescent

Purpose: Measures students' achievement in vocational industrial electronics programs. Used for grade assignment, identifying curriculum strengths and weaknesses, and evaluating job applicants.

Description: Two-part test of skills and knowledge in industrial electronics. The multiple-choice written test covers AC and DC concepts, fundamentals, semiconductor theory, solid state power control, digital/micro circuits, transducers, electronic circuits, ladder diagrams, motor circuits, test equipment, and safety. The performance test measures circuit construction, troubleshooting, semiconductor testing, soldering, desoldering, digital/micro gate logic, use of oscilloscope, use of equipment, and truth tables. Examiner required. Suitable for group use.
Timed: Written test 3 hours; performance test 3 hours
Scoring: Scoring service provided
Cost: Contact publisher
Publisher: National Occupational Competency Testing Institute

STUDENT OCCUPATIONAL COMPETENCY ACHIEVEMENT TESTING: MACHINE TRADES

Adolescent

Purpose: Measures students' achievement in vocational machine trades programs. Used for grade assignment, identifying curriculum strengths and weaknesses, and evaluating job applicants.

Description: Two-part test of skills and knowledge in machine trades. The multiple-choice written test covers bench work, sawing, drilling, lathes, milling, grinding, and related theory. The performance test measures abilities in layout, measurement, drilling and hole forming, lathe operations, milling machine operations, bench work, and safety. Examiner required. Suitable for group use.

Timed: Written test 3 hours; performance test 5 hours, 30 minutes

Scoring: Scoring service provided

Cost: Contact publisher

Publisher: National Occupational Competency Testing Institute

STUDENT OCCUPATIONAL COMPETENCY ACHIEVEMENT TESTING: PLUMBING

Adolescent

Purpose: Assesses competencies related to plumbing. Used for educational evaluation and employee screening.

Description: Multiple-item paper-pencil and task-performance test covering plumbing knowledge and skills. The multiple-choice written test (150 items) measures knowledge of assembly and layout, installation, planning, inspecting, evaluating, maintenance, and repair. The performance test measures drawing, layout, rough installation, and installation of a fixture. Examiner required. Suitable for group use.

Timed: Written test 3 hours; performance test 3 hours

Scoring: Scoring service provided

Cost: Contact publisher

Publisher: National Occupational Competency Testing Institute

STUDENT OCCUPATIONAL COMPETENCY ACHIEVEMENT TESTING: REFRIGERATION

Adolescent

Purpose: Measures students' achievement in vocational refrigeration programs.

Used for grade assignment, identifying curriculum strengths and weaknesses, and evaluating job applicants.

Description: Two-part test of skills and knowledge in refrigeration. The multiple-choice written test covers nomenclature; valves, gauges, and controls; electricity; related math and science; installation and service; and safety. The performance test is divided into three parts measuring different aspects of troubleshooting and repairing refrigeration systems. Examiner required. Suitable for group use.

Timed: Written test 3 hours; performance test 3 hours

Scoring: Scoring service provided

Cost: Contact publisher

Publisher: National Occupational Competency Testing Institute

STUDENT OCCUPATIONAL COMPETENCY ACHIEVEMENT TESTING: SMALL ENGINE REPAIR

Adolescent

Purpose: Measures students' achievement in vocational small engine repair programs. Used for grade assignment, identifying curriculum strengths and weaknesses, and evaluating job applicants.

Description: Two-part test of skills and knowledge in small engine repair. The multiple-choice written test covers ignition, fuel, governors, starters, valves-ports-exhaust, engine block components-cooling, compression-lubrication, powered equipment mechanisms, shop procedures-safety, and theory-shop arithmetic. The performance test measures abilities in checking engine, checking and measuring parts, valve service, carburetor service, ignition service, invoicing parts, and use of time. Examiner required. Suitable for group use.

Timed: Written test 3 hours; performance test 3 hours

Scoring: Scoring service provided

Cost: Contact publisher

Publisher: National Occupational Competency Testing Institute

STUDENT OCCUPATIONAL COMPETENCY ACHIEVEMENT TESTING: WELDING

Adolescent

Purpose: Measures students' achievement in vocational welding programs. Used for grade assignment, identifying curriculum strengths and weaknesses, and evaluating job applicants.

Description: Two-part test of skills and knowledge in welding occupations. The multiple-choice written test covers welding terms and symbols, electricity, basic metallurgy, shielded-metal arc welding, oxyfuel welding, gas metal arc welding, gas tungsten arc welding, and safety. The performance test measures abilities in oxyacetylene welding and brazing, shielded metal arc welding, gas metal arc welding, and gas tungsten arc welding. Examiner required. Suitable for group use.

Timed: Written test 3 hours; performance test 3 hours

Scoring: Scoring service provided

Cost: Contact publisher

Publisher: National Occupational Competency Testing Institute

Academic Subjects: Library and Media Skills

DIAGNOSTIC TEST OF LIBRARY SKILLS
Barbara Feldstein and Janet Rawdon

Child, adolescent
Grades 5–9

Purpose: Evaluates students' working knowledge of essential library skills.

Description: 50–item paper-pencil or computer-administered multiple-choice test measuring library skills in the following areas: definitions of library terms, use of the title page, use of the table of contents, use of an index, use of the card catalog, library arrangement, and use of reference materials. The results are recorded on an analytic sheet that indicates areas that require general class or small group attention. Further examination of individual answer sheets indicates specific needs. The test is available in equivalent forms A and B with interchangeable answer key. A bibliography of sources providing instruction and learning experiences for concepts included in this test is provided in the teacher's guide. The computer version operates on Apple II, Macintosh, and IBM PC and compatibles. Examiner required. Suitable for group use.

Untimed: Varies

Scoring: Hand key

Cost: Test kit, specify form (50 test booklets, 100 answer sheets, scoring key, teacher's guide) $26.95; computer version (disk, teacher's guide, student record sheet) $34.95

Publisher: Learnco, Inc.

LIBRARY SKILLS TEST
Illinois Association of College and Research Libraries

Adolescent
Grades 7–college

Purpose: Assesses students' skills in working with library materials.

Description: Multiple-item paper-pencil test covering current terminology, card catalog, classification systems, filing, parts of a book, indexes, reference tools, and bibliographic forms. The manual includes an answer key, content outline, and norms for Grades 7–12 and college freshmen. The scoring service provides three alphabetical lists and class summary data. Examiner required. Suitable for group use.

Timed: 45 minutes

Scoring: Computer scored

Cost: Test kit (manual, 20 test booklets) $19.50; scoring service $0.80 per student; specimen set $8.00

Publisher: Scholastic Testing Service, Inc.

Child, adolescent
Grades 4–12

Purpose: Measures a student's ability to use a school library effectively. Used by school library and media specialists to enhance instructional design, determine the effectiveness of library instruction, and identify general trends in student library/media ability.

Description: 53–item criterion-refer-enced paper-pencil multiple-choice test measuring knowledge of the organization of the library/media center, understanding of material selection, skills necessary for using print and nonprint resources, comprehension, and production/commu-nication. Examiner/self-administered. Suitable for group use.

Untimed: 50 minutes

Scoring: Hand key; may be machine scored

Cost: 30 reusable test booklets $30.00; manual $6.50

Publisher: Libraries Unlimited

TEST OF LIBRARY/STUDY SKILLS
Irene Gullette and Frances Hatfield

Child, adolescent
Grades 2–12

Purpose: Measures the basic essentials of library/media center skills.

Description: Multiple-item paper-pencil test measuring knowledge of book ar-rangement, parts of a book, the card catalog, indexes, and reference books. Available in three levels for different age groups: Level I (Grades 2–5), Level II (Grades 4–9), Level III (Grades 8–12). Self-administered. Suitable for group use.

Untimed: 50 minutes per level

Scoring: Hand key

Cost: Complete kit (50 test booklets, 100 answer cards, key) Level I $22.00, Level II or III $25.00
Publisher: Larlin Corporation
Information and availability unconfirmed; last verified in 1987.

Academic Subjects: Mathematics: Basic Math Skills

ARITHMETIC TEST A/8

Adolescent, adult

Purpose: Measures general arithmetic ability.

Description: Multiple-item paper-pencil test assessing arithmetic skills. Norms are available on request. Examiner required. Suitable for group use.
SOUTH AFRICAN PUBLISHER
Timed: 30–40 minutes
Scoring: Hand key
Cost: (In Rands) 25 booklets 20,25; key 0,60
Publisher: National Institute for Personnel Research

ASSESSMENT IN MATHEMATICS
R. W. Strong and
Somerset Local Education Authority

Child, adolescent

Purpose: Assesses the mathematics com-petencies of primary and lower secondary students. Determines readiness to pro-gress to new work.

Description: 86 multiple-item paper-pencil graded test sheets assessing student abilities in areas of work common to most instructional mathematics programs: number measure, probability and statis-tics, shape, and relations. The test sheets are printed as reproducible photocopy masters, providing a flexible assortment of graded tests for use in conjunction with existing instructional programs. The teacher's book provides the background

to the tests, objectives and information for each test, and scoring procedures, including reduced reproductions of the pupils' sheets with correct answers indicated. Record cards are available for systematically recording each child's achievement and progress. Examiner required. Suitable for group use.
BRITISH PUBLISHER

Untimed: Varies

Scoring: Examiner evaluated

Cost: Teacher's book, 86 pupils' sheets £21.50; 25 record cards £7.95

Publisher: Macmillan Education

BASIC MATHEMATICS TESTS SERIES
The National Foundation for Educational Research

Child, adolescent—Ages 6.9–14.6

Purpose: Measures understanding of basic mathematical principles. Used for diagnosing individual children's abilities.

Description: Five paper-pencil tests measuring understanding of fundamental relationships and processes in mathematics. Test A (40 items), for ages 6–8, measures a range of math skills. Test B (40 items), for ages 8–9, assesses more complex relationships. Test C (50 items), for ages 9–10, covers area, graphical representation, symmetry, inequality, elementary knowledge of sets, and decimals and fractions. Test DE, for ages 10–12, covers symmetry, tabulation, fractions, elementary algebra, basic spatial ability, and graphical representation. Test FG (55 items), for ages 12–14, covers a wide range of mathematical thinking. Examiner required. Suitable for group use.
BRITISH PUBLISHER

Untimed: 1 hour

Scoring: Hand key

Cost: Contact publisher

Publisher: NFER-NELSON Publishing Company Ltd.

BASIC NUMBER DIAGNOSTIC TEST
W.E.C. Gillham

Child—Ages 5–9

Purpose: Measures number skills of children ages 5–7 and of older children who are deficient in the use of numbers. Diagnoses children's strengths and weaknesses so that specific teaching objectives can be determined. Suitable for all children scoring below a 7½–year reading age on the Basic Number Screening Test.

Description: Multiple-item paper-pencil and oral-response test covering the basic number skills that a normally developing 7–year-old child should have mastered. The test items are arranged in approximate order of difficulty within 12 categories of skills progressing from reciting, copying, and writing numbers to dealing with simple addition and subtraction. The format allows close observation of the child's strategies and errors, thus providing a basis for remedial assistance. The test should be administered at regular intervals so that a child's progress can be charted and teaching requirements revised. Where appropriate, both test and retest items are provided. Approximate age-norms are provided. Examiner required. Not suitable for group use.
BRITISH PUBLISHER

Untimed: 15–25 minutes

Scoring: Examiner evaluated

Cost: Specimen set £2.50; 20 tests £5.50; manual £2.25

Publisher: Hodder & Stoughton

BASIC NUMBER SCREENING TEST
W.E.C. Gillham and K.A. Heese

Child—Ages 7–12

Purpose: Evaluates children's basic number skills. Used for survey and screening purposes. Identifies children needing further testing and possible remedial attention.

Description: Multiple-item paper-pencil test measuring proficiency with numbers and understanding of number concepts.

Two parallel forms, A and B, may be used simultaneously to minimize the risk of copying and for test-retest programs. Norms are presented as Number Ages (7:0 to 12:0). The manual contains instructions for administering and scoring the test. Examiner required. Suitable for group use.

BRITISH PUBLISHER

Untimed: 30 minutes

Scoring: Hand key

Cost: Specimen set £2.95; 20 tests (specify form) £3.50; manual £2.50

Publisher: Hodder & Stoughton

BASIC VISUAL-MOTOR ASSOCIATION TEST
Refer to page 610.

BASICS OF OPERATIONS (GRADES 1–3)
B. J. Beeson and Sam Adams

Child
Grades 1–3

Purpose: Measures the ability of third- and fourth-grade students to add and subtract. Used to assess student progress and determine remedial needs.

Description: 335–item paper-pencil test measuring basic knowledge of addition and subtraction, as well as readiness for multiplication and division. The teacher reads the directions/questions in the beginning sections. Other sections may be completed independently. Examiner required. Suitable for group use.

Untimed: 30 minutes

Scoring: Examiner evaluated

Cost: Contact publisher

Publisher: Dr. Charles Sauls

Information and availability unconfirmed; last verified in 1987.

CANADIAN TEST OF BASIC SKILLS: MATHEMATICS FRENCH EDITION (CTBS), LEVELS 9–14, FORM 7
E. King-Shaw and A. Hieronymus

Child
Grades 3–8

Purpose: Assesses students' abilities in mathematical concepts, problem solving, and computation.

Description: Series of paper-pencil multiple-choice subtests: Mathematics Concepts, Mathematics Problem Solving, and Mathematics Computation. Materials include test booklets, a multilevel teacher's guide, supplementary guide and key, and answer sheets. This test is an adaptation of the Iowa Tests of Basic Skills published by Riverside Publishing Company. Examiner must have a teaching certificate. Examiner required. Suitable for group use.

CANADIAN PUBLISHER

Timed: 66 minutes

Scoring: Hand key; machine scored; test scoring service available from publisher

Cost: Test booklets $2.70; teacher's guide $12.00; supplementary guide and key $4.95; 35 answer sheets $13.45

Publisher: Nelson Canada

COMMON FRACTIONS
Sam Adams

Child, adolescent
Grades 6–8

Purpose: Measures students' ability to work with common fractions. Diagnoses individual needs in this area.

Description: 172–item paper-pencil test measuring 49 concepts and computational skills necessary for understanding and working with common fractions. The student may complete the entire test or that portion related to a particular operation. Examiner required. Suitable for group use.

Untimed: 45 minutes

Scoring: Examiner evaluated

Cost: Contact publisher

Publisher: Dr. Charles Sauls

Information and availability unconfirmed; last verified in 1987.

DECIMAL FRACTIONS
B. J. Beeson and Lionel O. Pellegrin

Child, adolescent
Grades 6–8

Purpose: Measures students' ability to work with decimal fractions. Diagnoses individual needs in this area.

Description: 129–item paper-pencil test measuring 43 concepts and computational skills required to understand and work with decimal fractions. Examiner required. Suitable for group use.

Untimed: 45 minutes

Scoring: Examiner evaluated

Cost: Contact publisher

Publisher: Dr. Charles Sauls

Information and availability unconfirmed; last verified in 1987.

DIAGNOSTIC ABILITIES IN MATH (D.A.M. TEST)
Francis T. Sganga

Slow learners

Purpose: Measures knowledge of basic mathematics. Used for student placement and remediation.

Description: 220–item paper-pencil test in two sections. Part I is a timed test with 160 problems testing instant recall of fundamentals of addition, subtraction, multiplication, and division. Part II is a diagnostic test consisting of 60 problems covering whole numbers, fractions, and decimals. Examiner required. Suitable for group use.

Timed: Part I 30 minutes; Part II 3 hours

Scoring: Hand key

Cost: 10 test booklets, teacher instructions, answer key $22.95

Publisher: Mafex Associates, Inc.

Information and availability unconfirmed; last verified in 1987.

DIAGNOSTIC MATH TESTS

Child, adolescent

Purpose: Assesses skills in arithmetic. Used for determining nature of specific pupil problems.

Description: Three paper-pencil tests of math ability: Diagnostic Arithmetic Tests (Standards 2 to 8); Diagnostic Tests in Basic Algebra (Standards 7 and 8); and Mathematics Tests, Diagnostic, Primary

Level (Standards 1 to 5). Each test is divided into subtests. Aspects tested by the Diagnostic Tests in Basic Algebra are basic operations; simple algebraic expressions and linear equations; sets; exponents; number systems; ratio, rate, and proportion; substitution; and factors. Examiner required. Suitable for group use.

SOUTH AFRICAN PUBLISHER

Untimed: Not available

Scoring: Hand key; examiner evaluated

Cost: Contact publisher; orders outside the RSA will be dealt with on merit

Publisher: Human Sciences Research Council

DIAGNOSTIC SCREENING TEST: MATH, THIRD EDITION (DSTM)
Thomas D. Gnagey

Child, adolescent
Grades 1-10

Purpose: Determines a student's conceptual and computational mathematical skills.

Description: Multiple-item paper-pencil test in two sections: Basic Processes Section and Specialized Section. The Basic Processes Section consists of 36 items arranged developmentally within four major areas: addition skills, subtraction skills, multiplication, and division. Each area yields a separate Grade Equivalent Score and Consolidation Index Score and scores in nine supplemental categories: process, sequencing, simple computation, special manipulations, use of zero decimals, simple fractions, and manipulation in fractions. The Specialized Section consists of 37–45 items evaluating conceptual and computational skills in five areas: money, time, percent, U.S. measurement, and metric measurement. The examiner explains the procedure and students complete the problems. The test is available in alternate forms, A and B. Examiner required. Suitable for group use.

Untimed: 5–20 minutes

Scoring: Hand key

Cost: Manual, 25 Form A, 25 Form B $32.00

Publisher: Slosson Educational Publications, Inc.

DIAGNOSTIC TEST OF ARITHMETIC STRATEGIES (DTAS)
Herbert P. Ginsburg and Steven C. Mathews

Child
Grades 1–6

Purpose: Evaluates the strategies children in Grades 1–6 use to solve basic arithmetic problems. Used to plan instructional programs.

Description: Multiple-item paper-pencil test measuring the procedures children use to perform arithmetic calculations in addition, subtraction, multiplication, and division. Results provide a profile of each student's faulty calculational strategies and potential strengths. The examiner's manual covers the interpretation of test results as well as suggested remedial approaches. Examiner required. Suitable for group use.

Untimed: Varies
Scoring: Examiner evaluated
Cost: Complete kit (examiner's manual; 25 addition, subtraction, multiplication, and division answer sheets; student worksheets) $79.00
Publisher: PRO-ED

DMI MATHEMATICS SYSTEMS (DMI/MS)
CTB/McGraw-Hill

Child, adolescent
Grades K–8.9

Purpose: Identifies students' strengths in mathematics and diagnoses specific instructional needs.

Description: Multiple-item paper-pencil test measuring four strands of mathematics content: whole numbers, fractions and decimals, measurement and geometry, and problem solving and special topics. Each content area can be measured at two levels of specificity: category objectives assessment level and instructional objectives assessment level. The system is available on seven grade levels: Level A (Grades K.6–1.5), Level B (Grades 1.6–2.5), Level C (Grades 2.6–3.5), Level D (Grades 3.6–4.5), Level E (Grades 4.6–5.5), Level F (Grades 5.6–6.5), and Level G (Grades 6.6–8.9). The system is available in two formats. System 1, the graded approach, assesses skills by level, and materials are packaged according to the seven grade levels. System 2, the multigraded approach, assesses skills across levels, and materials are packaged according to the four strands of mathematics content. Classroom kits of instructional materials and mastery tests are available for both systems. Examiner required. Suitable for group use.

Untimed: Not available
Scoring: Hand key; may be computer scored
Cost: System 1, Graded Approach classroom kit, Level A and B each $230.70, Level C $246.40, Levels D-G $280.00
Publisher: CTB/Macmillan/McGraw-Hill

EARLY MATHEMATICS DIAGNOSTIC KIT
David Lumb and Margaret Lumb

Child—Ages 4–8

Purpose: Identifies problems related to learning mathematics. Used by teachers and educational psychologists for developing prescriptive programs.

Description: Multiple-item oral-response test assessing a child's understanding of mathematics-related concepts, including perception of color, shape, size, and space; counting; conservation of number; matching; classification; addition, subtraction, multiplication, and division; fractions; time; representation; and language. The test provides information on weaknesses in early mathematical experience and understanding that could impede progress in learning mathematics. Although designed for younger children, the test can be used with older children with specific learning difficulties in mathematics. Materials include a Book of Test Items, which contains 110 plates covering the major areas of the early mathematics curriculum, a set of 40 assorted colored cubes, and a set of 3 small boxes. Examiner required. Not suitable for group use.
BRITISH PUBLISHER

Untimed: 30 minutes

Scoring: Hand key

Cost: Contact publisher

Publisher: NFER-NELSON Publishing Company Ltd.

THE ENRIGHT® DIAGNOSTIC INVENTORY OF BASIC ARITHMETIC SKILLS
Brian E. Enright

Child
Grades 1–9

Purpose: Measures basic arithmetic computation skills and determines individual error patterns for skill-specific corrective instruction. Used for academic placement and to plan remedial instruction programs and establish IEPs for students with special arithmetic needs.

Description: Four sets of multiple-item paper-pencil tests assessing 144 arithmetic skills arranged in 13 computation skill sections: addition, subtraction, multiplication, and division of whole numbers, fractions, and decimals and conversion of fractions. The wide-range placement test (26 items) is available in two equivalent forms, A and B. The skill placement tests, one test for each of the 13 skill sections, are available in two alternate forms, A and B. The four basic facts tests (50 items each) measure basic facts in addition, subtraction, multiplication, and division. The skill tests contain five items for each of the 144 skills assessed. The examiner administers only the skill placement tests indicated by the wide-range placement test or the student's current classroom problems and then administers only the skill tests indicated by the student's performance on the skill placement tests. An instructional objective is listed for each of the 144 skills and the error patterns associated with that skill. Error analysis leads directly to planning and development of remedial instruction. An arithmetic record book and individual progress reports are available. A videotape for in-service training of examiners is available. Examiner required. Suitable for group use.

Untimed: Varies

Scoring: Examiner evaluated

Cost: Tester manual with 10 student tests and arithmetic record books $99.00; student test and arithmetic record book $4.65

Publisher: Curriculum Associates, Inc.

EXAM IN A CAN
Refer to page 333.

FUNDAMENTAL PROCESSES IN ARITHMETIC
Refer to page 635.

GRADED ARITHMETIC-MATHEMATICS TEST, METRIC EDITION
P.E. Vernon and K.M. Miller

Child, adolescent—Ages 6–16

Purpose: Measures children's arithmetic and mathematics skills. May be used with the visually impaired.

Description: Multiple-item paper-pencil test measuring achievement in arithmetic and mathematics. The test is available in a Junior Form (ages 6–12) and a Senior Form (ages 11–16). The manual provides relevant technical data and full instructions for administering the test, including an "oral" version for use with the visually impaired or pupils whose poor reading ability might handicap their completion of the test. The answers are clearly presented to facilitate scoring, and advice is given on the acceptability of various alternative forms of response. Norms are provided as mathematics ages (5:0–17:1) and as deviation quotients (for chronological ages 5.3–18+). Examiner required. Suitable for group use.
BRITISH PUBLISHER

Untimed: 30 minutes

Scoring: Hand key

Cost: Specimen set £2.95; 20 tests (specify form) £2.95; manual £2.50

Publisher: Hodder & Stoughton

GRADED ASSESSMENT IN MATHS DEVELOPMENTAL PACK (GAIM)

Inner London Education Authority, London and East Anglian Group for GCSE and King's College, London University, with the support of the Nuffield Foundation

Child, adolescent—Ages 11-16

Purpose: Assesses mathematical attainment and provides information for planning courses and attaining accreditation from the London and East Anglian Group for GCSE.

Description: Paper-pencil and oral-response criterion-referenced asssessment program utilizing 40 activities covering all areas of mathematics. Children in the classroom complete specific informal investigations as assembled by the teacher to meet the assessment criteria of the area of mathematics being taught. Profiles and reports are produced by the teacher. Examiner/self-administered. Suitable for group use.

Untimed: Varies

Scoring: Examiner evaluated; self-scored

Cost: Development pack £29.95

Publisher: Macmillan Education Ltd.

GROUP MATHEMATICS TEST: SECOND EDITION

Dennis Young

Child—Ages 6.5-8.10

Purpose: Measures children's mathematical understanding.

Description: Multiple-item paper-pencil test measuring simple mathematical skills and understanding. The item content of this second edition is the same as the first edition. The revised manual provides new norms and slightly revised instructions for administration. Separate tables of quotients are provided to cover a wide range of ability, from infants (ages 6.5-7.10) to first-year juniors (ages 6.5-7.10) to less able pupils up to age 12.10. Two parallel

forms are available. Examiner required. Suitable for group use.
BRITISH PUBLISHER

Untimed: Not available

Scoring: Examiner evaluated

Cost: Specimen set £3.25; 20 tests (specify form) £2.25; manual £2.95

Publisher: Hodder & Stoughton

HUDSON EDUCATION SKILLS INVENTORY-MATHEMATICS (HESI-M)

Refer to page 460.

INDIVIDUALIZED CRITERION REFERENCED TESTING (ICRT)

Refer to page 462.

INDIVIDUALIZED CRITERION REFERENCED TESTING— MATHEMATICS (ICRT—MATH)

Dale E. Strotman and Margaret T. Steen

Child, adolescent Grades 1-9

Purpose: Assesses mathematics performance of students. Provides information on skills mastered, skills for review, and skills to learn. Also used in adult basic education.

Description: Multiple-item paper-pencil power tests measuring student knowledge of operations, fractions, measurement, geometry, decimals and percentages, and special topics. The tests are based on a developmental continuum of 384 learning objectives for Grades 1-9. The tests are designed to be taken at each student's instructional level rather than grade level. The tests correlate to more than 115 math programs. Objectives are matched with current curricula and the content of newer textbooks. The results indicate resources for teaching and reinforcing skills, list names of all students who need instruction in each skill, and aid in grouping students according to their specific learning needs. Materials provide for interim testing and recording of progress. A program evaluation report provides criterion-referenced and norm-referenced information for each student, class, building, and district. The report includes scales scores, grade equivalents, percentiles, and NCEs. The testing program is used by administrators and teachers in city-wide instructional management systems, migrant and special education programs, and ECIA-Chapter projects. Examiner required. Suitable for group use.

Untimed: Varies

Scoring: Computer scored

Cost: Contact publisher

Publisher: Educational Development Corporation

KEYMATH REVISED: A DIAGNOSTIC INVENTORY OF ESSENTIAL MATHEMATICS
Austin J. Connolly

Child, adolescent
Grades K-9

Purpose: Measures students' understanding and application of important mathematics concepts and skills. Suggested for use by math specialists, educational diagnosticians, special education teachers, and Chapter I teachers.

Description: Three-category oral-response point-to and paper-pencil test covering basic concepts (numeration, rational numbers, geometry), operations (addition, subtraction, multiplication, division, mental computation), and applications (measurement, time and money, estimation, interpreting data, problem solving). Standard scores ($M=100$, $SD=15$), grade and age equivalents, percentile ranks, stanines, and NCEs are provided for three composites and total test. Scaled scores ($M=10$, $SD=3$), percentile ranks, stanines, and NCEs are provided for the individual subtests. Materials include Easels 1 and 2 and a test record form. This is a revision of the 1976 KeyMath Diagnostic Test. Examiners must have completed graduate training in measurement, guidance, and individual assessment. Two forms, A and B, are available. Computer software is available for score conversions and recommendations for remedial instruction. May

be used with individuals with physical and mental disabilities. Examiner required. Not suitable for group use.

Untimed: 35-50 minutes

Scoring: Examiner evaluated

Cost: Form A and Form B combined kit $235.00; Form A kit $125.00 Form B kit $125.00

Publisher: American Guidance Service

LEICESTER NUMBER TEST
W.E.C. Gillham and K.A. Hesse

Child—Ages 7.1–17.6

Purpose: Measures basic number skills of individual students and class groups. Identifies students needing special help. Indicates areas in which the class as a whole needs special attention.

Description: Multiple-item paper-pencil test assessing a child's understanding of basic concepts of the number system and grasp of the "four rules" of conventional calculation. The test is intended for general screening and should be administered at the beginning of the school year. Norms are provided for ages 7.1–9.0. Examiner required. Suitable for group use.
BRITISH PUBLISHER

Untimed: Not available

Scoring: Examiner evaluated

Cost: Specimen set £3.80; 20 tests £7.25; manual £2.95

Publisher: Hodder & Stoughton

MATH TESTS GRADE I/SUB A-STANDARD 10

Child, adolescent

Purpose: Measures understanding of mathematics. Used for educational evaluation and placement.

Description: 19 separate paper-pencil tests of mathematics achievement and understanding. Particular subtests vary, but generally they include Mechanical, Insight, and Problem Solving. Two alternate forms, A and B, are available for all standards except Grade I/Sub A. Examiner required. Suitable for group use.
SOUTH AFRICAN PUBLISHER

Untimed: Not available

Scoring: Hand key; examiner evaluated

Cost: Contact publisher; orders from outside the RSA will be dealt with on merit

Publisher: Human Sciences Research Council

MATHEMATICS ATTAINMENT TESTS SERIES

Child, adolescent—Ages 7–13.06

Purpose: Measures understanding of mathematics. Used to identify individual student strengths and weaknesses.

Description: Five paper-pencil tests measuring mathematics attainment: Test A (ages 7–8) Test B (ages 8–10), Test C1 (ages 9–12), Test DE2 (ages 10–11), and Test EF (ages 11–13). Tests A and B are administered orally and are varied in content and style. Tests C1 and DE2 are written tests in which computation is kept to a minimum. Questions cover graphs, simple geometry, base, series and number patterns, fractions, arithmetical processes, and equations. Test EF consists of 60 multiple-choice items measuring number concepts, space operations, geometry, and tabular/graphical representation. Examiner required. Suitable for group use.
BRITISH PUBLISHER

Untimed: 50 minutes per test

Scoring: Hand key; examiner evaluated

Cost: Contact publisher

Publisher: NFER-NELSON Publishing Company Ltd.

MATHEMATICS 7–12

National Foundation for Educational Research with Alan Brighouse, David Godber, and Peter Patilla

Child—Ages 7–12

Purpose: Assesses progress in the acquisition of mathematical skills and concepts taught in primary and first-year secondary-school programs. Administered at the end of the school year to measure individual and class achievement in mathematics.

Description: 50-item paper-pencil test measuring academic achievement in mathematics. The test items, many of which incorporate drawings or diagrams, measure four skill areas: understanding, computation, application, and factual recall. The test is available on six levels: Mathematics 7 (top infants or equivalent), Mathematics 8 (first-year junior), Mathematics 9 (second-year junior), Mathematics 10 (third-year junior), Mathematics 11 (fourth-year junior), and Mathematics 12 (first-year secondary). The test titles indicate the age ranges for which the tests were designed; for example, Mathematics 9 should be used towards the end of the academic year during which the pupils attain their ninth birthday. An overall standardized score compares each pupil's ability with the national average for the same age and with classmates of differing ages. Consistent use of the series enables progress to be monitored from year to year. Subscores for each of the four skill areas indicate individual strengths and weaknesses. The manual includes a discussion of the background, content, and use of tests; administration and scoring instructions; scoring keys; interpretation guidelines; conversion tables; and technical information. Examiner required. Suitable for group use.
BRITISH PUBLISHER

Untimed: Varies

Scoring: Examiner evaluated

Cost: Contact publisher

Publisher: NFER-NELSON Publishing Company Ltd.

MATHEMATICS TOPIC TESTS— ELEMENTARY LEVEL

Child, adolescent Grades 5–9

Purpose: Measures the degree to which students have attained or failed to attain stated mathematics objectives.

Description: Series of criterion-referenced tests focusing on specific topics rather than on the work of one grade level. Each test measures the degree to which students have attained or failed to attain stated educational objectives. The series also measures curricular objectives common to most Canadian courses from Grades 5–9. Tests include Number and Numeration; Addition and Subtraction with Whole Numbers; Multiplication and Division with Whole Numbers; Operations with Fractions; Multiplication and Division with Fractions; Measurement, Graphs, and Geometry; Operations with Decimals; Multiplication and Division with Decimals. Examiner required. Suitable for group use. CANADIAN PUBLISHER

Timed: Varies

Scoring: Hand key

Cost: Contact publisher

Publisher: Guidance Centre

Information and availability unconfirmed; last verified in 1987.

METROPOLITAN MATHEMATICS INSTRUCTIONAL TESTS
Thomas P. Hogan, Roger Farr, George A. Prescott, and Irving H. Balow

Child, adolescent
Grades K.5–9.9

Purpose: Assesses mathematics skills and competence. Used for providing prescriptive information on educational performance of individual pupils.

Description: Multiple-item series of paper-pencil tests measuring major components of mathematics skills, including numeration, geometry and measurement, problem solving and operations, whole numbers, laws and properties, fractions and decimals, and graphs and statistics. The test is divided into six levels: Primer (Grades K.5–1.4), Primary 1 (Grades 1.5–2.4), Primary 2 (Grades 2.5–3.4), Elementary (Grades 3.5–4.9), Intermediate (Grades 5.0–6.9), and Advanced 1 (Grades 7.0–9.9). Each level assesses four to seven of the above mathematic skills components. The test is one in a series of instructional tests related to the Metropolitan Achievement Test Survey Battery. This test has been superseded by the MAT 6 and is available only as long as supplies last. Examiner required. Suitable for group use.

Timed: Varies

Scoring: Hand key; may be machine scored; scoring service available

Cost: Specimen set, specify level (test, manual) $11.00; the Intermediate and Advanced 1 sets include a hand-scorable answer document

Publisher: The Psychological Corporation

Information and availability unconfirmed; last verified in 1988.

MICHIGAN PRESCRIPTIVE PROGRAM IN MATH
William E. Lockhart

Adolescent, adult
Grades 6 and above

Purpose: Measures mathematics skills and identifies skill deficits. Used to help students obtain a tenth-grade equivalency and pass the GED test in mathematics.

Description: Multiple-item paper-pencil test assessing the following high-school level mathematics skills: addition; subtraction; multiplication; division; fractions; averaging; decimals; changing decimals to percents; simple and compound interest; denominate numbers; reading line, bar, and circle graphs; finding perimeter, area, and volume; square roots; proportions; set theory; laws of operation; Roman numerals; exponents; signs; simple equations; inequalities; sum of angles; coordinate geometry; theorems; graphical solutions; and slope. The test booklet, answer key, and math study materials are reusable; the student response sheet and individual prescription sheet are consumed. Math study materials have allowed students 1.5 to 3.5 math grade gain in 24 clock hours of study. Examiner required. Suitable for group use.

Untimed: Varies

Scoring: Examiner evaluated

Cost: Test book $1.50; 7 response and prescription sheets $2.00; answer key $1.00; math study materials $7.00

Publisher: Academic Therapy Publications

MICROCOMPUTER MANAGED INFORMATION FOR CRITERION REFERENCED OBJECTIVES—MATH (MMICRO-MATH)
Ron Hambleton

Child, adolescent
Grades 1–9

Purpose: Assesses students' mathematics performance. Provides information on skills mastered, skills for review, and skills to learn. Also used in adult basic education.

Description: Multiple-item paper-pencil test measuring student knowledge of operations, fractions, measurement, geometry, decimals and percentages, and special topics. The test is based on the same 348 developmental learning objectives as those for the ICRT-Math Basic + With this computerized system, diagnostic and objective (mastery) tests are automatically scored in the school with a card or sheet reader recording information onto the software. Reports offer the same comprehensive diagnostic, prescriptive, and grouping information as the ICRT. However, the system does not include the norm-referenced data available from the mainframe computer, nor does it generate three selected correlations per teacher. Correlations may be purchased. Available for Apple, Commodore, and IBM microcomputers. Examiner required. Suitable for group use.

Untimed: Varies

Scoring: Computer scored

Cost: Contact publisher

Publisher: Educational Development Corporation

MONITORING BASIC SKILLS PROGRESS-MATH
Lynn S. Fuchs, Carol Hamlett, and Douglass Fuchs

Child

Purpose: Monitors progress in basic math.

Description: Computer-assisted measurement program that tests and monitors progress in basic math. Students are periodically tested at the computer on a different alternate test that includes each problem type to be taught during the school year. The computer generates and administers the tests and automatically scores the students' performance during administration. The computer shows the student the results of the testing and provides a graph of scores over time. The computer also generates a detailed skills analysis, which provides the teacher with specific ideas for program development. The complete program includes one master disk for student measurement and feedback, one teacher disk to view student assessment profiles with automatic graphed analysis and skills analysis, a manual containing blackline masters of each math test (30 alternate forms for each of Grades 1–6), a manual with a case study describing the use of the procedures, and instructions. Available for use with an Apple II family computer with 64K. Self-administered. Not suitable for group use.

Untimed: Varies

Scoring: Computer scored

Cost: Complete kit $98.00

Publisher: PRO-ED

MORETON MATHEMATICS TESTS: LEVEL II
R.J. Andrews, R.G. Cochrane, and J. Elkins

Child
Grades 3–5

Purpose: Measures the mathematical abilities of primary-school children.

Description: Multiple-item paper-pencil test consisting of two subtests, Form N and Form P. Form N measures numerical abilities. Form P measures mathematical operations. Metric measurement is used. Australian norms are provided in terms of arithmetic ages, 15–point scale scores, and percentiles for Grades 3, 4, and 5. Examiner required. Suitable for group use.

AUSTRALIAN PUBLISHER

Untimed: Varies

Scoring: Examiner required

Cost: Classroom kit (manual, 40 Form N, 40 Form P) $14.00

Publisher: Teaching and Testing Resources

Information and availability unconfirmed; last verified in 1987.

MORETON MATHEMATICS TESTS: LEVEL III
J. Elkins, R.J. Andrews, and R.G. Cochrane

Child
Grades 5-7

Purpose: Measures the mathematics abilities of primary-school children.

Description: Multiple-item paper-pencil test measuring mathematical abilities involving numerical operations. Metric measurement is employed. Australian norms are provided in terms of arithmetic ages, 15-point scale scores, and percentiles for Grades 5, 6, and 7. Examiner required. Suitable for group use. AUSTRALIAN PUBLISHER

Untimed: Varies

Scoring: Examiner evaluated

Cost: Standard kit (manual and 100 tests) $14.00

Publisher: Teaching and Testing Resources

Information and availability unconfirmed; last verified in 1987.

MULTILEVEL ACADEMIC SKILLS INVENTORY: MATH PROGRAM (MASI)
Kenneth W. Howell, Stanley H. Zucker, and Mada Kay Morehead

Child, adolescent
Grades 1-8

Purpose: Assesses student math performance in general and in detail to help teachers and school psychologists plan instructional strategies and refer students to remedial programs.

Description: Multiple-item reusable paper-pencil test on three levels measuring computation, application of skills with money, time and temperature, problem solving, metric measurement, addition,

subtraction, multiplication, division, fractions, decimals, ratios, percent, and geometry. A Survey Test samples performance over a wide range of objectives. The Placement Test assesses abilities in more detail with a content area, and a Specific Level Test examines subskills in detail. Materials include a manual, diagnostic batteries, survey and placement test booklets, response booklets, and record forms. Examiner required. Suitable for group use.

Untimed: Varies

Scoring: Examiner evaluated

Cost: Complete set $98.00

Publisher: The Psychological Corporation

Information and availability unconfirmed; last verified in 1988.

NATIONAL ACHIEVEMENT TESTS FOR ARITHMETIC AND MATHEMATICS—ALGEBRA TEST FOR ENGINEERING AND SCIENCE
Refer to page 473.

NATIONAL ACHIEVEMENT TESTS FOR ARITHMETIC AND MATHEMATICS—AMERICAN NUMERICAL TEST
Refer to page 474.

NATIONAL ACHIEVEMENT TESTS FOR ELEMENTARY SCHOOLS: ARITHMETIC AND MATHEMATICS—ARITHMETIC FUNDAMENTALS
Refer to page 474.

NATIONAL ACHIEVEMENT TESTS FOR ELEMENTARY SCHOOLS: ARITHMETIC AND MATHEMATICS—FUNDAMENTALS AND REASONING (GRADES 3-6)
Refer to page 475.

NATIONAL ACHIEVEMENT TESTS FOR ELEMENTARY SCHOOLS: ARITHMETIC AND MATHEMATICS— FUNDAMENTALS AND REASONING (GRADES 6–8)
Refer to page 475.

NATIONAL ACHIEVEMENT TESTS FOR ELEMENTARY SCHOOLS: ARITHMETIC AND MATHEMATICS—GENERAL MATH
Refer to page 475.

NATIONAL ACHIEVEMENT TESTS FOR ELEMENTARY SCHOOLS: ARITHMETIC AND MATHEMATICS—GENERAL MATHEMATICS
Refer to page 476.

NATIONAL PROFICIENCY SURVEY SERIES (NPSS): GENERAL MATH
Dale P. Scannell

Adolescent—Ages 12–18 Grades 8–12

Purpose: Measures end-of-course achievement in general mathematics courses.

Description: 42–item paper-pencil multiple-choice test used for evaluating student proficiency in general mathematics concepts. The test, which may be administered as a survey test or as an end-of-course test, is designed to assess 14 objectives. Each objective is tested by three questions. Normative and criterion-referenced data are available. One in a series of 13 NPSS tests. Examiner required. Suitable for group use.

Timed: 40 minutes

Scoring: Self-scored; hand key

Cost: Contact publisher for price and availability

Publisher: The Riverside Publishing Company

NOTTINGHAM NUMBER TEST
W.E.C. Gillham and K.A. Hesse

Child—Ages 9.1–11

Purpose: Measures children's basic knowledge of arithmetic. Identifies students needing further testing. Groups students according to ability for teaching purposes.

Description: Two multiple-item paper-pencil subtests measuring knowledge and understanding of basic arithmetic. The first test assesses basic number concepts (series and place value). The second test assesses basic calculation skills (the "four rules" of formal arithmetic). Items of each type are presented in varied order but are graded for difficulty and identified by symbols in the scoring column. Separate norms are provided for the two subtests, as well as for the test as a whole. Designed to be used as a follow-up to the Leicester Number Test. Examiner required. Suitable for group use.
BRITISH PUBLISHER

Untimed: Not available

Scoring: Examiner evaluated

Cost: Specimen set £3.80; 20 tests £5.00; manual £3.20

Publisher: Hodder & Stoughton

PROFICIENCY BATTERY IN ENGLISH AND MATHEMATICS FOR INDIAN SOUTH AFRICANS (PEMISA)
Refer to page 481.

PROFILE OF MATHEMATICAL SKILLS
Norman France

Child, adolescent—Ages 8–15

Purpose: Measures mathematics achievement. Used for diagnosis of specific student strengths and weaknesses.

Description: Multiple-item paper-pencil criterion-referenced tests of mathematics skills. The tests are divided into two levels. Level 1 (ages 8–13) measures addition, subtraction, multiplication, division, operations, measurement and money, and extensions. Level 2 (ages 10–15) measures fractions, decimal fractions and percentages, and diagrams in addition to the areas measured in Level 1. The tests are administered over the normal course of mathematics lessons. Examiner required. Suitable for group use. BRITISH PUBLISHER

Untimed: 30 minutes per test

Scoring: Hand key; examiner evaluated

Cost: Contact publisher

Publisher: NFER-NELSON Publishing Company Ltd.

PROGRESS TESTS IN MATHS
Roy Hollands

Child—Ages 7–12

Purpose: Assesses mathematics achievement throughout the primary and middle school years. Measures both individual and group performance. Used for program planning and assessment.

Description: Six multiple-item paper-pencil tests measuring children's yearly progress in mathematics. The test items measure achievement of particular skills and subskills in the following mathematical areas: number, measure, shape, and pictorial representations. Each of the six tests corresponds to one year's work in mathematics and is intended for use with a particular age group, ranging from age 7 (Math 1) to age 12 (Math 6). The tests also are suitable for diagnostic use with older students in remedial classes. Tests for the first three years can be read aloud by the teacher to minimize problems caused by the children's limited reading abilities. Test objectives are based on reference to existing math schemes, government and LEA guidelines, and the recommendations of a panel of teachers and advisors. Tests are scored on an A-E grading system. The teacher's manual provides information on the background of the series, objectives, administering the tests, modifying them to suit individual needs, and recording and interpreting the results. Suggestions also are provided for remedial and follow-up work where necessary. A secondary teacher's manual is available for use with tests 5 and 6 only. Examiner required. Suitable for group use.

Untimed: Varies

Scoring: Examiner evaluated

Cost: Evaluation pack (teacher's manual for Levels 1–6, copy of each test) £7.99; Maths 1 and 2 each £5.95; Maths 3–6 each £6.95

Publisher: Macmillan Education

READINESS FOR OPERATIONS (K–3)
Sam Adams and Charles Sauls

Child
Grades K–3

Purpose: Measures student understanding of math concepts that are prerequisite to addition and subtraction. Used to determine readiness for kindergarten mathematics and to assess remedial needs of first- and second-grade students.

Description: 48–item paper-pencil test measuring 16 concepts, including one-to-one correspondence (pictures of objects), one-to-one correspondence (symbols), matching equal sets, matching numerals, matching numerals and names, recognizing numerals, writing numbers, separating subsets, recognizing cardinal numbers, sequencing through 10, writing numerals for set, and basic meaning of addition. The examiner reads aloud the directions for each test item; no reading is required of the examinees. Examiner required. Suitable for group use.

Untimed: 30 minutes

Scoring: Examiner evaluated

Cost: Contact publisher

Publisher: Dr. Charles Sauls

Information and availability unconfirmed; last verified in 1987.

SKILLCORP COMPUTER MANAGEMENT SYSTEM—MATH

Child
Grades K–8

Purpose: Assesses math skill deficiencies. Used to diagnose individual deficiencies in math and prescribe resources for reteaching.

Description: 111 criterion-referenced tests determine math skill deficiencies. A microcomputer prints prescriptions for individual students or groups to reteach the skills not mastered. All skills tested are cross-referenced to major publisher materials. Materials include test administration manual and test cards for each grade level. Examiner required. Suitable for group use.
Timed: Varies, depending on test
Scoring: Hand key; may be computer scored
Cost: Contact publisher
Publisher: Skillcorp Software, Inc.

STANFORD MEASUREMENT SERIES—STANFORD DIAGNOSTIC MATHEMATICS TEST (SDMT): THIRD EDITION
Refer to page 489.

STEENBURGEN DIAGNOSTIC-PRESCRIPTIVE MATH PROGRAM AND QUICK MATH SCREENING TEST
Fran Steenburgen Gelb

Grades 1-6 and older students

Purpose: Determines an elementary school student's exact level of functioning in mathematics. Used to plan programs for children and older remedial students whose math skills are still at the elementary level.

Description: Multiple-item paper-pencil screening test measuring ability in simple addition, subtraction, one-digit carrying, addition of mixed numbers, and long division. The items are arranged in a sequential hierarchy according to the grade level at which each skill is introduced. For example, Level I includes problems appropriate for Grades 1-3, and Level II contains problems for Grades 4-6. Scores can be plotted on a profile sheet that graphically shows a student's progress from pre- to posttest. After the student's strengths and weaknesses are identified, the diagnostic-prescriptive

program consisting of 55 reproducible worksheets can be used by the student until skills are mastered. The format of the screening test does not overstimulate hyperactive or distractible children. Examiner required. Suitable for group use.
Untimed: 10 minutes
Scoring: Hand key
Cost: Manual $15.00; Level I 25 test forms, 25 profile sheets $15.00; Level II 25 test forms, 25 profile sheets $15.00
Publisher: Academic Therapy Publications

TEST OF COMPUTATIONAL PROCESSES
Neldon D. Kingston

Child, adolescent
Grades 1-8

Purpose: Determines strengths and weaknesses in mathematics computation. Used with students in Grades 1-8.

Description: Multiple-item paper-pencil test measuring computational skills in seven areas: addition, subtraction, multiplication, and division of whole numbers; fractions; decimals; and knowledge of essential measurement units. The test is norm-referenced. Examiner required. Suitable for group use.
Timed: 20-30 minutes for 1st grade; 80 minutes for 8th grade
Scoring: Examiner evaluated
Cost: Complete kit (25 8-page test booklets, manual) $50.00
Publisher: DLM Teaching Resources

TESTS OF COMPETENCE IN MATHEMATICS
Frances C. Morrison

Child, adolescent
Grades 4-9

Purpose: Assesses students' mathematics achievement. Provides information on specific areas of strengths and weaknesses. Used as a pre- or postcourse test.

Description: Three paper-pencil multiple-choice subtests of 50 items each measuring mastery of computational skills, mathematical concepts, and word problems. The material covered includes fractional and decimal knowledge, computational skills, geometry, and metric measurement. Subtest Level 4–5 is intended mainly for use at the end of Grade 4 or the beginning of Grade 5; Level 6–7 is designed for the end of Grade 6 or the beginning of Grade 7; and Level 8–9 is used at the end of Grade 8 or the beginning of Grade 9. Examiner required. Suitable for group use. CANADIAN PUBLISHER

Timed: 30 minutes per subtest

Scoring: Hand key

Cost: Specimen set, specify level (test booklets, answer sheet, key, manual) $5.25

Publisher: Guidance Centre

Information and availability unconfirmed; last verified in 1987.

WORKING WITH WHOLE NUMBERS
Sam Adams and Leslie Ellis

Child, adolescent
Grades 4–8

Purpose: Assesses ability to add, subtract, multiply, and divide. Used to plan remedial approaches for students in Grades 4–8.

Description: 575–item paper-pencil test in two sections measuring mastery of the four basic arithmetic operations using whole numbers. The survey portion measures concepts and is administered by the teacher. The second portion measures ability with facts and is completed independently. Examiner required. Suitable for group use.

Untimed: 45 minutes

Scoring: Examiner evaluated

Cost: Contact publisher

Publisher: Dr. Charles Sauls

Information and availability unconfirmed; last verified in 1987.

Y' MATHEMATICS SERIES
Dennis Young

Child—Ages 7.5–11.10

Purpose: Measures children's achievement in mathematics. Assesses individual and class progress in the study of mathematics and identifies strengths or weaknesses of curriculum and teaching methods.

Description: Four paper-pencil tests measuring mathematics achievement in four overlapping stages (Y1, Y2, Y3, and Y4) covering the overall age range from 7.5–11.10 years. Both Y1 (ages 7.5–8.10) and Y2 (ages 8.5–9.10) consist of three sections: orally presented items, computation, and written problems, a format that helps identify students whose mathematical ability is being underestimated because of reading difficulties. An additional table of quotients for Y2 is provided for use with older backward and slow-reading children up to age 14.10. Both Y3 (ages 9.5–10.10) and Y4 (ages 10.5–11.10) contain computation and written problems. The age ranges may be extended for special groups such as older, slow-learning pupils. Examiner required. Suitable for group use. BRITISH PUBLISHER

Timed: Single class period

Scoring: Examiner evaluated

Cost: Specimen set £6.50; 20 tests (specify form) £3.50; manual (specify level) £2.50

Publisher: Hodder & Stoughton

Academic Subjects: Mathematics: Upper Math Skills

ACER MATHEMATICS TESTS

Child, adolescent
Grades K–11

Purpose: Measures achievement in mathematics. Used for diagnosing individual student strengths and weaknesses.

Description: Six sets of multiple-choice and two sets of open-ended paper-pencil tests of basic mathematics skills: addition, subtraction, multiplication, and division.

Tests are ACER Class Achievement Test in Mathematics (CATIM), a criterion-referenced test for years 4–5; ACER Class Achievement Test in Mathematics (CATIM), years 6–7; ACER Review and Progress Tests in Mathematics (open-ended); ACER Mathematics Profile Series, measuring Operations at years 4–10 and Space, Measurement, and Number at years 7–10; Progressive Achievement Tests in Mathematics—Forms A or B, for years 3–8; Mathematics Evaluation Procedures K–2, years K–4 (open-ended). Examiner required. Suitable for group use.

AUSTRALIAN PUBLISHER

Timed: Varies

Scoring: Hand key

Cost: Contact publisher

Publisher: The Australian Council for Educational Research Limited

AMERICAN INVITATIONAL MATHEMATICS EXAMINATION (AIME)

Adolescent
Grades 9–12

Purpose: Measures mathematical achievement of high-school students with exceptional mathematical ability. Used to select students with the specific talents necessary for doing well on examinations such as the U.S.A. Mathematical Olympiad (USAMO).

Description: 15–item paper-pencil free-response test measuring mathematics abilities of selected high-school students. No multiple-choice questions are included. All problems can be solved using pre-calculus methods. Only students scoring above a cutoff score announced each fall on the American High School Mathematics Examination (ASHME) are invited to participate in the examination, which in turn serves as the qualifying examination for the USAMO. Participating schools must register each fall with the Regional Examination Coordinators. Examiner required. Suitable for group use.

Timed: 3 hours

Scoring: Scored by M.A.A. Committee on High School Contests

Cost: Contact Dr. Walter E. Mientka at M.A.A. address

Publisher: M.A.A. Committee on High School Examinations

ANNUAL HIGH SCHOOL MATHEMATICS EXAMINATION (AHSME)

Adolescent
Grades 7–12

Purpose: Assesses skills and conceptual knowledge of precalculus mathematical students. Designed to provide challenging problems to create and sustain an interest in mathematics.

Description: 30–item paper-pencil multiple-choice test assessing proficiency in the concepts and skills associated with precalculus mathematics with emphasis on intermediate algebra and plane geometry. Participating high schools must register each fall with the Regional Examination Coordinators. Each school makes its own decision as to the number of participants (for official status the minimum number of participants per school is three) although the test is open to all students with the necessary background. The test is administered in the U.S.A., Canada, England, Finland, Belgium, Hungary, Ireland, Israel, Italy, Jamaica, Luxembourg, Australia, Malaysia, and other American and foreign schools abroad. Examiner required. Suitable for group use. Available in Spanish, braille, and large-print editions.

Timed: 1 hour, 30 minutes

Scoring: Hand key

Cost: Specimen sets of prior examinations $.50 each

Publisher: M.A.A. Committee on High School Contests

CALIFORNIA DIAGNOSTIC MATHEMATICS TEST (CDMT)
CTB staff, Chapter I teachers

Grades 2–10

Purpose: Diagnoses mathematics strengths and needs of students ranking in the lower percentiles.

Description: Multiple-item criterion- and norm-referenced paper-pencil multiple-choice test available on six levels, A-F. Each level covers number concepts, computation, and mathematics application. At Level F, Life Shields are included. Consumable test books are available for Levels A-C and reusable test books and answer sheets for Levels D-F. The publisher provides a scoring service, and software for scoring is available for school use. Examiner required. Suitable for group use.

Untimed: Not available

Scoring: Computer scored; hand key; may be machine scored

Cost: 35 machine-scorable test books Levels A-C each $68.25; 35 hand-scorable test books Levels A-C each $41.65; 35 reusable test books Levels D-F each $31.15; hand scoring stencils Levels D-F each $9.10; 50 Compuscan machine-scorable answer sheets Levels D-F each $11.00; 50 hand-scorable answer sheets Levels D-F $14.25; 50 Scantron machine-scorable answer sheets $11.00

Publisher: CTB/Macmillan/McGraw-Hill

CHELSEA DIAGNOSTIC MATHEMATICS TESTS
Kathleen Hart, Margaret Brown, Dietmar Kuchemann, Daphne Kerslake, and Graham Ruddock

Child, adolescent—Ages 9–15

Purpose: Assesses students' level of mathematics achievement. Used by teachers for educational program planning and evaluation.

Description: Battery of 10 paper-pencil tests assessing levels of achievement in the following areas: algebra, fractions, graphs, measurement, number operations, place value and decimals, ratio and proportion, reflection and rotation, and vectors. Examiner required. Suitable for group use.
BRITISH PUBLISHER

Untimed: 30–60 minutes

Scoring: Hand key

Cost: Contact publisher

Publisher: NFER-NELSON Publishing Company Ltd.

CHELSEA DIAGNOSTIC MATHEMATICS TESTS: ALGEBRA
Kathleen Hart, Margaret Brown, Dietmar Kuchemann, Daphne Kerslake, and Graham Ruddock

Adolescent—Ages 12–15

Purpose: Assesses algebra abilities of students.

Description: Multiple-item paper-pencil test assessing a broad range of typical secondary school algebra tasks and focusing on different ways children use and interpret letters in generalized arithmetic. Practice items precede the main test to remind children of certain conventions. The test may be used with older children. One in a series of 10 tests in the Chelsea Diagnostic Mathematics Tests. Examiner required. Suitable for group use.
BRITISH PUBLISHER

Untimed: 30–60 minutes

Scoring: Hand key

Cost: Contact publisher

Publisher: NFER-NELSON Publishing Company Ltd.

CHELSEA DIAGNOSTIC MATHEMATICS TESTS: FRACTIONS 1
Kathleen Hart, Margaret Brown, Dietmar Kuchemann, Daphne Kerslake, and Graham Ruddock

Adolescent—Ages 11–13

Purpose: Measures students' ability to solve problems and compute fractions.

Description: Multiple-item paper-pencil test in two parts focusing on labeling fractions, adding and subtracting fractions, and solving problems using fractions. The main test is composed of problems, and a related section consists of fractional computations that mirror the problems. One in a series of 10 tests in the Chelsea Diagnostic Mathematics Tests. Examiner required. Suitable for group use. BRITISH PUBLISHER

Untimed: 30–60 minutes
Scoring: Hand key
Cost: Contact publisher
Publisher: NFER-NELSON Publishing Company Ltd.

CHELSEA DIAGNOSTIC MATHEMATICS TESTS: FRACTIONS 2
Kathleen Hart, Margaret Brown, Dietmar Kuchemann, Daphne Kerslake, and Graham Ruddock

Adolescent—Ages 13–15

Purpose: Measures students' ability to solve problems and do computations using fractions.

Description: Multiple-item paper-pencil test focusing on labeling fractions and adding, subtracting, multiplying, and dividing fractions. A related section deals with computation. One in a series of 10 tests in the Chelsea Diagnostic Mathematics Tests. Examiner required. Suitable for group use.
BRITISH PUBLISHER

Untimed: 30–60 minutes
Scoring: Hand key
Cost: Contact publisher
Publisher: NFER-NELSON Publishing Company Ltd.

CHELSEA DIAGNOSTIC MATHEMATICS TESTS: GRAPHS
Kathleen Hart, Margaret Brown, Dietmar Kuchemann, Daphne Kerslake, and Graham Ruddock

Adolescent—Ages 12–15

Purpose: Assesses students' understanding of graphs.

Description: Multiple-item paper-pencil test measuring understanding of bar charts, coordinates, scale, continuous graphs, and simple equations. One in a series of 10 tests in the Chelsea Diagnostic

Mathematics Tests. Examiner required. Suitable for group use. BRITISH PUBLISHER

Untimed: 30–60 minutes
Scoring: Hand key
Cost: Contact publisher
Publisher: NFER-NELSON Publishing Company Ltd.

CHELSEA DIAGNOSTIC MATHEMATICS TESTS: MEASUREMENT
Kathleen Hart, Margaret Brown, Dietmar Kuchemann, Daphne Kerslake, and Graham Ruddock

Adolescent—Ages 11–14

Purpose: Assesses students' ability to solve problems related to measurement.

Description: Multiple-item paper-pencil test involving mathematical computations of length, area, and volume. Practice questions describe common terms such as area and perimeter. One in a series of 10 tests in the Chelsea Diagnostic Mathematics Tests. Examiner required. Suitable for group use.
BRITISH PUBLISHER

Untimed: 30–60 minutes
Scoring: Hand key
Cost: Contact publisher
Publisher: NFER-NELSON Publishing Company Ltd.

CHELSEA DIAGNOSTIC MATHEMATICS TESTS: NUMBER OPERATIONS
Kathleen Hart, Margaret Brown, Dietmar Kuchemann, Daphne Kerslake, and Graham Ruddock

Adolescent—Ages 11–12

Purpose: Assesses conceptual understanding of the four basic number operations applied to whole numbers.

Description: Multiple-item paper-pencil test assessing whether children can recognize where each of the four basic number operations—addition, subtraction, multiplication, division—is applicable. The test

also requires children to provide a concrete example of each operation. The test can be used with younger and older students and with students ages 13–15 and older who have lower mathematical abilities. One in a series of 10 tests in the Chelsea Diagnostic Mathematics Tests. Examiner required. Suitable for group use.
BRITISH PUBLISHER
Untimed: 30–60 minutes
Scoring: Hand key
Cost: Contact publisher
Publisher: NFER-NELSON Publishing Company Ltd.

CHELSEA DIAGNOSTIC MATHEMATICS TESTS: PLACE VALUES AND DECIMALS
Kathleen Hart, Margaret Brown, Dietmar Kuchemann, Daphne Kerslake, and Graham Ruddock

Adolescent—Ages 11–15

Purpose: Assesses students' understanding of the base–10 place value notation system.

Description: Multiple-item paper-pencil test measuring students' understanding of the base–10 place value notation system for whole numbers and decimals and whether students can use it appropriately. One in a series of 10 tests in the Chelsea Diagnostic Mathematics Tests. Examiner required. Suitable for group use.
BRITISH PUBLISHER
Untimed: 30–60 minutes
Scoring: Hand key
Cost: Contact publisher
Publisher: NFER-NELSON Publishing Company Ltd.

CHELSEA DIAGNOSTIC MATHEMATICS TESTS: RATIO AND PROPORTION
Kathleen Hart, Margaret Brown, Dietmar Kuchemann, Daphne Kerslake, and Graham Ruddock

Adolescent—Ages 12–15

Purpose: Assesses students' conceptual understanding of ratio and proportion.

Description: Multiple-item paper-pencil test measuring understanding of ratio and proportion through a range of problems of varying complexity. The test also may be used with adults in higher education and some primary-school pupils. One in a series of 10 tests in the Chelsea Diagnostic Mathematics Tests. Examiner required. Suitable for group use.
BRITISH PUBLISHER
Untimed: 30–60 minutes
Scoring: Hand key
Cost: Contact publisher
Publisher: NFER-NELSON Publishing Company Ltd.

CHELSEA DIAGNOSTIC MATHEMATICS TESTS: REFLECTION AND ROTATION
Kathleen Hart, Margaret Brown, Dietmar Kuchemann, Daphne Kerslake, and Graham Ruddock

Adolescent—Ages 12–14

Purpose: Assesses students' understanding of reflection and rotation.

Description: Multiple-item paper-pencil test covering single reflections, single rotations (using a quarter turn), and combinations of reflections and rotations. The first two parts are preceded by trial items designed to remind students of terms such as "reflection," "mirror line," "rotation," and "quarter turn." One in a series of 10 tests in the Chelsea Diagnostic Mathematics Tests. Examiner required. Suitable for group use.
BRITISH PUBLISHER
Untimed: 30–60 minutes
Scoring: Hand key
Cost: Contact publisher
Publisher: NFER-NELSON Publishing Company Ltd.

COOPERATIVE MATHEMATICS TESTS
Educational Testing Service

Adolescent Grades 7–14

Purpose: Measures achievement in major mathematical content areas ranging from arithmetic to calculus.

Description: Multiple-item test assessing a student's comprehension of basic mathematical concepts, techniques, and unifying principles. The recommended grade levels for each subtest and the concepts it measures are Arithmetic (Grades 7–9), basic concepts without emphasis on commercial applications; Structure of the Number System (Grades 7–8), concepts underlying the structure of the real number system; Algebra (Grades 8–9), concepts and skills underlying quadratic equations, inequalities, number line, and field properties; Algebra II (Grades 9–12), concepts and skills underlying inequalities and absolute values; Geometry Part I (Grades 9–12), concepts in Euclidean geometry; Geometry Part II (Grades 9–12), advanced understanding, proof, spatial reasoning; Trigonometry (Grades 9–14), functional and numerical trigonometry; Algebra III (Grades 9–14), traditional topics and contemporary material, such as inequalities and functional notation; Analytic Geometry (Grades 9–14), suitable for one-semester course or combined analytic geometry-calculus course; Calculus Part I (Grades 9–14), algebraic functions, emphasis on differential calculus; Calculus Part II (Grades 9–14), transcendental functions, emphasis on integral calculus. Separate norms for college engineering, education, and liberal arts students are available. Subtests may be ordered independently. Examiner required. Suitable for group use.

Timed: 40–80 minutes

Scoring: Hand key; may be computer scored

Cost: 20 tests $12.80 (specify title); 100 answer sheets (specify hand- or machine-scorable) $18.00; manual $7.50; 10 scoring stencils $5.50

Publisher: CTB/Macmillan/McGraw-Hill

EXAM IN A CAN
IPS Publishing, Inc.

Ages 14 and older

Purpose: Evaluates math performance in the areas of basic math, geometry, algebra, precalculus, and calculus.

Description: Multiple-item paper-pencil free-response or multiple-choice assessment system measuring math skills in six areas: basic math, geometry, algebra, algebra II, precalculus, and calculus. Each area is comprised of 120 objectives. The teacher selects the targeted objectives and then an algorithm-driven generating program creates exams, quizzes, or worksheets comprised of items for each objective. Each printout provides the instructor with an answer sheet for students and an answer key with solutions. The program runs on Apple II, Macintosh, and IBM PC systems. Examiner/self-administered. Suitable for group use. Available in Spanish and French.

Untimed: Varies

Scoring: Hand key; machine scored; self-scored

Cost: Basic Math $79.95; Algebra I, Algebra II, Geometry, PreCalculus, Calculus each $89.95

Publisher: IPS Publishing, Inc.

METROPOLITAN MATHEMATICS INSTRUCTIONAL TESTS
Refer to page 322.

NATIONAL ACHIEVEMENT TESTS FOR ARITHMETIC AND MATHEMATICS—FIRST YEAR-ALGEBRA TEST
Refer to page 474.

NATIONAL ACHIEVEMENT TESTS FOR ARITHMETIC AND MATHEMATICS—PLANE GEOMETRY, SOLID GEOMETRY, AND PLANE TRIGONOMETRY TESTS
Refer to page 474.

NATIONAL PROFICIENCY SURVEY SERIES (NPSS): ALGEBRA 1
Dale P. Scannell

Adolescent—Ages 12–18
Grades 8–12

Purpose: Measures end-of-course achievement in beginning algebra courses.

Description: 45–item paper-pencil multiple-choice test used for evaluating student proficiency in basic algebra. The test, which may be administered as a survey test or as an end-of-course test, is designed to assess 15 objectives. Each objective is tested by three questions. Normative and criterion-referenced data are available. One in a series of 13 NPSS tests. Examiner required. Suitable for group use.

Timed: 40 minutes

Scoring: Self-scored; hand key

Cost: Contact publisher for price and availability

Publisher: The Riverside Publishing Company

NATIONAL PROFICIENCY SURVEY SERIES (NPSS): ALGEBRA 2
Dale P. Scannell

Adolescent—Ages 12–18
Grades 8–12

Purpose: Measures end-of-course achievement in upper-level algebra courses.

Description: 39–item paper-pencil multiple-choice test used for evaluating student proficiency in upper-level algebra. The test, which may be administered as a survey test or as an end-of-course test, is designed to assess 13 objectives. Each objective is tested by three questions. Normative and criterion-referenced data are available. One in a series of 13 NPSS tests. Examiner required. Suitable for group use.

Timed: 40 minutes

Scoring: Self-scored; hand key

Cost: Contact publisher for price and availability

Publisher: The Riverside Publishing Company

NATIONAL PROFICIENCY SURVEY SERIES (NPSS): GEOMETRY
Dale P. Scannell

Adolescent—Ages 12–18
Grades 8–12

Purpose: Measures end-of-course achievement in geometry courses.

Description: 39–item paper-pencil test used for evaluating student proficiency in geometry. The test, which may be administered as a survey test or as an end-of-course test, is designed to assess 13 objectives. Each objective is tested by three questions. Normative and criterion-referenced data are available. One in a series of 13 NPSS tests. Examiner required. Suitable for group use.

Timed: 40 minutes

Scoring: Self-scored; hand key

Cost: Contact publisher for price and availability

Publisher: The Riverside Publishing Company

NM CONSUMER MATHEMATICS TEST (NMCMT)
S. P. Klein

Adolescent
Grades 9–12

Purpose: Measures ability to solve consumer problems using basic arithmetic operations. Used for program evaluation and needs assessment.

Description: 20–item paper-pencil multiple-choice test measuring ability to solve problems involving measures and prices, addition, subtraction, multiplication, and division in a consumer context. The test booklets are reusable, and a lay-over stencil is used for scoring. Reliability and norms have been determined from samples of ninth- and twelfth-grade secondary students. Examiner required. Suitable for group use.

Timed: 20 minutes

Scoring: Hand key

Cost: Specimen set $6.00; 35 tests $12.00; 35 answer sheets $4.00; scoring stencil $3.00; manual $3.00

Publisher: Monitor

ORLEANS-HANNA ALGEBRA PROGNOSIS TEST (REVISED)
Refer to page 479.

STRUCTURE OF INTELLECT LEARNING ABILITIES TEST (SOI-LA): ARITHMETIC AND MATH SPLIT FORM (FORM M)
Mary Meeker and Robert Meeker

Adolescent, adult
Grades 7 and above

Purpose: Assesses the arithmetic and mathematics skills of intermediate, high-school, and college students.

Description: Multiple-item paper-pencil test assessing potential in arithmetic and mathematics. Discipline-focused test items are selected from the SOI-LA Basic Test. The Basic Test manual is required for administration. Materials are available to train any abilities not developed. See entry for Structure of Intellect (SOI) related tests. Examiner required. Suitable for group use.

Timed: 1 hour

Scoring: Hand key

Cost: Manual $35.00; 5 test forms $13.50; scoring keys $30.00

Publisher: Western Psychological Services

TEST OF COGNITIVE STYLE IN MATHEMATICS (TCSM)
John B. Bath, Stephen J. Chinn, and Dwight E. Knox

Ages 7–adult

Purpose: Identifies the cognitive-perceptual style of an individual's mathematical problem-solving skills.

Description: Multiple-item paper-pencil test assessing how an individual solves mathematical problems in four areas:

mental computation, arithmetic, geometry/visual, and algebra. The results are used to place the individual's problem-solving style on a continuum between two extremes: Gestalt thinker and stimulus bound. Examiner required. Not suitable for group use.

Timed: 20 minutes

Scoring: Examiner evaluated

Cost: Complete kit (manual, test questions, 50 profile record forms, 50 worksheets, 50 observation folders) $54.00

Publisher: Slosson Educational Publications, Inc.

TEST OF EARLY MATHEMATICS ABILITY–2 (TEMA–2)
Herbert P. Ginsburg and Arthur J. Baroody

Child—Ages 3–8

Purpose: Measures the mathematics performance of children. Diagnoses individual strengths and weaknesses. Used with mentally retarded and learning disabled children to measure progress, evaluate programs, screen for readiness, identify giftedness, guide instruction and remediation, and identify problems.

Description: 50–item oral-response or paper-pencil test assessing mathematical abilities in two domains: informal mathematics (concepts of relative magnitude, counting, and calculation) and formal mathematics (knowledge of convention number facts, calculation, and base-ten concepts). A picture card is used to present test items. Raw scores may be converted to standard scores, percentiles, and age equivalences. Criterion-referenced interpretation leads directly to instructional objectives. The examiner must be competent in the administration of educational, psychological, and language tests. Examiner required. Not suitable for group use.

Untimed: Varies

Scoring: Examiner evaluated

Cost: Complete kit (manual, 50 record forms, 26 picture cards) $54.00

Publisher: PRO-ED

TEST OF MATHEMATICAL ABILITIES (TOMA)
Virginia L. Brown and Elizabeth McEntire

Child, adolescent
Grades 3–12

Purpose: Assesses the mathematical attitudes and aptitudes of students. Used to plan and assess instructional programs in mathematics, identify gifted and learning disabled students, determine strengths and weaknesses, document progress, and conduct research.

Description: Five paper-pencil subtests assessing knowledge, mastery, and attitudes in two major skill areas: story problems (17 items) and computation (25 items). In addition to measuring the student's abilities, the following broad diagnostic areas are assessed: expressed attitudes toward mathematics (15 items), understanding of vocabulary as applied to mathematics (20 items), the functional use of mathematics as applied to our general culture, and the relationship between a student's attitudes and abilities and those of his peers. Normative information related to age and IQ, as well as graded mastery expectations for the "400" basic number facts, is provided for students ages 8–17. Scores differentiate diagnostically between students who have problems in mathematics and those who do not. Examiners must be competent in the administration of educational, psychological, and language tests. Examiner required. Suitable for group use.

Untimed: Varies

Scoring: Examiner evaluated

Cost: Complete kit (examiner's manual, 25 profile sheets, 25 student worksheets) $53.00

Publisher: PRO-ED

Reading: Elementary

AH1 X AND Y GROUP TESTS OF FORMAL REASONING
Refer to page 585.

ANALYTICAL READING INVENTORY, 2ND EDITION
Mary Lynn Woods and Alden J. Moe

Child, adolescent
Grades 1–9

Purpose: Analyzes reading skills to help classroom teachers and reading specialists make remediation decisions.

Description: 170 items of graded word lists and reading passages measuring strengths and weaknesses in word attack and comprehension skills, level of reading achievement, and potential for reading growth. Examiner required. Not suitable for group use.

Untimed: Varies

Scoring: Examiner evaluated

Cost: Complete package (student record summary sheets, qualitative analysis summary sheets, graded word lists, graded reading passages) $9.95

Publisher: Charles E. Merrill Publishing Company

Information and availability unconfirmed; last verified in 1987.

ASSESSING READING DIFFICULTIES: A DIAGNOSTIC AND REMEDIAL APPROACH, 2ND EDITION
Refer to page 675.

BASIC VISUAL-MOTOR ASSOCIATION TEST
Refer to page 610.

BOTEL READING INVENTORY
Morten Botel

Child

Purpose: Measures elementary school students' ability to read. Used for academic placement and measuring student progress throughout the school year.

Description: Four paper-pencil and oral-response tests assessing skills in three areas crucial to success in elementary reading and language arts: decoding, word recognition (oral reading ability), and word opposites (reading comprehension).

The Decoding Test measures decoding competency at seven levels ranging from the awareness of sounds and letter correspondences to decoding multisyllabic nonsense words. The seven levels are covered by 12 subtests of 10 items each. All responses are scored according to the following code: correct word, mispronunciation, substitution, or no response. As on all of the tests, the student's highest instructional level is considered to be the first level at which he falls below 80% correct answers.

The Spelling Test consists of five graded lists of 20 words each. The words are dictated, and the students are asked to spell them.

The Word Recognition Test consists of eight 20-word samples, spanning eight graduated reading levels from preprimer through fourth grade. As the student reads the words, responses are graded as correct word, mispronunciation, substitution, or no response.

The Word Opposites Test is a group test consisting of 10 scaled 10-word subtests that progress from first-reader level through senior high school. For each test item, the student is asked to select from four words the one that means the opposite. The Word Opposites Test may be administered both as a reading test and as a listening test. As a reading test, it indicates the student's current reading performance; as a listening test, it indicates the student's reading potential.

The reading placement tests yield three levels of reading competency: free reading level, instructional level, and frustration level. The Word Recognition and Word Opposites Tests are available in two forms, A and B, for pre- and posttesting. The administration manual includes information on administering, scoring, and interpreting the test, as well as technical data. Examiner required. Suitable for group use.

Untimed: Varies

Scoring: Examiner evaluated

Cost: Manual $12.45; 35 Decoding Tests $9.33; 35 Word Recognition Tests (A or B) $10.89 each; 35 Word Opposites Tests (A or B) $10.89

Publisher: Modern Curriculum Press, Inc.

BURT WORD READING TEST— NEW ZEALAND REVISION
Alison Gilmore, Cedric Croft, and Neil Reid

Child—Ages 5 and older

Purpose: Measures word reading skills of children.

Description: 110-item test of word reading skills in which the child reads from a test card containing 110 words printed in decreasing type size and graded in approximate order of difficulty. Used in conjunction with other information about the child, the test should allow the teacher to estimate the child's reading achievement and decide on appropriate teaching and reading materials, instructional groupings, and so forth. Normative data for 6–13-year-olds are presented in the form of equivalent age bands. Examiner required. Not suitable for group use. NEW ZEALAND PUBLISHER

Untimed: 5 minutes

Scoring: Examiner evaluated

Cost: Contact publisher

Publisher: New Zealand Council for Educational Research

CALIFORNIA DIAGNOSTIC READING TEST (CDRT)
CTB staff, Chapter I teachers

Grades 2–10

Purpose: Diagnoses reading strengths and needs of students ranking in the lower percentiles.

Description: Multiple-item criterion- and norm-referenced paper-pencil multiple-choice test available on six levels, A-F. Each level covers word analysis (except Level F), vocabulary, comprehension, and reading applications (Levels D, E, F). Consumable test books are available for

Levels A-C and reusable test books and answer sheets for Levels D-F. The publisher provides a scoring service, and software for scoring is available for school use. Examiner required. Suitable for group use.

Untimed: Not available

Scoring: Computer scored; hand key; may be machine scored

Cost: Contact publisher

Publisher: CTB/Macmillan/McGraw-Hill

CLYMER-BARRETT READINESS TEST
Refer to page 537.

COMPUTER CROSSROADS
*Stuart Paltrowitz and
Donna Paltrowitz*

Child

Purpose: Diagnoses weaknesses and strengths in reading comprehension skills of children with interest levels of Grades 2-5 and reading levels of Grades 1.8-2.8. Used in school settings.

Description: Computer-administered test of reading comprehension skills, including finding the main idea, sequencing, noting details, predicting outcomes, and inferring. The program allows students to create a story through which they journey with "computer pets," which the students also create. The program, which operates on Apple IIe computer systems, provides practice toward remediation and diagnostic information. Examiner required. Not suitable for group use.

Untimed: Varies

Scoring: Computer scored

Cost: Complete kit (3 diskettes, 3 back ups, management, documentation, and reproducible activity masters) $99.95

Publisher: Educational Activities, Inc.

Information and availability unconfirmed; last verified in 1988.

CONCISE WORD READING TESTS
R. J. Andrews

Child—Ages 7-12

Purpose: Measures the word reading skills of primary and lower secondary-school students. Used for class or school surveys and as a basis for grouping children for reading instruction.

Description: Four 20-item oral-response tests measuring the word recognition and word attack skills of children. Each test is suitable for use with more than one age level. Age norms and standardized scores are provided for Australian students. Examiner required. Suitable for group use.
AUSTRALIAN PUBLISHER

Untimed: Varies

Scoring: Examiner evaluated

Cost: Basic kit (test materials for 4 forms, 50 record forms with instructions and norms) $10.50

Publisher: Teaching and Testing Resources

Information and availability unconfirmed; last verified in 1987.

THE DELAWARE COUNTY SILENT READING TESTS: LEVEL 12
Delaware County Reading Council

Child
Grade 1

Purpose: Measures first-graders' ability to read and write. Used as a pretest to diagnose reading strengths and weaknesses and as a posttest of teaching effectiveness.

Description: 20-item paper-pencil multiple-choice and short-answer test covering four major areas: interpretation of ideas, organization of ideas, vocabulary, and structural analysis of words. The examiner distributes the story and test booklets and writes the following words on a chalkboard: "paragraph," "sentences," "word," "underline," "write," "letter," and "number." These words are not usually found in typical second-grade reading materials. The examiner guides the pupils in pronouncing the words and tells them they may ask for help in figuring out which words correspond to the appropriate constructions in the story. Examiner required. Suitable for group use.

Untimed: 45–50 minutes

Scoring: Hand key

Cost: Pupil test $0.10; story booklet $0.15; teacher's guide included with each order of 25; additional teacher guides and answer keys $0.10 each; specimen set $3.50

Publisher: Delaware County Reading Council

THE DELAWARE COUNTY SILENT READING TESTS: LEVEL 21 AND LEVEL 22
Delaware County Reading Council

Child
Grade 2

Purpose: Measures second-graders' ability to read and write. Used as a pretest to diagnose reading strengths and weaknesses and as a posttest of teaching effectiveness.

Description: 20–item paper-pencil multiple-choice and short-answer test covering four major areas: interpretation of ideas, organization of ideas, vocabulary, and structural analysis of words. The examiner distributes the story and test booklets and writes the following words on a chalkboard: "paragraph," "sentence," "question," "underline," "title," and "root." These words usually are not found in typical second-grade reading materials. The examiner guides the pupils in pronouncing the words and tells them they may ask for help in figuring out which words correspond to the appropriate constructions in the story. Examiner required. Suitable for group use.

Untimed: 45–50 minutes

Scoring: Hand key

Cost: Pupil test $0.10; story booklet $0.15; teacher's guide included with each order of 25; additional teacher's guides and answer keys $0.10 each; specimen set $3.50

Publisher: Delaware County Reading Council

THE DELAWARE COUNTY SILENT READING TESTS: LEVEL 31 AND LEVEL 32
Delaware County Reading Council

Child
Grade 3

Purpose: Measures third-graders' ability to read and write. Used as a pretest to diagnose reading strengths and weaknesses and as a posttest of teaching effectiveness.

Description: 20–item paper-pencil multiple-choice and short-answer test covering four major areas: interpretation of ideas, organization of ideas, vocabulary, and structural analysis of words. The examiner distributes the story and test booklets and writes the following words on a chalkboard: "sentences," "opposite," "paragraph," "syllable," "root," and "blank spaces." These words are not usually found in typical third-grade reading materials. The examiner guides the pupils in pronouncing the words and tells them they may ask for help in figuring out which words correspond to the appropriate constructions in the story. Examiner required. Suitable for group use.

Untimed: 45–50 minutes

Scoring: Hand key

Cost: Pupil test $0.10; story booklet $0.15; teacher's guide included with each order of 25; additional teacher guides and answer keys $0.10 each; specimen set $3.50

Publisher: Delaware County Reading Council

THE DELAWARE COUNTY SILENT READING TESTS: LEVELS 4–8
Delaware County Reading Council

Child, adolescent
Grades 4–8

Purpose: Measures intermediate-grade students' reading achievement and ability to express ideas in writing. Used to evaluate progress and for classroom placement and counseling.

Description: 20–item paper-pencil multiple-choice and short-answer test with separate forms for Grades 4–8. The student answers questions from a story booklet covering four areas: interpretation of ideas (8 items), organization of ideas (2 items), vocabulary (7 items), and structural analysis of words (3 items). Scores are ranked as excellent, good, average, poor, or very poor. Examiner required. Suitable for group use.

Untimed: 45–50 minutes

Scoring: Hand key

Cost: Pupil test $0.10; story booklet $0.15; teacher's guide included with each order of 25; additional teacher guides and answer keys $0.10 each; specimen set $3.50

Publisher: Delaware County Reading Council

DIAGNOSTIC READING SCALES, REVISED (DRS)
George D. Spache

Child

Purpose: Identifies a student's reading strengths and weaknesses. Used by educators to determine placement and to prescribe instruction.

Description: Multiple-item reading skills test consisting of a series of graduated scales containing 3 word-recognition lists, 22 reading selections, and 12 phonics and word analysis tests. The word-recognition list yields a tentative performance level and is used to determine the level at which the student begins the reading selections. The reading selections are used to establish three reading levels for the student: an instructional level, measuring oral reading and comprehension; an independent level, measuring silent reading and comprehension; and a potential level, measuring auditory comprehension. The word analysis and phonics tests measure the following skills: recognition of initial and final consonants, consonant digraphs and blends, short and long vowel sounds, vowels with *r*, vowel diphthongs and digraphs, common syllables and phonograms, initial consonants recognized auditorily; auditory discrimination of minimal word pairs; initial consonant

substitution; and blending of word parts. Examiner required. Not suitable for group use.

Timed: 1 hour

Scoring: Examiner evaluated

Cost: Specimen set, 1981 edition (test book, record book, manual, test reviewer's guide) $24.75

Publisher: CTB/Macmillan/McGraw-Hill

DOREN DIAGNOSTIC READING TEST OF WORD RECOGNITION SKILLS
Margaret Doren

Child
Grades K–4

Purpose: Assesses why a child has difficulty reading. Used with groups to identify the level from which reading instruction should proceed.

Description: 12–category paper-pencil measure of word recognition skills in the following areas: letter recognition, beginning sounds, whole word recognition, words within words, speech consonants, ending sounds, blending, rhyming, vowels, discriminate guessing, spelling, and sight words. The examiner reads the directions printed in the manual and encourages the students to follow the same directions in their test booklets. Sample questions are provided at the beginning of each subtest. Scores are graphed on an Individual Skill Profile for each student, and overall class performance is recorded on the Class Composite Record. The test is designed to provide, in a group situation, the detailed diagnosis that otherwise could be obtained only through individual testing. Examiner required. Suitable for group use.

Untimed: 1–3 hours

Scoring: Hand key; examiner evaluated

Cost: Manual $4.00; 25 test booklets $17.50; key $9.50

Publisher: American Guidance Service

DURRELL ANALYSIS OF READING DIFFICULTY: THIRD EDITION
Donald D. Durrell and Jane H. Catterson

Child
Grades 1–6

Purpose: Assesses reading behavior. Used for diagnosis, measurement of pre-reading skills, and planning remedial programs.

Description: Multiple-item series of tests and situations measuring 10 reading abilities: oral reading, silent reading, listening comprehension, listening vocabulary, word recognition/word analysis, spelling, auditory analysis of words and word elements, pronunciation of word elements, visual memory of words, and prereading phonics abilities. Supplementary paragraphs for oral and silent reading are provided for supplementary testing or retesting. Materials include a spiral-bound booklet containing items to be read and a tachistoscope with accompanying test card. Examiner required. Not suitable for group use.

Untimed: 30–45 minutes

Scoring: Examiner evaluated

Cost: Examiner's kit (5 record booklets, tachistoscope, reading booklet, manual) $45.00; manual $9.00

Publisher: The Psychological Corporation

Information and availability unconfirmed; last verified in 1988.

EARLY DETECTION OF READING DIFFICULTIES
M.M. Clay

Child
Years 1 and 2

Purpose: Assesses early reading and writing skills. Used for systematic recording of reading and writing achievements.

Description: Multiple-item test for observing the reading and writing behaviors of children in Years 1 and 2. Materials include a set of two test booklets, *Sands and Stones*, and a guide that presents the

theoretical background, administration details, and scoring interpretation of the tests. Examiner required. Not suitable for group use.

NEW ZEALAND PUBLISHER

Untimed: 30 minutes

Scoring: Hand key

Cost: $17.95 (New Zealand currency)

Publisher: Octopus Publishing Group Limited; distributed in U.S.A. by Heinemann Educational Books, Inc.

EFFECTIVE READING TESTS
Denis Vincent and Michael de la Mare with Helen Arnold

Child—Ages 7–12

Purpose: Screens for and monitors reading ability and special needs when used as a progress test. Diagnoses skill strengths and weaknesses and assists in formulating plans for remedial teaching when used as a skills test.

Description: Multiple-item paper-pencil multiple-choice test measuring reading comprehension on four levels. At each level, the test may be administered as a progress test or a skills test. As a progress test, reading comprehension is measured within a "real reading" context. When used as a skills test, reading comprehension is measured, but the results allow analysis of the following skills: using relationships within a text (following the thread of sentences and using context cues); acting upon the text (interpreting or reorganizing the text); employing reading strategies appropriate to the text and purpose (skimming and scanning); making an effective, imaginative, or personal response to reading; critical awareness and evaluation (distinguishing between fact and fiction); and location and selection (using alphabetical order and reference skills). The student is given a reader and either the progress test or the skills test and answers the test questions using the reader. The test ends when the student has completed all the questions or the questions become too difficult. The skills tests on all four levels begin with a timed skimming and scanning series of

questions. Examiner required. Suitable for group use.
BRITISH PUBLISHER

Untimed: Progress tests 45 minutes; skills tests 1 hour

Scoring: Progress tests, hand key; skills tests, examiner evaluated

Cost: Readers (six per level) £8.99; progress tests (25 per level) £5.50; skills tests (12 per level) £5.25; teacher's guide £10.99

Publisher: Macmillan Education

THE FLORIDA KINDERGARTEN SCREENING BATTERY
Paul Satz and Jack M. Fletcher

Child
Kindergarten

Purpose: Identifies kindergartners at high risk for later reading difficulties. Permits identification of learning problems prior to the beginning of reading instruction.

Description: Multiple-item battery of five tests screening children for potential reading problems. The battery includes the Peabody Picture Vocabulary Test-Revised, Beery Developmental Test of Visual-Motor Integration, Recognition-Discrimination Test, Finger Localization Test, and Alphabet Recitation. One total weighted score is yielded. The battery may be administered by supervised paraprofessionals. Examiner required. Not suitable for group use.

Untimed: 20 minutes

Scoring: Examiner evaluated

Cost: Expanded kit (all five tests, 50 record forms, manual) $135.00; basic kit (manual, 50 record forms, Recognition-Discrimination Test, Finger Localization Test, Alphabet Recitation) $55.00

Publisher: Psychological Assessment Resources, Inc.

FLOWERS-COSTELLO TESTS OF CENTRAL AUDITORY ABILITY
Refer to page 677.

GAP READING TEST

Child—Ages 7–12

Purpose: Assesses the reading comprehension of students. Used by teachers for planning instruction and checking progress.

Description: 45–item paper-pencil test in two alternate forms (R and B) consisting of several increasingly difficult paragraphs of information. The test uses a modified cloze technique in which students provide the missing words. Teachers can use the test for placement, information on a child's reading and spelling techniques, and retesting. Examiner required. Suitable for group use.
AUSTRALIAN PUBLISHER

Timed: 15 minutes

Scoring: Examiner evaluated

Cost: Complete kit (48 copies of Test R, 48 copies of Test B, manual) $24.95

Publisher: Heinemann Publishers Australia Pty Limited

GATES-MCKILLOP-HOROWITZ READING DIAGNOSTIC TESTS
Arthur I. Gates, Anne S. McKillop, and Elizabeth C. Horowitz

Child
Grades 1–6

Purpose: Evaluates children's oral reading, spelling, and writing skills, and diagnoses reading difficulties of older students. Used for class grouping and curriculum planning.

Description: 11–part verbal paper-pencil test measuring oral reading, isolated word recognition, knowledge of word parts, recognizing and blending common word parts, reading words, giving letter sounds, naming letters, identifying vowel sounds, auditory blending and discrimination, and writing through an informal sample. Not all parts need be given to every student. Materials include a test materials booklet containing a tachistoscope (for word flash tests), a pupil record book, and a manual. Examiner required. Not suitable for group use.

Untimed: 1 hour

Scoring: Examiner evaluated

Cost: Test materials (contains tachistoscope) $2.50; 30 pupil record booklets $7.50; manual of directions $1.00; specimen set (test materials, pupil record booklet, manual of directions) $3.50

Publisher: Teachers College Press

GILLINGHAM-CHILDS PHONICS PROFICIENCY SCALES: SERIES I, BASIC READING AND SPELLING; SERIES II, ADVANCED READING
Sally B. Childs and
Ralph de S. Childs

Child
Grades 1-8

Purpose: Evaluates student progress in the mastery of phonic and beginning reading skills to provide teachers with an index of remedial progress.

Description: Multiple-item primarily verbal examination in two series: Basic Reading and Spelling and Advanced Reading. Series I contains 12 scales dealing with basic reading and spelling skills: letter-sound relationships; three-letter words; consonant digraphs and blends; one-syllable words ending with *f*, *l*, or *s*; silent *e* words; syllabication rules; sight words; and suffix rules. The teacher uses the reading booklet for dictation of the spelling words because the reading and spelling words are the same. Series II contains 16 scales measuring advanced reading skills: alternating phonograms; hard and soft sounds of *c* and *g*; long vowel sounds; nonsense words; vowel diphthongs and digraphs; words irregular for reading; and more advanced syllabication rules. There is no spelling test in Series II. The teacher should be familiar with the pronunciation of nonsense words. The original version of the scales was developed by Anna Gillingham. The scales have been strengthened in their revised version and should be useful to anyone teaching phonics. Examiner required. Not suitable for group use.

Untimed: 30 minutes-1 hour

Scoring: Examiner evaluated

Cost: Series I scales book $6.50; reading record booklet $3.25; spelling record booklet $4.00; directions for use $0.50; Series II scales book $6.50; record booklet $2.50; directions for use $0.50

Publisher: Educators Publishing Service, Inc.

GILMORE ORAL READING TEST
John V. Gilmore and
Eunice C. Gilmore

Child
Grades 1-8

Purpose: Assesses the oral reading abilities of students. Used for program planning and academic placement.

Description: Oral-reading test measuring three aspects of oral reading ability: accuracy, comprehension, and rate. The spiral-bound booklet of reading paragraphs and the manual of directions are needed to administer the test. A separate record blank is needed for each child tested. A five-level classification of accuracy, rate, and comprehension is provided, as well as stanines and grade-equivalents for accuracy and comprehension scores. The test is available in two alternate and equivalent forms, C and D. A special edition is available for the visually handicapped. Examiner required. Not suitable for group use.

Untimed: 15-20 minutes

Scoring: Examiner evaluated

Cost: Examination kit (manual, record blank) $11.00; booklet of reading paragraphs $18.00; 35 record blanks (Form C or D) $30.00; manual $10.00

Publisher: The Psychological Corporation

Information and availability unconfirmed; last verified in 1988.

GROUP DIAGNOSTIC READING APTITUDE AND ACHIEVEMENT TESTS—INTERMEDIATE FORM
Marion Monroe and
Eva Edity Sherman

Child
Grades 3-9

Purpose: Measures reading aptitude and achievement. Diagnoses specific skill deficits that may impair reading performance.

Description: 391-item paper-pencil battery consisting of eight achievement tests (paragraph meaning, speed of reading, vowels, consonants, reversals, additions and omissions, arithmetic, and spelling) and seven aptitude tests (visual letter memory, visual form memory, auditory letter memory, auditory orientation and discrimination, copying text, cross-out letters, and vocabulary).

The Paragraph Reading Test (28 items; 7 minutes) requires students to read a question, read a paragraph containing the answer to the question, and select the appropriate one-word or short-phrase answer from five given choices.

The Speed of Reading Test (45 items; 1½ minutes) requires students to read through a one-page text and indicate comprehension by performing simple game-like tasks, such as "put a dot in this circle" or "cross out the three."

The vowels, consonants, reversals, and additions and omissions tests (24 items each; 2 minutes each) measure word discrimination skills by presenting three sentences for each test item, one of which is correct with the other two containing errors appropriate to the test (vowel substitution, consonant substitution, reversals, or additions or omissions). Students underline the correct sentence.

The Arithmetic Computation Test (30 items; 5 minutes) measures the ability to add, subtract, multiply, and divide with whole numbers, fractions, and decimals.

The Spelling Test (40 minutes; untimed) consists of sentences with blanks provided for missing words. The teacher reads the sentence with the missing word, and the students fill in the blank with the word pronounced by the teacher.

In the Visual Letter Memory Test (18 items), the teacher shows the students a card on which a nonsense word is printed. Each card is flashed for 5 seconds, and students are asked to write as much of the nonsense word from each card as they can remember.

In the Visual Form Memory Test (4 items), the teacher flashes cards with simple line-drawing designs for 10 seconds each and then asks the students to draw as much of each card as they can remember.

The Auditory Letter Memory Test (16 items) is similar to the visual test, except the teacher spells aloud the letters of some nonsense words for the students to copy down.

The Auditory Discrimination and Orientation Test (25 items) requires students to mark a grid of Xs in response to aural stimuli dictated by the teacher.

The Copying Text Test (1 item; 1½ minutes) measures fine-motor skills by requiring the students to copy a short story as quickly and plainly as they can.

In the Crossing-Out Letters Test (60 items; 1 minute), a text of nonsense words is provided in which every other word contains one letter *a*. Students are directed to cross out every *a* they can find.

The Vocabulary Test (28 items; untimed) provides four pairs of words for each test item. Only one of the pairs of words makes sense; the other three pairs are abstract combinations or obvious malapropisms. The teacher reads each pair aloud, and students are directed to underline the pair that makes the best sense to them.

The achievement tests are scored in terms of grade equivalents. The aptitude tests are scored in terms of percentiles by age. The front sheet of the 14–page test booklet provides forms for developing educational and diagnostic profiles and deriving a mental age for each student tested. Examiner required. Suitable for group use.

Timed: 9 timed tests 24 minutes

Untimed: 6 untimed tests varies

Scoring: Examiner evaluated

Cost: Test booklets each $0.25; 22 visual test cards $5.00; set of norms $1.00; directions to the examiner included free of charge

Publisher: C.H. Nevins Printing Company

GROUP READING ASSESSMENT
F.A. Spooncer

Child—Ages 8-9

Purpose: Measures group achievement of reading ability in the first two years of junior school (ages 8–9). Suitable for less able older juniors and the most backward entrants to secondary schools. Assesses performance of teaching programs at the classroom, school, or district level.

Description: Multiple-item paper-pencil test measuring achievement of reading skills that are taught in the first two years of junior school. Norms, derived from testing of over 3,000 children, are provided to cover reading ages 6.3–11.7. A table is provided for conversion of raw scores to standardized scores for children ages 8–9. Examiner required. Suitable for group use. BRITISH PUBLISHER

Untimed: 30 minutes

Scoring: Examiner evaluated

Cost: Specimen set £2.75; 20 tests £3.25; manual £2.50

Publisher: Hodder & Stoughton

GROUP READING TEST: SECOND EDITION
Dennis Young

Child—Ages 7–12.10

Purpose: Assesses children's reading achievement. Identifies children reading significantly above or below their age level.

Description: Multiple-item paper-pencil test of reading achievement available in two parallel forms, A and B, which remain unchanged from the original version. The two forms, along with template scoring methods, facilitate use of the test by one teacher with a full class. The second edition of the manual provides new norms for infants (ages 6.5–7.10), first-year juniors (7.10–8.10), and older, less able pupils up to age 12.10, increasing the accuracy of comparison between children of different ages. Examiner required. Suitable for group use. BRITISH PUBLISHER

Untimed: Not available

Scoring: Hand key

Cost: Specimen set £2.50; 20 tests (specify form) £1.85; template (specify form) £2.00 plus VAT; manual £1.95

Publisher: Hodder & Stoughton

HARRISON-STROUD READING READINESS PROFILE
M. Lucille Harrison and James B. Stroud

Child
Grades K–1

Purpose: Measures specific abilities and skills that children use in learning to read. Identifies areas in which children may need help before or during initial reading instruction.

Description: Five paper-pencil multiple-choice group tests assessing the following prereading skills: symbols, visual discriminations, context, auditory discriminations, and context and auditory clues. An optional sixth test, which is individually administered, identifies in approximately three minutes how well a student knows the names of the capital and lower-case letters. Raw scores are plotted on a chart that determines the percentile rank of each score and identifies the strengths and weaknesses of each student. Examiner required. Suitable for group (12–15 students) use.

Untimed: 80 minutes

Scoring: Examiner evaluated

Cost: Test kit (35 consumable test booklets, manual, class record sheet, letter card, scoring mask) $39.54

Publisher: The Riverside Publishing Company

INDIVIDUALIZED CRITERION REFERENCED TESTING (ICRT)
Refer to page 462.

INDIVIDUALIZED CRITERION REFERENCED TESTING— READING (ICRT—READING)
Dale E. Strotman and Margaret T. Steen

Child, adolescent
Grades K–8

Purpose: Assesses students' reading abilities. Provides information on skills mastered, skills requiring review, and

---

skills to learn. Also used in adult basic education.

Description: Multiple-item paper-pencil power test measuring phonetic analysis, structural analysis, word function, and comprehension. The test is based on a developmental continuum of 304 learning objectives for Grades K–8. Objectives are matched with current curricula and the content of newer textbooks. The results indicate resources for teaching and reinforcing skills, list names of students who need instruction in each skill, and aid in grouping students according to their specific learning needs. Materials provide for interim testing and recording of progress. The program evaluation report provides criterion-referenced and norm-referenced information for each class, student, building, and district. The report includes scale scores, grade equivalents, percentiles, and NCEs. The test is used by administrators and teachers in city-wide instructional management systems, migrant and special education programs, and ECIA-Chapter projects. Examiner required. Suitable for group use.

Untimed: Varies

Scoring: Computer scored

Cost: Computer scoring $1.75 per student; 10 booklets (specify level) $24.00

Publisher: Educational Development Corporation

Information and availability unconfirmed; last verified in 1988.

THE INFANT READING TESTS
Refer to page 549.

INFORMAL READING COMPREHENSION PLACEMENT TEST
Eunice Insel and Ann Edson

Child
Grades 1–8

Purpose: Measures reading comprehension. Determines students' instructional placement level.

Description: 68–item computer-administered test assessing word comprehension and passage comprehension. The 60–item word comprehension test uses a word

analogy format to measure students' knowledge of word meanings and thinking skills. The passage comprehension test consists of a series of eight graded selections and questions ranging in difficulty from the primary level through eighth grade. The level of difficulty for each of these selections was determined by using the Spache, Fry, and Dale-Chall readability formulas. Students are placed in an instructional reading range of first through eighth grade in word comprehension and passage comprehension. The test is totally administered, scored, and managed by the microcomputer. A cassette or diskette is available for the Apple II+ and IIe and TRS Models III and IV microcomputers. All diskette programs include backups. Examiner required. Not suitable for group use.

Untimed: Varies

Scoring: Computer scored

Cost: Cassette (specify model) $44.95; 1 diskette (specify model) $49.95

Publisher: Educational Activities, Inc.

JANSKY DIAGNOSTIC BATTERY
Jeannette J. Jansky

Child
Kindergarten

Purpose: Measures the reading readiness of kindergartners. Used for educational planning.

Description: Multiple-item battery of 15 verbal paper-pencil tests measuring reading readiness abilities. The battery is designed for kindergartners identified by the Jansky Screening Index as being at risk for not learning to read. The factors assessed are expressive and receptive language, verbal pattern matching, verbal memory, and graphomotor status. Instructions for administering and scoring are presented in Jansky and Hirsch's *Preventing Reading Failure*, published by Harper and Row. Examiner required. Not suitable for group use.

Untimed: 30 minutes

Scoring: Hand key; examiner evaluated

Cost: Complete kit (35 profile forms, 2 cartoon sequences, 35 nonsense word-matching forms, speech sound discrimination test, pattern tapper, word recognition and spelling cards) $30.00
Publisher: Jeannette J. Jansky

JANSKY SCREENING INDEX
Jeannette J. Jansky

Child
Kindergarten

Purpose: Identifies kindergartners who may show signs of failing to read by the time they finish second grade. Used to screen those in need of special educational help.

Description: 5 multiple-item paper-pencil and oral-language tests of basic readiness skills measuring ability in design copying, picture naming, lettering, naming, word matching, and sentence repetition. The Screening Index evolved after research on a preliminary longer battery, the Predictive Index by de Hirsch, Jansky, and Langford. Instructions for administering and scoring are included in *Preventing Reading Failure* by Jansky and de Hirsch, Harper and Row, 1972. Examiner required. Suitable for group use.
Untimed: 15–20 minutes
Scoring: Hand key; examiner evaluated
Cost: Complete kit $25.00
Publisher: Jeannette J. Jansky

LINGUISTIC AWARENESS IN READING READINESS
John Downing, Douglas Ayers, and Brian Schaefer

Child—Ages 4 and older

Purpose: Measures understanding of vocabulary and concepts related to reading and writing. Used for determining reading readiness of children. Also used with older children with reading difficulties.

Description: 75–item paper-pencil test in three parts assessing children's understanding of linguistic concepts. The test, available in two parallel forms, measures how well children recognize activities involved in reading and writing (22

items), their understanding of the uses of reading and writing (23 items), and their understanding of words related to literacy such as "word," "letter," and "sentence" (30 items). Examiner required. Suitable for group use.
BRITISH PUBLISHER
Untimed: 15–20 minutes per part
Scoring: Hand key
Cost: Contact publisher
Publisher: NFER-NELSON Publishing Company Ltd.

LONDON READING TEST (LRT)

Child—Ages 10.07–12.04

Purpose: Assesses reading level and pattern of abilities. Used to identify children needing remedial teaching.

Description: Multiple-item paper-pencil measure of reading abilities. The two alternate forms, A and B, contain three reading passages. Comprehension of the first two passages is tested using the cloze technique, and the third passage asks questions that tap a wide range of comprehension skills. Scores at both an independent and instructional level are obtained. Examiner required. Suitable for group use.
BRITISH PUBLISHER
Untimed: 1 hour
Scoring: Examiner evaluated
Cost: Contact publisher
Publisher: NFER-NELSON Publishing Company Ltd.

THE MACMILLAN DIAGNOSTIC READING PACK
Ted Ames

Child, adolescent—
Reading Ages 5–8

Purpose: Diagnoses children's reading problems. Suggests appropriate remedial programs. Used for in-service teacher training programs.

Description: 16 multiple-item paper-pencil and oral-response test cards presenting tests on specific reading skills and subskills, such as letter-matching and consonant blending. Checklists, for recording student performance on the tests and providing a detailed picture of individual ability, are available for four stages in the development of reading skills: reading ages 5–6, 6–7, 7–8, and 8–9. Together, the test cards and checklists provide a means of observing and testing reading skills from beginning reading to fluency. A teacher's manual provides clear instructions for testing and diagnosis and prescribes source references for further remedial procedures. Examiner required. Suitable for group use. BRITISH PUBLISHER

Untimed: Varies

Scoring: Examiner evaluated

Cost: Test kit (manual, 16 test cards, 10 copies each of 4 checklists) £21.50

Publisher: Macmillan Education

MACMILLAN GRADED WORD READING TEST
The Macmillan Test Unit

Child—Ages 6–14

Purpose: Measures the oral reading abilities of students. Also used for remedial work with older children.

Description: Two parallel tests of 50 words each on one card used by teachers for evaluating oral reading abilities. The tests are graded in difficulty, grouped in five levels, and accompanied by record sheets for marking and analyzing errors. Standardized scores and alternative reading ages are provided. Examiner required. Not suitable for group use. BRITISH PUBLISHER

Untimed: 5 minutes

Scoring: Examiner evaluated

Cost: Complete kit (word card, teacher's manual, 25 record sheets) £17.95

Publisher: Macmillan Education

MACMILLAN GROUP READING TEST
The Macmillan Test Unit

Child—Ages 7–11

Purpose: Assesses word recognition and reading comprehension of children.

Description: 48-item paper-pencil graded reading test in two similar forms assessing simple word recognition and full reading comprehension. Each form contains five picture-word recognition items and 43 sentence completion items. Standardized scores and alternative reading ages are provided. Examiner required. Suitable for group use. BRITISH PUBLISHER

Untimed: 30 minutes

Scoring: Hand key

Cost: Specimen set (copy Form A, copy Form B, teacher's manual) £5.99

Publisher: Macmillan Education

MICROCOMPUTER MANAGED INFORMATION FOR CRITERION REFERENCED OBJECTIVES— READING (MMICRO—READING)
Ron Hambleton

Child, adolescent
Grades 1–8

Purpose: Assesses students' reading abilities. Provides information on skills mastered, skills requiring review, and skills to learn. Also used in adult basic education.

Description: Multiple-item paper-pencil test measuring phonetic analysis, structural analysis, word function, and comprehension. The test is based on the same 304 developmental learning objectives grouped into four strands as those for the ICRT-Reading: phonetic analysis, structural analysis, word function, and comprehension. With this computerized system, diagnostic and objective (mastery) tests are automatically scored in the school with a card or sheet reader recording information onto the software. Reports offer the same comprehensive diagnostic, prescriptive, and grouping information as the ICRT. However, the system does not include the norm-referenced data available from the mainframe computer, nor does it generate three selected correlations per teacher. Correlations may be purchased. Available for Apple, Commodore, and IBM microcomputers. Examiner required. Suitable for group use.

Untimed: Varies

Scoring: Computer scored

Cost: Software $1,595.00; 10 booklets (specify level) $18.00; demonstration program $65.00
Publisher: Educational Development Corporation
Information and availability unconfirmed; last verified in 1987.

MONITORING BASIC SKILLS PROGRESS-READING (MBSP-R)
Lynn S. Fuchs, Carol Hamlett, and Douglass Fuchs

Child

Purpose: Monitors progress in basic reading.

Description: Computer-assisted measurement program that tests and monitors progress in basic reading. Students are routinely tested at the computer on instructional-level reading material using a multiple-choice cloze procedure. The program monitors and charts overall achievement gains. The complete program includes one master disk for student measurement and feedback; one teacher disk to view student assessment profiles, with automatic graphed analysis; and a manual with a case study and instructions. Available for use with an Apple II family computer with 64K. Self-administered. Not suitable for group use.
Untimed: Varies
Scoring: Computer scored
Cost: Complete kit $89.00
Publisher: PRO-ED

MONROE DIAGNOSTIC READING TEST
Marion Monroe

Child, adolescent
Grades 3-9

Purpose: Assesses reading deficiencies according to chronological and mental age. Used to diagnose special reading difficulties.

Description: 326–item card test comprised of nine analytic subtests. The analytic tests include the Alphabet Repeating and Reading Test; Iota Word Test; B, D, P, Q, U, N Test; Recognition of Orientation; Mirror Reading; Mirror Writ-

ing; Number Reversal; Word Discrimination; and Sounding and Handedness. The examiner can immediately tell if a child makes the usual mistakes for his grade level, or if he makes an excessive amount of a particular type of error. Examiner required. Not suitable for group use.
Timed: 30 minutes
Scoring: Hand key
Cost: Contact publisher
Publisher: C.H. Nevins Printing Company

MONROE READING APTITUDE TESTS
Marion Monroe

Child
Grades K–1

Purpose: Measures essential skills that determine reading ability. Used by schools to determine reading readiness.

Description: Five subtests assessing factors essential to success in reading: visual, auditory, motor control, oral speech and articulation, and language. Scores are presented in percentile terms for each half year. Examiner required. Suitable for group use.
Untimed: 10–15 minutes per subtest
Scoring: Examiner evaluated
Cost: Contact publisher
Publisher: C.H. Nevins Printing Company

MULTILEVEL ACADEMIC SKILLS INVENTORY: READING PROGRAM (MASI)
Kenneth W. Howell, Stanley H. Zucker, and Mada Kay Morehead

Child, adolescent
Grades 1–8

Purpose: Assesses student reading and language arts performance in general and in detail to help teachers and school psychologists plan instructional strategies and refer students to remedial programs.

Description: Multiple-item reusable paper-pencil test in three levels measuring decoding, reading comprehension, vocabulary, handwriting, and spelling. A Survey Test samples performance over a wide range of objectives. The Placement Test assesses abilities in more detail with a content area, and a Specific Level Test examines subskills in detail. Materials include a manual, diagnostic batteries, survey and placement test booklets, response booklets, and record forms. Examiner required. Suitable for group use.

Untimed: Varies

Scoring: Examiner evaluated

Cost: Complete set $89.00

Publisher: The Psychological Corporation

Information and availability unconfirmed; last verified in 1988.

NEALE ANALYSIS OF READING ABILITY
M.D. Neale

Child—Ages 6–12

Purpose: Assesses reading standard of children.

Description: Test booklet with three parallel forms, each containing reading passages standardized for six different grades. The test is printed in three different size types. Each left-hand page has a drawing that sets the scene for the passage to be read. British equivalent reading ages are provided for each raw score. Materials include a booklet, a manual, and record sheets for each form. Examiner required. Suitable for group use.
BRITISH PUBLISHER

Untimed: 10–15 minutes

Scoring: Examiner evaluated

Cost: Test booklet £11.99; manual £7.99; record sheets (specify form) £0.28 each

Publisher: Macmillian Education Ltd.

NEALE ANALYSIS OF READING ABILITY—REVISED
M.D. Neale

Child, adolescent—Ages 5.6–11.11

Purpose: Assesses the reading ability of children and adolescents. Used by teach-

ers for diagnostic purposes. Suitable for use with learning disabled students.

Description: Series of reading passages that the student reads aloud. The test is available in two parallel forms, Form 1 and Form 2, and a Diagnostic Tutor Form that extends test options. The test yields stanine and percentile rank and range scores, Neale (Rasch) scale scores, and reading ages. This test is a revised version of the Neale Analysis of Reading Ability published by Macmillan Education. Examiner required. Not suitable or group use.
AUSTRALIAN PUBLISHER

Untimed: 30 minutes

Scoring: Hand key; examiner evaluated

Cost: Contact publisher

Publisher: Australian Council for Educational Research Limited

---

THE NELSON READING SKILLS TESTS: FORMS 3 AND 4
Gerald S. Hanna, Leo M. Schell, and Robert L. Schreiner

Child
Grades 3–9

Purpose: Assesses student achievement and progress in word attack skills, vocabulary, reading comprehension, and reading rate. Diagnoses a student's reading strengths and weaknesses. Used with students in Grades 3–9 to meet Chapter 1 requirements.

Description: Paper-pencil multiple-choice test consisting of two subtests: Word Meaning and Reading Comprehension. The Word Meaning test measures three kinds of vocabulary items: words in isolation, words in phrases, and words in sentences. The Reading Comprehension test measures literal, relational, and higher-order tasks. The test is available on three levels: Level A (Grades 3–4), Level B (Grades 5–6), and Level C (Grades 7–9). All three levels are available in a single test booklet.
Two optional tests are available: the Word Parts test, available at Level A, diagnoses a student's decoding skills, including sound/symbol correspondence, root words, and syllabication; the Reading Rate test, available at Levels B and C,

includes a short subtest measuring comprehension of the reading rate passage. Test booklets are available in two parallel forms, 3 and 4.

Scores provided for the Word Parts, Word Meanings, and Reading Comprehension tests include raw scores, grade equivalent scores, national percentile ranks, national stanines, and normal curve equivalent scores. Verbal indicators of student performance on the Word Parts subtest are also provided. Words-per-minute and grade equivalent scores are provided for the Reading Rate test. Standardization and other studies are described in the technical manual. Administration and scoring procedures are described in the teacher's manual. Self-marking answer sheets are available for hand scoring; MRC answer sheets are available for machine scoring. Examiner required. Suitable for group use.

Timed: Word Parts 25 minutes; Word Meaning 8 minutes; Reading Comprehension 25 minutes; Reading Rate 3 minutes

Scoring: Hand key; may be machine scored

Cost: 35 test booklets (specify form) $30.36; 35 MRC answer sheets, teacher's manual, 35 student score report folders, materials for machine scoring $21.30; 35 self-marking answer sheets, teacher's manual, 35 student score report folders, 2 class record sheets $27.15; 2 scoring masks $7.86; technical manual $4.53

Publisher: The Riverside Publishing Company

NEW MACMILLAN READING ANALYSIS
Denis Vincent, Michael de la Mare, and Helen Arnold

Child—Ages 7–10

Purpose: Measures oral reading abilities of children ages 7–10 and older remedial students.

Description: Series of six graded oral reading passages in three parallel forms, combined with four-page analysis sheets, for determining oral reading comprehension, analyzing reading strategies, and monitoring progress. The progressively difficult passages allow the instructor to score reading accuracy and compare it with comprehension scores, as well as to classify errors, including reversals, mispronunciations, insertions, omissions, refusals, substitutions, and self-correction. The test also provides a miscues analysis of errors according to their semantic, graphophonic, or syntactic basis and an evaluation of the severity. Norms are expressed as age equivalent ranges. Examiner required. Not suitable for group use.

BRITISH PUBLISHER

Untimed: 15 minutes

Scoring: Examiner evaluated

Cost: Starter pack (reader, record sheets A, B, and C, manual) £26.95

Publisher: Macmillan Education

THE NEW SUCHER-ALLRED READING PLACEMENT INVENTORY
Floyd Sucher and Ruel A. Allred

Child, adolescent
Grades 1–6

Purpose: Assesses students' independent, instructional, and frustrational reading levels. Used for reading placement, identification of reading difficulties, and general screening for remedial reading.

Description: Multiple-item test measuring in two parts word recognition, oral reading, oral reading comprehension, and silent reading comprehension. In the Word-Recognition Test, which is administered first, the child orally reads a list of words. The teacher assesses word recognition and uses the results to select a starting point for administering the Oral Reading Test. Two forms, A and B, are available. Examiner required. Not suitable for group use.

Untimed: 20 minutes

Scoring: Examiner evaluated

Cost: One form and teacher's manual for class of 35 $17.49; two forms $27.48

Publisher: The Economy Company

Information and availability unconfirmed; last verified in 1987.

NON-VERBAL REASONING TESTS SERIES
Refer to page 595.

THE O'BRIEN VOCABULARY PLACEMENT TEST
Janet O'Brien

Child
Grades 1–6

Purpose: Measures the reading ability of elementary-school students. Used to identify children who have reading deficiencies.

Description: 10–item paper-pencil test in six sections, one for each grade through the sixth. Each test contains a list of words for which the student selects the antonym from four possible choices. The test enables a teacher to find the independent reading level of an entire class in 15 minutes. The test also can be used individually for new students and those in special education classes. Examiner required. Suitable for group use.

Untimed: 15 minutes

Scoring: Hand key

Cost: Apple IIe diskette $29.95

Publisher: Educational Activities, Inc.

Information and availability unconfirmed; last verified in 1988.

PREREADING EXPECTANCY SCREENING SCALE (PRESS)
Lawrence C. Hartlage and David G. Lucas

Child—Ages 6–9

Purpose: Assesses skills important in reading. Used for predicting reading problems for beginning readers.

Description: Multiple-item paper-pencil test measuring a child's recognition of the numbers 1–9 and the following shapes: cross, circle, star, square, and diamond. The scale consists of four subtests: Sequencing, Spatial, Memory, and Letter Identification. Items are read by the teacher. Examiner required. Suitable for group use.

Untimed: 35 minutes

Scoring: Hand key; examiner evaluated

Cost: Specimen set $9.00; 25 tests $15.00; 25 profile sheets (specify boys or girls) $6.75; manual $6.75

Publisher: Psychologists and Educators, Inc.

THE PRIMARY READING TEST
Norman Franck

Child—Ages 6–12

Purpose: Assesses reading comprehension. Used for individual pupil evaluations.

Description: Multiple-item paper-pencil test of reading comprehension. Items involve word recognition and sentence completion. The test is divided into two levels: Level 1 for children ages 6–10 and Level 2 for children ages 7–12. Two alternate forms, 1A and 2A, are available. Examiner required. Suitable for group use.

BRITISH PUBLISHER

Untimed: 20–30 minutes

Scoring: Hand key

Cost: Contact publisher

Publisher: NFER-NELSON Publishing Company Ltd.

PROFICIENCY BATTERY IN ENGLISH AND MATHEMATICS FOR INDIAN SOUTH AFRICANS (PEMISA)
Refer to page 481.

READING ABILITY SERIES
The National Foundation for Educational Research

Child, adolescent—Ages 7–13.75

Purpose: Assesses the reading skills children need in their school and home environments as well as information about reading difficulties.

Description: Multiple-item paper-pencil multiple-choice and open-ended tests assessing pupil's reading skills. The reading booklet contains a complete story and an expository piece that sometimes includes charts, diagrams, or graphs. In separate answer booklets, children respond to questions designed to retrieve specific information about the material they read in the reading booklet: background information, the intention or opinion of the author, and information provided in or suggested by any tables, graphs, or charts. The tests yield separate scores for the narrative and the expository pieces. The raw score, which is the sum of the separate scores, is converted to a SAS.

The Test of Initial Literacy, another component of the series, yields diagnostic information about specific reading difficulties. The questions, which become progressively more difficult, involve letter and word decoding, applying punctuation, copying short pieces of text, detecting spelling or graphical errors, writing down dictated words, and producing a short piece of free writing.

The series is available on six levels, A through F, determined by age group (first-year juniors to second-year secondary). A single manual provides administration, scoring, and interpretation instructions for all six test levels. Examiner required. Suitable for group use. BRITISH PUBLISHER

Untimed: 45 minutes

Scoring: Hand key

Cost: Contact publisher

Publisher: NFER-NELSON Publishing Company Ltd.

READING CLASSIFICATION TEST
H. J. Williamson and I.L. Ball

Child
Grades 2–6

Purpose: Measures reading skills of Australian children.

Description: Multiple-item test measures and provides ways of evaluating reading performance in Australian children. The packet includes diagnostic information, a pronunciation guide, test cards, a manual, and "links with readability of children's literature." Examiner required. Not suitable for group use. AUSTRALIAN PUBLISHER

Untimed: 15 minutes

Scoring: Examiner evaluated

Cost: Complete kit $3.00; 10 individualized record forms $0.60; (Australian currency)

Publisher: Educational Resources

Information and availability unconfirmed; last verified in 1987.

READING COMPREHENSION INVENTORY (RCI)
Gerard Giordano

Child
Grades K–6

Purpose: Assesses strengths and weaknessess in children's reading skills. Used by special educators, speech therapists, diagnosticians, and clinicians.

Description: Multiple-item reading test designed to determine a student's capacity for extracting meaningful information from narrative passages. The six progressively complex passages allow the instructor to determine the student's abilities to identify narrative elements and sequence information. The test also is used to determine the student's level of expected response to a particular passage. The structural elements of the passages (character, location, time, plot, and rationale) require the student to respond with a mixture of factual, critical, and extrapolative analyses. Because the development of the three major patterns of narrative elements, sequential information, and expected response is documented in the questions that correspond to each passage, a reading comprehension profile can be developed. Examiner required. Not suitable for group use.

Timed: Varies

Scoring: Hand key

Cost: Starter set $24.95; specimen set $13.00

Publisher: Scholastic Testing Service, Inc.

A READING READINESS TEST: REVERSAL TESTS (BILINGUAL)
Refer to page 709.

READING SKILLS CHECKLISTS

Child, adolescent

Purpose: Measures an individual student's growth in reading skills from kindergarten through junior high school. Used for program planning, parent conferences, and as a part of a transferring student's permanent file.

Description: Multiple-item paper-pencil checklist assessing student knowledge and mastery of important reading skills. Items on the list consist of descriptions of reading skills, which the teacher must rate according to the following scale: the skill has not been taught, the skill has been taught but not mastered, the skill has been taught and mastered. Checklists are presented in the form of file-sized folders and are available in three levels: primary, intermediate, and junior high. The checklists are suitable for use with most basal reading programs (phonics or sight-word based). Examiner required. Not suitable for group use.

Untimed: Varies

Scoring: Examiner evaluated

Cost: 30 primary checklists $15.00; 30 intermediate checklists $15.90; 30 junior high checklists $17.67

Publisher: Modern Curriculum Press, Inc.

THE READING SKILLS DIAGNOSTIC TEST III, 3RD REVISION (RSDT III)
Richard H. Bloomer

Child, adolescent
Grades 2–8

Purpose: Measures content, learning processes, and learning capacities necessary for learning how to read. Provides a structure for beginning reading instruction, as well as a model for diagnosis and treatment of early learning difficulties related to reading and writing.

Description: 48 paper-pencil subtests measuring mastery of beginning encoding-decoding and word recognition skills, basic processing skills, and learning processes. The subtests are arranged in four groups of 12 to measure four levels of response strength: reproduction, recognition, visual-oral, and auditory-motor. Each of the four levels measures content (letter knowledge, simple phonic knowledge, sight words, long vowels, consonant digraphs, and vowel diphthongs); basic processing skills (imitation, copying, multiple discrimination, consonant-vowel blending, and consonant-vowel-consonant blending); and learning capacities (short-term memory for words, short-term memory for letters and stimulus magnitude). Context clues at all four levels of response strength help teachers plan specific instructional and remedial approaches. Subtests and levels are arranged sequentially, and the test is designed to be administered one subtest at a time in a test-teach-test format. Examiner required. Levels 1 and 3 are individually administered; Levels 2 and 4 are group administered.

Untimed: Not available

Scoring: Hand key; examiner evaluated

Cost: Level 1 manual and answer sheets $16.40; Level 2 manual and answer sheets $19.70; Level 3 manual and test stimuli, record forms $25.50; Level 4 manual and answer sheets $21.80

Publisher: Brador Publications, Inc.

Information and availability unconfirmed; last verified in 1987.

READING TESTS SR-A AND SR-B

Child—Ages 7½–12

Purpose: Measures reading attainment of primary school children. Used for screening and surveying groups of pupils.

Description: Multiple-item paper-pencil tests measuring reading achievement. The items consist of sentence completion tasks. Examiner required. Suitable for group use.
BRITISH PUBLISHER

Timed: 20 minutes per test

Scoring: Examiner evaluated

Cost: Contact publisher

Publisher: NFER-NELSON Publishing Company Ltd.

READING YARDSTICKS

Child, adolescent
Grades K–8

Purpose: Assesses students' strengths and weaknesses in reading readiness, reading, and language skills. Used for grouping students for instruction and for helping teachers develop teaching strategies and materials.

Description: Paper-pencil multiple-choice test of reading ability divided into nine levels (6–14) corresponding to Grades K–8. At Level 6 (70 items), students are tested for visual and auditory discrimination, letter and word matching, vocabulary, and comprehension. Levels 7 (105 items) and 8 (135 items) test discrimination and study skills, phonic analysis, vocabulary, and comprehension. Level 8 also tests structural analysis. Levels 9–14 (210 items) test vocabulary, comprehension, structural analysis, and study skills. The test contains from four to nine subtests, depending on the test level. Available materials include a teacher's guide, technical report, and both class and student diagnostic reports. Machine-scorable test booklets are available for Levels 6–9. Answer folders are available for use with the reusable test booklets for Levels 9–14. Examiner required. Suitable for group use.

Untimed: Level 6 110 minutes; Level 7 150 minutes; Level 8 185 minutes; Levels 9–10 210 minutes; Levels 11–14 227 minutes

Scoring: Levels 6–9 machine scored; Levels 9–14 hand key; scoring service available

Cost: Examination kit, specify Levels 6–9, 9–12, or 13–14 (test booklets, directions for administration, teacher's guide, technical report) $3.51

Publisher: The Riverside Publishing Company

ROSWELL-CHALL AUDITORY BLENDING TEST
Florence Roswell and Jeanne Chall

Child
Grades 2–6

Purpose: Evaluates a child's ability to blend sounds when the sounds are presented orally. Used for classroom and remedial work in elementary and secondary schools.

Description: Multiple-item oral-response test assessing a child's ability to blend sounds auditorily into whole words, whether or not the association between the sounds and the corresponding letters has been learned. The test indicates the facility or difficulty students will encounter with phonics instruction. Examiner required. Not suitable for group use.

Untimed: 5 minutes

Scoring: Examiner evaluated

Cost: Get-acquainted set (manual, 2 copies of test) $4.50

Publisher: Essay Press

Information and availability unconfirmed; last verified in 1987.

ROSWELL-CHALL DIAGNOSTIC READING TEST OF WORD ANALYSIS SKILLS (REVISED AND EXTENDED)
Florence Roswell and Jeanne Chall

Child
Grades K–4

Purpose: Assesses a child's ability to use fundamental phonic and word recognition skills. Used for diagnostic and prescriptive teaching purposes in classrooms, tutorial work, and reading clinics.

Description: Multiple-item oral-response test containing the following subtests: sight recognition of high frequency words, naming capital and lowercase letters, consonant sounds, consonant blends and digraphs, short vowels, long vowels with *e*, long vowel combinations, writing and spelling CVC words. Appropriate subtests are indicated for different levels of reading ability. Results yield a comprehensive profile indicating a grade level and classifies skills as mastered, requiring review, or requiring systematic instruction. The test is available in Forms A and B for test-retest purposes. Suitable for use with older students whose phonic and word recognition skills are at a Grade 4 level or below. Examiner required. Not suitable for group use.

Untimed: 10–15 minutes
Scoring: Examiner evaluated
Cost: Get-acquainted set (manual, 2 copies Form A) $4.50
Publisher: Essay Press
Information and availability unconfirmed; last verified in 1987.

ST. LUCIA GRADED WORD READING TEST
R. J. Andrews

Child, adolescent

Purpose: Measures the word reading skills of primary and lower secondary-school students. Diagnoses specific skill deficits.

Description: Multiple-item oral-response reading test measuring word recognition skills. The test provides reading ages as well as diagnostic information on word attack skills and error patterns. Examiner required. Not suitable for group use. AUSTRALIAN PUBLISHER
Untimed: Varies
Scoring: Examiner evaluated
Cost: Basic kit (manual, test materials, 50 record forms) $11.00
Publisher: Teaching and Testing Resources
Information and availability unconfirmed; last verified in 1987.

ST. LUCIA READING COMPREHENSION TEST
J. Elkins and R. J. Andrews

Child
Grades 2–4

Purpose: Measures reading comprehension of children in the lower primary school.

Description: Multiple-item paper-pencil cloze-type test measuring the reading ability of students. The test is available in two alternate forms, A and B. Australian norms allow scores to be expressed as reading ages, percentiles, or 15-point scale scores. Examiner required. Suitable for group use. AUSTRALIAN PUBLISHER
Untimed: Varies

Scoring: Examiner evaluated
Cost: Basic kit (manual, 25 Form A, 25 Form B) $11.50
Publisher: Teaching and Testing Resources
Information and availability unconfirmed; last verified in 1987.

SALFORD SENTENCE READING TEST
G.E. Bookbinder

Child—Ages 6–12

Purpose: Measures reading achievement of children with reading ages between 6 and 10.6 years.

Description: Multiple-item oral-response test measuring reading achievement. The test form consists of a test card containing 13 sentences presented in order of increasing difficulty. Testing ceases when the child has completed the sentence in which the sixth reading error is made. The child's reading age can immediately be read off from the test card. Percentile scores for chronological ages 6.1–11.9 are listed separately in the manual. The test is available in three parallel forms, A, B, and C. The test cards are reusable and are available in sets containing one copy each of the three forms. Examiner required. Not suitable for group use. BRITISH PUBLISHER
Untimed: 2–3 minutes
Scoring: Examiner evaluated
Cost: Test cards Forms A, B, and C £3.25 per set of 3; manual £2.50
Publisher: Hodder & Stoughton

THE SCAN-TRON READING TEST
John W. Wick, Jeffrey K. Smith, Loyce D. Braun, Madelyn R. Smith, Dixie Lee Spiegel, and JoAnn Stevens

Child, adolescent
Grades 3–8

Purpose: Assesses the reading achievement of students.

Description: Multiple-item paper-pencil test assessing reading skills in four areas: literal comprehension, inferential comprehension, context clues, and main ideas. Items are presented in a four-option multiple-choice format. The test is available on six levels (Level 8: Grade 3, Level 9: Grade 4, Level 10: Grade 5, Level 11: Grade 6, Level 12: Grade 7, and Level 12: Grade 8). Level 8 is comprised of Word Attack (30 items; 20 minutes), Vocabulary (30 items; 20 minutes), and Reading Comprehension (35 items; 35 minutes) subtests. Levels 9–12 consist of two subtests: Vocabulary (30 items; 20 minutes) and Reading Comprehension (50 items; 50 minutes). The test yields a raw score, grade equivalent, normal curve equivalent, and percentile rank. Materials include a test booklet, answer sheet, examiner's manual, teacher's manual, norms booklet, out-of-level norms booklet, class list report, parent letter, student growth chart, hand-scoring template, answer key for use with the test scoring computer, and scoring software for use on IBM PC, Apple IIe, and TRS Models 3 and 4. Examiner required. Suitable for group use.

Timed: Level 8 1 hour, 15 minutes; Levels 9–12 1 hour, 10 minutes

Scoring: Hand key; computer scored

Cost: Contact publisher

Publisher: SCAN-TRON Corporation

SHORTENED EDINBURGH READING TEST
Godfrey Thomson Unit for Educational Research, Moray House College of Education, and Child Health and Education Study

Child—Ages 10–12

Purpose: Measures the reading standards of children and detects children needing remedial reading attention.

Description: 75–item paper-pencil test with three main subtests assessing written language attainment: Vocabulary (23 items), Syntax and Sequence (19 items), and Comprehension (25 items). Test items were selected from stages 1–4 of the Edinburgh Reading Tests. Contact the publisher for restrictions on the sale of the test. Examiner required. Suitable for group use.
BRITISH PUBLISHER

Untimed: 40 minutes

Scoring: Examiner evaluated

Cost: 20 test booklets £6.50; manual £3.25; specimen set £3.95

Publisher: Hodder & Stoughton

SKILLCORP COMPUTER MANAGEMENT SYSTEM— READING

Child
Grades 1–6

Purpose: Assesses reading skill deficiencies. Used to diagnose an individual student's reading base and prescribe resources for reteaching.

Description: 77 tests assessing five strands: phonetic analysis, structural analysis, vocabulary, comprehension, and study skills. All skills tested are cross-referenced to basal and supplementary reading programs. A microcomputer prints prescriptions for individual students or groups to reteach skills not mastered. Materials include a test administration manual and test cards for each grade level. Examiner required. Suitable for group use.

Untimed: Not available

Scoring: Hand key; may be computer scored

Cost: Contact publisher

Publisher: Skillcorp Software, Inc.

SOUTHGATE GROUP READING TESTS
Vera Southgate

Child—Ages 5–8

Purpose: Measures children's basic reading skills. Identifies students reading significantly above or below their expected age level.

Description: Paper-pencil test of reading ability measuring word selection. Norms are provided for ages 5.9–7.9. Two parallel forms of the test are available. Examiner required. Suitable for group use.
BRITISH PUBLISHER

Untimed: Not available

Scoring: Examiner evaluated

Cost: Specimen set £3.95; 20 copies Test 1 (specify form) £3.75; manual £3.75
Publisher: Hodder & Stoughton

STANDARDIZED READING INVENTORY (SRI)
Phyllis L. Newcomer

Child, adolescent
Grades 1-8

Purpose: Evaluates a student's idiosyncratic reading skills.

Description: 10-passage criterion-referenced reading test consisting of 10 graded passages containing key words designed to assess oral and silent reading from the preprimer to 8th-grade levels. After reading the passages, the student answers a series of comprehension questions. Each passage yields scores in word recognition and comprehension, revealing the student's independent, instructional, and frustration reading levels. The test is available in two forms, A and B. Examiner required. Not suitable for group use.
Untimed: Not available
Scoring: Hand key; examiner evaluated
Cost: Complete kit (manual, student booklet, 50 summary/record sheets, storage box) $59.00
Publisher: PRO-ED

STRUCTURE OF INTELLECT LEARNING ABILITIES TEST (SOI-LA): READING READINESS TEST (FORM RR)
SOI Institute Staff

Child

Purpose: Assesses the reading readiness of young children.

Description: Multiple-item oral-response test assessing abilities relating to reading readiness. The test includes instructions for administration. The basic test manual for the Stucture of Intellect (SOI) test is required for administration and scale interpretation. See entry for the Structure of Intellect (SOI) for related tests. Examiner required. Suitable for group use (some sections must be individually administered).

Untimed: 1 hour
Scoring: Examiner evaluated
Cost: 5 test booklets $14.40; manual $35.00
Publisher: Western Psychological Services

SUFFOLK READING SCALE
Fred Hagley

Child, adolescent—Ages
6-13

Purpose: Measures reading achievement and monitors the progress of individuals and groups. Used to identify children needing remediation and those whose development is normal.

Description: 80-item paper-pencil multiple-choice instrument screening for reading achievement. Items are divided among three levels, 1, 2, and 3, with some overlap between levels. Level 1, for top infants and first-year juniors, contains items 1-65. The first four items are pictorial, and the remaining items are printed in a large typeface. Level 2, for second- through fourth-year juniors, consists of items 6-75 in slightly smaller type. The third level, for fourth-year juniors and first- and second-year secondary students, contains items 11-80 in an A4 layout. Each level yields a raw score, standard age score, percentile rank, and age equivalent. The test is available in two parallel forms, A and B. Examiner required. Suitable for group use.
BRITISH PUBLISHER
Timed: 20 minutes
Scoring: Hand key (all levels); computer scored (Level 3)
Cost: Contact publisher
Publisher: NFER-NELSON Publishing Company Ltd.

TEST OF EARLY READING ABILITY-2 (TERA-2)
D. Kim Reid, Wayne P. Hresko, and Donald D. Hammill

Child—Ages 3-9.11

Purpose: Determines the actual reading ability (not "readiness") of preschool, kindergarten, and primary level students.

Used to identify problems, document progress, conduct research, and suggest instructional practices.

Description: Multiple-item paper-pencil test examining three areas related to early learning: contextual meaning, alphabet, and the conventions of reading (e.g., book orientation and format). Scaled scores, percentiles, age equivalents, and reading quotients are yielded. Results can be used to document early reading ability. Two equivalent forms (A and B) are available. Examiners must be competent in the administration of educational, psychological, and language tests. Examiner required. Not suitable for group use.

Untimed: Varies

Scoring: Examiner evaluated

Cost: Complete kit (manual, administration/picture book, 50 A and B profile/examiner record forms) $89.00

Publisher: PRO-ED

TEST OF INFERENCE ABILITY IN READING COMPREHENSION (TIA)
Linda M. Phillips and Cynthia C. Patterson

Adolescent—Ages 10–14 Grades 6–8

Purpose: Appraises students' inference ability in reading.

Description: 36–item paper-pencil multiple-choice test measuring a student's inference ability on the basis of full-length passages representative of the three kinds of discourse commonly found at the middle grade levels. Examiner required. Suitable for group use.
CANADIAN PUBLISHER

Untimed: 50 minutes

Scoring: Computer scored; hand key

Cost: 35 test booklets $35.00; 100 answer sheets $10.00; manual $5.00; technical report $10.00

Publisher: Institute for Educational Research and Development, Memorial University of Newfoundland

THACKRAY READING READINESS PROFILES
Derek V. Thackray and Lucy Thackray

Child—Ages 4–7

Purpose: Measures reading readiness of reception class children. Diagnoses prereading skill deficiencies of older nonreaders. Used to develop individualized prereading skill programs.

Description: Task-assessment and oral-response test measuring reading readiness indicators. Full instructions for interpreting the profiles and suggestions for developing specific reading readiness skills are contained in the manual. Examiner required. Suitable for group use.
BRITISH PUBLISHER

Untimed: Not available

Scoring: Examiner evaluated

Cost: Specimen set £4.50; 10 profiles £7.50; manual £3.75

Publisher: Hodder & Stoughton

VISUAL-AURAL DIGIT SPAN TEST (VADS)
Elizabeth M. Koppitz

Child—Ages 5½–12

Purpose: Diagnoses specific problems in reading recognition and spelling for children who can read and write digits. Used to develop individual educational programs for learning disabled children.

Description: Multiple-item test in which digit sequences on 26 test cards must be reproduced from memory, first orally; then in writing after being presented orally; and, finally, as a separate series, visually. The test measures auditory, visual, visual-auditory, and auditory-visual integration; sequence and recall of digits; and organization of written material. There are 11 scores, which are interpreted individually. Examiner required. Suitable for group use. Available in Spanish.

Untimed: 10 minutes

Scoring: Examiner evaluated

Cost: Manual $31.00; 100 tests $22.00
Publisher: The Psychological Corporation

Information and availability unconfirmed; last verified in 1988.

VISUAL DISCRIMINATION TEST
Joseph M. Wepman, Anne Morency, and Maria Seidl

Child—Ages 5–8

Purpose: Measures children's ability to discriminate visually between similar forms. Used to measure the skills necessary for learning to read.

Description: 20–item test in which the child responds by pointing to which of four nonalphabetic forms is the same as the example. No verbal responses are required. Separate norms are provided for ages 5, 6, 7, and 8. Adequacy threshold scores are provided to indicate the need for referral. Materials include a 24–page test booklet of original designs, a complete administration and scoring manual, and score sheets marked specifically for the test. Examiner required. Not suitable for group use.

Untimed: 10–15 minutes

Scoring: Hand key

Cost: Complete kit (1 set of reusable stimulus cards, 25 score sheets, manual) $55.00

Publisher: Western Psychological Services

VISUAL MEMORY SCALE (VMS)
James L. Carroll

Child—Ages 5–6

Purpose: Measures short-term visual memory. Used as an aid in diagnosing reading and spelling problems.

Description: 25–card examiner-led test of a child's ability to recognize patterns. The examiner gives the child a 5–second look at a card containing a complex geometric design and asks him to pick out the same design among four similar designs on a second card. Examiner required. Not suitable for group use.

Timed: Total test 5–7 minutes

Scoring: Hand key

Cost: Set of plates $6.00; manual $3.00; answer blanks $1.50

Publisher: Carroll Publications

Information and availability unconfirmed; last verified in 1987.

VISUAL MEMORY TEST
Joseph M. Wepman, Anne Morency, and Maria Seidl

Child—Ages 5–8

Purpose: Measures a child's ability to remember nonalphabetical, visual forms. Used to identify any perceptual inadequacy that might reduce the ability to learn to read.

Description: 16–item test measuring a child's ability to recall unfamiliar forms that cannot readily be named. The examiner shows the child a design on a target page, and the child chooses the design from four designs on a response page. Norms are provided for ages 5, 6, 7, and 8. Adequacy threshold scores indicate the need for additional evaluation. Examiner required. Not suitable for group use.

Untimed: 10–15 minutes

Scoring: Hand key

Cost: Complete kit (1 set of reusable stimulus cards, 25 score sheets, manual) $58.50

Publisher: Western Psychological Services

WIDE-SPAN READING TEST
Alan Brimer with Herbert Gross

Child, adolescent—Ages 7–15

Purpose: Measures sentence reading skills. Used to identify individual students' abilities.

Description: Multiple-item paper-pencil test of reading skills. Items consist of decoding printed symbols, fitting meanings to groups of sounds, and construing the structural relationship of meaning within the context of a sentence. Two parallel forms, A and B, are available.

Examiner required. Suitable for group use.

BRITISH PUBLISHER

Timed: 30 minutes

Scoring: Hand key

Cost: Contact publisher

Publisher: NFER-NELSON Publishing Company Ltd.

WORD ANALYSIS DIAGNOSTIC TESTS
Selma E. Herr

Child
Grades K–3

Purpose: Evaluates the word attack abilities of students in Grades K–3 and of remedial students in Grades K–12. Diagnoses skill deficiencies, assists in placement decisions, and serves as an achievement test.

Description: Multiple-item paper-pencil tests assessing proficiency in word analysis and phonics skills. The tests are arranged in four levels: Level A–1 (administered at the end of the reading readiness period), Level A–2 (Grade 1), Level B (Grade 2), and Level C (Grade 3). All levels may be used with students of any age for appropriate remedial purposes. Each level consists of four to six sections measuring skills appropriate to the student's grade level. Students are provided with a printed form containing familiar objects. Students respond by marking the appropriate symbol for material presented orally by an examiner or tape cassette. Examiner required. Suitable for group use.

Timed: 20–30 minutes per level

Scoring: Hand key

Cost: Comprehensive Teacher's Guide, cassette for each level $52.00

Publisher: Instructional Materials & Equipment Distributors

Information and availability unconfirmed; last verified in 1987.

WORD ANALYSIS DIAGNOSTIC TESTS—LEVEL A-1/READINESS
Selma E. Herr

Child
Grades K–1

Purpose: Assesses kindergartners' and first-graders' readiness to begin learning the printed symbols (letters and groups of letters) used in reading. Diagnoses skill deficiencies, assists in placement decisions, and measures reading readiness.

Description: 40–item paper-pencil test assessing students' readiness to apply printed symbols to phonetic units. Subtests include rhyming words, initial consonant sounds, ending consonant sounds, and digraph sounds. Students are provided with a printed form containing familiar objects. Students respond by marking the appropriate symbol for material presented orally by an examiner or tape cassette. Examiner required. Suitable for group use.

Timed: 20 minutes

Scoring: Hand key

Cost: Class packet (30 tests, teacher's guide/keys, cassette containing test) $16.00

Publisher: Instructional Materials & Equipment Distributors

Information and availability unconfirmed; last verified in 1987.

WORD ANALYSIS DIAGNOSTIC TESTS—LEVEL A-2/GRADE 1
Selma E. Herr

Child
Grades 1–2

Purpose: Measures word attack skills at the end of the first year of phonics instruction. Used with students at the end of Grade 1, beginning of Grade 2, or remedial students in Grades 3–4 to diagnose skill deficiencies, assist in placement decisions, and measure achievement.

Description: 79–item paper-pencil multiple-choice test assessing proficiency in word attack skills and phonics, including initial and final consonants, consonant digraphs, four consonant blends, short vowel sounds, and rhyming words. Students are provided with a printed form containing familiar objects. Students respond by marking the appropriate symbol for material presented orally by an examiner or tape cassette. Examiner required. Suitable for group use.

Timed: 20 minutes

Scoring: Hand key

Cost: Class packet (30 tests, teacher's guide/keys, cassette containing test) $16.00

Publisher: Instructional Materials & Equipment Distributors

Information and availability unconfirmed; last verified in 1987.

WORD ANALYSIS DIAGNOSTIC TESTS—LEVEL B/GRADE 2
Selma E. Herr

Child
Grades 2–3

Purpose: Measures word attack skills at the end of the second year of phonics instruction. Used with students at the end of Grade 2, the beginning of Grade 3, or remedial students in Grades 4–6 to diagnose skill deficiencies, assist in placement decisions, and measure achievement.

Description: 76–item paper-pencil multiple-choice test assessing proficiency in word attack skills and phonics, including long and short vowel sounds; vowels followed by *r*; the sounds *ou, ow, aw,* and *all*; hard and soft *c* and *g*; and the blends and digraphs. The test also assesses the ability to pronounce any phonetically based word, use context clues, and understand the meanings of words. Students are provided with a printed form containing familiar objects. Students respond by marking the appropriate symbol for material presented orally by an examiner or tape cassette. Examiner required. Suitable for group use.

Timed: 20 minutes

Scoring: Hand key

Cost: Class packet (30 tests, teacher's guide/keys, cassette containing test) $16.00

Publisher: Instructional Materials & Equipment Distributors

Information and availability unconfirmed; last verified in 1987.

WORD ANALYSIS DIAGNOSTIC TESTS—LEVEL C/GRADE 3
Selma E. Herr

Child
Grades 3–4

Purpose: Measures word attack skills at the end of Grade 3. Identifies students needing further training in word analysis before entering Grade 4. Used with older students in Grades 5–12 to diagnose reading disabilities related to word attack skills.

Description: 116–item paper-pencil test assessing proficiency in word analysis skills, including vowel sounds, silent letters, syllabications, and structural and phonetic analysis. Students are provided with a printed form containing familiar objects. Students respond by marking the appropriate symbol in response to material presented orally by an examiner or tape cassette. Examiner required. Suitable for group use.

Timed: 30 minutes

Scoring: Hand key

Cost: Class packet (30 tests, teacher's guide/keys, cassette containing test) $16.00

Publisher: Instructional Materials & Equipment Distributors

Information and availability unconfirmed; last verified in 1987.

WORD DISCRIMINATION TEST
Charles B. Huelsman, Jr.

Child
Grades 1.2–8.3

Purpose: Measures ability to recognize words. Identifies children with word-recognition skill deficiencies.

Description: 96–item paper-pencil multiple-choice test measuring how well students use length, internal design, and external configuration in perceiving words. Each test item consists of one word and four groups of letters that are not words. The students must draw a circle around the one word in each row. Grade equivalents are given for all raw scores. The test is available in two forms, A and B. Norms are based on 1,299 sets of scores from children in Grades 1-6. Examiner required. Suitable for group use.

Untimed: 15 minutes

Scoring: Hand key; examiner evaluated

Cost: Test $0.15

Publisher: Miami University Alumni Association

WORD RECOGNITION TEST
Clifford Carver

Child—Ages 4–8.6

Purpose: Assesses word recognition in children.

Description: Multiple-item paper-pencil test that indicates a child's overall word recognition ability and also analyzes errors and difficulties. Items cover the earliest stages of letter knowledge to levels generally achieved by age 8. Examiner required. Suitable for group use. BRITISH PUBLISHER

Untimed: Not available

Scoring: Not available

Cost: 20 tests £4.95; manual £2.95

Publisher: Hodder & Stoughton

Reading: High School and Above

BUFFALO READING TEST
Refer to page 871.

CALIFORNIA PHONICS SURVEY
Grace M. Brown and Alice B. Cottrell

Adolescent, adult Grades 7 and above

Purpose: Measures the overall phonic adequacy of a group, class, or school sys-

tem. Identifies individuals with some degree of phonic disability and determines the degree of impairment.

Description: 5–item oral-response test assessing a student's phonic adequacy. Items consist of exercises involving reading and listening that are constructed to reveal the most common reversals, confusions of blends and vowels, and other errors that reflect inability to relate letter combinations to spoken sounds. The student's pattern of errors is interpreted in terms of eight diagnostic categories related to skills necessary for adequate reading, spelling, and language. Four general levels of phonic adequacy are defined by raw scores: adequate phonics, some phonic disability, serious phonic disability, and gross phonic disability. Available in two forms for pre- and posttesting. A single test booklet is used to administer either form. A cassette tape is available. Examiner required. Suitable for group use.

Untimed: 45 minutes

Scoring: Examiner evaluated

Cost: Manual $10.50; 25 test booklets $9.00; 50 answer sheets (profiles on back) $12.50; scoring stencils (diagnostic set; form 1) $9.00; scoring stencils (retest score; form 2) $1.75; cassette tape $13.00

Publisher: Consulting Psychologists Press, Inc.

CLARKE READING SELF-ASSESSMENT SURVEY (SAS)
John H. Clarke and Simon Wittes

Grades 9–adult

Purpose: Measures student language skills prior to beginning the first semester in college. Used for self-assessment and counseling.

Description: Multiple-item paper-pencil instrument diagnosing strengths and weaknesses in reading, conceptualization, and written expression, with suggestions for skill improvement. The test booklet contains instructions for the student, multiple-choice questions, answers, scoring guide, and graphic profile. Self-administered. Suitable for group use.

Untimed: 1 hour

Scoring: Hand key

Cost: 10 surveys $25.00

Publisher: Academic Therapy
Publications

DIAGNOSTIC ANALYSIS OF
READING ERRORS (DARE)
*Jacquelyn Gillespie and
Jacqueline Shohet*

**Adolescent, adult—Ages
12 and older**

Purpose: Identifies adolescents and
adults with language-related problems,
diagnoses learning disabilities, and provides specific data on the visual-auditory
coding process for psychoeducational
diagnoses. Used to survey school and
community populations for educational
planning and research.

Description: 46–item paper-pencil multiple-choice test in which the examiner
dictates Wide Range Achievement Test
Level II spelling items and the individual
selects one of four choices as the correct
answer. Four measures of visual-auditory
transcoding ability are provided: Correct
(reading and spelling skills), Sound Substitution (phonic analysis skills), Omission
(word structure analysis), and Reversal
(sequencing efficiency). DARE coordinates with WRAT reading and spelling
tests in reading improvement programs
and attempts to provide a culture-fair
measure of English language skills. Scoring yields diagnostic error patterns, age
level norms (ages 12–adult), and standard
scores. Free computer scoring is available.
The test is restricted to educational and
psychological professionals. Examiner
required. Suitable for group use.

Untimed: 10 minutes

Scoring: Hand key; may be computer
scored

Cost: Manual $15.00; 50 answer sheets
$15.00

Publisher: Jastak Assessment Systems

EDINBURGH READING TESTS
*Godfrey Thomson Unit for
Educational Research and Moray
House College of Education*

**Child, adolescent—Ages
7–16**

Purpose: Measures students' general
reading abilities. Diagnoses the reading
strengths and weaknesses of each student
and identifies those needing special help.
Measures success of teaching methods in
classes, schools, or districts.

Description: Paper-pencil tests of reading achievement presented in four stages
for four different age groups. Each stage is
divided into four or more separately timed
subtests designed to assess different areas
of reading competence. An overall score
for the whole test and a separate score for
each subtest are obtained for each child.
The subtest scores are plotted on a profile, showing which relatively high or low
scores are significant and merit further
observation. Stage 1 (ages 7–9) is available
in two equivalent forms, A and B, for
test-retest programs. Practice items are
included in the test forms, which are
designed for administration in two sessions of 25 minutes. The profile is printed
on the back of each form. Stage 2 (ages
8.6–10.6) is presented in a single test
booklet. Stage 3 (ages 10.0–12.6) is served
by two parallel booklets, A and B. Stages
2 and 3 are designed for administration in
three sessions: Practice Test (30–35 minutes), Part I (40 minutes), and Part II (35
minutes). Stage 4 (ages 12–16) is designed
for administration in two sessions of 35
minutes. The profile is printed on the
back of the test booklet. Examiner
required. Suitable for group use.
BRITISH PUBLISHER

Timed: 25–35 minutes for each section

Scoring: Hand key

Cost: Stage 1 specimen set £3.95; Stage 2
specimen set £3.95; Stage 3 specimen set
£5.75; Stage 4 specimen set £4.50

Publisher: Hodder & Stoughton

MINNESOTA SPEED OF READING TEST
Alvia C. Eruich

Adolescent, adult
Grades 12 and above

Purpose: Measures reading speed. Designed for high-school seniors, college students, and college graduates.

Description: 38–item paper-pencil test in two forms, A and B, consisting of short paragraphs, each of which contains an "absurd" sentence or phrase that the subject is asked to cross out. The score depends on how many paragraphs are completed correctly within the time limit. Examiner required. Suitable for group use.

Timed: 6 minutes

Scoring: Hand key

Cost: 100 forms $5.00; specimen set $0.35

Publisher: University of Minnesota Press

NELSON-DENNY READING TEST: FORMS E AND F
James I. Brown, J. Michael Bennett, and Gerald S. Hanna

Adolescent, adult
Grades 9 and above

Purpose: Assesses student achievement and progress in vocabulary, comprehension, and reading rate.

Description: 136–item paper-pencil reading survey test in two parts. Part I, the vocabulary test, measures vocabulary development. Part II, the Comprehension test, assesses comprehension and reading rate. A standard score scale is provided. A special cut-time adult administration of 26 minutes is recommended for extension of graduate class testing. The test is available in two parallel forms, E and F. Examiner required. Suitable for group use.

Timed: 35 minutes

Scoring: Hand key; may be machine scored

Cost: 35 test booklets (specify form) $26.25; 35 MRC answer sheets $16.50; manual $6.00

Publisher: The Riverside Publishing Company

PSB READING COMPREHENSION EXAMINATION

Health occupations
students

Purpose: Measures individuals' ability to understand the material they read. Used to identify students in the health professions who need counseling or remedial assistance.

Description: Multiple-item paper-pencil test sampling essential functional elements of reading comprehension. It is specifically designed for secondary, post-secondary, and professional programs and may be used as an adjunct to PSB tests in practical nursing, health occupations, and nursing. Examiner required. Suitable for group use.

Timed: 30 minutes

Scoring: Machine scored

Cost: Reusable test booklets $5.00; answer sheets (scoring and reporting service) $3.00

Publisher: Psychological Services Bureau

READING/EVERYDAY ACTIVITIES IN LIFE (R/EAL)
Marilyn Lichtman

Adolescent, adult
Grades 10 and above

Purpose: Assesses whether an individual is functionally literate. Suitable for blacks, Puerto Ricans, Mexican Americans, rural groups, and other minority groups who have traditionally been singled out by the bias of standardized reading achievement tests, as well as for adults at basic educational levels and children ages 10 and older. Used for diagnostic and evaluative purposes.

Description: 45–item paper-pencil free-response test measuring an individual's ability to read and use language. The test consists of nine reading selections, each representing a general category of daily reading situations encountered by most individuals high-school age and older. The nine passages include a set of road signs, a TV schedule, a set of directions for preparing cheese pizza, a reading on narcotic drugs, a food market ad, an apartment lease or credit agreement, a road map, a want ad, and a job or credit application. Five questions, based on task analyses of the functions required to deal with the reading material, are asked for each selection. A cassette player, headphones (optional), a test booklet, and cassette are used to administer the test to insure that subjects' inability to understand written directions will not prevent them from understanding what is on the test. The test is available in two equivalent forms, A and B, for pre- and posttesting. Examiner required. Suitable for group use. Available in Spanish.

Untimed: 1 day

Scoring: Examiner evaluated

Cost: Specimen set (cassette, test, manual) $10.00; test booklet $1.50; cassettes $8.00 each; manual $8.50 each

Publisher: Westwood Press, Inc.

READING PROGRESS SCALE: COLLEGE VERSION
Ronald P. Carver

Adolescent, adult

Purpose: Estimates reading level of college students. Particularly appropriate for use with students who do not read well. Used for academic placement and referral.

Description: 80–item paper-pencil test assessing basic reading abilities. Scoring takes only seconds and provides immediate feedback to community-college students regarding which courses they should take. The test is available in two alternate forms: Form 2C and Form 5C. Examiner required. Suitable for group use.

Timed: 7 minutes

Scoring: Hand key

Cost: Specimen set $5.00; 100 tests $30.00; 1 manual free

Publisher: Revrac Publications, Inc.

SELF-OBSERVATION SCALES (SOS)
Refer to page 774.

Reading: Multilevel

THE ACCURACY LEVEL TEST (ALT)
Ronald P. Carver

Child, adolescent, adult
Grades 2–college

Purpose: Assesses reading accuracy level, rate level, and efficiency level. Also used with above-average readers in Grade 1.

Description: 100–item criterion-referenced paper-pencil vocabulary test designed to measure students' "rauding" ability; that is, their ability to read and comprehend. The test yields an Accuracy Level score in grade equivalents (GE). In addition, percentile ranks and standard score tables are provided for students in Grades 3–16. The ALT is available in two forms, A and B. This test is one of two tests that comprise The Reading Efficiency Level Battery (see separate entry). Examiner required. Suitable for group use.

Timed: 10 minutes

Scoring: Hand key

Cost: Examination kit (1 copy of test, User's Guide) $2.00; 100 tests (specify form) $25.00; User's Guide $2.00; technical manual $5.00

Publisher: Revrac Publications, Inc.

ACER READING TESTS

Child, adolescent
Grades 1–12

Purpose: Assesses reading skills. Used for diagnosis of individual strengths and weaknesses as part of an educational evaluation.

Description: 10 paper-pencil multiple-choice tests of skills important in reading achievement. Tests are ACER Paragraph

Reading Test, a screening test for years 6–8; ACER Primary Reading Survey Tests (Levels AA-BB), years 1 and 2. ACER Primary Reading Survey Tests (Levels A-D), years 3–6; ACER Primary Reading Survey Tests (Level D 1A–1C), a three-part test of reading achievement for year 6; Cooperative Reading Comprehension Test—L and M, years 8–10; English Skills Assessment, years 11 and 12; Progressive Achievement Tests-Form A or B; and Reading Appraisal Guide. Examiner required. Suitable for group use. AUSTRALIAN PUBLISHER

Timed: Varies

Scoring: Hand key; may be machine scored

Cost: Contact publisher

Publisher: The Australian Council for Educational Research Limited

---

BASIC READING RATE SCALE—BRAILLE AND LARGE TYPE EDITIONS
Adapted by Bill J. Duckworth and Hilda R. Caton

Ages 9–adult
Grades 4 and above

Purpose: Measures the reading speed of visually impaired individuals.

Description: 98–item paper-pencil (braille and large type) and oral-response test designed to measure reading speed. The examinee is directed to either circle or say the absurd word in a sentence. The test yields an accuracy score for speed of reading. The number of items attempted is divided into the number correct. A fourth-grade reading level is required. The test is adapted from the Basic Reading Rate Scale. The manuals are adapted for use with visually impaired individuals. Examiner required. Suitable for group use.

Timed: 5 minutes

Scoring: Hand key; examiner evaluated

Cost: Test $2.32; manual $34.28

Publisher: American Printing House for the Blind, Inc.

BIEMILLER TEST OF READING PROCESSES
Andrew Biemiller

Grades 2 and above

Purpose: Determines why a child is reading at a given level of proficiency and identifies strengths and weaknesses of a child's reading abilities.

Description: Multiple-item oral reading test monitoring letter speed, word speed out of context, and word speed in context. The test identifies individual differences in three kinds of reading processes: the ability to recognize print quickly, the ability to identify words quickly, and the ability to use context to facilitate word identification. A stopwatch is required. Examiner required. Not suitable for group use. CANADIAN PUBLISHER

Untimed: Not available

Scoring: Examiner evaluated

Cost: Examiner kit for 35 (administration booklet, test book, 35 record forms) $16.25

Publisher: Guidance Centre

Information and availability unconfirmed; last verified in 1987.

THE BODER TEST OF READING-SPELLING PATTERNS
Refer to page 631.

===============

BORMUTH'S READING PASSAGES AND CARVER'S QUESTIONS
Ronald P. Carver

Grades 1–college

Purpose: Measures reading comprehension. Used for research in reading.

Description: Multiple-item paper-pencil examination measuring reading comprehension. Questions cover 330 reading passages that are 100 words in length. Multiple-choice questions are used for 80 passages, and paraphrase questions are used for 160 passages. The passages were sampled from curriculum materials used with students in Grades 1–college. Examiner required. Suitable for group use.

Untimed: Not available

Scoring: Hand key

Cost: Examination kit (manual, price list for research materials that are available) $5.00

Publisher: Revrac Publications, Inc.

BRAILLE UNIT RECOGNITION BATTERY DIAGNOSTIC TEST OF GRADE 2 LITERARY BRAILLE
Bill J. Duckworth and Hilda R. Caton

Ages 9–adult
Grades 4 and above

Purpose: Measures visually handicapped individuals' knowledge of the literary braille code.

Description: 315–item paper-pencil multiple-choice test measuring knowledge of the literary braille code in seven contexts: Alphabet Letters (26 items); 1-, 2-, and 3–digit numbers (30 items); Phonograms (50 items); Morphograms (27 items); Letter Words (23 items); 1 to 5 shape wordlets (129 items); punctuation (30 items). A fourth-grade reading level is required. The test itself is administered in braille. Examiner required. Not suitable for group use.

Timed: 1 hour

Scoring: Hand key

Cost: Test $3.17; manual $17.07

Publisher: American Printing House for the Blind, Inc.

CLASSROOM READING INVENTORY, SIXTH EDITION
Nicholas J. Silvaroli

Child, adolescent
Grades 1 and above

Purpose: Assesses student's specific word-recognition and comprehension skills. Used for planning individual skills-oriented reading programs.

Description: Multiple-item paper-pencil and oral-response inventory measuring reading capabilities. The test is available in four forms: Forms A and B for students in Grades 1–6, Form C for junior high-school students, and Form D for high-school and adult students. Forms A and B consist of three parts: Graded Word Lists, Graded Oral Paragraphs, and Graded Spelling Survey. Forms C and D contain two parts, Graded Word Lists and Graded Oral Paragraphs. The inventory provides information on students' independent, instructional, and frustration reading levels and on their listening capacity levels. The test also provides specific subskill development information in the areas of word recognition (consonant, vowel, and syllable) and comprehension (literal, inference, and vocabulary). All four forms may be reproduced without the publisher's permission. Examiner required. Suitable for group use.

Untimed: 12 minutes

Scoring: Examiner evaluated

Cost: Contact publisher

Publisher: William C. Brown Company Publishers

CLOZE READING TESTS
D. Young

Child, adolescent—Ages 8-12.6

Purpose: Assesses students' reading skills.

Description: Multiple-item paper-pencil test utilizing the cloze technique to measure children's reading skills. Students read short passages and choose from a list those words that have been deleted from the passage. The test is available on levels 1, 2, and 3. Each level contains the same practice items and instructions and requires equal administration time, allowing the simultaneous use of more than one level in a classroom. Examiner required. Suitable for group use.
BRITISH PUBLISHER

Timed: 35 minutes

Scoring: Hand key

Cost: 20 tests (specify level) £3.50; manual £3.25

Publisher: Hodder & Stoughton

COGNITIVE SPEED BATTERY
Ronald P. Carver

Grades 2 and above

Purpose: Measures an individual's cognitive speed. Facilitates the diagnoses of individuals who could be helped to "raud" faster.

Description: Multiple-item paper-pencil battery of two tests measuring cognitive speed. The Speed of Thinking Test (STT) requires the individual to mark strings of paired letters of the alphabet, a variant of the letter-name task or Posner task. The Speed of Deciding Test (SDT) is administered to control for simple reaction time and the psychomotor speed of marking. The scores on both tests are used to derive a measure of cognitive speed (in grade equivalent units). When used in conjuction with the Rate Level Test (RLT; see separate entry), the Cognitive Speed Battery helps diagnose individuals whose reading and comprehension rate ("rauding") could be improved. Examiner required. Suitable for group use.

Timed: STT 2 minutes; SDT 1 minute

Scoring: Hand key

Cost: Examination kit (1 STT, 1 practice STT, 1 SDT, 1 practice SDT, manual) $5.00

Publisher: Revrac Publications, Inc.

DEGREES OF READING POWER® (DRP)

New York State Education Department, Carnegie Corporation, and Touchstone Applied Science Associates, Inc.

Child, adolescent, adult Grades 3–12, college

Purpose: Assesses reading comprehension of students. Used to identify and place students in reading programs, assess reading goals and standards, relate reading ability to functional reading situations, make admission decisions, and measure program evaluation outcomes. Also used to determine the English-language proficiency of bilingual students, to plan instruction for special education students, and to identify gifted students.

Description: Multiple-item paper-pencil multiple-choice text-referenced test in which students read a series of nonfiction prose passages, each with seven deleted

words. Students supply the missing words from among five choices provided for each deletion. The passages progress from easy to difficult.

The test yields six scores: raw score, independent level score (indicates the difficulty of textbooks the student can read with a 90% chance of understanding the material), three instructional level scores (70%, 75%, and 80% chance of student comprehending materials), and frustration level score (indicates probability of comprehension of 50% or less). Percentile ranks and NCEs are available for Grades 3–12.

The test is available in two alternate series, PA and PB, for Grades 3–12, with four levels available in each series. Forms PA-8 and PB-8 (8 passages, 56 items) are recommended for Grades 3–5; forms PA-6 and PB-6 (11 passages, 77 items) for Grades 5–7; forms PA-4 and PB-4 (11 passages, 77 items) for Grades 7–9; and forms PA-2 and PB-2 (11 passages, 77 items) for Grades 9–12. In addition, two alternate forms, CP-1A and CP-1B (9 passages, 63 items), are available for Grades 12–14. A handbook includes conversion and norms tables and interpretive information.

A Readability Report lists the difficulty of published instructional materials in DRP units. The report can be used to make decisions regarding textbook adoption, match reading assignments to student ability, and place transfer students familiar with different texts into the same level of difficulty in the texts used by the new school. In addition, a software program developed for schools and libraries allows the assignment of DRP readability levels for locally developed materials or other texts not listed in the Readability Report. Basic scoring service includes an alphabetical class roster, ranked grade roster, and summary statistics reports. Optional services include an individual report, student labels, a raw score summary, an item response summary, and research tapes or disks. Examiner required. Suitable for group use.

Untimed: About one class period

Scoring: Hand key; machine scored by publisher or locally

Cost: Examination set $15.00; 35 test booklets $47.30; 40 answer sheets $11.25; handbook $13.95; basic scoring (with norms) $1.35 per student

Publisher: Touchstone Applied Science Associates, Inc.

DIAGNOSTIC SCREENING TEST: READING, THIRD EDITION (DSTR)
Thomas D. Gnagey and Patricia A. Gnagey

Child, adolescent
Grades 1–13

Purpose: Determines reading achievement levels and diagnoses common reading problems by testing word recognition and reading and listening comprehension.

Description: 84–word paper-pencil test yielding two major scores (Word Recognition and Reading Comprehension Grade Equivalents) and eight diagnostic scores that reflect skills in using seven basic word attack skills, as well as sight vocabulary. The student reads a word list and comprehension passages aloud and answers prescribed questions. The examiner then reads a passage aloud and the student answers questions. The test yields a consolidation index that reflects how solid or spotty each skill is. The test is available in two equivalent forms, A and B. Examiner required. Not suitable for group use.

Untimed: 5–10 minutes

Scoring: Hand key

Cost: Manual, 25 Form A, 25 Form B $32.00

Publisher: Slosson Educational Publications, Inc.

DIAGNOSTIC WORD PATTERNS: TESTS 1, 2, AND 3
Evelyn Buckley

Grades 3 and above

Purpose: Assesses basic phonic knowledge. Used to help classroom teachers determine general word attack concepts to review with an entire class and to identify individual students' strengths and weaknesses in order to develop suitable reading programs.

Description: Three verbal paper-pencil 100–word tests, each of which can be used to test spelling and/or word recognition. When used as a spelling test, the words are dictated to the students, who write the words on their answer sheets. When used as a word recognition test, the same words are printed on cards for the students to read aloud. As a spelling test, the words can be administered to groups; as a word recognition test they must be administered individually. Test 1 deals with short vowels, nonphonetic words, and consonant digraphs. Test 2 covers vowel digraph and diphthong patterns, and nonphonetic words. Test 3 contains suffixes, two-syllable words, and more material from Tests 1 and 2. Materials include a teacher's manual. Examiner required. Word recognition test not suitable for group use.

Untimed: 20–45 minutes

Scoring: Examiner evaluated

Cost: Tests 1, 2, 3, teacher's manual $3.85; 50 student charts per test each $3.80; cards for word recognition test $4.40

Publisher: Educators Publishing Service, Inc.

FORMAL READING INVENTORY (FRI)
J. Lee Wiederholt

Child, adolescent
Grades 1–12

Purpose: Assesses silent reading comprehension and diagnoses the oral reading miscues of students. Used to develop teaching strategies.

Description: Multiple-item paper-pencil and oral-response test in four forms assessing reading comprehension and miscues. Each form contains 13 developmentally sequenced passages with five literal, inferential, critical, and affective multiple-choice questions following each story. Form A is used to derive a silent reading quotient. Form B, read orally by the student and marked by the examiner on a separate worksheet, is used to note reading behaviors, including comprehension strategies (meaning similarity), appropriate grammar forms (function similarity), word attack strategies (graphic/phonemic similarity), self-correction strategies, omissions, additions, dialect, and reversals. Form C (silent) and Form D (oral) are used as posttests. Examiner required. The silent reading forms are suitable for group use. The oral reading forms are not suitable for group use.

Untimed: Varies

Scoring: Hand key

Cost: Complete kit (examiner's manual, student book, 50 student record forms, storage box) $64.00

Publisher: PRO-ED

GAPADOL READING COMPREHENSION TESTS
J. McLeod and J. Anderson

Child, adolescent—Ages 7-16

Purpose: Measures reading comprehension. Used for identifying student achievement as part of an educational evaluation.

Description: Multiple-item paper-pencil tests of reading achievement using the cloze technique. The student fills in words omitted from reading passages. The test is useful for placement, information on a child's reading and spelling techniques, and retesting. Available in two alternate forms, G and Y. Examiner required. Suitable for group use.
AUSTRALIAN PUBLISHER

Timed: 15 minutes

Scoring: Examiner evaluated

Cost: Complete kit (25 copies Test G, 25 copies Test Y) $29.95

Publisher: Heinemann Publishers Australia Pty Limited

GATES-MACGINITIE READING TEST, CANADIAN EDITION (GMRT)
Walter MacGinitie

Child, adolescent Grades K-12

Purpose: Measures students' reading and vocabulary achievement levels. Used for placement and class planning.

Description: Multiple-item paper-pencil test of vocabulary and reading comprehension. The basic Level R contains 54 items. Levels A-F contain 85-89 items. Examiner required. Suitable for group use.
CANADIAN PUBLISHER

Timed: 55 minutes

Untimed: Level R 65 minutes

Scoring: Hand key; may be computer scored

Cost: 35 booklets $24.20; manual $13.00; key $2.30

Publisher: Nelson Canada

GATES-MACGINITIE READING TESTS, THIRD EDITION
Walter H. MacGinitie and Ruth K. MacGinitie

Child, adolescent Grades K-12

Purpose: Measures the reading achievement of students in Grades K-12. Used to identify students who would benefit from remedial or accelerated programs, to evaluate instructional programs, and to counsel students and report progress to parents.

Description: Multiple-item paper-pencil test assessing reading comprehension and vocabulary development. The test is available on nine levels: PRE (Grade K), R (Grade 1), 1 (Grade 1.3-1.9), 2 (Grade 2), 3 (Grade 3), 4 (Grade 4), 5/6 (Grades 5-6), 7/9 (Grades 7-9), 10/12 (Grades 10-12). Level PRE is a readiness test that assesses the student's knowledge of important background concepts on which beginning reading skills are built. Level R measures beginning reading achievement in four skill areas: initial consonants and consonant clusters, final consonant and consonant clusters, vowels, and use of context. Test levels 1 through 10/12 each include two tests—a vocabulary test and a comprehension test. Examiner required. Suitable for group use.

Timed: Levels 1-10/12 55 minutes

Untimed: Level PRE 85–105 minutes; Level R 55–70 minutes

Scoring: Hand key; may be computer scored

Cost: Contact publisher regarding price and availability

Publisher: The Riverside Publishing Company

GRAY ORAL READING TESTS— REVISED (GORT-R)
J. Lee Wiederholt and Brian R. Bryant

Child, adolescent—Ages 7–17

Purpose: Measures growth in oral reading and diagnoses reading difficulties in students.

Description: Multiple-item oral-response test in two alternate, equivalent forms. The student reads 13 developmentally sequenced passages and responds to five comprehension questions. The passage score, derived from reading rate and errors, is reported in standard scores and percentiles. This new test provides standard scores and percentiles for oral reading comprehension and a system for analyzing miscues in meaning similarity, function similarity, graphic/phonemic similarity, and self-correction. Examiner required. Not suitable for group use.

Untimed: 20–30 minutes

Scoring: Examiner evaluated

Cost: Complete kit (examiner's manual, student book, 25 profile/examiner record forms, storage box) $79.00

Publisher: PRO-ED

HUDSON EDUCATION SKILLS INVENTORY-READING (HESI-R)
Refer to page 461.

INFORMAL EVALUATION OF ORAL READING
Deborah Edel

All ages

Purpose: Measures reading ability of individuals of all ages. Used to estimate the student's reading level and diagnose

specific reading weaknesses. Also used with students learning English as a second language.

Description: Multiple-item oral-response test evaluating reading ability by informally surveying the student's reading performance. Eight reading passages measure the following factors: independent, instructional, frustration, oral comprehension, pattern of reading, type and frequency of reading error, reading style, and behavior. The test may be used at any level of oral-reading ability. Examiner required. Not suitable for group use.

Untimed: 15–35 minutes

Scoring: Examiner evaluated

Cost: Complete set (2 reading booklets, 25 evaluation forms, instructions) $9.95

Publisher: Book-Lab

Information and availability unconfirmed; last verified in 1988.

INTER-AMERICAN SERIES: TEST OF READING
Refer to page 577.

IOWA SILENT READING TESTS (ISRT)
Roger Farr, coordinating editor

Adolescent, adult Grades 6 and above

Purpose: Assesses ability to read. Used to diagnose student strengths and weaknesses and for implementation of remedial lesson plans.

Description: Multiple-item battery of paper-pencil tests measuring four reading skill areas. The subtests are Vocabulary, Comprehension, Directed Reading (work-study skills), and Reading Efficiency (rate with comprehension). Items in the Directed Reading subtest measure students' ability to use reference sources. The test is divided into three levels: Level 1 for Grades 6–9, Level 2 for Grades 9–community college, and Level 3 for accelerated students in Grades 11 and 12, college students, and professional groups. Level 3 does not include the Directed Reading subtest. Materials include two alternate and equivalent forms, E and F. Examiner required. Suitable for group use.

Timed: Level 1 1 hour, 31 minutes; Level 2 1 hour, 26 minutes; Level 3 56 minutes

Scoring: Hand key; may be machine scored; scoring service available

Cost: Specimen set, specify level (test, MRC answer document, hand-scorable answer document, class record, manual of directions, pupil profile) $10.00

Publisher: The Psychological Corporation

Information and availability unconfirmed; last verified in 1988.

MCCARTHY INDIVIDUALIZED DIAGNOSTIC READING INVENTORY
William G. McCarthy

Grades 2 and above

Purpose: Diagnoses the development of specific areas of reading skills for placement and the selection of appropriate instructional materials.

Description: 11 brief reading selections ranked from primer to Grade 12, read by the student to the examiner. Beginning with Part One, the student's skills are quickly measured by the Controlled Vocabulary List and Basal Reader Graded Selections. All reading errors can be marked on the Teacher Administration Booklet. Based on the student's performance in Part 1, the appropriate reading selections are administered for Parts 2, 3, and 4. The factors measured are oral reading, reading comprehension, critical thinking skills, vocabulary, phonics, word recognition, sight vocabulary, and study skills. Reading and other academic interests, psychosocial factors, and physical health also are evaluated. The last part of the test moves into prescription by providing structure to develop a preliminary plan for reading instruction based on the information gained in the inventory. Examiner required. Not suitable for group use.

Untimed: 1–1½ hours

Scoring: Examiner evaluated

Cost: Information booklet $2.40; teacher booklet $6.50; pupil booklet $1.60; 12 individual record forms and 1 class record sheet $7.50

Publisher: Educators Publishing Service, Inc.

METROPOLITAN READING INSTRUCTIONAL TESTS
Roger Farr, George A. Prescott, Irving H. Balow, and Thomas P. Hogan

---

Child
Grades K.5–9.9

Purpose: Measures reading skills. Used for providing prescriptive information on the educational performance of individual pupils.

Description: Multiple-item series of paper-pencil tests measuring major components of reading skills, including visual discrimination, letter recognition, auditory discrimination, sight vocabulary, phoneme/grapheme: consonants, phoneme/grapheme: vowels, vocabulary in context, word part clues, rate of comprehension, skimming and scanning, and reading comprehension. The test is divided into six levels: Primer (Grades K.5–1.4), Primary 1 (Grades 1.5–2.4), Primary 2 (Grades 2.5–3.4), Elementary (Grades 3.5–4.9), Intermediate (Grades 5.0–6.9), and Advanced 1 (Grades 7.0–9.9). Each level assesses four to seven of the above reading skills components. Materials include two alternate and equivalent forms, JI and KI. The test is one in a series of instructional tests related to the Metropolitan Achievement Tests Survey Battery. The test has been superseded by the MAT6 Reading Diagnostic Tests and is available only as long as supplies last. Examiner required. Suitable for group use.

Timed: Varies

Scoring: Hand key; may be machine scored; scoring service available

Cost: Specimen sets, specify level (test, manual) $17.00; the Intermediate and Advanced 1 sets include a hand-scorable document

Publisher: The Psychological Corporation

Information and availability unconfirmed; last verified in 1988.

NATIONAL ACHIEVEMENT TESTS: ENGLISH, READING, LITERATURE, AND VOCABULARY TESTS—READING

Refer to page 473.

POPE INVENTORY OF BASIC READING SKILLS
Lillie Pope

**Child, adolescent
Grades K–12**

Purpose: Evaluates basic reading skills. Appropriate for all students reading below the fourth-grade level. Used to plan reading instruction.

Description: Oral reading, verbal word recognition, and written responses measure 13 basic reading and word recognition skills, including the ability to match symbols with sounds, knowledge of right and left, and knowledge of basic sight words. The student's responses are evaluated and summarized in 12 areas. Examiner required. Not suitable for group use.

Untimed: 15–30 minutes

Scoring: Examiner evaluated

Cost: Complete kit (20 forms) $9.95

Publisher: Book-Lab

Information and availability unconfirmed; last verified in 1988.

PRESCRIPTIVE READING PERFORMANCE TEST: A SCALE FOR THE DIAGNOSIS OF DYSLEXIA (PRPT)
Janet B. Fudala

**Child, adolescent
Grades 1 and above**

Purpose: Assesses an individual's reading grade level and prereading readiness and diagnoses a student's strengths and weaknesses in word attack skills. Used for reading or learning disabilities programs and to comply with PL 94–142.

Description: Multiple-item paper-pencil and oral-response test assessing a student's reading and spelling performance and identifying four groups of readers:

normal readers, readers with auditory problems, readers with visual problems, and readers with auditory and visual problems. The student reads words presented on graded word lists. By evaluating words that are in the student's sight vocabulary and words that are not, the examiner documents strengths and weaknesses in the visual and auditory channels and identifies patterns of performance that have characteristic prescriptive educational implications. The manual presents standardization, validity and reliability data, and a number of case studies. Examiner required. Not suitable for group use.

Untimed: 15–20 minutes

Scoring: Hand key

Cost: Complete kit (one reusable set of word lists, 25 record forms, 25 answer sheets, manual) $45.00

Publisher: Western Psychological Services

PRI READING SYSTEMS (PRI/RS)
CTB/McGraw-Hill

**Child, adolescent
Grades K–9**

Purpose: Assesses reading and language arts skills.

Description: Multiple-item paper-pencil test measuring four language arts skill areas: oral language (language and comprehension), word attack and usage (word analysis, vocabulary, word usage), comprehension (literal, interpretive, and critical), and applications (study skills, content area reading).

The system is available on five grade levels: Level A (Grades K–1), Level B (Grades 1–2), Level C (Grades 2–3), Level D (Grades 4–6), and Level E (Grades 7–9). It is available in two formats: System 1 and System 2. System 1 uses a graded approach, which assesses skills by grade level. Each skill can be assessed at two levels of specificity: category objectives assessment level and instructional objectives assessment level. System 2 assesses skills across grade levels. Classroom kits of instructional materials and mastery tests are available for both systems. Examiner required. Suitable for group use.

Untimed: Not available

Scoring: Hand key; may be computer scored

Cost: Classroom kit (teacher resource files, mastery tests, mastery test reading passage book, tutor activity books, Student worksheet spirit masters, teacher's guide, continuous progress monitoring log, systems overview chart) Level A $246.40; Levels B-E each $280.00

Publisher: CTB/Macmillan/McGraw-Hill

THE RATE LEVEL TEST (RLT)
Ronald P. Carver

Child, adolescent, adult Grades 2–college

Purpose: Measures how quickly an individual can comprehend reading material.

Description: Multiple-item paper-pencil test measuring "rauding" rate, the rate at which an individual can read and comprehend material. The rauding rate does not measure comprehension of material that is skimmed or studied. The examiner first administers a practice form. After completing the practice form, the actual test is distributed, and the student reads a passage and answers questions. Scores yielded include the Rate Level Score (given in GE units) and a words-per-minute score. The RLT is available in two forms, A and B. The test is one of two tests that comprise The Reading Efficiency Level Battery (see separate entry). Examiner required. Suitable for group use.

Timed: 2 minutes

Scoring: Hand key

Cost: Examination kit (1 copy of test, User's Guide) $2.00; 100 tests and 100 practice forms (specify form) $25.00; User's Guide $2.00; technical manual $5.00

Publisher: Revrac Publications, Inc.

THE RAUDING EFFICIENCY LEVEL TEST (RELT)
Ronald P. Carver

Child, adolescent, adult

Purpose: Measures reading comprehension or general reading ability. Used with individuals reading at the second-grade level and above.

Description: Multiple-item computer-administered objective test measuring "rauding" efficiency, or general reading ability. The individual is administered three to seven reading passages from a total of 18 and then answers questions designed to measure the individual's comprehension of each passage. The program operates on IBM PC computers. Self-administered. Not suitable for group use

Untimed: 15–30 minutes

Scoring: Computer scored

Cost: Manual $2.00; computer disk (test, directions) $100.00

Publisher: Revrac Publications, Inc.

READING EFFICIENCY LEVEL BATTERY (RELB)
Ronald P. Carver

Child, adolescent, adult Grades 2–college

Purpose: Measures three factors involved in reading comprehension: accuracy level, rate level, and efficiency level. Used for placing students in instructional groups.

Description: Multiple-item paper-pencil battery composed of two instruments measuring levels of accuracy, rate, and efficiency of comprehension. The Accuracy Level Test (ALT; see separate entry) is a vocabulary test measuring the accuracy with which individuals comprehend the material they read. The Rate Level Test (RLT; see separate entry) measures the rate at which individuals comprehend reading material. An Efficiency Level Score is obtained by averaging the GE scores from the ALT and RLT. Percentile rank and standard score tables are provided for Grades 3–16. Both the ALT and the RLT are available in forms A and B. Examiner required. Suitable for group use.

Timed: ALT 10 minutes; RLT 2 minutes

Scoring: Hand key

Cost: Examination kit (1 ALT, 1 RLT, RELB manual) $5.00

Publisher: Revrac Publications, Inc.

READING EFFICIENCY TESTS
Lyle L. Miller

Adolescent, adult
Grades 7 and above

Purpose: Measures pre- and posttesting of reading rate, comprehension, and efficiency.

Description: Five multiple-item paper-pencil tests that include content on history, geography, government, culture, and the people of Brazil, Japan, India, New Zealand, and Switzerland. Each reading test contains 5,000 words, and each line of the test is numbered. Each answer sheet contains 50 items about the content of the reading selection. When the timed test is stopped, each student marks the line on which he was reading and is tested only on the material he has read. Examiner required. Suitable for group use.

Timed: 10 minutes per test

Scoring: Hand key

Cost: 20 booklets $15.00; 20 answer sheets $5.00; specimen set $5.00

Publisher: Developmental Reading Distributors

READING SPLIT FORM (FORM R)
Mary Meeker and Robert Meeker

Adolescent, adult
Grades 7 and above

Purpose: Assesses the reading ability of elementary, intermediate, high-school, and college students.

Description: Multiple-item paper-pencil test measuring reading ability. Discipline-focused test items are selected from the SOI-LA Basic Test. The Basic Test manual is required for administration. See

entry for the Structure of Intellect (SOI) test. Examiner required. Suitable for group use.

Timed: 1 hour

Scoring: Hand key

Cost: Examiner's manual $24.50; test form $1.95

Publisher: Western Psychological Services

READING TEST SERIES

Child, adolescent
Grades 1–12

Purpose: Assesses reading skills. Used to screen students and provide teachers with information regarding the overall reading performance of a class.

Description: Five multiple-item tests measuring reading comprehension. The tests are Reading Test A (ages 6–8), Reading Test AD (ages 8–10), Reading Test BD (ages 7–10), Reading Comprehension Test DE (ages 10–12), and Reading Test EH 1–2 (ages 11–15). Reading Tests A, AD, and BD consist of multiple-choice sentence-completion items. Reading Comprehension Test DE (50 items) measures understanding of complex reading passages. Test 1 of Reading Test EH 1–2 consists of 60 sentence-completion items. Test 2 contains 35 questions based on comprehension passages. Examiner required. Suitable for group use. BRITISH PUBLISHER

Timed: Varies

Scoring: Hand key

Cost: Contact publisher

Publisher: NFER-NELSON Publishing Company Ltd.

SLOSSON ORAL READING TEST-REVISED (SORT-R)
Richard L. Slosson

Child, adolescent
Grades 1–12

Purpose: Measures reading ability and identifies reading handicaps.

Description: Oral screening test providing an estimate of a person's word recognition level. The SORT-R is based upon the ability to pronounce words at different levels of difficulty, primer through high school. Examiner required. Not suitable for group use.

Untimed: 3–5 minutes

Scoring: Examiner evaluated

Cost: Complete kit $25.00; 50 answer sheets $13.00; manual $10.00; flipcard booklet $5.00

Publisher: Slosson Educational Publications, Inc.

SLOSSON SCREENING INTELLIGENCE TEST-REVISED (SSIT-R)
Refer to page 61.

SPADAFORE DIAGNOSTIC READING TEST (SDRT)
Gerald J. Spadafore

Child, adolescent, adult

Purpose: Assesses reading skills of students in Grades 1–12 and adults. Used as a screening and diagnostic instrument for academic placement and career guidance counseling.

Description: Four subtests assess word recognition, oral reading and comprehension, silent reading comprehension, and listening comprehension. Criterion-referenced test items are graded for difficulty. Independent, Instructional, and Frustration reading and comprehension levels are designated for performance at each grade level. Test results may be used for screening to determine whether reading problems exist at a student's current grade placement. Administration for screening requires 30 minutes for all four subtests and determines whether reading problems exist at a student's current grade placement. Administration for diagnostic purposes requires 60 minutes for all four subtests and yields a comparison of decoding reading skills. Guidelines are provided for interpreting performance in terms of vocational literacy. The test may be scored as it is administered. Provisions for conducting a detailed error analysis of oral reading are included. Examiner required. Not suitable for group use.

Untimed: Screening 30 minutes; diagnosis 1 hour

Scoring: Examiner evaluated

Cost: Test kit (manual, test plates, 10 test booklets) $55.00

Publisher: Academic Therapy Publications

STANFORD MEASUREMENT SERIES—STANFORD DIAGNOSTIC READING TEST (SDRT): THIRD EDITION
Refer to page 489.

TEST OF READING COMPREHENSION (TORC)
Virginia L. Brown,
Donald D. Hammill, and
J. Lee Wiederholt

Child, adolescent
Grades 2–12

Purpose: Assesses students' reading comprehension. Used to diagnose reading problems in terms of current psycholinguistic theories of reading comprehension as a constructive process involving both language and cognition.

Description: Eight multiple-item paper-pencil subtests measuring aspects of reading comprehension. Three of the subtests (General Vocabulary, Syntactic Similarities, and Paragraph Reading) are combined to determine a basic Comprehension Core, which is expressed as a Reading Comprehension Quotient (RCQ). Three subtests measure students' abilities to read the vocabularies of math, science, and social studies. Subtest #7, Reading the Directions of Schoolwork, is a diagnostic tool for younger or remedial students. The eighth subtest is Sentence Sequences. Scaled scores are provided for each subtest. Examiner required. Not suitable for group use.

Untimed: 1 hour, 45 minutes

Scoring: Hand key

Cost: Complete kit (examiner's manual, 10 student booklets, 50 answer sheets, 50 profile sheets, 50 Subtest 7) $89.00

Publisher: PRO-ED

TESTS OF READING COMPREHENSION (TORCH)
The Australian Council for Educational Research Limited

Child, adolescent Grades 3–10

Purpose: Measures reading ability.

Description: 14–passage reading test. Passages are of graded difficulty. After reading a specified passage, students are referred to an answer sheet that consists of a retelling of the passage read. The retelling contains gaps, corresponding to details in the original text, that students are required to complete using their own words. Australian data are presented as stanines and percentiles. A reading task analysis is also provided. Examiner required. Suitable for group use. AUSTRALIAN PUBLISHER

Untimed: 30 minutes

Scoring: Hand key

Cost: Contact publisher

Publisher: The Australian Council for Educational Research

WOODCOCK READING MASTERY TESTS-REVISED (WMRT-R)
Richard W. Woodcock

Ages 5–75 and older

Purpose: Assesses an individual's reading ability. Suggested for use by educational diagnosticians, reading specialists, and special education teachers.

Description: Oral-response point-to test assessing reading. Form G is comprised of six core subtests and one optional subtest: Visual-Auditory Learning (7 items), Letter Identification (51 items), Word Identification (106 items), Word Attack (45 items), Word Comprehension (146 items), Passage Comprehension (68 items), and Supplementary Letter Checklist (36 items). Form H is composed of four subtests: Word Identification (106 items), Word Attack (45 items), Word Comprehension (146 items), and Passage Comprehension (68 items). Age- and grade-based percentile ranks, standard scores ($M = 100$, $SD = 15$), NCEs (for

Chapter 1), and age and grade equivalents are provided. Materials include easel and test record form. This is a revision of the 1973 Woodcock Reading Mastery Tests. The examiner must have completed graduate training in measurement guidance and individual assessment. Computer software available for score conversions. May be used with individuals with physical and mental disabilities. Examiner required. Not suitable for group use.

Untimed: 10–30 minutes per cluster

Scoring: Examiner evaluated

Cost: Form G and Form H combined kit $198.00; Form G complete kit $125.00; Form H complete kit $120.00

Publisher: American Guidance Service

WORD SEARCH
Godfrey Thomson Unit for Educational Research

Child—Ages 7–12

Purpose: Assesses the reading level competence of children. Used to identify children with reading difficulties and who need remediation.

Description: Multiple-item paper-pencil test assessing children's reading levels. Children read short passages of whole stories or descriptions and supply the missing words by selecting from among several provided for each deletion. The test is available on two levels, 1 (ages 7–10) and 2 (ages 9–12), with alternate forms, A and B, provided at each level. Examiner required. Suitable for group use. BRITISH PUBLISHER

Untimed: 30 minutes

Scoring: Hand key

Cost: 20 test forms (specify level) £4.50; manual £3.25

Publisher: Hodder & Stoughton

Academic Subjects: Religious Education

CATHOLIC FAITH INVENTORY (CFI)
Kenneth Boyack, Robert D. Duggan, and Paul Huesing

Adult

Purpose: Measures attitudes, beliefs, and behaviors reflecting the integration of the Catholic faith into an individual's life. Used by pastors, catechists, pastoral counselors, and individuals who direct and develop lay ministry programs or spiritual programs for seminarians and religious persons. Used to enhance self-knowledge and spiritual growth and initiate pastoral dialogue.

Description: 108–item paper-pencil instrument surveying issues related to spiritual growth. The items are divided into three clusters: Spiritual Conversion, Moral Conversion, and Ecclesial Conversion. Spiritual Conversion (scripture, prayer, spiritual awareness) assesses an individual's awareness of life's spiritual meaning and committment to spiritual growth. Responses to the Moral Conversion cluster (conscience and morality, social justice) reflect the degree to which an individual's behaviors are rooted in Christian values and the moral teachings of the Catholic church. The third cluster, Ecclesial Conversion (basic Christian doctrine, Catholic identity, Catholic sacrament, community participation), reveals an individual's acceptance of, identification with, and involvement in the Catholic church. The instrument yields a CFI Total Score, which is based on a comparison of the subject's responses to preferred Catholic patterns of response. Materials consist of a guidebook, inventory booklet, answer sheet, scoring keys, minister's record form, participant's workbook, and group record form. Examiner required. Suitable for group use.

Untimed: 30 minutes

Scoring: Hand key

Cost: Contact publisher

Publisher: Paulist Press

NEW TESTAMENT DIAGNOSTIC
Fred R. Johnson

Adult—Ages 17 and older

Purpose: Measures and assesses New Testament knowledge.

Description: 150–item paper-pencil multiple-choice test with five subtests: Introduction to New Testament World and Records, Gospels, Acts, Epistles, and Revelation. Raw scores are converted to 100% scale and percentile ranks. Examiner required. Suitable for group use.

Timed: 1 hour

Scoring: Hand key

Cost: Test $1.00; 100 tests $75.00

Publisher: American Association of Bible Colleges

A PARTIAL INDEX OF MODERNIZATION: MEASUREMENT OF ATTITUDES TOWARD MORALITY
Panos D. Bardis

Adolescent, adult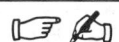

Purpose: Measures attitudes toward traditional concepts of sin. Used for clinical assessment, counseling, research on religion and morals, and discussions in religion and social science classes.

Description: 10–item paper-pencil test in which the subject rates 10 statements about sin and morality from 0 (least amount of agreement) to 10 (highest amount of agreement). The score equals the sum of the 10 numerical responses. The theoretical range of scores extends from 0 (least modern) to 100 (most modern). Examiner/self-administered. Suitable for group use.

Untimed: 5 minutes

Scoring: Examiner evaluated

Cost: Free

Publisher: Panos D. Bardis

A RELIGION SCALE
Refer to page 81.

STANDARDIZED BIBLE CONTENT TESTS
AABC Commission on Testing and Measurement

Adult

Purpose: Evaluates knowledge of the Bible. Used for college entrance examinations, class assignment, and comparing national and institutional norms.

Description: 150–item paper-pencil multiple-choice test measuring biblical knowledge: people, history, doctrine, geography, and quotations. The test is recommended for institutions of higher education and is available in six equivalent forms, A, B, C, D, E, F. Self-administered. Suitable for group use.
Timed: 45 minutes
Scoring: Hand key
Cost: Test (specify form) $1.00; answer sheet $0.10; scoring key $2.00; manual $5.00
Publisher: American Association of Bible Colleges

STANDARDIZED BIBLE CONTENT TESTS-FORM SP
Standardized Bible Content Test Committee

Adolescent, adult—Ages 15 and older

Purpose: Measures and assesses Bible knowledge for counseling.

Description: 150–item paper-pencil multiple-choice test. Scores are reported as percentiles relative to AABC member colleges. Examiner required. Suitable for group use.
Timed: 45 minutes
Scoring: Hand key
Cost: Test $1.00; 100 tests $75.00
Publisher: American Association of Bible Colleges

THANATOMETER
Panos D. Bardis

Adolescent, adult

Purpose: Measures awareness and acceptance of death.

Description: 20–item paper-pencil Likert scale assessing attitudes toward death and dying. Examinee responds by indicating degree of agreement with each item. Self-administered. Suitable for group use.
Untimed: 12 minutes
Scoring: Hand key
Cost: Free
Publisher: Panos D. Bardis

Academic Subjects: Science: General Science

ACER SCIENCE TESTS

Child—Years 7–12

Purpose: Measures achievement in science courses. Used for diagnosis of individual student strengths and weaknesses.

Description: Four paper-pencil multiple-choice tests of basic science subjects. Tests are Australian Biology Test Item Bank for year 11; Australian Biology Test Item Bank, year 12; ACER Chemistry Item Bank; and Test of Enquiry Skills (TOES), years 7 and 8. Examiner required. Suitable for group use.
AUSTRALIAN PUBLISHER
Timed: Varies
Scoring: Hand key
Cost: Contact publisher
Publisher: The Australian Council for Educational Research Limited

ADVANCED HIGH SCHOOL CHEMISTRY TESTS

Adolescent, adult Grades 10 and above

Purpose: Measures achievement in advanced or honors courses in high school chemistry. Evaluates student strengths and weaknesses and aids in assigning grades.

Description: 60–item paper-pencil multiple-choice test covering 10 areas of high-school chemistry: atomic structure; chemical bonding; thermodynamics; kinetics; solids, liquids, gases, and solutions; acid-base chemistry; electrochemistry; chemical periodicity; descriptive chemistry and stoichiometry; and laboratory procedures and techniques. Materials include 1986–ADV (60 items), Form 1988–ADV (60 items), and Form 1990 ADV (60 items). The tests are for use only by authorized chemistry teachers and administrators. Examiner required. Suitable for group use.

Timed: Form 1986–ADV 110 minutes; Form 1988–ADV 110 minutes; Form 1990–ADV 110 minutes

Scoring: Hand key

Cost: Specimen set $6.00; 25 to 100 tests $0.75 each; 25 answer sheets $3.00; scoring stencil $1.00

Publisher: American Chemical Society, Division of Chemical Education

BIOCHEMISTRY TESTS

Adolescent, adult
College students

Purpose: Measures achievement in undergraduate general biochemistry courses. Evaluates prospective graduate students and serves as a comprehensive final examination for undergraduate courses.

Description: 60–item paper-pencil test covering topics in general biochemistry. Forty percent of the items deal with the properties and structure-function relationships of biological molecules, and sixty percent of the questions cover intermediary metabolism and its control, the biochemistry of information macromolecules, and biochemical methods. Materials include Form 1977 and Form 1982. The test is for use only by authorized chemistry teachers and administrators. Examiner required. Suitable for group use.

Timed: Form 1982 120 minutes; Form 1977 120 minutes

Scoring: Hand key

Cost: Specimen set $6.00; 25 to 100 tests $0.90 each; 25 answer sheets $3.00; scoring stencil $1.00

Publisher: American Chemical Society, Division of Chemical Education

BRIEF ORGANIC CHEMISTRY TESTS

Adolescent, adult
College students

Purpose: Measures achievement in undergraduate organic chemistry courses. Evaluates student strengths and weaknesses and aids in assigning grades.

Description: 70–item paper-pencil test measuring topics in organic chemistry, including bonding, isomerism, functional group recognition, IUPAC nomenclature, physical properties, acidity and basicity, characteristic reactions of major functional groups, reaction mechanisms, qualitative organic analysis, applications, lipids, carbohydrates, and proteins. For use only by authorized chemistry teachers and administrators. Examiner required. Suitable for group use.

Timed: 90 minutes

Scoring: Hand key

Cost: Specimen set $6.00; 25 to 100 tests $0.90 each; 25 answer sheets $3.00; scoring stencils $1.00

Publisher: American Chemical Society, Division of Chemical Education

CALIFORNIA CHEMISTRY DIAGNOSTIC TEST

Adult

Purpose: Identifies which college chemistry courses are most appropriate for entering freshmen and/or prescribes remedial activities to develop necessary competencies.

Description: 44–item paper-pencil multiple-choice test providing information about the knowledge of chemistry retained by entering freshmen. Must be administered by a member of a college chemistry faculty. Examiner required. Suitable for group use.

Untimed: 45 minutes

general science

Scoring: Hand key; machine scored

Cost: Evaluation copy $6.00; test booklets $1.00–$0.80 each; scoring stencil $1.00; 25 answer sheets $3.00

Publisher: American Chemical Society, Division of Chemical Education

THE CULTURAL LITERACY TEST

Refer to page 452.

FIRST TERM GENERAL CHEMISTRY

Adult

Purpose: Assesses skill in topics most frequently covered during the first term of a two-term chemistry course.

Description: 80–item paper-pencil multiple-choice test consisting of six subtests: State of Matter (15 items), Stoichiometry and Thermochemistry (20 items), Atomic Structure and Periodicity (15 items), Molecular Structure and Intermolecular Forces (15 items), Solutions (5 items), and Descriptive Chemistry and Lab (10 items). The test is available in two forms, gray and blue, which differ only in the sequence of questions within subtest groupings. Must be administered by a member of a college chemistry faculty. Examiner required. Suitable for group use.

Timed: 110 minutes

Scoring: Hand key; machine scored

Cost: Evaluation copy $6.00; test booklets $1.00–$0.80 each; scoring stencil $1.00; 25 answer sheets $3.00

Publisher: American Chemical Society, Division of Chemical Education

GENERAL CHEMISTRY TESTS

**Adolescent, adult
College students**

Purpose: Measures achievement in first-year college chemistry courses. Evaluates student strengths and weaknesses and aids in assigning grades.

Description: Multiple-item paper-pencil test measuring the following chemistry subject areas: states of matter, stoichiome-

try, carbon chemistry, solutions, acid-based chemistry, equilibria, electrochemistry and redox, thermodynamics and kinetics, descriptive chemistry, special topics, and laboratory skills. Materials include Form 1985, Form 1985–B, Form 1987–B (50 items), Form 1987 (80 items), Form 1989–F (80 items), Form 1989 (75 items), and 1990–S (50 items). "Scrambled" forms, with items in different order, and brief forms, which are shortened versions of the tests, are also available. The tests are for use only by authorized chemistry teachers and administrators. Examiner required. Suitable for group use.

Timed: Form 1985 110 minutes; Form 1985–B 55 minutes; Form 1987–B 55 minutes; Form 1987 110 minutes; Form 1989–F 110 minutes; Form 1989 110 minutes; Form 1990–S 60 minutes

Scoring: Hand key; examiner evaluated; may be machine scored

Cost: Specimen set $5.00; 25 tests $18.00; 25 answer sheets $3.00; scoring stencils $1.00

Publisher: American Chemical Society, Division of Chemical Education

GENERAL-ORGANIC-BIOLOGICAL CHEMISTRY (FOR ALLIED HEALTH SCIENCES PROGRAM) TESTS

**Adolescent, adult
College students**

Purpose: Measures achievement in courses covering basic materials in general, organic, and biological chemistry. Used as a unit or end-of-semester examination.

Description: 180–item paper-pencil test measuring proficiency in three areas of chemistry: general, organic, and biological. Each subtest is divided into Part A (40 items) and Part B (20 items). Materials include Form 1979 and Form 1985. The test is for use only by authorized chemistry teachers and administrators. Examiner required. Suitable for group use.

Timed: Part A 35 minutes; Part B 20 minutes

Scoring: Hand key

Cost: Specimen set $6.00; 25 to 100 tests $0.90 each; 25 answer sheets $3.00; scoring stencil $1.00

Publisher: American Chemical Society, Division of Chemical Education

GENERAL SCIENCE TEST (A/107)

College students   

Purpose: Assesses scientific understanding of college entrants and higher.

Description: Multiple-item paper-pencil test in two parts assessing general scientific knowledge and understanding of technical materials. The first part contains questions on general science, and the second part consists of several paragraphs that determine the extent to which the examinee understands technical articles. Norms are available. Examiner required. Suitable for group use. SOUTH AFRICAN PUBLISHER

Timed: 55 minutes

Scoring: Hand key

Cost: (In Rands) reusable booklet 8,10; 25 answer sheets 4,10; scoring key 6,75; manual 16,30

Publisher: Human Sciences Research Council

GRADUATE LEVEL PLACEMENT EXAMINATIONS: ANALYTICAL CHEMISTRY

Adult
Graduate students   

Purpose: Measures achievement in college analytical chemistry courses. Used for placement of graduate students.

Description: 35- or 40-item paper-pencil multiple-choice test measuring knowledge of analytical chemistry. Materials include Form 1981-G (40 items) and Form 1985-G (50 items). The tests are for use only by authorized chemistry teachers and administrators. Examiner required. Suitable for group use.

Timed: Form 1985-G 120 minutes; Form 1981-G 90 minutes;

Scoring: Hand key

Cost: Specimen set $6.00; 25 to 100 tests $0.90 each; 25 answer sheets $3.00; scoring stencils $1.00

Publisher: American Chemical Society, Division of Chemical Education

GRADUATE LEVEL PLACEMENT EXAMINATIONS: INORGANIC CHEMISTRY

Adult
Graduate students   

Purpose: Measures achievement in college inorganic chemistry courses. Used for placement of graduate students.

Description: 60-item paper-pencil multiple-choice test measuring knowledge of inorganic chemistry. Materials include Forms 1976-I, 1981-I, and 1985-I. The test is for use only by authorized chemistry teachers and administrators. Examiner required. Suitable for group use.

Timed: Form 1985-I 120 minutes; Form 1981-I 110 minutes; Form 1976-I 110 minutes

Scoring: Hand key

Cost: Specimen set $6.00; 25 to 100 tests $0.90 each; 25 answer sheets $3.00; scoring stencils $1.00

Publisher: American Chemical Society, Division of Chemical Education

GRADUATE LEVEL PLACEMENT EXAMINATIONS: ORGANIC CHEMISTRY

Adult
Graduate students   

Purpose: Measures achievement in college organic chemistry courses. Used for placement of graduate students.

Description: 70- or 75-item paper-pencil multiple-choice test measuring knowledge of organic chemistry. Materials include 1981-G (70 items) and 1985-G (70 items). The test is for use only by authorized chemistry teachers and administrators. Examiner required. Suitable for group use.

Timed: Form 1985-G 90–120 minutes; Form 1981-G 90–120 minutes

Scoring: Hand key

Cost: Specimen set $6.00; 25 to 100 tests $0.90 each; 25 answer sheets $3.00; scoring stencils $1.00

Publisher: American Chemical Society, Division of Chemical Education

GRADUATE LEVEL PLACEMENT EXAMINATIONS: PHYSICAL CHEMISTRY

Adult
Graduate students

Purpose: Measures achievement in college physical chemistry courses. Used for placement of graduate students.

Description: 60–item paper-pencil multiple-choice test measuring knowledge of physical chemistry. Materials include Forms 1981–P and 1986–P. The test is for use only by authorized chemistry teachers and administrators. Examiner required. Suitable for group use.

Timed: 180 minutes

Scoring: Hand key

Cost: Specimen set $6.00; 25 to 100 tests $0.90 each; 25 answer sheets $3.00; scoring stencils $1.00

Publisher: American Chemical Society, Division of Chemical Education

HIGH SCHOOL CHEMISTRY TESTS

Adolescent
Grades 10–12

Purpose: Measures achievement in first-year high-school chemistry courses. Identifies student strengths and weaknesses and aids in assigning grades.

Description: 80–item paper-pencil test measuring understanding of fundamental concepts and application of basic principles in chemistry. Areas tested include introductory concepts, physical concepts, atomic and molecular concepts, and solutions concepts. Materials include Form 1985, Form 1985–S, Form 1987, Form 1987–S, Form 1989, and Form 1989–S. The "S" denotes scrambled versions, which contain items in a different order. The test is for use only by authorized

chemistry teachers and administrators. Examiner required. Suitable for group use.

Timed: 80 minutes

Scoring: Hand key

Cost: Specimen set $6.00; 25 to 100 tests $0.75 each; 25 answer sheets $3.00; scoring stencils $1.00

Publisher: American Chemical Society, Division of Chemical Education

INORGANIC CHEMISTRY TESTS

Adolescent, adult
College students

Purpose: Measures achievement in undergraduate inorganic chemistry courses. Assesses student strengths and weaknesses and assists graduate-level placement of entering students.

Description: 60–item paper-pencil test covering theoretical and descriptive inorganic chemistry. Topics include nomenclature, bonding, structure, reaction mechanisms, coordination chemistry, and thermodynamics of inorganic elements and compounds. Materials include Forms 1976, 1981, and 1985. The test is for use only by authorized chemistry teachers and administrators. Examiner required. Suitable for group use.

Timed: Form 1985 120 minutes; Form 1981 110 minutes; Form 1976 110 minutes

Scoring: Hand key

Cost: Specimen set $6.00; 25 to 100 tests $0.90 each; 25 answer sheets $3.00; scoring stencils $1.00

Publisher: American Chemical Society, Division of Chemical Education

INSTRUMENTAL DETERMINATIONS (ANALYSIS) TESTS

Adolescent, adult
College students

Purpose: Measures achievement in undergraduate instrumental determinations courses. Evaluates student strengths and weaknesses and aids in assigning grades.

Description: Multiple-item paper-pencil test assessing knowledge of instrumental methods. Form 1981 measures spectroscopy, electroanalytical chemistry, separations, instrumentation, thermal, NMR, mass spectroscopy, radioactivity, and choice of method, x-ray, internal standard methods, titration curves, and kinetics. The test is for use only by authorized chemistry teachers and administrators. Examiner required. Suitable for group use.

Timed: Form 1981 110 minutes

Scoring: Hand key

Cost: Specimen set $6.00; 25 to 100 tests $0.90 each; 25 answer sheets $3.00; scoring stencils $1.00

Publisher: American Chemical Society, Division of Chemical Education

MECHANICAL COMPREHENSION TEST A3/1

Adolescent

Purpose: Measures mechanical abilities.

Description: Multiple-item paper-pencil test assessing the ability to apply the laws and principles of physics and mechanics. The test is based on the secondary school syllabus. Examiner required. Suitable for group use.
SOUTH AFRICAN PUBLISHER

Untimed: 30–35 minutes

Scoring: Hand key

Cost: (In Rands) booklet 8,00; 25 answer sheets 4,10; set of keys 13,50; manual 16,30

Publisher: Human Sciences Research Council

NATIONAL PROFICIENCY SURVEY SERIES (NPSS): BIOLOGY
Dale P. Scannell

Adolescent—Ages 12–18
Grades 8–12

Purpose: Measures end-of-course achievement in biology courses.

Description: 45–item paper-pencil test used for evaluating student proficiency in biology. The test, which may be administered as a survey test or as an end-of-

course test, is designed to assess 15 objectives. Each objective is tested by three questions. Normative and criterion-referenced data are available. One in a series of 13 NPSS tests. Examiner required. Suitable for group use.

Timed: 40 minutes

Scoring: Self-scored; hand key

Cost: Contact publisher for price and availability

Publisher: The Riverside Publishing Company

NATIONAL PROFICIENCY SURVEY SERIES (NPSS): CHEMISTRY
Dale P. Scannell

Adolescent—Ages 12–18
Grades 8–12

Purpose: Measures end-of-course achievement in chemistry courses.

Description: 42–item paper-pencil test used for evaluating student proficiency in chemistry. The test, which may be administered as a survey test or as an end-of-course test, is designed to assess 14 objectives. Each objective is tested by three questions. Normative and criterion-referenced data are available. One in a series of 13 NPSS tests. Examiner required. Suitable for group use.

Timed: 40 minutes

Scoring: Self-scored; hand key

Cost: Contact publisher for price and availability

Publisher: The Riverside Publishing Company

NATIONAL PROFICIENCY SURVEY SERIES (NPSS): PHYSICS
Dale P. Scannell

Adolescent—Ages 12–18
Grades 8–12

Purpose: Measures end-of-course achievement in physics courses.

Description: 45–item paper-pencil test used for evaluating student proficiency in physics. The test, which may be administered as a survey test or as an end-of-course test, is designed to assess 15 objectives. Each objective is tested by three questions. Normative and criterion-referenced data are available. One in a series of 13 NPSS tests. Examiner required. Suitable for group use.

Timed: 40 minutes

Scoring: Self-scored; hand key

Cost: Contact publisher for price and availability

Publisher: The Riverside Publishing Company

NM CONCEPTS OF ECOLOGY TEST—LEVEL 1 (NMCET–1)
S.P. Klein

Child, adolescent
Grades 6–8

Purpose: Measures an individual's understanding of the concepts of ecology from micro to macro systems. Used for program evaluation and needs assessment.

Description: 20–item paper-pencil multiple-choice test measuring a student's understanding of natural resources, pollution, plant/animal dependencies, life processes, natural balance, geographic evolution and conservation, and natural adaptation. The test booklets are reusable, and a lay-over stencil is used for scoring. The reliability and norms have been determined from a sample of sixth-grade students. Examiner/self-administered. Suitable for group use.

Timed: 20 minutes

Scoring: Hand key

Cost: 35 tests (specify level) $12.00; 35 answer sheets (specify level) $4.00; scoring stencil $3.00; manual $3.00

Publisher: Monitor

NM CONCEPTS OF ECOLOGY TEST—LEVEL 2 (NMCET–2)
S.P. Klein

Adolescent
Grades 9–12

Purpose: Measures an individual's understanding of the basic concepts of ecology and conservation. Used for program evaluation and needs assessment.

Description: 20–item paper-pencil multiple-choice test measuring student's understanding of life processes, plant/animal dependencies, geographic evolution and conservation, soil conservation, and natural adaptation. The test booklets are reusable, and a lay-over stencil is used for scoring. Reliability and norms have been determined from samples of ninth- and twelfth-grade secondary students. Examiner/self-administered. Suitable for group use.

Timed: 20 minutes

Scoring: Hand key

Cost: Specimen set $6.00; 35 tests (specify level) $12.00; 35 answer sheets (specify level) $4.00; scoring stencil $3.00; manual $3.00

Publisher: Monitor

ORGANIC CHEMISTRY TESTS

Adolescent, adult
College students

Purpose: Measures achievement in undergraduate organic chemistry courses. Evaluates student strengths and weaknesses and aids in assigning grades.

Description: 70–item paper-pencil test measuring diverse aspects of organic chemistry, including theoretical concepts, acid and basic character of organic compounds, stereochemistry, various reaction types associated with organic molecules, reaction mechanisms, spectroscopic identification of organic structures, and synthetic sequences. Materials include Form 1986 and Form 1982. The test is for use only by authorized chemistry teachers and administrators. Examiner required. Suitable for group use.

Timed: Form 1986 115 minutes; Form 1982 115 minutes

Scoring: Hand key

Cost: Specimen set $6.00; 25 to 100 tests $0.90 each; 25 answer sheets $3.00; scoring stencils $1.00

Publisher: American Chemical Society, Division of Chemical Education

PHYSICAL CHEMISTRY FOR THE LIFE SCIENCES TEST

Adolescent, adult
College students

Purpose: Measures achievement in undergraduate courses in physical chemistry taught for life science students. Evaluates student strengths and weaknesses and aids in assigning grades.

Description: 50–item paper-pencil test measuring comprehension of principles of physical chemistry. Topic areas include thermodynamics, solutions and equilibria, dynamics, quantum chemistry, and macromolecules. The test is for use only by authorized chemistry teachers and administrators. Examiner required. Suitable for group use.

Timed: 100 minutes

Scoring: Hand key

Cost: Specimen set $6.00; 25 to 100 tests $0.90 each; 25 answer sheets $3.00; scoring stencils $1.00

Publisher: American Chemical Society, Division of Chemical Education

PHYSICAL CHEMISTRY TESTS

Adult
College students

Purpose: Measures achievement in undergraduate physical chemistry courses. Evaluates student strengths and weaknesses and aids in assigning grades.

Description: Three 45– to 50–item paper-pencil subtests measuring three aspects of physical chemistry: thermodynamics, chemical dynamics, and quantum chemistry. The subtests may be administered separately. The thermodynamics subtest covers fundamental laws, state functions, criteria for equilibrium, solutions, and electrochemistry. The chemical dynamics subtest covers rate theories, kinetic theory of gases, and transport phenomena. The quantum chemistry subtest covers fundamental laws of quantum mechanics and their applications. Each subtest is divided into Part A (30 items) and Part B (15 items). Three forms are available. Form 1976–T

contains only thermodynamics, Form 1981–D covers only chemical dynamics, and Form 1983–Q contains only quantum chemistry. The entire physical chemistry test may be given at the end of the physical chemistry course and covers chemical thermodynamics, chemical kinetics and transport phenomena, and quantum chemistry and spectroscopy. The test is for use only by authorized chemistry teachers and administrators. Examiner required. Suitable for group use.

Timed: 90–110 minutes

Scoring: Hand key

Cost: Specimen set $6.00; 25 to 100 tests $0.90 each; 25 answer sheets $3.00; scoring stencils $1.00

Publisher: American Chemical Society, Division of Chemical Education

POLYMER CHEMISTRY TEST

Adolescent, adult
College students

Purpose: Measures achievement in upper-level undergraduate and lower-level graduate courses in polymer chemistry. Evaluates student strengths and weaknesses and aids in placement and admission of graduate students.

Description: 70–item paper-pencil test covering five areas of polymer chemistry: organic, thermo-kinetics, characterization, physical behavior, and general. The test is for use only by authorized chemistry teachers and administrators. Examiner required. Suitable for group use.

Timed: 110 minutes

Scoring: Hand key

Cost: Specimen set $6.00; 25 to 100 tests $0.90 each; 25 answer sheets $3.00; scoring stencils $1.00

Publisher: American Chemical Society, Division of Chemical Education

QUANTITATIVE ANALYSIS (ANALYTICAL CHEMISTRY) TESTS

Adolescent, adult
College students

Purpose: Measures achievement in undergraduate analytical chemistry courses.

Evaluates student strengths and weaknesses and aids in assigning grades.

Description: 50–item paper-pencil test covering the following topics in analytical chemistry: gravimetric, volumetric, spectrophotometric, electrometric analysis, compleximetry, pH and buffers, solubility, analytical separations, data evaluation, oxidation-reduction, and indicators. Two forms are available, Form 1982 and Form 1988. The test is for use only by authorized chemistry teachers and administrators. Examiner required. Suitable for group use.

Timed: Form 1982 90 minutes; Form 1988 90 minutes

Scoring: Hand key

Cost: Specimen set $6.00; 25 to 100 tests $0.90 each; 25 answer sheets $3.00; scoring stencil $1.00

Publisher: American Chemical Society, Division of Chemical Education

SCIENCE TESTS—STANDARD 5 THROUGH STANDARD 8 HIGHER GRADE

Child, adolescent

Purpose: Assesses achievement in science courses. Used for educational evaluation and placement.

Description: Six paper-pencil tests of science knowledge in Standards 5 through 8 Higher Grade. General Science-Standard 5 consists of the following subtests: Measurement of Matter, Heat, Magnetism, and Biology. Physical Science-Standard 6 has three subtests: Matter Classification of Matter, Oxygen, Hydrogen, Carbon Dioxide; Water; and Force, Work, Energy, and Electricity. Physical Science-Standard 7 is very similar to Standard 6. Standard 8 and above measures eight aspects of physical science: light; sound; heat, light, and energy; electricity; atomic structure; chemical reactions; acids, bases, and salts; and chemical reactions and electricity. Biology tests for Standards 6 and 7 measure some of the following areas: reproduction, growth and development, nutrition, and gaseous exchange during respiration. Examiner required. Suitable for group use.
SOUTH AFRICAN PUBLISHER

Untimed: Not available

Scoring: Hand key; examiner evaluated

Cost: Contact publisher; orders from outside the RSA will be dealt with on merit

Publisher: Human Sciences Research Council

SCIENTIFIC KNOWLEDGE AND APTITUDE TEST
Refer to page 484.

TOLEDO CHEMISTRY PLACEMENT EXAMINATION

Adolescent, adult
College students

Purpose: Predicts performance in college chemistry. Used for placement in appropriate chemistry courses.

Description: 60–item paper-pencil multiple-choice test assessing readiness for college chemistry. Form 1981 (60 items) measures three areas: general mathematics, general chemical knowledge, and specific chemical knowledge. The test is for use only by authorized chemistry teachers and administrators. Examiner required. Suitable for group use.

Timed: 55 minutes

Scoring: Hand key

Cost: Specimen set $6.00; 25 to 100 tests $0.90; 25 answer sheets $3.00; scoring stencils $1.00

Publisher: American Chemical Society, Division of Chemical Education

Academic Subjects: Science: Health Science

FAST HEALTH KNOWLEDGE TEST FORM C, 1986 REVISION
Charles G. Fast

Adolescent, adult—Ages 15–22 Grades 10–14

Purpose: Measures discrimination and judgment in matters of personal health. Used to counsel high-school and college students, upgrade their health knowledge, and for pre- and posttesting in curriculum studies.

Description: 100–item paper-pencil multiple-choice test assessing a student's knowledge of factors contributing to personal health. Ten areas are covered: personal health, exercise, relaxation and sleep, nutrition, consumer health, contemporary health problems, safety and first aid, substances of abuse, disease control, mental health, family life and sex education. Norms are provided for college freshmen and high-school seniors. A scoring service is provided by the publisher. Examiner required. Suitable for group use.

Untimed: 40–50 minutes

Scoring: Hand key; may be computer scored

Cost: 50 copies $90.00; informational materials and copy of test $7.50; bulk rates available

Publisher: Charles G. Fast

Information and availability unconfirmed; last verified in 1988.

FEELING GREAT! A HEALTH AWARENESS SIMULATION
K. Ann Coleman

Adolescent
Grades 7–12

Purpose: Assesses students' health awareness. Used as a supplement in health and wellness courses.

Description: Multiple-item computer-administered health awareness simulation monitoring performance in eight areas: alcohol/drugs, exercise, nutrition, personal habits, safety, smoking, stress, and weight. The computer then presents a histogram that displays the student's performance in each of the categories. The Health Advisor component presents the student with information about behavior that can improve his or her Feeling Great Index. The program, which is available in both male and female versions, operates on Apple systems. Self-administered. Not suitable for group use.

Untimed: 1 hour

Scoring: Computer scored

Cost: Manual, unlimited disk administrations $42.90

Publisher: Laidlaw Brothers/Doubleday

Information and availability unconfirmed; last verified in 1988.

HUMAN REPRODUCTION
H. Frederick Kilander and Glenn C. Leach

Adolescent, adult
Grades 10 and above

Purpose: Measures high-school and college students' knowledge of the human reproductive system. Used for health and human sexuality courses.

Description: 33–item paper-pencil multiple-choice test assessing knowledge of human reproduction. Self-administered. Suitable for group use.

Timed: 30 minutes

Scoring: Hand key

Cost: Free

Publisher: Glenn C. Leach, Ed.D.

Information and availability unconfirmed; last verified in 1988.

INFORMATION TEST ON DRUGS AND DRUG ABUSE
Glenn C. Leach and Frederick H. Kilander

Adolescent, adult
Grades 10 and above

Purpose: Measures high-school and college students' knowledge of drugs and drug abuse. Used for drug abuse counseling.

Description: 30–item paper-pencil multiple-choice test covering legal and illegal drug use. Self-administered. Suitable for group use.

Timed: 30 minutes

Scoring: Hand key

Cost: Free

Publisher: Glenn C. Leach, Ed.D.

Information and availability unconfirmed; last verified in 1988.

KILANDER-LEACH HEALTH KNOWLEDGE
H. Frederick Kilander and Glenn C. Leach

Adolescent, adult
Grades 10 and above

Purpose: Measures high-school and college students' general knowledge of health. Used as a pre- or end-of-course exam in high-school health education classes and as a pre- or posttest for colleges and schools of nursing.

Description: 100–item paper-pencil multiple-choice test measuring health knowledge, including personal health, nutrition, community health, sanitation, communicable diseases, safety, first aid, family living, and mental health. Self-administered; proctor desirable. Suitable for group use.

Untimed: 45–50 minutes

Scoring: Hand key

Cost: 100 booklets $35.00; 35 copies $20.00 (prices include answer sheet and breakdown of questions by health areas)

Publisher: Glenn C. Leach, Ed.D.

Information and availability unconfirmed; last verified in 1988.

NATIONAL ACHIEVEMENT TESTS: HEALTH AND SCIENCE TESTS—HEALTH EDUCATION
John S. Shaw, Maurice E. Troyer, and Clifford L. Brownell

Adolescent
Grades 7 and above

Purpose: Assesses health knowledge. Used for educational evaluation.

Description: Paper-pencil test of newer phases of health information. The test contains problems with which students in high school and college should be familiar. Two equivalent forms, A and B, are available. Examiner required. Suitable for group use.

Timed: 40 minutes

Scoring: Hand key

Cost: Specimen set (test, manual, key) $4.00; 25 tests $8.75; 25 answer sheets $4.00

Publisher: Psychometric Affiliates

NUTRITION INFORMATION TEST
H. Frederick Kilander and Glenn C. Leach

Adolescent, adult
Grades 10 and above

Purpose: Determines nutrition knowledge and attitudes of high-school and college students.

Description: 33–item paper-pencil multiple-choice test covering various aspects of nutrition, including calories, diseases, physical health, and weight control. Self-administered. Suitable for group use.

Untimed: 15 minutes

Scoring: Hand key

Cost: Free

Publisher: Glenn C. Leach, Ed.D.

Information and availability unconfirmed; last verified in 1988.

THE OHIO VOCATIONAL ACHIEVEMENT TESTS IN HEALTH OCCUPATIONS EDUCATION: DENTAL ASSISTING
Refer to page 794.

THE OHIO VOCATIONAL ACHIEVEMENT TESTS IN HEALTH OCCUPATIONS EDUCATION: DIVERSIFIED HEALTH OCCUPATIONS
Refer to page 795.

THE OHIO VOCATIONAL ACHIEVEMENT TESTS IN HEALTH OCCUPATIONS EDUCATION: MEDICAL ASSISTING
Refer to page 795.

SMOKING AND HEALTH
H. Frederick Kilander and
Glenn C. Leach

Adolescent, adult
Grades 10–13

Purpose: Assesses an individual's commitment to and knowledge of smoking. Used for analysis of smoking behavior and research.

Description: 33–item paper-pencil multiple-choice and objective test on smoking. Self-administered. Suitable for group use.
Timed: 25 minutes
Scoring: Hand key
Cost: Free
Publisher: Glenn C. Leach, Ed.D.
Information and availability unconfirmed; last verified in 1988.

Academic Subjects: Social Studies

AMERICAN GOVERNMENT TESTS

Adolescent
Grades 8–12

Purpose: Evaluates high school students' understanding of government, with strong emphasis on political action and dynamics of American politics. Used for course testing and as a study guide.

Description: Seven 75–item paper-pencil multiple-choice matching true-false tests covering units on the Fundamentals of Government, the Executive Branch and Political Parties, the Legislative Branch, the Judicial Branch, and State and Local Government. A final examination is included also. Examiner required. Suitable for group use.
Untimed: Varies
Scoring: Hand key
Cost: Reproducible test book with response key $7.95
Publisher: The Perfection Form Company

AMERICAN HISTORY TESTS

Child, adolescent
Grades 7–9

Purpose: Evaluates junior high school students' knowledge of specific periods of American history. Used as pre- or post-tests and as study guides.

Description: 75–item paper-pencil multiple-choice matching true-false tests covering 12 periods from exploration and colonization of America to post-World War II. Unit tests, two semester tests, and a final examination are available. Examiner required. Suitable for group use.
Untimed: Varies
Scoring: Hand key
Cost: Reproducible test book with answer key $9.95
Publisher: The Perfection Form Company

AMERICAN HISTORY TESTS

Adolescent
Grades 10–12

Purpose: Evaluates senior high school students' knowledge of specific periods in American history. Used as pre- or post-tests and as study guides.

Description: 100–item paper-pencil multiple-choice matching true-false tests covering 11 periods in American history from the colonial period to contemporary times. Two semester tests and a final exam are included. Examiner required. Suitable for group use.
Untimed: Varies
Scoring: Hand key
Cost: Reproducible test book with response key $12.95
Publisher: The Perfection Form Company

BASIC ECONOMICS TEST (BET)
John F. Chizmar and
Ronald S. Halinski

Child
Grades 4–6

Purpose: Measures elementary-school students' understanding of economic principles. Used to assess curricular development and to determine the effectiveness of materials and teaching strategies.

Description: 38–item paper-pencil multiple-choice test covering basic economic concepts, economic systems, microeconomics, resource allocation, macroeconomics, and economic institutions. The test is available in two forms, A and B. Examiner required. Suitable for group use.
Timed: 50 minutes
Scoring: Hand key; may be computer scored
Cost: Manual and answer key $3.00; 25 test booklets (specify form) $6.00
Publisher: Joint Council on Economic Education

CONSERVATISM-RADICALISM OPINIONAIRE (C-R)
Refer to page 752.

CPRI QUESTIONNAIRES (Q–71, Q–74, Q–75, Q–76)
Refer to page 753.

THE CULTURAL LITERACY TEST
Refer to page 452.

ECONOMICS TESTS

Adolescent
Grades 10–12

Purpose: Measures high-school students' general knowledge of economics over a semester course. Used as pre- or posttests and study guides.

Description: 100–item paper-pencil multiple-choice matching true-false tests covering units on concepts in economics; price, income, supply and demand; labor and government's role; money, banking, and insurance; and international trade. A final examination and response key is included. Examiner required. Suitable for group use.
Untimed: Varies

Scoring: Hand key
Cost: Reproducible book with response key $7.95
Publisher: The Perfection Form Company

HUMAN LOYALTY EXPRESSIONAIRE
Theodore F. Lentz

Adolescent, adult
College students

Purpose: Measures human loyalty and global awareness. Used in peace and global studies courses.

Description: 172–item paper-pencil test in three sections. The subject agrees or disagrees with each statement. Examiner required. Suitable for group use.
Timed: 45 minutes
Scoring: Hand key
Cost: 3 forms of questionnaire, scoring keys, norms $7.00; questionnaires can be reproduced at no further charge
Publisher: Lentz Peace Research Laboratory

INFORMETER: AN INTERNATIONAL TECHNIQUE FOR THE MEASUREMENT OF POLITICAL INFORMATION
Panos D. Bardis

Adolescent
Grades 10 and above

Purpose: Measures political knowledge and awareness of local, national, and international affairs. Used for research on political information in the general population and discussion in social sciences classes.

Description: 100–item paper-pencil test in which the subject is asked to list important names, dates, events, and issues in response to specific questions about politics, government, and current events. Examiner/self-administered. Suitable for group use.
Untimed: 15 minutes
Scoring: Examiner evaluated
Cost: Free
Publisher: Panos D. Bardis

IRENOMETER
Panos D. Bardis

Adolescent, adult

Purpose: Measures attitudes and beliefs concerning peace. Used for discussion purposes.

Description: 10–item paper-pencil inventory in which an individual rates 10 statements about peace and its effects on individuals and society on a 5–point scale ranging from 0 (strongly disagree) to 4 (strongly agree). All statements express positive attitudes toward peace. The score equals the sum of the 10 numerical responses. Self-administered. Suitable for group use.

Untimed: Varies

Scoring: Self-scored

Cost: Free

Publisher: Panos D. Bardis

JUNIOR HIGH SCHOOL TEST OF ECONOMICS
Committee for the Development of a Junior High School Test of Economics

Adolescent
Grades 7–9

Purpose: Tests junior high-school students' understanding of economics. Used to evaluate classroom progress and effectiveness of teaching materials.

Description: 40–item paper-pencil examination of students' knowledge of economic facts and concepts. The concepts tested are scarcity, opportunity costs, supply and demands, GNP, money, prices and inflation, government taxation and spending, economic growth, and government policies to achieve full employment and price stability. Examiner required. Suitable for group use.

Timed: 40 minutes

Scoring: Hand key; may be computer scored

Cost: Manual with answer key $3.00; 25 tests $6.00

Publisher: Joint Council on Economic Education

NATIONAL PROFICIENCY SURVEY SERIES (NPSS): AMERICAN GOVERNMENT
Dale P. Scannell

Adolescent—Ages 12–18
Grades 8–12

Purpose: Measures end-of-course achievement in American government courses.

Description: 45–item paper-pencil test used for evaluating student proficiency in understanding American government. The test, which may be administered as a survey test or as an end-of-course test, is designed to assess 15 objectives. Each objective is tested by three questions. Normative and criterion-referenced data are available. One in a series of 13 NPSS tests. Examiner required. Suitable for group use.

Timed: 40 minutes

Scoring: Self-scored; hand key

Cost: Contact publisher for price and availability

Publisher: The Riverside Publishing Company

NATIONAL PROFICIENCY SURVEY SERIES (NPSS): U.S. HISTORY
Dale P. Scannell

Adolescent—Ages 12–18
Grades 8–12

Purpose: Measures end-of-course achievement in U.S. history courses.

Description: 42–item paper-pencil test used for evaluating student proficiency in U.S. history. The test, which may be administered as a survey test or as an end-of-course test, is designed to assess 14 objectives. Each objective is tested by three questions. Normative and criterion-referenced data are available. One in a series of 13 NPSS tests. Examiner required. Suitable for group use.

Timed: 40 minutes

Scoring: Self-scored; hand key

Cost: Contact publisher for price and availability

Publisher: The Riverside Publishing Company

NATIONAL PROFICIENCY SURVEY SERIES (NPSS): WORLD HISTORY
Dale P. Scannell

Adolescent—Ages 12–18
Grades 8–12

Purpose: Measures end-of-course achievement in world history courses.

Description: 45–item paper-pencil test used for evaluating student proficiency in world history. The test, which may be administered as a survey test or as an end-of-course test, is designed to assess 15 objectives. Each objective is tested by three questions. Normative and criterion-referenced data are available. One in a series of 13 NPSS tests. Examiner required. Suitable for group use.

Timed: 40 minutes

Scoring: Self-scored; hand key

Cost: Contact publisher for price and availability

Publisher: The Riverside Publishing Company

A PARTIAL INDEX OF MODERNIZATION: MEASUREMENT OF ATTITUDES TOWARD MORALITY
Refer to page 379.

PRIMARY TEST OF ECONOMIC UNDERSTANDING
Donald G. Davison and John H. Kilgore

Child
Grades 2–3

Purpose: Reveals a child's understanding of economic concepts typically taught in Grades 2 and 3. Used for diagnosis and to evaluate effectiveness of teaching materials.

Description: 32–item paper-pencil yes-no test. The child must answer both questions correctly to be scored correct. The

examiner reads the questions aloud, and the child writes "yes" or "no" for each one. Materials include a test and answer key. Examiner required. Suitable for group use.

Untimed: 40 minutes

Scoring: Hand key

Cost: Manual and answer key $3.00; 25 test booklets $6.00

Publisher: Bureau of Business and Economic Research/University of Iowa

Information and availability unconfirmed; last verified in 1987.

REVISED TEST OF UNDERSTANDING IN COLLEGE ECONOMICS
Phillip Saunders

Adolescent, adult

Purpose: Serves as a measuring instrument for controlled experiments in the teaching of introductory college economics. Used for research and to compare one college course with another.

Description: 90–item paper-pencil examination consisting of three subtests, each in comparable A and B forms. Each form contains 30 questions dealing with recognition and understanding and simple and complex application of macro-, micro-, and hybrid economic principles. The macro test covers the measurement of aggregate economic performance, aggregate supply, productive capacity and growth, income and expenditure approach to aggregate demand and fiscal policy, monetary approach to aggregate demand, policy combination, and practical problems of stabilization. The micro test covers basic economic problems, markets and market failure, externalities, government intervention and regulation, income distribution and government redistribution. The hybrid test covers material from both the macro and micro tests. Examiner required. Suitable for group use.

Timed: 45 minutes

Scoring: Hand key; may be computer scored

Cost: Manual $3.00; 25 test booklets $6.00 (specify form)

Publisher: Joint Council on Economic Education

TEST OF ECONOMIC LITERACY (TEL)
John C. Soper

Adolescent
Grades 11–12

Purpose: Measures senior high-school students' knowledge of economic systems and theory. Used to evaluate the quality of instruction and effectiveness of materials used.

Description: 46–item paper-pencil test covering seven content areas: basic economic problems, economic systems, microeconomics, resource allocation and economic distribution, macroeconomics, economic stability and growth, world economy, economic institutions, and concepts for evaluating economic actions and policies. The test is available in two forms, A and B. Examiner required. Suitable for group use. Available in Spanish.

Untimed: 40 minutes

Scoring: Hand key

Cost: Manual with answer key $3.00; 25 Form A $6.00; 25 Form B $6.00; single copy of Spanish language test $1.00

Publisher: Joint Council on Economic Education

TEST OF UNDERSTANDING IN PERSONAL ECONOMICS
Joint Council on Economic Education

Adolescent
Grades 9–12

Purpose: Measures high-school students' understanding of personal economics, including principles and operations. Used as course review and to determine effectiveness of instruction.

Description: 50–item paper-pencil multiple-choice test of the student's knowledge of economics. Examiner required. Suitable for group use.

Timed: 45 minutes

Scoring: Hand key

Cost: Manual with answer key $3.00; 25 test booklets $6.00

Publisher: Joint Council on Economic Education

A VIOLENCE SCALE
Refer to page 229.

WORLD GOVERNMENT SCALE
Refer to page 761.

WORLD HISTORY TESTS

Adolescent
Grades 8–12

Purpose: Measures high-school students' recall of factual information in world history. Used as unit tests, pre- or posttests, and study guides.

Description: 100–item reproducible paper-pencil multiple-choice matching true-false tests covering 10 historical periods from the earliest civilizations to new imperialism and the postwar world. Two semester tests, a final exam, and response key are included. Examiner required. Suitable for group use.

Untimed: Varies

Scoring: Hand key

Cost: Test and response key $10.95

Publisher: The Perfection Form Company

Academic Achievement and Aptitude

ACADEMIC APTITUDE TEST, STANDARD 10 (AAT)—1974

Adolescent

Purpose: Assesses academic abilities. Used for vocational guidance.

Description: Battery of 10 tests measuring specific academic aptitudes: Nonverbal Reasoning, Verbal Reasoning, English Vocabulary, English Reading Comprehension, Numerical Comprehension,

Afrikaans Vocabulary, Afrikaans Reading Comprehension, Squares, Spatial Perception (3D), and Mathematical Proficiency. Examiner required. Suitable for group use.
SOUTH AFRICAN PUBLISHER
Timed: 7 hours
Scoring: Hand key; examiner evaluated
Cost: (In Rands) test booklet 6,00; manual 7,00; demonstration model 4,00; 10 answer sheets 1,60; scoring stencil 6,00; orders from outside the RSA will be dealt with on merit
Publisher: Human Sciences Research Council

ACADEMIC APTITUDE TEST, UNIVERSITY (AAT)—1976

Adolescent, adult

Purpose: Assesses academic abilities at the university level. Used for vocational guidance.

Description: Multiple-item battery of tests measuring 10 specific academic aptitudes: Nonverbal Reasoning, Verbal Reasoning, English Vocabulary, English Reading Comprehension, Numerical Comprehension, Afrikaans Vocabulary, Afrikaans Reading Comprehension, Squares, Spatial Perception (3D), and Mathematical Proficiency. Examiner required. Suitable for group use.
SOUTH AFRICAN PUBLISHER
Timed: 7 hours
Scoring: Hand key; examiner evaluated
Cost: (In Rands) test booklet 6,40; manual 6,00; demonstration model 4,00; 10 answer sheets 1,60; scoring stencil 7,00; orders from outside the RSA will be dealt with on merit
Publisher: Human Sciences Research Council

ACADEMIC INSTRUCTIONAL MEASUREMENT SYSTEM (AIMS)

Child, adolescent
Grades 1–12

Purpose: Assesses mathematics, reading, and language arts skills. Used for achievement reporting, diagnosis, screening, and progress monitoring in school settings.

Description: 985–item paper-pencil item bank measuring curriculum-referenced, instructionally sequenced objectives. Reading/Language Arts content categories are phonic analysis, structural analysis, vocabulary, life study and reference, literal comprehension, inferential comprehension, critical comprehension, understanding literature, listening, spelling, mechanics, usage, grammar and syntax, proofreading, and composition. Mathematics content categories are numeration, whole numbers: addition, whole numbers: subtraction, whole numbers: multiplication, whole numbers: division, decimals, fractions, ratio/proportion/percent, measurement, geometry, problem solving, graphing/statistics, probability, prealgebra, and essential life skills. Materials include professionally prepared art and instructions. Test building software allows users to access, organize, and edit both AIMS and locally developed objectives. Examiner required. Suitable for group use.
Untimed: Not available
Scoring: Machine scored
Cost: Contact publisher
Publisher: The Psychological Corporation
Information and availability unconfirmed; last verified in 1988.

ACADEMIC-TECHNICAL APTITUDE TESTS FOR COLOURED PUPILS IN STANDARDS 6, 7, AND 8 (ATA)

Adolescent

Purpose: Measures the differential aptitudes of pupils in Standards 6–8. Used for vocational and educational guidance.

Description: Multiple-item battery of 10 paper-pencil tests, including verbal reasoning, nonverbal reasoning, computations, spatial perception (2D), mechanical reasoning, language comprehension, spatial perception (3D), comparison, coordination, and writing speed. Stanines and percentile ranks are available for each standard. Examiner required. Suitable for group use.
SOUTH AFRICAN PUBLISHER
Untimed: 4 hours
Scoring: Hand key

Cost: (In Rands) test booklet 5,00; manual 11,00; scoring stencil I 10,50; scoring stencil II 7,70; 10 answer sheets 1,50

Publisher: Human Sciences Research Council

ACER TESTS OF LEARNING ABILITY (TOLA)

Child, adolescent—Ages 8.6–13.2

Purpose: Measures the language and reasoning aspects of general intellectual ability important for academic success for students ages 8.6–13.2.

Description: Multiple-item paper-pencil test of general academic aptitude available at two levels: TOLA 4 (Year 4 of schooling or ages 8.6–11.5) and TOLA 6 (Year 6 of schooling or ages 10.3–13.2). Each level contains three separately timed subtests: Verbal Comprehension (vocabulary); General Reasoning (problem solving in a mathematical framework); and Syllogistic Reasoning (verbal analogies). Australian norms are provided in the form of stanines and percentile ranks. Examiner required. Suitable for group use.

AUSTRALIAN PUBLISHER

Timed: 33 minutes

Scoring: Hand key; may be machine scored

Cost: Contact publisher

Publisher: The Australian Council for Educational Research Limited

ACHIEVEMENT AND SPECIAL ABILITIES TESTING PROGRAMS: ADMISSIONS AND CREDENTIALING MEASUREMENT GROUP
The Psychological Corporation

Adolescent, adult

Purpose: Assesses special abilities and achievements of students and adults. Used for selection and admission of applicants and students to various programs and schools.

Description: Multiple-item paper-pencil multiple-choice tests of special ability and achievement. The Tests for Accounting (high school, college, and professional levels) assess the promise and achievement of prospective accounting students, enrolled accounting students, and graduate accountants. The Proficiency Test in Practical Nursing tests medical-surgical nursing, pharmacology, nutrition, maternal and child care, and general nursing information. The Qualifying Examination Services for Securities and Exchange Organizations is used by the National Association of Securities Dealers, New York Stock Exchange, American Stock Exchange, Pacific Coast Stock Exchange, and Chicago Board of Trade. Examiner required. Suitable for group use.

Timed: Varies, depending on exam

Scoring: Computer scoring service provided

Cost: Contact publisher

Publisher: Admissions and Credentialing Group/The Psychological Corporation

Information and availability unconfirmed; last verified in 1988.

ACHIEVEMENT TEST
College Board Achievement Test Development Committees

**Adolescent
Grades 10–12**

Purpose: Measures high-school students' knowledge of a particular subject and the ability to apply that knowledge in a specified subject area. Used to predict how well the student will do in a college-level course and for admissions selection and course placement.

Description: 15 paper-pencil multiple-choice tests, each one hour in length and containing from 60 to 100 questions, covering the following areas: English composition (with and without essay), literature, American history and social studies, European history and world cultures, mathematics level I, mathematics level II, French, German, Modern Hebrew, Italian, Latin, Spanish, biology, chemistry, and physics. The English composition test includes a 20–minute essay. One point is given for each correct answer, and a fraction of a point is deducted for each wrong answer. Scores are reported on a scale of 200 to 800. Most tests are administered five times a year, and the fee entitles a student to take as many as three tests on one date. The achievement tests, together with the Scholastic Aptitude Test (SAT), are offered through the Admissions Testing Program (ATP) of the College Board. For students with disabilities, the ATP offers special testing arrangements, including extended time administrations of the achievement tests. Examiner required. Suitable for group use.

Timed: 1 hour per test

Scoring: Computer scored

Cost: Contact publisher

Publisher: The College Board

ACHIEVEMENT TEST: ENGLISH—ENGLISH COMPOSITION
College Board Achievement Test Development Committees

Adolescent
Grades 10–12

Purpose: Measures high-school students' ability to write clear and effective prose in standard English. Used to predict college performance and by some schools for admissions selection and course placement.

Description: Multiple-item paper-pencil multiple-choice and essay test in two forms. One form is administered only in December and requires the student to answer approximately 70 multiple-choice questions and write a brief essay. The second form, offered at four other times during the year, consists of about 90 multiple-choice questions; no writing is involved. The various types of questions test the student's understanding of the relationship between ideas in a sentence, awareness of tone and meaning of words, sensitivity to wordiness and ambiguity, and knowledge of the structure and idiom of the written English that is acceptable to college teachers. The essay test (administered only in December) is a 20–minute assignment, preceded by a quotation or statement intended to stimulate the writer's thoughts on the subject. It gives the writer an opportunity to demonstrate quality of self-expression. Graded by

high-school and college English teachers, the essay comprises one-third of the total English Composition score, which is reported on a 200 to 800 scale. This achievement test, together with the Scholastic Aptitude Test (SAT), is offered through the Admissions Testing Program (ATP) of the College Board. For students with disabilities, the ATP has available special testing arrangements, including extended time administrations of the achievement test. Examiner required. Suitable for group use.

Timed: 1 hour

Scoring: Computer scored

Cost: Contact publisher

Publisher: The College Board

ACHIEVEMENT TEST: ENGLISH—LITERATURE
College Board Achievement Test Development Committees

Adolescent
Grades 10–12

Purpose: Assesses high-school students' understanding and interpretation of works of literature. Used to predict college performance and by some schools for admissions selection and course placement.

Description: 60–item paper-pencil multiple-choice test based on passages drawn from poetry, fiction, drama, and prose written in English from the Renaissance to the present. Some questions ask for analysis or summation of parts of or whole passages; others ask that elements of style (such as rhythm, rhyme, and metaphor) be related to the meaning, mood, or structure of the passage. The student is not expected to have read or studied any of the passages; he is expected to be able to examine them using developed skills. One point is given for each correct answer, and a fraction of a point is deducted for each wrong answer. Scores are reported on a scale of 200 to 800. This achievement test (offered five times a year), together with the Scholastic Aptitude Test (SAT), is offered through the Admissions Testing Program (ATP) of the College Board. For students with disabilities, the ATP has available special testing arrangements, including extended time administrations of the achievement test. Examiner required. Suitable for group use.

Timed: 1 hour

Scoring: Computer scored

Cost: Contact publisher

Publisher: The College Board

ACHIEVEMENT TEST: FOREIGN LANGUAGES—FRENCH
College Board Achievement Test Development Committees

Adolescent
Grades 10–12

Purpose: Measures high-school students' vocabulary mastery, grammatical control, and reading comprehension of French. Used to predict college performance and by some schools for admissions selection and course placement.

Description: Multiple-item paper-pencil multiple-choice test of ability and knowledge in three areas: vocabulary mastery, the knowledge of the meaning of words and idiomatic expressions as they appear in the written and spoken forms of the language; grammatical control, the identification of usage that is structurally correct and appropriate in context; and reading comprehension, the overall meaning of passages in various styles and levels of writing and recall of specific details. One point is given for each correct answer, and a fraction of a point is deducted for each wrong answer. Scores are reported on a scale of 200 to 800. This achievement test (administered five times a year), together with the Scholastic Aptitude Test (SAT), is offered through the Admissions Testing Program (ATP) of the College Board. For students with disabilities, the ATP has available special testing arrangements, including extended time administrations of the achievement test. Examiner required. Suitable for group use.

Timed: 1 hour

Scoring: Computer scored

Cost: Contact publisher

Publisher: The College Board

ACHIEVEMENT TEST: FOREIGN LANGUAGES—GERMAN
College Board Achievement Test Development Committees

Adolescent
Grades 10–12

Purpose: Measures high-school students' vocabulary mastery, grammatical control, and reading comprehension of German. Used to predict college performance and by some schools for admissions selection and course placement.

Description: Multiple-item paper-pencil multiple-choice test of ability and knowledge in three areas: vocabulary mastery, the knowledge of the meaning of words and idiomatic expressions as they appear in the written and spoken forms of the language; grammatical control, the identification of usage that is structurally correct and appropriate in context; and reading comprehension, the overall meaning of passages in various styles and levels of writing and recall of specific details. One point is given for each correct answer, and a fraction of a point is deducted for each wrong answer. Scores are reported on a scale of 200 to 800. This achievement test (administered two times a year), together with the Scholastic Aptitude Test (SAT), is offered through the Admissions Testing Program (ATP) of the College Board. For students with disabilities, the ATP has available special testing arrangements, including extended time administrations of the achievement test. Examiner required. Suitable for group use.

Timed: 1 hour

Scoring: Computer scored

Cost: Contact publisher

Publisher: The College Board

ACHIEVEMENT TEST: FOREIGN LANGUAGES—HEBREW
College Board Achievement Test Development Committees

Adolescent
Grades 10–12

Purpose: Measures high-school students' vocabulary mastery, grammatical control, and reading comprehension of Hebrew.

Used to predict college performance and by some schools for admissions selection and course placement.

Description: Multiple-item paper-pencil multiple-choice test of ability and knowledge in three areas: vocabulary mastery, the knowledge of the meaning of words and idiomatic expressions as they appear in the written and spoken forms of the language; grammatical control, the identification of usage that is structurally correct and appropriate in context; and reading comprehension, the overall meaning of passages in various styles and levels of writing and recall of specific details. One point is given for each correct answer, and a fraction of a point is deducted for each wrong answer. Scores are reported on a scale of 200 to 800. This achievement test (administered once a year), together with the Scholastic Aptitude Test (SAT), is offered through the Admissions Testing Program (ATP) of the College Board. For students with disabilities, the ATP has available special testing arrangements, including extended time administrations of the achievement test. Examiner required. Suitable for group use.

Timed: 1 hour
Scoring: Computer scored
Cost: Contact publisher
Publisher: The College Board

ACHIEVEMENT TEST: FOREIGN LANGUAGES—LATIN
College Board Achievement Test Development Committees

Adolescent
Grades 10–12

Purpose: Measures high-school students' vocabulary mastery, grammatical control, and reading comprehension of Latin. Used to predict college performance and by some schools for admissions selection and course placement.

Description: Multiple-item paper-pencil multiple-choice test of ability and knowledge in three areas: vocabulary mastery, the knowledge of the meaning of words and idiomatic expressions as they appear in the written and spoken forms of the language; grammatical control, the identification of usage that is structurally cor-

rect and appropriate in context; and reading comprehension, the overall meaning of passages in various styles and levels of writing and recall of specific details. One point is given for each correct answer, and a fraction of a point is deducted for each wrong answer. Scores are reported on a scale of 200 to 800. This achievement test (administered twice a year), together with the Scholastic Aptitude Test (SAT), is offered through the Admissions Testing Program (ATP) of the College Board. For students with disabilities, the ATP has available special testing arrangements, including extended time administrations of the achievement test. Examiner required. Suitable for group use.

Timed: 1 hour
Scoring: Computer scored
Cost: Contact publisher
Publisher: The College Board

ACHIEVEMENT TEST: FOREIGN LANGUAGES—SPANISH
College Board Achievement Test Development Committees

Adolescent
Grades 10–12

Purpose: Measures high-school students' vocabulary mastery, grammatical control, and reading comprehension of Spanish. Used to predict college performance and by some schools for admissions selection and course placement.

Description: Multiple-item paper-pencil multiple-choice test of ability and knowledge in three areas: vocabulary mastery, the knowledge of the meaning of words and idiomatic expressions as they appear in the written and spoken forms of the language; grammatical control, the identification of usage that is structurally correct and appropriate in context; and reading comprehension, the overall meaning of passages in various styles and levels of writing and recall of specific details. One point is given for each correct answer, and a fraction of a point is deducted for each wrong answer. Scores are reported on a scale of 200 to 800. This achievement test (administered five times a year), together with the Scholastic Aptitude Test (SAT), is offered through the Admissions Testing

Program (ATP) of the College Board. For students with disabilities, the ATP has available special testing arrangements, including extended time administrations of the achievement test. Examiner required. Suitable for group use.

Timed: 1 hour

Scoring: Computer scored

Cost: Contact publisher

Publisher: The College Board

ACHIEVEMENT TEST: HISTORY AND SOCIAL STUDIES— AMERICAN HISTORY AND SOCIAL STUDIES
College Board Achievement Test Development Committees

Adolescent
Grades 10–12

Purpose: Evaluates high-school students' knowledge of American history and social studies. Used to predict college performance and by some schools for admissions selection and course placement.

Description: 100–item paper-pencil multiple-choice test measuring knowledge of 19th- and 20th-century American history in the political, social, economic, diplomatic, intellectual, and cultural fields. The test also covers social studies concepts, methods, and generalizations as they are encountered in the study of history. One point is given for each correct answer, and a fraction of a point is deducted for each wrong answer. Scores are reported on a scale of 200 to 800. This achievement test (administered five times a year), together with the Scholastic Aptitude Test (SAT), is offered through the Admissions Testing Program (ATP) of the College Board. For students with disabilities, the ATP has available special testing arrangements, including extended time administrations of the achievement test. Examiner required. Suitable for group use.

Timed: 1 hour

Scoring: Computer scored

Cost: Contact publisher

Publisher: The College Board

ACHIEVEMENT TEST: HISTORY AND SOCIAL STUDIES— EUROPEAN HISTORY AND WORLD CULTURES
College Board Achievement Test Development Committees

Adolescent
Grades 10–12

Purpose: Measures high-school students' understanding of the development of Western and non-Western cultures, comprehension of fundamental social science concepts, and the ability to use basic historical techniques. Used to predict college performance and by some schools for admissions selection and course placement.

Description: 100–item paper-pencil multiple-choice test, half dealing with Western Europe and half with other areas. Most of the questions cover the period from the middle of the 15th century to the present, including political and diplomatic history, intellectual and cultural history, and social and economic history. One point is given for each correct answer, and a fraction of a point is deducted for each wrong answer. Scores are reported on a scale of 200 to 800. This achievement test (administered twice a year), together with the Scholastic Aptitude Test (SAT), is offered through the Admissions Testing Program (ATP) of the College Board. For students with disabilities, the ATP has available special testing arrangements, including extended time administrations of the achievement test. Examiner required. Suitable for group use.

Timed: 1 hour

Scoring: Computer scored

Cost: Contact publisher

Publisher: The College Board

ACHIEVEMENT TEST: MATHEMATICS—MATHEMATICS LEVEL I
College Board Achievement Test Development Committees

Adolescent
Grades 10–12

Purpose: Determines high-school students' level of skill in mathematics typical of three years of college preparatory work. Used to predict college performance and by some schools for admissions selection and course placement.

Description: Broad-range cumulative paper-pencil multiple-choice examination covering algebra, plane Euclidean geometry, coordinate geometry, trigonometry of the right triangle, functions and functional notation for composition and inverse, space perception of simple solids, mathematical reasoning, and the nature of proof. One point is given for each correct answer, and a fraction of a point is deducted for each wrong answer. Scores are reported on a scale of 200 to 800. This achievement test (administered five times a year), together with the Scholastic Aptitude Test (SAT), is offered through the Admissions Testing Program (ATP) of the College Board. For students with disabilities, the ATP has available special testing arrangements, including extended time administrations of the achievement test. Examiner required. Suitable for group use.
Timed: 1 hour
Scoring: Computer scored
Cost: Contact publisher
Publisher: The College Board

ACHIEVEMENT TEST: MATHEMATICS—MATHEMATICS LEVEL II
College Board Achievement Test Development Committees

Adolescent
Grades 10–12

Purpose: Determines the level of skill of high school students who have taken college preparatory level mathematics for 3½ years or more. Used to predict college performance and by some schools for admissions selection and course placement.

Description: Paper-pencil multiple-choice test overlapping the Mathematics Level I test. The questions in the Level II test concentrate on more advanced work, calling for a greater depth of understanding and sophistication and stressing as-

pects that are prerequisites for calculus. The Level II test is composed of nearly equal parts of algebra, geometry, trigonometry, functions, and a miscellaneous category consisting of such topics as sequences and limits, logic and proof, probability and statistics, and number theory. One point is given for each correct answer, and a fraction of a point is deducted for each wrong answer. Scores are reported on a scale of 200 to 800. This achievement test (administered five times a year), together with the Scholastic Aptitude Test (SAT), is offered through the Admissions Testing Program (ATP) of the College Board. For students with disabilities, the ATP has available special testing arrangements, including extended time administrations of the achievement test. Examiner required. Suitable for group use.
Timed: 1 hour
Scoring: Computer scored
Cost: Contact publisher
Publisher: The College Board

ACHIEVEMENT TEST: SCIENCES—BIOLOGY
College Board Achievement Test Development Committees

Adolescent
Grades 10–12

Purpose: Measures high school students' knowledge of biology and the skills of comprehension, application, analysis, synthesis, and evaluation that have been acquired for using that knowledge. Used to predict college performance and by some schools for admissions selection and course placement.

Description: Multiple-item paper-pencil multiple-choice test covering the following topics: cellular structure and function; organismal reproduction, development, growth, nutrition, structure, and function; genetics; evolution; systematics; ecology; and behavior. Some test questions require interpretation of experimental data, understanding of scientific methods and laboratory techniques, and knowledge of biology history. One point is given for each correct answer, and a fraction of a point is deducted for each wrong answer. Scores are reported on a scale of 200 to 800. This achievement test (administered five times a year), together with the Scholastic Aptitude Test (SAT), is offered through the Admissions Testing Program (ATP) of the College Board. For students with disabilities, the ATP has available special testing arrangements, including extended time administrations of the achievement test. Examiner required. Suitable for group use.

Timed: 1 hour
Scoring: Computer scored
Cost: Contact publisher
Publisher: The College Board

ACHIEVEMENT TEST: SCIENCES—CHEMISTRY
College Board Achievement Test Development Committees

Adolescent
Grades 10–12

Purpose: Measures high-school students' knowledge of chemistry and skills in comprehension, application, analysis, synthesis, and evaluation that have been acquired for using that knowledge. Used to predict college performance and by some schools for admissions selection and course placement.

Description: Multiple-item paper-pencil multiple-choice test covering areas such as kinetic-molecular theory and the three states of matter; atomic structure; quantitative relations; chemical bonding and molecular structure; the nature of chemical reactions; interpretation of chemical equilibria and reaction rates; electrochemistry; nuclear chemistry and radiochemistry; physical and chemical properties of the more familiar metals, transition elements, and nonmetals and of the more familiar compounds. One point is given for each correct answer, and a fraction of a point is deducted for each wrong answer. Scores are reported on a scale of 200 to 800. This achievement test (administered five times a year), together with the Scholastic Aptitude Test (SAT), is offered through the Admissions Testing Program (ATP) of the College Board. For students with disabilities, the ATP has available special testing arrangements, including

extended time administrations of the achievement test. Examiner required. Suitable for group use.

Timed: 1 hour
Scoring: Computer scored
Cost: Contact publisher
Publisher: The College Board

ACHIEVEMENT TEST: SCIENCES—PHYSICS
College Board Achievement Test Development Committees

Adolescent
Grades 10–12

Purpose: Measures high-school students' knowledge of physics and skills in comprehension, application, analysis, synthesis, and evaluation that have been acquired for using that knowledge. Used to predict college performance and by some schools for admissions selection and course placement.

Description: Multiple-item paper-pencil multiple-choice test covering mechanics, electricity and magnetism, geometric optics and waves, heat and kinetic theory, and modern physics. One point is given for each correct answer, and a fraction of a point is deducted for each wrong answer. Scores are reported on a scale of 200 to 800. This achievement test (administered five times a year), together with the Scholastic Aptitude Test (SAT), is offered through the Admissions Testing Program (ATP) of the College Board. For students with disabilities, the ATP has available special testing arrangements, including extended time administrations of the achievement test. Examiner required. Suitable for group use.

Timed: 1 hour
Scoring: Computer scored
Cost: Contact publisher
Publisher: The College Board

ACT ASSET PROGRAM
The American College Testing Program

Adult

Purpose: Measures academic preparation of entering community college students.

Used for academic advising, course placement, and retention services in 2–year institutions.

Description: Battery of seven tests: Writing Skills (36 items; 15–20 minutes), Reading Skills (24 items; 25 minutes), Numerical Skills (32 items; 25 minutes), Elementary Algebra Skills (25 items; 25 minutes), Intermediate Algebra Skills (25 items; 25 minutes), College Algebra Skills (25 items; 25 minutes), and Geometry Skills (25 items; 25 minutes). The student generally must take the first three tests, which cover basic skills; the last four tests, which cover advanced skills, are optional. Scored by Scan-Tron or NCS portable scanners, self-scoring answer folders, or immediately computer-scored by Scan-Tron or NCS. Examiner required. Suitable for group use.

Timed: Varies, depending on test

Scoring: Computer scored; hand key

Cost: Each participant (includes descriptive and follow-up research services) $2.50; reusable test booklet $0.50

Publisher: The American College Testing Program

ACT PROFICIENCY EXAMINATION PROGRAM (ACT PEP)
The American College Testing Program

Adult

Purpose: Assesses college-level academic achievement. Used to grant college credit and advanced placement in academic courses to students at over 700 colleges and universities, including the New York Regents College Degree Program.

Description: 42 paper-pencil tests measuring achievement in a wide range of fields: Arts and Sciences (6 tests), Business (15 tests), Education (4 tests), Nursing (17 tests). Most of the tests are objective (125–150 items) and some are essay. College-level achievement is measured from introductory to advanced levels of study. There are no restrictions on who may take the tests. The multiple-choice tests are administered nationwide up to six times yearly. Individuals seeking credit should contact their local colleges

for information. These tests are known as Regents College Examinations in New York State. Developed by the University of the State of New York, the tests are administered by ACT and accepted by over 700 participating colleges and universities. Examiner required. Suitable for group use.

Timed: 3–7 hours per test

Scoring: Examiner evaluated and computer scored by ACT

Cost: Varies in fee from $40.00–$125.00

Publisher: The American College Testing Program

ACT PROFICIENCY EXAMINATION PROGRAM—ARTS AND SCIENCES: ABNORMAL PSYCHOLOGY
The American College Testing Program

Adult

Purpose: Measures knowledge and understanding of abnormal psychology. Used to grant college credit and/or advanced placement in academic courses.

Description: Paper-pencil multiple-choice test assessing knowledge of the historical background of abnormal psychology, the major conceptualizations in the area, and the nature and description of abnormal disorders as well as their definitions, classification, etiology, and major treatments. The test assumes a familiarity with concepts typically learned in an introductory psychology course. Examiner required. Suitable for group use.

Timed: 3 hours

Scoring: Computer scored by ACT

Cost: Fee $40.00

Publisher: The American College Testing Program

ACT PROFICIENCY EXAMINATION PROGRAM—ARTS AND SCIENCES: ANATOMY AND PHYSIOLOGY
The American College Testing Program

Adult

Purpose: Measures knowledge and understanding of anatomy and physiology. Used to grant college credit and advanced placement in academic courses.

Description: Multiple-item paper-pencil multiple-choice test. Items are based on anatomical terminology and facts, physiological concepts and principles, and the structure and function of body cells, tissues, organs, and systems. Emphasis is placed on systems that maintain, integrate, and control bodily functions. Individuals seeking credit should contact their local colleges for information. Examiner required. Suitable for group use.

Timed: 3 hours

Scoring: Computer scored by ACT

Cost: Fee $40.00

Publisher: The American College Testing Program

ACT PROFICIENCY EXAMINATION PROGRAM—ARTS AND SCIENCES: FOUNDATION OF GERONTOLOGY
The American College Testing Program

Adult

Purpose: Measures knowledge and understanding of the biological, psychological, and social aspects of aging. Used to grant college credit and advanced placement in academic courses.

Description: Multiple-item paper-pencil multiple-choice test. Items are based on material normally taught in a one-semester introductory course in gerontology at the undergraduate level. Measures the ability to describe, understand, and analyze issues pertaining to the functioning and well-being of the elderly. Emphasis is placed on an awareness of the needs and realities involved in both the normal aspects of aging and problems associated with aging. Individuals seeking credit should contact their local colleges for information. Examiner required. Suitable for group use.

Timed: 3 hours

Scoring: Computer scored by ACT

Cost: Fee $40.00

Publisher: The American College Testing Program

ACT PROFICIENCY EXAMINATION PROGRAM—ARTS AND SCIENCES: MICROBIOLOGY
The American College Testing Program

Adult

Purpose: Assesses knowledge of microbiology. Used to grant college credit and advanced placement in academic courses.

Description: Paper-pencil multiple-choice test of knowledge and understanding of bacteria, algae, fungi, protozoa, viruses, and their relationships to humans. The test covers such areas as history, morphology, and ultrastructure, metabolism, growth and nutrition, genetics, physiological types, methods of control, and applied and environmental microbiology. Questions are based on material normally taught in a one-semester introductory course in microbiology at the undergraduate level. Examiner required. Suitable for group use.

Timed: 3 hours

Scoring: Computer scored by ACT

Cost: Fee $40.00

Publisher: The American College Testing Program

ACT PROFICIENCY EXAMINATION PROGRAM—ARTS AND SCIENCES: PHYSICAL GEOLOGY
The American College Testing Program

Adult

Purpose: Measures proficiency in the study of physical geology. Used to grant college credit and advanced placement in academic courses.

Description: Multiple-item paper-pencil multiple-choice test covering material normally taught in introductory undergraduate courses in physical geology. Measures knowledge and understanding of the following areas: the processes that form the earth through geologic time; the structure, composition, and evolution of the earth; and the landforms created by the processes that form the earth. Individuals seeking credit should contact their local colleges for information. Examiner required. Suitable for group use.

Timed: 3 hours

Scoring: Computer scored by ACT

Cost: Fee $40.00

Publisher: The American College Testing Program

ACT PROFICIENCY EXAMINATION PROGRAM—ARTS AND SCIENCES: STATISTICS
The American College Testing Program

Adult

Purpose: Assesses knowledge and understanding of the fundamental concepts of descriptive and inferential statistics. Used to grant college credit and advanced placement in academic courses.

Description: Paper-pencil multiple-choice test of material normally taught in a one-semester introductory course in mathematical statistics at the undergraduate level. Both the meaning and application of basic ideas are tested. Examiner required. Suitable for group use.

Timed: 3 hours

Scoring: Computer scored by ACT

Cost: Fee $40.00

Publisher: The American College Testing Program

ACT PROFICIENCY EXAMINATION PROGRAM— BUSINESS: ADVANCED ACCOUNTING
The American College Testing Program

Adult

Purpose: Measures knowledge and understanding of material taught in upper-level accounting courses at the undergraduate level. Used to grant college credit and advanced placement in academic courses.

Description: Essay test assessing various aspects of accounting, including partnerships; home and branch office relationships; business combinations and consolidated statements; foreign subsidiaries; reporting for estates, trusts, and nongoing concerns; and fund accounting for government units and not-for-profit organizations. A knowledge of generally accepted accounting principles (FASB statements), principles of economics, statistics, and basic computer science concepts is assumed. The test is scored on a pass/fail basis. Available in November, February, and May only. Examiner required. Suitable for group use.

Timed: 4 hours

Scoring: Examiner evaluated

Cost: $125.00

Publisher: The American College Testing Program

ACT PROFICIENCY EXAMINATION PROGRAM— BUSINESS: AUDITING
The American College Testing Program

Adult

Purpose: Measures knowledge and understanding of material taught in upper-level auditing courses at the undergraduate level. Used to grant college credit and advanced placement in academic courses.

Description: Essay test assessing various aspects of auditing, including professional responsibilities, internal control, audit evidence and procedures, reporting, and auditing aspects of specific topics. A knowledge of generally accepted accounting principles, statistics, and basic computer science concepts is assumed. The test is scored on a pass/fail basis. Available in November, February, and May only. Examiner required. Suitable for group use.

Timed: 4 hours

Scoring: Examiner evaluated

Cost: $125.00

Publisher: The American College Testing Program

ACT PROFICIENCY EXAMINATION PROGRAM— BUSINESS: BUSINESS POLICY
The American College Testing Program

Adult

Purpose: Measures knowledge and understanding of business policy. Used to grant college credit and advanced placement in academic courses.

Description: Essay test assessing knowledge and understanding of introductory business policy concepts, including those involving accounting, business law, corporation finance, economics, management, marketing, mathematics, production/operations management, and statistics. The test is scored on a pass/fail basis. Available in November, February, and May only. Examiner required. Suitable for group use.

Timed: 3 hours
Scoring: Examiner evaluated
Cost: $125.00
Publisher: The American College Testing Program

ACT PROFICIENCY EXAMINATION PROGRAM— BUSINESS: CORPORATION FINANCE
The American College Testing Program

Adult

Purpose: Measures knowledge and understanding of material taught in introductory corporation finance courses at the undergraduate level. Used to grant college credit and advanced placement in academic courses.

Description: Multiple-item paper-pencil multiple-choice test measuring eight areas of corporation finance: a) goals of financial management and introduction to strategic decisions of financial management, b) tools of financial analysis, c) management of current assets and liabilities, d) intermediate and long-term financial instruments, e) the investment decision, f) the financing decision, g) the

dividend decision, and h) international finance. The test yields a standard score. Examiner required. Suitable for group use.

Timed: 3 hours
Scoring: Computer scored
Cost: $50.00
Publisher: The American College Testing Program

ACT PROFICIENCY EXAMINATION PROGRAM— BUSINESS: COST ACCOUNTING AND ANALYSIS
The American College Testing Program

Adult

Purpose: Measures knowledge and understanding of material taught in upper-level accounting courses at the undergraduate level. Used to grant college credit and advanced placement in academic courses.

Description: Essay test assessing various aspects of cost accounting, including the internal uses of accounting information for purposes of planning, performance evaluation, decision making, and product costing. A knowledge of generally accepted accounting principles (FASB statements), statistics (including regression and probability), and linear programming is assumed. The test is scored on a pass/fail basis. Available in November, February, and May only. Examiner required. Suitable for group use.

Timed: 4 hours
Scoring: Examiner evaluated
Cost: $125.00
Publisher: The American College Testing Program

ACT PROFICIENCY EXAMINATION PROGRAM— BUSINESS: FEDERAL INCOME TAXATION
The American College Testing Program

Adult

Purpose: Measures knowledge and understanding of federal income tax system as taught in upper-level business courses at the undergraduate level. Used to grant college credit and advanced placement in academic courses.

Description: Essay test assessing various aspects of the federal income tax system, including taxation of individuals (gross income, adjusted gross income, taxable income, tax computation), taxation of corporations (tax treatments of income, deductions, losses, tax computation, corporate formation), and taxation of partnerships (partnership's tax treatment, tax year, organization). A knowledge of fundamental accounting principles is assumed. The test is scored on a pass/fail basis. Available in November, February, and May only. Examiner required. Suitable for group use.·

Timed: 4 hours
Scoring: Examiner evaluated
Cost: $125.00
Publisher: The American College Testing Program

ACT PROFICIENCY EXAMINATION PROGRAM— BUSINESS: INTERMEDIATE ACCOUNTING
The American College Testing Program

Adult

Purpose: Measures knowledge and understanding of material taught in upper-level accounting courses at the undergraduate level. Used to grant college credit and advanced placement in academic courses.

Description: Essay test assessing various areas of accounting, including theory and valuation, financial statements based on historical cost and alternatives to historical cost, statements of income and retained earnings, additional elements of measurement and disclosure, selection of alternatives allowable from generally accepted accounting principles, and accounting for unconsolidated investments in other companies. A knowledge of generally accepted accounting principles (FASB statements), principles of economics, statistics, and basic computer science concepts is assumed. The test is

scored on a pass/fail basis. Available in November, February, and May only. Examiner required. Suitable for group use.

Timed: 4 hours
Scoring: Examiner evaluated
Cost: $125.00
Publisher: The American College Testing Program

ACT PROFICIENCY EXAMINATION PROGRAM— BUSINESS: INTERMEDIATE BUSINESS LAW
The American College Testing Program

Adult

Purpose: Measures knowledge and understanding of materials taught in upper-level courses at the undergraduate level. Used to grant college credit and advanced placement in academic courses.

Description: Essay test assessing various aspects of business law, including legal aspects of the Uniform Commercial Code, business organizations, business legislation, insurance, legal liabilities of accountants, property rights, and personal property. A knowledge of basic contract law, torts, and the American legal system is assumed. The test is scored on a pass/fail basis. Available in November, February, and May only. Examiner required. Suitable for group use.

Timed: 4 hours
Scoring: Examiner evaluated
Cost: $125.00
Publisher: The American College Testing Program

ACT PROFICIENCY EXAMINATION PROGRAM— BUSINESS: INTRODUCTORY ACCOUNTING
The American College Testing Program

Adult

Purpose: Measures knowledge and understanding of basic accounting concepts, principles, and procedures. Used to grant college credit and advanced placement in academic courses.

Description: Multiple-item paper-pencil multiple-choice test covering six major categories: basic accounting concepts and principles; the accounting recording process; financial statements and analysis; accounting for assets, liabilities, owners equity, revenues, and expenses; manufacturing accounting; and analysis for managerial decision-making. Individuals seeking credit should contact their local colleges for information. Examiner required. Suitable for group use.

Timed: 3 hours
Scoring: Computer scored by ACT
Cost: Fee $50.00
Publisher: The American College Testing Program

ACT PROFICIENCY EXAMINATION PROGRAM— BUSINESS: PRINCIPLES OF MANAGEMENT
The American College Testing Program

Adult

Purpose: Measures proficiency in the principles of management. Used to grant college credit and advanced placement in academic courses.

Description: Multiple-item paper-pencil multiple-choice test covering the background of management thought, the planning function, the organizing function, the leading and influencing function, the controlling function, and special issues in management. Items are based on facts, terminology, concepts, and theories in the area of human relations as applied to individual and group behavior, organization dynamics, organizational development, functions of management, and the development of management thought. Individuals seeking credit should contact their local colleges for information. Examiner required. Suitable for group use.

Timed: 3 hours
Scoring: Computer scored by ACT
Cost: Fee $50.00
Publisher: The American College Testing Program

ACT PROFICIENCY EXAMINATION PROGRAM— BUSINESS: PRINCIPLES OF MARKETING
The American College Testing Program

Adult

Purpose: Assesses proficiency in principles of marketing. Used to grant college credit and advanced placement in academic courses.

Description: Multiple-item paper-pencil multiple-choice test measuring the following aspects of marketing: the role of marketing in the organization and society, analysis of markets, the functioning areas of marketing, and special topics. Those seeking credit should contact their local colleges for information. Examiner required. Suitable for group use.

Timed: 3 hours
Scoring: Computer scored by ACT
Cost: Fee $50.00
Publisher: The American College Testing Program

ACT PROFICIENCY EXAMINATION PROGRAM— BUSINESS: PRODUCTION/ OPERATIONS MANAGEMENT
The American College Testing Program

Adult

Purpose: Measures knowledge and understanding of material taught in introductory production/operations management courses at the undergraduate level. Used to grant credit and advanced placement in academic courses.

Description: Multiple-item paper-pencil multiple-choice test measuring four areas of production/operations management: a) definition and description of production/ operations management, b) design of the productive system, c) planning the use of the productive system, and d) control of the productive system. The test yields a standard score. Examiner required. Suitable for group use.

Timed: 3 hours

Scoring: Computer scored
Cost: $50.00
Publisher: The American College Testing Program

ACT PROFICIENCY EXAMINATION PROGRAM—EDUCATION: EDUCATIONAL PSYCHOLOGY

The American College Testing Program

Adult

Purpose: Assesses proficiency in the material covered by introductory college courses in educational psychology or in the psychological foundations of education. Used to grant college credit and advanced placement in academic courses.

Description: Multiple-item paper-pencil multiple-choice test. Covers terminology, concepts, theories, and principles in the following areas: individual growth and development; learning and instruction; the influence of social, cultural, and environmental factors; and measurement. No classroom or tutorial experience is assumed. Individuals seeking credit should contact their local colleges for information. Examiner required. Suitable for group use.
Timed: 3 hours
Scoring: Computer scored by ACT
Cost: Fee $40.00
Publisher: The American College Testing Program

ACT PROFICIENCY EXAMINATION PROGRAM—EDUCATION: READING INSTRUCTION IN THE ELEMENTARY SCHOOL

The American College Testing Program

Adult

Purpose: Assesses proficiency in elementary school reading instruction. Used to grant college credit and advanced placement in academic courses.

Description: Multiple-item paper-pencil multiple-choice test. Items are based on terms, concepts, and methods related to the following areas of reading instruction: assessment, goal setting, materials, methodologies, instructional management, instruction, evaluation, parental role, school support staff, and personal responsibilities of the teacher. Individuals seeking credit should contact their local colleges for information. Examiner required. Suitable for group use.
Timed: 3 hours
Scoring: Computer scored by ACT
Cost: Fee $40.00
Publisher: The American College Testing Program

ACT PROFICIENCY EXAMINATION PROGRAM—EDUCATION: THEORETICAL FOUNDATIONS

The American College Testing Program

Adult

Purpose: Assesses proficiency in corrective and remedial reading instruction. Used to grant college credit and advanced placement in academic courses. Also measures achievement typically expected of a student at the master's degree level who has completed a basic course sequence leading to a concentration in reading education.

Description: Multiple-item paper-pencil multiple-choice test consisting of four major categories: reading and writing as language processes; assessment and evaluation; teaching of reading; and professional role and ongoing professional development. Items are based upon the following aspects of teaching reading from the primary grades through secondary school: planning programs for pupils; parents' role; relationship between the reading teacher and the school support staff; and personal responsibilities of the reading teacher. Individuals seeking credit should contact their local colleges for information. Examiner required. Suitable for group use.
Timed: 3 hours
Scoring: Computer scored by ACT

Cost: Fee $40.00

Publisher: The American College Testing Program

ADMISSIONS EXAMINATIONS: ADMISSIONS AND CREDENTIALING GROUP: DOPPELT MATHEMATICAL REASONING TEST
J.E. Doppelt

Adult
Graduate students

Purpose: Measures mathematical reasoning ability. Assists in the selection of graduate students.

Description: Multiple-item paper-pencil test of mathematical reasoning ability. The test was developed to provide a high-level measure of mathematical skills comparable to the Miller Analogies Test and the Advanced Personnel Test. Examiner required. Suitable for group use.

Timed: 50 minutes

Scoring: Scoring service available

Cost: Contact publisher

Publisher: Admissions and Credentialing Group/The Psychological Corporation

Information and availability unconfirmed; last verified in 1988.

ADMISSIONS EXAMINATIONS: ADMISSIONS AND CREDENTIALING GROUP: MILLER ANALOGIES TEST
W.S. Miller

Adult
College students

Purpose: Assesses information and verbal reasoning ability. Used for admission of students to graduate school.

Description: 100–item paper-pencil test of verbal reasoning ability. Items are multiple-choice analogies. Braille and large-type editions are available. Distribution is restricted, and the test is administered at specified licensed university centers. Examiner required. Suitable for group use.

Timed: 50 minutes

Scoring: Not available

Cost: Contact publisher

Publisher: Admissions and Credentialing Group/The Psychological Corporation

Information and availability unconfirmed; last verified in 1988.

ADMISSIONS TESTING PROGRAM (ATP)

Adolescent
Grades 11–12

Purpose: Assists students, high schools, colleges, universities, and scholarship agencies with postsecondary educational planning and decision-making through a battery of aptitude and achievement tests.

Description: The ATP consists of the Scholastic Aptitude Test (SAT), the Test of Standard Written English (TSWE), the Achievement Tests, and the Student Descriptive Questionnaire (SDQ). Closely related to the ATP are the Student Search Service, the Summary Reporting Service, and the Validity Study Service. The SAT, TSWE, and Achievement Tests are described in separate entries. The Student Descriptive Questionnaire, answered by about 91% of all students who take the ATP, provides additional information about and specific characteristics of the student (background, academic record, extracurricular activities, etc.). The Student Search Service helps colleges and scholarship programs identify students with certain characteristics based on the SDQ. Students are included by their response on the SDQ and a search is conducted quarterly for colleges and programs requesting it. Handicapped students may be tested under special arrangements such as extended time administrations, with special editions of the SAT and TSWE (large type, braille, cassette) or with the use of a reader, manual translator, or an amanuensis. Tests for registered students are given at specified times at test centers, mostly located in high schools. Pre-enrollment is required. Examiner required. Suitable for group use.

Timed: See specific test

Scoring: Computer scored

Cost: Contact publisher

Publisher: The College Board

ADMISSIONS TESTING PROGRAM: PRELIMINARY SCHOLASTIC APTITUDE TEST/ NATIONAL MERIT (PSAT/NM)

Adolescent
Grade 11

Purpose: Assesses high-school students' verbal and mathematical reasoning abilities and evaluates readiness for college-level study. Used as a preview of the Scholastic Aptitude Test and serves as the qualifying test for student competitions conducted by the National Merit Scholarship Corporation: the National Merit Scholarship Program and the National Achievement Scholarship Program for Outstanding Negro Students.

Description: 115–item paper-pencil multiple-choice test measuring verbal and mathematical achievement and aptitude. The verbal section consists of 65 questions of four types: antonyms, sentence completions, analogies, and reading comprehension. The mathematical section consists of 50 questions applying graphic, spatial, numerical, symbolic, and logical techniques at a knowledge level no higher than elementary algebra and geometry. Special testing arrangements can be made for away-from-school testing, for students abroad, and for students with visual and other handicaps. Examiner required. Suitable for group use.

Timed: 1 hour, 40 minutes

Scoring: Computer scored

Cost: Contact publisher

Publisher: The College Board

ADMISSIONS TESTING PROGRAM: SCHOLASTIC APTITUDE TEST (SAT)

Adolescent
Grades 11–12

Purpose: Measures verbal and mathematic reasoning abilities related to successful performance in college. Used to supplement secondary-school records and

other information in assessing readiness for college-level work.

Description: 135–item paper-pencil multiple-choice test measuring reading comprehension, vocabulary, and mathematical problem-solving ability involving arithmetic reasoning, algebra, and geometry. The test consists of two verbal sections of 85 questions, including 25 antonyms, 20 analogies, 15 sentence completions, and 25 reading questions and two mathematical sections of 50 questions, including approximately two-thirds multiple-choice and one-third quantitative comparison questions. Examiner required. Suitable for group use.

Timed: 2½ hours

Scoring: Computer scored

Cost: Contact publisher

Publisher: The College Board

ADMISSIONS TESTING PROGRAM: TEST OF STANDARD WRITTEN ENGLISH (TSWE)

Adolescent
Grades 11–12

Purpose: Evaluates a student's ability to recognize standard written English. Used by colleges to help place students in appropriate freshman English courses.

Description: 50–item paper-pencil multiple-choice test measuring the basic principles of grammar and usage, as well as more complicated writing problems. This test is administered with the Scholastic Aptitude Test. Examiner required. Suitable for group use.

Timed: 30 minutes

Scoring: Computer scored

Cost: Contact publisher

Publisher: The College Board

ADULT BASIC LEARNING EXAMINATION SECOND EDITION (ABLE)
Bjorn Karlsen and Eric F. Gardner

Adult—Ages 17 and older

Purpose: Measures adult achievement in basic learning.

Description: Multiple-item paper-pencil measure of vocabulary knowledge, reading comprehension, spelling and arithmetic computation, and problem-solving skills. The test is divided into three levels. Level 1 is for adults with from 1 to 4 years of formal education. Level 2 is for adults with from 5 to 8 years of schooling. Level 3 is for those with at least 8 years of schooling and who may or may not have graduated from high school. Because the vocabulary test is dictated, no reading is required. The Arithmetic Problem-Solving test is dictated at Level 1. A short screening test, SelectABLE, is available for use in determining the appropriate level of ABLE for each applicant. The test is available in two alternate forms, E and F, at each level. SelectABLE is available in only one form. Examiner required. Suitable for group use.

Untimed: SelectABLE 15 minutes; Level 1 2 hours, 10 minutes; Levels 2 and 3 2 hours, 55 minutes

Scoring: Hand key; may be computer scored; Levels 2 and 3 self-scored

Cost: Specimen set (Level 1, 2, 3 test booklets for Form E; directions for administration for Levels 1, 2, 3; group record, hand-scorable answer sheet, and ready-score answer sheet for Level 2; SelectABLE ready-scale answer sheet) $23.00

Publisher: The Psychological Corporation

Information and availability unconfirmed; last verified in 1988.

AP EXAMINATION: ADVANCED PLACEMENT PROGRAM

**Adolescent
Grades 10–12**

Purpose: Measures academic achievement in a wide range of fields. Used by participating colleges to grant credit and placement in these fields to more gifted or advanced students and to measure the effectiveness of a school's Advanced Placement (AP) Program.

Description: The AP examinations are a part of the AP Program, which provides course descriptions, examinations, and curricular materials to high schools to allow those students who wish to pursue college-level studies while still in secondary school to receive advanced placement and/or credit upon entering college. The AP Program provides descriptions and examinations on 29 introductory college courses in the following 15 fields: art, biology, chemistry, computer science, economics, English, French, German, government and politics, history, Latin, mathematics, music, physics, and Spanish.

No test is longer than three hours, and some are shorter. All examinations are paper-pencil tests (except for the art portfolios) with an essay or problem-solving section and a multiple-choice section.

Using the operational services provided by the Educational Testing Service, the AP Examinations are administered in May by schools throughout the world. Any school may participate; it need only appoint an AP coordinator and order its examinations in time. The current fee for each examination is $62.00. Fee reductions are available for students with acute financial need. In June the examinations are graded on the following 5-point scale: 5=extremely well qualified, 4=well qualified, 3=qualified, 2=possibly qualified, 1=no recommendation. In July, the grades are sent to the students, their designated colleges, and their schools. Released examinations, *Teacher's Guides*, and booklets on grading the Advanced Placement Examination are available in most fields. Films and booklets describing the AP Program as a whole are available also. Available in braille and large print. Examiner required. Suitable for group use.

Timed: 3 hours maximum

Scoring: Computer scored; examiner evaluated

Cost: Per student $62.00

Publisher: The College Board

AP EXAMINATION: ART— HISTORY OF ART

**Adolescent
Grades 10–12**

Purpose: Measures academic achievement in the study of art history. Used by participating colleges to grant credit and placement to more gifted or advanced students. Also measures the effectiveness of a school's AP Program in art history.

Description: Multiple-item paper-pencil test arranged in two sections. Section I is a multiple-choice test of the student's acquisition of factual or objective aspects of history of art. Questions in this section test the student's knowledge about the history of Western art from antiquity to the present. Test items include names of artists, schools, movements, chronological periods and specific dates, and the subjects' styles, as well as the techniques of particular works of art. Section II has two parts. Part A is a series of short-answer questions testing the student's familiarity with a wide range of visual types and their historical significance. Test items in this part involve a comparison of related works of art. Section II, Part B is an essay test of the student's ability to deal with style development, treatment of a theme in art, the influence of historical context on works of art, and the influence of style from one given period to another. Examiners must have access to a slide projector. See AP Examination: Advanced Placement Program for administration time, scoring, and grade reporting. Examiner required. Suitable for group use.

Untimed: 3 hours

Scoring: Computer scored; examiner evaluated

Cost: Per student $62.00

Publisher: The College Board

AP EXAMINATION: ART—STUDIO ART (DRAWING)

Adolescent
Grades 10–12

Purpose: Evaluates academic achievement in the study of basic drawing skills. Used by participating colleges to grant credit and placement to more gifted or advanced students. Also measures the effectiveness of a school's AP Program in studio art.

Description: Student portfolios are evaluated according to criteria that parallel specialized drawing curricula at college and university levels. Students are asked to show evidence of experience and skill in perceptual and conceptual aspects of drawing. Portfolios are evaluated for quality, concentration (depth), and breadth. For evaluation of quality, students submit four original drawings to be judged in terms of their artistic "success." For evaluation of concentration, students submit up to 20 drawings (slides required) demonstrating in-depth work with a single concept or medium. For evaluation of breadth, students submit 14–20 additional slides to demonstrate exposure to and experience in a wide range of drawing alternatives. Detailed instructions for shipping, sizes of works to be submitted, and acceptable mediums are contained in the course description. See AP Examination: Advanced Placement Program for portfolio deadline, scoring, and grade reporting. Examiner/self-administered. Suitable for group use.

Untimed: Not available

Scoring: Examiner evaluated

Cost: Per student $62.00

Publisher: The College Board

AP EXAMINATION: ART—STUDIO ART (GENERAL PORTFOLIO)

Adolescent
Grades 10–12

Purpose: Evaluates general academic achievement in the study of studio art. Used by participating colleges to grant credit and placement to more gifted or advanced students. Also measures the effectiveness of a school's AP Program in studio art.

Description: Student portfolios are evaluated for three factors: quality, concentration (depth), and breadth. For evaluation of quality, students submit four original works in their original form to be judged in terms of artistic "success." For evaluation of concentration, students are asked to show evidence of work that reveals an in-depth artistic investigation (accompanied by a written commentary). For evaluation of breadth, students must submit slides of six drawings, as well as slides of six additional works addressing the following six artistic factors: technique, color, design, spatial content, and three-dimensional. Detailed instructions for shipping, size of works to be submitted, and acceptable mediums are included in the course description. See AP Examination: Advanced Placement Program for portfolio deadline, scoring, and grade reporting. Examiner/self-administered. Suitable for group use.

Untimed: Not available

Scoring: Examiner evaluated

Cost: Per student $62.00

Publisher: The College Board

AP EXAMINATION: BIOLOGY— GENERAL BIOLOGY

Adolescent
Grades 10–12

Purpose: Measures academic achievement in the study of biology. Used by participating colleges to grant credit and placement to more gifted or advanced students. Also measures the effectiveness of a school's AP Program in biology.

Description: Multiple-item paper-pencil test consists of a 90–minute multiple-choice section and a 90–minute free-response section. Both sections test the student's knowledge and understanding of the three major subdivisions of biology: molecular and cellular, organismal, and populational. Part of the multiple-choice section includes questions on experimental situations. In the free-response section, four required questions are presented. See AP Examination: Advanced Placement Program for administration time, scoring, and grade reporting. Examiner required. Suitable for group use.

Untimed: 3 hours maximum

Scoring: Computer scored; examiner evaluated

Cost: Per student $62.00

Publisher: The College Board

AP EXAMINATION: CHEMISTRY— GENERAL CHEMISTRY

Adolescent
Grades 10–12

Purpose: Measures academic achievement in the study of chemistry. Used by participating colleges to grant credit and placement to more gifted or advanced students. Also measures the effectiveness of a school's AP Program in chemistry.

Description: Multiple-item paper-pencil test in two parts. Part I (90 minutes) is a 75–item multiple-choice test, accounting for 45% of the final grade. Part II (90 minutes) consists of several comprehensive problems and essay topics that allow the student to demonstrate reasoning abilities by the application of chemical principles to problem solving. Part II accounts for 55% of the final grade. Both parts cover the following areas of fundamental chemistry: structure of matter, states of matter, reactions, descriptive chemistry, and laboratory work. Nonprogrammable hand calculators are allowed. See AP Examination: Advanced Placement Program for administration time, scoring, and grade reporting. Examiner required. Suitable for group use.

Untimed: 3 hours maximum

Scoring: Computer scored; examiner evaluated

Cost: Per student $62.00

Publisher: The College Board

AP EXAMINATION: COMPUTER SCIENCE A

Adolescent
Grades 10–12

Purpose: Measures academic achievement in the study of computer science. Used by participating colleges to grant credit and placement to more gifted or advanced students. Also measures the effectiveness of a school's AP Program in computer science.

Description: Multiple-item paper-pencil test consisting of equally weighted multiple-choice and free-response sections requiring students to design, write, and document programs and procedures. Section I (45 minutes) consists of 35 multiple-choice questions covering a) programming methodology, b) features of block-structured programming languages, c) fundamental data structures, d) algorithms, e) computer systems, and f) responsible use of computer systems. Section II (60 minutes) consists of three free-response questions. Those that require production of code must be written in standard Pascal.

Details on equipment needed are included in the course guide. See AP Examination: Advanced Placement Program for administration time, scoring, and grade reporting. Examiner required. Suitable for group use.

Timed: 105 minutes

Scoring: Computer scored; examiner evaluated

Cost: Per student $62.00

Publisher: The College Board

AP EXAMINATION: COMPUTER SCIENCE AB

Adolescent
Grades 10–12

Purpose: Measures academic achievement in the study of computer science. Used by participating colleges to grant credit and placement to more gifted or advanced students. Also measures the effectiveness of a school's AP Program in computer science.

Description: Multiple-item paper-pencil test consisting of equally weighted multiple-choice and free-response sections requiring the students to design, write, and document programs and procedures. Both sections include the following topics: programming methodology, features of programming languages, data types and structures, linear data structures, algorithms, and applications of computing. Knowledge of computer systems and social implications of computing are tested in questions on other topics. Details on equipment needed are included in the course guide. See AP Examination: Advanced Placement Program for admin-

istration time, scoring, and grade reporting. Examiner required. Suitable for group use.

Untimed: 3 hours maximum

Scoring: Computer scored; examiner evaluated

Cost: Per student $62.00

Publisher: The College Board

AP EXAMINATION: ECONOMICS: MACROECONOMICS

Adolescent
Grades 10–12

Purpose: Measures academic achievement in the study of macroeconomics. Used by participating colleges to grant credit and placement to more gifted or advanced students. Also measures the effectiveness of a school's AP Program in macroeconomics.

Description: Multiple-item paper-pencil test in two sections measuring a student's knowledge and understanding of economic principles as they apply to an economic system as a whole. Section I (60 minutes) covers a) basic economic concepts, b) measurement of economic performance, c) national income and price determination, and d) international economics and growth.

Section II (30 minutes) requires the student to answer one essay question in which he or she interrelates the different content areas, analyzes a given economic situation, and evaluates general macroeconomic principles and policies. See AP Examination: Advanced Placement Program for administration time, scoring, and grade reporting. Examiner required. Suitable for group use.

Timed: 90 minutes

Scoring: Computer scored; examiner evaluated

Cost: Per student $62.00

Publisher: The College Board

AP EXAMINATION: ECONOMICS: MICROECONOMICS

Adolescent
Grades 10–12

Purpose: Measures academic achievement in the study of microeconomics. Used by participating colleges to grant credit and placement to more gifted or advanced students. Also measures the effectiveness of a school's AP program in microeconomics.

Description: Multiple-item paper-pencil test in two sections measuring a student's knowledge and understanding of the principles of economics that apply to the functions of individual decision makers within the larger economic system. Section I (60 minutes) covers a) basic economic concepts, b) the nature and functions of product markets, c) factor markets, and d) efficiency, equity, and the role of government.

Section II (30 minutes) requires students to answer two short essay questions. The questions require the student to address the interrelationship of different content areas, analyze a given economic situation, and evaluate general microeconomic principles. See AP Examination: Advanced Placement Program for administration time, scoring, and grade reporting. Examiner required. Suitable for group use.

Timed: 90 minutes
Scoring: Computer scored; examiner evaluated
Cost: Per student $62.00
Publisher: The College Board

AP EXAMINATION: ENGLISH— ENGLISH LANGUAGE

Adolescent
Grades 10–12

Purpose: Measures academic achievement in the study of English language and composition. Used by participating colleges to grant credit and placement to more gifted or advanced students. Also measures the effectiveness of a school's AP Program in English language and composition.

Description: Multiple-item paper-pencil test arranged in two parts: Part I (60–75 minutes), which accounts for 40% of the final grade, employs multiple-choice questions testing a student's skill at recasting sentences and analyzing the

rhetoric of prose passages. Part II (105–120 minutes), which accounts for 60% of the final grade, requires students to directly demonstrate their skill at composition by writing several essays of varying lengths in various rhetorical modes. Both parts test abilities to recognize and work with the following factors: kinds and levels of diction, varieties of sentence structures, logical and functional semantic relationships, modes of discourse, aims of discourse, various rhetorical strategies, and appropriate relationships among author, audience, and subject. See AP Examination: Advanced Placement Program for administration time, scoring, and grade reporting. Examiner required. Suitable for group use.

Untimed: 3 hours maximum
Scoring: Computer scored; examiner evaluated
Cost: Per student $62.00
Publisher: The College Board

AP EXAMINATION: ENGLISH— ENGLISH LITERATURE

Adolescent
Grades 10–12

Purpose: Measures academic achievement in the study of English literature and composition. Used by participating colleges to grant credit and placement to more gifted or advanced students. Also measures the effectiveness of a school's AP Program in English literature and composition.

Description: Multiple-item paper-pencil test in two parts: Part I (60–75 minutes), which accounts for 40% of the final grade, employs multiple-choice questions testing the student's reading of selected passages. Part II (105–120 minutes), which accounts for 60% of the final grade, requires writing as a direct measure of the student's ability to read and interpret literature. Both parts measure the following critical and compositional skills: the use of modes of discourse, the recognition of assumptions underlying various rhetorical strategies, and the awareness of the resources of language (connotation, metaphor, irony, syntax, and tone). See AP Examination: Advanced Placement Program for administration time, scoring, and grade reporting. Examiner required. Suitable for group use.

Untimed: 3 hours maximum

Scoring: Computer scored; examiner evaluated

Cost: Per student $62.00

Publisher: The College Board

AP EXAMINATION: FRENCH LANGUAGE

Adolescent
Grades 10–12

Purpose: Measures academic achievement in the study of the French language. Used by participating colleges to grant credit and placement to more gifted or advanced students. Also measures the effectiveness of a school's AP Program in French language.

Description: Multiple-item paper-pencil and oral-response test evaluating level of performance in the use of the French language, both in understanding written and spoken French, and in responding with ease in correct and idiomatic French. Listening and reading skills are tested in the multiple-choice section. Writing and speaking skills are tested in the free-response section. The portion of the examination devoted to each skill accounts for 25% of the final grade. The examination as a whole tests the following objectives: ability to understand spoken French in both formal and conversational situations; the development of an ample vocabulary; and the ability to express ideas accurately and resourcefully, both orally and in writing. Students' oral responses are taped, requiring that all students have access to a tape recorder and be familiar with the equipment to be used in the examination. See AP Examination: Advanced Placement Program for administration time, scoring, and grade reporting. Examiner required. Suitable for group use.

Timed: 3 hours maximum

Scoring: Computer scored; examiner evaluated

Cost: Per student $62.00

Publisher: The College Board

AP EXAMINATION: FRENCH LITERATURE

Adolescent
Grades 10–12

Purpose: Measures academic achievement in the study of French literature and language. Used by participating colleges to grant credit and placement to more gifted or advanced students. Also measures the effectiveness of a school's AP Program in French literature.

Description: Multiple-item paper-pencil test in two sections. Section I (70–90 minutes), which accounts for 40% of the final grade, employs multiple-choice questions testing the student's ability to understand and analyze literary prose and poetry in French. Section II (90–100 minutes), which accounts for 60% of the final grade, consists of an essay and literary analysis. The examination as a whole measures understanding of the works of French literature on the reading list provided by the AP Program, the ability to interpret and analyze literary texts, and competence in the use of written French. See AP Examination: Advanced Placement Program for administration time, scoring, and grade reporting. Examiner required. Suitable for group use.

Timed: 3 hours maximum

Scoring: Computer scored; examiner evaluated

Cost: Per student $62.00

Publisher: The College Board

AP EXAMINATION: GERMAN LANGUAGE

Adolescent
Grades 10–12

Purpose: Measures academic achievement in the study of the German language. Used by participating colleges to grant credit and placement to more gifted or advanced students. Also measures the effectiveness of a school's AP Program in German.

Description: Multiple-item paper-pencil test consists of two sections. Section I (120 minutes), which accounts for two-thirds of the final grade, is a multiple-choice test for listening comprehension and reading skills. Section II (60 minutes), which accounts for one-third of the final grade, is a free-response essay test of writing skills. Speaking ability currently is not tested. The test evaluates level of performance in the use of the German language. See AP Examination: Advanced Placement Program for administration time, scoring, and grade reporting. Examiner required. Suitable for group use.

Timed: 3 hours maximum

Scoring: Computer scored; examiner evaluated

Cost: Per student $62.00

Publisher: The College Board

AP EXAMINATION: GOVERNMENT AND POLITICS

**Adolescent
Grades 10–12**

Purpose: Measures academic achievement in the study of government and politics. Used by participating colleges to grant credit and placement to more gifted or advanced students. Also measures the effectiveness of a school's AP Program in government and politics.

Description: Two 180–minute multiple-item paper-pencil tests: American Government and Politics and Comparative Government and Politics. (Students may take either test or both for a single fee, receiving a separate grade on each.) Each test is divided nearly equally between a multiple-choice section and a free-response section. Each test contributes 50% of the final grade. The topics covered in each test include the concepts and facts commonly covered in cognate introductory college courses. See AP Examination: Advanced Placement Program for administration time, scoring, and grade reporting. Examiner required. Suitable for group use.

Untimed: 3 hours maximum

Scoring: Computer scored

Cost: Per student $62.00

Publisher: The College Board

AP EXAMINATION: GOVERNMENT AND POLITICS: COMPARATIVE

**Adolescent
Grades 10–12**

Purpose: Measures academic achievement in the study of comparative government and politics. Used by participating colleges to grant credit and placement to more gifted or advanced students. Also measures the effectiveness of a school's AP Program in comparative government and politics.

Description: Multiple-item paper-pencil test arranged in two sections measuring the student's knowledge and understanding of the world's diverse political structures and practices. The examination is based on five countries. Four of those are Great Britain, France, the Soviet Union, and China. The student is allowed to choose from among India, Mexico, and Nigeria for the fifth country. Section I (45 minutes) covers a) the sources of public authority and political power, b) the relationship between state and society, c) the relationship between citizens and the state, d) political framework, e) political change, and f) introduction to comparative politics.

In Section II (45 minutes), the student is required to answer one of two essay questions in which he or she interrelates different content areas, discusses a developing nation, analyzes a case study, and evaluates general principles of comparative government and politics. See AP Examination: Advanced Placement Program for administration time, scoring, and grade reporting. Examiner required. Suitable for group use.

Timed: 90 minutes

Scoring: Computer scored; examiner evaluated

Cost: $62.00

Publisher: The College Board

AP EXAMINATION: GOVERNMENT AND POLITICS: UNITED STATES

**Adolescent
Grades 10–12**

Purpose: Measures academic achievement in the study of United States government and politics. Used by participating colleges to grant credit and placement to more gifted or advanced students. Also measures the effectiveness of a school's AP Program in art history.

Description: Multiple-item paper-pencil test arranged in two sections. Section I (45 minutes) is a multiple-choice test measuring the student's knowledge and understanding of a) the constitutional underpinnings of American democracy, b) the political beliefs and behaviors of individuals, c) political parties and interest groups (mechanisms that facilitate the communication of interests and preferences by like-minded citizens), d) the Congress, the presidency, the bureaucracy, and the federal courts: institutions and policy processes, and e) civil liberties and civil rights.

Section II (45 minutes) requires the student to answer one of two questions addressing the interrelationship of different content areas. Students also may be required to analyze case studies or to evaluate general principles of American government and politics. See AP Examination: Advanced Placement Program for administration time, scoring, and grade reporting. Examiner required. Suitable for group use.

Timed: 90 minutes
Scoring: Computer scored; examiner evaluated
Cost: Per student $62.00
Publisher: The College Board

AP EXAMINATION: HISTORY— AMERICAN HISTORY

Adolescent
Grades 10-12

Purpose: Measures academic achievement in the study of United States history. Used by participating colleges to grant credit and placement to more gifted or advanced students. Also measures the effectiveness of a school's AP Program in United States history.

Description: Multiple-item paper-pencil test consisting of two equally weighted sections. Section I (75 minutes) employs

multiple-choice questions testing the student's factual knowledge, breadth of preparation, and knowledge-based analytical skills. Section II consists of two parts: Part A (40 minutes), in which students answer a document-based essay question and Part B (50 minutes), in which students answer one of five standard essay questions. The essay questions test the student's mastery of historical interpretation and the ability to express views and knowledge in writing. Both sections cover the period from the earliest colonial settlements to the present (with emphasis on the 19th and 20th centuries) and cover the following topics: political institutions, behavior, public policy, social and economic change, diplomacy, international relations, and cultural and intellectual developments. See AP Examination: Advanced Placement Program for administration time, scoring, and grade reporting. Examiner required. Suitable for group use.

Timed: 3 hours maximum
Scoring: Computer scored; examiner evaluated
Cost: Per student $62.00
Publisher: The College Board

AP EXAMINATION: HISTORY— EUROPEAN HISTORY

Adolescent
Grades 10-12

Purpose: Measures academic achievement in the study of European history. Used by participating colleges to grant credit and placement to more gifted or advanced students. Also measures the effectiveness of a school's AP Program in European history.

Description: Multiple-item paper-pencil test in two equally weighted sections. Section I (75 minutes) is a multiple-choice test dealing with concepts, major historical facts, and historical analysis. Section II consists of two parts. Part A (45 minutes) is a document-based essay question, and Part B (45 minutes) requires the student to answer one of six standard essay questions. Students are expected to demonstrate a knowledge of basic chronology of major events and trends from approximately 1450 to the 1980s (high Renaissance to present). Test items cover the following historical themes: intellectual-cultural, social-economic, and political-diplomatic. See AP Examination: Advanced Placement Program for administration time, scoring, and grade reporting. Examiner required. Suitable for group use.

Timed: 3 hours maximum

Scoring: Computer scored; examiner evaluated

Cost: Per student $62.00

Publisher: The College Board

AP EXAMINATION: MATHEMATICS—CALCULUS AB

**Adolescent
Grades 10–12**

Purpose: Measures academic achievement in the study of calculus. Used by participating colleges to grant credit and placement to more gifted or advanced students. Also measures the effectiveness of a school's AP Program in calculus.

Description: Multiple-item paper-pencil test in two equally weighted parts: a multiple-choice test of proficiency covering a wide variety of topics and a problem section requiring students to demonstrate their ability to carry out proofs and solve problems involving a more extended chain of reasoning. The topics covered include elementary functions, differential calculus, and integral calculus. The use of specific functions, rather than their theoretical development and basis, is emphasized. Calculus AB level is not generally as advanced as Calculus BC level. See AP Examination: Advanced Placement Program for administration time, scoring, and grade reporting. Examiner required. Suitable for group use.

Timed: 3 hours maximum

Scoring: Computer scored; examiner evaluated

Cost: Per student $62.00

Publisher: The College Board

AP EXAMINATION: MATHEMATICS—CALCULUS BC

**Adolescent
Grades 10–12**

Purpose: Measures academic achievement in the study of calculus. Used by participating colleges to grant credit and placement to more gifted or advanced students. Also measures the effectiveness of a school's AP Program in calculus.

Description: Multiple-item paper-pencil test in two equally weighted parts: a multiple-choice test of proficiency covering a wide variety of topics and a problem section requiring students to demonstrate their ability to carry out proofs and solve problems involving a more extended chain of reasoning. The topics covered include elementary functions, differential calculus, integral calculus, sequences and series, and elementary differential equations. Calculus BC level is more advanced and involves more theoretical reasoning than Calculus AB level. See AP Examination: Advanced Placement Program for administration time, scoring, and grade reporting. Examiner required. Suitable for group use.

Timed: 3 hours maximum

Scoring: Computer scored; examiner evaluated

Cost: Per student $62.00

Publisher: The College Board

AP EXAMINATION: MUSIC—LISTENING AND LITERATURE

**Adolescent
Grades 10–12**

Purpose: Measures academic achievement in the study of music listening and literature. Used by participating colleges to grant credit and placement to more gifted or advanced students. Also measures the effectiveness of a school's AP Program in music.

Description: Multiple-item paper-pencil and aural stimuli test measuring knowledge of musical styles and forms. The test contains three types of questions: multiple-choice questions based on recorded music played within the examination (80%–85%); multiple-choice questions based on general musical knowledge rather than on aural materials (15%–20%); and free-response questions, some of which are based on recorded music. In the Aural Recognition of Musical Materials section, the student listens to examples of music from five periods (Middle Ages and Renaissance, Baroque, Classical, Romantic, and Twentieth Century—including jazz and popular) and answers questions regarding pitch content, rhythmic patterns and metric organization, compositional procedures and texture, medium and genre, and form. The non-aural Historical, Cultural, and Structural Aspects of Music section assesses general knowledge of composers and their works, knowledge of genres and their chronology, the cultural context of music, and musical terms. See AP Examination: Advanced Placement Program for administration time, scoring, and grade reporting. Examiner required. Suitable for group use.

Timed: 2 hours

Scoring: Computer scored; examiner evaluated

Cost: Per student $62.00

Publisher: The College Board

AP EXAMINATION: MUSIC— MUSIC THEORY

**Adolescent
Grades 10–12**

Purpose: Measures academic achievement in the study of music theory. Used by participating colleges to grant credit and placement to more gifted or advanced students. Also measures the effectiveness of a school's AP Program in music theory.

Description: Multiple-item paper-pencil and aural stimuli test measuring the student's understanding of musical structure and compositional procedures. Three kinds of questions are included: multiple-choice based on recorded music played within the examination; multiple-choice based on general musical knowledge rather than on aural materials; and free-

response questions of various lengths, some of which are based on recorded music.

Section I, Basic Terminology and Notational Skills, is a nonaural assessment of intervals, chords, scales, and modes; key signatures and clefs; rhythmic and metric notation; transposition skills, including knowledge of standard instrumental transpositions; and vocabulary relating to harmonic function, cadences and phrase structure, melodic variation, musical texture, and musical performance.

Section II, Writing Skills, is also nonaural and requires a four-part realization of figured bass symbols and/or Roman numerals, a two-voiced tonal counterpoint in 18th-century style, and writing a melody to specifications.

Section III, Visual Analysis, can be administered with or without aural stimuli. It covers large- and small-scale harmonic procedures, pitch organization and processes of melodic transformation or variation, rhythmic/metric organization, texture, and formal devices and/or procedures.

In Section IV, Aural Skills, while listening to musical selections, students answer questions regarding melodic dictation, harmonic dictation, cadence types and large-scale harmonic motions, recognition of performance errors, and musical processes and materials in the context of music literature. See AP Examination: Advanced Placement Program for administration time, scoring, and grade reporting. Examiner required. Suitable for group use.

Timed: 2 hours maximum

Scoring: Computer scored; examiner evaluated

Cost: Per student $62.00

Publisher: The College Board

AP EXAMINATION: PHYSICS B

**Adolescent
Grades 10–12**

Purpose: Measures academic achievement in the study of physics as a basis for more advanced work in the life sciences, medicine, geology, and related fields. Used by participating colleges to grant credit and placement to more gifted or advanced students. Also measures the effectiveness of a school's AP Program in physics.

Description: Multiple-item paper-pencil test consisting of two equally weighted sections (90 minutes each): one multiple-choice section and one free-response section. Five general topics are covered: mechanics, kinetic theory and thermodynamics, electricity and magnetism, waves and optics, and modern physics. Calculus is not required. See AP Examination: Advanced Placement Program for administration time, scoring, and grade reporting. Examiner required. Suitable for group use.

Timed: 3 hours maximum

Scoring: Computer scored; examiner evaluated

Cost: Per student $62.00

Publisher: The College Board

AP EXAMINATION: PHYSICS C

Adolescent
Grades 10–12

Purpose: Measures academic achievement in the study of physics as a basis for more advanced study in the physical sciences and engineering. Used by participating colleges to grant credit and placement to more gifted or advanced students. Also measures the effectiveness of a school's AP Program in physics.

Description: Multiple-item paper-pencil test in two parts (90 minutes each): one covering mechanics and one covering electricity and magnetism. Students may take one or both parts. Each part has a separate grade representing roughly one semester of college-level work. The parts are divided equally (in time and scoring weight) between a multiple-choice section and a free-response section. The mechanics part covers kinematics; Newton's Laws of Motion; work, energy, and power; systems of particles (statics); rotational motion; and oscillations and gravitation. The electricity and magnetism part covers electrostatics, electric current and circuits, capacitance and capacitors, magnetostatics, and electromagnetism. Use of calculus is required (when appropriate) for both parts. See AP Examination:

Advanced Placement Program for administration time, scoring, and grade reporting. Examiner required. Suitable for group use.

Timed: 3 hours maximum

Scoring: Computer scored; examiner evaluated

Cost: Per student $62.00

Publisher: The College Board

AP EXAMINATION: SPANISH— SPANISH LANGUAGE

Adolescent
Grades 10–12

Purpose: Measures academic achievement in the study of the Spanish language. Used by participating colleges to grant credit and placement to more gifted or advanced students. Also measures the effectiveness of a school's AP Program in Spanish.

Description: Multiple-item paper-pencil and oral-response test consisting of two sections. Section I (80–100 minutes) employs multiple-choice questions and tests listening and reading comprehension skills, including mastery of grammatical structure and vocabulary. Section II (75–85 minutes), a free-response section, tests the active skills of speaking and writing. The portion of the examination devoted to each skill counts for one-fourth of the composite score. The test evaluates general ability to understand written and spoken Spanish and to write and speak easily and idiomatically. Students must be trained in the use of the examination equipment in order to insure that their oral responses are properly recorded. See AP Examination: Advanced Placement Program for administration time, scoring, and grade reporting. Examiner required. Suitable for group use.

Timed: 3 hours maximum

Scoring: Computer scored; examiner evaluated

Cost: Per student $62.00

Publisher: The College Board

AP EXAMINATION: SPANISH— SPANISH LITERATURE

Adolescent
Grades 10–12

Purpose: Measures academic achievement in the study of Spanish literature. Used by participating colleges to grant credit and placement to more gifted or advanced students. Also measures the effectiveness of a school's AP Program in Spanish.

Description: Multiple-item paper-pencil test consisting of two parts: a) a multiple-choice section on aural comprehension, literary analysis, the reading comprehension of passages, and the analysis of two poems (counting 45%) and b) a free-response section on literary interpretation and analysis and skill in writing critical, expository prose in Spanish (counting 55%). Section 2 contains two essays, each dealing with two or more of the authors required by the AP Program in Spanish Literature. Students are asked to analyze and discuss, in Spanish, works that they have read (no choice of authors is given). See AP Examination: Advanced Placement Program for administration time, scoring, and grade reporting. Examiner required. Suitable for group use.

Timed: 3 hours maximum
Scoring: Computer scored; examiner evaluated
Cost: Per student $62.00
Publisher: The College Board

AP EXAMINATION: VERGIL AND CATULLUS-HORACE

Adolescent
Grades 10–12

Purpose: Measures academic achievement in the study of Latin. Used by participating colleges to grant credit and placement to more gifted or advanced students. Also measures the effectiveness of a school's AP Program in Latin.

Description: Multiple-item paper-pencil test consists of three parts: a multiple-choice section testing students' ability to read and understand Latin poetry at sight and two free-response sections measuring the students' ability to comprehend and interpret the material read in the two specific courses on Vergil and Catullus-Horace. Students may elect to take either or both of the free-response sections (each one represents roughly one semester of college work). Students are expected to be able to translate accurately from Latin into English the poetry they are reading and to demonstrate a grasp of the grammatical structures and vocabulary used. Other important factors include stylistic analysis; awareness of political, social, and cultural backgrounds of the works being read; and awareness of the classical influences of later literature. See AP Examination: Advanced Placement Program for administration time, scoring, and grade reporting. Examiner required. Suitable for group use.

Timed: 3 hours maximum
Scoring: Computer scored; examiner evaluated
Cost: Per student $62.00
Publisher: The College Board

APTITUDE TEST BATTERY FOR PUPILS IN STANDARDS 6 AND 7 (ATB)

Adolescent

Purpose: Measures aptitudes of students in Standards 6 and 7. Used in South Africa for educational placement and for identifying underachievement in black pupils.

Description: Multiple-item paper-pencil battery of multiple-choice tests for determining academic aptitude and achievement. The core battery of six tests includes English (reading comprehension and vocabulary), spatial perception, nonverbal reasoning, mathematics, Afrikaans (reading comprehension and vocabulary), and verbal reasoning. The supplementary tests are comparison, numerical, and mechanical insight. Stanines are calculated for the third term. Examiner required. Suitable for group use.
SOUTH AFRICAN PUBLISHER
Untimed: 5 hours
Scoring: Hand key; may be machine scored

Cost: Test booklet 7,50; manual 9,00; 10 answer sheets 1,80; scoring stencil 6,10
Publisher: Human Sciences Research Council

APTITUDE TEST FOR ADULTS (AA)

Child, adolescent

Purpose: Assesses scholastic aptitudes. Used for psychoeducational evaluation.

Description: 225-item paper-pencil test measuring nine scholastic aptitudes, including comparison, figural series, calculations, reasoning, mechanical insight, spatial visualization (2–D), classification, spatial visualization (3–D), and spare parts. Examiner required. Suitable for group use.
SOUTH AFRICAN PUBLISHER
Timed: 3½ hours
Scoring: Hand key; examiner evaluated
Cost: (In Rands) test booklet 4,50; manual 11,00; 10 answer sheets 1,20; scoring stencil 5,50; orders from outside the RSA will be dealt with on merit
Publisher: Human Sciences Research Council

APTITUDE TESTS FOR INDIAN SOUTH AFRICANS—JATISA AND SATISA

Child, adolescent

Purpose: Assesses aptitudes of Indian children. Used for vocational guidance.

Description: Multiple-item paper-pencil test batteries measuring scholastic and vocational attitudes. JATISA (Standards 6 to 8) consists of 10 subtests: Verbal Reasoning, Series Completion, Social Insight, Language Usage, Numerical Reasoning, Spatial Perception (2–D), Spatial Perception (3–D), Visual Arts, Clerical Speed and Accuracy, and Mechanical Insight. SATISA (Standards 9 and 10) consists of 11 subtests: Verbal Reasoning, Numerical Reasoning, Spatial Perception (3–D), Series Completion, Mechanical Insight, Classification, Spatial Perception (2–D), Comparison, Language Usage, Memory,

and Filing. Examiner required. Suitable for group use.
SOUTH AFRICAN PUBLISHER
Timed: Junior 3½ hours; Senior 4½ hours
Scoring: Hand key; examiner evaluated
Cost: (In Rands) Junior test plus photos 2,00; manual 10,00; scoring stencil 7,00; 10 answer sheets 1,60; Senior tests A or B 5,00 each; 10 answer sheets I 1,00; 10 answer sheets II 1,00; manual 10,00; scoring stencils I, II, III, IV 5,00 each; orders from outside the RSA will be dealt with on merit
Publisher: Human Sciences Research Council

APTITUDE TESTS FOR SCHOOL BEGINNERS (ASB)

Child—Ages 5–8

Purpose: Assesses aptitudes of children beginning school. Used for placement, program planning, and prediction of future achievement.

Description: Multiple-item paper-pencil test measuring eight areas important in the early school years: perception, spatial, reasoning, numerical, gestalt, coordination, memory, and verbal comprehension. The test yields a differential aptitude profile rather than IQ-type score. Administration during the first two months of the school year is recommended. Examiner required. Suitable for group use.
SOUTH AFRICAN PUBLISHER
Timed: 7 hours
Scoring: Hand key; examiner evaluated
Cost: Contact publisher; orders from outside the RSA will be dealt with on merit
Publisher: Human Sciences Research Council

BASIC ACHIEVEMENT SKILLS INDIVIDUAL SCREENER (BASIS)
The Psychological Corporation, Measurement Division Staff

Grades 1 and above

Purpose: Measures achievement in reading, mathematics, and spelling. Assesses individual students' academic strengths and weaknesses with both norm-referenced and criterion-referenced information. Used for program planning and evaluation, academic placement, and establishing IEPs.

Description: Three subtests assessing academic achievement in reading, mathematics, and spelling. Test items are grouped in grade-referenced clusters, which constitute the basic unit of administration. Testing begins at a grade cluster with which the student is expected to have little difficulty and continues until the student fails to reach the criteria for a particular cluster. The clusters range from Readiness through Grade 8 for reading and mathematics and from Grades 1–8 for spelling. The reading test assesses comprehension of graded passages. The student is required to read the passages aloud and supply the missing words. Comprehension at the lower levels is assessed by word reading and sentence reading, and readiness is measured by letter identification and visual discrimination. The mathematics test consists of a readiness subtest and assesses computation and problem solving above that level. The student works on the computation items directly in the record form. Word problems are dictated by the teacher and require no reading on the part of the student. The spelling test for Grades 1–8 consists of clusters of words that are dictated in sentence contexts. The student writes the words on the record form. An optional writing exercise (average samples provided for Grades 3–8) requires the student to write descriptively for 10 minutes. Samples are scored by comparison with criterion samples for each grade. Criterion-referenced scores for the subtests describe performance in basic skills and suggest grade and textbook placement. Raw scores can be converted to standard scores, age- and grade-based percentile ranks, stanines, grade equivalents, and age equivalents. The manual includes information for administering, scoring, and interpreting the tests. Examiner required. Not suitable for group use.

Untimed: 1 hour

Scoring: Hand key

Cost: Examiner's kit (manual, content booklet, 2 record forms) $45.00

Publisher: The Psychological Corporation

Information and availability unconfirmed; last verified in 1988.

BASIC EDUCATIONAL SKILLS TEST (BEST)
Ruth Segel and Sandra Golding

Child
Grades 1–5

Purpose: Determines perceptual abilities and reading, writing, and mathematical skills of elementary school children and older remedial students. Used to screen for group placement and program planning.

Description: 75–item paper-pencil examination consisting of three subtests: Reading, Writing/Spelling, and Mathematics. Materials include a manual, test plates, and recording forms, which correlate performance on each item with relevant perceptual modalities (auditory, visual, vocal, and haptic). Examiner required. Not suitable for group use.

Untimed: 20 minutes per subtest

Scoring: Hand key

Cost: Manual $12.00; test plates $23.00; 25 recording forms $11.00; kit $38.00

Publisher: United Educational Services, Inc.

BASIC SKILLS ASSESSMENT PROGRAM (BSAP)
Educational Testing Service

Ages 7–adult

Purpose: Evaluates an individual's ability to apply academic skills to everyday situations. Used to screen students who need special help in basic skills.

Description: 210–item paper-pencil multiple-choice test assessing an individual's ability to apply reading, writing, and mathematics skills to everyday tasks, such as understanding consumer information, reading newspapers, making simple calculations, writing letters, and completing job applications. The program can be used in high schools to judge attainment of minimal proficiency in basic skills before graduation. Examiner required. Suitable for group use.

Timed: 45 minutes

Scoring: Hand key; may be computer scored

Cost: Contact publisher

Publisher: CTB/Macmillan/McGraw-Hill

BOEHM TEST OF BASIC CONCEPTS—REVISED (BOEHM-R)
Ann E. Boehm

Child
Grades K–2

Purpose: Measures children's mastery of basic concepts used in classroom instruction. Identifies individual children with low level of concept development. Targets specific areas for basic concept remediation.

Description: 50–item paper-pencil multiple-choice picture test of concepts in such contexts as quantity, space, and time. The child responds to oral instructions by marking one of several pictures. Two alternate forms, C and D, measure the same concepts. A new 26–item Applications level for Grades 1 and 2 requires the child to respond to combinations of basic concepts. Examiner required. Suitable for small group use. Available in Spanish.

Untimed: 30 minutes

Scoring: Hand key

Cost: Examination kit (1 copy each booklet Form C, D, and Applications, directions, manual, class record, parent-teacher conference report, hand key) $19.00; 35 each of test booklets 1 and 2, directions, class record, key (specify form) $39.00; manual $15.00

Publisher: The Psychological Corporation

Information and availability unconfirmed; last verified in 1988.

THE BRIGANCE® DIAGNOSTIC COMPREHENSIVE INVENTORY OF BASIC SKILLS (CIBS)
Albert H. Brigance

Child, adolescent
Grades PreK–9

Purpose: Measures attainment of basic academic skills. Used to meet minimal competency requirements, develop IEPs, and determine academic placement.

Description: 203 skill sequences in the following 22 sections: readiness, speech, word recognition grade placement, oral reading, reading comprehension, listening, functional word recognition, word analysis, reference skills, graphs and maps, spelling, writing, math grade placement, numbers, number facts, computation of whole numbers, fractions and mixed numbers, decimals, percents, word problems, metrics, and math vocabulary. Assessment is initiated at the skill level at which the student will be successful and continues until the student's level of achievement for that skill is attained. The following assessment methods may be used to accommodate different situations: parent interview, teacher observation, group or individual, and informal appraisal of student performance in daily work. Two alternate forms, A and B, are available for pre- and posttesting for 51 skill sequences. All skill sequences are referenced to specific instructional objectives and grade-level expectations. The comprehensive record book graphically indicates at each testing the level of competency the student has achieved. An optional class record book tracks the progress of 30 students. IEP objective forms are available for readiness, reading, mathematics, and individual use (blank forms). A videotape for in-service training of examiners is available. Examiner required. Many sections are suitable for group use.

Untimed: Varies

Scoring: Examiner evaluated

Cost: Test book $113.00; class record book $9.95; 30 IEP objective forms $15.95; CIBS excerpts available at no charge; 10 comprehensive record books $22.95

Publisher: Curriculum Associates, Inc.

THE BRIGANCE® DIAGNOSTIC INVENTORY OF BASIC SKILLS
Albert H. Brigance

Child
Grades K–6

---

academic achievement and aptitude

Purpose: Measures students' mastery of basic academic skills. Used for academic placement, mainstreaming students, competency evaluations, and IEP development and evaluation.

Description: 143 paper-pencil or oral-response tests assessing student mastery in readiness, reading, language arts, and math. Test items are arranged in developmental and sequential order. Major skill sections include readiness, word recognition, reading (fluency and level), word analysis, vocabulary, handwriting, grammar and mechanics, spelling, reference skills, math placement, numbers, operations, measurement, and geometry. IEP objectives are included for each of the 143 academic skills assessed. The individual student record book graphically indicates at each testing the level of competency the student has achieved and identifies the student's current instructional goals. An optional class record book monitors the progress of 35 students and forms a comprehensive matrix of individual student's levels. IEP objective forms are available for reading, readiness, mathematics, and individual use (blank form). A videotape program for in-service training of examiners is available. Examiner required. Some sections are suitable for group use.

Untimed: Varies

Scoring: Examiner evaluated

Cost: Assessment book $99.00; class record book $9.95; free test excerpts available; 10 student record books $15.95

Publisher: Curriculum Associates, Inc.

THE BRIGANCE® DIAGNOSTIC INVENTORY OF ESSENTIAL SKILLS
Albert H. Brigance

Child, adolescent
Grades 4–12

Purpose: Measures a student's mastery of academic skills and skills essential to success as a citizen, consumer, worker, and family member. Used in secondary programs serving students with special needs. Used to develop IEPs.

Description: 186 paper-pencil or oral-response skill assessments measuring minimal academic and vocational compe-

tencies in the areas of reading, language arts, and math. The inventory includes rating scales to measure applied skills that cannot be assessed objectively, such as health and attitude, responsibility and self-discipline, job interview preparation, auto safety, and communication. Other practical assessments include sections on food and clothing, money and finance, travel and transportation, and communication and telephone skills.

Test results identify basic skills that have and have not been mastered, areas of strengths and weaknesses in academic and practical skills, and instructional objectives for a specified skill level. Individual record books graphically indicate at each testing the level of competency the student has achieved and the student's current instructional goals. An optional class record book monitors the progress of 15 students and forms a matrix of specific student competencies. IEP objective forms are available for reading, writing and spelling, mathematics, and individual use (blank form). Tests may be administered by teachers, aides, or parent volunteers. A videotape program for in-service training of examiners is available. Examiner required. Some sections are suitable for group use.

Untimed: Varies

Scoring: Examiner evaluated

Cost: Assessment book $139.95; class record book $9.95; free test excerpt available; 10 essential skills record books $24.95

Publisher: Curriculum Associates, Inc.

BRISTOL ACHIEVEMENT TESTS, REVISED EDITION
Alan Brimer, general editor

Child, adolescent—Ages
8–12

Purpose: Measures achievement in basic academic skills. Used for evaluation of student progress and identification of an individual's strengths and weaknesses.

Description: Multiple-item paper-pencil tests measuring achievement in English language, mathematics, and study skills. The English Language Tests measure word meaning, paragraph meaning, sen-

academic achievement and aptitude

tence organization, organization of ideas, and spelling and punctuation. The Mathematics Tests cover number, reasoning, space, measurement, and arithmetical laws and processes. The Study Skills Tests measure properties, structures, processes, explanations, and interpretation. The tests are available on five levels for individuals ages 8–12. Two parallel forms, A and B, are available. Examiner required. Suitable for group use. BRITISH PUBLISHER

Timed: 50–55 minutes per test

Scoring: Hand key; examiner evaluated

Cost: Contact publisher

Publisher: NFER-NELSON Publishing Company Ltd.

CALIFORNIA ACHIEVEMENT TESTS: FORMS C AND D (CAT/C&D)
CTB McGraw-Hill

Child, adolescent
Grades K–12.9

Purpose: Assesses achievement in basic academic skills. Used for making educational decisions leading to improvement in instruction.

Description: Multiple-item paper-pencil multiple-choice tests measuring a student's reading, spelling, language, reference, and mathematics skills. The tests are divided into 10 overlapping levels spanning Kindergarten through Grade 12. Level 10 is a kindergarten readiness instrument derived from Form S, Level A of the Comprehensive Tests of Basic Skills. Levels 11–19 are composed of separate tests that combine to yield the following scores: Total Reading, Spelling, Total Language, Total Mathematics, and Reference Skills. Spelling is not tested at Level 11; reference skills are tested only at Levels 14–19. Two alternate forms, C and D, are available. Levels 10–12 are available only in Form C; Levels 13–19 are available in both forms. Examiner required. Suitable for group use.

Timed: Complete battery 2–6 hours, depending on level

Scoring: Hand key; may be computer scored

Cost: Machine-scorable test books kit (examiner's manual, scoring key, 35 test books) Levels 10–13 each $85.40; reusable test books kit (examiner's manual, scoring key, 35 test books) Levels 14–19 each $85.40

Publisher: CTB/Macmillan/McGraw-Hill

CALIFORNIA ACHIEVEMENT TESTS: FORMS E AND F

Grades K–12.9

Purpose: Measures students' achievement. Used for evaluating educational programs and for instructional planning.

Description: Multiple-item paper-pencil multiple-choice battery of tests assessing student knowledge of reading, language, spelling, mathematics, study skills, science, and social studies. The battery is available in 11 overlapping levels ranging from Level 10 (Kindergarten) to Level 20 (Grades 10.6–12.9). Two scoring options are offered: the traditional number of correct responses (NCR) and a newer method based on item-response theory (IRT). Computer literacy, consumer economics, and high-school end-of-course tests (algebra, geometry, physics, chemistry, biology, world history, and American history) are also available. The test is linked statistically to the Spanish Assessment of Basic Education. Examiner required. Suitable for group use.

Timed: Complete battery 2–6 hours, depending on level

Scoring: Hand key; may be computer scored

Cost: Multilevel examination kit (Grades K–12) $37.45

Publisher: CTB/Macmillan/McGraw-Hill

CANADIAN ACHIEVEMENT TESTS (CAT)
Canadian Test Centre

Ages 6 and older
Grades 2–college level

Purpose: Assesses the educational achievement of students.

Description: Multiple-item paper-pencil multiple-choice test measuring the educational achievement of students in reading, language, mathematics, reference skills, and spelling on eight levels: Grade 2, Grade 3, Grade 4, Grade 5, Grade 6, Grade 7, Grades 8–9, and Grades 10–12. The test is an adaptation of the California Achievement Test. A machine-scoring service available from the publisher offers optional class, individual, and administrative reports. Examiner required. Suitable for group use.
CANADIAN PUBLISHER
Timed: 3 hours, 20 minutes
Scoring: Machine scored; may be hand scored
Cost: 35 machine-scorable test booklets (specify grade level): Grades 2–3 $59.95, Grades 4–12 $53.95; 50 machine-scorable answer sheets (Grades 4–12) $17.50; hand scorable answer sheets (25 per subtest) $12.50
Publisher: McGraw-Hill Ryerson

CANADIAN COGNITIVE ABILITIES TEST (CCAT), FORM 3
E. Wright, R. Thorndike, and Elizabeth P. Hagen

Child, adolescent
Grades K–12

Purpose: Measures students' cognitive development. Used for placement, counseling, and class planning.

Description: Multiple-item paper-pencil tests available in a primary battery (Grades K–3) and a multilevel battery (Grades 3–12). The primary battery (76–90 items) tests the following concepts: relational, multimental, quantitative, and oral. The multilevel battery (240 items) tests the following abilities: verbal (vocabulary, sentence completion, verbal classification, verbal analogies); quantitative (relations, number series, equations); and nonverbal (figure classification, analysis, and synthesis). This test is Canadian-normed and a Canadian adaptation of the Cognitive Abilities Test published by Riverside Publishing Company. Examiner required. Suitable for group use.
CANADIAN PUBLISHER

Timed: Multilevel battery 1 hour, 38 minutes
Untimed: Primary battery 54 minutes
Scoring: Hand key; may be computer scored
Cost: Multilevel Battery: booklet $7.85, 500 answer sheets $126.00, scoring mask $10.20, manual $13.90; Primary Battery: 35 booklets $33.00, scoring key $3.10, manual $8.50
Publisher: Nelson Canada

CANADIAN COMPREHENSIVE ASSESSMENT PROGRAM— ACHIEVEMENT SERIES

Child, adolescent
Grades PreK–9

Purpose: Evaluates students' achievement levels and development of learning processes and capabilities in the areas of reading, mathematics, and language.

Description: Multiple-item multiple-level paper-pencil test measuring student performance in reading, mathematics, and language. Some levels also measure performance in word attack, study skills, science, and social studies. Levels 4–6 (PreK-Grade 1) assess facility with language, ease in dealing with written symbols, and perception of quantity and applications of that perception. Level 4 contains 96 items divided among 10 subtests; Level 5 contains 96 items in 10 subtests; and Level 6 contains 128 items in 13 subtests. Levels 7 and 8 (Grades 2–3) measure achievement in reading, mathematics, and language. Level 7 contains 9 subtests; Level 8 contains 10 subtests. Two forms, A and B, are available at each level. Levels 9–12 (Grades 4–9) measures achievement in reading, mathematics, language, and study skills. Two forms, A and B, are available at each level, and each level contains 10 subtests. Examiner required. Suitable for group use.
CANADIAN PUBLISHER
Timed: Varies
Scoring: Hand key
Cost: Contact publisher
Publisher: Guidance Centre
Information and availability unconfirmed; last verified in 1987.

CANADIAN TESTS OF BASIC SKILLS: HIGH SCHOOL BATTERY (CTBS), LEVELS 15-18, FORM 7
E. King-Shaw and Dale Scannell

Adolescent Grades 9-12

Purpose: Assesses students' abilities in reading comprehension, mathematics, written expression, using sources of information, and applied proficiency skills.

Description: Four test levels (15-18) consisting of a series of paper-pencil multiple-choice subtests that include Reading Comprehension, Mathematics, Written Expression, Using Sources of Information, and Applied Proficiency Skills. This is an adaptation of the Tests of Achievement and Proficiency published by the Riverside Publishing Company. Examiner must have a teaching certificate. Examiner required. Suitable for group use. CANADIAN PUBLISHER

Timed: 160 minutes

Scoring: Hand key; machine scored; scoring service available from publisher

Cost: Examination kit $18.65

Publisher: Nelson Canada

CANADIAN TESTS OF BASIC SKILLS: HIGH SCHOOL EDITION (CTBS), FORM 5
E. King, D. Scannell, et al.

Adolescent—Ages 14-18

Purpose: Assesses high-school students' progress in developing basic educational skills. Used for class planning and counseling.

Description: 233-242-item paper-pencil test of achievement measuring reading comprehension, mathematics, using sources of information, and written expression. The test has a multilevel format with Canadian norms. This test is a Canadian adaptation of the Tests of Achievement and Proficiency published by Riverside Publishing Company. Examiner required. Suitable for group use. CANADIAN PUBLISHER

Timed: 2 hours, 40 minutes

Scoring: Hand key; may be computer scored

Cost: Booklet $7.75; 500 answer sheets $123.65; scoring masks $10.00; teacher's guide $13.50

Publisher: Nelson Canada

CANADIAN TESTS OF BASIC SKILLS: MULTILEVEL EDITION (CTBS), FORMS 5 AND 6
E. King, A.N. Hieronymus, et al.

Child, adolescent—Ages 8-14

Purpose: Assesses student progress in developing basic educational skills. Used for group placement and curriculum planning.

Description: 350-465-item paper-pencil measure of achievement in vocabulary, reading comprehension, spelling, capitalization, punctuation, usage, visual materials, reference materials, math concepts, math problems, and math computation. The test is timed, scaled to grade, and Canadian normed. One multilevel, reusable booklet is appropriate for students in Grades 3-8. This test is a Canadian adaptation of the Iowa Tests of Basic Skills published by Riverside Publishing Company. Examiner required. Suitable for group use. CANADIAN PUBLISHER

Timed: 4 hours, 40 minutes

Scoring: Hand key; may be computer scored

Cost: Booklet $7.85; 500 answer sheets $123.65; scoring mask $10.00; teacher's guide $13.20

Publisher: Nelson Canada

CANADIAN TESTS OF BASIC SKILLS: PRIMARY BATTERY (CTBS), FORM 5
E. King, A.N. Hieronymus, et al.

Child—Ages 5-8

Purpose: Assesses students' progress in developing basic educational skills. Used for class grouping and evaluation.

Description: 157-539-item paper-pencil test measuring vocabulary, reading com-

prehension, spelling, capitalization, punctuation, usage, visual materials, reference materials, mathematic concepts, problems, and computations. The test is scaled to grade and Canadian-normed. It is a Canadian adaptation of the Iowa Tests of Basic Skills published by Riverside Publishing Company. Examiner required. Suitable for group use.
CANADIAN PUBLISHER

Timed: 2 hours, 30 minutes–3 hours, 55 minutes

Scoring: Hand key

Cost: 25 booklets $33.85; scoring mask $17.75; teacher's guide $11.00

Publisher: Nelson Canada

CANADIAN TESTS OF BASIC SKILLS: PRIMARY BATTERY (CTBS) (LEVELS 5–8), FORM 7
E. King-Shaw and A. N. Hieronymus

Child
Grades K.2–3.5

Purpose: Assesses students' abilities in listening, vocabulary, word analysis, language, reading, mathematics, and work study.

Description: Four test levels (5–8) consisting of a series of paper-pencil multiple-choice subtests that include Listening, Vocabulary, Word Analysis, Language, Reading, Mathematics, and Work Study. Materials should include test booklets, scoring masks, a teacher's guide, and supplementary materials as required. Examiner must have a teaching certificate. This test is a Canadian adaptation of the Iowa Tests of Basic Skills published by Riverside Publishing Company. Examiner required. Suitable for group use.
CANADIAN PUBLISHER

Untimed: 115–235 minutes (varies according to level)

Scoring: Hand key

Cost: 25 test booklets $30.75; scoring mask $16.15; teacher's guide $9.85

Publisher: Nelson Canada

CATCH
Godfrey Thomson Unit for Educational Research

Child—Ages 6.6 to 8.6

Purpose: Screens for difficulty in mathematics and reading.

Description: Paper-pencil multiple-choice short-answer true-false test consisting of four subtests used to identify children with potential difficulties. The subtests are Reading: Shorter Pieces; Reading: Longer Pieces; Language of Early Mathematics; and Mathematical Procedures. Each subtest is available in Forms A and B. Available in large print. Restricted to authorized users. Examiner required. Suitable for group use.
BRITISH PUBLISHER

Untimed: 40 minutes

Scoring: Hand key

Cost: Contact publisher

Publisher: Hodder and Stoughton

THE CHILD CENTER OPERATIONAL ASSESSMENT TOOL (OAT)
CHILD Center Multidisciplinary Team

Child
Grades K–6—Special
Education Grades K–6

Purpose: Diagnoses the learning needs of elementary-school children. Identifies students needing further evaluation. Monitors educational progress during the course of the year. Used by both regular and special classroom teachers.

Description: Six subtests assess skills in reading, spelling, math concepts, math operations, language, and behavior. The criterion-referenced tests in reading, spelling, math concepts, and math operations present test items in logical sequence, from pre-academic to most complex. The language test assesses underlying learning abilities and identifies modality preferences. The behavior questionnaire identifies the child's profile in the following behavioral areas: learning, coordination, self-esteem, concentration, emotional lability, motor expression, involuntary behavior, and school attitude. Results yield precise instructional skill levels for each child in reading, spelling, and math and identify specific teaching objectives. Parents and aides may administer the test. *How to Use OAT Reading/Spelling Tests* and *The OAT Reading/Spelling Program* are available. Examiner required. Not suitable for group use.

Untimed: Varies

Scoring: Examiner evaluated

Cost: Specimen set (reading test, spelling test, examiner's manual-spelling tests, *How To Use the OAT Reading/Spelling Tests*) $10.00

Publisher: The CHILD Center

Information and availability unconfirmed; last verified in 1988.

CIRCUS

Grades PreK–3.5

Purpose: Diagnoses the instructional needs of children and monitors and evaluates early education programs.

Description: Multiple-item paper-pencil and oral-response tests available at four levels: CIRCUS A (Grades PreK-K.5; 14 tests), CIRCUS B (Grades K.5–1.5; 12 tests), CIRCUS C (Grades 1.5–2.5; 9 tests), and CIRCUS D (Grades 2.5–3.5; 10 tests). The tests comprising the battery are divided among three categories at each of the four levels: Basic Assessment Measures, Other Measures, and Measures for Special Purposes. Depending on the grade level, tests are provided for problem-solving skills, general information, productive language, visual discrimination, visual memory, perceptual motor coordination, interests and preferences, divergent production, auditory discrimination, oral reading, phonetic analysis, receptive vocabulary, functional language, and educational environment. Levels A and B contain scales for teacher rating of students. All four levels include a questionnaire for teacher rating of the educational environment. The test is a downward extension of the Sequential Tests of Educational Progress (STEP III; see separate entry). Examiner required. With the

exception of one test requiring oral responses, the battery is suitable for group use.

Untimed: Varies

Scoring: Computer scored

Cost: Contact publisher

Publisher: Educational Testing Service

Information and availability unconfirmed; last verified in 1988.

COGNITIVE ABILITIES TEST™: FORM 4 (COGAT®)
Robert L. Thorndike and Elizabeth P. Hagen

Child, adolescent
Grades K–12

Purpose: Assesses verbal, quantitative, and nonverbal cognitive skills important for academic success. Used to identify students who need help developing general cognitive skills, aid in the diagnosis of learning disabilities, and plan individualized instructional programs.

Description: Multiple-item paper-pencil multiple-choice test measuring the development of students' cognitive skills. The Primary Battery, organized into two levels (Level 1, 140 items, Grades K–1; Level 2, 165 items, Grades 2–3), measures the following factors: oral vocabulary, verbal classification, relational concepts, figure classification (multimental), figure matrices, and quantitative concepts. The Multilevel/Separate Level Editions are available for Levels A-H (Grades 3–12). Each level (200 items each) contains a verbal battery assessing sentence completion, verbal classification, and verbal analogies; a quantitative battery assessing quantitative relations, number series, and equation building; and a nonverbal battery measuring figure classification, figure analogies, and figure analysis. The CogAT Form 4 was normed concurrently with the Iowa Tests of Basic Skills® (Forms G and H) and the Tests of Achievement and Proficiency™ (Form S) to provide comparisons of achievement and abilities test scores. Examiner required. Suitable for group use.

Timed: Multilevel/Separate Level Editions 90 minutes

Untimed: Primary Battery 90 minutes

Scoring: Hand key; may be MRC or NCS machine scored

Cost: 35 Primary Battery machine-scorable test booklets (specify level), examiner's manual $57.00; Multilevel Edition Levels A-H $4.50 each; 35 Separate Level test booklets and directions for Levels A-H (specify level) $49.20 per package; 35 MRC answer sheets, examiner's manual $21.30 per level; examiner's manual $8.40

Publisher: The Riverside Publishing Company

COLLEGE BASIC ACADEMIC SUBJECTS EXAMINATION (CBASE)

Steven J. Osterlind and Center for Educational Assessment staff

---

College students

Purpose: Assesses college students' skills in English, mathematics, science, and social studies. Used to determine students' mastery of academic skills as well as the strengths and weaknesses of institutional programs.

Description: Multiple-item criterion-referenced multiple-choice and essay achievement test measuring subject-related skills, factual knowledge, and learning outcomes for three cross-disciplinary competencies (reading, mathematics, reasoning). The CBASE covers four subject areas: English, mathematics, science, and social studies. These four areas are divided into 13 cluster topics, which are then divided into 23 skills necessary for success in the topic areas.

English is divided into three cluster topics composed of seven skills: a) Reading and Literature (reading critically, reading analytically, understanding literature), b) Writing (writing as a process, conventions of written English, expository writing sample), and c) Language (levels of usage). The four cluster topics that comprise Mathematics are broken down into six skills: a) General Mathematics (practical applications, properties and notations), b) Statistics (statistical reasoning), c) Algebra (equations and inequalities, real numbers), and d) Geometry (geometric figures). Science consists of three clusters divided among five skills: a) Laboratory and Field Work (observation/

experimental design, laboratory/field techniques), b) Mathematical Skills (drawing conclusions, mathematical relationships), and c) Fundamental Concepts (life and physical sciences). Social Studies is divided into three cluster topics and five skills: a) World Geography (major societies and cultures, significance of world events), b) U.S. History (U.S. ethno-cultural interactions, significance of U.S. events, and c) Social Science (familiarity with social sciences).

Three forms are available. The Long Form, or the complete battery, contains 180 items, an essay, and a few demographic questions. This form is for use with individual students, whose scores are entered permanantly into a database maintained by the University of Missouri. The Institution Matrix Form yields aggregate data about institutions and should not be used to provide information about individual students. The Short Form (65 test items, demographic questions) assesses only English and mathematical skills.

The test yields composite, subject, cluster, skills, and competency scores. These scores are reported in the Examinee Score Report or the Institution Summary Report, depending on the type of information the individual or the institution seeks. Individual Examinee Score Reports are released only at the written request of the student. Institution Summary Reports are released only to authorized institution personnel. The University of Missouri-Columbia machine scores all Long Form and Institution Matrix Form booklets. Provisions may be made for scoring the Short Form locally.

New test forms of equal difficulty that reflect evolving curriculum are issued semiannually. The test may be purchased only by authorized institutions and agencies. Examiner required. Suitable for group use.

Timed: Long Form 3 hours, 30 minutes; Institution Matrix Form 1 hour or less; Short Form 60–100 minutes

Scoring: Machine scored

Cost: Contact publisher

Publisher: The Riverside Publishing Company

COLLEGE LEVEL EXAMINATION PROGRAM (CLEP)

Adolescent, adult
Grades 12 and above

Purpose: Enables both traditional and nontraditional students to earn college credit by recognizing college-level achievement acquired outside the conventional college classroom. Anyone may take the tests to demonstrate college-level competency, regardless of where or how this knowledge was acquired: through formal study, private reading, employment experience, noncredit courses, adult classes, TV/radio/cassette courses, military/industrial/business training, or advanced work in regular high-school courses. Also used by some businesses to allow employees to earn required continuing education credits.

Description: Five general examinations and 30 subject examinations assessing college-level proficiency in a wide range of fields. The general examinations measure achievement in five basic areas of the liberal arts: English composition, humanities, mathematics, natural sciences, and social sciences and history. The material tested in each area is usually covered in the first two years of college and is often referred to as the general or liberal education requirement. The subject examinations measure achievement in specific college courses and are used to grant exemption from and credit for these courses. The examinations are not based on a particular syllabus; they stress concepts, principles, relationships, and applications of course material. Constructed to differentiate among several levels of mastery, they contain questions of varying difficulty. All CLEP tests are constructed by committees composed of teachers and scholars from colleges and universities in all parts of the United States. Test content is based on a curriculum survey prepared by the Educational Testing Service and completed by colleges and universities throughout the country. The survey enables the committees to determine test specifications according to current curriculum standards, textbooks, and methods of teaching.

Examinations are administered each month at more than 1,000 test centers located on college and university campuses throughout the country (the General Examination in English Composition with essay is available in June, October, January, and April only). Approximately 48 hours after receipt of the answer sheets at ETS, test scores and a booklet explaining them are sent to the candidates and to colleges, universities, or other recipients specified by the candidates. If the optional essay section of a subject examination is taken, it is sent for grading to the institution receiving the score. Institutions honoring CLEP test scores for credit are listed in "CLEP Colleges," available free from the publisher. Examiner required. Suitable for group use.

Timed: 1 hour, 30 minutes per test

Scoring: Computer scored; free-response sections examiner evaluated locally

Cost: Contact publisher; examiner evaluated

Publisher: The College Board

COLLEGE LEVEL EXAMINATION PROGRAM (CLEP) GENERAL EXAMINATION: ENGLISH COMPOSITION

Adolescent, adult
Grades 12 and above

Purpose: Measures college-level competency in English composition. Also used by some businesses to allow employees to earn required continuing education credits.

Description: Multiple-item paper-pencil test available in two editions: Edition One (95 items) contains two 45–minute objective sections. Edition Two contains one 45–minute, 55–question objective section and one 45–minute essay section. Both editions measure competency in writing expository essays that follow the conventions of standard written English. The exam is concerned with freshman English students' acquired knowledge, not technical vocabulary or imaginative writing.

Section One of both editions deals primarily with logical and structural relationships within the sentence. Section Two of Edition One (multiple-choice items) deals with logical arrangement of ideas, use of evidence, and adaptation of language to purpose and audience. Section Two of Edition Two requires an expository essay to demonstrate skill at presenting a point of view, developing a logical argument, and providing supporting evidence. Examiner required. Suitable for group use.

Timed: 45 minutes each section

Scoring: Computer scored; essay section examiner evaluated locally

Cost: Contact publisher

Publisher: The College Board

COLLEGE LEVEL EXAMINATION PROGRAM (CLEP) GENERAL EXAMINATION: HUMANITIES

Adolescent, adult
Grades 12 and above

Purpose: Measures college-level knowledge of literature, art, and music. Also used by some businesses to allow employees to earn required continuing education credits.

Description: 150–item paper-pencil objective exam in two separately timed sections covering poetry, prose, philosophy, art history, visual arts, music, performing arts, and architecture. The test measures understanding of cultural interests and humanities subject matter in three ways: recollection or recognition of specific information; comprehension and application of concepts; and analysis and interpretation of various works of art. Examiner required. Suitable for group use.

Timed: 45 minutes each section

Scoring: Computer scored

Cost: Contact publisher

Publisher: The College Board

COLLEGE LEVEL EXAMINATION PROGRAM (CLEP) GENERAL EXAMINATION: MATHEMATICS

Adolescent, adult
Grades 12 and above

Purpose: Measures college-level competency in general mathematics. Also used by some businesses to allow employees to earn required continuing education credits.

Description: 90–item paper-pencil test consisting of two parts. Part A (40 questions) measures facility in arithmetic, elementary algebra, geometry, and data interpretation. Part B (50 objective questions) covers sets, logic, real number systems, functions and their graphs, probability and statistics, and miscellaneous topics. Calculators are not permitted. Examiner required. Suitable for group use.

Timed: Part A 30 minutes; Part B 60 minutes

Scoring: Computer scored

Cost: Contact publisher

Publisher: The College Board

COLLEGE LEVEL EXAMINATION PROGRAM (CLEP) GENERAL EXAMINATION: NATURAL SCIENCE

Adolescent, adult
Grades 12 and above

Purpose: Measures college-level competency in introductory biological and physical science areas. Also used by some businesses to allow employees to earn required continuing education credits.

Description: 120–item paper-pencil objective test consisting of two 45–minute timed sections—one concerning biological science, the other physical science. The exam should not be considered appropriate as a prerequisite for more advanced study in general biology and general chemistry. Emphasis is placed on the role of science in our contemporary society, the knowledge and application of the basic principles and concepts of science, and the understanding of scientific information and data that may be presented. The content covers origin and evolution of life, cell study, development in organisms, population biology with an emphasis in ecology, atomic and nuclear structure, chemical compounds/molecular structure, thermodynamics, classical mechanics and relativity, electrical and magnetism, the universe, and the Earth. Examiner required. Suitable for group use.

Timed: 45 minutes per section
Scoring: Computer scored
Cost: Contact publisher
Publisher: The College Board

COLLEGE LEVEL EXAMINATION PROGRAM (CLEP) GENERAL EXAMINATION: SOCIAL SCIENCE AND HISTORY

Adolescent, adult
Grades 12 and above

Purpose: Measures the level of knowledge and understanding expected of college students meeting a distributional or general education requirement in social sciences and history. Also used by some businesses to allow employees to earn required continuing education credits.

Description: 125–item paper-pencil multiple-choice test addressing a wide range of topics from the social sciences and history, including subject matter from introductory college courses in political science, economics, sociology, social psychology, United States history, Western civilization, and African-Asian civilizations. Test items assess knowledge of terminology, facts, conventions, methodology, concepts, principles, generalizations, and theories in the fields listed above, as well as the ability to apply these abstractions to particulars. Examiner required. Suitable for group use.
Timed: 1 hour, 30 minutes
Scoring: Computer scored
Cost: Contact publisher
Publisher: The College Board

COLLEGE LEVEL EXAMINATION PROGRAM (CLEP) SUBJECT EXAMINATION: BUSINESS: COMPUTERS AND DATA PROCESSING

Adolescent, adult
Grades 12 and above

Purpose: Measures proficiency in the material commonly taught in introductory one-semester college courses in computers and data processing. Also used by some

businesses to allow employees to earn required continuing education credits.

Description: 100–item paper-pencil multiple-choice test assessing knowledge and understanding of concepts of computer programming and data processing that are applicable to a variety of programming languages. Questions are divided nearly evenly between those that assess knowledge of terminology and basic concepts and those that require application of that knowledge. The test assumes a general knowledge of hardware and software but does not emphasize hardware design or language-specific programming techniques. Arranged in two separately timed sections of 50 items each, the test covers hardware, data, software, systems concepts, and miscellaneous historical and state-of-the-art topics. An optional essay section contains five in-depth questions about important topics in computer programming and data processing. Examiner required. Suitable for group use.
Timed: 45 minutes per section; optional essay 90 minutes
Scoring: Computer scored; essay section examiner evaluated locally
Cost: Contact publisher
Publisher: The College Board

COLLEGE LEVEL EXAMINATION PROGRAM (CLEP) SUBJECT EXAMINATION: BUSINESS: INTRODUCTION TO MANAGEMENT

Adolescent, adult
Grades 12 and above

Purpose: Measures understanding of the material taught in introductory courses on the essentials of management and organization. Also used by some businesses to allow employees to earn required continuing education credits.

Description: 100–item paper-pencil test in two separately timed sections assessing knowledge of manpower and human resources, operational aspects of management, functional aspects of management, and miscellaneous aspects of management. The optional essay section contains five questions measuring the ability to relate the concepts of management to cur-

---

rent issues and to bring together material drawn from different parts of the subject. Examiner required. Suitable for group use.

Timed: 45 minutes each section; essay 90 minutes

Scoring: Computer scored; essay section examiner evaluated locally

Cost: Contact publisher

Publisher: The College Board

COLLEGE LEVEL EXAMINATION PROGRAM (CLEP) SUBJECT EXAMINATION: BUSINESS: INTRODUCTORY ACCOUNTING

Adolescent, adult
Grades 12 and above

Purpose: Assesses the level of accounting skills expected of a person with one year (two semesters) of college accounting or equivalent on-the-job training. Also used by some businesses to allow employees to earn required continuing education credits.

Description: 80–item paper-pencil objective test in two separately timed sections measuring proficiency in financial accounting and managerial accounting, including familiarity with accounting concepts and terminology, the ability to prepare and use financial reports issued for internal and external purposes, and the ability to apply accounting techniques to simple problem situations involving computations. An optional six-item free-response section tests the candidates' abilities to apply general concepts and procedures to stated problems and to combine material from various areas of accounting. Silent hand calculators are allowed. Examiner required. Suitable for group use.

Timed: 45 minutes each section; free response 90 minutes

Scoring: Computer scored; free-response section examiner evaluated locally

Cost: Contact publisher

Publisher: The College Board

COLLEGE LEVEL EXAMINATION PROGRAM (CLEP) SUBJECT EXAMINATION: BUSINESS: INTRODUCTORY BUSINESS LAW

Adolescent, adult
Grades 12 and above

Purpose: Measures knowledge and understanding of American business law at the introductory undergraduate level. Also used by some businesses to allow employees to earn required continuing education credits.

Description: 100–item paper-pencil objective test in two separately timed sections assessing six major content categories: history and sources of American law, American legal systems and procedures, contracts, agency and employment, sales, and miscellaneous. The examination emphasizes the function of contracts. An optional five-item essay portion measures the ability to select pertinent material and present it in an organized manner dealing with case materials or business law concepts. Examiner required. Suitable for group use.

Timed: 45 minutes each section; essay 90 minutes

Scoring: Computer scored; essay section examiner evaluated locally

Cost: Contact publisher

Publisher: The College Board

COLLEGE LEVEL EXAMINATION PROGRAM (CLEP) SUBJECT EXAMINATION: BUSINESS: INTRODUCTORY MARKETING

Adolescent, adult
Grades 12 and above

Purpose: Measures proficiency in the material usually covered in introductory one-semester college courses on the fundamentals of marketing. Also used by some businesses to allow employees to earn required continuing education credits.

Description: 100–item paper-pencil multiple-choice test in two separately timed sections assessing knowledge and understanding of the principles of marketing.

The test assumes a basic knowledge of demographic and economic trends, wholesaling and retailing institutional structures, and the classification of consumer and industrial goods. Two optional essay questions test the ability to apply marketing principles to basic marketing problems. Examiner required. Suitable for group use.

Timed: 45 minutes each section; essay 90 minutes

Scoring: Computer scored; essay section examiner evaluated locally

Cost: Contact publisher

Publisher: The College Board

COLLEGE LEVEL EXAMINATION PROGRAM (CLEP) SUBJECT EXAMINATION: COMPOSITION AND LITERATURE: AMERICAN LITERATURE

Adolescent, adult
Grades 12 and above

Purpose: Measures knowledge of American prose and poetry from colonial time to present. Covers material usually taught in a two-semester college survey course. Also used by some businesses to allow employees to earn required continuing education credits.

Description: 100–item paper-pencil test in two separately timed sections measuring knowledge of the content, background, and authors of literary works. Knowledge of critical and historical literacy terms is assumed. The areas covered include the colonial and early national, romantic, realistic and naturalistic, modern, and contemporary periods. The remaining questions assess knowledge of content of particular literary works, including their characters, plots, settings, and themes. Some knowledge of historical and social settings, authors and their influence, and relations of literary works and traditions is required. The optional essay section contains three questions, two of which must be answered. The section tests the candidate's ability to make organized statements on American literature that are pertinent and informed. Examiner required. Suitable for group use.

Timed: 45 minutes per section; essay section 90 minutes

Scoring: Computer scored; essay section examiner evaluated locally

Cost: Contact publisher

Publisher: The College Board

COLLEGE LEVEL EXAMINATION PROGRAM (CLEP) SUBJECT EXAMINATION: COMPOSITION AND LITERATURE: ANALYSIS AND INTERPRETATION OF LITERATURE

Adolescent, adult
Grades 12 and above

Purpose: Measures college-level competency equivalent to a one-year (two-semester) undergraduate course in literature. Also used by some businesses to allow employees to earn required continuing education credits.

Description: 90–item paper-pencil objective test in two separately timed sections assessing a student's skills in literary analysis and interpretation, including the ability to read prose and poetry with understanding and respond to nuances of meaning, tone, mood, imagery, and style; interpret metaphors, recognize rhetorical and stylistic devices, perceive relationships, grasp authors' attitudes; and familiarity with basic literary terms. The examination covers both British and American poetry, prose, drama, and works in translation from the classical period to the 20th century. The optional essay section assesses the ability to write two well-organized critical essays on given passages of poetry and on general literary questions. Examiner required. Suitable for group use.

Timed: 45 minutes per section; essay section 90 minutes

Scoring: Computer scored; essay section examiner evaluated locally

Cost: Contact publisher

Publisher: The College Board

COLLEGE LEVEL EXAMINATION PROGRAM (CLEP) SUBJECT EXAMINATION: COMPOSITION AND LITERATURE: COLLEGE COMPOSITION

Adolescent, adult
Grades 12 and above

Purpose: Assesses knowledge of the theoretical aspects of expository writing and the ability to put into practice the principles of standard written English. Also used by some businesses to allow employees to earn required continuing education credits.

Description: 100–item paper-pencil objective test in two separately timed sections focusing on the elements of language, grammar, and logic required for expository writing. The examination covers application of the fundamentals of standard written English; the ability to recognize techniques and styles and logical development; and the ability to use resource material. An optional 90–minute essay section provides three questions, two of which must be answered. Examiner required. Suitable for group use.

Timed: 45 minutes per section; essay section 90 minutes

Scoring: Computer scored; essay section examiner evaluated locally

Cost: Contact publisher

Publisher: The College Board

COLLEGE LEVEL EXAMINATION PROGRAM (CLEP) SUBJECT EXAMINATION: COMPOSITION AND LITERATURE: ENGLISH LITERATURE

Adolescent, adult
Grades 12 and above

Purpose: Measures college-level competency in English literature. Also used by some businesses to allow employees to earn required continuing education credits.

Description: 105–item paper-pencil objective test in two separately timed sections assessing proficiency in the study of English literature. Knowledge of common literary terms and forms, as well as of major authors and texts is assumed. Many items are based on passages and poems. Other areas include literary background, content of major works, chronology, author identification, material patterns, and literary references. The candidate also is asked to analyze elements of form; perceive meanings; and identify tone, mood, imagery, and style. The optional 90–minute essay section requires the examinee to write a critical essay on an excerpt from a literary work as well as a second essay on one of two topics. Examiner required. Suitable for group use.

Timed: 45 minutes per section; essay section 90 minutes

Scoring: Computer scored; essay section examiner evaluated locally

Cost: Contact publisher

Publisher: The College Board

COLLEGE LEVEL EXAMINATION PROGRAM (CLEP) SUBJECT EXAMINATION: COMPOSITION AND LITERATURE: FRESHMAN ENGLISH

Adolescent, adult
Grades 12 and above

Purpose: Measures a candidate's ability to deal with various types of formal and informal writing as taught in first-year college English courses. Also used by some businesses to allow employees to earn required continuing education credits.

Description: 100–item paper-pencil objective test in two separately timed sections measuring sensitivity in reading as well as skill in judging and controlling language on the assumption that these abilities are closely related to writing ability. One third of the exam requires the analysis of short passages of prose and poetry, both for comprehension of content and for judgment of structure and style. One third of the test is devoted to considerations of style and logical development. The final third focuses on clear syntax, correct usage, correct punctuation, and sentence and paragraph organization. The optional essay section allows a candidate to demonstrate writing skills in three sustained writing tasks. The topics present concrete problems involving personal knowledge and require control and flexibility in the use of language. Examiner required. Suitable for group use.

Timed: 45 minutes per section; essay section 90 minutes

Scoring: Computer scored; essay section examiner evaluated locally

Cost: Contact publisher

Publisher: The College Board

COLLEGE LEVEL EXAMINATION PROGRAM (CLEP) SUBJECT EXAMINATION: FOREIGN LANGUAGES: COLLEGE FRENCH LEVELS 1 AND 2

Adolescent, adult
Grades 12 and above

Purpose: Measures knowledge and ability equivalent to that of students who have completed from two to four semesters of college-level French. Also used by some businesses to allow employees to earn required continuing education credits.

Description: Multiple-item paper-pencil test in two separately timed sections assessing proficiency in the skills typically achieved from the end of the first year through the second year of college-level French. In the 90–item Reading section (1 hour), examinees are assessed on vocabulary mastery, grammatical control, and reading comprehension. In the 55-item Listening section (30 minutes), items are presented orally via a tape and test phonemic discrimination, listening comprehension, and ability to understand native speakers in dialogues and narratives. Levels 1 and 2 are incorporated into a single examination. Examiner required. Suitable for group use.

Timed: 1 hour, 30 minutes

Scoring: Computer scored

Cost: Contact publisher

Publisher: The College Board

COLLEGE LEVEL EXAMINATION PROGRAM (CLEP) SUBJECT EXAMINATION: FOREIGN LANGUAGES: COLLEGE GERMAN LEVELS 1 AND 2

Adolescent, adult
Grades 12 and above

Purpose: Measures knowledge and ability equivalent to that of students who have completed from two to four semesters of college-level German. Also used by some businesses to allow employees to earn required continuing education credits.

Description: Multiple-item paper-pencil test in two separately timed sections assessing proficiency in the skills typically achieved from the end of the first year through the second year of college-level German. In the 80–item Reading section (1 hour), the examinee is assessed on vocabulary mastery, grammatical control, and reading comprehension. In the 60-item Listening section (30 minutes), items are presented orally via a tape and assess phonemic discrimination, listening comprehension, and the ability to understand native speakers in dialogues and narratives. Levels 1 and 2 are incorporated into a single examination. Examiner required. Suitable for group use.

Timed: 1 hour, 30 minutes

Scoring: Computer scored

Cost: Contact publisher

Publisher: The College Board

COLLEGE LEVEL EXAMINATION PROGRAM (CLEP) SUBJECT EXAMINATION: FOREIGN LANGUAGES: COLLEGE SPANISH LEVELS 1 AND 2

Adolescent, adult
Grades 12 and above

Purpose: Measures knowledge and ability equivalent to that of students who have completed from two to four semesters of college-level Spanish. Also used by some businesses to allow employees to earn required continuing education credits.

Description: Multiple-item paper-pencil test assessing proficiency in the skills typ-

---

ically achieved from the end of the first year through the second year of college-level Spanish. In the 70–item Reading section (45 minutes), examinees are assessed on vocabulary mastery, grammatical control, and reading comprehension. In the 70–item Listening section (45 minutes), items are presented orally via tape and assess phonemic discrimination, listening comprehension, and ability to understand native speakers in dialogues and narratives. Examiner required. Suitable for group use.

Timed: 1 hour, 30 minutes

Scoring: Computer scored

Cost: Contact publisher

Publisher: The College Board

COLLEGE LEVEL EXAMINATION PROGRAM (CLEP) SUBJECT EXAMINATION: HISTORY AND SOCIAL SCIENCES: AMERICAN GOVERNMENT

Adolescent, adult
Grades 12 and above

Purpose: Measures college-level competency in the study of American government and politics. Used by some businesses to allow employees to earn required continuing education credits.

Description: 100–item paper-pencil objective test in two separately timed sections of 50 items each. The areas tested include institutions and policy processes; presidency, bureaucracy, and Congress; federal courts and civil liberties; political parties and pressure groups; political beliefs and behavior; and constitutional underpinnings of American democracy. The optional essay section offers a choice of writing on any three of four topics offered. Examiner required. Suitable for group use.

Timed: 45 minutes per section; optional essay 90 minutes

Scoring: Computer scored; optional essay examiner evaluated locally

Cost: Contact publisher

Publisher: The College Board

COLLEGE LEVEL EXAMINATION PROGRAM (CLEP) SUBJECT EXAMINATION: HISTORY AND SOCIAL SCIENCES: AMERICAN HISTORY I: EARLY COLONIZATIONS TO 1877

Adolescent, adult
Grades 12 and above

Purpose: Measures proficiency in the material commonly covered in one-semester introductory college courses on the early period of American history. Also used by some businesses to allow employees to earn required continuing education credits.

Description: 120–item paper-pencil multiple-choice test assessing knowledge and understanding of American history from the Spanish and French colonizations to the end of Reconstruction (1877). About one third of the questions cover the period from 1500 to 1789 and two thirds the period between 1790 and 1877. Coverage of the colonial period emphasizes the development of the English colonies; the test as a whole emphasizes the period of nationhood. Candidates are expected to describe, characterize, analyze, and explain major historical phenomena in the following categories: political institutions and behavior and public policy, social and economic change, cultural and intellectual developments, and diplomacy and international relations. An optional essay section assesses the ability to present organized, logical historical arguments dealing with the topics covered in the objective section. Examiner required. Suitable for group use.

Timed: 45 minutes each section; essay 90 minutes

Scoring: Computer scored; free response section examiner evaluated locally

Cost: Contact publisher

Publisher: The College Board

COLLEGE LEVEL EXAMINATION PROGRAM (CLEP) SUBJECT EXAMINATION: HISTORY AND SOCIAL SCIENCES: AMERICAN HISTORY II: 1865 TO THE PRESENT

Adolescent, adult
Grades 12 and above

Purpose: Measures college-level competency in the study of American history from 1865 to the present. Also used by some businesses to allow employees to earn required continuing education credits.

Description: 120–item paper-pencil test in two separately timed sections covering the period of American history from the end of the Civil War to the present: from 1865 to 1914 (one third of test) and from 1915 to the present (two thirds of test). Content coverage emphasizes political institutions and behavior and public policy, social and economic change, cultural and intellectual developments, and diplomacy and international relations. An optional essay section also is offered. Examiner required. Suitable for group use.

Timed: 45 minutes each section; optional essay 90 minutes

Scoring: Computer scored; essay section examiner evaluated locally

Cost: Contact publisher

Publisher: The College Board

COLLEGE LEVEL EXAMINATION PROGRAM (CLEP) SUBJECT EXAMINATION: HISTORY AND SOCIAL SCIENCES: EDUCATIONAL PSYCHOLOGY

Adolescent, adult
Grades 12 and above

Purpose: Measures competency in educational psychology at the introductory college-course level. Also used by some businesses to allow employees to earn required continuing education credits.

Description: 100–item paper-pencil objective test in two separately timed sections assessing knowledge and comprehension of basic information, concepts, and principles pertaining to the psychology of education, including one's ability to integrate various aspects of this content as it applies to teaching situations and problems. The categories covered are theories and theorist, evaluation, teaching, education, development, motivation, and learning. The optional four-item essay section assesses factors such as accuracy of information, comprehensiveness and

relevance of treatment, organization of materials, approach to problems from a psychological frame of reference, and logic and imaginativeness. Examiner required. Suitable for group use.

Timed: 45 minutes each section; essay 90 minutes

Scoring: Computer scored; essay section examiner evaluated locally

Cost: Contact publisher

Publisher: The College Board

COLLEGE LEVEL EXAMINATION PROGRAM (CLEP) SUBJECT EXAMINATION: HISTORY AND SOCIAL SCIENCES: GENERAL PSYCHOLOGY

Adolescent, adult
Grades 12 and above

Purpose: Measures college-level competency in general psychology. Used by some businesses to allow employees to earn required continuing education credits.

Description: 100–item paper-pencil objective test in two separately timed sections assessing basic facts, concepts, and principles of general psychology, including physiology and behavior, perceptual and sensory experience, motivation and emotion, learning, cognition, life-span development, personality and adjustment, behavior disorders, social psychology, measurement and statistics, and history and philosophy. An optional essay section in which examinees answer three of four questions is included. Examiner required. Suitable for group use.

Timed: 45 minutes per section; optional essay 90 minutes

Scoring: Computer scored; optional essay examiner evaluated locally

Cost: Contact publisher

Publisher: The College Board

COLLEGE LEVEL EXAMINATION PROGRAM (CLEP) SUBJECT EXAMINATION: HISTORY AND SOCIAL SCIENCES: HUMAN GROWTH AND DEVELOPMENT

Adolescent, adult
Grades 12 and above

Purpose: Measures knowledge and understanding of the subject matter usually covered in introductory one-semester college courses in child psychology, child development, or developmental psychology with primary emphasis on infancy, early childhood, and middle childhood. Also used by some businesses to allow employees to earn required continuing education credits.

Description: 90–item paper-pencil multiple-choice test in two separately timed sections assessing proficiency in the field of child development with emphasis on the periods of early and middle childhood. Test items require examinees to demonstrate knowledge of facts, terminology, and theory; understanding of concepts and principles; and ability to apply what has been learned to particular problems or situations. The examination covers theoretical foundations (major views of development), research strategies and methodology, biological aspects of development, perceptual and sensorimotor development, cognitive development, language development, intelligence, social development, family and society, learning, and atypical behavior and development. An optional essay section consisting of four questions covers the same material as the objective section and measures the ability to select pertinent material and present it in an organized and logical manner. Examiner required. Suitable for group use.

Timed: 45 minutes each section; essay 90 minutes

Scoring: Computer scored; essay section examiner evaluated locally

Cost: Contact publisher

Publisher: The College Board

COLLEGE LEVEL EXAMINATION PROGRAM (CLEP) SUBJECT EXAMINATION: HISTORY AND SOCIAL SCIENCES: INTRODUCTORY MACROECONOMICS

Adolescent, adult
Grades 12 and above

Purpose: Measures college-level competency in introductory macroeconomics.

Used by some businesses to allow employees to earn required continuing education credits.

Description: 90–item paper-pencil objective test in two separately timed sections assessing knowledge and understanding of determinants of aggregate demand on the monetary and/or fiscal policies that are appropriate to achieve particular policy objectives, including basic or generic concepts and macroeconomic concepts. A 90–minute optional essay section in which students answer three of four questions is offered. Examiner required. Suitable for group use.

Timed: 45 minutes per section; optional essay 90 minutes

Scoring: Computer scored; optional essay examiner evaluated locally

Cost: Contact publisher

Publisher: The College Board

COLLEGE LEVEL EXAMINATION PROGRAM (CLEP) SUBJECT EXAMINATION: HISTORY AND SOCIAL SCIENCES: INTRODUCTORY MICROECONOMICS

Adolescent, adult
Grades 12 and above

Purpose: Measures college-level competency in introductory microeconomics. Used by some businesses to allow employees to earn required continuing education credits.

Description: 90–item paper-pencil objective test in two separately timed sections requiring students to apply analytical techniques to hypothetical situations and to analyze and evaluate interpretations or criticism of government policies on the basis of simple theoretical models. The test emphasizes analytical capabilities rather than factual understanding of United States institutions and policies. The test covers basic or generic concepts and microeconomic concepts. A 90–minute optional essay section in which students answer three of four questions is included. Examiner required. Suitable for group use.

Timed: 45 minutes per section; optional essay 90 minutes

Scoring: Computer scored; optional essay examiner evaluated locally

Cost: Contact publisher

Publisher: The College Board

COLLEGE LEVEL EXAMINATION PROGRAM (CLEP) SUBJECT EXAMINATION: HISTORY AND SOCIAL SCIENCES: WESTERN CIVILIZATION I: ANCIENT NEAR EAST TO 1648

**Adolescent, adult
Grades 12 and above**

Purpose: Measures college-level competency in the study of Western civilization from the ancient Near East to 1648. Used by some businesses to allow employees to earn required continuing education credits.

Description: 120–item paper-pencil objective test in two separately timed sections covering six broad historical periods: ancient Near East, ancient Greece and Hellenistic civilization, ancient Rome, medieval history, the Renaissance and Reformation, and early modern Europe (1560–1648). The optional essay section requires the candidate to answer two of four essays. Examiner required. Suitable for group use.

Timed: 45 minutes per section; optional essay 90 minutes

Scoring: Computer scored; optional essay examiner evaluated locally

Cost: Contact publisher

Publisher: The College Board

COLLEGE LEVEL EXAMINATION PROGRAM (CLEP) SUBJECT EXAMINATION: HISTORY AND SOCIAL SCIENCES: WESTERN CIVILIZATION II: 1648 TO THE PRESENT

**Adolescent, adult
Grades 12 and above**

Purpose: Measures college-level competency in the study of Western civilization from 1648 to the present. Used by some businesses to allow employees to earn required continuing education credits.

Description: 120–item paper-pencil objective exam in two separately timed sections covering 12 broad historical periods: absolutism and constitutionalism (1648–1715); competition for empire and economic expansion; the scientific view of the world; the Enlightenment and enlightened despotism; the French Revolution and Napoleonic Europe; the Industrial Revolution; political developments, 1815–1848; politics and diplomacy in the age of nationalism (1850–1914); economy, culture, and imperialism, 1850–1914; World War I, the Russian Revolution, and postwar Europe (1914–1924); Europe between the Wars; and World War II and contemporary Europe. The exam measures a person's ability to identify the causes and effects of major events in history; to analyze, interpret, and evaluate historical materials; and to reach conclusions. A 90–minute optional essay section in which examinees write essays on two of the four topics presented is included. Examiner required. Suitable for group use.

Timed: 45 minutes per section; optional essay 90 minutes

Scoring: Computer scored; optional essay examiner evaluated locally

Cost: Contact publisher

Publisher: The College Board

COLLEGE LEVEL EXAMINATION PROGRAM (CLEP) SUBJECT EXAMINATION: SCIENCE/MATHEMATICS: CALCULUS WITH ELEMENTARY FUNCTIONS

**Adolescent, adult
Grades 12 and above**

Purpose: Measures skills and concepts usually covered in a one-year college course in calculus with elementary functions. Also used by some businesses to allow employees to earn required continuing education credits.

Description: 45–item paper-pencil objective test in two separately timed sections assessing a person's intuitive understanding of calculus and experience with its methods and application. Knowledge of preparatory mathematics (algebra, plane and solid geometry, trigonometry, and analytical geometry) is assumed. The topics covered include elementary functions, differential calculus, and integral calculus. An optional six-item free-response section requiring the same knowledge as the multiple-choice portion of the test provides examinees with an opportunity to demonstrate their problem-solving abilities in depth. Examiner required. Suitable for group use.

Timed: 45 minutes per section; free-response section 90 minutes

Scoring: Computer scored; free-response section examiner evaluated locally

Cost: Contact publisher

Publisher: The College Board

COLLEGE LEVEL EXAMINATION PROGRAM (CLEP) SUBJECT EXAMINATION: SCIENCE/ MATHEMATICS: COLLEGE ALGEBRA

Adolescent, adult
Grades 12 and above

Purpose: Measures college-level competency equivalent to a one-semester college algebra course. Also used by some businesses to allow employees to earn required continuing education credits.

Description: 80–item paper-pencil objective exam in two separately timed sections consisting of questions that require the solution of routine or straightforward problems and application of concepts and skills in solving nonroutine problems. The exam assesses knowledge of basic algebraic operations; linear equations and inequities and their graphs; quadratic equations and their graphs; algebraic, exponential, and logarithmic functions; theory of equations; and a variety of related topics including sets, the real number system, complex numbers, systems of equations, sequence and series, matrix addition and multiplication, evaluation of determinants, and mathematical induction. Examiner required. Suitable for group use.

Timed: 45 minutes per section

Scoring: Computer scored

Cost: Contact publisher

Publisher: The College Board

COLLEGE LEVEL EXAMINATION PROGRAM (CLEP) SUBJECT EXAMINATION: SCIENCE/ MATHEMATICS: COLLEGE ALGEBRA/TRIGONOMETRY

Adolescent, adult
Grades 12 and above

Purpose: Measures college-level competency equivalent to a one-semester course that combines college algebra with trigonometry. Also used by some businesses to allow employees to earn required continuing education credits.

Description: 80–item paper-pencil multiple-choice test consisting of two 40–item sections. One section is devoted entirely to algebra, the other to trigonometry. The test as a whole provides a single score based on the entire 90–minute test. For descriptions of test content, refer to the college algebra and college trigonometry descriptions. Calculators are not permitted. Examiner required. Suitable for group use.

Timed: 45 minutes per section

Scoring: Computer scored

Cost: Contact publisher

Publisher: The College Board

COLLEGE LEVEL EXAMINATION PROGRAM (CLEP) SUBJECT EXAMINATION: SCIENCE/ MATHEMATICS: GENERAL BIOLOGY

Adolescent, adult
Grades 12 and above

Purpose: Measures proficiency in the material usually covered in a one-year biology course at the college level. Used by some businesses to allow employees to earn required continuing education credits.

Description: 120–item paper-pencil multiple-choice test in two separately timed sections assessing knowledge and understanding in three broad areas of the biological sciences: molecular and cellular, organismal, and populational. Test items require candidates to demonstrate knowledge of facts, principles, and processes of biology; understanding of the means by which information is collected, how it is interpreted, how one hypothesizes and synthesizes from available information, and how one draws conclusions and makes further predictions; and understanding that science is a human endeavor with social consequences. An optional essay section in which examinees must write three of four essays covers the same material and measures the ability to select pertinent material and present it in an organized and logical manner. Examiner required. Suitable for group use.

Timed: 45 minutes per section; optional essay 90 minutes

Scoring: Computer scored; optional essay examiner evaluated locally

Cost: Contact publisher

Publisher: The College Board

COLLEGE LEVEL EXAMINATION PROGRAM (CLEP) SUBJECT EXAMINATION: SCIENCE/MATHEMATICS: GENERAL CHEMISTRY

Adolescent, adult
Grades 12 and above

Purpose: Determines college-level competency in general chemistry. Used by some businesses to allow employees to earn required continuing education credits.

Description: 80–item paper-pencil objective test in two separately timed sections requiring the candidate to demonstrate knowledge of the material that constitutes the core topics of introductory college chemistry courses and to interpret and apply this material to new and unfamiliar material. The test measures structure of matter, states of matter, reaction types, equations and stoichiometry, kinetics, equilibrium, thermodynamics, descriptive chemistry, and experimental chemistry. The use of slide rules and calculators is permitted. The content of the optional free-response section includes essays, equations, and quantitative problems.

Examinees must respond to six of the nine items presented. Examiner required. Suitable for group use.

Timed: 45 minutes per section; optional free-response section 90 minutes

Scoring: Computer scored; optional free-response examiner evaluated locally

Cost: Contact publisher

Publisher: The College Board

COLLEGE LEVEL EXAMINATION PROGRAM (CLEP) SUBJECT EXAMINATION: SCIENCE/MATHEMATICS: TRIGONOMETRY

Adolescent, adult
Grades 12 and above

Purpose: Measures knowledge and ability equivalent to a one-semester college course with primary emphasis on analytical trigonometry. Also used by some businesses to allow employees to earn required continuing education credits.

Description: 80–item paper-pencil objective test in two separately timed sections assessing academic achievement in analytical trigonometry, including trigonometric functions and their relationships; trigonometric functions of angles with terminal sides in the various quadrants on the axes; trigonometric equations and inequalities; graphs of trigonometric functions; and trigonometry of the triangle, including the law of sines and cosines; and inverse functions and the trigonometric form of complex numbers. Examiner required. Suitable for group use.

Timed: 45 minutes per section

Scoring: Computer scored

Cost: Contact publisher

Publisher: The College Board

COLLEGE OUTCOME MEASURES PROGRAM (COMP)
The American College Testing Program

Adult
Grades 13–18

Purpose: Measures general education outcomes of college.

Description: 120–item paper-pencil multiple-choice test measuring six general outcome areas of college: a) communicating, b) solving problems, c) clarifying values, d) functioning within social situations, e) using science, and f) using the arts. Materials include TV documentaries, radio newscasts, magazine articles, ads, short stories, music. Three forms (8, 9, and 10) are available. Examiner required. Suitable for group use.

Timed: 129 minutes

Scoring: Computer scored

Cost: Contact publisher

Publisher: The American College Testing Program

COLLEGIATE ASSESSMENT OF ACADEMIC PROFICIENCY (CAAP)
The American College Testing Program

Adult
College Sophomores

Purpose: Assesses achievement and thinking skills. Used for program and individual student evaluation.

Description: Battery of six tests: Writing (essay), Writing Skills (72 items), Mathematics (35 items), Reading (36 items), Critical Thinking (32 items), and Science Reasoning (45 items). Two forms (88A, 88B) are available. Examiner required. Suitable for group use.

Timed: 40 minutes per test; additional 10 minutes for administration

Scoring: Multiple-choice tests; computer scored essay centrally rated

Cost: One test $6.00 per student; 2–4 objective/tests $10.00 per student; for other costs contact publisher

Publisher: The American College Testing Program

THE COMMUNITY COLLEGE ASSESSMENT PROGRAM (CCAP)

Adult—Community
college enrollees

Purpose: Measures abilities, background, and plans of community college students. Used for advisement and placement in serial English and math classes in community colleges in Washington. Also used as a diagnostic screening device for applicants to selected technical programs.

Description: Paper-pencil test of abilities and achievement predictive of performance in community college subjects. This is a modified version of the Washington Pre-College Test, which is somewhat shorter and designed to measure a broader range of ability. Examiner required. Suitable for group use.

Timed: 2 hours, 15 minutes

Scoring: Machine scored

Cost: Test booklet $2.00; answer sheet $2.00

Publisher: Washington Pre-College Program

Information and availability unconfirmed; last verified in 1988.

COMPREHENSIVE ASSESSMENT PROGRAM: ACHIEVEMENT SERIES
John W. Wick and Jefferey K. Smith

Child, adolescent—
Ages 4–18

Purpose: Assesses student achievement in basic academic areas. Used for evaluating individual or group status, planning instructional improvement, monitoring student progress, and evaluating program effectiveness.

Description: Multiple-item paper-pencil test available for 11 test levels. Levels 4–6 (PreK–Grade 1) emphasize children's capabilities to perform given tasks to ascertain their level of development. Levels 7–12 (Grades 2–8) measure achievement in reading, language, and mathematics. Levels 13 and 14 (Grades 9–12) test achievement in reading, language, writing, mathematics, science, and social studies. When combined with the Developing Cognitive Abilities Test, the level of student performance in relation to abilities can be determined. Examiner required. Suitable for group use.

Timed: Varies with level and test

Scoring: Hand key; may be computer scored

Cost: 35 test booklets $34.45–$46.65 (specify level and machine or hand-scorable); key $1.70 (specify level); manual $8.15

Publisher: American Testronics

COMPREHENSIVE ASSESSMENT PROGRAM: EARLY CHILDHOOD DIAGNOSTIC INSTRUMENT (ECDI)
Jana Mason and Janice Stewart

Child—Ages 4–6

Purpose: Identifies young children who may need additional services at the lower ends of the continuums of early literacy behaviors, conceptual development, and readiness skills.

Description: 133–item paper-pencil oral-response verbal point-to multiple-choice instrument consisting of three objective strands: Emergent Literacy, Language, and Basic Concepts. The instruments feature real tasks that young children learn in kindergarten. Children's responses indicate understandings of literacy and language when they enter school. In addition, a Social Competence strand assesses children's ability to communicate at a basic level about themselves. This is one test in the Comprehensive Assessment Program series. Examiner required. Not suitable for group use.

Untimed: 30 minutes

Scoring: Machine scored; hand key; scoring service available from publisher

Cost: Contact publisher

Publisher: American Testronics

COMPREHENSIVE ASSESSMENT PROGRAM: HIGH SCHOOL SUBJECT TESTS (HSST), FORM A
Louis A. Gatta

Adolescent
Grades 9–12

Purpose: Measures student's proficiency in common high-school courses. Also used to analyze instruction and planning.

Description: Multiple-item individual tests for the 15 most commonly taught courses at the secondary level: general mathematics, algebra, geometry, health,

consumer education, biology, chemistry, physical science, American history, American government, world geography, world history, language, literature and vocabulary, and writing and mechanics. Examiner required. Suitable for group use.

Timed: 40 minutes

Scoring: Hand key; may be computer scored

Cost: 35 test booklets $30.50; manual $9.00; directions for administration $2.40; 35 machine-scorable answer sheets (specify subject) $11.95

Publisher: American Testronics

COMPREHENSIVE ASSESSMENT PROGRAM: HIGH SCHOOL SUBJECT TESTS (HSST), FORM B
John W. Wick and Louis A. Gatta

Adolescent, adult

Purpose: Assesses high-school students' knowledge in the areas of mathematics, science, social studies, computer literacy, consumer economics, health, and English.

Description: Multiple-choice content-specific tests integrating both norm-referenced and criterion-referenced information. The titles available for these end-of-course tests are Language, Literature and Vocabulary, Writing and Mechanics, General Mathematics, Pre-Algebra, Advanced Algebra, Geometry, Computer Literacy, American Government, American History, World History, World Geography, Consumer Economics, Physical Science, Biology, Chemistry, Physics, and Health. Available in forms A and B. Examiner required. Suitable for group use.

Timed: 40 minutes

Scoring: Machine scored; hand key; scoring service available from publisher

Cost: 35 test booklets $30.50; 35 answer sheets $11.95; manual $9.00; directions $2.40

Publisher: American Testronics

COMPREHENSIVE TESTING PROGRAM (CTP)
Committees of Teachers and Curriculum Specialists

Child, adolescent Grades 1–12

Purpose: Measures the verbal and mathematical skills of students. Used for guidance counseling, the evaluation of student progress, and monitoring the effectiveness of instructional programs.

Description: Multiple-item paper-pencil multiple-choice tests arranged in five levels: Levels 1 and 2 for Grade 1 through early Grade 3; and Levels 3, 4, and 5 for the end of Grade 3 through Grade 12. Levels 1 and 2 (225 items) measure mathematics, reading, word analysis, and writing skills. Levels 3, 4, and 5 (300 items) measure verbal aptitude, quantitative aptitude, reading comprehension, mathematics, the mechanics of writing, vocabulary, and English expression. For Levels 1 and 2, students mark answers in machine-scorable test booklets; Levels 3, 4, and 5 use separate answer sheets. Use is restricted to schools with ERB membership. Examiner required. Suitable for group use.

Untimed: Levels 1 and 2 2 hours, 30 minutes

Timed: Levels 3, 4, and 5 4 hours, 20 minutes

Scoring: Hand key; may be computer scored

Cost: 20 booklets (Levels 1 and 2) $24.00; 20 booklets (Levels 3, 4, and 5) $38.00; manual $5.00

Publisher: Educational Records Bureau

COMPREHENSIVE TESTS OF BASIC SKILLS, FORMS S AND T

Child, adolescent Grades K–12.9

Purpose: Assesses basic skills in reading, language, mathematics, science, and social studies.

Description: Multiple-item paper-pencil multiple-choice test measuring basic academic skills. The test is available in Form S and Form T. Form S contains seven levels: Level A (Grades K–1.3), Level B (Grades K.6–1.9), Level C (Grades 1.6–2.9), Level 1 (Grades 2.5–4.9), Level 2 (Grades 4.5–6.9), Level 3 (Grades 6.5–8.9), and Level 4 (Grades 8.5–12.9). Levels A and B assess reading, language, and mathematics skills. Level C measures reading, language, mathematics, science, and social studies skills. Levels 1–4 assess reading, language, mathematics, social studies, and reference skills. Form T is available only for Levels 1–4. Forms S and T have been superseded by CTBS Forms U and V. Examiner required. Suitable for group use. Available in Spanish (CTBS-Español).

Timed: Complete battery 2–4 hours

Scoring: Hand key; may be computer scored

Cost: Contact publisher

Publisher: CTB/Macmillan/McGraw-Hill

COMPREHENSIVE TESTS OF BASIC SKILLS, FORMS U AND V

Child, adolescent Grades K–12.9

Purpose: Assesses basic skills in reading, language, mathematics, science, and social studies.

Description: Multiple-item paper-pencil multiple-choice test measuring basic academic skills. The test is available in Forms U and V. Form U contains 10 levels: Level A (Grades K.0–K.9), Level B (Grades K.6–1.6), Level C (Grades 1.0–1.9), Level D (Grades 1.6–2.9), Level E (Grades 2.6–3.9), Level F (Grades 3.6–4.9), Level G (Grades 4.6–6.9), Level H (Grades 6.6–8.9), Level J (Grades 8.6–12.9), and Level K (Grades 11.0–12.9). Level A tests reading and mathematics skills. Levels B and C test reading, language, and mathematics. Levels D and E assess reading, language, mathematics, science, social studies, and spelling. Levels F-K measure reading, language, mathematics, science, social studies, and reference skills. Form V is available only for Levels D-J. Forms U and V replace CTBS Forms S and T. This test is linked

academic achievement and aptitude

statistically to the Spanish Assessment of Basic Education. Examiner required. Suitable for group use.

Timed: Complete battery 1 hour, 8 minutes–4 hours, 50 minutes

Scoring: Hand key; may be computer scored

Cost: Multilevel examination kit (Grades K–12) $32.00

Publisher: CTB/Macmillan/McGraw-Hill

COOPERATIVE ENGLISH TESTS
Refer to page 282.

COOPERATIVE MATHEMATICS TESTS
Refer to page 333.

CORNELL CLASS REASONING TEST, FORM X
Robert H. Ennis,
William L. Gardiner,
Richard Morrow, Dieter Paulus, and
Lucille Ringel

Child, adolescent
Grades 4–12

Purpose: Assesses level of logical competence in deductive reasoning. Used for research in school systems.

Description: 72–item paper-pencil measure of class reasoning ability. One or two class relationship suppositionals are presented in each item, and the subject indicates whether a related statement then must be true, may be true, or must be false. Self-administered. Suitable for group use.

Timed: 50 minutes

Scoring: Hand key; may be computer scored

Cost: Test booklet with answer key $0.50

Publisher: Illinois Critical Thinking Project

Information and availability unconfirmed; last verified in 1988.

CORNELL CONDITIONAL REASONING TEST, FORM X
Robert H. Ennis,
William L. Gardiner, John Guzzetta,
Richard Morrow, Dieter Paulus, and
Lucille Ringel

Child, adolescent
Grades 4–12

Purpose: Assesses a subject's ability or level of conditional reasoning. Used for research in the areas of competence.

Description: 72–item paper-pencil measure of conditional reasoning. One or two conditionals and usually an additional supposition are presented in each item; the subject is asked to indicate whether a conclusion based on those assumptions would then have to be true, may be true, or would have to be false. Self-administered. Suitable for group use.

Timed: 50 minutes

Scoring: Hand key; may be computer scored

Cost: Test booklet with answer key $0.50

Publisher: Illinois Critical Thinking Project

Information and availability unconfirmed; last verified in 1988.

CORNELL CRITICAL THINKING TEST, LEVEL X
Robert H. Ennis and Jason Millman

Child, adolescent
Grades 4–14

Purpose: Assesses an individual's ability to think critically. Used for research, teaching of critical thinking, or as one of several criteria for admission to positions or areas requiring ability to think critically.

Description: 71–item paper-pencil multiple-choice measure of critical thinking divided into four sections. In the first section, the examinee reads a conclusion and decides which of several premises supports the conclusion. The second section measures the examinee's ability to judge the reliability of information. The third section tests the examinee's ability to judge whether a statement follows from premises. The fourth section involves the identification of assumptions. Level X is somewhat easier than Level Z. Examiner required for Grades 4–6. Suitable for group use.

Timed: 50–62 minutes

Scoring: Computer scored

Cost: Specimen set (tests, manual) $10.00; 10 tests $16.95; 10 machine-scorable answer sheets $4.95

Publisher: Midwest Publications Critical Thinking Press

CORNELL CRITICAL THINKING TEST, LEVEL Z
Robert H. Ennis and Jason Millman

Adolescent, adult
Grades 13 and above

Purpose: Assesses an individual's ability to think critically. Used for research, teaching of critical thinking, or as one of several criteria for admission to positions or areas requiring ability for critical thinking.

Description: 52–item paper-pencil multiple-choice measure of critical thinking divided into seven sections directed at assessing the examinee's ability to decide whether a statement follows from a given premise, detect equivocal arguments, judge reliability of observations and authenticity of sources, judge direction of support for a hypothesis, judge possible predictions for their value in guiding experiments, and find assumptions of various types. Level Z is somewhat more difficult than Level X. Self-administered. Suitable for group use.

Timed: 50 minutes

Scoring: Computer scored

Cost: Specimen set (manual, tests) $10.00; 10 tests $16.95; 10 machine-scorable answer sheets $4.95

Publisher: Midwest Publications Critical Thinking Press

CRITERION TEST OF BASIC SKILLS
Kerth Lundell, William Brown, and James Evans

Child
Grades 1–6

Purpose: Assesses reading and arithmetic skills of elementary school students. Used by teachers for classroom placement.

Description: Multiple-item paper-pencil criterion-referenced test covering reading and arithmetic skills. The Reading subtest measures letter recognition, letter sounding, blending, sequencing, special sounds, and sight words. The Arithmetic subtest measures number and numerical recognition, addition, subtraction, multiplication, and division. After scoring, both portions of the test can be transferred to a graphic profile of each student's strengths and weaknesses. Materials include recording forms, problem sheets, a stimulus card booklet, and a manual, which contains activities correlated to the skill areas assessed. Examiner required. Suitable for group use.

Untimed: 10–15 minutes

Scoring: Hand key

Cost: Manual $12.00; 25 arithmetic recording forms $8.00; 25 reading recording forms $8.00; 25 math problem sheets $4.00; stimulus cards booklet $8.00

Publisher: Academic Therapy Publications

THE CULTURAL LITERACY TEST
The Cultural Literacy Foundation

Adolescent—Ages 16–18
Grades 11–12

Purpose: Measures the extent of general knowledge 11th- and 12th-grade students have acquired in the humanities, social sciences, and sciences.

Description: 115–item paper-pencil multiple-choice test measuring general knowledge in the humanities (biblical references; mythology and folklore; conventions of written English; proverbs; idioms; literature in English; world literature, philosophy, and religion; visual and other arts), social sciences (American history to 1865; American history since 1865; world history to 1550; world history since 1550; anthropology, psychology, and sociology; business and economics; world politics; American politics; American geography; world geography), and sciences (earth sciences; physical sciences and mathematics; life sciences;

medicine, human body, health and disease; technology). Normative and criterion-referenced data are available for categories and total score. The test is available in parallel forms A and B. A scoring service is available through the publisher. Examiner required. Suitable for group use.

Timed: 50 minutes

Scoring: Machine scored

Cost: Contact publisher for price and availability

Publisher: The Riverside Publishing Company

DETROIT TESTS OF LEARNING APTITUDE–2 (DTLA–2)
Donald D. Hammill

Child, adolescent—Ages 6–17

Purpose: Measures general aptitude and discrete abilities of children and adolescents. Identifies students deficient in general or specific aptitude and serves as a standardized instrument in research.

Description: Multiple-item oral-response paper-pencil battery of 11 subtests yielding a detailed profile of a student's abilities and deficiencies. Subtests include word opposites, sentence imitation, word sequences, story construction, design reproduction, symbolic relations, picture fragments, story sequencing, basic information, design sequence, and letter sequence reversed. The abilities measured are vocabulary, grammar, following commands, repeating words, storytelling, drawing from memory, order recall, reasoning, relationship knowledge, Gestalt-closure function, and order recall. Nine composite scores—verbal, nonverbal, conceptual, structural, attention-enhanced, attention-reduced, motor-enhanced, and motor-reduced aptitudes, and the general intelligence quotient—provide information on linguistic, cognitive, attention, and motor abilities. The test is useful in diagnosing learning disabilities and mental retardation. The PRO-SCORE scoring system is available from the publisher for use with Apple II+, IIc, IIe, or IBM PC systems. Examiner required. Not suitable for group use.

Untimed: 1½ hours

Scoring: Hand key; may be computer scored

Cost: Complete kit (25 student response forms, 25 examiner record forms, 25 summary and profile sheets, picture book, examiner's manual, storage box) $98.00; PRO-SCORE scoring systems $69.00

Publisher: PRO-ED

DETROIT TESTS OF LEARNING APTITUDE–PRIMARY (DTLA-P)
Donald D. Hammill and Brian R. Bryant

Child—Ages 3.5–9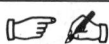

Purpose: Measures general and specific aptitudes of children. Identifies deficiencies in general and specific aptitudes and serves as a standardized instrument in research.

Description: 130–item oral-response paper-pencil battery yielding eight subtest scores (Verbal Quotient, Nonverbal Quotient, Conceptual Quotient, Structural Quotient, Motor-Enhanced Quotient, Motor-Reduced Quotient, Attention-Enhanced Quotient, Attention-Reduced Quotient) and one total score (General Intelligence Quotient) and providing a detailed profile of a student's abilities and deficiencies. The test is useful with low-functioning school-aged children. The PRO-SCORE scoring system is available from the publisher for use on the Apple II+, IIc, and IIe only. Examiner required. Not suitable for group use.

Untimed: 15–40 minutes

Scoring: Computer scored

Cost: Complete kit (examiner's manual, 25 student response forms, 25 profile/ examiner record forms, picture book, storage box) $89.00

Publisher: PRO-ED

DEVELOPING COGNITIVE ABILITIES (DCAT), 2ND EDITION
Refer to page 589.

---

academic achievement and aptitude

DIAGNOSTIC ABILITIES IN MATH (D.A.M. TEST)
Refer to page 316.

DIAGNOSTIC ACHIEVEMENT BATTERY–2 (DAB–2)
Phyllis L. Newcomer

Child, adolescent—Ages 6–14

Purpose: Assesses a child's ability to listen, speak, read, write, and perform simple mathematics operations. Diagnoses learning disabilities.

Description: Multiple-item paper-pencil and oral-response subtests assessing the following five components of a child's verbal and mathematical skills: Listening Component (Story Comprehension Test and Characteristics Test), Speaking Component (Synonyms Test and Grammatic Completion Test), Reading Component (Alphabet/Word Knowledge Test and Reading Comprehension Test), Writing Component (Capitalization Test, Punctuation Test, Spelling Test, and Writing Composition Test), and Math Component (Math Reasoning Test and Math Calculation Test). Results, converted to standard scores, provide a profile of the child's strengths and weaknesses on each of the five components, as well as on the 13 subtests. The components of the test may be administered independently, depending on the needs of the child being tested. The PRO-SCORE scoring system is available from the publisher for use on Apple II, IIe, II+; IBM PC; and MS-DOS systems. Examiner required. The written vocabulary, capitalization, punctuation, spelling, and math calculation subtests may be administered to small groups; the other subtests must be individually administered.

Untimed: 30 minutes–1 hour, 30 minutes

Scoring: Examiner evaluated; may be computer scored

Cost: Complete kit (manual, 25 student work sheets, 25 profile/answer sheets, picture book, storage box) $98.00; PRO-SCORE scoring systems $69.00

Publisher: PRO-ED

DIAGNOSTIC ACHIEVEMENT TEST FOR ADOLESCENTS (DATA)
Phyllis L. Newcomer and Brian R. Bryant

Adolescent Grades 7–12

Purpose: Measures the achievement level of secondary students.

Description: Multiple-item paper-pencil and oral-response test consisting of 10 subtests measuring achievement in reading, math, spelling, writing, science, and social studies. The subtests include Word Identification, Reading Comprehension, Math Calculations, Math Problem Solving, Spelling, and Writing Composition. Three supplemental subtests (Science, Social Studies, and Reference Skills) are also included. Subtest scores are converted to percentiles and standard scores. The PRO-SCORE scoring system is available from the publisher for use on Apple II, II+, and IIe; IBM PC; and MS-DOS computers. The system generates a four-page report providing background information on the student; raw scores, standard scores, percentiles, and descriptions for each subtest; standard score sums, percentiles, and descriptors for all composites and quotients; an optional cognitive aptitude score; subtest and composite profiles; intraindividual comparisons of all composites; and significance testing of all comparisons. Examiner required. Not suitable for group use.

Untimed: 1 hour, 30 minutes

Scoring: Computer scored

Cost: Complete kit (manual, 25 student response forms, 25 profile/examiner record forms, student booklet, storage box) $69.00; PRO-SCORE scoring system $69.00

Publisher: PRO-ED

DIFFERENTIAL APTITUDE TEST BATTERY
Manjula Mukerjee

Child, adolescent—Ages 11–13

Purpose: Identifies specific areas of students' academic aptitude.

Description: 547-item paper-pencil test consisting of seven subtests measuring aptitude in several academic fields. The subtests include English Knowledge and Comprehension, Clerical Aptitude I (speed), Clerical Aptitude II, Abstract Reasoning, Verbal Reasoning, Mathematics Knowledge and Comprehension, Scientific Aptitude, and Mechanical Comprehension. The scores from the subtests can be used to predict success in various education fields, such as the humanities, science, and commerce. An eighth-grade reading level is required. Examiner required. Suitable for group use.

PUBLISHED IN INDIA

Timed: 2 hours, 36 minutes

Scoring: Hand key; examiner evaluated

Cost: Contact distributor

Publisher: Manjula Mukerjee; exclusively distributed by Manasayan

---

DIFFERENTIAL APTITUDE TESTS (DAT): FORMS S AND T
G.K. Bennett, H.G. Seashore, and A.G. Wesman

**Adolescent
Grades 8–12**

Purpose: Assesses aptitude. Used for educational and vocational guidance in junior and senior high schools.

Description: Multiple-item paper-pencil test of eight abilities: verbal reasoning, numerical ability, abstract reasoning, clerical speed and accuracy, mechanical reasoning, space relations, spelling, and language usage. A ninth score is obtained by summing the verbal reasoning and numerical ability scores. Materials include two alternate forms, S and T. The Career Planning Questionnaire is optional. Forms S and T have been superseded by Forms V and W and are available only while supplies last. Examiner required. Suitable for group use.

Timed: Complete battery 3 hours or longer

Scoring: Hand key; may be machine scored; may be computer scored

Cost: Specimen set, specify Form S or Form T (test, various answer documents, directions, and norms) $25.00; Career Planning Service Information Packet (counselor's manual, questionnaire, glossary, interpretive report) $15.00

Publisher: The Psychological Corporation

Information and availability unconfirmed; last verified in 1988.

DIFFERENTIAL APTITUDE TESTS (DAT): FORMS V AND W
G.K. Bennett, H.G. Seashore, and A.G. Wesman

**Adolescent
Grades 8–12**

Purpose: Assesses aptitude. Used for educational and vocational guidance in junior and senior high schools.

Description: Multiple-item paper-pencil test of eight abilities: verbal reasoning, numerical ability, abstract reasoning, clerical speed and accuracy, mechanical reasoning, space relations, spelling, and language usage. A ninth score, an index of scholastic ability, is obtained by summing the verbal reasoning and numerical ability scores. Materials include two alternate and equivalent forms, V and W. The Career Planning Questionnaire is optional. Forms V and W supersede Forms S and T. Examiner required. Suitable for group use.

Timed: Complete battery 3 hours or longer

Scoring: Hand key; may be machine scored; may be computer scored

Cost: Specimen set (test, directions, administrator's handbook, MRC and NCS answer documents and sheets NC, list of correct answers, order for scoring service, sample profile forms) $13.00; Career Planning Service Information Packet (counselor's manual, directions, glossary, sample career planning report, explanation of school summary report, MRC answer document with MRC sheet NC, orientation booklet) $10.00

Publisher: The Psychological Corporation

Information and availability unconfirmed; last verified in 1988.

EDUCATIONAL ABILITIES SCALES

Adolescent—Ages 13–15

Purpose: Assesses abilities important to educational achievement. Used for identifying individual pupil strengths and weaknesses.

Description: Multiple-item battery of five pencil-paper tests covering the following abilities: mechanical, spatial, symbolic, scientific process and inference, and clerical speed and accuracy. The student uses a scraper to scratch away coating from answers; immediate feedback concerning accuracy is provided. Equivalent scores are provided for each ability, allowing comparison between different abilities. Examiner required. Suitable for group use.
BRITISH PUBLISHER

Untimed: Clerical Aptitude 20 minutes; other scales 40–45 minutes each

Scoring: Examiner evaluated

Cost: Contact publisher

Publisher: NFER-NELSON Publishing Company Ltd.

EDUCATIONAL DEVELOPMENT SERIES, REVISED 1984 EDITION
O. F. Anderhalter, R. H. Bauernfeind, Mary E. Greig, George Mallinson, Jacqueline Mallinson, Joseph Papenfuss, and Neil Vail

Child, adolescent
Grades K–12

Purpose: Assesses ability, achievement, and career interests of children and adolescents. Used by guidance counselors, teachers, and others for counseling, diagnosis, and instruction.

Description: Multiple-item paper-pencil battery of tests in four formats: Complete Battery, Core Achievement Battery, Basic Skills Battery, and Cognitive and Basic Skills Battery. The Complete Battery (Grades 4–12) contains 11 subtests: Career Interests and School Plans, School Interests, Non-Verbal Cognitive Skills, Verbal Cognitive Skills, Reference Skills, Reading, Language Arts, Mathematics,

Science, and Social Studies. The Core Achievement Battery (Grades 2–12) contains eight subtests: Career Interests and School Plans, School Interests, Reference Skills, Reading, Language Arts, Mathematics, Science, and Social Studies. Skills are assessed with five subtests in the Basic Skills Battery (Grades K–12): Career Interests and School Plans, School Interests, Reading, Language Arts, and Mathematics. The Cognitive and Basic Skills Battery (Grades K–12) contains seven subtests: Career Interests and School Plans, School Interests, Non-Verbal Skills, Verbal Skills, Reading, Language Arts, and Mathematics. The 1984 edition uses a single test level for each grade. Examiner required. Suitable for group use.

Timed: 6 hours or less

Scoring: Hand key; scoring service available

Cost: Specimen set (specify level and form) $12.00

Publisher: Scholastic Testing Service, Inc.

END-OF-COURSE TESTS

Adolescent
High school

Purpose: Assesses the end-of-course knowledge of students who have completed a course in one of several subject areas.

Description: 50–item paper-pencil tests assessing the knowledge students have acquired at the end of a course in any of nine subject areas. The tests are Algebra, Geometry, Physics, Chemistry, Biology, World History, American History, Consumer Economics, and Computer Literacy. A single manual contains administration instructions, norms tables, and scoring keys for all nine tests. Examiner required. Suitable for group use.

Timed: Varies, 40 minutes maximum

Scoring: Hand key

Cost: Multi-Subject Review Kit (manual with answer key, answer sheet, 1 of each test booklet) $14.85

Publisher: CTB/Macmillan/McGraw-Hill

THE ENHANCED ACT ASSESSMENT
The American College Testing Program

Adolescent, adult
Grades 7 and above

Purpose: Assesses the academic achievement of high-school students. The program is a comprehensive system of data collection, processing, and reporting designed to help students and counselors develop postsecondary plans and to help colleges develop instructional programs suited to the needs and characteristics of their applicants.

Description: 215–item paper-pencil assessment consisting of four separately timed sections: English test (45 minutes; 75 items); Mathematics test (60 minutes; 60 items); Reading test (35 minutes; 40 items); Science Reasoning test (35 minutes; 40 items). The student must take all four sections of the test. The test is administered five times each year at designated ACT test centers to college-bound students and is also available at certain college campuses under residual testing. The Enhanced ACT Assessment yields 12 scores: four test scores (scale 1–36), the composite score (scales 1–36), and seven subscores (scale 1–18). Examiner required. Suitable for group use.

Timed: 2 hours, 55 minutes; untimed for handicapped

Scoring: Hand key; may be computer scored

Cost: Basic test fee $11.50, New York $13.50 (includes 3 score reports); additional score reports $3.50 each

Publisher: The American College Testing Program

ERB COMPREHENSIVE TESTING PROGRAM (CTP II)

Child, adolescent

Purpose: Assesses general aptitude and achievement of students.

Description: Five-level multiple-choice test comprised of the following subtests:

Aptitude (Verbal and Quantitative), Vocabulary, Reading, Mechanics of Writing, English Expression, Mathematics Concepts (Levels 3 and 4 only), Mathematics Computation (Levels 3 and 4 only), Algebra (Levels 4 and 5 only), Geometry (Level 5 only), and General Mathematics (Level 5 only). Levels 1 and 2 are appropriate for students in Grades 1 to 3. Levels 3, 4, and 5 are designed for students in Grades 3–12. This is a revised version of the CTP. Available in Forms C and D. Suitable for use with individuals with visual impairments. Readers needed for the visually impaired. Examiner required. Suitable for group use.

Timed: Varies

Untimed: Varies

Scoring: Hand key; machine scored; scoring service available from publisher

Cost: 20 practice test booklets (reusable), set of directions $8.30; 50 practice answer sheets $4.20

Publisher: Educational Records Bureau

GENERAL ABILITY TESTS: NUMERICAL (GAT NUMERICAL)
Refer to page 974.

GENERAL ABILITY TESTS: PERCEPTUAL (GAT PERCEPTUAL)
Refer to page 974.

GENERAL ABILITY TESTS: VERBAL (GAT VERBAL)
Refer to page 975.

GOYER ORGANIZATION OF IDEAS TEST
Robert S. Goyer

Adolescent, adult
Grades 9–adult

Purpose: Measures the ability to organize ideas verbally and to assess an individual's general mental ability. Used to place undergraduates in upper-level courses and to screen students from areas in which they might not succeed.

Description: 30-item paper-pencil multiple-choice test of ability to perceive oral-visual-written stimuli and to analyze and synthesize the ideas selected. The total process applied involves the following identifiable skill categories: component (part-whole) relationships, including dependence-independence, significance-insignificance, and coordination of ideas; sequential relationships, including chronological, cause-to-effect, climax, and topical; material-to-purpose (relevance) relationships, including recognition of central or unifying idea and exclusion of ideas lacking consistency with total group; and transitional (connective) relationships, including use of relational words and phrases based on total pattern of communication. Examiner required. Suitable for group use. Available in Korean.

Untimed: 40–60 minutes

Scoring: Hand key; may be computer scored

Cost: Test booklet $2.00; answer key with normative summary $20.00

Publisher: Robert S. Goyer, Ph.D.

Information and availability unconfirmed; last verified in 1987.

GRADUATE AND MANAGERIAL ASSESSMENT
Psychometric Research Unit, The Hatfield Polytechnic

Adult

Purpose: Assesses numerical, verbal, and abstract reasoning abilities of adults. Used to select graduate-school job candidates and identify management potential of individuals.

Description: Three paper-pencil multiple-choice tests measuring the numerical, verbal, and abstract reasoning abilities of adults. The numerical test, used for recruiting graduates from general disciplines into finance-related occupations, presents realistic problems in commercial context and emphasizes problem-solving strategies rather than computational skills. The verbal test measures the capacity for detached critical appraisal of verbal material and is useful for assessing the ability of general arts graduates to evaluate semi-technical information. The abstract test assesses the flexibility and insight of individuals whose work is analytic, conceptual, and nonroutine. The tests may be used together or separately. Parallel forms are available. Examiner required. Suitable for group use.

BRITISH PUBLISHER

Timed: 30 minutes per test

Scoring: Hand key

Cost: Contact publisher

Publisher: NFER-NELSON Publishing Company Ltd.

GRADUATE MANAGEMENT ADMISSION TEST (GMAT)

Adult
College graduates

Purpose: Measures verbal and quantitative abilities related to success in graduate management schools. Used for admission to graduate management schools.

Description: Paper-pencil multiple-choice test measuring general verbal and quantitative abilities. It does not measure proficiency in undergraduate business or economics courses. The test is administered four times annually at centers established by the publisher, and registration materials are available at no charge. The test is not available for institutional use. Examiner required. Suitable for group use.

Untimed: 4 hours

Scoring: Computer scored

Cost: Contact publisher

Publisher: Educational Testing Service

Information and availability unconfirmed; last verified in 1988.

GRADUATE RECORD EXAMINATIONS (GRE)

Adult
College graduates

Purpose: Measures the academic abilities and knowledge of graduate school applicants. Used by graduate schools for screening the qualifications of applicants and by organizations for selecting fellowship recipients.

Description: Multiple-item paper-pencil multiple-choice battery of advanced achievement and aptitude tests. The General Test measures verbal, quantitative, and analytical abilities. The Subject Tests are available for the following 17 subjects: biology, chemistry, computer science, economics, education, engineering, French, geology, history, literature in English, mathematics, music, physics, political science, psychology, sociology, and Spanish. The tests are administered on specified dates at centers established by the publisher. Examiner required. Suitable for group use.

Timed: General test 3½ hours; subject tests 2 hours, 50 minutes each

Scoring: Computer scored

Cost: Contact publisher

Publisher: Educational Testing Service

Information and availability unconfirmed; last verified in 1988.

GUIDANCE TEST BATTERY FOR SECONDARY PUPILS (GBS)

Adolescent

Purpose: Measures scholastic achievement. Used for educational guidance.

Description: Paper-pencil test of pupils' proficiency in English, Afrikaans, Mathematics, Nonverbal Reasoning, and Verbal Reasoning. Two forms, A and B, are available. Suitable for group use. The test publisher notes that this test is "normed on Blacks only." Examiner required.
SOUTH AFRICAN PUBLISHER

Timed: 3½ hours

Scoring: Hand key; examiner evaluated; may be machine scored

Cost: (In Rands) test (A or B) 2,00 each; instructions and norms 1,70; scoring stencil 2,50; 10 answer sheets (machine and hand scoring) 2,00; manual 10,00; orders from outside the RSA will be dealt with on merit

Publisher: Human Sciences Research Council

HENMON-NELSON TEST OF MENTAL ABILITY (CANADIAN EDITION)
M. J. Nelson, Tom Lamke, and Joseph French

**Child, adolescent
Grades 3–12**

Purpose: Assesses students' academic aptitude.

Description: Series of paper-pencil multiple-choice subtests that test students' academic aptitude. This is a revision of the Henmon-Nelson Test of Mental Ability, Form 1 published by The Riverside Publishing Company (1973). Materials include test booklets, answer sheets, and record sheets. Examiner must have a teacher certificate. Examiner required. Suitable for group use.
CANADIAN PUBLISHER

Timed: 30 minutes

Scoring: Self-scored; hand key; scoring service available from publisher

Cost: Contact publisher

Publisher: Nelson Canada

HIGH LEVEL BATTERY B/75

Adult

Purpose: Assesses educational abilities of older students. Used with individuals entering college or higher.

Description: Multiple-item paper-pencil multiple-choice tests of academic abilities. The six tests are Mental Alertness, Language Ability in English and Afrikaans, Reading Comprehension, Vocabulary, Spelling, and Arithmetic. Examiner required. Suitable for group use.
SOUTH AFRICAN PUBLISHER

Timed: 1 hour, 53 minutes

Scoring: Hand key

Cost: (In Rands) booklet 13,20; 25 answer sheets 4,10; key 13,50; manual 16,30

Publisher: National Institute for Personnel Research

HUDSON EDUCATION SKILLS INVENTORY (HESI)

Floyd G. Hudson, Steven E. Colson, Doris L. Hudson Welch, Alison K. Banikowski, and Teresa A. Mehring

Child, adolescent
Grades K–12

Purpose: Assesses basic education skills, including mathematics, reading, and writing. Used to plan instruction for students with dysfunctional learning patterns.

Description: Multiple-item curriculum-based series of three separate tests for assessing mathematics, reading, and writing skills. (See separate entries on each test.) Each of the three curriculum skills tests is divided into specific subskills. A Student Book containing problems and items that require a visual stimulus is used to evoke the student's responses. The series is based on the Test-Down/Teach-Up model in which the examiner ends the test at the student's actual level of performance. Once the student's level of performance has been established, the teacher "teaches up" the Curriculum Skills Sequence. The series, which complies with assessment guidelines in PL 94–142, is designed so that all or only one of the tests may be administered as needed for planning instruction, selecting IEP goals and objectives, or measuring progress in a particular skill area.

The Examiner's Manual includes sample items and the Curriculum Skills Sequence. The Instructional Planning Form provides a detailed format for recording and monitoring assessment and instructional planning decisions. An optional software report system operating on Apple and IBM PC systems generates two report forms. The first, based on examiners' input about the students being tested, provides a report that indicates where testing should begin. The second form is the Instructional Planning Form described previously. Examiner required. Suitable for group use.

Untimed: Not available

Scoring: Computer scored

Cost: Complete HESI battery (1 each of complete Math, Reading, and Writing kits) $169.00

Publisher: PRO-ED

HUDSON EDUCATION SKILLS INVENTORY-MATHEMATICS (HESI-M)

Floyd G. Hudson, Steven E. Colson, Doris L. Hudson Welch, Alison K. Banikowski, and Teresa A. Mehring

Child, adolescent
Grades K–12

Purpose: Assesses students' mathematical skills. Used to plan instruction for students with dysfunctional learning patterns.

Description: Multiple-item curriculum-based test assessing mathematical skills, including numeration, addition, subtraction, multiplication, division, fractions, decimals, percentages, time, money, measurement, statistics, graphs, tables, geometry, and word problems. A Student Book containing problems and items that require a visual stimulus is used to evoke the student's responses. The test is based on the Test-Down/Teach-Up model in which the examiner ends the test at the student's actual level of performance. Once the student's level of performance has been established, the teacher "teaches up" the Curriculum Skills Sequence.

The Examiner's Manual includes sample items and the Curriculum Skills Sequence. The Instructional Planning Form provides a detailed format for recording and monitoring assessment and instructional planning decisions. An optional software report system operating on Apple and IBM PC systems generates two report forms. The first, based on examiners' input about the students being tested, provides a report that indicates where testing should begin. The second form is the Instructional Planning Form described previously. The test is one in a series assessing basic education skills. Other tests in the series assess reading and writing skills. (See separate entries on each test.) Examiner required. Suitable for group use.

Untimed: Not available

Scoring: Computer scored

Cost: Complete kit (examiner's manual, student book, 25 instructional planning forms) $59.00

Publisher: PRO-ED

Cost: Complete kit (examiner's manual, student book, 25 instructional planning forms) $59.00

Publisher: PRO-ED

HUDSON EDUCATION SKILLS INVENTORY-READING (HESI-R)
Floyd G. Hudson, Steven E. Colson, Doris L. Hudson Welch, Alison K. Banikowski, and Teresa A. Mehring

Child, adolescent
Grades K–12

Purpose: Assesses students' reading skills. Used to plan instruction for students with dysfunctional learning patterns.

Description: Multiple-item curriculum-based test assessing reading skills, including readiness, sight word vocabulary, phonic analysis, structural analysis, and comprehension. A Student Book containing problems and items that require a visual stimulus is used to evoke the student's responses. The test is based on the Test-Down/Teach-Up model in which the examiner ends the test at the student's actual level of performance. Once the student's level of performance has been established, the teacher "teaches up" the Curriculum Skills Sequence.

The Examiner's Manual includes sample items and the Curriculum Skills Sequence. The Instructional Planning Form provides a detailed format for recording and monitoring assessment and instructional planning decisions. An optional software report system operating on Apple and IBM PC systems generates two report forms. The first, based on examiners' input about the students being tested, provides a report that indicates where testing should begin. The second form is the Instructional Planning Form described previously. The test is one in a series assessing basic education skills. Other tests in the series assess mathematics and writing skills. (See separate entries on each test.) Examiner required. Suitable for group use.

Untimed: Not available

Scoring: Computer scored

HUDSON EDUCATION SKILLS INVENTORY-WRITING (HESI-W)
Floyd G. Hudson, Steven E. Colson, Doris L. Hudson Welch, Alison K. Banikowski, and Teresa A. Mehring

Child, adolescent
Grades K–12

Purpose: Assesses students' writing skills. Used to plan instruction for students with dysfunctional learning patterns.

Description: Multiple-item curriculum-based test assessing writing skills, including composition, spelling, and handwriting. A Student Book containing problems and items that require a visual stimulus is used to evoke the student's responses. The test is based on the Test-Down/Teach-Up model in which the examiner ends the test at the student's actual level of performance. Once the student's level of performance has been established, the teacher "teaches up" the Curriculum Skills Sequence.

The Examiner's Manual includes sample items and the Curriculum Skills Sequence. The Instructional Planning Form provides a detailed format for recording and monitoring assessment and instructional planning decisions. An optional software report system operating on Apple and IBM PC systems generates two report forms. The first, based on examiners' input about the students being tested, provides a report that indicates where testing should begin. The second form is the Instructional Planning Form described previously. The test is one in a series assessing basic education skills. Other tests in the series assess mathematics and reading skills. (See separate entries on each test.) Examiner required. Suitable for group use.

Untimed: Not available

Scoring: Computer scored

Cost: Complete kit (examiner's manual, student book, 25 instructional planning forms) $59.00

Publisher: PRO-ED

IDENTI-FORM: IDENTIFICATION, ASSESSMENT, AND BEYOND
Refer to page 624.

INDIVIDUALIZED CRITERION REFERENCED TESTING (ICRT)

Child

Purpose: Measures student progress and achievement against a specific set of objectives in reading and mathematics. Measures student mastery of specific skills. Used for program planning, instructional management, and program assessment.

Description: 718–item paper-pencil test assessing student skills in math and reading. The reading test (304 objectives) measures skills in the following areas: phonetic analysis, structural analysis, word function skills, and comprehension. Items are arranged in 38 color-coded test booklets divided into eight levels. The mathematics test (384 objectives) measures knowledge of whole number operations, fractions, measurement, geometry, decimals/percent, and special topics. Items are arranged in 51 test booklets divided into nine levels. The tests measure the students' mastery or lack of mastery for each skill or concept tested. Placement tests and procedures are provided for both reading and math to insure that students are tested at a level compatible with their abilities. These placement tests indicate which five reading tests and which five mathematics tests should be administered for the actual testing.

Three computer reports are provided. The student report identifies for each student which skills have been mastered, which skills need review, and which skills should be attempted next. Individual student records are kept in separate student profile folders for reading and mathematics. A teacher report and an administrative report are available. Benchmark tests also are provided for interim assessment of student progress. Objective-by-objec-

tive correlations are also provided for more than 275 reading materials and more than 130 mathematics materials. Examiner required. Suitable for group use.

Untimed: Varies

Scoring: Placement tests examiner evaluated; ICRT tests computer scored

Cost: Contact publisher

Publisher: Educational Development Corporation

INITIAL EVALUATION TESTS IN ENGLISH AND MATHEMATICS

Child, adolescent

Purpose: Measures achievement in English and math. Used for educational evaluation at the beginning of a new standard.

Description: Nine tests measuring achievement in English and mathematics. Initial Evaluation Tests in English are available at Standards 5 and 8. Seven Initial Evaluation Tests in Mathematics are available for Standards 1 to 7. Two alternate forms, A and B, are available for each of the nine tests. Tests should be administered as soon as possible after the beginning of the school year. Examiner required. Suitable for group use.

SOUTH AFRICAN PUBLISHER

Untimed: Not available

Scoring: Hand key; examiner evaluated

Cost: Contact publisher; orders from outside the RSA will be dealt with on merit

Publisher: Human Sciences Research Council

INTER-AMERICAN SERIES
Refer to page 576.

INTER-AMERICAN SERIES: TEST OF GENERAL ABILITY
Herschel T. Manuel

Ages 4–18
Grades PreK–12

Purpose: Assesses general educational abilities and achievement of students and adults enrolled in continuing education programs. Used for the individualization of instruction, the education of exceptional children, educational and vocational counseling, bilingual instruction and instruction in English or Spanish as a second language, basic and applied research, and entry and exit decision making regarding students in bilingual education programs.

Description: Multiple-item criterion-referenced paper-pencil test assessing general language and numerical abilities. Item formats are multiple-choice, short answer, true-false, and oral-response. The test is available on six levels. The Preschool level (80 items; PreK-K) assesses oral vocabulary, numerical reasoning, association, classification, and language dominance. Level 1 (80 items; Grades K-1) assesses oral vocabulary, verbal and numerical reasoning, association, classification, and language dominance. Level 2 (100 items; Grades 2-3) measures oral vocabulary, verbal and numerical reasoning, analogies, and classification. Levels 3 (Grades 4-6), 4 (Grades 7-9), and 5 (Grades 10-12) each contain 150 items covering sentence completion, analogies, computation, word relations, classification, and number series. Each level is available in parallel English and Spanish versions. The test is available in pre- and post-test forms to allow tracking of progress over a selected period of time. One of five tests in the Inter-American Series. Examiner required. Suitable for group use.

Untimed: Preschool varies

Timed: Level 1 25 minutes; Level 2 45 minutes; Levels 3-5 52 minutes

Scoring: Hand key

Cost: Contact publisher

Publisher: Guidance Testing Associates

Information and availability unconfirmed; last verified in 1988.

INTER-AMERICAN SERIES: TEST OF READING AND NUMBER
Herschel T. Manuel

Child—Ages 9–14
Grades 3–4

Purpose: Estimates achievement in reading and numerical operations. Used for placement.

Description: 100–item criterion-referenced paper-pencil test measuring achievement in reading and numerical operations. The test is available in parallel English and Spanish forms. Pre- and post-test forms are available to allow tracking of progress over a selected period of time. One of five tests in the Inter-American Series. Examiner required. Suitable for group use.

Timed: 34 minutes

Scoring: Hand key

Cost: Contact publisher

Publisher: Guidance Testing Associates

Information and availability unconfirmed; last verified in 1988.

INTERMEDIATE BATTERY B/77

Adult

Purpose: Assesses academic achievement and clerical aptitudes of individuals who have 10–12 years of schooling.

Description: Multiple-item paper-pencil set of seven subtests, six of which are similar to those in the High Level Battery (mental alertness, English, reading comprehension, vocabulary, spelling, and arithmetic). This battery does not include the Afrikaans reading comprehension, vocabulary, and spelling tests. However, it does include a clerical perception test. Examiner required. Suitable for group use.

SOUTH AFRICAN PUBLISHER

Timed: 2 hours, 45 minutes

Scoring: Hand key

Cost: (In Rands) booklet 13,20; 25 answer sheets 4,10; set of keys 13,50; manual 16,30

Publisher: National Institute for Personnel Research

IOWA TESTS OF BASIC SKILLS®, FORMS 7 AND 8 (ITBS®)
A. N. Hieronymus, E. F. Lindquist, and H.D. Hoover

Child, adolescent
Grades K–9

Purpose: Assesses the development of students' basic academic skills. Identifies strengths and weaknesses in basic academic skills and evaluates the effectiveness of instructional programs.

Description: Multiple-choice paper-pencil tests assessing proficiency in the basic skills required for academic success. The tests are organized into 10 levels. The Primary Battery (Levels 5–8) is used with students in Grades K–3. The Multilevel Edition/Separate Level Editions (Levels 9–14) are designed for students in Grades 3–9. All 10 levels assess combinations of the following skills: vocabulary, reading, language (spelling, capitalization, punctuation, language usage), work-study (visual materials, reference materials), and mathematics (concepts, problem solving, and computation). Listening and word analysis are also measured at the primary level. A separate Social Studies/Science supplement is available for Grades 3–9. The Early Primary Battery (Levels 5–6) is available only in a Basic Battery. The Primary Battery (Levels 7–8) and the Multilevel Edition (Levels 9–14) are available in a Basic Battery and a Complete Battery. The ITBS Forms 7 and 8 were normed concurrently with Form 3 of the Cognitive Abilities Test™ for reliable comparisons between attained and expected achievement scores. The Primary batteries use machine-scorable test booklets, and the Multilevel/Separate Level Editions use test booklets and separate answer sheets. Examiner required. Suitable for group use.

Timed: Multilevel/Separate Level Editions Basic Battery 139 minutes; Complete Battery 244 minutes

Untimed: Primary batteries 115–235 minutes, depending on form and level

Scoring: Hand key; may be machine scored (MRC or NCS)

Cost: 25 Level 5 MRC machine-scorable test booklets $51.00; 25 Level 6 MRC machine-scorable test booklets $59.10; 25 Level 7 or 8 Complete Battery MRC machine-scorable test booklets $66.96 per level; 25 Level 7 or 8 Basic Battery MRC machine-scorable test booklets, Teacher's Guide $59.10; Multilevel Edition Complete Battery $6.00; Basic Battery $4.65; 35 Social Studies/Science test booklets

$39.00; 35 Separate Level test booklets (specify level) $2.25 each; 35 MRC answer sheets, Teacher's Guide, $24.90 per level; Teacher's Guide $9.75

Publisher: The Riverside Publishing Company

IOWA TESTS OF BASIC SKILLS®, FORMS G, H, AND J (ITBS®)
A.N. Hieronymus, H.D. Hoover, and E.F. Lindquist

**Child, adolescent
Grades K–9**

Purpose: Assesses the development of basic academic skills. Identifies individual students' strengths and weaknesses and evaluates the effectiveness of instructional programs.

Description: Paper-pencil multiple-choice tests assessing proficiency in the basic skills required for academic success. The Multilevel/Separate Level Editions (Grades 3–9) measure the following skill areas at each level: vocabulary, reading, language, work study, and mathematics. Schools can track listening skills through junior high school and offer paper-pencil generative writing assessments for Grades 3–8. The Early Primary (Levels 5–6) and Primary (Levels 7–8) batteries (Grades K–3.5) include tests in listening, vocabulary, reading (except for Level 5), word analysis, language, and mathematics. The Primary Battery (Grades 1.7–3.5) also contains a work-study test. The Complete Battery Plus Social Studies and Science for Levels 7 and 8 contains all of the Complete Battery tests as well as tests in social studies and science. The tests were normed concurrently with Form 4 of the Cognitive Abilities Test™ for reliable comparisons between attained and expected achievement scores. All test levels (except Levels 5 and 6) are available in a Complete Battery and a Basic Battery. Examiner required. Suitable for group use.

Timed: Complete Battery 4 hours, 16 minutes; Basic Battery 2 hours, 15 minutes

Untimed: Primary batteries 115–326 minutes, depending on form and level

Scoring: Hand key; may be machine scored (MRC or NCS)

Cost: 35 Level 5 MRC machine-scorable test booklets $55.95; 35 Level 6 MRC machine-scorable test booklets $64.65; 35 Level 7 or 8 Complete Battery MRC machine-scorable test booklets $70.95; 35 MRC Basic Battery booklets for Level 7 or 8, Teacher's Guide $64.65; 35 Complete Battery Plus Social Studies and Science MRC machine-scorable test booklets $86.25; Multilevel Complete Battery test booklet $4.95; Multilevel Basic Battery test booklet $3.90; 35 Separate Level Complete Battery test booklets (specify level) $68.75; 35 MRC answer sheets, Teacher's Guide (specify level) $21.30; Teacher's Guide $8.40; Manual for School Administrators $21.00; contact publisher for Form J prices

Publisher: The Riverside Publishing Company

IOWA TESTS OF EDUCATIONAL DEVELOPMENT®, FORMS X-8 AND Y-8 (ITED®)
Leonard S. Feldt and
Robert A. Forsyth

Adolescent
Grades 9–12

Purpose: Assesses the intellectual skills that are important in adult life and provide the foundation for continued learning.

Description: 361–item paper-pencil battery of seven tests: Correctness and Appropriateness of Expression (Test E; Part 1, 54 items; Part 2, 15 items), Ability to Do Quantitative Thinking (Test Q; 40 items), Analysis of Social Studies Materials (Test SS; Part 1, 24 items; Part 2, 36 items), Analysis of Natural Science Materials (Test NS; Part 1, 24 items; Part 2, 36 items), Ability to Interpret Literary Materials (Test L; 46 items), Vocabulary (Test V; 40 items), and Use of Sources of Information (Test SI; 46 items). Scores for each of the seven tests, a composite score, and a reading total score are reported. Standard scores, national percentile ranks, local percentile ranks, stanines, and and a number of special norms are available for all nine scores. The battery is organized into two levels, Level I (Grades 9–10) and Level II (Grades 11–12). Both levels are

available in parallel Forms X–8 and Y–8. Examiner required. Suitable for group use.

Timed: 4 hours, 10 minutes

Scoring: Hand key; may be machine scored

Cost: 25 test booklets, Directions for Administration $49.80; 50 MRC answer sheets $17.70; Teacher, Administrator, and Counselor Manual $5.40; Norms Booklet $6.60

Publisher: The Riverside Publishing Company

JUNIOR APTITUDE TESTS (JAT)

Child, adolescent

Purpose: Measures scholastic aptitude. Used for educational counseling.

Description: Multiple-item paper-pencil test measuring specific scholastic aptitudes: classification, reasoning, number ability, synonyms, comparison, spatial (2D), spatial (3D), memory (paragraph), memory (words and symbols), and mechanical insight. Examiner required. Suitable for group use.
SOUTH AFRICAN PUBLISHER

Untimed: 2 hours, 45 minutes

Scoring: Hand key; examiner evaluated; may be machine scored

Cost: (In Rands) test booklet 3,00; 10 answer sheets (T1–T6), 1,00; 10 answer sheets (T7–T10) 1,00; scoring stencil for 1224 3,00; scoring stencil for 1225 5,50; manual 7,00; 10 machine answer sheets 2,00; orders from outside The RSA will be dealt with on merit

Publisher: Human Sciences Research Council

KAUFMAN TEST OF EDUCATIONAL ACHIEVEMENT (K-TEA)
Alan S. Kaufman and
Nadeen L. Kaufman

Child, adolescent
Grades 1–12

Purpose: Assesses educational achievement of students ages 6–18. Used for educational planning by school and clinical psychologists, educational diagnosticians, learning disabilities specialists, remedial reading teachers, counselors, and other specialists.

Description: Multiple-item oral-response paper-pencil test in two forms. The Brief Form measures global achievement in reading, mathematics, and spelling. The 52–item reading subtest assesses decoding of printed words and comprehension. The 52–item mathematics subtest measures basic arithmetic concepts, applications of mathematical principles to real-life situations, numerical reasoning, and simple and advanced computation skills. The 40–item spelling dictation subtest assesses ability using a steeply graded word list.

The Comprehensive Form provides a more thorough assessment of achievement through five subtests. The 60–item mathematics/applications subtest measures a wide variety of arithmetic concepts and extensive applications of mathematical principles and reasoning skills to real-life situations. The 60–item reading/decoding subtest measures the ability to identify letters and pronounce words of gradually increasing phonetic and non-phonetic difficulty. The 60–item spelling dictation subtest assesses ability using an increasingly difficult word list. The 50–item reading/comprehension subtest assesses literal and inferential comprehension. The 60–item mathematics/computation subtest assesses written computation skills, including the four basic operations and more complex computational abilities such as algebra.

Derived scores are age and grade standard scores (separate fall and spring norms), percentile ranks, stanines, and age and grade equivalents. Normal curve equivalent scores for Chapter 1 programs are available for Grades 1–12. The Error Analysis on the Comprehensive Form allows for identification of content area skill strengths and weaknesses. Examiner required. Not suitable for group use.

Timed: Brief form 20–30 minutes; comprehensive form 30–60 minutes

Scoring: Hand key; computer scored

Cost: Brief Form kit, regular edition (77 test plates in easel, manual, 25 record booklets, Report to Parents, shelf storage box) $59.00; Comprehensive form kit, regular edition (133 test plates in easel, manual, 25 record booklets, Report to Parents, shelf storage box) $99.00

Publisher: American Guidance Service

KUHLMANN ANDERSON TESTS (KA), 8TH EDITION
F. Kuhlmann and Rose Anderson

Child, adolescent
Grades K–12

Purpose: Evaluates students' academic ability and potential. Used for group placement and diagnosing individual learning abilities.

Description: 80– to 130–item paper-pencil test assessing academic potential. The test is available in eight booklets: K (Kindergarten), A (Grade 1), BC (Grades 2–3), CD (Grades 3–4), EF (Grades 5–7), G (Grades 7–9), and H (Grades 9–12). The test yields mental age, deviation IQ, grade percentile rank, IQ percentile rank, stanine, and separate verbal and quantitative grade percentile scores. Norms are based on a large national sampling of socioeconomic, ethnic, and social diversity. Only STS answer sheets may be machine scored. Examiner required. Suitable for group use.

Timed: 50–75 minutes

Scoring: Hand key; may be computer scored

Cost: 20 booklets $11.00–$17.60; 50 answer sheets $12.50; specimen set (specify level) $10.00

Publisher: Scholastic Testing Service, Inc.

LAW SCHOOL ADMISSION TEST (LSAT)

Adult
College students,
postgraduates

Purpose: Evaluates an individual's ability to undertake first-year law school work. Used with law school applicants.

Description: 100– to 120–item paper-pencil multiple-choice and writing test divided into six sections of four item types: Logical Reasoning (25–27 items; 35 minutes), Issues and Facts (40 items; 35 minutes), Analytical Reasoning (23–25 items; 35 minutes), and Reading Comprehension (27–29 items; 35 minutes).

academic achievement and aptitude

The Logical Reasoning section assesses the ability to recognize the point of an argument, perceive presuppositions supporting an argument, draw conclusions, infer missing material, apply principles that govern one argument to another argument, identify methods of argument or persuasion, evaluate arguments, differentiate between fact and opinion, analyze evidence, and assess claims critically. The Issues and Facts section measures the ability to work and reason with facts and rules. The Analytical Reasoning section presents the examinee with a set of several related conditions that describe a structure of relationships followed by at least five questions that test the examinee's understanding of that structure's implications. The Reading Comprehension section measures the examinee's ability to read with understanding and insight and to analyze written passages. A 30–minute, unscored Writing Sample is also part of the test. The test is available in large print and is suitable for use with physically, visually, and hearing-impaired individuals. Examiner required. Suitable for group use.

Timed: 3 hours, 30 minutes

Scoring: Machine scored

Cost: Contact publisher

Publisher: Law School Admission Council/Law School Admission Services

Information and availability unconfirmed; last verified in 1988.

LIFE SKILLS: FORMS 1 AND 2
Kenneth Majer and Dena C. Wadell

Adolescent
Grades 9–12

Purpose: Assesses student and group competency in basic reading and mathematics skills.

Description: Two multiple-item paper-pencil subtests measuring functional competencies in reading and mathematics. The Reading Test includes four objectives measuring the ability to follow directions (labels, signs); three objectives measuring locating and understanding references (phone books, catalogs); five objectives measuring interpretation and use of information (want ads, lease agreements); and

two objectives measuring the understanding of forms (taxes, installment purchases). The Mathematics Test objectives require the student to compute basic consumer problems; apply principles of percent, interest, and fractions; identify, estimate, and convert time, currency, and measurements; and interpret graphs, charts, and statistics. The manual includes test administration procedures, scoring, and basic technical data. The technical supplement provides comprehensive information. Two test forms, 1 and 2, are available for pretest-posttest experimental studies. Examiner required. Suitable for group use.

Timed: Reading test 40 minutes; mathematics test 40 minutes

Scoring: Examiner evaluated; may be computer scored

Cost: 35 test booklets (specify form) $55.32; 35 self-mark answer sheets $31.62; 35 MRC answer sheets $23.73; manual $4.20; technical supplement $16.95; examination kit (both test booklets, manual) $4.50

Publisher: The Riverside Publishing Company

METROPOLITAN ACHIEVEMENT TESTS: 5TH EDITION—SURVEY BATTERY
Irving H. Balow, Roger Farr, Thomas P. Hogan, and George A. Prescott

Child, adolescent
Grades K–12.9

Purpose: Assesses school achievement. Used for measuring performance of large groups of students.

Description: Multiple-item paper-pencil tests of school achievement divided into eight levels: Preprimer (Grade K.0–K.5), Primer (Grades K.5–1.4), Primary 1 (Grades 1.5–2.4), Primary 2 (Grades 2.5–3.4), Elementary (Grades 3.5–4.9), Intermediate (Grades 5.0–6.9), Advanced 1 (Grades 7.0–9.9), and Advanced 2 (Grades 10.0–12.9). The Basic Battery for all eight levels consists of tests in reading comprehension, mathematics, and language. The Complete Battery for the Primary 1 through the Advanced 1 levels also include social science and science tests. Materials include two alternate and equivalent forms, JS and KS. The Metropolitan instructional tests in reading, mathematics, and language provide more in-depth analyses than the Survey Battery. Examiner required. Suitable for group use.

Timed: Varies

Scoring: Hand key; may be machine scored; scoring service available

Cost: Specimen sets, specify level (test, manual) $17.00; the Preprimer set includes a practice test and directions, and the Intermediate and Advanced 1 and 2 sets include a hand-scorable answer document

Publisher: The Psychological Corporation

Information and availability unconfirmed; last verified in 1988.

METROPOLITAN ACHIEVEMENT TESTS: 6TH EDITION—SURVEY BATTERY

George A. Prescott, Irving H. Balow, Thomas P. Hogan, and Roger C. Farr

---

Child, adolescent
Grades K–12

Purpose: Assesses school achievement. Used for measuring performances of large groups of students.

Description: Multiple-item paper-pencil tests of school achievement divided into eight levels: Preprimer (Grades K.0–K.9), Primer (Grades K.5–1.9), Primary 1 (Grades 1.5–2.9), Primary 2 (Grades 2.5–3.9), Elementary (Grades 3.5–4.9), Intermediate (Grades 5.0–6.9), Advanced 1 (Grades 7.0–9.9), and Advanced 2 (Grades 10.0–12.9). The Basic Battery for all eight levels consists of tests in reading, mathematics, and language. The Complete Battery for the Primary 1 level through the Advanced 2 level also assesses social science and science. Research skills are measured at the Elementary level through the Advanced 2 level. The Metropolitan Reading, Mathematics, and Language Instructional tests provide more in-depth analyses than the Survey Battery. Examiner required. Suitable for group use.

Timed: Varies according to level

Scoring: Hand key; machine scoring available

Cost: Examination kit $15.00

Publisher: The Psychological Corporation

Information and availability unconfirmed; last verified in 1988.

METROPOLITAN LANGUAGE INSTRUCTIONAL TESTS

Refer to page 291.

METROPOLITAN MATHEMATICS INSTRUCTIONAL TESTS

Refer to page 322.

METROPOLITAN READINESS TESTS: FIFTH EDITION (MRT)

Refer to page 553.

MILL HILL VOCABULARY SCALE

J.C. Raven

Adolescent, adult—
Ages 6–adult

Purpose: Measures an individual's ability to recall information and state it verbally. Used for diagnosis, counseling, and school placement.

Description: Multiple-item paper-pencil vocabulary test consisting of two sets of words. In most common forms of the test, half the words are in multiple-choice format and half are in open-ended format. The scale can be used with an appropriate level of the Progressive Matrices Test. U.S. versions, with U.S. norms, are available. Materials include an expendable test booklet, a specimen set, and a manual. Examiner required. Suitable for group use.

BRITISH PUBLISHER

Untimed: 15 minutes

Scoring: Hand key; may be computer scored

Cost: 50 record forms £9.00; Section 5A of manual £3.20

Publisher: H.K. Lewis & Co., Ltd.; distributed in U.S.A. by The Psychological Corporation

Information and availability unconfirmed; last verified in 1988.

MINIMUM ESSENTIALS TEST (MET)
*William K. Rice, Jr.,
Thomas R. Guskey,
Carole Lachman Perlman, and
Marion F. Rice*

Adolescent, adult
Grades 8 and above

Purpose: Measures minimum basic academic skills. Used as a minimum competency test or as a final examination for basic essentials courses.

Description: 124-item paper-pencil test of basic skills in reading, language, and mathematics. The test provides information about students' ability to apply basic skills to life situations. An optional writing test requiring students to write a paragraph based on a given cartoon depiction is included. The academic and life skills sections may be used independently. Standards of acceptable performance are determined by local district. Examiner required. Suitable for group use.

Timed: Basic academic skills 45 minutes; basic life skills 45 minutes; writing sample 20 minutes

Scoring: Hand key; may be computer scored

Cost: 35 test booklets $32.35; 35 answer sheets $10.10; manual $5.60; key $1.70; directions for administration $2.70; norms booklet $5.65

Publisher: American Testronics

MONITORING BASIC SKILLS PROGRESS
*Lynn S. Fuchs, Carol Hamlett, and
Douglass Fuchs*

Child

Purpose: Monitors progress in three academic areas: basic reading, basic math, and basic spelling.

Description: Computer-assisted measurement series of three separate disks that test and monitor progress in basic reading, basic math, and basic spelling. With Basic Reading, students are routinely tested at the computer on instructional-level reading material using a multiple-choice cloze procedure. With Basic Math, students are periodically tested at the computer on a different alternate test that includes each problem type to be taught during the school year. With Basic Spelling, students' spelling proficiency is assessed by having them type words in the computer from a year-long curriculum. The computer generates and administers the tests and automatically scores the students' performance during administration. The computer shows students the results of the testing and provides a graph of scores over time. The complete MBSP program includes one each of Basic Reading, Basic Math, and Basic Spelling. Available for use with an Apple II family computer with 64K. Self-adminstered. Not suitable for group use.

Untimed: Varies

Scoring: Computer scored

Cost: Complete kit $249.00

Publisher: PRO-ED

MORAY HOUSE TESTS

Child, adolescent—Ages
7.3–14

Purpose: Assesses academic aptitude by measuring mathematic, English language, and verbal reasoning skills.

Description: 10 paper-pencil tests measuring mathematics, English, and verbal reasoning abilities at a number of different levels. Two tests cover mathematical reasoning and arithmetic computation. Achievement is effectively measured whether the children are taught by old or new methods.

Two tests measure the following English language skills: vocabulary, punctuation, semantics, syntax, and general comprehension of prose and poetry. The eight Verbal Reasoning Tests relate less directly to current attainment and schooling than the English and mathematics tests and as such have a semipredictive function. The MHT (Junior) 6 and 7 (ages 8.6–10.6), the MHT 82, 85, 86, 87, 88, and 89 (ages 10–12), the MHT 12/1 (ages 11–13), the MHT (Advanced) 10 (ages 12–14), and the MHT (Adult) 1 (ages 13.6–17.6) are standardized.

Normative data are available for all the tests but are derived from smaller samples (usually a single LEA) in the case of the unstandardized tests. The tests are available to schools with the permission of the local Chief Education Officer. Examiner required. Suitable for group use.
BRITISH PUBLISHER
Untimed: 45 minutes per test
Scoring: Examiner evaluated
Cost: 20 copies (specify test) £7.95–£10.25; contact publisher for further information
Publisher: Hodder & Stoughton

MULTILEVEL ACADEMIC SKILLS INVENTORY: MATH PROGRAM (MASI)
Refer to page 324.

MULTILEVEL ACADEMIC SKILLS INVENTORY: READING PROGRAM (MASI)
Refer to page 349.

MULTILEVEL ACADEMIC SURVEY TEST: CURRICULUM LEVEL TEST (MAST)
*Kenneth W. Howell,
Stanley H. Zucker, and
Mada Kay Morehead*

Child, adolescent
Grades K–12

Purpose: Identifies students' specific strengths and weaknesses in reading and mathematics skills.

Description: Multiple-item paper-pencil and oral reading test providing teachers with specific recommendations for additional testing, instruction, or progression to higher-level content in reading and mathematics. The reading portion includes oral reading (decoding) and silent reading (vocabulary and comprehension) on eight levels of graded passages. The

mathematics portion includes addition, subtraction, multiplication, and division of whole numbers, fractions, decimals, ratios, and proportions. This test complements the normative information obtained from the MAST Grade Level Test. Examiner required. Not suitable for group use.
Untimed: 10–30 minutes per subject
Scoring: Hand key
Cost: Specimen set (examiner's manual, grade level test booklet, curriculum level record form, answer sheet) $30.00
Publisher: The Psychological Corporation
Information and availability unconfirmed; last verified in 1988.

MULTILEVEL ACADEMIC SURVEY TEST: GRADE LEVEL TEST (MAST)
*Kenneth W. Howell,
Stanley H. Zucker, and
Mada Kay Morehead*

Child, adolescent
Grades K–12

Purpose: Assesses overall grade-level performance in mathematics and reading. Used by teachers, school psychologists, educational diagnosticians, and special education teachers.

Description: Multiple-item paper-pencil test of mathematics and reading performance available in a primary form for Grades K–2 and a short form and extended form for Grades 3–12. The test is standardized on a representative national sample and used primarily with students in Grades K–8 and high-school students with performance deficits reflecting inadequate skills. Two types of normed scores are reported: within-group norms and across-group norms. The within-group norms represent one-year age intervals from 5.0–17.0 and separate grade norms from K–12. Both age and grade norms tables include standard scores, percentile ranks, stanines, and normal curve equivalents. The across-grade norms are expressed as grade equivalents from K.1–12.9. Examiner required. Suitable for group use.
Untimed: 30 or 60 minutes, depending on form used

Scoring: Self-scored

Cost: Specimen set (examiner's manual, grade level test booklet, curriculum level record form, answer sheet) $30.00

Publisher: The Psychological Corporation

Information and availability unconfirmed; last verified in 1988.

MULTISCORE
The Riverside Publishing Company Staff and Consultants

Grades 1 and above

Purpose: Measures student proficiency in basic academic skills and the effectiveness of curricula and teaching materials. May be used as a minimum competency examination, as an exit test for measuring end-of-year proficiencies, and as a pretest or posttest for federal programs or other special projects.

Description: Customized paper-pencil multiple-choice test development service providing criterion-referenced assessment of reading, language arts, mathematics, science, social studies, and/or life skills. Educators may create their own customized criterion-referenced test booklets from a pool of over 5,500 items. Catalogs of instructional objectives allow educators to select the objectives most important to their schools. Educators also may choose the number of items (one, two, or three) to be used for testing each objective. Test booklets may be created to test one or more subject areas of one or more grade levels. Reusable test booklets and consumable machine-scorable booklets are available. Examiner required. Suitable for group use.

Untimed: Varies

Scoring: Hand key; may be machine scored; scoring service available

Cost: Examination kit (three objective catalogs, sample test booklets, performance objective selection booklet, technical handbook, and MULTISCORE brochure with sample scoring service report) $14.72

Publisher: The Riverside Publishing Company

NATIONAL ACADEMIC APTITUDE TESTS: NON-VERBAL INTELLIGENCE
Andrew Kobal, J. Wayne Wrightstone, and Karl R. Kunze; edited by A. J. MacElroy

Adolescent, adult Grades 10 and above

Purpose: Assesses mental abilities. Used to indicate aptitude for academic training in such areas as engineering, chemistry, and other sciences.

Description: Three nonverbal paper-pencil tests measuring mental aptitudes. The tests are Nonverbal Test of Spatial Relations, Comprehension of Physical Relations, and Graphic Relations. The test detects the ability to handle nonverbal materials at a high mental level. Items include pictorial and graphic work. Examiner required. Suitable for group use.

Timed: 26 minutes

Scoring: Hand key

Cost: Specimen set $4.00; 25 tests $13.75

Publisher: Psychometric Affiliates

NATIONAL ACADEMIC APTITUDE TESTS: VERBAL INTELLIGENCE
Andrew Kobal, J. Wayne Wrightstone, Karl R. Kunze; edited by A. J. MacElroy

Adolescent, adult Grades 12 and above

Purpose: Assesses mental aptitudes important in academic and professional work. Used for evaluation of applicants for employment and school programs.

Description: Three verbal paper-pencil tests measuring mental aptitudes. The tests cover general information, academic and general science, mental alertness, comprehension, judgment, arithmetic reasoning, comprehension of relations, logical selection, analogies, and classification. Norms are provided for Grades 7–12, college students, administrative and executive employees, physicians, lawyers, and other professionals. Examiner required. Suitable for group use.

Timed: 40 minutes
Scoring: Hand key
Cost: Specimen set $4.00; 25 tests $13.75
Publisher: Psychometric Affiliates

NATIONAL ACHIEVEMENT TEST (NAT), 2ND EDITION
John W. Wick, Donald L. Beggs, Marci Morrow Enos, Jack R. Fraenkel, Louis A. Gatta, Jana M. Mason, John T. Mouw, Jeffrey K. Smith, Janice Stewart, Thomas Valentin, and Norman E. Wallen

Child, adolescent

Purpose: Assesses achievement in basic skills, science, and social studies.

Description: 12–level multiple-choice comprehensive assessment program. Levels A and B (K–1) assess reading, language, and mathematics. Level C (Grade 1) assesses reading, language, mathematics, social studies, and science. Levels D, E, F-J, K, and L (Grades 2–12) assess reading, language, mathematics, reference skills, social studies, and science. Available in Forms 3 and 4. Examiner required. Suitable for group use.

Timed: Varies by level
Scoring: Machine scored; hand key; scoring service available from publisher
Cost: 25 test booklets Levels A and B $42.45, Levels C, D, E $57.90, Levels E-L $47.45; directions $6.00; 50 answer folders $17.70
Publisher: American Testronics

NATIONAL ACHIEVEMENT TESTS: ENGLISH, READING, LITERATURE, AND VOCABULARY TESTS—AMERICAN LITERACY TEST
John J. McCarty

Adult

Purpose: Assesses literacy in adults. Used for detecting the functionally illiterate.

Description: 50–item paper-pencil test measuring vocabulary or depth of literacy. Items require knowledge of approximate synonyms. The test discriminates degrees of literacy from the illiterate to the highly sophisticated. Examiner required. Suitable for group use.

Timed: 4 minutes
Scoring: Hand key
Cost: Specimen set (test, manual, key) $4.00; 25 scales $5.00
Publisher: Psychometric Affiliates

NATIONAL ACHIEVEMENT TESTS: ENGLISH, READING, LITERATURE, AND VOCABULARY TESTS—COLLEGE ENGLISH FOR HIGH SCHOOL AND COLLEGE
A.C. Jordon

Adolescent, adult
Grades 10 and above

Purpose: Assesses English achievement of high-school and college students. Used for evaluating prospective college students.

Description: Multiple-item paper-pencil test measuring a range of English skills, including the ability to use correct capitalization, punctuate correctly, use proper syntax, determine subject/verb agreement, vary sentence structure, use modifiers correctly, and apply language principles. Two equivalent forms, A and B, are available. Examiner required. Suitable for group use.

Timed: 45 minutes
Scoring: Hand key
Cost: Specimen set (test, manual, key) $4.00; 25 tests $8.75
Publisher: Psychometric Affiliates

NATIONAL ACHIEVEMENT TESTS: ENGLISH, READING, LITERATURE, AND VOCABULARY TESTS—ENGLISH
Robert K. Speer and Samuel Smith

Adolescent
Grades 7–12

Purpose: Assesses students' achievement in English. Used to identify students' strengths and weaknesses as part of an educational evaluation.

Description: Multiple-item paper-pencil test of knowledge and skill in English, including word usage, punctuation, vocabulary, the ability to select correct, sensible sentences, the ability to identify or express ideas, and the ability to identify or express feelings. The test emphasizes the power of self-expression and judgment. Two equivalent forms, A and B, are available. Examiner required. Suitable for group use.

Timed: 40 minutes

Scoring: Hand key

Cost: Specimen set (test, manual, key) $4.00; 25 tests $26.00

Publisher: Psychometric Affiliates

NATIONAL ACHIEVEMENT TESTS: ENGLISH, READING, LITERATURE, AND VOCABULARY TESTS—READING
Robert K. Speer and Samuel Smith

Adolescent, adult
Grades 7 and above

Purpose: Assesses students' reading achievement. Used to identify student strengths and weaknesses as part of an educational evaluation.

Description: Multiple-item paper-pencil test of reading skills important for achievement, including vocabulary, word discrimination, sentence meaning, noting details, and interpreting paragraphs. Two equivalent forms, A and B, are available. Examiner required. Suitable for group use.

Timed: 40 minutes

Scoring: Hand key

Cost: Specimen set (test, manual, key) $5.00; 25 tests $13.75

Publisher: Psychometric Affiliates

NATIONAL ACHIEVEMENT TESTS: ENGLISH, READING, LITERATURE, AND VOCABULARY TESTS—VOCABULARY (GRADES 3-8)
Robert K. Speer and Samuel Smith

Child, adolescent
Grades 3-8

Purpose: Assesses the vocabulary knowledge of children. Used as part of an educational evaluation.

Description: Multiple-item paper-pencil test of vocabulary knowledge. For each item, the base word is printed in capital letters in a meaningful sentence. The pupil selects a synonym for the base word from a group of words. The base words are more difficult than the synonyms. Two equivalent forms, A and B, are available. Examiner required. Suitable for group use.

Timed: 15 minutes

Scoring: Hand key

Cost: Specimen set (test, manual, key) $4.00; 25 tests $3.50

Publisher: Psychometric Affiliates

NATIONAL ACHIEVEMENT TESTS: ENGLISH, READING, LITERATURE, AND VOCABULARY TESTS—VOCABULARY (GRADES 7-COLLEGE)
Robert K. Speer and Samuel Smith

Adolescent
Grades 7 and above

Purpose: Assesses students' vocabulary knowledge. Used as part of an educational evaluation.

Description: Multiple-item paper-pencil test measuring knowledge and judgment related to word meaning and word discrimination. Two equivalent forms, A and B, are available. Examiner required. Suitable for group use.

Timed: 15 minutes

Scoring: Hand key

Cost: Specimen set (test, manual, key) $4.00; 25 tests $3.50

Publisher: Psychometric Affiliates

NATIONAL ACHIEVEMENT TESTS FOR ARITHMETIC AND MATHEMATICS—ALGEBRA TEST FOR ENGINEERING AND SCIENCE
A.B. Lonski; edited by John Kinsella

Adolescent, adult

Purpose: Assesses achievement in intermediate algebra. Used for screening students planning to register in an engineering college or technical school.

Description: Paper-pencil test of algebra knowledge. Items represent mistakes made in algebra by college freshmen who failed the subject in engineering and science courses. The test represents minimum essentials for entry into regular freshman mathematics. Examiner required. Suitable for group use.

Untimed: Not available

Scoring: Hand key

Cost: Specimen set (test, key, manual) $4.00; 25 tests $17.50; 25 answer sheets $3.00

Publisher: Psychometric Affiliates

NATIONAL ACHIEVEMENT TESTS FOR ARITHMETIC AND MATHEMATICS—AMERICAN NUMERICAL TEST
John J. McCarty

Adolescent, adult

Purpose: Assesses arithmetic and numerical ability. Used for educational evaluation and vocational guidance.

Description: 60–item paper-pencil test arranged in sequences of the four basic arithmetical operations. Items require numerical alertness and adaptation. Validity studies include specific fields of secretarial training, automotive, machine tools, construction technology, accounting, and machine drafting and design. Examiner required. Suitable for group use.

Timed: 4 minutes

Scoring: Hand key

Cost: Specimen set (test, key, manual) $4.00; 25 tests $5.00

Publisher: Psychometric Affiliates

NATIONAL ACHIEVEMENT TESTS FOR ARITHMETIC AND MATHEMATICS—FIRST YEAR-ALGEBRA TEST
Ray Webb and Julius H. Hlavaty

Adolescent

Purpose: Assesses achievement in first-year algebra. Used to identify strengths and weaknesses as part of an educational evaluation.

Description: Paper-pencil test measuring pupils' knowledge of first-year algebra. Two equivalent forms, A and B, are available. Examiner required. Suitable for group use.

Timed: 40 minutes

Scoring: Hand key

Cost: Specimen set (test, key, manual) $4.40; 25 tests $6.00; 25 answer sheets $4.50

Publisher: Psychometric Affiliates

NATIONAL ACHIEVEMENT TESTS FOR ARITHMETIC AND MATHEMATICS—PLANE GEOMETRY, SOLID GEOMETRY, AND PLANE TRIGONOMETRY TESTS
Ray Webb and Julius H. Hlavaty

Adolescent

Purpose: Assesses achievement in geometry and trigonometry. Used to identify strengths and weaknesses as part of an educational evaluation.

Description: Three paper-pencil tests measuring essential concepts, skills, and insight in three content areas: plane geometry, solid geometry, and plane trigonometry. Two equivalent forms, A and B, are available. Examiner required. Suitable for group use.

Timed: 40 minutes

Scoring: Hand key

Cost: Specimen set (test, key, manual) $4.00; 25 tests $8.75; 25 answer sheets $3.50

Publisher: Psychometric Affiliates

NATIONAL ACHIEVEMENT TESTS FOR ELEMENTARY SCHOOLS: ARITHMETIC AND MATHEMATICS—ARITHMETIC FUNDAMENTALS
Robert K. Speer and Samuel Smith

Child, adolescent
Grades 3–8

Purpose: Assesses students' achievement in basic arithmetic skills. Used to identify strengths and weaknesses as part of an educational evaluation.

Description: Multiple-item paper-pencil test covering three basic areas of arithmetic skills: speed and accuracy in computation; judgment, speed, and accuracy in comparing computations; and skill and understanding, without special reference to speed. Two equivalent forms, A and B, are available. Examiner required. Suitable for group use.

Timed: 45 minutes

Scoring: Hand key

Cost: Specimen set (test, key, manual) $4.00; 25 tests $5.00

Publisher: Psychometric Affiliates

NATIONAL ACHIEVEMENT TESTS FOR ELEMENTARY SCHOOLS: ARITHMETIC AND MATHEMATICS— FUNDAMENTALS AND REASONING (GRADES 3–6)
Robert K. Speer and Samuel Smith

Child
Grades 3–6

Purpose: Assesses students' achievement in arithmetic. Used to identify strengths and weaknesses as part of an educational evaluation.

Description: 5–part paper-pencil test of arithmetic reasoning and fundamentals, including computation, arithmetical judgments, problem reading, and problem solving. Special norms for students with high and low IQs are provided. Two equivalent forms, A and B, are available. Examiner required. Suitable for group use.

Timed: 30 minutes per part

Scoring: Hand key

Cost: Specimen set (test, key, manual) $4.00; 25 tests $5.00

Publisher: Psychometric Affiliates

NATIONAL ACHIEVEMENT TESTS FOR ELEMENTARY SCHOOLS: ARITHMETIC AND MATHEMATICS— FUNDAMENTALS AND REASONING (GRADES 6–8)
Robert K. Speer and Samuel Smith

Adolescent
Grades 6–8

Purpose: Assesses students' achievement in arithmetic. Used to identify strengths and weaknesses as part of an educational evaluation.

Description: 5–part paper-pencil test of arithmetic reasoning and fundamentals, including fundamentals, number comparisons, mathematical judgments, problem reading, and problem solving. Special norms for students with high and low IQs are provided. Two equivalent forms, A and B, are available. Examiner required. Suitable for group use.

Timed: 30 minutes per part

Scoring: Hand key

Cost: Specimen set (test, key, manual) $4.00; 25 tests $5.00

Publisher: Psychometric Affiliates

NATIONAL ACHIEVEMENT TESTS FOR ELEMENTARY SCHOOLS: ARITHMETIC AND MATHEMATICS—GENERAL MATH
Stanley J. Lejeune

Child
Grades 4–6

Purpose: Assesses students' achievement in general mathematics. Used to identify strengths and weaknesses as part of an educational evaluation.

Description: Multiple-item paper-pencil power test of student comprehension of 11 major topics in general mathematics: the numeration system; addition, subtraction, multiplication, and division; common fractions; decimal fractions and percentages; measurements; geometry; solving written problems; graphs and scale drawings; set terminology; mathematical structure; and money. Two equivalent forms, A and B, are available. Examiner required. Suitable for group use.

Untimed: Approximately 2–3 class periods

Scoring: Hand key

Cost: Specimen set (test, key, manual) $5.00; 25 tests $9.00; 25 answer sheets $3.50

Publisher: Psychometric Affiliates

NATIONAL ACHIEVEMENT TESTS FOR ELEMENTARY SCHOOLS: ARITHMETIC AND MATHEMATICS—GENERAL MATHEMATICS
Harry Eisner

Adolescent
Grades 7–9

Purpose: Assesses students' achievement in general mathematics. Used to identify strengths and weaknesses as part of an educational evaluation.

Description: Multiple-item paper-pencil test of student's knowledge of essential concepts, skills, and insights that should be developed in junior high school mathematics. The abilities measured are arithmetic, algebraic, and geometric concepts; applications; problem analysis; and reasoning. Two equivalent forms, A and B, are available. Examiner required. Suitable for group use.

Timed: Section 1 10 minutes; Section 2 15 minutes; Section 3 27 minutes

Scoring: Hand key

Cost: Specimen set (test, key, manual) $4.00; 25 tests $9.00

Publisher: Psychometric Affiliates

NATIONAL EDUCATIONAL DEVELOPMENT TEST (NEDT)
Science Research Associates and Thelma Gwinn Thurstone

Adolescent
Grades 9–10

Purpose: Assesses students' strengths and weaknesses in English, math, social studies, reading, natural sciences, and educational ability. Predicts success on

and serves as a practice instrument for college admissions exams.

Description: 209–item paper-pencil test measuring the ability to apply rules and principles of grammar and general English usage, understand mathematical concepts and apply principles in solving quantitative problems, comprehend reading selections, and apply critical reading skills. The test is semisecure (forms and keys are not released). The test is used only in schools that choose to serve as designated test centers. Examiner required. Suitable for group use.

Timed: 2 hours, 30 minutes

Scoring: Computer scored

Cost: Test materials and scoring service per student $3.65 for 1988–89 school year (prices change annually)

Publisher: SRA/London House

NATIONAL PROFICIENCY SURVEY SERIES (NPSS)
Dale P. Scannell

Adolescent—Ages 12–18
Grades 8–12

Purpose: Measures end-of-course achievement in selected high-school courses.

Description: 13 multiple-item paper-pencil multiple-choice tests used for evaluating student proficiency in mathematics (General Mathematics, 42 items; Algebra 1, 45 items; Algebra 2, 39 items; Geometry, 39 items), social studies (U.S. History, 42 items; World History, 45 items; American Government, 45 items), English (Literature, 39 items; Writing Fundamentals, 66 items; English IV, 42 items), and science (Biology, 45 items; Chemistry, 42 items; Physics, 45 items). The tests may be administered as survey tests or as end-of-course tests. Each test assesses 13 to 22 objectives that reflect the major content areas of the subject. Each objective is tested by three questions. Normative and criterion-referenced data are available. See separate entries for each of the 13 tests. Examiner required. Suitable for group use.

Timed: 40 minutes

Scoring: Self-scored; hand key

Cost: Contact publisher for price and availability
Publisher: The Riverside Publishing Company

THE NATIONAL TESTS OF BASIC SKILLS

PreK-college

Purpose: Measures basic skills taught by schools. Used to test achievement at individual, classroom, school, and district levels.

Description: Series of paper-pencil tests spanning 14 levels from preschool to college. Reading, language, mathematics, social studies, and science skills are measured by up to 11 subscales, depending on the level being tested. Score reporting includes both numerical and narrative material. Evaluations of student ability and attitudes may be obtained by using companion instruments, such as the Developing Cognitive Abilities Test and the School Attitude Measure. Examiner required. Suitable for group use.
Timed: 109–261 minutes depending on level
Scoring: All levels hand key; Levels A-D machine scoring available
Cost: Test review kit (all levels) $51.00; other prices available from publisher
Publisher: American Testronics

NEW JERSEY TEST OF REASONING SKILLS
Virginia Shipman

Child, adolescent—Ages 10–17 Grades 4–12

Purpose: Measures thinking and language-related reasoning skills.

Description: 50–item paper-pencil multiple-choice test of reasoning ability in 22 skill areas, including converting statements, analogical reasoning, detecting underlying assumptions, detecting ambiguities, distinguishing differences of kind and degree, recognizing dubious authority, contradicting statements, and discerning causal relationships. Examiner required. Suitable for group use.

Untimed: 40 minutes
Scoring: Computer scored; hand key
Cost: Contact publisher
Publisher: Institute for the Advancement of Philosophy for Children

---

NORMAL BATTERY A/76

Adult

Purpose: Assesses academic abilities of older students. Used with college entrants and higher.

Description: Multiple-item paper-pencil battery of six multiple-choice tests: Mental Alertness, Language Ability in English and Afrikaans, Reading Comprehension, Vocabulary, Spelling, and Arithmetic. Norms are available. Examiner required. Suitable for group use.
SOUTH AFRICAN PUBLISHER
Timed: 2 hours
Scoring: Hand key
Cost: (In Rands) booklet 11,80; 25 answer sheets 4,10; set of keys 13,50; manual 16,30
Publisher: National Institute for Personnel Research

OBJECTIVES-REFERENCED BANK OF ITEMS AND TESTS (ORBIT)

Grades K–12

Purpose: Allows the development of customized criterion-referenced tests. Offers objectives designed to meet educational needs, including diagnostic/prescriptive teaching, individual and small group evaluation, large-group program evaluation, and customized test development, scoring, and reporting services.

Description: Criterion-referenced bank of multiple-choice questions covering objectives in reading, language arts, mathematics, and social studies. The high-school competency component also includes listening, composition, consumerism, American government, and problem-solving objectives. School districts choose objectives that are best-suited for their districts' programs. Four test items are provided for each objective. Districts also may submit locally developed test

---

items to be incorporated with CTB items. Three test formats are available: a) machine-scorable books, b) hand-scorable books or reusable books with answer sheets, and c) single-sheet tests composed of one objective and four items. Customized scoring and reporting also are available. Examiner required. Suitable for group use.

Untimed: Varies

Scoring: Machine scored; hand key; computer scored

Cost: Contact publisher

Publisher: CTB/Macmillan/McGraw-Hill

OFFICIAL GED PRACTICE TEST
GED Testing Service of the American Council on Education

Adolescent, adult

Purpose: Determines readiness to take the full-length GED. Alleviates anxiety associated with taking the GED test.

Description: Paper-pencil test paralleling the content, format, and range of difficulty of the full-length GED tests. Five subtests cover the following academic areas: writing skills, social studies, science, literature and the arts, and mathematics. The answer sheet accommodates responses for all five subtests in a single sheet and contains a summary profile chart that identifies general strengths and weaknesses in various subject areas. Scoring templates and a detailed teacher's manual are provided in the Administrator's Set. The test is available in Forms AA and BB. All forms are statistically equated to a full-length secure GED test. An audiotape and large-print edition are available in English. Examiner required. Suitable for group use. Available in Spanish.

Timed: Varies

Scoring: Examiner evaluated

Cost: Single test and answer sheet, $2.50; 10 test booklets $16.00; 50 answer sheets $9.50; Administrator's Set $12.00

Publisher: American Council on Education; distributed by Prentice Hall/Cambridge

ONTARIO ASSESSMENT INSTRUMENT POOL (OAIP)

Adolescent Grades 4–13

Purpose: Evaluates student achievement and program effectiveness in Ontario Province Schools. Measures pupils' mastery of predetermined educational objectives. Used as a unit pre- or posttest. May be used with any other educational assessment device.

Description: 20 paper-pencil assessment instruments covering a variety of school subjects in both French and English. The following unit test titles are available: Chemistry I, II, III, and IV, Senior Division (Grades 11–13); English I and II, Intermediate Division (Grades 7–10); Anglais I, Junior Division Writing and Speaking (Grades 4–6); Anglais au cycle, Intermediate I Writing and Speaking (Grades 7–10); French as a Second Language, Junior and Intermediate Divisions (Grades 6–10); Français au cycle moyen I, Savoir écrire, savoir parler (Grades 4–6); Françcais au cycle intermédiaire I, Savoir écrire, savoir parler (Grades 7–10); Geography, Intermediate Division (Grades 7–10); Géographie (L'amérique du nord) au cycle intermédiaire (Grades 7–10); Geography (Canada) Intermediate Division (Grades 7–10); Géographie (le Canada) au cycle intermédiaire (Grades 7–10); History, Intermediate Division (Grades 7–10); History Part II, Intermediate Division (Grades 7–10); Mathematics, Intermediate Division (Grades 7–10); Mathématique au cycle intermédiaire (Grades 7–10); Physics, Senior Division (Grades 11–13); Physique au cycle supérieur (Grades 11–13).

The Pool will be made available to all teachers in systems within the Ontario province. The materials, which may be used separately or in groups, include test booklets, information sheets, and manuals. Examiner required. Suitable for group use.
CANADIAN PUBLISHER

Untimed: Varies

Scoring: Not available

Cost: $15.00 per package
Publisher: The Ontario Ministry of Education; distributed exclusively by The Ontario Institute for Studies in Education

Information and availability unconfirmed; last verified in 1988.

ORLEANS-HANNA ALGEBRA PROGNOSIS TEST (REVISED)
Gerald S. Hanna and Joseph B. Orleans

Adolescent
Grades 7 and above

Purpose: Identifies students likely to experience difficulties in an algebra course. Used in counseling, selecting, and grouping algebra students.

Description: Multiple-item test of three variables related to the prognosis of success in an algebra course: aptitude, achievement, and interest and motivation. Items include a questionnaire and work samples. Students complete the questionnaire by indicating recent grades and estimating their algebra grade. Then they complete the 60–item work sample. This test is a revision of the 1968 Orleans-Hanna Algebra Prognosis Test. Examiner required. Suitable for group use.

Timed: 40 minutes
Scoring: Hand key; may be machine scored; computer scoring service available
Cost: 35 tests with manual $39.00; 35 hand-scorable answer documents $15.00; keys $10.00; 35 NCS machine-scorable answer documents $15.00; 35 student report forms $13.00
Publisher: The Psychological Corporation

Information and availability unconfirmed; last verified in 1988.

OTIS-LENNON MENTAL ABILITY TEST
Arthur S. Otis and Roger T. Lennon

Child, adolescent
Grades K.5–12

Purpose: Assesses general mental ability or scholastic aptitude.

Description: Multiple-item test covering a broad range of cognitive abilities. The test is divided into six levels: Primary I and II (K-Grade 1), Elementary I and II (Grades 1–6), Intermediate (Grades 7–9), and Advanced (Grades 10–12). No reading is required for the first three levels. Materials include two alternate and equivalent forms, J and K. This test replaces the Otis Quick-Scoring Mental Ability Test. Examiner required. Suitable for group use.

Timed: Varies
Scoring: Hand key; may be machine scored; computer scoring service available
Cost: Examination kit, specify level (test, hand-scoring key, manual, norms, conversion booklet) $14.00
Publisher: The Psychological Corporation

Information and availability unconfirmed; last verified in 1988.

OTIS-LENNON SCHOOL ABILITY TEST (OLSAT)
Arthur S. Otis and Roger T. Lennon

Child, adolescent
Grades 1–12

Purpose: Measures abstract thinking and reasoning ability. Used for predicting success in cognitive, school-related activities.

Description: Multiple-item test covering abilities emphasized in school. Items use verbal, figural, and numerical stimuli. The test is divided into five levels: Primary I (Grade 1), Primary II (Grades 2–3), Elementary (Grades 4–5), Intermediate (Grades 6–8), and Advanced (Grades 9–12). No reading is required of pupils in Grades 1, 2, and 3. Materials include two alternate and equivalent forms, R and S. Form R may be used in conjunction with the Metropolitan Achievement Tests: 5th Edition. Form S may be used with SAT 7 to yield achievement/ability comparisons. Examiner required. Suitable for group use.

Timed: Varies
Scoring: Hand key; may be machine scored; computer scoring service available

Cost: Examination kit, specify level (test, manual, parent/teacher report) $10.00
Publisher: The Psychological Corporation
Information and availability unconfirmed; last verified in 1988.

PASSAGE 10-13
Godfrey Thomson Unit for Educational Research

Child—Ages 10-13

Purpose: Assesses skills in reading, mathematics, and reasoning.

Description: 137–item multiple-choice test consisting of three subtests: Reading, Mathematics, and Reasoning. The Reading subtest indicates performance in cloze comprehension, vocabulary, and understanding points-of-view. The Mathematics subtest includes number, fractions, measure, shapes, and pictorial representation. The Reasoning subtest uses verbal and nonverbal modes (numerical and visual) and differentiates between deductive and inductive reasoning ability. Each of the three subtests are available in equivalent forms A and B. Restricted to authorized users. Examiner required. Suitable for group use.
BRITISH PUBLISHER
Untimed: 35 minutes
Scoring: Hand key
Cost: Contact publisher
Publisher: Hodder and Stoughton

PEABODY INDIVIDUAL ACHIEVEMENT TEST-REVISED (PIAT-R)
Frederick C. Markwardt

Ages 5-18

Purpose: Provides an overview of individual scholastic achievement. Used in schools for academic achievement screening, instructional program planning, and program evaluation; in agencies and industry for obtaining an accurate picture of an individual's achievement; and in research for measuring levels of achievement.

Description: Oral-response point-to test comprised of five subtests: General Infor-

mation (100 items), Reading Recognition (100 items), Reading Comprehension (100 items), Mathematics (100 items), and Spelling (100 items). Optional subtests include Written Expression, Level 1 (18 items) and Written Expression, Level II (2 prompts). Age- and grade-based standard scores, age and grade equivalents, percentile ranks, NCEs, and stanines are provided for all subtests except Written Expression and for total reading and total test. Materials include four easels and a record booklet. This is a revision of the 1970 Peabody Individual Achievement Test. Examiner must have completed graduate training in measurement, guidance, and individual assessment. May be used with individuals with physical and mental disabilities. Examiner required. Not suitable for group use.
Untimed: 1 hour
Scoring: Examiner evaluated
Cost: Complete kit $175.00
Publisher: American Guidance Service

PRE-PROFESSIONAL SKILLS TEST (PPST)
Educational Testing Service

College students

Purpose: Measures the basic academic skills and achievement of individuals preparing for careers as elementary or high-school teachers.

Description: Multiple-item paper-pencil multiple-choice and essay test assessing proficiency in reading, writing, and mathematics. The 50–minute Reading test (40 questions) assesses the ability to understand, analyze, and evaluate short passages (100 words), long passages (200 words), and short statements. The 50–minute Mathematics test (40 questions) evaluates the ability to judge mathematical relations. The two-part Writing test consists of a 45–item multiple-choice test of functional written English (30 minutes) and an essay (30 minutes). Each part is graded separately and combined for a single Writing score. Examiner required. Suitable for group use
Timed: 3 hours
Scoring: Computer scored; examiner evaluated

Cost: Contact publisher

Publisher: Educational Testing Service

Information and availability unconfirmed; last verified in 1988.

PROFICIENCY BATTERIES—JSPB, SPB, APP AND SPT-HT

All ages

Purpose: Assesses achievement in scholastic fields. Used for selection and placement of students and applicants.

Description: Four paper-pencil measures of proficiency in a range of scholastic fields. The JSPB (Standards 5 to 7) measures proficiency in first language (English or Afrikaans), mathematics, natural sciences, geography, history, and second language. The SPB (Standards 8 to 10) measures social sciences, commercial sciences, natural sciences, arithmetic, and home language (English or Afrikaans). APP (first-year university students) tests proficiency in social sciences, commercial sciences, natural sciences, mathematical sciences, and their home language. The SPT-HP (adults whose proficiency is at the higher primary level) measures performance in mathematics, English, and Afrikaans. Examiner required. Suitable for group use.
SOUTH AFRICAN PUBLISHER

Timed: JSPB 2½ hours; SPB 1¾ hours; APB 1¾ hours

Scoring: Hand key; examiner evaluated

Cost: (In Rands) JSPB test 2,50; 10 answer sheets 1,50; scoring stencil 2,50; manual 9,00; SPB test 1,00; 10 answer sheets 1,50; scoring stencil and manual 1,50 each; APB test 1,10; 10 answer sheets 1,50; scoring stencil 1,50; manual 10,00; SPT-HP test 0,60; manual 2,50; scoring stencil 2,00; 10 answer sheets 1,20; orders from outside the RSA will be dealt with on merit

Publisher: Human Sciences Research Council

PROFICIENCY BATTERY IN ENGLISH AND MATHEMATICS FOR INDIAN SOUTH AFRICANS (PEMISA)

Adolescent Standards 6–7

Purpose: Evaluates the English and mathematics proficiency of Indian South African students. May be used to select and place students in courses.

Description: 120–item paper-pencil multiple-choice battery assessing students' skills in English and mathematics. The English Language Test is composed of two subtests. Language Usage (45 items) covers spelling, word usage, and the knowledge of the meaning of words, phrases, and sentences. Reading Comprehension (30 items) contains questions based on passages the student reads. The 45–item Mathematics Test measures factual knowledge, terminology and general principles, and general skills. The tests are available on two levels, Standard 6 and Standard 7, and in English only. Examiner required. Suitable for group use.
SOUTH AFRICAN PUBLISHER

Untimed: 2 hours, 30 minutes

Scoring: Hand key; machine scored

Cost: Contact publisher

Publisher: Human Sciences Research Council

PROGRESSIVE ACHIEVEMENT TESTS

Warwick Elley, Neil Reid, David Hughes, Cedric Croft, and Peter Jackson

Child, adolescent—Ages 7–15

Purpose: Measures school achievement. Used for educational assessment.

Description: Five paper-pencil tests measuring school achievement. The PAT: Reading Vocabulary test consists of multiple-choice items requiring the child to select the best synonym from five alternatives. The PAT: Listening Comprehension test measures the child's ability to understand material presented orally. The child chooses the best answer from four alternatives presented in multiple-choice format. The PAT: Reading Comprehension test consists of graded reading passages followed by five to seven multiple-choice questions. The PAT: Mathematics test is a 50–item multiple-choice test measuring achievement in knowledge, computation, understanding, and application.

The PAT: Study Skills test measures skills in three broad areas: knowledge and use of common reference materials, reading and interpreting graphic and tabular materials, and general reading study skills. Examiner required. Suitable for group use.

NEW ZEALAND PUBLISHER

Timed: 30–40 minutes

Scoring: Hand key; examiner evaluated

Cost: Contact publisher

Publisher: New Zealand Council for Educational Research

PSYCHO-EDUCATIONAL BATTERY (PEB)
Refer to page 639.

QUICK-SCORE ACHIEVEMENT TEST (Q-SAT)
Refer to page 559.

QUICKSCREEN
Refer to page 640.

RICHMOND TESTS OF BASIC SKILLS, SECOND EDITION
A.N. Hieronymus, E.F. Lindquist, and Norman France

Child, adolescent—Ages 8–14

Purpose: Assesses a child's progress in academic work. Used to diagnose areas of general strengths and weaknesses.

Description: Multiple-item paper-pencil profile measuring progress in five areas: vocabulary, reading comprehension, language skills, study skills, and mathematics. The instrument consists of 11 individual tests: Vocabulary, Reading Comprehension, Spelling, Use of Capital Letters, Punctuation, Usage, Map Reading, Reading Graphs and Tables, Knowledge and Use of Reference Materials, Mathematics Concepts, and Mathematics Problem Solving. The test is available in six levels for children ages 8–14. A 96–page book incorporating all 11 tests for all

six levels of difficulty is provided. Examiner required. Suitable for group use.

BRITISH PUBLISHER

Timed: Varies

Scoring: Hand key; computer scoring service available

Cost: Contact publisher

Publisher: NFER-NELSON Publishing Company Ltd.

SCHOLASTIC ABILITIES TEST FOR ADULTS (SATA)
Brian R. Bryant, James R. Patton, and Caroline Dunn

Adolescent, adult—Ages 16 and older

Purpose: Measures an individual's scholastic aptitude and achievement. Used to identify an individual's strengths and weaknesses and identify persons who may need special assistance in secondary and postsecondary training and educational settings.

Description: Multiple-item paper-pencil assessment battery consisting of nine subtests: Verbal Reasoning—understanding verbal analogies; Nonverbal Reasoning—using geometric forms to assess nonverbal problem solving; Quantitative Reasoning—determining problem-solving abilities using numbers; Reading Vocabulary—recognizing synonyms and antonyms in print; Reading Comprehension—reading passages silently and responding to multiple-choice items; Math Calculation—computing arithmetic, geometry, and algebra problems; Math Application—reading and computing story problems; Writing Mechanics—writing sentences that require spelling, capitalization, and punctuation skills; and Writing Composition—writing a story that is checked for content maturity and vocabulary.

Individual subtest raw scores are converted to estimated grade equivalents, standard scores ($M = 10$, $SD = 3$), and percentiles. Several composite scores are also generated: General Aptitude, Total Achievement, Reading, Mathematics, and Writing. Composite scores are reported as estimated grade equivalents, standard scores ($M = 100$, $SD = 15$), and percentiles. In addition, scores from the Reading Vocabulary, Math Calculation, and Writing Mechanics subtests are combined to obtain an Achievement Screener Quotient, which can be used for screening purposes.

Software scoring and report systems are available for use on Apple (II+, IIe, or IIc) and IBM computers. Examiner required. Suitable for group use.

Timed: Varies by subtest

Scoring: Hand key; may be computer scored

Cost: Complete kit (examiner's manual, 10 test books, 25 response booklets, 25 profile/examiner record forms, storage box) $109.00; software scoring and report system (specify IBM or Apple version) $69.00

Publisher: PRO-ED

SCHOLASTIC APTITUDE SCALE (SAS)
Brian R. Bryant and Phyllis Newcomer

Grades K–12

Purpose: Assesses general scholastic aptitude. Used in determinig aptitude-achievement discrepancy.

Description: 115–item oral-response test assessing three areas: Verbal Reasoning (35 items), Nonverbal Reasoning (40 items), and Quantitative Reasoning (40 items). Subtest raw scores are converted to percentiles and quotients. The Verbal Quotient, Nonverbal Quotient, and Quantitative Quotient can be combined to form a General Aptitude Quotient, which can be used as a predictor of school achievement. Materials include examiner's manual, picture book, and profile/ examiner record forms. A software scoring system is available for IBM compatibles and Apple II systems. Examiner required. Suitable for small group use.

Untimed: 30 minutes-1 hour, 30 minutes

Scoring: Hand key; may be computer scored

Cost: Complete kit $74.00

Publisher: PRO-ED

SCHOLASTIC APTITUDE TEST BATTERIES FOR STANDARDS 2, 3 AND 5–SATB AND JSATB

Child

Purpose: Assesses academic and scholastic aptitudes. Used for psychoeducational counseling.

Description: Multiple-item test batteries measuring a broad range of scholastic aptitudes. SATB (Standards 2 and 3) measures mathematics, nonverbal reasoning ability, and proficiency in English, Afrikaans, and one of seven mother tongues: Northern Sotho, Southern Sotho, Tswanga, Tsonga, Venda, Xhosa, and Zulu. JSATB (Standard 5) assesses abilities in language, mathematics, and verbal and nonverbal reasoning ability. Examiner required. Suitable for group use.
SOUTH AFRICAN PUBLISHER

Timed: SATB 3 hours; JSATB 2 hours, 30 minutes

Scoring: Hand key; examiner evaluated

Cost: (In Rands) SATB test booklet (specify language) 2,50; manual 7,00; 10 answer sheets 1,80; scoring stencil 5,00; JSATB test booklet 3,00; manual 8,00 net; 10 answer sheets 1,20; scoring stencil 1,00; orders from outside the RSA will be dealt with on merit

Publisher: Human Sciences Research Council

SCHOLASTIC PROFICIENCY TEST—HIGHER PRIMARY LEVEL (SPT-HP)

Adult

Purpose: Assesses proficiency in mathematics, English, and Afrikaans. Used in South Africa with adult blacks with an educational level of Standards 2-5 for selection and placement in training programs or occupations.

Description: Multiple-item paper-pencil test of scholastic proficiency in mathematics, English, and Afrikaans. Norms indicate the typical performance of people passing Standards 2-5. The test can be used for selecting and placing adults in training courses or occupations requiring a higher primary scholastic level. Examiner required. Suitable for group use. SOUTH AFRICAN PUBLISHER

Untimed: 3 hours, 15 minutes

Scoring: Hand key

Cost: (In Rands) Test booklet 0,60; manual 2,50; scoring stencil 2,00; 10 answer sheets 1,20

Publisher: Human Sciences Research Council

SCHOOL AND COLLEGE ABILITY TESTS, SERIES III (SCAT III)
Educational Testing Service

Child, adolescent
Grades 3.5–12.9

Purpose: Measures a student's basic verbal and quantitative abilities.

Description: 100–item two-part paper-pencil test measuring verbal and mathematical skills. The verbal portion of the test uses verbal analogies to assess a student's understanding of words. The quantitative section uses quantitative comparison items to measure a student's knowledge of basic number operations. The test yields verbal, quantitative, and total raw scores, which may be converted to standard scores, national percentile ranks, and stanines. Forms are available for three levels: Elementary (Grades 3–6), Intermediate (Grades 6–9), and Advanced (Grades 9–12). The SCAT III is a revision of the SCAT II; the metric system has been incorporated in the SCAT III and racial and ethnic biases have been reduced. Examiner required. Suitable for group use.

Timed: 40 minutes

Scoring: Hand key; may be computer scored

Cost: 35 reusable test books (specify level) $16.80; 100 answer sheets $18.00; scoring stencil $2.50

Publisher: CTB/Macmillan/McGraw-Hill

SCIENTIFIC KNOWLEDGE AND APTITUDE TEST
S. Chatterji and Manjula Mukerjee

Adolescent—Ages 15–16

Purpose: Measures the scientific knowledge and aptitude of high-school students.

Description: 72–item paper-pencil test assessing scientific knowledge and aptitude. The test may be used with students whose native language is not English but who have been taught in English-language schools. Examiner required. Suitable for group use. PUBLISHED IN INDIA

Timed: 1 hour

Scoring: Hand key; examiner evaluated

Cost: (In Rupees) complete kit (25 booklets, 100 answer sheets, manual, key) Rs90

Publisher: S. Chatterji and Manjula Mukerjee; distributed exclusively by Manasayan

SECONDARY SCHOOL ADMISSION TEST (SSAT)

Child, adolescent
Grades 5–10

Purpose: Measures the abilities of students applying for admission to Grades 6–11 of selective schools. Used by independent schools for student selection.

Description: Multiple-item paper-pencil multiple-choice test measuring verbal and quantitative abilities and reading comprehension. The test consists of four sections: one measuring verbal ability, two measuring mathematical ability, and one measuring reading comprehension. An upper level form is administered to students in Grades 8–10; a lower form is administered to students in Grades 5–7. Scores are normed on the student's grade level at the time of testing. Norms for each grade level are developed annually on the basis of the most recent three-year sample of candidates tested.

The test is administered on specific dates (six Saturdays during the school year and biweekly during the summer) at designated test centers. ETS publishes a *Bulletin of Information for Candidates,* which contains a list of test centers and dates, registration information, and a registration form. The *Bulletin* is mailed to score recipients in August for distribution to candidates, who complete the form and return it with the test fee to ETS. A booklet entitled *Preparing for the SSAT* is available for candidates who want to familiarize themselves with the test. The booklet contains a description of the test, examples and explanations of test questions, a sample test, and instructions for scoring the test and interpreting the scores.

Reading comprehension, verbal, quantitative, and total verbal and quantitative scaled scores, as well as program percentiles, are mailed to score recipients approximately 15 working days after each administration. Each score recipient receives a roster of scores for candidates who designated it as a score recipient, two gummed label reports for each candidate, current program norms, and an interpretive guide explaining how the information can be used. At the time of testing, students may designate up to six score recipients. A report of the candidate's scaled scores and percentiles, along with a booklet for interpreting scores, is sent to parents approximately four days after the reports are sent to the schools.

A program for the handicapped permits physically or visually handicapped students to take the test with up to double the amount of testing time per section. Examiner required. Suitable for group use.

Timed: Varies

Scoring: Computer scored; hand key

Cost: Domestic test fee (administration, parents' score report, six designated school reports) $25.00; foreign test fee (including Canada, Puerto Rico, U.S. territories) $45.00

Publisher: Educational Testing Service

Information and availability unconfirmed; last verified in 1988.

SENIOR ACADEMIC-TECHNICAL APTITUDE TESTS FOR COLOUREDS IN STANDARDS 8, 9, AND 10 (SATA)—1977

Adolescent, adult

Purpose: Measures the differential aptitudes of students and young adults with an educational level of Standards

8–10. Used for educational and occupational guidance.

Description: Multiple-item paper-pencil battery of tests in two forms assessing aptitudes. Forms A and B include 10 tests: Verbal Reasoning, Nonverbal Reasoning I (figure series), Nonverbal Reasoning II (dominoes), computations, reading comprehension, spelling and vocabulary, mechanical reasoning, spatial perception (3D), comparison, and price controlling. Form B has an additional filing test. Stanines and percentile ranks are available. Examiner required. Suitable for group use.

SOUTH AFRICAN PUBLISHER

Untimed: 4½ hours

Scoring: Hand key

Cost: (In Rands) Test booklet 2,00; manual 6,00; set of scoring stencils 2,50 each; 10 answer sheets 1,00

Publisher: Human Sciences Research Council

SENIOR APTITUDE TESTS (SAT)
F.A. Fouche and N.F Alberts

Adolescent, adult

Purpose: Measures scholastic aptitude. Used for educational counseling.

Description: Multiple-item paper-pencil test of 12 specific aptitudes: verbal comprehension, calculations, disguised words, comparison, pattern completion, figural series, spatial (2D), spatial (3D), memory (paragraph), memory (symbols), coordination, and writing speed. Examiner required. Suitable for group use.

SOUTH AFRICAN PUBLISHER

Timed: 2 hours

Scoring: Hand key; examiner evaluated; may be machine scored

Cost: (In Rands) test booklet 3,00; 10 answer sheets T11–T12 1,50; 10 answer sheets T1–T6, T7–T10 (specify form) 1,50; 10 profile sheets 1,00; scoring stencil (T1–T6) 3,00; scoring stencil (T7–T10) 3,00; manual 9,00; 10 machine answer sheets 2,00; appendix to manual (1978) 8,00; orders from outside the RSA will be dealt with on merit

Publisher: Human Sciences Research Council

---

academic achievement and aptitude

SEQUENTIAL TESTS OF EDUCATIONAL PROGRESS (STEP III)

Educational Testing Service

Child, adolescent
Grades PreK–12.9

Purpose: Measures achievement in language, mathematics, science, and social studies. Used to assess individual and group academic mastery and to evaluate curriculum programs.

Description: Multiple-item comprehensive testing program consisting of 10 levels: CIRCUS Preprimary and Primary Levels A-D (Grades PreK–3.5) and Intermediate and Advanced Levels E-J (Grades 3.5–12.9). The CIRCUS Preprimary and Primary levels assess pre-reading, reading, mathematics, and listening skills. Beginning with Grade 2, writing skills are measured. Study skills and social studies and science skills are tested beginning at Grade 3. The program also contains four end-of-course tests in algebra and geometry, biology, chemistry, and physics. Examiner required. Suitable for group use.

Timed: 40 minutes per test

Scoring: Hand key; may be computer scored

Cost: Multilevel specimen set (test booklet for Levels E-J, complete battery answer sheet, directions for administration, test development, and content) $25.65; Level B specimen sets (test books, teacher's editions, user's guides) $28.10; Levels C and D specimen sets (Basic Assessment tests, user's guide, directions for administration) $14.65

Publisher: CTB/Macmillan/McGraw-Hill

SPANISH ASSESSMENT OF BASIC EDUCATION (SABE)

Child, adolescent
Grades 1-8

Purpose: Assesses the basic reading and mathematics skills of Spanish-speaking LEP students.

Description: Multiple-item paper-pencil multiple-choice test covering word attack, vocabulary, reading comprehension, mathematics computation, and mathematics concepts and applications. The examiner must speak fluent Spanish. The test is linked statistically to the Comprehensive Tests of Basic Skills, Forms U and V and to the California Achievement Tests, Forms E and F. Examiner required. Suitable for group use. Available in Spanish only.

Timed: 2 hours

Scoring: Hand key; computer scored

Cost: Multilevel review kit $33.55

Publisher: CTB/Macmillan/McGraw-Hill

SRA ACHIEVEMENT SERIES, FORMS 1-2 (ACH 1-2)

Robert A. Naslund, Louis P. Thorpe, and D. Welty Lefever

Grades K-12

Purpose: Measures students' achievement. Used by teachers and administrators for program planning and evaluation, teachers to provide remediation, and parents and counselors to understand a student's performance as it relates to others across the country.

Description: Multiple-item paper-pencil battery of tests surveying general academic achievement. The lower battery of tests (Levels A-D), for Grades K–3, measures basic skills taught in reading (visual discrimination, auditory discrimination, letters and sounds, listening comprehension, vocabulary, comprehension); mathematics (concepts and computation); and language arts (mechanics, usage, spelling). The upper battery (Levels D-H), for Grades 4–12, measures basic skills in reading (vocabulary and comprehension); language arts (mechanics, usage, spelling); mathematics (concepts, computation, problem solving); use of reference materials; social studies; and science. For Level H, an additional Survey of Applied Skills score is reported, measuring knowledge of consumer economics, health and safety, employment, and community resources. An Education Ability Series also is available for use with the Survey of

Basic Skills. The EAS measures vocabulary, arithmetic computation, letter patterns, word differences, and manipulation of forms in space, and provides an estimate of educational ability. Examiner required. Suitable for group use.

Timed: Varies

Scoring: Hand key; may be computer scored; may be locally scored

Cost: 25 machine-scorable test booklets and examiner's manual: ACH with EAS at Levels A-D $42.50–$47.25, Levels D-H $35.25; 25 machine-scorable test booklets (ACH only) $33.50–$38.25 depending on level; 25 practice sheets (required at lower levels only) $2.65; booklet containing answer keys, norms, and conversion tables $19.50 all levels; 100 student profile sheets $15.25; 100 answer sheets for local scoring: SRA version $44.00, NCS version $61.50; sample sets $4.25 per level or $29.00 for all levels

Publisher: CTB/Macmillan/McGraw-Hill

SRA PAC PROGRAM
Robert A. Naslund, Louis P. Thorpe, and D. Welty Lefever

Child, adolescent Grades 4–10

Purpose: Assesses students' general academic achievement. Used for student screening, grade placement, and scheduling.

Description: Multiple-item paper-pencil test measuring academic achievement in reading, math, and language. Science, social studies, and knowledge of reference materials, the Educational Ability Series (EAS), and the Kuder General Interest Survey are available optionally. The test is a norm-referenced, shortened version of the SRA Achievement Series. Examiner required. Suitable for group use.

Timed: 3 hours

Scoring: Hand key; may be computer scored

Cost: 25 3R test books $22.25; 25 3R and optional tests $25.00; 25 optional EAS booklets $12.50; 100 answer sheets $24.25; scoring stencils $6.75 per level; answer keys, norms, and conversion tables $1.65 per level; sample set $4.00

Publisher: SRA/London House

SRA SURVEY OF BASIC SKILLS (SBS)

Grades K–12

Purpose: Measures students' achievement. Used by teachers and administrators for program planning and evaluation, teachers to provide remediation, and parents and counselors to understand a student's performance as it relates to others across the country.

Description: Multiple-item paper-pencil battery of tests surveying general academic achievement. The lower battery of tests (Levels 20–23), for Grades K–3, measures basic skills taught in reading (auditory discrimination, letters and sounds, decoding, listening comprehension, vocabulary, comprehension); mathematics (concepts/problem solving and computation); and language arts (mechanics, usage, spelling). The upper battery (Levels 34–37), for Grades 4–12, measures basic skills in reading (vocabulary and comprehension); language arts (mechanics, usage, spelling); mathematics (concepts, computation, problem solving); use of reference materials; social studies; and science. For Level 37, an additional Survey of Applied Skills score is reported, measuring knowledge of consumer economics, health and safety, employment, and community resources. An Education Ability Series also is available for use with the Survey of Basic Skills. The EAS measures vocabulary, arithmetic computation, letter patterns, word differences, and manipulation of forms in space, and provides an estimate of educational ability. Examiner required. Suitable for group use.

Timed: Varies

Scoring: Hand key; may be computer scored; may be locally scored

Cost: 25 machine-scorable test booklets and examiner's manual (SBS with EAS) $42.50–$47.25 depending on level; 25 machine-scorable test booklets (SBS only) $33.50–$38.25 depending on level; 25 practice sheets (required at lower levels only, available at upper levels) $2.65 all levels; booklet containing answer keys, norms, and conversion tables $5.50 at each level; 100 student profile sheets $15.25; 25 EAS booklets (Levels 23–37) $12.50; 100 answer sheets for local scoring: SRA version $44.00, NCS version $61.50; sample sets $16.25 for Levels 20–23 and $20.25 for Levels 34–37

Publisher: CTB/Macmillan/McGraw-Hill

STANFORD MEASUREMENT SERIES—STANFORD ACHIEVEMENT TEST: 7TH EDITION
Eric F. Gardner, Herbert C. Rudman, Bjorn Karlsen, and Jack C. Merwin

Child, adolescent Grades 1.5–9.9

Purpose: Assesses school achievement status of children.

Description: Multiple-item paper-pencil test measuring several aspects of school achievement. The test is divided into six levels: Primary 1, Primary 2, Primary 3, Intermediate 1, Intermediate 2, and Advanced. Primary 1 and 2 test nine achievement areas: word study skills, word reading, reading comprehension, vocabulary, listening comprehension, spelling concepts of number, mathematics computation, and environment. Primary 3 and Intermediate 1 and 2 measure the same areas as Primary 1 and 2, as well as language/English, mathematics applications, science, and social science. Word reading and environment are not assessed. The Advanced Level assesses every area except word study skills. Two alternate and equivalent forms, E and F, are available. Together with the Stanford Early School Achievement Test and the Stanford Test of Academic Skills, the test provides for continuous assessment throughout the school years. Examiner required. Suitable for group use.

Timed: Varies

Scoring: Hand key; computer scoring service available

Cost: Specimen set, specify level (complete battery booklet, teacher's directions, norms booklet) $16.00

Publisher: The Psychological Corporation

Information and availability unconfirmed; last verified in 1988.

STANFORD MEASUREMENT SERIES—STANFORD DIAGNOSTIC MATHEMATICS TEST (SDMT): THIRD EDITION
Leslie S. Beatty, Richard Madden, Eric F. Gardner, and Bjorn Karlsen

Child, adolescent Grades 1.5–12.8

Purpose: Identifies individual pupil needs in mathematics.

Description: Multiple-item paper-pencil test covering three mathematics skill areas: number system and numeration, computation, and applications. The test is divided into four levels: red (Grades 1.8–4.8), green (Grades 4.1–6.8), brown (Grades 6.1–8.0), and blue (Grades 8.1–12.8). Materials include manual with prescriptive teaching strategies and two alternate and equivalent forms, G and H. The test is linked statistically with the Stanford Achievement Test Series. Examiner required. Suitable for group use.

Timed: 85–100 minutes, depending on level

Scoring: Hand key; computer scoring available

Cost: Examination kit, specify level (test booklet, manual for interpreting order form, instructional placement report, directions for administering, a hand-scorable and MRC answer document for green, brown, and blue levels) $15.00

Publisher: The Psychological Corporation

Information and availability unconfirmed; last verified in 1988.

academic achievement and aptitude

STANFORD MEASUREMENT SERIES—STANFORD DIAGNOSTIC READING TEST (SDRT): THIRD EDITION
Bjorn Karlsen and Eric F. Gardner

Child, adolescent
Grades 1.5–12.8

Purpose: Measures major components of the reading process. Used for diagnosing specific student needs.

Description: Multiple-item paper-pencil test measuring four aspects of reading: comprehension, vocabulary, decoding, and rate. The test is divided into four levels: red (Grades 1.8–3.8), green (Grades 3.1–5.8), brown (Grades 5.1–8.8), and blue (Grades 8.8–12.8). Cutoff scores indicate the need for remedial instruction. Materials include handbooks with instructional suggestions and instructional materials. The brown and blue levels each include three kinds of answer documents: hand-scorable, MRC answer document, and ready score. The test is linked statistically with the Stanford Achievement Test Series. Two alternate and equivalent forms, G and H, are available. Examiner required. Suitable for group use.

Timed: 1 hour, 45 minutes–2 hours, 6 minutes, depending on level

Scoring: Hand key; machine scoring available

Cost: Examination kit, specify level (test booklet, instructional placement report, directions for administering, manual for interpreting order form) $15.00

Publisher: The Psychological Corporation

Information and availability unconfirmed; last verified in 1988.

STANFORD MEASUREMENT SERIES—STANFORD EARLY SCHOOL ACHIEVEMENT TEST: 2ND EDITION (SESAT)
Richard Madden, Eric F. Gardner, and Cathy S. Collins

Child
Grades K.0–1.9

Purpose: Assesses school achievement of children at the kindergarten and first-grade level.

Description: Multiple-item paper-pencil test measuring several aspects of school achievement. The test is divided into two levels: SESAT 1 for kindergartners and SESAT 2 for children from midkindergarten through first grade. Both levels assess sounds and letters, word reading, listening to words and stories, mathematics, and environment. SESAT 2 also tests sentence reading. Together with the Stanford Achievement Test: 7th Edition and the Stanford Test of Academic Skills, the SESAT provides for continuous assessment throughout the school years. Examiner required. Suitable for group use.

Timed: Total battery 2 hours, 25 minutes

Scoring: Hand key; computer scoring service available

Cost: Specimen set, specify level (complete battery book, teacher's directions, norms booklet) $15.00

Publisher: The Psychological Corporation

Information and availability unconfirmed; last verified in 1988.

STANFORD MEASUREMENT SERIES—STANFORD TEST OF ACADEMIC SKILLS: 2ND EDITION (TASK)
Eric F. Gardner, Robert Callis, Jack C. Merwin, and Herbert C. Rudman

Adolescent
Grades 8–13

Purpose: Assesses school achievement status of high-school students.

Description: Multiple-item paper-pencil test covering seven aspects of school achievement. The test is divided into two levels: TASK 1 and TASK 2. Both measure reading comprehension, vocabulary, spelling, language/English, mathematics, science, and social science. Two alternate and equivalent forms, E and F, are available. Together with the SESAT and the Stanford Achievement Test, the TASK provides continuous assessment throughout the school years. Examiner required. Suitable for group use.

Timed: Total battery 3 hours, 5 minutes

Scoring: Hand key; computer scoring service available

Cost: Specimen set (complete battery book, teacher's directions, norms booklet) $16.00

Publisher: The Psychological Corporation

Information and availability unconfirmed; last verified in 1988.

STEENBURGEN DIAGNOSTIC-PRESCRIPTIVE MATH PROGRAM AND QUICK MATH SCREENING TEST

Refer to page 327.

STS-HIGH SCHOOL PLACEMENT TEST (HSPT)

**Adolescent
Grades 8.3–9.3**

Purpose: Measures eighth-graders' ability to read, write, and solve arithmetic problems. Used for high-school placement.

Description: 298–item paper-pencil test measuring verbal cognitive skills (60 items), quantitative cognitive skills (52 items), reading skills (62 items), mathematics skills (64 items), and language skills (60 items). Optional tests include Mechanical Aptitude, Science, and Catholic Religion. For these closed edition tests, schools may purchase the test materials and hand score them, or they may lease the test materials and use the standard scoring service. The closed edition offers new materials each year, with security insured (no specimen sets are available). One of the optional tests may be selected free-of-charge with the closed edition. The open edition is a reprint of a recent closed edition, for which specimen sets are available. Optional materials available for both editions include student record cards, student score folders, an interpretive manual, and technical reports. Examiner required. Suitable for group use.

Timed: 2 hours, 30 minutes

Scoring: Hand key; may be computer scored

Cost: Specimen set $10.00

Publisher: Scholastic Testing Service, Inc.

SURVEY OF BASIC COMPETENCIES (SBC)
Jwalla P. Somwaru

Child, adolescent—Ages 3–15

Purpose: Measures children's ability to read, write, and solve arithmetic problems. Used to identify children with learning problems and screen for further testing with the Assessment of Basic Competencies diagnostic battery and for Chapter I assessment.

Description: 138–item verbal-response paper-pencil test consisting of four subtests: Information Processing (36 items), Language (36 items), Reading (30 items), and Mathematics (36 items). The test is individually administered, with the child and examiner on opposite sides of a desk. The test yields a raw score, developmental age score, grade equivalent score, and operating range (in terms of grade). The starter set includes the manual, a reusable test, 20 response forms, and a carrying case. Examiner required. Not suitable for group use.

Untimed: 30 minutes

Scoring: Hand key

Cost: Starter set $54.50

Publisher: Scholastic Testing Service, Inc.

THE TEST FOR ENTRANCE INTO TEACHER EDUCATION PROGRAMS (TETEP)

**Adult
College students**

Purpose: Measures abilities and achievement. Used with college students for admission and placement into schools of education in Washington.

Description: Paper-pencil test of abilities and achievement. The subtests include English Usage, Spelling, Reading Comprehension, Applied Mathematics, Vocabulary, and Mathematics Achievement. Test scores are returned to the institution in which the student desires entry into the teacher education program. The TETEP is a modified, shortened form of the Washington Pre-College Test. Examiner required. Suitable for group use.

Timed: 116 minutes

Scoring: Machine scored

Cost: $8.00 per student

Publisher: Washington Pre-College Program

Information and availability unconfirmed; last verified in 1988.

TEST OF COGNITIVE SKILLS (TCS)
CTB/McGraw-Hill

**Child, adolescent
Grades 2–12**

Purpose: Assesses skills important for success in school settings. Used for predicting school achievement and screening students for further evaluation.

Description: Multiple-item paper-pencil multiple-choice test consisting of four subtests (Sequences, Analogies, Memory, Verbal Reasoning) assessing cognitive skills. The Sequences test measures the student's ability to comprehend a rule or principle implicit in a pattern or sequence of figures, letters, or numbers. The Analogies test measures the student's ability to discern concrete or abstract relationships and to classify objects or concepts according to common attributes. The Memory test measures the student's ability to recall previously presented materials. The Verbal Reasoning test measures the student's ability to discern relationships and reason logically. The test is divided into five levels spanning Grades 2–12. The test yields the following scores: number of correct responses, age or grade percentile rank, stanine, scale score, and cognitive skills index. Examiner required. Suitable for group use.

Untimed: 1 hour

Scoring: Hand key; may be computer scored

Cost: Multilevel examination kit (assorted test booklets and answer sheets for different levels, handbook, record sheet) $37.45

Publisher: CTB/Macmillan/McGraw-Hill

TEST OF SCHOLASTIC ABILITIES (TOSCA)
Neil Reid, Peter Jackson, Alison Gilmore, and Cedric Croft

**Child, adolescent—
Ages 9–14**

Purpose: Measures a student's current status in broad language and numerical reasoning abilities. Used as a beginning step in educational assessment.

Description: 70–item paper-pencil test measuring basic scholastic abilities. Both multiple-choice and completion items are included. The abilities measured are school-related but do not involve skills taught directly in the classroom. The test is divided into three levels: primary, intermediate, and secondary. Examiner required. Suitable for group use.
NEW ZEALAND PUBLISHER

Timed: 30 minutes

Scoring: Examiner evaluated

Cost: Contact publisher

Publisher: New Zealand Council for Educational Research

TEST ON APPRAISING OBSERVATIONS
Stephen P. Norris and Ruth King

Adult

Purpose: Measures the ability of senior high-school and college students to appraise observations reported by others. Used in critical thinking research and evaluation, classroom instruction and evaluation, and selection and placement of students.

Description: 50–item paper-pencil test consisting of two stories and related items. Each item consists of two observation statements. Examinees decide which statement, if either, is more believable. The test is based on a set of principles for appraising observations related to charac-

---

teristics of the observer, the observation conditions, and the observation statement. The publisher offers a scoring service that generates a statistical report. Examiner/self-administered. Suitable for group use. CANADIAN PUBLISHER

Untimed: 50–60 minutes

Scoring: Hand key; may be computer scored

Cost: 35 test forms $35.00; 100 answer sheets (NCS General Purpose) $10.00; scoring key $1.00; manual $5.00; technical report of test design $10.00; scoring service $0.75 per answer sheet; standard statistical report $10.00; data diskette $10.00

Publisher: Institute for Educational Research and Development, Memorial University of Newfoundland

---

TEST ON APPRAISING OBSERVATIONS (CONSTRUCTED RESPONSE VERSION)
Stephen P. Norris

Adolescent, adult

Purpose: Measures an individual's ability to appraise observations reported by others. Used in teaching and diagnosis.

Description: 25–item paper-pencil short-answer test assessing an individual's ability to evaluate observations. The test is based on a set of principles for appraising observations related to characteristics of the observer, the observation conditions, and the observation statement. A sixth-grade reading level is required. Suitable for use with individuals with hearing and physical impairments. Examiner/self-administered. Suitable for group use. CANADIAN PUBLISHER

Untimed: 45 minutes

Scoring: Examiner evaluated

Cost: Contact publisher

Publisher: Institute for Educational Research and Development, Memorial University of Newfoundland

TESTS OF ACHIEVEMENT AND PROFICIENCY™: FORM T (TAP®)
Dale P. Scannell, Oscar M. Haugh, Alvin H. Schild, and Gilbert Ulmer

---

Adolescent
Grades 9–12

Purpose: Measures student progress in the basic skills and basic curricular areas. Used for evaluation and career planning.

Description: Multiple-item paper-pencil multiple-choice battery assessing student achievement in the basic skills. The tests are organized into four levels, Levels 15–18, which correspond to the four high-school grades. Each level is available in a Basic Battery and a Complete Battery. The Complete Battery (353–365 items) contains six tests covering reading comprehension, mathematics, written expression, using sources of information, social studies, and science. The Basic Battery (233–242 items) measures reading comprehension, mathematics, written expression, and sources of information. Objective, primarily norm-referenced score information allows students to compare their performances to those of other students in their grade and indicates areas where they have performed the most and least successfully. Information about students' general interests and future plans is provided through the TAP Questionnaire. An Applied Proficiency Skills score in practical skills and a Minimum Competency score in reading and mathematics are generated through a subset of items from the Basic Battery tests. The tests were normed concurrently with Form 3 of the Cognitive Abilities Test™ for reliable comparisons between attained and anticipated achievement test scores. Examiner required. Suitable for group use.

Timed: Complete Battery 4 hours; Basic Battery 2 hours, 40 minutes

Scoring: Hand key; may be machine (MRC or NCS) scored

Cost: Complete Battery test booklet for Levels 15–18 (single copy) $5.01; Basic Battery test booklet for Levels 15–18 (single copy) $3.81; 35 MRC answer sheets, teacher's guide (specify level) $20.46; scoring masks (specify level) $15.18; teacher's guide $8.64

Publisher: The Riverside Publishing Company

academic achievement and aptitude

TESTS OF ACHIEVEMENT AND PROFICIENCY™: FORMS G, H (TAP®)

Dale P. Scannell, Oscar H. Haugh, Alvin H. Schild, and Gilbert Ulmer

Adolescent Grades 9–12

Purpose: Measures student progress in the basic skills: reading, writing, listening, mathematics, using sources of information, social studies, and science. Used for evaluation and career planning.

Description: Paper-pencil multiple-choice battery assessing student achievement in the basic skills. The tests are organized into four levels, Levels 15–18, which correspond to the four high-school grades. Each level is available in a Basic Battery and a Complete Battery. The Basic Battery covers reading comprehension, mathematics, written expression, and using sources of information. The Complete Battery adds tests in science and social studies to the Basic Battery. Listening and Writing supplements are available. The Listening test evaluates students' abilities to remember exactly what they hear, identify word meanings in context, distinguish between fact and opinion, and remember main points and important details in a lecture. The Writing test measures skills in narration in Grade 9, explanation in Grade 10, analysis in Grade 11, and argumentation in Grade 12.

The Complete Battery is available in both a multilevel format with all four levels contained in a single test book and in a separate-level format. The Basic Battery is available in the multilevel format only. The multilevel format facilitates mixed-level testing in the same group.

The tests were normed concurrently with Form 4 of the Cognitive Abilities Test™ for reliable comparisons between attained and anticipated achievement test scores. Information about students' general interests and future plans is provided through the TAP Questionnaire. An Applied Proficiency Skills score in practical skills and a Minimum Competency score in reading and mathematics are gen-erated through a subset of items from the Basic Battery tests. Examiner required. Suitable for group use.

Timed: Complete Battery 4 hours; Basic Battery 2 hours, 40 minutes

Scoring: Hand key; may be MRC or NCS machine scored

Cost: Complete Battery Multilevel test booklet for levels 15–18 (single copy) $4.95; Basic Battery Multilevel test book-let for Levels 15–18 (single copy) $3.90; 35 Separate Level test booklets (specify level) $62.55; 35 MRC answer sheets, Teacher's Guide (specify level) $21.30; scoring masks (specify level and form) $16.35; Teacher's guide $8.40; Manual for School Administrators $21.00

Publisher: The Riverside Publishing Company

TESTS OF ACHIEVEMENT IN BASIC SKILLS (TABS)

EdITS Staff

Child, adolescent Grades 2–13

Purpose: Evaluates individual student progress in reading, mathematics, and geometry. Used to measure overall class and school achievement growth related to specific academic objectives.

Description: 66–item paper-pencil crite-rion-referenced tests measuring student achievement in mathematics and reading comprehension. Two parallel forms, 1 and 2, are available at four ability levels: Level A for Grades 2–4, Level B for Grades 4–6, Level C for Grades 7–9, and Level D for Grades 10–13. Test items are arranged in three parts. Part I, Arithmetic Skills, con-sists of 30 items measuring basic arith-metic skills. Part II, Geometry-Measure-ment-Application, consists of 25 items measuring basic geometric concepts, arithmetic measurements, and application to practical problems. Part III, Modern Concepts, consists of 11 items measuring modern mathematics concepts. Examiner required. Suitable for group use.

Untimed: One class period

Scoring: Scoring service available

Cost: Contact publisher

Publisher: EdITS/Educational and Industrial Testing Service

TESTS OF ADULT BASIC EDUCATION (TABE)
CTB/McGraw-Hill

Adult

Purpose: Measures adult proficiency in reading, mathematics, and language. Used by educators to identify individual weaknesses, establish the appropriate level of instruction, and measure growth after instruction.

Description: Multiple-item paper-pencil test measuring an adult's grasp of the reading, mathematics, and language skills required to function in society. The test is available on three levels: Level D, Difficult (Grades 6–9), Level M, Medium (Grades 4–6), and Level E, Easy (Grades 2–4). Levels D and M assess reading (vocabulary and comprehension), mathematics (computation, concepts, and problems), and language (mechanics and expression, spelling skills). Level E assesses only reading and math. A practice exercise is included to reduce anxiety and provide some experience in test-taking procedures. A Locator Test is administered to determine the appropriate test level. Although this 1976 edition of the TABE is still available, it has been superseded by the TABE, Forms 5 and 6, which is the 1987 revision. Examiner required. Suitable for group use.

Timed: Level D 2 hours, 17 minutes; Level M 2 hours, 29 minutes; Level E 1 hour, 28 minutes

Scoring: Hand key

Cost: Multilevel examination kit (descriptive brochure, practice exercise and locator test, practice exercise and locator test answer sheet, test books and manuals for all levels, complete battery answer sheet, group record sheet, test reviewer's guide) $8.95

Publisher: CTB/Macmillan/McGraw-Hill

TESTS OF ADULT BASIC EDUCATION (TABE), FORMS 5 AND 6

Adult

Purpose: Measures adult proficiency in reading, mathematics, and language. Used by educators to identify individual strengths and weaknesses, establish the appropriate level of instruction, and measure growth after instruction.

Description: Multiple-item paper-pencil multiple-choice test measuring an adult's grasp of the reading, mathematics, and language skills required to function in society. The test is available in four levels: Level A, Advanced (Grades 8.6–12.9), Level D, Difficult (Grades 6.6–8.9), Level M, Medium (Grades 4.6–6.9), and Level E, Easy (Grades 2.6–4.9). Subtests contained in each level are reading vocabulary, reading comprehension, mathematics computation, mathematics concepts and applications, language mechanics, language expression, and spelling. A practice test is included to reduce anxiety and to provide some experience in test-taking procedures. A locator test is administered to determine the appropriate test level. A short survey form is available for use when testing time is limited and diagnostic information is not required. A large-print edition is available for use with persons with vision impairments. Scores may be used to estimate performance on the GED tests. Software is available for microcomputer scoring. This 1987 edition is a revision of the 1976 TABE, which is still available. Examiner required. Suitable for group use.

Timed: Complete battery 3 hours, 30 minutes; Survey Form 1 hour, 30 minutes

Scoring: Hand key; may be computer scored

Cost: Multilevel test review kit (brochure; examination materials booklet; practice exercise and locator test, answer sheet; Survey Form booklet; booklet for each level of Complete Battery, Form 5; manual with answer keys for Survey and Complete Battery; Complete Battery hand-scorable answer sheet; SCAN-TRON answer sheets; group record sheet) $14.20

Publisher: CTB/Macmillan/McGraw-Hill

TESTS OF GENERAL EDUCATIONAL DEVELOPMENT (GED)
American Council on Education

Adolescent, adult

Purpose: Assesses an individual's attainment of the academic skills generally acquired upon graduation from high school. Used with individuals seeking a high-school equivalency diploma.

Description: Battery of five paper-pencil achievement tests measuring academic skills reflecting the objectives of secondary education: Writing Skills (55 multiple-choice items, 1 essay; 2 hours), Social Studies (64 items, 85 minutes), Science (66 items, 95 minutes), Interpreting Literature and the Arts (45 items, 65 minutes), and Mathematics (56 items, 90 minutes). Multiple-choice items are machine scored; essays are scored at central sites. The GED are secure exams available only to official GED testing centers. The tests are administered at designated times throughout the year to both civilians and military personnel. The battery has undergone several revisions. Examiner required. Suitable for group use. Available in French, Spanish, braille, large print, and on audiocassette.

Timed: 7 hours, 45 minutes

Scoring: Machine scored; examiner evaluated

Cost: Contact publisher

Publisher: General Educational Development Testing Service of the American Council on Education

THE 3-R'S® TEST
Nancy S. Cole, E. Roger Trent, Dena C. Wadell, Robert L. Thorndike, and Elizabeth P. Hagen

Child, adolescent
Grades K–12

Purpose: Measures achievement in basic reading, language, and mathematics skills as well as verbal and quantitative abilities.

Description: Three paper-pencil multiple-choice batteries assessing academic achievement and ability: the Achievement Edition for Grades K–12 (Levels 6–18), the Achievement/Abilities Edition for Grades 3–12 (Levels 9–18), and the Class-Period Edition for Grades K–12 (Levels 6–18). The Achievement Edition (Forms A and B) measures reading and mathematics abilities for students in Grades K–2, and reading, mathematics, and language skills for students in Grades 3–12. The Achievement and Abilities Edition (Form A) includes the tests in the Achievement Edition as well as tests measuring verbal and quantitative abilities. The Class-Period Edition (Form A) yields a single achievement score in just 50 minutes. La Prueba is the Spanish-language edition of The 3-R's Test, Form A for Grades K–9 (Levels 6–14). It is designed to determine the degree to which students are literate in Spanish and to assess the achievement of students whose primary language is Spanish. La Prueba also measures achievement in science and social studies. Examiner required. Suitable for group use.

Timed: 50–190 minutes depending on edition and grade level

Scoring: Hand key; may be MRC or NCS machine scored; self-scoring answer sheets for Levels 9–18

Cost: 25 Achievement MRC machine-scorable test booklets (Grades K–3); directions for administering $45.00–$55.80; 35 Achievement/Abilities test booklets (Grades 3–12), directions $76.95; teacher's manual $6.90; 35 MRC answer sheets $21.00; 35 self-scoring answer sheets $27.00; 25 Class-Period MRC machine-scorable test booklets (Grades K–3), directions $34.80; 35 Class-Period test booklets (Grades 3–12), directions $32.55; 35 self-scoring answer sheets (Grades 3–12) $33.00; 25 La Prueba MRC machine-scorable test booklets (Grades K–3), directions $56.40–$63.90; 35 La Prueba test booklets (Grades 4–8), directions $72.00; 35 La Prueba MRC answer sheets $18.00; La Prueba teacher's guide $14.60

Publisher: The Riverside Publishing Company

THE TWO CULTURES TEST
Edgar M. VanVleck et al.

Adolescent, adult

Purpose: Measures general knowledge in science and the humanities. Used primarily by adults for personal information or for class placement.

Description: 100–item paper-pencil multiple-choice test of general knowledge in the two knowledge "cultures" of Western civilization: science (50 questions) and the humanities (50 questions). Information tested is likely to be encountered in high-school and college curricula. A good knowledge of English and at least a high-school education are required. Self-administered. Suitable for group use.

Untimed: 1 hour

Scoring: Self-scored

Cost: Complete kit $6.00

Publisher: Polymath Systems

VERBAL REASONING TESTS SERIES

Child, adolescent—
Ages 8–15

Purpose: Measures general scholastic ability. Used for educational evaluation.

Description: Four paper-pencil tests of verbal reasoning. Items include analogies, similarities, opposites, codes, odd-man-out, jumbled sentences, classifications, and syllogisms. The six tests and the ages they are designed for are Verbal Test BC (ages 8–10), Verbal Test CD (ages 9–11), Verbal Test D (ages 10–12), and Verbal Test EF (ages 11–13). All tests require extensive use of written English and may not be suitable for poor readers. Verbal Test C and Verbal Test GH are out-of-print. Examiner required. Suitable for group use.
BRITISH PUBLISHER

Timed: Varies

Scoring: Hand key

Cost: Primary specimen set (1 pupil booklet BC, CD, C, D, and sample manual) £2.85; secondary specimen set (1 pupil booklet D, EF, GH, and sample manual) £2.25 (payment in sterling for all overseas orders)

Publisher: NFER-NELSON Publishing Company Ltd.

WASHINGTON PRE-COLLEGE PROGRAM

High-school juniors—
college transfer students

Purpose: Measures achievement, abilities, and interests and assesses values, personal background, and career plans. Used with Washington high-school students for admissions, guidance, and placement in colleges in Washington and nearby states. Used by high schools and state agencies for evaluation and policy making.

Description: Paper-pencil test of abilities and achievement. Includes English Usage, Spelling, Reading Comprehension, Mechanical Reasoning, Spatial Ability, Applied Mathematics, Vocabulary, and Mathematics Achievement subtests. The WPC program also includes the Registration Questionnaire, Vocational Interest Inventory (VII), standardized high-school records compiled from official transcripts, and exercises for collecting additional career guidance data. Results are returned via a Guidance Report containing test results, high-school record summary, 8 interest area scores, overall interest profile analysis, expectancies of success in 36 four-year college fields and 15 two-year training fields, and a summary of personal objectives. Available materials include a career planning guide that integrates the Guidance Report and additional personal data. Examiner required. Suitable for group use.

Timed: 3 hours, 30 minutes

Scoring: Machine scored

Cost: Test booklets, registration booklet, guidance report, student interpretation guide $13.00 per student

Publisher: Washington Pre-College Program

Information and availability unconfirmed; last verified in 1988.

WESTERN MICHIGAN UNIVERSITY ENGLISH QUALIFYING EXAM (EQE)
Refer to page 285.

WIDE RANGE ACHIEVEMENT TEST—REVISED (WRAT-R)
Sarah Jastak and Gary S. Wilkinson

Ages 5–adult

Purpose: Measures the basic educational skills of word recognition, spelling, and arithmetic and identifies individuals with learning difficulties. Used for educational placement, measuring school achievement, vocational assessment, and job placement and training.

Description: Three paper-pencil subtests (50–100 items per subtest) assessing coding skills: Reading (recognizing and naming letters and pronouncing printed words); Spelling (copying marks resembling letters, writing name, and printing words); and Arithmetic (counting, reading number symbols, oral and written computation). The test consists of two levels: Level I (ages 5–11) and Level II (ages 12–adult). Optional word lists for both levels of the reading and spelling tests are offered on plastic cards, and a recorded pronunciation of the lists is provided on cassette tape. The tape itself can be used to administer the spelling section. The test is normed for age rather than grade. For this revised version, norms are based on a national, stratified sample. In conjunction with other tests, such as the Wechsler Scales, WRAT-R is useful for determining personality structure. The test is restricted to educational and psychological professionals. A large-print edition is available for those who require magnification of reading material. Examiner required. The spelling and arithmetic subtests are suitable for group use. The reading subtest must be individually administered.

Timed: 10 minutes per subtest

Scoring: Examiner evaluated

Cost: Manual $22.00; 25 test forms $13.00

Publisher: Jastak Assessment Systems

WIDE RANGE ASSESSMENT OF MEMORY AND LEARNING (WRAML)
Refer to page 66.

WOODCOCK LANGUAGE PROFICIENCY BATTERY (WLPB)
Richard W. Woodcock

Ages 3–80 and older
Grades PreK and above

Purpose: Measures oral, reading, and written language in either English or Spanish. Used to diagnose language proficiency in children and adults and for instructional planning.

Description: Multiple-item battery of eight subtests taken from the Woodcock-Johnson Psycho-Educational Battery measuring the following factors: picture vocabulary, antonyms-synonyms, analogies, letter-word identification, word attack, passage comprehension, dictation, and proofing. Within the school-age range, the WLPB-English can be administered to students with English as their second language. If the Spanish form also is given, the overview can include a description of proficiency in each language in each area of skill. Materials, in both forms, include the battery, response booklets, and manual. Examiner required. Not suitable for group use. Available in Spanish.

Untimed: 45 minutes

Scoring: Examiner evaluated

Cost: English form $125.00; Spanish form $125.00

Publisher: DLM Teaching Resources

WOODCOCK-JOHNSON PSYCHO-EDUCATIONAL BATTERY-REVISED (WJ-R)
Richard W. Woodcock and Mary Bonner Johnson

Ages 2–90 and older
Grades PreK and above

Purpose: Evaluates individual cognitive ability, scholastic achievement, and interest level. Used to diagnose learning disabilities and for instructional planning, vocational rehabilitation counseling, and research.

Description: 39–test battery in two parts. The WJ-R may be administered in its entirety or as single tests or clusters to meet specific appraisal needs. Part One tests seven factors of long-term memory, short-term memory, processing speed, auditory processing, visual processing, comprehension knowledge, and fluid reasoning. Part Two (available in Forms A and B) tests the individual's achievement in five academic areas: reading, mathematics, written language, knowledge, and skills. Materials include test books, response booklets, cassette tape, and a technical manual, which also may be ordered separately. IBM and Apple computer scoring systems are available. Examiner required. Not suitable for group use. Available in Spanish.

Untimed: Varies

Scoring: Examiner evaluated; may be computer scored

Cost: Complete set with case $495.00

Publisher: DLM Teaching Resources

WORD AND NUMBER ASSESSMENT INVENTORY (WNAI)
Charles B. Johansson and Jean C. Johansson

Adolescent, adult
Grades 9 and above

Purpose: Measures individual verbal and numerical aptitude. Used for career and school counseling and employment screening.

Description: 80–item paper-pencil multiple-choice test consisting of 50 vocabulary and 30 mathematics items on combined question-answer forms. The scores are compared to those of individuals at several educational levels and in a number of occupations. The test may be computer scored via mail-in service or using Arion II Teleprocessing. Self-administered. Suitable for group use.

Untimed: 1 hour

Scoring: Computer scored

Cost: Manual $12.50; interpretive report $5.05–$8.80 depending on quantity; profile report $3.15–4.35 depending on quantity

Publisher: National Computer Systems/PAS Division

Achievement in Health-Related Curricula

ACT PROFICIENCY EXAMINATION PROGRAM—NURSING: ADULT NURSING
The American College Testing Program

Adult

Purpose: Assesses proficiency in adult nursing care. Used to grant college credit and advanced placement in academic courses.

Description: Multiple-item paper-pencil multiple-choice test. Items are based on material normally taught in an upper-division sequence of courses in medical-surgical nursing or adult nursing at the baccalaureate level. Designed for and standardized at the B.S. degree level. Individuals seeking credit should contact their local colleges for information. Examiner required. Suitable for group use.

Timed: 3 hours

Scoring: Computer scored by ACT

Cost: Fee $40.00

Publisher: The American College Testing Program

ACT PROFICIENCY EXAMINATION PROGRAM— NURSING: COMMONALITIES IN NURSING CARE: AREA A
The American College Testing Program

Adult

Purpose: Assesses proficiency in dealing with basic nursing problems. Used to grant college credit and advanced placement in academic courses.

Description: Multiple-item paper-pencil multiple-choice test. Items are based on common nursing problems and nursing care as they are related to the health continuum, communication and interpersonal relations, asepsis, comfort, rest and activity, and safety. Knowledge and understanding of technical vocabulary, anatomy, physiology, emotional and physical development, and pharmacology is assumed. Designed for and standardized at the A.S. degree level. Those seeking credit should contact their local colleges for information. Examiner required. Suitable for group use.

Timed: 3 hours
Scoring: Computer scored by ACT
Cost: Fee $50.00
Publisher: The American College Testing Program

ACT PROFICIENCY EXAMINATION PROGRAM— NURSING: COMMONALITIES IN NURSING CARE: AREA B
The American College Testing Program

Adult

Purpose: Assesses proficiency in dealing with common nursing problems. Used to grant college credit and advanced placement in academic courses.

Description: Multiple-item paper-pencil multiple-choice test. Items are based on common nursing problems and nursing care as they are related to nutrition, elimination, oxygenation, and fluid and electrolyte balance. Knowledge and understanding of technical vocabulary, anatomy,

physiology, emotional and physical development, nutrition, and pharmacology are assumed. Designed for and standardized at the A.S. degree level. Individuals seeking credit should contact their local colleges for information. Examiner required. Suitable for group use.

Timed: 3 hours
Scoring: Computer scored by ACT
Cost: Fee $50.00
Publisher: The American College Testing Program

ACT PROFICIENCY EXAMINATION PROGRAM— NURSING: DIFFERENCES IN NURSING CARE: AREA A
The American College Testing Program

Adult

Purpose: Assesses proficiency in the nursing care of children and adult patients with common diseases and health-care problems, particularly those problems relating to oxygenation and cell growth. Used to grant college credit and advanced placement in academic courses.

Description: Multiple-item paper-pencil multiple-choice test measuring knowledge and understanding relating to the various different health-care problems frequently encountered by the associate degree nurse. Questions concern aspects of acute and long-term health problems; comprehension of the causes, symptoms, and relationships between common and specific manifestations involving oxygenation and cell growth; comprehension of the effects and relative advantages and disadvantages of various treatments; and ability to apply knowledge of differences in nursing care related to oxygenation and cell growth and resulting from specific health problems and the individual's response to clinical situations. Knowledge of anatomy, physiology, pharmacology, and nutrition is assumed. Designed for and standardized at the A.S. degree level. Individuals seeking credit should contact their local colleges for information. Examiner required. Suitable for group use.

Timed: 3 hours
Scoring: Computer scored by ACT

Cost: Fee $50.00

Publisher: The American College Testing Program

ACT PROFICIENCY EXAMINATION PROGRAM— NURSING: DIFFERENCES IN NURSING CARE: AREA B
The American College Testing Program

Adult

Purpose: Assesses proficiency in the nursing care of children and adults with common diseases and health problems, particularly those problems relating to behavioral responses and endocrine/regulatory mechanisms. Used to grant college credit and advanced placement in academic courses.

Description: Multiple-item paper-pencil multiple-choice test measuring four areas of basic nursing care: knowledge of anatomy, physiology, pathophysiology, physical and emotional development, and psychosocial aspects of acute and long-term health problems; comprehension of the causes, symptoms, and relationships between common and specific manifestations involving behavioral responses and endocrine/regulatory mechanisms; comprehension of the effects and relative advantages and disadvantages of various treatments; and ability to apply knowledge of differences in nursing care related to behavioral responses and endocrine/regulatory mechanisms resulting from specific health problems and the individual's response to clinical settings. Knowledge of anatomy, physiology, pharmacology, and nutrition is assumed. Designed for and standardized at the A.S. degree level. Individuals seeking credit should contact their local colleges for information. Examiner required. Suitable for group use.

Timed: 3 hours

Scoring: Computer scored by ACT

Cost: Fee $50.00

Publisher: The American College Testing Program

ACT PROFICIENCY EXAMINATION PROGRAM— NURSING: DIFFERENCES IN NURSING CARE: AREA C
The American College Testing Program

Adult

Purpose: Assesses proficiency in nursing care of children and adults with diseases and common health problems, particularly those relating to the infectious process, tissue trauma, and neuromuscular dysfunctions. Used to grant college credit and advanced placement in academic courses.

Description: Multiple-item paper-pencil multiple-choice test measuring four areas of basic nursing care: knowledge of anatomy, physiology, pathophysiology, physical and emotional development, and psychosocial aspects of acute and long-term health problems; comprehension of the causes, symptoms, and relationships between common and specific manifestations involving the infectious process, tissue trauma, and neuromuscular dysfunctions; comprehension of the effects and relative advantages and disadvantages of various treatments; and ability to apply knowledge of differences in nursing care related to the infectious process, tissue trauma, and neuromuscular dysfunctions resulting from specific health problems and the individual's response to clinical situations. Knowledge of anatomy, physiology, pharmacology, and nutrition is assumed. Designed for and standardized at the A.S. degree level. Individuals seeking credit should contact their local colleges for information. Examiner required. Suitable for group use.

Timed: 3 hours

Scoring: Computer scored by ACT

Cost: Fee $50.00

Publisher: The American College Testing Program

ACT PROFICIENCY EXAMINATION PROGRAM— NURSING: FUNDAMENTALS OF NURSING
The American College Testing Program

Adult

Purpose: Assesses proficiency in nursing skills and procedures. Measures knowledge and understanding of the nursing process, assessment, and implementation. Used to grant college credit and advanced placement in academic courses.

Description: Multiple-item paper-pencil multiple-choice test measuring terms, facts, and trends and the ability to apply principles and theories to nursing situations. Examination is based on conventional nursing content. Designed for and standardized for the A.S. degree level. Individuals seeking credit should contact their local colleges for information. Examiner required. Suitable for group use.
Timed: 3 hours
Scoring: Computer scored by ACT
Cost: Fee $40.00
Publisher: The American College Testing Program

ACT PROFICIENCY EXAMINATION PROGRAM— NURSING: HEALTH RESTORATION: AREA I
The American College Testing Program

Adult

Purpose: Assesses proficiency in nursing care and intervention aimed at health restoration for individuals, families, and communities. Used to grant college credit and advanced placement in academic courses.

Description: Multiple-item paper-pencil multiple-choice test. Items are based on the interrelationship of the nursing process and changes in the client system (individual, family, community). The nursing process is emphasized as the framework for assisting client adaptation to change in a way that promotes restoration, palliation, habilitation, and rehabilitation. This exam focuses on selected health problems: cardiovascular, respiratory, endocrine, and autoimmune problems; neoplasms; and accidents and disasters. Designed for and standardized at the B.S. degree level. Individuals seeking credit should contact their local colleges for information. Examiner required. Suitable for group use.

Timed: 3 hours
Scoring: Computer scored by ACT
Cost: Fee $50.00
Publisher: The American College Testing Program

ACT PROFICIENCY EXAMINATION PROGRAM— NURSING: HEALTH RESTORATION: AREA II
The American College Testing Program

Adult

Purpose: Assesses proficiency in nursing care and intervention aimed at health restoration of individuals, families, and communities. Used to grant college credit and advanced placement in academic courses.

Description: Multiple-item paper-pencil multiple-choice test. Items are based on the interrelationship between the nursing process and changes in the client system (individual, family, community). The nursing process is emphasized as the framework for assisting client adaptation to change in a way that promotes restoration, palliation, habilitation, and rehabilitation. Questions cover emotional and behavioral problems, neurological and sensory health problems, infections and communicable diseases, complications of pregnancy and problems of the high-risk neonate, birth defects, and genetic problems. Designed for and standardized at the B.S. degree level. Individuals seeking credit should contact their local colleges for information. Examiner required. Suitable for group use.
Timed: 3 hours
Scoring: Computer scored by ACT
Cost: Fee $50.00
Publisher: The American College Testing Program

ACT PROFICIENCY EXAMINATION PROGRAM— NURSING: HEALTH SUPPORT: AREA I
The American College Testing Program

Adult

Purpose: Assesses proficiency in health support approaches. Used to grant college credit and advanced placement in academic courses.

Description: Multiple-item paper-pencil multiple-choice test. Items cover the patterns that influence wellness and the understanding of health promotion and prevention of illness in the nursing care of the client. The examination emphasizes use of the nursing process to support health of the client throughout the life cycle. Client spectrum includes individuals, families, and communities. Specific areas tested are theoretical and philosophical concepts; ecological and epidemiological concepts; individual, family, and community assessment; community resources and dissemination of health case information; and patterns of risk specific to problems of environmental safety, nutrition, and childbearing and child rearing. Designed for and standardized at the B.S. degree level. Individuals seeking credit should contact their local colleges for information. Examiner required. Suitable for group use.

Timed: 3 hours
Scoring: Computer scored by ACT
Cost: Fee $50.00
Publisher: The American College Testing Program

ACT PROFICIENCY EXAMINATION PROGRAM— NURSING: HEALTH SUPPORT: AREA II
The American College Testing Program

Adult

Purpose: Assesses the use of the nursing process in supporting the health of the client throughout the life cycle. Used to grant college credit and advanced placement in academic courses.

Description: Multiple-item paper-pencil multiple-choice test. Items focus on alterations of developmental, sustenal, activity, or life-space patterns that place the client (individual, family, community) at high risk for major health problems. Emphasis is placed on nursing actions related to prevention, teaching and coun-

seling, screening, and early detection with regard to the need of the clients. The major health problems covered are cardiovascular and respiratory problems, neoplasms, infections, and communicable diseases, neuromuscular and endocrine problems, autoimmune/hypersensitivity problems, and birth defects and genetic problems. Designed for and standardized at the B.S. degree level. Individuals seeking credit should contact their local colleges for information. Examiner required. Suitable for group use.

Timed: 3 hours
Scoring: Computer scored by ACT
Cost: Fee $50.00
Publisher: The American College Testing Program

ACT PROFICIENCY EXAMINATION PROGRAM— NURSING: MATERNAL AND CHILD NURSING: ASSOCIATE DEGREE
The American College Testing Program

Adult

Purpose: Assesses proficiency in maternal and child nursing. Used to grant college credit and advanced placement in academic courses.

Description: Multiple-item paper-pencil multiple-choice test. Items are based on knowledge of facts, trends, and terminology and on the ability to recognize and apply theories of nursing care and principles of interpersonal relationships, nutrition, and pharmacology to a variety of health-care situations. The test also assesses the ability to utilize the nursing process (assessment, planning, implementation, and evaluation) as it relates to the nursing care of the family during the childbearing cycle. Designed for and standardized at the A.S. degree level. Individuals seeking credit should contact their local colleges for information. Examiner required. Suitable for group use.

Timed: 3 hours
Scoring: Computer scored by ACT
Cost: Fee $40.00
Publisher: The American College Testing Program

ACT PROFICIENCY EXAMINATION PROGRAM— NURSING: MATERNAL AND CHILD NURSING: BACCALAUREATE DEGREE
The American College Testing Program

Adult

Purpose: Measures proficiency in maternal and child nursing. Used to grant college credit and advanced placement in academic courses.

Description: Multiple-item paper-pencil multiple-choice test. Items are based on the physiology and pathophysiology of maternal and child nursing, the theoretical framework of family functioning, and the application of the nursing process to practical situations. Designed for and standardized at the B.S. degree level. Individuals seeking credit should contact their local colleges for information. Examiner required. Suitable for group use.

Timed: 3 hours
Scoring: Computer scored by ACT
Cost: Fee $40.00
Publisher: The American College Testing Program

ACT PROFICIENCY EXAMINATION PROGRAM— NURSING: MATERNITY NURSING
The American College Testing Program

Adult

Purpose: Assesses knowledge and understanding of maternity nursing and normal health care maintenance for the well and ill child at birth.

Description: 85–100–item paper-pencil multiple-choice test. Items are based on terminology, facts, principles, theories, and trends in the areas of nutrition, pharmacology, familial interrelationships, pregnancy periods, and child care and development from birth through adolescence. The test yields a standard score. Designed for and standardized at the A.S. degree level. Those seeking credit should

contact their local colleges for information. Examiner required. Suitable for group use.

Timed: 3 hours
Scoring: Computer scored by ACT
Cost: Fee $40.00
Publisher: The American College Testing Program

ACT PROFICIENCY EXAMINATION PROGRAM— NURSING: OCCUPATIONAL STRATEGIES IN NURSING
The American College Testing Program

Adult

Purpose: Assesses an individual's knowledge and understanding of the roles and functions of the technical nurse as that individual contributes to the current practice of nursing within the legal limitations placed on the profession. Used to grant college credit and advanced placement in academic courses.

Description: Multiple-item paper-pencil multiple-choice test covering the health team, nursing team, and legal guidelines to nursing practice within both the context of the history and the current framework of the health care delivery system. The test covers knowledge and understanding of how licensure, nursing organizations, and education influence the technical nurse's function, as well as ethical guidelines for nursing practice. Designed for and standardized at the A.S. degree level. Individuals seeking credit should contact their local colleges for information. Examiner required. Suitable for group use.

Timed: 3 hours
Scoring: Computer scored by ACT
Cost: Fee $50.00
Publisher: The American College Testing Program

ACT PROFICIENCY EXAMINATION PROGRAM— NURSING: PROFESSIONAL STRATEGIES IN NURSING
The American College Testing Program

Adult

Purpose: Measures knowledge and understanding of the professional role in nursing. Used to grant college credit and advanced placement in academic courses.

Description: Multiple-item paper-pencil multiple-choice test focused on professional practice and the health-care delivery system. Other areas tested include understanding of the development of the profession of nursing, professional organizations, and the evolution of nursing practice and education. Designed for and standardized at the B.S. degree level. Individuals seeking credit should contact their local colleges for information. Examiner required. Suitable for group use.

Timed: 3 hours

Scoring: Computer scored by ACT

Cost: Fee $50.00

Publisher: The American College Testing Program

ACT PROFICIENCY EXAMINATION PROGRAM—NURSING: PSYCHIATRIC/MENTAL HEALTH NURSING
The American College Testing Program

Adult

Purpose: Assesses proficiency in psychiatric and mental health nursing. Used to grant college credit and advanced placement in academic courses.

Description: Multiple-item paper-pencil multiple-choice test. Items are based on terminology, principles, and dynamics in the areas of personality development, family development, and psychological dysfunctions as they relate to nursing assessment, planning, intervention, and evaluation. Designed for and standardized at the B.S. degree level. Individuals seeking credit should contact their local colleges for information. Examiner required. Suitable for group use.

Timed: 3 hours

Scoring: Computer scored by ACT

Cost: Fee $40.00

Publisher: The American College Testing Program

ADMISSIONS EXAMINATIONS: ADMISSIONS AND CREDENTIALING GROUP
The Psychological Corporation

Adolescent, adult
Grades 10 and above

Purpose: Assesses students' readiness to enter various health and medical schools and colleges. Used for admission and guidance of students seeking to enter posthigh-school studies.

Description: 10 paper-pencil admissions examinations: Allied Health Professions Admissions Test (AHPAT), Entrance Examination for Schools of Health Related Technologies (EESRT), Pharmacy College Admissions Test (PCAT), Optometry College Admission Test (OCAT), Veterinary Aptitude Test (VAT), Dental Hygiene Candidate Aptitude Test (DHCAT), Entrance Examination for Schools of Nursing, Entrance Examination for Schools of Practical/Vocational Nursing, Aptitude Test for Allied Health Programs, and Allied Health Entrance Examination. The Admissions and Credentialing Group provides testing services to certification boards, professional registries, and national associations in connection with professional licensing, certification, counseling, admissions, scholarships, and personnel selection. It also offers related consulting services. Applicants must complete and file an application and the appropriate fee by specific deadlines. Results are sent to the applicant and schools or colleges designated by the applicant approximately three to six weeks following the date of testing. Tests are given at designated test centers. For specific content and cost information, contact the publisher. Examiner required. Suitable for group use.

Timed: Approximately 4 hours per test

Scoring: Computer scoring service provided

Cost: Contact publisher

Publisher: Admissions and Credentialing Group/The Psychological Corporation

Information and availability unconfirmed; last verified in 1988.

ADMISSIONS EXAMINATIONS: ADMISSIONS AND CREDENTIALING GROUP: ALLIED HEALTH ENTRANCE EXAMINATION
The Psychological Corporation

Adolescent, adult
Grades 10 and above

Purpose: Assesses aptitude and achievement of students seeking admission to short-term assistant and technician educational programs. Used for admissions and selection.

Description: Multiple-item paper-pencil multiple-choice test for applicants to short-term assistant and technician educational programs. See Admissions Examinations: Admissions and Credentialing Group of The Psychological Corporation. Examiner required. Suitable for group use.

Untimed: Not available

Scoring: Scoring service provided by publisher

Cost: Contact publisher

Publisher: Admissions and Credentialing Group/The Psychological Corporation

Information and availability unconfirmed; last verified in 1988.

ADMISSIONS EXAMINATIONS: ADMISSIONS AND CREDENTIALING GROUP: ALLIED HEALTH PROFESSIONS ADMISSIONS TEST (AHPAT)
The Psychological Corporation

Adolescent, adult
Grades 10 and above

Purpose: Assesses students' readiness for entering upper division majors in programs leading to baccalaureate and postbaccalaureate degrees in allied health professions. Used for admissions and selection.

Description: Multiple-item paper-pencil multiple-choice test measuring verbal ability, quantitative ability, biology principles and concepts, chemistry principles, including inorganic and organic chemistry, and reading comprehension. See

Admissions Examinations: Admissions and Credentialing Group of The Psychological Corporation. Examiner required. Suitable for group use.

Timed: Not available

Scoring: Scoring service provided by publisher

Cost: Contact publisher

Publisher: Admissions and Credentialing Group/The Psychological Corporation

Information and availability unconfirmed; last verified in 1988.

ADMISSIONS EXAMINATIONS: ADMISSIONS AND CREDENTIALING GROUP: APTITUDE TEST FOR ALLIED HEALTH PROGRAMS
The Psychological Corporation

Adolescent, adult
Grades 10 and above

Purpose: Assesses aptitude and achievement of students seeking admission to one- and two-year allied health education programs. Used for admissions and selection.

Description: Multiple-item paper-pencil multiple-choice test designed for students applying to allied health education programs. See Admissions Examinations: Admissions and Credentialing Group of The Psychological Corporation. Examiner required. Suitable for group use.

Timed: Not available

Scoring: Scoring service provided by publisher

Cost: Contact publisher

Publisher: Admissions and Credentialing Group/The Psychological Corporation

Information and availability unconfirmed; last verified in 1988.

ADMISSIONS EXAMINATIONS: ADMISSIONS AND CREDENTIALING GROUP: ENTRANCE EXAMINATION FOR SCHOOLS OF HEALTH RELATED TECHNOLOGIES (EESRT)
The Psychological Corporation

Adolescent, adult
Grades 10 and above

Purpose: Measures general academic and scientific knowledge with emphasis on the physical sciences for applicants seeking admission to one- or two-year posthigh-school programs in health-related technologies. Used for admissions and selection.

Description: Multiple-item paper-pencil multiple-choice test measuring verbal ability, quantitative ability, science, reading comprehension, and space relations. See Admissions Examinations: Admissions and Credentialing Group of The Psychological Corporation. Examiner required. Suitable for group use.

Timed: Not available

Scoring: Scoring service provided by publisher

Cost: Contact publisher

Publisher: Admissions and Credentialing Group/The Psychological Corporation

Information and availability unconfirmed; last verified in 1988.

ADMISSIONS EXAMINATIONS: ADMISSIONS AND CREDENTIALING GROUP: ENTRANCE EXAMINATION FOR SCHOOLS OF NURSING
The Psychological Corporation

Adolescent, adult
Grades 10 and above

Purpose: Assesses students' readiness for entering a posthigh-school nursing school. Used for admissions and selection.

Description: Multiple-item paper-pencil test designed to assist in the admission and guidance of students entering nursing school. See Admissions Examinations: Admissions and Credentialing Group of The Psychological Corporation. Examiner required. Suitable for group use.

Timed: Not available

Scoring: Scoring service provided by publisher

Cost: Contact publisher

Publisher: Admissions and Credentialing Group/The Psychological Corporation

Information and availability unconfirmed; last verified in 1988.

ADMISSIONS EXAMINATIONS: ADMISSIONS AND CREDENTIALING GROUP: ENTRANCE EXAMINATION FOR SCHOOLS OF PRACTICAL/ VOCATIONAL NURSING
The Psychological Corporation

Adolescent, adult
Grades 10 and above

Purpose: Assesses aptitude and achievement of students seeking admission to schools of practical or vocational nursing. Used for admissions and selection.

Description: Multiple-item paper-pencil multiple-choice test designed for programs admitting students being prepared to become practical or vocational nurses. See Admissions Examinations: Admissions and Credentialing Group of The Psychological Corporation. Examiner required. Suitable for group use.

Timed: Not available

Scoring: Scoring service provided by publisher

Cost: Contact publisher

Publisher: Admissions and Credentialing Group/The Psychological Corporation

Information and availability unconfirmed; last verified in 1988.

ADMISSIONS EXAMINATIONS: ADMISSIONS AND CREDENTIALING GROUP: OPTOMETRY COLLEGE ADMISSION TEST
The Psychological Corporation

Adolescent, adult
Grades 10 and above

Purpose: Assesses aptitude and achievement of students seeking admission to colleges of optometry. Used for admissions and selection.

Description: Multiple-item paper-pencil multiple-choice test measuring verbal ability, quantitative ability, biology principles and concepts, organic and inorganic chemistry knowledge, physics knowledge with emphasis on light, and study-reading ability. See Admissions Examinations:

Admissions and Credentialing Group of The Psychological Corporation. Examiner required. Suitable for group use.
Timed: 3 hours
Scoring: Scoring service provided by publisher
Cost: Contact publisher
Publisher: Admissions and Credentialing Group/The Psychological Corporation
Information and availability unconfirmed; last verified in 1988.

ADMISSIONS EXAMINATIONS: ADMISSIONS AND CREDENTIALING GROUP: PHARMACY COLLEGE ADMISSION TEST (PCAT)
The Psychological Corporation

Adolescent, adult
Grades 10 and above

Purpose: Assesses aptitude and achievement of students seeking admission to colleges of pharmacy. Used for admissions and selection.

Description: Multiple-item paper-pencil multiple-choice test designed to assist in the admission and guidance of students seeking admission to pharmacy colleges. The test measures verbal ability, quantitative ability, chemistry knowledge, biology knowledge, and reading comprehension. See Admissions Examinations: Admissions and Credentialing Group of The Psychological Corporation. Examiner required. Suitable for group use.
Timed: 2 hours, 30 minutes
Scoring: Scoring service provided by publisher
Cost: Contact publisher
Publisher: Admissions and Credentialing Group/The Psychological Corporation
Information and availability unconfirmed; last verified in 1988.

ADMISSIONS EXAMINATIONS: ADMISSIONS AND CREDENTIALING GROUP: VETERINARY APTITUDE TEST (VAT)
The Psychological Corporation

Adolescent, adult
Grades 10 and above

Purpose: Assesses aptitude and achievement of students seeking admission to colleges of veterinary medicine. Used for admissions and selection.

Description: Five multiple-item paper-pencil tests measuring abilities related to scholastic performance: reading comprehension, quantitative ability, biology, chemistry, and study reading. In addition, applicant performance on these measures is combined in a total score to provide a single index of scholastic aptitude. See Admissions Examinations: Admissions and Credentialing Group of The Psychological Corporation. Examiner required. Suitable for group use.
Timed: 4 hours
Scoring: Scoring service provided by publisher
Cost: Contact publisher
Publisher: Admissions and Credentialing Group/The Psychological Corporation
Information and availability unconfirmed; last verified in 1988.

DENTAL ADMISSION TEST (DAT)
American Dental Association

Adult
Grades 14 and above

Purpose: Measures general academic ability, scientific understanding, and perceptual ability of potential dental school students. Required of all candidates for admission to U.S. dental schools.

Description: 290–item paper-pencil competitive examination in four sections: Quantitative Reasoning (50 items); Reading Comprehension (50 items); Natural Sciences, including biology and general and organic chemistry (100 items); and Perceptual Ability (90 items). The test is administered only to individuals who have completed at least one year of college, including courses in natural sciences, although two or more years of college experience are recommended. No books, slide rules, paper, calculators, or other resource materials are permitted in the exam room. Administered biannually in specific cities only. Examiner required (provided through the American Dental Association). Suitable for group use.

Timed: ½ day
Scoring: Computer scored
Cost: Fee $60.00
Publisher: American Dental Association

LUTHER HOSPITAL SENTENCE COMPLETIONS (LHSC)

Refer to page 768.

MEDICAL COLLEGE ADMISSION TEST

Adolescent, adult
Grades 13 and above

Purpose: Assists medical school admission committees in the evaluation of candidates primarily applying to medical school.

Description: One full day of examinations assessing academic achievement of medical school applicants. The examinations are administered in four sections: Science Knowledge (presents biology, chemistry, and physics in separate assessment areas as a partial assessment of science achievement), Science Problems (intermingles biology, chemistry, and physics to assess the application of knowledge in solving problems), Skills Analysis: Reading (presents information in reading passages to assess analytical and reasoning skills), and Skills Analysis: Quantitative (assesses analytical and reasoning skills using questions involving quantitative material). The student manual includes test day schedule, a complete practice test, descriptions of the tests, and comprehensive guidelines for preparing for the test. Prerequisite subjects for the science subtests are usually covered in one-year introductory courses in biology, general chemistry, organic chemistry, and physics. The examinations are administered in the spring and fall of each year at centers established and supervised by the American College Testing Program. Examiner required. Suitable for group use.

Timed: 7 hours
Scoring: Computer scored

Cost: Regular exam (on Saturday) $95.00; student manual $10.00 plus postage
Publisher: Association of American Medical Colleges

NCLEX-RN SUCCESS TEST

Graduate nurses

Purpose: Assesses nursing ability, skill, and knowledge at the RN entry level.

Description: 200–item paper-pencil multiple-choice test measuring nursing ability, skill, and knowledge at the RN entry level. Percent correct and percentile scores are provided for total score and two subscales. Materials include the test and answer sheet included in the book *American Nursing Review for NCLEX-RN.* Self-administered. Not suitable for group use.

Untimed: 3½ hours
Scoring: Computer scored; scoring service available from publisher
Cost: $23.00 per answer sheet scored
Publisher: National League for Nursing

NLN ACHIEVEMENT TESTS FOR PRACTICAL NURSING

Practical nursing students

Purpose: Measures individual student achievement in practical/vocational nursing programs and enables faculty to evaluate specific course or program objectives in terms of nationally accepted objectives in nursing and compare the scores of students in a nursing program with those of students throughout the country.

Description: Seven paper-pencil multiple-choice tests consisting of 80–170 questions each. The following tests are available: Comprehensive Nursing Achievement Test for Practical Nursing Students, Fundamentals for Practical Nursing Students, Medical-Surgical Nursing for Practical Nursing Students, Maternity Nursing for Practical Nursing Students, Mental Health Concepts for

Practical Nursing Students, Nursing of Children for Practical Nursing Students, and Pharmacology for Practical Nursing Students. Test items have been developed in cooperation with faculty members throughout the United States, reflecting the objectives and subject-matter content of practical/vocational nursing programs from all geographic areas.

All test papers must be returned to NLN Test Service for scoring. Reports on test results are returned to the nursing program within 10 working days after NLN receives the answer sheets. Reports include raw scores and percentiles, item descriptors, a list of omitted or incorrectly answered items for each student, and an additional group analysis when more than 10 students are tested as a group. NLN encourages faculty members to review the tests before ordering them to insure that appropriate subject-matter content areas have been covered. NLN achievement tests may be used in the United States, its territories, and Canada by state- or province-approved programs preparing students for nursing practice; by hospitals and colleges that are approved to provide instruction to students from such programs; and by nurse licensing authorities in the United States and Canada or their agents. Requests for use by any other program are evaluated individually. The tests are available in English only. Examiner required. Suitable for group use.

Untimed: 1 hour, 30 minutes–3 hours per test

Scoring: Computer scored

Cost: Test service (test booklets, answer sheets, directions for administration, scoring service) $5.00–$10.00 per student per test

Publisher: National League for Nursing

NLN ACHIEVEMENT TESTS FOR PRACTICAL NURSING: COMPREHENSIVE NURSING ACHIEVEMENT TEST FOR PRACTICAL NURSING STUDENTS (FORM 3513)

Practical nursing students

Purpose: Measures the full range of knowledge needed by graduating students in practical/vocational nursing programs

for beginning practice. Assesses readiness for the nurse licensure examination.

Description: Approximately 170–item paper-pencil multiple-choice test measuring the full range of material presented in programs preparing students for practical nursing. Questions pertain to case situations representative of conditions commonly encountered by the beginning practitioner in health-care settings, including care of the adult, care of the elderly, nursing during childbearing, and nursing of children. The questions call for the application of knowledge in the assessment of client status, planning, intervention in basic nursing situations, evaluating, recording, and reporting. Questions related to growth and development, mental health concepts, basic communication techniques, medication administration and effects, as well as nutrition are integrated. A total score, along with subscores in broad clinical areas, are reported in the form of individual diagnostic profiles. Two copies are provided: one for distribution to students and one for faculty analysis. Norms are provided for practical nursing students. The test should be administered at the end of the program to assess readiness for the nurse licensure examination and to provide practice in taking a nationally standardized test of nursing knowledge. The test is available for faculty review. Examiner required. Suitable for group use.

Untimed: 3 hours

Scoring: Computer scored

Cost: Test service (test booklets, answer sheets, directions for administration, scoring service) $10.00 per student

Publisher: National League for Nursing

NLN ACHIEVEMENT TESTS FOR PRACTICAL NURSING: FUNDAMENTALS FOR PRACTICAL NURSING STUDENTS (FORM 4616)

Practical nursing students

Purpose: Measures individual achievement of practical/vocational nursing students in body structure and function, nursing procedures, and normal nutrition.

Description: Approximately 100–item paper-pencil multiple-choice test measuring the ability to identify basic bodily structures and functions, select appropriate measures for giving care to patients, and identify nutritional requirements and the nutritional elements of food. Items on nursing practice include principles of therapeutic communication, the nursing process, vital signs, body mechanics, and aseptic technique. A total score and three subscores (Anatomy and Physiology, Normal Nutrition, Nursing Practice) are provided. Norms are reported for practical nursing students. The test should be administered early in the program, after completion of the areas covered by the test. The test is available for faculty review. Form 4616 supersedes NLN Achievement Tests for Practical Nursing: Three Units of Content (Form 1482). Examiner required. Suitable for group use.

Untimed: 2 hours

Scoring: Computer scored

Cost: Test service (test booklets, answer sheets, directions for administration, scoring service) $5.00 per student

Publisher: National League for Nursing

NLN ACHIEVEMENT TESTS FOR PRACTICAL NURSING: MATERNITY NURSING FOR PRACTICAL NURSING STUDENTS (FORM 4019)

Practical nursing students

Purpose: Measures the individual achievement of practical/vocational nursing students in objectives related to maternity nursing.

Description: Approximately 110–item paper-pencil multiple-choice test measuring student knowledge of the objectives of maternity nursing related to nursing measures, including medications, nutrition, and communication. A total score and three subscores (antepartum, intra- and post-partum, neonate) are reported. Norms are reported for practical nursing students. The test should be administered after completion of the course in maternity nursing. This form supercedes NLN Achievement Tests for Practical Nursing: Maternity Nursing for Practical Nursing Students (Form 1182). The test is available for faculty review. Examiner required. Suitable for group use.

Untimed: 2 hours

Scoring: Computer scored

Cost: Test service (test booklets, answer sheets, directions for administration, scoring service) $5.00 per student

Publisher: National League for Nursing

NLN ACHIEVEMENT TESTS FOR PRACTICAL NURSING: MEDICAL-SURGICAL NURSING FOR PRACTICAL NURSING STUDENTS (FORM 4218)

Practical nursing students

Purpose: Measures individual achievement of practical/vocational nursing students in medical-surgical nursing.

Description: Approximately 120–item paper-pencil multiple-choice test measuring knowledge and application of the facts and principles related to the care of patients with medical and surgical conditions. Questions refer to patient situations and represent a variety of ages and common conditions. Items relating to the practical nurse's role in drug and diet therapy, communications, and patient teaching are integrated. A total score and two subscores (medical nursing and surgical nursing) are reported based on the number of questions answered correctly. Norms are reported for practical nursing students. The test should be administered when the student's program is near completion. The test is available for faculty review. Form 4218 supersedes Form 1982. Examiner required. Suitable for group use.

Untimed: 2 hours

Scoring: Computer scored

Cost: Test service (test booklets, answer sheets, directions for administration, scoring service) $5.00 per student

Publisher: National League for Nursing

NLN ACHIEVEMENT TESTS FOR PRACTICAL NURSING: MENTAL HEALTH CONCEPTS FOR PRACTICAL NURSING STUDENTS (FORM 4415)

Practical nursing students

Purpose: Measures practical nursing students' understanding of the principles of mental health and their application to the general practice of practical/vocational nursing.

Description: 102–item paper-pencil test focusing on the mental health concepts applicable to the basic care of persons with physical impairment and mental illness. The test also includes questions on the psychological aspects of children. A total score and two subscores (behaviors/concepts and nursing interventions) are reported. Scores are based on the number of questions answered correctly. Norms for practical nursing students are provided. The test is available for faculty review. Examiner required. Suitable for group use.

Untimed: 2 hours

Scoring: Computer scored

Cost: Test service (test booklets, answer sheets, directions for administration, scoring service) $4.00 per student

Publisher: National League for Nursing

NLN ACHIEVEMENT TESTS FOR PRACTICAL NURSING: NURSING OF CHILDREN FOR PRACTICAL NURSING STUDENTS (FORM 4119)

Practical nursing students

Purpose: Measures individual achievement of practical/vocational nursing students in pediatric nursing.

Description: 107–item paper-pencil multiple-choice test measuring achievement of major objectives related to the nursing of children. Questions assess knowledge of normal growth and development in children and nursing measures based on age-related needs, including preventive measures; knowledge and recognition of various pathophysiological processes and treatments, including nutrition and expected outcomes and knowledge of nursing measures commonly used in the care of children who are ill, including drug administration and communication skills. Questions about teaching and providing emotional support to family members are included also. A total score is reported in addition to three subscores (Normal Growth and Development, Pathophysiology and Treatment, and Nursing Measures). Scores are based on the number of questions answered correctly. Norms are reported for practical nursing students. The test should be administered to students who have completed their major learning experience in the content area of the test. The test is available for faculty review. This form supercedes Nursing of Children for Practical Nursing Students (Form 4113). Examiner required. Suitable for group use.

Untimed: 2 hours

Scoring: Computer scored

Cost: Test service (test booklets, answer sheets, directions for administration, scoring service) $5.00 per student

Publisher: National League for Nursing

NLN ACHIEVEMENT TESTS FOR PRACTICAL NURSING: PHARMACOLOGY FOR PRACTICAL NURSES (FORM 4519)

Practical nursing students

Purpose: Measures practical/vocational nursing student's knowledge of facts and principles related to drugs and drug administration.

Description: Approximately 100–item paper-pencil multiple-choice test measuring general knowledge of pharmacology, chiefly through the interpretation of orders and observations necessary for detecting the effects of common drugs and assessing the basic principles of drug administration. A total score is reported together with two subscores (Principles of Drug Administrations, Calculations, and Other Implications for Nursing; and Effects, Therapeutic and Other). Scores are based on the number of questions answered correctly. Norms are reported for practical nursing students. The test should be administered when the program is completed. The test is available for faculty review. Form 4519 supercedes Form 1782 of Pharmacology for Practical Nurses. Examiner required. Suitable for group use.

Untimed: 1 hour, 30 minutes

Scoring: Computer scored

Cost: Test service (test booklets, answer sheets, directions for administration, scoring service) $5.00 per student

Publisher: National League for Nursing

NLN ACHIEVEMENT TESTS FOR REGISTERED NURSING

Registered nursing students

Purpose: Appraises individual achievement in all programs preparing students for RN practice. Enables faculty to evaluate specific course or program objectives in terms of nationally accepted objectives in nursing and compare the scores of students in a nursing program with those of students throughout the country.

Description: Paper-pencil multiple-choice tests consisting of approximately 80–215 questions. The following tests are available: Anatomy and Physiology; Basic Nursing Care I, II, III; Chemistry; Comprehensive Nursing Achievement; Diagnostic Readiness Test for RN Licensure; Diet Therapy and Applied Nutrition; Fundamentals of Drug Therapy; Maternity and Child Nursing; Microbiology; Natural Sciences in Nursing; Normal Nutrition; Nursing Care of Adults I, II; Nursing Care of Adults in Special Care Units; Nursing of Children; Nursing the Childbearing Family; Pharmacology in Clinical Nursing; and Psychiatric Nursing.

Test items have been developed in cooperation with faculty members throughout the United States, reflecting the objectives and subject-matter emphases of teachers from all geographic areas. Some achievement tests are designed to be administered at the end of a course; others are administered after the completion of major learning experiences that may include more than one course or toward

the end of the program. The timing of administration depends on the individual school's curriculum organization.

All test papers must be returned to NLN Test Service for scoring. Reports on test results are returned to the program within 10 working days after NLN receives the answer sheets. Reports include raw scores and percentiles, item descriptors, a list of omitted or incorrectly answered items for each student, and an additional group analysis when more than 10 students are tested as a group. NLN encourages faculty members to review the tests before ordering to ensure that appropriate subject-matter content areas have been covered.

NLN achievement tests may be used in the United States, its territories, and Canada by state- or province-approved programs preparing students for nursing practice; by hospitals and colleges approved to provide instruction to students from such programs; and by nurse licensing authorities in the United States and Canada or their agents. Requests for use by any other program are evaluated individually. The tests are available in English only. Examiner required. Suitable for group use.

Untimed: 1½–3½ hours per test

Scoring: Computer scored

Cost: Test service (test booklets, answer sheets, directions for administration, scoring of answer sheets, reporting of test results) $5.00–$27.50 per student per test

Publisher: National League for Nursing

NLN ACHIEVEMENT TESTS FOR REGISTERED NURSING: ANATOMY AND PHYSIOLOGY (FORM 1213)

Registered nursing students

Purpose: Measures individual achievement of registered nursing students in anatomy and physiology.

Description: Approximately 115–item paper-pencil multiple-choice test measuring knowledge of anatomy and physiology in the following subject-matter areas: cellular metabolism and integumentary system; musculoskeletal system; circulatory system (including lymphatics and fetal circulation); respiratory system; gastrointestinal system; endocrine system; reproductive system; nervous system; special senses; urinary system; and water, electrolyte, and acid-base regulation. For the 105 items scored, total score and two subscores (anatomy and physiology) are reported based on the number of questions answered correctly. Separate norms are reported for students in associate degree, baccalaureate, and diploma programs. The test is available for faculty review. Examiner required. Suitable for group use.

Untimed: 2 hours

Scoring: Computer scored

Cost: Test service (test booklets, answer sheets, directions for administration, scoring service) $5.00 per student

Publisher: National League for Nursing

NLN ACHIEVEMENT TESTS FOR REGISTERED NURSING: BASIC NURSING CARE I, II, III (FORMS 0416, 0426, 0436)

Registered nursing students

Purpose: Measures individual achievement of registered nursing students in the basics of nursing care and attainment of nationally accepted objectives in nursing.

Description: Series of three 100–item paper-pencil multiple-choice tests that may be administered separately or in combination.

Basic Nursing Care I, Form 0416, emphasizes nursing process, nursing diagnosis, and the nursing care plan. Items are included that test basic nursing measures for the care of dependent clients with stable conditions, including hygiene, positioning, nutrition, hydration, vital signs, skin care, application of heat or cold, catheter care, and other basic nursing skills.

Basic Nursing Care II, Form 0426, consists of questions that pertain to the calculation of dosages and principles of administration of common medications (oral, parenteral, opthalmic, and rectal); such nursing measures as preoperative care, aseptic technique, assessment and

management of pain, oxygen therapy, blood transfusion; and common laboratory tests.

Basic Nursing Care III, Form 0436, requires considerable use of judgment, decision-making skills, and determination of priorities for care. The nursing measures tested include those related to fluid and electrolyte balance, CPR, patient teaching, effects of bedrest, and effects of illness on significant others. Much of the content relates to psychosocial aspects of care, including principles of interviewing and ethical/legal implications of nursing actions. Included are items that test nutritional assessment, planning, and evaluation, as well as knowledge of the nutritional value of foods.

A total score and three subscores (Core Concepts, Physiological Needs, and Psychological Needs) are provided for each test. Scores are based on the number of items answered correctly. Separate norms are reported for students in associate degree, baccalaureate, and diploma programs. The test is available for faculty review. Examiner required. Suitable for group use.

Untimed: 2 hours

Scoring: Computer scored

Cost: Test service (test booklets, answer sheets, directions for administration, scoring service) $5.00 per student

Publisher: National League for Nursing

NLN ACHIEVEMENT TESTS FOR REGISTERED NURSING: CHEMISTRY (FORM 1013)

Registered nursing students

Purpose: Measures individual achievement of students in registered nursing programs in the principles and concepts of chemistry as it applies to human functioning and the health sciences.

Description: Approximately 120–item paper-pencil multiple-choice test measuring recognition of the concepts and principles of general chemistry that pertain to the health sciences, organic compounds and structures that form the basis for understanding physiological reactions, and concepts and principles of biochemistry as they relate to human functioning. A total score and three subscores (general chemistry, organic chemistry, and biochemistry) are provided based on the number of questions answered correctly. Separate norms are reported for students in associate degree, baccalaureate, and diploma programs. The test is available for faculty review. Examiner required. Suitable for group use.

Untimed: 2 hours

Scoring: Computer scored

Cost: Test service (test booklets, answer sheets, directions for administration, scoring service) $5.00 per student

Publisher: National League for Nursing

NLN ACHIEVEMENT TESTS FOR REGISTERED NURSING: COMPREHENSIVE NURSING ACHIEVEMENT TEST (FORM 3019)

Registered nursing students

Purpose: Measures achievement of graduating students in registered nursing programs in a range of knowledge needed by the beginning practitioner. Assesses readiness for the nurse licensure examination.

Description: Approximately 210–item paper-pencil multiple-choice test of a graduating student's knowledge of human functioning, the nursing process, and clinical content. This test assesses readiness for the registered nurse licensure examination, NCLEX-RN. Questions are presented as case situations drawn from a variety of clinical areas and are written within the nursing process framework. A total raw score is reported with an indication of the likelihood of passing NCLEX-RN for students performing at the same level. A variety of subscores are reported as well to complete the individual diagnostic profiles. A copy is provided for the student and another for faculty analysis. This form supercedes NLN Achievement Tests for Registered Nursing: Comprehensive Achievement Test (Form 3017). Examiner required. Suitable for group use.

Untimed: 3 hours, 30 minutes

Scoring: Computer scored

Cost: Test service (test booklets, answer sheets, directions for administration, scoring service) $17.00 per student

Publisher: National League for Nursing

NLN ACHIEVEMENT TESTS FOR REGISTERED NURSING: DIAGNOSTIC TEST FOR RN LICENSURE (FORM 3518)
National League for Nursing

Registered nursing students

Purpose: Assesses knowledge and skills needed for entry-level practice as measured by the RN licensing examination.

Description: 172–item paper-pencil multiple-choice test identifying areas of strength and weakness for students preparing for RN licensure. An individualized performance profile provides an estimate of the student's probability of success on the licensing examination NCLEX-RN. In addition, the profile indicates in 31 separate graphs the student's relative strengths and weaknesses in several categories, including nursing process (5 areas), client needs (4 areas), human functioning (8 areas), health alterations (10 areas), and clinical nursing (4 areas). A customized study guide is included. Content frameworks are described on the report. Class summary reports are provided for educators returning groups of answer sheets. Examiner/self-administered. Suitable for group use.

Untimed: 3 hours

Scoring: Computer scored

Cost: $27.50 per answer sheet returned for scoring

Publisher: National League for Nursing

NLN ACHIEVEMENT TESTS FOR REGISTERED NURSING: DIET THERAPY AND APPLIED NUTRITION (FORM 3313)

Registered nursing students

Purpose: Measures individual achievement of registered nursing students in diet therapy and applied nutrition.

Description: Approximately 120–item paper-pencil multiple-choice test measuring knowledge of the facts and principles of nutrition and the ability to apply that knowledge to situations involving patients who have specific nutritional problems. A total score, a facts and principles subscore, and an application of knowledge subscore are provided based on the number of questions answered correctly. Separate norms are reported for students in associate degree, baccalaureate, and diploma programs. The test should be administered at the end of the students' program and is not a substitute for the NLN achievement test in normal nutrition. The test is available for faculty review. Examiner required. Suitable for group use.

Untimed: 2 hours

Scoring: Computer scored

Cost: Test service (test booklets, answer sheets, directions for administration, scoring service) $5.00 per student

Publisher: National League for Nursing

NLN ACHIEVEMENT TESTS FOR REGISTERED NURSING: FUNDAMENTALS OF DRUG THERAPY (FORM 1414)

Registered nursing students

Purpose: Measures individual achievement of registered nursing students in drug therapy.

Description: Approximately 110–item paper-pencil multiple-choice test measuring knowledge of the general principles of drug administration, calculations, and drug effects. A total score and three subscores (calculations, principles of drug administration, and drug effects) are reported based on the number of questions answered correctly. Separate norms are reported for associate degree, baccalaureate, and diploma programs. The test is intended for use relatively early in the program (knowledge of clinical nursing is not required) and is not a substitute for the NLN achievement test in pharmacology in clinical nursing. The test is available for faculty review. Examiner required. Suitable for group use.

Untimed: 2 hours

Scoring: Computer scored

Cost: Test service (test booklets, answer sheets, directions for administration, scoring service) $5.00 per student

Publisher: National League for Nursing

NLN ACHIEVEMENT TESTS FOR REGISTERED NURSING: MATERNITY AND CHILD NURSING (FORM 0519)

Registered nursing students

Purpose: Measures individual achievement of registered nursing students in maternal and child nursing.

Description: Approximately 115–item paper-pencil multiple-choice test measuring understanding of the facts and principles of maternal and child nursing and the ability to apply them. Test items include case situations. Some cases are structured to follow a family over a period of time and require the student to apply principles from both maternal and child nursing to a particular situation. A total score and two subscores (nursing care during the pregnancy cycle and nursing care of children) are provided based on the number of questions answered correctly. Separate norms are reported for students in associate degree, baccalaureate, and diploma programs. The test should be administered late in the program, after completion of all major areas that contribute to the understanding of maternity and child nursing. It is not a replacement for NLN's separate achievement tests in nursing the childbearing family and nursing of children, which are designed for use relatively early in the program. This form supercedes NLN Achievement Tests for Registered Nursing: Maternity and Child Nursing (Form 0513). The test is available for faculty review. Examiner required. Suitable for group use.

Untimed: 2 hours

Scoring: Computer scored

Cost: Test service (test booklets, answer sheets, directions for administration, scoring service) $5.00 per student

Publisher: National League for Nursing

NLN ACHIEVEMENT TESTS FOR REGISTERED NURSING: MICROBIOLOGY (FORM 1113)

Registered nursing students

Purpose: Measures individual achievement of registered nursing students in microbiology as it applies to nursing.

Description: Approximately 115–item paper-pencil multiple-choice test measuring the nursing student's understanding of facts and principles related to the causative microorganisms of infectious diseases. For the 89 items scored, a total score and subscores for three areas are provided: the basic processes occurring during the cellular activity of microorganisms, the structural and functional differences of the microorganisms, techniques and measures for studying and culturing microorganisms that cause infectious disease; substances developed for immunization, the body's immunological response to foreign substances, and the antimicrobials used in controlling diseases; and the transmission of organisms, the incidence, manifestation, and progression of communicable diseases, as well as methods used to destroy microorganisms. Each score is based on the number of questions answered correctly. Separate norms are provided for students in associate degree, baccalaureate, and diploma programs. The test is available for faculty review. Examiner required. Suitable for group use.
Untimed: 2 hours
Scoring: Computer scored
Cost: Test service (test booklets, answer booklets, directions for administration, scoring service) $5.00 per student
Publisher: National League for Nursing

NLN ACHIEVEMENT TESTS FOR REGISTERED NURSING: NATURAL SCIENCES IN NURSING (FORM 3213)

Registered nursing students

Purpose: Measures individual achievement of registered nursing students in the natural sciences as necessary for understanding client's physical conditions and providing appropriate nursing care.

Description: Approximately 110–item paper-pencil multiple-choice test measuring understanding of natural science facts and principles related to client care. Questions cover the areas of physiology, chemistry, physics, microbiology, and anatomy. For the 72 items scored, total score, a facts and principles subscore, and an application of knowledge subscore are provided based on the number of questions answered correctly. Separate norms are reported for students in associate degree, baccalaureate, and diploma programs. The test should be administered after students have completed science courses pertaining to the fields listed. The test is available for faculty review. Examiner required. Suitable for group use.
Untimed: 2 hours
Scoring: Computer scored
Cost: Test service (test booklets, answer sheets, directions for administration, scoring service) $5.00 per student
Publisher: National League for Nursing

NLN ACHIEVEMENT TESTS FOR REGISTERED NURSING: NORMAL NUTRITION (FORM 1313)

Registered nursing students

Purpose: Measures individual achievement of registered nursing students in normal nutrition.

Description: Approximately 110–item paper-pencil multiple-choice test measuring knowledge of the facts and principles of normal nutrition and the ability to apply those principles. Test items cover nutrients, the bodily processes involved in the utilization of nutrients in food, and the role of nutrition in health. A total score, a knowledge and interpretation of information basic to normal nutrition subscore, and an application of knowledge of normal nutrition subscore are provided based on a correction-for-guessing formula. Separate norms are reported for students in associate degree, baccalaureate, and diploma programs. This test should be administered after the student completes initial major learning experience in normal nutrition (knowledge of clinical nursing is not required). The test is available for faculty review. Examiner required. Suitable for group use.

Untimed: 2 hours

Scoring: Computer scored

Cost: Test service (test booklets, answer sheets, directions for administration, scoring service) $5.00 per student

Publisher: National League for Nursing

NLN ACHIEVEMENT TESTS FOR REGISTERED NURSING: NURSING CARE OF ADULTS IN SPECIAL CARE UNITS (FORM 0214)

Registered nursing students

Purpose: Assesses knowledge related to the nursing care of adults with acute physical impairment due to disease or accident. Used with registered nursing students completing this nursing sequence.

Description: Approximately 100–item paper-pencil multiple-choice test measuring knowledge related to the nursing care of adults who require complex nursing care, patients in a rehabilitation unit, and the dying. Emphasis is on pathophysiological conditions and the nursing measures required. Questions on pharmacology, nutrition, and the psychosocial aspects of patient care are integrated. Questions reflect the steps of the nursing process. A total score and three subscores (Pathophysiological Alterations, Nursing Measures, and Therapeutic Management) are reported. Each score is based on the number of questions answered correctly. Separate norms are reported for students in associate degree, baccalaureate, and diploma programs. The test is available for faculty review. Examiner required. Suitable for group use.

Untimed: 2 hours

Scoring: Computer scored

Cost: Test service (test booklets, answer sheets, directions for administration, scoring service) $5.00 per student tested

Publisher: National League for Nursing

NLN ACHIEVEMENT TESTS FOR REGISTERED NURSING: NURSING CARE OF ADULTS, PARTS I AND II (FORMS 0217 AND 0227)

Registered nursing students

Purpose: Measures individual achievement of registered nursing students in nursing care of adults with pathophysiological disturbances and attainment of nationally accepted objectives in nursing.

Description: Two approximately 130–item paper-pencil multiple-choice tests measuring knowledge of the nursing care of adults with pathophysiological disturbances. Part I (Form 0217) measures knowledge of problems related to deficiencies in providing oxygen or nutrients to cells, alterations in patterns of elimination, and failures in regulation of metabolism. Part II (Form 0227) measures alterations in urinary functions, impaired mobility, impaired skin integrity, and alterations in sensory and perceptual functions. Most of the questions are presented as case situations and relate to hospitalized patients. The health problems selected reflect those occurring most frequently in the adult population of the United States. The questions emphasize the nursing care demanded by the patient's condition and are written to reflect the nursing process. Questions to measure knowledge of pharmacology and nutrition are integrated.

For each test, a total score and two sets of subscores are reported based on the number of questions answered correctly. One set of subscores reflects the objectives of the test: pathophysiology, nursing measures, and therapeutic management (including drugs and diet). The second set of subscores reflects the nursing process: assessing, analyzing, and evaluating—steps that require the ability to gather and interpret information about a patient; and planning and implementing—steps that require the ability to select appropriate measures for providing care to a patient. Norms are reported for all students preparing for registered nurse practice, in addition to separate norms for associate degree and diploma students.

These tests are intended as end-of-course tests after students have completed the major learning experiences in the content described. Tests are available for faculty review. These tests supersede the NLN Achievement Tests for Registered Nursing: Nursing Care of Adults with Pathophysiological Disturbances—Parts I and II (Form 0217 and 0227). Examiner required. Suitable for group use.

Untimed: Part I 2 hours; Part II 2 hours

Scoring: Computer scored

Cost: Test service, specify Part I or Part II (test booklets, answer sheets, directions for administration, scoring service) $5.00 per student

Publisher: National League for Nursing

NLN ACHIEVEMENT TESTS FOR REGISTERED NURSING: NURSING OF CHILDREN (FORM 0118)

Registered nursing students

Purpose: Measures individual achievement of registered nursing students in nursing care for children.

Description: Approximately 120–item paper-pencil multiple-choice test measuring understanding of facts and principles related to the nursing care of children and the ability to apply those principles. Questions relating to growth and development, teaching, interpersonal relations, nutrition, pharmacology, and the basic sciences are integrated. A total score and three subscores (care of infants, care of toddlers and preschoolers, and care of school-age children and adolescents) are reported based on the number of questions answered correctly. Separate norms are reported for students in associate degree, baccalaureate, and diploma programs. The test is available for faculty review. Form 0118 supersedes Form 0113. Examiner required. Suitable for group use.

Untimed: 2 hours

Scoring: Computer scored

Cost: Test service (test booklets, answer sheets, directions for administration, scoring service) $5.00 per student

Publisher: National League for Nursing

NLN ACHIEVEMENT TESTS FOR REGISTERED NURSING: NURSING THE CHILDBEARING FAMILY (FORM 0015)

Registered nursing students

Purpose: Assesses knowledge related to nursing the childbearing family. Used with registered nursing students completing the maternity nursing sequence.

Description: 123–item paper-pencil multiple-choice test measuring understanding of the facts and principles related to nursing the childbearing family and the ability to apply them. Questions on nutrition, pharmacology, the basic sciences, and interpersonal relations are integrated. While emphasis is on the normal, questions dealing with common health problems of the mother and newborn are included. Questions are written in the framework of the nursing process. A total score and three subscores (antepartal care; intrapartal and postpartal care; and fetal and newborn development and care) are provided. Scores are based on the number of questions answered correctly. Separate norms are reported for students in associate degree, baccalaureate, and diploma programs. The test is available for faculty review. Examiner required. Suitable for group use.

Untimed: 2 hours

Scoring: Computer scored

Cost: Test service (test booklet, answer sheets, directions for administration, scoring service) $5.00 per student

Publisher: National League for Nursing

NLN ACHIEVEMENT TESTS FOR REGISTERED NURSING: PHARMACOLOGY IN CLINICAL NURSING (FORM 3418)

Registered nursing students

Purpose: Measures individual achievement of registered nursing students in applied pharmacology.

Description: Approximately 110–item paper-pencil multiple-choice test measur-

achievement in health-related curricula

ing understanding of facts and principles related to drugs and drug administration, including the actions of pharmacologic agents, undesirable effects of drugs and their control, drug administration, and the calculation of dosages. Case situations are drawn from maternity nursing, nursing care of children, nursing care of adults with mental illness, nursing care of adults with pathophysiological disturbances, and geriatric nursing. A total test score based on the number of questions answered correctly is reported. Norms are reported for students in all registered nursing programs, in addition to separate norms for associate and baccalaureate degree students. The test should be administered late in the nursing program, after students have considerable clinical experience. The test is available for faculty review. Form 3418 supersedes form Form 0982. Examiner required. Suitable for group use.

Untimed: 2 hours

Scoring: Computer scored

Cost: Test service (test booklets, answer sheets, directions for administration, scoring service) $5.00 per student

Publisher: National League for Nursing

NLN ACHIEVEMENT TESTS FOR REGISTERED NURSING: PSYCHIATRIC NURSING (FORM 0314)

Registered nursing students

Purpose: Measures individual achievement of registered nursing students in psychiatric nursing.

Description: Approximately 110–item paper-pencil multiple-choice test measuring knowledge of theory and practice in psychiatric nursing, including patient situations. The therapeutic role of the nurse in the care of patients with mental disorders is emphasized. For the 100 items scored, a total score and two subscores (concept/process and planning/intervention) are reported based on the number of questions answered correctly. Separate norms are reported for students in associate degree, baccalaureate, and diploma programs. The test should be admin-

istered after students have completed their major learning experiences in psychiatric nursing. This form is a revision of Form 0781. The test is available for faculty review. Examiner required. Suitable for group use.

Untimed: 2 hours

Scoring: Computer scored

Cost: Test service (test booklets, answer sheets, directions for administration, scoring service) $5.00 per student

Publisher: National League for Nursing

NLN BACCALAUREATE-LEVEL ACHIEVEMENT TESTS FOR REGISTERED NURSING

Baccalaureate-level registered nursing students

Purpose: Appraises individual achievement of students in baccalaureate-level registered nursing programs and attainment of nationally accepted objectives in nursing.

Description: Five paper-pencil multiple-choice tests consisting of 80–210 questions. The following tests are available: Community Health Nursing, Comprehensive Nursing Achievement Test for Baccalaureate Students, Health and Illness: Adult Care, Nursing Care in Mental Health and Mental Illness, and Parent-Child Care. Test items were developed in cooperation with faculty members throughout the United States, reflecting the objectives and subject-matter content of baccalaureate programs from all geographic areas. All test papers must be returned to NLN Test Service for scoring. Reports on test results are returned to the program within 10 working days after NLN receives the answer sheets. Reports include raw scores and percentiles, item descriptors, a list of omitted and incorrectly answered items for each student, and an additional group analysis when more than 10 students are tested as a group. NLN encourages faculty members to review the tests before ordering to ensure that appropriate subject-matter content areas are covered. Examiner required. Suitable for group use.

Untimed: 1½–4 hours per test

Scoring: Computer scored

Cost: Test service (test booklets, answer sheets, directions for administration, scoring service) $5.00–$8.00 per student per test

Publisher: National League for Nursing

NLN BACCALAUREATE-LEVEL ACHIEVEMENT TESTS FOR REGISTERED NURSING: COMMUNITY HEALTH NURSING (FORM 2314)

Baccalaureate-level registered nursing students

Purpose: Measures individual student achievement in community health nursing in baccalaureate-level registered nursing programs.

Description: Approximately 100–item paper-pencil multiple-choice test measuring students' ability to apply the principles of community health planning and organization of health-care services in contemporary society and knowledge of the nursing process as it is applied to the community and to family groups and individuals in community settings. The test is based on an approach to community health nursing that stresses promotion of maximum health with respect for cultural differences and individual values and with recognition of the ethical-legal constraints within which the community health nurse functions. Knowledge basic to nursing practice in any setting, such as communication, nutrition, and pharmacology, is tested within the context of the community settings where nurses practice. A total score and three subscores (human ecology, individual in systems, community health planning/health care system) are provided based on the number of questions answered correctly. Norms are reported for baccalaureate-level students only. The test should be administered to students in baccalaureate programs who have completed a major learning experience in community health nursing. The test is available for faculty review. Examiner required. Suitable for group use.

Untimed: 1 hour, 30 minutes

Scoring: Computer scored

Cost: Test service (test booklets, answer sheets, directions for administration, scoring service) $5.00 per student

Publisher: National League for Nursing

NLN BACCALAUREATE-LEVEL ACHIEVEMENT TESTS FOR REGISTERED NURSING: COMPREHENSIVE NURSING ACHIEVEMENT TEST FOR BACCALAUREATE NURSING STUDENTS (FORM 3113)

Baccalaureate-level registered nursing students

Purpose: Measures individual achievement of students ready to graduate from baccalaureate-level registered nursing programs.

Description: Approximately 210–item paper-pencil multiple-choice test measuring students' ability to apply knowledge derived from nursing science, as well as from the natural, behavioral, and social sciences. The test focuses on the cumulative results of the educational program rather than on the content of individual clinical components. To accommodate the heterogeneity of baccalaureate nursing curricula, an attempt has been made to construct a test that reflects a number of representative conceptual frameworks. Performance reports are based on 200 items scored. Subscores are reported for each of the following content areas: clients being assessed for health status, including risk factors; clients experiencing a knowledge deficit; clients experiencing maturational or situational crisis; clients experiencing alteration of physiological functioning; clients with dysfunctional patterns of behavior; and leadership and research process. The six subscores reflect the percentage of questions answered correctly within the diagnostic cluster. The total score, based on the number of questions answered correctly, is a standard score. The score report includes information about individual student performance, as well as group performance. Norms are reported for baccalaureate students. The test should be administered to students about to graduate from a baccalaureate program in registered nursing. The test is available for faculty review. Examiner required. Suitable for group use.

Untimed: 4 hours

Scoring: Computer scored

Cost: Test service (test booklets, answer sheets, directions for administration, scoring services) $8.00 per student

Publisher: National League for Nursing

NLN BACCALAUREATE-LEVEL ACHIEVEMENT TESTS FOR REGISTERED NURSING: HEALTH AND ILLNESS: ADULT CARE (FORM 2117)

Baccalaureate-level registered nursing students

Purpose: Measures individual achievement in medical-surgical nursing for students in baccalaureate-level registered nursing programs.

Description: Approximately 120–item paper-pencil test measuring students' knowledge of facts and principles related to medical-surgical nursing and the ability to apply them to patient-care situations. The questions relate to adult patients in a variety of age groups. The client situations represent the health-illness continuum. The questions emphasize assessment, decision-making, and teaching skills of the nurse. A total score and two subscores are provided: a) care of healthy patients and patients with early changes in health status and b) care of acutely ill patients and patients in need of rehabilitation. Norms are reported for baccalaureate students. The test should be administered after students in baccalaureate programs complete their major learning experience in the care of adults in health and illness. The test is available for faculty review. Examiner required. Suitable for group use.

Untimed: 2 hours

Scoring: Computer scored

Cost: Test service (test booklets, answer sheets, directions for administration, scoring service) $5.00 per student

Publisher: National League for Nursing

NLN BACCALAUREATE-LEVEL ACHIEVEMENT TESTS FOR REGISTERED NURSING: NURSING CARE IN MENTAL HEALTH AND MENTAL ILLNESS (FORM 2214)

Baccalaureate-level registered nursing students

Purpose: Measures individual achievement in psychiatric nursing in baccalaureate-level registered nursing programs.

Description: Approximately 120–item paper-pencil multiple-choice test measuring knowledge of the concepts and principles essential in the care of clients with a variety of mental disorders. The case situations cover a number of different settings, and questions covering primary and tertiary prevention are included. Although the test focuses on the knowledge required for caring for clients with mental disorders, questions covering new approaches to treatment and concepts of a broader nature are integrated. A total score and three subscores (knowledge/concepts, assessing/analyzing/evaluating, planning/implementing) are reported based on the number of questions answered correctly. Norms are reported for baccalaureate students. The test should be administered to students who have completed their major learning experience in psychiatric nursing. The test is available for faculty review. Examiner required. Suitable for group use.

Untimed: 2 hours

Scoring: Computer scored

Cost: Test service (test booklets, answer sheets, directions for administration, scoring service) $5.00 per student

Publisher: National League for Nursing

NLN BACCALAUREATE-LEVEL ACHIEVEMENT TESTS FOR REGISTERED NURSING: PARENT-CHILD CARE (FORM 2019)

Baccalaureate-level registered nursing students

Purpose: Measures individual achievement in parent-child nursing care in baccalaureate-level registered nursing programs.

Description: Approximately 110–item paper-pencil multiple-choice test measuring knowledge of nursing interventions for individuals during infancy, childhood, and adolescence and for families during the childbearing and child rearing years. In addition to measuring the achievement of learning objectives pertinent to all areas of nursing practice, such as principles of communication, the test measures learning objectives specific to the nursing of parents and children, including psychosocial and physical development of children and parents and normal and unexpected physical changes related to childhood and childbearing. The test presents nursing situations in a variety of inpatient and outpatient settings where parents and children requiring health care are encountered. A total score and two subscores (childbearing, including fetal development and the neonate to one month of age; and care of the child from one month to young adulthood, including family health concepts) are provided based on the number of questions answered correctly. Norms are reported for baccalaureate students. The test assesses students' knowledge of all steps of the nursing process and should be administered to baccalaureate students who have completed all of the major learning experiences in the content area. The test is available for faculty review. This test supercedes NLN Baccalaureate-Level Achievement Tests for Registered Nursing: Parent-Child Care (Form 0822). Examiner required. Suitable for group use.

Untimed: 2 hours

Scoring: Computer scored

Cost: Test service (test booklets, answer sheets, directions for administration, scoring service) $5.00 per student

Publisher: National League for Nursing

NLN EMPLOYEE ASSESSMENT SERIES: BASIC PROFICIENCY IN MEDICATION ADMINISTRATION

Nurses (RN and LPN/ LVN)

Purpose: Identifies nursing staff needs for instruction in pharmacology. Used to assess need for in-service education.

Description: 60–item paper-pencil multiple-choice test covering dosage calculations (15 items), principles of drug administration (about 20 items), and effects of commonly used drugs (about 25 items). Subscores can be obtained for each of the three areas assessed. Two forms of the test are available. Available only to nursing practice agencies. Examiner required. Suitable for group use.

Untimed: 1 hour

Scoring: Hand key

Cost: Package (25 test booklets, manual, scoring key) $75.00

Publisher: National League for Nursing

NLN EMPLOYEE ASSESSMENT SERIES: CARING FOR PERSONS WITH AIDS

Registered nurses

Purpose: Measures the nurse's knowledge and ability to apply basic principles necessary to provide safe care to persons with AIDS. Used to assess need for in-service education.

Description: 60–item paper-pencil multiple-choice test including etiology and epidemiology; prevention and education for community and family; infection control; clinical nursing management; and ethical-legal issues for persons with AIDS and for health-care workers. Two subscores are available: Knowledge (21 items) and Application (39 items). This test was designed to conform to the Centers for Disease Control-MMWR publication "Recommendations for Prevention of HIV Transmission in Health-Care Settings," August 21, 1987, Vol. 36, No. 2S. Available only to nursing practice agencies. Examiner required. Suitable for group use.

Untimed: 1 hour

Scoring: Hand key

Cost: 25 test booklets, manual, scoring key $75.00

Publisher: National League for Nursing

NLN EMPLOYEE ASSESSMENT SERIES: HOME HEALTH AIDE SKILLS ASSESSMENT

National League for Nursing

Adult
Home health aides

Purpose: Measures the ability to apply the basic principles needed for safe patient care.

Description: 60–item paper-pencil multiple-choice test covering the home health aide's role and function (15 items), the basic care needs of patients (25 items), and caring for patients with special needs (20 items). Subscores are yielded for each of the three areas assessed. Examiner required. Suitable for group use.

Untimed: 1 hour

Scoring: Hand key

Cost: 10 test booklets, manual, scoring key $50.00

Publisher: National League for Nursing

NLN EMPLOYEE ASSESSMENT SERIES: LONG-TERM CARE NURSING ASSISTANT TEST

Nursing assistants

Purpose: Measures knowledge and ability to apply the basic principles necessary for providing safe care to residents in long-term care facilities. Used to assess need for in-service education.

Description: 60–item paper-pencil multiple-choice test of content on normal aging; psychological needs of residents; basic personal care for residents; care for residents who are disabled, ill, or dying; resident safety; observing and reporting signs and symptoms; and the nursing assistant's role and function. Two subscores are provided: Knowledge (23 items), and Application (37 items). Available only to nursing practice agencies. Examiner required. Suitable for group use.

Untimed: 1 hour

Scoring: Hand key

Cost: Package (10 test booklets, manual scoring key) $50.00

Publisher: National League for Nursing

NLN EMPLOYEE ASSESSMENT SERIES: MEDICATIONS FOR CORONARY CARE

Registered nurses

Purpose: Measures nurse's knowledge and skills related to drugs used in the care of patients with coronary problems. Used to assess need for in-service education.

Description: 60–item paper-pencil multiple-choice test covers the major groups of coronary care medications and asks for interpretation of selected EKG rhythm strips. Subscores are available for calculations (11 items), therapeutic effects and actions (29 items), and side and untoward effects (20 items). Available only to nursing practice agencies. Examiner required. Suitable for group use.

Untimed: 1 hour

Scoring: Hand key

Cost: 10 test booklets, manual, scoring key $50.00

Publisher: National League for Nursing

NLN EMPLOYEE ASSESSMENT SERIES: PSYCHOTROPIC DRUG ADMINISTRATION

Registered nurses

Purpose: Measures registered nurse's knowledge of drugs used in the treatment of patients with psychiatric disorders. Used to assess need for in-service education.

Description: 60–item paper-pencil multiple-choice test covering the major groups of psychotropic medications in terms of actions, untoward effects, interactions, and implications for nursing interventions. A small number of items deal with some commonly abused substances. Subscores are available for actions (13 items), untoward effects and interactions (24 items), and nursing implications (23 items). Available only to nursing practice agencies. Examiner required. Suitable for group use.

Untimed: 1 hour

Scoring: Hand key

Cost: Package (10 test booklets, manual, scoring key) $50.00

Publisher: National League for Nursing

NLN NURSING MOBILITY PROFILE I

Registered nursing students

Purpose: Evaluates previous learning and experience in order to establish credit and placement in programs preparing individuals for registered nursing practice. Administered to licensed practical nurses.

Description: Approximately 400–item paper-pencil multiple-choice battery assessing three content areas: foundations of nursing (200 items), nursing care during childbearing (100 items), and nursing care of the child (100 items). Book One (foundations of nursing) includes questions related to nursing care to meet basic physiological and psychosocial needs of clients with stable conditions. The first section of Book Two (nursing care during childbearing) includes questions related to nursing care during antepartal, intrapartal, and neonatal periods. The second section of Book Two (nursing care of the child) includes questions related to nursing care of the hospitalized infant, toddler, preschooler, school-age child, and adolescent. The two test books may be administered separately or together as determined by individual needs. Questions are based on the nursing care of clients in health-care settings and are presented in case situations representative of those commonly encountered in nursing practice. Test items are written within the framework of the steps of the nursing process.

To safeguard the security of the examination, the tests may be administered by faculty at individual schools of nursing on uniform test dates selected by NLN Test Service. (Contact NLN Test Service to arrange alternate dates.) The tests should be administered in a one-day session to be scheduled by faculty at participating schools of nursing during the restricted periods.

A total score (decision score) is reported for each of the three content areas.

Diagnostic scores are also provided as a supplement to faculty evaluations of students and students' self-assessments of strengths and weaknesses. An information bulletin providing more detailed information about the content, scoring, and administration of the examination is available upon request. Suggested methods for institutional standard setting are available upon request. Examiner required. Suitable for group use.

Timed: Book One 3½ hours; Book Two 3½ hours

Scoring: Computer scored

Cost: Test service, specify book (test booklets, answer sheets, directions for administration, scoring service) $34.50 per book administered

Publisher: National League for Nursing

NLN NURSING MOBILITY PROFILE II

Registered nursing students

Purpose: Evaluates previous learning and experience in order to establish credit and placement in baccalaureate nursing programs. Administered to registered nurses seeking placement in a baccalaureate nursing program.

Description: Approximately 560–item paper-pencil multiple-choice battery assessing four content areas: care of the adult client (220 items), care of the client during childbearing (110 items), care of the child (110 items), and care of the client with mental disorder (120 items). Test books may be administered in any order or combination as determined by individual needs. Book One (care of the adult client) includes content related to the nursing care of individual clients whose delivery of oxygen to the cells is deficient; clients with digestive and metabolic problems and difficulty providing nutrients to the cells; clients with sensorimotor function impairment; and clients with genitourinary or reproductive system dysfunctions. The first section of Book Two (care of the client during childbearing) includes content related to nursing care during the antepartal, intrapartal, postpartal, and neonatal periods. The second section of

Book Two (care of the child) includes content related to nursing care of the infant, the toddler and preschooler, and the school-age child and adolescent. Book Three (care of the client with mental disorder) contains content related to nursing care of adults with psychological, adjustmental, and organic mental disorders. Most of the questions on the profile are presented in case situations representative of health problems and conditions commonly encountered in nursing practice. The questions relate to the promotion, maintenance, and restoration of health. Items emphasize normal findings, deviations from normal, and treatment modalities, including drugs, nutrition, and nursing interventions.

The tests should be administered in a one-and-a-half-day session to be scheduled by faculty at participating schools of nursing during the restricted periods selected by NLN Test Service to safeguard the security of the examination. Contact NLN Test Service to arrange alternate dates.

Standardized scores for each of the four tests are reported to faculty for use in making decisions about placement or awarding/denying specific course credits. Subscores for content and nursing process are reported also to provide additional advisory information. Two copies of the performance report are provided: one for student use and a second for faculty use. An information bulletin providing more detailed information about the scoring, content, and administration of the examination is available. Examiner required. Suitable for group use.

Timed: Book One 4 hours; Book Two 4 hours; Book Three 2 hours

Scoring: Computer scored

Cost: Test service, specify book (test booklets, answer sheets, directions for administration, scoring service) $34.50 per book administered

Publisher: National League for Nursing

NLN PRE-ADMISSION EXAMINATION-PN (PAX-PN)

Nursing program
applicants

Purpose: Measures ability and scholastic achievement in specific content areas that predict academic success in practical nursing programs. Assists in admissions and placement decisions by schools preparing students for practical nursing.

Description: Battery of three paper-pencil multiple-choice tests measuring ability in the following areas: verbal ability, science achievement, and mathematics achievement. The verbal ability test consists of word knowledge and reading comprehension sections. The word knowledge section measures the ability to recognize the meaning of a word as it is used in a sentence. Applicants choose the answer that best completes a statement. The reading section is composed of passages of a scientific or general nature and associated questions suitable for measuring reading comprehension skills. The mathematics test measures the ability to solve computational or word problems involving proportions, ratios, decimals, fractions, percentages, and elementary algebraic concepts. The science test measures knowledge of general principles of chemistry, physics, biology, and health. Most of the questions test knowledge of information from secondary-school general science and health classes that has useful applications to practical nursing. Experimental questions are included for test development purposes only and are not scored.

The tests, administered as a single battery, are administered at scheduled sessions throughout the country at test sites established by NLN Test Service. Contact NLN if alternate dates are required.

The test performance of each applicant is reported in terms of raw scores and percentiles. Percentile norms are provided for applicants to all registered nursing programs in addition to separate norms for applicants to associate degree programs and diploma programs. A standardized composite score based on a weighted combination of subscores is also reported. Interpretive material is provided with each report. Examiner required. Suitable for group use.

Timed: 3 hours, 30 minutes

Scoring: Computer scored

Cost: One administration with two score reports (one for applicant and one for designated school of practical nursing) $20.00; additional reports $8.00

Publisher: National League for Nursing

NLN PRE-ADMISSION EXAMINATION-RN (PAX-RN)

Nursing program applicants

Purpose: Measures ability and academic achievement in specific content areas that predict academic success in programs preparing students for beginning registered nursing practice. Assists schools in making admissions and placement decisions.

Description: Battery of three multiple-item paper-pencil multiple-choice tests measuring ability in the following areas: verbal ability, mathematics achievement, and science achievement. The verbal ability test consists of word knowledge and reading comprehension sections. The word knowledge section measures the ability to recognize the meaning of a word as it is used in a sentence. Applicants choose the answer that best completes a statement. The reading section is composed of passages of a scientific or general nature with associated questions suitable for measuring reading comprehension skills. The mathematics test measures skills in basic arithmetic calculations, as well as elementary algebraic and geometric concepts. Straight computational, as well as reading problems, are included. The science test evaluates knowledge of high-school-level general science, chemistry, physics, and biology, with particular emphasis on areas most applicable to the nursing curriculum. Experimental questions are included for test development purposes only and are not included in scoring.

The test is administered at scheduled sessions throughout the country at test sites established by NLN Test Service. Contact NLN if alternate dates are required. The test performance of each applicant is reported in terms of raw scores and percentiles.

Percentile norms are provided for applicants to associate degree programs, diploma programs, and all registered nursing programs. A standardized composite score based on a weighted combination of subscores is also reported. Interpretive material is provided with each report. Examiner required. Suitable for group use.

Timed: 3 hours, 30 minutes

Scoring: Computer scored

Cost: One administration with two score reports (one for the applicant and one for a designated school of nursing) $20.00; additional reports $8.00

Publisher: National League for Nursing

NURSE ATTITUDES INVENTORY (NAI)
Refer to page 769.

NURSING SENTENCE COMPLETIONS (NSC)
Refer to page 769.

NURSING TESTS
Thelma Hunt

Adolescent Grades 12 and above

Purpose: Measures aptitude for nursing. Used to select applicants for nursing or practical nursing schools or for assistance in guidance and counseling of prenursing students.

Description: Four paper-pencil multiple-choice tests assessing aptitude for nursing: the Nursing Aptitude Test (specialized general ability test), the Arithmetic Test for Prospective Nurses, the General Science Test for Prospective Nurses, and the Interest-Preference Test for Prospective Nurses. The tests may be administered separately or as a complete battery. Norms are available for high-school seniors. Examiner required. Suitable for group use.

Timed: Varies

Scoring: Examiner evaluated

Cost: 25 aptitude tests $6.00; 25 arithmetic tests $3.00; 25 general science tests $4.00; 25 interest-preference tests $5.00; specimen set for all four tests $5.00

Publisher: The Center for Psychological Service

Information and availability unconfirmed; last verified in 1987.

PSB APTITUDE FOR PRACTICAL NURSING EXAMINATION

Adult—Practical nursing students

Purpose: Measures abilities, skills, knowledge, and attitudes important to successful performance as a practical nurse. Used as an admission test for schools and programs of practical nursing.

Description: Multiple-item paper-pencil battery of five tests assessing areas important for performance as a practical nurse: General Mental Ability, Spelling, the Natural Sciences, Judgment in Practical Nursing Situations, and Personal Adjustment. The battery predicts an individual's readiness for specialized instruction in practical nursing. Examiner required. Suitable for group use.

Timed: 2 hours, 45 minutes

Scoring: Machine scored

Cost: Reusable test booklets $5.00; answer sheets (scoring and reporting service) $5.00

Publisher: Psychological Services Bureau

PSB HEALTH OCCUPATIONS APTITUDE EXAMINATION

Adult—Health occupations students

Purpose: Measures abilities, skills, knowledge, and attitudes important to successful performance in various health-care occupations. Used as an admission test for schools and programs in health occupations.

Description: Multiple-item paper-pencil battery of five tests assessing areas important to performance in health-care occupations: academic aptitude, spelling, reading comprehension, the natural sciences, and vocational adjustment. The test predicts an individual's readiness for specialized instruction in numerous health-care positions, including medical record technician, dental assistant, psychiatric aide, histologic technician, nursing assistant, respiratory therapy technician, and radiologic technologist. Examiner required. Suitable for group use.

Timed: 2 hours

Scoring: Machine scored

Cost: Reusable test booklets $5.00; answer sheets (scoring and reporting service) $5.00

Publisher: Psychological Services Bureau

PSB NURSING SCHOOL APTITUDE EXAMINATION (RN), 1988 REVISION

Adult—Nursing school candidates

Purpose: Measures abilities, skills, knowledge, and attitudes important to successful performance as a nurse. Used as an admission test for schools and departments of nursing.

Description: Multiple-item paper-pencil battery of five tests assessing areas important for performance as a nurse: academic aptitude, spelling, reading comprehension, information in the natural sciences, and vocational adjustment. The battery predicts readiness for instruction in nursing at the diploma or associate degree levels. Both the original version and the revised versions are available. Examiner required. Suitable for group use.

Timed: 2 hours, 45 minutes

Scoring: Machine scored

Cost: Reusable test booklets $5.00; answer sheets (scoring and reporting service) $5.00

Publisher: Psychological Services Bureau

PSB READING COMPREHENSION EXAMINATION
Refer to page 365.

STUDENT OCCUPATIONAL COMPETENCY ACHIEVEMENT TESTING: PRACTICAL NURSING

Adolescent

Purpose: Measures students' achievement in vocational practical nursing programs. Used for grade assignment, identifying curriculum strengths and weaknesses, and evaluating job applicants.

Description: Two-part test of skills and knowledge in practical nursing. The multiple-choice written test covers anatomy and physiology, medical/surgical nursing, basic nursing, maternal and child health, and personal/vocational relationships. The performance test measures abilities in making an occupied bed, taking vital signs, demonstrating sterile technique/ indwelling catheter, administration of oral medication, administration of an intramuscular injection, administration of subcutaneous medication, tube feeding, perineal care, collection of clean catch/ midstream urine specimen, and transferring patients from a bed to a wheelchair. Examiner required. Suitable for group use.

Timed: Written test 3 hours; performance test 3 hours

Scoring: Scoring service provided

Cost: Contact publisher

Publisher: National Occupational Competency Testing Institute

Driving and Safety Education

HOW TO DRIVE
American Automobile Association

Adolescent, adult—Ages 16 and older

Purpose: Measures students' knowledge of many aspects of the safe operation of an automobile. Used by driver education teachers and driver improvement program directors.

Description: 178 multiple-choice items in 12 paper-pencil tests accompanying the book *How to Drive* published by the American Automobile Association. Each test consists of 12 to 20 items and covers one chapter of the book. The chapters are "Driving Laws and Controls," "Car Control, Skills and Habits," "Basic Maneuvers," "Driving an Automobile with a Manual Shift," "Vision and Perception," "Management of Time and Space," "Interacting with Other Users," "Adverse Driving Conditions and Emergencies," "Keeping Fit to Drive," "Consumer's Guide to Trouble-Free and Economical Driving," "Driving with a Trailer," and "Collisions and Insurance." Self-administered. Suitable for group use.

Untimed: 20 minutes per chapter

Scoring: Hand key; examiner evaluated

Cost: 24 test booklets $10.00; 100 answer sheets $2.75

Publisher: American Automobile Association

PSEUDOISOCHROMATIC PLATES
Refer to page 729.

SAFE DRIVER ATTITUDE TEST (SDAT)
Russell L. Carey, Dawn Bashara, and Harry Schmadeke

Adult

Purpose: Measures attitudes of drivers, including handicapped and learning disabled adolescents, toward certain driving situations.

Description: 19–item paper-pencil multiple-choice test measuring drivers' attitudes toward certain driving situations. The test is designed to reflect such attitudes as self-centeredness, egoism, cautiousness, rashness, and general acceptance of and compliance with the law. In each of two filmstrips, actual and model simulation of driving dilemmas are shown, followed by three illustrative, narrated alternatives. Students view the filmstrips at separate sittings and enter responses on an answer sheet. Examiner required. Suitable for group use.

Untimed: 10–11 minutes

Scoring: Hand key

Cost: Program (2 full-color filmstrips, cassette, teacher's guide, ditto for student answers and profiles) $49.00

Publisher: Educational Activities, Inc.

Information and availability unconfirmed; last verified in 1988.

THEORY TESTS FOR LICENSES

Adult

Purpose: Assesses knowledge of driving skills. Used for issuance of driver's and learner's licenses.

Description: Multiple-item paper-pencil measures of vehicle driver's knowledge of the rules of the road, road traffic signs, and vehicle controls. The test also covers relevant portions of the Road Traffic Ordinances of the Provinces. Three equivalent forms are available. These tests are available only to licensing authorities with the power to issue learner's and driver's licenses and who have examiners with certificates of competency issued by the HSRC. Examiner required. Suitable for group use. SOUTH AFRICAN PUBLISHER

Untimed: Driver's 45 minutes; learner's 1 hour

Scoring: Hand key; examiner evaluated

Cost: Contact publisher; orders from outside the RSA will be dealt with on merit

Publisher: Human Sciences Research Council

TITMUS II-S STANDARD VISION TESTER DRIVER ED MODEL, MANUAL CONTROL
Refer to page 732.

WILSON DRIVER SELECTION TEST
Clark L. Wilson

Adult

Purpose: Evaluates visual attention, depth visualization, eye-hand coordination, steadiness, and recognition of details. Used by driver selection and evaluation companies and schools to screen per-

sonnel in order to reduce the risk of operator-caused accidents.

Description: Six-part paper-pencil nonverbal test measuring visual attention, depth perception, recognition of simple and complex details, eye-hand coordination, and steadiness. The booklet includes norms for males and females, as well as items on the subject's accident record and personal history. Examiner required. Suitable for group use.

Timed: 26 minutes

Scoring: Hand key

Cost: Manual $14.50; key $1.95; package of tests $52.50; specimen set $33.50

Publisher: Martin M. Bruce, Ph.D., Publishers

Education Development and School Readiness

THE ABC INVENTORY
Normand Adair and George Blesch

Child—Ages 3½–6½

Purpose: Assesses the school readiness of preschoolers and provides an index of a child's maturity upon entering school. Identifies children needing further evaluation and assistance. Provides a basis for better parent-teacher understanding.

Description: Oral-response and task-performance test assessing a child's general level of maturity and development. The four sections of the test require the child to draw a man; answer language questions, such as "what has wings" or "tell me the color of grass"; answer cognitive questions, such as "what is ice when it melts" or "how do we hear"; and perform motor activity tasks, such as counting four squares, folding a paper triangle, repeating four digits, and copying a square. Examiner required. Not suitable for group use.

Untimed: 8–9 minutes

Scoring: Examiner evaluated

Cost: 50 inventories, manual $8.00
Publisher: Educational Studies and Development

Information and availability unconfirmed; last verified in 1987.

ACER CHECKLISTS FOR SCHOOL BEGINNERS

Child
Grades PreK–1

Purpose: Measures the school readiness of preschool and kindergarten children. Identifies children in need of further evaluation and developmental assistance.

Description: Multiple-item paper-pencil checklist consisting primarily of single-task activities covering the following areas: social development, motor skills, memory and attention, and language skills. Each item is scored plus or minus, depending on whether the child has displayed the developmental behavior presented in the item. The items may be checked in any order, and most may be evaluated through informal observation. Based on the results of the checklist, the child's behavioral development is assessed to provide a measure of the child's readiness for participation in formal school situations. The checklist is available in two forms: one for teachers and one for parents. Materials include the checklist in its alternate forms, a class record sheet, and a manual. Examiner required. Not suitable for group use. The parent checklist is available in Arabic, Greek, Italian, Maltese, Serbo-Croatian (Yugoslav), Spanish, and Turkish.
AUSTRALIAN PUBLISHER
Untimed: Varies
Scoring: Examiner evaluated
Cost: Contact publisher
Publisher: The Australian Council for Educational Research Limited

ACER EARLY SCHOOL SERIES

Child
PreK–Grade 1

Purpose: Measures the perceptual, verbal, and numerical skills needed by children entering kindergarten. Used for readiness screening and to identify children in need of further evaluation and assistance.

Description: Multiple-item paper-pencil tests of nine readiness skills: auditory discrimination, recognition of initial consonant sounds, numbers, figure formation, prepositions, pronouns, verb tense, negation, and comprehension. An overall Word Knowledge score is also obtained. Materials include separate administration booklets for each test and the handbook *Early Identification and Intervention.* Examiner required. Suitable for group use.
AUSTRALIAN PUBLISHER
Untimed: Varies
Scoring: Hand key
Cost: Contact publisher
Publisher: The Australian Council for Educational Research Limited

ACHIEVEMENT IDENTIFICATION MEASURE (AIM)
Refer to page 761.

ADAPTIVE BEHAVIOR SCALE FOR INFANTS AND EARLY CHILDHOOD (ABSI)
Henry Leland, Mandana Shoaee, Douglas McElwain, and Rachael Christie

Child—Ages 0–6

Purpose: Describes the adaptive behavior of infants and young children. Aids effective program planning and preschool placement. May be used with the mentally retarded, developmentally disabled, and physically handicapped.

Description: 63–item interview examination covering seven domains and an 80–item review test of potential maladaptive social behavior. The domains measured are adaptive behavior, independent functioning and physical development, communication skills, conceptual skills, play skills, self-direction and personal responsibility, and socialization. The test may be used to detect major psychological problems that may be developing, indications of possible brain damage or other sensorimotor problems, and indications of possible delays in cognitive and communication development. The test is administered by an examiner acting as a third party to a parent, teacher, or other individual who has thorough knowledge of the child. Examiner required. Not suitable for group use.

Untimed: 45 minutes

Scoring: Examiner evaluated

Cost: Specimen set $9.00

Publisher: The Nisonger Center, Ohio State University

Information and availability unconfirmed; last verified in 1987.

ADELPHI PARENT ADMINISTERED READINESS TEST (A.P.A.R.T.)
Pnina S. Klein

Child—Ages 5.2–6.3

Purpose: Identifies learning disabilities and language problems of preschoolers. Used for counseling and helping parents understand the relationship between ability and academic achievement.

Description: 42–item paper-pencil examination consisting of 10 subtests covering concept formation, letter form recognition, writing ability, knowledge of numbers, visual perception, visual memory, comprehension and memory, auditory sequential memory, recognition of facial expressions of emotion, and creative ability. The parent reads directions to the child, records responses, and scores the test. The test is to be administered 4–6 months before the child enters first grade. Examiner required. Not suitable for group use. May be administered in languages other than English.

Untimed: 20 minutes

Scoring: Hand key; examiner evaluated

Cost: 10 tests $24.95

Publisher: Mafex Associates, Inc.

Information and availability unconfirmed; last verified in 1987.

ANALYSIS OF READINESS SKILLS
Mary C. Rodriques,
William H. Vogler, and
James F. Wilson

Child
Grades K–1

Purpose: Measures a child's reading and mathematics readiness.

Description: 30–item oral-response test consisting of three subtests (10 items each): visual perception of letters, letter identification, and mathematics (identification of numerals and counting numerals). The teacher's manual provides directions for administering the tests in English or Spanish and includes norms for both English-speaking and Spanish-speaking children. Examiner required. Suitable for group use.

Untimed: 35 minutes

Scoring: Examiner evaluated

Cost: Test kit (25 test booklets, teacher's manual, scoring key, class record sheet, sample item chart) $20.61

Publisher: The Riverside Publishing Company

ANTON BRENNER DEVELOPMENTAL GESTALT TEST OF SCHOOL READINESS
Anton Brenner

Child—Ages 5–6

Purpose: Assesses a child's readiness for kindergarten or first grade. Used to identify children requiring special attention.

Description: Multiple-item oral-response and task-assessment test using Gestalt and developmental principles to measure children's conceptual and perceptual differentiating abilities. The test provides a quantitative and qualitative evaluation of a child's perceptual-conceptual development and identifies three special groups: early maturing and/or gifted; slowly maturing and/or retarded; and emotionally disturbed. The test is designed to be almost "culture free" and can be used with non-English-speaking and culturally deprived children. Examiner required. Not suitable for group use.

Untimed: 5 minutes

Scoring: Hand key; examiner evaluated

Cost: Complete kit (25 booklets, manual, set of test materials) $35.00

Publisher: Western Psychological Services

ASSESSMENT IN NURSERY EDUCATION
Margaret Bate and Marjorie Smith

Child—Ages 3–5　

Purpose: Assesses development of children. Used for identifying strengths and weaknesses and for monitoring progress.

Description: Multiple-item observational assessment of five major developmental areas: social skills and social thinking, talking and listening, thinking and doing, manual and tool skills, and physical skills. The child is assessed on observed and demonstrated ability to perform special tasks. Materials include outlines of model people, pictures and picture story cards, a set of shapes for copying, a set of shapes for cutting out, and guideline patterns for drawing. Videotapes demonstrating assessment are also available. Examiner required. Not suitable for group use. BRITISH PUBLISHER

Untimed: Varies

Scoring: Examiner evaluated

Cost: Contact publisher

Publisher: NFER-NELSON Publishing Company Ltd.

ATTITUDE TOWARD SCHOOL QUESTIONNAIRE (ASQ)
Refer to page 750.

AUTISM SCREENING INSTRUMENT FOR EDUCATIONAL PLANNING (ASIEP)
Refer to page 231.

THE BARBER SCALES OF SELF-REGARD FOR PRESCHOOL CHILDREN
Refer to page 26.

BASIC SCHOOL SKILLS INVENTORY—DIAGNOSTIC (BSSI-D)
Donald D. Hammill and James E. Leigh

Child—Ages 4–7.5　

Purpose: Determines the special learning needs of children by pinpointing both the general areas and the specific readiness skills that need remedial attention. Results of this testing-for-teaching-approach-to-assessment provide practical knowledge for teaching children the items they do not know.

Description: 110–item paper-pencil test enabling the examiner to view a child's performance individually or compared with his peers. The test measures six areas of school performance: daily living skills, spoken language, reading readiness, writing readiness, math readiness, and classroom behavior. A companion test is the Basic School Skills Inventory—Screen. Examiner required. Not suitable for group use.

Untimed: Varies

Scoring: Examiner evaluated

Cost: Complete (examiner's manual, 50 answer sheets, picture book, storage box) $54.00

Publisher: PRO-ED

BASIC SCHOOL SKILLS INVENTORY—SCREEN (BSSI-S)
Donald D. Hammill and James E. Leigh

Child—Ages 4–6.11　

Purpose: Diagnoses children who are "high risk" for school failure, need more in-depth assessment, and should be referred for further evaluation. Assesses a child's overall readiness for school.

Description: 20–item paper-pencil observational screening device that examines daily living skills, spoken language, reading readiness, writing readiness, math readiness, and classroom behavior. The examiner checks off the answers he knows about the child; further investigation may be needed for some items. A companion test is the Basic School Skills Inventory—Diagnostic. Examiner required. Not suitable for group use.

Untimed: 5–8 minutes

Scoring: Examiner evaluated

Cost: Complete (examiner's manual, 50 answer sheets) $19.00

Publisher: PRO-ED

BATTELLE DEVELOPMENTAL INVENTORY (BDI)
Jean Newborg, John R. Stock, Linda Wnek, John Guidubaldi, and John Svinicki

Child—Ages 0–8

Purpose: Evaluates the development of children from infant to primary levels. Screens and diagnoses developmental strengths and weaknesses. Used to establish IEPs and aid in placement and eligibility decisions.

Description: Multiple-item test assessing key developmental skills in five domains: personal-social, adaptive, motor, communication, and cognition. Information is obtained through structured interactions with the child in a controlled setting, observation of the child, and interviews with the child's parents, caregivers, and teachers. Test items contain content and sequence directly compatible with infant and preschool curricula for use in generating IEPs. The test yields standard scores, percentile ranks, and age equivalent scores. The test may be administered by a teacher or trained paraprofessional. Various modifications are required when administering the test to handicapped children. A screening examination is included or is available separately. (See entry for Battelle Developmental Inventory Screening Test for details.) Examiner required. Suitable for group use if the station procedure is used.

Untimed: Screening examination 10–30 minutes; diagnostic evaluation 1–2 hours

Scoring: Examiner evaluated

Cost: Test kit (15 scoring booklets, 30 screening test booklets, test item booklets, manual) $175.00

Publisher: DLM Teaching Resources

BATTELLE DEVELOPMENTAL INVENTORY (BDI) SCREENING TEST

Child—Ages 0–8

Purpose: Screens developmental behaviors and identifies areas needing in-depth evaluation with the complete BDI.

Description: 96–item test assessing developmental behaviors along personal-social, adaptive, motor, communication, and cognitive domains. The test, which is a short form of the Battelle Developmental Inventory, yields cutoff scores and age equivalents. Examiner required. Not suitable for group use.

Untimed: 10–30 minutes

Scoring: Examiner evaluated

Cost: Complete kit (30 screening test booklets, test item book, examiner's manual) $65.00

Publisher: DLM Teaching Resources

BEHAVIOUR STUDY TECHNIQUE
Refer to page 27.

THE BINGHAM BUTTON TEST
Refer to page 27.

BIRTH TO THREE DEVELOPMENTAL SCALE— SCREENING TEST
Tina E. Bangs and Susan Dodson

Child—Ages 0–3

Purpose: Assesses developmental delay in the behavioral categories of language comprehension, oral language, problem solving, social/personal, and motor activities. Used for educational planning and diagnosis.

Description: 85–item scale for early identification of developmental delay. The factors measured include basic skills/perceptual motor, social/emotional/interest, auditory skills, reception, and expression. Materials include a manual and record form. Data derived from the scale provide norm-referenced feedback. Scores ob-

---

tained are percentiles, standard scores, and stanines. Examiner required. Not suitable for group use.

Untimed: Varies

Scoring: Examiner evaluated

Cost: Screening test $60.00

Publisher: DLM Teaching Resources

BOEHM TEST OF BASIC CONCEPTS—PRESCHOOL VERSION
Ann E. Boehm

Child—Ages 3–5

Purpose: Measures young child's knowledge of 26 basic relational concepts. Used to identify weaknesses in basic concept comprehension for development of appropriate remediation.

Description: 52–item test utilizing a pictorial booklet to display the concepts to be tested. The child responds to oral instructions by pointing to one of several pictures. The examiner records the child's responses on the record form. Each concept is tested twice. Examiner required. Not suitable for group use.

Untimed: 10–15 minutes

Scoring: Hand key

Cost: Complete kit (picture book, manual, 35 individual record forms, class record) $49.00

Publisher: The Psychological Corporation

Information and availability unconfirmed; last verified in 1988.

BRACKEN BASIC CONCEPT SCALE (BBCS)
Bruce A. Bracken

Child—Ages 2½–8

Purpose: Measures a child's acquisition of basic concepts. Used with both regular and special education populations.

Description: 258–item verbal "point-to" test using picture stimuli to evaluate 11 categories of basic concept acquisition, including color, shape, size, quantity, counting, letter identification, direction/ position, time/sequence, texture, comparisons, and social/emotional responses.

The four-option multiple-choice items are intended to reduce the probability of guessing. The instrument is available as a complete diagnostic scale that measures 258 basic concepts and as a screening test. Results of the diagnostic scale can be applied in planning therapy or lessons. The screening test (see separate description) identifies kindergarten and first-grade students whose concept development is below age-level expectations. Two alternate forms facilitate pre- and posttest assessment. Examiner required. Not suitable for group use.

Untimed: 20–40 minutes

Scoring: Hand key

Cost: Complete program $98.00; examiner's manual $15.00; stimulus manual $60.00; 25 diagnostic record forms $13.00; 12 screening tests (specify Form A or B) $13.00

Publisher: The Psychological Corporation

Information and availability unconfirmed; last verified in 1988.

BRACKEN BASIC CONCEPT SCALE—SCREENING TEST (BBCS-SCREENING)
Bruce A. Bracken

Child

Purpose: Helps identify kindergartners and first-graders whose ability to distinguish concepts is below age-level expectations. Used as a guide for further testing.

Description: 30–item paper-pencil multiple-choice test in which books of picture stimuli assess different concepts of approximately equal difficulty in eight categories of basic concept acquisition. The test yields a single norm-referenced standard score. Two alternate forms are available for pre- and posttesting. Examiner required. Suitable for group use.

Timed: 5–10 minutes

Scoring: Hand key

Cost: 12 Form A (includes 1 directions booklet) $13.00; 12 Form B $13.00

Publisher: The Psychological Corporation

Information and availability unconfirmed; last verified in 1988.

BRIEF INDEX OF ADAPTIVE BEHAVIOR (BIAB)
R. Steve McCallum,
Maurice S. Herrin,
Jimmy P. Wheeler, and
Jeanette R. Edwards

Child, adolescent—Ages 5-17

Purpose: Evaluates the development of adaptive behavior in children and adolescents. Used for counseling purposes.

Description: 39-item paper-pencil observational inventory assessing three domains of adaptive behavior: independent functioning, socialization, and communication. The inventory is completed and scored by either a parent or teacher. The manual includes a discussion of the test and procedures for administration and scoring. Self-administered. Not suitable for group use.

Untimed: Varies

Scoring: Examiner evaluated

Cost: Starter set (manual, 20 response sheets) $8.00; specimen set $6.00

Publisher: Scholastic Testing Service, Inc.

THE BRIGANCE® DIAGNOSTIC INVENTORY OF EARLY DEVELOPMENT
Albert H. Brigance

Child—Developmental ages 0-7

Purpose: Measures the development of children functioning below the developmental age of seven years. Diagnoses developmental delays and monitors progress over a period of time. Used to develop IEPs.

Description: 200 paper-pencil oral-response and direct-observation skill assessments measuring psychomotor, self-help, communication, general knowledge and comprehension, and academic skill levels. Test items are arranged in developmental sequential order in the following major skill areas: preambulatory, gross motor, fine motor, prespeech, speech and language, general knowledge and comprehension, readiness, basic reading,

manuscript writing, and basic math skills. An introductory section outlines how to administer the tests, assess skill levels, record the results, identify specific instructional objectives, and develop IEPs. Results, expressed in terms of developmental ages, are entered into the individual record book, which indicates graphically at each testing the level of competency the individual has achieved. An optional group record book monitors the progress of 15 individuals. Examiner required. Not suitable for group use.

Untimed: Varies

Scoring: Examiner evaluated

Cost: Assessment book $95.00; group record book $9.95; free test excerpts available; 10 pack developmental record books $19.95

Publisher: Curriculum Associates, Inc.

THE BRIGANCE® K & 1 SCREEN
Albert H. Brigance

Child
Grades K-1

Purpose: Screens the basic skills necessary for success in Grades K-1. Identifies students needing special service referral, determines appropriate pupil placement, and assists in planning instructional programs and developing IEPs.

Description: Multiple-item paper-pencil oral-response and direct-observation assessments measuring the following basic skills: personal data response, color recognition, picture vocabulary, visual discrimination, visual-motor skills, standing gross-motor skills, draw-a-person (body image), rote counting, identification of body parts, reciting the alphabet, following verbal directions, numeral comprehension, recognizing lowercase letters (uppercase alternate), auditory discrimination, printing personal data, syntax and fluency, and numerals in sequence. Five optional advanced assessments are included for students scoring 95 percent or above on the basic first-grade assessment: response to picture, articulation of sounds, basic preprimer vocabulary, pre-primer/primer oral reading, and basic number skills. Personal information, assessment results, scoring, testing observations, comparative summary of the screening, and recommendations are all recorded on the pupil data sheet. An optional class summary record folder collects and summarizes data for 30 pupils. Optional forms for teacher rating, parent rating, and examiner observations are reproducible. Separate pupil data sheets are required, and class summary record folders are available. Criterion-referenced results are translated directly into curriculum or program objectives to meet the needs of individual pupils. Test items are cross-referenced to the BRIGANCE® Inventory of Basic Skills and the Inventory of Early Development to facilitate further evaluation of skill deficiencies. Examiner required. Not suitable for group use.

Untimed: 12 minutes

Scoring: Examiner evaluated

Cost: Assessment manual $49.00; 30 pupil data sheets, class summary record folder for Grade K $15.95; 30 pupil data sheets, class summary record folder for Grade 1 $16.00

Publisher: Curriculum Associates, Inc.

BRIGANCE® PRESCHOOL SCREEN
Albert H. Brigance

Child—Ages 3–4

Purpose: Evaluates basic developmental and readiness skills of children. Used for program planning, placement, and special service referrals.

Description: Multiple-item oral-response and task-performance test evaluating basic developmental and readiness skills. Children identify body parts, objects, and colors; demonstrate gross and visual motor skills; match colors; explain the use of objects; repeat sentences; build with blocks; and provide personal data. Number concepts, picture vocabulary, use of plural *s*, *-ing*, prepositions, and irregular plural nouns are tested also. Rating forms and supplementary skill assessments allow for additional observations and extended screening options. Examiner required. Suitable for group use.

Untimed: 12 minutes

Scoring: Examiner evaluated

Cost: SCREEN (with building blocks for tests) $48.50; 30 three-year-old child data forms $15.90; 30 four-year-old child data forms $15.50

Publisher: Curriculum Associates, Inc.

THE BURY INFANT CHECK
Lea Pearson and John Quinn

Child

Purpose: Identifies children with special needs requiring intervention. Used by teachers with children in their second or third school term.

Description: Multiple-item paper-pencil test measuring language skills, learning style, memory, number, and perceptual motor skills in compliance with the 1981 Education Act. The test consists of both teacher-rated and child-completed items and is available in a Quick Check and Full Check version. The Quick Check version consists of 13 teacher-rated items from the Language Skills and Learning Style subtests. Children scoring below an established cutoff point are administered the Full Check. Examiner required. Suitable for group use.

BRITISH PUBLISHER

Untimed: Quick Check 3–4 minutes; Full Check 20 minutes

Scoring: Hand key; examiner evaluated

Cost: Contact publisher

Publisher: NFER-NELSON Publishing Company Ltd.

CALIFORNIA PRESCHOOL SOCIAL COMPETENCY SCALE
Samuel Levine, Freeman F. Elzey, and Mary Lewis

Child—Ages 2.6–5.6

Purpose: Assesses the social competency of preschool children. Used by teachers for diagnosis, placement, or measurement of the development of young children.

Description: 30–item paper-pencil rating scale providing objective, numerical evaluations of the social competency of preschool children. The items call for specific behaviors (preschool children's interpersonal behavior and the degree to which they assume social responsibility). The manual provides percentile norms for children from high and low occupational levels for four age groups (by sex) from ages 2.6–5.6. Examiner required. Not suitable for group use.

Untimed: Not available

Scoring: Hand key

Cost: Specimen set (manual, scale) $3.00; manual $2.75; 25 tests $9.25

Publisher: Consulting Psychologists Press, Inc.

CANADIAN COGNITIVE ABILITIES TEST: PRIMARY BATTERY (CCAT), LEVELS 1 & 2, FORM 7
Refer to page 588.

CANADIAN TESTS OF BASIC SKILLS: MULTILEVEL (CTBS), LEVELS 5–18, FORM 7/8
E. King-Shaw, A. N. Hieronymus, and D. Scannell

Child, adolescent
Grades K.2–12

Purpose: Assesses students' abilities in vocabulary, reading comprehension, spelling, capitalization, punctuation, usage, visual materials, reference materials, mathematics concepts, mathematics problem solving, and mathematics computation.

Description: Three test levels (primary, multilevel, and high school), each consisting of a series of multiple-choice paper-pencil subtests that include Vocabulary, Reading Comprehension, Spelling, Capitalization, Punctuation, Usage, Visual Materials, Reference Materials, Mathematics Concepts, Mathematics Problem Solving, and Mathematics Computation. Materials include test booklets, answer sheets, scoring masks, teacher's guide, and supplementary materials as required. This is an adaptation of the Iowa Tests of Basic Skills published by Riverside Publishing Company. Examiner must have a teaching certificate. Examiner required. Suitable for group use. The mathematics subtests are available in French.
CANADIAN PUBLISHER

Timed: Primary 235 minutes; Multilevel 256 minutes; High School 160 minutes

Scoring: Hand key; machine scored; scoring service available from publisher

Cost: Test booklets $7.15; 35 answer sheets $13.45; scoring masks $9.25; teacher's guide $12.00

Publisher: Nelson Canada

CANADIAN TESTS OF BASIC SKILLS: PRIMARY BATTERY (CTBS) (LEVELS 5–8), FORM 7
Refer to page 432.

CENTRAL INSTITUTE FOR THE DEAF PRESCHOOL PERFORMANCE SCALE (CID PRESCHOOL PERFORMANCE SCALE)
Refer to page 662.

CHILDPACE—CHILD DEVELOPMENT PROGRAM
Refer to page 30.

CIRCUS
Refer to page 433.

CLYMER-BARRETT READINESS TEST
Theodore Clymer and Thomas C. Barrett

Child
Grades K–1

Purpose: Measures the important skills and background necessary for success in beginning instruction, especially in reading. Identifies students with serious skill deficits. Used at the end of Kindergarten to assess the results of a readiness program and at the beginning of Grade 1 to group students and determine instructional goals.

Description: 116–item paper-pencil multiple-choice test and 24–item observational inventory (completed by the child's classroom teacher) assessing readiness for first-grade instruction. Six tests measure three types of skills: Recognizing

Letters (35 items) and Matching Words (20 items) measure visual discrimination; Beginning Sounds (20 items) and Ending Sounds (20 items) measure auditory discrimination; and Completing Shapes (20 items) and Copy-A-Sentence (1 item) measure visual-motor coordination. The tests are administered during three separate periods, one period for each skill area assessed. The first test of visual discrimination, Recognizing Letters, and the first test of auditory discrimination, Beginning Sounds, may be administered in a short form for screening purposes. The readiness survey collects teacher observations concerning oral language facility, concept development, listening and thinking skills, social and emotional development, and work habits.

All six tests, the readiness survey, and a student summary page are contained in one 16–page booklet and are available in equivalent forms, A and B, for pre- and posttesting. The test also includes a class record sheet and a manual. The test is a revised version of the Clymer-Barrett Pre-reading Battery. Examiner required. Suitable for group use.

Untimed: Varies

Scoring: Examiner evaluated

Cost: Contact publisher

Publisher: Chapman, Brook & Kent

Information and availability unconfirmed; last verified in 1987.

COGNITIVE ABILITIES SCALE (CAS)
Sharon Bradley-Johnson

Child—Ages 2–3

Purpose: Identifies children with cognitive development deficiencies. Used for planning instructional programs and as an overall performance measure for children who will not talk or whose speech is unintelligible.

Description: 88–item test in which toys are used as stimuli to assess language, imitation, reading, memory, mathematics, handwriting, and other skills important for school success. A total score, five subtest scores, and percentile and standard scores are obtained. Examiner required. Not suitable for group use.

Untimed: 30–45 minutes

Scoring: Examiner evaluated

Cost: Complete kit (manual, child's book, 25 examiner record books, picture cards, toys, storage box) $99.00

Publisher: PRO-ED

COGNITIVE CONTROL BATTERY: THE FRUIT DISTRACTION TEST
Refer to page 632.

COGNITIVE CONTROL BATTERY: THE LEVELING-SHARPENING HOUSE TEST
Refer to page 632.

COGNITIVE CONTROL BATTERY: THE SCATTERED SCANNING TEST
Refer to page 632.

COGNITIVE SKILLS ASSESSMENT BATTERY
Ann E. Boehm and Barbara Slater

Child
Grades PreK-K

Purpose: Assesses preschool and kindergarten children's progress relative to teaching goals in cognitive and physical-motor areas. Used by teachers for curriculum planning and to match classroom goals with cognitive skills.

Description: 64–item verbal test using easel cards to measure orientation towards environment, discrimination of similarities and differences, comprehension and concept formation, coordination, and immediate and delayed memory. The easel is placed between the examiner and the child, and the child is introduced to the task. The examiner goes through the cards, asking questions and recording the responses. Materials include an easel and 64 cards, response sheets, manual, eight blocks, watch, and paper and pencils. The test does not provide criteria levels and no total score is obtained. The examiner should be a teacher, learning disability specialist, or school psychologist. Examiner required. Not suitable for group use. Available in Japanese.

Untimed: 20–25 minutes

Scoring: Examiner evaluated

Cost: Complete kit (card easel, assessor's manual, class record sheet, 30 pupil response sheets) $49.95; manual $3.50

Publisher: Teachers College Press

COMPREHENSIVE ASSESSMENT PROGRAM: BEGINNING EDUCATION ASSESSMENT (BEA)

Child—Ages 4–6

Purpose: Assesses children's educational development. Used for screening children for learning problems.

Description: Multiple-item paper-pencil measure of students' cognitive growth with reading-, language-, and mathematics-related tasks. The test consists of three separate but related test levels. All tasks are examiner-paced to reduce anxiety and respond to individual needs. The test may be used with the CAP Achievement Series to provide continuous assessment from prekindergarten through high school. Examiner required. Suitable for group use.

Untimed: Open ended

Scoring: Hand key; may be machine scored; may be computer scored

Cost: 35 hand-scorable test booklets Level 4 $44.55; Levels 5 and 6 $34.45; 35 machine-scorable test booklets Levels 5 and 6 $46.65; manual $8.15; hand key (specify level) $1.70

Publisher: American Testronics

COMPREHENSIVE ASSESSMENT PROGRAM: EARLY CHILDHOOD DIAGNOSTIC INSTRUMENT (ECDI)
Refer to page 449.

COMPREHENSIVE IDENTIFICATION PROCESS (CIP)
R. Reid Zehrbach

Child—Ages 2.5–5.5

Purpose: Evaluates the mental and physical development of young children. Used to identify those in need of special medical, psychological, or educational help before entering Kindergarten or the first grade.

Description: Multiple-item verbal-response and task-assessment test of eight areas of child development: cognitive-verbal, fine motor, gross motor, speech and expressive language, hearing, vision, social/affective, and medical history. The screening kit contains administrator's and interviewer's manuals, a screening booklet, 35 parent interview forms, 35 observation of behavior forms, 35 speech and expressive language forms, 35 record folders, and the materials required for the tasks (blocks, balls, beads, buttons, crayons, etc.). The test can be administered by trained paraprofessionals supervised by professionals in the preschool area. Suggestions for dealing with various cultural and language backgrounds are included. The test helps meet the Child Find requirements of PL 94–142. Examiner required. Not suitable for group use. Available in Spanish.

Untimed: 30 minutes

Scoring: Examiner evaluated

Cost: CIP screening kit $90.00

Publisher: Scholastic Testing Service, Inc.

CONCEPT ASSESSMENT KIT— CONSERVATION (CAK)
Marcel L. Goldschmid and Peter M. Bentler

Child—Ages 4–7

Purpose: Assesses the cognitive development of preschool and early school-age children. Used to assess the effect of training based on Piaget's theories.

Description: Multiple-item task-assessment and oral-response test measuring the development of the concept of conservation. Two parallel forms, A and B, measure conservation in terms of two-dimensional space, number, substance, continuous quantity, discontinuous quantity, and weight. Form C measures conservation in terms of area and length. Test items are constructed to assess the child's conservation behavior and comprehension of the principle involved. The items require the child to indicate the presence or absence of conservation and specify the reason for his judgment. CAK is relatively independent of IQ but correlates significantly with school performance. The two parallel forms assess the effect of training, and Form C tests the transfer effects of the training. Norms are provided separately for boys and girls ages 4–7. Examiner required. Not suitable for group use.

Untimed: 15 minutes per form

Scoring: Hand key

Cost: Complete kit (Forms A, B, C, manual) $43.50

Publisher: EdITS/Educational and Industrial Testing Service

DABERON SCREENING FOR SCHOOL READINESS-2
Virginia A. Danzer,
Mary Frances Gerber, and
Theresa M. Lyons with
Judith K. Voress

Handicapped children—
Ages 4–6

Purpose: Assesses the school readiness of children and other handicapped and difficult-to-manage children. Used to develop IEPs.

Description: Multiple-item oral-response and task-performance test assessing language skills, knowledge of body parts, color and number concepts, functional use of prepositions, plurals, ability to follow directions, general knowledge, visual perception, gross-motor development, and the ability to categorize. A high percentage of accurate responses indicates school readiness. Inaccurate responses indicate future problem areas, the need for further diagnostic and prognostic study, and information that needs to be taught. The results yield a Learning Readiness Equivalency age score to identify children with learning difficulties. A *Report On Readiness* is provided for parent and teacher discussion. The manual includes information regarding administration and assessment procedures and instructional objectives for writing IEPs. Examiner required. Not suitable for group use.

Untimed: 20–40 minutes

Scoring: Examiner evaluated

Cost: Complete test kit (manual, materials needed for administration, 25 screening forms, 25 Report On Readiness, 5 classroom summary forms) $79.00

Publisher: PRO-ED

THE DALLAS PRE-SCHOOL SCREENING TEST—REVISED

Child—Ages 3–6

Purpose: Assesses learning disabilities of preschool children. Identifies children in need of special education assistance.

Description: Measures level of development in six learning areas: auditory (listening, discrimination, memory), language (receptive, expressive, communication), motor (gross and fine), visual (drawings, color discrimination, geometric designs), psychological (vocabulary and number concepts), and articulation (phonemes, initial and final positions). Examiner required. Not suitable for group use. Available in Spanish.

Untimed: Not available

Scoring: Hand key; examiner evaluated

Cost: Complete kit (manual, cards, 25 pupil record forms and profile sheets) $27.50

Publisher: Dallas Educational Services

DEGANGI-BERK TEST OF SENSORY INTEGRATION (TSI)
Refer to page 611.

DEVELOPMENTAL ACTIVITIES SCREENING INVENTORY-II (DASI-II)
Rebecca R. Fewell and
Mary Beth Langley

Child—Ages 0–60 months

Purpose: Detects early developmental disabilities in children.

Description: 67–item oral-response and task-performance test assessing 15 developmental skills categories ranging from sensory intactness, means-end relationships, and causality to memory, seriation, and reasoning. Test items may be administered in different sequences in one or two sittings. Instructions are given either verbally or visually. Each test item includes adaptations for use with visually impaired children. The following stimulus items are included in the test kit: 37 picture cards, 5 set-configuration cards, 2 pairs of numeral cards, 3 pairs of word cards, and 4 shape cards. The manual includes a matrix for identifying the concepts tapped by each test item, simple instructional programs for teaching the specific skills assessed by the test items, and an example of the type of program that might be used for a child assessed with this instrument. The test may be administered by classroom teachers with a minimum of testing experience. Examiner required. Not suitable for group use.

Untimed: Varies

Scoring: Examiner evaluated

Cost: Complete kit (manual, 50 record forms, stimulus items in storage box) $54.00

Publisher: PRO-ED

THE DEVELOPMENTAL PROFILE II (DP-II)
Gerald D. Alpern, Thomas Boll, and Marsha Shearer

Child—Ages 0–9

Purpose: Evaluates the age-equivalent physical, social, and mental development of normal or handicapped children. Used for counseling, school planning, and research.

Description: 186–item paper-pencil or computer-administered interview test covering five areas: physical, self-help, social, academic, and communication. Developmental age scores are derived by interviewing a parent or through teacher observation. From birth to age 4, the scales are graded by half-year increments. From Ages 5–9, they are graded in yearly increments. The test also provides an IQ equivalency score. Materials include test books, profile and scoring forms, a manual, and step-by-step procedures for test administration and interpretation. The computer version is suitable for use with IBM PC or compatible systems. The manual must be purchased separately for the computer version. A computer report is available through mail-in service or on-site (if the computer version is used). Examiner required. Suitable for group use.

Untimed: 20–40 minutes

Scoring: Examiner evaluated; may be computer scored

Cost: Paper-pencil version complete kit (25 scoring/profile forms, manual) $60.00; disk for administration and scoring (25 uses) $149.50

Publisher: Western Psychological Services

DEVELOPMENTAL TASKS FOR KINDERGARTEN READINESS (DTKR)
Walter J. Lesiak

Child—Ages 4½–6½

Purpose: Assesses a child's skills and abilities as they relate to performance in kindergarten. Aids curriculum planning by providing school personnel with profiles of children entering kindergarten.

Description: Multiple-item test consisting of 12 subtests utilizing auditory and visual stimuli to assess the following areas: social development, receptive and expressive oral language, visual-motor skills, and cognitive development. The examiner asks questions, arranged in order of difficulty, and/or presents stimulus cards to the child. The child responds, and the examiner records judgments and observations of the response for diagnostic and prescriptive use. Examiner required. Not suitable for group use.

Untimed: 20 minutes

Scoring: Hand key; examiner evaluated

Cost: Complete kit $40.00; manual $10.00; cards $9.75; 25 record booklets $22.50

Publisher: Clinical Psychology Publishing Co., Inc.

EARLY LEARNING ASSESSMENT AND DEVELOPMENT
Audrey Curtis and Mary Wignall

Child

Purpose: Assesses developmental skills and capacities of children in the first years of school. Identifies appropriate remedial activities for children who need to practice and develop certain skills.

Description: Multiple-item task-performance and teacher-observation instrument assessing five developmental areas: motor skills (fine motor and gross motor), perceptual skills (visual, auditory, and tactile perception), communication skills, learning and memory, and emotional and social development. Each area is considered under two headings: assessing strengths and weaknesses and developing skills.

Eleven cards (for sequencing and auditory perception activities) and nine spirit duplicator masters (for individual child profile and visual perception activities) are provided for eliciting activities that allow teachers to observe and pinpoint children's individual developmental abilities. Using guidelines presented in the handbook, teachers can identify and remedy areas of weakness in the first year of infant school, before the child becomes used to failure. The materials also are useful for older children who have specific learning difficulties. Specific remedial suggestions are provided in the handbook. Record sheets are provided to monitor class progress. Examiner required. Not suitable for group use. BRITISH PUBLISHER

Untimed: Varies

Scoring: Examiner evaluated

Cost: Test kit (handbook, 11 cards, 9 spirit duplicating masters, 5 record sheets, ring-binding folder) £24.95

Publisher: Macmillan Education

EARLY SCHOOL INVENTORY (ESI-D)
Joanne R. Nurss and Mary E. McGauvran

Child
Grades PreK–1

Purpose: Collects information about a child's development in order to help the teacher effectively plan instruction.

Description: 82–item checklist for recording observed physical, language, socio-emotional, and cognitive development. The teacher indicates whether the child demonstrates each behavior. The inventory is an integral part of the Metropolitan Readiness Test. Examiner required. Not suitable for group use.

Untimed: Open ended

Scoring: Examiner evaluated

Cost: 35 inventories with Directions for Administering $25.00

Publisher: The Psychological Corporation

Information and availability unconfirmed; last verified in 1988.

EARLY SCHOOL INVENTORY— PRELITERACY (ESI-P)
Joanne R. Nurss and Mary E. McGauvran

Child
Grades PreK–1

Purpose: Obtains information about a child's concept of print, writing, and storytelling.

Description: Three-section inventory examining a child's progress in acquiring preliteracy skills: What You Read, Why You Read, and How You Read. The test also measures the child's ability to communicate through writing, retell a familiar story, and include basic story structural concepts in telling a story. Examiner required. Not suitable for group use.

Timed: 20 minutes

Scoring: Examiner evaluated

Cost: 35 self-scoring sheets, directions and 1 set of 4 cards $30.00; manual $30.00

Publisher: The Psychological Corporation

Information and availability unconfirmed; last verified in 1988.

EARLY SCREENING INVENTORY (ESI)
Samuel J. Meisels and
Martha Stone Wiske

Child—Ages 4–6

Purpose: Assesses children's ability to acquire new skills. Designed to identify children who may need further evaluation and special educational services.

Description: Multiple-item task-performance and oral-response screening instrument assessing the development of kindergarten-aged children. The test is divided into four sections. The initial screening items section assesses the child's ability to respond to an unstructured drawing task and fine-motor control. The visual-motor/adaptive section examines fine-motor control, eye-hand coordination, the ability to remember visual sequences, the ability to draw visual forms, and the ability to reproduce three-dimensional structures. The language and cognition section assesses language comprehension and verbal expression, the ability to reason and count, and the ability to remember auditory sequences. The gross-motor/body awareness section assesses balance, large-motor coordination, and the ability to imitate body positions from visual cues. Nonconsumable stimuli for all tests are provided. The manual includes directions for administering, scoring, and interpreting the tests and statistical information. The parent questionnaire provides relevant information about the child's family, medical, and developmental history. Examiner required. Suitable for group use.

Untimed: Varies

Scoring: Examiner evaluated

Cost: Test kit (manual, screening materials, 30 score sheets, 30 parent questionnaires) $43.95

Publisher: Teachers College Press

EDINBURGH PICTURE TEST
Godfrey Thomson Unit for
Educational Research, University of
Edinburgh

Child—Ages 6.6–8.0

Purpose: Assesses the nonverbal reasoning abilities of children. Identifies children needing further evaluation. Used to measure achievement in the infant school and to aid in selection procedures.

Description: Multiple-item paper-pencil test consisting of five subscales: doesn't belong, classification, reversed similarities, analogies, and sequences. Each subscale is separately timed with its own instructions and examples. Pictures and shapes are used to present tasks similar to those used in verbal reasoning tests. Items are based on ideas used in the former Moray House Picture Tests, but have been completely redrawn and retested. The manual contains information for administering and scoring the test and details of the test's construction and standardization. Examiner required. Suitable for group use.

Timed: 30–40 minutes

Scoring: Examiner evaluated

Cost: 20 test booklets £5.95; manual £3.25; specimen set £3.95

Publisher: Hodder & Stoughton

THE FIRST GRADE READINESS CHECKLIST
John J. Austin

Child Kindergarten

Purpose: Evaluates a child's readiness for first-grade work. Used for determining the learning experiences at which the child can be expected to succeed and for school placement.

Description: 54-item paper-pencil yes-no test measuring the subject's comprehension, age and growth, practical skills, attitudes and interests, memory for numbers, and general knowledge. Self-administered by parents or teachers. Suitable for group use.

Untimed: 15 minutes

Scoring: Examiner evaluated

Cost: Parent's kit (condensed version of handbook, 2 each of 4 sample checklists) $7.00; 50 checklists $9.00; manual $8.95

Publisher: Research Concepts

Information and availability unconfirmed; last verified in 1987.

THE FIVE P'S: PARENT/ PROFESSIONAL PRESCHOOL PERFORMANCE PROFILE
Judith Simon Bloch

Child—Ages 1-7

Purpose: Assesses the development of young handicapped children with learning, language, and behavior problems in two major natural environments, home and school. Used as a means for implementing PL 99-457, preparing Individual Education Programs (IEPs), classroom objectives and programs, and implementing the child assessment component of the Individualized Family Service Plans (IFSP).

Description: 458-item observational assessment instrument consisting of 13 scales grouped in six developmental areas: a) Classroom Adjustment; b) Self-Help Skills (Toileting and Hygiene, Mealtime Behaviors, Dressing); c) Language Development (Communicative Competence, Receptive Language, Expressive Language); d) Social Development (Emerging Self, Relationships to Adults, Relationships to Children); e) Motor Development (Gross Motor/Balance/Coordination Skills, Perceptual/Fine Motor Skills); and f) Cognitive Development. Scale items describe developmental skills and interfering behaviors. Items are observed by teacher and parent at school and at home, respectively, and are rated "yes," "sometimes," or "no." The assessment is completed twice yearly, at 6-month intervals, to provide a means of ongoing assessment linked to remediation. The assessment is used to collect and organize material; provide a database for the IEP; identify a child's needs and strengths; set goals; measure change; and contribute to parent education and involvement. Examiner required. Not suitable for group use. Available in Spanish and Hebrew.

Untimed: Varies

Scoring: Examiner evaluated

Cost: Specimen set (scale booklets, IEP forms, graphic profile, manual) $34.95; materials for class of 10 $80.00; technical manual $3.00

Publisher: Variety Pre-Schooler's Workshop

FROSTIG DEVELOPMENTAL TEST OF VISUAL PERCEPTION (DTVP)
Marianne Frostig and Associates

Child
Grades PreK-3

Purpose: Evaluates children referred for learning difficulties or neurological handicaps by assessing perceptual skills.

Description: 41-item paper-pencil test of five operationally defined perceptual skills: eye-motor coordination, figure-ground, constancy of shape, position in space, and spatial relationships. The test is correlated with reading achievement in a normal first-grade classroom. Materials include 11 demonstration cards showing various shapes and figures. The examiner provides regular and colored pencils and crayons. A blackboard is necessary for group administration. Examiner required. Suitable for group use. Available in Spanish, French, German, Italian, Dutch, Japanese, and Swedish.

Untimed: 30-45 minutes

Scoring: Hand key

Cost: Specimen set (test booklet, manual, monograph, demonstration cards, set of score keys) $14.75; 25 tests $23.50

Publisher: Consulting Psychologists Press, Inc.

THE GESELL PRESCHOOL TEST
Gesell Institute

Child—Ages 2½-6

Purpose: Assesses the behavioral, emotional, and physical development of children. Used for screening, early intervention, or diagnosis depending on the qualifications of the examiner. Meets Child Find Requirements of PL 94-142.

Description: 13 tests assessing a wide range of developmental factors in preschoolers. The Cube Test measures eye-hand coordination, motor skill, attention span, level of functioning in a structured fine-motor task, and ability to understand and follow directions. The Interview Questions test assesses clarity of speech and accuracy of information. The Pencil and Paper Tests (Name, Numbers, and Copy Form) assess visual perception and neuromuscular and eye-hand coordination. The Incomplete Man test assesses perceptual functioning by requiring the child to draw additional parts to a partially drawn human figure. The Discriminates Prepositions test measures understanding of words and concepts related to spatial position. The Digit Repetition test assesses the ability to focus attention, hold information, repeat information in order given, and short-term memory. The Picture Vocabulary test assesses verbal intelligence. The Color Forms test measures recognition of similar shapes. The Action Agent test assesses language comprehension. The Three-Hole Formboard test measures form discrimination ability and general adaptability. The Identifying Letters and Numbers test measures academic abilities against standard norms. The Motor test assesses patterns of comprehension, manipulation, and gross-motor activity. The Developmental Schedules section provides behavioral age-level in all areas tested. The test yields an effective personality profile. Materials include test manual, 50 pre-collated test recording sheets, developmental schedules, Typical Response Cards to help evaluate the Copy Form and Incomplete Man tests, 10 cubes, bean bag, picture vocabulary booklet, two-sided chart of letters and numbers, three-hole formboard, color forms, copy forms, nontoxic pellets and bottle, and complimentary case. Examiner required. Not suitable for group use.

Untimed: 40 minutes

Scoring: Examiner evaluated

Cost: Complete kit $153.00

Publisher: Programs for Education, Inc.

THE GESELL SCHOOL READINESS TEST—COMPLETE BATTERY
Gesell Institute

Child—Ages 4½–9

Purpose: Determines whether a child is ready to begin Kindergarten, assesses a child's readiness for grade promotion (Grades 1–3), and evaluates whether a child has been placed at the proper grade level for his abilities. Used by school psy-

chologists, educators, early childhood specialists, and child development professionals.

Description: Seven subtests measuring the adaptive behavior and visual-perceptual skills necessary for successful performance in Kindergarten to Grade 3. The Cube Test measures eye-hand coordination, motor skills, attention span, and level of functioning in a structured fine-motor task. The Interview Questions test assesses clarity of speech and accuracy of information. The Pencil and Paper Tests (Name, Numbers, and Copy Forms) assess visual perception, neuromuscular and eye-hand coordination, and general level of maturity. The Incomplete Man test measures perceptual functioning by asking the child to draw additional parts to an incomplete human figure. The Right and Left test measures the ability to name parts of the body, distinguish right from left, and follow single and double commands. The Visual Tests assess understanding of directions, ability to carry out orders, and the ability to hold and recall information. The Animals and Interests test measures verbal abilities while providing clues about the child's tempo, organization of thinking, and capacity to attend.

Materials include pre-collated recording sheets for 50 students; a textbook of administration procedures and background information; Typical Response Cards to help evaluate the Copy Form and Incomplete Man tests; visual stimuli cards, cubes, and cylinders required for the various tests; a sample School Readiness Test (for practice and preparation); and carrying case. Examiner required. Not suitable for group use.

Untimed: 40 minutes

Scoring: Examiner evaluated

Cost: Complete kit $115.00

Publisher: Programs for Education, Inc.

GOODMAN LOCK BOX
Joan Goodman

Child
PreK

Purpose: Screens preschool children for mental retardation, fine-motor problems, and distractibility/hyperactivity. Used as a nonthreatening warm-up instrument for more extensive preschool screening.

Description: Multiple-task assessment of a preschooler's ability to organize a free-choice situation. The child is presented with a box with 10 locked doors to open and investigate. A toy is behind each door. The manner in which the child removes the toys is observed to determine whether the child is systematic and organized or poorly focused and distractible. The test relies entirely on spontaneous behavior (no questions are asked). It supplements, without duplicating, other intelligence tests. Norms are provided at 6–month intervals for normally developing children and at yearly intervals for mentally retarded children. Examiner required. Not suitable for group use.

Timed: 6½ minutes

Scoring: Examiner evaluated

Cost: Complete kit (testing materials, manual, record forms) $375.00

Publisher: Stoelting Co.

GROUP TESTS FOR 5/6 AND 7/8 YEAR OLDS—1960

Child—Ages 5–8　　

Purpose: Assesses intellectual ability. Used for measurement of school readiness.

Description: 6–subtest measure of general intellectual ability. Materials include bilingual (English, Afrikaans) test booklets. The child should be able to handle a pencil and follow instructions without emotional distress. Examiner required. Suitable for group use.
SOUTH AFRICAN PUBLISHER

Untimed: No time limit

Scoring: Hand key; examiner evaluated

Cost: (In Rands) 10 tests for 5/6 2,00; 10 tests for 7/8 3,00; manual 7,00; orders from outside the RSA will be dealt with on merit

Publisher: Human Sciences Research Council

HANNAH-GARDNER TEST OF VERBAL AND NONVERBAL LANGUAGE FUNCTIONING
Elaine P. Hannah and Julie O. Gardner

Child—Ages 3½–5½　　

Purpose: Assesses the verbal and nonverbal language of preschoolers. Used for identifying language deficits.

Description: Multiple-item test consisting of five subtests utilizing picture stimuli. The Visual Perception subtest assesses visual comprehension, visual reception, visual discrimination, visual memory, visual closure, visual sequencing, auditory comprehension, auditory reception, classification and categorization, eye-hand coordination, and ability to verbalize. The Concepts subtest measures visual comprehension, visual reception, visual discrimination, auditory comprehension, auditory reception, auditory discrimination, space, time, quantity, and colors. The Auditory Perception subtest covers auditory comprehension, auditory reception, auditory discrimination, auditory memory, auditory closure, ability to verbalize, space, time, quantity, and color. The Receptive Language Development subtest measures auditory comprehension, auditory perception, auditory discrimination, and eye-hand coordination. The Expressive Language subtest covers auditory comprehension, auditory reception, auditory discrimination, auditory closure, ability to verbalize, and colors. In addition, the test identifies familiarity with and usage of verbs and adverbs, plural forms of regular nouns, past tense, negatives, verbs and prepositional phrases, conjunctions, embedding one idea into another, and imperatives. The test yields percentiles and verbal and nonverbal scores. Examiner required. Not suitable for group use. Available in Spanish with Spanish normative data.

Untimed: Varies

Scoring: Examiner evaluated

Cost: $80.00

Publisher: Lingua Press

Information and availability unconfirmed; last verified in 1988.

HARRISON-STROUD READING READINESS PROFILE
Refer to page 345.

HAWAII EARLY LEARNING PROFILE (HELP)
Refer to page 33.

HELP FOR SPECIAL PRESCHOOLERS—CHECKLIST
The Santa Cruz County Office of Education

Child—Ages 3-6 Preschoolers

Purpose: Assesses developmental skills. Used with disabled and normal children in special education, Head Start, child care centers, preschools, and other programs.

Description: Multiple-item paper-pencil 20-page checklist of more than 500 behaviorally written skills grouped according to 40 goals and covering the areas of self-help, motor, communication, and social and learning skills. The checklist also provides columns for recording assessment dates, checking age references, and commenting on parent needs and child progress. A supplemental activities binder, which is ordered separately, provides thousands of activities correlated to the assessment skills covered on the checklist. The activities are designed for developing IEPs and as home support materials for parents. Examiner required. Not suitable for group use.

Untimed: Not available

Scoring: Examiner evaluated

Cost: Checklist $2.95; activities binder $34.95

Publisher: VORT Corporation

Information and availability unconfirmed; last verified in 1988.

HESS SCHOOL READINESS SCALE (HSRS)
Richard J. Hess

Child—Ages 3.5-7

Purpose: Measures the general mental ability of young children. Used to determine readiness to enter school and to predict classroom success.

Description: 45–item paper-pencil verbal test consisting of 12 subtests: Pictoral Identification, Discrimination of Animal Pictures, Picture Memory, Form Perception and Discrimination, Comprehension and Discrimination, Copying Geometric Forms, Paper Folding, Number Concepts, Digital Memory Span, Opposite Analogies, Comprehension, and Sentence Memory Span. All subtests are presented with verbal instructions. Materials include the manual, a guide for administering, a counting frame, 4″ x 4″ paper package, triangle paper package, 5½″ x 8½″ paper package, scoring forms, pencil, and case. Examiner required. Not suitable for group use.

Timed: 2 hours

Scoring: Hand key; examiner evaluated

Cost: Complete kit $34.95

Publisher: Mafex Associates, Inc.

Information and availability unconfirmed; last verified in 1987.

HOWELL PREKINDERGARTEN SCREENING TEST
Joseph P. Ryan, Ronald Mead, and Howell Township Schools, Howell, N.J.

Child—Ages 4-5

Purpose: Measures the school readiness of children entering kindergarten. Identifies children with learning disabilities, special talents, and English language deficiencies. Used for academic placement at the kindergarten level.

Description: Battery of oral-response and task-performance subtests assessing 21 critical skills related to school readiness, including shape and letter identification; listening comprehension; visual, motor, and fine coordination; auditory memory; and prereading and math skills. Scoring provides a profile of each child's strengths and weaknesses and identifies children needing special placement: learning disabled, gifted and talented, and ESL programs. Consumable student test booklets are scored according to guidelines provided in the manual. Individual record sheets are included in each test booklet for teacher reference. The test may be administered by teachers, paraprofessionals, or volunteers. Examiner required. Suitable for group use.

Timed: 1 hour (maximum)

Scoring: Examiner evaluated

Cost: 10 student test booklets $17.95; user's guide and technical manual $12.95; specimen set (student test booklet, user's guide) $14.95

Publisher: Book-Lab

Information and availability unconfirmed; last verified in 1988.

HUMANICS NATIONAL CHILD ASSESSMENT FORMS: AGES 0-3 YEARS

Child—Ages 0-3

Purpose: Records children's skills and behaviors. Used by parents and teachers for planning educational and developmental experiences.

Description: 90–item paper-pencil checklist for assessing the development of a child's skills and behaviors in five areas: social-emotional, language, cognitive, gross motor, and fine motor. Items are arranged in developmental sequence. Space is provided for recording observations three times during one year. Examiner required. Not suitable for group use.

Untimed: Varies

Scoring: Examiner evaluated

Cost: 25 forms $24.95

Publisher: Humanics Psychological Corporation, A Division of Humanics Limited

Information and availability unconfirmed; last verified in 1988.

HUMANICS NATIONAL CHILD ASSESSMENT FORMS: AGES 3-6 YEARS

Child—Ages 3-6

Purpose: Records children's skills and behaviors. Used by parents and teachers for planning educational activities.

Description: Multiple-item paper-pencil checklist for measuring skills and behaviors of children. Teachers or teacher aides record observations for educational planning. The checklist is useful in helping parents understand their child's growth and development. Examiner required. Not suitable for group use.

Untimed: Varies

Scoring: Examiner evaluated

Cost: 25 forms $24.95

Publisher: Humanics Psychological Test Corporation, A Division of Humanics Limited

Information and availability unconfirmed; last verified in 1988.

ILLINOIS TEST OF PSYCHOLINGUISTIC ABILITIES (ITPA)
Samuel A. Kirk, James J. McCarthy, and Winifred D. Kirk

Child—Ages 2-10

Purpose: Assesses specific psycholinguistic abilities and disabilities in young children; facilitates assessment of a child's abilities for purposes of remediation.

Description: 300–item test evaluating a child's cognitive and perceptual abilities in three areas: communication, psycholinguistic processes, and levels of organization. There are 12 subtests: Auditory Reception, Visual Reception, Auditory Association, Visual Association, Verbal Expression, Manual Expression, Grammatic Closure, Visual Closure, Auditory Sequential Memory, Visual Sequential Memory, Auditory Closure, and Sound Blending. The test kit includes an examiner's manual, Visual Sequential Memory booklet, two picture books, chips and tray for visual sequences, picture strips, objects for the verbal and manual expression test, audiocassette, and carrying case. Examiner required. Not suitable for group use. Available in Spanish (from the author only).

Untimed: 1 hour

Scoring: Hand key

Cost: Kit $110.00; record forms and picture strips $15.75; *Aids and Precautions in Administering the ITPA* $4.95; *Psycholinguistic Learning Disabilities* $6.95

Publisher: University of Illinois Press

Information and availability unconfirmed; last verified in 1988.

INFANT RATING SCALE (IRS)
G.A. Lindsay

Child—Ages 5–7½

Purpose: Evaluates a child's developing skills and behavior and provides an overall picture of the child's developmental progress compared with his peer group. Identifies children "at risk" in one or more areas and helps the teacher respond appropriately.

Description: 25–item paper-pencil observational instrument rating a child's strengths and weaknesses on a 5–point scale in the following developmental areas: language, early learning and motor skills, behavior, social integration, and general development. The scale is available on two levels: Level 1 (ages 5–5½) and Level 2 (ages 7–7½). The teacher completes a form for each pupil and enters the ratings on a separate profile/record sheet, providing a broad overview of the child's areas of strength and weakness and a comparison of the child with other children the same age, in terms of subtests and total scores. When Level 2 is used later with the same pupil, the scale forms part of a consecutive monitoring procedure to facilitate the planning of an individualized educational strategy as the child progresses from the Infants to the Junior School. Full statistical details, together with practical illustrations of the uses and interpretations of the IRS, are given in the manual. Self-administered. Suitable for group use.
BRITISH PUBLISHER

Untimed: Not available

Scoring: Examiner evaluated

Cost: Specimen set (Levels 1 and 2) £4.00; manual £3.25; 20 rating scales (specify level) £3.50; 20 profile/record forms £3.50

Publisher: Hodder & Stoughton

THE INFANT READING TESTS
M.A. Brimer and B. Raban

Child—Ages 4–6

Purpose: Assesses the reading-related skills of children.

Description: Multiple-item task-performance diagnostic tests measuring reading-related abilities. The three pre-reading tests, used with children who have not begun formal reading instruction, examine linguistic competence, the ability to use printed symbols, recognition of speech sounds, and discrimination of printed shapes. The three reading tests examine word recognition, sentence completion, and reading comprehension skills. Together, the tests yield a profile of maturation and learning. Rather than standardized scores and reading ages, the tests provide a scale ranging from 1–7, derived in the same manner as the new British Ability Scales. A score of two or lower indicates that a child lacks the skill tested. A score of five or higher indicates that a child possesses the required processes. Tests may be administered on separate days. Examiner required. Suitable for group use.
BRITISH PUBLISHER

Untimed: 20 minutes

Scoring: Not available

Cost: Contact publisher

Publisher: Educational Evaluation Enterprises

Information and availability unconfirmed; last verified in 1988.

INFANT SCREENING
Humberside Local Education Authority

Child—Ages 5 and older

Purpose: Identifies children who are "at risk" in terms of educational, social, or emotional failure in their early school years. Diagnoses exact areas where problems exist. Suggests appropriate teaching programs to deal with the problems. Used for in-service training of teachers of young children.

Description: Two multiple-item paper-pencil observational checklists and one multiple-item paper-pencil test assessing developmental areas of ability ranging from visual and auditory discrimination to managing behavior. Checklist 1 is completed for children ages 5 and older; Checklist 2 is completed for children ages 6 and older. The test booklet is administered to children ages 6 and older and is used in conjunction with the second checklist. Individual pupil profiles record children's progress and problems, forming a basis from which decisions about remedial work can be made. The teacher's book explains use of the materials for initial screening and provides ideas for follow-up diagnosis and remediation throughout the infant and lower junior years. Examiner required. Suitable for group use. BRITISH PUBLISHER

Untimed: Varies

Scoring: Examiner evaluated

Cost: 20 Checklists 1 or 2 £3.25; 10 test booklets £3.25; 25 pupil profiles £3.25; teacher's book and 8 diagnostic test cards £10.95

Publisher: Macmillan Education

KAUFMAN DEVELOPMENTAL SCALE (KDS)
Harvey Kaufman

Child

Purpose: Evaluates school readiness, developmental deficits, and all levels of retardation for normal children through age nine and the mentally retarded of all ages. Used in programming accountability.

Description: 270–item task-assessment test consisting of behavioral evaluation items that are actually expandable teaching objectives. The KDS yields a Developmental Age and Developmental Quotient, as well as individual age-scores and quotients for the following areas of behavioral development: gross motor, fine motor, receptive, expressive, personal behavior, and interpersonal behavior. Examiner required. Not suitable for group use.

Untimed: Not available

Scoring: Examiner evaluated

Cost: Complete kit (testing materials, manual, 25 record forms, carrying case) $210.00

Publisher: Stoelting Co.

KAUFMAN INFANT AND PRESCHOOL SCALE (KIPS)
Refer to page 34.

KEELE PRE-SCHOOL ASSESSMENT GUIDE
Stephen Tyler

Child
Preschool

Purpose: Assesses child development. Used for identifying strengths and weaknesses and for individual program planning.

Description: Two-part instrument outlining a child's developmental abilities. Section I assesses social behavior, and Section II covers cognition, language, socialization, and physical skills. Performance may be plotted on a circular chart. Examiner required. Not suitable for group use. BRITISH PUBLISHER

Untimed: Completed in stages over a number of days

Scoring: Examiner evaluated

Cost: Contact publisher

Publisher: NFER-NELSON Publishing Company Ltd.

KENT INFANT DEVELOPMENT SCALE (KID SCALE)
Refer to page 35.

KINDERGARTEN INVENTORY OF DEVELOPMENTAL SKILLS (KIDS)
State Task Force on Early Childhood Screening

Child—Ages 4-6

Purpose: Assesses the development of children. Used by teachers and screening teams for prekindergarten screening.

Description: Multiple-item response test assessing the number, auditory, paper-pencil, language, visual, and gross-motor skills of prekindergarten children or children entering kindergarten. The 1978 Revised Edition is used with children ages 4.5–6 during the spring or summer preceding kindergarten entrance. The 1980 Alternate Edition is used with children ages 4–6 anytime during the year preceding kindergarten entrance. The screening battery includes an optional parent questionnaire. Examiner required. Not suitable for group use.

Untimed: 35 minutes

Scoring: Hand key

Cost: Specimen set (pupil record sheet, response sheets 1 and 2, parent questionnaire, administration and scoring manual, instructional guide book, technical report) 1978 Edition $15.00; alternate edition $12.50

Publisher: Center for Educational Assessment

KINDERGARTEN LANGUAGE SCREENING TEST (KLST)
Refer to page 700.

KOHN PROBLEM CHECKLIST (KPC) RESEARCH EDITION
Refer to page 742.

KOHN SOCIAL COMPETENCE SCALE (KSC) RESEARCH EDITION
Refer to page 742.

KOONTZ CHILD DEVELOPMENTAL PROGRAM: TRAINING ACTIVITIES FOR THE FIRST 48 MONTHS
Charles W. Koontz

Child—Developmental ages 1–48 months

Purpose: Evaluates the development of normal and retarded children who are functioning at developmental levels of 1–48 months. Used for evaluating and developing skills. May be modified for use with the hearing- and visually impaired.

Description: 550–item paper-pencil inventory of observable performance items arranged to parallel development in a normal child. A parent, teacher, or therapist checks off the specific behaviors that have been observed in the child's routine activities in order to establish the level of functioning in each of four areas of evaluation (gross motor, fine motor, social, and language). Progress is recorded in relation to performance items, and the training activities are designed to reinforce and develop each skill. The test pages, which are made of cardboard, are organized so that different developmental age levels of each of the four areas appear at the same time. Consequently, an examiner working with a child functioning at different levels in any of the four areas has all the appropriate activities visible simultaneously. Examiner required. Not suitable for group use.

Untimed: Not available

Scoring: Hand key

Cost: Complete kit (50 record cards, manual) $37.50

Publisher: Western Psychological Services

LEARNING INVENTORY OF KINDERGARTEN EXPERIENCE (LIKE)
Nathaniel O. Owings, Paulette Mills, and Cynthia Best O'Dell

Child—Ages 4–6 Kindergarten

Purpose: Screens developmental skills of kindergarten students.

Description: 51–item paper-pencil oral-response short-answer point-to test with five subtests assessing gross motor, fine motor, conceptual: aural/oral, comprehension, and miscellaneous skills. Percentiles are reported for each of the five subscores. The test is a formal database procedure and can be used as a standardized test to satisfy PL 94–142. The procedure has high internal consistency reliability based on developmental norms and appropriate item difficulty relative to item analysis. The test is suitable for use with

---

individuals with mental impairments, so that further evaluation can be pursued. A few items from the Miller-Yoder are included in the test. Examiner required. Not suitable for group use.

Untimed: 20 minutes

Scoring: Hand key

Cost: Complete kit $175.00

Publisher: University of Washington Press

LEXINGTON DEVELOPMENTAL SCALES (LDS)
Child Development Centers of the Bluegrass, Inc. Staff

Child—Ages 2–6

Purpose: Assesses the development of handicapped and nonhandicapped preschool children. Identifies a child's needs and abilities. Used to plan programs and evaluate the effectiveness of classroom and child instruction.

Description: Multiple-item observational inventory assessing development in the following areas: gross and fine motor, language, personal and social, and cognitive. Test items are organized according to developmental area and are listed by age. The results are plotted on an interpretive chart, and age norms are arranged in sequence denoting four continuous stages of development. The LDS Long Form provides an in-depth assessment and requires approximately 2 hours to administer. The LDS Short Form is a screening tool that takes 30–45 minutes to administer. Examiner required. Not suitable for group use.

Untimed: Long Form 2 hours; Short Form 30–45 minutes

Scoring: Examiner evaluated

Cost: Long Form manual $6.00; Long Form chart $1.25; Short Form manual $4.00; Short Form chart $1.00

Publisher: Child Development Centers of the Bluegrass, Inc.

Information and availability unconfirmed; last verified in 1987.

LINGUISTIC AWARENESS IN READING READINESS
Refer to page 347.

THE LOLLIPOP TEST: A DIAGNOSTIC SCREENING TEST OF SCHOOL READINESS, REVISED 1988
Alex L. Chew

Child
PreK-Grade 1

Purpose: Evaluates the school readiness of preschoolers, kindergartners, and first-graders. Used to plan individualized programs in Grades K–1.

Description: Multiple-item oral-response and task-assessment measuring a preschooler's attainment of the developmental skills necessary for success in Grades K–1. Test items are culture-free. Results identify both deficiencies and strengths for each child tested. The test may be administered before and after preschool programs to assess progress in readiness skills. Examiner required. Suitable for group use. Available in Spanish.

Untimed: 15–20 minutes

Scoring: Examiner evaluated

Cost: Test kit (manual, 7 cards, 5 booklets) $29.95

Publisher: Humanics Psychological Test Corporation, A Division of Humanics Limited

Information and availability unconfirmed; last verified in 1988.

MAXFIELD-BUCHOLZ SOCIAL MATURITY SCALE FOR BLIND PRE-SCHOOL CHILDREN
Refer to page 665.

MCCARTHY SCALES OF CHILDREN'S ABILITIES
Refer to page 36.

MCCARTHY SCREENING TEST
Dorothea McCarthy

Child—Ages 4–6.5

Purpose: Predicts a child's ability to cope with school work in the early grades. For use in early identification of children at risk for school problems.

Description: Six-task test measuring the following mental abilities: right-left orientation, verbal memory, draw-a-person, numerical memory, conceptual grouping, and leg coordination. Children with learning disabilities or other handicaps perform less well than children without problems. Materials include card for right-left orientation, tape, and blocks. The tasks are taken from the McCarthy Scales of Children's Abilities. Examiner required. Not suitable for group use.

Untimed: 20 minutes

Scoring: Examiner evaluated

Cost: Complete set (all necessary equipment, manual, 25 record forms, 25 drawing booklets, carrying case) $115.00

Publisher: The Psychological Corporation

Information and availability unconfirmed; last verified in 1988.

THE MEASUREMENT OF SELF-CONCEPT IN KINDERGARTEN CHILDREN (MSCKC)
Lucienne Y. Levin and J. Clayton Lafferty

Kindergarten

Purpose: Assesses self-concept of kindergartners by analyzing their drawings.

Description: Multiple-item paper-pencil instrument used by kindergarten teachers for measuring children's self-concept. The objective evaluation system applied to the children's drawings and paintings is a tool for predicting probable academic success and indicating problem areas for correction by curriculum design and alternative teaching methods. The instrument provides a means of comparing a child to his own self rather than to other children. Self-administered. Suitable for group use.

Untimed: 10–20 minutes

Scoring: Hand key

Cost: Complete set (general manual, scoring manual, 100 score sheets) $26.00

Publisher: Research Concepts

Information and availability unconfirmed; last verified in 1987.

MEETING STREET SCHOOL SCREENING TEST
Peter Hainsworth and Marion Siqueland

Child—Ages 5–7½

Purpose: Identifies kindergartners and first-graders with learning disorders. Used to minimize subsequent learning failure and behavioral upset.

Description: 15–item paper-pencil test containing three subtests (5 items each). The Motor Patterning subtest assesses the ability to hop, skip, move on command, imitate the examiner's hand gestures, and fine-finger dexterity. The Visual-Perceptual subtest assesses copying geometric and letter forms, drawing when commanded, and tapping block patterns in sequence. The Language subtest assesses repetition of short phrases, sentences, and nonsense words; counting forward and backward; sequencing time concepts; and describing an abstract picture. The examiner uses a spiral-bound manual and a record booklet containing a worksheet, scoresheet, behavior rating scale, and performance grid. Normative tables for tests and scores are provided at one-half year levels based on 1966 census figures. Examiner required. Not suitable for group use.

Untimed: 20 minutes

Scoring: Hand key; examiner evaluated

Cost: Manual $12.00; 50 record forms $5.00; 100 record forms $9.00

Publisher: Meeting Street School, Easter Seal Society of Rhode Island, Inc.

Information and availability unconfirmed; last verified in 1987.

METROPOLITAN READINESS TESTS: FIFTH EDITION (MRT)
Joanne R. Nurss and Mary E. McGauvran

Child
Grades PreK–1

Purpose: Assesses underlying skills important for early school learning. For use in identifying each individual child's needs.

Description: Multiple-item paper-pencil test of skills important for learning reading and mathematics and for developing language. The test is divided into two levels. Level I yields four scores: Auditory, Visual Area, Language Area, and Pre-Reading Skills Composite. Level II yields scores in Auditory Area, Visual Area, Language Area, Quantitative Area, Pre-Reading Skills Composite, and Battery Composite. The test is also available in a 1976 edition. The test is available only as long as supplies last. Examiner required. Suitable for group use.

Timed: Level 1 80–90 minutes; Level II 100 minutes

Scoring: Computer scoring service available

Cost: Examination kit, 1986 edition, specify level (test booklet, manual, Parts I and II; parent-teacher report, Early School Inventory-Developmental, Early School Inventory-Preliteracy, class record, practice booklet) $17.00; Examination kit, 1976 edition $18.00

Publisher: The Psychological Corporation

Information and availability unconfirmed; last verified in 1988.

MINNESOTA CHILD DEVELOPMENT INVENTORY (MCDI)
Refer to page 36.

MINNESOTA PREKINDERGARTEN INVENTORY (MPI)
Harold Ireton and Edward Thwing

Child—Ages 4½–5½

Purpose: Measures a child's readiness for kindergarten. Used by educators, psychologists, physicians, and other professionals to assess the child's current development, readiness skills, social and emotional adjustment, and symptoms.

Description: 150–item paper-pencil inventory completed by the mother. The inventory measures self-help, fine-motor, expressive language, comprehension, memory, letter recognition, number comprehension, immaturity, hyperactivity,

behavior problems, emotional problems, motor, language, somatic, and sensory symptoms. Intended for mothers with a high-school education. Self-administered. Suitable for group use.

Untimed: 15 minutes

Scoring: Hand key

Cost: 10 reusable booklets $7.00; 25 answer sheets $7.00; 25 profile forms $7.00; scoring templates $12.00; manual $14.00

Publisher: Behavior Science Systems, Inc.

MOTOR SKILLS INVENTORY (MSI)
Refer to page 614.

MUMA ASSESSMENT PROGRAM (MAP)—REVISED SECOND EDITION
John R. Muma

Preschoolers

Purpose: Assesses the cognitive, linguistic, and communication domains of preschoolers and early school-aged children. Used by speech and language clinicians and teachers for developing IEPs. May also be used with adults.

Description: Criterion-referenced stimulus-response test utilizing card decks to assess learning styles, sensorimotor skills, rule and nonrule governed learning, and the concepts of conservation, quantity, and likeness. Examiner required. Not suitable for group use.

Untimed: Not available

Scoring: Examiner evaluated

Cost: Complete kit (manual, 6 card decks, 6 pads of response forms, storage box) $79.00

Publisher: PRO-ED

PACE
Lisa K. Barclay and James R. Barclay

Preschoolers

Purpose: Identifies learning skills deficits in preschool children. Used by school psychologists, special educators, teachers, and other professionals involved in preschool screening, educational placement, and remediation.

Description: 68–item paper-pencil or computer-administered task-performance instrument in which the examiner observes the child's behavior in 12 areas: motor coordination, eye-hand coordination, small-muscle coordination, visual perception, rhythm recognition, listening, visual matching, tactile skills, motor behavior memory, verbal memory, attending, and social development. Parents' observations may be integrated and compared with classroom results. A short form (FAST PACE) that includes 18 of the original items can be used as a brief, preliminary screening device. The computer software operates on Apple II and IBM PC systems. As many as 100 individual cases can be stored on disk at one time. The disk has unlimited uses. Examiner required. Suitable for small group use.

Untimed: Not available

Scoring: Examiner evaluated

Cost: $165.00

Publisher: MetriTech, Inc.

PARENT READINESS EVALUATION OF PRESCHOOLERS (PREP)
A. Edward Ahr

Child—Ages 3.9–5.5

Purpose: Evaluates the verbal and mental abilities of preschool children. Used to assess educational readiness.

Description: 190–item verbal and manual test to help parents ascertain their preschoolers' educational readiness. The test aids parents helping their children learn at home by pointing out strengths and weaknesses. Used in conjunction with the handbook *Developing Your Child's Skills and Abilities at Home*. Examiner required. Not suitable for group use.

Untimed: 30 minutes

Scoring: Hand key

Cost: Specimen set $2.50

Publisher: Priority Innovations, Inc.

Information and availability unconfirmed; last verified in 1988.

PEABODY DEVELOPMENTAL MOTOR SCALES AND ACTIVITY CARDS
Refer to page 615.

PEDIATRIC EXAMINATION OF EDUCATIONAL READINESS (PEER)
Melvine D. Levine

Child—Ages 4–6

Purpose: Detects high-prevalence low-severity disabilities in young children that are critical to success in school. Used for diagnosis, screening, research, and professional training.

Description: Verbal paper-pencil show-tell measure of six developmental areas: orientation, gross-motor, visual-fine motor, sequential, linguistic, and pre-academic skills. The child is asked to identify pictures and copy some of them with a pencil; tasks are presented to the child using numerous miscellaneous items (keys, tennis balls, blocks) contained in the kit; sentences are provided for language assessment. The examination produces an empirical description of what occurred when a child was asked to perform age-appropriate tasks. The information then can be used to help plan health, education, and developmentally oriented services. Examiner required. Not suitable for group use.

Untimed: 1 hour

Scoring: Examiner evaluated

Cost: Record forms and stimulus booklet $27.00; examiner's manual $9.00; stimulus booklet $7.50; kit $8.50; complete set $52.00; specimen set (manual, record forms) $9.50

Publisher: Educators Publishing Service, Inc.

THE PORTAGE EARLY EDUCATION PROGRAMME—UK VERSION
Refer to page 653.

PRE-ACADEMIC LEARNING INVENTORY (PAL)
Mildred H. Wood and Fay M. Layne

Child—Ages 4½–6

Purpose: Assesses readiness of young children to handle academic tasks. Used to diagnose strengths and weaknesses in order to plan educational and remedial programs.

Description: Multiple-item checklist examining nine areas: language development, speech development, concept development, body concept, auditory channel development, visual channel development, visual-motor integration, eye-hand coordination, and gross-motor coordination. Materials include stimulus pictures and cards, record booklets and sheets, eye-hand coordination activity sheets, and parent-child activity leaflets. Scoring is by the checklist method. Examiner required. Not suitable for group use.

Untimed: 30–35 minutes
Scoring: Hand key; examiner evaluated
Cost: Test kit $35.00
Publisher: United Educational Services, Inc.

PRESCHOOL AND KINDERGARTEN INTEREST DESCRIPTOR (PRIDE)
Refer to page 625.

PRESCHOOL AND KINDERGARTEN PERFORMANCE PROFILE
Alfred J. DiNola, Bernard Kaminsky, Allen E. Sternfeld

Child
Grades Prek-K

Purpose: Assesses the developmental levels of preschool and kindergarten children.

Description: 50–item paper-pencil inventory of the social, intellectual, and physical development of children in preschool and kindergarten. The items are grouped in 10 areas: interpersonal rela-

tions, emotional behavior, safety, communication, basic concepts, perceptual development, imagination and creative expression, self-help, gross-motor skills, and fine-motor skills. Each item is rated on a 7–point scale. The test helps teachers identify students with low developmental levels or possible learning disabilities, indicates strengths and weaknesses, and determines readiness for new learning. Examiner required. Not suitable for group use.

Untimed: Varies
Scoring: Examiner required
Cost: Class kit (teacher's manual, 25 record booklets, 25 progress report folders) $25.00
Publisher: Educational Performance Associates

PRESCHOOL EMBEDDED FIGURES TEST (PEFT)
Susan W. Coates

Child—Ages 3–6

Purpose: Assesses individual perceptual processes, including field dependence. Used for counseling and research.

Description: 24–item nonverbal test of cognitive functioning and styles. Items are complex black-and-white line drawings in which the subject must find an embedded triangle. Materials include plates with complex figures, clear plastic envelopes, and one simple figure. Examiner required. Not suitable for group use.

Timed: 15 minutes
Scoring: Examiner evaluated
Cost: Complete kit (manual, plates, 25 record sheets) $17.50
Publisher: Consulting Psychologists Press, Inc.

PRESCHOOL LANGUAGE SCALE (PLS)
Refer to page 707.

PRESCHOOL SCREENING INSTRUMENT
Stephen Paul Cohen

Child—Ages 4–5.3

Purpose: Identifies prekindergarten children with learning disabilities. Used to meet PL 94–142 screening requirements.

Description: Multiple-item task-assessment test in which the child is told he will be "playing some games" with the examiner, who administers the following subtests: Figure Drawing, Circle Drawing, Tower Building, Cross Drawing, Block Design, Square Drawing, Broad Jumping, Balancing, Ball Throwing, Hopping, Whole Name, Picture Responses, Comprehension, and Oral Vocabulary. The child's responses are evaluated in seven developmental areas: visual-motor perception, fine-motor development, gross-motor skills, language development, verbal fluency, conceptual skills, and speech and behavioral problems. Examiner required. Not suitable for group use.

Untimed: 5–8 minutes

Scoring: Examiner evaluated

Cost: Complete kit (25 student record books, manual, 16 wooden blocks, picture story card, 6 kindergarten-size pencils) $51.00

Publisher: Stoelting Co.

PRESCHOOL SELF-CONCEPT PICTURE TEST (PS-CPT)
Refer to page 771.

PRESCREENING DEVELOPMENTAL QUESTIONNAIRE (PDQ)
William F. Frankenburg, W. VanDoorninck, T. Liddell, and N. Dick

Child—Ages 3 months–6 years

Purpose: Determines whether children can perform certain skills performed by most children their age. Used as an indicator for further testing.

Description: 97–item paper-pencil test administered by the parents, who are given response forms color-coded by age with 10 questions appropriate for each age group. Forms are available for the following age groups: 3–8 months, 9–15 months, 16–24 months, 2 years 1

month–4 years 9 months, and 5–6 years. Examiners must have at least a high-school education. Examiner required. Suitable for group use. Available in Spanish and French.

Untimed: 2–5 minutes

Scoring: Hand key

Cost: 100 forms (specify age group) English $10.50; Spanish $11.50; French $11.50; directions and interpretive instructions included

Publisher: Denver Developmental Materials, Inc.

PRESCRIPTIVE TEACHING SERIES
Sue Martin

Child, adolescent Grades 1–8

Purpose: Measures individual child development. Used for assessment of a child's strengths and weaknesses and for planning educational experiences.

Description: Six-scale test of development in the following areas: visual, visual-motor, motor, auditory, reading and language, and math. The Visual Skills Test is composed of 22 skills with 104 subitems. The Visual-Motor Skills Booklet is composed of 28 items in four areas: body imagery, spatial orientation, visual-motor discrimination, and writing skills. The Motor Skills booklet consists of 166 items. The Auditory Skills Booklet consists of 31 items in several areas: auditory stimuli, speech response to auditory stimuli, oral reading, and phonetic analysis. The Reading and Language Skills booklet is composed of 152 skills, and Math Skills is composed of 315 skills. Examiner required. Not suitable for group use.

Untimed: Each rating period 15 minutes

Scoring: Hand key; examiner evaluated

Cost: Examiner's set (10 copies all booklets, manual) $40.00; 25 Visual Skills, 25 Visual-Motor Skills each $15.00; 25 Motor Skills, 25 Auditory Skills, 25 Reading and Language Skills each $20.00; 25 Math Skills $35.00

Publisher: Psychologists and Educators, Inc.

PRIMARY ACADEMIC SENTIMENT SCALE (PASS)
Glen Robbins Thompson

Child—Ages 4.4–7.3

Purpose: Assesses a child's motivation for learning, level of maturity, and parental independence. Used to screen for school readiness and develop academic motivation plans.

Description: 38–item verbal scale yielding two scores: sentiment quotient (interest in academics) and dependency stanine (child's interdependence on parents). The child is shown pictures of various activities and asked to point to a happy, neutral, or sad face, depending on how he feels about the activity. Examiner required. Suitable for group use.

Untimed: 30 minutes

Scoring: Hand key

Cost: Specimen set $4.00; tests $1.50 in quantity, with one manual for every 35 tests

Publisher: Priority Innovations, Inc.

Information and availability unconfirmed; last verified in 1988.

PRIMARY EDUCATION PROGRAM: DIAGNOSTIC TEST FOR CLASSIFICATION/ COMMUNICATION SKILLS (PEP)
Margaret C. Wang and Lauren B. Resnick

Child—Ages 3–6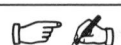

Purpose: Measures the ability of young children to match, sort, and name things. Used by teachers for individual curriculum planning.

Description: Multiple-item picture-book verbal test of a child's ability to match like objects, discriminate shapes and sizes, name colors and shapes, and handle descriptions of size, length, width, and height. One test is provided for each objective. Materials include a progress chart and a manual. Examiner required. Not suitable for group use.

Untimed: Not available

Scoring: Hand key; examiner evaluated

Cost: Complete kit $27.95

Publisher: Mafex Associates, Inc.

Information and availability unconfirmed; last verified in 1987.

PRIMARY EDUCATION PROGRAM: DIAGNOSTIC TESTS FOR QUANTIFICATION SKILLS
Margaret C. Wang and Lauren B. Resnick

Child—Ages 3–6

Purpose: Assesses entry-level quantification skills of preschool and primary-grade children. Used for group placement and checking instructional progress.

Description: 8–unit verbal test covering 56 objectives: nine in counting and comprehending one-to-one correspondences to the number 5; nine in counting and comprehending one-to-one correspondences to the number 10; seven in numerals to the number 5; seven in numerals 6–10; seven in comparison of sets; four in seriation and ordinal position; seven in addition and subtraction; and six in adding and subtracting equations. Materials include a manual, progress chart, and handbook with all the necessary instructions. Examiner required. Not suitable for group use.

Untimed: Not available

Scoring: Hand key; examiner evaluated

Cost: Complete kit $22.95

Publisher: Mafex Associates, Inc.

Information and availability unconfirmed; last verified in 1987.

PRIMARY MENTAL ABILITIES (PMA) READINESS LEVEL, REVISED
L.L. Thurstone and Thelma Gwinn Thurstone

Child
Grades K–1

Purpose: Assesses learning readiness of kindergartners and first-graders. Provides information about level of development compared with other children. Used to plan materials and instruction rates, identify special needs, facilitate grouping, and communicate with parents.

Description: 90–item paper-pencil test measuring auditory discrimination, verbal meaning, perceptual speed, number facility, and spatial relations. Grade-based normative information is available. Examiner required. Suitable for group use.

Untimed: 1 hour

Scoring: Hand key

Cost: Complete set (30 copies each of 4 test booklets and student profile folders, examiner's manual, and user's manual) $32.00

Publisher: SRA/London House

PSYCHOEDUCATIONAL PROFILE—REVISED (PEP-R)
Eric Schopler, Robert J. Reichler, Ann Bashford, Margaret D. Lansing, and Lee M. Marcus

Developmentally disabled children

Purpose: Measures the learning abilities and characteristics of autistic and related developmentally disordered children. Used to establish individualized special education curricula or home programs for developmentally disabled children who were previously regarded as untestable.

Description: Multiple-item task-performance test assessing the learning abilities of autistic and developmentally disabled children. The test results comprise a learning profile reflecting the individual characteristics of the child. This profile is translated into an appropriately individualized special education curriculum or home program according to the teaching strategies described in Volume II of the manual. The manual, *Individualized Assessment for Autistic and Developmentally Disabled Children,* is published in two volumes by PRO-ED. Volume I describes the psychoeducational profile, and Volume II discusses teaching strategies for parents and professionals. Examiner required. Not suitable for group use.

Untimed: Varies

Scoring: Examiner evaluated

Cost: Volume I complete program (manual, 10 profile sheets) $39.00; Volume II $24.00

Publisher: PRO-ED

PSYCHOLOGICAL EVALUATION OF CHILDREN'S HUMAN FIGURE DRAWINGS (HFD)
Refer to page 148.

THE PYRAMID SCALES
Refer to page 672.

QUICK-SCORE ACHIEVEMENT TEST (Q-SAT)
Donald D. Hammill, Jerome J. Ammer, Mary E. Cronin, Linda H. Mandlebaum, and Sally S. Quinby

Child, adolescent
Grades 1–12

Purpose: Identifies students with subject matter content difficulties. Used by teachers, psychologists, and diagnosticians.

Description: Multiple-item paper-pencil test measuring student proficiency in reading, writing, arithmetic, and facts about science, social studies, health, and language arts. Results are reported as standard scores and percentiles. The test is available in two equivalent forms, A and B, and is suited for English-speaking children regardless of nationality. The PRO-SCORE scoring system is available from the publisher for use on Apple IIc, II+, and IIe and IBM PC and MS-DOS computers. The system generates a four-page report providing background information on the student; raw scores, standard scores, percentiles, and descriptions for each subtest; standard score sums, percentiles, and descriptors for all composites and quotients; an optional cognitive aptitude score; subtest and composite profiles; intraindividual comparisons of all composites; and significance testing of all comparisons. Examiner required. Not suitable for group use.

Untimed: 40 minutes

Scoring: Hand key; may be computer scored

Cost: Complete kit (manual, 50 summary/profile sheets, 25 student record forms for each form A and B, storage box) $63.00; PRO-SCORE scoring systems $69.00

Publisher: PRO-ED

RATING INVENTORY FOR SCREENING KINDERGARTNERS (RISK)
J. Michael Coleman and G. Michael Dover

Child
Kindergarten

Purpose: Assesses likelihood of future supplemental educational assistance.

Description: 34–item computer-administered questionnaire covering school competence, task orientation, sociability, behavior, and motor skills. The computer program records teacher ratings, calculates local norms, and provides a list of students who are at risk for developing future educational problems. Performance in skill areas are reported as Z-scores. May be used with Apple IIe, IIc, or IIgs with 64K memory or IBM PC or compatibles with 256K memory. Examiner required. Not suitable for group use.

Untimed: Varies

Scoring: Examiner evaluated

Cost: $190.00

Publisher: PRO-ED

READINESS FOR OPERATIONS (K–3)
Refer to page 326.

REVISED PRE-READING SCREENING PROCEDURES TO IDENTIFY FIRST GRADE ACADEMIC NEEDS
Beth H. Slingerland

Child
Grades K–1

Purpose: Evaluates young children of average to superior intelligence in order to locate individuals with hearing, seeing, or moving difficulties that might indicate a language disability. Used to determine what kinds of special instruction/counseling are needed.

Description: Series of 12 verbal-visual subtests measuring visual perception; visual discrimination; visual recall; visual-motor skills; auditory recall; auditory discrimination; auditory perception; letter knowledge; and language skills, such as vocabulary, enunciation, comprehension of oral directions, oral expression, and recall of new words. The test also evaluates the child's motor coordination, hobbies and interests, attention span, and mental growth.

The test identifies children who are ready for formal instruction in reading, writing, and spelling and are able to learn through conventional methods; children who, while appearing to be ready, reveal indications of a language disability and need immediate multisensory instruction; children who show language confusion or possible developmental lag but whose maturity indicates a need to begin strengthening their language background; children who, regardless of age, are unready to begin reading instruction and who would benefit from more readiness and social development training. Materials consist of a test booklet (including 12 teacher observation/summary sheets and 12 practice pages), teacher's manual (including instructions and detachable answer key), and teacher's cards and chart (two sets of cards and two copies of a wall chart used in the tests). Many of the tests require students to use a pencil for marking. The examiner explains the directions to the students before they proceed with the task. Examiner required. Suitable for group use.

Untimed: 2–3 hours

Scoring: Hand key; examiner evaluated

Cost: 12 test booklets $14.00; teacher's manual $5.00; teacher's cards and chart $6.50; specimen set (teacher's manual, test booklet) $5.25

Publisher: Educators Publishing Service, Inc.

REVISED PRESCREENING DEVELOPMENTAL QUESTIONNAIRE (R-PDQ)

Child—Ages 0–6

Purpose: Determines whether a child possesses developmental skills acquired by most other children of his age. Used to indicate further testing.

Description: 105–item paper-pencil pre-screening test administered by the child's parents. This updated version is designed to include more age-appropriate items, simplified parent scoring, and easier norm comparisons. Forms are available for the following age ranges: 0–9 months, 9–24 months, 2–4 years, and 4–6 years. Examiners must have at least a high school education. Examiner required. Suitable for group use.

Untimed: Office assistant 2 minutes; parents 10 minutes

Scoring: Hand key

Cost: 100 forms $10.50

Publisher: Denver Developmental Materials, Inc.

REYNELL-ZINKIN DEVELOPMENT SCALES FOR YOUNG VISUALLY HANDICAPPED CHILDREN
Joan Reynell and P. Zinkin

Child

Purpose: Assesses development of blind and partially sighted babies and young children. Used for planning management and early education programs.

Description: Performance test of intellectual development with separate subscales for the following areas: social adaptation, sensorimotor understanding, exploration of environment, response to sound and verbal comprehension, and expressive language and communication. The assessment yields a profile detailing strong and weak areas. The provided tables allow comparisons to blind, partially sighted, and sighted children. The test is designed for professionals responsible for the assessment and education of the handicapped (doctors, psychologists, and teachers of blind and partially sighted children). The examiner provides toys and other necessary materials. Examiner required. Not suitable for group use.
BRITISH PUBLISHER

Untimed: Not available

Scoring: Examiner evaluated

Cost: Contact publisher

Publisher: NFER-NELSON Publishing Company Ltd.

RILEY PRESCHOOL DEVELOPMENTAL SCREENING INVENTORY
Clara M.D. Riley

Child
Grades PreK–1

Purpose: Measures readiness to attend school and identifies children most likely to need assistance adjusting to normal school situations. Used for counseling and to meet the requirements of PL 94–142.

Description: Multiple-item observational test providing a child's developmental age and self-concept and determining serious developmental and maturational problems. The instrument can be administered at the beginning of preschool, kindergarten, or first grade. It was developed and has been used widely in Head Start programs. Suggested cutoff scores are provided. Examiner required. Suitable for group use. Test instructions are in both Spanish and English.

Untimed: 15–20 minutes

Scoring: Examiner evaluated

Cost: Complete kit (25 tests, manual) $19.00

Publisher: Western Psychological Services

ROCKFORD INFANT DEVELOPMENTAL SCALES (RIDES)
Project RHISE

Child—Ages 0–4

Purpose: Evaluates the level of a child's skill and behavioral development. Used for initial assessment by special education teachers to guide and objectify their observations of a child.

Description: Multiple-item paper-pencil evaluation of 308 developmental behaviors arranged by age into five skill areas: personal-social/self-help, fine motor/adaptive, receptive language, expressive language, and gross motor. Each behavioral item is determined to be present, emerging, or absent in the child. Test results relate these single items to major developmental patterns and competencies. The format calls for one eight-page booklet per child. An Individual Child Progress Graph on the back page shows progress and allows comparison of levels across developmental areas. The manual contains a section detailing development, use, and interpretation of the test. The entries for all 308 behaviors provide scoring criteria, developmental significance, equipment specifications, and references to further information. An appendix containing master equipment list, skill group listings, notes, and bibliography are included. The Starter Set includes the manual and 20 checklists. Examiner required. Not suitable for group use.

Untimed: Varies

Scoring: Hand key

Cost: Starter set $40.00

Publisher: Scholastic Testing Service, Inc.

SANTA CLARA PLUS COMPUTER MANAGEMENT SYSTEM

Child—Ages 3½–7

Purpose: Assesses cognitive and affective skills of children. Used for diagnostic and prescriptive mastery of objectives for kindergarten and special education students.

Description: Multiple-test kit assessing 60 cognitive and 12 affective skills (one item per objective). The examiner directs the child to perform an activity, monitors the task, and rates the child's performance. Results are transferred to a profile chart or microcomputer diskette for analysis and prescription. Prescriptive materials are provided. Examiner required. Suitable for group use.

Untimed: Not available

Scoring: Hand key; may be computer scored

Cost: Complete $160.00 and $50.00 per diskette for each additional classroom; package of test cards $4.00

Publisher: Skillcorp Software, Inc.

SCHOOL ENTRANCE CHECKLIST
John McLeod

Child
Grades K–1

Purpose: Gathers relevant social data about a child just entering school for routine survey and screening purposes.

Description: 18–item paper-pencil questionnaire completed by parents or guardians at the time a child enters school. The questionnaire is recommended for routine survey and screening. The School Entrance Checklist contains the most pertinent questions from the Dyslexia Schedule, but contains only 18 of the Dyslexia Schedule's 89 questions to avoid overwhelming the parent. The School Entrance Checklist may be sent home for the parents to complete and return. Examiner required. Not suitable for group use.

Untimed: 20–30 minutes

Scoring: Examiner evaluated

Cost: Less than 100 each $0.90; 100 or more each $0.75; manual $3.25

Publisher: Educators Publishing Service, Inc.

THE SCHOOL READINESS CHECKLIST
John J. Austin and J. Clayton Lafferty

Child—PreK

Purpose: Determines a child's readiness for kindergarten work. Used to educate parents about learning patterns and to help with preschool clinics and meetings.

Description: 43–item paper-pencil yes-no test measuring the subject's comprehension, age and growth, practical skills, attitudes and interests, memory for numbers, and general knowledge. Materials include booklets with white child or black child illustrations. Self-administered by parents and teachers. Not suitable for group use. Manual available in Spanish.

Untimed: 15 minutes

Scoring: Examiner evaluated

Cost: Specimen set (condensed version of handbook, 2 kindergarten, 2 first grade) $7.00; manual $8.95; 50 checklists $9.00
Publisher: Research Concepts
Information and availability unconfirmed; last verified in 1987.

SCHOOL READINESS EVALUATION BY TRAINED TESTERS (SETT)—1984

Child

Purpose: Evaluates the developmental level of children about to begin school. Used by teachers for classifying entering students and by psychologists for diagnostic purposes.

Description: 36–item test evaluating the language and general, physical and motor, and emotional and social development of children entering school. Items are constructed to create learning situations similar to those that occur in the classroom and to promote interaction between the teacher and the student. Scores yield five groups of beginners distinguished according to the types of problems that may interfere with academic development. Examiner required. Not suitable for group use.
SOUTH AFRICAN PUBLISHER
Untimed: 30 minutes
Scoring: Examiner evaluated
Cost: Contact publisher
Publisher: Human Sciences Research Council

SCHOOL READINESS SCREENING TEST
Gesell Institute

Child—Ages 4½–5

Purpose: Measures coordination, motor skills, and verbal ability of young children. Used to determine developmental readiness for Kindergarten.

Description: Multiple-task verbal and manual paper-pencil examination containing five subtests measuring predominant adaptive behavior. The Cube Test measures eye-hand coordination, motor skills, attention span, and level of functioning in a structured fine-motor task. The Interview Questions reveal speech clarity and accuracy of information. The Paper and Pencil Tests reveal visual perception, neuromuscular and eye-hand coordination, and general maturity level. The Incomplete Man test provides clues to perceptual functioning by requiring the child to complete a human figure. The Animals and Interests test assesses verbal abilities and provides clues about a child's tempo, organization of thinking, and capacity to attend.

Materials include pre-collated recording sheets for 50 students; a textbook of administration procedures and background information; cubes, visual stimuli cards, and cylinders required for the various tests; Typical Response Cards to help evaluate the Copy Form and Incomplete Man tests; a sample School Readiness Test (for practice and preparation); and carrying case. Examiner required. Not suitable for group use.
Untimed: 20 minutes
Scoring: Examiner evaluated
Cost: Complete kit $99.50
Publisher: Programs for Education, Inc.

SCHOOL READINESS SURVEY
F.L. Jordan and James Massey

Child—Ages 4–6

Purpose: Assesses a child's understanding of numbers, colors, words, and forms. Used to determine readiness for kindergarten.

Description: 95–item paper-pencil verbal test consisting of eight school readiness subtests: Number Concept, Discrimination of Form, Color Naming, Symbol Matching, Speaking Vocabulary, Listening Vocabulary, General Information, and General Readiness. The test may be administered by parents or an examiner. Parent-administered scores are correlated with teacher-administered scores. Materials include suggestions to parents for developing the child's skill areas. Parents must supply two pencils and a marker. Examiner required. Not suitable for group use.
Untimed: Not available
Scoring: Examiner evaluated

Cost: Manual $1.75; 25 surveys $19.00
Publisher: Consulting Psychologists Press, Inc.

SCHOOL READINESS TEST (SRT)
Oliver F. Anderhalter

Child
Grades K-1

Purpose: Determines individual and group readiness for first grade. Used to identify and diagnose students with skill deficiencies.

Description: Multiple-item paper-pencil verbal test designed for children entering the first grade. The test reveals readiness for formal instruction by assessing seven skill areas: word recognition, identifying letters, visual discrimination, auditory discrimination, comprehension and interpretation, handwriting readiness, and number readiness. The test results, which can be used as the basis for placement, show each child at one of six readiness levels. Examiner required. Suitable for group use. Manual available in Spanish.
Timed: 1 hour
Scoring: Hand key; examiner evaluated
Cost: Complete set (35 booklets, manual, scoring key, class record sheet) $24.95; specimen set $9.00
Publisher: Scholastic Testing Service, Inc.

SCHOOL READINESS TESTS FOR BLIND CHILDREN (STBC)

Blind children

Purpose: Assesses cognitive abilities of blind children. Used for determining school readiness.

Description: Seven-subtest measure of cognitive skills important to school readiness, including Information Test, Kinesthesis Test, Vocabulary Test, Number Concept Test, Motor Development Test, Memory Test, and Reasoning Test. The examiner may make subjective evaluations of the child's perseverance, readiness to follow instructions, and social adjustment. Examiner required. Not suitable for group use.
SOUTH AFRICAN PUBLISHER

Untimed: 1½ hours
Scoring: Examiner evaluated
Cost: (In Rands) complete kit (10 biographical questionnaires, 10 answer sheets, container, apparatus, manual) 103,70; orders from outside the RSA will be dealt with on merit
Publisher: Human Sciences Research Council

SCREENING CHILDREN FOR RELATED EARLY EDUCATIONAL NEEDS (SCREEN)
Wayne P. Hresko, D. Kim Reid, Donald D. Hammill, Herbert P. Ginsburg, and Arthur J. Baroody

Child—Ages 3-7

Purpose: Identifies intraindividual abilities in educationally relevant areas. Used to identify mildly handicapped students and to document student growth and program effectiveness.

Description: Multiple-item picture-response test identifying intraindividual abilities in the areas of language, reading, written language, and mathematics achievement. Standard scores and percentiles are reported for the overall test and each of its four components. The test consists of selected items from the Test of Early Language Development, Test of Early Mathematical Ability, Test of Early Reading Ability, and Test of Early Written English.
The PRO-SCORE scoring system is available from the publisher for use on Apple II, II+, and IIe and IBM PC and MS-DOS computers. The system generates a four-page report providing background information on the student; raw scores, standard scores, percentiles, and descriptions for each subtest; standard score sums, percentiles, and descriptors for all composites and quotients; an optional cognitive aptitude score; subtest and composite profiles; intraindividual comparisons of all composites; and significance testing of all comparisons. Examiner required. Not suitable for group use.
Untimed: 15–40 minutes
Scoring: Hand key; may be computer scored

Cost: Complete kit (manual, 25 profile/record forms, 25 student workbooks, picture book, storage box) $79.00; PRO-SCORE scoring system $69.00

Publisher: PRO-ED

SCREENING TEST FOR THE ASSIGNMENT OF REMEDIAL TREATMENT
A. Edward Ahr

Child—Ages 4.5-6.5

Purpose: Assesses the skill development of children. Identifies children needing evaluation for potential learning difficulties. Also used to evaluate Kindergarten and Grade 1 instructional programs.

Description: 50-item orally administered test assessing the basic skills required for successful performance in Kindergarten and first grade. The test measures the following factors: visual memory, auditory memory, visual-motor coordination, and visual discrimination. Each test item consists of four pictures presented on one page in the test booklet. The examiner instructs the child to look at each page and then asks the child to select the correct answer, copy the pictures, or remember what is pictured (for delayed response) for the pictures presented for each test item. Examiner required. Suitable for group use.

Timed: 45 minutes

Scoring: Hand key

Cost: Specimen set $4.00; test $1.50; manual included with order of 35 tests

Publisher: Priority Innovations, Inc.

Information and availability unconfirmed; last verified in 1988.

SCREENING TEST OF ACADEMIC READINESS (STAR)
A. Edward Ahr

Child—Ages 4-6

Purpose: Measures mental ability and emotional development of young children. Used to determine school readiness.

Description: 50-item paper-pencil test consisting of eight subtests: Picture Vocabulary, Letters, Picture Completion, Copying, Picture Description, Human

Figure, Relationships, and Numbers. The examiner asks the child to point to the correct answer or mark it in the answer book. The child's understanding of the world is evaluated by asking him or her to identify objects, copy simple figures, or identify an object among other items in a picture after hearing a description of the object. Examiner required. Suitable for group use.

Untimed: 1 hour

Scoring: Hand key

Cost: Specimen set $4.00; test $1.50; manual included with 35 tests

Publisher: Priority Innovations, Inc.

Information and availability unconfirmed; last verified in 1988.

SLOSSON ARTICULATION, LANGUAGE TEST WITH PHONOLOGY (SALT-P)
Wilma Jean Tade

Child—Ages 3-5.11

Purpose: Assesses articulation, phonology, and language in children. Used in educational, clinical, private practice, Head Start, and other preschool settings.

Description: Multiple-item oral-response test using stimulus pictures to measure communicative competence in preschool children. The test features a prescreening segment that identifies children in need of further testing. Children recommended for further testing are simultaneously screened for articulation, phonology, and language. The articulation section is composed of 22 initial and 18 final consonant sounds and 10 consonant blends or clusters. The test contains provisions that allow the examinee to demonstrate ability to use selective vowels and dipthongs. Five phonological processes are measured: initial consonant omission, final consonant omission, fronting, stopping, and cluster reduction. The language subscore reflects errors on 31 language barriers. The test yields a single score that indicates communicative competence. The score can be compared to an index of scores denoting normal performance with respect to chronological age. An instructional video is available for examiners and students. Examiner required. Not suitable for group use.

Untimed: 7–10 minutes

Scoring: Examiner evaluated

Cost: Complete kit (manual, test book, 50 scoring forms) $48.00

Publisher: Slosson Educational Publications, Inc.

THE SOI CREATIVITY TEST
J.P. Guilford et al.

Child
Grades 4–7

Purpose: Measures creative thinking among children by assessing verbal and nonverbal modes of expression. Used for counseling, group placement, and research.

Description: 10 paper-pencil tests measuring different aspects of divergent production. Both semantic (verbal) and visual-figural abilities are tested in the battery. The tests are Names for Stories, What to Do with It, Similar Meanings, Writing Sentences, Kinds of People, Make Something Out of It, Different Letter Groups, Making Objects, Hidden Letters, and Adding Decorations. It is recommended that the entire battery be used. The tests are adaptations of adult forms for the same factors. The manual of interpretations, profile chart, and review set cover the entire battery. The tests, scoring guides, and administratives manuals may be ordered for individual tests. Alternate forms are available. Norms are provided for fourth- and sixth-grade students. The tests are restricted to APA members. Examiner required. Suitable for group use.

Timed: 1 hour, 40 minutes

Scoring: Examiner evaluated

Cost: Test $3.00

Publisher: SOI Institute; distributed by M & M Systems

STRUCTURE OF INTELLECT LEARNING ABILITIES TEST (SOI)
Mary Meeker and Robert Meeker

Grades K-adult

Purpose: Measures an individual's learning abilities. Used for cognitive clinical assessment, diagnosis, screening for giftedness, and to identify specific learning deficiencies.

Description: 430–item paper-pencil multiple-choice free-response test. The test measures 26 factors identified by Guilford's Structure-of-Intellect model. The operations of cognition, memory, evaluation, convergent production, and divergent production are applied to figural, symbolic, and semantic content. The test is available in two equivalent forms, A and B, and five shorter forms (gifted-screening, math, reading, primary screening, and reading readiness). The shorter forms use 10–12 subtest factors, printed test forms, and a manual with visual aids for group presentations. Training in administration and usage is required. Examiner required. Suitable for group use in some situations.

Untimed: 2½ hours

Scoring: Hand key

Cost: Complete kit (10 test booklets, 5 each of Form A and Form B, manual, set of scoring keys, set of stimulus cards, 10 worksheets and profile forms) $125.00; contact publisher for costs of shorter forms

Publisher: Western Psychological Services

STUDY OF CHILDREN'S LEARNING BEHAVIORS
Refer to page 783.

SURVEY OF EARLY CHILDHOOD ABILITIES (SECA)
Karen Gardner Codding

Child—Ages 3.5–7

Purpose: Measures the learning skills of children. Used by principals, resource specialists, admissions personnel, psychologists, counselors, elementary school teachers, and other professionals to determine kindergarten and first-grade readiness.

Description: Multiple-item test battery consisting of four individual tests evaluating skills necessary for school readiness:

a) Visual Motor (eye-hand coordination), b) Kindergarten/First Grade Readiness (reading, spelling, arithmetic), c) Auditory Perception (number memory, sentence memory, word memory, interpretation of directions, word discrimination, processing), and d) Visual Perception: Non-Motor (discrimination, memory, spatial relationships, form constancy, sequential memory, figure-ground, closure). Results are provided in age equivalents, scaled scores, percentiles, and stanines. Examiner required. Not suitable for group use.

Untimed: 40 minutes

Scoring: Examiner evaluated

Cost: Complete kit (manual, 25 profile sheets, 25 record booklets, 25 test booklets, test plates) $79.95

Publisher: Children's Hospital of San Francisco, Publications Department

---

THE TACTILE TEST OF BASIC CONCEPTS

Visually handicapped children—Grades K–2

Purpose: Assesses the visually handicapped child's mastery of concepts commonly found in preschool and primary-grade instructional materials and essential to understanding oral communications from teachers and fellow pupils. Used with children in Grades K–2 who require braille and other tactile media.

Description: 50-item tactile test of verbal comprehension and conceptual development of visually handicapped children. Five practice cards are provided to familiarize the child with the test task and to determine if he is familiar with the raised outline forms used in the test (circle, square, triangle, rectangle). The test is a tactile analog of the Boehm Test of Basic Concepts, Form A, presented with raised outline forms. A few items consist of simple raised outline drawings. The BTBC test manual is included for use in interpreting the test results. Examiner required. Not suitable for group use.

Untimed: Not available

Scoring: Hand key; examiner evaluated

Cost: Complete set (5 practice cards, 50 test cards, 1 class record form, TTBC test manual, BTBC test manual) $26.49

Publisher: American Printing House for the Blind, Inc.

TEST OF EARLY WRITTEN LANGUAGE (TEWL)
Wayne P. Hresko

Child—Ages 3–7

Purpose: Measures the emerging written language skills of young children. Used to identify mildly handicapped students and to document student growth and program effectiveness.

Description: Multiple-item paper-pencil test covering areas with a direct relationship to a young child's school-related activities, including transcription, conventions of print, communication, creative expression, and record keeping. Picture cards are used to prompt writing samples. The test yields standard scores and percentiles, which can be used with other cognitive and academic measures to identify intraindividual abilities. Examiner required. Not suitable for group use.

Untimed: 10–30 minutes

Scoring: Examiner evaluated

Cost: Complete kit (manual, 25 profile/record forms, 25 student workbooks, 7 picture cards, storage box) $69.00

Publisher: PRO-ED

TEST OF KINDERGARTEN/FIRST GRADE READINESS SKILLS (TKFGRS)
Karen Gardner Codding

Child—Ages 3.5–7

Purpose: Evaluates a child's basic reading, spelling, and arithmetic skills. Used by principals, elementary school teachers, psychologists, counselors, admissions personnel, resource specialists, and other professionals to assess academic readiness for kindergarten and first grade.

Description: Standardized test determining academic readiness and areas of low functioning in reading, spelling, and mathematics. Results show whether remedial intervention is required in order for the child to develop the skills necessary to progress academically. Age equivalents, standard scores, percentiles, and stanines are provided. Examiner required. Not suitable for group use.

Untimed: 20 minutes

Scoring: Examiner evaluated

Cost: Complete kit (manual, 25 record booklets, 8 cards) $29.95

Publisher: Children's Hospital of San Francisco, Publications Department

TEST OF RELATIONAL CONCEPTS (TRC)
Nellie K. Edmonston and Nancy Litchfield Thane

Child—Ages 3.0–7.11

Purpose: Identifies deficits in children's understanding of relational concepts. Used by speech pathologists, psychologists, and special primary and early childhood teachers for identifying children needing remediation.

Description: Multiple-item picture test assessing 56 relational concepts, including dimensional adjectives and spatial, temporal, and quantitative words. Examiner required. Not suitable for group use.

Untimed: 15 minutes

Scoring: Hand key; examiner evaluated

Cost: Complete kit (manual, picture book, 50 record forms, storage box) $64.00

Publisher: PRO-ED

TESTS OF BASIC EXPERIENCES, SECOND EDITION (TOBE 2)
Margaret H. Moss

Child
Grades K–1

Purpose: Measures the degree to which young children have acquired concepts and experiences related to effective school participation. Used for evaluation of school readiness.

Description: Multiple-item battery of paper-pencil tests measuring quantity and quality of children's early learning experiences. The test is divided into two overlapping levels, K and L, covering programs from preschool through first grade. Each level contains a language, mathematics, science, and social studies test. Each test item consists of a verbal stimulus and four pictured responses. As the examiner reads the stimulus aloud, the child responds by marking one of the pictures. Level K can be used in the spring of prekindergarten, the fall and spring of kindergarten, and the fall of first grade. Level L is for use in the spring of kindergarten and the fall and spring of first grade. An Instructional Activities Kit contains materials for teaching concepts and skills. Examiner required. Suitable for group use. Available in Spanish.

Untimed: 45 minutes per test

Scoring: Hand key; may be computer scored

Cost: Specimen set, specify level (machine- and hand-scorable test books, manual, answer key, norms and technical data book, practice test, class evaluation record, test reviewer's guide) $15.60

Publisher: CTB/Macmillan/McGraw-Hill

VALETT INVENTORY OF CRITICAL THINKING ABILITIES (VICTA)
Robert E. Valett

Ages 4–15 and older
exceptional pupils

Purpose: Assesses problem-solving skills and abilities of children and older exceptional pupils with developmental difficulties. Used at the beginning of a diagnostic session to establish rapport with a child.

Description: 100–item verbal-response examination of sensory-perceptual exploration, intuitive organization, concrete relationships, representational concepts, and propositional logic. The test consists of problems dealing with 10 critical thinking abilities: knowledge, analysis, calculation, verbal conceptualization, synthesis, comprehension, application, humor, evaluation, and imagination. A quantitative evaluation of the student's critical thinking ability is provided by determining the percentage of tasks the student passes at each of the five developmental stages and comparing that figure with the child's age. Only items of appropriate difficulty for a child are tested. Examiner required. Not suitable for group use.

Untimed: 40 minutes

Scoring: Examiner evaluated

Cost: Manual $15.00; 50 record forms $17.00

Publisher: Academic Therapy Publications

THE VANE KINDERGARTEN TEST (VKT), 1984 REVISION
Julia R. Vane

Child
Kindergarten

Purpose: Evaluates the academic potential of young children and identifies those for whom remedial help may be necessary.

Description: Three-part multiple-item task-assessment oral-response test assessing eye-hand coordination, vocabulary development, emotional adjustment, and hearing deficiency. In Part I, the child is presented with pictures of three shapes (circle, square, hexagon) and copies them on a sheet of paper. In Part II, the child turns the paper over and draws a picture of a man. In Part III, the child identifies as many words as possible from a list of 12 words arranged in order of difficulty. The words generally are used only by exceptionally bright children. Examiner required. Suitable for group use.

Untimed: 10 minutes

Scoring: Examiner evaluated

Cost: Manual $7.50; 50 record sheets $8.50; sample kit $8.00

Publisher: Clinical Psychology Publishing Co., Inc.

VOCABULARY COMPREHENSION SCALE (VCS)
Refer to page 280.

English as a Second Language and Bilingualism

BASIC ENGLISH SKILLS TEST (BEST)
Center for Applied Linguistics

Adult

Purpose: Measures basic oral and literacy skills in adults who are learning English as a second language.

Description: 86–item multiple-choice short-answer paper-pencil and oral-response test measuring oral and literacy skills. The Oral Interview section (49 items) measures listening comprehension, communication, fluency, and pronunciation. The Literacy Skills section (37 items) measures reading and writing. Scores are yielded for each area measured. Examiner required. Suitable for group use.

Timed: Literacy Skills 1 hour

Untimed: Oral Interview 15 minutes

Scoring: Examiner evaluated; hand key

Cost: Manual $20.00; 2 picture cue books $11.00; 5 interviewer's booklets $12.00; 100 interview scoring sheets $25.00; 20 Literacy Skills tests $45.00; complete kit $125.00

Publisher: Center for Applied Linguistics

BASIC INVENTORY OF NATURAL LANGUAGE (BINL)
CHECpoint Systems, Inc.

Child, adolescent
Grades K–12

Purpose: Measures students' language proficiency. Used in bilingual, ESL, language development, and speech and language remediation programs.

Description: Oral-response test in which each test item consists of a color photograph that is used to elicit language samples from the students. The language samples are transcribed and analyzed at three levels: word class (determiner, noun, verb, adjective, adverb, preposition, etc.); type of phrase employed (noun, verb, prepositional, gerund, etc.); and sentence type (simple, compound, compound/complex, etc.).

Four BINL kits are available. Forms A and B are elementary kits for use with Grades K–6. Forms C and D are secondary kits for use with Grades 7–12. The kits include an instructions manual, 20 full-color photographs on heavy posterboard, 400 individual oral scoring sheets, class profile cards, sorting envelopes to prepare the tests for machine scoring, and materials for teaching the prescription activities included in the instructions manual.

Three BINL computer-scoring programs are available. BINL I scoring is available from the publisher. The reports from this program include individual scores, class and grade level, graphs of student placement, and classification of students into four categories: Non, Limited, Functional, and Proficient. The program is available in English, Spanish, and 24 other languages. BINL II SDS (Same Day Scoring) and BINL II LPS (Language Profile Scoring) are available for the Apple IIe and IIc computers only. Use is limited by licensing to one machine per program. BINL II SDS is an on-site program in which language samples may be entered and holistically scored by up to three persons. The following scores are obtained: Listening Comprehension, Fluency, Vocabulary, Pronunciation, and Grammar.

A detailed report and a summary report are available. The BINL II SDS diskettes may be sent to the publisher for scoring by the BINL II LPS, a language analysis program that produces a detailed profile of the language sample produced during the test. The profile shows variety of vocabulary, sentence length, total words, total unique words, number of nouns, verbs, modals, prepositions, complexity level of each sentence, and average complexity level for the sample. The profiles are used as data for planning lessons for oral language development and remediation. Examiner required. Not suitable for group use.

Untimed: Varies

Scoring: Computer scored

Cost: BINL kit A, B, C, or D $59.00 each

Publisher: CHECpoint Systems, Inc.

BILINGUAL ORAL LANGUAGE TEST: BOLT-ENGLISH AND BOLT-SPANISH
Sam Cohen, Roberto Cruz, and Raul Bravo

Adolescent
Grades 7–12

Purpose: Measures English and Spanish oral language skills. Determines a student's level of bilingualism. Used for academic placement and planning and for reporting accurate results on enrollment and language dominance to federal and state agencies.

Description: Two multiple-item oral-response tests assessing oral language skills in English (BOLT-English) or Spanish (BOLT-Spanish). The tests assess oral language skills from simple sentence patterns to more complex syntactical forms of the language. Students are classified into one of four language categories: non-English/Spanish-speaking, very limited English/Spanish-speaking, limited English/Spanish-speaking, and English/Spanish-speaking. The two tests are independent components of the same instrument and based on the same organization. Results of both tests are combined to determine a student's level of bilingualism. The summary page is used to record the level of bilingualism and to organize data for enrollment and language dominance reports. The test may be used on a pre- or posttest basis to determine gain of proficiency in English and/or Spanish. Information concerning the results of field testing are presented in the technical reports. Examiner required. Not suitable for group use.

Untimed: 6 minutes

Scoring: Examiner evaluated

Cost: Classroom packets: English or Spanish (manual, picture booklet, 30 answer sheets, class record chart) $25.00; bilingual test summary page $0.50; technical reports $1.75

Publisher: Bilingual Media Productions, Inc.

Information and availability unconfirmed; last verified in 1987.

BILINGUAL SYNTAX MEASURE I AND II (BSM)
Marina K. Burt, Heidi C. Dulay, and Eduardo Hernandez

Child, adolescent
Grades K–12

Purpose: Measures children's mastery of basic oral syntactic structures in both English and Spanish. Used for diagnosis and placement in bilingual and other special language programs.

Description: Multiple-item measure testing strengths and weaknesses in basic language construction by using cartoon-type pictures and simple questions to elicit natural speech patterns. The test also places pupils in a proficiency level category (in both English and Spanish). Scores may be used for determining English readiness or program exit in bilingual and other special programs. The test is available on two levels: BSMI for Grades K–2 and BSMII for Grades 3–12. The manual provides proficiency ratings and equivalent LAU categories established by federal guidelines. Examiner required. Not suitable for group use. Available in English and Spanish.

Untimed: 10–15 minutes

Scoring: Hand key

Cost: Complete set (picture booklet, 35 English child/student response booklets, English manual, 35 Spanish child/student response booklets, Spanish manual, class records, technical handbook, expanding envelope) BSMI $155.00; BSMII $165.00

Publisher: The Psychological Corporation

Information and availability unconfirmed; last verified in 1988.

BILINGUAL TWO LANGUAGE BATTERY OF TESTS
Adolph Caso

All ages

Purpose: Measures language proficiency in English and five native languages: Spanish, Italian, Portuguese, Vietnamese, and French. Assesses language dominance and determines point of bilinguality. Used with students and adults at any level of language proficiency for academic placement and evaluation and to determine LAU categories.

Description: Battery of criterion-referenced paper-pencil and oral-response tests comparing proficiency in English with proficiency in any of five native languages. Tests for all languages consist of four parts (although the content in English is not necessarily the same as that in the native languages): phonetics (letter recognition and spelling), comprehension situations (opposites, similarities, comparisons, reading, and listening), writing sentences related to pictures, and an optional supplement measuring oral language proficiency (questions related to Limited English Proficiency Students). Students listen to directions presented on a pre-recorded tape (English on one side and the native language on the other) and write their answers in the student booklet of the appropriate language. The native language test is given first and the English test must be administered within two weeks. The battery may be administered at any time during the year, but optimal administration is in two sessions per school year (spring-fall) for three consecutive years. Results for both language tests are recorded on the student score profile card, which includes the following charts: composite scores, proficiency levels, language dominance, point of bilinguality, and LAU category. A cassette player is required. Examiner required. Suitable for group use.

Timed: English test 21 minutes; native language test 21 minutes

Scoring: Examiner evaluated

Cost: Contact publisher

Publisher: Branden Press

Information and availability unconfirmed; last verified in 1988.

THE BRIGANCE® DIAGNOSTIC ASSESSMENT OF BASIC SKILLS— SPANISH EDITION
Albert H. Brigance

Child, adolescent
Grades PreK–9

Purpose: Measures the academic skills of Spanish-speaking students. Distinguishes language barriers from learning disabilities. Used by bilingual, ESL, migrant, and bilingual special educators to identify, develop, implement, and evaluate appropriate academic programs for Spanish-speaking students.

Description: 102 skill sequences assessing Spanish-speaking students' abilities in the following areas: readiness, speech, functional word recognition, oral reading, reading comprehension, word analysis, listening, writing and alphabetizing, numbers and computation, and measurement. Directions to the examiner are written in English; directions to the student are written in Spanish. Assessments used for dominant language screening present directions to the student in English and Spanish. The diagnostic tests identify skills the student has and has not mastered and students who might have learning disabilities. The diagnostic tests also help to determine individual instructional objectives. The dominant language screening form provides a means of comparing a student's performance in English and Spanish on all of the oral language and literacy diagnostic assessments. Results of the screening are used to place students in appropriate ESL and bilingual programs. The seven grade-level screens assess skills that indicate grade-level competency in Grades K–6. The results are used to place students at their appropriate instructional levels and to identify students who need further evaluation. Individual student record books graphically record at each testing the level of competency the student has achieved. An optional class record book tracks the progress of 35 students. A videotape program for in-service training of examiners is available. Examiner required. Many sections are suitable for group use.

Untimed: Varies

Scoring: Examiner evaluated

Cost: Assessment book $99.00; class record book $9.95; 10 student record books $22.95

Publisher: Curriculum Associates, Inc.

BRISTOL LANGUAGE DEVELOPMENT SCALES
Refer to page 688.

COMPTON PHONOLOGICAL ASSESSMENT OF FOREIGN ACCENT
Arthur J. Compton

Child

Purpose: Analyzes English pronunciation errors of individuals born outside the United States.

Description: Oral-response test utilizing a step-by-step approach for analyzing pronunciation errors. A phonetically balanced sampling of speech sounds in single words, sentences and phrases, oral reading, and conversational speech comprise the analysis. The information obtained is organized into a visual display of error patterns according to phonological feature groupings. Examiner required. Not suitable for group use.

Untimed: 90 minutes

Scoring: Examiner evaluated

Cost: Kit (manual, 65 stimulus words, oral reading passage, 25 response-analysis booklets) $45.00

Publisher: Carousel House

Information and availability unconfirmed; last verified in 1988.

CRANE ORAL DOMINANCE TEST (CODT)
Barbara J. Crane

Child, adolescent
Grades PreK–12

Purpose: Determines whether a student has a dominant language (Spanish/English) or is bilingual. Used to help instructors prescribe appropriate instructional materials and identify bilingual special education students.

Description: Multiple-item oral-response test identifying which language a student retains best, English or Spanish. The examiner reads from four (preschool) to eight (school age) words. Some of the words are in English and some are in Spanish. The student responds by repeating as many words as he can remember. Based on the results of 64 word-pair sets, the student is classified as monolingual non-English, dominant non-English, functionally bilingual, dominant English, or monolingual English. Examiner required. Not suitable for group use.

Untimed: 20 minutes

Scoring: Examiner evaluated

Cost: Complete kit (30 test booklets, 30 score sheets, manual) $32.07

Publisher: Crane Publishing Co.

DOS AMIGOS VERBAL LANGUAGE SCALES
Donald E. Critchlow

Child, adolescent—Ages 5-13

Purpose: Measures a child's ability to understand English and Spanish words. Used to determine dominant language proficiency so that primary-language instruction, ESL programs, or remediation may be planned.

Description: 85-item verbal test in English and Spanish consisting of 85 word scales and their opposites. The examiner dictates each stimulus word, and the examinee responds with a word that has the opposite meaning. So that the test can be used in other English-speaking countries, words that have unique American-English spellings are excluded. The examiner must be fluent in English and Spanish. Not suitable for group use.

Untimed: 20 minutes

Scoring: Hand key

Cost: Manual $11.00; 25 recording forms $9.00; kit $18.00

Publisher: United Educational Services, Inc.

EL CIRCO
Educational Testing Service

Child
Grades PreK-1

Purpose: Identifies Spanish-speaking children's instructional needs in the areas of language and math. Used to evaluate early childhood bilingual curricula.

Description: Four paper-pencil tests assessing the language and mathematics skills of Spanish-speaking children. The Language Check is a pretest that deter-

mines whether the child's Spanish proficiency is sufficient to complete the exam. Para Que Sirven Las Palabras is a 38–item measure of the child's receptive language skills in Spanish. What Words Are For is a 30–item measure of receptive language skills in English. Cuanto y Cuantos is a 39–item measure of mathematical skills (counting, relationships, and numerical concepts). Examiner required. Suitable for group use.

Untimed: 15–30 minutes

Scoring: Hand key

Cost: Specimen set (copy of each measure, administration directions, and user's guide) $15.25

Publisher: CTB/Macmillan/McGraw-Hill

ENGLISH FIRST AND SECOND LANGUAGE TESTS

All ages

Purpose: Measures understanding of English as a first or second language. Used for educational placement and guidance.

Description: 19 separate paper-pencil tests of English comprehension for each standard or level of pupil. Particular subtests vary but generally include Language Usage, Vocabulary, Reading Comprehension, and Spelling. Two alternate forms, A and B, are available for each standard. Examiner required. Suitable for group use.

SOUTH AFRICAN PUBLISHER

Untimed: Not available

Scoring: Hand key; examiner evaluated

Cost: Contact publisher; orders from outside the RSA will be dealt with on merit

Publisher: Human Sciences Research Council

ENGLISH KNOWLEDGE AND COMPREHENSION
S. Chatterji and Manjula Mukerjee

Adolescent—Ages 14–16

Purpose: Measures students' knowledge and comprehension of English.

Description: 67–item paper-pencil test arranged in two separately timed parts assessing knowledge and comprehension of the English language. Part I (20 minutes) consists of 29 items. Part II (1 hour) consists of 38 items. The test may be used with students whose native language is not English but who have been taught in English-language schools. Examiner required. Suitable for group use. PUBLISHED IN INDIA

Timed: 1 hour, 20 minutes

Scoring: Hand key; examiner evaluated

Cost: (In Rupees) Complete kit (25 booklets, 100 answer sheets, key, manual) Contact distributor

Publisher: S. Chatterji and Manjula Mukerjee; distributed by Manasayan

---

ENGLISH LANGUAGE SKILLS ASSESSMENT IN A READING CONTEXT (ELSA)
Donna Ilyin, Cecelia Doherty, Laurie Freid Lee, and Lynn Levy

Adolescent, adult　　　

Purpose: Measures student understanding of the meaning and grammatical correctness of English language statements. Used to assess English as a second language.

Description: 25–item paper-pencil multiple-choice test in six versions: beginning conversation, beginning narration, intermediate conversation, intermediate narration, advanced narration, and advanced letter. The student selects one of four words that best completes the sentence in the conversation or story. The test has been used in federal accountability reports for funding. Examiner required. Suitable for group use.

Untimed: 30 minutes

Scoring: Hand key; machine scored

Cost: Contact publisher

Publisher: Newbury House Publishers, Inc.

Information and availability unconfirmed; last verified in 1987.

ENGLISH PLACEMENT TEST (EPT)
Mary Spaan, with Laura Strowe, A. Corrigan, B. Dobson, E. Kellman, and S. Tyma

Adult　　　

Purpose: Assesses facility with the English language. Used to group low to intermediate proficiency adult nonnative speakers of English into homogenous ability levels as they enter an intensive English course.

Description: 100–item paper-pencil multiple-choice test of listening comprehension, grammar in conversational contexts, vocabulary recognition, and reading comprehension of sentences. A tape is available for use with the listening comprehension items. Three forms (A, B, C) are available. Examiner required. Suitable for group use.

Timed: 1 hour, 5 minutes

Scoring: Hand key

Cost: Testing package (examiner's manual, scoring stencil, 20 test booklets, 100 answer sheets) $20.00

Publisher: English Language Institute

EXPRESSIVE ONE-WORD PICTURE VOCABULARY TEST: UPPER EXTENSION (EOWPVT: UE)
Refer to page 696.

HENDERSON-MORIARTY ESL-LITERACY PLACEMENT TEST (HELP)
Cindy Henderson and Pia Moriarty

Adult—Ages 16–80　　　

Purpose: Assesses English literacy skills of individuals with limited English proficiency. Used for placement.

Description: 40–item criterion-referenced paper-pencil and oral-response test consisting of short answer, verbal, show-tell, point-to, and true-false questions assessing oral (24 items) and written (16 items) language skills. A Global score provides an overall indication of the examinee's level of proficiency. The examiner must have a TESOL certificate or a master's degree in psychology or applied linguistics. Examiner required. Not suitable for group use.

Untimed: 30 minutes
Scoring: Hand key
Cost: Manual $16.95
Publisher: Alemany Press

HOWELL PREKINDERGARTEN SCREENING TEST
Refer to page 547.

IDEA ORAL LANGUAGE PROFICIENCY TEST (IPT I)— ENGLISH
Wanda S. Ballard, Phyllis L. Tighe, and Henry F. Dalton

ESL students
Grades K and above

Purpose: Evaluates language proficiency, determines language classifications, and yields diagnostic information. Used for initial identification of limited-proficient students for Language Census and for reclassification purposes.

Description: 83–item short-answer oral-response show-tell and point-to test assessing a broad range of skills in the general areas of vocabulary, comprehension, grammatical structure, and verbal expression, including articulation. At the end of the test, a chart helps the examiner determine the student's designation: a) non-English-speaking (NES), b) limited-English-speaking (LES), or c) fluent-English-speaking (FES). The test is available on six levels, A-F, in two versions, A and B, for test-retest purposes. The test is one in a series of IDEA Oral Language Proficiency Tests. Examiner required. Not suitable for group use. Available in Spanish.

Untimed: 15 minutes
Scoring: Hand key
Cost: 50 tests $22.00; pictures $29.00; examiner's manual $12.00; technical manual $20.00; 50 level summaries $6.00; 10 group lists $3.00 (specify form A or B for each element ordered)
Publisher: Ballard & Tighe, Inc.

IDEA ORAL LANGUAGE PROFICIENCY TEST (IPT II)— ENGLISH
Henry F. Dalton and Beverly Amori

Adolescent, adult
Grades 7 and above

Purpose: Evaluates language proficiency, determines language classifications, and yields diagnostic information. Used for initial identification of limited-proficient students for Language Census and for reclassification systems.

Description: 91–item short-answer oral-response show-tell and point-to test assessing a broad range of skills in the general areas of vocabulary, comprehension, grammatical structure, and verbal expression, including articulation. At the end of the test, a chart helps the examiner determine the student's designation: a) non-English-speaking (NES), b) limited-English-speaking (LES), or c) fluent-English-speaking (FES). The test is available on six levels, A-F, in two versions, A and B, for test-retest purposes. The test is one in a series of IDEA Oral Language Proficiency Tests. Examiner required. Not suitable for group use. Available in Spanish.

Untimed: 15 minutes
Scoring: Hand key
Cost: 50 tests $22.00; pictures $29.00; examiner's manual $12.00; technical manual $20.00; 50 level summaries $6.00; 10 group lists $3.00 (specify form A or B for each element ordered)
Publisher: Ballard & Tighe, Inc.

ILYIN ORAL INTERVIEW TEST
Donna Ilyin

Adolescent, adult
Grades 10 and above

Purpose: Measures the ability of secondary and adult students to communicate accurately in English. Used to assess abilities in English as a first or second language.

Description: 50–item verbal test in which the examiner shows paired pictures to the student, asks questions about them, and requires the student to respond, enabling the examiner to assess student comprehension and ability to use proper English grammar. Examiner required. Not suitable for group use.

Untimed: 30 minutes

Scoring: Examiner evaluated

Cost: Contact publisher

Publisher: Newbury House Publishers, Inc.

Information and availability unconfirmed; last verified in 1987.

INFORMAL EVALUATION OF ORAL READING
Refer to page 372.

INTER-AMERICAN SERIES
Herschel T. Manuel et al.

All ages
Grades K–12 and above

Purpose: Assesses and compares the abilities and educational achievements of students of different languages and cultures. Used for the individualization of instruction, the education of exceptional children, educational and vocational counseling, bilingual instruction and instruction in English or Spanish as a second language, basic and applied research, and entry and exit decision making regarding students in bilingual education programs.

Description: 5 criterion-referenced multiple-level multiple-item paper-pencil tests assessing students' abilities and educational achievements. The five tests are Test of Reading (5 levels), Test of General Ability (6 levels), Test of Oral Comprehension (1 level), Test of Reading and Number (1 level), and Inventory of Interests (1 level). Item formats are multiple-choice, oral-response, true-false, and short answer. Each test at each level is available in both English and Spanish. Both the English and Spanish forms are parallel in content in order to provide comparable scores when the Spanish form is administered to Spanish-speaking students and the English form is administered to English-speaking students, particularly within the same classroom. Tests may also be used in one language alone.

In addition, both forms of the tests may be administered to the same student in order to compare the student's ability in the two languages. See separate descriptions of individual tests in the series. Examiner required. Suitable for group use.

Untimed: Varies

Timed: Varies

Scoring: Hand key

Cost: Varies according to test and level; contact publisher

Publisher: Guidance Testing Associates

Information and availability unconfirmed; last verified in 1988.

INTER-AMERICAN SERIES: INVENTORY OF INTERESTS
Refer to page 825.

INTER-AMERICAN SERIES: TEST OF GENERAL ABILITY
Refer to page 462.

INTER-AMERICAN SERIES: TEST OF ORAL COMPREHENSION
Herschel T. Manuel

Child—Ages 5–6
Grades K–1

Purpose: Assesses oral comprehension of English or Spanish. May be used to determine language dominance. Used for the individualization of instruction, the education of exceptional children, educational and vocational counseling, bilingual instruction and instruction in English or Spanish as a second language, basic and applied research, and entry and exit decision making regarding students in bilingual education programs.

Description: 35–item criterion-referenced orally administered test measuring a child's understanding of expressions read in English or Spanish. The test is available in pre- and posttest forms to allow tracking of progress over a selected period of time. One of five tests in the Inter-American Series. Examiner required. Suitable for group use. Available in Spanish and English.

Timed: 35 minutes

Scoring: Hand key

Cost: Contact publisher

Publisher: Guidance Testing Associates

Information and availability unconfirmed; last verified in 1988.

INTER-AMERICAN SERIES: TEST OF READING
Herschel T. Manuel

Child, adolescent—
Ages 6–18

Purpose: Assesses reading ability and achievement in students and adults enrolled in continuing education courses. Used for the individualization of instruction, the education of exceptional children, educational and vocational counseling, bilingual instruction and instruction in English or Spanish as a second language, basic and applied research, and entry and exit decision making regarding students in bilingual education programs.

Description: Multiple-item criterion-referenced paper-pencil test assessing various areas of reading achievement. Item formats are multiple-choice, true-false, oral-response, and short answer. The test is available on five levels. Level 1 (80 items; Grades 1–2) assesses vocabulary and reading comprehension. Level 2 (110 items; Grades 2–3) assesses level of comprehension, speed of comprehension, and vocabulary. Levels 3 (Grades 4–6), 4 (Grades 7–9), and 5 (Grades 10–12) each contain 125 items assessing vocabulary, speed of comprehension, and level of comprehension. Each level is available in parallel English and Spanish forms. The test is available in pre- and posttest forms to allow tracking of progress over a selected period of time. One of five tests in the Inter-Amerian Series. Examiner required. Suitable for group use.

Timed: Level 1 18 minutes; Level 2 23 minutes; Levels 3–5 41 minutes

Scoring: Hand key

Cost: Contact publisher

Publisher: Guidance Testing Associates

Information and availability unconfirmed; last verified in 1988.

INVENTORY OF LANGUAGE ABILITIES
Refer to page 699.

LANGUAGE ASSESSMENT BATTERY
Staff of the New York City Board of Education

Child, adolescent
Grades K–12

Purpose: Assesses students' verbal abilities in English and/or Spanish. Identifies Spanish-speaking students who cannot participate effectively in English-speaking classrooms and provides a comparable measure of their communication skills in Spanish. Used for academic evaluation and placement of Spanish-speaking students.

Description: Multiple-item paper-pencil and oral-response subtests measuring students' achievement of basic language skills: reading, writing, listening, comprehension, and speaking. The battery is available in an English edition and a Spanish edition. Test item difficulties are low in order to differentiate among students in the lower quartile. All items in both editions were reviewed for vocabulary load, grammatical construction, appropriateness of Spanish usage, racial and gender bias, and correctness of item content. Both editions are presented in three levels: Level I for Grades K–2, Level II for Grades 3–6, and Level III for Grades 7–12. All Level I subtests are individually administered. The speaking subtests for Levels II and III are individually administered so the teacher can accommodate regional differences in vocabulary usage or dialect. The use of criterion-referenced interpretation and locally developed cutoff scores is recommended. Test development and related research are described in the technical manual. Examiner required. Levels II and III (except the speaking subtests) are suitable for group use.

Untimed: 41 minutes per edition

Scoring: Hand key

Cost: 35 Level I test booklets (specify English or Spanish Edition), examiner's directions, picture stimulus booklet $15.60; 35 Level II or Level III test booklets (specify edition), examiner's directions, picture stimulus card $27.54; 35 Digitek answer sheets (specify level and edition) $12.81; Digitek scoring masks (specify Spanish Levels II or III, English Level III) $2.73; 250 NCS answer sheets $90.93; technical manual $7.86; examination kit $16.08

Publisher: The Riverside Publishing Company

LANGUAGE FACILITY TEST
Refer to page 700.

LANGUAGE PROFICIENCY TEST (LPT)
Joan E. Gerald and Gloria Weinstock

Grades 7–adult

Purpose: Evaluates an individual's ability to use the English language, especially those individuals whose lack of skill prevents them from succeeding at work or school. Used to identify competency levels and to detect specific deficiencies of ESL students.

Description: Multiple-item paper-pencil criterion-referenced test in three major sections: aural/oral, reading, and writing. The test covers nine areas of language functioning, including an optional translation section for ESL students. Each section was designed with subtests of increasing difficulty to provide scores indicating the most appropriate levels of instruction for the student. Scores for each subtest are converted to a percentage and plotted on a profile chart that indicates the level of proficiency. Materials are appropriate in content for the mature student who has low-level skills. Examiner required. Most of the nine subtests can be group administered; the two that measure low-level functioning require individual administration and are optional for native English students. Other subtests may be group administered.

Untimed: 1 hour, 30 minutes
Scoring: Hand key

Cost: Manual $12.00; 20 test booklets $30.00
Publisher: Academic Therapy Publications

LISTENING COMPREHENSION GROUP TEST (LCGT)
Donna Ilyin

Adolescent, adult—Ages 14–85

Purpose: Measures the ability of non-native speakers of English to comprehend and write English. Used as an aid to student placement, screening, and diagnosis.

Description: Two-part verbal-picture paper-pencil test used in English as a Second Language (ESL) and bilingual programs. The picture test (LCPT) measures listening comprehension by requiring the subject to look at a picture or series of pictures. The examiner makes a statement about each picture and then asks questions. The subject answers each question by selecting one of three pictures and either "yes" or "no," which are written on a separate piece of paper. The written test (LCWT) is intended for intermediate and advanced ESL students. Students look at a picture series, listen to a story, look at other related pictures, listen to the examiner's questions, and write one-sentence answers. Examiner required. Suitable for group use.

Untimed: Picture test 30 minutes; written test 45 minutes
Scoring: Hand key
Cost: Contact publisher
Publisher: Newbury House Publishers, Inc.

Information and availability unconfirmed; last verified in 1987.

LISTENING COMPREHENSION TEST (LCT)
John Upshur, H. Koba, Mary Spaan, and Laura Strowe

Adult

Purpose: Measures an individual's understanding of spoken English. Used to predict the academic success of nonnative speakers of English.

Description: 45–item paper-pencil multiple-choice test of aural comprehension of English. The student is read a short question or statement and responds by marking the appropriate written answer. A tape recording of the verbal questions and statements is available. The test is available in three forms: 4, 5, and 6. This test is a retired, nonsecure component of the Michigan Test Battery. It is sold only to educational institutions for internal use (e.g., to measure the learning progress of ESL/EFL students who have already been admitted to a program or to confirm the level of proficiency of matriculated students). The tests are not to be used for initial university admission purposes or to report scores to other institutions. Examiner required. Suitable for group use.

Timed: 20 minutes

Scoring: Hand key

Cost: Testing package (manual, 20 test booklets, 100 answer sheets, 3 scoring stencils) $18.50

Publisher: English Language Institute

MACULAITIS LANGUAGE ASSESSMENT PROGRAM (MAC K–12)
Jean D. Maculaitis

Child, adolescent—Ages 4–19
Grades PreK–12

Purpose: Assesses the English language proficiency of children and adolescents with limited English proficiency. Used for placement.

Description: 200–item criterion-referenced paper-pencil and oral-response test consisting of multiple-choice, short answer, essay, verbal, show-tell, and point-to questions assessing listening, speaking, reading, and writing proficiency. The test yields scores in each of the four areas of assessment. The examiner must have a TESOL certificate or a master's degree in bilingual education, teaching English as a second language, applied linguistics, or psychology. APA certification standards apply to all purchases. A computer scoring service is available from B. Cohen and Associates or Data Scan. Examiner required. Suitable for group use.

Untimed: 2 hours

Scoring: Hand key; examiner evaluated; computer scored

Cost: Specimen kit (manuals, forms) $232.25

Publisher: Alemany Press

MICHIGAN TEST OF AURAL COMPREHENSION (MTAC)
John Upshur

Adult

Purpose: Measures an individual's understanding of spoken English. Used to predict the academic success of nonnative speakers of English.

Description: 90–item paper-pencil multiple-choice test of aural comprehension in which the student hears either a question or a statement and responds by marking the appropriate written answer choice. Three alternate forms (1, 2, 3), each accompanied by a tape recording, are available. The test may be used in conjunction with the Michigan Test of English Language Proficiency. These materials are retired, nonsecure components of the Michigan Test Battery and should not be used for initial admission. They are suitable for placement of students who already have been admitted. Examiner required. Suitable for group use.

Timed: 25 minutes

Scoring: Hand key

Cost: Testing package (examiner's manual, 3 scoring stencils, 20 test booklets, 100 answer sheets) $23.50

Publisher: English Language Institute

MICHIGAN TEST OF ENGLISH LANGUAGE PROFICIENCY (MTELP)
John Upshur

Adult

Purpose: Assesses an individual's facility with the English language. Used to predict the academic success of advanced proficiency adult nonnative speakers of English.

Description: 100–item paper-pencil multiple-choice test of grammar, reading comprehension, and vocabulary. Available in nine alternate forms (F, G, H, J, K, L, P, Q, R). These materials are retired, non-secure components of the Michigan Test Battery and should not be used as an admission test; however, it is suitable for placement of students who already have been admitted. Examiner required. Suitable for group use.

Timed: 1 hour, 15 minutes

Scoring: Hand key

Cost: Testing package (manual, scoring stencil, 20 test booklets, 100 answer sheets) $20.00

Publisher: English Language Institute

ORAL LANGUAGE EVALUATION (OLE)
Nicholas J. Silvaroli, Jann T. Skinner, and J.O. "Rocky" Maynes

Child

Purpose: Assesses the English and Spanish language development of bilingual children. Used for academic planning and placement. Used by teachers with limited language evaluation experience and/or structural linguistic training.

Description: Multiple-item oral-response test assessing English and Spanish oral-language skills. Development is classified along a 6–point continuum of language development: labeling, basic sentences, language expansion, connecting-relating-modifying, storytelling-concrete, and storytelling-abstract. Part I (assessment) establishes a beginning oral language level in either English or Spanish. Part II (diagnosis) identifies pre-post test data and specific language responses that pinpoint specific oral language needs. Part II (prescription) provides the teacher with general and specific instructional activities and/or suggestions for helping students develop their oral language. Examiner required. Not suitable for group use.

Untimed: Varies

Scoring: Examiner evaluated

Cost: Manual $7.95

Publisher: EMC Publishing

Information and availability unconfirmed; last verified in 1987.

PRAGMATICS PROFILE OF EARLY COMMUNICATION SKILLS
Refer to page 706.

PRESCHOOL IDEA ORAL LANGUAGE PROFICIENCY TEST (PRE-IPT)
Connie Williams, Wanda S. Ballard, and Phyllis L. Tighe

Child—Ages 3-5
PreK

Purpose: Evaluates language proficiency, determines language classifications, and yields diagnostic information. Used for initial identification of limited-proficient students for Language Census and for reclassification purposes.

Description: 42–item short-answer oral-response show-tell and point-to test assessing a broad range of skills in the general areas of vocabulary, comprehension, grammatical structure, and verbal expression. At the end of the test, a chart helps the examiner determine the student's designation: a) non-English-speaking, b) limited-English-speaking, or c) fluent-English-speaking. The test is available on six levels, A-F. The test is one in a series of IDEA Oral Language Proficiency Tests. Examiner required. Not suitable for group use. Available in Spanish.

Untimed: 3–10 minutes

Scoring: Hand key

Cost: 50 test booklets $22.00; background board $16.00; story pieces $13.00; examiner's manual $12.00; technical manual $20.00; 50 level summaries $6.00; 10 group lists $3.00

Publisher: Ballard & Tighe, Inc.

SANDWELL BILINGUAL SCREENING ASSESSMENT
Refer to page 710.

SECOND LANGUAGE ORAL TEST OF ENGLISH (SLOTE)
Ann K. Fathman

Child—Ages 4-12

Purpose: Measures the oral language structure of children with limited English proficiency. Used for placement.

Description: 60–item criterion-referenced oral-response test measuring oral language structure. The test yields 20 subscores and 1 global score. The examiner must have a TESOL certificate or a master's degree in psychology. Examiner required. Not recommended for group use.

Untimed: 20 minutes

Scoring: Hand key

Cost: Manual, answer sheet, black line master of answer sheet $18.95

Publisher: Alemany Press

SECONDARY LEVEL ENGLISH PROFICIENCY TEST (SLEP)
Educational Testing Service

Adolescent—Ages 12–17 Grades 7–12

Purpose: Assesses English language proficiency of nonnative speakers. Used as an admissions test by private secondary schools and as a placement test by both public and private secondary schools.

Description: 150–item paper-pencil multiple-choice test measuring two components (75 items each) of English proficiency: listening comprehension and reading comprehension (structure and vocabulary). The test does not measure productive language skills. A tape recorder is required to administer the listening comprehension sections. A cassette tape is included. Raw and converted scores are provided for both the listening comprehension and reading comprehension sections. The test is available in three equivalent forms. Examiner required. Suitable for group use.

Timed: 1 hour, 20 minutes

Scoring: Hand key

Cost: Complete kit (reusable materials, 25 test booklets, 100 answer sheets, cassette, 2 keys, manual) $100.00

Publisher: Educational Testing Service

Information and availability unconfirmed; last verified in 1988.

TEST OF ENGLISH AS A FOREIGN LANGUAGE (TOEFL)
Educational Testing Service

Adult

Purpose: Assesses proficiency in English for nonnative speakers. Used as a college admission and placement test.

Description: 150–item paper-pencil multiple-choice test measuring three aspects of English ability: listening comprehension, structure and written expression, and vocabulary and reading comprehension. Items involve comprehension of spoken and written language. The test is administered monthly on either International (Saturday) Test Dates or Special Center (Friday) Test Dates.

The Test of Written English (TWE) is a required part of the TOEFL at the September, October, March, and May administrations. This essay test is designed to allow the examinee to demonstrate his or her ability to compose in English, including organizing ideas on paper, supporting those ideas with examples or evidence, and composing in standard written English. The examinee writes for 30 minutes on a given topic. The essay then is reviewed by a committee of composition specialists who score it holistically on a 1–6 scale. The TWE score is reported separately on the TOEFL score report and is not added to the TOEFL score.

In addition to the TOEFL International and Special Center Testing Programs, the TOEFL Institutional Testing Program (TOEFL ITP) is available. Under this program, qualified educational and commercial institutions may arrange to test their own students, applicants, or employees with their own staffs and facilities at any time. The TOEFL tests offered under this arrangement are forms previously used in the International and Special Center Testing Programs. Scores obtained through TOEFL ITP may be compared to those obtained in the other programs. The TOEFL ITP also offers the Preliminary Test of English as a Foreign Language (PRE-TOEFL) to measure English proficiency at the lower range of the lower-level TOEFL scale score. Originally, PRE-TOEFL was designed to measure the English proficiency of students needing some knowledge of English but not planning to study in the United States. The preliminary test also is used with students for whom the TOEFL would be too difficult. Like the TOEFL, the PRE-TOEFL uses a paper-pencil multiple-choice format to measure listening comprehension, structure and written expression, and vocabulary and reading comprehension. Examiner required. Suitable for group use.

Timed: TOEFL 3 hours; TWE 30 minutes; TOEFL ITP 2 hours

Scoring: Computer scored

Cost: TOEFL: International (Saturday) Test Dates $27.00 per student, Special Center (Friday) Test Dates $35.00 per student, overseas $29.00 and $37.00, respectively; TOEFL ITP: $12.00 per examinee tested, minimum $120.00 charge; PRE-TOEFL: $9.00 per examinee tested, minimum $90.00 charge

Publisher: Educational Testing Service

Information and availability unconfirmed; last verified in 1988.

TEST OF ENGLISH PROFICIENCY LEVEL (TEPL)
George Rathmell

Adolescent, adult—Ages 12–30
Grades 6 and above

Purpose: Measures the English proficiency of individuals with limited English proficiency. Used for placement.

Description: Criterion-referenced paper-pencil and oral-response test consisting of 74 multiple-choice, short-answer, essay, and verbal items assessing oral (30 items) and reading and structural (44 items) English language skills. The examiner must have a TESOL certificate or a master's degree in psychology. Examiner required. Suitable for group use.

Timed: Not available

Scoring: Hand key; may be machine scored

Cost: $49.95 (includes black line masters of test booklet and answer sheets)

Publisher: Alemany Press

TEST OF SPOKEN ENGLISH (TSE)
Educational Testing Service

Adult

Purpose: Assesses nonnative speakers' proficiency in spoken English. Used to evaluate applicants for graduate-level teaching assistantships and for certification in health-related professions.

Description: 24–item oral-response test consisting of seven sections assessing nonnative speakers' proficiency in spoken English. A test tape and a test book are used as stimulus material. The tape leads the examinee through questions requiring controlled responses to less structured free answers that demand more active use of English. The subject's answers are taped and evaluated by two raters at ETS. The test yields scores in three areas: grammar, fluency, and pronunciation. TSE is part of the Test of English as a Foreign Language (TOEFL) program and is designed to compliment the TOEFL, which does not measure oral English proficiency. The institutional version, the Speaking Proficiency English Assessment Kit (SPEAK), is available for local testing. Two additional test forms, SPEAK II and SPEAK III, are available. Examiner required. Suitable for group use.

Untimed: 20 minutes

Scoring: Computer scored; examiner evaluated

Cost: Academic purposes $60.00; professional purposes $85.00

Publisher: Educational Testing Service

Information and availability unconfirmed; last verified in 1988.

Intelligence and Related

ACER ADVANCED TEST AL-AQ (SECOND EDITION) AND BL-BQ

Adolescent, adult—Ages 15 and older

Purpose: Measures intelligence of students ages 15 and older at secondary and tertiary levels.

Description: Multiple-item paper-pencil intelligence test available in two parallel forms: AL-AQ (Second Edition) and BL-BQ. The L section of both forms contains linguistic items, and the Q section contains quantitative items. Norms are presented for upper secondary level and first-year samples from TAFE colleges and Colleges of Advanced Education. Materials include expendable booklets for each section (AL, BL, AQ, or BQ), scoring keys for each section, manual, and specimen set. Examiner required. Suitable for group use.
AUSTRALIAN PUBLISHER

Timed: AL, BL 15 minutes; AQ, BQ 20 minutes

Scoring: Hand key; examiner evaluated

Cost: Contact publisher

Publisher: The Australian Council for Educational Research Limited

---

ACER ADVANCED TEST B40 (REVISED)

Adolescent, adult—Ages 15 and older

Purpose: Measures intelligence of students ages 15 years and older.

Description: 77–item paper-pencil test measuring general mental abilities, including both verbal and numerical reasoning. The revised manual includes norms for adults and supplementary data for 15–year-olds and first-year college students. Materials include an expendable booklet, score key, manual, and specimen set. Examiner required. Suitable for group use.
AUSTRALIAN PUBLISHER

Untimed: 1 hour

Scoring: Hand key

Cost: Contact publisher

Publisher: The Australian Council for Educational Research Limited

---

ACER ADVANCED TEST BL-BQ— NEW ZEALAND REVISION

Adolescent, adult

Purpose: Measures broad aspects of general linguistic and quantitative abilities. Used with students in Form 7, with students undertaking tertiary courses, or with adults with superior verbal or quantitative skills.

Description: Multiple-item paper-pencil test measuring general intellectual skills as demonstrated by the ability to see relationships and solve problems. Both verbal and numerical abilities are tested. The instrument has applications for the prediction of achievement, educational and vocational counseling, and selection of occupations demanding high-level verbal and numerical reasoning ability. Because the test emphasizes verbal and numerical problem-solving abilities, it is inappropriate for use with individuals whose cultural, linguistic, or educational backgrounds could be considered disadvantaged. Separate linguistic and quantitative scores are provided. New Zealand norms are presented as percentile ranks and stanines for tests BL and BQ and total score for 16–17–year-olds, a group of officer cadets from the armed forces, and selected tertiary students. This test is a higher level measure than the ACER Higher Test PL-PQ: New Zealand Revision. Examiner required. Suitable for group use.
NEW ZEALAND PUBLISHER

Untimed: BL 20 minutes; BQ 25 minutes

Scoring: Hand key; examiner evaluated

Cost: Contact publisher

Publisher: New Zealand Council for Educational Research

ACER HIGHER TEST PL-PQ—NEW ZEALAND REVISION

Adolescent, adult

Purpose: Measures general linguistic and quantitative abilities. Used with students in Form 5 and above, individuals who have left school, and adults who have not begun tertiary education at an advanced level.

Description: Multiple-item paper-pencil test measuring general intellectual skills as demonstrated by the ability to see relationships and solve problems. Both verbal and numerical abilities are tested. The instrument has applications for the prediction of achievement, educational and vocational counseling, and selection of occupations demanding high-level verbal and numerical reasoning ability. Because the test emphasizes verbal and numerical problem-solving abilities, it is inappropriate for use with individuals whose cultural, linguistic, or educational backgrounds could be considered disadvantaged. Separate linguistic and quantitative scores are provided. New Zealand norms are presented as percentile ranks and stanines for tests PL and PQ and total score for 15-, 16-, and 17-year-olds, a group of recruits from the armed forces, and selected short-course apprentices from polytechnics. This test is less demanding than the ACER Advanced Test BL-BQ—New Zealand Revision. Examiner required. Suitable for group use.
NEW ZEALAND PUBLISHER
Timed: PL 20 minutes; PQ 25 minutes
Scoring: Hand key; examiner evaluated
Cost: Contact publisher
Publisher: New Zealand Council for Educational Research

ACER HIGHER TESTS: WL-WQ, ML-MQ (SECOND EDITION) AND PL-PQ

Adolescent, adult—Ages 13 and older

Purpose: Measures the intelligence of students.

Description: 72-item paper-pencil tests of general mental abilities available in three forms: WL-WQ for students ages 13 and older and parallel forms ML-MQ and PL-PQ for students ages 15 and older. The L section (36 items) of each form has a linguistic bias; the Q section (36 items) is quantitative. Australian norms are provided for both sections sep-

arately and for a combined score. Examiner required. Suitable for group use.
AUSTRALIAN PUBLISHER
Timed: L section 15 minutes; Q section 20 minutes
Scoring: Hand key; examiner evaluated
Cost: Contact publisher
Publisher: The Australian Council for Educational Research Limited

---

ACER INTERMEDIATE TEST F

Child, adolescent—Ages 10-14

Purpose: Measures the intelligence of students.

Description: 80-item pencil-paper test measuring general mental abilities in the following areas: classification, jumbled sentences, number series, synonyms and antonyms, arithmetical and verbal problems, and proverbs. Materials include a four-page booklet, scoring key, manual, and specimen set. Australian norms are provided. Examiner required. Suitable for group use.
AUSTRALIAN PUBLISHER
Timed: 30 minutes
Scoring: Hand key
Cost: Contact publisher
Publisher: The Australian Council for Educational Research Limited

---

ACER INTERMEDIATE TEST G

Child, adolescent—Ages 10-15

Purpose: Measures intelligence of students.

Description: 75-item paper-pencil test measuring general mental abilities: verbal comprehension, verbal reasoning, and quantitative reasoning. Australian age and grade norms are provided. Not available to Australian government schools. Examiner required. Suitable for group use.
AUSTRALIAN PUBLISHER
Timed: 30 minutes
Scoring: Hand key
Cost: Contact publisher
Publisher: The Australian Council for Educational Research Limited

ACER JUNIOR A TEST

Child—Ages 8.6–11.11

Purpose: Measures intelligence of children.

Description: 75–item paper-pencil test measuring verbal, nonverbal, and quantitative reasoning abilities. Materials include an eight-page booklet, scoring key, manual, and specimen set. Examiner required. Suitable for group use. AUSTRALIAN PUBLISHER

Timed: 30 minutes

Scoring: Hand key

Cost: Contact publisher

Publisher: The Australian Council for Educational Research Limited

ADVANCED PROGRESSIVE MATRICES (APM)
Refer to page 49.

AH1 X AND Y GROUP TESTS OF FORMAL REASONING
A. W. Heim, K. P. Watts, and V. Simmonds

Child—Ages 5–11

Purpose: Assesses perceptual or nonverbal reasoning skills. Used for classroom evaluation of poor readers.

Description: Four-subtest paper-pencil multiple-choice measure of nonverbal reasoning. The subtests cover series, likes, analogies, and differents. Items are presented in pictorial or diagrammatic format. Two parallel forms, X and Y, are available. Examiner required. Suitable for group use. BRITISH PUBLISHER

Timed: 35–45 minutes

Scoring: Hand key

Cost: Contact publisher

Publisher: NFER-NELSON Publishing Company Ltd.

AH2/AH3 GROUP TESTS OF GENERAL REASONING
A. W. Heim, K. P. Watts, and V. Simmonds

Ages 10–adult

Purpose: Assesses general reasoning ability. Used for evaluating intelligence.

Description: 120–item paper-pencil multiple-choice test consisting of three subtests (40 items each) measuring reasoning ability: Verbal (V), Numerical (N), and Perceptual (P). The Perceptual subtest presents items in diagrammatic and pictorial formats. A profile of the subject, showing areas of strength and weakness, may be constructed. Two parallel forms, AH2 and AH3, are available. The test was developed as an alternative to the AH4 Group Tests of Intelligence. Examiner required. Suitable for group use. BRITISH PUBLISHER

Timed: 14 minutes per subtest

Scoring: Hand key

Cost: Contact publisher

Publisher: NFER-NELSON Publishing Company Ltd.

AH4 GROUP TEST OF GENERAL INTELLIGENCE (REGULAR EDITION)
A. W. Heim

Ages 10–adult

Purpose: Measures general intellectual ability. Used for evaluation of children, adults, or selected groups with below-average levels of intelligence.

Description: Multiple-item paper-pencil test measuring general intelligence. The first section tests verbal and numerical skills, and the second section contains items, presented in diagrammatic form, requiring deductive reasoning, the understanding of everyday words, accurate observance of details, and the following of simple instructions exactly. Although most items are multiple-choice, a few require more extensive answers. Examiner required. Suitable for group use. BRITISH PUBLISHER

Timed: 35–45 minutes

Scoring: Hand key
Cost: Contact publisher
Publisher: NFER-NELSON Publishing
Company Ltd.

AH5 GROUP TEST OF HIGH GRADE INTELLIGENCE
A. W. Heim

Adolescent, adult—Ages
13–college

Purpose: Assesses general intellectual ability. Used for evaluating subjects of above-average intelligence.

Description: Two-part paper-pencil test measuring intelligence. The first part contains verbal and numerical problems, and the second part contains problems in diagrammatic form. The items, the majority of which are multiple-choice, emphasize deductive reasoning, but they also require accurate observation, attention to detail, and the ability to appreciate shades of meaning. Examiner required. Suitable for group use.
BRITISH PUBLISHER
Timed: 20 minutes per part
Scoring: Hand key
Cost: Contact publisher
Publisher: NFER-NELSON Publishing
Company Ltd.

AH6 GROUP TESTS OF HIGH LEVEL INTELLIGENCE
A. W. Heim, K. P. Watts, and V. Simmonds

Adolescent, adult—Ages
16–college

Purpose: Assesses general learning ability. Used for evaluating above-average subjects.

Description: Two separate paper-pencil tests of general reasoning. Form SEM (Scientists, Engineers, and Mathematicians) is used with scientists, engineers, and mathematicians (whether potential or qualified). Form AG (Arts and General) is used with historians, linguists, teachers, economists, other candidates in arts courses and management, and applicants for management training positions. Both

tests include verbal, numerical, and diagrammatic items, but the proportion of each item type differs. Form AG contains half verbal items, and Form SEM contains equal proportions of the three item types. The test is similar in concept to the AH5 but is suitable for a somewhat higher age range. Examiner required. Suitable for group use.
BRITISH PUBLISHER
Timed: Form AG 35 minutes; Form SEM 40 minutes
Scoring: Hand key
Cost: Contact publisher
Publisher: NFER-NELSON Publishing
Company Ltd.

ARLIN TEST OF FORMAL REASONING (ATFR)
Patricia Kennedy Arlin

Child, adolescent
Grades 6–12

Purpose: Assesses student's cognitive abilities. Used by teachers to plan curriculum, modify teaching techniques, and identify gifted students.

Description: 32–item paper-pencil multiple-choice test assessing students' cognitive abilities at one of five levels: concrete, high concrete, transitional, low formal, and high formal reasoning in the application of Piaget's developmental theory. The interpretation of both the total test score and the subtest scores is based on Inhelder and Piaget's description of formal operational thought and the eight schemata associated with that thought (multiplicative compensation, probability, correlations, combinational reasoning, proportional reasoning, forms of conservation beyond direct verification, mechanical equilibrium, and coordination of two or more systems or frames of reference).

Two computer scoring packages are available. Package 1 provides an alphabetical pupil list indicating subtest scores, total test scores, and cognitive level designation. Package 2 includes summary item statistics, coefficients of correlations, means, total test statistics, subtest statistics, total test report, number tested, grade, mean, standard deviation, highest and lowest scores, Hoyt reliability, standard error of measurement statistics, and a total test histogram. Individual, class, group, grade level, and school statistics are available for total test, subtest, and items. A sixth-grade reading level is required. Examiner required. Suitable for group use.

Untimed: 1 hour

Scoring: Hand key; may be computer scored

Cost: Test kit (manual, 35 test booklets, 35 answer sheets, template) $48.00

Publisher: Slosson Educational Publications, Inc.

BLOOMER LEARNING TEST (BLT)
Richard H. Bloomer

**Child, adolescent
Grades 1.5–11 and
above**

Purpose: Determines strengths and weaknesses in learning patterns of individual pupils for purposes of planning remedial or compensatory educational programs. Used with special groups such as the learning disabled, emotionally disturbed, and gifted, as well as with normal students.

Description: 10 multiple-item paper-pencil multiple-choice subtests, each of which may be used alone and in any order. The subtests measure activity, visual and auditory short-term memory, visual apprehension, serial learning, recall, relearning, association, paired associate learning, concept recognition and production, and problem solving. The test also evaluates simple-learning IQ, problem-solving IQ, and full-learning IQ. The 10 subtests are contained in a loose-leaf binder. Scores are calculated on a student record form. Examiner required. Suitable for group use.

Timed: Rate of Responding 8 minutes; Association 5 minutes

Scoring: Hand key; examiner evaluated

Cost: Manual, test stimuli, answer forms, record forms, scoring key $78.00

Publisher: Brador Publications, Inc.

Information and availability unconfirmed; last verified in 1987.

THE BRITISH ABILITY SCALES, REVISED EDITION
Colin D. Elliott, David J. Murray, and Lea S. Pearson

**Child, adolescent—Ages
2.5–17**

Purpose: Assesses cognitive ability. Used for individual, educational, and clinical evaluations.

Description: 23 scales measuring cognitive ability. The scales are classified along three major dimensions: stimulus presentation mode, response mode, and behavioral characteristics. The behavioral characteristics dimension is divided into speed of information processing and five major areas of processes. Each scale may be administered on its own or in combination with the other scales. A short-form version is available for most of the scales. Examiner required. Not suitable for group use.

BRITISH PUBLISHER

Timed: Open ended

Scoring: Examiner evaluated

Cost: Contact publisher

Publisher: NFER-NELSON Publishing Company Ltd.

BRITISH PICTURE VOCABULARY SCALES
Lloyd M. Dunn, Leota M. Dunn, Chris Whetton, and David Pintilie

**Child, adolescent—Ages
2.6–18**

Purpose: Measures receptive vocabulary of children. Used with physically disabled, mentally handicapped, disturbed, retarded, speech-impaired, and learning disabled children.

Description: Multiple-item response test assessing receptive vocabulary of children. Test plates are set up on a stand, and the examiner pronounces a stimulus word from the manual. The subject, looking at the test plate, indicates by nodding or gesturing which picture best indicates the meaning of that word. The results indicate above- or below-average ability and problems that may require special

---

attention. The test is used for screening new school entrants or measuring child development in the early years. A short and a long form are available. Examiner required. Not suitable for group use. BRITISH PUBLISHER

Untimed: Varies

Scoring: Hand key

Cost: Contact publisher

Publisher: NFER-NELSON Publishing Company Ltd.

CANADIAN COGNITIVE ABILITIES TEST: MULTILEVEL EDITION (CCAT), LEVELS A-H, FORM 7
E. Wright, R. Thorndike, and E. Hagen

Child, adolescent
Grades 3-12

Purpose: Assesses students' abilities in three parallel batteries: verbal, nonverbal, and quantitative.

Description: Series of paper-pencil multiple-choice subtests for three parallel batteries: Verbal, Nonverbal, and Quantitative. Materials include test booklets, examiner's manual, and answer sheets. A consumable booklet for Level A for younger children is also available. It is accompanied by a supplementary manual with key. This test is a Canadian adaptation of the Cognitive Abilities Test published by Riverside Publishing Company. Examiner must have a teaching certificate. Examiner required. Suitable for group use. CANADIAN PUBLISHER

Timed: 90 minutes

Scoring: Scoring service available from publisher; hand key

Cost: Test booklets $7.15; 35 answer sheets $13.45; scoring mask $9.25; teacher's guide $12.00

Publisher: Nelson Canada

CANADIAN COGNITIVE ABILITIES TEST: PRIMARY BATTERY (CCAT), LEVELS 1 & 2, FORM 7
E. Wright, R. Thorndike, and E. Hagen

Child
Grades K.5-3

Purpose: Assesses students' verbal, non-verbal, and quantitative abilities.

Description: Series of three multiple-choice paper-pencil subtests: Verbal, Nonverbal, and Quantitative. Materials include test booklets, an examiner's manual, and a score key for each level tested. This test is a Canadian adaptation of the Cognitive Abilities Tests published by Riverside Publishing Company. Examiner must have a teaching certificate. Examiner required. Suitable for group use. CANADIAN PUBLISHER

Untimed: Varies

Scoring: Hand key

Cost: 35 test booklets $30.00; examiner's manual $7.65; scoring key $2.80

Publisher: Nelson Canada

CHILDREN'S ABILITIES SCALES

Child—Ages 11-12½

Purpose: Assesses children's intellectual abilities. Used for describing individual strengths and weaknesses and for identifying learning difficulties.

Description: Battery of paper-pencil tests covering verbal, nonverbal, and spatial abilities. The manual explains the relationship between the tests, allowing the teacher to build a profile of the child's abilities. Examiner required. Suitable for group use. BRITISH PUBLISHER

Untimed: 15-35 minutes per test

Scoring: Hand key; examiner evaluated

Cost: Contact publisher

Publisher: NFER-NELSON Publishing Company Ltd.

COLOURED PROGRESSIVE MATRICES
Refer to page 50.

COLUMBIA MENTAL MATURITY SCALE (CMMS)
Refer to page 50.

COMPOUND SERIES TEST (CST)
Refer to page 972.

COMPREHENSIVE ASSESSMENT PROGRAM: DEVELOPING COGNITIVE ABILITIES TEST, FORMS A AND B
Donald L. Beggs and John T. Mouw

Child, adolescent
Grades 2–12

Purpose: Identifies intellectual strengths and weaknesses in groups and individuals. Used to compare learning ability to academic achievement. Identifies students for gifted programs and evaluates curricular alternatives.

Description: 80–item paper-pencil test measuring verbal, quantitative, and spatial abilities. Tests for Grades 3–12 provide information about the individual's skills in application, analysis, synthesis; knowledge; and comprehension. When administered with the Comprehensive Assessment Program: Achievement Series, the test shows the level of student performance in relation to abilities. Examiner required. Suitable for group use.

Timed: 50 minutes

Scoring: Hand key; may be computer scored

Cost: 35 test booklets $24.40–$34.00 (specify level and machine or hand-scorable); 35 answer sheets $10.80; directions for administration $2.75; manual $18.70; key $5.30

Publisher: American Testronics

CREATIVE REASONING TEST
John H. Doolittle

Ages 8 and older

Purpose: Assesses creative, associative thinking.

Description: Three 20–item tests (Levels A–1, B–1, and B–2) in paper-pencil problem-solving riddle format measuring associative thinking and the ability to generate categories. Levels B–1 and B–2 can be used as pre- or posttests. Used in ongoing data collection. An elementary

reading level is required. Teacher certification is required for the examiner. Examiner required. Suitable for group use.

Timed: 30 minutes

Scoring: Hand key

Cost: Set $5.95

Publisher: Midwest Publications Critical Thinking Press

CREATIVITY ASSESSMENT PACKET
Refer to page 621.

THE CULTURE FAIR SERIES: SCALES 1, 2, 3
Refer to page 51.

DEVELOPING COGNITIVE ABILITIES (DCAT), 2ND EDITION
Donald L. Beggs and John T. Mouw

Child, adolescent—Ages
5–18
Grades 1–12

Purpose: Assesses cognitive characteristics that can be altered in the school environment, identifies intellectual strengths and weaknesses, identifies students for gifted programs, and evaluates curricular alternatives.

Description: Multiple-choice test available in 8 levels, C/D to L, for students in Grades 1–12. The test was developed along a format that includes both a cognitive taxonomy (Bloom et al., 1956) and a content area taxonomy. The content areas are verbal, quantitative, and spatial. The three cognitive levels are Basic Cognitive Abilities, Application Abilities, and Critical Thinking Abilities. The test results can be used to identify strengths, weaknesses, and areas for potential school remediation activities. The three cognitive dimensions provide information that can assist teachers in identifying level of thinking ability across the traditional content areas. This is one test in the Comprehensive Assessment Program series and a revision of the 1980 DCAT. Examiner required. Suitable for group use.

Timed: Varies by level

intelligence and related

Scoring: Machine scored; hand key; scoring service available from publisher

Cost: 25 machine-scorable test booklets Levels C/D and E $37.10; 25 reusable test booklets Levels E-L $28.75; 35 answer sheets $12.40; directions $3.90

Publisher: American Testronics

FOSTER MAZES
Refer to page 612.

FULL-RANGE PICTURE VOCABULARY TEST (FRPV)
Refer to page 52.

GROUP TEST FOR INDIAN PUPILS—1968

Child, adolescent

Purpose: Measures general mental ability. Used for psychoeducational evaluation.

Description: 6–subtest paper-pencil measure of general mental ability. Three subtests are verbal and three are nonverbal. Tests provide three scores: verbal, nonverbal, and total. The test is divided into three series: Junior, Intermediate, and Senior. Two alternative forms are available for the Junior and Intermediate Series. Examiner required. Suitable for group use.
SOUTH AFRICAN PUBLISHER

Timed: 2 hours

Scoring: Hand key; examiner evaluated

Cost: (In Rands) Junior Form A test booklet 2,40; Junior Form B test booklet 2,00; Intermediate Form A test booklet 2,00; Intermediate Form B 2,00; Senior test booklets 2,00; manual 5,50; scoring stencils-Junior A 2,50; Junior B 2,50; Intermediate A and B 2,50 each; Senior 2,50; orders from outside the RSA will be dealt with on merit

Publisher: Human Sciences Research Council

GROUP TESTS—1974
Refer to page 53.

HARDING SKYSCRAPER FORM B-C
Christopher P. Harding

Adult

Purpose: Measures mental abilities at a high level of achievement. Originally developed to serve the selection needs of the International Society for Philosophical Enquiry. Used with candidates in the 140–173 Ability Quotient range, with a ceiling of 181+.

Description: 40–item paper-pencil test measuring the integration of thinking, creative, and informational abilities to yield a single unified score called the Ability Quotient (AQ). Using multiple-choice and short-answer questions for Section B and incomplete analogies (each with four choices) for Section C, the test measures convergent, divergent, and condivergent thinking processes. Examiner required. Suitable for group use.
AUSTRALIAN PUBLISHER

Untimed: 1½–2 hours

Scoring: Scored by publisher

Cost: Test scoring $35.00

Publisher: Harding Tests

HARDING W87 TEST
Christopher P. Harding

Adult

Purpose: Measures mental abilities at a high level of achievement. Developed to replace the Harding Skyscraper as the entrance test of the International Society for Philosophical Enquiry (ISPE). Suitable for individuals with Ability Quotient 140–173.

Description: 64–item paper-pencil test measuring the integration of thinking, creative, and informational abilities. The test consists of two parts. Set I (34 items) uses multiple-choice and free-response questions to test verbal, numerical, and logical reasoning abilities. Set II (30 items) provides incomplete word analogies, requiring the subject to choose from 10 possible words to complete the analogy. The test as a whole measures convergent, divergent, and condivergent thinking processes. This test may be obtained only from ISPE. Examiner required. Suitable for group use. AUSTRALIAN PUBLISHER

Untimed: 3 hours

Scoring: Publisher scored

Cost: Contact ISPE

Publisher: Harding Tests

HEALY PICTORIAL COMPLETION TEST I
William Healy

Child

Purpose: Measures mental ability and intelligence based on an individual's apperceptive ability. Used with all ages, primarily with individuals with a child-type mind.

Description: 10–item task-assessment test using a picture board with 10 pieces missing so that the scene is incomplete. The missing pieces are of uniform size and shape, and the subject must select the 10 correct insets from the 50 choices presented and insert them in their proper places to complete the scene. Errors are rated as logical errors and total errors. Observation of the child's approach to the task provides information about the child's mental control and processes of association. The instrument is particularly useful with defectives and aberrational individuals. This test also is included in the Arthur Point Scale of Performance, Form I. Examiner required. Not suitable for group use.

Timed: 20 minutes

Scoring: Examiner evaluated

Cost: Test, manual, carrying case $150.00

Publisher: Stoelting Co.

HENMON-NELSON TESTS OF MENTAL ABILITY
Joseph L. French, Tom A. Lamke, and Martin J. Nelson

Child, adolescent
Grades K–12

Purpose: Measures the general mental abilities of elementary and high-school students.

Description: Battery of paper-pencil multiple-choice tests assessing the cognitive abilities of students. The tests are available on four levels designed for use in the following grade ranges: Grades K–2 (Primary Battery), Grades 3–6, Grades 6–9, and Grades 9–12. The Primary Battery consists of three subtests (listening, picture vocabulary, and size and number), which measure nine abilities and require no reading on the part of the students. The tests for Grades 3–12 contain items, arranged in omnibus-cycle form, related to academic success (vocabulary, sentence completion, opposites, general information, verbal analogies, verbal classification, verbal inference, number series, arithmetic reasoning, and figure analogies). The following scores are available: raw score, Deviation IQ (a standard score by age), age percentile rank and stanine, and grade percentile rank and stanine.

Consumable test booklets are available for all levels. Reusable test booklets and MRC answer cards (for use with scoring service) are available for Grades 3–12 only. The Primary Battery examiner's manual includes directions for administering each test, information about the nature and purposes of the tests, and guidelines for interpreting and using the test results. The examiner's manual for Grades 3–12 includes information for administering, understanding, and using the tests, technical information, and norms tables. Examiner required. Suitable for group use.

Timed: Grades K–2 25–30 minutes; Grades 3–12 30 minutes

Scoring: Examiner evaluated; may be computer scored (Grades 3–12 only)

Cost: 35 Primary Battery test booklets, manual, class record sheet $38.61; 35 test booklets (specify consumable or reusable) for Grades 3–6, 6–9, or 9–12, manual, class record sheet $28.83; 100 MRC answer cards (includes all materials needed to obtain scoring service) $19.92; examiner's manual (Grades K–2 or 3–12) $3.84; 35 class record sheets $9.99

Publisher: The Riverside Publishing Company

INDIVIDUAL SCALE FOR INDIAN SOUTH AFRICANS (ISISA)—1971

Child, adolescent—Ages 8–17

Purpose: Assesses intelligence in Indian pupils. Used for psychological-educational evaluation.

Description: 10–subtest measure of general intellectual ability. Five subtests are verbal; five are nonverbal. Scores obtained include Vocabulary, Comprehension, Similarities, Problems, Memory, Pattern Completion, Blocks, Absurdities, Formboard, and Mazes. The test may be administered in an abbreviated form. The test was adapted for Indians from the New South African Individual Scale. Examiner required. Not suitable for group use.
SOUTH AFRICAN PUBLISHER
Untimed: 1 hour, 20 minutes
Scoring: Hand key; examiner evaluated
Cost: (In Rands) complete specimen set (2 pattern completions, 2 mazes, 2 answer sheets) 134,20; orders from outside the RSA will be dealt with on merit
Publisher: Human Sciences Research Council

INTELLIGENCE TESTS

Child, adolescent

Purpose: Measures general intelligence of secondary-school pupils.

Description: Several tests assessing the reasoning abilities of secondary-school pupils. The Cotswold Tests provide measures of mental ability and English ability for two age levels: 10–12½ years and 8½–9½ years. The Kelvin Tests include infant, reading, and mental tests. The Ryburn Tests are available for two levels: junior and senior. The Cotswold Personality Assessment provides three preference scores (things, people, ideas) and three attitude scores (using one's hands, being with other people, talking about school) for students ages 11–16. The last test of the battery is the Orton Intelligence Test for students ages 9–14 years.

Instructions, norms, and a booklet entitled *Spotlight on Reasoning* are available for all tests. Examiner required. Not suitable for group use.
BRITISH PUBLISHER
Timed: Varies
Scoring: Not available
Cost: 20 Cotswold tests (specify title) £1.60; 20 Kelvin tests (specify title) £1.60; 20 Ryburn tests (specify junior or senior) £1.60; 100 Cotswold Personality Assessment £7.95; 20 Orton Intelligence tests £1.40; instructions and norms for all tests 20p.
Publisher: Robert Gibson Publisher
Information and availability unconfirmed; last verified in 1987.

INTERNATIONAL SOCIETY FOR PHILOSOPHICAL ENQUIRY VOCABULARY FORM A
Refer to page 289.

INTERNATIONAL SOCIETY FOR PHILOSOPHICAL ENQUIRY VOCABULARY FORM B
Refer to page 289.

JUNIOR SOUTH AFRICAN INDIVIDUAL SCALES (JSAIS)— 1979
Refer to page 54.

KNOX'S CUBE TEST (KCT)
Mark Stone and Benjamin Wright

Child, adolescent

Purpose: Measures children's and adult's short-term memory and attention span, which together constitute the most elementary stage of mental activity. Used to evaluate deaf, language-impaired, and foreign-speaking persons.

Description: Multiple-task assessment of attention span and short-term memory measuring how accurately an individual can repeat simple rhythmic figures tapped out for him by the examiner. Test materials include four cubes attached to a wooden base and a separate tapping block. Directions can be delivered in pantomime. The manual provides procedures and rationale for administering, scoring, and interpreting a comprehensive version of KCT, which incorporates all previous versions. This revision utilizes Rasch measurement procedures to develop an objective psychometric variable, along which both items and persons can be positioned. Two versions are available: KCT JR (ages 2–8) and KCT SR (ages 8 and above). Examiner required. Not suitable for group use.

Timed: Not available

Scoring: Examiner evaluated

Cost: Both versions complete (testing materials, manual, record forms) $24.50 each

Publisher: Stoelting Co.

KOHS BLOCK DESIGN TEST
S.C. Kohs

Mental ages 3–19

Purpose: Measures intelligence of persons with a mental age of 3–19 years. Used for testing individuals with language and hearing handicaps, the disadvantaged, and non-English-speaking individuals.

Description: Multiple-item task-assessment test consisting of 17 cards containing colored designs and 16 colored blocks that the subject uses to duplicate the designs on the cards. Performance is evaluated for attention, adaptation, and auto-criticism. This test also is included in the Merrill-Palmer and Arthur Performance scales. The complete set includes cubes, cards, a manual, and 50 record blanks. Examiner required. Suitable for group use.

Timed: 40 minutes or less

Scoring: Examiner evaluated

Cost: Complete kit $85.00

Publisher: Stoelting Co.

LANGDON ADULT INTELLIGENCE TEST (LAIT)
Refer to page 55.

MATRIX ANALOGIES TEST— EXPANDED FORM (MAT-EF)

Child, adolescent—Ages 5–17

Purpose: Measures nonverbal reasoning ability of students.

Description: 64–item paper-pencil multiple-choice test consisting of abstract designs or matrices from which an element in a progression is missing. The child chooses the missing element from six alternatives. Items are organized in four groups: pattern completion, reasoning by analogy, serial reasoning, and spatial visualization. The test yields standard scores, percentile ranks, age equivalents for the total score, and item group scores. Since minimal verbal comprehension and response are required, the test can be used for assessment of bilingual, gifted, learning disabled, mentally retarded, hearing- and/or language-impaired, and physically disabled persons with limited response capabilities. The test can be administered by psychologists, counselors, school psychologists and diagnosticians, rehabilitation psychologists, and other professionals with proper training and experience in testing. Examiner required. Not suitable for group use.

Untimed: 30 minutes

Scoring: Hand key

Cost: Specimen set (examiner's manual, stimulus manual, 50 answer sheets, case) $69.00

Publisher: The Psychological Corporation

Information and availability unconfirmed; last verified in 1988.

MATRIX ANALOGIES TEST— SHORT FORM (MAT-SF)
Jack A. Naglieri

Child, adolescent—Ages 5–17.11

Purpose: Measures nonverbal reasoning abilities of students. Designed to screen large numbers of children with learning difficulties or potentially gifted bilingual or educationally disadvantaged students whose school performance may be poor due to limited English language proficiency.

Description: 35–item paper-pencil test consisting of abstract designs with missing elements and matrices containing progressive elements that predict the next element in a progression. Test items are part of the larger MAT—Expanded Form. The test features norms on a large nationally representative U.S. sample and a six-option, multiple-choice format. When used with the Multi-Level Academic Survey Test, this test also may be used to screen for learning-disabled children identified on the basis of an ability-achievement discrepancy. The test yields percentile ranks, stanines by half-year age intervals, and age equivalents from 5.0–17.11. Examiner required. Suitable for group use. May be administered individually to a child with a physically handicapping condition.

Untimed: 20 minutes

Scoring: Hand key

Cost: Specimen set (examiner's manual, reusable test booklet, self-scoring answer sheet) $17.00

Publisher: The Psychological Corporation

Information and availability unconfirmed; last verified in 1988.

MULTIDIMENSIONAL APTITUDE BATTERY—FORM L
Refer to page 57.

NEW SOUTH AFRICAN GROUP TEST (NSAGT)—1965

Child, adolescent—Ages 8–17

Purpose: Assesses intellectual ability. Used for psychological and educational evaluation.

Description: 6–subtest measure of general intellectual ability. Three subtests are verbal, and three are nonverbal. The test is available at three levels: Junior, Intermediate, and Senior. Two equivalent forms are available for the Junior and Senior Series. The test is available only to departments of education and private schools or to schools training teachers for the purpose of training and research. Examiner required. Not suitable for group use.
SOUTH AFRICAN PUBLISHER

Timed: 2 hours

Scoring: Hand key; examiner evaluated; may be machine scored

Cost: (In Rands) Form J test 1,20; Form G test 3,10; Form S/T test 1,20; Intermediate manual 8,60; Junior and Senior manual 13,00; scoring stencils (specify form) 3,00 each; 10 answer sheets 1,50; orders from outside the RSA will be dealt with on merit

Publisher: Human Sciences Research Council

NON-LANGUAGE LEARNING TEST
Refer to page 58.

NON-LANGUAGE TEST OF VERBAL INTELLIGENCE
S. Chatterji and Manjula Mukerjee

Child—Ages 8–12

Purpose: Measures verbal intelligence of children using a nonlanguage medium. Used to test groups of children with differing linguistic or cultural backgrounds. Also identifies children whose academic backwardness is due to linguistic difficulty rather than to lack of verbal ability.

Description: 62–item paper-pencil multiple-choice test consisting entirely of pictured test items. The test consists of four parts: analogy, classification, opposites, and picture arrangement. The candidates are required to record their answers on a separate answer sheet. The test booklets are reusable. The examiner's manual includes detailed instructions for administration, evaluation, and interpretation of the test. Examiner required. Suitable for group use.
PUBLISHED IN INDIA

Timed: 45 minutes

Scoring: Hand key; examiner evaluated

Cost: Contact publisher

Publisher: Statistical Publishing Society

Information and availability unconfirmed; last verified in 1987.

NON-READERS INTELLIGENCE TEST (THIRD EDITION) AND ORAL VERBAL INTELLIGENCE TEST
Dennis Young

Child, adolescent—Ages 6.7–14.11

Purpose: Measures intelligence of students whose performance would be underestimated if they were required to read the questions. Used with children suspected of or diagnosed as Educationally Subnormal (ESN). Identifies children needing special educational assistance.

Description: Multiple-item paper-pencil intelligence test orally administered to slow or nonreaders. The test is available in two forms. The Non-Readers Intelligence Test is for use with unstreamed children ages 6.7–8.11 and with less able children up to the age of 13.11. The Oral Verbal Intelligence Test is for use with unstreamed children ages 7.6–10.11 and with less able children up to the age of 14.11. The third edition of the Non-Readers Intelligence Test manual offers revised items (replacing words like "pop" that have acquired new meanings) and new norms. The manual for the Oral Verbal Intelligence Test contains details of test construction and full instructions for administering and scoring the test. Both tests employ the same scoring template. Examiner required. Suitable for group use.

BRITISH PUBLISHER

Untimed: Not available

Scoring: Hand key

Cost: NRIT manual £2.50; specimen set £3.20; template £3.25; 20 answer sheets £1.50 plus VAT; OVIT manual £2.75; specimen set £3.20; 20 answer sheets £1.90 plus VAT; template £3.25

Publisher: Hodder & Stoughton

NON-VERBAL ABILITY TESTS (NAT)
H.A.H. Rowe

Child, adolescent—Ages 8–adult

Purpose: Measures general ability of the "g" type as well as perceptual, conceptual, and attention and concentration skills.

Description: Domain-referenced battery of 18 nonverbal paper-pencil tests assessing general and specific abilities. The tests cover matching shapes, matching directions, categorization, picture completion, embedded figures, figure formation, mazes, sequencing, picture arrangement, visual search, simple key tests, complex key tests, code tracking, and visual recall. The tests do not require verbalization, reading, or writing in either the administration or the completion of the largely diagrammatic stimulus materials. The battery yields an ability profile, the level and shape of which can be interpreted for each individual. Materials include test forms, a manual, and a monograph entitled *Language-Free Evaluation of Cognitive Development*. Examiner required. Suitable for group use.

AUSTRALIAN PUBLISHER

Untimed: Varies

Scoring: Hand key; examiner evaluated

Cost: Contact publisher

Publisher: The Australian Council for Educational Research Limited

NON-VERBAL REASONING TESTS SERIES

Child, adolescent—Ages 7–15

Purpose: Assesses nonverbal reasoning ability. Used for evaluation of poor readers.

Description: Three paper-pencil tests of basic reasoning using geometric shapes and pictures. All questions appear in pictorial or diagrammatic form. Pictures Test A (ages 7–8) uses three types of questions in picture form. In the first section, the child chooses the picture different from a set; in the second section, the child chooses one of five alternative patterns to complete a story or pattern; the third section presents analogues in pictorial form. Non-Verbal Test BD (ages 8–11) consists of questions relating to geometric shapes, cyphers, similarities, analogues, and series. Non-Verbal Test DH (ages 10–15)

contains two main types of questions. The first requires the child to select one of five small squares that will complete the overall series or pattern contained in a larger square. Other questions are series type. The test may be administered in the full 96–question form or in the shorter 64–question form. Examiner required. Suitable for group use.
BRITISH PUBLISHER
Timed: Varies, depending on test
Scoring: Hand key
Cost: Contact publisher
Publisher: NFER-NELSON Publishing Company Ltd.

NONVERBAL TEST OF COGNITIVE SKILLS (NTCS)
G. Orville Johnson and Herbert F. Boyd

Child
Grades K–7

Purpose: Measures the cognitive abilities of students with limited verbal ability.

Description: Multiple-item nonverbal test in which the examiner uses pantomime to guide the child in the manipulation of blocks, color cubes, dominos, picture stimuli, and Knox cubes to measure the following skills and abilities: reasoning, rote memory, recognition and memory of patterns, visual memory, discrimination, space and spatial relationships, conceptual thinking, recognition of and ability to deal with quantities, quantitative memory, and visual motor perception. Examiner required. Not suitable for group use.
Timed: 25–35 minutes
Scoring: Examiner evaluated
Cost: Test kit $150.00
Publisher: The Psychological Corporation
Information and availability unconfirmed; last verified in 1988.

PEABODY PICTURE VOCABULARY TEST-REVISED (PPVT-R)
Lloyd M. Dunn and Leota M. Dunn

Ages 2½–adult

Purpose: Measures receptive vocabulary for Standard American English, estimates verbal ability, and assesses academic aptitude. Used with English as a Second Language students, mentally retarded and gifted students, and applicants for jobs requiring good aural vocabulary.

Description: 175–item "point-to" response test measuring receptive vocabulary in English. Test items, arranged in order of increasing difficulty, consist of plates of four pictures. Subjects are shown a plate and asked to point to the picture that corresponds to the stimulus word. Only those plates within a subject's ability range are administered. Age-based norms include standard scores, percentile ranks, stanines, and age equivalents. The complete kit includes 175 test plates bound in an easel, manual, 25 individual record forms, and shelf box. Available in two forms, L and M. A special plastic plate edition is available. Examiner required. Not suitable for group use.
Untimed: 10–20 minutes
Scoring: Examiner evaluated
Cost: Complete kit (Form L or M): regular edition $46.00; special plastic edition $59.00
Publisher: American Guidance Service

PICTORIAL TEST OF INTELLIGENCE
Joseph L. French

Child—Ages 3–8

Purpose: Measures children's general ability. Used for curriculum planning and evaluation.

Description: Multiple-item oral picture test in six sections. The subtests are Picture Vocabulary, Information and Comprehension, Form Discrimination, Similarities, Size and Number, and Immediate Recall. The examiner presents picture cards on which four possible answers are represented and asks questions of the child. The cards are designed so that the examiner, by observing eye movement, also can determine the response of children who are physically handicapped. Materials include cards, a manual, and record forms. Examiner required. Not suitable for group use. CANADIAN PUBLISHER

Untimed: 45 minutes
Scoring: Hand key
Cost: Contact publisher
Publisher: Institute of Psychological Research, Inc.

PROVERBS TEST
Donald R. Gorham

All ages

Purpose: Assesses abstract verbal functioning. Used for individual clinical evaluation, screening, and clinical research.

Description: 12– or 40–item power test measuring verbal comprehension. The subject is required to explain the meanings of proverbs. The 12–item free-answer format allows the subject to respond in his or her own words. A 40–item multiple-choice format is also available. The free-response forms are scored for abstractness and pertinence on a 3–point scale. The multiple-choice form is scored with a hand stencil. Forms I, II, and III are available for free-answer administration. Examiner required. Only the multiple-choice form is suitable for group use.

Untimed: Individual test 10–30 minutes; group multiple-choice test 20–40 minutes
Scoring: Hand key; examiner evaluated
Cost: Complete kit (general manual; clinical manual; 10 each of Forms I, II, III; scoring cards; 10 free-response form booklets; scoring stencils) $13.00; 100 test blanks $8.00; 25 test booklets (specify Form I, II, or III) $28.00; 100 answer sheets $8.00
Publisher: Psychological Test Specialists

ROSS TEST OF HIGHER COGNITIVE PROCESSES (ROSS TEST)
John D. Ross and Catherine M. Ross

Child
Grades 4–6

Purpose: Assesses abstract and critical thinking skills among gifted and non-

gifted intermediate grade students. Used to screen students for special programs and to evaluate program effectiveness.

Description: 105–item paper-pencil multiple-choice test in eight sections, each dealing with a specific level of higher cognitive processes within the areas of analysis, synthesis, and evaluation. Test is taken in two sittings. Responses may be recorded directly in the student test booklet or on an optional answer sheet. Materials include overlays for the scoring of answer sheets and a cassette tape of the test. Examiner required. Suitable for group use.

Timed: First sitting 50 minutes; second sitting 55 minutes
Scoring: Hand key
Cost: Manual $15.00; 10 test booklets $15.00; 25 answer sheets/profile forms $10.00; hand key $5.00; cassette tape test $10.00
Publisher: Academic Therapy Publications

SCHUBERT GENERAL ABILITY BATTERY
Herman J.P. Schubert

Adolescent, adult

Purpose: Measures general mental abilities. Used for scholastic and industrial placement and guidance in high school, college, and industry.

Description: Multiple-item paper-pencil battery of tests assessing general mental abilities in order to predict educational and employment success. The battery yields scores for verbal skills, precise thinking, arithmetic reasoning, and logical analysis. Examiner required. Suitable for group use.

Timed: Varies
Scoring: Hand key
Cost: Kit (25 tests, answer key, manual) $45.00
Publisher: Slosson Educational Publications, Inc.

SENIOR SOUTH AFRICAN INDIVIDUAL SCALE (SSAIS)—1964
Refer to page 60.

SOI PRIMARY FORM (FORM P)
SOI Institute Staff

Child
Grades K-3

Purpose: Assesses the learning abilities of young children. Screens for special education or gifted placement. Used for early testing of bilingual and disadvantaged students in order to identify special needs or giftedness.

Description: Eleven subtests evaluating the processing abilities required for success in Grades K-3. Six subtests test processing abilities; the remaining five are diagnostic subtests. The test is designed for screening all students in Grades K-3 before an in-depth testing by a competency team for PL 94-142 or gifted placement. The test includes auditory sequencing. The basic test manual is required for interpretation of scales. See entry for Structure of Intellect (SOI) test for related tests. Suitable for teacher administration to groups; some subtests are administered individually to students who cannot write. Examiner required. Suitable for group use. Available in Spanish.

Untimed: Processing 30 minutes; diagnostic 25 minutes

Scoring: Hand key

Cost: 5 test booklets $17.25; scoring keys $28.75; SOI test manual $35.00

Publisher: Western Psychological Services

THE SOUTH AFRICAN INDIVIDUAL SCALE FOR THE BLIND (SAISB)—1979

Child, adolescent—Ages 6-18

Purpose: Measures general intelligence of blind children. Used for psychological and educational evaluations.

Description: 9-subtest measure of general intellectual ability. Five subtests are verbal, and four are nonverbal. Materials include Braillon sheets for the Pattern Completion and Dominos subtests, a form board, and wooden blocks. The test

was adapted from the New South African Individual Scale (NSAIS). Examiner required. Not suitable for group use. SOUTH AFRICAN PUBLISHER

Untimed: Not available

Scoring: Hand key; examiner evaluated

Cost: Complete specimen set (Pattern Completion, Rubberboard, Subtest 7, 8, 9, Form Board B, manual, vulvalite case, 2 sheets of cellophane paper, 2 general answer sheets, 137,40; orders from outside the RSA will be dealt with on merit

Publisher: Human Sciences Research Council

THE STANDARD PROGRESSIVE MATRICES (SPM-1956)
Refer to page 61.

THE STANFORD-BINET INTELLIGENCE SCALE, FORM L-M
Refer to page 62.

THE STANFORD-BINET INTELLIGENCE SCALE, FOURTH EDITION
Refer to page 62.

SYSTEM OF MULTICULTURAL PLURALISTIC ASSESSMENT (SOMPA)
Jane R. Mercer and June F. Lewis

Child—Ages 5-11

Purpose: Assesses cognitive abilities, sensorimotor abilities, and adaptive behavior of children. Used for assessing children of diverse cultural backgrounds.

Description: Multiple-instrument measure covering various aspects of functioning of children from diverse cultural backgrounds. The test has two major components: The Parent Interview and Student Assessment Materials. The Parent Interview is conducted in the home and requires the administration of the Adaptive Behavior Inventory for Children (ABIC), Sociocultural Scales, and Health History Inventories. Student Assessment Materials data are collected in the school and include administration or completion of the following tests and tasks: Physical Dexterity Tasks, Weight by Height, Visual Acuity, Auditory Acuity, Bender Visual Motor Gestalt Test (sold separately), and the WISC-R or WPPSI (sold separately). The test should be interpreted by a psychologist or a qualified team. Normative data are provided for black, Hispanic, and white children. Examiner required. Not suitable for group use. The Parent Interview is available in Spanish.

Untimed: Parent interview 60 minutes; Student Assessment Materials 20 minutes in addition to time required for the Wechsler and Bender-Gestalt tests

Scoring: Examiner evaluated

Cost: Basic kit (parent interview manual, 25 parent interview record forms, set of 6 ABIC scoring keys, student assessment manual, 25 student assessment record forms, 25 profile folders, technical manual) $99.00

Publisher: The Psychological Corporation

Information and availability unconfirmed; last verified in 1988.

TEST OF CONCEPT UTILIZATION (TCU)
Richard L. Crager

Child, adolescent—Ages 5–18

Purpose: Measures the ability of children and adolescents to think conceptually. Used by teachers to identify children's conceptual strengths, especially underachievers and children with learning disabilities.

Description: 50–item oral-response test consisting of 50 pairs of colored pictures of common objects. The child indicates how the objects are alike. Analysis of the responses provides qualitative and quantitative assessments of five areas of conceptual thinking: color, shape, relational function, homogeneous function, and abstract function. Norms are provided for individuals ages 5–18. *The Development of Concepts: A Manual for the Test of Concept Utilization* (104 pages) includes all scoring instructions, standardization, normative

data, and chapters on clinical and educational uses of the test. The new (1980) manual, *Concepts in the Classroom: A Manual for the Educational Use of the Test of Conceptual Utilization,* provides instructions for a short scoring procedure. New studies are presented in the revised manual, but it does not include administration instructions or normative data. The original manual is still needed to administer and interpret the test. Examiner required. Not suitable for group use.

Untimed: 10 minutes

Scoring: Hand key

Cost: Complete kit (set of test plates, 25 protocol sheets, 25 scoring booklets, 2 manuals, 25 short-scoring forms) $95.00

Publisher: Western Psychological Services

THE TEST OF NONVERBAL INTELLIGENCE–2 (TONI–2)
Refer to page 63.

TEST OF PROBLEM SOLVING (TOPS)
Linda Zachman, Carol Jorgensen, Rosemary Huisingh, and Mark Barrett

Child—Ages 6–12

Purpose: Assesses the verbal reasoning and problem-solving abilities of children.

Description: 50–item oral-response test assessing the ability to use expressive language to think logically and solve problems. The problems, which are presented with picture stimuli, test thinking skills, such as determining causes, answering negative why questions, determining solutions, avoiding problems, and explaining inferences. The results yield age equivalencies, percentile ranks, standard scores, and standard deviations. Examiner required. Not suitable for group use.

Untimed: Varies

Scoring: Examiner evaluated

Cost: Test kit (examiner's manual, book of visual stimuli, 20 test forms) $57.95

Publisher: LinguiSystems, Inc.

TEST ON APPRAISING OBSERVATIONS
Refer to page 492.

THE TITAN TEST
Refer to page 63.

WECHSLER SCALES: WECHSLER ADULT INTELLIGENCE SCALE (WAIS)
Refer to page 64.

WECHSLER SCALES: WECHSLER ADULT INTELLIGENCE SCALE—REVISED (WAIS-R)
Refer to page 64.

WECHSLER SCALES: WECHSLER INTELLIGENCE SCALE FOR CHILDREN—1949 EDITION (WISC)
Refer to page 64.

WECHSLER SCALES: WECHSLER INTELLIGENCE SCALE FOR CHILDREN—REVISED (WISC-R)
Refer to page 65.

WECHSLER SCALES: WECHSLER INTELLIGENCE SCALE FOR CHILDREN—REVISED (WISC-R) SPLIT-HALF SHORT FORM
Refer to page 65.

WECHSLER SCALES: WECHSLER PRESCHOOL AND PRIMARY SCALE OF INTELLIGENCE (WPPSI)
Refer to page 66.

WHIMBEY ANALYTICAL SKILLS INVENTORY (WASI)
Arthur Whimbey

Adolescent, adult
Grades 9 and above

Purpose: Assesses the analytical reasoning ability of high-school and college students and adults.

Description: 38–item paper-pencil test assessing analytical reasoning ability and measuring academic aptitude. The test, which is incorporated in Arthur Whimbey and Jack Lochhead's book *Problem Solving and Comprehension* (4th ed.), can be used to indicate a student's potential for college success. After administration, students discuss and compare solutions to test items. A fourth-grade reading level is required. A table is provided to compute IQ. Self-administered. Suitable for group use.

Untimed: 50 minutes
Scoring: Hand key
Cost: *Problem Solving and Comprehension* (4th ed.) $13.50
Publisher: Lawrence Erlbaum Associates, Inc.

WIDE RANGE ASSESSMENT OF MEMORY AND LEARNING (WRAML)
Refer to page 66.

WIDE RANGE INTELLIGENCE-PERSONALITY TEST (WRIPT)
Refer to page 258.

School and Institutional Environments

ACADEMIC ADVISING INVENTORY
Roger B. Winston, Jr. and Janet A. Sandor

College students

Purpose: Assesses undergraduate academic advising programs. Used with college students.

Description: Multiple-item paper-pencil inventory for evaluating advising programs from a theoretical perspective, making comparisons across institutions.

The inventory is used in various advising delivery systems, including college departments and campus-wide advising centers. The inventory has five parts. The Developmental-Prescriptive Advising Scale and Subscales, Part I (14 items), allows the student to describe the nature of the advising relationship and the quality of activities in which the student and advisor engage. In the Advisor-Advisee Activities (30 items), Part II, students report the frequency of advising activities during an academic year. Part II is composed of five scales: Exploring Institutional Policies, Academic Majors and Courses, Personal Development and Interpersonal Relationships, Teaching Personal Skills, and Registration and Scheduling Classes. In Part III, Satisfaction with Advising, students answer five questions related to their satisfaction with advice during the academic year. Demographic information on the student is requested in Part IV. Part V is made up of optional locally generated items. Self-administered. Suitable for group use.

Untimed: 20 minutes

Scoring: Machine scored

Cost: 50 reusable test forms $17.50; manual $5.50

Publisher: Student Development Associates, Inc.

CLASS ACTIVITIES QUESTIONNAIRE (CAQ)
Refer to page 855.

THE CLASSROOM ENVIRONMENT INDEX (CEI)
George Stern and Associates

Grades 5 and above

Purpose: Measures the psychological environment of a classroom (Grades 5–12 and certain college classes) in terms of the need-press paradigm of human behavior as conceptualized by Henry Murray. Used for research and teacher development purposes.

Description: 300–item paper-pencil true-false inventory assessing the environment of a classroom in terms of 30 press scales reflecting the 30 basic need scales estab-

lished on the Stern Activities Index (AI). The test items refer to classroom environment, teacher personality, teaching style, creativity, and other facets of the teaching-learning process. Scores are provided for six first-order dimensions (humanistic intellectual climate, group intellectual life, achievement standards, personal dignity, orderliness, and science) and two second-order dimensions (development press and control press). The questionnaire is designed so that it can be divided into two parts, requiring each student to answer only half of the 300 questions. Item content has been kept as similar as possible to that of the other Syracuse Indexes (especially the High School Characteristics Index). A number of revisions make the instrument applicable to the individual classroom rather than to the institution as a whole. Analysis differentiates between classrooms, subjects, grades, and educational levels. Self-administered. Suitable for group use.

Untimed: 40 minutes

Scoring: Examiner evaluated; may be computer scored

Cost: Test booklet $0.50; answer sheet $0.10; profile form $0.10; technical manual $7.50; prices for computer scoring and analysis available on request

Publisher: FAAX Corporation

CLASSROOM ENVIRONMENT SCALE (CES)
Rudolf H. Moos and Edison J. Trickett

Adolescent
Grades 7–12

Purpose: Assesses the teaching atmosphere of junior and senior high-school classrooms in order to evaluate the effects of course content, teaching methods, teacher personality, and class composition.

Description: 90–item paper-pencil test measuring nine dimensions of classroom atmosphere: involvement, affiliation, teacher support, task orientation, competition, order and organization, rule clarity, teacher control, and innovation. These dimensions are grouped into four sets: relationship, personal development, system maintenance, and system change. Materials include four forms: The Real Form (Form R), which measures current perceptions of classroom atmosphere; the Ideal Form (Form I), which measures conceptions of the ideal classroom atmosphere; the Expectations Form (Form E), which measures expectations about a new classroom; and a 36–item Short Form (Form S). Forms I and E are not published, although reworded instructions and items are listed in the manual. Examiner required. Suitable for group use.

Untimed: Not available

Scoring: Examiner evaluated

Cost: Specimen set (user's guide, manual, scoring key, test booklet, answer sheet, profile) $15.00; 1987 manual $9.50

Publisher: Consulting Psychologists Press, Inc.

THE COLLEGE
CHARACTERISTICS INDEX (CCI)
George Stern and Associates

College student

Purpose: Measures the perceived press found in college environments in terms of the need-press paradigm of human behavior as conceptualized by Henry Murray. Used for student survey and research purposes.

Description: 300–item (long form) or 92–item (short form) paper-pencil true-false inventory assessing the atmosphere of a college in terms of 30 scales reflecting the 30 basic need scales established on the Stern Activities Index (AI). The test items refer to curriculum, teaching and classroom activities, rules, regulations, policies, student organizations, activities, interests, features of the campus, services and facilities, and relationships among students and faculty. The long form provides scores on the 30 basic press scales (10 items per scale), 11 first-order dimensions (aspiration level, intellectual climate, student dignity, academic climate, academic achievement, self-expression, group life, academic organization, social form, play-work, and vocational climate), and three second-order dimensions (intellectual climate, non-intellectual climate, and impulse control).

The short form provides scores on 11 first-order dimensions and three second-order dimensions. Self-administered. Suitable for group use.

Untimed: Long form 40 minutes; short form 20 minutes

Scoring: Examiner evaluated; may be computer scored

Cost: Test booklet $0.50; answer sheet $0.10; profile form $0.10; technical manual $7.50; prices for computer scoring and analysis available on request

Publisher: FAAX Corporation

COMMUNITY COLLEGE GOALS
INVENTORY (CCGI)
*Research Staff of
Educational Testing Service*

Adolescent, adult
College students

Purpose: Assesses the educational goals of community colleges. Used to establish priorities and to provide direction to present and future planning.

Description: 90–item paper-pencil test assessing the educational goals of community colleges. The 20 goal areas are divided into two types, outcome goals and process goals. The outcome goals are academic development, intellectual orientation, individual personal development, humanism/altruism, cultural/aesthetic awareness, traditional religiousness, vocational preparation, advanced training, research, meeting local needs, public service, social egalitarianism, and social criticism/activism. The process goals are freedom, democratic governance, community, intellectual/aesthetic environment, innovation, off-campus learning, and accountability/efficiency. The inventory is distributed to a random sample of students, faculty, and administrators at community colleges. Materials include space for 20 additional locally written goals. Self-administered. Suitable for group use.

Untimed: 45 minutes

Scoring: Computer scored

Cost: Booklet $0.65; processing $1.75

Publisher: Educational Testing Service

Information and availability unconfirmed; last verified in 1988.

COUNSELING SERVICES ASSESSMENT BLANK (CSAB)
Refer to page 753.

COUNTRY SCHOOL EXAMINATIONS
Michigan Department of Public Instruction

All ages

Purpose: Compares current elementary-school examinations of basic skills and competency with similar tests given in the early 20th century. Used to develop student, parent, and community appreciation for early standards of educational achievement.

Description: Paper-pencil collection of six reprints from historic educational achievement tests given in the early 1900s in a one-room schoolhouse in Michigan. One is the State of Michigan Examination Questions of 1921 for a city teachers' examination, and three are the State of Michigan Examination Questions used in 1919, 1920, and 1921 for eighth-grade graduation. The other two are the Michigan Winter Term Examination of 1913 and the Michigan Fall Term Examination of 1914, for Grades 1–8. Self-administered. Suitable for group use.

Untimed: 45 minutes

Scoring: Examiner evaluated

Cost: Specimen set (includes all examinations) $8.95; 25 individual test booklets $8.75

Publisher: Research Concepts

Information and availability unconfirmed; last verified in 1987.

EARLY CHILDHOOD ENVIRONMENT RATING SCALE
Thelma Harms and Richard M. Clifford

Adult

Purpose: Evaluates the adequacy of preschool child care settings. Used to assess class day care, Headstart, nursery school, and kindergarten programs.

Description: 37–item paper-pencil test in which the examiner rates child-care environments in terms of use of space, materials and experiences to enhance child development, and daily schedule and level of supervision provided. A room-by-room evaluation covers routines for the personal care of the children, room furnishing and display, language-reasoning experiences, fine- and gross-motor activities, creative activities, social development activities, and adult needs. Materials include a rating scale book and a scoring sheet. Examiner required. Not suitable for group use.

Untimed: Not available

Scoring: Examiner evaluated

Cost: Rating scale $7.95; 30 additional scoring sheets $6.95

Publisher: Teachers College Press

EFFECTIVE SCHOOL BATTERY (ESB)
Gary D. Gottfredson

Adolescent
Grades 7–12

Purpose: Assesses the school environment of middle, junior, and senior high schools. Used by administrators, board members, and teachers to identify excellence, diagnose problems, plan and develop programs, monitor progress, and research specific aspects of the school.

Description: Multiple-item paper-pencil survey used with students and teachers for determining perceptions about school climate and characteristics of students and teachers in the school. Results describe 34 specific aspects of school climate and student and teacher characteristics. Four profiles that describe the school and can be used to compare any school to other schools are produced. Examiner required. Suitable for group use.

Untimed: 50 minutes

Scoring: Computer scored

Cost: Introductory kit (user's manual, coordinator's manual, survey administrator's instructions, one each of student and teacher survey booklets, answer sheets) $25.00; user's manual $20.00

Publisher: Psychological Assessment Resources, Inc.

THE HIGH SCHOOL CHARACTERISTICS INDEX (HSCI) AND THE ELEMENTARY AND SECONDARY SCHOOL INDEX (ESI)
George Stern and Associates

Child, adolescent

Purpose: Measures the psychological characteristics of the academic environments of elementary and secondary schools in terms of the need-press paradigm of human behavior as conceptualized by Henry Murray. Used for student survey and research purposes.

Description: 300–item (HSCI) and 61–item (ESI) paper-pencil true-false inventories assessing the atmosphere of elementary and secondary schools along 30 basic press scales reflecting the 30 basic need scales established on the Stern Activities Index (AI). Both scales provide seven first-order scores (intellectual climate, expressiveness, group social life, personal dignity/supportiveness, achievement standards, orderliness/control, and peer group dominance) and three second-order dimensions (development press, orderliness/control, and peer group dominance). The 300–item HSCI contains 10 items for each of the press scales, which are identical in name and parallel in meaning to those used for the College Characteristics Index. Factor analysis was used to develop the ESI, which is essentially a short form of the HSCI. In addition to its use for secondary schools, the ESI can be used at the elementary level down to Grade 4. The HSCI should not be used below the secondary-school level. Self-administered. Suitable for group use.

Untimed: HSCI 40 minutes; ESI 15 minutes

Scoring: Examiner evaluated; may be computer scored

Cost: Test booklet $0.50; answer sheet $0.10; profile form $0.10; technical manual $7.50; prices for computer scoring and analysis available on request

Publisher: FAAX Corporation

INSTITUTIONAL FUNCTIONING INVENTORY
Research Staff at Educational Testing Services and Earl J. McGrath

Adult

Purpose: Evaluates functioning of educational institutions. Used in self-studies for accreditation, planning, and research.

Description: 132–item paper-pencil test assessing 11 dimensions of institutional functioning: intellectual-aesthetic, extra-curriculum, freedom, human diversity, concern for undergraduate learning, democratic governance, meeting local needs, self-study and planning, concern for advanced knowledge, concern for innovation, and institutional esprit. The inventory is distributed to a random sample of college community members, including the faculty, administration, and students. Self-administered. Suitable for group use. Available in French for Canadian institutions.

Untimed: 45 minutes

Scoring: Computer scored

Cost: Reusable faculty booklet $0.50; reusable student booklets $0.35; answer sheet $0.10 each

Publisher: Educational Testing Service

Information and availability unconfirmed; last verified in 1988.

INSTITUTIONAL GOALS INVENTORY (IGI)
Research Staff of Educational Testing Service

Adolescent, adult College students

Purpose: Assesses the educational goals of educational institutions. Used to establish priorities and to provide direction to present and future planning.

Description: 90–item paper-pencil test assessing the educational goals of educational institutions. The 20 goal areas are divided into two types, outcome goals and process goals. The outcome goals are academic development, intellectual orientation, individual personal development, humanism/altruism, cultural/aesthetic awareness, traditional religiousness, vocational preparation, advanced training, research, meeting local needs, public service, social egalitarianism, and social criticism/activism. The process goals are freedom, democratic governance, community, intellectual/aesthetic environment, innovation, off-campus learning, and accountability/efficiency. The inventory is distributed to a random sample of students, faculty, and administrators at educational institutions. Materials include space for 20 additional locally written goals. Self-administered. Suitable for group use. Available in French (for Canadian universities) and Spanish.

Untimed: 45 minutes

Scoring: Computer scored

Cost: Booklet $0.65; processing $1.75

Publisher: Educational Testing Service

Information and availability unconfirmed; last verified in 1988.

THE INSTRUCTIONAL ENVIRONMENT SCALE (TIES)
James E. Ysseldyke and Sandra L. Christenson

School administrators

Purpose: Analyzes a student's instructional environment. Used to identify the student's instructional needs and plan instructional interventions in order to improve the student's instructional outcome.

Description: Paper-pencil system utilizing teacher and student interviews and observations to assess 12 components of a student's instructional environment: instructional presentation, classroom environment, teacher expectations, cognitive emphasis, motivational techniques, relevant practice, academic engaged time, informed feedback, adaptive instruction, progress evaluation, instructional planning, and student understanding. Self-administered. Not suitable for group use.

Untimed: Not available

Scoring: Examiner evaluated

Cost: Complete kit (manual, 25 instructional rating forms, 25 summary/profile sheets, 25 data record forms, storage box) $54.00

Publisher: PRO-ED

LIGHT'S RETENTION SCALE (LRS)
Refer to page 743.

PARENT OPINION INVENTORY
National Study of School Evaluation

Adult

Purpose: Evaluates parents' opinions of their children's school and its programs. Provides an opportunity for parents to make direct recommendations. Used by school personnel to make decisions regarding program development, policy formulation, administrative organization, faculty development, and community relations. Also used as part of a complete school evaluation process.

Description: 55–item paper-pencil multiple-choice opinion survey consisting of two parts. Part A contains 51 multiple-choice items assessing parent opinion of various aspects of the school. Part B contains four open-ended items constructed for parents to make recommendations for school improvement. The Administrator's Manual describes the development of the instrument, provides instructions for administering the inventory, and contains a single copy of both Parts A and B. A seventh-grade reading level is required. This version is the 1988 revised edition of the Parent Opinion Inventory. The inventory may be administered independently or in conjunction with the Student Opinion Inventory, the Teacher Opinion Inventory, or as part of a complete school evaluation program. Individuals with physical, visual, or hearing impairments may complete the test with the assistance of a non-impaired individual. A computer scoring service is available from the Bureau of Evaluative Studies and Testing, Indiana University, Bloomington, IN 47405 (812) 335–1595. Self-administered. Suitable for group use.

Untimed: Varies

Scoring: Computer scored; may be machine scored; may be self-scored

Cost: 25 copies Part A $4.00; 25 copies Part B $3.00; Administrator's Manual $3.00

Publisher: National Study of School Evaluation

Information and availability unconfirmed; last verified in 1988.

PERFORMANCE LEVELS OF A SCHOOL PROGRAM SURVEY (PLSPS)
Refer to page 857.

THE PURDUE TEACHER EVALUATION SCALE (PTES)
Refer to page 854.

SCHOOL CLIMATE INVENTORY
Larry A. Braskamp and Martin L. Maehr

Grades 3 and above　

Purpose: Assesses school culture. Used by elementary and secondary school administrators to assess student and teacher attitudes toward the school and its instructional learning climate.

Description: Multiple-item paper-pencil multiple-choice test assessing four dimensions of school culture: excellence, recognition, power, and affiliation. The test is available in two forms, teacher (60 items) and student (22 items). The teacher version contains additional scales measuring strength of culture, degree of commitment or loyalty to the school, and job satisfaction. Items for the entry were adapted from SPECTRUM (see separate entry). Examiner/self-administered. Suitable for group use.

Untimed: Teacher version 15 minutes; student version 5–10 minutes

Scoring: Computer scored

Cost: Contact publisher

Publisher: MetriTech, Inc.

SCHOOL PRINCIPAL JOB FUNCTIONS INVENTORY (SP-JFI)
Melany E. Baehr, Frances M. Burns, R. Bruce McPherson, and Columbus Salley

Adult　

Purpose: Assesses the relative importance of functions performed in a particular type of principalship and the principal's ability to perform the functions. Used to clarify a school principal's job responsibilities and to diagnose individual and group training needs.

Description: Multiple-item paper-pencil inventory assessing the relative importance of 17 basic functions for overall successful performance in a given principalship: personal handling of student adjustment problems, organizations and extracurricular activities, individual student development, utilization of specialized staff, evaluation of teacher performance, collegial contacts, racial and ethnic group problems, troubleshooting and problem solving, community involvement and support, dealing with gangs, curriculum development, instructional materials, staffing, working with unions, working with central office, safety regulations, and fiscal control. Items are rated by the incumbent principal. The inventory also may be used to have incumbents rate their relative ability to perform these functions. Separate forms are available for rating the importance of various functions and for self-rating of the incumbent's abilities. Examiner required. Suitable for group use.

Untimed: 40–60 minutes

Scoring: Hand key; may be computer scored

Cost: Specimen set $8.00; 25 test booklets $20.00

Publisher: London House, Inc.

SMALL COLLEGE GOALS INVENTORY (SCGI)
Research Staff of Educational Testing Service

Adolescent, adult
College students

Purpose: Assesses the educational goals of small colleges. Used to establish priorities and to provide direction for present and future planning.

Description: 90–item paper-pencil test assessing the educational goals of small colleges. The 20 goal areas are divided into two types, outcome goals and process goals. The outcome goals are academic development, intellectual orientation, individual personal development, humanism/altruism, cultural/aesthetic awareness, traditional religiousness, vocational preparation, advanced training, research, meeting local needs, public service, social egalitarianism, and social criticism/activism. The process goals are freedom, democratic governance, community, intellectual/aesthetic environment, innovation, off-campus learning, and accountability/efficiency. The inventory is distributed to a random sample of students, faculty, and administrators. Materials include space for 20 additional locally written goals. Self-administered. Suitable for group use.

Untimed: 45 minutes
Scoring: Computer scored
Cost: Booklets $0.65; processing $1.75
Publisher: Educational Testing Service
Information and availability unconfirmed; last verified in 1988.

STUDENT OUTCOMES INFORMATION SERVICE (SOIS) STUDENT OUTCOMES QUESTIONNAIRES

College students

Purpose: Collects, analyzes, and evaluates the experiences, goals, accomplishments, and attitudes of college students. Used by college and university administrators to study retention, review program utilization, assess trends in needs for student services, and aid unit-level decision making and planning.

Description: Series of six paper-pencil multiple-item instruments, administered to college students at six intervals before and after college, covering experiences, goals, accomplishments, and attitudes. Each questionnaire is available in a 2–year and 4–year version. Materials include a

manual, data processing, and questionnaire analysis. Self-administered. Suitable for group use.

Untimed: Not available
Scoring: Computer scored
Cost: Contact publisher
Publisher: The College Board

STUDENT REACTIONS TO COLLEGE: FOUR YEAR COLLEGE EDITION (SRC/4)
Research Staff of Educational Testing Service

Adolescent, adult
College students

Purpose: Assesses the needs and concerns of students enrolled in four-year colleges. Used in institutional self-assessment for developing programs and services for students.

Description: 150–item paper-pencil test assessing four dimensions of student concerns: processes of instruction, program planning, administrative affairs, and out-of-class activities. These four dimensions are divided further into such areas as content of courses, appropriateness of course work to occupational goals, satisfaction with teaching procedures, student-faculty relations, educational and occupational decisions, effectiveness of advisors and counselors, registration, regulations, availability of classes, housing, employment, financial aid, and satisfaction with campus environment. The test is distributed to random samples of students. Self-administered. Suitable for group use.

Untimed: 50 minutes
Scoring: Computer scored
Cost: Booklet $0.65; processing $1.75
Publisher: Educational Testing Service
Information and availability unconfirmed; last verified in 1988.

STUDENT REACTIONS TO COLLEGE: TWO YEAR COLLEGE EDITION (SRC/2)
Research Staff of Educational Testing Service

Adolescent, adult
College students

Purpose: Assesses the needs and concerns of students enrolled in two-year colleges. Used in institutional self-assessment for developing programs and services for students.

Description: 150–item paper-pencil test assessing four dimensions of student concerns: processes of instruction, program planning, administrative affairs, and out-of-class activities. These four dimensions are divided further into such areas as content of courses, appropriateness of course work to occupational goals, satisfaction with teaching procedures, student-faculty relations, educational and occupational decisions, effectiveness of advisors and counselors, registration, regulations, availability of classes, housing, employment, financial aid, and satisfaction with campus environment. The test is distributed to a random sample of students. Self-administered. Suitable for group use.

Untimed: 50 minutes

Scoring: Computer scored

Cost: Booklet $0.65; processing $1.75

Publisher: Educational Testing Service

Information and availability unconfirmed; last verified in 1988.

TEACHER OPINION INVENTORY
Refer to page 859.

THINKING ABOUT MY SCHOOL
Joanne Rand Whitmore

Child
Grades 4–6

Purpose: Measures students' perceptions of their school environment and their feelings about their school.

Description: 47–item paper-pencil questionnaire measuring students' perceptions of their school. The test is used to increase teachers' understanding of pupils as a group and as individuals, to stimulate classroom analysis of problems and discussions of attitudes and behavior at school, and to provide student government leaders or other groups with information to study school problems. Examiner required. Suitable for group use.

Untimed: Varies

Scoring: Examiner evaluated

Cost: Complete kit $19.95

Publisher: D.O.K. Publishers, Inc.

TROUBLE-SHOOTING CHECKLIST (TSC) FOR HIGHER EDUCATIONAL SETTINGS
B.A. Manning

Adult

Purpose: Measures organizational variables that predict an educational institution's potential for successfully adopting innovations. Identifies areas of acceptance and resistance. Used by personnel involved in implementing innovations in higher educational settings.

Description: 100–item paper-pencil questionnaire assessing an institution's potential for adopting innovations along the following five scales: organizational climate, organizational staff, communications, innovative experience, and students. The scores on the five scales provide a profile of an institution's particular strengths and weaknesses with respect to the adoption process. Self-administered. Suitable for group use.

Untimed: Varies

Scoring: Examiner evaluated

Cost: Instrument and manual $2.50

Publisher: Distributed by ERIC Document Reproduction Service

Information and availability unconfirmed; last verified in 1987.

TROUBLE-SHOOTING CHECKLIST (TSC) FOR SCHOOL-BASED SETTINGS
B.A. Manning

Adult

Purpose: Measures organizational variables that predict a school's potential for successfully adopting and implementing educational innovations. Identifies areas of acceptance and resistance. Used by school personnel involved in implementing educational innovations.

Description: Multiple-item paper-pencil checklist assessing a school's potential for adopting innovations along the following seven scales: communication patterns, innovative experience, school-based staff, central administration, relations with the community, organizational climate, and students. The scores on the seven scales provide a profile of a school's particular strengths and weaknesses with respect to the adoption process. Self-administered. Suitable for group use.

Untimed: Varies

Scoring: Examiner evaluated

Cost: Instrument and manual $2.50

Publisher: Distributed by ERIC Document Reproduction Service

Information and availability unconfirmed; last verified in 1987.

UNIVERSITY RESIDENCE ENVIRONMENT SCALE (URES)
Rudolf H. Moos and Marvin S. Gerst

College students, adult

Purpose: Assesses the social environment of university residence halls and dormitories.

Description: 100–item paper-pencil true-false test of 10 dimensions of the social climate of college dormitories: involvement, emotional support, independence, traditional social orientation, competition, academic achievement, intellectuality, order and organization, student influence, and innovation. Materials include the Real Form (Form R), which measures current perceptions of a residence; the 40–item Short Form (Form S); the Expectations Form (Form E), which measures expectations of a new residence; and the Ideal Form (Form I), which measures conceptions of an ideal residence hall environment. Forms I and E are not in published form, but items and instructions appear in the Appendix of the URES manual. One in a series of nine Social Climate scales. Examiner required. Suitable for group use.

Untimed: Not available

Scoring: Hand key; examiner evaluated

Cost: 25 reusable tests $8.50; 50 answer sheets $5.50; 50 profiles $3.75; key $1.75; manual $15.00

Publisher: Consulting Psychologists Press, Inc.

Sensorimotor Skills

ADOLESCENT AND ADULT PSYCHOEDUCATIONAL PROFILE (AAPEP)
Refer to page 660.

ANN ARBOR LEARNING INVENTORY AND REMEDIATION PROGRAM
Barbara Meister Vitale and Waneta Bullock

Child
Grades K–8

Purpose: Evaluates the central processing and perceptual skills necessary for reading, writing, and spelling. Identifies learning difficulties and deficits and suggests appropriate remedial strategies. Used to establish IEPs.

Description: Multiple-item task-performance oral-response and paper-pencil test measuring the following central processing skills: visual discrimination, visual memory, auditory discrimination, auditory memory, and modality strength (auditory or visual). Also identifies specific visual and auditory perceptual problems, such as rotations, closure, omissions, directionality, and sequencing problems. Test items are presented in order of natural cognitive development, beginning with pictures, proceeding to objects and geometric forms, and finally to letters, words, and phrases. Tasks involve listening, manipulating, showing, matching, visualizing, telling, and writing. In addition to information on central processing skills and perceptual abilities, results also provide objective data on developmental levels for prereading readiness, precomputational skills, kinesthetic and motor skills, and comprehension and critical thinking. Available for three levels: Level A (Grades K–1), Level B (Grades 2–4), and Level C (Grades 5–8). Manual provides remedial suggestions for immediate classroom use. Examiner required. Suitable for group use.

Untimed: Varies

Scoring: Examiner evaluated

Cost: Teacher's manual for Levels A-C each $8.00; 10 student booklets for Levels A-C $10.00; stimulus cards for Level C (optional) $8.00

Publisher: Academic Therapy Publications

BASIC VISUAL-MOTOR ASSOCIATION TEST
James Battle

Child
Grades 1–9

Purpose: Measures visual short-term memory. Predicts students' skills in reading, spelling, and arithmetic. Used by classroom teachers, resource teachers, school psychologists, and remedial therapists.

Description: 120–item paper-pencil symbol-copying test in two forms assessing the following visual-motor skills: recall of visual symbols, visual sequencing ability, visual association skills, visual-motor ability, visual integrative ability, and symbol-integration skills. Students are asked to copy 60 symbols (uppercase letters) on Form A and 60 symbols (lowercase letters) on Form B. Conversion tables provide percentile ranks and T-scores derived from raw scores. Examiner required. Suitable for group use in Grades 2–9 and for individual use in Grade 1.

Timed: 3 minutes per form

Scoring: Examiner evaluated

Cost: Test kit (manual, 25 forms A and B, scoring acetate) $19.50; specimen set (manual, sample test form) $12.50

Publisher: Special Child Publications

Information and availability unconfirmed; last verified in 1988.

BENDER-PURDUE REFLEX TEST AND TRAINING MANUAL
Miriam Bender

Child—Ages 6–12

Purpose: Determines the presence and/or level of symmetric tonic neck reflex activity in children who are suspected of having learning disabilities. Used to diag-

nose whether the response interferes with learning and to plan motor-training programs.

Description: Six-task motor performance test in which the child participates in a variety of movement tasks (such as rocking and creeping backward and forward on hands and knees) as the examiner physically resists the student's progress from varying points of leverage. Scoring is based on the number of deviations from a standard, "perfect" posture and pattern of locomotion. Materials include illustrated instructions for a motor-training program and a book of spirit masters for parents' use at home. The test is also available on videotape. Examiner required. Not suitable for group use.

Untimed: 20 minutes

Scoring: Examiner evaluated

Cost: Manual $12.00; 25 recording forms $8.00; 12 spirit masters $8.00; kit $22.00

Publisher: United Educational Services, Inc.

BENDER VISUAL MOTOR GESTALT TEST
Refer to page 96.

BENTON REVISED VISUAL RETENTION TEST
Refer to page 96.

BRUININKS-OSERETSKY TEST OF MOTOR PROFICIENCY
Robert H. Bruininks

Child, adolescent—Ages 4½–14½

Purpose: Determines a child's level of motor proficiency. Used for educational placement, assessing neurological development, and evaluating motor training programs.

Description: 46–item physical-performance and paper-pencil battery grouped into eight subtests: Running Speed and Agility, Balance, Bilateral Coordination, Strength, Upper-Limb Coordination, Response Speed, Visual-Motor Control, and Upper-Limb Speed and Dexterity. The examiner records the child's performance on given tasks, and the child uses a student booklet for cutting and paper-pencil responses. Two forms are available: the complete battery and a short form. The complete battery yields three scores: Gross Motor Composite (large muscles of the shoulders, trunk, and legs), Fine Motor Composite (small muscles of the fingers, hand, and forearms), and Battery Composite (general motor performance). Subtest and composite scores can be converted to age-based standard scores, percentile ranks, stanines, and age equivalents. The short form of the test includes 14 items from the complete battery to yield a single score of general motor proficiency, which can be converted to an age-based standard score, percentile rank, and stanine. Materials include a manual, 25 individual record forms, a sample of the alternate Short Form, 25 student booklets, and a set of testing equipment, all in a metal case. Examiner required. Not suitable for group use.

Untimed: Short form 15–20 minutes; complete battery 45–60 minutes

Scoring: Examiner evaluated

Cost: Complete battery $295.00

Publisher: American Guidance Service

THE BURY INFANT CHECK
Refer to page 536.

DEGANGI-BERK TEST OF SENSORY INTEGRATION (TSI)
Georgia A. DeGangi and Ronald A. Berk

Child—Ages 3–5

Purpose: Measures overall sensory integration in preschool children. Screens for young children with delays in sensory, motor, and perceptual skills in order to facilitate intervention programs.

Description: 36–item performance test of three subdomains of sensory integration: postural control, bilateral motor integration, and reflex integration. The examiner rates the child's response to each item on a numerical scale indicating abnormal to normal development. Examiner required. Not suitable for group use.

Untimed: 30 minutes

Scoring: Examiner required

Cost: Complete kit (test materials, 25 star design sheets, 25 protocol booklets, manual, and carrying case) $42.75

Publisher: Western Psychological Services

DENVER HANDWRITING ANALYSIS (DHA)
Peggy L. Anderson

Child
Grades 3–8

Purpose: Assesses the general quality of a student's cursive handwriting and provides detailed information related to handwriting instruction.

Description: Multiple-item paper-pencil test consisting of five areas: near-point copying, writing the alphabet from memory, far-point copying, manuscript-cursive transition, and dictation. Each subtest yields a Mastery Level score that allows intra-individual comparisons to be made across varying task formats. The DHA Scoring Profile includes a subskill analysis section that classifies errors by type and a performance analysis section that yields more general information about spatial organization, speed, slant, and appearance. The manual includes interpretive guidelines, samples of written reports summarizing student performance, and remedial suggestions related to each subtest. Examiner required. Suitable for group use.

Untimed: 20–60 minutes

Scoring: Examiner evaluated

Cost: Test kit (manual and wall chart, 25 record forms, 25 scoring profiles, 50 remedial checklists, in vinyl folder) $32.00

Publisher: Academic Therapy Publications

DEVELOPMENTAL TEST OF VISUAL-MOTOR INTEGRATION (VMI)
Refer to page 101.

EARLY LEARNING ASSESSMENT AND DEVELOPMENT
Refer to page 542.

EARLY SCREENING INVENTORY (ESI)
Refer to page 543.

FOSTER MAZES

Adult

Purpose: Measures nonverbal intelligence.

Description: Task-performance test assessing spatial orientation and spatial reasoning ability. A blindfolded individual must find his way out of a grooved maze pattern using a stylus or pencil. Mazes are presented in the form of grooves etched into 8½″ x 11″ boards, which are available in two equivalent forms, A and B. The manual provides scoring guidelines. Examiner required. Not suitable for group use.

Untimed: Varies

Scoring: Examiner evaluated

Cost: Maze (specify form A or B) $97.50

Publisher: Stoelting Co.

FROSTIG MOVEMENT SKILLS TEST BATTERY (EXPERIMENTAL EDITION)
Russel E. Orpet

Child—Ages 6–12

Purpose: Evaluates the development of sensorimotor skills in children. Diagnoses areas of sensorimotor development requiring special attention.

Description: 12 task-performance tests providing scaled scores on five factors: hand-eye coordination, strength, balance, visually guided movement, and flexibility. Norms by sex are provided for normally developing children ages 6–12. The manual provides a rationale for the battery, statistical information, and instructions for administration and scoring. The equipment required for the test can be assembled or built from specifications provided in the manual or purchased in the standard equipment kit, which includes the manual, 50 recording sheets, wooden blocks, block transfer kit, bean bags, floor targets, carpenter's rule, and brackets for walking board. The equipment kit does not include the two 12–foot 2x4s and stopwatch that are required. Examiner required. Suitable for group use.

Untimed: Single child 20 minutes; group of 3 or 4 45 minutes

Scoring: Examiner evaluated

Cost: Standard equipment kit $99.00; manual, including sample recording sheet $5.50; 50 recording sheets $6.00

Publisher: Consulting Psychologists Press, Inc.

GIBSON SPIRAL MAZE
Refer to page 104.

HUGHES BASIC GROSS MOTOR ASSESSMENT (HBGMA)
Jeanne E. Hughes

Child—Ages 5 years, 6 months–12 years, 5 months

Purpose: Detects motor problems in children with minor motor dysfunction. Used to identify children needing in-depth physical therapy or physical education. Also suitable for use with mentally, visually, physically, and hearing-impaired children. The test should not be used to assess developmental delay.

Description: 8 criterion-referenced balance-locomotor and eye-hand coordination tasks measuring the quality of movement of basic gross-motor skills normally present in 5– to 6–year-old children. Materials required (but not provided) are six bean bags, two playground balls, tape, a stopwatch, and a teacher-made item. Scores are interpreted on the basis of performance and are not to be used as developmental age scores. An 88–page manual contains detailed directions for administration and interpretation as well as drawings that interpret the subtests; a bibliography supporting rationale underlying the HBGMA development; statistical information regarding the standardization and norming procedures used with 1,260 regular school children ages 5 years, 6 months to 12 years, 5 months; and details of both the reliability and the validity studies. Examiner required. Not suitable for group use.

Untimed: Varies

Timed: Not available

Scoring: Examiner evaluated

Cost: Manual $12.00

Publisher: Jeanne E. Hughes, Ph.D.; distributed exclusively by G.E. Miller, Inc.

Information and availability unconfirmed; last verified in 1988.

LATERAL AWARENESS AND DIRECTIONALITY TEST (LAD)
August J. Mauser and Joseph F. Loackavitch

Child, adolescent Grades 1-12

Purpose: Determines lateral awareness and directional skills of elementary and secondary school children. Used to identify high-risk, medium-risk, and low-risk students for possible program intervention.

Description: 35-illustration paper-pencil test measuring right-left labeling ability at two levels: lateral awareness and directionality. Items range from single to double commands that require either a unilateral, contralateral, or cross diagonal response. Also measured are such spatial concepts as same direction, 180-degree inversion, 90-degree rotation, and person-to-person orientation. Materials consist of test plates, recording forms, a scoring template, and a manual, which includes information on screening, diagnosis, and potential program modification. Examiner required. Suitable for group use.

Untimed: 20 minutes

Scoring: Hand key

Cost: Test kit $43.00

Publisher: United Educational Services, Inc.

LINCOLN-OSERETSKY MOTOR DEVELOPMENT SCALE
William Sloan

Child, adolescent

Purpose: Measures motor development of children. Used to supplement information obtained from other techniques concerning intellectual, social, emotional, and physical development.

Description: 36-item task assessment of a child's motor development. The areas covered are static coordination, dynamic coordination, speed of movement and asynkinesia (finger dexterity), eye-hand coordination, and gross activity of the hands, arms, legs, and trunk. Both unilateral and bilateral tasks are involved. The test items, arranged in order of difficulty, include walking backwards, crouching on tiptoe, standing on one foot, touching nose, touching fingertips, tapping rhythmically with feet and fingers, jumping over a rope, finger movement, standing heel to toe, close and open hands alternately, making dots, catching a ball, making a ball, winding thread, balancing a rod crosswise, describing circles in the air, tapping, placing coins and matchsticks, jump and turn about, putting matchsticks in a box, winding thread while walking, throwing a ball, sorting matchsticks, drawing lines, cutting circle, putting coins in a box, tracing mazes, balancing on tiptoe, tapping with feet and fingers, jumping and touching heels, tapping feet and describing circles, standing on one foot, jumping and clapping, balancing on tiptoe and opening and closing hands, and balancing a rod vertically. The manual includes a complete analysis of test results obtained from boys and girls ages 6–14 for each item of the scale; percentages passing each item at each age level; correlation of item-scores with age; percentile norms of both sexes, separately and combined; and odd-even reliability for boys and girls. Examiner required. Not suitable for group use.

Untimed: Not available

Scoring: Examiner evaluated

Cost: Complete kit (test materials, 50 record blanks, manual) $125.00

Publisher: Stoelting Co.

MEMORY-FOR-DESIGNS TEST (MFD)

Refer to page 111.

MINNESOTA SPATIAL RELATIONS TEST

American Guidance Service
Test Division

Adolescent, adult—Ages 16 and older

Purpose: Assesses an individual's ability to visualize spatial relations. Used for vocational education, rehabilitation counseling, and personnel selection.

Description: Manual test measuring an individual's accurate perception of relationships and speed in manipulating three-dimensional objects. The test requires four form boards, A-B and C-D paired. Each board has a different arrangement of 58 cutouts, into which blocks of various shapes are fitted. The individual transfers blocks from Board A to the proper places on Board B and then repeats the process with Boards C and D. The kit includes four board blocks, two carrying cases, 50 record forms, and a manual. Time scores are converted to standard scores and percentile ranks, and error scores are expressed as a percentile rank. Examiner required. Not suitable for group use.

Timed: 10–20 minutes
Scoring: Examiner evaluated
Cost: Complete $650.00
Publisher: American Guidance Service

MKM PICTURE ARRANGEMENT TEST (PAT)

Leland Michael and James W. King

Child
Grades K–6

Purpose: Measures the extent to which the subject places information and objects in the left-right sequence common to the United States. Useful in diagnosing poor reading skills and learning disabilities related to directionality problems.

Description: 5–item visual-manual sequencing test in which a poem entitled "A Great Gray Elephant" is read to the subject. Five pictures illustrating the poem are placed before the subject in random order, and as the poem is read, the subject is asked to place the pictures in the order in which they occur in the poem. The examiner records the subject's actions. A left-right movement is expected. Examiner required. Not suitable for group use.

Untimed: 3 minutes
Scoring: Examiner evaluated
Cost: Complete kit (instruction sheet, 5 picture cards, 5 poems) $10.00
Publisher: MKM

MOTOR SKILLS INVENTORY (MSI)

John Aulenta

Child

Purpose: Evaluates the motor functioning of normal and handicapped preschool and primary-age children. Establishes motor functioning age levels and identifies children needing further evaluation. Used by trained diagnostic personnel as part of a comprehensive psychological or developmental evaluation.

Description: 85–item paper-pencil observational inventory assessing fine-motor (40 items) and gross-motor (45 items) skill development. Test items represent individual motor abilities (e.g., "lifts cup with handle" or "turns single pages in book"), which are scored "plus" or "minus" according to the child's success or failure at performing the described task. Test items for the two areas are presented in order of normal development. Basal and ceiling levels are established using a guideline of five consecutive successes or failures. Examiners are encouraged to utilize information from parental reports and the results of other tests in completing the inventory. Intended for use with children ages six months to seven years, the inventory also may be used with older handicapped children functioning within that developmental age range. Results of the inventory can contribute to the diagnosis of retardation, developmental language delays, learning disability, specific motor deficit, and general or specific developmental immaturities. It can also clarify developmental discrepancies among cognitive, linguistic, social, and motor areas. The manual includes directions for administration and interpretation of results. Examiner required. Not suitable for group use.

Untimed: 5–15 minutes

Scoring: Examiner evaluated

Cost: Complete test kit (manual, 15 administration booklets) $9.00; manual $5.00; 15 administration booklets $5.00

Publisher: Stoelting Co.

MOTOR-FREE VISUAL PERCEPTION TEST (MVPT)
Ronald R. Colarusso and Donald D. Hammill

Ages 4–8 and older individuals with motor problems

Purpose: Assesses visual perception in children and older individuals who have motor problems. Used for screening and diagnostic and research purposes, especially with individuals who are learning disabled, motorically impaired, physically handicapped, or mentally retarded.

Description: 36–item point-and-tell test in which the subject is shown a line drawing and asked to match the stimulus by pointing to one of a multiple-choice set of other drawings. Materials consist of test plates and recording forms. Instructions are reproduced in the test plates for convenience in administering the test. Examiner required. Not suitable for group use.

Untimed: 10 minutes

Scoring: Hand key

Cost: Manual $15.00; test plates $24.00; 50 recording forms $8.00

Publisher: Academic Therapy Publications

MUMA ASSESSMENT PROGRAM (MAP)—REVISED SECOND EDITION
Refer to page 554.

PEABODY DEVELOPMENTAL MOTOR SCALES AND ACTIVITY CARDS
M. Rhonda Folio and Rebecca R. Fewell

Child—Ages 0–83 months

Purpose: Assesses the motor development of children during the first seven years of life. Identifies children whose gross- or fine-motor skills are delayed or abnormal. Used to establish IEPs.

Description: Multiple-item task-performance test consisting of a comprehensive sequence of gross- and fine-motor skills from which the child's relative developmental skill level can be determined. The test may be used to analyze a wide range of skills identified as questionable by prior screening or to diagnose specific characteristics of a motor problem. Norms are provided for each skill category at each level and for the total test. The instructional program components include a tab-indexed card file of 170 gross-motor and 112 fine-motor activities referenced to the items on the test. These activity cards provide an instructional curriculum to fill developmental gaps, strengthen emerging skills, and set objectives for skills not yet attained. Examiner required. May be administered individually or to groups of children using a station-testing procedure.

Untimed: 20–30 minutes per scale

Scoring: Examiner evaluated

Cost: Test kit (manual, 15 scoring booklets, 282 activity cards, cubes, pegboard, pegs, formboard and shapes, bottle, beads and laces, box, dowel and string, etc.) $180.00

Publisher: DLM Teaching Resources

PHOTOELECTRIC ROTARY PURSUIT

Adolescent, adult—Ages 15 and older

Purpose: Measures general perceptual-motor learning across such parameters as handedness, transfer of training, and distribution of practice. Used for vocational evaluation, research, and classroom demonstration of learning principles.

Description: Manual nonverbal test in which the subject uses a rotary pursuit apparatus to follow a moving light around a pattern (square, circle, or triangle). The light moves in either a clockwise or counterclockwise direction at a fixed or variable speed for either a fixed time or a fixed number of revolutions. "On target" time, hits, and total test time are measured. Examiner required. Not suitable for group use.

Untimed: Time not standardized

Scoring: Examiner evaluated

Cost: Budget Photoelectric Rotary Pursuit (Model 30020) $620.00; Photoelectric Rotary Pursuit (Model 30014) $1,255.00; Basic accessory package (Model 30025) $350.00; Deluxe accessory package (Model 30028) $975.00

Publisher: Lafayette Instrument Company, Inc.

THE PREVERBAL ASSESSMENT-INTERVENTION PROFILE (P.A.I.P.)
Patricia Connard

All ages

Purpose: Assesses communication and motor performance of students and adults whose communication performance is between the developmental range of 0–9 months. Diagnoses communication needs and evaluates prelinguistic behavior of preverbal individuals.

Description: Multiple-item three-stage observational procedure for observing and reporting performance in a natural environment. The test assesses the sensori-motor domains of auditory, visual, vocal/oral, and motor in a manner that yields an individualized preverbal/motor assessment profile. The examiner records information supplied by parents, caregivers, and teachers; observes behaviors during eating, bathing, dressing, and playing; and presents structured tasks using spoons, mirrors, lights, spinning and pull toys, and so forth. The test, used primarily with severely retarded, profoundly retarded, or multihandicapped

individuals, can be adapted for stroke patients. Examiner required. Not suitable for group use.

Untimed: Not available

Scoring: Examiner evaluated

Cost: Complete kit $44.90

Publisher: PRO-ED

THE PRIMARY VISUAL MOTOR TEST
Mary R. Haworth

Mental ages 4–8

Purpose: Assesses visual-motor functioning in preschool and primary-grade children. Used as a rough measure of intellectual performance skills in deaf or speech-handicapped children.

Description: Multiple-task nonverbal test in which the examiner presents 16 geometrical and simple representational designs for the child to copy in designated rectangular spaces marked off on the test sheets. The test screens for reading-related difficulties, determines the extent of visual-motor deficiencies in retarded children, and assesses the general level of functioning in deaf or speech-handicapped children. Test data are also available on 130 psychotic children ages 6–12. The test must be administered by persons trained in test administration and interpretation. Suitable for group use. Examiner required.

Untimed: 10–15 minutes

Scoring: Examiner evaluated

Cost: Manual $45.00; test cards $10.50; 100 tests $16.50; 50 scoring forms $24.00

Publisher: The Psychological Corporation

Information and availability unconfirmed; last verified in 1988.

PURDUE PERCEPTUAL-MOTOR SURVEY (PPMS)
Eugene G. Roach and Newell C. Kephart

Child, adolescent
Grades PreK–8

Purpose: Identifies children with perceptual-motor disabilities by tracing a child's development to the point where developmental dysfunction occurs. Assists teachers in developing remedial programs.

Description: 22–item task assessment measuring laterality, directionality, and perceptual-motor matching skills. The walking board and jumping tests measure balance and posture. The body image and differentiation tests include naming 10 parts of the body, imitation of movements, obstacle course, the Krauss-Weber test, and angels in the snow. A chalkboard test for rhythmic writing, ocular control, and form perception measures perceptual-motor matching skills. Examiner required. Not suitable for group use.

Untimed: Varies

Scoring: Examiner evaluated

Cost: Manual $30.00; score forms $23.00

Publisher: The Psychological Corporation

Information and availability unconfirmed; last verified in 1988.

QUICK NEUROLOGICAL SCREENING TEST—REVISED (QNST)
Refer to page 120.

THE RAIL-WALKING TEST
Refer to page 120.

REACTION TIME TESTING

Ages 5 and older

Purpose: Measures the reaction time component of perceptual motor coordination. Used for psychological research, drug screening, reaction training, and vocational guidance.

Description: Manual nonverbal test in which the subject faces various stimulus presentations and trials incorporated with the stimulus-response device controlled by the examiner, who is seated across the table. The devices vary in resolution, stimulus presentation, and response requirements and test auditory or visual simple reaction time, visual discrimination reaction time, and reaction-movement time. Examiner required. Not suitable for group use.

Untimed: 1–15 minutes

Scoring: Examiner evaluated

Cost: Multi-choice Reaction time apparatus with Ready signal and digital $1/1000$ seconds (Model 63014) $990.00, with Voice activated RT Control (Model 63013) $1,345.00; Reaction/Movement timer digital $1/1000$ second (Model 63017) $1,450.00

Publisher: Lafayette Instrument Company, Inc.

RECEPTIVE-EXPRESSIVE OBSERVATION (REO)
Joan M. Smith

Ages 6–adult

Purpose: Assesses simple memory and memory coding across sensory channels: visual-motor, visual-vocal, auditory-vocal, and auditory-motor. Identifies student deficiencies in the perceptual areas addressed.

Description: Multiple-task test assessing performance in labeling, discrimination, sequencing, and short-term memory. Eighteen visual-vocal and 18 visual-motor cards are provided. The examiner reads each item to the subject, and the subject answers with auditory-vocal and auditory-motor responses. Items are increased progressively in length in each of the four cross-channel perceptual areas. Responses are observed and entered on the recording form. Conversion tables are provided for scores. The test manual includes suggestions for remediation. Examiner required. Not suitable for group use.

Untimed: 15 minutes

Scoring: Examiner evaluated

Cost: Test kit (manual, two sets of visual-motor and visual-vocal cards, reproducible response form) $45.00

Publisher: Learning Time Products

RILEY MOTOR PROBLEMS INVENTORY
Refer to page 123.

ROEDER MANIPULATIVE APTITUDE TEST
Wesley S. Roeder

Adolescent, adult—Ages 15 and older

Purpose: Assesses eye, hand, and finger coordination. Used to screen employees and trainees for jobs requiring eye-hand coordination, including typing, mechanics, radio/TV repair, machinists, draftsmen, and machine operators.

Description: Task-performance test measuring speed and dexterity in executing certain movements with the hands, arms, and fingers, particularly thrusting and twisting movements. Four tasks are provided using the following materials: one styrene-plexiglass board with T-Bar, four trays containing 10 sockets each, and a supply of rods, caps, washers, and nuts. Part 1 requires the subject to insert and twist a rod into a socket on the board and place a cap on the top of each rod, completing as many assemblies as possible in 3 minutes. Part 2 involves alternately sliding a washer and nut on each side of the T-bar as quickly as possible for 40 seconds. Part 3 repeats the washer/nut task, using the left hand only. Part 4 repeats the washer/nut task with the right hand only. Examiner required. Suitable for group use (limited only by availability of materials).

Timed: 5 minutes

Scoring: Hand key

Cost: Board and parts (Model 32026) $195.00; 50 score sheets (Model 32026 RB) $10.50

Publisher: Lafayette Instrument Company, Inc.

SENSORY INTEGRATION AND PRAXIS TESTS (SIPT)
A. Jean Ayres

Child—Ages 4–8.11

Purpose: Measures sensory integration processes that underlie learning problems and emotional disorders. Used for analyzing sensory integrative dysfunction and planning treatment strategies.

Description: Seventeen tests assessing aspects of sensory processing in the vestibular, proprioceptive, kinesthetic, tactile, and visual systems as well as the behavior and learning disorders (including learning disabilities, emotional disorders, and minimal brain dysfunction) associated with inadequate integration of sensory input from these systems. The subtests are Space Visualization, Figure-Ground Perception, Manual Form Perception, Kinesthesia, Finger Identification, Graphesthesia, Localization of Tactile Stimuli, Praxis on Verbal Command, Design Copying, Constructional Praxis, Postural Praxis, Oral Praxis, Sequencing Praxis, Bilateral Motor Coordination, Standing and Walking Balance, Motor Accuracy, and Postrotary Nystagmus.

Computer scoring and interpretation are available only through Western Psychological Services. Users record examinees' performances on WPS TEST REPORT answer sheets and send them to WPS, where they are scored within 8 hours of receipt. WPS immediately returns an interpretive report that provides the total score for each subtest and specific content scores for many of the subtests. In addition, the WPS ChromaGraph for SIPT provides an eight-color single-page visual summary of major testing and statistical results, including deviant scores, score patterns expected for both dysfunctional children and those who exhibit average and superior patterns of sensory integration, and score comparisons to six prototypic diagnostic groups: generalized sensory integrative dysfunction, visuo- and somatodyspraxia, dyspraxia on verbal command, low average bilateral integration and sequencing, low average sensory integration and praxis, and high average sensory integration and praxis. The test is a validated revision of the Southern California Sensory Integration Tests (SCSIT). Examiner required. Not suitable for group use.

Untimed: Varies

Scoring: Computer scored

Cost: Set $985.00

Publisher: Western Psychological Services

THE SOUTHERN CALIFORNIA ORDINAL SCALES OF DEVELOPMENT
California State Department of Education: Diagnostic School for the Neurologically Handicapped, Southern California

All ages

Purpose: Assesses all levels of Piagetian development from sensorimotor through formal operations. Used especially with multihandicapped, developmentally delayed, and learning disordered children for comparative assessments, ability grouping, research, and IEP development.

Description: Six separately bound scales measuring the quality of the child's sensory and information processing in the following areas: cognition, communication, social-affective behavior, practical abilities, fine-motor abilities, and gross-motor abilities. The procedures are easily adapted to meet the needs of each child and require no special setting. Examiner required. Not suitable for group use.

Untimed: 45–90 minutes per scale

Scoring: Examiner evaluated; hand key

Cost: Scale of Cognition $20.00; Scale of Communication $25.00; Scale of Social-Affective Behavior, Scale of Practical Abilities, Scale of Fine Motor Abilities, Scale of Gross Motor Abilities $18.00 each; complete set $117.00

Publisher: Foreworks Publications

STANDARDIZED ROAD-MAP TEST OF DIRECTION SENSE
John Money

Ages 7–adult

Purpose: Assesses directional orientation in children and adults. Used as a quick measure of disability and as part of a full neuropsychological battery to evaluate children suspected of underachieving.

Description: With a marker, the student traces a path through a maze consisting of 32 possible turns. The test is scored on the basis of items-correct-to-total. Conversion tables for percentiles are provided for males and females for three age groupings within the 7–18–year-old range. Examiner required. Not suitable for group use.

Untimed: 10 minutes

Scoring: Hand key

Cost: Manual $16.95; 50 test forms $10.00; scoring template $4.00; kit $24.95

Publisher: United Educational Services, Inc.

SYSTEM OF MULTICULTURAL PLURALISTIC ASSESSMENT (SOMPA)
Refer to page 598.

TEST OF GROSS MOTOR DEVELOPMENT (TGMD)
Dale A. Ulrich

Child—Ages 3–10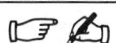

Purpose: Assesses common motor skills of children. Used for educational planning and research and to evaluate existing special education programs.

Description: Multiple-item task-performance test consisting of two subtests. The Locomotor Skills subtest measures the run, gallop, hop, skip, horizontal jump, leap, and slide. The Object Control Skills subtest measures the two-hand strike, stationary bounce, catch, kick, and overhand throw. The examiner records observations in a student record book. Examiner required. Not suitable for group use.

Timed: 15 minutes

Scoring: Examiner evaluated

Cost: Complete kit (examiner's manual, 50 student record books) $44.00

Publisher: PRO-ED

TEST OF LEGIBLE HANDWRITING (TOLH)
Stephen C. Larsen and Donald D. Hammill

Grades 2–12

Purpose: Assesses the legibility of an individual's handwriting.

Description: Paper-pencil test evaluating a minimum of two samples of a child's handwriting. Examinees write one creative essay. They are also instructed to write on an additional topic (e.g., biographical sketch, correspondence), ensuring that a variety of themes and settings are represented. Legibility is rated on a scale from 1 to 9. Five types of scores are yielded: raw scores, percentiles, standard scores, composite quotients, and grade equivalents. Examiner required. Suitable for group use.

Untimed: Each writing prompt 15 minutes

Scoring: Hand key

Cost: $39.00

Publisher: PRO-ED

TEST OF MOTOR IMPAIRMENT—HENDERSON REVISION (TOMI-R)
D.H. Stott, F.A. Moyes, and S.E. Henderson

Child—Ages 5 and older

Purpose: Identifies and describes impairments of gross- and fine-motor functioning in children.

Description: Multiple-task test measuring a child's ability to perform tasks requiring manual dexterity, ball skills, and dynamic and static balance. Suitable for children in five designated age bands, with eight tasks in each band. Two separate tasks are provided in each area. The test also assesses factors of attitude and temperament as they influence performance. Materials include a manual, record form, and other task aids. Examiner required. Not suitable for group use.

Timed: 35–40 minutes

Scoring: Examiner evaluated

Cost: Complete set (all necessary equipment, manual, 25 record forms at each grade level, carrying case) $250.00

Publisher: The Psychological Corporation

Information and availability unconfirmed; last verified in 1988.

TEST OF VISUAL-MOTOR SKILLS (TVMS)
Morrison F. Gardner

Child—Ages 2–13

Purpose: Provides an accurate measurement of a child's eye-hand coordination (how a child motorically translates with his hand what he visually perceives). Helps determine whether a child has a neurosensory integration dysfunction. Used by teachers, occupational therapists, psychologists, pediatricians, resource specialists, counselors, and other professionals.

Description: 26 designs in a single test booklet, arranged progressively according to difficulty, assessing a child's eye-hand-motor accuracy, motor control, motor coordination, and/or gestalt interpretation. The test is standardized so that results may be converted to motor ages, standard scores, and percentiles. Examiner required. Suitable for group use.

Untimed: 3–5 minutes

Scoring: Hand key; examiner evaluated

Cost: Kit (manual, 15 test booklets with 26 designs each) $29.95

Publisher: Children's Hospital of San Francisco, Publications Department

---

Special Education: Gifted

ARLIN TEST OF FORMAL REASONING (ATFR)
Refer to page 586.

BARCLAY CLASSROOM ASSESSMENT SYSTEM (BCAS)
Refer to page 763.

BIOGRAPHICAL INVENTORY, FORM U
Institute for Behavioral Research in Creativity Staff

Adolescent—Ages 11–18
Grades 6–12

Purpose: Identifies gifted and talented students.

Description: 150-item paper-pencil multiple-choice test assessing academic performance, creativity, artistic potential, leadership, vocational maturity, and educational orientation. The inventory is based on life history experiences and provides an alternate approach or supplement to standardized achievement measures. The test may be read aloud to students with reading difficulties. Scores are designed to be race-fair. Raw scores and percentile ranks based on grouped grade-level norms are generated by the computer scoring service provided by the publisher. A sixth-grade reading level is required. Examiner/self-administered. Suitable for group use.

Untimed: 30–60 minutes

Scoring: Computer scored

Cost: Specimen set $10.00; 35 booklets $30.00; answer sheets each $0.05; contact publisher for scoring costs

Publisher: Institute for Behavioral Research in Creativity

BLOOMER LEARNING TEST (BLT)
Refer to page 587.

CARTOON CONSERVATION SCALES (CCS)

Child, adolescent
Grades K–6

Purpose: Assesses students' intellectual development.

Description: Multiple-item paper-pencil neo-Piagetian test identifying gifted or special education students. The scales may be scored in two ways. The first method is based on the simple addition of the correct responses within and across subscales. The second method is based on probability and is used to determine which of the subscales the student actually passed. The test was designed without cultural or language bias and may be administered in any language to individuals or small groups. Examiner required. Suitable for group use.

Untimed: 20–25 minutes

Scoring: Hand key

Cost: Complete kit $79.00

Publisher: Linguametrics Group

Information and availability unconfirmed; last verified in 1988.

COMPREHENSIVE ASSESSMENT PROGRAM: DEVELOPING COGNITIVE ABILITIES TEST, FORMS A AND B
Refer to page 589.

CREATIVE REASONING TEST
Refer to page 589.

CREATIVITY ASSESSMENT PACKET
Frank E. Williams

Child, adolescent—Ages 6–18

Purpose: Measures cognitive and affective factors related to the creative process. Identifies gifted students.

Description: Two multiple-item paper-pencil tests assessing eight general areas of cognitive and affective behavior. The Test of Divergent Thinking measures fluency, flexibility, elaboration, and originality. Test items require semantic transformation, thus combining right-left brain abilities. The Divergent Feelings Test measures curiosity, imagination, complexity, and risk-taking (affective traits measured in a verbal analysis mode also requiring left-right brain synthesis). A parent-teacher inventory (the Williams scale) asks parents and teachers to rate each child on various manifestations of the eight subscores, providing a means of comparing observed behavior with measured potential. The manual includes directions for administering and scoring the tests, scoring templates, and a list of teaching strategies related to the creative processes measured by the test. On the back of the Test of Divergent Thinking is a pupil assessment matrix for profiling results of all three tests. The tests are available in two alternate forms, A and B. Examiner required. Suitable for group use.

Untimed: Varies

Scoring: Examiner evaluated

Cost: Complete kit (manual, 25 each Form A and B divergent thinking tests, 25 divergent feelings tests, 25 Williams scale booklets) $40.00

Publisher: D.O.K. Publishers, Inc.

CREATIVITY ATTITUDE SURVEY (CAS)
Charles E. Schaefer

Child
Grades 4–6

Purpose: Assesses attitudes important for creative thinking. Used in the evaluation of training programs in creativity.

Description: 32–item paper-pencil test measuring five dimensions associated with creative thinking: confidence in own ideas; appreciation of fantasy; theoretical and aesthetic orientation; openness to impulse expression; and desire for novelty. The items are statements to which the child indicates agreement or disagreement. Examiner required. Suitable for group use.

Untimed: 10 minutes

Scoring: Hand key

Cost: Specimen set $5.00; manual $4.50; 25 tests $15.00

Publisher: Psychologists and Educators, Inc.

CREATIVITY CHECKLIST (CCH)
David L. Johnson

Grades K–graduate school

Purpose: Evaluates creativity in people of all educational levels, in any social setting. Used in school, business, family, free play, and training settings to identify gifted individuals and to evaluate creativity programs.

Description: 8–item paper-pencil questionnaire used by an examiner to record observations of eight categories of the subject's creative behavior. The categories are sensitivity or preference for complexity, fluency, flexibility, resourcefulness, constructional skill, ingenuity or productiveness, independence, and positive self-ref-

erencing behavior. The examiner (parent, teacher, counselor) indicates the extent to which he or she has observed (consistently, frequently, occasionally, seldom, never) examples of these characteristics in the individual being evaluated. The sum of the eight items provides a total creativity score. Cutoff points for different levels of creative performance are provided. Examiner required. Suitable for group use.

Untimed: 15 minutes

Scoring: Examiner evaluated

Cost: Complete kit (30 record forms, manual) $9.50

Publisher: Stoelting Co.

DEGREES OF READING POWER® (DRP)
Refer to page 369.

EBY ELEMENTARY IDENTIFICATION INSTRUMENT (EEII)
Judy W. Eby

Child, adolescent
Grades K–8

Purpose: Measures academic talent and gifted behavior. Used to select students for gifted programs.

Description: Multiple-item paper-pencil inventories assessing academic performance and classroom behavior in order to identify gifted students. The identification model consists of the following three components: general selection matrix, teacher recommendation form, and unit selection matrix. Together they provide a profile of the child's potential for academically challenging educational experiences. Examiner required. Suitable for group use.

Untimed: Varies

Scoring: Examiner evaluated

Cost: Test kit (manual, 50 general selection matrix forms, 50 teacher recommendation forms, 50 unit selection matrix forms) $24.50

Publisher: Slosson Educational Publications, Inc.

EBY GIFTED BEHAVIOR INDEX
Judy W. Eby

All ages

Purpose: Assesses giftedness for placement in gifted programs. Used in IEP development.

Description: Paper-pencil rating scale assessing giftedness in six talent fields: Verbal, Social/Leadership, Visual/Special, Math/Science Problem Solving, Mechanical/Technical, and Musical. Examiner required. Suitable for group use.

Untimed: Varies

Scoring: Examiner evaluated

Cost: $24.95

Publisher: D.O.K. Publishers

EVALUATING EDUCATIONAL PROGRAMS FOR INTELLECTUALLY GIFTED STUDENTS (EEPIGS)
Joanne Rand Whitmore

Child, adolescent
Grades K–12

Purpose: Evaluates educational programming for gifted students. Used by administrators, school psychologists, and teachers.

Description: Multiple-item paper-pencil process tool for evaluating whether programs for intellectually gifted students are meeting the students' needs, especially those needs that influence socioemotional and cognitive development. Educators may add their own specific curriculum content-related questions appropriate to the specific areas of giftedness of a particular student or the goals of a particular program. Examiner required. Suitable for group use.

Untimed: Varies

Scoring: Examiner evaluated

Cost: Complete kit $24.00

Publisher: D.O.K. Publishers, Inc.

GIFTED AND TALENTED SCALE

Child
Grades 4–6

Purpose: Assesses abstract and reasoning abilities in gifted children. Can be used to screen for placement.

Description: Paper-pencil multiple-choice test of five categories of abstract and reasoning abilities: numerical reasoning, vocabulary, synonyms and antonyms, similarities, and analogies. The test was normed on students in gifted programs in Grades 4–6. Examiner/self-administered. Suitable for group use.

Untimed: Not available

Scoring: Hand key

Cost: Complete kit (manual, 25 pupil record forms) $50.00

Publisher: Dallas Educational Services

GIFTED AND TALENTED SCREENING FORM (GTSF)
David L. Johnson

Child, adolescent
Grades K–9

Purpose: Identifies gifted and talented children. Used in educational, family, and social settings and by school districts initiating formal, federally funded programs.

Description: 24–item paper-pencil inventory measuring the following talent areas: academics, intelligence, creativity, leadership, visual-performing arts, and psychomotor ability. The respondent (parent, teacher, or anyone familiar with the child) is asked to indicate the extent to which he or she has observed (consistently, frequently, occasionally, seldom, never) gifted and talented characteristics in the child being evaluated. Cutoff criterion points are suggested for each of the talent areas. Examiner required. Suitable for group use.

Untimed: 20 minutes

Scoring: Examiner evaluated

Cost: Complete kit (30 record forms, score keys, manual) $14.25

Publisher: Stoelting Co.

GROUP INVENTORY FOR FINDING CREATIVE TALENT (GIFT)
Sylvia B. Rimm

Child
Grades K–6

Purpose: Assesses creativity. Used to identify gifted students.

Description: Multiple-item paper-pencil test of interests and attitudes related to creativity. The test yields the following dimension scores: Imagination, Independence, and Many Interests. Validation groups include minorities, urban and suburban students, learning disabled, and gifted students. Self-administered. Suitable for group use. Available in Spanish.
Untimed: 20–40 minutes
Scoring: Machine scored
Cost: Specimen set $12.00; class set of 30 $44.00 (indicate grade level); scoring included in price
Publisher: Educational Assessment Service, Inc.

GROUP INVENTORY FOR FINDING INTERESTS (GIFFI)
Sylvia B. Rimm and Gary A. Davis

Child, adolescent
Grades 6–12

Purpose: Assesses creativity in children. Used to identify gifted children.

Description: Multiple-item paper-pencil test of interests and attitudes related to creativity. The test yields the following dimension scores: Creative Art and Writing, Confidence, Imagination, Challenge-Inventiveness, and Many Interests. Validation groups include minorities, urban and suburban students, learning disabled, and gifted children. Self-administered. Suitable for group use. Available in Spanish.
Untimed: 20–40 minutes
Scoring: Machine scored
Cost: Specimen set $12.00; class set of 30 tests and scoring $60.00 (indicate grade level)
Publisher: Educational Assessment Service, Inc.

HOWELL PREKINDERGARTEN SCREENING TEST
Refer to page 547.

IDENTI-FORM: IDENTIFICATION, ASSESSMENT, AND BEYOND
Patricia Weber and Cathy Battaglia

Adult

Purpose: Assesses students for educational placement. Used by educators primarily to identify gifted students.

Description: Multiple-item prescriptive assessment system incorporating test, performance, and anecdotal data. The system is used for developing individualized educational programs and selecting students for programs for gifted children. Information also can be used for educational planning for students not selected for special programs for the gifted. Examiner required. Suitable for group use.
Untimed: Varies
Scoring: Examiner evaluated
Cost: $25.00
Publisher: D.O.K. Publishers, Inc.

INTER-AMERICAN SERIES
Refer to page 576.

INTER-AMERICAN SERIES: TEST OF GENERAL ABILITY
Refer to page 462.

INTER-AMERICAN SERIES: TEST OF ORAL COMPREHENSION
Refer to page 576.

INTER-AMERICAN SERIES: TEST OF READING
Refer to page 577.

LANGDON ADULT INTELLIGENCE TEST (LAIT)
Refer to page 55.

LEARNING STYLE IDENTIFICATION SCALE (LSIS)

Refer to page 754.

MATRIX ANALOGIES TEST— EXPANDED FORM (MAT-EF)

Refer to page 593.

MATRIX ANALOGIES TEST— SHORT FORM (MAT-SF)

Refer to page 593.

PRESCHOOL AND KINDERGARTEN INTEREST DESCRIPTOR (PRIDE)

Sylvia B. Rimm

Child—Ages 3-6

Purpose: Identifies creatively gifted preschool and kindergarten children. Used for academic placement in gifted programs.

Description: 50–item paper-pencil inventory in which parents assess their child's attitudes and interests by responding "no," "to a small extent," "average," "more than average," or "definitely" to each item. Scores are provided on four dimensions: Many Interests, Independence-Perseverance, Imagination-Playfulness, and Originality. All scoring is completed by Educational Assessment Service, Inc. Self-administered. Suitable for group use.

Untimed: 20–35 minutes

Scoring: Computer scored

Cost: Specimen set $12.00; class set of 30 tests and computer scoring $60.00

Publisher: Educational Assessment Service, Inc.

ROSS TEST OF HIGHER COGNITIVE PROCESSES (ROSS TEST)

Refer to page 597.

SCALES FOR RATING THE BEHAVIORAL CHARACTERISTICS OF SUPERIOR STUDENTS (SRBCSS)

Joseph S. Renzulli, Linda H. Smith, Alan J. White, Carolyn M. Callahan, and Robert K. Hartman

Child, adolescent

Purpose: Assesses the behavioral characteristics related to the objectives of gifted and talented elementary and junior high-school programs. Used to supplement measures of intelligence, achievement, and creativity in selecting students for gifted and talented programs.

Description: 95–item paper-pencil inventory consisting of 10 subscales, each of which assesses a different dimension of behavioral characteristics related to gifted and talented educational objectives. The following 10 dimensions are evaluated: learning, motivation, creativity, leadership, art, music, dramatics, planning, precise communication, and expressive communication. Each scale consists of 4–15 statements describing behaviors attributed to gifted and talented students. The teacher rates each item on a 4–point scale from "seldom" to "almost always," reflecting the degree to which the presence or absence of each characteristic has been observed. The 10 subscales represent 10 distinct sets of behavioral characteristics; therefore, no total score is derived. Only scales relevant to program objectives should be selected for use in a given program. Self-administered by teacher. Suitable for group use.

Untimed: Varies

Scoring: Examiner evaluated

Cost: Test kit $8.95; additional sets of 100 tests $49.95

Publisher: Creative Learning Press, Inc.

SCALES OF CREATIVITY AND LEARNING ENVIRONMENT (SCALE)

Steven W. Slosson

Child, adolescent
Grades 1-12

Purpose: Aids teachers in recognizing gifted attributes and characteristics in students.

Description: 170–item descriptive rating scale composed of the Scale of Gifted Students and the Scale of Divergent/Convergent Thinking. The Scale of Gifted Students assesses attributes and characteristics in the following areas: cognitive (19 items), comprehension (15 items), language (11 items), affective (14 items), behavioral (13 items), problem-solving (21 items), and hobbies and play (12 items). The Scale of Divergent/Convergent Thinking assesses attributes and characteristics in six areas: knowledge (9 items), ability (9 items), task commitment (15 items), synthesis (12 items), creativity (11 items), and evaluation (9 items). Raw scores are converted to ordinal scale scores. Ratings are based on a 5–point Likert scale and month-long observation of student behavior. Examiner required. Not suitable for group use.

Timed: 10 minutes
Scoring: Examiner evaluated
Cost: Complete kit (manual, 25 of each scale in vinyl binder) $35.00
Publisher: Slosson Educational Publications, Inc.

SCREENING ASSESSMENT FOR GIFTED ELEMENTARY STUDENTS (SAGES)
Susan K. Johnsen and Anne Corn

Child—Ages 7.0–12.11

Purpose: Assesses aptitude, achievement, and creativity. Used to identify gifted children.

Description: Multiple-item paper-pencil test consisting of three subtests. The Reasoning subtest, which measures aptitude, requires the child to solve problems by identifying relationships among pictures and figures. In the School Acquired Information subtest, the child answers multiple-choice questions assessing social studies, science, and math achievement. The Divergent Production subtest measures ideational fluency, an aspect of creativity. Standard scores and percentile ranks are provided for each subtest. Examiner required. The Divergent Pro-

duction subtest must be administered individually. Reasoning and School Acquired Information subtests suitable for group use.

Untimed: 30–50 minutes
Scoring: Hand key
Cost: Complete kit (manual, picture book, 50 profile and response sheets) $74.00
Publisher: PRO-ED

SEQUENTIAL ASSESSMENT OF MATHEMATICS INVENTORY— INDIVIDUAL ASSESSMENT BATTERY (SAMI)
Refer to page 804.

THE SOI CREATIVITY TEST
Refer to page 566.

SOI-LEARNING ABILITIES TEST: SCREENING FORM FOR ATYPICAL GIFTED
Mary Meeker

Grades 2–adult

Purpose: Identifies gifted students who do not fit the typical gifted pattern of high semantic and verbal abilities. Used primarily with minority, culturally different populations, and disadvantaged children who do not enter school with expected verbal/language concepts.

Description: 161–item paper-pencil set of 10 subtests selected from the SOI-LA Test, which contains 26 subtests measuring structure of intellect abilities: constancy of objects in space (CFS), understanding abstract information (CSR), auditory attention (MSU—auditory), judging similarities and matching of concepts (EFC), word recognition and speed of reading (NST), psychomotor readiness (NFU), auditory concentration for sequencing (MSS—auditory), judgment of arithmetic similarities (ESC), and symbolic problem solving (NSI). The examiner may begin with any subtest; the test may be given in parts on different days. The test is based on the Structure of Intellect Theory of Human Intelligence. Results reflect students' intellectual abilities rather than knowledge of content. The test is recommended for use when the whole SOI-LA Test cannot be administered. The entire SOI-LA Test should be administered when developing comprehensive educational programs. Examiner required. Suitable for group use.

Timed: 3–10 minutes per subtest

Scoring: Hand key; may be computer scored

Cost: Test form $1.90; examiner's manual $35.00

Publisher: M & M Systems

SOI PRIMARY FORM (FORM P)
Refer to page 598.

STRUCTURE OF INTELLECT LEARNING ABILITIES TEST (SOI)
Refer to page 566.

STRUCTURE OF INTELLECT LEARNING ABILITIES TEST (SOI-LA): SCREENING FORM FOR GIFTED
Mary Meeker and Robert Meeker

Grades 2–adult

Purpose: Screens for gifted students as potential candidates for gifted educational programs. Identifies children at risk for learning problems and is used to develop educational plans.

Description: 155–item paper-pencil test identifying children from larger populations or groups who show gifted abilities and should be considered for gifted programs. The 12 subtests measure visual closure (16 items), verbal relations (25 items), visual attending and auditory attention (4 items each), word recognition and speed of reading (27 items), creativity with things (1 item), vocabulary (30 items), understanding extended verbal information (18 items), visual concentration for sequencing and auditory concentration for sequencing (4 items each), symbolic problem solving (21 items), and creativity with words and ideas (1 item). The basic test manual is required for administration. The test is recommended for use when the entire SOI-LA Test can-

not be administered. See entry for Structure of Intellect (SOI) for related tests. Examiner required. Suitable for group use.

Timed: 1–2 hours

Scoring: Hand key

Cost: Kit $125.00

Publisher: Western Psychological Services

A SURVEY OF STUDENTS' EDUCATIONAL TALENTS AND SKILLS (ASSETS)
Grand Rapids Public School System

Child
Grades K–6

Purpose: Identifies gifted and talented students in order to individualize study programs and planning and to help parents and teachers discuss students' needs.

Description: 35–item paper-pencil test in three parts: one for the student, one for the parent, and one for the teacher. The students respond to statements as "almost," "sometimes," and "never" and fill in blanks about their favorite books, hobbies, and activities. Self-administered. Suitable for group use.

Untimed: 40 minutes

Scoring: Computer scored

Cost: Specimen set $5.95; 30 tests, specify early (Grades K–3) or later (Grades 4–6) elementary $39.60

Publisher: Learning Publications

TEST OF CREATIVE POTENTIAL (TCP)
R. Hoepfner and J. Hemenway

Grades 2–adult

Purpose: Measures general creative potential. Used for individual and program evaluation and for research.

Description: Multiple-item paper-pencil examination in three separate subtests assessing fluency, flexibility, and elaboration of verbal, symbolic, and figural materials. The Writing Words subtest asks the subject to write many words that mean the same as the given words. The Picture Decoration section requires the takers to elaborately decorate simplified pictures. The License Plate Words subtest asks the subject to make many words that have certain literal qualities. All items are open-ended and restricted only by time. Scoring procedures, reliability estimates, and norms have been developed on samples of subjects ranging from Grades 2–12. Examiner required. Suitable for group use.

Timed: 22 minutes

Scoring: Hand key; examiner evaluated; scoring service available

Cost: Specimen set (specify form) $8.00; 35 tests $30.00; manual $4.00; 10 score rosters $3.00; scoring service $2.50 per booklet

Publisher: Monitor

THINKING CREATIVELY IN ACTION AND MOVEMENT (TCAM)
E. Paul Torrance

Child—Ages 3–8

Purpose: Identifies creative children. Used as part of a program to keep alive and further develop promising creative talent among young children.

Description: Nonverbal movement test assessing the creativity of young children, especially preschoolers. The responses are appropriate to the developmental characteristics of the younger child and are physical in nature, although verbal responses are acceptable. A standard scoring service (raw scores and T-scores are entered on scoring worksheets) is available. The manual contains a scoring guide for those who wish to self-score the test. Examiner required. Not suitable for group use.

Timed: 10–30 minutes

Scoring: Hand key; examiner evaluated

Cost: 20 tests $15.75; specimen set $12.00

Publisher: Scholastic Testing Service, Inc.

THINKING CREATIVELY WITH SOUNDS AND WORDS (TCSW)
E. Paul Torrance, Joe Khantena, and Bert F. Cunnington

Grades 3–adult

Purpose: Measures ability to create images for words and sounds. Used to identify gifted and creative individuals and to teach imagery.

Description: Two-test battery assessing creativity by measuring the originality of ideas stimulated by abstract sounds and spoken onomatopoeic words. The two tests are Sounds and Images and Onomatopeia and Images. The battery is available in equivalent forms (A and B) on two levels: Level I (Grades 3–12) and Level II (Adult). Two long-playing records provide the stimuli for each level. The test may be scored by the examiner with the help of the scoring guide included in the manual; the standard scoring service is also available. Examiner required. Suitable for group use.

Timed: 30 minutes per test

Scoring: Hand key; examiner evaluated

Cost: 20 tests $15.00; specimen set $12.00

Publisher: Scholastic Testing Service, Inc.

TORRANCE TESTS OF CREATIVE THINKING (TTCT)
E. Paul Torrance

Grades K-adult

Purpose: Assesses the ability to visualize and transform words, meanings, and patterns. Used to identify gifted, creative individuals.

Description: Multiple-task paper-pencil measure of an individual's creativity. It assesses four mental characteristics: fluency, flexibility, originality, and elaboration. The test is available in two editions. The Verbal TTCT uses seven word-based exercises. The Figural TTCT uses three picture-based exercises. The Verbal TTCT can be administered orally to students in Kindergarten through Grade 3 and is easily administered and scored.

Individuals with psychometric training should interpret the subtest and total scores. "Streamlined" scoring of the figural forms of the overall test is available. This alternative scoring yields norm-referenced measures for fluency, originality, abstractness of titles, elaboration, and resistance to premature closure. It provides an overall Creativity Index and criterion-referenced scores for several creativity indicators. This test is available in two equivalent forms (A and B) for both the verbal and the figural editions. A scoring guide is available in the directions manual. The TTCT standard scoring service and streamlined scoring for figural tests are also available. Examiner required. Suitable for group use.

Timed: Figural TTCT 30 minutes; Verbal TTCT 45 minutes

Scoring: Examiner evaluated

Cost: 20 tests (specify edition and form) $15.00; specimen set (specify form) $12.00

Publisher: Scholastic Testing Service, Inc.

WATSON-GLASER CRITICAL THINKING APPRAISAL
*Goodwin Watson and
Edward M. Glaser*

Adolescent, adult
Grades 9 and above

Purpose: Assesses critical thinking abilities. Used for evaluation of gifted and talented individuals. Used to select candidates for positions in which analytic reasoning is an important part of the job.

Description: 80–item paper-pencil test measuring five aspects of the ability to think critically: inference, recognition of assumptions, deduction, interpretation, and evaluation of arguments. The subject responds to the exercises, which include problems, statements, arguments, and interpretation of material encountered on a daily basis. Two alternate and equivalent forms, A and B, are available. Examiner required. Suitable for group use.

Untimed: 50 minutes

Scoring: Hand key; may be machine scored

Cost: 35 tests $59.00; 35 OPScan answer documents $19.00; key $10.00; manual $12.00; class record $3.00 (specify form for each item ordered); specimen kit (test booklet, answer document, key, manual, class record) $20.00

Publisher: The Psychological Corporation
Information and availability unconfirmed; last verified in 1988.

Special Education: Learning Disabled

ADD-H COMPREHENSIVE TEACHER'S RATING SCALE (ACTERS)
Refer to page 646.

ADELPHI PARENT ADMINISTERED READINESS TEST (A.P.A.R.T.)
Refer to page 531.

ANALYTIC LEARNING DISABILITY ASSESSMENT (ALDA)
*Thomas D. Gnagey and
Patricia D. Gnagey*

Child, adolescent—Ages
8–14

Purpose: Measures the skills necessary to read, spell, write, and work with numbers. Aids in the neuropsychological evaluation of learning disabled, educable mentally retarded, and behaviorally disturbed students.

Description: Multiple-item test assessing a student's strengths and weaknessess in 77 skills underlying basic school subjects. The strengths and weaknessess are matched with the student's most appropriate learning method for each subject: 11 reading methods, 23 spelling methods, 6 math computation methods, and 8 handwriting methods. The results are transferred to the Recommendation Pamphlet to create an individualized teaching plan providing specific procedures and methods for teachers. Materials include a scoring sheet, student worksheets with tear-out sections, an individualized student learning plan, a teacher recommendation pamphlet, also with tear-out sections, four colored scoring pencils, tape, and a straight-edge ruler in a leather carrying case. The test should not be used unless a learning dysfunction is suspected. Examiner required. Not suitable for group use.

Untimed: 75 minutes

Scoring: Hand key

Cost: Complete kit (test book, manual, scoring straight edge, four colored scoring pencils, tape, chalk, 20 complete testing forms, teaching plan, carrying case) $96.00

Publisher: Slosson Educational Publications, Inc.

ANN ARBOR LEARNING INVENTORY AND REMEDIATION PROGRAM
Refer to page 609.

THE ANSER SYSTEM-AGGREGATE NEUROBEHAVIORAL STUDENT HEALTH AND EDUCATIONAL REVIEW
Melvin D. Levine

Child, adolescent—Ages 3–18

Purpose: Gathers information from parents and teachers for the educator or clinician who has questions about a child with learning and/or behavioral problems. Used in schools, health-care, and counseling centers to evaluate children with low severity, high prevalence disabilities. Follow-up questionnaires assist in monitoring progress.

Description: Three separate short-answer paper-pencil questionnaires for parents and school personnel to evaluate three age groups: Form 1 (ages 3–5), Form 2 (ages 6–11), and Form 3 (ages 12 and older). Form 4 is a self-administered student profile to be completed by students ages 9 and older. The parent questionnaire (Form 5P) surveys family history, possible pregnancy problems, health

problems, functional problems, early development, early educational experience, skills and interests, activity-attention problems, associated behaviors, and associated strengths. The school questionnaire (Form 5S) covers the educational program and setting, special facilities available, and the results of previous testing. The self-administered Student Profile (Form 6) asks the student to rate himself on a series of statements in the following categories: fine motor, gross motor, memory, attention, language, general efficiency, visual-spatial processing, sequencing, general academic performance, and social interaction. Examiner required. Not suitable for group use.

Untimed: 30–60 minutes

Scoring: Examiner evaluated

Cost: Interpreter's guide (Forms 1–6) $8.00; specimen set Forms 1–4 (guide, sample of each form) $8.00; specimen set Forms 5–6 (guide for 5–6, sample forms) $4.00

Publisher: Educators Publishing Service, Inc.

AUDITORY POINTING TEST
Janet B. Fudala, LuVern H. Kunze, and John D. Ross

All ages
Grades K–adult

Purpose: Measures short-term memory in children and adults through visual-motor responses. Used for remedial planning, especially with individuals with oral communication problems.

Description: Multiple-item cross-modal test in which the teacher/clinician shows the student 10 different stimulus cards, each of which contains eight simple line drawings (from a total stimulus pool of 32 separate drawings). The child is asked to point to the item mentioned by the examiner. Two forms are provided for test and retest. Scoring is on the basis of items-correct-to-ceiling. Norms are available for students in Grades K–5. The test has not been normed on older students and adults. Materials include recording forms, summary sheets, set of test cards and plates, and manual. Examiner required. Not suitable for group use.

Untimed: 20 minutes

Scoring: Hand key

Cost: Manual $10.00; 25 recording forms (specify A or B) $10.00; 25 student summary sheets $7.00; set of test cards and plates $10.00; kit $31.00

Publisher: United Educational Services, Inc.

AUTISTIC BEHAVIOR COMPOSITE CHECKLIST AND PROFILE
Refer to page 135.

BARCLAY CLASSROOM ASSESSMENT SYSTEM (BCAS)
Refer to page 763.

BASIC NUMBER DIAGNOSTIC TEST
Refer to page 314.

BENDER-PURDUE REFLEX TEST AND TRAINING MANUAL
Refer to page 610.

THE BODER TEST OF READING-SPELLING PATTERNS
Elena Boder and Sylvia Jarrico

All ages

Purpose: Differentiates specific reading disability (developmental dyslexia) from nonspecific reading disability through reading and spelling performance. Used to classify dyslexic readers into one of three subtypes, each with its own prognostic and remedial implications.

Description: 300–item paper-pencil tests of reading and spelling ability. The Reading Test uses 13 graded word lists of 20 words each, half of which are phonetic and half of which are nonphonetic. The words, which are presented flash and untimed, require sight vocabulary and phonic word analysis skills. The Spelling Test uses two individualized spelling lists (10 known words and 10 unknown) based on the student's reading performance. Both the reading and spelling tests tap the central visual and auditory processes

required for reading and spelling, making it possible to diagnose developmental dyslexia by the joint analysis of reading and spelling as interdependent functions. The results should be supplemented with testing that uses instructional materials to which the child already has been and will be exposed. Examiner required. Not suitable for group use.

Timed: 30 minutes

Scoring: Examiner evaluated

Cost: Complete kit $67.00

Publisher: The Psychological Corporation

Information and availability unconfirmed; last verified in 1988.

THE BRIGANCE® DIAGNOSTIC ASSESSMENT OF BASIC SKILLS—SPANISH EDITION
Refer to page 571.

CAREER ASSESSMENT INVENTORIES: FOR THE LEARNING DISABLED (CAI)
Carol Weller and Mary Buchanan

LD students

Purpose: Assesses the personality, abilities, and interests of learning disabled students. Used to help learning disabled students make intelligent and realistic career choices.

Description: Multiple-item paper-pencil test consisting of three inventories. The Attributes Inventory assesses the examinee's dominant personality characteristics. The Ability Inventory provides a profile of strengths and weaknesses across the auditory, visual, and motor areas. The Interest Inventory determines whether the examinee's career goals are realistic. The inventories are completed by the examiner after observing the examinee. However, the Interest Inventory may be completed by the examinee. Each inventory presents a list of descriptors that are evaluated using a numerical scale. The results are profiled and used to locate appropriate career options in the Job Finder section of the manual. The attributes and interests inventories are keyed

special education: learning disabled

education **631**

to John I. Holland's theory of careers. Examiner required. Suitable for group use.

Untimed: 20–30 minutes

Scoring: Examiner evaluated

Cost: Test kit (manual, 50 attributes/ability inventories, 50 interest inventories) $40.00

Publisher: Academic Therapy Publications

CATCH
Refer to page 432.

COGNITIVE ABILITIES TEST™: FORM 4 (COGAT®)
Refer to page 433.

COGNITIVE CONTROL BATTERY: THE FRUIT DISTRACTION TEST
Sebastiano Santostefano

Child, adolescent—Ages 4–12

Purpose: Predicts the presence of learning disabilities and assesses the role of cognitive dysfunctions in school and adjustment problems.

Description: Verbal measure of an individual's ability to selectively attend even when there is interference from competing stimuli. The child responds by naming a series of colors presented with and without distractions or contradictions. This test, along with the Leveling-Sharpening House Test and the Scattered Scanning Test, comprise the Cognitive Control Battery. Examiner required. Not suitable for group use.

Untimed: Not available

Scoring: Examiner required

Cost: Complete kit (stimulus materials, 100 record sheets, manual) $92.00

Publisher: Western Psychological Services

COGNITIVE CONTROL BATTERY: THE LEVELING-SHARPENING HOUSE TEST
Sebastiano Santostefano

Child, adolescent—Ages 4–12

Purpose: Predicts the presence of learning disabilities and assesses the role of cognitive dysfunctions in school adjustment problems.

Description: 60–item verbal-response measure of the manner in which a child organizes memory images and relates them to current perceptions. Items consist of two-dimensional line drawings of a house printed on separate cards. The child examines each card and describes how the drawing is different, if it is at all, from the previous card. This test, along with the Fruit Distraction Test and the Scattered Scanning Test, comprise the Cognitive Control Battery. Examiner required. Not suitable for group use.

Untimed: Not available

Scoring: Examiner evaluated

Cost: Complete kit (picture book, 100 record sheets, manual) $135.00

Publisher: Western Psychological Services

COGNITIVE CONTROL BATTERY: THE SCATTERED SCANNING TEST
Sebastiano Santostefano

Child, adolescent—Ages 4–12

Purpose: Predicts the presence of learning disabilities and assesses the role of cognitive dysfunctions in school and adjustment problems.

Description: Paper-pencil test of an individual's preferred way of scanning information (broad vs. narrow). The child scans a display of geometric shapes randomly scattered over a sheet of paper and marks certain ones. This test, along with the Leveling-Sharpening House Test and the Fruit Distraction Test, comprise the Cognitive Control Battery. The test is available in two forms: Form 1 (ages 3–8) and Form 2 (ages 9–12). Examiner required. Not suitable for group use.

Untimed: Not available

Scoring: Examiner evaluated

Cost: Complete kit (100 Form 1 test sheets, 25 Form 2 test sheets, 1 line measure, 100 record sheets, manual) $98.00

Publisher: Western Psychological Services

COMPREHENSIVE ASSESSMENT PROGRAM: BEGINNING EDUCATION ASSESSMENT (BEA)
Refer to page 539.

CONTACT WITH DISABLED PERSONS SCALE (CDP)
Refer to page 662.

THE DECODING SKILLS TEST (DST)
Ellis Richardson and Barbara DiBenedetto

Child, adolescent, adult

Purpose: Measures decoding skills used in reading. Used to pinpoint specific problems in the development of decoding skills and is particularly suitable for children with developmental dyslexia. May be used with any individual with a reading level ranging from Grades 1–5.

Description: Multiple-item oral-response test consisting of three subtests measuring a child's vocabulary and use of letter-sound patterns. Subtest I, Basal Vocabulary, measures the ability to decode words representative of the reader levels (pre-primer to five-two reader) of most basal reader programs. Items are presented as 11 word lists each containing 10 words selected from 10 standard or basal reader programs. Subtest II, Phonic Patterns, assesses phonics ability along four dimensions: single and multiple consonant arrangements, vowel patterns, monosyllabic and polysyllabic patterns, and use of spelling patterns, including nonsense words. The third subtest, Oral Reading, consists of 11 passages corresponding to each of the word lists in Subtest I and five

comprehension questions. The test yields more than 40 criterion-referenced scores. Examiner required. Not suitable for group use.

Untimed: Not available

Scoring: Examiner evaluated

Cost: Kit (manual, presentation book, 24 scoring booklets) $64.50

Publisher: York Press, Inc.

THE DEVEREUX ELEMENTARY SCHOOL BEHAVIOR RATING SCALE (DESB-II)
Refer to page 739.

DIAGNOSIS AND REMEDIATION OF HANDWRITING PROBLEMS (DRHP)
Denis H. Stott, Fred A. Moyes, and Sheila E. Henderson

Child, adolescent—Ages 7½–18

Purpose: Evaluates children's handwriting skills. Identifies children with possible learning disabilities. Used in regular classrooms, remedial clinics, and work with individual children.

Description: Multiple-item paper-pencil test assessing handwriting problems. Objective analysis of handwriting faults distinguishes between faults that should yield to regular teaching procedures and those of a more serious nature requiring special treatment. Also measures fine-motor problems due to unknown or suspected neurological dysfunction or associated with stress. The manual includes programs of remediation that can be adapted to the type of fault and ages of the children involved. Examiner required. Suitable for group use. CANADIAN PUBLISHER

Untimed: 20 minutes

Scoring: Examiner evaluated

Cost: Contact publisher

Publisher: Brook Educational Publishing Ltd., Canada

DIAGNOSTIC ACHIEVEMENT BATTERY–2 (DAB–2)
Refer to page 454.

---

special education: learning disabled

DIAGNOSTIC ANALYSIS OF READING ERRORS (DARE)
Refer to page 364.

DYSLEXIA DETERMINATION TEST (DDT)
*John R. Griffin and
Howard N. Walton*

Child, adolescent
Grades 2-12

Purpose: Evaluates learning disorders in reading, writing, and spelling; differentiates dyslexic patterns from other disorders. Used for diagnostic purposes and to suggest appropriate remedial approaches.

Description: Multiple-item paper-pencil test measuring and evaluating a student's ability to decode and encode the English language. The test identifies seven specific dyslexic patterns and provides suggestions for therapy. The test may be used with students who have normal sensory-perceptual, cognitive, and motor abilities, yet have difficulty reading and writing. Examiner required. Not suitable for group use.

Untimed: 20-25 minutes

Scoring: Examiner evaluated

Cost: Complete kit (examiner's instructional manual; decoding word list booklet; instructional audiocassette; 60 interpretation recording forms; decoding patterns checklists, 30 Form A, 30 Form B; Therapy in Dyslexia and Reading Problems) $66.95

Publisher: Instructional Materials & Equipment Distributors

Information and availability unconfirmed; last verified in 1987.

DYSLEXIA SCHEDULE
John McLeod

Child
Grades K-1

Purpose: Gathers relevant social data and developmental information from parents or guardians about a child who has been referred to a specialist due to a reading disability.

Description: 89-item paper-pencil questionnaire completed by the parents or guardians before the child visits a clinic. The results provide the clinician with background data to help evaluate characteristics associated with childhood dyslexia before testing begins. Examiner required. Not suitable for group use.

Untimed: 20-30 minutes

Scoring: Examiner evaluated

Cost: Less than 24 each $1.80; 24 or more each $1.60; manual $3.25

Publisher: Educators Publishing Service, Inc.

THE DYSLEXIA SCREENING SURVEY (DSS)
Refer to page 102.

EARLY LEARNING ASSESSMENT AND DEVELOPMENT
Refer to page 542.

EINSTEIN ASSESSMENT OF SCHOOL RELATED SKILLS
*Ruth L. Gottesman and
Frances M. Cerullo*

Child
Grades K-5

Purpose: Helps identify children at risk for or experiencing mild learning difficulties.

Description: Multiple-item paper-pencil and oral-response test measuring the major skill areas that underlie school achievement. The test consists of from five to seven subtests (Language/Cognition, Word Recognition, Oral Reading, Reading Comprehension, Auditory Memory, Arithmetic, Visual-Motor Integration) depending on the test level administered. Six test levels, corresponding to grade levels kindergarten to Grade 5 are available. The test yields scores indicating acceptable performance levels as well as individuals needing further evaluation. The four-page test booklet contains the student's worksheet, biographical data, and test score summary. The eight-page examiner's form provides directions for administering, scoring, and interpreting the test. A technical manual is also available. May be used with physically and mentally impaired children. Examiner required. Not suitable for group use.

Untimed: 7–10 minutes

Scoring: Examiner evaluated

Cost: 10 tests (levels K–5) $18.12 each; technical manual free

Publisher: Modern Curriculum Press, Inc.

ENGLISH PICTURE VOCABULARY TESTS (EPVTS)
Refer to page 694.

EVALUATING COMMUNICATIVE COMPETENCE: A FUNCTIONAL PRAGMATIC PROCEDURE (REVISED EDITION)
Refer to page 695.

EXPRESSIVE ONE-WORD PICTURE VOCABULARY TEST (EOWPVT)
Refer to page 696.

FLORIDA INTERNATIONAL DIAGNOSTIC-PRESCRIPTIVE VOCATIONAL COMPETENCY PROFILE
Refer to page 844.

FUNDAMENTAL PROCESSES IN ARITHMETIC
G. T. Buswell and L. John

Ages 6–adult
Grades 1–12

Purpose: Determines an individual's approach to solving computation problems in addition, subtraction, multiplication, and division. Used with learning disabled, emotionally disabled, and MIMH children and adults.

Description: 172–item paper-pencil and oral-response test assessing computation skills in addition (46 items), subtraction (44 items), multiplication (44 items), and

division (42 items). Each operation is tested with problems that are graded in difficulty. Students work the problems and verbalize the processes they employ to arrive at the solutions. Examiner required. Not suitable for group use.

Untimed: Varies

Scoring: Examiner evaluated

Cost: Manual $3.00; pupil work sheet $0.75; teacher's diagnostic chart $1.00

Publisher: Allen House

GORDON DIAGNOSTIC SYSTEM (GDI)
Michael Gordon

Ages 4 and older

Purpose: Assesses attention deficits and impulsiveness. Used by clinicians, educators, and physicians.

Description: Microprocessor-based assessment device designed to aid in the diagnosis of attention deficits, especially ADHD/Hyperactivity and AIDS Dementia Complex, and provide information about an individual's ability to sustain attention and exert self-control. The microprocessor administers a series of tasks, most representing a variant of the continuous performance test paradigm. The Vigilance Task requires the examinee to respond only to a particular combination of numbers embedded in a random digit series. A more complex version of the task, The Distractibility Task, is suitable for older children and adults. The Delay Task requires the examinee to inhibit responding in order to earn points.

The microprocessor records various quantitative features of the examinee's performance, including errors of omission and commission and correct responses. Error analyses and reaction times also are provided. The system, which is portable, also may be used for assessing response to stimulant medication. Examiner required. Not suitable for group use.

Timed: 9 minutes per task

Scoring: Microprocessor scored

Cost: GDS unit, manual, record forms $1,395.00

Publisher: Gordon Systems, Inc.

Information and availability unconfirmed; last verified in 1988.

HOWELL PREKINDERGARTEN SCREENING TEST
Refer to page 547.

HUDSON EDUCATION SKILLS INVENTORY (HESI)
Refer to page 460.

HUDSON EDUCATION SKILLS INVENTORY-MATHEMATICS (HESI-M)
Refer to page 460.

HUDSON EDUCATION SKILLS INVENTORY-READING (HESI-R)
Refer to page 461.

HUDSON EDUCATION SKILLS INVENTORY-WRITING (HESI-W)
Refer to page 461.

ILLINOIS TEST OF PSYCHOLINGUISTIC ABILITIES (ITPA)
Refer to page 548.

THE INFORMAL WRITING INVENTORY
Gerard Giordano

Grades 3–12, reading handicapped adults

Purpose: Measures a person's ability to communicate by writing. Focuses on formation (handwriting and spelling), grammatical, and communication skills. Enables clinicians or teachers to analyze the abilities of potentially disabled writers.

Description: Paper-pencil inventory utilizing pictures that stimulate students to write. A simple notation system is used to annotate the writing samples and identify the types of writing problems. Errors are summarized on a profile sheet and a communication index is calculated. Based on this information, remedial exercises are suggested. The manual contains information on administering, scoring, and profiling the inventory and its results and information on remedial writing exercises. Examiner required. Not suitable for group use.

Timed: Varies
Scoring: Hand key; examiner evaluated
Cost: Specimen set $17.50
Publisher: Scholastic Testing Service, Inc.

JORDAN LEFT-RIGHT REVERSAL TEST (JLRRT)–1990 REVISION
Brian T. Jordan

Child—Ages 5–12

Purpose: Assesses the extent to which a child reverses letters, numbers, and words. Used as a screening device by classroom teachers or as one part of a full diagnostic battery.

Description: Multiple-item paper-pencil examination on two levels. Level 1 tests reversals of letters, numerals, and words. Level 2 reveals reversed lowercase letters within words and whole-word reversals within sentences. The manual includes detailed remediation exercises and a conversion table based on new, more conservative norms to determine developmental age. Examiner required. Suitable for group use.

Untimed: 20 minutes
Scoring: Hand key
Cost: Manual $13.00; 50 test forms $8.00
Publisher: Academic Therapy Publications

JOSEPH PRESCHOOL AND PRIMARY SELF-CONCEPT SCREENING TEST (JPPSST)
Jack Joseph

Child—Ages 3.5–9

Purpose: Measures social-emotional development of children. Used to identify children who may have learning difficulties due to negative self-appraisals and to monitor progress in early childhood programs and special education classes. Used to meet requirements of PL 94–142.

Description: 16–item paper-pencil and oral-response test in two parts. First, the child draws his own face on a blank figure of the corresponding sex. Next, the child answers two simple oral-response questions and 13 questions asking the child to select from pairs of pictures the one with which he identifies more closely. The face drawing is evaluated qualitatively, and the 15 questions are scored objectively. The test generates a Global Self-Concept Score based on five dimensions and provides objective high-risk cutoff points. The effects of socially desirable responses are corrected for at upper ranges (ages 5–9). Both quantitative and qualitative indices regarding possible cognitive deficits and experiential or receptive language lags are developed. The manual provides normative data, measures of validity and reliability, item analysis, specific case illustrations, and research considerations. Examiner required. Not suitable for group use.

Untimed: 5–7 minutes

Scoring: Examiner evaluated

Cost: Complete kit $60.00

Publisher: Stoelting Co.

KAUFMAN TEST OF EDUCATIONAL ACHIEVEMENT (K-TEA)
Refer to page 465.

KERBY LEARNING MODALITY TEST, REVISED 1980
Maude L. Kerby

Child—Ages 5–11

Purpose: Measures the learning abilities of children in terms of visual, auditory, and motor activity skills. Used to identify children with learning disabilities, to plan teaching strategies, and to comply with PL 94–142.

Description: Multiple-item paper-pencil test measuring strengths and weaknesses in three primary learning modalities: visual, auditory, and motor activity. The test consists of a variety of classroom work samples in eight subtests: visual and auditory discrimination, visual and auditory closure, visual and auditory memory, and visual and auditory motor coordination. Kits are available for three age levels:

kindergarten, age 5; primary, ages 6–8; and intermediate, ages 8–11. Examiner required. Suitable for group use.

Timed: 15 minutes

Scoring: Hand key

Cost: Kindergarten kit (10 test booklets, tape cassette, 10 record sheets, manual) $29.50; primary kit (10 test booklets, scoring keys, tape cassette, 10 record sheets, manual) $37.50; intermediate kit (10 test booklets, 10 answer sheets, scoring keys, tape cassette, 10 record sheets, manual) $39.50; complete kit (kindergarten kit, primary kit, intermediate kit) $98.00

Publisher: Western Psychological Services

LANGUAGE INVENTORY FOR TEACHERS (LIT)
Arlene Cooper and Beverly A. School

Grades PreK–9 and older students

Purpose: Assesses the language ability of students who have difficulties in reading and writing. Used to determine areas of deficiency requiring remedial intervention and to help teachers write comprehensive Individualized Education Programs.

Description: Multiple-item paper-pencil sequence of more than 500 language tasks corresponding to 13 long-range goals, five for spoken language and eight for written language. The tasks are ordered by type and difficulty to correspond to the hierarchical development of language concepts. Testing begins at a point where the examinee is expected to succeed and is discontinued when the examinee has made several errors. The examiner may translate the items the student misses into instructional objectives by following the guidelines in the manual. Examiner required. Not suitable for group use.

Untimed: 30 minutes

Scoring: Hand key

Cost: Manual $13.00; 50 record forms $18.00; specimen set $13.00

Publisher: Academic Therapy Publications

LANGUAGE-STRUCTURED AUDITORY RETENTION SPAN TEST (LARS)
Luis Carlson

Ages 3.7–adult

Purpose: Assesses the ability of children and adults to maintain short-term memory for linguistically significant information. Used to detect the inability to recall when there is an unfamiliar or nonsense word in an otherwise familiar sentence.

Description: 58–item test determining recall of information in a linguistic context when there are two conditions of familiar words, an unfamiliar word, or two nonsense words in the stimuli. The test provides an estimate of the optimum length of an aural message from which a person may profit during a learning experience. Two equivalent forms allow test-retest without learning effect. Examiner required. Not suitable for group use.

Untimed: 12–15 minutes
Scoring: Hand key
Cost: Manual $12.00; 50 test forms (A or B) $18.00
Publisher: Academic Therapy Publications

LEARNING DISABILITY RATING PROCEDURE (LDRP)
Gerald J. Spadafore and Sharon J. Spadafore

Child, adolescent
Grades 1–12

Purpose: Helps evaluate the general mental and social abilities of elementary and secondary school students. Used to determine LD placement.

Description: Multiple-item paper-pencil evaluation in which the examiner rates the examinee on each of 10 indicators ranging from general intelligence and listening comprehension to socially inappropriate behavior and learning motivation. The test provides a basis for discussion during placement meetings as each participant completes the rating form. Total scores are averaged and compared to the criteria that describe each student as a poor, fair, good, or excellent candidate for LD placement. The manual outlines necessary testing and observations that should be made before the meeting. Examiner required. Not suitable for group use.

Untimed: 15 minutes
Scoring: Examiner evaluated
Cost: Test kit (manual, 50 rating forms in vinyl folder) $30.00
Publisher: Academic Therapy Publications

MATRIX ANALOGIES TEST— EXPANDED FORM (MAT-EF)
Refer to page 593.

MATRIX ANALOGIES TEST— SHORT FORM (MAT-SF)
Refer to page 593.

MCCARRON-DIAL SYSTEM (MDS)
Refer to page 847.

MEASUREMENT OF LANGUAGE DEVELOPMENT
Refer to page 702.

MINNESOTA PERCEPTO-DIAGNOSTIC TEST (MPD), 1982 REVISION
Refer to page 112.

MULLEN SCALES OF EARLY LEARNING (MSEL)
Refer to page 37.

MULTILEVEL INFORMAL LANGUAGE INVENTORY (MILI)
Refer to page 703.

NEALE ANALYSIS OF READING ABILITY—REVISED
Refer to page 350.

NEW MACMILLAN READING ANALYSIS
Refer to page 351.

THE O'BRIEN VOCABULARY PLACEMENT TEST
Refer to page 352.

PERCEPTUAL MEMORY TASK (PMT)
Refer to page 670.

THE POLLACK-BRANDEN BATTERY: FOR IDENTIFICATION OF LEARNING DISABILITIES, DYSLEXIA, AND CLASSROOM DYSFUNCTION

Child, adolescent—Ages 6–18

Purpose: Diagnoses students' learning disabilities. Used by clinicians and special education teachers to establish treatment plans or educational programs (IEPs).

Description: Multiple-item paper-pencil battery assessing receptive and expressive language skills. The battery diagnoses and classifies learning disabilities, dyslexia, and other classroom dysfunctions. The test consists of two subbatteries. The clinical battery informs clinicians of weaknesses and strengths in cognitive and emotional areas of development and is used as a basis for developing treatment plans. The classroom battery informs the educator of an individualized educational program (IEP) and identifies individual problem areas. Both subbatteries are based on the application of Luria's neuropsychological theories of functional learning systems in the brain. Criterion-referenced scoring and interpretation offers a direct guide to effective remedial approaches. Examiner required. Classroom battery suitable for group use.

Untimed: Varies

Scoring: Examiner evaluated

Cost: 10 tests $18.95; user's guide $14.95; specimen set $19.95

Publisher: Book-Lab

Information and availability unconfirmed; last verified in 1988.

PORTABLE TACTUAL PERFORMANCE TEST (P-TPT)
Refer to page 119.

PRESCHOOL SCREENING INSTRUMENT
Refer to page 556.

PRESCRIPTIVE READING PERFORMANCE TEST: A SCALE FOR THE DIAGNOSIS OF DYSLEXIA (PRPT)
Refer to page 374.

THE PREVERBAL ASSESSMENT-INTERVENTION PROFILE (P.A.I.P.)
Refer to page 616.

PSYCHO-EDUCATIONAL BATTERY (PEB)
Lillie Pope

All ages

Purpose: Identifies learning problems of children and adults. Used to develop individualized teaching plans.

Description: Multiple-item paper-pencil observational instrument measuring the following aspects of a student's functioning: motor performance; sensory and perceptual performance; language cognition and memory; and reading, spelling, and arithmetic skills. The examiner completes the inventory based on observations of the student. Some additional probing by the evaluator may be necessary. Interpretation of the inventory yields a psycho-educational assessment of skills and deficits in young children and all age groups for special needs populations. The subjects should be within a normal range of behavior and gross-motor skills. Two forms are available: Level Y (Grades K–6) and Level O (junior high to adult). The PEB consists of five components: a student recording form; evaluator recording form; a family, social, and medical history; a visual pack; and a teacher's referral form. Examiner required. Not suitable for group use.

Untimed: 1–2 hours

Scoring: Examiner evaluated

Cost: Complete kit (specify Level Y or O) $29.95; part A, recording forms $7.95; part B, evaluator's form $14.95; part C, family, social, and medical history $9.95; part D, visual pack $9.95; part E, teacher's referral form $6.95

Publisher: Book-Lab

Information and availability unconfirmed; last verified in 1988.

PSYCHOEDUCATIONAL PROFILE—REVISED (PEP-R)
Refer to page 559.

THE PUPIL RATING SCALE (REVISED): SCREENING FOR LEARNING DISABILITIES
Helmer R. Myklebust

Child
Grades K–6

Purpose: Measures hearing, speech, motor, and social behavior of elementary school children. Used to screen for learning disabilities.

Description: 24–item rating scale covering auditory comprehension, spoken language, orientation, motor coordination, and personal-social behavior. The test provides objective data for language disorders as well as for nonverbal behavior. Teachers must be familiar with the children they are rating. Examiner required. Suitable for group use.

Untimed: 5–10 minutes

Scoring: Examiner evaluated

Cost: Scale and manual $25.99; 50 record forms $15.95

Publisher: The Psychological Corporation

QUICKSCREEN
Janet B. Fudala

Child
Grades K–2

Purpose: Measures young children's ability to read, write, and use numbers in order to identify students who may have speech, language, or learning problems. Used to implement PL 94–142.

Description: Multiple-item paper-pencil verbal test available at three levels: kindergarten, first grade, and second grade. The kindergarten level, which is available in parallel forms A, B, C, and D, consists of four subtests: Name Writing, Figure Copying, Story, and Sentence Repetition. The first-grade level, available in parallel forms A and B, consists of five subtests: Name Writing, Figures, Words, Story, and Sentences. The second-grade level, available in parallel forms A and B, consists of five subtests: Name Writing, Figures, Story, Cognitive, and Sentences. Cutoff scores are provided to identify students with a high or possible risk of potential learning disability so they can be referred for more detailed evaluation. The manual provides evidence of reliability and validity, detailed instructions for administration and scoring, case studies, and recommended materials and tests for subsequent evaluation and remediation. The Score Sheet provides a summary of the entire classroom, and the Scoring Summary Card for the first-grade and second-grade levels summarizes scoring procedures on an easy-to-refer-to card to facilitate scoring. Examiner required. Suitable for group use.

Untimed: 15–25 minutes

Scoring: Hand key

Cost: Complete kit $92.50

Publisher: Western Psychological Services

READING COMPREHENSION INVENTORY (RCI)
Refer to page 353.

READING FREE VOCATIONAL INTEREST INVENTORY—REVISED (R-FVII REVISED)
Refer to page 834.

THE REVERSALS FREQUENCY TEST
Richard A. Gardner

Child, adolescent—Ages 5–15½

Purpose: Assesses a child's letter and number reversals frequency. Identifies children needing further evaluation for a neurologically based learning disability.

Description: Three multiple-item paper-pencil tests of letter and number reversals frequency. In the Reversals Execution Test, the child writes a specific list of numbers and letters, and the examiner records the number of items written in reversed orientation. The Reversals Recognition Test presents the child with an array of numbers and letters, some of which are correctly oriented and some of which are presented as mirror images. The child places a cross over the reversed items, and the examiner records the number of errors. In the Reversals Matching Test, each item consists of a model number or letter followed by four samples of the same letter or number. One of the four samples is correctly oriented, like the model. The child places a circle around the number or letter that matches the model, and the examiner records the number of errors. Each test is scored separately. Means, standard deviations, and percentile ranks are provided for both normal children and those known to have neurologically based learning disabilities. The manual provides tabulated data, graphs, and theoretical material that enable the examiner to ascertain the significance of a child's score in learning disability assessment. Examiner required. Suitable for group use.

Untimed: Varies

Scoring: Examiner evaluated

Cost: Test $15.00

Publisher: Creative Therapeutics

SCHOOL PROBLEM SCREENING INVENTORY, FIFTH EDITION
Thomas D. Gnagey

Child, adolescent
Grades PreK–12

Purpose: Diagnoses and classifies learning and behavior problems. Used for teacher planning and evaluation and to verify the continued eligibility of previously placed special education students.

Description: 37-item paper-pencil test consisting of 10 empirically derived

scales. Six scales assess the following specific diagnostic categories: learning disabilities (visual-motor and auditory-verbal), mental retardation, behavior disorder (overcontrolled and undercontrolled), and educational handicap. The four less differentiated scales that follow are used to determine the broad problem area in which to initiate further diagnostic evaluation when a child's problem does not fall within the six specific categories listed above: learning disabilities (general nonspecific), general learning skill deficit, behavior disorder (general nonspecific), and general maladjustment. The teacher uses an inventory sheet to rate the student on the 37 characteristics and sums the scores in each of the diagnostic categories to obtain ratings of "not likely," "possible," and "very likely." Examiner required. Not suitable for group use.

Untimed: 7–10 minutes

Scoring: Hand key

Cost: Manual, 20 analysis worksheets $16.00

Publisher: Slosson Educational Publications, Inc.

SCREENING TEST FOR THE ASSIGNMENT OF REMEDIAL TREATMENT
Refer to page 565.

SEARCH: A SCANNING INSTRUMENT FOR THE IDENTIFICATION OF POTENTIAL LEARNING DISABILITY
Archie A. Silver and Rosa A. Hagin

Child—Ages 5–6

Purpose: Detects learning difficulties and identifies specific skill deficits in children. Used to establish educational objectives for individual students and groups of students.

Description: Multiple-item oral-response and task-performance test consisting of 10 subtests: three tests of visual perception (matching, recall, and visual-motor), two auditory tests (discrimination and sequencing), two intermodal tests (articulation and initial consonants), and three body-image tests (directionality, finger schema, and pencil grip).

The total score indicates the degree of each child's vulnerability to learning failure in the early grades. The subtest scores yield a profile of the child's perceptual skills (assets and deficits), which is used in guiding subsequent educational intervention. Specific intervention procedures may be found in the test's companion program TEACH. Test scores are interpreted by means of VABs (vulnerable ranges for each component) and stanines for completion of the student's profile. Two kinds of norms may be used: age norms and local norms. The manual includes age norms ranging from 63–80 months for specific samples, such as inner-city, small-town rural, suburban, and selected independent schools, as well as instructions for computing local norms. The test may be used independently or in conjunction with TEACH. Examiner required. Not suitable for group use.

Untimed: 20 minutes

Scoring: Examiner evaluated

Cost: Complete kit (manual, 30 record blanks, 12 miniature identification toys) $47.50

Publisher: Walker Educational Book Corporation

SENSORY INTEGRATION AND PRAXIS TESTS (SIPT)
Refer to page 618.

SLINGERLAND SCREENING TESTS FOR IDENTIFYING CHILDREN WITH SPECIFIC LANGUAGE DISABILITY
Refer to page 713.

SOUTHGATE GROUP READING TESTS
Refer to page 357.

SPATIAL ORIENTATION MEMORY TEST
Joseph M. Wepman and D. Turaids

Child—Ages 5–9

Purpose: Measures a child's ability to retain and recall the orientation of visually presented forms. Used to identify children facing potential learning difficulties.

Description: Multiple-item oral-response test. The examiner presents a target page with a nonalphabetic design to the child and asks the child to select the same design from the response page, which contains four or five samples of the same design in different rotational positions. Spatial orientation ability prepares the child for individual letter discrimination recall, sequential ordering of letters in words, and related skills essential for reading. Adequacy scores are indicated for ages 5, 6, 7, 8, and 9. The test is available in two forms for retesting. Examiner required. Not suitable for group use.

Untimed: 10–15 minutes

Scoring: Hand key

Cost: Complete kit (reusable test booklet, 25 score sheets, manual) $60.00

Publisher: Western Psychological Services

THE SPELLMASTER ASSESSMENT AND TEACHING SYSTEM
Refer to page 279.

STANDARDIZED ROAD-MAP TEST OF DIRECTION SENSE
Refer to page 619.

STRUCTURE OF INTELLECT LEARNING ABILITIES TEST (SOI)
Refer to page 566.

SYMBOL DIGIT MODALITIES TEST
Refer to page 130.

THE TACTILE TEST OF BASIC CONCEPTS
Refer to page 567.

TEACHER ASSESSMENT OF GRAMMATICAL STRUCTURES
Refer to page 680.

TEST OF ADOLESCENT LANGUAGE-2 (TOAL-2)
Refer to page 716.

TEST OF CONCEPT UTILIZATION (TCU)
Refer to page 599.

TEST OF PRAGMATIC SKILLS (REVISED)
Refer to page 720.

TEST OF WORD FINDING (TWF)
Refer to page 721.

UNIFORM PERFORMANCE ASSESSMENT SYSTEM (UPAS)
Owen R. White, Norris G. Haring, Eugene B. Edgar, James Q. Affleck, and Alice H. Hayden

All ages

Purpose: Monitors a student's developmental progression in the basic skills normally acquired during the first six years of life.

Description: 250-item verbal-response test using stimulus cards to introduce tasks for measuring four categories of performance: preacademic/fine-motor skills, communication skills, social/self-help skills, and gross-motor development. Examiner required. Not suitable for group use.

Untimed: Varies; some subtests timed

Scoring: Examiner evaluated

Cost: Complete $98.00

Publisher: The Psychological Corporation

Information and availability unconfirmed; last verified in 1988.

VISCO CHILD DEVELOPMENT SCREENING TEST (THE CHILDS TEST)
Susan J. Visco and Carmela R. Visco

Child—Ages 3–7

Purpose: Assesses the development of learning abilities and skills in children. Identifies children with possible learning disabilities who should be referred for diagnostic evaluation.

Description: 118–item task-performance test measuring the basic skills and abilities required in the learning process. The following factors are evaluated: processing functions (visual perceptuomotor, auditory-visual-motor integration, visual vocal, and auditory vocal); abilities (sequencing, language, numerical, syntax, and articulation); and cognition (cognitive efficiency). In addition to the materials included in the kit, a stopwatch, a small table, 2 chairs, a tape for a line, a small cup, and a flight of stairs are required. Examiner required. Not suitable for group use.

Untimed: 25–30 minutes

Scoring: Hand key; examiner evaluated

Cost: Program (overview manual, test administration and scoring manual, 20 individualized record booklets, nine 1-inch cubes, 7 numerical Gestalt cards, 25 labels and functions picture cards, felt strip with 4 buttons, felt strip with 4 button holes) $59.00; 10 extra record booklets $11.95; orientation and training sound filmstrip $29.00

Publisher: Educational Activities, Inc.

Information and availability unconfirmed; last verified in 1988.

VISUAL SKILLS APPRAISAL (VSA)
Refer to page 733.

WELLER-STRAWSER SCALES OF ADAPTIVE BEHAVIOR: FOR THE LEARNING DISABLED (WSSAB)
Carol Weller and Sherri Strawser

**Child, adolescent
Grades 1–12**

Purpose: Assesses the adaptive behavior of elementary and secondary school learning disabled students. Used to determine severity of disabilities and to identify areas requiring remedial attention.

Description: Multiple-item paper-pencil norm-referenced scales covering social coping, relationships, pragmatic language, and production. The scales are completed by a teacher or diagnostician following a period of observation of the student. The total score and subtest scores define behavior problems as mild to moderate or moderate to severe. Using the results and following suggestions in the manual, the examiner may develop compensatory teaching techniques to help the student cope with situations in school, home, social, and job environments. Examiner required. Not suitable for group use.

Untimed: 15 minutes

Scoring: Examiner evaluated

Cost: Manual $15.00; 50 forms (specify elementary or secondary) $18.00

Publisher: Academic Therapy Publications

WOODCOCK LANGUAGE PROFICIENCY BATTERY (WLPB)
Refer to page 497.

THE WORD TEST
Refer to page 722.

Special Education: Mentally Handicapped

AAMD ADAPTIVE BEHAVIOR SCALE—RESIDENTIAL AND COMMUNITY EDITION
Kazuo Nihira, Ray Foster,
Max Shellhaas, and Henry Leland

Ages 3 and older

Purpose: Assesses the social and daily living skills of children and adults who are mentally retarded or emotionally disturbed.

Description: Two-part 110–item paper-pencil scale measuring the social and daily living skills and behaviors of children and adults who are mentally retarded or emotionally disturbed. Part One is organized along developmental lines and includes 10 domains covering skills considered important to personal independence: Independent Functioning, Physical Development, Economic Activity, Language Development, Numbers and Time, Domestic Activity, Vocational Activity, Self-Direction, Responsibility, and Socialization. Part Two measures 14 maladaptive behaviors related to personality and behavior disorders: Violent and Destructive Behavior, Antisocial Behavior, Rebellious Behavior, Untrustworthy Behavior, Withdrawal, Stereotyped Behavior and Odd Mannerisms, Inappropriate Interpersonal Manners, Unacceptable Vocal Habits, Unacceptable or Eccentric Habits, Self-Abusive Behavior, Hyperactive Tendencies, Sexually Aberrant Behavior, Psychological Disturbances, and Use of Medications. The manual includes instructions for administering, scoring, profiling, and interpreting, in addition to discussions of reliability, validity, and suggested administrative applications. The instructional planning profile summarizes an individual's scores on the 21 domains and yields a graphic profile. Examiner required. Not suitable for group use.

Untimed: 30 minutes

Scoring: Examiner evaluated

Cost: Starter kit $19.00

Publisher: PRO-ED

AAMD ADAPTIVE BEHAVIOR SCALE—SCHOOL EDITION (ABS-SE)
Nadine M. Lambert,
Myra Windmiller, Linda Cole, and
Deborah Tharinger

Child, adolescent—
Ages 3–16

Purpose: Assesses the social and daily living skills of children whose adaptive behavior indicates possible mental retardation, emotional disturbance, or other learning handicaps. Used for screening and instructional planning.

Description: 95–item paper-pencil scale measuring the social and daily living skills and behaviors of children. The instrument, which is completed by the examiner, yields five factor scores and one comparison score. Scores are converted to profiles that are used in diagnostic and placement decisions and in formulating general educational goals. Examiner required. Not suitable for group use.

Untimed: 30 minutes

Scoring: Examiner evaluated; may be computer scored

Cost: Starter set (manuals, 2 assessment booklets, 2 instructional planning profiles, 2 diagnostic profiles, 2 parent guides) $31.00

Publisher: PRO-ED

ABERRANT BEHAVIOR CHECKLIST (ABC)
Refer to page 230.

ADAPTIVE BEHAVIOR INVENTORY (ABI)
Linda Brown and James E. Leigh

School-aged children

Purpose: Evaluates the functional, daily living skills of school-aged children. Used to identify mentally retarded and emotionally disturbed children.

Description: 150–item paper-pencil tests assessing functional skills in the following five scale areas: Self-Care Skills (30 items), Communication Skills (30 items), Social Skills (30 items), Academic Skills (30 items), and Occupational Skills (30 items). The test yields an Adaptive Behavior Quotient, standard scores, and percentiles. The ABI-Short Form, which contains 50 items and yields the same scores as the complete form, is also available.

The PRO-SCORE scoring system is available from the publisher for use on Apple II, II +, and IIe and IBM PC and MS-DOS computers. The system generates a four-page report providing background information on the student; raw scores, standard scores, percentiles, and descriptions for each subtest; standard score sums, percentiles, and descriptors

for all composites and quotients; an optional cognitive aptitude score; subtest and composite profiles; intraindividual comparisons of all composites; and significance testing of all comparisons. Examiner required. Not suitable for group use.

Untimed: Not available

Scoring: Computer scored

Cost: Complete kit (25 profile and response sheets, 25 short form response sheets, manual, storage box) $49.00; PRO-SCORE scoring system (specify computer) $69.00

Publisher: PRO-ED

ADAPTIVE FUNCTIONING INDEX (AFI)
Nancy J. Marlett

Adult

Purpose: Measures a developmentally disabled or mentally retarded individual's ability to function independently in the community.

Description: 410–item criterion-referenced oral-response test assessing independent functioning. Items are grouped according to three categories: social education (180 items), vocational (80 items), and residential (150 items). Examiner required. Not suitable for group use. Available in French.

CANADIAN PUBLISHER

Untimed: 45–90 minutes

Scoring: Examiner evaluated

Cost: Complete kit $55.00

Publisher: The Vocational and Rehabilitation Research Institute

Information and availability unconfirmed; last verified in 1988.

ADAPTIVE FUNCTIONING OF THE DEPENDENT HANDICAPPED
Nancy J. Marlett, S. Cameron, S. Douglas, E. Hooper, and G. Long

All ages—Profoundly mentally retarded

Purpose: Identifies training and medical needs of the profoundly mentally retarded in the areas of nursing care, physical development, awareness, and self-help.

Description: 20–item paper-pencil test composed of four categories identifying the medical and training needs of the profoundly mentally retarded: Nursing Care (5 items), Physical Development (5 items), Awareness (5 items), and Self-Help (5 items). Examiner required. Suitable for group use.
CANADIAN PUBLISHER

Untimed: Varies

Scoring: Examiner evaluated

Cost: 10 tests $5.20; 50 tests $22.00 (Canadian rates)

Publisher: The Vocational and Rehabilitation Research Institute

Information and availability unconfirmed; last verified in 1988.

ADD-H COMPREHENSIVE TEACHER'S RATING SCALE (ACTERS)
Rina K. Ullmann, Ester K. Sleator, and Robert L. Sprague

**Child
Grades K–5**

Purpose: Aids in diagnosis of Attention Deficit Disorder with or without Hyperactivity. Used as a screening device to differentiate between ADD-H children and those who may be otherwise learning disabled, to help determine children who may benefit from therapeutic intervention, and to monitor medication dosages of ADD-H children.

Description: 24–item paper-pencil or computer-administered multiple-choice test assessing behavior relevant to the diagnosis of Attention Deficit Disorder. The four scales are Attention (6 items), Hyperactivity (5 items), Social Skills (7 items), and Oppositional (6 items). The classroom teacher rates items on a 5–point scale ranging from "almost never" to "almost always." An ACTeRS Profile (Boys or Girls forms) is generated. The computer version operates on IBM PC and compatible systems. APA purchase restrictions apply. Examiner required. Not suitable for group use.

Untimed: 15 minutes

Scoring: Self-scored; computer scored

Cost: Kit (manual, 100 rating forms/profiles) $48.00; computer version $75.00

Publisher: MetriTech, Inc.

ANALYTIC LEARNING DISABILITY ASSESSMENT (ALDA)
Refer to page 629.

BALTHAZAR SCALES OF ADAPTIVE BEHAVIOR I: SCALES OF FUNCTIONAL INDEPENDENCE
Earl E. Balthazar

Mentally retarded of all ages

Purpose: Evaluates the self-help skills of the profoundly or severely mentally retarded. Used to plan and monitor goal-directed remedial programs.

Description: Multiple-item paper-pencil observational inventory assessing the functional independence of profoundly and severely handicapped individuals. Data derived from direct observation of the individual are used to determine objective performance levels, which in turn identify appropriate remedial programs for developing self-help skills. The scoring form includes nighttime supplements. Program effectiveness can be evaluated by readministering the scales. Personnel in residential treatment facilities can be trained within a week to become observers and raters. The inventory is also helpful in explaining the development of self-help skills to families. Examiner required. Not suitable for group use.

Untimed: Varies

Scoring: Examiner evaluated

Cost: 2–volume 1983 manual $12.50; 25 scoring forms $10.00

Publisher: Consulting Psychologists Press, Inc.

BALTHAZAR SCALES OF ADAPTIVE BEHAVIOR II: SCALES OF SOCIAL ADAPTATION
Earl E. Balthazar

Mentally retarded children and adults

Purpose: Evaluates the coping behaviors of profoundly retarded adults and children. Used for program planning and progress evaluation.

Description: Multiple-item paper-pencil observational inventory assessing eight categories of social adaptation and coping behaviors: unadaptive self-directed behaviors, unadaptive interpersonal behaviors, adaptive self-directed behaviors, adaptive interpersonal behaviors, verbal communication, play activities, response to instructions, and checklist items. Ratings are based on direct observation of the individual in his own environment. Readministration of the scales is sensitive to changes in the individual's behavior. The manual provides instructions for use by technicians, teachers, and other paraprofessionals. Examiner required. Not suitable for group use.

Untimed: Varies

Scoring: Examiner evaluated

Cost: Complete kit (manual and materials for 25 subjects) $22.00

Publisher: Consulting Psychologists Press, Inc.

BAY AREA FUNCTIONAL PERFORMANCE EVALUATION, 2ND EDITION (BAFPE)
Refer to page 158.

BECKER WORK ADJUSTMENT PROFILE (BWAP)
Ralph L. Becker

Adolescent, adult—Ages 15 and older

Purpose: Assesses the vocational adjustment and competency of individuals with mental retardation, cerebral palsy, cultural disadvantage, learning disabilities, emotional disturbance, and physical disabilities.

Description: 63–item Likert-type paper-pencil questionnaire completed by an individual familiar with the examinee's work. Vocational adjustment and competency are evaluated in four domains: Work-Habits/Attitudes (10 items), Interpersonal Relations (12 items), Cognitive Skills (19 items), and Work Performance skills (22 items).

In addition to scores in each domain, a global score is obtained. The raw scores are converted to percentiles, T-scores, and stanines using an appropriate norm for the mentally retarded, physically disabled, emotionally disturbed, or learning disabled. Two profiles are available: a Peer Profile to interpret an individual's work adjustment compared with other people who have the same disability and an Employability Status Profile that provides a graphic picture of the person's vocational competency for placement in one of five program tracks: Day Care, Work Activity, Sheltered Workshop, Transitional, and Community-Competitive. Two editions of the questionnaire are available: a short scale and a full scale. Examiner required. Not suitable for group use.

Untimed: 10–20 minutes

Scoring: Examiner required

Cost: Starter set (2 short scales, 2 full scales, 2 profiles, manual) $15.25

Publisher: Elbern Publications

BEHAVIORAL CHARACTERISTICS PROGRESSION (BCP)
Refer to page 660.

BEREWEEKE SKILL TEACHING SYSTEM—REVISED EDITION
D. Felce, J. Mansell, J. Jenkins, and U. de Kock

Severely and moderately mentally handicapped children and adults

Purpose: Assesses the behavioral capabilities of mentally handicapped individuals. Used by residential and day care staff, including nurses, occupational therapists, and social workers, to monitor progress and plan teaching programs designed to promote self-sufficiency.

Description: Multiple-item paper-pencil checklist used by caregivers to assess a patient's everyday living skills and weaknesses. The checklist provides space for recording the patient's present behavior and for formulating long-term goals. Patient progress in the daily teaching program is monitored by a nursing officer or senior social worker. The revised edition features age-appropriate items and an updated handbook. The test is available in two versions: children and adult. Examiner required. Not suitable for group use.
BRITISH PUBLISHER
Untimed: Continuous teaching and monitoring program
Scoring: Examiner evaluated
Cost: Contact publisher
Publisher: NFER-NELSON Publishing Company Ltd.

BRISTOL LANGUAGE DEVELOPMENT SCALES
Refer to page 688.

BRISTOL SOCIAL ADJUSTMENT GUIDES, AMERICAN EDITION (BSAG)
Refer to page 737.

BRITISH PICTURE VOCABULARY SCALES
Refer to page 587.

CAIN-LEVINE SOCIAL COMPETENCY SCALE
Leo F. Cain, Samuel Levine, and Freeman F. Elzey

**Child, adolescent—
Ages 5–13**

Purpose: Measures the social competence of trainable mentally retarded children. Used for diagnosis, placement, planning, and training evaluation.

Description: 44–item scale of four aspects of social competence: self-help,

initiative, social skills, and communication. Items are administered and evaluated by interviewing the child's parents. Four subscale scores and a total score are yielded. Percentile norms based on mentally retarded children are offered for chronological ages 5–13. The manual includes instructions for use of the scales by teachers and clinicians. Examiner required. Not suitable for group use.

Untimed: Open ended
Scoring: Examiner evaluated
Cost: Manual $7.00; 25 scales $18.00
Publisher: Consulting Psychologists Press, Inc.

CALLIER AZUZA SCALE: H-EDITION
Refer to page 688.

CAMELOT BEHAVIORAL CHECKLIST
Ray W. Foster

All ages

Purpose: Evaluates adaptive behavior skills in mentally retarded persons. Used to plan and monitor educational programs for such individuals.

Description: 399–item paper-pencil checklist in 10 categories and 40 subcategories measuring the following skills: self-help, physical development, home, duties, vocational and economic behaviors, independent travel, numerical and communication skills, and social behavior responsibility. The examiner assigns each description a plus or minus value, which is transferred to a profile sheet that records and displays the student's progress and aids in the sequencing of training objectives. The test is of limited use to the severely retarded. Examiner required. Not suitable for group use.

Untimed: 20 minutes
Scoring: Hand key
Cost: Manual $3.50; checklist $0.45 each
Publisher: Camelot Behavioral Systems

CHART OF INITIATIVE AND INDEPENDENCE
J. Whitehouse

All ages—Mentally handicapped individuals

Purpose: Assesses present behavior, potential, and level of opportunity. Used by hospital, day care, and residential staffs to set future goals for mentally handicapped individuals in their care.

Description: Two multiple-item paper-pencil appraisals designed to increase a mentally handicapped individual's opportunities by encouraging initiative and independence. First, the examiner uses the Individual Assessment Form to record the individual's current levels of behavior, opportunity, and potential. Next, the Developmental Program Form is used to suggest goals. The Residential Policy Form is completed next to form a background for examining the feasibility of the goals. It is used to record institutional policy as well as entry and exit criteria. The Preliminary Assessment Form, which is a shortened version of the Individual Assessment Form, is available for social workers. Examiner required. Not suitable for group use.

Untimed: Continuous recording and goal-setting system

Scoring: Examiner evaluated

Cost: Contact publisher

Publisher: NFER-NELSON Publishing Company Ltd.

COGNITIVE DIAGNOSTIC BATTERY (CDB)
Stanley R. Kay

All ages

Purpose: Evaluates the nature and degree of intellectual disorders. May be used with intellectually limited, nonverbal, inattentive, overtly psychotic, or otherwise untestable patients for purposes of diagnostic evaluation and monitoring treatment progress.

Description: Multiple-item nonverbal-response and task-performance tests assessing cognitive deficits due to im-paired development versus later regression. Five tests utilize a Piagetian developmental framework to assess early conceptual maturation, higher order concept utilization, egocentric versus socialized thinking, perceptual motor development, attention span, arousal-related cognitive disturbance, and psychomotor rate. Normative data are provided for schizophrenics, mentally retarded psychotics, normal adults, children, and the elderly. The results differentially diagnose mental retardation from psychosis. The manual includes technical data. Examiner required. Not suitable for group use.

Untimed: 10–30 minutes

Scoring: Hand key

Cost: Test kit (5 tests, manual, 50 record forms, 50 span-of-attention forms) $44.95

Publisher: Psychological Assessment Resources, Inc.

COMPREHENSIVE LANGUAGE PROGRAM (CLP)
Peoria Association for Retarded Citizens

Mental ages 0–5

Purpose: Evaluates the language and pre-language skills of retarded and handicapped individuals who have language development problems. Used for diagnosis and remediation.

Description: Multiple-item oral-response and task-assessment test covering eight areas of language development: attending, manipulation of objects, mimicking, matching, identifying, labeling, following directions, and word combinations. A checklist records the student's entry-level achievement. The results provide a basis for subsequent instruction. There are 285 detailed lesson plans, designed for use 20 to 30 minutes daily, 5 days a week, covering the eight areas. Record sheets record incremental progress. Examiner required. Not suitable for group use.

Untimed: Varies

Scoring: Hand key

Cost: Starter set $190.00

Publisher: Scholastic Testing Service, Inc.

COMPREHENSIVE TEST OF ADAPTIVE BEHAVIOR
Gary Adams

All ages

Purpose: Aids in the precise evaluation of handicapped individual's adaptive abilities. Used for placement and to determine where an individual stands in relation to others of the same age or handicap. Also helps in establishing the scope and sequence of training.

Description: 527–item paper-pencil inventory of adaptive behavior in six skill categories: self-help (with separate subtests for male and female), home living, independent living, social, sensorimotor, and language concepts/academic skills. The examiner checks off the skills the individual has mastered based on observation of the individual, parent/guardian report, and formal testing. Because skills are sequenced in the order that handicapped individuals acquire them, not in normal developmental order, the test is inappropriate for normally developing individuals. Examiner required. Not suitable for group use.

Untimed: Variable

Scoring: Examiner evaluated

Cost: Complete program $59.00; components available individually

Publisher: The Psychological Corporation

Information and availability unconfirmed; last verified in 1988.

DEVELOPMENTAL ASSESSMENT OF LIFE EXPERIENCES, 1986 REVISED (DALE)
*Gertrude A. Barber,
John P. Mannino, and Robert J. Will*

All ages

Purpose: Assesses skill development in individuals who have been withdrawn from the mainstream of society for long durations of time at institutions for developmental and/or physical handicaps.

Description: A systemized approach to monitoring skill development in school-age children and in adults. Five basic processes are employed during habilitation: a) assessment to determine behavioral strengths and needs, b) discussion and planning of the assessment results to determine the direction intervention goals should take, c) program development to establish specific intervention goals and objectives, d) plan implementation for carrying out the program, and e) evaluation of the plan's success or failure.

Two inventories include lists of items covering a spectrum of self-care and community living skills. The Level I inventory, for severely mentally retarded individuals (A.A.M.S. Classification), lists 258 items describing tasks reflecting the following areas of self-help skills: sensorimotor, language, self-help, cognition, and socialization. Level II (509 items) lists behaviors that are of a higher functioning nature and assess the following community living skills: personal hygiene, personal management, communications, residence/home maintenance, and community access. The items describe skills in terms of the ways in which specific tasks are approached or completed and are expressed in positive terminology. The items within each skill area are listed in order of increasing difficulty.

Two types of scores are utilized in rating every item on the inventory. A quantitative score indicates the frequency of the response; items are rated as responds less than 50%, responds approximately 50%, responds 90% or greater, N/A (not applicable), N/O (never observed), or INCAP (incapable of responding). Qualitative ratings identify responses for each behavioral item as inappropriate/incorrect, fair approximation with reminders, or excellent approximation with few reminders.

Initial evaluation identifies an individual's competencies (require a "3c" rating), which can then serve as a basis for determining the skills that need to be expanded or developed. A series of graphs is provided to summarize this evaluative information by subscale (bathing, money concepts, etc.), priority (personal hygiene, sensorimotor, etc.), and full-scale (all items on the inventory). Although the skills are recommended to be rated and graphed semiannually, items on which the individual has achieved competency are graphed immediately on the cumulative chart, showing on any given day all the areas in which an individual has exhibited competency. The manual provides an instructional narrative, which serves as a guide in the use of the system and presents sample copies of pertinent data recording forms. Examiner required. Not suitable for group use.

Untimed: Ongoing

Scoring: Examiner evaluated

Cost: Manual $5.00; Level I booklet $3.50; Level II booklet $3.50

Publisher: Barber Center Press Publications

THE DEVEREUX CHILD BEHAVIOR RATING SCALE (DCB)
George Spivack and Jules Spotts

Child—Ages 6–12

Purpose: Assesses symptomatic behaviors of children. Used with mentally retarded and emotionally disturbed children for diagnostic and screening procedures, group placement decisions, and assessment of progress in response to specific programs or procedures.

Description: 97–item paper-pencil inventory assessing overt behavior patterns of children. The evaluator (parent or child-care worker living with the child) rates each item according to how he feels the subject's behavior compares to the behavior of normal children of the same age. The test yields 17 scores: Distractibility, Poor Self-Care, Pathological Use of Senses, Emotional Detachment, Social Isolation, Poor Coordination and Body Tonus, Incontinence, Messiness-Sloppiness, Inadequate Need for Independence, Unresponsiveness to Stimulation, Proneness to Emotional Upset, Need for Adult Contact, Anxious-Fearful Ideation, "Impulse" Ideation, Inability to Delay, Social Aggression, and Unethical Behavior. Examiner required. Not suitable for group use.

Untimed: 10–15 minutes

Scoring: Examiner evaluated

Cost: Contact publisher

Publisher: The Devereux Foundation

EINSTEIN ASSESSMENT OF SCHOOL RELATED SKILLS
Refer to page 634.

FLORIDA INTERNATIONAL DIAGNOSTIC-PRESCRIPTIVE VOCATIONAL COMPETENCY PROFILE
Refer to page 844.

FUNCTIONAL PERFORMANCE RECORD
D. Mulhall

All ages—Handicapped individuals

Purpose: Assesses the degree to which an individual can independently perform a wide range of daily living skills and aids in program planning and evaluation. Used by care staffs, health visitors, doctors, occupational therapists, nursing officers, speech therapists, health authorities, and social service departments with physically and mentally handicapped, elderly, and other residential/day care clients.

Description: 600–item paper-pencil or computer-administered checklist divided into 27 functional areas: activity level; aggression; attention span; domestic/survival skills; dressing (female); dressing (male); feeding; fits and faints; hearing; incontinence; memory; mobility; motor coordination and loss of balance; muscular function; number skills; personal hygiene; personal safety; reading skill; social behavior; socially unacceptable behavior; speech and language production; speech and language reception; toileting; touch, temperature, and hypothermia; transportation; vision; and writing skills. The client's caregiver completes the questionnaire by using the paper-pencil version, entering data directly onto a record disk that collates results on an IBM microcomputer, or transferring data from the paper-pencil version to the record disk. Scores are provided for each of the 27 areas of functioning. When used in conjunction with a special database, the checklist allows analysis of group results that can aid in staffing, bud-

---

geting, and resource allocation. On an individual level, the assessment can be used to prepare individuals for discharge from special education programs, mental and psychiatric hospitals, and other institutions and to monitor therapy progress. Examiner required. Suitable for group use.

Untimed: Varies

Scoring: Computer scored; may be hand scored

Cost: Contact publisher

Publisher: NFER-NELSON Publishing Company Ltd.

GOODMAN LOCK BOX
Refer to page 545.

GRASSI BASIC COGNITIVE EVALUATION
Refer to page 105.

HUGHES BASIC GROSS MOTOR ASSESSMENT (HBGMA)
Refer to page 612.

INDEPENDENT LIVING BEHAVIOR CHECKLIST (ILBC)
Richard T. Walls, Thomas Zane, and John E. Thvedt

Adult—Ages 16 and older

Purpose: Assesses independent living skills, progress in reaching goals, and program effectiveness. Used to develop objectively specified curriculum for programming independent living skills for individuals with mental and physical limitations.

Description: 343–item criterion-referenced checklist used to assess the independent living skills of individuals. The items cover six domains: a) mobility skills (42 items), b) self-care skills (63 items), c) home maintenance and safety skills (46 items), d) food skills (75 items), e) social and communication skills (69 items), and f) functional academic skills (48 items). Each item includes a condition, behavior, and standard for performance. The examiner rates each item as mastered (+), to be

trained (–), or not applicable based on prior knowledge of the client, observation on-the-job or in a training setting, or the examinee's performance in a simulated environment. A skills profile is developed. Examiner required. Not suitable for group use.

Untimed: Varies

Scoring: Hand key

Cost: Manual with skill summary chart $8.00; 10 summary charts $1.00

Publisher: Research and Training Center Press

INVENTORY FOR CLIENT AND AGENCY PLANNING (ICAP)
Refer to page 665.

KAUFMAN DEVELOPMENTAL SCALE (KDS)
Refer to page 550.

KAUFMAN INFANT AND PRESCHOOL SCALE (KIPS)
Refer to page 34.

KEY EDUCATIONAL VOCATIONAL ASSESSMENT SYSTEM (KEVAS)
Refer to page 846.

KOONTZ CHILD DEVELOPMENTAL PROGRAM: TRAINING ACTIVITIES FOR THE FIRST 48 MONTHS
Refer to page 551.

LANGUAGE FACILITY TEST
Refer to page 700.

LEITER INTERNATIONAL PERFORMANCE SCALE (ARTHUR ADAPTATION)
Refer to page 56.

LEITER INTERNATIONAL PERFORMANCE SCALE (LIPS)
Refer to page 56.

MCCARRON-DIAL SYSTEM (MDS)
Refer to page 847.

MOTOR-FREE VISUAL PERCEPTION TEST (MVPT)
Refer to page 615.

MULLEN SCALES OF EARLY LEARNING (MSEL)
Refer to page 37.

NISONGER QUESTIONNAIRE FOR PARENTS
Refer to page 666.

NON-READERS INTELLIGENCE TEST (THIRD EDITION) AND ORAL VERBAL INTELLIGENCE TEST
Refer to page 595.

OARS MULTIDIMENSIONAL FUNCTIONAL ASSESSMENT QUESTIONNAIRE
Refer to page 114.

PATHWAYS TO INDEPENDENCE
Refer to page 667.

PERCEPTUAL MEMORY TASK (PMT)
Refer to page 670.

PHONOLOGICAL PROCESS ANALYSIS
Refer to page 705.

THE PORTAGE EARLY EDUCATION PROGRAMME—UK VERSION

Child—Ages 0-6

Purpose: Assesses and monitors children's developmental skills. Used by teachers to set teaching goals and develop teaching activities for children whose developmental age is 0–6.

Description: A checklist containing 624 behaviors covering infant stimulation, self-help, motor skills, cognitive, socialization, and language skills forms the initial phase of the program. The checklist incorporates both the original checklist of behaviors and the Wessex Revised Portage Language Checklist, which is no longer available as a separate instrument. This revised checklist lists the 624 behaviors according to years or stages of development. Revised activity cards (incorporates original cards and the Wessex cards) present suggestions for teaching each behavior on the checklist. An activity chart for record keeping and planning individualized training programs is available. The manual presents instructions for setting up and administering a Portage scheme. Examiner required. Not suitable for group use.

Untimed: Continuous assessment and teaching program

Scoring: Examiner evaluated

Cost: Contact publisher

Publisher: NFER-NELSON Publishing Company Ltd.

PRAGMATICS PROFILE OF EARLY COMMUNICATION SKILLS
Refer to page 706.

PRE-MOD II
Refer to page 745.

THE PREVERBAL ASSESSMENT-INTERVENTION PROFILE (P.A.I.P.)
Refer to page 616.

PRE-VERBAL COMMUNICATION SCHEDULE
Refer to page 708.

READING FREE VOCATIONAL INTEREST INVENTORY— REVISED (R-FVII REVISED)
Refer to page 834.

SCALES OF INDEPENDENT BEHAVIOR (SIB)
Robert H. Bruininks,
Richard W. Woodcock,
Richard F. Weatherman, and
Bradley K. Hill

Infant-adult

Purpose: Measures adaptive and problem behavior. Used in school, community, and institutional settings to determine personal and community independence of nonhandicapped and handicapped individuals with varying degrees of mental, emotional, behavioral, or physical disability. Helps determine eligibility for special services, program planning, and individual and program evaluation.

Description: Multiple-item structured interview guide with 14 subtests assessing motor skills, social interaction and communication skills, personal independence skills, and problem behaviors. In addition, four maladaptive behavior indexes measure the frequency and severity of problem behaviors: General Maladaptive Index, Internalized Maladaptive Index, Externalized Maladaptive Index, and Asocial Maladaptive Index. Age scores, percentile ranks, standard scores, relative performance index, expected range of independence, and instructional range are obtained. The examiner uses an easel-binder for interviewing the examinee. Information also may be obtained from the parent, caregiver, or teacher. The SIB offers five administration options: full battery, short form, early development scale, individual clusters, and a problem behavior scale. This test is related structurally and statistically to the Woodcock-Johnson Psycho-Educational Battery (1977). Because common norms are provided for the two tests, an individual's adaptive behavior may be interpreted in relation to cognitive ability. Examiner required. Not suitable for group use.

Untimed: Complete battery 45–60 minutes; other forms 10–15 minutes

Scoring: Examiner evaluated; may be computer scored

Cost: Complete program (test book, interviewer's manual, 25 response booklets) $125.00

Publisher: DLM Teaching Resources

SCHOOL CHILD STRESS SCALE (SCSS)
Refer to page 150.

SCHOOL READINESS TESTS FOR BLIND CHILDREN (STBC)
Refer to page 564.

SCREENING CHILDREN FOR RELATED EARLY EDUCATIONAL NEEDS (SCREEN)
Refer to page 564.

SEQUENCE RECALL (SEQREC)
Refer to page 126.

SEQUENCED INVENTORY OF COMMUNICATION DEVELOPMENT, REVISED EDITION
Refer to page 712.

SKILLS ASSESSMENT MODULE (SAM)
Refer to page 804.

SOCIAL AND PREVOCATIONAL INFORMATION BATTERY, REVISED (SPIB-R)
Andrew Halpern, Paul Raffeld,
Larry K. Irvin, Robert Link, and
Ardan Munkres

EMR students in junior and senior high school, adults

Purpose: Assesses an educable mentally retarded student's knowledge of skills and competencies important for community adjustment. Used by educators as an evaluative device in programs for EMR students.

Description: 277–item orally administered paper-pencil test consisting of nine subtests (Job Search Skills, Job Related Behavior, Banking, Budgeting, Purchasing, Home Management, Physical Health Care, Hygiene and Grooming, Functional Signs) measuring a student's attainment of five long-range goals of work-study or work experience programs in secondary schools: employability, economic self-sufficiency, family living, personal habits, and communication. The student responds to each item by marking it true-false or by selecting an appropriate picture. Results can be used to place students in the Skills for Independent Living resource kit curriculum. Examiner required. Suitable for use with groups not exceeding 20 students.

Untimed: 15–25 minutes per subtest

Scoring: Hand key; may be computer scored

Cost: Specimen set (both a machine-scorable and hand-scorable test book, manual, answer key, user's guide, class record sheet, test reviewer's guide) $14.60

Publisher: CTB/Macmillan/McGraw-Hill

SOCIAL AND PREVOCATIONAL INFORMATION BATTERY-T (SPIB-T)
Andrew Halpern, Paul Raffeld, Larry K. Irvin, Robert Link, and Jacqueline D. Beckland

TMR students in junior and senior high school, adults

Purpose: Assesses a mild to moderately mentally retarded student's knowledge of skills and competencies important for community adjustment. Used by educators to evaluate students and programs.

Description: 291–item orally administered paper-pencil test consisting of nine subtests (Job Search Skills, Job Related Behavior, Banking, Budgeting, Purchasing, Home Management, Physical Health Care, Hygiene and Grooming, and Functional Signs) measuring a student's attainment of five long-range goals of work-study or work experience programs in secondary schools: employability, economic self-sufficiency, family living, personal habits, and communication. The

results can be used to place students in the Skills for Independent Living resource kit curriculum. Examiner required. Suitable for use with groups not exceeding 20 students.

Untimed: 15–25 minutes per subtest

Scoring: Hand key

Cost: Specimen set (hand-scorable test book, pretest, manual, answer key, technical summary) $14.60

Publisher: CTB/Macmillan/McGraw-Hill

SOCIO-SEXUAL KNOWLEDGE AND ATTITUDES TEST (SSKAT)
Refer to page 93.

STREET SURVIVAL SKILLS QUESTIONNAIRE (SSSQ)
Refer to page 673.

STYCAR HEARING TESTS
Refer to page 680.

STYCAR LANGUAGE TEST
Refer to page 715.

SYSTEM FOR ASSESSMENT AND GROUP EVALUATION (SAGE)
Refer to page 806.

TARC ASSESSMENT SYSTEM FOR SEVERELY HANDICAPPED CHILDREN
Wayne Sailor and Bonnie Jean Mix

Severely handicapped children

Purpose: Measures the self-help, motor communication, and social skills of severely handicapped children. Used to evaluate rehabilitation programs and to assess the effectiveness of specific instruction.

Description: Multiple-item observational examination in which the examiner spends several weeks observing a child's behavior in group situations and then uses an assessment inventory to score specific behaviors. The scores are transferred to a profile display sheet that relates behavior to both the child and a standard sample, pointing out undeveloped and strong skills. The examiner must have professional training. Examiner required. Not suitable for group use.

Untimed: Open ended

Scoring: Examiner evaluated

Cost: Manual, 10 assessment sheets $16.00

Publisher: PRO-ED

TEST OF ADOLESCENT LANGUAGE-2 (TOAL-2)
Refer to page 716.

TEST OF EARLY WRITTEN LANGUAGE (TEWL)
Refer to page 567.

TEST OF PRAGMATIC SKILLS (REVISED)
Refer to page 720.

TEST OF WORD FINDING (TWF)
Refer to page 721.

T.M.R. PERFORMANCE PROFILE FOR THE SEVERELY AND MODERATELY RETARDED
Alfred J. DiNola, Bernard Kaminsky, and Allen E. Sternfeld

Mentally retarded individuals

Purpose: Assesses the adaptive behavior of severely and moderately retarded individuals. Used by teachers for curriculum planning.

Description: 240–item paper-pencil inventory assessing six areas of behavior: social, self-care and safety, communication, basic knowledge, practical skills, and body usage and health. Individual performance is measured against specific developmental items on a 5–point rating scale. Examiner required. Not suitable for group use.

Untimed: Varies

Scoring: Examiner evaluated

Cost: Class kit (teacher's manual, 10 record booklets, and 10 yearly comparative charts) $20.00

Publisher: Educational Performance Associates

T.M.R. SCHOOL COMPETENCY SCALES
Samuel Levine, Freeman F. Elzey, Paul Thormahlen, and Leo F. Cain

Child, adolescent—Ages 5 and older

Purpose: Assesses students' adaptive skills in trainable mentally retarded (TMR) classroom settings. Used to evaluate strengths and weaknesses and to measure progress.

Description: 91– or 103–item paper-pencil rating scale measuring five school competence skill areas: perceptual-motor, initiative-responsibility, cognition, personal-social, and language. Items are rated on a 4–point scale by the classroom teacher. Materials include separate scales for each of five age groups: 5–7, 8–10, 11–13, 14–16, and 17 and older. Scales are published in two forms: one for the two younger age groups (91 items) and one for the three older age groups (103 items). Examiner required. Not suitable for group use.

Untimed: Not available

Scoring: Examiner evaluated

Cost: Specimen set (manual, Scales I and II) $8.50; manual $6.50; 25 scales (specify form) $37.00

Publisher: Consulting Psychologists Press, Inc.

VALETT INVENTORY OF CRITICAL THINKING ABILITIES (VICTA)
Refer to page 568.

VCWS 1—SMALL TOOLS (MECHANICAL)
Refer to page 1074.

VCWS 2—SIZE DISCRIMINATION
Refer to page 1074.

VCWS 4—UPPER EXTREMITY RANGE OF MOTION
Refer to page 1075.

VCWS 6—INDEPENDENT PROBLEM SOLVING
Refer to page 924.

VCWS 7—MULTI-LEVEL SORTING
Refer to page 1075.

VCWS 11—EYE-HAND-FOOT COORDINATION
Refer to page 1076.

VCWS 17—PRE-VOCATIONAL READINESS BATTERY

Adult

Purpose: Measures an individual's ability to function independently. May be used with mentally retarded individuals to determine whether the individual requires a sheltered environment or can function independently.

Description: Assessment and training tool containing five subtests: Developmental Assessment, Workshop Evaluation, Vocational Interest Screening, Interpersonal/Social Skills, and Independent Living Skills. The Developmental Assessment subtest contains functional nonmedical measures of physical and mental abilities. Workshop Evaluation is a simulated assembly process designed to determine whether the examinee is appropriately placed in a work or training setting. The Vocational Interest Screening subtest, presented in an audiovisual format, identifies job interests. The Interpersonal/Social Skills subtest identifies barriers to employment or independent living. The Independent Living Skills subtest measures skill and knowledge in transportation, money handling, grooming, and living environment. The tasks in each subtest vary in difficulty from very simple

recognition of rooms to more complex processes relating to work. The test is designed in such a way that a lack of language or reading skills does not present a barrier to evaluation. The test should not be administered to individuals with severe impairment of the upper extremities. Examiner required. Not suitable for group use.

Timed: Not available

Scoring: Examiner evaluated

Cost: $3,595.00

Publisher: Valpar International Corporation

VINELAND ADAPTIVE BEHAVIOR SCALES
Refer to page 257.

VOCATIONAL ADAPTATION RATING SCALES (VARS)
Robert G. Malgady, Peter R. Barcher, John Davis, and George Towner

Mentally retarded

Purpose: Measures problem behaviors among mentally retarded adolescents and adults in vocational settings. Used for curriculum development, Individualized Education Programs (IEPs) placement, and evaluating readiness for mainstreaming.

Description: 133–item paper-pencil inventory measuring the kind of maladaptive behavior likely to occur in vocational settings, such as sheltered workshops, job facilities, or vocational training programs. The examiner (a teacher, nurse, parent, or other adult familiar with the individual) uses a scale ranging from "never" to "regularly" to indicate the frequency with which the individual displays the behavior described in the statement. Six scales are measured: Verbal Manners; Communication Skills; Attendance and Punctuality; Interpersonal Behavior; Respect for Property, Rules and Regulations; and Grooming and Personal Hygiene. All six scales and the total score are profiled for both frequency and severity (a useful indicator of potential job impairment) in deciles and T-scores. Examiner required. Suitable for group use.

Untimed: 20–30 minutes

Scoring: Hand key

Cost: Complete kit (25 booklets, manual) $30.00

Publisher: Western Psychological Services

VOCATIONAL BEHAVIOR CHECKLIST (VBC)
Refer to page 851.

VOCATIONAL INFORMATION AND EVALUATION WORK SAMPLES (VIEWS)
Refer to page 837.

VOCATIONAL INTEREST AND SOPHISTICATION ASSESSMENT (VISA)
J.J. Parnicky, H. Kahn, and A.D. Burdett

Adolescent, adult

Purpose: Determines the vocational interests and job information of mildly retarded adolescents and young adults. Used for counseling, training projections, and job placement.

Description: Verbal picture-book examination. The book for men evaluates aptitudes for work in garages, laundries, food service, maintenance, farm/grounds, materials handling, and industry. The book for women evaluates interests in business/clerical, housekeeping, food service, laundry, and sewing. Examiner required. Not suitable for group use.

Untimed: 30–45 minutes

Scoring: Examiner evaluated

Cost: Specimen set $15.00; manual $4.00; male picture book $5.00; female picture book $4.00; 50 inquiry forms $5.00; 25 male or female response forms $2.00; 25 male or female profile forms $3.00

Publisher: The Nisonger Center, Ohio State University

Information and availability unconfirmed; last verified in 1987.

VOCATIONAL INTEREST, TEMPERAMENT, AND APTITUDE SYSTEM (VITAS)

Adult
High school students

Purpose: Assesses aptitudes, vocational interests, and work-related temperaments of disadvantaged and educable mentally retarded persons. Used for vocational guidance.

Description: Performance test of vocational aptitudes consisting of work samples in 21 areas: nuts, bolts, and washers assembly; packing matchbooks; tile sorting and weighing; collating material samples; verifying numbers; pressing linens; budget book assembly; nail and screw sorting; pipe assembly; filing by letters; lock assembly; circuit board inspection; calculating; message taking; bank teller; proofreading; payroll computation; census interviewing; spot welding; laboratory assistant; and drafting. The assessment process includes orientation, assessment, a motivational group session, feedback, and an interest interview. The test requires less than a sixth-grade reading level. Individually packaged hardware is provided for all work samples. Examiner required. Suitable for group use (10 persons per week).

Untimed: 2½ days

Scoring: Examiner evaluated

Cost: Contact publisher

Publisher: Vocational Research Institute—J.E.V.S.

VOCATIONAL TRANSIT
Howard C. Dansky, Jeffrey A. Harris, Mary E. Konefsky, and Lisa S. Student

Adolescent, adult—Ages 14 and older
Grades 9 and above

Purpose: Assesses vocational potential: aptitudes, learning style, and work rate stability. Used for vocational counseling and placement of individuals who are mentally retarded, brain injured, or severely learning disabled.

Description: Computer-driven vocational assessment system for measurement of motor coordination (60 seconds), manual dexterity (90 seconds), finger dexterity (without assembly—60 seconds; with assembly—90 seconds), and form perception. Each motor test has a demonstration, practice, and testing phase. The Form Perception test incorporates a multiple-choice format and is preceded by three pretest phases: form-board, flip-chart, and attribute orientation. Formal testing involves three phases during which interventions are progressively introduced to provide cognitive structure. Testing yields raw scores, aptitude levels (1–5), percentiles using MR and/or non-impaired norm bases, and work rate stability scores. This test is suitable for individuals with hearing and mental impairments. The computer version is suitable for IBM PCs and compatibles, Apple IIgs, and MACs. Examiner required. Not suitable for group use.

Untimed: 1–3 hours

Scoring: Computer scored

Cost: $5,850.00

Publisher: Vocational Research Institute—J.E.V.S.

WASHER VISUAL ACUITY SCREENING TECHNIQUE (WVAST)
Refer to page 734.

WIDE RANGE EMPLOYABILITY SAMPLE TEST (WREST)
Refer to page 852.

THE WISCONSIN BEHAVIOR RATING SCALE (WBRS)
Refer to page 669.

WORK ADJUSTMENT RATING FORM (WARF)
Refer to page 927.

Y.E.M.R. PERFORMANCE PROFILE FOR THE YOUNG MODERATELY AND MILDLY RETARDED
Alfred J. DiNola, Bernard Kaminsky, and Allen E. Sternfeld

Mentally retarded children

Purpose: Assesses the adaptive behavior of moderately and mildly retarded children. Used by teachers for planning and reporting.

Description: 100–item paper-pencil inventory of 10 areas of behavior: social, self-help, safety, communication, motor skills, manipulative skills, perceptual and intellectual development, academics, imagination and creative expression, and emotional behavior. The profile can be used for educational planning and for reporting strengths and needs to parents. Examiner required. Not suitable for group use.

Untimed: Varies

Scoring: Examiner evaluated

Cost: Class kit (teacher's manual, 15 record booklets, and 15 yearly comparative charts) $25.00

Publisher: Educational Performance Associates

Special Education: Physically Handicapped: Auditory, Orthopedic, and Visual

---

AN ADAPTATION OF THE WECHSLER INTELLIGENCE SCALE FOR CHILDREN—REVISED FOR THE DEAF
Refer to page 48.

AN ADAPTATION OF THE WECHSLER PRESCHOOL AND PRIMARY SCALE OF INTELLIGENCE FOR DEAF CHILDREN
Refer to page 49.

ADOLESCENT AND ADULT PSYCHOEDUCATIONAL PROFILE (AAPEP)
Gary B. Mesibov, Eric Schopler, Bruce Schaffer, and Rhoda Landrus

Handicapped adolescents and adults

Purpose: Measures the learning abilities and characteristics of severely handicapped adolescents and adults. Used by service providers, teachers, and parents for preparing and maintaining autistic and developmentally handicapped individuals in community-based programs. Used with individuals previously regarded as untestable.

Description: Multiple-item task-performance test assessing the learning abilities of autistic and developmentally handicapped individuals. The test results comprise a profile reflecting the individual characteristics of the person. The profile is translated into an appropriately individualized set of goals and objectives for each individual. Examiner required. Not suitable for group use.

Untimed: Varies

Scoring: Examiner evaluated

Cost: Manual $29.00

Publisher: PRO-ED

ADOLESCENT EMOTIONAL FACTORS INVENTORY
Refer to page 153.

ATTITUDE TOWARDS DISABLED PERSONS SCALE (ATDP)
Refer to page 750.

BASIC READING RATE SCALE— BRAILLE AND LARGE TYPE EDITIONS
Refer to page 367.

BECKER WORK ADJUSTMENT PROFILE (BWAP)
Refer to page 647.

BEHAVIOR ASSESSMENT BATTERY: SECOND EDITION
Chris Kiernan and Malcolm Jones

Handicapped children and adults

Purpose: Assesses handicapped individuals' ability to function in their environment.

Description: Battery of tests providing a range of assessment procedures for use with profoundly handicapped individuals. The tests, which are presented in book form, identify an individual's developmental strengths and weaknesses and may be used as a basis for educational planning. Each section consists of a set of items aimed at certain criterion behaviors. Successful completion of the items is an indication of the person's ability to function adequately in his or her environment. This revision includes a chapter on the use and interpretation of the battery and material on sign language. Examiner required. Not suitable for group use. BRITISH PUBLISHER

Untimed: Varies

Scoring: Examiner evaluated

Cost: Contact publisher

Publisher: NFER-NELSON Publishing Company Ltd.

BEHAVIORAL CHARACTERISTICS PROGRESSION (BCP)
The Santa Cruz County Office of Education

Ages 1 year-adult

Purpose: Assesses developmental skills. Used by professionals working with severely handicapped, mentally retarded, autistic, and physically disabled children and adults.

Description: 183–page observation booklet for assessing 2,400 criterion-referenced self-help, visual/motor, speech and language, cognitive, personal and social, and academic and prevocational skills organized into 59 goal areas. Each of the goal areas contains "identifying behaviors" designed for quick screening of the examinee's needs and graded from primary skills (age 1) to socially acceptable adult behaviors. The booklet provides space for assessing six individuals for each behavior or for assessing one individual six times. A binder format, which is more suitable for individualized planning and quicker visual tracking of progress, is available. Five separately ordered BCP Method books (self-help, motor skills, communication skills, social skills, learning/academic skills) that provide thousands of instructional activities correlated to the BCP skills are also available. Examiner required. Not suitable for group use.

Untimed: Not available

Scoring: Examiner evaluated

Cost: Booklet $10.95; binder $12.95; method books $24.95–$27.95

Publisher: VORT Corporation

Information and availability unconfirmed; last verified in 1988.

THE BLIND LEARNING APTITUDE TEST (BLAT)
T. Ernest Newland

Child, adolescent— Ages 6–16

Purpose: Evaluates the academic aptitude of blind children.

Description: 61–item nonverbal test of tactile discrimination involving patterned dots and lines on 61 embossed plastic pages. The examiner guides the child's hand over the pages, and the child describes what is felt. Materials include a 39–page examiner's manual, testing book, embossed pages, and 30 record forms. Examiner required. Not suitable for group use.

Untimed: 20–45 minutes

Scoring: Hand key

Cost: Complete $50.00; manual $7.50

Publisher: University of Illinois Press

Information and availability unconfirmed; last verified in 1988.

THE BODY IMAGE OF BLIND CHILDREN
Bryant J. Cratty and Theresa A. Sams

Blind children—Ages 5–15

Purpose: Evaluates the extent to which a blind child is able to identify his body parts and respond to requests for various types of movements.

Description: Multiple-item oral-response and task-performance assessment procedure measuring the body image of blind children in the following areas: body parts, body planes, body movements, laterality, and directionality. The manual includes norms for comparison among various subpopulations of blind children, suggested applications, interpretive guidelines, and a discussion of body-image training for blind children. Examiner required. Not suitable for group use.

Untimed: Varies

Scoring: Examiner evaluated

Cost: Manual $7.95

Publisher: The American Foundation for the Blind

BRAILLE UNIT RECOGNITION BATTERY DIAGNOSTIC TEST OF GRADE 2 LITERARY BRAILLE
Refer to page 368.

BRITISH PICTURE VOCABULARY SCALES
Refer to page 587.

THE BZOCH-LEAGUE RECEPTIVE-EXPRESSIVE EMERGENT LANGUAGE SCALE (REEL)
Refer to page 28.

CALLIER-AZUSA SCALE: G-EDITION
Refer to page 29.

CENTRAL INSTITUTE FOR THE DEAF PRESCHOOL PERFORMANCE SCALE (CID PRESCHOOL PERFORMANCE SCALE)
Ann E. Geers and Helen S. Lane

Hearing- and language-impaired preschoolers

Purpose: Measures intellectual potential using completely nonverbal testing procedures. Predicts school achievement in hearing-impaired and language-impaired preschoolers.

Description: Multiple-item task-performance test assessing the intellectual abilities of preschoolers without requiring a single spoken word from either the examiner or the child (optional verbal clues are provided for hearing children). Six subtests assess intellectual abilities in the following areas: manual planning (block building, Montessori cylinders, and two-figure formboard); manual dexterity (buttons and Wallin pegs); form perception (Decroly pictures, Seguin formboard); perceptual/motor skills (Knox cube, drawing, and paper folding); preschool skills (color sorting and counting sticks); and part/whole relations (Manikin and Stutsman puzzles). Test materials were selected from existing mental tests for children ages 2–5 to obtain a broad, clinical picture of the child's ability and a numerical rating (Deviation IQ) that would correlate with a Stanford-Binet IQ. The test is an adaptation of the early Randall's Island Performance Series. Examiner required. Not suitable for group use.

Untimed: Varies

Scoring: Examiner evaluated

Cost: Complete kit (manual, record forms, manipulatives for subtests) $395.00; manual $4.50; 30 record forms $10.50

Publisher: Stoelting Co.

COLUMBIA MENTAL MATURITY SCALE (CMMS)
Refer to page 50.

CONTACT WITH DISABLED PERSONS SCALE (CDP)
H.E. Yuker and M.A. Hurley

Child, adolescent, adult

Purpose: Measures the quantity and quality of an individual's prior contact with disabled persons.

Description: 20–item paper-pencil Likert-type instrument assessing an individual's amount and type of prior contact with a disabled person. Examinees use a 5–point scale ranging from "never" to "very often" to respond to items. Some items contain an affective component. Items may be modified to refer to persons with specific disabilities or to members of minority or ethnic groups. Examiner required. Suitable for group use.

Untimed: 8 minutes

Scoring: Hand key

Cost: Free

Publisher: Center for the Study of Attitudes Toward Persons with Disabilities, Hofstra University

DEVELOPMENTAL ASSESSMENT FOR THE SEVERELY HANDICAPPED (DASH)
Mary K. Dykes

Child—Developmental ages 0–8

Purpose: Assesses the development of severely handicapped individuals functioning between the developmental ages of birth to eight years. Used to establish IEPs.

Description: Five multiple-item paper-pencil observational scales assessing development in the following domains: sensorimotor, language, preacademic, activities of daily living, and social-emotional. The five Pinpoint Scales are sensitive to small changes in skill performance. The skills assessed are identified as either present, emerging, task-resistive, nonrelevant, or unknown. Examiner required. Not suitable for group use.

Untimed: Varies

Scoring: Examiner evaluated

Cost: Complete kit (manual, 5 each of 5 pinpoint scales, 25 daily plan sheets, 25 comprehensive program records, 25 individualized education plans) $89.00

Publisher: PRO-ED

DEVELOPMENTAL ASSESSMENT OF LIFE EXPERIENCES, 1986 REVISED (DALE)

Refer to page 650.

EINSTEIN ASSESSMENT OF SCHOOL RELATED SKILLS

Refer to page 634.

EMOTIONAL FACTORS INVENTORY

Refer to page 239.

FULL-RANGE PICTURE VOCABULARY TEST (FRPV)

Refer to page 52.

FUNCTIONAL SKILLS SCREENING INVENTORY (FSSI)

Heather Becker, Sally Schur, Michele Paoletti-Schelp, and Ed Hammer

All ages

Purpose: Assesses the critical living and working skills of moderately to severely handicapped and multiply handicapped children and adults. Used by teachers, trainers, parents, occupational therapists, instructional aides, social workers, houseparents, vocational evaluators, counselors, and others working in private homes, schools, group homes, rehabilitation centers, sheltered workshops, work activity centers, nursing homes, institutions, and hospitals.

Description: 343–item paper-pencil and computer-administered domain-referenced behavioral checklist assessing the

skills necessary for various levels of independent functioning. The items, which are chronological age-appropriate, are divided into 8 scales and 27 subscales: Basic Skills and Concepts (36 items; basic motor skills, sensory discrimination, using objects, spatial relations and mobility), Communication (27 items; receptive, expressive), Personal Care (50 items; eating, dressing, toileting, body care, health care, leisure), Homemaking (33 items; cleaning, food preparation, clothing care), Work Skills and Concepts (64 items; work awareness, social skills in the work setting, work skills, work habits), Community Living (68 items; reading/writing, numbers, money, shopping, time, telephone/TTY, community access, personal knowledge), Social Awareness (35 items), and Problem Behaviors (30 items).

Items are prioritized on three levels that relate an individual's skills to environmental requirements: autonomy in any setting, supervision in a group home and supported employment, and independent living and competitive community employment. For each item, independence, competence, and frequency of performance are rated on a 5-point scale. The examiner observes the individual in a familiar, unstructured environment conducive to spontaneous behavior. Information from an informant familiar with the examinee may be used for items the examiner is unable to observe firsthand.

Scores are reported across content area scales and within priority levels. The computer program is for use with Apple IIe, Apple IIgs, and IBM PC and compatible systems. Examiner required. Not suitable for group use.

Untimed: Several days to several weeks

Scoring: Examiner evaluated; computer or hand scored

Cost: Contact distributor

Publisher: Functional Assessments and Training Consultants

FUNCTIONAL SKILLS SCREENING INVENTORY: EMPLOYMENT EDITION (FSSI: EE)

Heather Becker, Sally Schur, Michele Paoletti-Schelp, and Ed Hammer

Adolescent, adult

Purpose: Measures skills required for employment in specific positions at various work sites.

Description: 343-item paper-pencil or computer-administered domain-referenced behavioral checklist. The items, which are identical to those of the FSSI, are rated on a 5-point scale ranging from 0 (no competence on this skill is required for employment in the position under consideration) to 4 (mastery of the skill is a requirement for the position under consideration). The inventory is used by a) counselors and placement specialists to determine the most appropriate work for clients, b) vocational educators/trainers to identify clients' specific skill needs for various positions, c) training program administrators to evaluate appropriate training for preparing clients for future employment, and d) state-level service coordinators to identify possible employment options for their target populations. Profile sheets are identical to those of the FSSI, which allows for direct comparison. The program operates on IBM PC and compatible systems. Examiner required. Not suitable for group use.

Untimed: Several days to several weeks

Scoring: Examiner evaluated; computer or hand scored

Cost: Contact publisher

Publisher: Functional Assessments and Training Consultants

FUNCTIONAL SKILLS SCREENING INVENTORY: TRAINING PROGRAM EDITION (FSSI: TPE)
Heather Becker, Sally Schur, Michele Paoletti-Schelp, and Ed Hammer

Adolescent, adult

Purpose: Assesses the amount and level of functional skills training provided by educational, rehabilitation, and residential programs serving moderately and severely handicapped individuals.

Description: 343-item paper-pencil and computer-administered domain-referenced behavioral checklist. The items, which are identical to those on the Functional Skills Screening Inventory (FSSI),

are rated on a 5-point scale ranging from 0 (program does not provide training for the skill) to 4 (program provides extensive, regular training on the skill). The instrument is used by a) program administrators to describe their training programs and to identify the programs' strengths and weaknesses, b) vocational counselors and placement specialists to identify training programs that best meet client needs, c) educational personnel to facilitate transition to adult living and working, and d) state-level service coordinators to identify the range and appropriateness of services available to their target populations. Profile sheets are identical to those used for the FSSI, which allows for direct comparison. The computer program operates on IBM PC and compatible systems. Examiner required. Not suitable for group use.

Untimed: Several days to several weeks

Scoring: Examiner evaluated; computer scored

Cost: Contact publisher

Publisher: Functional Assessments and Training Consultants

HAPTIC INTELLIGENCE SCALE
Refer to page 53.

HELP FOR SPECIAL PRESCHOOLERS—CHECKLIST
Refer to page 547.

HISKEY-NEBRASKA TEST OF LEARNING APTITUDE
Marshall S. Hiskey

Child, adolescent—Ages 2¹/₂–18¹/₂

Purpose: Evaluates learning potential of deaf children and those with hearing, speech, or language handicaps.

Description: Battery of 12 subtests measuring visual-motor coordination, sequential memory, visual retention or stimuli in a series, visual discrimination and matching, and awareness of environment. The tests are Bead Patterns, Memory for Color, Picture Identification, Picture Association, Paper Folding Patterns,

Visual Attention Span, Block Patterns, Completion of Drawings, Memory for Digits, Puzzle Blocks, Picture Analogies, and Spatial Reasoning. The scales are nonverbal and have norms for evaluating either hearing or deaf children. Examiner required. Not suitable for group use.

Untimed: 50–60 minutes

Scoring: Examiner evaluated

Cost: Complete set $120.00

Publisher: The Hiskey-Nebraska Test

HUGHES BASIC GROSS MOTOR ASSESSMENT (HBGMA)
Refer to page 612.

INVENTORY FOR CLIENT AND AGENCY PLANNING (ICAP)
Robert H. Bruininks,
Bradley K. Hill,
Richard F. Weatherman, and
Richard W. Woodcock

Infant-adult

Purpose: Measures the adaptive and problem behaviors and service needs of moderately to severely disabled or mentally retarded individuals in residential, rehabilitation, education, and human service programs. Also used by geriatric service agencies.

Description: Multiple-item paper-pencil self-report inventory providing client information in the following areas: diagnostic and health status, adaptive behavior, problem behavior, service history, residential placement, projected service needs, functional limitations, and social-leisure history. The results can be used by administrators and supervisors to determine the client's current status and eligibility for services and to manage programs and facilities by assisting in their accreditation, coordinating and planning project costs and reimbursement, and obtaining funding. Age scores, adaptive behavior percentile ranks, problem behavior indexes, standard scores, and service level index scores are obtained. Examiner required. Not suitable for group use.

Untimed: 20 minutes

Scoring: Examiner evaluated; may be computer scored

Cost: Complete kit (manual, 25 inventory record forms) $75.00

Publisher: DLM Teaching Resources

KAHN INTELLIGENCE TEST (KIT:EXP): A CULTURE-MINIMIZED EXPERIENCE
Refer to page 54.

KEELER ACUITY CARD-INFANT ASSESSMENT SET
Refer to page 727.

KNOX'S CUBE TEST (KCT)
Refer to page 592.

LEITER INTERNATIONAL PERFORMANCE SCALE (ARTHUR ADAPTATION)
Refer to page 56.

LEITER INTERNATIONAL PERFORMANCE SCALE (LIPS)
Refer to page 56.

MAXFIELD-BUCHOLZ SOCIAL MATURITY SCALE FOR BLIND PRE-SCHOOL CHILDREN
Kathryn E. Maxfield and
Sandra Bucholz

Blind children—Ages 0–8

Purpose: Measures the social maturity of blind children.

Description: Multiple-item paper-pencil observational inventory and parent-interview guide assessing the developmental skills and social maturity of blind infants and preschool children. The objective is to find a means of comparing the present status and/or the progress of a given blind child's acquisition of personal and social independence and competence with that of other blind children of the same age. The examiner's ratings are based on personal observations in the home setting and supplemented by parent interview. This scale is an adaption of the Vineland Social Maturity Scale. Examiner required. Not suitable for group use.

Untimed: Varies

Scoring: Examiner evaluated

Cost: 10 record blanks $2.00; manual $6.95

Publisher: The American Foundation for the Blind

MCCARRON-DIAL SYSTEM (MDS)
Refer to page 847.

THE MOSSFORD ASSESSMENT CHART OF THE PHYSICALLY HANDICAPPED
Janet Whitehouse

Handicapped individuals—Ages 5–18

Purpose: Evaluates the daily living skills of physically handicapped children. Used in schools, hospitals, and residential and assessment centers for the physically handicapped and by social workers making placement or employment decisions.

Description: Multiple-item paper-pencil checklist of daily living skills relevant to children and adolescents with mild to severe degrees of physical handicap. Items cover mobility, dressing, manipulative skills, personal hygiene, health, communicating, reading, writing, mathematics, financial and domestic skills, and leisure activities. Results are presented on a pie chart depicting the skills that are being learned, those already mastered, and those that may have been overlooked entirely. The chart enables annual comparisons of progress to be made and forms a visual record of the child's progress. Examiner required. Not suitable for group use.
BRITISH PUBLISHER

Untimed: Varies

Scoring: Examiner evaluated

Cost: Contact publisher

Publisher: NFER-NELSON Publishing Company Ltd.

MOTOR-FREE VISUAL PERCEPTION TEST (MVPT)
Refer to page 615.

MOTOR SKILLS INVENTORY (MSI)
Refer to page 614.

NISONGER QUESTIONNAIRE FOR PARENTS
W. Loadman, F.A. Benson, and Douglas McElwain

Handicapped children

Purpose: Gathers preliminary information on a handicapped child from the perspective of the parents.

Description: Multiple-item paper-pencil questionnaire consisting of nontechnical questions concerning the status of a handicapped child. Parents complete the form, which emphasizes current rather than historical information. A pocket is provided on the form for the child's picture. Self-administered. Suitable for group use.

Untimed: Varies

Scoring: Examiner evaluated

Cost: 20 questionnaires $20.00; user's guide $0.75; specimen set (user's guide, one questionnaire) $3.00

Publisher: The Nisonger Center, Ohio State University

Information and availability unconfirmed; last verified in 1987.

NON-LANGUAGE LEARNING TEST
Refer to page 58.

OARS MULTIDIMENSIONAL FUNCTIONAL ASSESSMENT QUESTIONNAIRE
Refer to page 114.

PAIRED WORD MEMORY TASK (PAIRMEM)
Refer to page 115.

PATHWAYS TO INDEPENDENCE
Dorothy M. Jeffree and
Sally Cheseldine

All ages

Purpose: Assesses the ability of disadvantaged school-aged children and mentally and physically handicapped adults in training programs to live independently.

Description: Series of multiple-item checklists assessing the strengths and weaknesses of individuals desiring to live independently within the community. The results may be used to identify areas where further help may be needed and to suggest opportunities. Examiner required. Not suitable for group use. BRITISH PUBLISHER

Untimed: Not available

Scoring: Examiner evaluated

Cost: 10 checklists £14.00 plus VAT

Publisher: Hodder & Stoughton

PERCEPTUAL MEMORY TASK (PMT)
Refer to page 670.

PICTORIAL TEST OF INTELLIGENCE
Refer to page 596.

PRE-MOD II
Refer to page 745.

PRE-VERBAL COMMUNICATION SCHEDULE
Refer to page 708.

PRG INTEREST INVENTORY
Refer to page 833.

THE PRIMARY VISUAL MOTOR TEST
Refer to page 616.

RECEPTIVE ONE-WORD PICTURE VOCABULARY TEST (ROWPVT)
Refer to page 709.

RECEPTIVE ONE-WORD PICTURE VOCABULARY TEST—UPPER EXTENSION (ROWPVT-UE)
Refer to page 709.

SCALES OF INDEPENDENT BEHAVIOR (SIB)
Refer to page 654.

S.E.E.D. DEVELOPMENTAL PROFILES
Refer to page 42.

SELF-OBSERVATION SCALES (SOS)
Refer to page 774.

THE SOUTH AFRICAN INDIVIDUAL SCALE FOR THE BLIND (SAISB)—1979
Refer to page 598.

THE SOUTHERN CALIFORNIA ORDINAL SCALES OF DEVELOPMENT
Refer to page 619.

STROMBERG DEXTERITY TEST (SDT)
Refer to page 1073.

STYCAR CHART OF DEVELOPMENTAL SEQUENCES (REVISED 1975 EDITION)
Refer to page 43.

STYCAR HEARING TESTS
Refer to page 680.

STYCAR VISION TESTS
Refer to page 731.

SYSTEM FOR ASSESSMENT AND GROUP EVALUATION (SAGE)
Refer to page 806.

TEST FOR EXAMINING EXPRESSIVE MORPHOLOGY (TEEM)
Refer to page 716.

TEST OF SYNTACTIC ABILITIES
Refer to page 721.

VCWS 1—SMALL TOOLS (MECHANICAL)
Refer to page 1074.

VCWS 2—SIZE DISCRIMINATION
Refer to page 1074.

VCWS 3—NUMERICAL SORTING
Refer to page 924.

VCWS 4—UPPER EXTREMITY RANGE OF MOTION
Refer to page 1075.

VCWS 5—CLERICAL COMPREHENSION AND APTITUDE
Refer to page 950.

VCWS 6—INDEPENDENT PROBLEM SOLVING
Refer to page 924.

VCWS 7—MULTI-LEVEL SORTING
Refer to page 1075.

VCWS 9—WHOLE BODY RANGE OF MOTION
Refer to page 1076.

VCWS 11—EYE-HAND-FOOT COORDINATION
Refer to page 1076.

VCWS 12—SOLDERING AND INSPECTION (ELECTRONIC)
Refer to page 925.

VCWS 18—CONCEPTUAL UNDERSTANDING THROUGH BLIND EVALUATION (CUBE)

Blind adults

Purpose: Measures the perceptive abilities that help a person compensate for visual handicaps. Used with the congenitally and adventitiously blind.

Description: Performance-based battery of six tests assessing a person's perceptual skills in meeting the basic needs of judgment, mobility, orientation, discrimination, and balance. The subtests are Tactual Perception, Mobility/Discrimination Skills, Spatial Organization and Memory, Assembly and Packaging, and Audile Perception. Administration of the tests varies according to the factors being assessed: mobility or job skills. Examiner required. Not suitable for group use.

Timed: Not available

Scoring: Examiner evaluated

Cost: $3,995.00

Publisher: Valpar International Corporation

VINELAND ADAPTIVE BEHAVIOR SCALES
Refer to page 257.

VOCATIONAL BEHAVIOR CHECKLIST (VBC)
Refer to page 851.

VOCATIONAL EDUCATION READINESS TEST IN AUTO MECHANICS (VERT-AM)
Refer to page 809.

VOCATIONAL EDUCATION READINESS TEST IN BASIC WIRING (VERT-BW)
Refer to page 810.

VOCATIONAL EDUCATION READINESS TEST IN QUANTITY FOODS (VERT-QF)
Refer to page 810.

WALKER-MCCONNELL SCALE OF SOCIAL COMPETENCE AND SCHOOL ADJUSTMENT
Refer to page 777.

THE WISCONSIN BEHAVIOR RATING SCALE (WBRS)
Agnes Y. Song and
Central Wisconsin Center
for the Developmentally Disabled staff

Developmental ages 0–3

Purpose: Assesses the adaptive behavior of any individual between the developmental ages of 0 and 3. Also estimates the level of retardation in adaptive behavior. Suitable for use with the visually, mentally, physically, or hearing impaired.

Description: 218–item paper-pencil interviewer or observer rating scale assessing adaptive behavior. The 11 subscales are Gross Motor, Fine Motor, Expressive Language, Receptive Language, Play Skills, Socialization, Domestic Activity, Eating, Toileting, Dressing, and Grooming. The test yields a Behavioral Age Equivalent for each of the subscales and for the total scale. Examiner required. Not suitable for group use.

Untimed: 15 minutes

Scoring: Examiner evaluated

Cost: 100 scales $40.00; manual $2.50

Publisher: Central Wisconsin Center for the Developmentally Disabled

Special Education: Special Education

ADOLESCENT AND ADULT PSYCHOEDUCATIONAL PROFILE (AAPEP)
Refer to page 660.

BATTELLE DEVELOPMENTAL INVENTORY (BDI)
Refer to page 533.

THE BEHAVIOR EVALUATION SCALE–2 (BES–2)
Refer to page 736.

BENCH MARK MEASURES
Refer to page 286.

BESSEMER SCREENING TEST
Evelyn V. Jones and Gary L. Sapp

Child, adolescent—Ages 7–14

Purpose: Identifies children who may require special education services. Used to screen the learning disabled, emotionally disturbed, mentally retarded, and academically gifted.

Description: Five paper-pencil subtests requiring the student to write his own name, produce a human figure drawing, read words or symbols, reproduce abstract designs, and perform mathematic computations. The subtests are arranged in order of increasing difficulty and are similar to tasks the student would encounter in a regular classroom. Examiner required. Suitable for group use.

Timed: Maximum 15 minutes

Scoring: Examiner evaluated

Cost: Complete kit (15 student booklets, 30 scoring sheets, manual) $13.00

Publisher: Stoelting Co.

THE BRIGANCE® DIAGNOSTIC INVENTORY OF ESSENTIAL SKILLS
Refer to page 428.

BRISTOL SOCIAL ADJUSTMENT GUIDES
Refer to page 737.

CARTOON CONSERVATION SCALES (CCS)
Refer to page 621.

THE CHILD CENTER OPERATIONAL ASSESSMENT TOOL (OAT)
Refer to page 432.

DABERON SCREENING FOR SCHOOL READINESS-2
Refer to page 540.

DIAGNOSTIC SCREENING TEST: ACHIEVEMENT (DSTA)
Thomas D. Gnagey and Patricia A. Gnagey

Child, adolescent
Grades K–14

Purpose: Measures basic knowledge of science, social studies, and literature and the arts to help determine a course of study for special education students.

Description: 108–item multiple-choice paper-pencil test measuring a student's conceptual level in science, social studies, and literature and the arts. Scores are obtained for practical knowledge and estimated mental age. The manual discusses subtest pattern analysis of student motivation, cultural versus organic retardation, cultural deprivation, reading and study skill problems, and possession of practical versus formal knowledge. The examiner explains the procedure to individuals or groups and reads the test if the students have poor reading skills. Examiner required. Suitable for group use.

Untimed: 5–10 minutes

Scoring: Hand key

Cost: Manual and 50 test forms $35.00

Publisher: Slosson Educational Publications, Inc.

THE DYSINTEGRAL LEARNING CHECKLIST FOR DYSLEXIA
Refer to page 102.

EFFECTIVE READING TESTS
Refer to page 341.

EMOTIONAL/BEHAVIORAL SCREENING PROGRAM (ESP)
Refer to page 740.

EXPLORE THE WORLD OF WORK (E-WOW)
Refer to page 821.

THE FLOWERS AUDITORY PROCESSING TEST (F.A.S.T.)
Refer to page 676.

HELP FOR SPECIAL PRESCHOOLERS—CHECKLIST
Refer to page 547.

KAUFMAN ASSESSMENT BATTERY FOR CHILDREN (K-ABC)
Refer to page 55.

PERCEPTUAL MEMORY TASK (PMT)
Lawrence T. McCarron

Ages 4 and older
Grades PreK and above

Purpose: Assesses individual learning style. Used with special education and rehabilitation populations at any level of intellectual functioning and with physical, mental, emotional, or functional behavior disabilities. Target disability groups include the learning disabled, emotionally disabled, mentally retarded, cerebral palsied, closed head injured, socially handicapped, and culturally disadvantaged.

Description: 62–item oral-response and show-tell test utilizing stimulus materials to assess fundamental information processing skills essential for learning and performance, including perception and memory for spatial relationships; visual and auditory sequential memory, intermediate term memory, and discrimination of detail. The Spatial Relations subtest (12 items) measures memory for spatial relations. Examinees use cubes to reconstruct printed cube patterns that progress from simple to complex. In the Visual Designs subtest (12 items), the examinee utilizes multicolored design blocks to match from memory a sequence of designs presented visually. In the Auditory-Visual Colors subtest (14 items), which measures auditory recognition and sequential memory, the examinee uses basic color blocks to match a sequence of colors presented orally. The Discrimination Recall subtest (24 items) uses duplications of the previously used stimulus designs and cube patterns mixed with similar distractor materials to measure intermediate term memory and visual discrimination. The instrument also provides for behavioral observations of focused attention, cognitive flexibility, sequential organization, and depth perception.

To test hearing- and visually impaired examinees (those with visual acuity of 20/400 or worse in either eye), supplementary procedures involving two alternate subtasks are provided. The instrument also assesses information processing skills dependent on right and left cerebral functioning.

Age-corrected norm tables are used to convert each subtest score to a standard score that can be profiled on the PMT Score Form to portray graphically the individual's relative strengths and/or weaknesses. Factor scores also may be determined and compared to indicate relative strengths and weaknesses in specific memory processes. Examiner required. Not suitable for group use.

Untimed: Varies

Scoring: Hand key

Cost: Complete set $280.00

Publisher: McCarron-Dial Systems

Information and availability unconfirmed; last verified in 1988.

PERCEPTUAL-MOTOR ASSESSMENT FOR CHILDREN (P-MAC)
Jack G. Dial,
Lawrence T. McCarron, and
Garry Amann

Child, adolescent—Ages 4–15 years, 11 months Grades PreK and above

Purpose: Screens perceptual-motor skills. Used by diagnosticians and classroom teachers to identify needs and provide educational management for the special needs students.

Description: Mulitple-item oral-response point-to task-performance battery of perceptual-motor skills. The battery consists of selected subtests from the McCarron Assessment of Neuromuscular Development (MAND), Haptic Visual Discrimination Test (HVDT), and Perceptual Memory Task (PMT). See separate descriptions of each of these instruments. The MAND subtests administered are Beads in Box, Finger Tapping, Nut & Bolt, Hand Strength, Standing on One Foot, and Finger-Nose-Finger. The HVDT subtests involved are Shape, Size, and Texture. The PMT subtests are Spatial Relations and Auditory-Visual Colors Recognition/Sequencing.

The P-MAC Computer Program provides scores for each area assessed. In addition, various other information available from the examinee's file and/or personal interviews (WISC-R, BVMGT, PPVT, academic achievement scores, background information, adaptive behavior scores and professional opinions and observations regarding adaptive behavior) can be entered and included in the computer analysis. Four types of printed reports are offered: a) Educational Analysis Report, b) Classroom Report, c) Report of Trait Scores, and d) Comprehensive Evaluation Report. The computer program operates on Apple, IBM PC and compatible, and Macintosh systems. Examiner required. Not suitable for group use.

Timed: Not available

Untimed: Varies

Scoring: Examiner evaluated; hand key; may be computer scored

Cost: Complete set (assessment battery in single case, comprehensive manual, scoring forms, 5-volume set of *Guides for Educational Management*, computer program and operating manual) $1,375.00

Publisher: McCarron-Dial Systems

Information and availability unconfirmed; last verified in 1988.

PERFORMANCE ASSESSMENT OF SYNTAX: ELICITED AND SPONTANEOUS (PASES)
Refer to page 705.

THE PYRAMID SCALES
John D. Cone

Ages birth–78

Purpose: Assesses adaptive behavior in moderately to severely handicapped persons of all ages. Used to plan appropriate intervention programs, monitor changes in adaptive functioning over long periods of time, and establish relevant training priorities.

Description: 20 multiple-item paper-pencil scales assessing a handicapped individual's adaptive functioning skills. The scales are completed by the examiner using one or all of the following three modes: interview with the handicapped individual, interview with an informant, or direct observation. The 20 skills areas assessed are arranged in three scale categories: sensory (24 items), primary (71 items), and secondary (63 items). Sensory scales assess tactile, auditory, and visual responsiveness skills. Items in this category are appropriate for very young and/ or low-functioning individuals. Primary scales assess nine basic skills: gross motor, eating, fine motor, toileting, dressing, social interaction, washing and grooming, and receptive and expressive language. Secondary scales assess eight skills appropriate for older, higher-functioning individuals: recreation and leisure, writing, domestic behavior, reading, vocational, time, numbers, and money. Items in the scale were selected from and curriculum-referenced to such sources as the Brigance Inventory, the Behavior Characteristics

Progression (BCP), the Learning Accomplishment Profile (LAP), and the Uniform Performance Assessment System (UPAS). Tables are provided in the manual showing correlations between the scores of this test and those of other measures of adaptive ability. The test formerly was known as The West Virginia Assessment and Tracking System. The test may be administered in sign language to accomodate impaired individuals. Examiner required. Not suitable for group use.

Untimed: Varies

Scoring: Examiner evaluated; computer scored

Cost: Complete kit (manual, 50 answer sheets, storage box) $39.00

Publisher: PRO-ED

RECEPTIVE ONE-WORD PICTURE VOCABULARY TEST (ROWPVT)
Refer to page 709.

RECEPTIVE ONE-WORD PICTURE VOCABULARY TEST—UPPER EXTENSION (ROWPVT-UE)
Refer to page 709.

SANTA CLARA PLUS COMPUTER MANAGEMENT SYSTEM
Refer to page 562.

SCREENING TEST OF ADOLESCENT LANGUAGE (STAL)
Refer to page 711.

SOI PRIMARY FORM (FORM P)
Refer to page 598.

THE SPELLMASTER ASSESSMENT AND TEACHING SYSTEM
Refer to page 279.

STREET SURVIVAL SKILLS QUESTIONNAIRE (SSSQ)
*Dan Linkenhoker and
Lawrence T. McCarron*

**Ages 9 and older
Grades 2 and above**

Purpose: Measures specific aspects of the adaptive behavior of special education students, particularly the mentally retarded. Used as a baseline behavioral measure of the effects of training and to predict an individual's potential for successfully adapting to community living conditions and vocational placement. Provides curriculum guides for directing the individual from baseline behaviors to higher levels of functioning required for community living.

Description: 216–item oral-response and point-to test consisting of nine subtests, each presented in a separate booklet containing 24 picture plates. Basic Concepts assesses color matching, color recognition, and knowledge of quantitative concepts. Functional Signs deals with the individual's ability to recognize basic signs and symbols used in workshops, schools, public facilities, and other public services. Tool Identification and Use measures recognition and knowledge of the function of specific tools commonly used in sheltered workshops or for minor home repairs. Domestic Management tests familiarity with the requirements for successfully managing an apartment, specifically the ability to use utensils or appliances for food preparation and clothing maintenance. Health, First Aid and Safety assesses understanding of personal health care, hygiene, first aid, and safety skills needed in daily living. Public Services measures knowledge of a wide range of public services utilized in community living, including public transportation, store recognition, post office, banking, and telephone and telephone directory. Time deals with the ability to tell time and understand time-related concepts (clock time, digital clocks, calendar time, and figuring time requirements). Money assesses skill in recognizing and handling money, including coins and currency, recognizing money equivalence, and making change. Measurement examines the ability to use common measurements such as temperature measures, liquid measures, and linear measures.

During administration, the examiner orally presents the question, and the examinee responds by pointing to one of the four pictures presented. Specific items involving the use of a telephone directory and the identification of signs, products, and currency require fundamental reading skills. The large print and graphic format is designed for use with individuals with visual acuity of 20/200 or better in either eye. A booklet of instructions for administering the SSSQ in sign language is available.

For each subtest, the examiner enters and profiles a scale on the SSSQ Score Form, which depicts relative strengths and weaknesses in each area tested and provides information for individual program planning. A Survival Skills Quotient (SSQ), based on a mean of 100 and a standard deviation of 15, may be used to compare SSSQ scores with intelligence. A computer software scoring program that totals subtest scores and plots them according to age-appropriate norms is available for use on Apple, IBM PC and compatibles, and Macintosh systems. The SSSQ Report that is generated also provides narrative interpretations of the examinee's performance in each area as well as more specific area analyses. Examiner required. Not suitable for group use.

Untimed: 30–45 minutes

Scoring: Hand key; may be computer scored

Cost: Complete $210.00

Publisher: McCarron-Dial Systems

Information and availability unconfirmed; last verified in 1988.

TARC ASSESSMENT SYSTEM FOR SEVERELY HANDICAPPED CHILDREN
Refer to page 655.

THE TEST OF PRACTICAL KNOWLEDGE (TPK)
*J. Lee Wiederholt and
Stephen C. Larsen*

**Adolescent—Ages
12.11–18.8
Grades 8–12**

Purpose: Identifies high-school students who are less knowledgeable than their peers about important daily living skills. Determines strengths and weaknesses of an individual's practical knowledge. Used to document student's progress in special programs, assess program effectiveness, document progress, and conduct research.

Description: 105–item paper-pencil test consisting of three subtests: Personal Knowledge (35 items relating to information needed to deal independently with day-to-day living), Social Knowledge (35 items relating to social interactions, community services, and leisure activities), and Occupational Knowledge (30 items relating to information needed to operate successfully in job situations). Subtest raw scores, percentiles, stanines, and a Practical Knowledge Quotient are yielded. The examiner must be competent in the administration of educational, language, and vocational psychology tests. Individuals with visual and physical handicaps may provide oral responses. Examiner required. Suitable for group use.

Untimed: 35–40 minutes

Scoring: Hand key; examiner evaluated

Cost: Complete kit (examiner's manual, 25 student booklets, 50 profile sheets, scoring stencil, storage box) $59.00

Publisher: PRO-ED

TESTS FOR EVERYDAY LIVING (TEL)
Andrew Halpern, Larry K. Irvin, and Janet T. Landman

Child, adolescent, adult
Grades 7–12

Purpose: Measures low-functioning students' knowledge of skills necessary for performing everyday activities. Also used by educators as a curriculum guide.

Description: 245–item orally administered paper-pencil multiple-choice test consisting of seven subtests: Job Search Skills, Job Related Behavior, Health Care, Home Management, Purchasing Habits, Banking, and Budget. A few performance items require reading skill. Results can be used to place students in the Skills for Independent Living resource kit curriculum. The test may be used at the junior high-school level with regular, remedial, and learning-disabled students. At the senior high-school level, it is most effective when used with average or low-functioning students. Examiner required. Suitable for use with groups not exceeding 20 students.

Untimed: Varies

Scoring: Hand key

Cost: Specimen set (test book, manual, answer key, technical report) $14.60

Publisher: CTB/Macmillan/McGraw-Hill

Speech, Hearing, and Visual: Auditory

ADVANCED TESTS OF CENTRAL AUDITORY ABILITIES
Arthur Flowers

Grades 2 and above

Purpose: Measures central auditory abilities of low-achieving children and adults. Screens for general hearing-perception problems and isolates specific auditory phonemic identification deficiencies.

Description: 56–item two-part verbal test measuring auditory closure and figure-ground (ability to listen selectively against background noise). Test I, Competing Messages, is comprised of 31 items. Test II, Low Pass Filtered Speech, is comprised of 31 items also. All test items, including practice items, and directions to examiner are included on audiotape. Examiner required. Not suitable for group use.

Untimed: 8–10 minutes

Scoring: Examiner evaluated

Cost: Kit $79.00; pad of 30 score sheets $4.00

Publisher: Perceptual Learning Systems

ASSESSING READING DIFFICULTIES: A DIAGNOSTIC AND REMEDIAL APPROACH, 2ND EDITION
Lynette Bradley

Child

Purpose: Identifies children whose reading difficulties are the result of poor auditory organization and children who are likely to encounter future reading and spelling problems.

Description: Multiple-item paper-pencil test assessing the problems of children who are making little or no progress towards learning to read. Test items are based on extensive longitudinal research that proved the close relationship between the inability to rhyme or identify rhyming words and reading failure. A section for recording teacher observations is included. The manual provides full details for administering the schedule and interpreting the results. Guidelines for appropriate remedial action are provided also. Examiner required. Not suitable for group use. BRITISH PUBLISHER

Untimed: Varies

Scoring: Examiner evaluated

Cost: Manual £4.95; 25 test sheets £4.95

Publisher: Macmillan Education

AUDITORY DISCRIMINATION AND ATTENTION TEST
R. Morgan-Barry

Child, adolescent—
Ages 3–12

Purpose: Assesses a child's ability to discriminate between sounds. Used by speech therapists, teachers in language units and special schools, and educational and clinical psychologists to determine whether listening or auditory deficits are contributing to a child's expressive language problems.

Description: Verbally administered test in which the examiner uses 18 colored test plates, each containing two pictures, to assess a child's ability to discriminate between sounds. The examiner presents the test plates one at a time to the child and names one of the two pictures on each plate. The child is to place a counter under the picture named by the examiner. Each of the 18 test plates is presented six times to prevent random response. Norm tables are used to convert error scores to percentages and standard scores. Examiner required. Not suitable for group use.

Untimed: 20 minutes

Scoring: Hand key

Cost: Contact publisher

Publisher: NFER-NELSON Publishing Company Ltd.

AUDITORY INTEGRATIVE ABILITIES TEST (AIAT)
Carole Grote

Child—Ages 6–9

Purpose: Diagnoses auditory perceptual disorders as they relate to language-based learning disabilities in children. Used in conjunction with other tests to develop a remedial program.

Description: 30–item paper-pencil test consisting of three subtests. The auditory-motor subtest requires the student to clap his hands to sound patterns. The auditory-graphic subtest requires the student to chart sound patterns on index cards. The auditory-verbal subtest requires the student to orally reproduce sound patterns. A cassette tape, included with the material, is used to administer the test. The student uses score sheets to record his responses. Since the tasks involved may be new and unfamiliar, some pretest training is recommended and provided for in the manual. Examiner required. Suitable for group use.

Untimed: Not available

Scoring: Hand key

Cost: Program (cassette tape, 25 individual scoring sheets, index cards, examiner's manual) $14.50; 25 additional score sheets $3.30

Publisher: Educational Activities, Inc.

Information and availability unconfirmed; last verified in 1988.

AUDITORY MEMORY SPAN TEST
*Joseph M. Wepman and
Anne Morency*

Child—Ages 5–8

Purpose: Measures the ability of children ages 5–8 to retain and recall words as auditory units, an essential capacity for learning how to speak and read accurately. Used to identify specific auditory learning disabilities.

Description: Oral-response test assessing the development of a child's ability to retain and recall familiar, isolated words received aurally. The test items are based on the most frequently used words in the spoken vocabulary of five-year-old children. Norms are provided for children ages 5, 6, 7, and 8. Available in two equivalent forms, 1 and 2. Examiner required. Not suitable for group use.

Untimed: 5–10 minutes

Scoring: Hand key

Cost: Complete kit (includes 100 each of Forms 1 and 2, manual) $47.50

Publisher: Western Psychological Services

AUDITORY POINTING TEST
Refer to page 630.

AUDITORY SEQUENTIAL MEMORY TEST
*Joseph M. Wepman and
Anne Morency*

Child—Ages 5–8

Purpose: Measures the ability of children ages 5–8 to remember and repeat what they have just heard. Used to diagnose specific auditory learning disabilities.

Description: Oral-response test assessing a child's ability to repeat from immediate memory an increasing series of digits in the exact order of their verbal presentation. The test is useful for determining a child's readiness for learning to read and speak with accuracy and is also a determinant of spelling and arithmetic achievement. Norms are provided for children

ages 5, 6, 7, and 8. Available in two equivalent forms, 1 and 2. Examiner required. Not suitable for group use.

Untimed: 5 minutes

Scoring: Hand key

Cost: Complete kit (100 each of Forms 1 and 2, manual) $47.50

Publisher: Western Psychological Services

CARROW AUDITORY-VISUAL ABILITIES TEST (CAVAT)
Refer to page 724.

DENVER AUDIOMETRIC SCREENING TEST (DAST)
*William K. Frankenburg,
Marion Dreris, and Elinor Kuzuk*

Ages 3 and older

Purpose: Detects children with hearing deficiencies. Used to screen for 25dB loss. Those who fail the test are referred for additional examination.

Description: Function test in which a trained examiner creates a tone with an audiometer and checks the child's response. The child indicates whether the tone can be heard at different decibel levels. Examiner and audiometer required. Not suitable for group use.

Untimed: 5–10 minutes

Scoring: Examiner evaluated

Cost: 25 tests $4.00; manual/workbook $10.25

Publisher: Denver Developmental Materials, Inc.

EXPRESSIVE ONE-WORD PICTURE VOCABULARY TEST: UPPER EXTENSION (EOWPVT: UE)
Refer to page 696.

THE FLOWERS AUDITORY PROCESSING TEST (F.A.S.T.)
Arthur Flowers

**Child—Ages 6–11
Grades 1–6**

Purpose: Helps identify children with potential central auditory problems for further testing. Used in clinical and school settings by speech-language therapists, LD resource specialists, audiologists, reading specialists, psychologists, diagnosticians, psychometricians, classroom teachers, special education teachers, school administrators, Chapter I teachers and specialists, and supervised paraprofessionals.

Description: Multiple-item auditory screening test administered without earphones via a cassette player. Test stimuli represent the central auditory factor of selective listening, or auditory-figure ground. Overlapping single word presentations are utilized along with a nonverbal, picture-pointing response mode. The test has been used with the neurologically handicapped, autistic, hearing-impaired, educationally disadvantaged, mentally handicapped, orthopedic and multiply handicapped, visually impaired, and emotionally handicapped as well as English as a Second Language and Head Start children. Examiner required. Not suitable for group use.

Untimed: 5 minutes

Scoring: Examiner evaluated

Cost: Test kit (cassette, manual with picture response mode, test record form pad) $69.00

Publisher: Perceptual Learning Systems

FLOWERS-COSTELLO TESTS OF CENTRAL AUDITORY ABILITY
*Arthur Flowers and
Mary Rose Costello*

**Child
Grades K–6**

Purpose: Identifies kindergartners and first-graders who have hearing-perception problems and establishes probabilities for future reading success. For low-achieving elementary school students, it measures central auditory abilities in order to isolate specific auditory phonemic identification deficiencies.

Description: 48–item two-part verbal test measuring auditory closure and figure-ground (ability to listen selectively against background noise). Part I (24

items) deals with low-pass filtered speech. Part II (24 items) assesses how the child handles competing messages. All the items and examiner instructions are on audiotape. The examiner plays the tape, and the taker responds verbally. For kindergarten students, pictures are shown, a statement (i.e., "We put a shoe on our . . .") is made, pictures are shown, and the child points to the object not mentioned. The test is designed for low-achieving children whose CAA scores suggest a specific learning disability that may interfere with the child's progress. Examiner required. Not suitable for group use.

Untimed: 15 minutes

Scoring: Examiner evaluated

Cost: Basic kit $125.00; 30 test score sheets $4.00

Publisher: Perceptual Learning Systems

GOLDMAN-FRISTOE-WOODCOCK AUDITORY SKILLS TEST BATTERY
*Ronald Goldman, Macalyne Fristoe,
and Richard W. Woodcock*

Ages 3–adult

Purpose: Diagnoses an individual's ability to hear clearly under difficult conditions. Used for instructional planning.

Description: Twelve subtests measuring auditory selective attention, diagnostic auditory discrimination, auditory memory, and sound-symbol skills. The examiner presents a test plate to the subject and records the subject's response. The Auditory Selective Attention Test assesses the ability to attend under increasingly difficult listening conditions. The Diagnostic Auditory Discrimination Test—Part I assesses the individual's ability to discriminate between specific speech sounds that are frequently confused. The Diagnostic Auditory Discrimination Test—Part II is used with individuals who experience difficulty with speech-sound discrimination in Part I. The Auditory Memory Tests assess three aspects of auditory memory performance: recognition memory, memory for content, and memory for sequence. The Sound Symbol Tests assess several abilities underlying the development of written language skills. Scores derived are age equivalents, age-based percentile ranks, standard scores, and stanines. Materials include four manuals, 25 response forms in each of the five easels (diagnostic auditory discrimination tests are in two easels), test plates bound into five easels, one test tape per easel, 25 battery profile forms, and a technical manual. Examiner required. Not suitable for group use.

Untimed: 15 minutes per subtest

Scoring: Examiner evaluated

Cost: Complete test battery (5 easel kits) $250.00

Publisher: American Guidance Service

GOLDMAN-FRISTOE-WOODCOCK TEST OF AUDITORY DISCRIMINATION
Ronald Goldman, Macalyne Fristoe, and Richard W. Woodcock

All ages

Purpose: Assesses an individual's ability to discriminate speech sounds in quiet and in noise. Screens for deficiencies in speech-sound discrimination that may contribute to learning difficulties.

Description: 2–part test in which the examiner presents a test plate containing four drawings to the subject. The subject responds to a stimulus word (presented via audiocassette to ensure standardized presentation) by pointing to one of the drawings on the plate. Total error scores can be converted to age-based percentile ranks and standard scores. An error analysis may be completed to explore further the types of errors made on either subtest. Materials include test plates bound in an easel, manual, 50 response forms, and the audiocassette. Examiner required. Not suitable for group use.

Untimed: 20–30 minutes

Scoring: Examiner evaluated

Cost: Contact publisher

Publisher: American Guidance Service

THE HEARING MEASUREMENT SCALE
William G. Noble

Hearing-impaired individuals

Purpose: Measures degree of hearing impairment as reported by the hearing-impaired individual.

Description: Multiple-item interview or paper-pencil self-report questionnaire assessing the degree to which an individual's hearing is impaired. The scale yields eight scores: Speech Hearing, Hearing for Nonspeech Sounds, Spatial Localization, Emotional Response to Hearing Impairment, Speech Distortion, Tinnitus, Personal Opinion of Hearing, and Total. Self-administered. Paper-pencil version suitable for group use. AUSTRALIAN PUBLISHER

Untimed: Varies

Scoring: Examiner evaluated

Cost: Test kit (manual, 50 questionnaires, transparent scoring matrix) $17.50

Publisher: University of New England (Australia)

Information and availability unconfirmed; last verified in 1988.

INVENTORY OF PERCEPTUAL SKILLS (IPS)
Refer to page 727.

KERBY LEARNING MODALITY TEST, REVISED 1980
Refer to page 637.

LANGUAGE-STRUCTURED AUDITORY RETENTION SPAN TEST (LARS)
Refer to page 638.

LINDAMOOD AUDITORY CONCEPTUALIZATION TEST (LAC)
Charles H. Lindamood and Patricia C. Lindamood

All ages

Purpose: Measures an individual's ability to discriminate one speech sound from another and to perceive the number, order, and sameness or difference of speech sounds in sequences. Used to diagnose auditory-conceptual dysfunctions and to determine the need for remedial training.

Description: 40–item criterion-referenced test in which the subject arranges colored blocks (each symbolizing one speech sound) in a row to represent a sound pattern spoken by the examiner. The color of the blocks indicates sameness or difference with a repeated sound symbolized by the same color block and a different sound by a different color. Materials include the manual, cassette, 24 wooden blocks in six colors, test forms, and examiner's cue sheets. A separate product, "Auditory Discrimination in Depth," provides a training program. The LAC, which is not appropriate for deaf subjects, is to be administered individually by an examiner. Not suitable for group use. Available in Spanish.

Untimed: 10 minutes
Scoring: Examiner evaluated
Cost: Complete set $46.00
Publisher: DLM Teaching Resources

OLIPHANT AUDITORY DISCRIMINATION MEMORY TEST
Genevieve Oliphant

Child
Grades 1–8

Purpose: Evaluates the ability of grade-school students to hear and discriminate sounds and words. Used to identify students needing further testing and to diagnose the relationship between perceptual problems and learning disabilities.

Description: 20–item paper-pencil test measuring how well students discriminate sounds and remember what they hear. Each item presents the student with two words, which are either alike or minimally different. The examiner then presents a third word, and the student is asked to decide whether that word is the same as the first or second word or whether all three words are the same. The

words are all single-syllable in a consonant-vowel-consonant format. Examiner required. Suitable for group use.

Untimed: 30–45 minutes
Scoring: Examiner evaluated
Cost: Complete kit (12 tests, 2 sheets of teacher directions) $3.30
Publisher: Educators Publishing Service, Inc.

SCREENING TEST FOR AUDITORY PERCEPTION (STAP)
Geraldine M. Kimmel and Jack Wahl

Child
Grades 1–6 and
remedial students

Purpose: Assesses weaknesses in five areas of auditory perception in elementary school and remedial students. Used to identify those who are performing below grade or age level.

Description: Series of multiple-item paper-pencil subtests measuring ability to discriminate among long versus short vowels, single versus blend initial consonants, rhyming versus nonrhyming words, same versus different rhythmic patterns, and same versus different words. Abnormal limits indicating a student's need for remedial attention or further testing are provided. Materials include suggested remedial activities for each of the five skill areas tapped. Available on cassette tape for uniform administration. Examiner required. Suitable for group use.

Untimed: 45 minutes
Scoring: Hand key
Cost: Manual $12.00; 50 record forms $10.00; scoring template $3.00
Publisher: Academic Therapy Publications

A SCREENING TEST FOR AUDITORY PROCESSING DISORDERS (SCAN)
Robert W. Keith

Child—Ages 3–11

Purpose: Identifies central auditory disorders in children.

Description: Multiple-item standardized response test consisting of four subtests of auditory abilities. In the Filtered Words subtest, the child hears words in which high frequency sounds have been filtered. In the Auditory Figure Ground subtest, the child hears words with background noise. In the Auditory Fusion subtest, the child hears words that consist of low and high pass filtered bands presented to both ears separately, then split and presented to different ears simultaneously. In the Competing Words subtest, the child hears a different word in each ear simultaneously. Examiner required. Not suitable for group use.

Untimed: 15 minutes

Scoring: Not available

Cost: Set (examiner's manual, test audio-cassette, 25 record forms, vinyl case) $59.00

Publisher: The Psychological Corporation

Information and availability unconfirmed; last verified in 1988.

SEQUENCED INVENTORY OF COMMUNICATION DEVELOPMENT, REVISED EDITION
Refer to page 712.

SKLAR APHASIA SCALE— REVISED 1983
Refer to page 128.

SMITH-JOHNSON NONVERBAL PERFORMANCE SCALE
Refer to page 42.

STYCAR HEARING TESTS
Mary D. Sheridan

Child—Ages 6 months–7 years

Purpose: Assesses child's capacity to hear with comprehension in commonplace situations. Used for preliminary screening of very young or mentally handicapped children.

Description: Multiple-item series of simple clinical auditory screening tests. The child responds to toys and pictures. Materials include a manual, vocabulary cards, toy blocks, rattle, plane, boat, cars, and dolls. The tests are available to medical doctors, speech therapists, and teachers of the deaf, blind, and physically handicapped. Examiner required. Not suitable for group use.

BRITISH PUBLISHER

Untimed: Not available

Scoring: Examiner evaluated

Cost: Contact publisher

Publisher: NFER-NELSON Publishing Company Ltd.

TEACHER ASSESSMENT OF GRAMMATICAL STRUCTURES
Jean S. Moog and Victoria J. Kozak

Child

Purpose: Evaluates a hearing-impaired child's understanding and use of grammatical structures. Used for developing teaching plans. May also be used with normal children whose English syntax development is delayed.

Description: Series of three multiple-item paper-pencil forms assessing grammatical structure and use. The Pre-Sentence form, designed for hearing-impaired children younger than age 6 and normal children ages 2–4 with language impairments, covers receptive and expressive skills as well as pre-sentence structure. The Simple Sentence form assesses the expressive language skills and simple sentence structures of hearing-impaired children ages 5–9 and normal children ages 3 and older. The Complex Sentence form, which covers expressive skills and complex sentence structures, is intended for hearing-impaired children ages 8 and older and normal children ages 3.6 and older. The forms should be used as a supplement to standardized testing. Examiner required. Not suitable for group use.

Untimed: Varies

Scoring: Examiner evaluated

Cost: Contact publisher

Publisher: Central Institute for the Deaf

TEST FOR AUDITORY COMPREHENSION OF LANGUAGE—1985 REVISED EDITION (TACL-R)
Elizabeth Carrow-Woolfolk

Ages 3.9–11

Purpose: Measures auditory comprehension of children. Also used with adults.

Description: Multiple-item response test assessing auditory understanding of word classes and relations, grammatical morphemes, and elaborated sentence constructions. The test requires no oral response. This revised edition provides high reliability and validity, a more efficient scoring system, and a variety of normative comparisons. The test yields percentile ranks, standard scores, and age equivalents. Guidelines for administering the test to adults are provided. Examiner required. Not suitable for group use.

Untimed: 10–20 minutes

Scoring: Examiner evaluated; may be computer scored

Cost: Complete kit (test book, manual, record forms) $120.00

Publisher: DLM Teaching Resources

TEST FOR AUDITORY FIGURE-GROUND DISCRIMINATION (TAFD)—1981

Child—Ages 5–10

Purpose: Measures ability to attend to one sound and to perceive it in relation to, but separate from, competing sounds. Used for educational evaluation.

Description: 7–subtest measure of auditory perception of specific sounds against a variety of background sounds (e.g., a bicycle bell against traffic noise or speech against background music). The child responds verbally to tape-recorded stimuli. Materials include a cassette tape recording of the TAFD. Available to professional personnel attached to education departments and others who can document their expertise. Examiner required. Not suitable for group use.
SOUTH AFRICAN PUBLISHER

Timed: 1 hour

Scoring: Examiner evaluated

Cost: Contact publisher; all orders from outside the RSA will be dealt with on merit

Publisher: Human Sciences Research Council

TEST OF AUDITORY COMPREHENSION (TAC)
Los Angeles County Schools

Hearing-impaired—Ages 4–17

Purpose: Assesses comprehension in hearing-impaired children. Used for academic placement and instructional planning.

Description: Ten subtests measuring auditory comprehension. The subtests begin with simple auditory discrimination tasks and conclude by assessing the child's understanding of complex stories given with a competing message background. The child responds to recorded messages by pointing to one of several pictures. The test results produce a profile of the child's performance on a continuum of auditory tasks, provide a basis for instruction, and allow comparison of results by age, degree of hearing loss, and type of placement. Administration requires the child's usual amplification, a quiet room, and a program-stop or cassette player. Norms are provided for individuals ages 4–17 with moderate to profound hearing losses. The test is directly correlated to a curriculum and training program and also may be used to assess auditory processing of the learning disabled. Examiner required. Not suitable for group use.

Untimed: 30 minutes

Scoring: Examiner evaluated; hand key

Cost: Test, manual $75.00

Publisher: Foreworks Publications

TEST OF AUDITORY-PERCEPTUAL SKILLS (TAPS)
Morrison F. Gardner

Child—Ages 4–12

Purpose: Assesses the auditory functions of children. Used by psychologists, speech pathologists, language specialists,

---

learning specialists, diagnosticians, and other professionals.

Description: Multiple-item response test consisting of six subtests measuring auditory discrimination, auditory sequential memory, auditory word memory, auditory interpreting directions, auditory sentence memory auditory processing, and hyperactivity. The test is used for diagnosing auditory perceptual difficulties, imperceptions of auditory modality, language problems, and learning problems. Raw scores can be converted to stanines, percentiles, auditory age equivalents, and auditory standard scores for each subtest. Examiner required. Not suitable for group use.

Untimed: 10–15 minutes

Scoring: Hand key

Cost: Test kit (manual, 35 test booklets) $59.50

Publisher: Children's Hospital of San Francisco, Publications Department

---

TESTING-TEACHING MODULE OF AUDITORY DISCRIMINATION (TTMAD)
Victoria Risko

Child
Grades K–6

Purpose: Determines auditory discrimination in elementary school children and increases proficiency in those skills. Used in developmental, corrective, or remedial programs that focus on auditory discrimination and blending.

Description: Multiple-item paper-pencil verbal assessment in two sections. Section 1 is a 125–item diagnostic instrument consisting of subtests in six areas: initial and final consonants, initial and final blends and diagraphs, vowels and vowel combinations. The second section is a series of 450 games and activities to increase proficiency. When skill deficiencies are detected by diagnostic testing, the examiner refers to the teaching activities in the manual. The games and activities, which correspond directly to each skill assessed, are coded by whether they are appropriate for individualized or group

instruction or both. Individual item analysis sheets are provided. Examiner required. Suitable for group use.

Untimed: 20–30 minutes

Scoring: Examiner evaluated

Cost: Complete kit $18.00

Publisher: United Educational Services, Inc.

TREE/BEE TEST OF AUDITORY DISCRIMINATION (TREE/BEE TEST)
Janet B. Fudala

Ages 3–adult

Purpose: Measures auditory discrimination abilities in children and adults. Used as a basis for further testing and remediation.

Description: Multiple-item oral-response test in which the examinees are shown stimulus pictures and point to or mark the proper picture as the examiner says the word or phrase (e.g., a tree, a bee, or a key). Four equivalent forms are provided for test-retest situations. There are two sets of stimulus pictures and two sets of stimulus items, which can be mixed. A flip-flop book is available for individual administration. No reading or writing is required of the examinee. The test has been normed for children ages 3–9, but not for older children or adults. Examiner required. Suitable for group use.

Untimed: 10 minutes

Scoring: Hand key

Cost: Test kit $42.00

Publisher: United Educational Services, Inc.

WEPMAN'S AUDITORY DISCRIMINATION TEST, 2ND EDITION
Joseph M. Wepman

Child—Ages 4–8

Purpose: Measures the auditory discrimination ability of children ages 4–8. Used to identify specific auditory learning disabilities for possible remediation.

Description: Oral-response test in which children are verbally presented pairs of words and asked to discriminate between them. The test predicts articulatory speech defects and certain remedial reading problems. The second edition is identical to the original edition except for scoring. In the second edition, scoring is based on a correct score rather than on the "error" basis of the original edition. The 1987 manual contains standardization tables for children ages 4–8, a 5–point qualitative rating scale, an interpretation section discussing how the test results may be used, reports on research using the test, and selected references. Examiner required. Not suitable for group use.

Untimed: 10–15 minutes

Scoring: Hand key

Cost: Complete kit (100 each of form 1A or 2A, manual) $62.50

Publisher: Western Psychological Services

WRITTEN LANGUAGE SYNTAX TEST
Refer to page 294.

Speech, Hearing, and Visual: Speech and Language

ADAPTED SEQUENCED INVENTORY OF COMMUNICATION DEVELOPMENT FOR ADOLESCENTS AND ADULTS WITH SEVERE HANDICAPS
Sandra E. McClennen

Adolescent, adult

Purpose: Evaluates the communication abilities of severely handicapped adolescents and adults whose language skills are in the range of birth to four years. Used for remedial programming by speech-language pathologists, audiologists, psychologists, and teachers trained in speech and language assessment techniques.

Description: 76–item inventory assessing and diagnosing language disorders in ado-

lescents and adults. The receptive communication section (27 items) includes a processing profile for auditory perception, pragmatic, semantic, and syntactic language as well as a concepts profile for awareness, words, directions, questions, and attributes. The expressive communication section (31 items) includes a processing profile for pragmatic and semantic/syntactic language and imitation and for motor and/or vocal/verbal initiating behavior. An observation/interview section (18 items) is also included. The test approach is based on the order of difficulty concept, and mode of expression is defined to recognize alternatives to vocal communication. The resulting Communication Profile provides guidelines for developing remedial programs for adolescents and adults who have little or no speech or who are understood only by those closest to them. Handicapping conditions represented in the norm group include severe hearing loss, legal blindness, epilepsy, spastic quadriplegic, and non-ambulation. Adaptations are described for clients with cerebral palsy and other motor handicaps. The test kit includes over 60 age-appropriate objects used as stimuli for test items. Examiner required. Not suitable for group use.

Untimed: Varies

Scoring: Examiner evaluated

Cost: Complete kit (manuals, 50 receptive skills checklists and profiles, 50 expressive skills checklists and profiles, 50 assessment booklets stimulus objects, plastic carrying case) $250.00

Publisher: University of Washington Press

THE ALPHA TEST OF PHONOLOGY (ALPHA)
Robert J. Lowe

Child—Ages 3–9

Purpose: Assesses articulation and phonological process errors simultaneously.

Description: 50–item delayed sentence-imitation test using picture stimuli to elicit a target word. The word can be analyzed for either phoneme errors or phonological process errors. The examiner presents 50 three- to four-word sentences. A summary chart of phonological processes and articulation errors are included in the manual. Norms are provided for children ages 3–9, including age equivalencies, percentile ranks, standard scores, and standard deviations. Norms also are available for articulation-disordered children. Examiner required. Not suitable for group use.

Untimed: 15–20 minutes

Scoring: Examiner evaluated

Cost: Test kit (manual with pictures, 20 test forms) $44.90

Publisher: LinguiSystems, Inc.

ANALYSIS OF THE LANGUAGE OF LEARNING
Elizabeth G. Blodgett and Eugene B. Cooper

Child—Ages 5–10

Purpose: Determines a child's metalinguistic abilities. Identifies children who may have difficulty with the language used in the classroom or for instruction.

Description: 88–item test of metalinguistic abilities identifying a child's ability to define, give examples of, and recognize the concepts of letters, words, syllables, sentences, nouns, spelling, questions, and stories, including the ability to segment sentences into words and words into phonemes. The test also assesses the ability to repair sentences containing word order errors, semantic errors, grammatical errors, and phonological errors. Norms are provided for children ages 5–10. The test yields standard scores, age equivalencies, percentile ranks, and standard deviations. In addition, norms for a language-disordered population are provided for comparison. Examiner required. Not suitable for group use.

Untimed: Varies

Scoring: Examiner evaluated

Cost: Test kit (manual, 20 test forms) $44.90

Publisher: LinguiSystems, Inc.

APRAXIA BATTERY FOR ADULTS (ABA)
Refer to page 95.

ARIZONA ARTICULATION PROFICIENCY SCALE: SECOND EDITION
Janet Barker Fudala and William M. Reynolds

Child—Ages 1½–13 years

Purpose: Measures the speaking abilities of children. Used to identify children requiring speech therapy.

Description: 48–item oral-response measure of articulation performance in which the child responds to pictures and sentences presented on stimulus cards. The examiner records all errors in the protocol booklet. A sentence test is provided as an alternative for use with older children. Scores provided include total articulatory proficiency and percentage of improvement. Norms are provided for children ages 1½–13 years. A Survey Form is available for compiling an abbreviated articulation record of 10 children on a single sheet. Examiner required. Suitable for group use.

Untimed: 10–15 minutes

Scoring: Hand key

Cost: Kit (set of reusable picture test cards, 25 protocol booklets, 10 survey forms, manual) $64.00

Publisher: Western Psychological Services

ASSESSING SEMANTIC SKILLS THROUGH EVERYDAY THEMES (ASSET)
Mark Barrett, Linda Zachman, and Rosemary Huisingh

Child—Ages 3–10

Purpose: Assesses the receptive and expressive vocabulary and semantic skills of preschool and early elementary children.

Description: 150–item test examining semantics through a theme approach that utilizes 20 pictures depicting the day-to-day life experiences of preschool and early elementary children. The themes include learning and playing, shopping, around the house, working, eating, and health and fitness. The types of tasks that are evaluated receptively and expressively are labeling, categorizing, attributes, functions, and definitions. The test provides standardized analyses of a child's strengths and weaknesses as well as an overall estimate of the individual child's semantic and vocabulary abilities in relation to other children the child's age. Standard scores, percentile ranks, age equivalents, and standard deviations are available. In addition, the normative data from a sample of language-disordered children who were administered the test is available. Examiner required. Not suitable for group use.

Untimed: Varies

Scoring: Examiner evaluated

Cost: Test kit (manual, picture stimuli book, 20 test forms) $57.95

Publisher: LinguiSystems, Inc.

ASSESSMENT AND THERAPY PROGRAMME FOR DYSFLUENT CHILDREN
L. Rustin

Child—Ages 7–13

Purpose: Assesses and manages dysfluency in children. Used by speech therapists and psychologists.

Description: Multiple-item structured interview conducted with both child and parents to assess fluency and to gather information about the child's behavior and social and emotional background. The results of this assessment aid in developing a therapy program involving both the clinician and the parents. The clinician uses task sheets to set goals for parents to work towards during teaching at home. Child and adult workbooks contain exercises relative to the training program. Both the task sheets and workbooks are used to record progress. Although the system is designed for children ages 7–13, the assessment phase may be used with children as young as 2½. Examiner required. Suitable for group use.
BRITISH PUBLISHER

Untimed: Continuous assessment and teaching system

Scoring: Examiner evaluated

Cost: Contact publisher

Publisher: NFER-NELSON Publishing Company Ltd.

ASSESSMENT OF APHASIA AND RELATED DISORDERS, SECOND EDITION
Refer to page 95.

ASSESSMENT OF CHILDREN'S LANGUAGE COMPREHENSION (ACLC)
Rochana Foster, Jane J. Giddan, and Joel Stark

Child—Ages 3–6.5

Purpose: Identifies receptive language difficulties in young children in order to provide guidelines for remediation of language disorders.

Description: 41–item verbal test of language comprehension measuring understanding of core vocabulary and combination of language elements. The test uses 50 common words combined into two-, three-, and four-element phrases. Each of the 41 spiral-bound stimulus cards is presented to the child, who points to an appropriate picture in response to a word or phrase from the examiner. A 17–item ACLC Group Form has been developed for classroom screening. Examiner required. Not suitable for group use. Available in Spanish.

Timed: 10–15 minutes

Scoring: Examiner evaluated

Cost: Complete kit (card set, manual, pad of recording sheets) $23.50

Publisher: Consulting Psychologists Press, Inc.

ASSESSMENT OF FLUENCY IN SCHOOL-AGE CHILDREN (AFSC)
Julia Thompson

Child, adolescent
Grades K–12

Purpose: Evaluates speech deficiencies. Used to assess individuals who stutter and for therapy and school programs.

Description: 37–item paper-pencil test measuring expressive language, physiological components (oral motor and breath control), and self-awareness of dysfluencies. Materials needed (but not included) are a tape recorder, picture stimuli, and stop watch. The test must be administered by a speech pathologist. Examiner required. Not suitable for group use.

Untimed: 45 minutes

Scoring: Examiner evaluated

Cost: Complete set (resource guide, 32 assessment forms, 32 parent interview forms, 32 teacher evaluation forms, 32 dismissal forms, carrying case) $49.00

Publisher: PRO-ED

ASSESSMENT OF INTELLIGIBILITY OF DYSARTHIC SPEECH (AIDS)
Kathryn Yorkston, David Beukelman, and Charles Traynor

Adolescent, adult

Purpose: Assesses the single-word intelligibility, sentence intelligibility, and speaking rates of dysarthric adolescents and adults.

Description: Multiple-item verbal and listening test measuring single-word intelligibility, sentence intelligibility, and speaking rates of dysarthric individuals. A computer version that operates on an Apple 48K system with single disk drive and monochrome monitor automatically selects at random 50 words and 20 sentences from hundreds of stimuli. All of the data are then stored and scored automatically. Examiner required. Not suitable for group use.

Untimed: Not available

Scoring: Examiner evaluated

Cost: Complete paper-pencil version (manual, picture book of stimulus words and sentences, pocket portfolio) $69.00; complete computer version (manual, 2 software disks, storage container) $149.00

Publisher: PRO-ED

THE ASSESSMENT OF PHONOLOGICAL PROCESSES— REVISED (APP-R)
Barbara Williams Hodson

Child—Ages 3–8

Purpose: Evaluates the ability of children with severe speech disorders to use phonetics. Used for early childhood intervention and placement.

Description: 50–item test measuring spontaneous utterances naming three-dimensional stimuli. The examiner records speech deviations using narrow phonetic transcription. Materials include recording, analysis, summary, and preschool and multisyllabic screening forms, as well as 12 pictures for multisyllabic screening and 12 picture cards for hard-to-find objects. The revised edition replaces the original test, The Assessment of Phonological Processes. Examiner required. Not suitable for group use.

Untimed: 20 minutes

Scoring: Examiner evaluated; may be computer scored

Cost: Complete kit (manual, 50 recording forms, 50 analysis sheets, 50 analysis summary sheets, 50 preschool screening forms, 50 multisyllabic screening forms) $69.00

Publisher: PRO-ED

AUDITORY DISCRIMINATION AND ATTENTION TEST
Refer to page 675.

AUDITORY-VISUAL, SINGLE-WORD PICTURE VOCABULARY TEST—ADOLESCENT
Morrison F. Gardner

Adolescent—Ages 12–17
Grades 7–11

Purpose: Measures vocabulary through auditory-visual stimuli. Used by counselors, teachers, speech therapists, language pathologists, and psychologists.

Description: 75–item test in which the examinee points to the correct picture of a word both heard (auditory stimuli) and seen (visual stimuli). The examinee must choose the word from among four pictures. The plates are arranged in progressive order of difficulty. Receptive language standard scores, receptive language ages, percentiles, and stanines are determined from the raw scores. Examiner/self-administered. Suitable for group use.

Untimed: 10–15 minutes

Scoring: Examiner evaluated

Cost: Test kit (manual, test plates, 25 record forms) $44.95

Publisher: Children's Hospital of San Francisco, Publications Department

BANKSON LANGUAGE SCREENING TEST–2 (BLT–2)
Nicholas W. Bankson

Child—Ages 3–7

Purpose: Measures psycholinguistic and perceptual skills. Determines the need for further diagnostic assessment. Used to plan language intervention programs.

Description: Multiple-item oral-response test measuring three general categories of a child's language competence: Semantic Knowledge, Morphological/Syntactical Rules, and Pragmatics. Scores are reported in standard scores and percentile ranks. A 20–item short form is also available for screening purposes. Examiner required. Not suitable for group use.

Untimed: Varies

Scoring: Examiner evaluated

Cost: Complete kit (examiner's manual, 25 profile/examiner's record booklets, 25 screen record forms, picture book) $77.00

Publisher: PRO-ED

BASIC INVENTORY OF NATURAL LANGUAGE (BINL)
Refer to page 569.

BASIC LANGUAGE CONCEPTS TEST (BLCT)
Siegfried Engelmann, Dorothy Ross, and Virginia Bingham

Child—Ages 4–6.5

Purpose: Assesses the language competence of children ages 4–6.5 and older language-deficient children. Used by teachers, special educators, speech-language pathologists, school psychologists, or supervised nonprofessionals to diagnose specific skill deficiencies, to serve as a basis for developing IEPs, and to obtain baseline measures against which to evaluate progress.

Description: Multiple-item three-part oral-response test assessing receptive and expressive deficiencies, the representational character of language, and the recognition of sequence and pattern in language. Part I (32 items) measures receptive language skills; Part II (35 items) measures expressive language skills; Part III assesses analogy skills. Results provide diagnostic information for the teacher/clinician to distinguish between children with language disorders and disadvantaged children who develop more slowly and to set goals for individual education programs. Examiner required. Not suitable for group use.

Untimed: 15 minutes

Scoring: Hand key

Cost: Test kit (includes manual, 15 test forms) $35.00

Publisher: SRA/London House

THE BER-SIL SPANISH TESTS: ELEMENTARY TEST 1987 REVISION
Refer to page 300.

THE BER-SIL SPANISH TESTS: SECONDARY TEST
Refer to page 301.

BILINGUAL SYNTAX MEASURE I AND II (BSM)
Refer to page 571.

BRACKEN BASIC CONCEPT SCALE (BBCS)
Refer to page 534.

BRACKEN BASIC CONCEPT SCALE—SCREENING TEST (BBCS-SCREENING)
Refer to page 534.

BRISTOL LANGUAGE DEVELOPMENT SCALES
M. Gutfreund

Child—Ages 15 months–5 years

Purpose: Provides differential diagnosis of children's expressive language problems. Used by speech therapists, specialist language teachers, educational psychologists, and teachers of the deaf with language delayed, bilingual, and mentally handicapped children to plan management programs and set therapy goals.

Description: Multiple-item assessment system examining a child's expressive language problems. The system focuses on three areas fundamental to the emergence of language: pragmatics (how language is used), semantics (the meaning of language), and syntax (the form of language). The items within each of these three sections are divided into 10 stages of development. To begin the assessment, the examiner obtains a sample of the child's speech using any instrument designed for that purpose. The sample then is analyzed using one of two scales: the Main Scale or the Syntax Free Scale. The Main Scale assesses the developmental level of the child's expressive language and identifies deficits that warrant further attention. The Syntax Free Scale, originally developed for use with deaf children, also is used with bilingual or mentally handicapped children, who use a combination of words and signs to communicate. The examiner then uses the Therapy Planning Form to plan long- and short-term therapy goals. Examiner required. Not suitable for group use.
BRITISH PUBLISHER

Untimed: Varies

Scoring: Examiner evaluated

Cost: Contact publisher

Publisher: NFER-NELSON Publishing Company Ltd.

CALLIER AZUZA SCALE: H-EDITION
Robert D. Stillman and Christy W. Battle

Child, adolescent

Purpose: Assesses communication abilities in individuals with severe or multiple disabilities.

Description: Criterion-referenced test with four subtests: Representational and Symbolic Development (63 items), Receptive Communication (46 items), Development of Intentional Communication (35 items), and Reciprocity (48 items). Scores yield age equivalences. The examiner must be familiar with the student. This test is suitable for individuals with visual, hearing, physical, and mental impairments. Examiner required. Not suitable for group use.

Untimed: Varies

Scoring: Examiner evaluated

Cost: $12.00

Publisher: Callier Center for Communication Disorders

CAMBRIDGE KINDERGARTEN SCREENING TEST
Ann M. Shahzade

Child—Kindergarten

Purpose: Measures the speech and language abilities of kindergartners. Identifies children needing further evaluation or observation.

Description: Multiple-item oral-response and task-performance test screening all major areas of speech and language. The various subtests are administered by means of realistic, full-color photographs of common objects and with the use of 10 wooden color cubes. The test may be administered by a speech pathologist, classroom teacher, aide, or volunteer. Step-by-step directions for administering the test are provided in the spiral-bound testing book. The screener's manual contains instructions for administering, scoring, and record keeping. Examiner required. Suitable for screening groups of children.

Untimed: 10–20 minutes

Scoring: Examiner evaluated

Cost: Test kit (testing book, manual, wooden color cubes, vinyl carrying case) $75.00

Publisher: DLM Teaching Resources

CARROW AUDITORY-VISUAL ABILITIES TEST (CAVAT)
Refer to page 724.

CARROW ELICITED LANGUAGES INVENTORY (CELI)
Elizabeth Carrow-Woolfolk

Child—Ages 3 to 7.11

Purpose: Measures the productive control of grammar in young children and diagnoses expressive language delays and disorders. Used to obtain data on a child's grammatical structure.

Description: 52-item norm-referenced test of oral stimuli based on the technique of eliciting imitation of a sequence of sentences that include basic construction types and specific grammatical morphemes. The stimuli (51 sentences and one phrase) are presented by the examiner. The child's responses are recorded and transcribed from the tape onto a scoring/analysis form, which provides a format for analyzing errors of substitution, addition, omission, transposition, and reversal. A separate verb protocol sheet allows an analysis of the production of verb forms. Materials include the test manual, a training guide with practice exercises, the analysis forms, and a cassette or reel training tape. The test is not appropriate for nonverbal subjects. Examiner required. Not suitable for group use.

Untimed: 25 minutes

Scoring: Examiner evaluated

Cost: Complete $69.00

Publisher: DLM Teaching Resources

CHILD LANGUAGE ABILITY MEASURES (CLAM)
Albert Mehrabian and Christy Floynihan

Child—Ages 2–7

Purpose: Measures the language production and language comprehension abilities of children. Identifies linguistic abilities and difficulties. Used by educators, speech-language pathologists, testers, and child psychologists to plan language development programs.

Description: Six multiple-item oral-response and nonverbal task-performance tests measuring a child's expressive and receptive language abilities, including vocabulary comprehension, grammar comprehension, inflection production, grammar imitation, "grammar formedness" judgment, and grammar equivalence judgment. The tests assess a child's language development, including knowledge of syntactic, semantic, and phonological rules rather than intellectual skills such as memory span, knowledge of real world facts, or ability to form abstract relationships. Administration procedures contain built-in safeguards against tester bias (such as encouraging one child more than another). The six tests may be administered separately or together, depending on the needs of the child in question (a selected pair of tests is usually sufficient to obtain a reliable and valid measure of a child's language skills).

Norms are provided to calculate standardized scores for each test and for combinations of tests. In addition, norms are included to provide the age level corresponding to a child's language skills. The manual (for all six tests) includes details regarding the construction of the tests, statistics on item selection and test reliabilities, appropriate age ranges for each test, and scoring procedures and norms. Two administration books are available. Sample answer sheets are provided at the end of each test administration booklet and can be copied by the examiner for use in recording children's answers during testing. Examiner required. Not suitable for group use.

Untimed: 15 minutes per test

Scoring: Examiner evaluated

Cost: Manual $12.00; test administration booklets $20.00 each

Publisher: Albert Mehrabian

CLARK-MADISON TEST OF ORAL LANGUAGE
*John B. Clark and
Charles L. Madison*

Child—Ages 4-8

Purpose: Evaluates the expressive capacity of children. Diagnoses language disorders.

Description: 66–item oral-response test utilizing a nonimitative elicitation technique and assessing responses in seven categories: syntax, modifiers, determiners, prepositions, verbs, pronouns, and inflections. Ninety-seven targets are elicited in the context of a 66–sentence communicative exchange. The test is cross-referenced to create specific multiple-response eliciting probes. Examiner required. Not suitable for group use.

Untimed: 10–20 minutes

Scoring: Examiner evaluated

Cost: Test kit (examiner's manual, stimulus material and picture book, 50 response and analysis forms) $69.00

Publisher: PRO-ED

CLINICAL EVALUATION OF LANGUAGE FUNCTIONS (CELF)
Eleanor Semel and Elisabeth H. Wiig

**Child, adolescent
Grades K-12**

Purpose: Yields detailed diagnostic information on language processing and production skills to identify children with language disabilities.

Description: Multiple-item oral-response assessment consisting of two screening tests (Elementary for Grades K–5 and Advanced for Grades 5–12) and a diagnostic battery. The Elementary screening test is administered using a "Simon Says" format. The Advanced screening test utilizes playing cards to elicit language processing skills. The Diagnostic Battery employs 13 criterion- and norm-referenced subtests to probe language processing, language production, and receptive and expressive phonological factors. These 13 subtests can be administered in their entirety, in part, or in any sequence. Examiner required. Not suitable for group use.

Untimed: 1–2 hours

Scoring: Examiner evaluated

Cost: Complete diagnostic battery $189.00; screening package $45.00

Publisher: The Psychological Corporation

Information and availability unconfirmed; last verified in 1988.

CLINICAL EVALUATION OF LANGUAGE FUNCTIONS— ELEMENTARY AND ADVANCED LEVEL SCREENING (CELF)
Eleanor Semel and Elisabeth H. Wiig

**Child, adolescent
Grades K-12**

Purpose: Evaluates a student's language processing and production abilities. Used to help teachers and school psychologists identify students with potential language problems.

Description: Multiple-item tests probing accuracy in phoneme discrimination, sentence formation rules (morphology and syntax), interpretation of words and logical relationships among sentence components and linguistic concepts, and retention and recall of word and action sequences. Production screening items probe agility and accuracy in phoneme production; ability to recall, identify, and retrieve words and concepts; accuracy in serial recall; and immediate recall of model sentences. The Grades K–5 version contains 48 items in a "Simon Says" format, and the Grades 6–12 test contains 52 items in a card-playing format. Examiner required. Not suitable for group use.

Untimed: 20 minutes

Scoring: Examiner evaluated

Cost: Elementary package $29.00; advanced level package $29.00

Publisher: The Psychological Corporation

Information and availability unconfirmed; last verified in 1988.

CLINICAL PROBES OF ARTICULATION CONSISTENCY (C-PAC)
Wayne Secord

Ages 5 and older

Purpose: Provides an in-depth picture of how well an individual speaks and articulates specific sounds; used for planning and evaluating speech therapy.

Description: Verbal response test of 25 illustrated stories, adult-level reading passages, and duplicating-master articulation probes to elicit responses and check for articulation of target sounds. Specific sounds are assessed in a wide range of contexts: consonants in isolated words, clusters, sentences, and conversational speech; vowels and diphthongs in single words and minimal contrast pairs; and vocalic *r* sounds. Examiner evaluated. Not suitable for group use.

Untimed: 5–10 minutes per probe

Scoring: Examiner evaluated

Cost: Complete program $79.00; story manual $25.00; spirit masters $29.00; manual $25.00

Publisher: The Psychological Corporation

Information and availability unconfirmed; last verified in 1988.

COMMUNICATIVE ABILITIES IN DAILY LIVING (CADL)
Audrey L. Holland

Aphasic adults

Purpose: Assesses the functional communication skills of aphasic adults. Used for planning treatment programs.

Description: Multiple-item oral-response test assessing functional communication disorders. Descriptive data are provided in 10 categories: reading/writing/calculating; speech acts; content utilization; role playing; sequential relationships; social conventions; divergences; nonverbal symbols; deixis (movement-related communicative behavior); and humor, metaphor, and absurdity. The test employs both traditional (usual examiner roles) and nontraditional (role playing) methods. Pro-

vides cutoff scores for determining functional communication disorders. Examiner required. Not suitable for group use.

Untimed: Not available

Scoring: Examiner evaluated

Cost: Complete kit (administration booklet, scoring kit, audiotape cassette, storage box) $98.00

Publisher: PRO-ED

COMMUNICATIVE EVALUATION CHART
Refer to page 30.

COMPREHENSIVE SCREENING TOOL FOR DETERMINING OPTIMAL COMMUNICATION MODE (CST)
Linda I. House and Brenda S. Rogerson

Developmental ages 6 months-adult

Purpose: Assesses the communication mode of children and adults. Used by speech and language pathologists.

Description: Multiple-item battery of response tests used by clinicians for systematically and objectively determining what the examinee's potential is for use of an augmentative system, its mode, and code. The test also helps determine whether augmentative communication is needed to support or substitute for vocal communication. Three subtests assess oral skills, manual skills, and pictographic skills. The Oral Skills Battery consists of three subtests addressing the following areas: prespeech and oral awareness, prearticulatory and articulatory skills, and auditory awareness. The Manual Skills Battery covers prerequisite skills for manual training, movement patterning, and cognitive correlates for manual communication. The Pictographic Skills Battery assesses prerequisites for visual training, attending behaviors and accuracy of movement, and cognitive correlates for pictographic skills. Scoring is completed on a 5–point scale. Examiner required. Not suitable for group use.

Untimed: Varies

Scoring: Examiner evaluated

Cost: Complete kit $53.00

Publisher: United Educational Services, Inc.

COMPTON PHONOLOGICAL ASSESSMENT OF CHILDREN
Arthur J. Compton

Child—Ages 3–6

Purpose: Assesses and analyzes children's misarticulations.

Description: Multiple-item oral-response test in six parts using picture stimuli to assess initial and final single consonants, consonant blends, and vowels. Part 1 is an optional screening test consisting of 15 stimulus words testing initial and final consonants. Part 2 (30 minutes) contains 51 black-and-white line drawings of objects, people, and situations. The examinee repeats each item twice to test for consistency of production, and the examiner transcibes all sounds in each word each time it is repeated. Most of the items are one-syllable words beginning and ending with one consonant. Part 3 detects error patterns in the examinee's spontaneous speech. Part 4 (10 minutes) is a pattern analysis based on the results of parts 2 and 3. Part 5 (15 minutes) is a phonological rule analysis based on misarticulation results. In Part 6 (10 minutes), the examiner correlates the rule analysis of Part 5 with the basic processes in the examinee's deviant system. Materials for administration include response-analysis booklets and a spiral-bound manual containing instructions and 51 stimulus pictures. The test is a revision of the 1978 Compton-Hutton Phonological Assessment. The revision includes the screening section, the assessment of vowels, a section for transcribing spontaneous speech errors, new normative data, and specification and cross-referencing of deviant rules with corresponding phonological process. Examiner required. Suitable for group use.

Untimed: 1 hour

Scoring: Examiner evaluated

Cost: Manual, 25 response-analysis booklets $45.00

Publisher: Carousel House

Information and availability unconfirmed; last verified in 1988.

COMPTON SPEECH AND LANGUAGE SCREENING EVALUATION
Arthur J. Compton

**Child
PreK-Grade 1**

Purpose: Estimates articulation and language development of young children.

Description: Multiple-item oral-response test utilizing common objects to elicit verbal responses from the child. The test, which measures both production and comprehension, covers the following areas: articulation, vocabulary, colors, shapes, memory span, language (plurals, opposites, progressive and past tenses, prepositions, multiple commands, possessive pronouns), spontaneous language, fluency, voice, and oral mechanism. The materials include revised response forms with age profiles, pass/fail guidelines, and an audiogram. Examiner required. Not suitable for group use. Available in Spanish.

Untimed: 6–10 minutes

Scoring: Examiner evaluated

Cost: Kit (manual, carrying case, stimulus objects, pictures for eliciting conversational speech, 25 response forms) $50.00

Publisher: Carousel House

Information and availability unconfirmed; last verified in 1988.

COMPUTER MANAGED ARTICULATION DIAGNOSIS
James L. Fitch

Language age 4–adult

Purpose: Assesses the articulation skills of individuals with a language age of 4–adult. Used for preparing individual education programs.

Description: 46–item computer-administered oral-response test analyzing articulation errors. Using an elicited sentence format for nonreaders or stimulus sentences on the screen, examiners can test single phonemes, blends, or both, as well as stimulatability. Each sound is presented in pre- and postvocalic position, and no consonants are abutting the consonants tested. A computer-generated, four-page analysis of error patterns by distinctive feature is available in 5 minutes. The software operates on Apple II+, IIe, and IIc systems. Examiner required. Not suitable for group use.

Untimed: 5 minutes

Scoring: Computer scored

Cost: Complete kit (20–page manual, 1 diskette and 1 backup, storage folder) $69.00

Publisher: Communication Skill Builders, Inc.

COMPUTER MANAGED SCREENING TEST
James L. Fitch

Child—Ages 3–8

Purpose: Assesses articulation, expressive and receptive language, voice, and fluency in children. Used for language development and early childhood education.

Description: 32–item oral-response test using manipulative objects to assess children's language abilities. The examiner reads instructions displayed on a computer screen and keys the child's responses. The program runs on Apple II+, IIe, and IIc computers with DOS 3.3, 48K RAM, disk drive, and a compatible printer. Examiner required. Not suitable for group use.

Untimed: 2½–4 minutes

Scoring: Not available

Cost: Complete kit $85.00

Publisher: Communication Skill Builders, Inc.

A DEEP TEST OF ARTICULATION: PICTURE FORM
Eugene T. McDonald

Child
Grades K–4

Purpose: Assesses a child's ability to produce sounds in various phonetic combinations. Useful for planning therapy.

Description: Verbal test with longitudinal norms measuring a child's articulatory proficiency by assessing 13 sounds. Each sound is tested by 60 items. The examiner places two sets of picture cards mounted side by side before the child. The child names the two pictures, and the examiner determines whether the sounds made by the child were correct. A trained examiner is required. Not suitable for group use.

Untimed: 15–20 minutes

Scoring: Examiner evaluated

Cost: Test kit (instructions, sample cards) $19.95

Publisher: Communication Skill Builders, Inc.

A DEEP TEST OF ARTICULATION: SENTENCE FORM
Eugene T. McDonald

Grades 3 and above

Purpose: Assesses a child's ability to produce sounds in a sentence. Used to determine for which sounds the child needs remedial work.

Description: Multiple-item verbal test measuring a child's articulatory proficiency. The examiner flips the pages of a booklet, and the child reads sentences containing sound combinations. A trained examiner is required. Not suitable for group use.

Untimed: Not available

Scoring: Examiner evaluated

Cost: Test kit (test booklet, instructions) $15.95

Publisher: Communication Skill Builders, Inc.

DENVER ARTICULATION SCREENING EXAM (DASE)
Amelia F. Drumwright

Child—Ages 2.5–7

Purpose: Detects speech articulation problems in children. Screens for more sophisticated testing.

Description: 22–picture test measuring a child's intelligibility (does not assess language ability, vocabulary, school readiness, or intelligence). The examiner shows the pictures, displayed on 11 cards, to the child, says a word, and the child repeats it. The test is not recommended for shy or younger children. Examiner required. Not suitable for group use.

Untimed: 5 minutes

Scoring: Examiner evaluated

Cost: 25 tests $4.00; manual/workbook $10.25; picture cards $4.25

Publisher: Denver Developmental Materials, Inc.

DIAGNOSTIC SCREENING TEST: LANGUAGE, SECOND EDITION (DSTL)
Refer to page 287.

DYSARTHRIA PROFILE
S.J. Robertson

Adolescent, adult

Purpose: Identifies the presence and severity of dysarthria. Used with adolescents and adults to make treatment recommendations.

Description: Series of activities evaluating various aspects of dysarthria, including respiration, phonation, articulation, facial musculative movement, diadochokinesis, reflex activity, intelligibility, and prosody and rate. Examiner required. Not suitable for group use.

Untimed: Not available

Scoring: Examiner evaluated

Cost: Complete kit (manual, 5 stimulus cards, scoring form, profile summary form) $19.95

Publisher: Communication Skill Builders, Inc.

ELICITED ARTICULATORY SYSTEM EVALUATION (EASE)
Susie Finn Steed and
William O. Haynes

All ages

Purpose: Assesses articulation in individuals of all ages. Used as an initial

assessment tool and/or to assess the effects of therapy.

Description: Multiple-item verbal stimulus-response test assessing 337 consonants, 187 vowel productions, and 10 phonological processes, including deletion of final consonants, fronting of fricatives, stopping, and vocalization. The examiner reads a sentence about a picture, and the examinee repeats it. Certain words in each sentence are targeted for evaluation. The examiner enters the analysis of the words on a score sheet, and later uses a color-coding system for transferring the information to an analysis booklet where test results can be analyzed for articulatory and phonological strengths and weaknesses. Examiner required. Not suitable for group use.

Untimed: 15 minutes

Scoring: Examiner evaluated

Cost: Complete kit (manual, 25 score sheets, 25 analysis booklets, picture book, storage box) $89.00

Publisher: PRO-ED

ENGLISH PICTURE VOCABULARY TESTS (EPVTS)
M.A. Brimer and C.M. Dunn

Ages 2.9–adult

Purpose: Assesses listening vocabulary. Used by teachers and speech therapists for identifying reading difficulty and other verbal learning handicaps.

Description: Multiple-item response test measuring verbal comprehension in which the examinee matches a picture with a spoken word. The test is available on five levels: Test 1 (40 items) for ages 5–8.11; Test 2 (40 items) for ages 7–11.11 (group and individual versions); Test 3 (48 items) for ages 11–18; and a full-range version (125 items arranged in order of increasing difficulty) for ages 3–18. No reading is required. Examiner required. Suitable for group use depending on level. BRITISH PUBLISHER

Untimed: Varies

Scoring: Hand key

Cost: Contact publisher

Publisher: Educational Evaluation Enterprises

Information and availability unconfirmed; last verified in 1987.

EVALUATING ACQUIRED SKILLS IN COMMUNICATION (EASIC)
Anita Marcott Riley

Ages 3 months–8 years　

Purpose: Assesses the language abilities of individuals with a language age of 3 months–8 years and an interest level age of 4–20 years. Used for planning speech-language therapy programs for severely language-impaired clients.

Description: Multiple-item oral-response test consisting of five inventories assessing an individual's abilities in semantics, syntax, morphology, and pragmatics. The examiner uses picture stimuli to elicit spontaneous, cued, imitated, manipulated, noncompliant, or incorrect responses. The test helps determine emerging communication skills, including before meaningful speech; understanding of simple noun labels, action verbs, and basic concepts; emerging modes of communication; understanding of more complex language functions; and use of more complex communication. The test includes goals for individual education prescriptions. It is used with autistic, mentally impaired, developmentally delayed, and preschool language-delayed children and adolescents. Examiner required. Not suitable for group use.

Untimed: Not available

Scoring: Hand key

Cost: Complete kit $75.00

Publisher: Communication Skill Builders, Inc.

EVALUATING COMMUNICATIVE COMPETENCE: A FUNCTIONAL PRAGMATIC PROCEDURE (REVISED EDITION)
Charlann S. Simon

Adolescent—Ages 9–17　

Purpose: Assesses auditory and expressive language skills. Used with language and learning-impaired adolescents.

Description: Series of 21 tasks designed to measure language processing abilities, metalinguistic skills, and functional use of language. The tasks include comprehension of directions, giving directions, creative storytelling, maintenance of tense in storytelling, stating similarities and differences, barrier games, and expression and justification of an opinion. Each task is designed so that examinees demonstrate competency in both listener and speaker roles. Stimulus materials are included. Examiner required. Not suitable for group use.

Untimed: Not available

Scoring: Examiner evaluated

Cost: Complete kit (manual, 59 pages of stimulus materials, 6 blocks, 12 picture cards, 10 scoring forms, 3-ring binder) $65.00

Publisher: Communication Skill Builders, Inc.

EXAMINING FOR APHASIA: SECOND EDITION
Jon Eisenson

Adolescent, adult　

Purpose: Assesses language functioning of aphasics.

Description: Multiple-item procedure for systematically exploring language functioning in aphasics. Materials include a manual detailing issues in the assessment of aphasics and 14 plates of stimulus materials in black and white. The examiner assembles other common objects required for the examination. Examiner required. Not suitable for group use.

Untimed: 30–120 minutes

Scoring: Examiner evaluated

Cost: Complete set (manual, 25 record forms) $60.00; manual $35.00; record forms $29.00

Publisher: The Psychological Corporation

Information and availability unconfirmed; last verified in 1988.

EXPRESSIVE ONE-WORD PICTURE VOCABULARY TEST (EOWPVT)
Morrison F. Gardner

Child—Ages 2–12

Purpose: Assesses a child's verbal intelligence. Used to screen for possible speech defects, to evaluate bilingual student fluency in English, and to determine preschool placement.

Description: 110–item verbal test of definitional and interpretational skills. The test consists of 100 pictures presented one at a time to the examinee, who names each picture while the examiner records the response. Scoring tables yield deviation IQs, percentiles, and mental age equivalents. Materials include test plates and a set of Spanish recording forms. Examiner required. Not suitable for group use. Available in Spanish.

Untimed: 20 minutes

Scoring: Hand key

Cost: Test kit (manual, test plates, 50 English record forms in vinyl folder) $63.00

Publisher: Academic Therapy Publications

EXPRESSIVE ONE-WORD PICTURE VOCABULARY TEST: UPPER EXTENSION (EOWPVT: UE)
Morrison F. Gardner

Adolescent—Ages 12–15

Purpose: Assesses the expressive vocabulary of students ages 12–15 as a measure of verbal intelligence. Used to detect speech defects and learning disabilities.

Description: Multiple-item oral-response test in which the student demonstrates his ability to understand and use words by naming pictures that range from simple objects to representations of abstract concepts. Each test item consists of one picture stimulus that requires a single-word answer. Test results yield mental ages, percentiles, stanines, and deviation IQ scores, which allow for the comparison of expressive language skills to other measures of receptive language, the detection of speech defects, the identification of learning disorders related to hearing loss and imperceptions of the auditory modality, the assessment of auditory-visual association ability, and the evaluation of a bilingual student's English/Spanish fluency. Examiner required. Suitable for use with small groups that respond in writing. Available in Spanish.

Untimed: 5–10 minutes

Scoring: Examiner evaluated

Cost: Test kit (manual, test plates, 50 English record forms, vinyl folder) $58.00

Publisher: Academic Therapy Publications

FLETCHER TIME-BY-COUNT TEST OF DIADOCHOKINETIC SYLLABLE RATE
Samuel G. Fletcher

Child, adolescent—Ages 6–13

Purpose: Assesses oral motor coordination.

Description: Multiple-item test assessing oral motor coordination, which may reflect residual impairment of speech structure or function. The test provides a method for recording diadochokinetic syllable rate and comparing results to norms by age for children ages 6–13. Examiner required. Not suitable for group use.

Untimed: Not available

Scoring: Hand key

Cost: 3 pads of 50–page forms $19.00

Publisher: PRO-ED

FLUHARTY PRESCHOOL SPEECH AND LANGUAGE SCREENING TEST
Nancy Buono Fluharty

Child—Ages 2–6

Purpose: Evaluates the language performance of preschoolers. Identifies children with delayed or abnormal language development.

Description: Multiple-item oral-response test assessing syntax, articulation, and auditory comprehension. Picture stimuli (ten 8⅜" x 5") cards are used to elicit language samples. Cutoff scores are provided for each age level of each area screened. Examiner required. Not suitable for group use.

Untimed: 5–10 minutes

Scoring: Examiner evaluated

Cost: Complete program (10 picture cards, 2 pads of 50 response forms, guide) $45.00

Publisher: DLM Teaching Resources

FRENCHAY DYSARTHRIA ASSESSMENT
P. Enderby

Adolescent, adult—Ages 12 and older

Purpose: Assesses dysarthria—speech impairment due to neuromuscular disorders—resulting from such conditions as cerebral palsy, Parkinson's disease, head injury, and stroke. Used by speech therapists, doctors, psychiatrists, and clinical psychologists to select and monitor appropriate treatment programs.

Description: 29–item task-performance and behavioral-observation test measuring speech impairment due to neuromuscular disorders. The test items cover reflex, respiration, lips, jaw, palate, larynx, tongue, intelligibility, influencing factors (sight, teeth, language, mood, posture), rate, and sensation. The results are recorded graphically on multicopy forms using a 9–point rating scale. Examiner required. Not suitable for group use.

Untimed: Varies

Scoring: Examiner evaluated

Cost: Contact publisher

Publisher: College Hill Press; co-published in the United Kingdom and Western Europe by NFER-NELSON Publishing Company Ltd.; distributed in Canada by Copp Clark, Pitman Ltd.; distributed worldwide by Whurr Publishers Ltd.

FULLERTON LANGUAGE TEST FOR ADOLESCENTS (EXPERIMENTAL EDITION)
Arden R. Thorum

Ages 11–adult

Purpose: Measures receptive and expressive language skills. Identifies language-impaired adolescents.

Description: 142–item verbal test of eight functions important in the acquisition and effective use of language skills: auditory synthesis, morphology competency, oral commands, convergent production, divergent production, syllabication, grammatic competency, and idioms. Each function is scored according to three language performance levels: competency, instruction, or frustration. Materials include a set of stimulus items. Examiner required. Not suitable for group use.

Untimed: 45 minutes

Scoring: Hand key; examiner evaluated

Cost: Examiner's kit (stimulus items, 25 scoring forms and profiles, manual) $30.50

Publisher: Consulting Psychologists Press, Inc.

FULLERTON LANGUAGE TEST FOR ADOLESCENTS, 2ND EDITION
Arden R. Thorum

Adolescent, adult—Ages 11–18 and older

Purpose: Measures expressive and receptive language skills, distinguishes normal from language-impaired individuals, and diagnoses language strengths and weaknesses.

Description: Multiple-item verbal test consisting of eight subtests measuring various language skills: Auditory Synthesis, Morphology Competency, Oral Commands, Convergent Production, Divergent Production, Syllabication, Grammatic Competency, and Idioms. The profile is based on three language performance levels. This revised edition of the test includes an updated performance profile, an optional descriptive scoring method, expanded scoring instructions, and a summary of the research conducted on the test. Examiner required. Not suitable for group use.

Untimed: 35 minutes

Scoring: Examiner evaluated

Cost: Examiner's kit (manual, stimulus items, 25 each of scoring forms and profiles) $30.50

Publisher: Consulting Psychologists Press, Inc.

GOLDMAN-FRISTOE TEST OF ARTICULATION
Ronald Goldman and
Macalyne Fristoe

Child, adolescent—Ages 2-16 and older

Purpose: Assesses an individual's ability to speak clearly. Used as a basis for remedial planning.

Description: Three verbal subtests of articulation of major speech sounds in the initial, medial, and final positions; articulatory skills used in connected speech; and articulation of sounds known to be difficult for the student. In the Sounds-in-Words subtest, the student names the pictures of 35 familiar objects. In the Sounds-in-Sentences subtest, the student retells two stories the examiner has just read. In the Stimulability subtest, the examiner tests the student on the sounds misarticulated in the Sounds-in-Words subtest. Percentile ranks are provided by age for the Sounds-in-Words and Stimulability subtests. However, the interpretation of the test lies more in knowing which sounds the individual produces incorrectly and the type of misproduction than in an overall quantitative score that shows performance in relation to that of other individuals. Materials include test plates in an easel, 25 response forms, and a manual. No reading is required. The picture format enables the examiner to use the test with retarded or easily distractible children. Examiner required. Not suitable for group use.

Untimed: Sounds-In-Words subtest 15 minutes; varies for other two subtests

Scoring: Examiner evaluated

Cost: Complete test kit $75.00

Publisher: American Guidance Service

HANNAH-GARDNER TEST OF VERBAL AND NONVERBAL LANGUAGE FUNCTIONING
Refer to page 546.

INTERPERSONAL LANGUAGE SKILLS ASSESSMENT—FINAL EDITION
Carolyn M. Blagden and
Nancy L. McConnell

Child, adolescent—Ages 8-14

Purpose: Determines how effectively students use language to participate in social situations. Identifies students with inadequate communication skills and pinpoints specific communication behavior problems.

Description: Multiple-category paper-pencil observational inventory assessing a student's use of the linguistic social skills necessary for successful interpersonal interactions. The student being tested is observed interacting in a group with two or three of his peers. His interpersonal language skills are assessed according to percentage of utterances by age for comment type: presence of negation and/or sarcasm; creative language use; type of semantic, grammatic or production efficiency errors; and comment category for commanding, criticizing, informing, justifying, requesting and supporting. One to four students may be evaluated simultaneously. The results identify students with inadequate communication skills. Norms are provided for students ages 8-14. Examiner required. Suitable for small group use.

Untimed: Varies

Scoring: Examiner evaluated

Cost: Test kit (manual, 20 test forms) $34.90

Publisher: LinguiSystems, Inc.

speech, hearing, and visual: speech and language

INVENTORY OF LANGUAGE ABILITIES
Esther H. Minskoff,
Douglas E. Wiseman, and
J. Gerald Minskoff

Grades PreK–2

Purpose: Assesses language abilities of preschool and early primary-school children. Used by teachers and educational specialists for identifying language learning disabilities. Also used in bilingual or ESL programs.

Description: 132–item paper-pencil inventory based on the Illinois Test of Psycholinguistic Abilities and used to screen language disabilities. The test covers auditory reception, visual memory, grammatic closure, visual closure, and auditory closure and sound blending. The 11 checklists each contain 12 social and academic behaviors observable by a teacher. If more than 50% of the behaviors in a category are checked, a possible learning disability in that area is indicated. Examiner required. Not suitable for group use.

Untimed: Varies

Scoring: Examiner evaluated

Cost: 25 record booklets $15.00

Publisher: Educational Performance Associates

IOWA'S SEVERITY RATING SCALE
Iowa Department of Education

Child, adolescent

Purpose: Assesses the severity of speech and language disorders.

Description: Likert-type scale evaluating a student's speech and language in four areas: articulation, language, voice, and fluency. The student's speech and language is rated on a continuum from 0 (adequate speech and language) to 4 (speech and language disorder). May be used with students af all ages and with those whose mutiple handicaps include speech and language impairments. Examiner required. Not suitable for group use.

Untimed: Varies

Scoring: Examiner evaluated

Cost: $24.00

Publisher: PRO-ED

THE JOLIET 3–MINUTE SPEECH AND LANGUAGE SCREEN (JMSLS)
Mary C. Kinzler and
Constance Cowing Johnson

Child
Grades K–5

Purpose: Measures the speech and language development of school-age children. Identifies children with speech and language disorders. Used to screen large numbers of children.

Description: Multiple-item individually administered oral-response test assessing receptive vocabulary, expressive syntax, voice, fluency, and phonological competence. Line drawings are used to elicit receptive vocabulary. Sentences are used to identify expressive syntax, morphology, and phonological competence. Norms are provided for Grades K, 2, and 5. Examiner required. Suitable for group use.

Untimed: 3 minutes

Scoring: Examiner evaluated

Cost: Test kit (manual, 20 vocabulary plates, 2 scoring sheets) $25.00

Publisher: Communication Skill Builders, Inc.

KHAN-LEWIS PHONOLOGICAL ANALYSIS (KLPA)
Linda Khan and Nancy Lewis

Child—Ages 2–5 years, 11 months

Purpose: Assesses the phonological processes of children ages 2–5 years, 11 months. Also used with older children with articulation problems. Used by speech language pathologists with training in phonetic transcription.

Description: Multiple-item paper-pencil assessment identifying specific phoneme errors and determining speech simplification patterns. This test is used following administration of the Sounds-in-Words subtest of the Goldman-Fristoe Test of Articulation. The examiner completes the

---

KLPA analysis form, which lists over 1,200 sound changes occuring when responses to the Sounds-in-Words subtest are mispronounced. Norms are based on a representative national sample of children ages 2–5 years, 11 months. Scores include an index of individual usage for each of the 12 developmental phonological processes; a percentage-of-occurrence score for each of three nondevelopmental phonological processes; an index of overall phonological process usage expressed as a percentile rank, a speech simplification rating, and an age equivalent; and an inventory of phonemes the child produces, which may be used for developing treatment programs. Examiner required. Not suitable for group use.

Untimed: 5–10 minutes

Scoring: Hand key

Cost: Complete kit (manual, 25 analysis forms in folder) $42.50

Publisher: American Guidance Service

KINDERGARTEN LANGUAGE SCREENING TEST (KLST)
Sharon V. Gauthier and Charles L. Madison

Child—Ages 4–7 Kindergarten

Purpose: Tests receptive and expressive language competency and assesses language deficits that may cause kindergartners to fail academically.

Description: 8–item oral-response test identifying children for further diagnostic testing for language deficits that may accelerate academic failure. The examiner assesses expressive and receptive language competence through identification of name, age, colors, body parts, number concepts, commands, sentence repetition, and spontaneous speech. The test is based on the verbal language abilities considered average for children of kindergarten age. Examiner required. Not suitable for group use.

Untimed: 4–5 minutes

Scoring: Examiner evaluated

Cost: Portfolio (examiner's manual, picture cards, 50 test forms) $34.00

Publisher: PRO-ED

LANGUAGE ASSESSMENT SCALES (LAS)

Child, adolescent Grades K–12

Purpose: Assesses students' oral language abilities.

Description: Multiple-item paper-pencil test available in two parallel forms (A and B), two levels (Level 1 for Grades K–5 and Level 2 for Grades 6–12+), and two formats (multicopy scoresheets and student test booklets). The Multi-Copy Scoresheets (MSC) for the SCAN-TRON Optical Readers format consists of two parts. Part 1 is hand or machine-scorable and administered with reusable cue pictures for testing or placement. Part 2 is a separate tear-off sheet for the teacher and provides specific assignments for language arts activities, an individual student academic profile and performance record, and a five-level checklist for placement based on communicative competence and linguistic proficiency. Examiner required. Not suitable for group use. Available in Spanish.

Untimed: Short form 10 minutes; long form 20 minutes

Scoring: Hand key; may be machine scored

Cost: Complete kit $63.95

Publisher: Linguametrics Group

Information and availability unconfirmed; last verified in 1988.

LANGUAGE FACILITY TEST
John T. Dailey

Child, adolescent—Ages 3–15

Purpose: Evaluates how well children speak in the language or dialect in which they were reared. Assesses gains in language ability. Used for bilingual, early and special education programs, as well as programs for the deaf and physically or mentally handicapped.

Description: 12–item oral-response test in which children are asked to tell stories about or describe each of three pictures in four forms. Responses are assigned scores on a 9-point scale according to detailed scoring criteria and examples at each level. The scores measure how well children use the language or dialect to which they have been exposed in the home or school environment. Provides a measure of language facility that is relatively independent of vocabulary, information, pronunciation, and grammar. Norms are available for ages 3 to 15. Normative data also are reported for many subgroups, such as the mentally retarded, deaf, physically handicapped, poor readers, and children with behavior problems. Not suitable for adults with better-than-average language facility. The test kit includes 12 picture plates, test administrator's manual, SPANISH supplement to the manual, and Manual Supplement II (Selected Dissertations and other Reports). The test can be administered in Spanish, sign language, or other languages or dialects. Examiner required. Not suitable for group use.

Untimed: 10 minutes

Scoring: Examiner evaluated

Cost: Complete kit $25.00; 100 answer booklets $15.00

Publisher: The Allington Corporation

LANGUAGE INVENTORY FOR TEACHERS (LIT)
Refer to page 637.

LANGUAGE PROCESSING TEST
Gail Richard and Mary Anne Hanner

Child—Ages 5-12

Purpose: Assesses a child's ability to process language and provides insight into how the child organizes information.

Description: Multiple-item verbally administered oral-response test using common vocabulary known to children to provide a hierarchical evaluation of language processing skills. The test identifies the child's strengths and weaknesses in the areas of association, categorization, similarities and differences, attributes, and multiple meaning words. The test assesses how the child organizes information and identifies behaviors associated with processing disorders such as word

retrieval difficulties, nonspecific word usage, rehearsing responses, and inappropriate word order substitutions. Norms are provided for children ages 5-12. The test yields age equivalencies, percentile ranks, standard scores, and standard deviations. Examiner required. Not suitable for group use.

Untimed: Varies

Scoring: Examiner evaluated

Cost: Test kit (manual with pictures, 20 test forms) $44.90

Publisher: LinguiSystems, Inc.

"LET'S TALK" INVENTORY FOR ADOLESCENTS
Elisabeth H. Wiig

Adolescent, adult
Grades 9 and above

Purpose: Evaluates students' ability to communicate by talking; used by speech pathologists, special educators, and psychologists to identify and diagnose students who have social communication problems.

Description: 40-item verbal test in which the examiner gives the description and context of a picture and asks the student to formulate appropriate speech acts for the context, thereby probing four communication functions: ritualizing, informing, controlling, and feeling. Scoring reflects the register and appropriateness of the speech acts formulated. "Drop back" of extension items are included. Subsequent use provides data on progress as a result of intervention. The test may be followed by the instructional program "Let's Talk": Developing Prosocial Communication Skills. Examiner required. Not suitable for group use.

Timed: 30-45 minutes

Scoring: Examiner evaluated

Cost: Complete kit $79.00

Publisher: The Psychological Corporation

Information and availability unconfirmed; last verified in 1988.

THE LISTENING FOR MEANING TEST
Refer to page 290.

MEASUREMENT OF LANGUAGE DEVELOPMENT
Carol Melnick

Child—Ages 3.0–7.11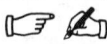

Purpose: Measures progress of therapy programs for language-impaired children, including presentence level children. Used with language-delayed (with normal intelligence), mentally retarded, hearing-impaired, and emotionally disturbed children to assess effects of language intervention programs.

Description: 186–item "point-to" and oral-response test covering eight subtasks: primary verbs, personal pronouns, negatives, indefinite pronouns, interrogative reversals, who-questions, secondary verbs, and conjunctions. The items consist of familiar objects and situations pictured in the stimulus book. The examiner describes the stimulus pictures and asks the child to point to the one that has been described. The examiner then describes pictures and asks the child to describe them in his own words. The responses are evaluated for both receptive and expressive language, mean length of utterance, word order, and semantic relations. The complete test kit includes a manual, receptive-expressive picture plates, and 25 record forms. Examiner required. Not suitable for group use.

Untimed: Not available

Scoring: Examiner evaluated

Cost: Complete kit $49.50

Publisher: Stoelting Co.

MERRILL LANGUAGE SCREENING TEST (MLST)
Myrna Mumm, Wayne Secord, and Katherine Dykstra

Child
Grades K–1

Purpose: Identifies language problems in kindergartners and first-graders.

Description: Six picture stimulus cards, a manual, and an audiocassette are used to elicit responses from children in order to assess receptive and expressive language skills in five areas: production of complete sentences, utterance length, verb-tense agreement, elaboration, and communication competence. The optional Articulation Screening Inventory can be used to test 16 phonemes. The components are available individually. Examiner required. Suitable for use in group screening.

Untimed: 5 minutes

Scoring: Examiner evaluated

Cost: Complete kit $69.00

Publisher: The Psychological Corporation

Information and availability unconfirmed; last verified in 1988.

MILLER-YODER LANGUAGE COMPREHENSION TEST (MY)
Jon F. Miller and David Yoder

Child—Developmental ages 4–8

Purpose: Assesses language comprehension of children. Used by speech clinicians.

Description: Picture-book test assessing children's understanding of short, simple sentences in a variety of grammatical structures. The test helps determine similarity of language comprehension in same-age peers and comprehension difficulties. The test is designed for normal, developmentally delayed, and mentally retarded children between the developmental ages of 4–8. Three sets of picture plates provide selection for different populations. Examiner required. Not suitable for group use.

Untimed: 10–30 minutes

Scoring: Hand key

Cost: Complete kit (examiner's manual, 25 scoring forms, picture book) $79.00; scoring forms $11.00

Publisher: PRO-ED

MINNESOTA TEST FOR DIFFERENTIAL DIAGNOSIS OF APHASIA
Mildred Schuell

Adult

Purpose: Assesses language disturbance due to brain damage; aids in classifying patients and determining prognosis.

Description: The subject responds to questions and cards presented by the examiner, who then evaluates disturbances in hearing, seeing, and reading; speech and language; visuomotor and writing; and disturbances of numerical relationships and arithmetic processes. The test may be administered over several sessions, depending on patient's fatigue. Examiner required. Not suitable for group use.

Untimed: Open ended

Scoring: Hand key; examiner evaluated

Cost: Manual $2.00; Differential Diagnosis of Aphasia with the Minnesota test $7.95

Publisher: University of Minnesota Press

MULTILEVEL INFORMAL LANGUAGE INVENTORY (MILI)
Candace L. Goldsworthy

Child, adolescent
Grades K–6

Purpose: Assesses three distinct levels of oral language. Provides an informal measure of the child's level of functioning in the production of critical semantic relations and syntactic constructions.

Description: Verbal test assessing three levels of language (spontaneous evoked, indirect imitation, and receptive) in eight semantic and syntactic categories (verbs, nouns, modification, interrogatives, negations, combining prepositions, adverbs and prepositions, associative language). Using the manual and picture stimuli provided in the test kit, specific types of responses are obtained. Survey scenes elicit short, spontaneous language samples; survey stories elicit more complex language forms through storytelling and paraphrasing; and specific probes focus on key syntactic constructions. Examiner required. Not suitable for group use.

Untimed: 45 minutes

Scoring: Examiner evaluated

Cost: Complete $69.00; 12 record forms $15.00; picture manual $45.00; examiner's manual $25.00

Publisher: The Psychological Corporation

Information and availability unconfirmed; last verified in 1988.

MUMA ASSESSMENT PROGRAM (MAP)—REVISED SECOND EDITION
Refer to page 554.

NEW ENGLAND PANTOMIME TESTS: ASSESSMENT OF NONVERBAL COMMUNICATION
Robert J. Duffy and Joseph R. Duffy

Adolescent, adult

Purpose: Assesses the gestural expressive and receptive abilities of language-disordered clients. Used as a standardized measure of therapy effectiveness.

Description: Multiple-item test diagnosing communication disorders common to aphasics and other brain-injured adults and adolescents. The program consists of four distinct pantomime tests: Pantomime Recognition Test (forms A and B), a nonverbal test assessing an individual's ability to recognize pantomime acts associated with common pictured objects; Pantomime Expression Test, evaluating the simple pantomimic performance of aphasic individuals; and Pantomime Referential Abilities Test, measuring the communicative effectiveness of a client on a simple pantomimic referential task. Results help clinicians determine appropriate treatment. Examiner required. Not suitable for group use.

Untimed: Varies

Scoring: Examiner evaluated

Cost: Test kit (examiner's manual, picture book) $69.00

Publisher: PRO-ED

NON-LANGUAGE TEST OF VERBAL INTELLIGENCE
Refer to page 594.

NORTHWESTERN SYNTAX SCREENING TEST (NSST)
Laura L. Lee

Child—Ages 3–7

Purpose: Measures a child's syntactic development. Used to identify deficient children needing further evaluation.

Description: Screening test in which the child is asked to respond to short verbal statements by picking out a picture that the statement best describes or by repeating an appropriate statement pertaining to the picture. Receptive and expressive language abilities are evaluated. Examiner required. Not suitable for group use.

Untimed: 15–25 minutes

Scoring: Examiner evaluated

Cost: Test, 100 answer forms $19.95

Publisher: Northwestern University Press

Information and availability unconfirmed; last verified in 1987.

ORAL LANGUAGE EVALUATION (OLE)
Refer to page 580.

ORAL SPEECH MECHANISM SCREENING EXAMINATION— REVISED (OSMSE-R)
Kenneth O. St. Louis and Dennis M. Ruscello

All ages

Purpose: Evaluates speech, language, and other related skills. Used for examining oral speech mechanisms in language and speech clients of all ages.

Description: Oral-response instrument examining the lips, tongue, jaw, teeth, hard palate, soft palate, pharynx, velopharyngeal function, breathing, and diadochokinetic rates. The revised edition yields separate numerical scores for Structure and Function in addition to the total score. Examiner required. Not suitable for group use.

Untimed: 5–10 minutes

Scoring: Examiner evaluated

Cost: Complete kit (manual, 50 scoring forms, storage box) $39.00

Publisher: PRO-ED

THE PATTERNED ELICITATION SYNTAX TEST (PEST)
Edna Carter Young and Joseph J. Perachio

Child—Language age 3–7.5 years

Purpose: Determines whether a child's expressive grammatical skills are age appropriate. Identifies children needing further evaluation.

Description: Multiple-item oral-response test using the delayed imitation technique to assess a child's use of 44 syntactic structures. The child listens to three consecutive modeled sentences with a common syntactic pattern but varying vocabulary while looking simultaneously at corresponding line illustrations. The child then repeats the sentences with the aid of the drawings. The first two sentences serve as carriers. The third sentence, which is most distant from the examiner's model, is used in scoring. In addition to determining the child's language age, criterion-referenced interpretation of the child's responses provides an in-depth analysis of the child's use of grammatical structures. The manual includes stimulus pictures, a demonstration page, normative data, and instructions for administration and scoring. The response form is used to record the child's utterances, the assessment form includes grammatical analysis, and the individual data form is used for recordkeeping. Examiner required. Not suitable for group use.

Untimed: 20 minutes

Scoring: Examiner evaluated

Cost: Test kit (stimulus pictures, demonstration page, normative data, instructions, response sheets, assessment sheets, individual data form) $24.95

Publisher: Communication Skill Builders, Inc.

speech, hearing, and visual: speech and language

PERFORMANCE ASSESSMENT OF SYNTAX: ELICITED AND SPONTANEOUS (PASES)
Lila Coughran

Child—Ages 3-8

Purpose: Assesses a child's ability to produce key syntactic structures. May be used with young, severely impaired children or children with short attention spans.

Description: Multiple-item oral-response test measuring the 11 most frequently exhibited errors in children's syntax: articles, personal pronouns, possessive pronouns, adjectives, verbs (is/are and present progressive), verbs (has/have), verbs (past tense, regular, and irregular), plurality, negation, interrogation, and conjunctions. The child's spontaneous use of language is assessed when possible, but in the event of failure, stimulus items are provided for eliciting appropriate responses. The criterion-referenced nature of the test allows specific subtests rather than the entire battery to be administered. The test may be used with language-impaired and normally developing children functioning within the 3–8-year age-range. Examiner required. Not suitable for group use.

Untimed: Varies

Scoring: Examiner evaluated

Cost: Complete kit (manual, stimulus items, easel binder, 10 response forms) $80.00

Publisher: Exceptional Resources, Inc.

Information and availability unconfirmed; last verified in 1987.

PHONEMIC SYNTHESIS: BLENDING SOUNDS INTO WORDS
Jack Katz and Cornelia Harmon

Child, adolescent
Grades 1-4

Purpose: Identifies and evaluates auditory processing difficulties and provides materials for remediation.

Description: Multiple-item response test and instructional package for diagnosing and remediating speech problems, including discrimination, sequencing, and/or blending. Although the program was designed for children in Grades 1-4, it can be used with slow learners in Grades 5-12. The package includes the test, 15 progressively more difficult lessons, 9 audiocassette tapes, a 52–page picture book, and 12 picture cards. Examiner required. Not suitable for group use.

Untimed: Varies

Scoring: Not available

Cost: Complete package $105.00

Publisher: DLM Teaching Resources

PHONOLOGICAL ASSESSMENT OF CHILD SPEECH
Pamela Grunwell

Child

Purpose: Assesses sound system of children. Used by clinicians and therapists to diagnose problems and develop treatment programs.

Description: Multiple-item oral-response test providing a comprehensive assessment of children's speech. The detailed phonological analysis aids clinicians in obtaining a representative sample of a child's speech, recording the sample in analyzable form, analyzing data obtained, interpreting the analysis, and designing effective treatment programs. The test compares a child's sound system to that of an adults' and with a normal developmental stage. The test provides a diagnostic indication of the type and severity of speech problems. Examiner required. Not suitable for group use.
BRITISH PUBLISHER

Untimed: Not available

Scoring: Examiner evaluated

Cost: Contact publisher

Publisher: NFER-NELSON Publishing Company Ltd.

PHONOLOGICAL PROCESS ANALYSIS
Frederick F. Weiner

Child—Ages 2-5

Purpose: Assesses articulation and guides intervention strategies. Identifies phonological disorders. Used with unintelligible children.

Description: 136–item oral-response delayed-imitation test measuring syllable structure processes, harmony processes, and feature contrast processes. A percent accuracy score is yielded. Materials include an examiner's manual, pictures, and record forms. Examiner required. Not suitable for group use.

Untimed: Varies

Scoring: Examiner evaluated

Cost: Complete kit $28.00

Publisher: PRO-ED

PHOTO ARTICULATION TEST, 2ND EDITION (PAT)
K. Pendergast, S. Dickey, J. Selmar, and A. Soder

Child—Ages 3–11

Purpose: Measures articulation skills. Used for screening and analysis in schools and clinics and for therapy.

Description: 72 color photographs arranged with nine pictures on each of eight sheets to measure articulation of consonants, consonant blends, vowels, and diphthongs. The test categorizes defective sounds as tongue, lip, or vowel sounds. The subject names the items in the color photographs as the examiner points to the pictures and records responses on the recording sheet. Materials include a supplementary test words list. This revised edition replaces the 1969 edition.

An extension of this revised edition, Computer Graphics for the Photo Articulation Test (CGPAT), was developed by the Phonology Project to provide microcomputer stimuli for assessing young children as well as children who are difficult to test. The CGPAT is not a computer-scoring version of the PAT. The program operates on Apple IIc and IIe systems manufactured after mid–1985 or Apple IIe systems produced prior to mid–1985 that have enhancements and a color monitor. Examiner required. Not suitable for group use.

Untimed: 5 minutes

Scoring: Examiner evaluated

Cost: Complete $59.00; 100 recording sheets $19.00; photo articulation cards $19.00; software program $79.00

Publisher: PRO-ED

PICTURE ARTICULATION AND SCREENING TEST (PALST)
Word Making Productions

Child
Grades PreK–6

Purpose: Screens articulation and language skills of children. Identifies children needing further evaluation and assistance.

Description: 13–item oral-response test assessing strengths and weaknesses in articulation. Each test item consists of a picture card showing an activity or scene, such as an Indian shooting an arrow at a rabbit or a child brushing his teeth. The child is asked to describe each card. The examiner evaluates the responses based on the completeness of the child's articulation. Six sounds are emphasized: *sh, r, th, s, l,* and *t.* Examiner required. Suitable for group use.

Untimed: 2–3 minutes

Scoring: Examiner evaluated

Cost: Complete kit (test, recording forms) $25.30

Publisher: Word Making Productions

PRAGMATICS PROFILE OF EARLY COMMUNICATION SKILLS
H. Dewart and S. Summers

Child—Ages 9 months–5 years

Purpose: Assesses the pragmatic aspects of a child's language. Used by speech therapists, educational psychologists, nursery teachers, and health visitors with normal, bilingual, mentally handicapped, and hearing-impaired children.

Description: Structured interview in which the child's parent or caregiver describes the child's behavior in a wide range of communicative settings in order to provide the examiner with the pragmatic aspects of the child's language, or the way in which the child uses language. The program is contained in a handbook that includes a record form that can be photocopied. The results, which provide an overview of the way the child expresses communicative intentions, responds to communication, participates in conversations, and is affected by situational contexts, help the examiner decide whether further assessment is needed and which elements of pragmatics should be incorporated into the child's therapy program. Examiner required. Not suitable for group use.

Untimed: 30 minutes

Scoring: Examiner evaluated

Cost: Contact publisher

Publisher: NFER-NELSON Publishing Company Ltd.

PRAGMATICS SCREENING TEST (PST)
Philip M. Prinz and Frederick F. Weiner

Child—Ages 3.5–8.5

Purpose: Evaluates the communication skills of children. Used with children who may have language delays.

Description: Multiple-item response test made up of three gamelike tasks: Absurd Requests, Ghost Trick, and Referential Communication. The standardized test covers pragmatic skills, including maintaining a topic; returning to a topic; formulating speech acts (e.g., making statements or requests); modifying a request in terms of politeness; narrating a story; revising a directive when the listener appears not to understand; and establishing a referent for a listener. Examiner required. Not suitable for group use.

Untimed: 15 minutes

Scoring: Hand key

Cost: Contact publisher

Publisher: The Psychological Corporation

Information and availability unconfirmed; last verified in 1988.

PRE-LAS
S. Duncan and E. De Avila

Child—Ages 4–6

Purpose: Assesses children's oral-language abilities.

Description: Multiple-item response test measuring the expressive and receptive language skills of preschool and kindergarten children. The six subtests are What's in the House (lexical), Choose a Picture (sentence comprehension), Simon Says (following instructions), Say What You Hear (sentence imitation/morphemes), Let's Tell Stories (story retelling), and Finishing Stories (sentence completion/clauses). Results are used for educational planning. Materials include colored cue pictures and an audio cassette. Examiner required. Not suitable for group use.

Untimed: 15 minutes

Scoring: Hand key

Cost: Examiner's kit $63.95

Publisher: Linguametrics Group

Information and availability unconfirmed; last verified in 1988.

PRESCHOOL LANGUAGE SCALE (PLS)
Irla Lee Zimmerman, Violette G. Steiner, and Robert Evatt Pond

Child—Ages 1–7

Purpose: Provides a diagnostic measure of receptive and expressive language.

Description: Multiple-item test assessing both auditory comprehension and verbal ability. Items measure sensory discrimination, logical thinking, grammar and vocabulary, memory and attention span, temporal/spatial relations, and self-image at most age levels in each of the two domains. Examiner required. Not suitable for group use. Available in Spanish.

Untimed: 20 minutes

Scoring: Examiner evaluated

Cost: Complete $45.00

Publisher: The Psychological Corporation

Information and availability unconfirmed; last verified in 1988.

PRE-VERBAL COMMUNICATION SCHEDULE
C. Kiernan and B. Reid

All ages—Nonverbal individuals

Purpose: Assesses preverbal communication skills. Used by teachers, speech therapists, instructors in adult training centers, and nurses to assess severely mentally handicapped individuals, normal infants, nonspeaking deaf children, and severely handicapped individuals.

Description: 195–item paper-pencil checklist covering precommunicative and formal and informal communicative and receptive skills. An individual's particular strengths and weaknesses are identified so that appropriate intervention can be planned. A 35–item short form is also included. Examiner required. Not suitable for group use.
BRITISH PUBLISHER

Untimed: 1 hour

Scoring: Examiner evaluated

Cost: Contact publisher

Publisher: NFER-NELSON Publishing Company Ltd.

THE PRIMARY LANGUAGE SCREEN
Diane L. Eger

Child Grades K–1

Purpose: Assesses language skills. Used in screening.

Description: Paper-pencil oral-response criterion-referenced test with two subtests: Expressive Language and Receptive Language. Scores are used to generate language profiles. Examiner must be a speech pathologist. Examiner required. Suitable for group use.

Untimed: 30 minutes

Scoring: Examiner evaluated; hand key

Cost: $25.00

Publisher: United Educational Service, Inc.

PSYCHOLINGUISTIC RATING SCALE (PRS)
Kenneth L. Hobby

Child, adolescent Grades K–8.9

Purpose: Measures psycholinguistic behaviors relevant to classroom performance of students. Used to screen students for special attention under PL 94–142.

Description: Multiple-item paper-pencil inventory in which a teacher familiar with the child uses a 5–point scale ranging from "seldom" to "frequently" to respond to statements about the frequency of classroom behaviors. The scale is available on four levels: readiness (Grades K–1.4), elementary (Grades 1.5–2.9), intermediate (Grades 3.0–5.9), and advanced (Grades 6.0–8.9). The readiness, elementary, and intermediate levels include the following 10 subscales containing 4–5 items each: auditory reception, auditory association, auditory memory, auditory closure, verbal expression, visual reception, visual association, visual memory, visual closure, and manual expression. The Advanced Level does not include the visual closure or manual expression subscales. The scales are based on the same theoretical structure as the Illinois Test of Psycholinguistic Abilities (ITPA). Scoring yields subscores and a total score. Norms are provided by sex for each of the four levels. Examiner required. Not suitable for group use.

Untimed: 5 minutes

Scoring: Hand key

Cost: Complete kit (25 booklets for each level, manual) $50.00

Publisher: Western Psychological Services

THE PUPIL RATING SCALE (REVISED): SCREENING FOR LEARNING DISABILITIES
Refer to page 640.

READING COMPREHENSION INVENTORY (RCI)
Refer to page 353.

A READING READINESS TEST: REVERSAL TESTS (BILINGUAL)
Ake W. Edfeldt

Child
Grade 1

Purpose: Measures degree of speech reversal tendencies in young children before they learn to read. Used by educators and speech therapists to predict reading problems in first grade.

Description: Oral-response test based on research into the cause and effect of word transposition tendencies of children. The test was developed to diagnose and prevent these difficulties. A child who is scored either as "control case" or as "not yet ready to read" is not considered ready to master reading and, therefore, should postpone instruction. Examiner required. Not suitable for group use. CANADIAN PUBLISHER

Untimed: Not available

Scoring: Hand key; examiner evaluated

Cost: Contact publisher

Publisher: Institute of Psychological Research, Inc.

RECEPTIVE ONE-WORD PICTURE VOCABULARY TEST (ROWPVT)
Morrison F. Gardner

Child—Ages 2–11.11

Purpose: Assesses receptive vocabulary of bilingual, speech-impaired, immature, withdrawn, and emotionally and physically impaired children.

Description: 100–item response test using 100 picture plates, each with four illustrations presented horizontally across the page. The child identifies the illustration that matches the word presented by the examiner. When used with the Expressive One-Word Picture Vocabulary Test, comparisons can be made between a student's receptive and expressive vocabulary skills. Examiner required. Not suitable for group use.

Untimed: 20 minutes

Scoring: Hand key

Cost: Test kit (manual, test plates, 50 English record forms) $63.00

Publisher: Academic Therapy Publications

RECEPTIVE ONE-WORD PICTURE VOCABULARY TEST—UPPER EXTENSION (ROWPVT-UE)
Rick Brownell

Adolescent—Ages 12.0–15.11

Purpose: Assesses receptive vocabulary. Used with bilingual, speech-impaired, immature and withdrawn, and emotionally and physically impaired children.

Description: Multiple-item nonverbal assessment of receptive vocabulary. The examinee points to an illustration that matches the word presented by the examiner. The test is an upward extension of the Receptive One-Word Picture Vocabulary Test. When the ROWPVT-UE is used with the Expressive One-Word Picture Vocabulary Test—Upper Extension, the two measures evaluate differences in speaking and hearing vocabularies. Tables for converting raw scores to Language Standard Scores, percentile ranks, stanines, and Language Ages are provided. Examiner required. Not suitable for group use.

Untimed: 20 minutes

Scoring: Examiner evaluated

Cost: Kit (manual, test plates, 50 English record forms, vinyl folder) $63.00

Publisher: Academic Therapy Publications

REVISED PRE-READING SCREENING PROCEDURES TO IDENTIFY FIRST GRADE ACADEMIC NEEDS
Refer to page 560.

REYNELL DEVELOPMENTAL LANGUAGE SCALES—SECOND REVISION
Refer to page 40.

RHODE ISLAND TEST OF LANGUAGE STRUCTURE (RITLS)
Elizabeth Engen and Tryg̱ Engen

Ages 3-20

Purpose: Measures English language development in hearing children ages 3–6 or hearing-impaired children and adults ages 3–20. Used for educational planning.

Description: 100–item multiple-choice verification test assessing understanding of language structure (syntax). The test presents 20 sentence types, both simple and complex. The test is used for educational planning, such as determination of school readiness, bilingual programming, and language introduction procedures. It can also be used where language development is a concern, including mental retardation, learning disability, and bilingual programs. Examiner required. Not suitable for group use.

Timed: 30 minutes

Scoring: Hand key

Cost: Complete kit (test booklet, 10 analysis sheets, 10 response sheets, manual, storage box) $84.00

Publisher: PRO-ED

RILEY ARTICULATION AND LANGUAGE TEST: REVISED
Glyndon D. Riley

Child
Grades K–2

Purpose: Measures the language proficiency of young children. Used to identify children most in need of speech therapy.

Description: Oral-response screening test consisting of three subtests (Language Proficiency and Intelligibility, Articulation Function, and Language Function) measuring phonemic similarity, stimulability, number of defective sounds, error consistency, frequency of occurrence, and developmental expectancy. The test yields an objective articulation loss score and standardized language loss and language function scores. Examiner required. Not suitable for group use.

Untimed: 2–3 minutes

Scoring: Hand key

Cost: Complete kit (25 tests, manual) $20.00

Publisher: Western Psychological Services

ROSWELL-CHALL AUDITORY BLENDING TEST
Refer to page 355.

SANDWELL BILINGUAL SCREENING ASSESSMENT
D. Duncan, D. Gibbs, N. Singh Noor, and H. Mohammed Whittaker

Child—Ages 6-9

Purpose: Determines whether expressive language problems are the result of a second language learning problem or of pathological causes. Used by teachers, ESL teachers, and speech therapists in making decisions regarding ESL remediation and speech therapy.

Description: 44–item picture-based orally administered verbal-response test that isolates the nature of language acquisition problems. The examinee responds verbally to questions based on 44 line drawings presented on an easel. Because the questions are read in both Panjabi and English, the examiner must be fluent in Panjabi. Examiner required. Not suitable for group use.
BRITISH PUBLISHER

Timed: 20 minutes per scale

Scoring: Hand key

Cost: Contact publisher

Publisher: NFER-NELSON Publishing Company Ltd.

SCREENING DEEP TEST OF ARTICULATION
Eugene T. McDonald

Child
Grades K–3

Purpose: Assesses a child's ability to produce commonly misarticulated consonant sounds. Used to determine whether a child needs further testing.

Description: 90–item verbal test assessing a child's ability to produce nine consonant sounds in a variety of phonetic contexts. The examiner displays pairs of pictures to elicit the child's production of bisyllables. Selected consonants occur in different consonant types (single, abutting, in compounds) and in a variety of contexts requiring overlapping articulatory movements. A trained examiner is required. Not suitable for group use.

Untimed: 5 minutes

Scoring: Hand key; examiner evaluated

Cost: 50 individual record sheets $4.95; 50 teacher report forms $4.95

Publisher: Communication Skill Builders, Inc.

SCREENING KIT OF LANGUAGE DEVELOPMENT (SKOLD)
Lynn S. Bliss and Doris V. Allen

Child—Ages 2–5

Purpose: Assesses language disorders and delays in young children. Used by speech-language pathologist paraprofessionals in day care and by health care, nursing, and preschool specialists.

Description: 135–item oral-response test measuring language development in children speaking either black English or standard English. Picture stimuli are used to assess vocabulary, comprehension, story completion, individual and paired sentence repetition with pictures, individual sentence repetition without pictures, and comprehension of commands. The test consists of six subtests, three for black English and three for standard English, in each of the following age ranges: 30–36 months, 37–42 months, and 43–48 months. Norms are provided for speakers of Black and Standard English. The manual includes guidelines for administration and scoring and appendices covering normal language development, disordered language, and the linguistic characteristics of black English. Examiner required. Not suitable for group use.

Untimed: 15 minutes

Scoring: Examiner evaluated

Cost: Test kit (manual, stimulus book, set of either black or standard English scoring forms) $52.50

Publisher: Slosson Educational Publications, Inc.

SCREENING TEST FOR DEVELOPMENTAL APRAXIA OF SPEECH
Robert W. Blakeley

Child—Ages 4–12

Purpose: Assists in the differential diagnosis of developmental apraxia of speech.

Description: Multiple-item test diagnosing the developmental apraxia of speech through eight subtests. The subtests are Expressive Language Discrepancy, Vowels and Diphthongs, Oral Motor Movement, Verbal Sequencing, Motorically Complex Words, Articulation, Transpositions, and Prosody. The testing results of 169 children of normal intelligence with multiple articulation errors are reported. Examiner required. Not suitable for group use.

Untimed: 10 minutes

Scoring: Examiner evaluated

Cost: Test kit (examiner's manual, 50 response record forms) $54.00

Publisher: PRO-ED

SCREENING TEST OF ADOLESCENT LANGUAGE (STAL)
Elizabeth M. Prather,
Sheila Van Ausdal Breecher,
Marimyn Lee Stafford, and
Elizabeth Matthews Wallace

Adolescent
Grades 6 and above

Purpose: Assesses linguistic development and identifies junior and senior high-school students needing further testing. Used with large populations of students in public school settings by speech-language pathologists, classroom teachers, school counselors and psychologists, and teachers of special education.

Description: 23–item oral-response screening instrument consisting of four subtests assessing language skills often associated with learning/language disabilities. The Vocabulary subtest (12 items) assesses comprehension of word meaning, substitution of a synonym in a grammatically correct form, and word finding and retrieval competencies. The Auditory Memory Span subtest (3 items) requires repetition of a sentence in its original syntactical form and measures the aspect of memory span associated with related semantic and syntactic stimuli. The Language Processing subtest (5 items) requires the student to decode a message and use language for reasoning and problem solving. The Proverb Explanation subtest (3 items) assesses paraphrasing and cognitive skills needed for verbal clarity. Standard instructions are given at the beginning of each subtest, and the student's oral responses are recorded and evaluated in accordance with the instructions included in the manual. Cutoff scores based on normative studies of sixth- and ninth-grade students identify students needing further testing. The newly revised STAL includes a miniscreen that may be used for testing large groups of students. This brief version can be used to project scores on the complete STAL. Examiner required. Not suitable for group use.

Untimed: 7 minutes

Scoring: Examiner evaluated

Cost: Complete kit (manual, 50 test forms, laminated cards summarizing administration and scoring procedures) $40.00

Publisher: University of Washington Press

SENTENCE COMPREHENSION TEST: REVISED EDITION AND PANJABI VERSION
K. Wheldall, P. Mittler,
A. Hobsbaum, D. Gibbs,
D. Duncan, and S. Jit Saund

Child—Ages 3–5

Purpose: Assesses children's comprehension of English and/or Panjabi. Used by speech therapists and teachers to pinpoint particular sentence structure difficulties and to aid in decisions regarding referrals to speech therapists.

Description: Multiple-item orally administered picture-based screening test assessing language comprehension in the absence of contextual clues usually present in ordinary conversations. The

examiner reads a stimulus sentence, and the examinee chooses the set of pictures that best illustrates the sentence's meaning. The pictures in the revised test have been redrawn and the manual has been updated. When used as a comparative measure, the Panjabi version can help to establish whether a child has difficulty acquiring English as a second language or has a pathological language difficulty that requires speech therapy. Examiner required. Not suitable for group use. BRITISH PUBLISHER

Untimed: 15 minutes

Scoring: Hand key

Cost: Contact publisher

Publisher: NFER-NELSON Publishing Company Ltd.

SEQUENCED INVENTORY OF COMMUNICATION DEVELOPMENT, REVISED EDITION
Dona Lea Hedrick,
Elizabeth M. Prather, and
Annette R. Tobin

Child—Ages 4 months–4 years

Purpose: Evaluates the communication abilities of normal and retarded children functioning between the ages of four months and four years. Used for remedial programming by speech-language pathologists, audiologists, psychologists, and teachers trained in speech and language assessment techniques.

Description: 210–item inventory assessing and diagnosing language disorders in young children. The receptive language section (92 items) includes behavioral items that test sound and speech discrimination and awareness and understanding. The expressive language section (118 items) includes three types of expressive behaviors (imitating, initiating, and responding) and measures verbal output for length, grammatical and syntactic structure, and articulation. The resulting Communication Profile provides guidelines for developing remedial programs for young children with language disorders, mental retardation, specific language problems, and hearing or visual impairments. Some items have been adapted from the REP Scale, the Denver Developmental Scale, and the Illinois Test of Adaptive Abilities. The test kit includes over 100 objects used as stimuli for test items. The test has been used with autistic and other difficult-to-test children, hearing-impaired children, and Yup'ik-speaking Eskimo children. A Cuban Spanish edition is available. Examiner required. Not suitable for group use.

Untimed: Varies

Scoring: Examiner evaluated

Cost: Complete kit (manual, 50 receptive test booklets, 50 expressive test booklets, stimulus objects, plastic carrying case) $275.00

Publisher: University of Washington Press

SKLAR APHASIA SCALE—REVISED 1983
Refer to page 128.

SLINGERLAND SCREENING TESTS FOR IDENTIFYING CHILDREN WITH SPECIFIC LANGUAGE DISABILITY
Beth H. Slingerland

Child
Grades 1–6

Purpose: Screens elementary-school children for indications of specific language disabilities in reading, spelling, handwriting, and speaking in order to identify those needing special tutoring and further evaluation and to show teachers the strengths and weaknesses in the perceptual-motor functions of their pupils.

Description: Multiple-item verbal paper-pencil examination containing eight subtests. Five of the subtests evaluate visual-motor coordination and visual memory linked with motor coordination. Three subtests evaluate auditory-visual discrimination or auditory memory-to-motor ability. The test is available in four forms, A, B, C for Grades 1–4 and D for Grades 5–6. Form D, which contains a ninth subtest evaluating personal orientation in time and space and the ability to express ideas in writing, helps identify children

whose specific language difficulties may have become persistent. All the forms contain separate Echolalia tests and include individual auditory tests to identify students who have difficulty recalling words and pronouncing words correctly or who are unable to express their ideas in an organized manner. Examiner required. Suitable for group use, except Echolalia Test. Also available in a Spanish adaptation.

Untimed: 1½ hours

Scoring: Examiner evaluated

Cost: 12 screening tests (Forms A, B, C) each $5.40, (Form D) $7.00; teacher's manual (Forms A, B, C) $5.50, (Form D) $4.50; cards and charts (Forms A, B, C) each $8.00, (Form D) $11.00

Publisher: Educators Publishing Service, Inc.

SLOSSON ARTICULATION, LANGUAGE TEST WITH PHONOLOGY (SALT-P)
Refer to page 565.

SMITH-JOHNSON NONVERBAL PERFORMANCE SCALE
Refer to page 42.

SPECIFIC LANGUAGE DISABILITY TESTS
Neva Malcomesius

Adolescent
Grades 6–8

Purpose: Screens entire classroom groups or individual students and identifies those who show specific language disability. Used to help design remedial programs and indicate the need for further testing.

Description: 10 paper-pencil subtests identifying perceptual language problems through analysis of written performance. Subtests I-V evaluate visual perception: visual discrimination, visual memory, and visual-motor coordination. Subtests VI-X evaluate auditory perception: auditory discrimination, auditory memory, auditory-motor coordination, and comprehension. All tests check handwriting and the ability to follow directions. Materials include the teacher's manual, test booklet, and cards and charts. Examiner required. Suitable for group use.

Untimed: 1–1½ hours

Scoring: Examiner evaluated

Cost: 12 tests $8.00; charts and cards $8.00; teacher's manual $1.50; specimen set (teacher's manual, test) $1.75

Publisher: Educators Publishing Service, Inc.

SPEECH-EASE SCREENING INVENTORY (K–1)
Speech-Ease (Teryl Pigott, Jane Barry, Barbara Hughes, Debra Eastin, Patricia Titus, Harriett Stensel, Kathleen Metcalf, and Belinda Porter)

Child
Grades K–1

Purpose: Assesses the articulation and language development of children. Used to identify students needing speech-language services.

Description: Multiple-item response test evaluating the speech and language development of children. The basic section assesses articulation, language association, auditory recall, expressive vocabulary, and concept development. An optional section includes additional auditory items, a section on similarities and differences, a language sample, and a section on linguistic relationships. Examiner required. Not suitable for group use.

Untimed: 7–10 minutes

Scoring: Examiner evaluated

Cost: Complete $39.00; 96 screening forms $4.00; 48 kindergarten summary sheets $4.00; 48 first-grade summary sheets $4.00

Publisher: PRO-ED

STIM-CON
Ronald K. Sommers

Child
Grades K–1

Purpose: Identifies children whose articulation may be deficient and therefore require speech correctional services.

Description: Multiple-item verbal and picture-response test measuring both stimulability for defective phonemes and consistency of misarticulation of phonemes. Examiner required. Not suitable for group use.

Untimed: Not available

Scoring: Examiner evaluated

Cost: Complete kit (administration and picture assessment manuals, 25 kindergarten summary forms, 25 first-grade summary forms, 25 stimulability assessment forms) $42.00

Publisher: United Educational Services, Inc.

STUTTERING PREDICTION INSTRUMENT FOR YOUNG CHILDREN (SPI)
Glyndon D. Riley

Child—Ages 3–8

Purpose: Determines whether a child should be scheduled for therapy to treat stuttering.

Description: Diagnostic test utilizing pictures, parent interview, observation, and taped recordings of the child's speech to assess the child's history, reactions, part-word repetitions, prolongations, and frequency of stuttered words. Examiner required. Not suitable for group use.

Untimed: Not available

Scoring: Examiner evaluated

Cost: Complete kit (manual with picture plates, 50 test/tracking forms, storage box) $44.00

Publisher: PRO-ED

STUTTERING SEVERITY INSTRUMENT FOR CHILDREN AND ADULTS (SSI)
Glyndon D. Riley

All ages

Purpose: Measures the severity of stuttering and evaluates the effects of treatment. Used by clinicians and researchers.

Description: Oral-response test utilizing pictures to measure the frequency of repetition and prolongation of sounds and syllables, estimated duration of the longest stuttering events, and observable concomitants. Examiner required. Not suitable for group use.

Untimed: Not available

Scoring: Examiner evaluated

Cost: Complete kit (manual, picture plates, 50 test/tracking forms, storage box) $39.00

Publisher: PRO-ED

STYCAR CHART OF DEVELOPMENTAL SEQUENCES (REVISED 1975 EDITION)
Refer to page 43.

STYCAR LANGUAGE TEST
Mary D. Sheridan

Child—Ages 1–7

Purpose: Assesses language development. Used for differential diagnosis and management of speech disorders in young children and mentally retarded individuals.

Description: Multiple-item series of clinical testing procedures for assessing language and speech skills. The test is divided into three overlapping procedures: The Common Objects Test (ages 1–2), The Miniature Toys Test (ages 21 months–4 years), and the Picture Book Test (ages 2½–7). The tests do not provide pass/fail results. Descriptive recording and rating on a 3- to 5-point scale is recommended. The test is available to speech therapists, medical doctors, and specialist language teachers. Examiner required. Not suitable for group use.
BRITISH PUBLISHER

Untimed: 30 minutes

Scoring: Examiner evaluated

Cost: Contact publisher

Publisher: NFER-NELSON Publishing Company Ltd.

SYMBOLIC PLAY TEST—SECOND EDITION (SPT: 2 ED)
Marianne Lowe and Anthony Costello

Child—Ages 1–3

Purpose: Assesses the conditions necessary for meaningful language development. Used for evaluating the language potentialities of very young children.

Description: Multiple-item test measuring early concept formation and symbolization. The examiner presents objects to the child and rates meaningful responses and connections that the child makes as expressed in spontaneous nonverbal play activities. Materials include a set of toys. A videotape for the SPT is available. The test is used by speech therapists and pediatricians. A new edition with a revised manual is available. Examiner required. Not suitable for group use.
BRITISH PUBLISHER

Untimed: 10–15 minutes

Scoring: Examiner evaluated

Cost: Contact publisher

Publisher: NFER-NELSON Publishing Company Ltd.

TEMPLE UNIVERSITY SHORT SYNTAX INVENTORY (TUSSI)
Adele Gerber and Henry Goehl

Mental ages 5–7

Purpose: Assesses patterns of syntax and morphology in individuals with a mental age of 5–7 and in older language-delayed individuals. Used for creating therapy goals and in writing individual preschool programs and individual education plans.

Description: Multiple-item test analyzing basic sentence elements and morphemes for both initiated and elicited responses. The test contains a broad range of evaluation items and compares language knowledge and use. The test also can be used with individuals who are mentally, emotionally, or physically handicapped. Examiner required. Not suitable for group use.

Untimed: 10–15 minutes

Scoring: Examiner evaluated

Cost: Complete kit (manual, TUSSI–2, 4 multipicture boards, and 32 picture cards) $44.00

Publisher: Slosson Educational Publications, Inc.

TEST FOR EXAMINING EXPRESSIVE MORPHOLOGY (TEEM)
Kenneth G. Shipley, Terry A. Stone, and Marlene B. Sue

Child, adolescent

Purpose: Assesses the expressive morpheme development of children (language age 3–8 years; interest level 3–16 years), measures general language level, and monitors student progress. Used in language remediation, hearing-impaired, early childhood, special education, and speech therapy classes.

Description: 54–item oral-response sentence-completion test assessing the allomorphic variations of six major morphemes: present progressives, plurals, possessives, past tenses, third-person singulars, and derived adjectives. The examiner presents each stimulus picture while reading the stimulus phrase, and the child completes the phrase while viewing the picture. Results identify specific morphemes and allomorphic variations requiring stimulation or instruction. The manual includes administration and scoring instructions and technical data. Examiner required. Not suitable for group use.

Untimed: 7 minutes

Scoring: Examiner evaluated

Cost: Test kit (manual, 25 scoring forms, test book) $29.95

Publisher: Communication Skill Builders, Inc.

TEST FOR ORAL LANGUAGE PRODUCTION (TOLP)—1980

Child—Ages 4.5–10.5

Purpose: Measures oral language ability. Used for educational evaluation.

Description: Multiple-item verbal test of 16 aspects of language production covering productivity, syntactic complexity, correctness, fluency, and content. Materials include stimulus materials that the subject responds to orally. The TOLP is available only to professional personnel attached to education departments and others with sufficient knowledge of sentence analysis to score the test. Examiner required. Not suitable for group use. SOUTH AFRICAN PUBLISHER

Untimed: 30 minutes–1 hour, 30 minutes

Scoring: Hand key; examiner evaluated

Cost: (In Rands) stimulus material 7,00; manual 16,00; 10 scoring sheets 2,50; orders from outside the RSA will be dealt with on merit

Publisher: Human Sciences Research Council

TEST OF ADOLESCENT LANGUAGE–2 (TOAL–2)
Donald D. Hammill, Virgnia L. Brown, Stephen C. Larsen, and J. Lee Wiederholt

Adolescent—Ages 12–18.5

Purpose: Assesses the language abilities of adolescents. Specifies where intervention is needed.

Description: Multiple-item paper-pencil and oral-response test assessing a broad range of language abilities. Composite scores are yielded for listening, speaking, reading, writing, spoken language, written language, vocabulary, grammar, receptive language, and expressive language. The test also yields an Adolescent Language Quotient (ALQ). The revised version of the test includes easier items for use with mentally retarded, learning disabled, language-disordered, and slow learning students.

The PRO-SCORE scoring system is available from the publisher for use on Apple II+, IIc, and IIe computers. The system generates a four-page report providing background information on the student; raw scores, standard scores, percentiles, and descriptions for each subtest; standard score sums, percentiles, and descriptors for all composites and quotients; an optional cognitive aptitude score; subtest and composite profiles; intraindividual comparisons of all composites; and significance testing of all comparisons. Examiner required. Not suitable for group use.

Untimed: 1–3 hours

Scoring: Hand key; may be computer scored

Cost: Complete kit (manual, 50 student answer booklets, 10 student books, 50 profile sheets, storage box) $94.00; PRO-SCORE scoring system $69.00

Publisher: PRO-ED

TEST OF ARTICULATION PERFORMANCE—DIAGNOSTIC (TAP-D)
Brian R. Bryant and Deborah L. Bryant

Child—Ages 3–8

Purpose: Assesses a child's articulatory strengths and weaknesses. Used for educational planning and diagnostic evaluation.

Description: Multiple-item oral-response test assessing the following components of a child's articulatory performance: isolated words (phonetic inventory, percent correct, error analysis of substitutions, omissions, and distortions), distinctive features (place, manner, and voicing), selective deep test (adjacent sounds), continuous speech (key phonemes in sentences), stimulability (syllables, words, and sentences), and verbal communication scales (parent, teacher, and student). Picture stimuli are used to elicit responses. The examiner selects the components needed to provide a comprehensive analysis of the child's articulatory performance. The test kit includes the Verbal Communication Scales as a measure of the child's practical use of language. Examiner required. Not suitable for group use.

Untimed: Varies

Scoring: Examiner evaluated

Cost: Complete kit (manual, 82 picture cards, 25 profile forms, complete VCS, storage box) $88.00

Publisher: PRO-ED

TEST OF ARTICULATION PERFORMANCE—SCREEN (TAPS-S)
Brian R. Bryant and Deborah L. Bryant

Child—Ages 3–8.11

Purpose: Identifies children with articulation problems who need further evaluation. Used where large numbers of children must be screened in a short period of time.

Description: 31–item oral-response test assessing the articulation performance of children. Picture stimuli are used to elicit both spontaneous and imitative production. Visually impaired individuals use sentence prompts or imitation without pictures. Quotients, percentiles, and age equivalents are available for children ages 3 years to 8 years, 11 months. Examiner required. Individually administered. Suitable for use with large groups.

Untimed: 3–5 minutes

Scoring: Examiner evaluated

Cost: Complete kit (manual, picture book, 50 answer sheets, storage box) $54.00

Publisher: PRO-ED

TEST OF AWARENESS OF LANGUAGE SEGMENTS (TALS)
Diane J. Sawyer

Grades K-older students with learning problems

Purpose: Assesses an individual's ability to segment stream of spoken language.

Description: 46–item test assessing an individual's awareness of the units of language as meaning (i.e., word units, syllable units, phonemic units). Three subtests (Sentences-to-Words, Words-to-Syllables, and Words-to-Sounds) assess which units of language a child can explicitly manipulate.

The test provides information that will help teachers plan reading instruction for students in kindergarten and first grade by a) indicating whether a child's language has developed to meet the instructional demands of a beginning reading program, b) helping teachers decide which reading approach to use with a student (whole word, phonogram patterns, or phonics), and c) providing clues for selecting materials and activities appropriate to the language awareness level of the student.

Cutoff scores are available based on inferences drawn from research studies involving more than 1,000 children at each grade level (kindergarten and first grade). Examiner required. Not suitable for group use.

Untimed: 15–30 minutes

Scoring: Examiner evaluated

Cost: Contact publisher

Publisher: PRO-ED

TEST OF EARLY LANGUAGE DEVELOPMENT (TELD)
Wayne P. Hresko, D. Kim Reid, and Donald D. Hammill

Child—Ages 3–7.11

Purpose: Measures content and form in the receptive and expressive language abilities of children. Used to identify problems, document progress, conduct research, and guide instructional practices.

Description: 38–item oral-response and point-to test using a variety of semantic and syntactic tasks to assess different aspects of receptive/expressive language. Standard scores, percentiles, age equivalents, and language quotients are calculated. Examiners must be competent in the administration of educational, psychological, and language tests. Examiner required. Not suitable for group use.

Untimed: 15 minutes

Scoring: Examiner evaluated

Cost: Complete kit (manual, 11 picture cards, 50 record forms) $44.00

Publisher: PRO-ED

TEST OF LANGUAGE COMPETENCE (TLC)
Elisabeth H. Wiig and Wayne Secord

Child, adolescent—Ages 9–19

Purpose: Measures language competence of students.

Description: Multiple-item response test for diagnosing language disabilities by assessing language strategies rather than language skill. The Recreating Sentences subtest examines the ability to perceive the nature of a communication and recreate a semantically, syntactically, and pragmatically appropriate sentence. The Understanding Metaphoric Expressions subtest has students interpret an expression and select another one with the same meaning. The Understanding Ambiguous Sentences subtest evaluates the ability to recognize and interpret alternative meanings of lexical and structural ambiguities. The Making Inferences subtest has students identify permissible inferences based on causal relationships or chains. The test's features include norm-referenced scores, extension teaching and testing formats for each subtest, and individual education program guidelines. Examiner required. Not suitable for group use.

Untimed: 1 hour

Scoring: Hand key

Cost: Complete program (administration manual, technical manual, stimulus manual, record forms, canvas carrying case) $89.00

Publisher: The Psychological Corporation

Information and availability unconfirmed; last verified in 1988.

TEST OF LANGUAGE DEVELOPMENT-2 INTERMEDIATE (TOLD-2 INTERMEDIATE)
Donald D. Hammill and Phyllis L. Newcomer

Child—Ages 8.6–12.11
Grades 3–6

Purpose: Assesses the expressive and receptive language abilities of children. Identifies children with language problems.

Description: Multiple–item oral-response test consisting of six subtests measuring different aspects of spoken language. The Generals (25 items), Vocabulary (35 items), and Malapropisms (30 items) subtests assess the understanding and meaningful use of spoken words. The Sentence Combining (20 items), Word Ordering (25 items), and Grammatic Comprehension (40 items) subtests assess different aspects of grammar. Test results are reported in terms of raw scores, standard scores, percentiles, and age equivalents. By combining various subtest scores, it is possible to diagnose a child's abilities in relation to specific language skills, including overall spoken language, listening (receptive language), speaking (expressive language), semantics (the meaning of words), and syntax (grammar). Examiner required. Suitable for group use.

Untimed: 40 minutes

Scoring: Hand key; may be computer scored

Cost: Complete kit (examiner's manual, 50 profile/examiner record forms, storage box) $56.00

Publisher: PRO-ED

TEST OF LANGUAGE DEVELOPMENT–2 PRIMARY (TOLD–2 PRIMARY)
Phyllis L. Newcomer and Donald D. Hammill

Child—Ages 4–8.11
Grades K–3

Purpose: Assesses the expressive and receptive abilities of children. Used as a language achievement test and to identify children with language problems, including mental retardation, learning disabilities, reading disabilities, speech delays, and articulation problems.

Description: 190–item oral-response and point-to test consisting of seven subtests measuring different components of spoken language. The Picture Vocabulary (35 items) and Oral Vocabulary (30 items) subtests assess the understanding and meaningful use of spoken words. The Grammatic Understanding (25 items), Sentence Imitation (30 items), and Grammatic Completion (30 items) subtests assess different aspects of grammar. The Word Articulation (20 items) and Word Discrimination (20 items) subtests are

supplemental tests measuring the ability to pronounce words correctly and distinguish between words that sound familiar. Test results are reported in terms of standard scores, percentiles, age equivalents, Spoken Language Quotient, Listening Quotient, Speaking Quotient, Semantics Quotient, and Phonology Quotient. By combining various subtest scores, it is possible to diagnose a child's abilities in relation to specific language skills, including overall spoken language, listening (receptive language), speaking (expressive language), semantics (the meaning of words), and syntax (grammar). The examiner must have formal training in assessment. Examiner required. Not suitable for group use.

Untimed: 40 minutes

Scoring: Examiner evaluated; computer scored

Cost: Complete kit (examiner's manual, picture book, 50 profile/examiner record forms, storage box) $98.00

Publisher: PRO-ED

TEST OF MINIMAL ARTICULATION COMPETENCE (T-MAC)
Wayne Secord

Ages 3–adult

Purpose: Assesses the severity of articulation disorders. Used to identify children needing therapy, monitors speech development in terms of research-based minimal expectations for age level, and targets the most trainable phonemes for remediation.

Description: Multiple-item verbal-response test using one of the following procedures: picture identification, sentence reading, or sentence repetition. The test provides a flexible format for obtaining a diagnostic measure of articulation performance on 24 consonant phonemes; frequently occurring s, r, and l blends; 12 vowels; 4 diphthongs; and variations of vocalic r. The test kit includes a manual and 25 record forms. Examiner required. Not suitable for group use.

Untimed: 10 minutes

Scoring: Examiner evaluated

Cost: 25 record forms $17.00; manual $30.00; complete program $45.00

Publisher: The Psychological Corporation

Information and availability unconfirmed; last verified in 1988.

TEST OF ORAL STRUCTURES AND FUNCTIONS (TOSF)
Gary J. Vitali

Ages 7–adult

Purpose: Assesses oral structures, non-verbal oral functioning, and verbal oral functioning. Used by speech pathologists for screening, differential diagnosis, case-load management decisions, and pre- and posttreatment assessment.

Description: Multiple-item paper-pencil and oral-response test assessing oral structures and motor integrity during verbal and nonverbal oral functioning and establishing the nature of structural, neurological, or functional disorders. The test is composed of five subtests: Speech Survey, Verbal Oral Functioning, Nonverbal Motor Functioning, Orofacial Structures, and History/Behavioral Survey.

The Speech Survey targets articulation, rate/prosody, fluency, and voice during spontaneous or elicited speech. The Verbal Oral Functioning subtest assesses the integrity of oral-nasal resonance balance during imitated and spontaneous speech and articulatory precision and rate/prosody during tests that control for performance loading effects, syllable position effects, voicing, manner of articulation, and placement of articulation. The Nonverbal Motor Functioning subtest assesses volitional and automatic oral functioning during essentially static and sequenced activities controlled for general anatomic site of functioning. The Orofacial Structures subtest is an observational survey of intraoral and orofacial structures at rest. The History/Behavioral Survey is a questionnaire addressing the presence of historical information and behaviors often occurring with disorders of oral structures and functions.

Descriptive information and expected subtest performance is given for dysarthria, apraxia, Broca's aphasia, velo-pharyngeal incompetence-insufficiency, and functional disorders. Examiner required. Not suitable for group use.

Timed: 20 minutes

Scoring: Examiner evaluated

Cost: Complete kit (manual, 25 test booklets, finger cots, tongue blades, balloons, oroscope penlight) $60.00

Publisher: Slosson Educational Publications, Inc.

TEST OF PRAGMATIC SKILLS (REVISED)
Brian Shulman

Child—Ages 3–8

Purpose: Assesses the functional communication abilities of children. Used with language-disordered, learning disabled, and mentally handicapped children to determine the direction of therapy.

Description: Series of four guided play interactions utilizing manipulative objects to assess how a child uses language to serve a variety of functions. The child demonstrates verbal and nonverbal communication intentions in 10 categories, including naming and labeling, reasoning, requesting, and denying. Materials include the manual, instructions for administering the play sequences, manipulatives, scoring sheets, and summary sheets. A computerized administration and scoring system is available for Apple II+, IIe, IIc, and IIg computers. The program administers the test, calculates test scores, prints test data, and provides information about extension testing and intervention programs. Examiner required. Not suitable for group use.

Untimed: Not available

Scoring: Examiner evaluated; may be computer scored

Cost: Complete kit (manual, 25 test booklets, 2 toy telephones, 10 wooden cubes, 2 puppets) $65.00; computer vesion (disk and back-up, manual, folder) $39.95

Publisher: Communication Skill Builders, Inc.

TEST OF RELATIONAL CONCEPTS (TRC)
Refer to page 568.

TEST OF SYNTACTIC ABILITIES
Stephen P. Quigley,
Marjorie W. Steinkamp,
Desmond J. Power, and
Barry W. Jones

Child, adolescent—Ages 10–19

Purpose: Measures the difficulties that profoundly, prelingually deaf students may experience in comprehending and using the syntactic structure of standard English. Used for clinical diagnosis and placement in special education programs.

Description: 20 tests measuring an individual's skill in using nine major syntactic structures: negation, conjunction, determiners, question formation, verb processes, pronominalization, relativization, complementation, and nominalization. A screening test containing items selected from the diagnostic battery is available in two parallel forms to provide a profile of strengths and weaknesses on individual structures and to determine need for further testing or instruction. The test has been standardized on deaf children, but it may also be suitable for diagnostic and normative evaluation of individuals with language problems resulting from other causes. Examiner required. Not suitable for group use.

Untimed: Not available

Scoring: Examiner evaluated

Cost: Contact publisher

Publisher: DORMAC, Inc.

Information and availability unconfirmed; last verified in 1987.

TEST OF WORD FINDING (TWF)
Diane J. German

Child, adolescent—Ages 6.6–12.11

Purpose: Diagnoses expressive language problems resulting from word retrieval difficulties. Used in educational and clinical settings with normal, language-

disordered, learning disabled, and mentally retarded children for planning remediation, evaluating progress, and researching the nature of word-finding disorders in special populations.

Description: Multiple-item test in which a child responding to naming tasks is scored for accuracy and item response time, resulting in one of four profiles of word-finding patterns: fast and accurate, slow and accurate, fast and inaccurate, slow and inaccurate. Percentile ranks, standard scores, and means and standard deviations for response and completion times are obtained. An easel-binder test book is used for administration. Examiner required. Not suitable for group use.

Untimed: 20–30 minutes

Scoring: Examiner evaluated

Cost: Complete kit (test book; administration, interpretation, and scoring manual; technical manual; 25 response booklets) $110.00

Publisher: DLM Teaching Resources

THE TOKEN TEST FOR CHILDREN
Frank DiSimoni

Child—Ages 3–12.5

Purpose: Measures functional listening ability in children and identifies receptive language dysfunction. Used in language therapy.

Description: 61–item test in which the child arranges wooden tokens in response to the examiner's oral directions. The results can be used to indicate a need for further testing of lexicon and syntax or to rule out language impairment in a child with reading difficulties. Materials include the tokens, manual, and scoring forms. Age and grade scores available. The test is not appropriate for deaf subjects. Examiner required. Not suitable for group use.

Untimed: 10 minutes

Scoring: Examiner evaluated

Cost: Complete $45.00

Publisher: DLM Teaching Resources

UTAH TEST OF LANGUAGE DEVELOPMENT-3 (UTLD-3)
Merlin J. Mecham

Child, adolescent—Ages 1-14

Purpose: Identifies children with language-learning disabilities who may need further assistance.

Description: 51–item task-assessment oral-response test measuring the following factors: receptive semantic language, expressive semantic language, receptive sequential language, and expressive sequential language. Test items are arranged in developmental order. The examiner begins testing at or just below a child's expected level of ability and works down until eight consecutive correct answers are obtained, whereupon he works upward from the starting point. When eight consecutive incorrect answers are obtained, the test is discontinued. Items are scored as correct (plus) or incorrect (minus). The total score is the total number of pluses. Results are presented as percentiles, stanines, language-age equivalents, and raw scores. Restricted to persons trained in psychological or educational testing. Examiner required. Not suitable for group use.

Untimed: 20–30 minutes

Scoring: Examiner evaluated

Cost: Complete kit $59.00

Publisher: PRO-ED

WEISS COMPREHENSIVE ARTICULATION TEST (WCAT)
Curtis E. Weiss

Ages 3–adult

Purpose: Determines articulation disorders or delays and identifies misarticulation patterns and other problems. Used in articulation therapy.

Description: Multiple-item criterion-referenced test in two forms: an easel-stand flip book of 85 pictures for subjects who cannot read and a card with 38 sentences for those who can. With the pictures, the child supplies the missing word in a sentence spoken by the examiner; with the

sentences, the child does the reading. Materials include the picture cards and sentence card, a manual, and response forms. The test is not appropriate for non-verbal subjects and can be individually administered only by an examiner.

Untimed: 20 minutes

Scoring: Examiner evaluated

Cost: Complete $60.00

Publisher: DLM Teaching Resources

THE WESTERN APHASIA BATTERY (WAB)
Refer to page 134.

THE WORD TEST
Carol Jorgensen, Mark Barrett, Rosemary Huisingh, and Linda Zachman

Child—Ages 7-12

Purpose: Assesses students' expressive vocabulary and semantic abilities. Used with language-disabled, learning-disabled, mentally disabled, and other exceptional children as a basis for planning therapy programs.

Description: Multiple-item oral-response test assessing vocabulary and semantic abilities in six tasks: associations, synonyms, semantic absurdities, antonyms, definitions, and multiple definitions. All tasks are presented auditorily; no reading or pictures are involved. The vocabulary of the test items is related to school curricula. The test results yield age equivalencies, percentile ranks, standard scores, and standard deviations for students ages 7–12. Ceilings and demonstration items are provided. Examiner required. Not suitable for group use.

Untimed: 30 minutes

Scoring: Examiner evaluated

Cost: Test kit (manual, 20 test forms) $44.90

Publisher: LinguiSystems, Inc.

THE WORD TEST—ADOLESCENT
Linda Zachman, Rosemary Huisingh, Mark Barrett, Jane Orman, and Carolyn Blagden

Ages 12–18

Purpose: Assesses students' expressive vocabulary and semantic skills using common as well as unique contexts. Tasks reflect language usage typical of school assignments and life experiences.

Description: 60–item oral-response test assessing a student's facility with language and word meaning. The four subtests assess the following expressive vocabulary and semantic tasks: Brand Names, Synonyms, Sign of the Times, and Definitions. Tasks are presented both auditorily and in printed or graphic form. Test results yield age equivalencies, standard scores, standard deviations and percentile ranks for students ages 12 to 18. Demonstration items are provided. A discussion of performance and suggestions for remediation are included in the test manual. Examiner required. Not suitable for group use.

Untimed: Varies

Scoring: Examiner evaluated

Cost: Test kit (manual, 20 test forms) $44.90

Publisher: LinguiSystems, Inc.

WRITTEN LANGUAGE SYNTAX TEST
Refer to page 294.

Speech, Hearing, and Visual: Visual

ALLEN PICTURE TESTS
Henry F. Allen

Child—Ages 3½–6

Purpose: Measures visual acuity of children. Used in Headstart programs, kindergarten and the primary grades, and pediatricians' offices to identify children needing further diagnosis and assistance.

Description: One test slide, used with a vision screening instrument, measuring preschoolers' binocularity and visual acuity. Slides measure 20/100, 20/50, 20/40, and 20/30 levels of acuity for both right and left eyes. A training card is used to familiarize the child with the names of the objects used on the test cards (jeep, birthday cake, telephone, and man on a horse). The test is an alternative to the Michigan Pre-School Acuity Tests. A Titmus II Vision Tester is required. Examiner required. Not suitable for group use.

Untimed: 3–5 minutes

Scoring: Hand key; examiner evaluated

Cost: Slide for Vision Tester II $35.00

Publisher: Titmus Optical, Inc.

AMSLER CHART
Marc Amsler

All ages

Purpose: Analyzes disturbances of visual function.

Description: Oral-response and point-to vision test consisting of seven subtests: a) Standard, b) Central Scotoma, c) Color Scotoma, d) Scotoma, e) Metamorphosia, f) Metamorphosia—more detailed, and g) Limits of Fovea. The test is suitable for use with impaired individuals and geriatric patients. Written instructions are provided for the hearing impaired. The examiner must be an O.D. or M.D. Examiner required. Not suitable for group use.
BRITISH PUBLISHER

Untimed: Varies

Scoring: Self-scored; examiner evaluated

Cost: Manual with pad $46.00; pad $4.75; 100 patient grids $25.00

Publisher: Keeler Limited; distributed in the U.S. by Keeler Instruments, Inc.

BASIC READING RATE SCALE— BRAILLE AND LARGE TYPE EDITIONS
Refer to page 367.

BIEGER TEST OF VISUAL DISCRIMINATION
Elaine Bieger

All ages　　　

Purpose: Measures visual discrimination abilities using letters and words.

Description: 112–item paper-pencil multiple-choice test consisting of seven subtests measuring levels of mastery in the following areas: larger and lesser contrasts in letters and words, orientation reversal in letters and words, and sequence reversals in words. The test may be administered independently or in conjunction with the Visual Discrimination of Words Training Program. Following the format of the test, the training program starts with contrasting words and systematically progresses to words with almost identical features. The whole word and parts of the word are presented to provide systematic experiences relating parts of the word and the gestalt simultaneously. The individual is taught to scan words that are simultaneously positioned further and further apart. The test is available in two forms, A and B. Examiner required. Suitable for group use.

Untimed: 5 minutes per subtest; 35 minutes total

Scoring: Examiner evaluated

Cost: Complete kit (manual, test record forms, workbook) $20.50; manual (for both test and training program) $5.50; 30 record forms (15 of each form) $9.75; training program workbook $6.50

Publisher: Stoelting Co.

BRAILLE UNIT RECOGNITION BATTERY DIAGNOSTIC TEST OF GRADE 2 LITERARY BRAILLE
Refer to page 368.

THE BZOCH-LEAGUE RECEPTIVE-EXPRESSIVE EMERGENT LANGUAGE SCALE (REEL)
Refer to page 28.

CALLIER-AZUSA SCALE: G-EDITION
Refer to page 29.

CARROW AUDITORY-VISUAL ABILITIES TEST (CAVAT)
Elizabeth Carrow-Woolfolk

Child—Ages 4–10　　

Purpose: Measures auditory and visual perceptual, motor, and memory skills in children. Used to identify language/learning problems, analyze sources of auditory and/or visual difficulties, and for instructional programming.

Description: Multiple-item set of two norm-referenced paper-pencil verbal-visual batteries containing 14 subtests. They allow comparison of individual performances in auditory and visual abilities by providing data on interrelationships among discrimination, memory, and motor skills. In the Visual Abilities battery, the categories are visual discrimination matching, visual discrimination memory, visual-motor copying, visual-motor memory, and motor speed. In the Auditory Abilities battery, the categories are picture memory, picture sequence selection, digits forward, digits backward, sentence repetition, word repetition, auditory blending, auditory discrimination in quiet, and auditory discrimination in noise. Materials include test books, response/scoring booklets, cassette, manual, and an entry test for determining which subtests or battery to administer. The Visual battery is not appropriate for blind subjects; the Auditory is not appropriate for the deaf. Examiner required. Not suitable for group use.

Timed: 90 minutes for entire test; 2–13 minutes per test

Scoring: Examiner evaluated

Cost: Complete $135.00

Publisher: DLM Teaching Resources

CITY UNIVERSITY COLOR VISION TEST
Robert Fletcher

All ages　　　

Purpose: Diagnoses all types of color deficiencies, including the blue/yellow range. Used to assess the depth and degree of color deficiencies.

Description: 10–item paper-pencil test assessing color deficiencies in children and adults. Four color standards are arranged in a diamond form around a central standard. One of the outer spots is a match or near match to the central one for a color normal. The other three standards are matches for protan, deutan, and tritan defectives. Examiner required. Not suitable for group use.

Untimed: 5 minutes

Scoring: Hand key; examiner evaluated

Cost: Complete kit (two-ring binder, instructions, scoring key, black cards, record charts) $163.00

Publisher: Keeler Instruments, Inc.

DENVER EYE SCREENING TEST (DEST)
William K. Frankenburg, J. Goldstein, and A. Barker

Child—Ages 6 months–7 years

Purpose: Helps evaluate vision problems in children to determine if a child needs specialized testing.

Description: Performance test in which the examiner shows seven picture cards and asks the child to name the picture at 15 feet. For children age six months to two years-five months, the examiner uses an "E" card and a spinning toy to attract the child's attention and examines its eyes to see if they track; first one eye is tested, then the other. Materials consist of picture cards, cord, toy, plastic occluder, and "E" card. A flashlight is required. Examiner required. Not suitable for group use.

Untimed: 10 minutes

Scoring: Examiner evaluated

Cost: Complete kit $14.00; manual/workbook $10.00; 25 test forms $4.00

Publisher: Denver Developmental Materials, Inc.

DEVELOPMENTAL VISION TEST
SOI Institute Staff

Child

Purpose: Assesses 10 visual functions of young children. Used by teachers, nurses, and health service personnel to screen all students before vision problems cause academic problems.

Description: Screening instrument for detecting vision problems that may affect learning. The nine subtests are taken from the basic SOI Learning Abilities test, and the SOI-LA manual is used for administration. Scoring is keyed to the *Developmental Vision Guide* for complete interpretation. The test includes a vision checklist. Computer analysis is available. Examiner required. Suitable for group use.

Untimed: Varies

Scoring: Examiner evaluated; may be computer scored

Cost: Test form $1.90

Publisher: M & M Systems

DVORINE COLOR VISION TEST
Israel Dvorine

All ages

Purpose: Identifies individuals with defective color vision. Used for screening for color blindness in schools and industrial settings.

Description: 15–item test for determining the type and degree of color vision defect. The subject reads numbers or traces paths consisting of multicolored dots presented against a background of contrasting dots. Materials include 15 plates and 8 auxiliary plates for verification. Examiner required. Not suitable for group use.

Untimed: 2–3 minutes

Scoring: Examiner evaluated

Cost: Booklet of color plates $175.00; 35 record forms $16.50

Publisher: The Psychological Corporation

Information and availability unconfirmed; last verified in 1988.

EFRON VISUAL ACUITY TEST
Marvin Efron

Child, adolescent, adult

Purpose: Measures visual acuity (20/20 to 20/200).

Description: Oral-response show-tell test using a total of 19 cards: 15 cards measure far vision, 1 card measures near vision, and 3 cards are used for matching. This test is suitable for use with individuals with visual, hearing, physical, and mental impairments. Examiner required. Not suitable for group use.
Untimed: 5–10 minutes
Scoring: Examiner evaluated
Cost: $35.00
Publisher: Titmus Optical, Inc.

EFRON VISUAL ACUITY TEST SLIDES
Marvin Efron

Child—Ages 2–5

Purpose: Measures visual acuity (20/30 and 20/40). Must be used with Titmus II Vision Tester.

Description: Oral-response point-to test in two series (20/30 and 20/40) measuring visual acuity. Each series has one demonstration slide, three test slides, five sets of training cards, and three cards for matching. This test is suitable for use with individuals with visual, hearing, physical, and mental impairments. Examiner required. Not suitable for group use.
Untimed: 3–5 minutes
Scoring: Examiner evaluated
Cost: $113.40 per series
Publisher: Titmus Optical, Inc.

ERROR DETECTION IN TEXTS (DETECT)
Refer to page 103.

FARNSWORTH DICHOTOMOUS TEST FOR COLOR BLINDNESS
Dean Farnsworth

Adolescent, adult

Purpose: Provides a clear and quick indication of color blindness. Separates individuals unable to perform work involving color codes from those who are normal or moderately color effective.

Description: One-task test of color vision in which the applicant arranges colored caps according to color on a hinged rack. The pattern of responses is compared to that of normal subjects. Materials include a hinged rack with one permanently mounted reference color cap and fifteen movable color caps. Examiner required. Not suitable for group use.
Untimed: 5 minutes
Scoring: Hand key; examiner evaluated
Cost: Complete set (caps, rack, manual, 100 analysis sheets) $350.00; manual $25.00; 100 analysis sheets $26.00
Publisher: The Psychological Corporation
Information and availability unconfirmed; last verified in 1988.

FARNSWORTH-MUNSELL 100 HUE TEST
Refer to page 883.

HILL PERFORMANCE TEST OF SELECTED POSITIONED CONCEPTS
Everett Hill

Child—Ages 6–10

Purpose: Measures the development of spatial concepts in visually impaired children. Used by teachers and mobility specialists to diagnose visually impaired children.

Description: 72–item task-assessment of basic spatial concepts such as front, back, left, and right. The development of these positional concepts is tested through performance on four types of tasks: identifying body relationships, demonstrating positional concepts of body parts to one another, demonstrating positional concepts of body parts to other objects, and forming object-to-object relationships. The test may be used as a criterion-referenced instrument to identify individual strengths and weaknesses in the area of spatial concepts or as a norm-referenced test. Examiner required. Not suitable for group use.

Untimed: Not available

Scoring: Examiner evaluated

Cost: Complete kit (20 record forms, manual) $16.00

Publisher: Stoelting Co.

INVENTORY OF PERCEPTUAL SKILLS (IPS)
Donald R. O'Dell

Child

Purpose: Assesses visual and auditory perceptual skills and provides the structure for individual remedial programs. Aids in instructional planning for students at all age levels and in the development of IEPs.

Description: 79-item oral-response and task-performance test assessing perceptual skills in the following areas: visual discrimination, visual memory, object recognition, visual-motor coordination, auditory discrimination, auditory memory, auditory sequencing, and auditory blending. Once scored and recorded on the student profile (included in the student record booklet), a graphic comparison can be made of all of the subtests. A score below the mean on any subtest indicates a weakness in that area. The test may be administered by teachers, aides, or specialists without special training. The teacher's manual contains many educational activities in visual and auditory perception. Games, exercises, and activities provide the teacher with a variety of approaches and materials to use with the student. The student workbook includes 18 exercises to improve the areas in need of remediation. Examiner required. Not suitable for group use.

Untimed: Varies

Scoring: Examiner evaluated

Cost: Complete set (manual, student workbook, 10 student record booklets, stimulus cards) $16.25; manual $3.25; student workbook $1.75; 10 student record booklets $10.00; stimulus cards $2.25

Publisher: Stoelting Co.

ISHIHARA'S TEST FOR COLOUR BLINDNESS
Shinobu Ishihara

All ages

Purpose: Determines whether a patient has normal color vision. Used for school and employee screening.

Description: 24-item visual identification test measuring normal color perception. Each test item consists of a plate of pseudo-isochromatic colors with a number or pattern on each plate. The patient is asked to read the number or trace the pattern on each plate. Children who do not know numbers may trace the numbers. The test identifies both protan- and deutan-type color deficiencies with an indication of whether they are strong or mild. Test materials include a 24-page book of color plates, an informational guide, and a scoring key. Not limited to English language administration. Examiner required. Suitable for group use.

Untimed: 1 minute or less

Scoring: Hand key; examiner evaluated

Cost: 24 plates $100.00

Publisher: Kanehara & Co. Ltd., Japan; distributed in the U.S. by Titmus Optical, Inc.

KEELER ACUITY CARD-INFANT ASSESSMENT SET

Infant, young child

Purpose: Assesses the visual acuity of infants and young children within a variety of clinical settings.

Description: Acuity cards that provide a method of determining the visual acuity of infants and young children. The standard procedure is based on infants' known "preference" for patterned stimuli as indicated by their looking behavior. The results can be converted to an approximate Snellen equivalent. Use is restricted to optometrists and ophthalmologists. Examiner required. Not suitable for group use.
BRITISH PUBLISHER

Untimed: 2-5 minutes

Scoring: Examiner evaluated

Cost: Infant set $1,200.00; child set $1,400.00

Publisher: Keeler Limited; distributed in the U.S. by Keeler Instruments, Inc.

MICHIGAN PRE-SCHOOL ACUITY AND BINOCULARITY TEST

Child—Ages 3½–6

Purpose: Measures acuity and screens for binocular vision of children in Headstart, preschool programs, and primary grades. Identifies children needing further evaluation. Used with both handicapped and normally developing children.

Description: Vision tester and four slides comprise two tests: one for visual acuity and one for binocular vision. The test for visual acuity consists of three slides and four training cards. The child is familiarized with the task of determining "which way the table legs point" using the training cards and then takes the test using the vision tester. The Acuity Test measures both right eye and left eye acuity. Two levels are available. The Standard Test level is 20/30 on a pass/fail basis. A 20/40 level is also available. The Binocularity Test consists of one slide and uses the "which way do the table legs point" task. It identifies children with amblyopia, suppression, and other binocularity problems. The tests are used by pediatricians, family physicians, medical specialists, and school screening programs for purposes of screening and referral. A Titmus II Vision Tester is required. Examiner required. Not suitable for group use.

Untimed: Acuity 5 minutes; binocularity 2 minutes

Scoring: Hand key; examiner evaluated

Cost: Complete (3 acuity slides, 1 binocularity slide, manual, accessories) $135.00

Publisher: Titmus Optical, Inc.

MKM BINOCULAR PRESCHOOL TEST
Leland Michael and James W. King

Child—PreK

Purpose: Helps evaluate the near-point visual performance of preschool and other nonreading children. Used to demonstrate how learning lenses can improve performance and to monitor progress of visual therapy cases.

Description: One-card visual-verbal test. The card, used with a stereoscope, contains an array of geometric symbols. Some symbols are presented to both eyes and others are presented to the right or left eye alone. If the child has good binocular performance, the symbols will be read in the proper sequence without undue hesitation. A child's tendency to see double might suppress the vision of one eye, thus omitting the symbols presented to that eye. Binocular problems then can be identified. A stereoscope is needed. Examiner required. Not suitable for group use.

Untimed: 2–3 minutes

Scoring: Examiner evaluated

Cost: Complete kit (50 score sheets, instructions, cards) $10.00

Publisher: MKM

MKM MONOCULAR AND BINOCULAR READING TEST
Leland Michael and James W. King

Child
Grades 1–2

Purpose: Helps identify children with reading problems related to subtle differences in the vision of one eye or the other. Used to demonstrate how learning lenses can improve performance and to monitor progress of visual therapy cases.

Description: Six-card visual-verbal test. The cards are divided into two sets. The first set contains 110 words known by most children by the end of the first grade; the second set contains an additional 110 words children are expected to know by the end of the second grade. Each set contains three cards. The child reads the first card with the left eye alone. The second card presents the same words in reverse order for the right eye alone. The examiner records errors and time on a score sheet, determining which errors were common to both eyes and which were made with the right or left eye alone. Word reversals, improper vowel sounds, and other errors are expected to be about the same for each eye, but if the time for one eye exceeds the other by 20% or more, a binocular visual problem should be suspected. The third card contains the same words as the first two cards. Some words are presented to both eyes and others are presented just to the right or the left eye alone. A stereoscope is needed. Examiner administered. Not suitable for group use.

Untimed: 5–10 minutes

Scoring: Examiner evaluated

Cost: Complete kit (cards, score pads) $30.00; additional score pads $3.50

Publisher: MKM

PEEK-A-BOO TEST
Pat Hill

Child—Ages 3-7

Purpose: Determines vision impairment in normal and retarded children not yet able to read.

Description: Eight-target set that presents nonlanguage tests in six areas: acuity, vertical and lateral eye coordination, fusion, depth perception, and color discrimination. The cards, which are modern illustrations of familiar objects, are shown one at a time in the Telebinocular (refer to the Visual Survey Telebinocular). The examiner asks specific questions and records answers on a corresponding record form, which is ordered separately. Examiner required. Not suitable for group use.

Timed: 5 minutes

Scoring: Hand key

Cost: Complete kit $54.00; contact publisher for record forms price

Publisher: Keystone View, Division of Mast Development Company

---

PROFESSIONAL VISION TESTER

Ages 5 and older

Purpose: Measures an individual's visual performance. Used to detect vision deficiencies.

Description: 11-test nonverbal battery measuring phoria-vertical and lateral at near and far distances (4 tests), acuity of right and left eyes at near and far distances (6 tests), and stereopsis and color discrimination (1 test). Materials include a precision stereoscopic instrument equipped with adjustable viewing aperture height, constant illumination, and a revolving drum to hold test slides. All controls are on the right side of the machine and require a minimum number of manipulations. Questions are simple and direct, and the routine can be learned with minimal training. Examiner required. Not suitable for group use.

Untimed: 10 minutes

Scoring: Hand key

Cost: Instrument (Model 14019) $1,550.00

Publisher: Lafayette Instrument Company, Inc.

PSEUDOISOCHROMATIC PLATES

Grades PreK-adult

Purpose: Tests for protanoid and deuteranoid types of red-green color blindness. Used for perceptual screening, vision testing, and drivers' tests.

Description: 15-item oral-response test assessing red-green color perception. Plates consisting of patterns of colored dots revealing numbers are held 30 inches in front of the subject, who is given approximately 2 seconds to call out the number formed by the pattern on each plate. Materials consist of a single booklet of color plates containing a demonstration plate and 14 number plates. Examiner required. Not suitable for group use.

Untimed: 3 minutes

Scoring: Hand key

Cost: Plates (Model 14017) $90.00

Publisher: Lafayette Instrument Company, Inc.

RANDOT STEREOPSIS TEST

All ages

Purpose: Determines whether a patient has stereo-depth perception and/or binocular vision. Screens children and adults for further evaluation and treatment.

Description: Two stereo vectographs (dot patterns on a homogeneous background) and polaroid glasses are used to measure children's stereo depth perception and gross depth perception. More definitive tests are included for adult patients. Wearing the polaroid glasses, the patient views the vectographs and picks out the characters formed by the dot patterns. The test is not practical with very young children and provides no monocular clues. Examiner required. Suitable for group use.

Untimed: 10–15 minutes

Scoring: Hand key; examiner evaluated

Cost: Complete $99.00

Publisher: Stereo Optical Co.; distributed by Titmus Optical, Inc.

REACTION TIME MEASURE OF VISUAL FIELD (REACT)
Refer to page 121.

REYNELL-ZINKIN DEVELOPMENT SCALES FOR YOUNG VISUALLY HANDICAPPED CHILDREN
Refer to page 561.

RICHMOND PSEUDO-ISOCHROMATIC COLOR TEST

All ages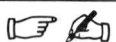

Purpose: Assesses color perception.

Description: 15-plate test determines red-green vision deficiency. The test utilizes a demonstration plate to explain the numerical plate design. Subject must be able to read. Examiner required. Not suitable for group use.

Untimed: 5 minutes

Scoring: Examiner evaluated

Cost: 15 plates $55.00

Publisher: Richmond Products

SEARCHING FOR SHAPES (SEARCH)
Refer to page 126.

SINGLE AND DOUBLE SIMULTANEOUS STIMULATION (SDSS)
Refer to page 128.

SKLAR APHASIA SCALE—REVISED 1983
Refer to page 128.

SLOAN ACHROMATOPSIA TEST
Refer to page 266.

SONKSEN-SILVER ACUITY SYSTEM

Child—Ages 3 and older

Purpose: Assesses the visual acuity of individuals with communication problems.

Description: Point-to vision test measuring distance and near acuity. May be used with individuals with visual, hearing, physical, or mental impairments. Examiner required. Not suitable for group use. BRITISH PUBLISHER

Untimed: Varies

Scoring: Examiner evaluated

Cost: Basic Screening test $190.00

Publisher: Keeler Limited; distributed in the U.S. by Keeler Instruments, Inc.

THE SOUTH AFRICAN INDIVIDUAL SCALE FOR THE BLIND (SAISB)—1979
Refer to page 598.

SPEEDED READING OF WORD LISTS (SRWL)
Refer to page 129.

STEREO FLY STEREOPSIS TEST

All ages

Purpose: Determines whether a patient has stereo depth perception and/or binocular vision. Screens children and adults for further evaluation and treatment.

Used with very young children to determine binocular vision.

Description: Two stereo vectographs and polaroid glasses are used to measure children's stereo depth perception and gross depth perception. More definitive tests are included for adult patients. Wearing the polaroid glasses, the patient views the vectographs and identifies the objects illustrated. The test contains a picture of a large housefly, which is particularly effective with very young children. Used as a screening aid but not for diagnosis. Examiner required. Not suitable for group use.

Untimed: 5–10 minutes

Scoring: Hand key; examiner evaluated

Cost: Complete $99.00

Publisher: Stereo Optical Co.; distributed by Titmus Optical, Inc.

STYCAR VISION TESTS
Mary D. Sheridan

Child—Ages 6 months–7 years

Purpose: Assesses vision in children. Used for evaluating very young and handicapped children.

Description: Multiple-item three-performance test of vision. The Stycar Vision Test (ages 2–7) uses toys and laminated cards and charts. The Graded Balls Test (ages 6 months–2 years) assesses the visual competence of motorically impaired children and those with language difficulties. Use of a reversible occluder is recommended. The Panda Test is used with children with severe visual or other handicaps. The tests are available to medical doctors and teachers of the blind. Examiner required. Not suitable for group use. BRITISH PUBLISHER

Untimed: Not available

Scoring: Examiner evaluated

Cost: Contact publisher

Publisher: NFER-NELSON Publishing Company Ltd.

TEST OF VISUAL-PERCEPTUAL SKILLS (NON-MOTOR) (TVPS N-M)
Morrison F. Gardner

Child—Ages 4–12

Purpose: Measures visual-perceptual skills.

Description: 112–item test measuring a child's visual-perceptual skills in seven areas: visual discrimination, visual memory, visual-spatial relationships, visual form constancy, visual sequential memory, visual figure-ground, and visual closure. A "point-to" format is utilized. Perceptual ages, scaled scores, and percentiles are available for each subtest; perceptual quotients, percentiles, and median perceptual ages are obtained by combining all subtest scores. The test is available in male and female forms. May be used with individuals with visual, hearing, physical, and mental impairments. Examiner required. Not suitable for group use.

Untimed: 10–20 minutes

Scoring: Hand key

Cost: Complete kit (manual, test plates, 25 record forms) $59.95

Publisher: Children's Hospital of San Francisco

TITMUS II VISION TESTER: PEDIATRIC MODEL

Child—Grades PreK–6

Purpose: Screens visual skills of preschool, Head Start, and primary grade students. Identifies students with visual defects that may affect their performance in school.

Description: Vision tester with eight test slides screening the visual abilities of young children. Preschool children are tested for acuity far, right eye, left eye, and binocularity. Primary-grade students are tested for acuity far, right eye, left eye, hyperopia, heterophorias, and color vision. Test materials include the vision tester with eight slides, a training manual, record forms, and a lens unit. Examiner required. Not suitable for group use.

Untimed: 3–5 minutes

Scoring: Hand key; examiner evaluated

Cost: Remote control $1,395.00; manual control $1,095.00; for built-in perimeter to test peripheral vision, add $100.00 to each model

Publisher: Titmus Optical, Inc.

TITMUS II VISION TESTER: PROFESSIONAL MODEL

All ages

Purpose: Screens visual skills of preschool, primary, and secondary students and adults. Identifies individuals with visual deficiencies.

Description: Vision tester with eight slides screening visual skills. Preschool children are tested for acuity far, right eye, left eye, and binocularity. Primary-grade students are tested for acuity far, right eye, left eye, hyperopia, heterophorias, and color vision. Secondary-grade students and adults are tested for acuity far and near, right eye, left eye, both eyes, vertical and lateral heterophorias, and color vision. Test materials include eight slides and vision tester, a training manual, record forms, and a lens unit. Examiner required. Not suitable for group use.

Untimed: 3–5 minutes

Scoring: Hand key; examiner evaluated

Cost: Remote control $1,395.00; manual control $1,095.00; for built-in perimeter to test peripheral vision, add $100.00 to each model

Publisher: Titmus Optical, Inc.

TITMUS II-S STANDARD VISION TESTER DRIVER ED MODEL, MANUAL CONTROL
Titmus Optical, Inc.

Adolescent, adult

Purpose: Screens vision skills of drivers and driver license applicants to determine whether or not they meet their state requirements for licensing.

Description: Precision stereoscopic instrument with eight test slides. Tests visual acuities at far with letters or num-

bers, color identification, highway sign identification, and heterophorias. Available with or without perimeter for testing of peripheral vision. Examiner required. Not suitable for group use.

Untimed: 3–5 minutes

Scoring: Examiner evaluated

Cost: $1,395.00; with perimeter $1,495.00

Publisher: Titmus Optical, Inc.

TITMUS II-S STANDARD VISION TESTER SCHOOL MODEL, MANUAL CONTROL
Titmus Optical, Inc.

Child, adolescent

Purpose: Screens visual skill of preschool and elementary-grade students. Identifies students with visual deficiencies that may affect their performance in school.

Description: Precision stereoscopic instrument with eight test slides testing preschool children for acuity, right and left eye, and binocularity. Elementary-grade children are tested for binocularity; acuity far, right eye, and left eye; hyperopia; vertical and lateral phorias at far and near; and color perception, far and near. Test materials include Titmus II-S Vision Tester with eight test slides, training manual, record forms, and a lens unit. Some special test slides are available to accommodate individuals with visual impairments. Examiner required. Not suitable for group use.

Untimed: 3–5 minutes

Scoring: Hand key; examiner evaluated

Cost: $1,095.00

Publisher: Titmus Optical, Inc.

VISION TESTING OF YOUNG CHILDREN

Child—Ages 30 months-PreK

Purpose: Tests vision in young children.

Description: Eight colorful plastic alphabet letters used for assessing vision in young children. These symbols replace the usual linear chart of letters used with school-age children and adults and help to sustain cooperation of young children. Examiner required. Not suitable for group use.

BRITISH PUBLISHER

Untimed: Not available

Scoring: Examiner evaluated

Cost: $9.00

Publisher: The Test Agency Ltd.

VISUAL DISCRIMINATION TEST
Refer to page 360.

VISUAL FUNCTIONING ASSESSMENT TOOL (VFAT)
Kathleen Costello, Patricia Pinkney, and Wendy Scheffero

All ages

Purpose: Assesses visual functioning in the educational setting. Used to instruct low-vision individuals of all ages and levels, including the severely handicapped, and to help establish IEPs.

Description: Observation test using common classroom materials to assess the following areas of visual functioning: appearance of eyes, basic responses, fixation tracking, saccadic movement, scanning, visual accuity, visual field, depth perception, eye-hand and eye-foot coordination, visual imitation and memory, visual discrimination, visual perception, and concepts of self and others in space, pictures, visual environment, and mobility. It is not necessary to administer the entire VFAT to every student. Specific appropriate areas may be used independently. The test is designed to be administered by an eye specialist or a teacher of the visually impaired. Examiner required. Not suitable for group use.

Untimed: Not available

Scoring: Examiner evaluated

Cost: Complete kit (recording forms, manual) $41.50

Publisher: Stoelting Co.

VISUAL SCANNING (SCAN)
Refer to page 133.

VISUAL SKILLS APPRAISAL (VSA)
Regina G. Richards and Gary S. Oppenheim in consultation with G.N. Getman

Child
Grades K–4

Purpose: Assesses visual skills of students in Grades K–4. Used by teachers who may not have specialized training in visual skills assessment for identifying visual inefficiencies that affect school performance.

Description: Multiple-item task-performance test assessing pursuit, scanning, alignment, and locating movements; eye-hand coordination; and fixation unity. The test identifies students who should be referred for a comprehensive visual examination. The test is self-contained and does not require the use of other equipment. The manual includes many visual training techniques keyed to each subtest. Examiner required. Not suitable for group use.

Untimed: 10–15 minutes

Scoring: Hand key

Cost: Test kit (manual, stimulus cards, 25 design completion forms, 25 red/green trail forms, 25 score sheets, red/green glasses) $55.00

Publisher: Academic Therapy Publications

VISUAL SKILLS TEST SET #5100

Ages 8–adult

Purpose: Determines basic visual patterns, binocular acceptance of prescriptions, and need for orthoptic training. Used for vision screening of school children.

Description: Vision test using 15 stereo targets to screen the following visual skills: phorias, fusion readiness, binocular visual efficiency at near and far points, stereopsis, and color discrimination. Cards are shown to the child one at a time in the telebinocular (refer to the Visual Survey Telebinocular), specific questions are asked, and answers are recorded on a corresponding form, which is ordered

---

separately. The test may be too difficult for young children and slow learners. Examiner required. Not suitable for group use.

Untimed: 5 minutes

Scoring: Hand key

Cost: Complete kit $91.00

Publisher: Keystone View, Division of Mast Development Company

---

VISUAL SURVEY TELEBINOCULAR (VISION SCREENING TELEBINOCULAR)

Ages 3–adult

Purpose: Measures near- and far-point vision. Used for remediation screening.

Description: Vision test using a general purpose telebinocular equipped with the same lens system as the opthalmic telebinocular, as well as occluder paddles, adjustable viewing head height, and built-in internal slide illumination. During testing, target slides are placed in the instrument, and the individual is asked specific questions about each card. For slide description, refer to the Visual Skills Test Set. The telebinocular can accommodate the Plus Lens attachment. Examiner required. Not suitable for group use.

Untimed: 5 minutes

Scoring: Hand key

Cost: Complete kit $640.00

Publisher: Keystone View, Division of Mast Development Company

---

WASHER VISUAL ACUITY SCREENING TECHNIQUE (WVAST)
Rhonda Wiczer Washer

Mentally handicapped

Purpose: Measures the visual abilities of severely handicapped (mental age 2.6 years to adult), low-functioning, and very young children. Used for screening groups of children to identify those with possible visual impairments.

Description: Multiple-item vision test screening both near- and far-point acuity. The testing procedure omits as many perceptual, motor, and verbal skills as possi-

ble. A conditioning process is outlined for familiarizing individuals with the symbols, matching skills, and eye occlusion used in the screening. The test may be administered by trained volunteers. Examiner required. Suitable for screening groups of children.

Untimed: Varies

Scoring: Examiner evaluated

Cost: Starter set (manual, symbol cards, stimulus cards, occluders, near-point panel, 20 screening records) $49.00; specimen set $9.00

Publisher: Scholastic Testing Service, Inc.

Student Evaluation and Counseling: Behavior Problems and Counseling Tools

ADOLESCENT CHEMICAL DEPENDENCY INVENTORY (ACDI)
Refer to page 17.

ADOLESCENT-COPING ORIENTATION FOR PROBLEM EXPERIENCES (A-COPE)
Refer to page 153.

AMERICAN DRUG AND ALCOHOL SURVEY (ADAS)
RMBSI, Inc.

Adolescent—Ages 11–19
Grades 6–12

Purpose: Assesses drug and alcohol use, peer use, and sanctions. Used by school districts for assessment of school and district drug use levels.

Description: 57–item paper-pencil multiple-choice test measuring drug and alcohol use. The survey yields the American Drug and Alcohol Survey Report that provides information about lifetime prevalence, last year and last month levels of drug and alcohol use, risk levels, perceived harm of drugs, and peer usage. The test is updated yearly. A scoring service is available from the publisher. A fourth-grade reading level is required. Self-administered. Suitable for group use.

Untimed: 20 minutes

Scoring: Computer scored

Cost: Approximately $1.00 per student; $150.00 per report; contact publisher for estimate

Publisher: Rocky Mountain Behavioral Science Institute, Inc.

AMERICAN DRUG AND ALCOHOL SURVEY (ADAS)— CHILDREN'S FORM
RMBSI, Inc.

Adolescent—Ages 9–14 Grades 4–8

Purpose: Assesses alcohol, marijuana, inhalant, and other drug use. Used by schools and school districts for assessment of drug and alcohol problems and for program evaluation.

Description: 35–item paper-pencil multiple-choice test assessing drug and alcohol use. The survey yields an American Drug and Alcohol Survey Report. A scoring service is provided by the publisher. A third-grade reading level is required. Self-administered. Suitable for group use.

Untimed: 20 minutes

Scoring: Computer scored

Cost: Approximately $1.00 per student; $100.00 per report

Publisher: Rocky Mountain Behavioral Science Institute, Inc.

ANALYSIS OF COPING STYLE (ACS)
Herbert F. Boyd and G. Orville Johnson

Child, adolescent Grades K–12

Purpose: Identifies coping styles being used by children to deal with problems related to interpersonal relationships with peers and authorities. Allows school psychologists, educators, or guidance coun-

selors to screen and develop appropriate intervention programs.

Description: 20–item paper-pencil test in which the examiner presents pictures of school situations (with peers and adults), and the students choose one of six possible responses. The responses are analyzed for patterns of coping styles: externalized attack, internalized attack, avoidance, or denial. The test discriminates between normal and disturbed populations. Two versions are available: one for elementary-school children and one for high-school students. Materials include picture stimuli (sheets or overhead transparencies), response forms, and manual. Examiner required. Suitable for group use.

Untimed: 10–20 minutes

Scoring: Hand key

Cost: 25 individual record forms $12.00; 100 group response forms $12.00; elementary transparencies $30.00; secondary transparencies $30.00; manual $29.00

Publisher: The Psychological Corporation

Information and availability unconfirmed; last verified in 1988.

THE ANSER SYSTEM-AGGREGATE NEUROBEHAVIORAL STUDENT HEALTH AND EDUCATIONAL REVIEW
Refer to page 630.

ATTENTION DEFICIT DISORDER BEHAVIOR RATING SCALES (ADDBRS)
Ned Owens and Betty White Owens

Child, adolescent—Ages 6–16 Grades 1–12

Purpose: Identifies children and adolescents with Attention Deficit Disorder. Used for referral to a medical doctor and as a follow-up to measure academic and behavioral improvement.

Description: 50–item paper-pencil rating scale identifying Attention Deficit Disorder. Teachers or parents rate items on a 5–point scale ranging from "You have not noticed this behavior before" to "You have noticed this behavior to a very large degree." The test contains three primary, or organic, scales (Inattention, Impulsivity, Hyperactivity) and seven secondary, or emotional, scales (Anger Control, Academics, Anxiety, Confidence, Aggressiveness, Resistance, Social). Results distinguish between individuals with Attention Deficit Disorder without Hyperactivity and Attention Deficit Disorder with Hyperactivity. Self-administered. Not suitable for group use.

Untimed: 15–30 minutes

Scoring: Examiner evaluated

Cost: Kit (25 rating sheets, 25 profile sheets, manual) $15.00

Publisher: Ned Owens, M.Ed., Inc.

THE BEHAVIOR EVALUATION SCALE—2 (BES-2)
Stephen B. McCarney and James E. Leigh

Child, adolescent
Grades K–12

Purpose: Assesses the behavioral problems of students. Used by school personnel to make decisions about eligibility, placement, and programming for students with behavior problems.

Description: Multiple-item paper-pencil observational inventory assessing the behavioral problems of students regardless of primary handicapping conditions. The instrument may be used with students who have learning disabilities, mental retardation, physical handicaps, or other handicapping conditions. Examiner/self-administered. Not suitable for group use.

Untimed: Varies

Scoring: Examiner evaluated

Cost: Complete kit (manual, 50 student record forms, 1 sample data collection form) $50.00

Publisher: PRO-ED

BEHAVIOR RATING PROFILE (BRP)–2
Linda L. Brown and Donald D. Hammill

Child, adolescent
Grades 1–12

Purpose: Identifies elementary and secondary students thought to have behavior problems and the settings in which those problems seem prominent. Also identifies individuals who have differing perceptions about the behavior of a student.

Description: Multiple-item paper-pencil battery consisting of six independent, individually normed measures: three Student Rating Scales (Home, School, and Peer), Parent Rating Scale, Teacher Rating Scale, and the Sociogram. May be used with emotionally disturbed and learning disabled students. Examiner required. Not suitable for group use.

Untimed: Varies

Scoring: Hand key

Cost: Complete kit (examiner's manual; 50 each of teacher, parent, and student rating forms; 50 profile sheets; storage box) $106.00

Publisher: PRO-ED

BEHAVIORAL INTERVENTION PLAN
Refer to page 232.

BEHAVIOUR PROBLEMS: A SYSTEM OF MANAGEMENT
Peter Galvin and Richard Singleton

Child, adolescent

Purpose: Assesses and monitors the behavior of problem children. Used in the classroom by specialist and nonspecialist teachers.

Description: Three paper-pencil record forms providing a framework for assessing and monitoring the classroom behavior of up to eight children over a 6–month period. The Behaviour Checklist enables the teacher to identify and describe inappropriate behaviors, note specific problems, and select two priority behaviors on which future work will concentrate. The Daily Record Sheet provides a record of observed classroom behavior and notes details concerning priority behaviors (frequency, duration), positive behaviors, and other significant items. The observations help assess the success of the long-term program. The Monthly Progress Chart records information about the child (age,

IQ, reading age) and provides a systematic account of the behavior management strategies adopted. The manual explains the rationale behind the system and includes guidelines for the system's use and references to books on appropriate remedial programs. Examiner required. Suitable for group use.

BRITISH PUBLISHER

Untimed: Varies

Scoring: Examiner evaluated

Cost: Contact publisher

Publisher: NFER-NELSON Publishing Company Ltd.

BRIEF LIFE HISTORY INVENTORY
Refer to page 233.

BRISTOL SOCIAL ADJUSTMENT GUIDES
D.H. Stott and N.C. Marston

Child, adolescent—Ages 5–15

Purpose: Evaluates the behavior patterns of children and adolescents. Identifies maladjusted and disturbed children needing further testing and assistance. Used for clinical diagnosis.

Description: Paper-pencil checklist consisting of statements about a child's habits of response to his environment. The checklist should be filled out by a teacher, social worker, or other adult familiar with the child's behavior. The inventory provides the clinician with a picture of the child's day-to-day behavior and a system for interpreting that behavior by means of diagnostic forms. Development of the guides, theoretical implications, and related studies are described in the manual. Not for sale in the United States. Self-administered by the evaluator under supervision of a psychologist. Not suitable for group use.

BRITISH PUBLISHER

Untimed: Open ended

Scoring: Examiner evaluated

Cost: Specimen set (includes manual) £8.95 plus VAT; manual £5.50

Publisher: Hodder & Stoughton

BRISTOL SOCIAL ADJUSTMENT GUIDES, AMERICAN EDITION (BSAG)
D.H. Stott

Child, adolescent—Ages 5–16

Purpose: Diagnoses the nature and extent of behavioral disturbances and social adjustment in children. Used by teachers and school psychologists.

Description: Multiple-item paper-pencil observational instrument consisting of short phrases describing a child's behavior. The phrases that apply to the child being evaluated are underlined by an adult familiar with the child. The guides are concerned with observable behavior rather than with inferences based on projective techniques or the child's self-assessment. An overall assessment of maladjustment, subscores for five core syndromes (unforthcomingness, withdrawal, depression, inconsequence, hostility), and four additional associated groupings (peer-maladaptiveness, nonsyndromic overreaction, nonsyndromic underreaction, and neurological symptoms) are provided. The test is available in separate forms for boys and girls. Separate norms based on students from city, county, and church schools are provided for boys and girls. Examiner required. Suitable for group use.

Untimed: 10–15 minutes

Scoring: Hand key

Cost: Specimen set (includes manual, all forms) $5.50; 25 booklets (specify male or female) $13.75; 50 profile sheets (expendable) $8.50; hand scoring keys (set of 7) $14.75; manual $2.75; specimen set (manual and 1 copy of all forms) $5.50

Publisher: Educational and Industrial Testing Service

BURKS' BEHAVIOR RATING SCALES, PRESCHOOL AND KINDERGARTEN EDITION
Refer to page 136.

CHILD ANXIETY SCALE (CAS)
Refer to page 137.

CHILD BEHAVIOR CHECKLIST AND REVISED CHILD BEHAVIOR PROFILE
Refer to page 138.

CHILDREN'S ADAPTIVE BEHAVIOR SCALE
Refer to page 764.

CHILDREN'S INTERACTION MATRIX (CIM)
Refer to page 235.

CHILDREN'S VERSION/FAMILY ENVIRONMENT SCALE (CV/FES)
Refer to page 68.

A CLASS PLAY
E.M. Bower

Child
Grades 3–7

Purpose: Evaluates the peer perceptions and self-images of children. Identifies children with low self-images and children whose self-image does not correspond to the perceptions of their peers. Used by classroom teachers to identify children needing further assistance or evaluation.

Description: 50–item paper-pencil test consisting of two sections. Section I (20 items) contains descriptions of 20 hypothetical roles in a play, with instructions directing each student to choose the classmate who would be most suitable and natural in each of the roles. Odd-numbered items present positive roles such as "a class president" or "a very fair person who plays games fairly." Even-numbered items present negative roles such as "a bully who picks on smaller boys and girls."
Section II (30 items) consists of multiple-choice questions in which students are presented with four of the roles from the play (two positive and two negative) with instructions such as "Which of these four roles would a teacher pick for you to play?" Students are asked to indicate the roles they would pick for themselves, as

well as the roles their peers or teacher would (or would not) pick for them to play. Scoring for both sections consists of computing the proportion of positive and negative perceptions for each child within each of the two sections. A comparison of the students' peer-perceptions (the score from Section I) with their self-perceptions (the score from Section II) indicates the congruence or incongruence between the students' perceptions of themselves and the way they are perceived by others. Examiner required. Suitable for group use.

Untimed: Varies

Scoring: Examiner evaluated

Cost: Contact publisher

Publisher: Charles C. Thomas, Publisher

DECISION MAKING ORGANIZER (DMO)
Anna Miller-Tiedeman and Patricia Elenz-Martin

Adolescent, adult
Grades 10 and above

Purpose: Diagnoses decision-making problems of high-school and college students. Used for counseling and guidance.

Description: 36–item paper-pencil multiple-choice test measuring self-understanding; educational, career, and vocational plans; time use; and barriers to decision making. The subjects are presented with questions and asked to check from five responses those that apply to them (more than one response may be checked for each question). Self-administered. Suitable for group use.

Timed: 10 minutes

Scoring: Examiner evaluated

Cost: Starter set (manual, 20 organizers) $17.50

Publisher: Scholastic Testing Service, Inc.

DEMOS D (DROPOUT) SCALE
George D. Demos

Adolescent
Grades 7–12

Purpose: Identifies students who are probable school drop-outs. Used for preventive counseling.

Description: 29–item paper-pencil questionnaire measuring attitudes in four areas: toward teachers, toward education, influences by peers or parents, and school behavior. The questionnaire yields a total score and basic area scores, which are converted to probabilities of dropping out of school. A fifth-grade reading level is required. Self-administered. Suitable for group use.

Untimed: 15–20 minutes
Scoring: Hand key
Cost: Complete kit (25 forms, manual) $14.75
Publisher: Western Psychological Services

THE DEVEREUX ADOLESCENT BEHAVIOR RATING SCALE
George Spivack, Peter Haimes, and Jules Spotts

Adolescent—Ages 13–18

Purpose: Assesses the behavior symptoms of normal and emotionally disturbed adolescents. Used for diagnostic and screening procedures, group placement decisions, and assessment of progress in response to specific programs or procedures.

Description: 84–item paper-pencil test assessing symptomatic behaviors of adolescents. The evaluator (someone living with the youth) rates each item according to how he feels the subject's behavior compares with the behavior of normal children of the same age. The test yields 12 factor scores (Unethical Behavior, Defiant-Resistive, Domineering-Sadistic, Heterosexual Interest, Hyperactive Expansive, Poor Emotional Control, Need Approval and Dependency, Emotional Distance, Physical Inferiority-Timidity, Schizoid Withdrawal, Bizarre Speech and Cognition, Bizarre Action), 3 cluster scores (Inability to Delay, Paranoid Thought, Anxious Self-Blame), and 11 item scores (Persecution, Plotting, Bodily Concern, External Influences, Compulsive Acts, Avoids Competition, Withdrawn, Socialization, Peer Domi-

nance, Physical Coordination, Distraction). Examiner required. Not suitable for group use.

Untimed: 10–15 minutes
Scoring: Examiner evaluated
Cost: Contact publisher
Publisher: The Devereux Foundation

THE DEVEREUX ELEMENTARY SCHOOL BEHAVIOR RATING SCALE (DESB-II)
Marshall Swift

Child—Ages 6–12

Purpose: Assesses overt classroom behaviors at the elementary-school level. Diagnoses problem behaviors that interfere with classroom performance. Used for screening procedures, group placement decisions, and assessment of progress in response to specific programs or procedures.

Description: 52–item paper-pencil inventory assessing the symptomatic classroom behavior patterns of children. The classroom teacher rates each item according to how he feels the subject's behavior compares to the behavior of normal children his age. The test yields 10 behavior factors (Work Organization, Creative Initiative/Involvement, Positive Toward Teacher, Need for Direction in Work, Socially Withdrawn, Failure Anxiety, Impatience, Irrelevant Thinking/TALK, Blaming, Negative/Aggressive) and 4 behavior clusters (Perseverance, Peer Cooperation, Confusion, and Inattention). Self-administered by teacher. Not suitable for group use.

Untimed: 10–15 minutes
Scoring: Examiner evaluated
Cost: Contact publisher
Publisher: The Devereux Foundation

DIMENSIONS OF SELF-CONCEPT (DOSC)
William B. Michael and Robert A. Smith

Child, adolescent Grades 4 and above

Purpose: Identifies students who might have difficulty with schoolwork due to low self-esteem and diagnoses factors contributing to low self-esteem.

Description: Multiple-item paper-pencil questionnaire assessing level of aspiration, anxiety, academic interest and satisfaction, leadership and initiative, and identification vs. alienation. Form E is available for Grades 4–6, Form S for Grades 7–12, Form H for College. Percentile ranks are presented for Grades 4–6, 7–9, and 10–12. Examiner required. Suitable for group use.

Untimed: Form E 20–40 minutes; Form S 15–35 minutes; Form H 15–35 minutes

Scoring: Machine scored by publisher

Cost: 25 test forms $7.75; manual $2.75; specimen set $5.50

Publisher: EdITS/Educational and Industrial Testing Service

EDUCATION APPERCEPTION TEST
Jack M. Thompson and Robert A. Sones

Child, adolescent
Grades PreK–8

Purpose: Assesses students' attitudes toward school and education. Used to work with acting-out and problem children, including some adolescents.

Description: 10–item projective test in which the examiner uses 18 pictures (8 for boys, 8 for girls, 2 for both boys and girls) to evoke responses in four major areas: reaction to authority, reaction toward learning, peer relationships, and home attitude toward school. Responses to each photograph include "What took place before?," "What is going on now?," "What feelings are involved?," and "What is the outcome?" The test is not normed. Examiner required. Not suitable for group use.

Untimed: 20–30 minutes

Scoring: Examiner evaluated

Cost: Complete set (pictures, manual) $29.50

Publisher: Western Psychological Services

EMOTIONAL/BEHAVIORAL SCREENING PROGRAM (ESP)
Jack G. Dial and Garry Amann

Child, adolescent—Ages 9
and older

Purpose: Analyzes emotional and behavioral functioning. Used with special needs students.

Description: 35–item paper-pencil checklist for rating an individual on the basis of observed behavior, reliable case history reports, or information provided by a reliable informant. The checklist, called the Behavioral Checklist for Students (BCS), contains seven categories of items: Impulsivity-Frustration, Anxiety, Depression-Withdrawal, Socialization, Self-Concept, Aggression, and Reality Discrimination.

Raw subtest scores are entered into the computer. Users may choose from types of reports. The Analysis Report is an analysis of emotional/behavioral functions with possible diagnostic categories. The Classroom Report describes emotional/behavioral characteristics the teacher may anticipate and lists specific recommendations for educational management. The Comprehensive Report integrates features of both the Analysis Report and the Classroom Report. The software operates on Apple and IBM PC and compatible systems. Examiner/self-administered. Not suitable for group use.

Untimed: Varies

Scoring: Examiner evaluated; may be computer scored

Cost: Complete kit (comprehensive manual, 25 copies of BCS, computer program with operating manual) $200.00

Publisher: McCarron-Dial Systems

Information and availability unconfirmed; last verified in 1988.

THE FORTY-EIGHT ITEM COUNSELING EVALUATION TEST: REVISED
Refer to page 173.

HAHNEMANN ELEMENTARY SCHOOL BEHAVIOR RATING SCALE (HESB)
George Spivack and Marshall Swift

Elementary-school students

Purpose: Assesses classroom behavior relevant to academic achievement and behavioral adjustment during the elementary school years. Used in education, research, and counseling.

Description: 60–item teacher rating instrument consisting of 14 scales: originality, independent learning, involvement, productive with peers, intellectual dependency, failure anxiety, unreflectiveness, irrelevant talk, social over-involvement, negative feelings, holding back/withdrawn, critical/competitive, blaming, and approach to teacher. Of the 14 behavioral factors, 4 tap positive coping behaviors and 10 tap negative coping behaviors. The scale is based on factor analytic studies of normal and deviant children in regular, special, and open classrooms. Factors relate to academic achievement and controlling for IQ. Norms are provided. Examiner required. Not suitable for group use.

Untimed: 15 minutes

Scoring: Examiner evaluated

Cost: Manual $12.00; 50 scales $0.30 each; 500 scales $0.24 each

Publisher: George Spivack and Marshall Swift

HAHNEMANN HIGH SCHOOL BEHAVIOR RATING SCALE (HHSB)
George Spivack and Marshall Swift

High-school students

Purpose: Assesses classroom behaviors that abet positive coping in the classroom and behaviors that indicate poor coping. Used in education, research, and counseling.

Description: 45–item teacher rating scale consisting of 13 scales: reasoning ability, originality, verbal interaction, rapport with teacher, anxious producer, general anxiety, quiet-withdrawn, poor work hab-

its, lack of intellectual independence, dogmatic-inflexible, verbal negativism, disturbance-restless, and expressed inability. The scale has been used to predict adjustment in young adulthood and as an outcome measure for educational and therapeutic interventions. The scale is based on analytic studies of normal and deviant children. Norms are provided. Examiner required. Not suitable for group use.

Untimed: 10 minutes

Scoring: Examiner evaluated

Cost: Manual $12.00; 50 scales each $0.30; 500 scales each $0.24

Publisher: George Spivack and Marshall Swift

HILSON ADOLESCENT PROFILE (HAP)
Refer to page 178.

HOME INDEX
Harrison G. Gough

Grades 6 and above

Purpose: Gathers information from junior-high and high-school students concerning their home backgrounds and socioeconomic status. Used to forecast educational achievement, dropout, and other academic criteria, and to gather biographical data on delinquents and children with behavioral problems.

Description: 22–item paper-pencil yes-no information blank for surveying students' home and family backgrounds. The information draws on four categories: social status of family, ownership and material possessions, socio-civic involvement, and cultural-aesthetic involvement. Scores may be obtained for each of the categories and also for the total to reflect overall socioeconomic status. The validity of these five scores depends on the accuracy of the information reported by the students. College students should be asked to report on their family/home life at the time they were in junior or senior high school. Not meaningful for adults except for Retrospective Appraisal of Childhood Status of Home. The norms provided are based on 4,381 junior and

---

senior high-school students in a nation-wide sample. Test users are furnished with copies of the manual, several reprints, and a copy of the blank from which additional copies can be made. Self-administered. Suitable for group use.

Untimed: 10 minutes

Scoring: Hand key

Cost: Free

Publisher: Harrison G. Gough/Institute of Personality Assessment and Research, University of California

---

HOW WELL DO YOU KNOW YOURSELF
Refer to page 180.

INFERRED SELF-CONCEPT SCALE
E.L. McDaniel

Child
Grades 1-6

Purpose: Evaluates the self-concept of children based on their behavior in school.

Description: 30–item paper-pencil inventory evaluating a child's self-concept. Based on observation of the child, a teacher or counselor familiar with the child rates him on a 5–point scale ranging from "never" to "always." With the aid of standardized scoring and interpretation, the child's self-concept is assessed based on this behavior profile. Administered by a teacher or counselor familiar with the child. Examiner required. Not suitable for group use.

Untimed: 15–20 minutes

Scoring: Hand key

Cost: Complete kit (100 scales, manual) $18.00

Publisher: Western Psychological Services

INTERPERSONAL COMMUNICATION INVENTORY (ICI)
Refer to page 182.

INVENTORY OF INDIVIDUALLY-PERCEIVED GROUP COHESIVENESS
Refer to page 1005.

KOHN PROBLEM CHECKLIST (KPC) RESEARCH EDITION
Martin Kohn

Child
Prek-K

Purpose: Assesses the presence or absence of behavior problems in children.

Description: 49–item paper-pencil unipolar behavior rating scale measuring the presence or absence of pathological behavior. The ratings of two teachers are combined to yield angry-defiant and apathetic-withdrawn behavior dimension scores. These scores can be merged with scores obtained on the Kohn Social Competence (KSC) Scale to yield pooled-instrument scores across the two scales. The test is available only to institutions with a staff member who has completed an advanced level course in testing from an accredited college or university. Registration is required. Examiner required. Not suitable for group use.

Untimed: 10 minutes or less

Scoring: Hand key

Cost: Complete kit (25 Ready-Score KPC answer sheets, 25 Ready-Score KSC answer sheets, 1 reusable item booklet with both KPC and KSC items, manual) $59.00

Publisher: The Psychological Corporation

Information and availability unconfirmed; last verified in 1988.

KOHN SOCIAL COMPETENCE SCALE (KSC) RESEARCH EDITION
Martin Kohn

Child
Prek-K

Purpose: Assesses the social-emotional functioning of young children.

Description: 64– or 73–item paper-pencil bipolar behavior rating scale measuring social competency along the following dimensions: cooperative-compliant versus angry-defiant and interest-participation versus apathetic-withdrawn. One or two teachers evaluate the child. Their scores are combined to produce scores along the bipolar behavior dimensions. Scores can be merged with scores from the Kohn Problem Checklist to yield pooled-instrument scores across the two scales. The 64–item version is designed for children enrolled in half-day programs, and the 73–item version for children in full-day programs. The test is available only to institutions with a staff member who has completed an advanced level course in testing from an accredited college or university. Registration is required. Examiner required. Not suitable for group use.

Untimed: 5–10 minutes

Scoring: Hand key

Cost: Manual $20.00; 25 Ready-Score answer sheets $17.00

Publisher: The Psychological Corporation

Information and availability unconfirmed; last verified in 1988.

LEWIS COUNSELING INVENTORY
Refer to page 188.

LIFE ADJUSTMENT INVENTORY
Ronald C. Doll and
J. Wayne Wrightstone

Adolescent
Grades 9–12

Purpose: Measures general adjustment to high-school curriculum. Used for curriculum surveys and diagnosis of maladjusted pupils for individual guidance.

Description: Multiple-item paper-pencil test of general adjustment to the high-school curriculum. The test measures the feeling of needing additional experiences in 13 specific areas, such as consumer education; religion, morals, and ethics; family living; vocational orientation and preparation; reading and study skills; and citizenship education. The test conforms

with the United States Office of Education's Life Adjustment Program. Examiner required. Suitable for group use.

Untimed: 25 minutes

Scoring: Hand key

Cost: Specimen set $5.00; 25 inventories $8.75

Publisher: Psychometric Affiliates

LIGHT'S RETENTION SCALE (LRS)
H. Wayne Light

Child, adolescent
Grades 1–12

Purpose: Determines whether an elementary- or secondary-school student would benefit from grade retention. Used for counseling and to guide parents and school staff.

Description: 19–category paper-pencil scale pinpointing such areas of concern as age, emotional and behavior problems, motivation, absenteeism, and presence of learning disabilities. Each factor is evaluated on a 5–point scale, and the total score is reduced to several "retention candidacy" categories that indicate whether the student is likely to benefit from retention. Materials include the Parent Guide to Grade Retention, a statement of factors to consider when deciding whether to retain a child. Examiner required. Not suitable for group use.

Untimed: 10–15 minutes

Scoring: Examiner evaluated

Cost: Manual $15.00; 50 recording forms $18.00; 50 parent guides $18.00

Publisher: Academic Therapy Publications

MISSOURI COMPREHENSIVE STUDENT NEEDS SURVEY

Adolescent
Grades 8–12

Purpose: Identifies the needs of high-school students so that guidance programs can be developed for individual students and groups of students with common needs.

Description: Multiple-item paper-pencil inventory providing information on the needs of students. Students rank 16 common needs on a scale of 1 (high) to 5 (low). Four reports are issued: classroom roster, individual student profile, group data (ranking of needs by category form), and group data (ranking of needs by item form). Self-administered. Suitable for group use.

Untimed: 1 hour

Scoring: Computer scored

Cost: Survey instrument $0.20; scoring service $0.24

Publisher: Center for Educational Assessment

NORMATIVE ADAPTIVE BEHAVIOR CHECKLIST (NABC)
Gary Adams

Ages 0–21 years

Purpose: Identifies individuals with adaptive behavior deficits, provides a norm-referenced evaluation of skills and abilities, and identifies individuals needing more comprehensive evaluation. Used for evaluation and placement in special programs and rounding out psychoeducational files.

Description: 120–item paper-pencil checklist of adaptive behavior skills in six categories: self-help skills, home living skills, independent living skills, social skills, sensorimotor skills, and language concepts/academic skills. The examiner checks off the skills the individual has mastered. Most of the checklist can be completed from memory; some interviews may be needed. The test may be administered by a classroom teacher or school psychologist. Examiner required. Not suitable for group use.

Untimed: 30 minutes

Scoring: Examiner evaluated

Cost: Complete program $23.00; components available individually

Publisher: The Psychological Corporation

Information and availability unconfirmed; last verified in 1988.

PHSF RELATIONS QUESTIONNAIRE—1970
A. Fouche and P.E. Grobbelaar

Child, adolescent

Purpose: Assesses adjustment level of high-school students. Used for counseling and guidance.

Description: Paper-pencil questionnaire of 12 aspects of personal adjustment, including self-confidence, self-esteem, self-control, nervousness, health, family influences, personal freedom, sociability-G, sociability-S, moral sense, formal relations, and a desirability scale. Examiner required. Suitable for group use.
SOUTH AFRICAN PUBLISHER

Untimed: 30 minutes

Scoring: Hand key; examiner evaluated; may be machine scored

Cost: (In Rands) test booklet 0,50; 10 answer sheets 1,00; 10 answer sheets (machine–3881) 2,10; scoring stencil 1, 2,50; scoring stencil 2, 3,00; manual 7,00; annexure to manual 4,00; appendix to manual 7,00; manual (Indian South African norms) 6,00; orders from outside the RSA will be dealt with on merit

Publisher: Human Sciences Research Council

PIKUNAS GRAPHOSCOPIC SCALE (PGS)
Refer to page 249.

===

PORTEOUS PROBLEM CHECKLIST
M. Porteous

Adolescent—Ages 11–17

Purpose: Assesses social, emotional, and personal problems of adolescents. Used by teachers, counselors, educational psychologists, and youth workers.

Description: 68–item paper-pencil screening and diagnostic test in nine sets assessing the degree and focus of young people's concerns. Using colloquial language, the tests center on problems related to parents, peers, employment, authority, symptoms, boy-girl, oppres-

sion, delinquency, and image. Examiner required. Suitable for group use.
BRITISH PUBLISHER
Untimed: 20–30 minutes
Scoring: Hand key
Cost: Contact publisher
Publisher: NFER-NELSON Publishing Company Ltd.

THE PORTLAND PROBLEM BEHAVIOR CHECKLIST—REVISED (PPBC-R)
Steven Waksman

Child, adolescent
Grades K–12

Purpose: Identifies problem behaviors of students. Used by teachers, mental health personnel, counselors, and childcare workers for evaluation, referral, or planning individual education programs or intervention programs.

Description: 29–item paper-pencil rating scale used by the examiner to identify conduct, academic, anxiety, peer, and personal problems of individual students. The results provide information for research and program evaluation, counseling or diagnostic services, parent conferences, and screening programs. Examiner required. Not suitable for group use.
Untimed: 5–10 minutes
Scoring: Examiner evaluated
Cost: Complete kit $49.00
Publisher: PRO-ED

PRE-MOD II
Joseph Kaplan and Sandy Kent

Handicapped students

Purpose: Diagnoses behavior problems and prescribes appropriate interventions. Used by teachers or specialists working with mildly to moderately handicapped children; also used by teachers of normal and slow learners in the regular classroom. Used to establish IEPs in the affective domain and social skills areas.

Description: Multiple-item computer-administered assessment instrument diagnosing the underlying causes of 10 of the most common behavior problems found in the classroom, including physical aggression, abusive-provocative language, noncompliance, and hyperactive-impulsive and withdrawn behavior. The program presents the teacher with a list of the 10 behaviors, from which the individual student's basic problems are identified. For each behavior identified, the program provides a socially appropriate behavior that is incompatible with the student's maladaptive behavior. The teacher then is presented with a list of prerequisite skills, knowledge, and attitudes necessary for the student to engage in the socially appropriate behavior. The teacher then identifies the prerequisites the student lacks and is provided with corresponding performance objectives and suggested interventions for each prerequisite the student lacks. Additional assessments are provided for determining the status of the prerequisites. The accompanying operator's manual is written in plain English.

The program may be used independently or in conjunction with the textbook *Beyond Behavior Modification* (Kaplan, 1983) as an instructional aid in teaching behavior management strategies. Examiner required. Not suitable for group use.
Untimed: Varies
Scoring: Computer scored
Cost: Software package for Apple II+ or IIe microcomputers (diskette, backup diskette, user's manual, 10 test sheets) $119.00
Publisher: PRO-ED

PRE-SCHOOL BEHAVIOUR CHECKLIST
J. McGuire and N. Richman

Child—Ages 2–5

Purpose: Identifies behavioral and emotional problems in preschoolers. Used in classroom settings by nursery school staffs to plan behavioral management programs. Also used by nurses and nursing assistants and clinical and educational psychologists.

Description: 22–item paper-pencil checklist in which the examiner assesses from four alternatives the degree to which the child exhibits behavior such as feeding, sleeping, soiling, tempers, fears, worries, and moods. Items are scored numerically for frequency and severity. Examiner required. Not suitable for group use. BRITISH PUBLISHER

Untimed: 10 minutes
Scoring: Examiner evaluated
Cost: Contact publisher
Publisher: NFER-NELSON Publishing Company Ltd.

PURPOSE IN LIFE (PIL)
Refer to page 213.

THE REVISED BEHAVIOR PROBLEM CHECKLIST (RBPC)
*Herbert C. Quay and
Donald R. Peterson*

Child, adolescent

Purpose: Assesses the nature of problem behavior. Used in educational, mental health, pediatric, and correctional settings as well as for research purposes.

Description: 85–item paper-pencil observational inventory consisting of statements about problem behaviors commonly seen in children and adolescents. Each item on the inventory is rated by a knowledgeable observer (parent, teacher, child-care worker, correctional staff member). Scores are provided for six subscales: conduct disorder, socialized aggression, attention problems-immaturity, anxiety-withdrawal, psychotic behavior, and motor excess. The 1987 manual provides a description of the test's development, data on reliability and validity, and means and standard deviations from various normal and clinical samples. Examiner required. Not suitable for group use.
Untimed: 15 minutes
Scoring: Hand key
Cost: Test kit (1987 manual, 50 tests, scoring stencil) $25.00
Publisher: Herbert C. Quay

REYNOLDS ADOLESCENT DEPRESSION SCALE (RADS)
Refer to page 214.

SCHOOL ENVIRONMENT PREFERENCE SURVEY
Refer to page 835.

SCHOOL INTEREST INVENTORY
Refer to page 757.

THE SCHOOL PLAY
E.M. Bower

**Child
Grades 3–7**

Purpose: Evaluates the peer perceptions and self-images of children. Identifies children with a low self-image and children whose self-image does not correspond to the perceptions of their peers. Used by classroom teachers to identify children needing further assistance or evaluation.

Description: 38–item paper-pencil peer-rating instrument in two sections. Section I (14 items) contains descriptions of 14 hypothetical roles in a play and instructions directing each student to choose the classmate who would be most suitable and natural in each of the roles. In Section II (24 items), students answer multiple-choice questions eliciting how the students see themselves in relation to each role. This test is the 1980 revision of A Class Play and is contained in *Early Identification of Emotionally Handicapped Children in School*, 3rd Edition. Examiner required. Suitable for group use.
Untimed: Varies
Scoring: Examiner evaluated
Cost: *Early Identification of Emotionally Handicapped Children in School*, 3rd Edition, 1982 $26.75
Publisher: Charles C. Thomas, Publisher

SCHOOL PROBLEM SCREENING INVENTORY, FIFTH EDITION
Refer to page 641.

SEARCH INSTITUTE PROFILES OF STUDENT LIFE: ATTITUDES AND BEHAVIORS
Refer to page 773.

THE SELF-PERCEPTION INVENTORY (SPI)
*Anthony T. Soares and
Louise M. Soares*

Grades 1–adult

Purpose: Assesses how an individual sees self, how the individual thinks others see him, and how others do see him. Used to determine the need for counseling and as a counseling tool for personality assessment.

Description: Multiple-item paper-pencil test in four categories: students (10 forms), adults (11 forms), nurses (7 forms), and teachers (10 forms). The student forms are self-concept—how the individual sees self; reflected self-classmates—how the individual thinks classmates see him; reflected self-teachers—how the individual thinks teachers see him; reflected self-parents—how the individual thinks parents see him; ideal concept—the kind of person the individual would like to be; perceptions of others—others rate the male individuals, others rate the female individuals; student-self—how the individual sees self as a student; perceptions of others-student-self—how others see the individual as a student (male and female). The adult, nursing, and teacher forms are similar. Students are measured against 20 pairs of bipolar traits; adults, nurses, and teachers are measured against 36 pairs of traits. The subject rates the subject on each pair of traits by marking appropriately within a four-space scale. Self-administered. Suitable for group use. Available in French, Italian, and Spanish.

Untimed: 5–10 minutes per scale

Scoring: Hand key

Cost: Specimen set (indicate level) $14.00

Publisher: SOARES Associates

SELF PROFILE Q-SORT (SPQS)
Alan J. Politte

Child, adolescent
Grades 2 and above

Purpose: Assesses student's feelings toward self. Used for elementary-school counseling.

Description: 63–item test of self-perception in which the child indicates whether or not each item describes his feelings. The test is administered orally to younger children; older children may read the items themselves. Examiner required. Suitable for group use.

Untimed: 10 minutes

Scoring: Examiner evaluated

Cost: Specimen set $4.50; 25 forms $6.75

Publisher: Psychologists and Educators, Inc.

SIXTEEN PERSONALITY FACTOR QUESTIONNAIRE
Refer to page 221.

SOCIAL BEHAVIOR ASSESSMENT (SBA)
Refer to page 774.

SOCIAL-EMOTIONAL DIMENSION SCALE (SEDS)
*Jerry B. Hutton and
Timothy G. Roberts*

Child, adolescent—Ages
5.5–18.5

Purpose: Identifies students who may have conduct disorders or emotional disturbance behavior problems. Used by teachers, counselors, and psychologists.

Description: 32–item test assessing inappropriate behaviors of students, including physical/fear reaction, depressive reaction, avoidance of peer interaction, avoidance of teacher interaction, inappropriate behaviors, and aggressive interaction. The test provides percentiles and standard scores. Examiner required. Not suitable for group use.

Timed: Not available

Scoring: Examiner evaluated

Cost: Complete kit (examiner's manual, 50 profile/record sheets, storage box) $44.00

Publisher: PRO-ED

SOCIAL RETICENCE SCALE (SRS)
Refer to page 223.

STRESS RESPONSE SCALE
Louis A. Chandler

Child, adolescent—Ages 5–14

Purpose: Assesses the emotional status of children ages 5–14 with nonorganic and mild to moderate emotional problems. Used in schools and clinics for screening and diagnosis.

Description: 40–item paper-pencil inventory indicating the maladaptive coping efforts of children. Adults rate children on a 6–point scale. The test is based on a model that predicts five behavior styles: acting out, overactive, passive-aggressive, repressed, and dependent. Test results may be profiled to suggest the child's preferred response pattern. The test should not be used with the mentally retarded, psychoneurologically learning disabled, or severely emotionally handicapped. A computer scoring program is available for IBM PC or Apple II systems. Examiner required. Not suitable for group use.

Untimed: Varies

Scoring: Hand key; may be computer scored

Cost: Sample kit (manual, set of forms) $18.50

Publisher: Louis A. Chandler, Ph.D.

STUDENT EVALUATION SCALE (SES)
Refer to page 758.

SUICIDAL IDEATION QUESTIONNAIRE (SIQ)
Refer to page 225.

SURVEY OF PERSONAL VALUES
Refer to page 1030.

TASKS OF EMOTIONAL DEVELOPMENT TEST (TED)
Haskel Cohen and Geraldine Weil

Child, adolescent—Ages 6–18

Purpose: Detects potential child behavior problems. Used to determine reasons for student learning difficulties.

Description: Multiple-item oral-response projective test consisting of 49 photographs of children, each designed to represent a selected task of emotional development. The test measures 13 factors: socialization, aggression, trust, academic learning, conscious of property of others, identification with same-sex parent, separation from mother figure, acceptance of limits from adults, acceptance of siblings, acceptance of affection between parents, attitudes toward orderliness/cleanliness, positive self-concept, and positive heterosexual socialization. Responses are rated in five dimensions: perception, outcome, affect, motivation, and spontaneity. Four sets of photographs are provided: 12 photographs each for boys and girls ages 6–11 and 13 photographs each for boys and girls ages 12–18. Each set provides essentially the same stimuli with variations for age and sex. The test kit includes 49 photo cards and a manual containing instructions and rating scales for each photo. The book *Tasks of Emotional Development*, which discusses construction of the test and rating scales and includes sample stories scored according to the rating scales, is available also. Examiner required. Not suitable for group use.

Untimed: Not available

Scoring: Examiner evaluated

Cost: Complete set $35.00; textbook $18.00

Publisher: T.E.D. Associates

Information and availability unconfirmed; last verified in 1987.

TEST ANXIETY INVENTORY (RESEARCH EDITION) (TAI)
Charles D. Spielberger

Adolescent, adult
Grades 10 and above

Purpose: Measures individual differences in test-taking anxiety. Used for research.

Description: 20–item paper-pencil test of two major components of test anxiety: worry and emotionality. Respondents report how frequently they experience specific anxiety symptoms in examination situations. Similar in structure and concept to the T-Anxiety scale of the State-Trait Anxiety Inventory. May be self-administered. Suitable for group use.

Untimed: 5–10 minutes

Scoring: Hand key

Cost: Manual $4.50; key $1.25; 25 expendable tests $3.50

Publisher: Consulting Psychologists Press, Inc.

TEST OF EARLY SOCIOEMOTIONAL DEVELOPMENT (TOESD)
Wayne P. Hresko and Linda Brown

Child—Ages 3–7.11

Purpose: Evaluates the behavior of children. Identifies children with behavior problems and the setting in which the problems most often occur. Also used with children who are learning disabled and mentally retarded.

Description: Four multiple-item paper-pencil and oral-response components assessing problem behaviors in children. The 30–item Student Rating Scale is completed by the student; the 34–item Parent Rating Scale is completed by the parent(s); and the 36–item Teacher Rating Scale is completed by the teacher or other professionals who interact with the child in a school setting. A sociogram provides information about peer perceptions of the child being evaluated. Results discriminate among normal, behavior-disordered, learning-disabled, and mentally retarded children. All four components yield percentile ranks, standard scores, and scale raw scores. This instrument is a downward extension of the Behavior Rating Profile (BRP) and resembles the BRP in both form and content. Examiner required. Not suitable for group use.

Untimed: Varies

Scoring: Examiner evaluated

Cost: Complete kit (manual, 50 student rating forms, 50 parent rating forms, 50 teacher rating forms, storage box) $67.00

Publisher: PRO-ED

THERAPY ATTITUDE INVENTORY (TAI)
Refer to page 81.

WALKER-MCCONNELL SCALE OF SOCIAL COMPETENCE AND SCHOOL ADJUSTMENT
Refer to page 777.

WALKER PROBLEM BEHAVIOR IDENTIFICATION CHECKLIST, REVISED 1983
Hill M. Walker

Child
Grades PreK–6

Purpose: Identifies children with behavior problems. Used to evaluate children for counseling and possible referral.

Description: 50–item paper-pencil true-false inventory consisting of behavior statements that are applied to the child being rated. The checklist can be completed by anyone familiar with the child, although it is used primarily by teachers. The test provides a Total Score, a cutoff score for classifying children as disturbed, and scores for the following five scales: Acting-Out, Withdrawal, Distractibility, Disturbed Peer Relations, and Immaturity. Examiner required. Suitable for group use.

Untimed: 5 minutes

Scoring: Hand key

Cost: Complete kit (pad of 200 checklists—100 each male and female, manual) $40.00

Publisher: Western Psychological Services

Student Evaluation and Counseling: Student Attitudes

ARLIN-HILLS ATTITUDE SURVEYS
Marshall Arlin and David Hills

Child, adolescent
Grades K–12

Purpose: Assesses student attitudes. Used for research on student attitudes.

Description: Four 15–item paper-pencil questionnaires measuring student attitudes in the following areas: attitude toward teachers, attitude toward learning, attitude toward language, and attitude toward arithmetic. Items are presented in a cartoon format. Because group results are used, the four instruments may be distributed at random to students within a classroom. Each instrument is divided into three levels: Primary for Grades K–3, Elementary for Grades 4–6, and High School for Grades 7–12. Computer scoring is recommended for groups. Examiner required. Suitable for group use.

Untimed: 5–10 minutes

Scoring: Hand key; may be computer scored

Cost: Contact publisher

Publisher: Psychologists and Educators, Inc.

ATTITUDE TOWARD SCHOOL QUESTIONNAIRE (ASQ)
G.P. Strickland, R. Hoepfner, and S.P. Klein

Child
Grades K–3

Purpose: Assesses children's attitudes toward school. Used to evaluate affective programs and for research on young children's attitudes toward school.

Description: 15–item paper-pencil test measuring attitudes toward school, school work, show-and-tell activities, reading, math, authority, peers, and playing. Children view cartoons depicting school situations while English narrations are read. The children then are asked how they feel about each situation and respond by circling a happy, neutral, or unhappy face. Reading and number skills are not required because each item is on a separate page that is colored rather than numbered. The child must know the five basic colors in order to follow along. The colored pages aid teachers in ensuring that all students are working on the same item. The people in the cartoons are racially ambiguous so children of various racial groups can equally identify with the figures. The girls' form and the boys' form feature same-sex main characters. Examiner required. Suitable for group use.

Timed: 20 minutes

Scoring: Hand key

Cost: Specimen set $10.00; 20 questionnaires (10 female, 10 male) $28.00; manual $5.00

Publisher: Monitor

ATTITUDE TOWARDS DISABLED PERSONS SCALE (ATDP)
H.E. Yuker and J.R. Block

Students, adults

Purpose: Assesses attitudes toward disabled persons. Used to evaluate mainstreaming in the schools, hiring of disabled persons, and methods of changing attitudes toward the disabled. Used with teachers, employers, counselors, physicians, and students who interact with disabled individuals.

Description: Multiple-item paper-pencil inventory assessing the attitudes of either disabled or nondisabled persons toward disabled persons. The inventory is available in three forms: Form O (20 items), Form A (30 items), and Form B (30 items). Examiner required. Suitable for group use.

Untimed: 15 minutes

Scoring: Hand key; may be computer scored

Cost: Complete manual (copies of three forms, scoring instructions, literature review) $10.00

Publisher: Center for the Study of Attitudes Toward Persons with Disabilities, Hofstra University

BLOOM SENTENCE COMPLETION ATTITUDE SURVEY
Refer to page 160.

CANADIAN COMPREHENSIVE ASSESSMENT PROGRAM: SCHOOL ATTITUDE MEASURE (SAM)

Child, adolescent Grades 4-9

Purpose: Evaluates students' affective responses to their school experience. Used for program development, individual education planning, selection and placement of students for particular programs, guidance planning, and developing instructional standards and objectives.

Description: Multidimensional self-report survey instrument developed to evaluate students' affective responses to their school experience and to establish students' self-perception as competent learners. The instrument's three levels provide information on five attitude levels: motivation for schooling, academic self-concept, reference-based, student's sense of control over performance, and student's instructional mastery. Examiner required. Suitable for group use.
CANADIAN PUBLISHER
Timed: Varies
Scoring: Machine scored
Cost: Review kit $12.25
Publisher: Guidance Centre

Information and availability unconfirmed; last verified in 1987.

CHAPIN SOCIAL INSIGHT TEST
F. Stuart Chapin

High-school students, adult

Purpose: Measures the social insight of high-school and college students and adults.

Description: 25-item paper-pencil test assessing an individual's ability to diagnose a situation involving human interaction. Individuals with this ability recognize the dynamics underlying a described behavior or choose the wisest course of action to resolve a difficulty. The test was devised in 1942, first published in 1968, and currently is distributed with a reprint summarizing recent validation studies. Available until present supply is exhausted. Examiner required. Suitable for group use.
Untimed: Not available
Scoring: Hand key
Cost: 25 situations booklets $8.00; 50 response booklets $11.50; manual $5.25
Publisher: Consulting Psychologists Press, Inc.

CLASSROOM SOCIOMETRIC ANALYSIS KIT
E. Myers

Child, adolescent Grades 3-12

Purpose: Measures students' attitudes of social acceptance or rejection based on the expressed preferences of their classmates. Used by classroom teachers.

Description: Multiple-item paper-pencil test assessing the sociometric aspect of classroom dynamics. The test is available in two forms, A and B. Form A contains one work and one play question already printed on the pupil questionnaires. In Form B, the sociometric questions are blank to allow the teacher to develop questions and print them on the questionnaire. A manual is available. Examiner required. Suitable for group use.
Untimed: Not available
Scoring: Examiner evaluated
Cost: Contact publisher
Publisher: Educational Research Council of America

Information and availability unconfirmed; last verified in 1987.

COMPREHENSIVE ASSESSMENT PROGRAM: SCHOOL ATTITUDE MEASURE, FORM A

*Lawrence J. Dolan and
Marci Morrow Enos*

**Child, adolescent
Grades 4–12**

Purpose: Evaluates students' views of their academic environment and of themselves as competent students.

Description: Multiple-item measure of five affective dimensions of the student: motivation for schooling; academic self-concept, performance-based; academic self-concept, reference-based; sense of control over performance; and sense of instructional mastery. The test is available for three levels: Grades 4–6, Grades 7–8, and Grades 9–12. Items may be read to young students provided no interpretive comment is made. National and local percentile ranks are provided. Examiner required. Suitable for group use. Available in Spanish.

Untimed: Not available

Scoring: Computer scored

Cost: 5 pupil booklets (specify level) $30.10; 35 answer sheets $10.80; manual $8.75; 35 profiles $8.20

Publisher: American Testronics

COMPREHENSIVE ASSESSMENT PROGRAM: SCHOOL ATTITUDE MEASURE (SAM), 2ND EDITION

Marci M. Enos

**Child, adolescent—Ages
5–18**

Purpose: Assesses student attitude as it relates to school achievement. Used for identifying students at risk.

Description: Five-level multiple-choice paper-pencil test divided into five scales: Motivation for Schooling, Academic Self-Concept—Performance Based, Academic Self-Concept—Reference Based, Student's Sense of Control over Performance, and Student's Instructional Mastery. Each scale consists of a set of statements followed by four response choices: never agree, sometimes agree, usually agree, and always agree. Level C/D is used with Grades 1–2, Level E/F with Grades 3–4, Level G/H with Grades 5–6, Level I/J with Grades 7–8, and Level K/L with Grades 9–12. Raw scores are transformed by statistical analysis using the Rasch model, providing the user with both raw scores and logit scores derived through the Rasch analysis, facilitating comparison between student scores and the scores on the five scales. This is one test in the Comprehensive Assessment Program series and is a revision of the 1980 SAM. Examiner required. Suitable for group use.

Timed: Varies by level

Scoring: Machine scored; hand key; scoring available through publisher

Cost: 25 machine-scorable test booklets Levels C/D and E $37.10; 25 reusable test booklets Levels E–L $28.75; 35 answer sheets $12.40; directions $3.90

Publisher: American Testronics

CONSERVATISM-RADICALISM OPINIONAIRE (C-R)

Theodore F. Lentz and colleagues

**Adolescent, adult
Grades 13 and above**

Purpose: Measures character and disposition along conservatism-radicalism dimension. Used in college and adult courses in political psychology and political science.

Description: 60–item paper-pencil test measuring the conservative-radical attitudes of the subject, who is asked to agree or disagree with each statement by marking it plus or minus. Self-administered. Suitable for group use.

Untimed: 30 minutes

Scoring: Hand key

Cost: Manual, sample of opinionaire $1.00; quantity discounts available upon request

Publisher: Lentz Peace Research Laboratory

COUNSELING SERVICES ASSESSMENT BLANK (CSAB)
James C. Hurst and Richard G. Weigel

College student

Purpose: Assesses client reaction to counseling services. Used in the evaluation of counseling centers.

Description: Paper-pencil test providing client assessment and feedback about counseling services. Materials include a manual providing information about the use and interpretation of results of the CSAB. Examiner/self-administered. Suitable for group use.

Untimed: 15 minutes

Scoring: Hand key

Cost: 100 test blanks $14.00; manual $15.00

Publisher: Rocky Mountain Behavioral Science Institute, Inc.

CPRI QUESTIONNAIRES (Q-71, Q-74, Q-75, Q-76)
William Eckhardt

Adolescent, adult Grades 10 and above

Purpose: Measures personality, ideology, and philosophy. Used by high schools, colleges, churches, and civic clubs.

Description: 240-item paper-pencil test in four sections covering the following categories: conformity, nationalism, responsibility, religiosity, impulsivity, bureaucracy, neuroticism, militarism, misanthropy, morality, discipline, capitalism, humanism, egoism, authoritarianism, fatalism, justice, imperialism, and mysticism. The person rates each item on a 5-point scale ranging from "strongly disagree" to "strongly agree." Self-administered. Suitable for group use. Available in Spanish, German, Hindi, Dutch, Belgian, Urdu, and Bengali.

Untimed: 15-30 minutes

Scoring: Hand key

Cost: Manual (including background and interpretive material), 4 questionnaires, answer sheets, scoring instructions, norms $5.00; questionnaires and answer sheets may be reproduced at no further charge

Publisher: Lentz Peace Research Laboratory

CULTURE-FREE SELF-ESTEEM INVENTORIES
Refer to page 236.

THE EDUCATIONAL PROCESS QUESTIONNAIRE (EPQ)
Refer to page 853.

EVALUATED DISPOSITION TOWARD THE ENVIRONMENT (EDEN)
Norman J. Milchus

Adolescent Grades 7-13

Purpose: Assesses the strength of a student's environmental values. Used for self-insight and program evaluation.

Description: 70-item paired-comparison test measuring the following values: aesthetic, experiential, knowledge-seeking, responsible, prudent (conservation ethic), active, and practical. Students pick one of the pair of activities they prefer. The test uses a 5-point Likert-type scale. Examiner required. Suitable for group use.

Untimed: 30-40 minutes

Scoring: Computer scored

Cost: Specimen set $3.25; 20 inventory booklets $22.00; 20 response sheets $3.25; computer scoring $1.00 (minimum $60.00)

Publisher: Person-O-Metrics, Inc.

THE INTEREST-A-LYZER
Joseph S. Renzulli

Child, adolescent

Purpose: Examines the present and potential interests of upper-elementary and junior high-school students. Used as a basis for group discussions and in-depth counseling.

Description: Multiple-item paper-pencil instrument consisting of a series of open-ended questions structured to highlight general patterns of interest. Items cover mathematical, historical, political, scientific, artistic, and technical interest areas. Examiner required. Suitable for group use.

Untimed: Varies

Scoring: Examiner evaluated

Cost: 100 questionnaires $25.95

Publisher: Creative Learning Press, Inc.

INTERPERSONAL STYLE INVENTORY (ISI)
Refer to page 183.

IRENOMETER
Refer to page 393.

KATZ-ZALK OPINION QUESTIONNAIRE
Phyllis Katz and Sue Rosenberg Zalk

Child
Grades 1–6

Purpose: Measures racial attitudes in children. Used in research to assess change in attitudes.

Description: 55–item paper-pencil test measuring the racial attitudes of children. The test contains 38 race-related questions and 17 buffer items that provide a measure of gender attitudes. The child is shown a slide of two or four children interacting and is asked to mark the box under the child credited with a positive or negative act or attribute. The test only assesses attitudes towards black children and white children. Examiner required. Suitable for group use.

Untimed: 30–60 minutes

Scoring: Hand key

Cost: Booklet $1.00; slides $75.00; large orders are discounted

Publisher: Sue Rosenberg Zalk and Phyllis Katz

LEADERSHIP SKILLS INVENTORY
Frances A. Karnes and Jane C. Chauvin

Child, adolescent
Grades 4–12

Purpose: Assesses leadership abilities of students. Used by students, teachers, consultants, curriculum planners, and teacher-trainers.

Description: Multiple-item paper-pencil or computer-administered inventory assessing fundamentals of leadership, written and oral communication, group dynamics, problem-solving, personal development, decision-making, and planning abilities. The results help students understand and develop leadership abilities. The inventory may be used for pre- and postevaluation. An activities manual is included. Self-administered. Suitable for group use.

Untimed: Varies

Scoring: Self-scored

Cost: Complete kit $45.95; computer version $19.95

Publisher: D.O.K. Publishers, Inc.

LEARNING STYLE IDENTIFICATION SCALE (LSIS)
Paul J. Malcom, William C. Lutz, Mary A. Gerken, and Gary M. Hoeltke

Child

Purpose: Assesses the manner in which students prefer to learn. Used with low-functioning, average, and gifted students for academic planning.

Description: 24–item paper-pencil observational inventory assessing classroom behaviors related to students' preferred learning styles. The scale measures the extent to which a student relies on internal sources of information (feelings, beliefs, and attitudes) and external sources of information (other people, events, and social institutions). It also identifies five learning styles based on the student's preferred manner of reacting to situations and solving problems. The handbook contains directions for administering, scoring, and profiling the scale; teaching guidelines, techniques, and activities for each learning style; data on test development, reliability, and validity; factor analyses; and rating differences by grade and sex. Examiner required. Suitable for group use.

Untimed: 15 minutes

Scoring: Examiner evaluated

Cost: Handbook and 30 rating, scoring, and profiling forms $30.00; 30 rating, scoring, and profiling forms $11.00

Publisher: CTB/Macmillan/McGraw-Hill

LEARNING STYLE INVENTORY (LSI)
Rita Dunn, Kenneth Dunn, and Gary E. Price

Child, adolescent
Grades 3–12

Purpose: Identifies students' preferred learning environments. Used for designing instructional environments and counseling.

Description: 104–item paper-pencil or computer-administered Likert scale test assessing the conditions under which students prefer to learn. Individual preferences are measured in the following areas: immediate environment (sound, heat, light, and design), emotionality (motivation, responsibility, persistence, and structure), sociological needs (self-oriented, peer-oriented, adult-oriented, or combined ways), and physical needs (perceptual preferences, time of day, food intake, and mobility). Test items consist of statements about how people like to learn. Students indicate whether they agree or disagree with each item.

Results identify student preferences and indicate the degree to which a student's responses are consistent. Suggested strategies for instructional and environmental alternatives are provided to complement the student's revealed learning style.

Computerized results are available in three forms: individual profile (raw scores for each of the 22 areas, standard scores, and a plot for each score in each area),

group summary (identifies students with significantly high or low scores and groups individuals with similar preferences), and a subscale summary.

The computer-administered version (LSI-C) operates on Apple or IBM PC or compatible systems. Items are presented via the screen. The profile is available on-screen and in hard copy format if the student has access to a printer. The program records responses, enabling testing to resume at the point at which it was interrupted. Several additional options are available for the Group Summary when the inventory is computer-administered. Users with access to a 3000 or 3051 NCS scanner may purchase a program that scans completed LSI forms and generates an on-site printout of results. The scanner must be hooked up to an IBM PC or compatible computer.

The test is available on two levels: Grades 3–4 and Grades 5–12. Self-administered. Suitable for group use. Available in French, Hindi, and Spanish.

Untimed: 30 minutes

Scoring: Computer scored

Cost: Specimen set (manual, research report, inventory booklet, answer sheet) $12.00; diskette (100 administrations per licensing agreement) $295.00; each additional 100 administrations $60.00; NCS scanner program $395.00; 100 answer sheets for NCS scanner program $60.00

Publisher: Price Systems, Inc.

Information and availability unconfirmed; last verified in 1988.

LEARNING STYLES INVENTORY (LSI)
Albert A. Canfield

Adolescent, adult

Purpose: Identifies an individual's preferred learning methods. Identifies individuals with little or no interest in independent or unstructured learning situations. Used in conjunction with the Canfield Instructional Style Inventory to maximize teaching and learning efficiency.

Description: 30–item paper-pencil forced-rank inventory measuring individual learning needs (interacting with others, goal setting, competition, friendly relations with instructor, independence in study, classroom authority); preferred mediums (listening, reading, viewing pictures, graphs, slides, or direct experience); and areas of interest (numeric concepts, qualitative concepts, working with inanimate things and people). The inventory also indicates student perceptions as to how they will perform in the learning situation and identifies learning problems associated with either traditional or innovative teaching methods. The test is available in two forms: Form S-A for use with most adults and Form E for use with persons whose reading level is as low as the fifth grade. The test booklets are reusable. Separate norms are available for males and females. Self-administered. Suitable for group use.

Untimed: 30 minutes

Scoring: Self-scored

Cost: Kit $55.00

Publisher: Western Psychological Services

MINNESOTA SCHOOL ATTITUDE SURVEY (MSAS)
Andrew Ahlgren

Child, adolescent
Grades 1–12

Purpose: Measures students' feelings and attitudes toward a range of school experiences. Shows way to identify problems and suggests changes.

Description: Multiple-item paper-pencil survey in two levels: a lower level for Grades 1–3 and an upper level for Grades 4–12. Each level has two parts. Part 1 assesses affective reactions to academic subjects, school personnel, self-expression, peers, and various learning modes and situations. Part 2 assesses feelings of support, pressure, motivation, acceptance/exclusion, cooperation/competition, and self-worth. The survey provides information on the impact of instructional programs and school climate on attitudes and feelings, helps with understanding of learning patterns and behavior, and indicates problem areas. No printed score reports are available. A microcomputer display package is available for Apple II,

II+, and IIe with 48K memory, DOS 3.3, and a single disk drive. Color monitor and an Apple Silentype or graphics printer with a Grappler Plus interface also is required. Examiner required. Suitable for group use.

Untimed: 30–40 minutes

Scoring: Computer scoring by publisher only

Cost: Complete kit (scoring, general manual, instructions for administrators per 25 answer sheets) $1.60 per student; $180.00 per diskette for microcomputer display of results

Publisher: SRA/London House

MOTIVATION ANALYSIS TEST (MAT)
Refer to page 1013.

PURDUE STUDENT-TEACHER OPINIONAIRE—FORM B (PSTO)
Refer to page 858.

QUALITY OF SCHOOL LIFE SCALE (QSL)
Joyce L. Epstein with
James M. McPartland

Child, adolescent
Grades 4–12

Purpose: Assesses student's feelings about the school environment. Used to study and evaluate the social, task, and authority structures of schools and classrooms.

Description: Multiple-item paper-pencil test measuring student's school satisfaction, commitment to classwork, and reactions to teachers. Subscores are provided for each area. The technical manual summarizes research on the scale, provides reliability and validity data, and item-to-scale and item-to-test correlations. The scale is intended for use with local norms or in a criterion-referenced framework. Examiner required. Suitable for group use.

Untimed: 20 minutes

Scoring: Hand key

Cost: Test kit (35 questionnaire folders, manual, scoring key) $13.47

Publisher: The Riverside Publishing Company

QUEST: A LIFE CHOICE INVENTORY
Norman J. Milchus, D. Rodwell, and O. Mumey

Child, adolescent
Grades 9–12

Purpose: Measures the impact of value clarification in career education, substance abuse prevention, and positive group mental health programs on high-school students. Used to provide an overall assessment of school climate.

Description: 40–item paper-pencil Likert-type scale measuring needs recognition, value clarification, adaptive autonomy, perception of reality, and self-worth. Self-administered. Suitable for group use.

Untimed: 30 minutes

Scoring: Computer scored

Cost: Specimen set $3.00; computer scoring $1.25 each (minimum $75.00)

Publisher: Person-O-Metrics, Inc.

SCHOOL INTEREST INVENTORY
William C. Cottle

Adolescent
Grades 7–12

Purpose: Assesses an adolescent's school-related attitudes and interests. Identifies potential school dropouts. Used for counseling and program planning.

Description: 150–item paper-pencil inventory surveying student attitudes and interests in order to identify students with a high potential for dropping out of school. Weighted and unweighted scores may be obtained for males and females by using the appropriate scoring mask. The manual contains information about the development of the test, validity studies used to develop the scale, scoring, interpretation, and use. Examiner required. Suitable for group use.

Untimed: 20 minutes

Scoring: Hand key

Cost: 100 test booklets $52.38; manual $3.63; set of 2 scoring masks $5.31

Publisher: The Riverside Publishing Company

SEARCH INSTITUTE PROFILES OF STUDENT LIFE: ALCOHOL AND OTHER DRUGS
Refer to page 24.

SEARCH INSTITUTE PROFILES OF STUDENT LIFE: ATTITUDES AND BEHAVIORS
Refer to page 773.

SEARCH INSTITUTE PROFILES OF STUDENT LIFE: SEXUALITY
Search Institute

Adolescent—Ages 11–18
Grades 6–12

Purpose: Assesses student attitudes, knowledge, and behaviors concerning sexuality. Used as baseline information for programming in public and private schools and youth-serving agencies.

Description: 111–item paper-pencil survey on sexuality-related issues such as reproductive facts and myths, students' values, and other predictors of health and well-being. The test assesses students' understanding of the risks involved in too-early sexual activity. It also considers patterns of decision-making and student interest in programs that schools and communities might provide. This is one survey in the Search Institute Profiles of Student Life Series. It is a modified version of a test created as part of a 5–year study funded by the U.S. Department of Health and Human Services. Examiner required. Suitable for group use.

Untimed: 30 minutes

Scoring: Machine scored

Cost: System $2,500.00; charge per student $1.25

Publisher: Search Institute

SELF-ESTEEM QUESTIONNAIRE (SEQ-3)
Refer to page 252.

STUDENT ADJUSTMENT INVENTORY
James R. Barclay

**Child, adolescent
Grades 5–14**

Purpose: Assesses students' understanding of their own attitudes and feelings that may interfere with learning and school adjustment.

Description: 78–item computer-administered or paper-pencil inventory yielding scores in self-esteem, group interaction, self-discipline, communication, energy/effort, learning/studying, and attitude towards the learning environment. This test is a revision of The Barclay Learning Needs Assessment Inventory. Materials include test booklet, answer sheet, and IBM PC compatible computer software. Self-administered. Suitable for group use.

Untimed: 30 minutes

Scoring: Computer scored; hand key; mail-in service

Cost: Complete kit (disk, 10 reusable booklets, 50 answer sheets) $213.00; mail-in report kit (manual, 2 booklets, 5 answer sheets, 5 report processings) $29.75

Publisher: MetriTech, Inc.

STUDENT EVALUATION SCALE (SES)
William T. Martin and Sue Martin

Ages 6–21

Purpose: Assesses attitudes and behaviors of elementary- and secondary-school children. Used to evaluate educational and social-emotional responses to school.

Description: 52–item paper-pencil test of two areas of student attitudes: educational response and social-emotional response. Items are rated by teachers or guidance personnel after observing students for a

2– to 3–week period. The rating scale ranges from 0 (never) to 3 (always). Self-administered. Suitable for group use.

Untimed: 5 minutes

Scoring: Examiner evaluated

Cost: Specimen set (includes manual) $5.00; 25 rating and profile forms $6.75

Publisher: Psychologists and Educators, Inc.

STUDENT MOTIVATION DIAGNOSTIC QUESTIONNAIRE
*Kevin M. Matthews and
Carvin L. Brown*

**Child, adolescent—Ages
5–18
Grades K–12**

Purpose: Assesses student motivation.

Description: 64–item paper-pencil multiple-choice test assessing student motivation. Each of the student's subject area's are assessed by four subtests: Teacher Expectation, Student Self-Concept of Ability, Future Utility of Subject, and Student Attitude Toward Teacher. The test is used by schools to determine teacher motivation, which also affects student motivation. Examiner required. Suitable for group use.

Untimed: Varies

Scoring: Machine scored; may be computer scored

Cost: 25 forms $24.95

Publisher: Humanics Psychological Test Corporation, A Division of Humanics Limited

Information and availability unconfirmed; last verified in 1988.

STUDENT OPINION INVENTORY
National Study of School Evaluation

**Child, adolescent—Ages
9–20
Grades 4–12**

Purpose: Assesses students' opinions of their school and its programs. Provides students with an opportunity to make direct recommendations. Used by school personnel as part of a complete school evaluation process.

Description: 46–item multiple-choice paper-pencil opinion survey consisting of two parts. Part A contains 38 multiple-choice items assessing students' attitudes toward various aspects of the school. Part B contains 8 open-ended questions constructed for students to make direct recommendations for school improvement. The Administrator's Manual describes the development of the instrument, provides instructions for administering the inventory, and includes single copies of both Parts A and B. The inventory may be administered independently as a measure of student attitudes and morale or in conjunction with the Teacher Opinion Inventory, the Parent Opinion Inventory, or as a part of a complete school evaluation process. Individuals with physical, hearing, or visual impairments may complete the inventory with the assistance of a non-impaired individual. A seventh-grade reading level is required. A scoring service is available from the Bureau of Evaluative Studies and Testing, Indiana University, Bloomington, Indiana 47405 (812) 335–1595. This test is the 1988 revision of the Student Opinion Inventory. Examiner/self-administered. Suitable for group use.

Untimed: Varies

Scoring: Computer scored; may be machine scored; may be self-scored

Cost: 50 copies Part A $6.50; 50 copies of Part B $4.50; manual $4.50

Publisher: National Study of School Evaluation

Information and availability unconfirmed; last verified in 1988.

STUDENT ORIENTATIONS SURVEY (S.O.S.)
Barry R. Morstain

Adolescent, adult

Purpose: Assesses students' attitudes toward educational policies. Used for research on orientations toward philosophies, purposes, and processes related to a college education.

Description: 80–item paper-pencil measure of 10 aspects of student orientations toward college: achievement, assignment learning, assessment, affiliation, affirma-

tion, inquiry, independent study, interaction, informal association, and involvement. Items are statements that are rated on a modified Likert scale. Self-administered. Suitable for group use. Available in Spanish.

Untimed: 20 minutes

Scoring: Computer scored

Cost: S.O.S. OpScan form scoring (researcher receives an overall group printout and a scored data deck) $0.50

Publisher: Barry R. Morstain, Ph.D.

Information and availability unconfirmed; last verified in 1987.

STUDENT PROFILE AND ASSESSMENT RECORD (SPAR)
Theodore K. Miller and Roger B. Winston, Jr.

College students—Ages 17–23

Purpose: Assesses perceptions of entering college students. Used by academic advisors, counselors, residence hall staff, and others.

Description: Multiple-item paper-pencil comprehensive self-assessment tool providing information in six categories: general (home address, marital status, disabilities, need for financial assistance, emergency contact person); academic (perceptions of subjects, decision about major, noncredit academic interests and long-range plans, instructional approach preference, academic strengths and weaknesses); career; health and wellness; activities and organizations; and special concerns and other considerations. The SPAR folder has space for recording the student's test profile, high-school academic record, and other pertinent information, including educational goals and objectives. The instrument is useful in the initial phases of orientation. It is recommended for use in conjunction with the Student Developmental Task Inventory. Self-administered. Not suitable for group use.

Untimed: Varies

Scoring: Self-scored

Cost: 50 folders $20.00

Publisher: Student Development Associates, Inc.

SURVEY OF SCHOOL ATTITUDES (SSA)
Thomas P. Hogan

Child, adolescent
Grades 1–8

Purpose: Assesses children's reaction to major areas of school curriculum. Used for determining instructional presentation in curriculum programs.

Description: Multiple-item paper-pencil test of reactions to four areas of school curriculum: reading and language arts, mathematics, science, and social studies. Each area is represented by 15 activities characteristic of the curriculum. Students indicate whether they like, dislike, or feel neutral toward each activity. The test is divided into two levels: Primary (Grades 1–3) and Intermediate (Grades 4–8). The primary-level items are dictated by the teacher. The intermediate-level items are sentence stems read by the student. Two alternate and equivalent forms, A and B, are available. Examiner required. Suitable for group use.

Untimed: Primary 40 minutes in two sittings; Intermediate 30 minutes

Scoring: Hand key; scoring service available

Cost: Specimen set (test booklets, manual for each level) $10.00; 35 tests with manual and class record $29.00; keys $5.00; 35 hand-scorable answer documents for Intermediate level $11.00; 35 MRC machine-scorable tests for Primary level $43.00; 100 MRC machine-scorable tests for Intermediate level $36.00

Publisher: The Psychological Corporation

Information and availability unconfirmed; last verified in 1988.

TEST OF ATTITUDE TOWARD SCHOOL (TAS)
Guy Thibaudeau

Child, adolescent
Grades 1–12

Purpose: Assesses an individual's attitude toward school.

Description: Oral-response test assessing two principle components of scholastic attitude: emotional disposition toward school and tendencies to action. The administrator presents to the child drawings showing situations that arise at school and notes how the examinee interprets the situations depicted. The number of situations liked and hated are calculated. Examiner required. Not suitable for group use. Available in French.
CANADIAN PUBLISHER

Untimed: Varies

Scoring: Examiner evaluated

Cost: Manual $15.00; set of drawings $12.00; 25 questionnaires $18.00

Publisher: Institute of Psychological Research, Inc.

TLC-LEARNING PREFERENCE INVENTORY KIT

Students

Purpose: Assesses the manner in which students prefer to learn. Used for classroom planning and management.

Description: 144–item paper-pencil inventory assessing individual student preferences for perception and judgment and providing insights into students' attitudes toward things and ideas in their world. The test items and assessment procedures are based on Jung's Theory of Psychological Type. One Adult Learning Style Inventory is included to allow teachers to compare their own preferred learning style with their preferred teaching style. The manual includes guidelines for collecting student data and for scoring, analyzing, and plotting student learning styles; guidelines for classroom planning and management based on test results; and sample lesson plans outlining how to use each of the four learning styles for maximum learning. Examiner required. Suitable for group use.

Untimed: Varies

Scoring: Examiner evaluated

Cost: Test kit (manual, 30 student inventories and scoring sheets, 30 student diagnostic folders, student learning behavior checklist, adult learning style inventory, teaching style inventory) $59.00

Publisher: Mafex Associates, Inc.

Information and availability unconfirmed; last verified in 1987.

TLC-LEARNING STYLE INVENTORY

Adult

Purpose: Assesses the manner in which an individual prefers to learn. Used for adult self-assessments.

Description: Multiple-item paper-pencil test measuring individual preferences for how information is collected and how judgments are made about its significance. The test items and scoring procedures are based on Jung's Theory of Personality Type. The words/terms that individuals select to describe their learning styles correspond to the four distinct styles of learning. Self-administered. Suitable for group use.

Untimed: Varies

Scoring: Self-scored

Cost: Six inventories $21.00

Publisher: Mafex Associates, Inc.

Information and availability unconfirmed; last verified in 1987.

WORLD GOVERNMENT SCALE
Panos D. Bardis

Adolescent, adult

Purpose: Measures attitudes and beliefs concerning world government and the possible effects world government might have on society. Used for discussion and educational purposes.

Description: 6–item paper-pencil inventory in which individuals rate six statements about world government and its effects on society on a 5–point scale from 0 (strongly disagree) to 4 (strongly agree). All statements express positive attitudes toward world government. The score equals the sum of the six numerical responses. The theoretical range extends from 0 (complete rejection of the concept of world government) to 24 (complete acceptance). Self-administered. Suitable for group use.

Untimed: Varies

Scoring: Self-scored

Cost: Free

Publisher: Panos D. Bardis

Student Evaluation and Counseling: Student Personality Factors

AAMD ADAPTIVE BEHAVIOR SCALE—SCHOOL EDITION (ABS-SE)

Refer to page 644.

ACHIEVEMENT IDENTIFICATION MEASURE (AIM)
Sylvia B. Rimm

Grades K–12

Purpose: Identifies characteristics contributing to underachievement in students. Used by teachers and parents for communication and intervention.

Description: 77–item paper-pencil inventory in which parents assess their child's characteristics in five areas (Competition, Responsibility, Independence/Dependence Achievement, Achievement Communication, Respect/Dominance) by responding "no," "to a small extent," "average," "more than average," or "definitely" to each item. The test distinguishes between achievers and underachievers. Parents receive a computer-scored report with a manual that explains the meaning of the scores. Self-administered. Suitable for group use.

Untimed: 20 minutes

Scoring: Computer scored

Cost: Class set of 30 tests and computer scoring $85.00; specimen set $12.00

Publisher: Educational Assessment Service, Inc.

ACHIEVEMENT IDENTIFICATION MEASURE-TEACHER OBSERVATION (AIM-TO)
Sylvia B. Rimm

Child, adolescent Grades K–12

Purpose: Identifies characteristics contributing to achievement in students. Used by teachers.

Description: 70–item paper-pencil inventory completed by teachers to assess competition, responsibility, achievement communication, independence/dependence, respect, and dominance. The test is available in both male and female forms. A computer scoring service is available. Examiner required. Not suitable for group use.

Timed: 20 minutes

Scoring: Examiner evaluated

Cost: 30 tests $85.00; specimen set $12.00

Publisher: Educational Assessment Services, Inc.

ADAPTIVE BEHAVIOR INVENTORY (ABI)
Refer to page 645.

ADAPTIVE BEHAVIOR INVENTORY OF CHILDREN (ABIC)
Refer to page 66.

THE ADJECTIVE CHECK LIST (ACL)
Refer to page 152.

THE ADJUSTMENT INVENTORY: STUDENT FORM
Hugh M. Bell

Adolescent, adult

Purpose: Measures the personal and social adjustment of students in junior high school through college.

Description: Multiple-item paper-pencil self-report inventory assessing six scales of adjustment: home adjustment, health

adjustment, submissiveness (formerly social adjustment), emotionality (formerly emotional adjustment), hostility, and masculinity-femininity. Norms are provided for high-school and college students. Self-administered. Suitable for group use.

Untimed: 25 minutes

Scoring: Hand key

Cost: Manual $4.75; 25 reusable test booklets $5.50; 50 answer sheets (includes profile) $10.50; scoring stencils $9.00

Publisher: Consulting Psychologists Press, Inc.

ADOLESCENT ALIENATION INDEX (AAI)
Refer to page 152.

ADULT PERSONALITY INVENTORY
Refer to page 154.

THE AFFECTIVE PERCEPTION INVENTORY (API)
Anthony T. Soares and Louise M. Soares

Grades 1–12, college

Purpose: Assesses a student's feelings about self regarding general school experiences and specific curriculum areas. Used by educators, sociologists, counselors, and psychologists interested in subject's view of academic world.

Description: Multiple-item paper-pencil test for four levels: primary (Grades 1–3), intermediate (Grades 4–8), advanced (Grades 9–12), and college. Each level is comprised of nine scales: Self as a Person, Student Self, English, Math, Science, Social Sciences, The Arts, Physical Education, and School. Other scales include Humanities Perceptions, Business Perceptions, and Foreign Language Perceptions. The student rates self by marking perceptions in the appropriate space on a scale for the various traits. The examiner may need to read the test to young children. Examiner required. Suitable for group use. Available in Spanish, Italian, and French.

Untimed: 30 minutes

Scoring: Hand key
Cost: Specimen set (indicate level) $14.00
Publisher: SOARES Associates

ATHLETIC MOTIVATION INVENTORY (AMI)
Refer to page 157.

BARCLAY CLASSROOM ASSESSMENT SYSTEM (BCAS)
James R. Barclay

Child
Grades 3–6

Purpose: Evaluates children in relation to their classroom situations, peers, and teachers. Used by educators and counselors to identify gifted children and children with learning disabilities, plan Individualized Educational Plans, and facilitate compliance with PL 94–142.

Description: Multiple-entry paper-pencil screening procedure identifying children who are at high risk for learning-related problems. The examiner uses an Evaluation Booklet to collect information from the teacher and each child in the class. The results provide a comprehensive report for each child based on computer processing of the data gained from the child, classroom peers, and the teacher (who provides demographic information and responds to a brief adjective checklist for each child). The computer report provides the following information for each child: factor scores for task-order achievement, control-predictability, reserved-internal, physical-activity, sociability-affiliation, and enterprising-dominance; a narrative report of the child's self-estimates of his self-competency skills, vocational awareness, reinforcers, and attitude toward school; peer and teacher estimates; suspected difficulties with problem analysis; general intervention direction; and prescriptions. When stanine scores for standardized tests are provided by the teacher, additional relationships between psychosocial variables and academic achievement can be obtained. Computer scoring is available via mail-in services. Examiner required. Suitable for group use.

Untimed: 30–45 minutes
Scoring: Computer scored
Cost: Complete kit (evaluation booklets, computer processing for 36 students, class summary sheet, manual) $135.00
Publisher: Western Psychological Services

BASIC LIVING SKILLS SCALE

Child
Grades 3–6

Purpose: Assesses basic skills necessary for daily living.

Description: Paper-pencil test of six categories of basic living skills: self-concept, interpersonal relations, responsibility, decision making, study skills, and career planning. Materials include pupil task books to assist in skill improvement and strategies handbooks for facilitators. Examiner/self-administered. Suitable for group use.
Untimed: Not available
Scoring: Hand key; may be machine scored; scoring service available
Cost: Complete kit (manual, 35 pupil record forms and profile sheets) $30.80
Publisher: Dallas Educational Services

THE BASIC PERSONALITY INVENTORY (BPI)
Refer to page 157.

BEHAVIORAL ACADEMIC SELF-ESTEEM (BASE)
Stanley Coopersmith and Ragnar Gilberts

Child, adolescent
Grades PreK–8

Purpose: Measures academic self-esteem. Used for counseling and research.

Description: 16–item paper-pencil test consisting of a behavioral rating scale assessing five factors related to self-esteem: student initiative, social attention, success/failure, social attraction, and self-confidence. The test may be used with children as young as 4 years of age and by teachers, parents, and other professionals

---

student personality factors

who can observe the child directly. May be used in conjunction with The Coopersmith Self-Esteem Inventory to improve the accuracy and stability of self-esteem measurements. Self-administered. Suitable for group use.

Untimed: 5 minutes

Scoring: Hand key; examiner evaluated

Cost: 25 rating scales $6.00; manual $9.00

Publisher: Consulting Psychologists Press, Inc.

CALIFORNIA PSYCHOLOGICAL INVENTORY, 1987 REVISED EDITION
Refer to page 161.

CHILD & ADOLESCENT ADJUSTMENT PROFILE (CAAP)
Refer to page 137.

CHILD BEHAVIOR RATING SCALE
Refer to page 139.

CHILDREN'S ADAPTIVE BEHAVIOR SCALE
Bert O. Richmond and Richard H. Kicklighter

Child—Ages 5-11

Purpose: Assesses the adaptive behavior of children. Used to plan remediation programs.

Description: Multiple-item paper-pencil observational inventory covering five areas of adaptive behavior: language development, independent functioning, family role performance, economic vocational activity, and socialization. A teacher or school psychologist completes the inventory based on direct observation of the child and evaluates the results according to guidelines presented in the manual. Self-administered. Suitable for group use.

Untimed: Varies

Scoring: Examiner evaluated

Cost: Test kit (manual, picture book, 5 record forms) $29.95

Publisher: Humanics Psychological Test Corporation, A Division of Humanics Limited

---

CHILDREN'S APPERCEPTIVE STORY-TELLING TEST (CAST)
Refer to page 141.

CHILDREN'S PERSONALITY QUESTIONNAIRE (CPQ)
Refer to page 142.

CHILDREN'S VERSION/FAMILY ENVIRONMENT SCALE (CV/FES)
Refer to page 68.

A CLASS PLAY
Refer to page 738.

COMREY PERSONALITY SCALES (CPS)
Refer to page 165.

COOPERSMITH SELF-ESTEEM INVENTORIES (CSEI)
Refer to page 236.

THE COPING INVENTORY
Shirley Zeitlin

Grades PreK-12

Purpose: Assesses the behavior patterns and skills that are resources a person uses to meet personal needs and to adapt to the demands of his environment. Provides information about level of effectiveness, general coping style, and specific resources and vulnerabilities.

Description: 48-item paper-pencil inventory in two categories: Coping with Self and Coping with Environment. The items in each category are divided into three dimensions that describe coping style: productive, active, and flexible. The Adaptive Behavior Summary is used to describe how effectively a person copes, and Behavior Lists are used to identify strengths and weaknesses in a person's coping actions. The inventory is available in two forms: Observation (ages 3–16) and Self-Rated (adolescents and adults). The manuals for each level contain instructions for rating, scoring, and implementing the results. Examiner required. The Self-Rated form is suitable for group use.

Timed: Varies

Scoring: Hand key; examiner evaluated

Cost: Starter set (manual, 20 forms) $25.00; self-rated specimen set $9.00; observation specimen set $14.00

Publisher: Scholastic Testing Service, Inc.

CURTIS COMPLETION FORM
Refer to page 168.

DIMENSIONS OF SELF-CONCEPT (DOSC)
Refer to page 739.

EARLY SCHOOL PERSONALITY QUESTIONNAIRE (ESPQ)
Refer to page 143.

EDUCATION APPERCEPTION TEST
Refer to page 740.

EYSENCK PERSONALITY QUESTIONNAIRE (EPQ)
Refer to page 172.

FROST SELF-DESCRIPTION QUESTIONNAIRE
Refer to page 144.

GROUP ACHIEVEMENT IDENTIFICATION MEASURE (GAIM)
Sylvia B. Rimm

Child, adolescent—Ages 10–18 Grades 5–12

Purpose: Identifies students with characteristics that may contribute to under-

achievement. Used by classroom teachers to help underachieving students.

Description: 90–item paper-pencil inventory assessing achievement characteristics. The inventory directs both teachers and parents to the areas in which the child must change in order to achieve in school. The test yields a Total Score as well as five dimension scores: Competition, Responsibility, Achievement Communication, Independence/Dependence, and Respect Dominance. The test is available for both male and female forms. A computer scoring service is available from the publisher. Self-administered. Suitable for group use.

Untimed: Varies

Scoring: Computer scored

Cost: Specimen set $12.00; class set of 30 tests and computer scoring $85.00

Publisher: Educational Assessment Service, Inc.

GUILFORD-ZIMMERMAN TEMPERAMENT SURVEY (GZTS)
Refer to page 177.

HARTMAN VALUE PROFILE (HVP)
Refer to page 242.

HIGH SCHOOL PERSONALITY QUESTIONNAIRE (HSPQ)
Refer to page 178.

HOUSE-TREE-PERSON (H-T-P) PROJECTIVE TECHNIQUE
Refer to page 244.

INCOMPLETE SENTENCES TASK
Refer to page 182.

INDEX OF PERSONALITY CHARACTERISTICS (IPC)
Linda Brown and Margaret C. Coleman

Child, adolescent—Ages 8–17 years, 11 months

Purpose: Measures personality characteristics. Discriminates between normal,

---

nonhandicapped behavior disordered, learning disabled, and emotionally disturbed students.

Description: 75–item paper-pencil test measuring personality characteristics in eight areas. The subtests embedded within the items are Academic (pervasiveness of personality characteristics in school), Nonacademic (pervasiveness of personality characteristics out of school), Perception of Self, Perception of Others, Acting In (behavioral manifestations of personality), Acting Out (behavioral manifestations of personality), Internal Locus of Control (ability to accept responsibility for feelings and behaviors), External Locus of Control (ability to accept responsibility for feelings and behaviors). Standard scores, percentile ranks, and a personality quotient are reported. Self-administered. Suitable for group use.

Untimed: 30 minutes

Scoring: Examiner evaluated

Cost: Complete kit (examiner's manual, 50 student response booklets, 50 profile and record forms, storage box) $59.00

Publisher: PRO-ED

INSTITUTE OF CHILD STUDY SECURITY TEST—ELEMENTARY FORM
Michael F. Grapko

Child, adolescent
Grades 4–8

Purpose: Measures child's personal security and behavior patterns. Provides teachers with a better understanding of children and recognition of the kind of direction and encouragement children need to develop sound mental health habits.

Description: The test is presented in story form *(The Story of Jimmy)* and deals with significant areas of the child's life. The test is based on Dr. W.E. Blatz's theory of security. Examiner required. Suitable for group use.
CANADIAN PUBLISHER

Untimed: 25 minutes

Scoring: Hand key

Cost: Specimen set (manual, scoring form, test) $5.25

Publisher: Guidance Centre
Information and availability unconfirmed; last verified in 1987.

INSTITUTE OF CHILD STUDY SECURITY TEST—PRIMARY FORM
Michael F. Grapko

Child
Grades 1–3

Purpose: Measures child's personal security and behavior patterns. Provides teachers with a better understanding of children and recognition of the kind of direction and encouragement children need to develop sound mental health habits.

Description: The test is presented in story form *(The Story of Timmy)* and deals with significant areas of the child's life. A consistency score and a security scale are provided, indicating the child's consistency in mode of response to a variety of life situations and his pattern of security development. Examiner required. Suitable for group use.
CANADIAN PUBLISHER

Timed: 20 minutes

Scoring: Hand key

Cost: Specimen set (manual, scoring form, test) $4.50

Publisher: Guidance Centre
Information and availability unconfirmed; last verified in 1987.

INTERMEDIATE PERSONALITY QUESTIONNAIRE FOR INDIAN PUPILS (IPQI)—1974

Child, adolescent

Purpose: Assesses personality. Used for guidance of children with social and emotional problems. Used in vocational guidance.

Description: Multiple-item paper-pencil measure of 10 aspects of personality, including social extraversion, verbal intelligence, emotional stability, adventuresomeness, creativity, dominance, perseverance, relaxedness, spirit of enterprise, and environment relatedness. Examiner required. Suitable for group use.

SOUTH AFRICAN PUBLISHER

Untimed: 30–45 minutes

Scoring: Hand key

Cost: (In Rands) test booklet 2,50; manual 2,00; scoring stencil 0,50; 10 answer sheets 1,50; orders from outside the RSA will be dealt with on merit

Publisher: Human Sciences Research Council

INVENTORY FOR COUNSELING AND DEVELOPMENT
Norman S. Giddan, F. Reid Creech, and Victor R. Lovell

College students

Purpose: Identifies the strengths, assets, and coping skills of college students. Used in on-campus counseling centers, private and community mental health centers, college health centers, and hospitals as a predictor of personal, social, and academic functioning and in research to predict student retention and to identify the personality characteristics of a student body.

Description: 449–item paper-pencil true-false test consisting of 23 scales. The 15 substantive scales measure personality dimensions affecting an individual's personal, social, and academic functioning. The four criterion scales measure academic characteristics. A criterion scale measures stereotypes related to sex role, and three validity scales assess response-style characteristics. A profile report is available. Examiner/self-administered. Suitable for group use.

Untimed: 1 hour

Scoring: Computer scored; hand key

Cost: Specimen set (test booklet, profile report answer sheet, manual) $12.60

Publisher: National Computer Systems/PAS Division

IPAT ANXIETY SCALE (OR SELF-ANALYSIS FORM)
Refer to page 9.

JACKSON PERSONALITY INVENTORY (JPI)
Refer to page 185.

JESNESS BEHAVIOR CHECK LIST
Refer to page 186.

JOSEPH PRESCHOOL AND PRIMARY SELF-CONCEPT SCREENING TEST (JPPSST)
Refer to page 636.

KINETIC DRAWING SYSTEM FOR FAMILY AND SCHOOLS (KFD AND KSD) (COMBINED KFD AND KSD 1985)
Howard M. Knoff and H. Thompson Prout

Child, adolescent—Ages 5–20

Purpose: Provides personalized themes within school and family contexts. Used for school psychology referrals.

Description: Paper-pencil oral-response projective system integrating Kinetic Family Drawing and Kinetic School Drawings covering a broad range of the most frequent areas of child and adolescent distress—family and school. It consists of two drawings with a series of suggested projective questions relating to the action between figures; figure characteristics; position, distance, and barriers style; and symbols. Each has a projective interpretation for family and school forms and a variable number of items subject to examiner discretion. Examiner required. Not suitable for group use.

Untimed: Varies

Scoring: Examiner evaluated

Cost: Kit (handbook, scoring booklet) $35.00

Publisher: Western Psychological Services

LEADERSHIP ABILITY EVALUATION
Refer to page 1046.

LEADERSHIP SKILLS INVENTORY
Refer to page 754.

LUTHER HOSPITAL SENTENCE COMPLETIONS (LHSC)
John R. Thurston

Adolescent, adult

Purpose: Evaluates attitudes and emotional reactions of nursing students and nursing school applicants. Used to predict probable success or failure in nursing school.

Description: 90–item paper-pencil sentence completion test measuring six attitudes related to nursing school performance: nursing, self, home and family, responsibility, academics, and others-love-marriage. Materials consist of a self-directing test booklet. A comprehensive manual covering this and other NRA tests is available also. The manual includes a scoring key, and the publisher offers a scoring service. Self-administered. Suitable for group use.

Untimed: 30 minutes

Scoring: Hand key

Cost: Specimen set $5.00; 25 tests $10.00; manual $20.00

Publisher: Nursing Research Associates

Information and availability unconfirmed; last verified in 1988.

MARTINEK-ZAICHKOWSKY SELF-CONCEPT SCALE FOR CHILDREN (MZSCS)
Thomas J. Martinek and Leonard D. Zaichkowsky

Child, adolescent Grades 1–8

Purpose: Measures the global self-concept of children, identifies children with low self-esteem, and evaluates the impact of the educational process on a child's self-perception. May be used with non-English-speaking children. Used for research and referral.

Description: 25–item paper-pencil forced-choice test measuring physical, behavioral, and emotional aspects of a child's self-confidence. Five factors are covered: satisfaction and happiness; home and family relationships and circumstances; ability in games, recreation, and sports; personality traits and emotional tendencies; and behavioral and social characteristics in school. Each test item consists of a page in the test booklet that presents the child with a pair of pictures representing positive and negative roles. The child circles the picture he considers to be most like himself. The test requires little or no reading ability and is culture-free. Examiner required. Suitable for group use.

Untimed: 10–15 minutes

Scoring: Hand key; examiner evaluated

Cost: Specimen set $10.00; 25 tests $35.00; manual $6.75

Publisher: Psychologists and Educators, Inc.

MATHEMATICS ANXIETY RATING SCALE-A (MARS-A)
Richard M. Suinn

Child, adolescent Grades 7–12

Purpose: Measures students' anxieties regarding situations involving the use of mathematics. Used for screening and diagnostic purposes and research on mathematics anxiety and as a means for developing anxiety hierarchies for desensitization therapy.

Description: 98–item paper-pencil test assessing the level of a student's mathematics anxiety. Test items refer to situations involving the use of mathematics. Students are asked to rate on a 5–point scale ranging from "not at all" to "very much" how anxious they are made by each situation. Norms are available for junior and senior high-school students by grade and by sex. Use is restricted to APA membership guidelines. Self-administered. Suitable for group use.

Untimed: 20–30 minutes

Scoring: Hand key

Cost: 100 scales $60.00

Publisher: Rocky Mountain Behavioral Science Institute, Inc.

MAUDSLEY PERSONALITY INVENTORY (MPI)
Refer to page 191.

THE MEASUREMENT OF SELF-CONCEPT IN KINDERGARTEN CHILDREN (MSCKC)
Refer to page 553.

MILLON ADOLESCENT PERSONALITY INVENTORY (MAPI)
Refer to page 193.

MODES OF EXISTENCE TEST
Refer to page 248.

MOONEY PROBLEM CHECKLIST
Refer to page 197.

MULTIPLE AFFECT ADJECTIVE CHECK LIST (MAACL)
Refer to page 198.

MURPHY-MEISGEIER TYPE INDICATOR FOR CHILDREN (MMTIC)
Refer to page 782.

NEUROTICISM SCALE QUESTIONNAIRE (NSQ)
Refer to page 201.

NURSE ATTITUDES INVENTORY (NAI)
John R. Thurston

Adolescent, adult

Purpose: Evaluates attitudes and emotional reactions of nursing students and nursing school applicants. Used to predict probable success or failure in nursing school.

Description: 70–item paper-pencil multiple-choice test in two forms evaluating six attitudes related to nursing school performance: nursing, self, home and family, responsibility, academics, and others-love-marriage. The scales evaluate positive and negative attitudes. Materials include a self-directing test booklet, answer sheet, and scoring key. A comprehensive manual covering this and other NRA tests is available. Self-administered. Suitable for group use.

Untimed: 30 minutes

Scoring: Hand key; examiner evaluated; scoring service available

Cost: Specimen set (excluding key) $10.00; 50 answer sheets $5.00; scoring key $15.00; manual $20.00; scoring service $5.00 per test

Publisher: Nursing Research Associates

Information and availability unconfirmed; last verified in 1988.

NURSING SENTENCE COMPLETIONS (NSC)
John R. Thurston

Adolescent, adult

Purpose: Evaluates attitudes and emotions of nursing students and applicants to nursing school. Used to predict probable success or failure in nursing school.

Description: 40–item paper-pencil sentence completion test measuring six attitudes related to nursing school performance: nursing, self, home and family, responsibility, academics, and others-love-marriage. Materials consist of a self-directing test booklet. A comprehensive manual covering this and other NRA tests is available also. The manual also includes a scoring key. The test can be scored with the Nursing Education Scale. The publisher offers a scoring service. Examiner/self-administered. Suitable for group use.

Untimed: 20 minutes

Scoring: Hand key

Cost: Specimen set $10.00; 25 tests $10.00; comprehensive manual $15.00; scoring service $5.00 per test

Publisher: Nursing Research Associates

Information and availability unconfirmed; last verified in 1988.

OETTING'S COMPUTER ANXIETY SCALE (COMPAS)
E.R. Oetting

Adolescent, adult

Purpose: Assesses general computer anxiety.

Description: 48–item (long form) or 10–item (short form) multiple-choice test assessing general computer anxiety. May be used with individuals with physical impairments. Examiner required. Suitable for group use.

Untimed: Short form 5 minutes; long form 20 minutes

Scoring: Hand key

Cost: 100 long forms $30.00; 100 short forms $15.00; manual $12.00

Publisher: Rocky Mountain Behavioral Science Institute, Inc.

OMNIBUS PERSONALITY INVENTORY (OPI)
P.A. Histe, T.R. McConnell, H.D. Webster, and G.D. Yonge

Adolescent, adult
Grades 11 and above

Purpose: Assesses selected personality factors, values, and interests of students relevant to an academic activity. Used to understand and differentiate among students in an educational context.

Description: 385–item paper-pencil inventory of 14 aspects of personality, including thinking introversion, theoretical orientation, aestheticism, complexity, autonomy, religious orientation, social extraversion, impulse expression, personal integration, anxiety level, altruism, practical outlook, masculinity-femininity, and response bias. An Intellectual Disposition Category is determined for each individual by combining his standings on six of the regular scales. Examiner required. Suitable for group use.

Untimed: 45–60 minutes

Scoring: Hand key

Cost: 25 inventory booklets $29.00; 50 hand-scorable answer sheets $23.00; manual $25.00; specimen set $21.00

Publisher: The Psychological Corporation

Information and availability unconfirmed; last verified in 1988.

PATHWAYS TO INDEPENDENCE
Refer to page 667.

THE PERSONAL AUDIT
Refer to page 1017.

PERSONAL QUESTIONNAIRE RAPID SCALING TECHNIQUE (PQRST)
Refer to page 206.

PERSONALITY INVENTORY FOR CHILDREN (PIC), REVISED FORMAT
Refer to page 146.

PERSONALITY RATING SCALE
Refer to page 146.

POLITTE SENTENCE COMPLETION TEST (PSCT)
Alan J. Politte

Child, adolescent
Grades 1–12

Purpose: Evaluates personality traits and adjustment of children. Used to assess personality in educational, counseling, and clinical areas.

Description: 35–item paper-pencil free-response projective test measuring personality. Students are told that the test is a "questionnaire" or an "exercise" in which they are to read the stems and then complete the sentences. The test serves as a screening device through which the examiner can gain further insight into the thinking processes of the student. It is not an instrument that provides a "score" or normative reference for the student. Persons without training in clinical psychology should use the test as an aid in interview or counseling settings. Clinically trained psychologists can base their interpretations from a psychoanalytic, social, behavioral, or similar approach. The test is available in two forms: Elementary for Grades 1–6 and Secondary for Grades 7–12. Examiner/self-administered. Suitable for group use.

Untimed: 15 minutes

Scoring: Examiner evaluated

Cost: Specimen set $4.50; 25 tests (manual included; specify form) $8.25

Publisher: Psychologists and Educators, Inc.

THE PRESCHOOL BEHAVIOR QUESTIONNAIRE
Refer to page 147.

PRESCHOOL SELF-CONCEPT PICTURE TEST (PS-CPT)
Rosestelle B. Woolner

Child—Ages 4–5

Purpose: Assesses a preschooler's opinions of himself in terms of how he perceives himself to be and the way he would like to be. Used to design curricula that enhance a preschooler's self-concept.

Description: 10–item oral-response test measuring a preschooler's opinion of himself in regard to 10 pairs of bipolar characteristics: dirty/clean, active/passive, aggressive/nonaggressive, afraid/unafraid, strong/weak, acceptance/rejection, unhappy/happy, group rejection/group acceptance, sharing/nonsharing, and dependence/independence. A set of 10 picture plates presents drawings of children representing each of the bipolar characteristics. The child is shown the plates and asked to indicate the drawing with which he identifies and the drawing with which he would like to identify. Variances between the two responses provide the teacher with an opportunity to help the child reduce the degree of difference between the way he sees himself and the way he would like to see himself. Retesting reveals progress in this direction. Available in four forms: male, female, black, white. Examiner required. Not suitable for group use.

Untimed: 15 minutes

Scoring: Hand key

Cost: Complete (4 subtests, manual, 25 score sheets) $15.00 plus postage and handling

Publisher: Rosestelle B. Woolner, Ed.D.

PSYCHOEPISTEMOLOGICAL PROFILE (PEP)
Refer to page 212.

PSYCHOLOGICAL DISTRESS INVENTORY (PDI)
Applied Innovations

College students

Purpose: Measures life stress in college students. Used as a screening device for students seeking psychological services from counseling centers.

Description: 50–item paper-pencil or computer-administered measure of depression, anxiety, somatic discomfort, and stress in college students requesting psychological services from counseling centers. Students rate life events occurring in the past 12 months on a 5–point, Likert-type scale indicating stressfulness or aversiveness of the event. The results are used for deciding whether more extensive psychological evaluation is needed. Self-administered. Suitable for group use.

Untimed: 10–20 minutes

Scoring: Hand key; may be computer scored

Cost: Computer version $275.00

Publisher: Applied Innovations, Inc.

Information and availability unconfirmed; last verified in 1987.

PSYCHOLOGICAL SCREENING INVENTORY (PSI)
Refer to page 212.

QUALITY OF SCHOOL LIFE SCALE (QSL)
Refer to page 756.

REYNOLDS ADOLESCENT DEPRESSION SCALE (RADS)
Refer to page 214.

ROGERS PERSONAL ADJUSTMENT INVENTORY—UK REVISION
Refer to page 149.

SCALES FOR RATING THE BEHAVIORAL CHARACTERISTICS OF SUPERIOR STUDENTS (SRBCSS)
Refer to page 625.

SCAMIN: A SELF-CONCEPT AND MOTIVATION INVENTORY: EARLY ELEMENTARY
Norman J. Milchus,
George A. Farrah, and William Reitz

Child
Grades 1–3

Purpose: Measures self-concept and assesses the motivation inventory of students.

Description: 24–item test in which items are responded to on a machine-scorable scale of five sad to happy faces to ascertain the child's self-concept strength and to develop a motivational inventory. Examiner required. Suitable for group use.

Untimed: 25 minutes

Scoring: Hand key; may be computer scored

Cost: Specimen set $7.00; manual $1.25; key $4.00

Publisher: Person-O-Metrics, Inc.

SCAMIN: A SELF-CONCEPT AND MOTIVATION INVENTORY: LATER ELEMENTARY
Norman J. Milchus,
George A. Farrah, and William Reitz

Child
Grades 3–6

Purpose: Measures self-concept and assesses the motivational inventory of students.

Description: 48–item paper-pencil test measuring achievement needs, achievement investment, role expectations, and self-adequacy. The examiner reads the items to the class. Examiner required. Suitable for group use.

Untimed: 30 minutes

Scoring: Hand key; may be computer scored

Cost: Specimen set $7.00; manual $1.25; key $4.00

Publisher: Person-O-Metrics, Inc.

SCAMIN: A SELF-CONCEPT AND MOTIVATION INVENTORY: PRESCHOOL/KINDERGARTEN
Norman J. Milchus,
George A. Farrah, and William Reitz

Child
Grades PreK-K

Purpose: Measures self-concept and assesses the motivation of preschool and kindergarten children.

Description: 24–item test using three sad to happy face responses to evaluate self-concept strength. Examiner required. Suitable for group use.

Untimed: 30 minutes

Scoring: Hand key; may be computer scored

Cost: Specimen set $7.00; manual $1.25; key $4.00

Publisher: Person-O-Metrics, Inc.

SCAMIN: A SELF-CONCEPT AND MOTIVATION INVENTORY: SECONDARY FORM
Norman J. Milchus,
George A. Farrah, and William Reitz

Adolescent
Grades 7–12

Purpose: Determines an individual's self-concept and motivation in an academic context.

Description: 64–item paper-pencil test measuring achievement needs, achievement investment, role expectation, and self-adequacy. Four levels of the test, each with a different number of items and administration times, are available. Examiner required. Suitable for group use. Available in Spanish.

Untimed: 30–40 minutes

Scoring: Hand key; may be computer scored

Cost: Specimen set $7.00; manual $1.25; key $4.00

Publisher: Person-O-Metrics, Inc.

SCHOOL MOTIVATION ANALYSIS TEST (SMAT)
Refer to page 217.

THE SCHOOL PLAY
Refer to page 746.

SCHOOL SOCIAL SKILLS RATING SCALE (S3 RATING SCALE)
Laura Brown, Donald Black, and John Downs

Child, adolescent

Purpose: Identifies strengths and deficits in school-related social behaviors of elementary and high-school students.

Description: 40–item paper-pencil criterion-referenced inventory assessing student social skills needed for success in school and employment. Using a 6–point Likert scale and month-long observation of student behavior, teachers rate students on adult relations (12 items), peer relations (16 items), school rules (6 items), and classroom behaviors (6 items). The test can be used for social skills instruction, discussion of student behavior with parents and other school personnel, and development and monitoring of social behavior goals for individual education plans. The test can be used with residential, special education, and regular education students. Examiner required. Not suitable for group use.

Untimed: 10 minutes

Scoring: Examiner evaluated

Cost: Complete kit (S3 manual, SSS–2 in vinyl binder) $35.00

Publisher: Slosson Educational Publications, Inc.

SEARCH INSTITUTE PROFILES OF STUDENT LIFE: ATTITUDES AND BEHAVIORS
Search Institute

Adolescent—Ages 11–18
Grades 6–12

Purpose: Assesses the behaviors and attitudes that affect student motivation and achievement. Used as baseline information for programming in public and private schools and youth-serving agencies.

Description: 152–item paper-pencil survey that includes topics such as student attitudes and efforts in school, prosocial and antisocial behavior, sexuality, peer and parent relationships, self-esteem, alienation, alcohol and other drug use and non-use, stress, abuse, eating disorders, general well-being, and program interests. Yields a comprehensive report of students' attitudes, understandings, and responses to student life. This is one survey in the Search Institute Profile of Student Life series. Examiner required. Suitable for group use.

Untimed: 35 minutes

Scoring: Machine scored; scoring service available from publisher

Cost: System $2,500.00; charge per student $1.25

Publisher: Search Institute

SELF-CONCEPT SCALE

Adolescent
Grades 7–12

Purpose: Assesses self-concept in students.

Description: Paper-pencil test of five areas of student self-concept: decision-making skills, interpersonal relations, responsibility, study skills, and career planning. Materials include pupil task books to assist in skill development and a strategies handbook providing pupil activities for facilitators. Examiner/self-administered. Suitable for group use.

Untimed: Not available

Scoring: Hand key; may be machine scored; scoring service available

Cost: Complete kit (manual, 35 pupil record forms and profile sheets) $30.80

Publisher: Dallas Educational Services

SELF-OBSERVATION SCALES (SOS)
William G. Katzenmeyer and A. Jackson Stenner

Child, adolescent—Ages 5–19
Grades K–12

Purpose: Assesses the social maturity, self-acceptance, self-security, and affiliations of children and handicapped subjects. Used by schools and hospitals and in research.

Description: Multiple-item paper-pencil test measuring the areas of social maturity, social confidence, self-acceptance, self-security, school affiliation, teacher affiliation, and peer affiliation. Four forms are available: Primary (Grades K–3; 50 items), Intermediate (Grades 4–6; 60 items), Junior High (Grades 7–9; 72 items), and Senior High (Grades 10–12; 72 items). Subjects respond "yes" or "no" to each item. The Primary Form uses smiling/frowning faces to portray yes/no alternatives. T-scores are factor analytically derived. A scoring service is available from the publisher. Examiner required for Primary Form; other forms are self-administered. Suitable for group use.

Untimed: 25–30 minutes

Scoring: Computer scored

Cost: Complete kit (30 test booklets, scoring, manual) $55.00

Publisher: NTS Research Corporation

THE SELF-PERCEPTION INVENTORY (SPI)
Refer to page 747.

SELF PROFILE Q-SORT (SPQS)
Refer to page 747.

SENTENCE COMPLETION TEST
Refer to page 220.

SOCIAL BEHAVIOR ASSESSMENT (SBA)
T.M. Stephens

Child
Grades K–8

Purpose: Assesses the school-related social skills of students. Used in research and education to diagnose behavior deficits, provide classification and descriptive information on social behaviors, and select students who need social skills training.

Description: 136–item teacher-rated observation tool assessing school-related social skills and containing 30 subcategories arranged under four behavior categories: environmental, interpersonal, task-related, and self-related. Using observation or recall, teachers rate each student on each item (0=not observed or applicable, 1=at acceptable level, 2=lower than acceptable level, 3=never exhibited). Examiner required. Suitable for group use.

Untimed: 22 minutes

Scoring: Examiner evaluated

Cost: Packet of 25, with prescriptions $5.00; without prescriptions $6.50

Publisher: Cedars Press

Information and availability unconfirmed; last verified in 1987.

SOCIAL INTELLIGENCE TEST
F.A. Moss, Thelma Hunt, and K. Omwake

Adolescent, adult
Grades 10 and above

Purpose: Assesses basic social perceptions and judgments of students.

Description: Multiple-item paper-pencil test measuring five factors: judgment in social situations, recognition of mental state of speaker, observation of human behavior, memory for names and faces, and sense of humor. Percentile norms are provided for high-school, college, and adult populations. Three editions are available: Second Edition (Long Form);

Shortened Edition (omits Memory for names and Faces factor); and Special Edition (contains only Judgment in Social Situations and Observation of Human Behavior). A complete specimen set contains all three forms. Examiner required. Suitable for group use.
CANADIAN PUBLISHER
Timed: 50 minutes
Scoring: Hand key
Cost: Specimen set $5.00
Publisher: The Center for Psychological Service

SOCIAL RETICENCE SCALE (SRS)
Refer to page 223.

STRESS IMPACT SCALE (SIS)
Jerry B. Hutton and
Timothy G. Roberts

Ages 8–19½

Purpose: Screens students for potentially stressful events and conditions.

Description: 70–item paper-pencil self-report rating scale covering stress occurrence and stress impact. Percentiles and quotients are provided for stress occurrence, stress impact, and stress impact differential. Self-administered. Suitable for group use.
Untimed: 20 minutes
Scoring: Hand key
Cost: $44.00
Publisher: PRO-ED

STUDENT ADAPTATION TO COLLEGE QUESTIONNAIRE (SACQ)
Robert W. Baker and Bohad Siryk

Adult

Purpose: Measures overall student adjustment to college. Used for college counseling.

Description: 67–item multiple-choice questionnaire with four subscales that measure academic adjustment, social adjustment, personal-emotional adjustment, and attachment to the college. Yields T-scores. A computer version for IBM and compatible personal computers is available. Self-administered. Suitable for group use.
Untimed: 30 minutes
Scoring: Machine scored; computer scored; self-scored; scoring service available from publisher
Cost: Kit (25 questionnaires, 2 computer scannable answer sheets, manual) $60.00; computer disk (25 uses) $125.00
Publisher: Western Psychological Services

STUDENT ADJUSTMENT INVENTORY
Refer to page 758.

STUDENT DEVELOPMENTAL TASK AND LIFESTYLE INVENTORY (SDTLI)
Roger B. Winston, Jr.,
Theodore K. Miller, and
Judith S. Prince

Adult—Ages 17–24
College students

Purpose: Measures the psychosocial development of traditional-aged college students.

Description: 140–item paper-pencil true-false test covering the following psychosocial areas: Establishing and Clarifying Purpose Task (educational involvement, career planning, lifestyle planning, cultural participation, life management), Developing Mature Interpersonal Relationships (tolerance, peer relationships, emotional autonomy), Academic Autonomy Task, Salubrious Lifestyle Scale, Intimacy Scale, and Response Bias Scale. A 12th-grade reading level is required. This inventory is an adaptation of the Student Developmental Task Inventory (see separate entry). Suitable for the visually, hearing, and physically impaired. Materials include booklets, answer sheets, and interpretive guides, all of which must be purchased in packages of 50. Self-administered. Suitable for group use.
Untimed: 20–30 minutes
Scoring: Self-scored

Cost: 50 booklets $45.00; 50 answer sheets $20.00; 50 interpretive guides $12.50

Publisher: Student Developmental Associates, Inc.

STUDY OF VALUES
Gordon W. Allport, Phillip E. Vernon, and Gardner Lindzey

Adolescent, adult
Grades 10 and above

Purpose: Measures the relative prominence of an individual's basic interests or personality motives. Used for educational planning, vocational planning and guidance, personnel selection, and research.

Description: 45–item paper-pencil test measuring six values: theoretical, economic, aesthetic, social, political, and religious. The test is designed primarily for use with college students or adults with some college education. It should be used only when the interpretation is supervised and guided by individuals who have had considerable experience in psychological testing and personality theory. Self-administered. Suitable for group use.

Untimed: 20 minutes
Scoring: Hand key
Cost: 35 hand-scorable test booklets, manual $22.29
Publisher: The Riverside Publishing Company

SUICIDAL IDEATION QUESTIONNAIRE (SIQ)
Refer to page 225.

SUINN TEST ANXIETY BEHAVIOR SCALE (STABS)
Richard M. Suinn

Adolescent, adult
Grades 7 and above

Purpose: Measures a person's anxiety regarding academic testing situations. Used for screening and diagnostic purposes and for research on test anxiety and as a tool in developing anxiety hierarchies for desensitization therapy.

Description: 50–item paper-pencil test assessing the level of a person's test anxiety. Test items refer to experiences related to academic testing that may cause fear or apprehension. The subject rates his anxiety concerning each test item on a 5–point scale ranging from "not at all" to "very much." Norms are available for college students, adult nonstudents, and males and females. Use is restricted to APA membership guidelines. Self-administered. Suitable for group use.

Untimed: 20 minutes
Scoring: Hand key
Cost: 100 scales $45.00
Publisher: Rocky Mountain Behavioral Science Institute, Inc.

TEMPERAMENT ASSESSMENT BATTERY FOR CHILDREN (TABC)
Refer to page 150.

TEST ANXIETY PROFILE (TAP)
E.R. Oetting and C.W. Cole

Adolescent, adult
Grades 7 and above

Purpose: Measures a person's anxieties regarding academic testing situations. Used for screening and counseling purposes.

Description: 77–item paper-pencil test assessing a person's feelings and thoughts in regard to six academic testing situations: multiple-choice exams, math exams, essay exams, unannounced tests, talking in front of a class, and tests with time limits. Each test item consists of a pair of bipolar adjectives separated by a 7–point scale. The subject rates himself on each pair of adjectives according to his thoughts or feelings in each of the testing situations. Two anxiety scores are derived for each testing situation: Feelings of Anxiety (FA) and Thought Interference (TI). Use is restricted to APA membership guidelines. Self-administered. Suitable for group use.

Untimed: 10–15 minutes
Scoring: Hand key; examiner evaluated
Cost: 100 tests $60.00; manual $15.00
Publisher: Rocky Mountain Behavioral Science Institute, Inc.

THE TEST OF SOCIAL INSIGHT: YOUTH AND ADULT EDITIONS

Refer to page 255.

THE WAKSMAN SOCIAL SKILLS RATING SCALE (WSSRS)

Steven Waksman

Child, adolescent
Grades K–12

Purpose: Assesses social skills deficits of students. Used by teachers and clinicians for selecting students for social skills training or special counseling programs and for evaluating the effectiveness of those programs.

Description: 21–item rating scale identifying specific social skill deficits in children and adolescents by surveying aggressive and passive domains. The examiner rates the behavior of the "targeted" student or students on a scale ranging from 0 (never) to 3 (usually). The assessment permits clinicians to compare the students with a normative sample for identification or classification purposes and to set criteria for social skills training, counseling, and program evaluation. Examiner required. Not suitable for group use.

Untimed: 5–10 minutes
Scoring: Examiner evaluated
Cost: Complete kit $32.95
Publisher: PRO-ED

WALKER-MCCONNELL SCALE OF SOCIAL COMPETENCE AND SCHOOL ADJUSTMENT

*Hill M. Walker and
Scott R. McConnell*

Child
Grades K–6

Purpose: Measures social skills of students, including teacher-preferred social behavior, peer-preferred social behavior, and school adjustment. Screens for and identifies social skills deficits. Used for school evaluations, for developing IEPs, to facilitate MDT certification and re-placement decisions, and to guide development of social skills training programs. May be used for identifying social compe-

tence deficits among handicapped and at-risk populations.

Description: 43–item rating scale used by teachers to measure the social skills of students. The first two scales focus on peer relations, and the third emphasizes adjustment to the behavioral demands of the classroom. Items are rated on a 4–point Likert scale format. Teachers should observe students for 2 months prior to using the scale with those students. Results are reported as standard scores. The total score is reported as a quotient. Examiner required. Not suitable for group use.

Untimed: 5 minutes per child
Scoring: Examiner evaluated
Cost: Complete kit (examiner's manual, 50 profile/rating forms, storage box) $44.00
Publisher: PRO-ED

Student Evaluation and Counseling: Study Skills Attitudes

CAI STUDY SKILLS TEST

William F. Brown

Adolescent, adult
Grades 11 and above

Purpose: Measures a student's knowledge of efficient study skills and effective academic attitudes. Used to identify students who need help and, when used as a posttest, students who fail to learn adequate skills.

Description: 200–item paper-pencil or computer-administered true-false test of student's knowledge in 10 areas: managing time, improving memory, taking lecture notes, reading texts, taking exams, writing themes and reports, giving oral reports, improving scholastic motivation, improving interpersonal relations, and improving concentration. The test also is available on a computer diskette for Apple II and IBM PC computers. Self-administered. Suitable for group use.

Untimed: 50 minutes

Scoring: Hand key

Cost: Test $0.85; 100 tests $75.00; answer sheet $0.35; 250 answer sheets $75.00; hand key stencil $5.00; direction manual $3.50; computer disk $200.00

Publisher: WFB Enterprises

Information and availability unconfirmed; last verified in 1987.

CANADIAN COMPREHENSIVE ASSESSMENT PROGRAM: DEVELOPING COGNITIVE ABILITIES TEST (DCAT)

Child, adolescent
Grades 2–9

Purpose: Measures learning characteristics of students.

Description: Multiple-item paper-pencil test measuring students' learning characteristics. Items involve both a content area and a cognitive level. Student performance is evaluated in three content areas: verbal ability, quantitative ability, and spatial ability. Information is provided on the five cognitive levels of Bloom's taxonomy: knowledge, comprehension, application, analysis, and synthesis. Examiner required. Suitable for group use.
CANADIAN PUBLISHER

Timed: Varies

Scoring: Hand key

Cost: Review kit $15.00

Publisher: Guidance Centre

Information and availability unconfirmed; last verified in 1987.

CHILDREN'S ACADEMIC INTRINSIC MOTIVATION INVENTORY (CAIMI)
Adele E. Gottfried

Child
Grades 4–8

Purpose: Assesses academic motivation in children. Used to identify students with academic difficulties and to differentiate motivation from achievement and ability factors. Also used in course selec-

tion and individual and district level program planning.

Description: 122–item paper-pencil instrument measuring motivation for learning in both general and specific areas. The 44 questions comprise five scales: Reading, Math, Social Studies, Science, and General. A profile form is provided. Results are reported as T-scores or percentiles. Examiner/self-administered. Suitable for group use.

Untimed: 20–30 minutes

Scoring: Not available

Cost: Kit (manual, 25 test booklets, 25 profile forms) $39.95

Publisher: Psychological Assessment Resources, Inc.

CORNELL LEARNING AND STUDY SKILLS INVENTORY
Walter Pauk and Russell Cassel

Adolescent, adult
Grades 7–12, college

Purpose: Assesses skills important to effective learning in high school and college. Used for educational counseling.

Description: 120–item paper-pencil test of study skills yielding scores in seven areas: goal orientation, activity structure, scholarly skills, lecture mastery, textbook mastery, examination mastery, self-mastery, and study efficiency. Twenty-two of the items are included in a Reading Validity Index, which determines whether the student has responded thoughtfully. Two forms, the College Form and the Secondary School Form, are available. College Form items are answered on a 5–point ordinal scale ranging from seldom to always. The Secondary School Form items are written in a true-false format. Self-administered. Suitable for group use.

Untimed: 30–45 minutes

Scoring: Hand key

Cost: Specimen set $9.00; 25 tests $20.00; 25 answer sheets, 25 profile sheets $6.75 each; keys $6.75; manual $6.75 (specify Secondary or College form)

Publisher: Psychologists and Educators, Inc.

EFFECTIVE STUDY TEST (EST)
William F. Brown

Adolescent, adult
Grades 9–college

Purpose: Identifies students needing counseling for their study skills and habits. Used to monitor student progress in response to counseling and instruction intended to improve study methods.

Description: 125–item paper-pencil true-false test assessing students' knowledge of effective study methods. The test contains five subscales: reading behavior, reality orientation, study organization, writing behavior, and examination behavior. The test yields a total score for study effectiveness. Use is restricted to professional educators. Self-administered. Suitable for group use.

Untimed: 35–45 minutes

Scoring: Hand key

Cost: 25 reusable test booklets $7.50; 25 answer sheets $3.00; scoring stencil $0.70; direction manual $0.70

Publisher: The American College Testing Program

LEARNING BEHAVIORS SCALE
Denis H. Stott, Paul A. McDermott, Leonard F. Green, and Jean Francis

Child
Kindergarten

Purpose: Identifies a child's learning behaviors. Used to determine how a child will perform academically.

Description: 23–item paper-pencil questionnaire completed by the classroom teacher to assess learning behaviors to determine a child's probable academic performance. For each statement, the teacher indicates whether the behavior described "usually," "sometimes," or "doesn't" apply to the child. Items are worded both positively and negatively. The test yields three learning style dimension scores: Avoidant—Rejecting, Inattentive—Distractible, and Apprehensive—Unresponsive. This test formerly was known as the Guide to the Child's Learning Style (GCLS). Examiner required. Suitable for group use.

Untimed: 1–2 minutes per child

Scoring: Hand key

Cost: Complete kit (25 questionnaires, 1 set of 4 keys, manual) $59.00

Publisher: The Psychological Corporation

Information and availability unconfirmed; last verified in 1988.

LEARNING EFFICIENCY TEST (LET)
Raymond E. Webster

Child, adolescent, adult—
Ages 6 and older

Purpose: Measures visual and auditory memory characteristics of children and adults. Used to determine deficits that may be related to classroom learning problems and for academic placement, identification of learning-handicapped students, and identification of students' preferred learning style.

Description: Multiple-item paper-pencil norm-referenced measure of visual memory and auditory memory. Two subtests assess both ordered and unordered recall under three conditions: immediate recall, short-term recall, and long-term recall. In the Visual Memory subtest, the examiner shows the examinee nonrhyming letters on stimulus cards. For the Auditory Memory subtest, the examiner reads the letters to the examinee. Sequences to be remembered range in length from two to nine items. The manual includes an interpretation of memory performance and describes remedial activities that can be used to improve learning efficiency. Examiner required. Not suitable for group use.

Untimed: 10–15 minutes

Scoring: Hand key

Cost: Test kit (manual, stimulus cards, 50 record forms in vinyl folder) $46.00

Publisher: Academic Therapy Publications

LEARNING PREFERENCE INVENTORY
Harvey F. Silver and J. Robert Hanson

Students

Purpose: Identifies the learning preferences or styles of students. Used by educators for diagnosing student learning styles, curriculum planning, and selection of appropriate teaching strategies.

Description: 144–item paper-pencil inventory assessing an individual's learning preferences. The instrument is based on Jung's Theory of Psychological Type and indicates how an individual perceives (through sensing or intuition), makes judgments (through thinking or feeling), and processes data (through introversion or extroversion). Teachers receive learning style profiles on each student and the class. The inventory was developed with inner-city, urban, and suburban students. Examiner/self-administered. Suitable for group use.

Untimed: 30 minutes

Scoring: Hand key; may be computer scored

Cost: $2.50 per copy; computer-scorable copy (includes full diagnostic printout and class plot) $5.00

Publisher: Hanson, Silver, Strong and Associates, Inc.

Information and availability unconfirmed; last verified in 1987.

LEARNING PROCESS QUESTIONNAIRE (LPQ)
J. Biggs

Adolescent Grades 8–12

Purpose: Assesses a student's general orientation towards learning by identifying the motives and strategies that comprise an approach to learning. Used by teachers and counselors.

Description: 36–item paper-pencil test identifying the motives and strategies that comprise a student's approach to learning. Items are rated in a Likert-scale format. Stanine and percentile rank scores

are yielded for total raw score conversion. Separate profiles are provided for motive and strategy subscales. One of two tests in a series (see entry for Study Process Questionnaire). Examiner required. Suitable for group use.

AUSTRALIAN PUBLISHER

Timed: 20 minutes

Scoring: Hand key; may be machine scored

Cost: Contact publisher

Publisher: Australian Council for Educational Research Limited

LEARNING STYLE INVENTORY
Harvey F. Silver and J. Robert Hanson

Student, adult

Purpose: Identifies learning styles of students and adults.

Description: 80–item paper-pencil self-assessment tool for identifying learning preferences. The inventory includes behaviors for four different learning styles: sensing-thinkers (factual, memory-based mastery learning); sensing-feelers (involvement and motivation for learning); intuitive thinkers (understanding, critical and conceptual thinking); and intuitive feelers (creative, innovative synthesizing-type thinking). The instrument includes detailed descriptions of the four styles. Individuals draw their own profiles. Results can help teachers understand their own and their students' learning styles. Self-administered. Suitable for group use.

Untimed: 30 minutes

Scoring: Self-scored

Cost: $3.50 per copy

Publisher: Hanson, Silver, Strong and Associates, Inc.

Information and availability unconfirmed; last verified in 1987.

LEARNING STYLES INVENTORY
Richard M. Cooper and Jerry F. Brown

Adolescent

Purpose: Assesses learning styles.

Description: 45–item paper-pencil or computer-administered multiple-choice and Likert-scale test assessing learning styles through the following subtests: Visual Language, Visual Numeric, Auditory Language, Auditory Numeric, Tactile Concrete, Social Individual, Social Group, Oral Expressiveness, and Written Expressiveness. The test yields several scores, including Class Composite, Individual vs. Class, Teacher vs. Class, Class Prescriptive Information, and Individual Prescriptive Information. The computer program operates on Apple and Commodore computer systems using MS DOS. Self-administered. Suitable for group use.

Untimed: Varies

Scoring: Computer scored

Cost: 2 diskettes and back-ups, documentation $98.00

Publisher: Educational Activities, Inc.

Information and availability unconfirmed; last verified in 1988.

LEARNING STYLES INVENTORY
Al Babich, CITE Version;
Helena Hendrix-Frye,
Vocational Version

Adolescent, adult—Ages
12 and older

Purpose: Assesses individual learning style.

Description: Computer-administered or paper-pencil multiple-choice test with four subtests: Cognitive Learning Style, Social Learning Style, Expressive Learning Style, and Vocational (Environmental) Learning Style. A Learning Style Computerized Reporting service is available. All reproducible forms are included. The computer version is available in Apple (ProDos) and IBM (MS-DOS). The test is available in large print, audiocassette, and videocassette. Examiner/self-administered. Suitable for group use.

Untimed: 45 minutes

Scoring: Computer scored; hand key

Cost: $395.00 Cite version; $495.00 Vocational version

Publisher: Piney Mountain Press, Inc.

LEARNING STYLES INVENTORY (LSI)
Refer to page 755.

LEARNING STYLES INVENTORY (LSI)
Joseph S. Renzulli and
Linda H. Smith

Child
Grades 4–12

Purpose: Assesses the methods through which students prefer to learn. Used to assist teachers in individualizing the instructional process.

Description: 65–item paper-pencil inventory assessing student attitudes toward nine modes of instruction: projects, drill and recitation, peer teaching, discussion, teaching games, independent study, programmed instruction, lecture, and stimulation. Various classroom learning experiences associated with these nine teaching/learning style approaches are described, and students use a 5–point scale ranging from "very unpleasant" to "very pleasant" to indicate their reaction to each activity. A teacher form is included with each set of student materials. Teachers respond to items that parallel those on the student form in terms of how frequently each activity occurs in the classroom. The resulting profile of instructional styles can be compared to individual student preferences and serve to facilitate a closer match between how teachers instruct and the styles to which students respond most favorably. Examiner required. Suitable for group use.

Untimed: Varies

Scoring: Computer scored

Cost: Class set (30 student forms, teacher form, computer scoring) $22.95; specimen set (manual, teacher form, student form) $8.50

Publisher: Creative Learning Press, Inc.

MATHEMATICS ANXIETY RATING SCALE
Refer to page 190.

---

study skills attitudes

MURPHY-MEISGEIER TYPE INDICATOR FOR CHILDREN (MMTIC)
Charles Meisgeier and Elizabeth Murphy

Child
Grades 2–8

Purpose: Determines the Jungian types of children in order to identify individual learning styles.

Description: 70–item paper-pencil test measuring four preference scales: Extraversion-Introversion (16 items), Sensing-Intuition (18 items), Thinking-Feeling (18 items), and Judgment-Perception (18 items). The inventory is designed to affirm the child's strengths to increase self-esteem; contribute to the rearing, teaching, counseling; and overall understanding of children; and provide a means through which children can understand individual differences. The manual contains statistical information as well as descriptions of learning styles associated with each type. Three booklets introducing type to children, parents, and teachers are available. The computer report identifies the individual preferences and reports information on learning styles. The reading level of the items is most appropriate for students in Grades 3–6; however, teachers may read the items aloud to second graders or any examinee with reading difficulties. Examiner required. Suitable for group use.

Untimed: Not available

Scoring: Hand key; may be computer scored

Cost: Manual $13.50; 25 test booklets $15.00; 10 prepaid answer sheets $25.00; 50 non-prepaid answer sheets $18.00; 50 scoring report forms (specify Grades 2–5 or Grades 5–8) $17.50; scoring keys $12.50

Publisher: Consulting Psychologists Press, Inc.

MY BOOK OF THINGS AND STUFF: AN INTEREST QUESTIONNAIRE FOR YOUNG CHILDREN
Ann McGeevy

Child—Ages 6–11

Purpose: Assesses the interests of young children.

Description: Multiple-item paper-pencil questionnaire including over 40 illustrated items focusing on the special interests and learning styles of students. The book also includes a teacher's section, an interest profile sheet, sample pages from a journal, and bibliographies of interest-centered books and magazines for children. All questionnaire pages are perforated and prepared on blackline masters so that copies can be made for an entire class. Examiner required. Suitable for group use.

Untimed: Varies

Scoring: Examiner evaluated

Cost: Questionnaire booklet $13.95

Publisher: Creative Learning Press, Inc.

SELF-DIRECTED LEARNING READINESS SCALE (SDLRS)
Lucy M. Guglielmino

Adult

Purpose: Assesses an individual's learning preferences and attitudes toward learning. Used to measure readiness for self-directed learning.

Description: 58–item paper-pencil or computer-administered self-report multiple-choice test assessing readiness for self-directed learning. The test is available on two levels, Elementary (E) and Adult (A). A Business (B) form and a Self-Scoring (S) form are available at the adult level. A sixth-grade reading level is required. Form ABE, suitable for adults with lower reading levels (Grade 3.7 reading level required) and non-native speakers of English, is also available. The software program operates on Apple IIc systems. Raw scores may be converted to percentile rankings. Self-administered. Suitable for group use. Adult form available in Spanish, French, German, Chinese, Japanese, and Finnish. Form ABE available in Spanish.

Untimed: 20 minutes

Scoring: Computer scored (except self-scoring form)

Cost: $3.00 per copy including scoring; $3.95 for self-scoring form; quantity discounts available

Publisher: Guglielmino & Associates, Inc.

STUDY ATTITUDES AND METHODS SURVEY (SAMS)
William B. Michael, Joan J. Michael, and Wayne S. Zimmerman

Adolescent, adult
Grades 7 and above

Purpose: Diagnoses habits and attitudes that may be preventing junior high school, high-school, and college students from achieving full academic potential. Used in the classroom and for school-wide screening to identify students most likely to benefit from individual counseling.

Description: Multiple-item paper-pencil inventory assessing dimensions of a motivational, noncognitive nature that relate to school achievement and contribute to a student's performance beyond those measured by traditional ability tests. The student's profile can provide the requisite insights and guidelines for study habit improvement. Scales measured by the SAMS are Academic Interest/Love of Learning, Academic Drive, Study Methods, Lack of Anxiety, Lack of Manipulation, and Lack of Alienation Toward Authority. Norms are provided for high-school and college level. Examiner required. Suitable for group use.

Untimed: 20–30 minutes

Scoring: Hand key; may be computer scored

Cost: Specimen set (manual, all forms) $5.50; 25 booklets and answer sheets $9.50; 25 profile interpretive guides $3.25; keys $10.75; manual $2.75

Publisher: EdITS/Educational and Industrial Testing Service

STUDY HABITS EVALUATION AND INSTRUCTION KIT
Peter Jackson, Neil Reid, and Cedric Croft

Child, adolescent—Ages 14–17

Purpose: Measures and provides instruction on study habits. Used for educational guidance.

Description: Two-part paper-pencil test measuring study habits. Part 1, the Inventory of Study Habits, assists pupils in measuring study habits. The second part, consisting of self-instructional booklets, allows students to work on improving study habits in seven areas: study environment, study time, study organization, reading skills, notetaking skills, exam preparation, and exam technique. Self-administered. Suitable for group use. NEW ZEALAND PUBLISHER

Untimed: 45 minutes

Scoring: Hand key; examiner evaluated

Cost: Contact publisher

Publisher: New Zealand Council for Educational Research

STUDY OF CHILDREN'S LEARNING BEHAVIORS
Denis H. Stott, Paul A. McDermott, Leonard F. Green, and Jean Francis

---

Child
PreK-Grade 4

Purpose: Identifies a child's learning style. Used to determine how a child will perform academically.

Description: Multiple-item paper-pencil questionnaire completed by the classroom teacher to identify a student's patterns of learning-related behaviors and problem-solving strategies. Three learning style dimension scores are yielded: Avoidant, Inattentive, and Overly Independent. Examiner required. Suitable for group use.

Untimed: 1–2 minutes per child

Scoring: Hand key

Cost: Complete kit (25 questionnaires, 1 set of 3 keys, manual) $59.00

Publisher: The Psychological Corporation

Information and availability unconfirmed; last verified in 1988.

STUDY PROCESS QUESTIONNAIRE (SPQ)
J. Biggs

Tertiary students

Purpose: Assesses a student's general orientation towards learning by identifying the motives and strategies that comprise an approach to learning. Used by teachers or counselors.

Description: 42–item paper-pencil test identifying the motives and strategies that comprise the student's approach to learning. Items are rated on a Likert-scale format. Stanine and percentile rank scores are presented for total raw score conversion. Separate profiles are presented for motive and strategy subscales. The test is one of two in a series (see entry for Learning Process Questionnaire). Examiner required. Suitable for group use. AUSTRALIAN PUBLISHER

Timed: 20 minutes

Scoring: Hand key; may be machine scored

Cost: Contact publisher

Publisher: Australian Council for Educational Research Limited

STUDY SKILLS COUNSELING EVALUATION
George D. Demos

Adolescent, adult
Grades 10–college

Purpose: Evaluates the study habits and attitudes of high-school and college students.

Description: 50–item paper-pencil questionnaire in which students use a scale ranging from "very often" to "very seldom" to rate themselves on time distribution, study conditions, taking notes, examinations, and habits and attitudes. The questionnaire contains "critical items" that differentiate between B and C students. Self-administered. Suitable for group use.

Untimed: 10–20 minutes

Scoring: Hand key

Cost: Complete kit (25 forms, manual) $17.50

Publisher: Western Psychological Services

STUDY SKILLS SURVEYS (SSS)
William F. Brown

Adolescent, adult
Grades 9–13, college

Purpose: Identifies study skill problems likely to hinder academic achievement. Used to counsel students about effective study habits and attitudes.

Description: 60–item paper-pencil "yes-no" test containing three scales designed to evaluate organization, study techniques, and study motivation. The test helps students recognize and change poor study habits. Self-administered. Suitable for group use. Available in Spanish.

Untimed: 15–20 minutes

Scoring: Hand key

Cost: 25 reusable test booklets $7.50; 25 answer sheets $3.00; 25 student workbooks $5.00; directions manual $0.35

Publisher: The American College Testing Program

SUBSUMED ABILITIES TEST—A MEASURE OF LEARNING EFFICIENCY (SAT)
Martin M. Bruce

Adolescent, adult
Grades 6 and above

Purpose: Measures the subject's ability and willingness to learn; used for student placement, vocational counseling, and job selection.

Description: 60–item nonverbal paper-pencil test consisting of 30 pairs of items, each of which is composed of four line drawings. The student analyzes one with three others, resulting in a Potential Abilities Score and a Demonstrated Abilities Score based on the student's ability to conceptualize, form abstractions, and recognize identicals. Designed for individuals with at least a sixth-grade education. Examiner/self-administered. Suitable for group use.

Timed: 30 minutes

Scoring: Hand key

Cost: Pkg. of tests $43.00; manual $13.50; manual's supplement (1984) $14.50; package of scoring key-tabulation sheets $18.00; specimen set $32.50

Publisher: Martin M. Bruce, Ph.D., Publishers

SURVEY OF STUDY HABITS AND ATTITUDES (SSHA)
W.F. Brown and W.H. Holtzman

Adolescent, adult
Grades 7–college

Purpose: Measures study methods, motivation for studying, and certain attitudes toward scholastic activities that are important in the classroom.

Description: 100–item paper-pencil test measuring four basic aspects of study habits and attitudes: delay avoidance, work methods, teacher approval, and education acceptance. Students rate themselves according to their own habits and attitudes. The test yields a Study Habits subtotal, a Study Attitude subtotal, and total study Orientation scores. Two forms, Form H (Grades 7–12) and Form C (college students), are available. Self-administered. Suitable for group use. Available in Spanish.

Untimed: 20–25 minutes

Scoring: Hand key; may be machine scored

Cost: Examination kit (survey, IBM 805 answer document, key, manual) $15.00; 25 surveys $21.00; 50 IBM 805 answer documents $19.00; manual and keys $12.00

Publisher: The Psychological Corporation

Information and availability unconfirmed; last verified in 1988.

WRENN STUDY HABITS INVENTORY
C. Gilbert Wrenn

Adolescent, adult
Grades 10 and above

Purpose: Identifies student study habits and attitudes. Used for academic counseling.

Description: 28–item paper-pencil test of habits and attitudes by which high and low scholarship students are distinguished. A negative item score means response is closer to response given by low scholarship students. Self-administered. Suitable for group use.

Untimed: 10–20 minutes

Scoring: Hand key

Cost: Specimen set (test, manual, key) $1.75; manual and scoring stencil $1.50; 25 tests $4.25

Publisher: Consulting Psychologists Press, Inc.

Student Evaluation and Counseling: Vocational Guidance: Achievement and Aptitude

ACADEMIC-TECHNICAL APTITUDE TESTS—ATA AND SATA

Child, adolescent

Purpose: Assesses differential job aptitudes. Used for vocational and educational guidance.

Description: Multiple-item paper-pencil batteries measuring occupational aptitudes. The ATA battery (for pupils in Standards 6, 7, and 8) consists of 10 tests: Verbal Reasoning, Nonverbal Reasoning, Computations, Spatial Perceptions (2–D), Mechanical Reasoning, Language Comprehension, Spatial Perception (3–D), Comparison, Coordination, and Writing Speed. SATA (for pupils in Standards 8, 9, and 10) is available in two forms, A and B. Form A consists of the following 10 tests: Verbal Reasoning, Nonverbal Reasoning I: Figure Series, Nonverbal Reasoning II: Dominoes, Computations,

Reading Comprehension, Spelling and Vocabulary, Mechanical Reasoning, Spatial Perception (3–D), Comparison, and Price Controlling. Form B has one additional subtest, Filing. Examiner required. Suitable for group use. SOUTH AFRICAN PUBLISHER

Timed: ATA 4 hours; SATA 4½ hours

Scoring: Hand key; examiner evaluated

Cost: (In Rands) ATA test 5,00; manual 11,00; scoring stencil I 10,50; scoring stencil II 7,50; 10 answer sheets I 1,50; 10 answer sheets II 1,50; SATA test (specify A or B) 2,00; manual 6,00; scoring stencils I, II (specify A or B) 2,50 each; 10 answer sheets I 1,00; 10 answer sheets II 1,00; orders from outside the RSA will be dealt with on merit

Publisher: Human Sciences Research Council

THE APPLIED KNOWLEDGE TEST (AKT)
M.A. Brimer

Adolescent—Ages 14–18

Purpose: Measures the ability to use knowledge of mathematics, English, science, and spatial relationships. Used for vocational guidance.

Description: Multiple-item paper-pencil measures of a student's competence in the four employment-related subject areas of mathematics, English, science, and spatial relationships. Results can be used to validate interest scores from the Occupational Interest Rating Scale (OIRS). Examiner/self-administered. Suitable for group use. BRITISH PUBLISHER

Untimed: 60 minutes

Scoring: Hand key

Cost: Contact publisher

Publisher: Educational Evaluation Enterprises

Information and availability unconfirmed; last verified in 1987.

APTITUDE INTEREST MEASUREMENT (AIM)
Refer to page 866.

APTITUDE TESTS FOR INDIAN SOUTH AFRICANS—JATISA AND SATISA
Refer to page 425.

ARMED SERVICES VOCATIONAL APTITUDE BATTERY (ASVAB)
Department of Defense

Adolescent, adult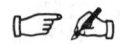
Grades 10 and over

Purpose: Evaluates high-school students' vocational interests and aptitudes. Used for counseling and by the military services to identify eligible graduates for possible recruitment.

Description: 334–item paper-pencil test of aptitudes in various vocational and technical fields. Factors measured include electronics, mechanical comprehension, general science, automotive and shop information, numerical operations, coding speed, word knowledge, arithmetic, reasoning, paragraph comprehension, and mathematics knowledge. Indicates ability in the following areas: verbal; math; academic; mechanical and crafts; business and clerical; electronics and electrical; and health, social, and technologies. A military service recruiter will assist each school in administering the test, and the U.S. Military Entrance Processing Command (USMEPCOM) provides the examiner. Individual test results are delivered to school counselors, and copies of the scores are given to the recruiting services. Examiner required. Suitable for group use.

Timed: 3 hours

Scoring: Computer scored

Cost: No charge to schools for administration, materials, and scoring

Publisher: U.S. Department of Defense

Information and availability unconfirmed; last verified in 1987.

BALL APTITUDE BATTERY™
Refer to page 869.

THE BRIGANCE® DIAGNOSTIC INVENTORY OF BASIC SKILLS
Refer to page 427.

BUSINESS ENGLISH TEST (BET)
John T. Dailey

Adolescent, adult
Grades 9 and above

Purpose: Assesses knowledge in business English skills. Used in career counseling.

Description: 111–item paper-pencil test measuring vocational aptitude for trade, technical, and business careers. The BET yields a single score, but subscores in spelling, punctuation, capitalization, and grammar can be obtained for local interpretation by using the BET scoring mask. Together, the Technical and Scholastic Test (TST) and the BET make up the Dailey Vocational Tests. The examiner's manual includes information for administering, scoring, and interpreting both the BET and the TST. The individual profile sheet and group report form are designed for use with both tests. The Spatial Visualization Test (SVT) is no longer published. However, for those who already have the SVT booklets, combined BET/SVT answer sheets are available. Examiner required. Suitable for group use.

Timed: 30 minutes

Scoring: Hand key

Cost: 35 test booklets $19.50; examiner's manual $4.50; 100 answer sheets $23.85

Publisher: The Riverside Publishing Company

CAREER AND VOCATIONAL FORM OF THE SOI-LA BASIC TEST

Adolescent, adult

Purpose: Measures cognitive abilities patterned to predict career and vocational options.

Description: Multiple-item paper-pencil test measuring 24 cognitive abilities patterned to predict career and vocational options. The test consists of subtests

taken from the SOI-LA Basic Test. The MSI subtest has been replaced with a test of MMI. Instructions for self-administration are included with each form. The scoring keys and instructions in the Basic Test manual apply. Career and vocational choices are listed on an accompanying sheet for selection. A *Career and Vocation Choice Guide* is included. Materials are available for training any low abilities required for a desired occupation. Computer analysis is available. Self-administered. Suitable for group use.

Timed: 3–5 minutes per test

Scoring: Hand key; may be computer scored

Cost: Examiner's manual $35.00; test form $2.85

Publisher: M & M Systems

COMPREHENSIVE ABILITY BATTERY (CAB)
Refer to page 875.

COMPUTER APTITUDE, LITERACY, AND INTEREST PROFILE (CALIP)
Mary S. Poplin, David E. Drew, and Robert S. Gable

Ages 12–60

Purpose: Assesses computer-related abilities of children and adults. Used by school vocational counselors, school psychologists, administrators, and junior and senior high-school and college instructors. Also used in business and industry to make personnel decisions.

Description: Multiple-item paper-pencil test consisting of six subtests: estimation, graphic patterns, logical structures, series, computer interest, and computer literacy. The test measures computer programming aptitudes; computer use aptitudes, including systems analysis, graphics, and repair; and computer literacy, interest, and experience. Examiner/self-administered. Suitable for group use.

Untimed: 45 minutes

Scoring: Hand key

Cost: Complete kit (examiner's manual, 50 answer sheets, 10 test booklets, storage box) $59.00

Publisher: PRO-ED

A CREATIVITY MEASURE—THE SRT SCALE
Refer to page 998.

DIFFERENTIAL APTITUDE TESTS (DAT): FORMS S AND T
Refer to page 455.

DIFFERENTIAL APTITUDE TESTS (DAT): FORMS V AND W
Refer to page 455.

GUIDEPAK
Refer to page 984.

INTER-AMERICAN SERIES: TEST OF ORAL COMPREHENSION
Refer to page 576.

INTUITIVE MECHANICS (WEIGHTS AND PULLEYS)
Refer to page 1066.

THE MAJOR-MINOR-FINDER
Arthur Cutler, Francis Ferry, Robert Kauk, and Robert Robinett

Adolescent, adult
Grades 10 and above

Purpose: Assesses an individual's aptitudes and interests and identifies appropriate college major choices. Used in college orientation courses at the upper high-school and college level.

Description: Multiple-item paper-pencil or computer-administered college major exploration instrument matching student aptitudes and interests with 120 college majors. The test includes information concerning jobs related to 120 college majors, skills and interests required of the 120 majors, and college majors most compatible with educational goals and career interests.

Reusable assessment booklets are used in conjunction with consumable insert answer folders for paper-pencil administration. Microcomputer programs are available for TRS–80 Models I and III, Commodore PET/CBM, Commodore 64, Apple II+ and IIe, and IBM personal computers. Software packages include instructions, printed inventories, and additional information. An optional introductory filmstrip is available. A supplement, the *College-Major Handbook*, includes further data on each college major, a definition of the major, courses required, aptitudes most needed, job activities associated with the major, chances for employment in jobs associated with the major, related career opportunities, and where to write for further information. The paper-pencil version may be self-administered. Suitable for group use.

Untimed: Varies

Scoring: Self-scored; may be computer scored

Cost: Reusable test booklet, answer folder $1.45; additional answer folders $0.25; manual $3.50; *College-Major Handbook* $4.00; diskettes $89.95; filmstrip $32.95

Publisher: CFKR Career Materials, Inc.

Information and availability unconfirmed; last verified in 1988.

MINNESOTA ENGINEERING ANALOGIES TEST
M.D. Dunnette

Engineering and graduate
school applicants

Purpose: Measures engineering achievement and mathematical reasoning ability. Used for selection and placement of engineers and admission of graduate students.

Description: Multiple-item paper-pencil test of engineering skills and potential. Items are multiple-choice analogies. The test can be taken at one of over 600 licensed testing centers throughout the United States, Canadian provinces, Puerto Rico, the Philippines, England, and Australia. Scores will be reported to graduate admission officers and faculty advisors or to personnel offices. Examiner required. Suitable for group use.

Timed: 45 minutes

Scoring: Scoring service available

Cost: Contact publisher

Publisher: Admissions and Credentialing Group/The Psychological Corporation

Information and availability unconfirmed; last verified in 1988.

MISSOURI APTITUDE AND CAREER INFORMATION INVENTORY (MACII)
Refer to page 829.

NIIP ENGINEERING SELECTION TEST BATTERY

Adult

Purpose: Assesses general intellectual ability and specific skills. Used for selecting student, professional, and industrial engineering applicants.

Description: Battery of paper-pencil tests measuring general and specific intellectual abilities. The manual provides administration details and scoring procedures for tests GT82, GT90A/B, GT70/70B, EA4, and VMD (1979 revision).

Group Test 90A (GT90A) is a 4–part test of general intelligence and verbal aptitude for adults of above-average educational attainment. Group Test 90B (GT90B) is an alternative to GT90A, containing similar but different items. Group Test 70 (GT70) is a 3–part general intelligence test for use with groups of above-average educational attainment. Group Test 70B (GT70B) is a similar but alternative test to GT70. Engineering Arithmetic Test 4 (EA4) is a metricated test. Group Test 82 (GT82) is a 4–part test measuring comprehension of shapes and spatial relationships. The Vincents Mechanical Diagrams Test—1979 Revision contains four subtests containing mechanical problems. Examiner required. Suitable for group use.

BRITISH PUBLISHER

Timed: Varies, depending on test

Scoring: Hand key

Cost: Contact publisher

Publisher: NFER-NELSON Publishing Company Ltd.

NIIP ENGINEERING SELECTION TEST BATTERY: ENGINEERING ARITHMETIC TEST EA4

Ages 15–adult

Purpose: Identifies engineering-related abilities of students. Used in counseling for selecting courses, apprenticeships, and occupations.

Description: Multiple-item paper-pencil test identifying candidates for engineering-related courses, apprenticeships, and occupations. One in a series of five tests in the NIIP Engineering Selection Battery. Examiner required. Suitable for group use.

BRITISH PUBLISHER

Timed: 22 minutes

Scoring: Hand key

Cost: Contact publisher

Publisher: NFER-NELSON Publishing Company Ltd.

NIIP ENGINEERING SELECTION TEST BATTERY: GROUP TEST 82

Adolescent, adult—Ages 15–adult

Purpose: Assesses the conceptual ability to rotate and turn over two-dimensional shapes. Used for selecting job applicants in engineering-related fields.

Description: Multiple-item four-part paper-pencil test assessing candidate's ability to rotate and turn over two-dimensional shapes in the mind's eye. The test booklet is reusable. One in a series of five tests in the NIIP Engineering Selection Battery. Examiner required. Suitable for group use.

BRITISH PUBLISHER

Timed: 30 minutes

Scoring: Hand key

Cost: Contact publisher

Publisher: NFER-NELSON Publishing Company Ltd.

NIIP ENGINEERING SELECTION TEST BATTERY: GROUP TESTS 70 AND 70B

Adolescent, adult—Ages 15–adult

Purpose: Measures general intelligence of applicants for apprentice, managerial, supervisory, skilled, and clerical positions in engineering-related fields.

Description: Two paper-pencil tests assessing general intelligence through nonverbal questions. Each test contains three subtests: Coding, Matrices, and Series. Because the tests are not precisely parallel, separate norms are provided. One in a series of five tests in the NIIP Engineering Selection Battery. Examiner required. Suitable for group use. BRITISH PUBLISHER

Timed: 30 minutes

Scoring: Hand key

Cost: Contact publisher

Publisher: NFER-NELSON Publishing Company Ltd.

NIIP ENGINEERING SELECTION TEST BATTERY: GROUP TESTS 90A AND 90B

Adolescent, adult—Ages 15–adult

Purpose: Assesses the verbal abilities of adults with a fair level of educational achievement. Used for evaluating applicants for apprentice, management, supervisory, and skilled technical posts.

Description: Two paper-pencil tests of intelligence and verbal aptitude used for evaluating applicants for higher-level positions in engineering-related fields. One in a series of five tests in the NIIP Engineering Selection Battery. Examiner required. Suitable for group use. BRITISH PUBLISHER

Timed: 30 minutes

Scoring: Hand key

Cost: Contact publisher

Publisher: NFER-NELSON Publishing Company Ltd.

NIIP ENGINEERING SELECTION TEST BATTERY: VINCENT MECHANICAL DIAGRAMS TEST (REVISED)

Adolescent, adult—Ages 15–adult

Purpose: Assesses individual's ability to understand the concepts of cog, pulley, and lever systems.

Description: Multiple-item paper-pencil test using diagrams for assessing the mechanical understanding of candidates for positions in engineering-related fields. One in a series of five tests in the NIIP Engineering Selection Battery. Examiner required. Suitable for group use. BRITISH PUBLISHER

Timed: 15 minutes

Scoring: Hand key

Cost: Contact publisher

Publisher: NFER-NELSON Publishing Company Ltd.

OFFICE SKILLS ACHIEVEMENT TEST

Refer to page 939.

THE OHIO VOCATIONAL ACHIEVEMENT TEST PROGRAM

Adolescent, adult Grades 11–12 and postsecondary

Purpose: Measures high-school and postsecondary students' abilities and understanding of specific vocational areas. Used to evaluate teaching objectives and materials and for counseling and program improvement.

Description: Tests junior, senior, and postsecondary vocational students in 38 vocational areas. The program is part of a test battery package that includes the Test of Cognitive Skills (TCS). The complete battery is to be administered on any three consecutive days during the first three weeks of March (at other times for an additional cost). The tests reveal the correlation of student academic aptitude and vocational achievement. The test measures students' ability to solve problems, analyze data, use abstractions in specific situations, and assemble parts to form a complete structure. The test also assesses student knowledge of principles and specifics. The test booklets are controlled and must be returned after use. Examiner required. Suitable for group use.

Timed: TCS 1 hour; Parts I and II 2 hours each

Scoring: Computer scored

Cost: Testing loan service (test booklets, answer sheets, scoring service) Ohio students $1.50 each; out-of-state students $2.50 each for March administration, $3.50 at other times

Publisher: Instructional Materials Laboratory, The Ohio State University

---

THE OHIO VOCATIONAL ACHIEVEMENT TESTS IN AGRICULTURAL EDUCATION: AGRICULTURAL BUSINESS

Adolescent, adult
Grades 11–12 and
postsecondary

Purpose: Evaluates and diagnoses achievement for instructional improvement in agricultural business. May be used for vocational guidance in an overall program.

Description: 328–item paper-pencil multiple-choice test in two parts. Part I (170 items) covers retail sales, maintaining stock, storage and distribution, marketing, and office functions. Part II (158 items) covers establishing and managing agribusiness, agricultural skills, and personal development. Examiner required. Suitable for group use.

Timed: 2 hours per part

Scoring: Computer scored

Cost: Testing loan service (test booklets, answer sheets, scoring service) Ohio students $1.25 each; out-of-state students $2.50 each for March administration, $3.50 at other times

Publisher: Instructional Materials Laboratory, The Ohio State University

---

THE OHIO VOCATIONAL ACHIEVEMENT TESTS IN AGRICULTURAL EDUCATION: AGRICULTURAL EQUIPMENT MECHANICS

Adolescent, adult
Grades 11–12 and
postsecondary

Purpose: Evaluates and diagnoses achievement for instructional improvement in agricultural equipment mechanics. May be used for vocational guidance in an overall program.

Description: 381–item paper-pencil multiple-choice test in two parts. Part I (192 items) covers intake and exhaust systems, fuel systems, electrical systems, power trains, engine lubrication systems, agricultural equipment assembly, and personal development. Part II (189 items) covers cooling systems; compression section; hydraulic systems; braking systems; steering and wheel systems; welding, fabricating, and refinishing; and heating, air conditioning, and ventilation systems. Examiner required. Suitable for group use.

Timed: 2 hours per part

Scoring: Computer scored

Cost: Testing loan service (test booklets, answer sheets, scoring service) Ohio students $1.50 each; out-of-state students $2.50 each for March administration, $3.50 at other times

Publisher: Instructional Materials Laboratory, The Ohio State University

---

THE OHIO VOCATIONAL ACHIEVEMENT TESTS IN AGRICULTURAL EDUCATION: FARM MANAGEMENT

Adolescent, adult
Grades 11–12 and
postsecondary

Purpose: Evaluates and diagnoses achievement for instructional improvement in farm management. May be used for vocational guidance in an overall program.

Description: 340–item paper-pencil multiple-choice test in two parts. Part I (161 items) covers seven areas: performing general office work, operating the computer, planning and organizing the farm business, marketing agricultural products, planning the crop and livestock program, planning the equipment and machinery program, and planning buildings and structures. Part II (179 items) covers financing the farm business, purchasing and storing supplies, keeping enterprise records, planning and supervising labor, summarizing and analyzing farm business records, protecting and transferring assets, being aware of farm law, and securing real estate resources. Examiner required. Suitable for group use.

Timed: 2 hours per part

Scoring: Computer scored

Cost: Testing loan service (test booklets, answer sheets, scoring service) Ohio students $1.50 each; out-of-state students $2.50 each for March administration, $3.50 at other times

Publisher: Instructional Materials Laboratory, The Ohio State University

THE OHIO VOCATIONAL ACHIEVEMENT TESTS IN AGRICULTURAL EDUCATION: HORTICULTURE

Adolescent, adult
**Grades 11–12 and
postsecondary**

Purpose: Evaluates and diagnoses achievement for instructional improvement in horticulture. May be used for vocational guidance in an overall program.

Description: 363–item paper-pencil multiple-choice test in two parts. Part I (179 items) covers soil and plant science, greenhouse operations, interior plantscape services, landscape services, and turf services. Part II (184 items) covers retail floriculture, nursery, garden center, fruit and vegetable production, equipment and mechanics, and personal development. Examiner required. Suitable for group use.

Timed: 2 hours per part

Scoring: Computer scored

Cost: Testing loan service (test booklets, answer sheets, scoring service) Ohio students $1.50 each; out-of-state students $2.50 each for March administration, $3.50 at other times

Publisher: Instructional Materials Laboratory, The Ohio State University

THE OHIO VOCATIONAL ACHIEVEMENT TESTS IN AGRICULTURAL EDUCATION: PRODUCTION AGRICULTURE

Adolescent, adult
**Grades 11–12 and
postsecondary**

Purpose: Evaluates and diagnoses achievement for instructional improvement in production agriculture. May be used for vocational guidance in an overall program.

Description: 349–item paper-pencil multiple-choice test in two parts. Part I (175 items) covers beef production, small grain production, sheep production, soybean production, crop chemical application, and agricultural construction. Part II (174 items) covers operator equipment maintenance, dairy production, corn production, swine production, forage production, and employment procedures. Examiner required. Suitable for group use.

Timed: 2 hours per part

Scoring: Computer scored

Cost: Testing loan service (test booklets, answer sheets, scoring service) Ohio students $1.50 each; out-of-state students $2.50 each for March administration, $3.50 at other times

Publisher: Instructional Materials Laboratory, The Ohio State University

THE OHIO VOCATIONAL ACHIEVEMENT TESTS IN BUSINESS EDUCATION: ACCOUNTING/COMPUTING CLERK

Adolescent, adult
**Grades 11–12 and
postsecondary**

Purpose: Evaluates and diagnoses achievement for instructional improvement in the accounting/computing clerk area. May be used for vocational guidance in an overall program.

Description: 375–item paper-pencil multiple-choice test in two parts. Part I (192 items) covers purchases and payables, receipts and payments, specialized accounting functions, and payroll records. Part II (183 items) covers sales and receivables, maintaining files and inventory records, general office duties, electronic accounting functions, and personal development and employment. Examiner required. Suitable for group use.

Timed: 2 hours per part

Scoring: Computer scored

Cost: Testing loan service (test booklets, answer sheets, scoring service) Ohio students $1.50 each; out-of-state students $2.50 each for March administration, $3.50 at other times

Publisher: Instructional Materials Laboratory, The Ohio State University

---

THE OHIO VOCATIONAL ACHIEVEMENT TESTS IN BUSINESS EDUCATION: ADMINISTRATIVE SUPPORT OCCUPATION

Adolescent, adult Grades 11–12 and postsecondary

Purpose: Evaluates and diagnoses achievement for instructional improvement in clerk typing. May be used for vocational guidance in an overall program.

Description: 367–item paper-pencil multiple-choice test in two parts. Part I (178 items) covers four areas: preparing business documents, managing records, processing mail and shipments, and performing telephone duties. Part II (189 items) covers seven areas: using human relations skills, performing financial functions, obtaining employment, performing administrative tasks, managing personal resources and time, utilizing communication skills, and operating and maintaining office equipment. Examiner required. Suitable for group use.

Timed: 2 hours per part

Scoring: Computer scored

Cost: Testing loan service (test booklets, answer sheets, scoring service) Ohio students $1.50 each; out-of-state students $2.50 each for March administration, $3.50 at other times

Publisher: Instructional Materials Laboratory, The Ohio State University

---

THE OHIO VOCATIONAL ACHIEVEMENT TESTS IN BUSINESS EDUCATION: CLERK-STENOGRAPHER

Adolescent, adult Grades 11–12 and postsecondary

Purpose: Evaluates and diagnoses achievement for instructional improvement in the clerk-stenographer area. May be used for vocational guidance in an overall program.

Description: 386–item paper-pencil multiple-choice test in two parts. Part I (187 items) covers keyboarding, handling mail, taking dictation and transcribing documents, and personal development. Part II (199 items) covers performing accounting functions, communicating with others, reproducing copy and word processing, managing records, and expediting administrative responsibility. Examiner required. Suitable for group use.

Timed: 2 hours per part

Scoring: Computer scored

Cost: Testing loan service (test booklets, answer sheets, scoring service) Ohio students $1.50 each; out-of-state students $2.50 each for March administration, $3.50 at other times

Publisher: Instructional Materials Laboratory, The Ohio State University

---

THE OHIO VOCATIONAL ACHIEVEMENT TESTS IN BUSINESS EDUCATION: DATA PROCESSING

Adolescent, adult Grades 11–12 and postsecondary

Purpose: Evaluates and diagnoses achievement for instructional improvement in data processing. May be used for vocational guidance in an overall program.

Description: 380–item paper-pencil multiple-choice test in two parts. Part I (187 items) covers performing data entry, providing clerical support, using software, and performing business applications. Part II (193 items) covers operating computer systems, performing accounting functions, analyzing and designing business systems, and progressing in the work environment. Examiner required. Suitable for group use.

Timed: 2 hours per part

Scoring: Computer scored

Cost: Testing loan service (test booklets, answer sheets, scoring service) Ohio students $1.50 each; out-of-state students $2.50 each for March administration, $3.50 at other times

Publisher: Instructional Materials Laboratory, The Ohio State University

THE OHIO VOCATIONAL ACHIEVEMENT TESTS IN BUSINESS EDUCATION: GENERAL OFFICE CLERK

Adolescent, adult Grades 11–12 and postsecondary

Purpose: Evaluates and diagnoses achievement for instructional improvement in the general office area. May be used for vocational guidance in an overall program.

Description: 374–item paper-pencil multiple-choice test in two parts. Part I (192 items) covers reception, telephone, and electronic communications; financial records; preparing typewritten copy; and records management. Part II (182 items) covers reprographics, mailing, and shipping; accounting functions; information processing and transcription; composition and editing; and personal development and human relations. Examiner required. Suitable for group use.

Timed: 2 hours per part

Scoring: Computer scored

Cost: Testing loan service (test booklets, answer sheets, scoring service) Ohio students $1.50 each; out-of-state students $2.50 each for March administration, $3.50 at other times

Publisher: Instructional Materials Laboratory, The Ohio State University

THE OHIO VOCATIONAL ACHIEVEMENT TESTS IN BUSINESS EDUCATION: WORD AND INFORMATION PROCESSING

Adolescent, adult Grades 11–12 and postsecondary

Purpose: Evaluates and diagnoses achievement for instructional improvement in the area of word processing. May by used for vocational guidance in an overall program.

Description: 362–item paper-pencil multiple-choice test in two parts. Part I (178 items) covers preparing information, inputting information, and producing information. Part II (184 items) covers managing records, performing accounting functions, maintaining equipment, performing administrative functions, and personal development. Examiner required. Suitable for group use.

Timed: 2 hours per part

Scoring: Computer scored

Cost: Testing loan service (test booklets, answer sheets, scoring service) Ohio students $1.50 each; out-of-state students $2.50 each for March administration, $3.50 at other times

Publisher: Instructional Materials Laboratory, The Ohio State University

THE OHIO VOCATIONAL ACHIEVEMENT TESTS IN HEALTH OCCUPATIONS EDUCATION: DENTAL ASSISTING

Adolescent, adult Grades 11–12 and postsecondary

Purpose: Evaluates and diagnoses achievement for instructional improve-

ment in dental assisting. May be used for vocational guidance in an overall program.

Description: 376–item paper-pencil multiple-choice test in two parts. Part I (185 items) covers dental anatomy, dental emergencies, preventive dentistry, infection control, and chairside assisting. Part II (191 items) covers dental specialties, dental laboratory, radiology, dental office management, and personal development. Examiner required. Suitable for group use.

Timed: 2 hours per part

Scoring: Computer scored

Cost: Testing loan service (test booklets, answer sheets, scoring service) Ohio students $1.50 each; out-of-state students $2.50 each for March administration, $3.50 at other times

Publisher: Instructional Materials Laboratory, The Ohio State University

---

THE OHIO VOCATIONAL ACHIEVEMENT TESTS IN HEALTH OCCUPATIONS EDUCATION: DIVERSIFIED HEALTH OCCUPATIONS

Adolescent, adult
Grades 11–12 and
postsecondary

Purpose: Evaluates and diagnoses achievement for instructional improvement in health occupation areas. May be used for vocational guidance in an overall program.

Description: 340–item paper-pencil multiple-choice test in two parts. Part I (162 items) covers anatomy and physiology, asepsis and sterilization, vital signs, acute care nursing, and ward clerk. Part II (178 items) covers emergency first aid; long-term care nursing; home health aide; medical assisting and laboratory; dental assisting; and personal development, employment skills, and ethics. Examiner required. Suitable for group use.

Timed: 2 hours per part

Scoring: Computer scored

Cost: Testing loan service (test booklets, answer sheets, scoring service) Ohio students $1.50 each; out-of-state students $2.50 each for March administration, $3.50 at other times

Publisher: Instructional Materials Laboratory, The Ohio State University

---

THE OHIO VOCATIONAL ACHIEVEMENT TESTS IN HEALTH OCCUPATIONS EDUCATION: MEDICAL ASSISTING

Adolescent, adult
Grades 11–12 and
postsecondary

Purpose: Evaluates and diagnoses achievement for instructional improvement in medical assisting. May be used for vocational guidance in an overall program.

Description: 396–item paper-pencil multiple-choice test in two parts. Part I (206 items) covers establishing a database and assisting with physical exam, maintaining asepsis, assisting with specialty exam, maintaining and administering medication, assisting with medical emergencies, and assisting with laboratory procedures. Part II (190 items) covers assisting with specialized diagnostic tests and procedures, managing medical records, performing receptionist duties, performing bookkeeping duties, processing insurance forms, and meeting professional responsibilities. Examiner required. Suitable for group use.

Timed: 2 hours per part

Scoring: Computer scored

Cost: Testing loan service (test booklets, answer sheets, scoring service) Ohio students $1.50 each; out-of-state students $2.50 each for March administration, $3.50 at other times

Publisher: Instructional Materials Laboratory, The Ohio State University

---

THE OHIO VOCATIONAL ACHIEVEMENT TESTS IN HOME ECONOMICS EDUCATION: CHILD CARE SERVICES

Adolescent, adult
Grades 11–12 and
postsecondary

Purpose: Evaluates and diagnoses achievement for instructional improvement in child care services. May be used for vocational guidance in an overall program.

Description: 360–item paper-pencil multiple-choice test in two parts. Part I (182 items) covers four areas: assist with preschool; assist with routine activities; assist with elementary school; and assist with maintenance of facility, equipment, and supplies. Part II (178 items) covers five areas: assist with program planning, assist in managing the center, assist with infants and toddlers, assist wtih exceptional children, and personal development. Examiner required. Suitable for group use.

Timed: 2 hours per part

Scoring: Computer scored

Cost: Testing loan service (test booklets, answer sheets, scoring service) Ohio students $1.50 each; out-of-state students $2.50 each for March administration, $3.50 at other times

Publisher: Instructional Materials Laboratory, The Ohio State University

---

THE OHIO VOCATIONAL ACHIEVEMENT TESTS IN HOME ECONOMICS EDUCATION: COMMUNITY AND HOME SERVICES

Adolescent, adult Grades 11–12 and postsecondary

Purpose: Evaluates and diagnoses achievement for instructional improvement in community and home services. May be used for vocational guidance in an overall program.

Description: 367–item paper-pencil multiple-choice test in two parts. Part I (189 items) covers communicating information; giving personal care; taking vital signs; lifting, moving, and transporting patients; assisting with special care procedures; assisting with patients' nutritional needs; and caring for infants and children. Part II (178 items) covers assisting with recreational activities, bed making and laundry care, providing housekeep-

ing services, and personal development. Examiner required. Suitable for group use.

Timed: 2 hours per part

Scoring: Computer scored

Cost: Testing loan service (test booklets, answer sheets, scoring service) Ohio students $1.50 each; out-of-state students $2.50 each for March administration, $3.50 at other times

Publisher: Instructional Materials Laboratory, The Ohio State University

---

THE OHIO VOCATIONAL ACHIEVEMENT TESTS IN HOME ECONOMICS EDUCATION: FABRIC TECHNOLOGY

Adolescent, adult Grades 11–12 and postsecondary

Purpose: Evaluates and diagnoses achievement for instructional improvement in fabric services. May be used for vocational guidance in an overall program.

Description: 406–item paper-pencil multiple-choice test in two parts. Part I (203 items) covers operating power machines; caring for fabrics; tailoring, dressmaking, and altering; and coordinating wardrobe. Part II (203 items) covers designing interiors, designing window treatments, coordinating fabrics, and operating a business. Examiner required. Suitable for group use.

Timed: 2 hours per part

Scoring: Computer scored

Cost: Testing loan service (test booklets, answer sheets, scoring service) Ohio students $1.50 each; out-of-state students $2.50 each for March administration, $3.50 at other times

Publisher: Instructional Materials Laboratory, The Ohio State University

---

THE OHIO VOCATIONAL ACHIEVEMENT TESTS IN HOME ECONOMICS EDUCATION: HOME ECONOMICS FOOD SERVICES

Adolescent, adult Grades 11–12 and postsecondary

Purpose: Evaluates and diagnoses achievement for instructional improvement in home economics food services. May be used for vocational guidance in an overall program.

Description: 355–item paper-pencil multiple-choice test in two parts. Part I (182 items) covers cook/chef, sanitation and safety, dietary aide, pantry worker, and steward worker. Part II (173 items) covers baker, front of the house, caterer, management and supervision, and personal development. Examiner required. Suitable for group use.

Timed: 2 hours per part

Scoring: Computer scored

Cost: Testing loan service (test booklets, answer sheets, scoring service) Ohio students $1.50 each; out-of-state students $2.50 each for March administration, $3.50 at other times

Publisher: Instructional Materials Laboratory, The Ohio State University

THE OHIO VOCATIONAL ACHIEVEMENT TESTS IN MARKETING EDUCATION: APPAREL AND ACCESSORIES

**Adolescent, adult
Grades 11–12 and
postsecondary**

Purpose: Evaluates and diagnoses achievement for instructional improvement in apparel and accessories. May be used for vocational guidance in an overall program.

Description: 342–item paper-pencil multiple-choice test in two parts. Part I (172 items) covers cashiering, merchandise display, sales, stockkeeping and inventory control, and first-line management. Part II (170 items) covers product knowledge, receiving and marking merchandise, support functions, customer services, and obtaining employment. Examiner required. Suitable for group use.

Timed: 2 hours per part

Scoring: Computer scored

Cost: Testing loan service (test booklets, answer sheets, scoring service) Ohio students $1.50 each; out-of-state students $2.50 each for March administration, $3.50 at other times

Publisher: Instructional Materials Laboratory, The Ohio State University

THE OHIO VOCATIONAL ACHIEVEMENT TESTS IN MARKETING EDUCATION: FOOD MARKETING

**Adolescent, adult
Grades 11–12 and
postsecondary**

Purpose: Evaluates and diagnoses achievement for instructional improvement in food marketing. May be used for vocational guidance in an overall program.

Description: 361–item paper-pencil multiple-choice test in two parts. Part I (172 items) covers receiving and storing, operations, front end operations, product and service technology, selling, and advertising. Part II (189 items) covers display/merchandising; communications; human relations; economics, marketing, and entrepreneurship; and personal development. Examiner required. Suitable for group use.

Timed: 2 hours per part

Scoring: Computer scored

Cost: Testing loan service (test booklets, answer sheets, scoring service) Ohio students $1.50 each; out-of-state students $2.50 each for March administration, $3.50 at other times

Publisher: Instructional Materials Laboratory, The Ohio State University

THE OHIO VOCATIONAL ACHIEVEMENT TESTS IN MARKETING EDUCATION: GENERAL MERCHANDISE RETAILING

**Adolescent, adult
Grades 11–12 and
postsecondary**

Purpose: Evaluates and diagnoses achievement for instructional improve-

ment in general merchandise retailing. May be used for vocational guidance in an overall program.

Description: 358–item paper-pencil multiple-choice test in two parts. Part I (182 items) covers selling, cashiering, store security, housekeeping and safety, and human relations. Part II (176 items) covers merchandise display; receiving, stocking, and inventory control; marketing; and personal development. Examiner required. Suitable for group use.

Timed: 2 hours per part

Scoring: Computer scored

Cost: Testing loan service (test booklets, answer sheets, scoring service) Ohio students $1.50 each; out-of-state students $2.50 each for March administration, $3.50 at other times

Publisher: Instructional Materials Laboratory, The Ohio State University

---

THE OHIO VOCATIONAL ACHIEVEMENT TESTS IN MARKETING EDUCATION: RESTAURANT MARKETING AND MANAGEMENT

Adolescent, adult
Grades 11–12 and
postsecondary

Purpose: Evaluates and diagnoses achievement for instructional improvement in restaurant marketing and management. May be used for vocational guidance in an overall program.

Description: 374–item paper-pencil multiple-choice test in two parts. Part I (186 items) covers host, hostess, cashier; server and table attendant; food bar worker; pantry worker; cook; and establishing and controlling stock, cost, and prices. Part II (188 items) covers utility worker, sales promotion, personnel management, store operational and maintenance policies, and personal development. Examiner required. Suitable for group use.

Timed: 2 hours per part

Scoring: Computer scored

Cost: Testing loan service (test booklets, answer sheets, scoring service) Ohio students $1.50 each; out-of-state students $2.50 each for March administration, $3.50 at other times

Publisher: Instructional Materials Laboratory, The Ohio State University

---

THE OHIO VOCATIONAL ACHIEVEMENT TESTS IN TRADE AND INDUSTRIAL EDUCATION: AUTO BODY MECHANIC

Adolescent, adult
Grades 11–12 and
postsecondary

Purpose: Evaluates and diagnoses achievement for instructional improvement in auto body mechanics. May be used for vocational guidance in an overall program.

Description: 365–item paper-pencil multiple-choice test in two parts. Part I (184 items) covers welding, repair and straightening, patch and fill, fiberglass and plastic repair, panel replacement, reconditioning, and refinishing. Part II (181 items) covers trim, hardware, and glass; frame and unit body repair; suspension systems; engine cooling systems; heating and air conditioning; electrical systems; and personal development and shop management. Examiner required. Suitable for group use.

Timed: 2 hours per part

Scoring: Computer scored

Cost: Testing loan service (test booklets, answer sheets, scoring service) Ohio students $1.50 each; out-of-state students $2.50 each for March administration, $3.50 at other times

Publisher: Instructional Materials Laboratory, The Ohio State University

---

THE OHIO VOCATIONAL ACHIEVEMENT TESTS IN TRADE AND INDUSTRIAL EDUCATION: AUTOMOTIVE MECHANICS

Adolescent, adult
Grades 11–12 and
postsecondary

Purpose: Evaluates and diagnoses achievement for instructional improvement in automotive mechanics. May be used for vocational guidance in an overall program.

Description: 364–item paper-pencil multiple-choice test in two parts. Part I (183 items) covers lubrication and preventive maintenance; engine service and repair, cooling systems, fuel and exhaust systems, ignition systems, and personal development. Part II (181 items) covers charging systems; accessory systems; transmissions and drive line; emission systems; brake systems; steering and suspension systems; and heating, ventilation, and air conditioning systems. Examiner required. Suitable for group use.

Timed: 2 hours per part

Scoring: Computer scored

Cost: Testing loan service (test booklets, answer sheets, scoring service) Ohio students $1.50 each; out-of-state students $2.50 each for March administration, $3.50 at other times

Publisher: Instructional Materials Laboratory, The Ohio State University

---

THE OHIO VOCATIONAL ACHIEVEMENT TESTS IN TRADE AND INDUSTRIAL EDUCATION: BUILDING MAINTENANCE

Adolescent, adult
Grades 11–12 and
postsecondary

Purpose: Evaluates and diagnoses achievement for instructional improvement in building maintenance. May be used for vocational guidance in an overall program.

Description: 325–item paper-pencil multiple-choice test in two parts. Part I (164 items) covers carpentry, masonry, electrical, heating and air conditioning, and painting and decorating. Part II (161 items) covers plumbing, welding, flooring, custodial, grounds and landscape, and personal development. Examiner required. Suitable for group use.

Timed: 2 hours per part

Scoring: Computer scored

Cost: Testing loan service (test booklets, answer sheets, scoring service) Ohio students $1.50 each; out-of-state students $2.50 each for March administration, $3.50 at other times

Publisher: Instructional Materials Laboratory, The Ohio State University

---

THE OHIO VOCATIONAL ACHIEVEMENT TESTS IN TRADE AND INDUSTRIAL EDUCATION: CARPENTRY

Adolescent, adult
Grades 11–12 and
postsecondary

Purpose: Evaluates and diagnoses achievement for instructional improvement in carpentry. May be used for vocational guidance in an overall program.

Description: 377–item paper-pencil multiple-choice test in two parts. Part I (188 items) covers blueprint reading, surveying, footers and foundations, floor framing, stairs, wall and ceiling framing, and roof framing. Part II (189 items) covers roofing, exterior finish, insulation, interior finish, special applications, energy efficient construction, and personal development. Examiner required. Suitable for group use.

Timed: 2 hours per part

Scoring: Computer scored

Cost: Testing loan service (test booklets, answer sheets, scoring service) Ohio students $1.50 each; out-of-state students $2.50 each for March administration, $3.50 at other times

Publisher: Instructional Materials Laboratory, The Ohio State University

---

THE OHIO VOCATIONAL ACHIEVEMENT TESTS IN TRADE AND INDUSTRIAL EDUCATION: COMMERICAL ART

Adolescent, adult
Grades 11–12 and
postsecondary

Purpose: Evaluates and diagnoses achievement for instructional improvement in commercial art. May be used for vocational guidance in an overall program.

Description: 364–item paper-pencil multiple-choice test in two parts. Part I (181 items) covers illustration, lettering, layout, photography, specialized functions, and business functions. Part II (183 items) covers design, mechanical, typography, reproduction, and personal development. Examiner required. Suitable for group use.

Timed: 2 hours per part

Scoring: Computer scored

Cost: Testing loan service (test booklets, answer sheets, scoring service) Ohio students $1.50 each; out-of-state students $2.50 each for March administration, $3.50 at other times

Publisher: Instructional Materials Laboratory, The Ohio State University

THE OHIO VOCATIONAL ACHIEVEMENT TESTS IN TRADE AND INDUSTRIAL EDUCATION: COSMETOLOGY

Adolescent, adult
Grades 11–12 and
postsecondary

Purpose: Evaluates and diagnoses achievement for instructional improvement in cosmetology. May be used for vocational guidance in an overall program.

Description: 367–item paper-pencil multiple-choice test in two parts. Part I (184 items) covers manicuring, facials and skin care, hair shaping, hairstyling, and hair color. Part II (183 items) covers sanitation and safety, scalp care, permanent waving, shop management and customer relations, and personal development. Examiner required. Suitable for group use.

Timed: 2 hours per part

Scoring: Computer scored

Cost: Testing loan service (test booklets, answer sheets, scoring service) Ohio students $1.50 each; out-of-state students $2.50 each for March administration, $3.50 at other times

Publisher: Instructional Materials Laboratory, The Ohio State University

THE OHIO VOCATIONAL ACHIEVEMENT TESTS IN TRADE AND INDUSTRIAL EDUCATION: DIESEL MECHANIC

Adolescent, adult
Grades 11–12 and
postsecondary

Purpose: Evaluates and diagnoses achievement for instructional improvement in diesel mechanics. May be used for vocational guidance in an overall program.

Description: 350–item paper-pencil multiple-choice test in two parts. Part I (176 items) covers service and repair engines, fuel systems, cooling systems, electrical systems, exhaust intake systems, and lubrication and preventive maintenance. Part II (174 items) covers drive lines, suspension systems, brake systems, heating and air conditioning systems, cabs and chassis, hydraulic systems, service management and records, and personal development. Examiner required. Suitable for group use.

Timed: 2 hours per part

Scoring: Computer scored

Cost: Testing loan service (test booklets, answer sheets, scoring service) Ohio students $1.50 each; out-of-state students $2.50 each for March administration, $3.50 at other times

Publisher: Instructional Materials Laboratory, The Ohio State University

THE OHIO VOCATIONAL ACHIEVEMENT TESTS IN TRADE AND INDUSTRIAL EDUCATION: DRAFTING

Adolescent, adult
Grades 11–12 and
postsecondary

Purpose: Evaluates and diagnoses achievement for instructional improvement in drafting. May be used for vocational guidance in an overall program.

Description: 347–item paper-pencil multiple-choice test in two parts. Part I (171 items) covers geometric shapes and construction, orthographic and auxiliary projection, pictorial drawing, sectional views, production/working drawings, fastening methods, and industrial materials and processes. Part II (176 items) covers dimensions and tolerances, intersections and developments, mechanics, architectural drawings, structural and civil drawings, electrical and electronic drawings, and personal development. Examiner required. Suitable for group use.

Timed: 2 hours per part

Scoring: Computer scored

Cost: Testing loan service (test booklets, answer sheets, scoring service) Ohio students $1.50 each; out-of-state students $2.50 each for March administration, $3.50 at other times

Publisher: Instructional Materials Laboratory, The Ohio State University

THE OHIO VOCATIONAL ACHIEVEMENT TESTS IN TRADE AND INDUSTRIAL EDUCATION: ELECTRICAL TRADES

Adolescent, adult
Grades 11–12 and
postsecondary

Purpose: Evaluates and diagnoses achievement for instructional improvement in construction electricity. May be used for vocational guidance in an overall program.

Description: 360–item paper-pencil multiple-choice test in two parts. Part I (188 items) covers six areas: estimating the job, selecting tools and equipment, roughing in residential wiring, roughing in commercial wiring, finishing residential wiring, and finishing commercial wiring. Part II (172 items) covers installing residential equipment; installing commercial services; installing motors, generators, and controls; servicing electrical equipment; installing and servicing low-voltage systems; installing and servicing security, fire, alarm, and energy management systems; developing shop management skills; rewiring electrical systems; installing programmable machine controls; installing and servicing transformers; and meeting professional responsibility. Examiner required. Suitable for group use.

Timed: 2 hours per part

Scoring: Computer scored

Cost: Testing loan service (test booklets, answer sheets, scoring service) Ohio students $1.50 each; out-of-state students $2.50 each for March administration, $3.50 at other times

Publisher: Instructional Materials Laboratory, The Ohio State University

THE OHIO VOCATIONAL ACHIEVEMENT TESTS IN TRADE AND INDUSTRIAL EDUCATION: ELECTRONICS

Adolescent, adult
Grades 11–12 and
postsecondary

Purpose: Evaluates and diagnoses achievement for instructional improvement in electronics. May be used for vocational guidance in an overall program.

Description: 373–item paper-pencil multiple-choice test in two parts. Part I (190 items) covers DC circuits, AC circuits, solid state circuits, and analog circuits. Part II (183 items) covers digital circuits, control/processor operations, test equipment, electrical/electronic systems and subassemblies, and personal development. Examiner required. Suitable for group use.

Timed: 2 hours per part

Scoring: Computer scored

Cost: Testing loan service (test booklets, answer sheets, scoring service) Ohio students $1.50 each; out-of-state students $2.50 each for March administration, $3.50 at other times

Publisher: Instructional Materials Laboratory, The Ohio State University

THE OHIO VOCATIONAL ACHIEVEMENT TESTS IN TRADE AND INDUSTRIAL EDUCATION: HEATING, AIR CONDITIONING, AND REFRIGERATION

Adolescent, adult
Grades 11–12 and
postsecondary

Purpose: Evaluates and diagnoses achievement for instructional improve-

ment in heating, air conditioning, and refrigeration. May be used for vocational guidance in an overall program.

Description: 358–item paper-pencil multiple-choice test in two parts. Part I (183 items) covers installing heating systems, installing refrigeration and air conditioning equipment, and troubleshooting refrigeration and air conditioning equipment. Part II (175 items) covers service and repair of refrigeration and air conditioning equipment-mechanical; service and repair of refrigeration and air conditioning equipment-electrical; troubleshooting, service, and repair of gas heating systems; troubleshooting, service, and repair of oil heating systems; troubleshooting, service, and repair of alternate heating systems; and personal development. Examiner required. Suitable for group use.

Timed: 2 hours per part

Scoring: Computer scored

Cost: Testing loan service (test booklets, answer sheets, scoring service) Ohio students $1.50 each; out-of-state students $2.50 each for March administration, $3.50 at other times

Publisher: Instructional Materials Laboratory, The Ohio State University

THE OHIO VOCATIONAL ACHIEVEMENT TESTS IN TRADE AND INDUSTRIAL EDUCATION: LITHOGRAPHIC PRINTING

Adolescent, adult
Grades 11–12 and
postsecondary

Purpose: Evaluates and diagnoses achievement for instructional improvement in lithographic printing. May be used for vocational guidance in an overall program.

Description: 329–item paper-pencil multiple-choice test in two parts. Part I (176 items) covers layout and design, composing, proofing, paste-up, camera and film processing, and personal development. Part II (153 items) covers stripping, platemaking and proofs, offset presses, and finishing operations. Examiner required. Suitable for group use.

Timed: 2 hours per part

Scoring: Computer scored

Cost: Testing loan service (test booklets, answer sheets, scoring service) Ohio students $1.50 each; out-of-state students $2.50 each for March administration, $3.50 at other times

Publisher: Instructional Materials Laboratory, The Ohio State University

THE OHIO VOCATIONAL ACHIEVEMENT TESTS IN TRADE AND INDUSTRIAL EDUCATION: MASONRY

Adolescent, adult
Grades 11–12 and
postsecondary

Purpose: Evaluates and diagnoses achievement for instructional improvement in masonry. May be used for vocational guidance in an overall program.

Description: 387–item paper-pencil multiple-choice test in two parts. Part I (193 items) covers preparing materials and establishing the work area, laying brick and blocking to a line, laying brick and blocking with a plumb rule, constructing fireplaces and chimneys, and constructing arches. Part II (194 items) covers miscellaneous masonry construction, concrete masonry, surveying, welding and cutting, and personal development. Examiner required. Suitable for group use.

Timed: 2 hours per part

Scoring: Computer scored

Cost: Testing loan service (test booklets, answer sheets, scoring service) Ohio students $1.50 each; out-of-state students $2.50 each for March administration, $3.50 at other times

Publisher: Instructional Materials Laboratory, The Ohio State University

THE OHIO VOCATIONAL ACHIEVEMENT TESTS IN TRADE AND INDUSTRIAL EDUCATION: PRECISION MACHINE TRADES

Adolescent, adult
Grades 11–12 and
postsecondary

Purpose: Evaluates and diagnoses achievement for instructional improvement in precision machine trades. May be used for vocational guidance in an overall program.

Description: 370–item paper-pencil multiple-choice test in two parts. Part I (169 items) covers performing benchwork, setting up and operating a drilling machine, setting up and operating power saws, performing layout, measuring workpieces, inspecting workpieces, and setting up and operating lathes and turning machines. Part II (201 items) covers setting up and operating a milling machine; setting up and operating abrasive machines; performing heat treating; programming, setting up, and operating CNC lathe; programming, setting up, and operating CNC mill; setting up and operating electrical discharge machines; and obtaining and maintaining employment. This test formerly was called The Ohio Vocational Achievement Tests in Metal Trades: Machine Trades. Examiner required. Suitable for group use.

Timed: 2 hours per part

Scoring: Computer scored

Cost: Testing loan service (test booklets, answer sheets, scoring service) Ohio students $1.50 each; out-of-state students $2.50 each for March administration, $3.50 at other times

Publisher: Instructional Materials Laboratory, The Ohio State University

---

THE OHIO VOCATIONAL ACHIEVEMENT TESTS IN TRADE AND INDUSTRIAL EDUCATION: SMALL ENGINE TECHNICIAN

Adolescent, adult
Grades 11–12 and
postsecondary

Purpose: Evaluates and diagnoses achievement for instructional improvement in small engine repair. May be used for vocational guidance in an overall program.

Description: 369–item paper-pencil multiple-choice test in two parts. Part I (169 items) covers four areas: operate business; operate shop; perform setup, preservice, and storage; and service engine. Part II (200 items) covers three areas: service

equipment, perform setup, and recondition equipment. Examiner required. Suitable for group use.

Timed: 2 hours per part

Scoring: Computer scored

Cost: Testing loan service (test booklets, answer sheets, scoring service) Ohio students $1.50 each; out-of-state students $2.50 each for March administration, $3.50 at other times

Publisher: Instructional Materials Laboratory, The Ohio State University

---

THE OHIO VOCATIONAL ACHIEVEMENT TESTS IN TRADE AND INDUSTRIAL EDUCATION: WELDING

Adolescent, adult
Grades 11–12 and
postsecondary

Purpose: Evaluates and diagnoses achievement for instructional improvement in welding. May be used for vocational guidance in an overall program.

Description: 369–item paper-pencil multiple-choice test in two parts. Part I (187 items) covers oxyfuel welding, shielded metal arc welding, fabrication and assembly, and personal development. Part II (182 items) covers gas tungsten arc welding, gas metal arc welding, specialized welding process (resistance, plasma, and submerged arc). Examiner required. Suitable for group use.

Timed: 2 hours per part

Scoring: Computer scored

Cost: Testing loan service (test booklets, answer sheets, scoring service) Ohio students $1.50 each; out-of-state students $2.50 each for March administration, $3.50 at other times

Publisher: Instructional Materials Laboratory, The Ohio State University

---

RIVERMEAD PERCEPTUAL ASSESSMENT BATTERY
Refer to page 124.

SCHUBERT GENERAL ABILITY BATTERY
Refer to page 597.

SENIOR ACADEMIC-TECHNICAL APTITUDE TESTS FOR COLOUREDS IN STANDARDS 8, 9, AND 10 (SATA)—1977
Refer to page 485.

SEQUENTIAL ASSESSMENT OF MATHEMATICS INVENTORY— INDIVIDUAL ASSESSMENT BATTERY (SAMI)
Fredricka K. Reisman

Child, adolescent
Grades K–8

Purpose: Provides a comprehensive profile of a student's overall standing in the mathematics curriculum, including the specific strengths and weaknesses that affect the student's performance.

Description: 243–item paper-pencil test measuring math performance in eight content areas: math language, ordinality, number/notation, measurement, geometry, computation, word problems, and math applications. Norms reported include standard scores, percentile ranks, stanines, and grade equivalents. Examiner required. Not suitable for group use.

Untimed: 30–60 minutes

Scoring: Hand key

Cost: Complete program $59.00; components available individually

Publisher: The Psychological Corporation

Information and availability unconfirmed; last verified in 1988.

SKILLS ASSESSMENT MODULE (SAM)
Michelle Rosinek

Adolescent—Ages 13–18
Grades 8–12

Purpose: Assesses skills and abilities related to vocational training. Used with the mildly handicapped and disadvantaged.

Description: Multiple-item paper-pencil and task-performance test assessing vocational skills and abilities. SAM contains three paper-pencil tests and 12 activities.

The Learning Style Inventory (15 minutes) is administered first to determine preference in the areas of information gathering, working conditions, and expression. The Revised Beta Examination (20 minutes) measures nonverbal general learning abilities. The Auditory Directions Screen (8 minutes) assesses the ability to follow directions.

The 12 hands-on activities are mail sort (17 minutes), alphabetizing (10 minutes), etch-a-sketch maze (16 minutes), payroll computation (10 minutes), patient information memo (27 minutes), small parts (19 minutes), ruler reading (7.5 minutes), pipe assembly (12 minutes), O-rings (7 minutes), block designs (5 minutes), color sort (2 minutes), and circuit board (8 minutes).

Scores are reported as percentiles, MTM-I Conversions, and a profile graph of time and error percentiles. A correlation report compares students' performance to local training requirements. Forms are available for average high-school students and for mildly handicapped, disadvantaged, and MTM-I children and adolescents. Examiner required. Suitable for group use.

Untimed: 2 hours, 30 minutes

Scoring: Computer scored; examiner evaluated; hand key

Cost: $1,695.00

Publisher: Piney Mountain Press, Inc.

SRA VERBAL FORM
Refer to page 915.

STUDENT OCCUPATIONAL COMPETENCY ACHIEVEMENT TESTING (SOCAT)
Refer to page 306.

STUDENT OCCUPATIONAL COMPETENCY ACHIEVEMENT TESTING: ACCOUNTING/ BOOKKEEPING
Refer to page 274.

STUDENT OCCUPATIONAL COMPETENCY ACHIEVEMENT TESTING: AGRICULTURE MECHANICS
Refer to page 307.

STUDENT OCCUPATIONAL COMPETENCY ACHIEVEMENT TESTING: AUTO BODY
Refer to page 307.

STUDENT OCCUPATIONAL COMPETENCY ACHIEVEMENT TESTING: AUTO MECHANICS
Refer to page 307.

STUDENT OCCUPATIONAL COMPETENCY ACHIEVEMENT TESTING: CARPENTRY
Refer to page 307.

STUDENT OCCUPATIONAL COMPETENCY ACHIEVEMENT TESTING: COMMERCIAL FOODS
Refer to page 305.

STUDENT OCCUPATIONAL COMPETENCY ACHIEVEMENT TESTING: COMPUTER PROGRAMMING
Refer to page 274.

STUDENT OCCUPATIONAL COMPETENCY ACHIEVEMENT TESTING: CONSTRUCTION ELECTRICITY
Refer to page 308.

STUDENT OCCUPATIONAL COMPETENCY ACHIEVEMENT TESTING: CONSTRUCTION MASONRY
Refer to page 308.

STUDENT OCCUPATIONAL COMPETENCY ACHIEVEMENT TESTING: DRAFTING
Refer to page 308.

STUDENT OCCUPATIONAL COMPETENCY ACHIEVEMENT TESTING: ELECTRONICS
Refer to page 309.

STUDENT OCCUPATIONAL COMPETENCY ACHIEVEMENT TESTING: GENERAL MERCHANDISING
Refer to page 305.

STUDENT OCCUPATIONAL COMPETENCY ACHIEVEMENT TESTING: GENERAL OFFICE
Refer to page 274.

STUDENT OCCUPATIONAL COMPETENCY ACHIEVEMENT TESTING: GRAPHIC ARTS
Refer to page 298.

STUDENT OCCUPATIONAL COMPETENCY ACHIEVEMENT TESTING: HEATING AND AIR CONDITIONING
Refer to page 309.

STUDENT OCCUPATIONAL COMPETENCY ACHIEVEMENT TESTING: HOME ENTERTAINMENT EQUIPMENT REPAIR
Refer to page 309.

STUDENT OCCUPATIONAL COMPETENCY ACHIEVEMENT TESTING: HORTICULTURE
Refer to page 310.

STUDENT OCCUPATIONAL COMPETENCY ACHIEVEMENT TESTING: INDUSTRIAL ELECTRICITY

Refer to page 310.

STUDENT OCCUPATIONAL COMPETENCY ACHIEVEMENT TESTING: INDUSTRIAL ELECTRONICS

Refer to page 310.

STUDENT OCCUPATIONAL COMPETENCY ACHIEVEMENT TESTING: MACHINE TRADES

Refer to page 310.

STUDENT OCCUPATIONAL COMPETENCY ACHIEVEMENT TESTING: PLUMBING

Refer to page 311.

STUDENT OCCUPATIONAL COMPETENCY ACHIEVEMENT TESTING: PRACTICAL NURSING

Refer to page 528.

STUDENT OCCUPATIONAL COMPETENCY ACHIEVEMENT TESTING: REFRIGERATION

Refer to page 311.

STUDENT OCCUPATIONAL COMPETENCY ACHIEVEMENT TESTING: SEWN PRODUCTS

Refer to page 305.

STUDENT OCCUPATIONAL COMPETENCY ACHIEVEMENT TESTING: SMALL ENGINE REPAIR

Refer to page 311.

STUDENT OCCUPATIONAL COMPETENCY ACHIEVEMENT TESTING: WELDING

Refer to page 312.

SYSTEM FOR ASSESSMENT AND GROUP EVALUATION (SAGE)

Schaeber & Associates,
Creative Development, Inc.

Ages 14 and older
Grades 8 and above

Purpose: Measures educational development, vocational aptitudes, vocational interests, temperaments, and work attitudes. Used with the physically or mentally disabled, the disadvantaged, and dislocated or injured workers for vocational planning and guidance.

Description: Multiple-item paper-pencil multiple-choice battery consisting of five tests. The Cognitive and Conceptual Abilities Test (CCAT; 45 minutes) measures general educational development in reasoning, math, and language. The Vocational Aptitude Battery (VAB; 2 hours) measures the Department of Labor's (DOL) 11 vocational aptitudes. The Vocational Interest Inventory (VII; 30 minutes) measures the DOL's 12 interest areas. The Temperament Factor Assessment (TFA; 20 minutes) measures the DOL's 10 temperament factors. The Assessment of Work Attitudes (AWA; 30 minutes) measures the individual's knowledge of employer expectations and attitudes about the world of work.

The CCAT yields raw scores that are converted to GED and approximate grade levels. The VAB yields raw scores that are converted to aptitude levels. The VII yields a graphical presentation of an individual's top interest and experience areas. The TFA yields the positive adaptability traits of an individual. The AWA yields a raw score that is converted to an attitudinal index (band). All test scores are interpreted and presented on an Individualized Detailed Profile. Examiner required. Suitable for group use.

Timed: CCAT and VAB Not available

Untimed: VII, TFA, and AWA Varies

Scoring: Hand key; computer scored

Cost: $8,395.00

Publisher: PESCO, International

Information and availability unconfirmed; last verified in 1988.

vocational guidance: achievement and aptitude

TECHNICAL AND SCHOLASTIC TEST (TST)
John T. Dailey

Adolescent, adult
Grades 9 and above

Purpose: Assesses knowledge and potential in electrical, mechanical, and scholastic skills. Used in career counseling and vocational guidance settings.

Description: 150–item paper-pencil test measuring knowledge and abilities that relate to success in trade, technical, and business careers. The TST includes items that yield scores for seven subtests: electricity, electronics, mechanical information, physical sciences, arithmetic reasoning, algebra, and vocabulary. The examiner's manual provides information for administering, scoring, and interpreting both the TST and the Business English Test (BET). Together, the BET and the TST make up the Dailey Vocational Tests. The individual report profile sheet and group report form are designed for use with both tests. Examiner required. Suitable for group use.

Timed: 65 minutes

Scoring: Hand key

Cost: 35 test booklets $45.00; examiner's manual $5.70; 100 answer sheets $30.00

Publisher: The Riverside Publishing Company

TRADE APTITUDE TEST (TRAT)—1983

Adolescent, adult

Purpose: Assesses aptitudes of adult blacks for training in trades. Used for screening prospective trade-school students.

Description: 16–subtest paper-pencil measure of skills important to trade training, including skill, coordination, patterns, spare parts, classification, assembling, calculations, inspection, graphs, mechanical insight, mathematics, spatial perception (2–D), vocabulary, figure series, and spatial perception (3–D).

Examiner required. Suitable for group use.
SOUTH AFRICAN PUBLISHER

Untimed: 4 hours, 45 minutes

Scoring: Hand key; examiner evaluated; may be machine scored

Cost: (In Rands) test booklet 4,00; manual 15,00; 10 answer sheets 1,60 (specify hand key or machine score); scoring stencil for answer sheet 4,00; scoring stencil for machine answer sheets 4,50; orders from outside the RSA will be dealt with on merit

Publisher: Human Sciences Research Council

VCWS 8—SIMULATED ASSEMBLY
Refer to page 1075.

VCWS 10—TRI-LEVEL MEASUREMENT
Refer to page 924.

VCWS 14—INTEGRATED PEER PERFORMANCE
Refer to page 1035.

VCWS 17—PRE-VOCATIONAL READINESS BATTERY
Refer to page 657.

VCWS 18—CONCEPTUAL UNDERSTANDING THROUGH BLIND EVALUATION (CUBE)
Refer to page 668.

VCWS 19—DYNAMIC PHYSICAL CAPACITIES
Valpar International Corporation

Adult

Purpose: Measures the Physical Demands factor of the Worker Qualifications Profile of the *Dictionary of Occupational Titles* (DOT). Evaluates an individual's endurance and strength. May be used in post-injury cases.

Description: Objective measure of functional capacity in terms of strength. The exercise measures each of the strength levels represented in the Physical Demands factor of the Worker Qualifications Profile of the DOT: sedentary, light, medium, heavy, and very heavy. The examinee, who assumes the role of a shipping and receiving clerk, handles materials varying in weight from 5 pounds to 115 pounds. The examinee begins with exercises on the sedentary level and gradually moves through the range of strengths until he reaches his capacity. The test may be discontinued at any time. The test should be administered only to individuals who are able to walk, are free of visual handicaps, and who have use of their upper extremities. Examiner required. Not suitable for group use.

Timed: Not available

Scoring: Examiner evaluated

Cost: $3,995.00

Publisher: Valpar International Corporation

VCWS 201—PHYSICAL CAPACITIES/MOBILITY SCREENING
Valpar International Corporation

Adolescent, adult—Ages 13 and older

Purpose: Screens physical demands required in work/training settings. Used for placement and career planning.

Description: Criterion-referenced test consisting of demonstrated performance of lifting, continuous lifting, two-handed grip, palm press, horizontal press, vertical press, balancing, walk forward, walk backward, walk heel-toe, and climbing. The examiner must meet the qualifications required by the testing site. Materials include weight scale, standing platform, lifting apparatus, hinged climbing board, and tape measure. This test is suitable for individuals with hearing, physical, and mental impairments. Signing for hearing impairment necessary. Examiner required. Not suitable for group use.

Untimed: 10–15 minutes

Scoring: Examiner evaluated

Cost: $695.00

Publisher: Valpar International Corporation

VCWS 202—MECHANICAL ASSEMBLY/ALIGNMENT AND HAMMERING
Valpar International Corporation

Adolescent, adult—Ages 13 and older

Purpose: Assesses worker qualification profile factors for job/curricula placement and career planning.

Description: Criterion-referenced test consisting of demonstrated performance of block assembly, alignment driving, block disassembly, and hammering. Spatial aptitude, motor coordination, finger dexterity, and manual dexterity are measured. The test yields MTM standard and percentile scores. Materials include assembly block, assorted small tools and parts, and hammering cards. This test is suitable for individuals with hearing, physical, and mental impairments. Signing for hearing impairment necessary. Examiner required. Not suitable for group use.

Timed: 10–15 minutes

Scoring: Examiner evaluated

Cost: $995.00

Publisher: Valpar International Corporation

VCWS 203—MECHANICAL REASONING AND MACHINE TENDING
Valpar International Corporation

Adolescent, adult—Ages 13 and older

Purpose: Assesses worker qualification profile factors for job/curricula placement and career planning.

Description: Criterion-referenced test consisting of demonstrated performance of platform assembly, disassembly using fingers, and small tools. Measures vocational reasoning, motor coordination, manual dexterity, finger dexterity, and general learning ability. The test yields MTM standard and percentile scores. Materials include four-legged platform, machine tending board, nut driver, and felt marker. This test is suitable for individuals with hearing, physical, and mental impairments. Signing for hearing impairment is necessary. Examiner required. Not suitable for group use.

Timed: 10–15 minutes

Scoring: Examiner evaluated

Cost: $995.00

Publisher: Valpar International Corporation

VCWS 204—FINE FINGER DEXTERITY
Valpar International Corporation

Adolescent, adult—Ages 13 and older

Purpose: Assesses worker qualification profile factors for job/curricula placement and career planning.

Description: Criterion-referenced test consisting of demonstrated performance of dominant and nondominant fine finger dexterity. The test yields MTM standard and percentile scores. Materials include wiring box and tweezers. This test is suitable for individuals with hearing, physical, and mental impairments. Signing for hearing impairment necessary. Examiner required. Not suitable for group use.

Timed: 10–15 minutes

Scoring: Examiner evaluated

Cost: $695.00

Publisher: Valpar International Corporation

VCWS 205—INDEPENDENT PERCEPTUAL SCREENING (SPECIAL APTITUDE)
Valpar International Corporation

Adolescent, adult—Ages 13 and older

Purpose: Assesses worker qualification profile factors for job/curricula placement and career planning.

Description: Criterion-referenced test consisting of demonstrated performance of pin placement, pin assembly, six-part assembly, and three-dimensional assembly. Measures special aptitude, reasoning, general learning ability, form perception,

motor coordination, and finger and manual dexterity. The test yields MTM standard and percentile scores. Materials include assembly board, parts bin, and assorted assembly parts. This test is suitable for individuals with hearing, physical, and mental impairments. Signing for hearing impairment necessary. Examiner required. Not suitable for group use.

Timed: 25–30 minutes

Scoring: Examiner evaluated

Cost: $595.00

Publisher: Valpar International Corporation

VOCATIONAL EDUCATION READINESS TEST IN AUTO MECHANICS (VERT-AM)
Lynn W. McBroom, Sam Chen, Steven Machalow, John Seaman, and Vicky Robbins

Adolescent, adult, visually impaired

Purpose: Assesses the readiness of individuals who are blind or visually impaired to enter an auto mechanics training program. Used for vocational evaluation.

Description: 10 multiple-item paper-pencil multiple-choice and oral-response criterion-referenced tests measuring the psychomotor skills required for the following tasks involved in auto mechanics: measuring; sorting nuts and assembling nuts and bolts; using open-end wrench, box-end wrench, ratchet wrench, torque wrench, flathead screwdriver, and Phillips screwdriver; and answering basic terminology, math computation, and reading problem questions.

The test yields a composite percentile score (made up of performance time and number of errors) for each subtest and an overall percentile score for total performance. Reading materials for the test may be reproduced in braille, large print, and cassette tape versions by the local examiner. Instructions for equipment construction and the tools needed are included in the manual. This test is one in the Vocational Education Readiness Tests series. The manual is available in regular print or on cassette tape. Examiner required. Not suitable for group use.

Timed: Varies

Scoring: Examiner evaluated; hand key

Cost: Manual $10.00

Publisher: Mississippi State University Rehabilitation Research and Training Center on Blindness and Low Vision

---

VOCATIONAL EDUCATION READINESS TEST IN BASIC WIRING (VERT-BW)
Lynn W. McBroom, John Seaman, Sam Chen, Steven Machalow, and Vicky Robbins

---

Adolescent, adult, visually impaired

Purpose: Assesses the readiness of individuals who are blind or visually impaired to enter a basic wiring training program. Used for vocational evaluation.

Description: Seven verbally administered and oral-response criterion-referenced tests measuring the psychomotor skills required for the following tasks involved in basic wiring: measuring; using a crimper-stripper tool, lineman's pliers, PVC electrical tape, insulated plastic solderless connectors, and noninsulated Type-B solderless connectors; and wiring a duplex wall receptacle.

The test yields a composite percentile score (made up of performance time and number of errors) for each subtest and an overall percentile score for total performance. Instructions for equipment construction and the tools needed are included in the manual. This test is one in the Vocational Education Readiness Tests series. The manual is available in regular print or on cassette tape. Examiner required. Not suitable for group use.

Timed: Varies

Scoring: Examiner evaluated; hand key

Cost: Manual $10.00

Publisher: Mississippi State University Rehabilitation Research and Training Center on Blindness and Low Vision

VOCATIONAL EDUCATION READINESS TEST IN QUANTITY FOODS (VERT-QF)
Lynn W. McBroom, Sam Chen, and John Seaman

Adolescent, adult, visually impaired

Purpose: Assesses the readiness of individuals who are blind or visually impaired to enter a quantity foods training program. Used for vocational evaluation.

Description: 10 multiple-item paper-pencil multiple-choice and oral-response criterion-referenced tests measuring the psychomotor skills required for the following tasks involved in food preparation: measuring; oven control and timer; proportional servings; recipes; dry measure by volume; liquid measure by volume; dry measure by weight; basic terminology; computation skills; and reading problems. The test yields a composite percentile score (made up of performance time and number of errors) for each subtest and an overall percentile score for total performance. Reading materials for the test may be reproduced in braille, large print, and cassette tape versions by the local examiner. Instructions for equipment construction and the tools needed are included in the manual. This test is one in the Vocational Education Readiness Tests series. The manual is available in regular print or on cassette tape. Examiner required. Not suitable for group use.

Timed: Varies

Scoring: Examiner evaluated; hand key

Cost: Manual $10.00

Publisher: Mississippi State University Rehabilitation Research and Training Center on Blindness and Low Vision

---

VOCATIONAL TRANSIT
Refer to page 658.

VOC-TECH QUICK SCREENER
Refer to page 840.

WORK APTITUDE: PROFILE AND PRACTICE SET
Saville and Holdsworth Ltd.

Adolescent—Ages 15–17

Purpose: Assesses occupational aptitude in various career-related areas.

Description: 132–item paper-pencil multiple-choice true-false and short-answer test assessing an adolescent's occupational aptitude with six subtests: Using Words (16 items), Using Your Eyes (20 items), Working with Numbers (25 items), How Things Work (15 items), Being Accurate (40 items), and Thinking Logically (16 items). Scores are available for each of the six tests. A diagnostic and formative profile is also available. Examiner required. Suitable for group use.

Timed: 5 minutes per test

Scoring: Hand key

Cost: Specimen set £19.99; 5 test booklets £29.99; 30 answer sheets £4.99; teacher's manual £14.99; scoring keys £12.99

Publisher: Macmillan Education Ltd.

WORK SAMPLES
Refer to page 928.

Student Evaluation and Counseling: Vocational Guidance: Interests and Attitudes

ARMED SERVICES-CIVILIAN INTEREST SURVEY (ASCVIS)
Refer to page 982.

ASSESSMENT OF CAREER DECISION MAKING (ACDM)
Vincent A. Harren and Jacqueline N. Buck

Adolescent, adult
Grades 9 and above

Purpose: Assesses the factors involved in the career decision making of high-school, community college, and college students.

Description: 94–item paper-pencil true-false test based on Harren's model of career decision making. It assesses a student's decision-making style, satisfaction with and adjustment to school, and progress in the selection of a college major and in formulating occupational plans. A special counselor's report and a group summary report are provided for each student. Mail-in computer scoring is available. Self-administered. Suitable for group use.

Untimed: 10–15 minutes

Scoring: Computer scored

Cost: Complete kit (manual, two ACDM answer sheets including scoring service) $40.00

Publisher: Western Psychological Services

BASS ORIENTATION INVENTORY (ORI)
Bernard M. Bass

Adolescent, adult
Grades 10 and above

Purpose: Measures attitudes toward achievement and rewards. Used for personnel assessment, high-school and college vocational counseling, and group research.

Description: 27–item paper-pencil forced-choice test of three types of orientation toward satisfaction and rewards: self-orientation, interaction-orientation, and task-orientation. Results help to predict an individual's success and performance in various types of work. The inventory is based on Bass's theory of interpersonal behavior in organizations. Examiner required. Suitable for group use.

Untimed: 10–15 minutes

Scoring: Hand key

Cost: Specimen set (manual, scoring key, test booklet) $6.50

Publisher: Consulting Psychologists Press, Inc.

CALIFORNIA LIFE GOALS EVALUATION SCHEDULES
Refer to page 161.

CANADIAN OCCUPATIONAL INTEREST INVENTORY (COII)
Refer to page 982.

CAREER AND VOCATIONAL INTEREST INVENTORY

Adolescent, adult

Purpose: Measures an individual's career and vocational interests. Used to assist high-school students and adults in making educational and/or career decisions.

Description: Multiple-item paper-pencil or computer-administered inventory assessing over 30 basic vocational interest scales and providing scores on the six Holland theme scales. Narrative statements, as well as a list of occupations that match the subject's interests, are presented. Examiner required. Suitable for group use.

Untimed: Varies

Scoring: Computer scored

Cost: Contact publisher

Publisher: Integrated Professional Systems, Inc.

Information and availability unconfirmed; last verified in 1987.

CAREER ASSESSMENT INVENTORIES: FOR THE LEARNING DISABLED (CAI)
Refer to page 631.

CAREER ASSESSMENT INVENTORY—THE ENHANCED VERSION
Charles B. Johansson

Adolescent, adult
Grades 9 and above

Purpose: Assesses the career interests of students and individuals re-entering the job market or considering a career change. Used for making decisions about career interest, screening job applicants, and providing career and vocational assistance.

Description: 370–item paper-pencil test in which items are answered on a 5–point Likert-type scale ranging from "like very much" to "dislike very much." Items are divided into three major categories: activities, school subjects, and occupations. The test, which focuses on careers requiring up to and including 4 years of college, covers 111 occupations. Six General Occupational Theme scores (Holland's RIASEC) and 25 Basic Interest scale scores that divide the 6 general scores into specific areas are provided. A narrative report, profile report, and optional group reports are available. Items are written at an 8th-grade reading level. This is a revision of the Career Assessment Inventory—The Vocational Version, which focuses on skilled trade occupations and careers requiring little or no postsecondary education. The inventory may be computer scored in one of three ways: via mail-in services, Arion II teleprocessing, or MICROTEST™ assessment system. Self-administered. Suitable for group use.

Untimed: 40 minutes

Scoring: Computer scored by NCS

Cost: Manual $16.50; narrative report $5.90–$8.75 depending on quantity; profile report $3.40–$4.50 depending on quantity

Publisher: National Computer Systems/ PAS Division

CAREER ASSESSMENT INVENTORY—VOCATIONAL VERSION
Charles B. Johansson

Adolescent, adult
Grades 8 and above

Purpose: Measures occupational interests of high-school students who want immediate, noncollege-graduate business or technical training. Used for employment decisions, vocational rehabilitation, and self-employment.

Description: 305–item paper-pencil test in a five-response Likert format. The inventory covers six general occupational themes (Holland's RIASEC), 22 basic interest scales, and 91 occupational scales. The test may be computer scored by NCS in one of three ways: via mail-in service, Arion II Teleprocessing, or MICRO-TEST™ assessment system. Self-administered. Suitable for group use. Available in French and Spanish.

Untimed: 25–30 minutes

Scoring: Computer scored by NCS

Cost: Manual $16.50; narrative report $5.50–$8.35 depending on quantity; profile report $3.05–$4.20 depending on quantity

Publisher: National Computer Systems/PAS Division

CAREER DECISION SCALE (CDS), 2ND EDITION

Refer to page 996.

CAREER DEVELOPMENT INVENTORY (COLLEGE AND UNIVERSITY FORM)

Refer to page 843.

CAREER DEVELOPMENT INVENTORY (SCHOOL FORM)

Refer to page 843.

CAREER DIRECTIONS INVENTORY
Douglas N. Jackson

Adolescent, adult

Purpose: Helps evaluate career interests of high-school and college students and adults. Used for educational and vocational planning and counseling.

Description: 100–item paper-pencil or computer-administered inventory consisting of a triad of statements for each item, describing job-related activities. The examinee marks the most and least preferred activities. Computer scoring yields a sex-fair profile of 15 basic interest scales. The pattern of these interests is compared to the interest patterns shown by individuals in a wide variety of occupations. This new test evolved from the Jackson Vocational Interest Survey; the content and vocabulary are easier and more emphasis is placed on activities involved in nonprofessional occupations. Extended and Basic Reports are available through the mail-in batch scoring service. The computer version operates on IBM PC and compatible systems. Examiner required. Suitable for group use.

Untimed: 30–45 minutes

Scoring: Computer scored by publisher

Cost: Examination kit (manual, question and answer document, computerized scoring for one individual) $15.00; computer version (licensing agreement with 25 scorings) $150.00

Publisher: SIGMA Assessment Systems, Inc., Research Psychologists Press Division

---

CAREER EXPLORATION PROFILE (CEP)
Gary Harr

High-school students, adults

Purpose: Assesses career-related attitudes, interests, and abilities of high-school students and adults. Used in career exploration, counseling, and training.

Description: Computer-administered tool assessing attitudes, interests, and abilities. The instrument may be used in either an INTERACTIVE mode (using self-estimated aptitudes) or a BATCH mode (based on objective test scores). As many as 50 profiles may be generated in one run. The CEP is compatible with Holland interest code categories and allows direct integration of aptitude and interest data and Holland code type categories and worker trait groups. Materials include a user's manual and masters for transparencies used in interpreting results. Self-administered. Not suitable for group use.

Untimed: Not available

Scoring: Computer scored

Cost: $175.00

Publisher: Precision People, Inc.

Information and availability unconfirmed; last verified in 1987.

CAREER EXPLORATION SERIES (CES)
Arthur Cutler, Francis Ferry, Robert Kauk, and Robert Robinett

Adolescent, adult

Purpose: Assesses an individual's job-related interests and identifies appropriate vocational choices. Used in vocational education programs.

Description: Six multiple-item paper-pencil or computer-administered inventories matching job interests with job characteristics in the following fields: AG-O (agriculture, conservation, forestry); BIZ-O (business, sales, management, clerical); CER-O (consumer/home econ-related fields); DAC-O (design, performing arts, communication); IND-O (industrial, mechanics, construction); and SCI-O (scientific, mathematical, health). Each of the inventories includes reusable booklets for self-assessment and self-scoring of job matches; answer insert folders that give job information for exploration and decision making; matching of job interests with the job characteristics of selected jobs in each field; listings of 300–500 related job titles in each field; and job duties, pay range, and outlook of job titles within each occupational field. Microcomputer programs are available for TRS–80 Models I and III, Commodore PET/CBM, Commodore 64, Apple II+ and IIe, and IBM personal computer. Software packages include instructions, printed inventories, and additional information. An introductory filmstrip is also available. The paper-pencil version may be self-administered. Suitable for group use.

Untimed: Varies

Scoring: Self-scored; may be computer scored

Cost: Class set (materials for 35 students) $45.00; additional answer folders to use with reusable booklets $0.25; diskettes (complete series) $249.95

Publisher: CFKR Career Materials, Inc.

Information and availability unconfirmed; last verified in 1988.

CAREER GUIDANCE INVENTORY
James E. Oliver

Adolescent
Grades 7–13

Purpose: Measures comparative strength of interests in 25 trades, services, and technologies. Used to counsel noncollege-bound students.

Description: 240–item paper-pencil test covering 14 engineering-related trades and 11 others: carpentry, masonry, mechanical repair, painting and decorating, plumbing-pipefitting, printing, tool and die making, sheet metal and welding, drafting and design technology, mechanical engineering technology, and industrial production. Students rate their interest in each area on a scale from 1 (very low) to 20 (very high). Examiner required. Suitable for group use.

Untimed: 1 hour, 30 minutes

Scoring: Hand key

Cost: Specimen set $3.00; booklet $1.25; manual $1.00; 25 self-scoring answer sheets and profiles $20.00

Publisher: Educational Guidance, Inc.

Information and availability unconfirmed; last verified in 1987.

CAREER INTEREST TEST (CIT)
Refer to page 983.

CAREER MATURITY INVENTORY (CMI)
John O. Crites

Adolescent
Grades 6–12

Purpose: Measures a student's maturity with respect to attitudes and competencies regarding career decisions. Used by vocational counselors and educators in planning programs.

Description: Two paper-pencil invento-ries assessing attitudes and competencies important for mature career decision making. The Attitude Scale measures the student's maturity with respect to de-cisiveness, involvement, independence, orientation, and compromise toward mak-ing a career choice. The Competency Test contains five subtests measuring compe-tencies that are important in making career decisions. See the individual descriptions of the CMI: Attitude Scale and the CMI: Competence Test. Exam-iner required. Suitable for group use.

Untimed: 3 hours, 5 minutes

Scoring: Hand key; may be computer scored

Cost: Specimen set (Attitude Scale book, Competence Test book, manual, theory and research handbook, computer-scora-ble answer sheet, maturity profile, and test reviewer's guide) $14.60

Publisher: CTB/Macmillan/McGraw-Hill

CAREER MATURITY INVENTORY: ATTITUDE SCALE

Adolescent
Grades 6–12

Purpose: Measures a student's maturity with respect to attitudes regarding career decisions. Used by vocational counselors and educators in planning programs.

Description: Multiple-item paper-pencil test measuring a student's maturity with respect to feelings, subjective reactions, and dispositions toward making a career choice. The test is available in two forms: Screening Form A–2 and Counseling Form B–1. The screening form provides an overall measure and is used for screen-ing or survey purposes. The counseling form provides scores for five variables: decisiveness, involvement, independence, orientation, and compromise. Examiner required. Suitable for group use.

Untimed: Screening form 25 minutes; counseling form 35 minutes

Scoring: Hand key; may be computer scored

Cost: 35 test books (specify screening or counseling) $46.90; 50 CompuScan answer sheets $11.50; 50 hand-scorable answer sheets $19.50

Publisher: CTB/Macmillan/McGraw-Hill

CAREER MATURITY INVENTORY: COMPETENCE TEST

Adolescent
Grades 6–12

Purpose: Measures a student's maturity with respect to competencies regarding career decisions. Used by vocational coun-selors and educators in planning pro-grams.

Description: Multiple-item paper-pencil test containing five subtests: Self-Ap-praisal, Occupational Information, Goal Selection, Planning, and Problem Solv-ing. Each test item presents a hypothet-ical situation, and the student must choose one of five answer choices. Exam-iner required. Suitable for group use.

Untimed: 25 minutes per subtest

Scoring: Hand key; may be computer scored

Cost: 35 test books $77.35; 50 Com-puScan answer sheets $11.00; 50 hand-scorable answer sheets $19.50

Publisher: CTB/Macmillan/McGraw-Hill

CAREER ORIENTATION PLACEMENT AND EVALUATION SURVEY (COPES)

Adolescent, adult
Grades 8 and above

Purpose: Measures personal values related to the type of work an individual chooses and the satisfactions derived from the occupation. Used for career evaluation and guidance and to supplement other types of information used in industrial or educational counseling situations in which the goal is improved self-awareness.

Description: Multiple-item paper-pencil inventory measuring the following eight value dimensions related to career evalua-tion and selection: investigative, practical, independent, leadership, orderliness, recognition, aesthetic, and social. The COPES value dimensions are based on theoretical and factor analytic research and are keyed to the COPSystem Career Clusters. Norms are provided for high-school and college levels. Self-admin-istered. Suitable for group use.

Untimed: 30 minutes

Scoring: Self-scored; may be computer scored

Cost: Specimen set (manual, all forms) $4.75

Publisher: EdITS/Educational and Industrial Testing Service

CAREER PATH STRATEGY
Refer to page 843.
===

CAREER PLANNING PROGRAM (CPP)
Refer to page 844.
===

CAREER PROBLEM CHECKLIST
Tony Crowley

Adolescent—Ages 14–17

Purpose: Identifies the problems second-ary-school and college students may experience when making career plans. Used by careers teachers, officers, and counselors in lessons, interviews, and careers programs.

Description: 100–item four-page paper-pencil questionnaire identifying the prob-lems individual students or groups of students may experience in career plan-ning. Students identify the kinds of problems they are experiencing from the 100 examples listed. Items cover informa-tion about school, home, getting informa-tion about jobs, starting work, applying for a job, and decision making. The test is used to identify the instructional needs of individuals and groups of students, pro-vide structure in guidance interviews, help form discussion groups in structured careers lessons, and plan and monitor the effects of careers programs. Examiner required. Suitable for group use. BRITISH PUBLISHER

Untimed: Varies

Scoring: Examiner evaluated

Cost: Contact publisher

Publisher: NFER-NELSON Publishing Company Ltd.

CAREER QUEST
Chronicle Guidance Development Staff

Adolescent, adult—Ages 12 and older Grades 7 and above

Purpose: Assesses career interests. Aids in career exploration and decision mak-ing. Suitable for use with physically and hearing-impaired individuals.

Description: Multiple-item paper-pencil multiple-choice test assessing career inter-ests according to the 12 interest areas of the U.S. Department of Labor's *Guide for Occupational Exploration (GOE)*. The inventory is available in two forms. Form S (108 items) is designed for initial career exploration and planning. Form L (144 items) offers detailed career exploration and planning. The *Interpretive Guide* leads users to their top three interest areas, and the *Career Paths* booklet provides infor-mation for further career exploration. Other materials include an administra-tor's guide and a *Career Crosswalk* booklet listing over 1,100 occupations related to the inventory and cross-refer-encing them to the *Guide for Occupational Exploration, Dictionary of Occupational Titles, Standard Occupational Classifica-tions*, and *Chronicle Occupational Briefs*. The test requires a sixth-grade reading level. Examiner/self-administered. Suit-able for group use.

Untimed: 10–15 minutes

Scoring: Self-scored

Cost: Form S kit (material for 25 uses) $51.25; Form L kit (material for 25 uses) $57.50

Publisher: Chronicle Guidance Publications, Inc.

CAREER SURVEY

Adolescent, adult Grades 7 and above

Purpose: Measures interests of people in careers. Used in guidance and vocational counseling.

Description: 132–item paper-pencil Likert-scale test covering 12 areas of career interest: accommodating/entertaining, humanitarian/caretaking, plant/animal/caretaking, mechanical, business detail, sales, numerical, communications/promotion, science/technology, artistic expression, educational/social, and medical. The interest scales were built around a two-dimensional model: people-things and data-ideas. Also included is a 40–item ability survey measuring verbal and nonverbal reasoning ability. Explanatory material for the client is available in the orientation booklet and the career planning booklet. Examiner/self-administered. Suitable for group use.

Timed: Ability scales 24 minutes total

Untimed: Interest scales 20–25 minutes

Scoring: Machine scored

Cost: 35 test booklets, 35 orientation booklets, directions for administration $28.10; scoring and reporting services extra

Publisher: American Testronics

CAREER SURVEY, VOCATIONAL EDITION

Adolescent, adult—Ages
13 and older
Grades 7–12

Purpose: Measures an individual's vocational interests and abilities.

Description: Multiple-choice guidance instrument consisting of two parts: the Ohio Career Interest Survey and the Career Ability Survey. The interest survey includes 132 items organized into 12 scales that cover the world of work and is based upon a two-dimensional model: people-things and data-ideas. The 40–item ability survey contains a Verbal Reasoning Ability subtest (verbal analogies) and a Nonverbal Reasoning Ability subtest (number series and concept relationships).

A variety of score reports are available. The Career Profile and the Counselor's

List Report are provided as a part of the basic scoring services; the Label, the Group Guidance Report, and the Educational Planning Report are optional. Scores are reported as percentile ranks and are interpreted in a graphic and a narrative format. Examiner required. Suitable for group use.

Timed: Ability Survey 24 minutes

Untimed: Interest Survey 20 minutes

Scoring: Machine scored; hand key; scoring service available from publisher

Cost: Kit (35 test booklets, directions) $28.10

Publisher: American Testronics

CAREERS

Refer to page 997.

CHATTERJI'S NON-LANGUAGE PREFERENCE (CNPR)
S. Chatterji

Child, adolescent—Ages
10–16

Purpose: Determines individual areas of interest for students. Used for educational counseling, vocational guidance, and career planning.

Description: 150–item paper-pencil multiple-choice test assessing interest in 10 broad interest areas: fine arts, literary work, scientific, medical, agricultural, technical, craft, outdoor, sports, and household work. Each test item consists of a three-choice question presented with stick-figure drawings. The nonlanguage presentation is suitable for use with non-English-speaking students. The manual provides information on administering, scoring, and interpreting the test. Examiner required. Suitable for group use.
PUBLISHED IN INDIA

Untimed: 45 minutes

Scoring: Hand key; examiner evaluated

Cost: Contact distributor (in Rupees) specimen set; complete kit (25 booklets, 100 answer sheets, 100 profile charts, scoring stencils, manual)

Publisher: S. Chatterji; distributed exclusively by Manasayan

---

CHOOSING A CAREER

Refer to page 997.

COLORADO EDUCATIONAL INTEREST INDICATOR (CEII)

*Robert D. Whetstone and
Ronald G. Taylor*

High-school and college students

Purpose: Identifies the interests of high-school upperclassmen and college freshmen and sophomores. Used for choosing colleges and majors and planning educational programs.

Description: 399–item paper-pencil inventory identifies the interests of high-school and college students. The inventory yields scores for 63 academic majors, 33 educational clusters, as well as for scales that predict academic achievement, personal characteristics, and other information. Examinees respond by marking the items "like," "dislike," or "indifferent." A three-page printout rank orders the scores and provides brief interpretive comments. Self-administered. Suitable for group use.

Untimed: 35–45 minutes

Scoring: Computer scored

Cost: Specimen set (interpretive manual, test booklet, answer sheet) $3.50

Publisher: Consulting Psychologists Press, Inc.

COPSYSTEM CAREER OCCUPATIONAL PREFERENCE SYSTEM

Robert R. Knapp and Lila F. Knapp

**Adolescent, adult
Grades 7 and above**

Purpose: Measures the interests, abilities, and work values of junior high, high-school, and college students. Used for occupational and career planning and guidance.

Description: The COPSystem consists of three measuring instruments, COPS Interest Inventory, CAPS Ability Battery, and COPES Values Survey, which may be combined and analyzed in two distinct manners. The three (or any two) instruments may be administered and then interpreted on the Comprehensive Career Guide, or they may be interpreted separately and then summarized on the Summary Guide. The Comprehensive Career Guides and the separate Self-Interpretation Profile and Guides contain brief descriptions of the 14 clusters. For career and educational planning, sample occupations are presented separately for the 14 clusters. In addition, suggested activities for obtaining experience, college majors and school courses related to the clusters, a decision-making worksheet for career exploration, and a 4–year program planning guide and courses are provided. All instruments are related to the following COPSystem Career Clusters: science, professional and skilled; technology, professional and skilled; consumer economics; outdoor; business, professional and skilled; clerical; communication; arts, professional and skilled; and service, professional and skilled. Self-administered. Suitable for group use.

Untimed: 2 hours

Scoring: Self-scored; may be computer scored

Cost: Specimen set $9.75

Publisher: EdITS/Educational and Industrial Testing Service

COPSYSTEM INTEREST INVENTORY (COPS)

Robert R. Knapp and Lila F. Knapp

**Adolescent, adult
Grades 7 and above**

Purpose: Measures job activity interests related to occupational clusters appropriate for college- and vocationally-oriented individuals. Used for academic counseling, career planning, and vocational guidance.

Description: Multiple-item paper-pencil inventory measuring interests related to both professional and skilled positions in science, technology, business, arts, and service and to occupations in communication, consumer economics, clerical, and outdoor fields. Each cluster is keyed to curriculum choice and major sources of detailed job information, including the *Dictionary of Occupational Titles*, VIEW, and the *Occupational Outlook Handbook*. On-site scoring provides immediate feedback of results. The instrument may be used with the CAPS and COPES as part of the COPSystem. Percentile norms are presented separately for high-school and college levels. Self-administered. Suitable for group use. Available in a Spanish and a Canadian version.

Untimed: 20 minutes

Scoring: Hand key; may be computer scored

Cost: Specimen set (all forms, technical manual) $6.75; 25 expendable self-scoring test booklets $9.25; 25 self-interpretation guides and profile sheets $9.00; 25 machine-scoring booklets and answer sheets $9.50; hand-scoring keys $14.00; examiner's manual $1.75; technical manual $6.00

Publisher: EdITS/Educational and Industrial Testing Service

COPSYSTEM INTEREST INVENTORY FORM R (COPS-R)
Lila F. Knapp and Robert R. Knapp

Adolescent
Grades 6–12

Purpose: Measures job activity interests related to occupational clusters. Used for academic counseling, career planning, and vocational guidance.

Description: Multiple-item paper-pencil inventory measuring interests related to both professional and skilled positions in science, technology, business, arts, and service and to occupations in communication, consumer economics, clerical, and outdoor fields. COPS Form R is parallel to the COPS Interest Inventory but uses simpler language and a single norms profile. Items are written at a sixth-grade reading level, and the whole unit is presented in a single booklet. The instrument may be used with CAPS and COPES as a part of the COPSystem. A self-scoring form and a machine-scoring form for processing and scoring by EdITS are available. Percentile norms are provided at the high-school level. Self-administered. Suitable for group use.

Untimed: 20 minutes

Scoring: Self-scored; may be computer scored

Cost: Specimen set (manual, all forms) $4.75; 25 self-scoring forms (includes self-scoring booklet and self-interpretation guide) $18.25; 25 machine-scoring booklets and answer sheets $9.50; examiner's manual $1.75; technical manual $3.75

Publisher: EdITS/Educational and Industrial Testing Service

COPSYSTEM INTERMEDIATE INVENTORY (COPS II)
Lila F. Knapp and Robert R. Knapp

Adolescent
Grades 4–7

Purpose: Measures the career-related interests of students in Grades 4–7 and older students for whom language or reading might present more difficulty. Used for academic counseling and guidance.

Description: Multiple-item paper-pencil inventory providing a rating of student's job-related interests based to a large extent on knowledge of school activities. COPS II extends interest measurement to younger students and to older students with reading or language difficulties or for whom motivational considerations are of special concern. Items are written at a fourth-grade reading level. Self-administered. Suitable for group use.

Untimed: Response 20–30 minutes; scoring 15–20 minutes

Scoring: Self-scored

Cost: Specimen set (includes manual) $2.75; 25 self-scoring forms (combined self-scoring booklet and self-interpretation guide) $19.25; set of 14 COPSystem occupational cluster charts with COPSystem II cartoons $40.00; 25 pocket-size cluster charts $5.50

Publisher: EdITS/Educational and Industrial Testing Service

COPSYSTEM PROFESSIONAL LEVEL INTEREST INVENTORY (COPS-P)
Lisa Knapp-Lee, Lila F. Knapp, and Robert R. Knapp

Adolescent, adult
Grades 7 and above

Purpose: Measures the career-related interests of professionally minded high-school and college students. Used for college major and occupational selection and orientation.

Description: Multiple-item paper-pencil inventory measuring interests related to professional level occupations in the following career clusters: Science medical-life, physical; Technology civil, electrical, mechanical; Outdoor agribusiness, nature; Business management, finance; Computation; Communication written, oral; Arts design, performing; and Service social, instructional. Separate percentile norms are provided for high-school and college levels. Self-administered. Suitable for group use.

Untimed: 30–40 minutes

Scoring: Self-scored; may be computer scored

Cost: Specimen set $6.50; 25 expendable self-scoring test booklets $9.25; 25 self-interpretation guides and profile sheets $9.00; 25 machine-scoring booklets and answer sheets $9.50

Publisher: EdITS/Educational and Industrial Testing Service

CURTIS INTEREST SCALE
Refer to page 984.

THE DECISION MAKING INVENTORY
Refer to page 999.

DF OPINION SURVEY: AN INVENTORY OF DYNAMIC FACTORS (DFOS)
J.P. Guilford, Paul R. Christensen, and Nicholas A. Bond, Jr.

Adolescent, adult
Grades 10 and above

Purpose: Measures general motivational factors. May be used for personnel selection, counseling, and guidance.

Description: Multiple-item paper-pencil inventory measuring 10 general motivational factors that were found in an analysis of interest variables: need for attention, liking for thinking, adventure vs. security, self-reliance vs. dependence, aesthetic appreciation, cultural conformity, need for freedom, realistic thinking, need for precision, and need for diversion. The factors have general implications for personality and are related to broad vocational interests. Norms are provided for high-school and college students. The test is restricted to APA members. Examiner required. Suitable for group use.

Untimed: 45 minutes

Scoring: Hand key; may be computer scored

Cost: Contact publisher

Publisher: Sheridan Psychological Services, Inc.

DOLE VOCATIONAL SENTENCE COMPLETION BLANK
Arthur A. Dole

Adolescent
Grades 7–12

Purpose: Evaluates an individual's career-related interests and abilities. Used with high-school students for educational and vocational counseling, rehabilitation, diagnosis, or therapy.

Description: 21–item paper-pencil projective inventory assessing a student's concerns, emphases, and preferences concerning future vocational choices. Test items consist of sentence stems to be completed in the student's own words. Results yield 29 scores, including Problems, Achievement, Independence, Satisfaction, Material Possessions, Vocation, Effectiveness, Recognition From Others, Relaxation, Intellectual Qualities, Activity, Relationships with Other People, Recreation, Outdoor Activities, Mechanical Interest, Computational Interest, Scientific Interest, Persuasive Influence, Artistic Interest, Literary Interest, Musical Activities, Social Service, Clerical Interests, Domestic Interests, Academic

Interests, Armed Forces, and Homemaking Interests (household arts). Scores also are available for nine optional categories: Peace of Mind, Security, Value, Obligation, Health, Religion, Social Studies, Negative Academic, and Unclassifiable. The test supplements and amplifies, in the student's own words, the results of standardized inventories such as the Kuder or Strong. Examiner required. Suitable for group use.

Untimed: 20 minutes

Scoring: Examiner evaluated

Cost: Test kit (manual, 30 record forms, 30 individual score profiles) $16.25

Publisher: Stoelting Co.

EDUCATIONAL DEVELOPMENT SERIES, REVISED 1984 EDITION
Refer to page 456.

EDUCATIONAL INTEREST INVENTORY
James E. Oliver

Adolescent, adult
Grades 10 and above

Purpose: Measures comparative strength of interests in 22 major areas of study leading to B.A. degrees in colleges and universities. Used for educational guidance counseling and career planning.

Description: 250–item paper-pencil inventory consisting of forced-choice pairs of statements related to interests in fine arts, applied arts, physical and biological science, and social science. The inventory measures interests in the following major areas of study: music, art, communication, education, business administration, engineering, industrial arts, agriculture, nursing, library arts, home economics, botany, zoology, physics, chemistry, geology, earth science, history, political science, sociology, psychology, and economics. Self-administered. Suitable for group use.

Untimed: 1 hour, 30 minutes

Scoring: Self-scored

Cost: Specimen set $3.00; booklet $1.25; manual $1.00; 25 self-scoring answer sheets and profiles $20.00

Publisher: Educational Guidance, Inc.

Information and availability unconfirmed; last verified in 1987.

EMPLOYABILITY ATTITUDES
Refer to page 1000.

EXPLORE THE WORLD OF WORK (E-WOW)
Arthur Cutler, Francis Ferry, Robert Kauk, and Robert Robinett

---

Child
Grades 4–6

Purpose: Measures vocational interests for students in Grades 4–6, special education students at any level, and students who read at the third- to fifth-grade level. Used for early introduction to vocational education.

Description: 36–item paper-pencil rating inventory assessing students' interests in 36 job activities in the following job clusters: business-office-sales, industry-mechanics-transportation-construction, art-communication-design, health-education-social service, forestry-agriculture-natural resources, and scientific-technical-health. Thirty-six pictures with brief captions identify the job activities. Students use colored pencils or crayons to color the drawings green (like), yellow (not sure), or red (don't like). Six activities are listed for each of the six job clusters. After indicating preferred job activities within the clusters, students select preferred job titles and explore one job in-depth by following an exploration process outlined in the folder (including a visit to workers on the job). For further job research, two copies of the *JOB-O Dictionary* are included with each class set. The test also may be used with *Exploring Careers*, a junior edition of the *Occupational Outlook Handbook*. A computer version is available. Self-administered. Suitable for group use.

Untimed: Varies

Scoring: Hand key

Cost: Class set (35 folders, 2 JOB-O dictionaries, user's guide) $16.00; individual folders $0.40; diskettes $89.95

Publisher: CFKR Career Materials, Inc.

Information and availability unconfirmed; last verified in 1988.

FORER VOCATIONAL SURVEY: MEN-WOMEN
Bertram R. Forer

Adolescent, adult

Purpose: Evaluates attitudes and goals related to work situations among adolescents and adults; useful for career planning, vocational guidance, and employee selection and placement.

Description: 80–item paper-pencil multiple-choice test in which the subject completes structured sentence stems measuring three areas of occupational activity: reactions to specified situations, causes of feelings and actions, and vocational goals. Results reveal interpersonal behavior, attitudes toward work, supervision, authority, people, and work dynamics. Self-administered. Suitable for group use.

Untimed: 20–30 minutes

Scoring: Examiner evaluated

Cost: Complete kit (25 men and 25 women forms, 50 record forms, manual) $42.50

Publisher: Western Psychological Services

GEIST PICTURE INTEREST INVENTORY
Harold Geist

Adolescent, adult
Grades 8 and above

Purpose: Identifies an individual's vocational and avocational interests. Used for vocational guidance and placement, especially with culture-limited and educationally deprived individuals.

Description: Multiple-item paper-pencil multiple-choice test requiring minimal language skills. The subject circles one of three pictures depicting the vocational and avocational scenes he prefers. Occupational norms are provided for Grades 8–12, college, and adult. A Motivation

Questionnaire can be administered separately to explore motivations behind occupational choices. Examiner/self-administered. Suitable for group use.

Untimed: 20–30 minutes

Scoring: Hand key

Cost: Complete kit (10 male and 10 female tests, 10 male and 10 female motivation questionnaires, manual) $42.50

Publisher: Western Psychological Services

GORDON OCCUPATIONAL CHECK LIST II
Leonard V. Gordon

Adolescent, adult
Grades 8 and above

Purpose: Identifies areas of job interest. Used for counseling of noncollege-bound high-school students.

Description: Multiple-item paper-pencil test consisting of 240 activities, each related to a different occupation within six broad vocational interest categories: business, arts, outdoors, technical-mechanical, technical-industrial, and service. The categories are further divided into the area and work group classifications used in the Department of Labor's *Guide for Occupational Exploration*. Examiner required. Suitable for group use.

Untimed: 20–25 minutes

Scoring: Examiner evaluated

Cost: 35 checklists, manual, 35 Job Title supplements $42.00; manual $12.00; examination kit (checklist, manual, Job Title supplement) $15.00

Publisher: The Psychological Corporation

Information and availability unconfirmed; last verified in 1988.

HALL OCCUPATIONAL ORIENTATION INVENTORY (HALL)
Lacy G. Hall and
Randolph B. Tarrier

Grades 3 and above

Purpose: Emphasizes the student's future possibilities and encourages the student to broaden his perceptions of his potentials and priorities. Used for career planning and vocational guidance.

Description: Multiple-item paper-pencil test based on the personality-need theory inspired by Abraham Maslow and adapted by Anne Roe to the area of occupational choice. The inventory assesses psychological needs, which are correlated to worker traits and job characteristics identified by the U.S. Department of Labor. The inventory focuses on 22 job and personality characteristics: creativity, independence, risk, information-knowledge, belongingness, security, aspiration, esteem, self-actualization, personal satisfaction, routine-dependence, data-orientation, things orientation, people orientation, location concern, aptitude concern, monetary concern, physical abilities concern, environment concern, co-worker concern, qualifications concern, time concern, and defensiveness.

The inventory is available in three levels. Intermediate HALL (Grades 3–7) is a shorter inventory with school-focused items designed to complement awareness/development programs. The Young Adult/College HALL Revised 3rd Edition (high-school and college students and professionals) focuses on jobs and occupations. Adult Basic HALL (reading-handicapped adults) is a shorter inventory with a world-of-work orientation and controlled readability levels. Separate inventory booklets, interpretive folders, and response sheets are available for each of the three levels.

A counselor's manual, the HALL Career Education Reader, a videotape training film, and the STS scoring service are also available. Self-administered. Suitable for group use.

Timed: 30–40 minutes

Scoring: Hand key; examiner evaluated; may be computer scored

Cost: 20 inventory booklets $17.00; 20 interpretive folders $10.00; 20 response sheets $10.00; specimen set (specify level) with manual $12.00, without manual $8.50

Publisher: Scholastic Testing Service, Inc.

THE HARRINGTON-O'SHEA CAREER DESCISION-MAKING SYSTEM (CDM)
Thomas F. Harrington and Arthur J. O'Shea

Adolescent, adult
Grades 7 and over

Purpose: Evaluates the interests and abilities of high-school and college students and adults. Used with students to guide study for future occupations and with adults to identify new careers and skills.

Description: Multiple-item short-answer examination in which an individual records information about occupational choices, school subject preferences, job values, abilities, and plans for further education or training. The survey includes a list of 120 work activity items. The responses contribute to one of six interest scales: Crafts, Science, Arts, Social, Business, and Clerical. Raw scores on the highest two interest scales are used to identify three or four career clusters for exploration. A Career Clusters Chart shows typical jobs in each cluster, as well as related school subjects and abilities. Occupational outlook and training requirements are given for each job listed. The jobs are keyed to the *Dictionary of Occupational Titles*.

The test is available in three editions. In the self-scored edition, the student records information in a survey booklet, and an interpretive folder shows the student how to compare the career cluster with the self-reported information. The machine-scored edition reports results in a profile report or in a detailed 12–page individualized narrative report, and the student and examiner arrange a counseling session to discuss appropriate careers. Machine-scored users can also order a Group Summary Report, which compiles responses by sex within grade or counselor group. Up to 10 locally-developed questions can be included in this report. Interpretation is via the raw scores used to find appropriate career clusters. Optional percentile-rank norms are available for Grades 7–12 and college freshmen. The microcomputer edition can be used with the TRS–80 Model III, TRS–80 Model 4, and Apple II +, IIc, and IIe. The student types responses directly into the computer. Results are presented both on the screen and on a printout. The Interpretive Folder explains the career clusters. When a printer is not available, results can be transferred from the screen to the folder. The Interpretive Report, which includes the Summary Profile and Exploring Your Career Clusters, is included with the microcomputer edition.

A seventh-grade reading level is required. An audiocassette is available for students whose reading ability may interfere with completion of the questions. Self-administered. Suitable for group use. Self-scored edition available in Spanish.

Untimed: 30–40 minutes

Scoring: Self-scored; machine scored; computer scored

Cost: Specimen set (includes self-scored survey booklet, interpretive folder, machine-scored survey booklet) $3.00; contact publisher for price of microcomputer edition

Publisher: American Guidance Service

HIDDEN TALENTS TEST
Ronald R. McCormick

Adult—Ages 16 and older
Grades 11-12

Purpose: Assesses an individual's perceived talents, needs for developing the talent, and an activity that most meaningfully expresses the talent. Used for career counseling.

Description: Paper-pencil test in which the examinee is presented with a line drawing of a three-way mirror. In the left panel, the examinee is instructed to draw a picture of a talent he or she possesses. In the right panel, the examinee draws a picture of what he or she will need or own to develop the talent. In the center panel, the examinee illustrates an activity that would meaningfully express the talent. Finally, the examinee writes captions for each of the three drawings. The test is designed to provide the examinee with insight into what his or her talents may be. Self-administered. Suitable for group use.

Untimed: 5–10 minutes

Scoring: Self-scored; examiner evaluated

Cost: 25 forms $15.00

Publisher: Dr. R.R. McCormick and Associates

Information and availability unconfirmed; last verified in 1988.

HIGH SCHOOL CAREER-COURSE PLANNER
Arthur Cutler, Francis Ferry, Robert Kauk, and Robert Robinett

Adolescent

Purpose: Evaluates career interests of junior high and high-school students. Used to develop a course plan that is consistent with self-assessed career goals.

Description: 6–item paper-pencil test measuring interests in the following six occupational areas: working with tools, working with people, creating new things, solving problems, and doing physical work. Students rate each area on a 3–point scale from one (high interest) to three (low interest). A profile of the six ratings is compared with similar profiles from the following 16 occupational clusters: industrial production, clerical, computer, banking-insurance-administrative, service (food, personal, protective), education, sales, construction, transportation, scientific-technical, mechanics-repairers, health, social scientists-social service, performing arts-communications-design, agriculture-forestry-conservation, and mining petroleum. Related job titles, suggested course work, and job entry requirements are included for each of the 16 occupational clusters, providing a basis for developing course plans. For further job research, each class set includes two copies of the *JOB-O Dictionary*. A computer version is available. Self-administered. Suitable for group use.

Untimed: Varies

Scoring: Hand key

Cost: Class set (35 folders, 2 JOB-O dictionaries, user's guide) $16.00; individual folders $0.40; diskettes $79.95

Publisher: CFKR Career Materials, Inc.

Information and availability unconfirmed; last verified in 1988.

HIGH SCHOOL INTEREST QUESTIONNAIRE (HSIQ)—1973

Adolescent
Grades 10–12

Purpose: Measures vocational interests of coloured students. Used for vocational guidance.

Description: 200–item paper-pencil test of eight interest areas: language, performing arts, fine arts, social, science, technical, business, and office work. The pupil responds like, indifferent, or dislike to each item. Examiner required. Suitable for group use.
SOUTH AFRICAN PUBLISHER

Untimed: 45–60 minutes

Scoring: Hand key; examiner evaluated

Cost: (In Rands) questionnaire 1,50; manual 9,80; 10 answer sheets 1,00; orders from outside the RSA will be dealt with on merit

Publisher: Human Sciences Research Council

HOW WELL DO YOU KNOW YOUR INTERESTS
Thomas N. Jenkins

Adolescent, adult
Grades 10 and above

Purpose: Assesses attitudes toward work activities. Used for vocational guidance.

Description: Multiple-item paper-pencil test measuring interests in 10 vocational areas: business, mechanical, outdoor, service, research, visual art, amusement, literacy, music, and general work attitudes. Items are rated on a 6–point scale ranging from "like tremendously" to "dislike tremendously." Examiner required. Suitable for group use.

Untimed: 10 minutes

Scoring: Hand key

Cost: Complete kit (3 test booklets of each edition and manual) $10.00; 25 tests (specify secondary, college, or personnel) $20.00; keys $6.75; handbook of interpretations $6.75; manual $6.75

Publisher: Psychologists and Educators, Inc.

INDIVIDUAL CAREER EXPLORATION (ICE)
Anna Miller-Tiedeman in consultation with Anne Roe

Child, adolescent
Grades 3–12

Purpose: Identifies career areas of interest to students.

Description: Multiple-item paper-pencil inventory designed to help students focus on future occupations in relation to their current interests, experiences, abilities, and ambitions in the following areas: service, business contact, organization, technology, outdoor, science, general culture, and arts and entertainment. It is based on the Roe theory of occupations. Two forms are available: Verbal ICE (Grades 8–12) and Picture ICE (Grades 3–7). Picture ICE also may be used with special education classes. Self-administered. Suitable for group use.

Timed: 2 hours

Scoring: Self-scored; hand key

Cost: Starter set (20 inventory booklets, 20 classification of occupation by group and level for Picture Form, 20 job trends, 60 job information checklists, manual of directions, technical supplement) $60.00; specimen set (specify form) $12.95

Publisher: Scholastic Testing Service, Inc.

INTER-AMERICAN SERIES: INVENTORY OF INTERESTS
Herschel T. Manuel

Adolescent, adult
Junior high and above

Purpose: Assesses individuals' occupational interests. Used by counselors.

Description: Multiple-item paper-pencil inventory measuring the examinee's degree of interest in more than 100 occupations. The test is available in parallel Spanish and English forms. Examiner required. Suitable for group use.

Untimed: Varies

Scoring: Hand key

Cost: Contact publisher

Publisher: Guidance Testing Associates

Information and availability unconfirmed; last verified in 1988.

INTEREST DETERMINATION, EXPLORATION, AND ASSESSMENT SYSTEM (IDEAS)
Charles B. Johansson

Adolescent
Grades 6–12

Purpose: Measures career-related interests of junior high and high-school students. Used in career planning and occupational exploration at the junior high and high-school level.

Description: 112–item paper-pencil inventory assessing a range of career interests. Test items present five response choices. The areas covered are mechanical/fixing, electronics, nature/outdoors, science/numbers, writing, arts/crafts, social service, child care, medical service, business, sales, office practices, and food service. The test is scored on a 5–point Likert-type scale and is sold in a self-contained package that can be scored and interpreted by the student. A sixth-grade reading level is required. Self-administered. Suitable for group use.

Untimed: 30–40 minutes

Scoring: Hand key

Cost: Manual $5.50; 25 booklets $19.50–$24.75 depending on quantity

Publisher: National Computer Systems/PAS Division

INTEREST QUESTIONNAIRE FOR INDIAN SOUTH AFRICANS (IQISA)—1969
S. Oosthuizen

Adolescent

Purpose: Assesses interests of Indian pupils. Used for vocational guidance.

Description: 210–item paper-pencil measure of seven categories of interests: language, art, social service, science, mechanical, business, and office work. The subject responds like, indifferent, or

dislike for each item. Examiner required. Suitable for group use.
SOUTH AFRICAN PUBLISHER

Untimed: 2 hours

Scoring: Hand key; examiner evaluated

Cost: (In Rands) questionnaire 2,00; manual 2,00; 10 answer sheets 0,50; orders from outside the RSA will be dealt with on merit

Publisher: Human Sciences Research Council

INVENTARIO INVESTIGATIVO DE INTERÉS VOCACIONAL (IIIV)
Jeffrey A. Harris and Howard C. Dansky

Adolescent, adult—Ages
14 and older
Grades 8 and above

Purpose: Assesses vocational interest for Spanish-speaking individuals. Used in vocational counseling.

Description: 162–item paper-pencil multiple-choice test with 12 subscales: Artistic, Scientific, Plants/Animals, Protective, Mechanical, Industrial, Business Detail, Selling, Accommodating, Humanitarian, Leading-Influencing, and Physical Performing. The test yields raw scores, percentiles (total), percentile (male), and percentile (female). This is a Spanish adaptation of the Vocational Research Interest Inventory (VRII). A fourth-grade reading level is required. Examiner must be bilingual in English and Spanish. The VRII is available for Apple IIe and IIgs and IBM compatibles (only for scoring and reporting, not for administration). Examiner required. Suitable for group use.

Untimed: 10–15 minutes

Scoring: Hand key; computer scored; self-scored

Cost: Kit $12.50; manual $12.00; 25 forms $15.00–$17.25

Publisher: Vocational Research Institute—J.E.V.S.

INVENTORY OF RELIGIOUS ACTIVITIES AND INTERESTS
Sam C. Webb and Richard A. Hunt

**Adolescent, adult
Grades 10 and above**

Purpose: Measures interest in church-related careers, self-rated abilities, and career values. Form M is used in the candidacy program of the United Methodist Church as a counseling guide.

Description: 240–item paper-pencil inventory of interest in 10 church career areas: counselor, administrator, teacher, scholar, evangelist, spiritual guide, preacher, reformer, priest, and musician. Form M also measures background, family influence values, and self-rated abilities. Examiner required. Suitable for group use.

Untimed: 45 minutes

Scoring: Hand key; may be computer scored

Cost: Specimen set $6.00; Form A hand scoring stencil set $5.00; Form M computer scoring $2.00 per answer sheet

Publisher: Datascan

Information and availability unconfirmed; last verified in 1987.

INVENTORY OF VOCATIONAL INTERESTS
Andrew Kobal, J. Wayne Wrightstone, Karl R. Kunze, edited by Andrew J. MacElroy

**Adolescent, adult
Grades 10 and above**

Purpose: Assesses vocational interests. Used for vocational guidance.

Description: 25–subject paper-pencil test of occupational interests. Each of the 25 topics contains 10 responses. The test, which provides insight into both major and minor interests, measures academic, artistic, mechanical, business and economic, and farm-agricultural areas. Materials include an inventory and occupation index arranged by vocational categories in the manual. Examiner required. Suitable for group use.

Timed: 35 minutes

Scoring: Examiner evaluated

Cost: Specimen set $4.00; 25 tests $5.00; 25 answer sheets $5.00

Publisher: Psychometric Affiliates

IRRATIONAL BELIEFS TEST
Refer to page 185.

JACKSON VOCATIONAL INTEREST SURVEY (JVIS)
Douglas N. Jackson

**Adolescent, adult
Grades 10 and above**

Purpose: Helps evaluate career interests of high-school and college students. Used for educational and vocational planning and counseling and for personnel placement.

Description: 289–item paper-pencil or computer-administered inventory consisting of paired statements covering 10 occupational themes: expressive, logical, inquiring, practical, assertive, socialized, helping, conventional, enterprising, and communicative. The subject marks one of two responses. Scoring yields a sex-fair profile of 34 basic career clusters. A seventh-grade reading level is required. The computer version operates on IBM PC and compatible systems. Examiner required. Suitable for group use. Available in French.

Untimed: 45–60 minutes

Scoring: Hand key; may be computer scored

Cost: Examination kit $17.50; manual $10.50; 25 test booklets $19.00; 25 hand-scorable answer sheets $4.75; 25 profile sheets $4.75; mail-in batch-scored reports: Extended $7.00, Basic $3.50; computer version (licensed package with 25 scorings) $150.00

Publisher: SIGMA Assessment Systems, Inc., Research Psychologists Press Division

JOB MATCHING II
Refer to page 986.

JOB-O

Arthur Cutler, Francis Ferry, Robert Kauk, and Robert Robinett

Adolescent, adult
Grades 7 and above

Purpose: Assesses an individual's aspirations and interests and identifies appropriate career and occupational choices. Used in career counseling and vocational guidance.

Description: Multiple-item paper-pencil or computer-administered career exploration instrument assessing nine variables related to educational aspirations, occupational interests, and interpersonal and physical characteristics of occupations. The *Dictionary of Occupational Titles*, the *Occupational Outlook Handbook*, and Dr. William B. Schutz's FIRO-B provide the theoretical basis relating test responses to current labor statistics, trends, and predictions for 120 job titles. The reusable assessment booklet contains complete directions and guides the student in recording responses in the consumable answer folder. The folder displays information on the number of people employed, job outlook, training requirements, and job clusters for the 120 job titles. The *JOB-O Dictionary* contains precise definitions of all job titles, related job titles, and unusual jobs and indicates which characteristics are related to each job. The manual includes information on development and rationale and instructions for administration and use. Computer programs are available for TRS-80 Models I and III, Commodore PET/CBM, Commodore 64, Apple II + and IIe, and IBM personal computers. An optional introductory filmstrip is also available. The paper-pencil version may be self-administered. Suitable for group use.

Untimed: Varies

Scoring: Hand key; may be computer scored

Cost: Reusable test booklet, answer folder $1.45; additional answer folders $0.25; manual $3.50; JOB-O Dictionary $1.75; filmstrip $32.95; diskettes $89.95

Publisher: CFKR Career Materials, Inc.

Information and availability unconfirmed; last verified in 1988.

JUNG PERSONALITY QUESTIONNAIRE (JPQ)—1983

Refer to page 246.

KUDER GENERAL INTEREST SURVEY, FORM E, REVISED 1988

Frederic Kuder

Adolescent
Grades 6–12

Purpose: Assesses students' preferences for various activities related to general interest areas. Used to guide educational planning toward future employment.

Description: 168–item paper-pencil inventory measuring preferences in 10 general interest areas: outdoor, mechanical, scientific, computational, persuasive, artistic, literary, musical, social science, and clerical. Scoring and profile construction can be done by the student in the hand-scored version. A narrative report form, accompanied by an interpretive leaflet, is provided for the machine-scored version. The revised General Manual contains general, technical, and interpretive information, including a script from a sample counseling session. The 1988 revision includes updated norms, report forms, and manual as well as the addition of interpretive leaflets and optional ancillary materials (Job and College Majors Charts). A sixth-grade reading level is required. Examiner required. Suitable for group use.

Untimed: 45–60 minutes

Scoring: Hand key; may be machine scored or computer scored locally

Cost: Complete set (materials and scoring for 25 students, machine-scored version) $66.25; complete set (25 booklets and answer pads, hand-scored version) $41.25; software for computer-scored version $300.00; Job and College Majors Charts $10.00; specimen set each version $7.00; general manual included in order

Publisher: CTB/Macmillan/McGraw-Hill

KUDER OCCUPATIONAL INTEREST SURVEY, FORM DD (KOIS), REVISED
Refer to page 986.

KUDER PREFERENCE RECORD, VOCATIONAL, FORM CP
Frederic Kuder

Adolescent, adult
Grades 9 and above

Purpose: Evaluates occupational interests of students and adults. Used for vocational counseling and employee screening and placement.

Description: 168–item paper-pencil survey measuring interests in 10 occupational areas: outdoor, mechanical, scientific, computational, persuasive, artistic, literary, musical, social science, and clerical. The subject uses a pin to indicate a "most liked" and "least liked" activity for each group of three activities. A high-school reading level is required. Self-administered. Suitable for group use.

Untimed: 30–40 minutes

Scoring: Hand key

Cost: Specimen set $7.00; 25 booklets $40.70; no charge for manual if requested when ordering

Publisher: CTB/Macmillan/McGraw-Hill

LEISURE ACTIVITIES BLANK (LAB)
George E. McKechnie

Adult

Purpose: Assesses an individual's past and future leisure and recreation activities. Used for research and counseling.

Description: 120–item paper-pencil test of recreational time use. Items are a list of recreational activities. Respondents indicate the extent of past participation and expected future participation in each activity. The test yields six past factor scores: mechanics, crafts, intellectual, slow living, sports, and glamour sports; eight future factor scores: adventure, mechanics, crafts, easy living, intellec-

tual, ego-recognition, slow living, and clean living; and two validity scales. Self-administered. Suitable for group use.

Untimed: 15–20 minutes

Scoring: Hand key

Cost: Manual $7.50; 25 tests $4.75; 50 profiles $12.50; scoring stencils $24.00

Publisher: Consulting Psychologists Press, Inc.

MILWAUKEE ACADEMIC INTEREST INVENTORY
Andrew R. Baggaley

Adolescent, adult
Grades 12–14

Purpose: Measures academic study interests. Used to help college-bound high-school seniors and college freshmen and sophomores select college majors.

Description: 150–item paper-pencil test comparing a student's academic interests with those of typical students in specified fields. Scores provide stanine ranking for six major areas: physical science (physics, chemistry, mathematics, engineering); healing occupations (medicine, medical technology, pharmacy); behavioral science (psychology, sociology, anthropology, social work); economics (economics, commerce); humanities-social studies (political science, history, philosophy, languages, journalism); and elementary education. Items are designed to minimize response patterns adapted to social desirability rather than to the student's real feelings. Self-administered. Suitable for group use.

Untimed: 20 minutes

Scoring: Hand key

Cost: Complete kit (10 reusable tests, 100 answer sheets, manual, key) $50.00

Publisher: Western Psychological Services

MISSOURI APTITUDE AND CAREER INFORMATION INVENTORY (MACII)

Adolescent
Grades 9.5–12

Purpose: Assesses the verbal and quantitative aptitudes and career interests of students.

Description: Multiple-item paper-pencil test combining Form X of the School and College Ability Test—Series III (SCAT III) with a career information inventory. The SCAT III portion measures a student's understanding of words and their relationship through verbal analogies and of fundamental number operations through quantitative comparisons. The career inventory indicates occupational preferences using a list of 250 occupations, interests, and future plans. Examiner/self-administered. Suitable for group use.

Timed: 80 minutes

Scoring: Computer scored

Cost: Answer sheets $0.15; test booklet rental $0.12; scoring service $0.35

Publisher: Center for Educational Assessment

---

19 FIELD INTEREST INVENTORY (19 FII)—1970

Adolescent, adult

Purpose: Assesses vocational interests of high-school students. Used for vocational guidance.

Description: Multiple-item paper-pencil measure of 19 broad areas of vocational interest: fine arts, performing arts, language, historical, service, social work, sociability, public speaking, law, creative thought, science, practical-male, practical-female, numerical, business, clerical, travel, nature, and sport. Scores on two aspects of interests, work-hobby and active-passive, also are obtained. Examiner required. Suitable for group use. SOUTH AFRICAN PUBLISHER

Untimed: 45 minutes

Scoring: Hand key; examiner evaluated; may be machine scored

Cost: (In Rands) test booklet 2,00; manual 7,00; 10 answer sheets 2,50; 10 machine answer sheets 2,00; student norms 5,00; orders from outside the RSA will be dealt with on merit

Publisher: Human Sciences Research Council

NM ATTITUDE TOWARD WORK TEST (NMATWT)
C.C. Healy and S.P. Klein

Adolescent
Grades 9–12

Purpose: Measures individual appreciation of the personal and social significance of work. Used for career counseling and program evaluation.

Description: 25–item paper-pencil multiple-choice test evaluating attitudes toward preparing for an occupation; the feeling that work contributes to self-confidence, self-esteem, and self-actualization; the belief that work leads to many benefits, such as security, interpersonal contacts, friends, and things money can buy; acceptance of the desirability of the interdependence of people, of people all "pulling together"; and the belief in the value of work for our society. Reliability and norms have been determined from samples of 9th- and 12th-grade secondary students. Examiner required. Suitable for group use.

Timed: 15 minutes

Scoring: Hand key

Cost: Specimen set $6.00; 35 tests $12.00; 35 answer sheets $4.00; scoring stencil $3.00; manual $4.00

Publisher: Monitor

OCC-U-SORT
Lawrence K. Jones

Adolescent, adult
Grades 7 and above

Purpose: Helps an individual clarify his interests and values in order to make career decisions. Used by education counselors.

Description: Self-administered career intervention instrument utilizing a deck of 60 cards, each of which contains the name of an occupation, to identify and clarify an individual's thoughts about an occupation. The subject sorts the cards, choosing the 12 occupations he considers most appropriate for himself. Each occupation is coded, using John Holland's six interest categories, according to the interest category it primarily and secondarily represents. Each interest category receives a numerical score based on the number of times it was a primary or secondary code among the 12 occupations the individual chose. The three categories with the highest scores form the individual's interest code, which the individual uses to explore occupations in the *Guide to Occupations*. Card sets are available in three different levels based on the educational background required for the jobs. Self-administered. Suitable for group use.

Untimed: Not available

Scoring: Self-scored; examiner evaluated

Cost: Specimen set (manual, booklet, *Guide to Occupations*, four sort cards, poster) $14.60

Publisher: CTB/Macmillan/McGraw-Hill

OCCUPATIONAL APTITUDE SURVEY AND INTEREST SCHEDULE—APTITUDE SURVEY (OASIS-AS)
Randall M. Parker

Adolescent Grades 8–12

Purpose: Evaluates a high-school student's aptitude for various occupations. Used for occupational guidance and counseling.

Description: 245–item paper-pencil survey measuring general, verbal, numerical, spatial, perceptual, and manual abilities through five subtests: a) Vocabulary (40 items, 9 minutes), b) Computation (30 items, 12 minutes), c) Spatial Relations (20 items, 8 minutes), d) Word Comparison (95 items, 5 minutes), e) Making Marks (60 items, 1 minute). Subtest raw scores, percentiles, stanines, and 5–point scores are yielded. A companion test to the Interest Schedule, scores for both surveys are keyed directly to the *Dictionary of Occupational Titles, Guide for Occupational Exploration,* and the *Worker Trait Group Guide.* Examiner required. Suitable for group use.

Timed: 35 minutes

Scoring: Examiner evaluated

Cost: Complete set (examiner's manual, 25 test booklets, 50 answer sheets, 50 profile sheets, storage box) $62.00

Publisher: PRO-ED

OCCUPATIONAL APTITUDE SURVEY AND INTEREST SCHEDULE—INTEREST SCHEDULE (OASIS-IS)
Randall M. Parker

Adolescent Grades 8–12

Purpose: Evaluates a high-school student's areas of interest, as related to various occupations. Used for occupational guidance and counseling.

Description: 240–item paper-pencil or computer-administered self-rating scale measuring the following interest areas: artistic, scientific, nature, protective, mechanical, industrial, business detail, selling, accommodating, humanitarian, leading/influencing, and physical performing. The test yields scale raw scores, percentiles, and stanines. A companion test is the Aptitude Survey. Scores for both surveys are keyed directly to the *Dictionary of Occupational Titles, Guide for Occupational Exploration,* and the *Worker Trait Group Guide.* The computer version operates on Apple II+, IIe, IIc, or compatible systems. Questions may be read aloud to the visually impaired. Examiner required. Suitable for group use.

Untimed: 30 minutes

Scoring: Examiner evaluated; may be computer scored

Cost: Complete set (examiner's manual, 25 test booklets, 50 answer sheets, 50 profile sheets, storage box) $67.00

Publisher: PRO-ED

THE OCCUPATIONAL INTEREST RATING SCALE (OIRS)
M.A. Brimer

Adolescent—Ages 14–18

Purpose: Identifies the vocational interests of adolescents. Used for vocational counseling.

Description: Multiple-item paper-pencil instrument using a two-way classification

system for determining vocational interests. Seven occupational areas (business, technical, care, aesthetic, scientific, numerical, and field) and five directions of involvement (persuasive, operational, empathic, making, and intellectual) are covered in the inventory. The test provides two forms in the same booklet for examining the stability of interest. Used with the Applied Knowledge Tests (AKT), expressed interests can be matched with performance in the cognitive domain. This test minimizes the need to know specific terminology and uses a sample-free item analysis system and test-free ability scale scoring system. Each area and direction of involvement is measured on a scale of 0–10 based on techniques adopted for the new British Intelligence Scale. Strengths of interests between areas and between persons can be compared. Self-administered. Suitable for group use.
BRITISH PUBLISHER

Untimed: Varies

Scoring: Not available

Cost: Contact publisher

Publisher: Educational Evaluation Enterprises

Information and availability unconfirmed; last verified in 1987.

OHIO VOCATIONAL INTEREST SURVEY (OVIS)
Ayres G. D'Costa,
David W. Winefordner,
John G. Odgers, and Paul B. Koons, Jr.

Adolescent
Grades 8–13

Purpose: Assesses occupational and vocational interests. Used to assist students with educational and vocational plans.

Description: 280–item paper-pencil test of job-related interests. Items are work activities to which the student indicates his degree of interest. Materials include a Student Information Questionnaire, which gathers background information about the student's plans, preferences, and interests. This test has been superceded by 1981 OVIS II. Examiner required. Suitable for group use.

Timed: 60–90 minutes

Scoring: Scoring service available

Cost: Manual $22.00

Publisher: The Psychological Corporation

Information and availability unconfirmed; last verified in 1988.

OHIO VOCATIONAL INTEREST SURVEY: SECOND EDITION (OVIS II)

Adolescent, adult
Grades 7 and above

Purpose: Assesses occupational and vocational interests. Used for educational and vocational counseling.

Description: 253–item paper-pencil test of job-related interests. Items are job activities to which the student responds on a 5–point scale ranging from "like very much" to "dislike very much." Used in conjunction with the *Dictionary of Occupational Titles*, OVIS II classifies occupations according to three elements: data, people, and things. Materials include a *Career Planner Workbook, Handbook for Exploring Careers*, and filmstrips to aid counselors in administering and interpreting the test. OVIS II supersedes the 1969 OVIS. A microcomputer version is available. Examiner required. Suitable for group use.

Untimed: 45 minutes

Scoring: Hand key; may be machine scored; MRC scoring service available

Cost: 35 tests $42.00; 35 hand-scorable answer documents $36.00; 35 MRC machine-scorable answer documents $23.00; 35 NCS machine-scorable answer documents $23.00; basic scoring service $2.55 per pupil

Publisher: The Psychological Corporation

Information and availability unconfirmed; last verified in 1988.

PERSONAL QUESTIONNAIRE/ OCCUPATIONAL VALUES
Educational and Industrial Test Services Ltd. Staff

Child, adolescent

Purpose: Provides comprehensive details of a person's background. Used for vocational and educational guidance and to supplement interviews.

Description: Multiple-item paper-pencil questionnaire covering the following areas: physical, educational (formal and informal), home and family, social, hobbies, occupational attitudes, occupational achievements (adult form only), occupational checklist, and occupational values. The Occupational Values form is a scale measuring eight important factors in the work situation that indicate the individual's attitude toward various aspects of job security or achievement and risk. The Personal Questionnaire also is available in a juvenile version. Self-administered. Suitable for group use.
BRITISH PUBLISHER

Untimed: Not available

Scoring: Examiner evaluated

Cost: Contact publisher

Publisher: Educational and Industrial Test Services, Ltd.

PICTURE VOCATIONAL INTEREST QUESTIONNAIRE FOR ADULTS (PVI)—1981

Adolescent, adult

Purpose: Assesses vocational interests. Used for vocational guidance.

Description: 110-item measure of interest in 11 areas: clerical work, advanced engineering trades, lower engineering trades, woodwork, painting trades, building, domestic work, food preparation, agriculture, tailoring, and leatherwork. The subject indicates preference, dislike, or neutral for each item. Examiner required. Suitable for group use.
SOUTH AFRICAN PUBLISHER

Untimed: 30–45 minutes

Scoring: Hand key; examiner evaluated

Cost: (In Rands) manual 8,50; questionnaire 4,50; 10 answer sheets 2,50; orders from outside the RSA will be dealt with on merit

Publisher: Human Sciences Research Council

PLANNING CAREER GOALS (PCG)
American Institutes for Research

Adolescent Grades 8–12

Purpose: Provides information to help students make career plans. Used by guidance and counseling personnel.

Description: 906–item paper-pencil tests consisting of an Interest Inventory (300 items), Information Measures (240 items), and Ability Measures (366 items). The Interest Inventory consists of three sections: occupations, occupational activities, and current activities. The student indicates his interest in each of 12 career groups by rating job titles, job activities, or job-related youth activities on a 5–point scale. The items contained in Information Measures sample the student's knowledge of various occupations. The items contained in Ability Measures evaluate the student in 10 areas: reading comprehension, mathematics, abstract reasoning, creativity, mechanical reasoning, English, quantitative reasoning, vocabulary, visualization, and computation. A Life and Career Plans Survey is used to determine the student's present educational and career plans and values. Examiner required. Suitable for group use.

Untimed: Not available

Scoring: Hand key; may be computer scored

Cost: Examination kit (Ability Measure, Interest Inventory, Information Measure, answer booklet, handbook, student guide, test reviewer's guide) $14.60

Publisher: CTB/Macmillan/McGraw-Hill

PRG INTEREST INVENTORY

Visually handicapped individuals

Purpose: Measures the vocational/occupational interests of visually handicapped individuals.

Description: 150–item paper-pencil questionnaire assessing interests in the following 10 areas: mechanical, computational, scientific, persuasive, artistic, literary, musical, social service, clerical, and outdoor. The questionnaire and answer sheet are presented in large-print format. Examiner required. Suitable for group use.

Untimed: Varies

Scoring: Examiner evaluated

Cost: Test kit (test booklet, 10 answer sheets, instructions for administration and scoring) $20.00

Publisher: Associated Services for the Blind

READING FREE VOCATIONAL INTEREST INVENTORY—REVISED (R-FVII REVISED)
Ralph Leonard Becker

Adolescent, adult—Ages 13 and older

Purpose: Measures vocational preferences of mentally retarded, learning disabled, and disadvantaged persons in job areas that are realistically within the individuals' capabilities. Used for vocational guidance counseling, selection of prospective job trainees, and job placement.

Description: 165–item paper-pencil forced-choice test measuring the vocational preferences of the educable mentally retarded (EMR), learning disabled (LD), trainable mentally retarded (TMR), and adult disadvantaged. The test items consist of 55 sets of three drawings each, depicting job tasks from the unskilled, semiskilled, and skilled levels. Each artist-drawn picture is typical of the kind and type of job in which EMR, LD, and TMR individuals are known to be proficient and productive. From the three alternatives in each set, individuals select the one picture or job task they most prefer. The examiner may describe the pictorial items for examinees requiring assistance.

Scores are obtained for 11 vocational interest clusters: automotive, building trades, clerical, animal care, food service, patient care, horticulture, housekeeping, personal service, laundry service, and materials handling. The test yields standard scores, percentiles, stanines, and individual vocational profiles using percentiles.

A single test booklet is used for both males and females in compliance with federal Title IX requirements. Test booklets include a detachable scoring sheet and individual profile sheet. For each interest cluster, a list of appropriate job titles is suggested for individuals who score high in each occupational category. The drawings in this revised edition have been modified to avoid persons appearing in stereotypic occupational roles. The updated 1988 manual includes additional norms, a glossary, and profiles of incumbent mentally retarded workers in each of the 11 interest areas as status validity of the scales. The *Occupational Title Lists (OTL)* provides an expanded description of the occupational categories and subcategories of the R-FVII as well as a list of job titles within each category. Examiners may use the OTL to match job titles with their clients' R-FVII scores. This revised version of the R-FVII supersedes all earlier versions, which are no longer available. Examiner required. Suitable for group use.

Untimed: 20 minutes or less

Scoring: Hand key; self-scored

Cost: Sample set (10 test booklets, 1 manual) $22.75

Publisher: Elbern Publications

SAFRAN STUDENTS INTEREST INVENTORY (THIRD EDITION)
C. Safran

Adolescent Grades 5–12

Purpose: Assesses occupational interests of students.

Description: Multiple-item three-part paper-pencil inventory determining the relationship of students' interests and occupational characteristics. Section 1 requires students to choose one alternative from 168 pairs of occupational alternatives categorized in the areas of economic, technical, outdoor, service, humane, artistic, and scientific preferences. Section II measures school subject interests, and Section III contains a self-rated Levels of Ability Chart (academic, mechanical, social, and clerical). Student interests are referenced to the *Canadian Classification and Dictionary of Occupations* (CCDO) and the Student Guidance Information System (SGIS). The inventory is available on two levels: Level 1 (Grades 5–9) and Level 2 (Grades 8–12). Reading levels are matched to the grades indicated for test levels. For remedial and special education students in Grades 8–9, the Level 1 instrument should be used. This new edition includes occupational selections designed to be relevant to a student's world. Examiner/self-administered. Suitable for group use. CANADIAN PUBLISHER

Untimed: 40 minutes

Scoring: Hand key

Cost: Specimen set (test booklets Levels 1 and 2, student manual, counselor's manual) $11.00; 35 student booklets $32.90

Publisher: Nelson Canada

SCHOOL ENVIRONMENT PREFERENCE SURVEY
Leonard V. Gordon

Child, adolescent
Grades 1–12

Purpose: Measures work role socialization as it occurs in the traditional school setting. Used for academic and disciplinary student counseling, vocational counseling, and instructional planning.

Description: 24–item paper-pencil test measuring a student's levels of commitment to the set of attitudes, values, and behaviors necessary for employment and that are fostered and rewarded in most school settings. The scales measured are structured role orientation, self-subordination, traditionalism, rule conformity, and uncriticalness. High and low scores have differential behavioral implications. Norms are provided for high-school level. Examiner required. Suitable for group use.

Untimed: 10–15 minutes

Scoring: Hand key; may be computer scored

Cost: Specimen set $5.20; 25 forms $7.00; keys $10.75; manual $2.75

Publisher: EdITS/Educational and Industrial Testing Service

THE SELF-DIRECTED SEARCH, CANADIAN EDITION
John L. Holland

Adolescent, adult
Grades 7 and above

Purpose: Stimulates students' involvement in an active exploration of the world of work through self-evaluation of abilities and interests.

Description: Multiple-item paper-pencil career-search tool encourages student involvement in vocational guidance. The assessment booklet is a self-evaluation of interests and abilities. The Occupations Finder is designed to stimulate active exploration of career possibilities. The Occupations Finder of this Canadian edition contains job titles and numbers from the *Canadian Classification and Dictionary of Occupations (CCDO)* but retains the Holland's coding system. The SDS can be used at home or in schools. Examiner/ self-administered. Suitable for group use. CANADIAN PUBLISHER

Timed: Varies

Scoring: Self-scored

Cost: Specimen set (test booklet, test booklet Form E, Occupations Finder, Jobs Finder Form E, Counselor's Guide, and Understanding Yourself and Your Career) $4.00

Publisher: Guidance Centre

Information and availability unconfirmed; last verified in 1987.

THE SELF-DIRECTED SEARCH— NEW ZEALAND REVISION
Brian Keeling and Bryan Tuck

Adolescent, adult

Purpose: Assesses the abilities and interests of adolescents and adults. Used as a career counseling aid.

Description: Multiple-item paper-pencil instrument evaluating a client's interests and competencies. The test incorporates John L. Holland's theory of vocational choice and is, therefore, organized in terms of his six personality types: Realistic, Investigative, Artistic, Social, Enterprising, and Conventional. The assessment booklet provides the evaluation, and the Occupations Finder lists approximately 450 occupational titles encompassing descriptions of most jobs in the New Zealand labor force. The individual jobs are arranged according to the six personality types, and each occupational subclass is arranged according to the minimum educational level required. In addition, most occupations are designated by a 4–digit New Zealand Standard Classification of Occupations code. Examiner/self-administered. Suitable for group use.

Untimed: 30–45 minutes
Scoring: Self-scored
Cost: Contact publisher
Publisher: New Zealand Council for Educational Research

THE SELF-DIRECTED SEARCH, 1985 REVISION (SDS)
Refer to page 989.

SIX-FACTOR AUTOMATED VOCATIONAL ASSESSMENT SYSTEM (SAVAS)
Bruce Duthie

Adolescent, adult

Purpose: Assesses client interest patterns and matches them to occupations in the *Occupational Outlook Handbook*. Used by counselors and clients.

Description: Vocational guidance system matching client interest patterns with occupations listed in the *Occupational Outlook Handbook*. The client completes the Six-Factor Vocational Interest Inventory—a forced-choice test using an ipsative procedure for determining the occupational code—or other interest tests using the six factors of Holland's vocational theory. The six factors represented are realistic, investigative, artistic, social, enterprising, and conventional. All occupations in the system are arranged in order based on their similarity to the cli-

ent's interest profile from the results of the Six-Factor Vocational Interest Inventory. The report classifies occupations from very similar to very dissimilar compared to the client's interest pattern. The general, verbal, and numerical ability needed for each occuption, a three-letter interest code, educational level, salary range, job outlook in the 1990s, and the page number for each occupation in the *Occupational Outlook Handbook* are in the printout. Examiner/self-administered. Suitable for group use.

Untimed: Varies
Scoring: Computer scored
Cost: Software, manual $195.00
Publisher: Pacific Psychological

STUDY OF VALUES
Refer to page 776.

SUBSUMED ABILITIES TEST—A MEASURE OF LEARNING EFFICIENCY (SAT)
Refer to page 784.

SYSTEM FOR ASSESSMENT AND GROUP EVALUATION (SAGE)
Refer to page 806.

TAYLOR-JOHNSON TEMPERAMENT ANALYSIS
Refer to page 226.

THEOLOGICAL SCHOOL INVENTORY (TSI)
Richard A. Hunt, Fred R. King, and James Dittes

Adult

Purpose: Provides information about background, perceptions of the ministry as a career, motivation for ministry, and interest in specific areas of professional ministry.

Description: 165–item paper-pencil inventory consisting of the following scales: Call Concept, Special Leading, Natural Leading, Acceptance, Intellectual Concern, Self-Fulfillment, Leadership, Evangelical Outreach, Social Concern, Service to Persons, Definiteness, and Flexibility. When computer scored, the inventory yields a summary of group results in addition to individual profiles. Self-administered. Suitable for group use.

Untimed: 40–50 minutes

Scoring: Hand key; may be computer scored

Cost: Specimen set (manual, test booklet, guide to interpretation) $15.00; computer scoring $2.00 per individual

Publisher: Ministry Inventories

Information and availability unconfirmed; last verified in 1987.

VOCATIONAL ADAPTATION RATING SCALES (VARS)
Refer to page 657.

VOCATIONAL APPERCEPTION TEST: ADVANCED FORM (VAT:ADV)
R.B. Ammons, M.N. Butler, and S.A. Herzig

Adolescent, adult
Grades 10 and above

Purpose: Assesses vocational interests and attitudes. Used for vocational guidance and research on development of occupational interests.

Description: 8– or 10–item projective measure of occupational attitudes. Items are cards, 8 for males and 10 for females, showing persons engaged in common occupations. Subjects are asked to tell a story about each picture. Responses are rated for general preference for occupation, areas of concern to the individual, reason for entering occupation, and outcomes. Materials include a set of plates and a manual. Examiner required. Not suitable for group use.

Untimed: 25–40 minutes

Scoring: Examiner evaluated

Cost: Plates, manual $14.50

Publisher: Psychological Test Specialists

VOCATIONAL INFORMATION AND EVALUATION WORK SAMPLES (VIEWS)

Adult
High-school students

Purpose: Assesses vocational interests and abilities of the mentally retarded. Used for vocational guidance.

Description: Work simulating tests of abilities. The 16 work samples include the following tasks: sorting, cutting, collating, assembling, weighing, tying, measuring, using hand tools, tending a drill press, and electric machine feeding. The assessment process includes client orientation, demonstration by the examiner, training, and timed assessment. A separate training phase and observation of the client help distinguish between learning and performance and provide information about learning, quality of work, and productivity. The test requires no reading ability. VIEWS is normed on a national sample of mentally retarded individuals with a mean IQ of 52. MODAPTS, or industrial performance comparisons, are computed for each sample to indicate the ability to perform at a competitive level of work. Examiner required. Suitable for small group use.

Untimed: 4–5 days

Scoring: Examiner evaluated

Cost: Contact publisher

Publisher: Vocational Research Institute—J.E.V.S.

VOCATIONAL INFORMATION PROFILE (VIP)
National Computer Systems (NCS) and the United States Employment Service (USES)

Adolescent, adult—Ages
16 and older
Grades 9–12 and above

Purpose: Assesses aptitudes and interest levels as they relate to occupational success/career choice for vocational and career counseling and job placement of displaced workers.

Description: Series of multiple-item subtests that includes the General Aptitude Test Battery (GATB) and the United States Employment Service (USES) Interest Inventory. The GATB is divided into 12 timed sections. Parts 1–7 consist of 434 multiple-choice questions. Parts 8–12 require special apparatus for testing motor coordination, finger dexterity, and manual dexterity. The USES Interest Inventory consists of 162 statements to which respondents indicate they "Like," "Dislike," or are "Not Sure." The GATB yields 12 raw scores that convert to 9 aptitude scores: General Learning Ability, Verbal Aptitude, Numerical Aptitude, Special Aptitude, Form Perception, Clerical Perception, Motor Coordination, Finger Dexterity, and Manual Dexterity.

The USES Interest Inventory yields standard scores for 12 interest areas: artistic, scientific, plants and animals, protective, mechanical, industrial, business detail, selling, accommodating, humanitarian, leading/influencing, and physical performing. Reports generated include the Vocational Information Profile Narrative Report and the Vocational Information Profile Counselor's Summary Report. Forms B, C, and D are available, and male and female percentile scores for the Interest Inventory portion of the test are provided. Materials include an administration manual, test booklets, answer sheets, pencils, peg boards, and finger dexterity boards. A sixth-grade reading level is required. The examiner must be certified by the State Employment Service Office. Users must obtain a GATB Release Agreement from the State Employment Service office. Examiner required. Suitable for group use.

Timed: Varies

Untimed: Varies

Scoring: Machine scored; hand key; computer scored

Cost: $2.15 per individual

Publisher: National Computer Systems/PAS Division

VOCATIONAL INTEREST AND SOPHISTICATION ASSESSMENT (VISA)

Refer to page 658.

===

VOCATIONAL INTEREST INVENTORY (VII)
Patricia W. Lunneborg

Adolescent, adult
Grades 11 and above

Purpose: Measures high-school students' interests in a number of vocational areas. Used for vocational and educational guidance.

Description: 112–item paper-pencil or computer-administered inventory measuring the relative strengths of students' interests in eight occupational areas: service, business contact, organization, technical, outdoor, science, general culture, and arts and entertainment. Each item is a forced-choice statement that pulls interests apart.

Two copies of a narrative report are provided for each student. The report includes a profile of scores by percentile; a summary of percentiles and T-scores for each scale; an analysis and discussion of all scores at or above the 75th percentile; a college majors profile, which compares a student's scores with the mean scores of college majors who took the VII when they were in high school; and a discussion of nontraditional areas for exploration for students who scored between the 50th and 75th percentiles in an area that, in the past, has been considered nontraditional for his or her sex (test items are controlled for sex bias and mixed-sex norms are used).

An eight-page *Guide to Interpretation* describes the types of people typical of each of the eight interest groups and gives examples of jobs typical of each group for five levels of education and training: on-the-job training, technical school, community college, bachelor's degree, and postgraduate degree. The microcomputer version is available for IBM PC or compatible systems. Self-administered. Suitable for group use.

Untimed: 20 minutes

Scoring: Computer scored

Cost: Paper-pencil version complete kit (2 tests, computer processing, manual) $37.50; IBM version (25 uses) $125.00

Publisher: Western Psychological Services

VOCATIONAL INTEREST, EXPERIENCE & SKILL ASSESSMENT (VIESA), CANADIAN EDITION
ACT Career Planning Services

Grades 8 and above

Purpose: Measures vocational interests, experiences, and skills of individuals. Used by educators and professionals in career counseling with individuals and for group programs.

Description: Multiple-item two-part paper-pencil assessment providing career counseling information. Individuals link personal characteristics determined using the *Career Guidebook* to more than 500 occupations on a World of Work Map that shows how occupations relate to each other. The Job Family Charts list occupations according to typical preparation level, including high-school courses, post high-school preparation, and college majors. Occupations are referenced to the *Canadian Classification and Dictionary of Occupation (CCDO)* and the Student Guidance Information System (SGIS). The test is available on two levels: Level 1 (Grades 8–10) and Level 2 (Grades 11–adult). A seventh-grade reading level is required. Examiner/self-administered. Suitable for group use.
CANADIAN PUBLISHER

Untimed: 40–45 minutes

Scoring: Hand key

Cost: Examination kit Level 1 and 2 $12.65; 25 student booklets $46.50

Publisher: Nelson Canada

VOCATIONAL INTEREST, EXPERIENCE & SKILL ASSESSMENT (VIESA), SECOND EDITION
The American College Testing Program

Adolescent, adult
Grades 8 and above

Purpose: Summarizes high-school students' and adults' career interests and experiences. Used for career counseling.

Description: 129–item paper-pencil questionnaire measuring career-related interests, experiences, and skills in terms of work tasks involving data, ideas, people, and things. The test is designed to help students expand their self-awareness and to identify career options. A World-of-Work Map is used to relate information concerning 500 occupations employing over 95% of the U.S. labor force. A 16–page "Career Guidebook" is used for the test, and an eight-page "Job Family Charts" is provided to identify occupational options. The test is available on two levels: Level I (Grades 8–10) and Level II (Grades 11–adult). Self-administered. Suitable for group use.

Untimed: 45 minutes

Scoring: Self-scored

Cost: Participant material $0.95; specimen set $4.50

Publisher: The American College Testing Program

VOCATIONAL INTEREST QUESTIONNAIRE FOR PUPILS IN STANDARDS 6–10 (VIQ)—1974

Adolescent

Purpose: Assesses vocational interests. Used for vocational and study guidance.

Description: Multiple-item paper-pencil test of 10 fields of vocational interest, including technical, outdoor, social service, natural sciences, office work (clerical), office work (numerical), music, art, commerce, and language. Examiner required. Suitable for group use.
SOUTH AFRICAN PUBLISHER

Untimed: 1 hour–1 hour, 30 minutes

Scoring: Hand key; examiner evaluated; may be machine scored

Cost: (In Rands) questionnaire 1,20; manual 6,00; 10 answer sheets 1,00; 10 machine answer sheets 1,60; orders from outside the RSA will be dealt with on merit

Publisher: Human Sciences Research Council

VOCATIONAL INTEREST, TEMPERAMENT, AND APTITUDE SYSTEM (VITAS)
Refer to page 658.

VOCATIONAL PREFERENCE INVENTORY, 1985 REVISION (VPI)
Refer to page 991.

VOCATIONAL RESEARCH INTEREST INVENTORY (VRII)
*Howard C. Dansky and
Jeffrey A. Harris*

Adolescent, adult

Purpose: Identifies the interests of high-school juniors and seniors and adults. Used for vocational counseling and job exploration.

Description: 162–item paper-pencil or computer-administered inventory assessing an individual's interests in 12 areas tied to the jobs listed in the *Dictionary of Occupational Titles* and the *Guide for Occupational Exploration*: artistic, scientific, plants/animals, protective, mechanical, industrial, business detail, selling, accommodating, humanitarian, lead/ influence, and physical performing. Each form includes score profiles and explanations of the U.S. Department of Labor's *Occupational Exploration System*. Separate norms are provided for prevocational and vocational students.

The computer version runs on Apple IIe, Apple II+, Apple IIgs, IBM, and IBM compatible systems with one disc drive. The examinee uses only the arrow and return keys to respond. All responses can be either scored automatically or stored on disk for later scoring and evaluation. In addition, the program allows reports to be generated based on data manually entered from the paper-pencil version. Free demonstration disks of the software are available upon request.

The Spanish translation, Inventario Investigativo de Interes Vocacional (IIIV), is designed to be accessible to native speakers of Spanish in all regions of the United States. For some items in which a single usage would not convey the intended meaning in all dialects, alternative usages are included in parentheses. The IIIV has been normed on native Spanish-speaking U.S. residents. The VRII norms also are provided with the IIIV.

Both the VRII and the IIIV yield standard and percentile scores, the latter against the total norm sample and against those of the same sex in the norm sample. In addition, both tests provide an Individual Profile Analysis (IPA), an ideographic interpretation that reveals areas that stand out within the examinee's own profile without regard for normative scores. A fourth-grade reading level is required. Self-administered. Suitable for group use.

Untimed: 15–20 minutes

Scoring: Hand key; computer scored on site

Cost: Specimen kit, paper-pencil version (manual, 5 test forms) $12.50; software package $295.00

Publisher: Vocational Research Institute—J.E.V.S.

VOCATIONAL TRAINING INVENTORY AND EXPLORATION SURVEY (VOC-TIES)
Nancy Scott

Adolescent, adult—Ages 13 and older

Purpose: Identifies vocational interests.

Description: Paper-pencil multiple-choice survey generating a descriptive report of vocational interest for junior high, high school, and pre-vocational students. Test is available in large print, on audiocassette, and on videocassette. This test is suitable for individuals with physical or mental impairments with instructor's assistance. Examiner required. Suitable for group use.

Untimed: 45 minutes

Scoring: Computer scored

Cost: $495.00

Publisher: Piney Mountain Press, Inc.

VOC-TECH QUICK SCREENER
CFKR Career Materials

Adolescent, adult

Purpose: Assesses career aptitudes, interests, and training plans of high-school students and adults. Used with individuals not planning to attend 4–year college.

Description: Multiple-item paper-pencil or computer-administered test surveying 400 traditional and nontraditional careers demanding high-tech literacy to extreme physical activity. The inventory consists of 14 vocational-technical job clusters based upon the latest information in the *Occupational Outlook Handbook* and other sources. This screening tool helps match career goals with jobs and identify job options and training programs. The computer version operates on Apple IIe and IBM PC systems. Self-administered. Suitable for group use.

Untimed: Varies

Scoring: Self-scored; may be computer scored

Cost: VTQS individual folders $0.50; class set of 35 $16.00; *Occupational Outlook Handbook* $17.75; VTQS computer program diskette $79.95

Publisher: CFKR Career Materials, Inc.

Information and availability unconfirmed; last verified in 1988.

WIDE RANGE ACHIEVEMENT TEST—REVISED (WRAT-R)
Refer to page 497.

WIDE RANGE INTEREST-OPINION TEST (WRIOT)
Joseph F. Jastak and Sarah Jastak

Ages 5–adult

Purpose: Provides information about vocational interests (without language requirements). Assesses levels of self-projected ability, aspiration level, and social conformity. Used in vocational and career planning and counseling and employee selection and placement and to coordinate instruction/therapy plans with interest/attitude patterns.

Description: 150–item paper-pencil test measuring an individual's occupational motivation according to his likes and dislikes. The test booklet contains 150 pages with three pictures on each page. Each picture shows an individual or group performing a specific job. The subject must select the picture he likes the most and the picture he likes the least for each page. The results are presented on a report form that graphically shows an individual's strength of interest in 18 interest and 8 attitude clusters (normed on seven age groups from ages 5–adult, separately for males and females). The occupational range is from unskilled labor to the highest levels of training. The test may be used with the educationally and culturally disadvantaged, the learning disabled, the mentally retarded, and the deaf. The picture titles can be read to the blind. Individual administration is necessary for those unable to complete a separate answer sheet. A 35mm film strip (used instead of the picture book) and supplementary job title lists are available. Personal computer software is available for scoring and reporting of results. Examiner required. Suitable for group use (except where noted).

Untimed: 40 minutes

Scoring: Hand key; may be computer scored

Cost: Manual $27.00; 50 test forms $15.00; 50 report forms $15.00; key $35.95; stencils $15.00; film strip $85.00

Publisher: Jastak Assessment Systems

WORD AND NUMBER ASSESSMENT INVENTORY (WNAI)
Refer to page 498.

WORK ASPECT PREFERENCE SCALE (WAPS)
Refer to page 1036.

WORK VALUES INVENTORY
Donald E. Super

Adolescent, adult
Grades 7 and above

Purpose: Measures values that are particularly important for determining an individual's vocational satisfaction and success. Used for career counseling and vocational guidance.

Description: 45–item paper-pencil inventory measuring 15 values related to vocational satisfaction and success: intellectual stimulation, job achievement, way of life, economic returns, altruism, creativity, relationships with associates, job security, prestige, management of others, variety, aesthetics, independence, supervisory relations, and physical surroundings. Students rate 45 statements pertaining to work values, and the strength of each value is determined from the weighted ratings. Norms are provided by sex for junior and senior high-school students. Examiner required. Suitable for group use.

Untimed: 15 minutes

Scoring: Hand key; may be computer scored

Cost: Test kit (100 MRC machine-scorable test booklets, manual, materials needed to obtain scoring services) $75.12

Publisher: The Riverside Publishing Company

THE WORLD OF WORK INVENTORY
Refer to page 991.

Student Evaluation and Counseling: Vocational Guidance: Occupational Knowledge and Skills

---

CAREER ABILITY PLACEMENT SURVEY (CAPS)
Lila F. Knapp and Robert R. Knapp

Adolescent, adult
Grades 7 and above

Purpose: Measures abilities keyed to entry requirements for the majority of jobs in each of the 14 COPSystem Career Clusters. Used with students for career and vocational guidance and academic counseling.

Description: Eight paper-pencil subtests measuring career-related abilities. The

tests are Mechanical Reasoning, Spatial Relations, Verbal Reasoning, Numerical Ability, Language Usage, Word Knowledge, Perceptual Speed and Accuracy, and Manual Speed and Dexterity. The eight tests are keyed to the COPSystem Career Clusters. A cassette tape of recorded instructions is available. Examiner/self-administered. Suitable for group use.

Timed: 51 minutes

Scoring: Self-scoring; may be computer scored

Cost: Specimen set (one copy of each test, manual) $7.00

Publisher: EdITS/Educational and Industrial Testing Service

CAREER AWARENESS INVENTORY (CAI)
LaVerna M. Fadale

Child, adolescent
Grades 3–12

Purpose: Helps students assess how much they know about careers and their own career choices. Used for group discussion and as a pre- and posttest for career awareness.

Description: Multiple-item paper-pencil multiple-choice test covers seven areas of career knowledge: related occupations, contact with occupations, job characteristics, functions of occupations, grouping of occupations, work locations of occupations, and self-assessment of career awareness. The Elementary CAI may be used with pupils in Grades 3–6, and the Advanced CAI may be used with pupils in Grades 7–12. The inventory was developed under the sponsorship of the Cornell Institute for Research and Development in Occupational Education. Examiner/self-administered. Suitable for group use.

Timed: 60–90 minutes

Scoring: Hand key; examiner evaluated; may be computer scored

Cost: Complete kit (20 reusable booklets, manual, class record sheet) $25.00; 50 answer sheets $12.50

Publisher: Scholastic Testing Service, Inc.

CAREER DEVELOPMENT INVENTORY (COLLEGE AND UNIVERSITY FORM)
Donald E. Super,
Albert S. Thompson,
Richard H. Lindeman,
Jean P. Jordaan, and Roger A. Myers

College students

Purpose: Assesses knowledge and attitudes about career choices. Used with college and university students for guidance and for designing and evaluating career counseling programs.

Description: Multiple-item paper-pencil inventory for determining knowledge and attitudes of college and university students regarding careers. Students respond on computer-scored answer sheets. The computer scoring service provides individual student profiles, a group roster, response analysis by occupational group, and response analysis of the Career Planning and Career Exploration items. The User's Manual contains information on development, use, and interpretation of the test, as well as case studies and norms. The Technical Manual contains statistical and research information. Test booklets are reusable. Also available in a high-school version. Examiner required. Suitable for group use.

Untimed: 55–65 minutes

Scoring: Computer scored

Cost: 25 test booklets $20.00; 10 prepaid answer sheets $35.00; 2–volume manual $22.00

Publisher: Consulting Psychologists Press, Inc.

CAREER DEVELOPMENT INVENTORY (SCHOOL FORM)
Donald E. Super,
Albert S. Thompson,
Richard H. Lindeman,
Jean P. Jordaan, and Roger A. Myers

Adolescent
Grades 10–12

Purpose: Assesses individual attitudes, knowledge, and skills related to vocational decisions. Used in career counseling courses.

Description: 120–item paper-pencil test covering eight dimensions of vocational decision-making: career planning, career exploration, decision-making, world-of-work information, knowledge of preferred occupational group, career development attitudes, career development knowledge and skills, and career orientation total. The scoring service offered by the publisher consists of individual student profiles, a group roster, a response analysis by occupation, and a response analysis of the Career Planning and Career Direction items. May be administered in one 65–minute session or two—one 40–minute and one 25–minute—sessions. Examiner required. Suitable for group use.

Untimed: 55–65 minutes

Scoring: Computer scored

Cost: Specimen set (includes test booklet, prepaid answer sheet, manual) $18.00

Publisher: Consulting Psychologists Press, Inc.

CAREER PATH STRATEGY
Jeffery Siegel

Adolescent, adult—Ages
16 and older

Purpose: Evaluates a person's career potential. Used to develop career guidance programs, recommend career choices or changes, and monitor progress toward career goals.

Description: 75–item paper-pencil interview guide assessing an individual's career strategies. The guide examines the following factors: mental ability; vocational interests; personality testing; ideal career and ideal life-style; personal background data, such as educational and employment history; cultural, geographic, and economic opportunities and limitations; preliminary career decisions; and strategies for achieving career goals. The program includes homework assignments and forms for reassessment and follow-up. The clinician completes the inventory during the counseling session, evaluates the results, and makes appropriate suggestions. Examiner required. Not suitable for group use.

Untimed: 30 minutes
Scoring: Examiner evaluated
Cost: 50 strategy forms $15.00
Publisher: The Wilmington Press
Information and availability unconfirmed; last verified in 1987.

CAREER PLANNING PROGRAM(CPP)
The American College Testing Program

**Adolescent, adult
Grades 8 and above**

Purpose: Evaluates an individual's career-related abilities, interests, and experiences. Used for vocational counseling and course placement.

Description: 436–item paper-pencil test on two levels designed to help the examinee identify and explore personally relevant occupations and educational programs. Six factors are measured in each of three areas: career-related abilities, interests, and experiences. Level I is used with students in Grades 8–10, and Level II is suitable for use with high-school juniors and seniors and adults. Examiner required. Suitable for group use.
Timed: 2½ hours
Scoring: Computer scored by ACT
Cost: Examination kit $10.00; assessment booklet $0.50
Publisher: The American College Testing Program

FLANAGAN APTITUDE CLASSIFICATION TESTS (FACT)
Refer to page 883.

FLORIDA INTERNATIONAL DIAGNOSTIC-PRESCRIPTIVE VOCATIONAL COMPETENCY PROFILE
Howard Rosenberg and Dennis G. Tesolowski

Adolescent, adult

Purpose: Evaluates vocational behaviors related to work adjustment, job readiness, and employability. Used with mentally retarded, specific learning-disabled,

seriously emotionally disturbed, and economically disadvantaged adolescents and adults.

Description: 70–item paper-pencil rating scale assessing an individual's development in terms of job readiness and employability. The test contains the following subscales: vocational self-help skills, social-emotional adjustment, work attitudes-responsibility, cognitive-learning ability, perceptual-motor skills, and general work habits. Performance on each of the test items is assessed on a 5–point rating scale representing five developmental levels of vocational competency. The profile assists in the selection of training programs and determines an individual's present vocational functional level. The profile is used in special education classes, work-study programs, and vocational education classes, as well as in sheltered workshops, work activities centers, rehabilitation facilities, adult education classes, and vocational schools. Self-administered by examiner. Not suitable for group use.
Untimed: Varies
Scoring: Examiner evaluated
Cost: Test kit (manual, 10 record forms, 10 individualized vocational prescription forms) $27.00
Publisher: Stoelting Co.

FUNCTIONAL SKILLS SCREENING INVENTORY: EMPLOYMENT EDITION (FSSI: EE)
Refer to page 663.

JOB AWARENESS INVENTORY
Teen Makowski

Adolescent—Ages 15–17

Purpose: Evaluates student understanding of common occupations. Used as a prevocational test for special needs students, especially those who are slow or nonreaders.

Description: 100–item paper-pencil test measuring knowledge of the world of work, occupations, abilities, general information, and interview procedures. Materials include two forms, A and B; test booklet; and manual. The test may be read to students. Examiner required. Suitable for group use.

Untimed: Not available

Scoring: Hand key

Cost: Class set for 10 students $32.95; 20 students $55.95

Publisher: Mafex Associates, Inc.

Information and availability unconfirmed; last verified in 1987.

JOB SEARCH ASSESSMENT

Adolescent, adult

Purpose: Assesses an individual's understanding of the processes involved in successfully seeking and getting a job. Used for guidance and counseling and in conjunction with job search training programs.

Description: 80–item multiple-choice A-V format instrument assessing the following 20 areas related to job seeking: identifying skills, tasks, and qualities; writing resumes; clarifying values; setting goals; applying grammatical rules; completing application forms; planning the job search; making cold calls; establishing referral/support networks; knowledge of employee responsibility; communicating with others; dealing with employment agencies; the interview; cold canvassing for potential employment; using newspapers and the Yellow Pages; spelling words correctly; knowledge of legal and illegal items; taking employment tests; writing letters in response to want ads; and using interpersonal skills on the job. Items are presented by means of four characters as they face relevant job search situations. Responses are recorded in a booklet for computer scoring or on a card for on-site scoring. Pre- and post-assessment options are available for use with Prep's Job Search or other related curriculum. Examiner/self-administered. Suitable for group use.

Untimed: 2 hours

Scoring: Computer scored on-site or by publisher

Cost: Contact publisher

Publisher: Prep, A Division of Educational Technologies Inc.

JOB SEEKING SKILLS SURVEY (JSSS)
Donald S. Tackley

Adolescent, adult—Ages
16 and older
Grades 10 and above

Purpose: Measures job-seeking knowledge. Used in individual counseling, group counseling, screening, research, and career guidance to increase an individual's effectiveness in securing and retaining employment. Also used in instructional programs as a pre- and post-test in order to measure the effectiveness of job-seeking skills instruction.

Description: Multiple-item paper-pencil or computer-administered multiple-choice and true-false survey measuring an individual's knowledge of the basic steps involved in the job-seeking, getting, and retention process. Items are related to the following topic areas: luck vs. planning; sources of job openings; job applications; resume, cover letter, letter of application; job interviews; and the future: work habits/attitudes and continuing education.

The survey is available in three forms. The 106–item Instructional Needs Assessment Edition (INAE) is designed for individuals and institutions planning instructional programs based on item analysis of survey results or whose instructional or counseling time with individual students is limited. Forms A and B (53 items each) are designed to measure the effectiveness of instructional programs. All three forms are available as paper-pencil booklets. Forms A and B are also available on diskettes operating on Apple II systems.

Self-scored answer sheets printed on two layers of sealed paper are required for Form INAE. Responses recorded on the top layer transfer to the bottom layer. When the sheets are separated, the responses on the bottom sheet appear on the same line as the employers' preferred answer (preferred responses were established by submitting the survey to 200 employers in two states).

The paper-pencil versions of Forms A and B must be scored by hand unless optical test scoring equipment is available. The computer version of these two forms allows microcomputer scoring and prints results in terms of total percent correct and specific survey items incorrect. It also can generate results for an individual or for each person in a group and perform group and item analysis.

A 10th-grade reading level is required. The examiner may read the survey aloud to individuals with reading comprehension deficiencies. The JSSS is a revision of the Work-Seeking and Work-Getting Skills Survey. Examiner/self-administered. Suitable for group use.

Untimed: INAE 40 minutes; Form A or B 20 minutes

Scoring: Computer scored; hand key; may be machine scored; self-scored

Cost: Specimen set $19.95; diskette $48.95

Publisher: D.S. Transition Associates, Inc.

JOB TRAINING ASSESSMENT PROGRAM (JOBTAP)

Adult

Purpose: Assesses the general knowledge and job-related skills of youths and adults. Used with displaced, unskilled, unemployed, or entry-level workers for career planning and placement.

Description: Multiple-item battery of guidance tests and inventories yielding information on an individual's job search skills; general job knowledge; interest; work experience; and verbal, numerical, spatial, and basic work skills. Two of these assessments include Job Finder Tests—Book 1 containing the Basic Work Skills Test (45 minutes) and the Inspection/Visualization Test (20 minutes) and Job Finder Tests—Book 2 containing the Training and Work Manuals Test, Work Rules and Procedures Test, Follow-the-Rule Basic Arithmetic Test, and Follow-the-Rule Arithmetic Test. Results from these assessments (phase 1 of the program) are presented in three client information reports and two administrator information reports used for planning (phase 2) and implementation (phase 3). Examiner/self-administered. Suitable for group use.

Untimed: Complete test 1 hour, 30 minutes

Scoring: Computer scored

Cost: Contact publisher

Publisher: Educational Testing Service

Information and availability unconfirmed; last verified in 1988.

KEY EDUCATIONAL VOCATIONAL ASSESSMENT SYSTEM (KEVAS)
Key Education, Inc.

**Adolescent, adult—Ages 13 and older
Grades 8 and above**

Purpose: Measures a broad range of perceptual and psychomotor functions, basic skills competencies, social functioning, temperament factors, and vocational interests related to job performance. Used with in-school handicapped and special needs youths and adults, and vocational rehabilitation clients for vocational planning, career evaluation, and vocational rehabilitation.

Description: Multiple-item norm-referenced system consisting of 20 subtests measuring psychophysical functioning, motivational factors, problem-solving ability, vocational interests, math skills, language skills, social competency, and supervisory potential.

Eight of the subtests, measuring 13 functions (auditory acuity, auditory localization, auditory memory, visual reaction time, auditory reaction time, combined visual/auditory reaction time with hand, combined visual/auditory reaction time with foot, hand strength, manual persistence, fine-motor skills, abstract reasoning, visual memory, nonverbal problem solving), are administered using the KEVAS P.T.S., a portable, computerized test station consisting of a microcomputer and specialized test hardware. A response panel allows interaction between the KEVAS P.T.S. and the examinee. All KEVAS P.T.S. subtests are timed, but no limits are imposed.

The Ciba-Geigy vision and color charts are used to screen visual acuity and color blindness. The paper-pencil Key Functional Literacy Test measures word knowledge and language usage skills. The Key Arithmetic Test evaluates arithmetic and spatial problem-solving skills. Reading grade level is assessed using the Wide Range Achievement Test—Reading Scale. Several measures of vocational interest are used to generate a vocational interest profile.

Subtests administered via the KEVAS P.T.S. are scored internally, results are interpreted, and an individualized profile is produced. The paper-pencil subtests are scored by hand. Raw scores are entered manually into the KEVAS P.T.S., which integrates the data into the interpretive report.

A third-grade reading level is required. The publisher can provide certified examiners or train designated agency personnel. Examiner/self-administered. Suitable for group use.

Untimed: 2 hours, 30 minutes

Scoring: Computer scored; hand key; examiner evaluated

Cost: Contact publisher

Publisher: Key Education, Inc.

KNOWLEDGE OF OCCUPATIONS TEST
Leroy G. Baruth

Adolescent
Grades 10–12

Purpose: Assesses high-school students' knowledge of occupations. Used for vocational guidance.

Description: 96–item paper-pencil multiple-choice measure of what students know about occupations. Item content was drawn from sources including the *Occupational Outlook Handbook* and *The Encyclopedia of Career and Vocational Guidance*. Examiner required. Suitable for group use.

Timed: 40 minutes

Scoring: Hand key; may be machine scored

Cost: Specimen set $9.00; 25 tests $20.00; 25 profile sheets, 25 answer sheets $8.25 each; key $2.75; manual $6.75

Publisher: Psychologists and Educators, Inc.

LIVING SKILLS
Refer to page 899.

MCCARRON-DIAL SYSTEM (MDS)
Lawrence T. McCarron and Jack G. Dial

Adolescent, adult—Ages 16 and older

Purpose: Assesses verbal-spatial-cognitive, sensory, motor, emotional, and integration-coping factors. Used primarily in educational and vocational programming, development, and placement of special education and rehabilitation populations at any level of intellectual functioning and with physical, mental, emotional, or functional behavior disabilities.

Description: Multiple-item paper-pencil oral-response point-to task-performance battery consisting of six separate instruments: a) Peabody Picture Vocabulary Test—Revised (PPVT-R), b) Bender Visual Motor Gestalt Test (BVMGT), c) Behavior Rating Scale (BRS), d) Observational Emotional Inventory (OEI), e) Haptic Visual Discrimination Test (HVDT), and f) McCarron Assessment of Neuromuscular Development (MAND).

The verbal-spatial-cognitive factor is assessed through the PPVT and, if available, the Wechsler Scales: Wechsler Adult Intelligence Scale (WAIS) and measures of academic achievement. The sensory factor is tested by the BVMGT and the HVDT. Motor functioning is assessed with the MAND. Emotional factors are measured with the OEI. Integration-Coping is tested with the BRS and, if available, the Street Survival Skills Questionnaire (SSSQ). See separate entries for each of these instruments.

The standard format for comprehensive reporting includes specific scores, vocational and residential placement scores, behavioral observations, case history information, lists of strengths and weaknesses, programming priorities, and programming recommendations. The Individual Evaluation Profile allows recording and profiling of the total score of each test administered. The Individual

Program Plan allows recording of subtest scores and right/left measures. The scores are then profiled for each of the five factors.

Four computer software programs, each operating on IBM PC and compatibles, Apple, and Macintosh systems, assist in the analysis and interpretation of MDS data. The Computer Assessment Program (CAP) generates a vocational evaluation/consultive report. The Individualized Trait Analysis for Program Planning (ITAPP) is a resource for writing individual program plans in a vocational or prevocational context. The Occupational Exploration System (OES) provides a list of occupations suitable for vocational exploration, planning, or development. Remedial Motor Training (RMT) provides activities and strategies for remediating the examinee's specific motor deficits.

The system is designed to predict the level of vocational and residential functioning the individual may achieve after training. This predicted level can be used to establish vocational goals and/or appropriate vocational program placement. The system is targeted especially toward the learning disabled, emotionally disturbed, mentally retarded, cerebral palsied, closed head-injured, socially handicapped, and culturally disadvantaged. It also can be adapted for use with blind (requires administration of the Haptic Memory Matching Test) or deaf persons. In addition, it is appropriate for the neuropsychological assessment and evaluation of sensorimotor development of children.

The examiner's commitment to pursue training is a purchase prerequisite. A Spanish version of the administration instructions is available. Examiner required. Not suitable for group use.

Timed: Not available

Untimed: Varies

Scoring: Hand key; examiner evaluated

Cost: Complete MDS $1,625.00; HVDT only $615.00; MAND only $745.00; CAP $775.00; ITAPP $1,250.00; OES $775.00; RMT $250.00; additional manuals and scoring forms may be purchased separately

Publisher: McCarron-Dial Systems

Information and availability unconfirmed; last verified in 1988.

MESA

Adolescent, adult

Purpose: Provides baseline data for the development of an individual's education, training, or employment plan or for more extensive vocational evaluation. May be used with individuals contemplating entering the labor market for the first time or changing fields of work.

Description: Multiple-item computer-administered test measuring 21 factors of the Worker Qualifications Profile as defined in the U.S. Department of Labor's *Dictionary of Occupational Titles*. The test consists of the following six subtests: Hardware Exercises, which measures the ability to use tools, machine-tending, instruction following, finger dexterity, problem solving, and assembly; Computer Exercises, which screens vision, size-color-shape discrimination, eye-hand coordination, and academic skills; Perceptual Screening, which assesses spatial aptitudes; Talking/Persuasive Screening, which measures the ability to communicate verbally; Physical Capacities and Mobility, which measures dynamic strength; and Vocational/Interest Awareness, which consists of two exercises assessing vocational interests and knowledge of the world of work. The test may be used with Apple and IBM computers. Examiner/self-administered. Suitable for group use.

Timed: 4½ hours

Scoring: Hand key; examiner evaluated; computer scored

Cost: 1 station $3,975.00; 2 stations $5,150.00; 4 stations $7,450.00

Publisher: Valpar International Corporation

MESA SF2

Adolescent, adult

Purpose: Provides baseline data for the development of an individual's education, training, or employment plan or for more extensive vocational evaluation. May be used with individuals contemplating entering the labor market for the first time or changing fields of work.

Description: Multiple-item computer-administered test containing the following two subtests: Hardware Exercises, which measures the ability to use tools, machine tending, instruction following, finger dexterity, problem solving, and assembly; and Computer Exercises, which screens vision, size-color-shape discrimination, eye-hand coordination, memory, reasoning, eye-hand-foot coordination, and academic skills. Computer-generated reports are available. The test is a shortened version of MESA. Examiner/self-administered. Suitable for group use.

Timed: 1½ hours

Scoring: Hand key; examiner evaluated; computer scored

Cost: $2,995.00

Publisher: Valpar International Corporation

NM CAREER DEVELOPMENT TEST (NMCDT)
C.C. Healy and S.P. Klein

**Adolescent
Grades 9–12**

Purpose: Measures an individual's knowledge of what is required to hold a job and to advance in an occupation. Used for career counseling and program evaluation.

Description: 25–item paper-pencil multiple-choice test measuring student's feelings about whether success or failure is a function of one's own actions rather than luck. It also measures knowledge of how to conduct oneself properly on the job and of factors that influence advancement in a chosen field or occupation. The test booklets are reusable, and a lay-over stencil is used for scoring. Reliability and norms have been determined from samples of 9th- and 12th-grade secondary students. Examiner required. Suitable for group use.

Timed: 20 minutes

Scoring: Hand key

Cost: Specimen set $6.00; 35 tests $12.00; 35 answer sheets $4.00; scoring stencil $3.00; manual $4.00

Publisher: Monitor

NM CAREER ORIENTED ACTIVITIES CHECKLIST (NMCOAC)
C.C. Healy and S.P. Klein

**Adolescent
Grades 9–12**

Purpose: Evaluates an individual's experience in consulting sources of information necessary to plan a career. Used for vocational counseling and planning.

Description: 25–item paper-pencil multiple-choice test evaluating a student's experience in consulting various sources of information about occupations, acting to provide information about occupations the student is considering, obtaining the high-school training needed for occupations being considered, and making definite plans regarding what will be done upon graduation. The test is designed for 12th-graders, but has been administered successfully to 9th-graders. Test booklets are reusable, and a lay-over stencil is used for scoring. Reliability and norms have been determined from samples of 9th- and 12th-grade students. Examiner required. Suitable for group use.

Timed: 20 minutes

Scoring: Hand key

Cost: Specimen set $6.00; 35 tests $12.00; 35 answer sheets $4.00; scoring stencils $5.00; manual $4.00

Publisher: Monitor

NM CAREER PLANNING TEST (NMCPT)
C.C. Healy and S.P. Klein

**Adolescent
Grades 9–12**

Purpose: Measures an individual's ability to make appropriate decisions about preparing for and selecting an occupation. Used for career counseling and program evaluation.

Description: 20–item paper-pencil multiple-choice test measuring student knowledge of informational sources to consult to obtain knowledge about various occupations and of what actions should be taken in order to make a decision related to selecting and preparing for an occupation. Test booklets for the two equivalent forms, A and B, are reusable. A lay-over stencil is used for scoring. Reliability and norms for both forms of this test have been determined from samples of 9th- and 12th-grade secondary students. Examiner required. Suitable for group use.

Timed: 20 minutes

Scoring: Hand key

Cost: Specimen set $6.00; 35 tests (specify form) $12.00; 35 answer sheets (specify form) $4.00; scoring stencil (specify form) $3.00; manual $4.00

Publisher: Monitor

NM JOB APPLICATION PROCEDURES TEST (NMJAPT)
C.C. Healy and S.P. Klein

Adolescent Grades 9–12

Purpose: Assesses an individual's knowledge of how to apply for a job. Used for career counseling and program evaluation.

Description: 20–item paper-pencil multiple-choice test of student ability to make inquiries, read advertisements, and use employment agencies. It also measures the ability to complete a job application form satisfactorily and knowledge of how to conduct oneself during an interview. The test booklets are reusable, and a lay-over stencil is used for scoring. Reliability and norms have been determined from samples of 9th- and 12th-grade secondary students. Examiner required. Suitable for group use.

Timed: 20 minutes

Scoring: Hand key

Cost: Specimen set $6.00; 35 tests $12.00; 35 answer sheets $4.00; scoring stencil $3.00; manual $4.00

Publisher: Monitor

NM KNOWLEDGE OF OCCUPATIONS TEST (NMKOOT)
C.C. Healy and S.P. Klein

Adolescent Grades 9–12

Purpose: Measures an individual's knowledge of the characteristics and requirements of various occupations. Used for vocational counseling and program evaluation.

Description: 25–item paper-pencil multiple-choice test measuring a student's knowledge of job characteristics (hours of work, pay, work environment, tasks, and demand) and of job and personal requirements (training, abilities, and interests). The test booklets are reusable, and a lay-over stencil is used for scoring. Reliability and norms have been determined from samples of 9th- and 12th-grade secondary students. Self-administered. Suitable for group use.

Timed: 20 minutes

Scoring: Hand key

Cost: Specimen set $6.00; 35 tests $12.00; 35 answer sheets $4.00; scoring stencil $3.00; manual $4.00

Publisher: Monitor

PROGRAM FOR ASSESSING YOUTH EMPLOYMENT SKILLS (PAYES)
Educational Testing Service

Adolescent

Purpose: Measures the attitudes, knowledge, and interests of students preparing for entry-level employment. Used by program directors, counselors, and teachers working with dropouts, potential dropouts, and disadvantaged youth in government training programs, skill centers, vocational high schools, ABE centers, and correctional institutions.

Description: Three orally administered paper-pencil tests assessing attitudes, knowledge, and interests related to entry-level employment. Test Booklet I measures attitudes toward job-holding skills (supervisor's requests, appropriate dress, punctuality), attitudes toward supervision by authority figures (judge, supervisor, teacher, police officer, and parent), and self-confidence in social and employment situations. Measurements are made by assessing responses to multiple-choice questions based on statements, real-life situations, and scenes. Test Booklet II provides cognitive measures, including job knowledge (understanding of education required, salary, task performed, location of work, working hours, and tools), job seeking skills (interpretation of newspaper want ads and job application forms), and practical job-related reasoning in situations that require following directions. Test Booklet III measures seven vocational interest clusters (aesthetic, business, clerical, outdoor, service, science, technical). Respondents indicate their degree of interest in specific job tasks that are described verbally and pictured. Students mark answers directly in test booklets. Examiner required. Suitable for group use.

Untimed: Varies

Scoring: Examiner evaluated

Cost: Complete set (20 each of Test Booklets I, II, and III, score sheets) $90.00; user's guide $4.50; administrators' manual $5.50

Publisher: Educational Testing Service

SPACE RELATIONS (PAPER PUZZLES)
Refer to page 914.

SPACE THINKING (FLAGS)
Refer to page 914.

SWEET'S TECHNICAL INFORMATION TEST (STIT)
R. Sweet

Adolescent—Ages 13.6–18

Purpose: Measures the technical knowledge of students. Used in counseling settings to assess suitability for technical and practical occupations at trade and subprofessional levels.

Description: 55–item paper-pencil multiple-choice test measuring three areas of technical knowledge: electricity and electronics, woodwork and general tool use, and mechanics. Items are of four main types: identification, use, operation, and component. The test is designed to measure the type of technical information that might be acquired through an interest in the three areas, rather than as a measure of mechanical aptitude. Australian norms are provided for males and females separately. Materials include a reusable test booklet, answer sheet, scoring key, manual, and specimen set. Examiner evaluated. Suitable for group use.

AUSTRALIAN PUBLISHER

Timed: 20 minutes

Scoring: Hand key; examiner evaluated; may be machine scored

Cost: Contact publisher

Publisher: The Australian Council for Educational Research Limited

---

TECHNICAL AND SCIENTIFIC INFORMATION TEST, TECHNICAL READING COMPREHENSION TEST AND GENERAL SCIENCE TEST
Refer to page 919.

VCWS 15—ELECTRICAL CIRCUITRY AND PRINT READING
Refer to page 925.

VCWS 16—DRAFTING
Refer to page 925.

VOCATIONAL BEHAVIOR CHECKLIST (VBC)
Richard T. Walls, Thomas Zane, and Thomas J. Werner

Adolescent, adult—Ages 16–65

Purpose: Assesses prevocational and vocational skills, assists in planning individualized programming, and assesses the effectiveness of rehabilitation programs. Used in classroom, home, and work environments.

Description: 344-item criterion-referenced checklist used by an observer to rate the examinee's vocational skills both on-the-job and in simulated environments. Skills are categorized along seven domains: a) prevocational skills (194 items), b) job-seeking skills (20 items), c) interview skills (21 items), d) job-related skills (21 items), e) work performance skills (47 items), f) on-the-job social skills (19 items), and g) union-financial-security skills (22 items). The examiner may delete inappropriate skill objectives, add objectives, or modify objectives by adapting the conditions, instructions, behaviors, or standards to suit individual needs. Examiner required. Not suitable for group use.

Untimed: Varies

Scoring: Hand key

Cost: Manual with summary chart $8.00; extra summary charts $1.00 per package of 10

Publisher: Research and Training Center Press

VOCATIONAL INTEREST, EXPERIENCE & SKILL ASSESSMENT (VIESA), CANADIAN EDITION
Refer to page 839.

VOCATIONAL INTEREST, EXPERIENCE & SKILL ASSESSMENT (VIESA), SECOND EDITION
Refer to page 839.

WEBER ADVANCED SPATIAL PERCEPTION TEST (WASP)
P.G. Weber

Adolescent, adult—Ages 13½ and older

Purpose: Measures spatial perception abilities of individuals ages 13½ and older. Used in counseling to assess an individual's suitability for technical and practical occupations at trade and subprofessional levels.

Description: Four paper-pencil subtests measuring spatial abilities in four dimensions. The Form Recognition Test measures the ability to identify a stimulus figure that is combined with other figures similar in shape. The Pattern Perception Test requires the examinee to draw a line around those crosses in a complex pattern that correspond to crosses in a simpler given pattern; the Shape Analysis Test requires the examinee to indicate which of five small shapes are used to compose a larger shape. In the Reflected Figure Test, the examinee draws a given figure upside down. Australian norms are provided. Materials include a reusable test booklet for the Form Recognition Test, a separate answer booklet containing an answer sheet for a Form Recognition Test and questions and answer space for the remaining tests, a set of score keys, a manual, and specimen set. Examiner required. Suitable for group use. AUSTRALIAN PUBLISHER

Timed: 45 minutes

Scoring: Hand key; examiner evaluated

Cost: Contact publisher

Publisher: The Australian Council for Educational Research Limited

---

WIDE RANGE EMPLOYABILITY SAMPLE TEST (WREST)
Joseph F. Jastak and Sarah Jastak

Adolescent, adult—Ages 16–adult

Purpose: Measures a person's ability to work at routine manual tasks. Assists in diagnosis of mental retardation and determines the feasibility of competitive employment of the severely handicapped. Used for placement in sheltered workshops or daily activities programs.

Description: 10-item test in which individuals complete simple manual tasks, including folding, stapling, packaging, measuring, assembling, tag stringing, gluing, collating, and color or shade and pattern matching. Each of the tasks is carefully taught prior to testing. The tasks measure "horizontal" achievement (the capacity to do the routine operations involved in all jobs regardless of level). Persons with average or above-average scores on WREST are not mentally retarded, even if their scores on "vertical" achievement or intelligence tests rate them as retarded. Scored for speed and accuracy, the results are expressed in scaled scores for each item. Standard scores are provided for total production quantity and quality and for a combined technical productivity rating. Norms are provided for three populations: general, sheltered workshop, and industrial. Examiner required. Not suitable for group use.

Timed: 1 hour

Scoring: Examiner evaluated

Cost: Complete $1,600.00

Publisher: Jastak Assessment Systems

Teacher Evaluation: Student Opinion of Teachers

ACADEMIC ADVISING INVENTORY
Refer to page 600.

CLASSROOM ENVIRONMENT SCALE (CES)
Refer to page 601.

DIAGNOSTIC TEACHER-RATING SCALE
Sister Mary Amatora

Adolescent, adult
Grades 7 and above

Purpose: Measures students' perceptions of their teachers. Used to analyze and improve student-teacher relations.

Description: 56–item paper-pencil inventory consisting of two scales. The Area Scale (7 items) consists of a list of attributes related to effective teaching and good student-teacher relations. Students rate their teacher for each attribute on a 5–point scale from "worst" to "best." The Diagnostic Checklist (49 items) consists of true-false statements assessing seven factors: liking for teacher; ability to

explain; kindness, friendliness, and understanding; fairness in grading; discipline; amount of work required; and liking for lessons. The checklist is available in two similar forms, A and B. Examiner required. Suitable for group use.

Untimed: Not available

Scoring: Hand key; examiner evaluated

Cost: Specimen set $5.00; complete kit (35 record sheets for scale, checklist, manual) $12.00

Publisher: Educators/Employers' Tests & Services Associates

THE EDUCATIONAL PROCESS QUESTIONNAIRE (EPQ)
Institute for Behavioral Research in Creativity

Child, adolescent
Grades 3 and above

Purpose: Gathers student descriptions of classroom activities, providing information on key educational processes.

Description: 54–item paper-pencil multiple-choice instrument consisting of five scales: Development of Multiple Talents, Reinforcement of Self-Concept, Expectations, Feedback, and Academic Learning Time. Examiner required. Suitable for group use.

Untimed: Varies

Scoring: Computer scored; scoring service available from publisher

Cost: Contact publisher

Publisher: Institute for Behavioral Research in Creativity

ENDEAVOR INSTRUCTIONAL RATING SYSTEM
Peter W. Fry

Adolescent, adult
College students

Purpose: Measures teacher effectiveness at the college and university level.

Description: 7–item paper-pencil measure of the instructor's organizational, communication, and interpersonal skills and the difficulty of the course. A brief rating form is distributed to each student, and the students respond to each item. The test requires advanced planning and is limited to classes with five or more students. The publisher no longer provides a scoring service. Self-administered. Suitable for group use.

Untimed: 5–7 minutes

Scoring: Not available

Cost: Contact publisher

Publisher: Endeavor Information Systems, Inc.

Information and availability unconfirmed; last verified in 1987.

IDEA—INSTRUCTIONAL DEVELOPMENT AND EFFECTIVENESS ASSESSMENT
Center for Faculty Evaluation and Development, Kansas State University

College students

Purpose: Assesses teaching effectiveness. May be used within departments or throughout institutions.

Description: 38–item paper-pencil four-part instrument in which students and faculty rate teaching effectiveness. The system is based on the assumption that effective teaching is best assessed through instructional goals rather than teacher behavior. For each class, the faculty member completes a Faculty Information Sheet with name grid, department code, course number, enrollment, time and day of class, and ratings (essential, important, of minor importance) of each instructional goal. Students complete the Response Card and the Survey Form, which consists of five sections. Section I (items 1–20) requires students to rate the frequency of teacher behaviors or methods. In Section II (items 21–30), students rate their own progress toward each of the instructional goals. The third section (items 31–34) requires students to rate specific course characteristics. In Section IV (items 35–38), students rate their own characteristics. A fifth section contains items that are used only for research. The Response Card, which is completed in conjunction with the Survey Form, may contain up to 25 additional questions developed by the instructor.

The test yields a three-page, seven-part computerized report that summarizes and interprets students' responses on the survey forms. A short form consisting of a 14–item sheet is available for use in one or two courses to gather information for personnel decisions. Computer analysis controls for level of student motivation (the student's desire to take the course) and size of class. Comparative data for 44 different academic fields are available in table form. Examiner/self-administered. Suitable for group use.

Untimed: 10–20 minutes

Scoring: Computer scored

Cost: $0.12–$0.20 per student; $3.00–$5.00 per class

Publisher: Center for Faculty Evaluation and Development, Kansas State University

Information and availability unconfirmed; last verified in 1988.

THE PURDUE TEACHER EVALUATION SCALE (PTES)
Ralph R. Bentley and Allan R. Starry

Adolescent Grades 7–12

Purpose: Measures student opinions of teachers. Used to provide teachers with information for a program of self-improvement and development.

Description: Multiple-item paper-pencil measure of six dimensions of student attitudes toward teachers: ability to motivate students, ability to control students, subject matter orientation of teacher, student-teacher communication, teaching methods and procedures, and fairness of teacher. Examiner required. Suitable for group use.

Untimed: 20 minutes

Scoring: Hand key; may be computer scored

Cost: Contact publisher

Publisher: Purdue Research Foundation

STUDENT INSTRUCTIONAL REPORT (SIR)
Research staff of Educational Testing Service

Adolescent, adult
College students

Purpose: Measures teacher performance. Used for instructional improvement, administrative decisions, and student course selection.

Description: 39–item paper-pencil test assessing six aspects of teacher performance: course organization and planning, faculty/student interaction, communication; course difficulty and workload, textbooks and readings, and tests and exams. The instrument is administered to students during regular class sessions. Examiner required. Suitable for group use. Available in French (for Canadian universities) and Spanish.

Untimed: 50 minutes

Scoring: Computer scored

Cost: First 20,000 forms $0.18 each; processing first 5,000 forms $0.35 each

Publisher: Educational Testing Service

Information and availability unconfirmed; last verified in 1988.

STUDENT MOTIVATION DIAGNOSTIC QUESTIONNAIRE
Refer to page 758.

STUDENT OPINION INVENTORY
Refer to page 758.

THINKING ABOUT MY SCHOOL
Refer to page 608.

THE WILSON TEACHER-APPRAISAL SCALE
Howard Wilson

Adolescent, adult
Grades 7–16

Purpose: Allows teachers to see how they are perceived by their students. Used at the close of an academic term, often in conjunction with A Self-Appraisal Scale for Teachers, to aid in the professional development of classroom instructors.

Description: 16–item paper-pencil rating scale allowing students to rate the performance of their classroom instructors. Students rate the teacher as a person and as an instructor compared to other instructors. Course content and assignments are also rated. The scale is purchased and supplied by the institution and voluntarily used by teachers as a tool to increase their effectiveness. Self-administered. Suitable for group use.

Untimed: 5 minutes

Scoring: Examiner evaluated

Cost: 50 scales $2.50

Publisher: Administrative Research Associates

Information and availability unconfirmed; last verified in 1988.

Teacher Evaluation: Teacher Attitudes

CHANGE AGENT QUESTIONNAIRE (CAQ)
Refer to page 997.

CLASS ACTIVITIES QUESTIONNAIRE (CAQ)
Joe M. Steele

Adolescent, adult

Purpose: Assesses the instructional climate of upper-elementary and high-school classrooms. Enables teachers to determine whether goals and expectations are clearly defined in the classroom. Assesses affective factors, such as openness, independence, divergence, and emphasis on grades.

Description: 30–item paper-pencil questionnaire assessing five dimensions of instructional climate in the classroom: lower thought processes, higher thought processes, classroom focus, classroom climate, and student opinions. Items 1–27 assess cognitive emphasis and classroom conditions by asking students to rate statements about their classroom experiences on a 4–point scale ranging from "strongly agree" to "strongly disagree." Items 28–30 allow the students to describe in their own words what they perceive to be the strengths and weaknesses of their class. Teachers complete the questionnaire twice, once to indicate what they intend to emphasize in the classroom and a second time to indicate what they predict the students as a group will say. Computer scoring compares the teacher's responses to those provided by the students. Examiner required. Suitable for group use.

Untimed: 20–30 minutes

Scoring: Computer scored

Cost: Test kit (30 student forms, two teacher forms, manual, and computer analysis) $22.95; specimen set $8.95

Publisher: Creative Learning Press, Inc.

EDUCATIONAL VALUES (VAL-ED)
Will Schutz

Adult

Purpose: Assesses an individual's attitudes towards education. Used to evaluate the working relationships of students, teachers, administrators, or community members.

Description: Multiple-item paper-pencil survey of values regarding interpersonal relationships in school settings. The factors included relate to inclusion, control, and affection at both the feeling and the behavioral levels and to the purpose and importance of education. Examiner/self-administered. Suitable for group use.

Untimed: Not available

Scoring: Hand key

Cost: Specimen set (test booklet, scoring key) $4.50

Publisher: Consulting Psychologists Press, Inc.

EMPATHY INVENTORY (EI)
John R. Thurston

Adult

Purpose: Measures ability of nursing faculty, counselors, and others to empathize

with nursing students. Used for self-evaluation.

Description: 75–item paper-pencil test with a dual-choice format providing interested individuals an opportunity to check their empathic ability. Materials include a self-directing booklet, answer sheet, and scoring key. A comprehensive manual covering this and other NRA tests is available. Self-administered. Suitable for group use.

Untimed: 30 minutes

Scoring: Hand key; scoring service available

Cost: Specimen set (including scoring, key) $10.00; 50 answer sheets $5.00; scoring key $5.00; comprehensive manual $20.00; scoring service $2.00 per test

Publisher: Nursing Research Associates

Information and availability unconfirmed; last verified in 1988.

IDEA—INSTRUCTIONAL DEVELOPMENT AND EFFECTIVENESS ASSESSMENT
Refer to page 854.

INSTRUCTIONAL LEADERSHIP INVENTORY
Martin L. Maehr, Russell Ames, and MetriTech, Inc. staff

Adult

Purpose: Evaluates the leadership goals and behaviors of school administrators.

Description: 188–item paper-pencil multiple-choice inventory evaluating the leadership goals and behaviors of school administrators within the context of the individual's current school, district, and community situation. A mail-in scoring service is available from the publisher. APA purchase guidelines apply. Self-administered. Suitable for group use.

Untimed: 1 hour

Scoring: Computer scored

Cost: Contact publisher

Publisher: MetriTech, Inc.

INSTRUCTIONAL STYLES INVENTORY (ISI)
Albert A. Canfield and
Judith S. Canfield

Adult

Purpose: Identifies a teacher's preferred instructional methods. Used in conjunction with the Learning Styles Inventory to maximize teaching and learning efficiency.

Description: 25–item paper-pencil forced-rank inventory assessing a teacher's preferences concerning learning environments, instructional modalities, and topical interests. The inventory also measures how much responsibility the instructor will assume for student learning (instead of measuring performance expectancy), identifies areas where instructional training would be most beneficial, provides information to help instructors interpret classroom problems and student reactions, and measures the same dimensions as the Canfield Learning Styles Inventory to allow for one-to-one comparison between the two inventories. The test booklets are reusable. Separate norms are provided for male and female instructors. Self-administered. Suitable for group use.

Untimed: 20–30 minutes

Scoring: Self-scored

Cost: Kit $35.00

Publisher: Western Psychological Services

MASLACH BURNOUT INVENTORY, 2ND EDITION
Refer to page 1010.

OPINIONS TOWARD ADOLESCENTS (OTA SCALE)
William T. Martin

Adolescent, adult
Grades 5–7

Purpose: Evaluates attitudes and personality factors that may help or inhibit interpersonal relationships between adults and adolescents. Used to screen persons

who will be working with adolescents and to educate current staff members.

Description: 89–item paper-pencil inventory examining bipolar attitudes on the following subscales: conservative-liberal, permissive-punitive, morally accepting-morally restrictive, democratic-authoritarian, trust-mistrust, acceptance-prejudice, misunderstanding-understanding, and sincerity-skepticism (a validity scale reflecting test-taking attitude). Norms are provided for various adult and college groups. A fifth- to seventh-grade reading level is required. Self-administered. Suitable for group use.

Untimed: 20 minutes

Scoring: Hand key

Cost: Examiner's set (manual, keys, 25 test books, 25 answer sheets, 25 profile sheets) $40.00; 25 tests $15.00; 25 profile sheets $8.25; 25 answer sheets $6.75; keys $6.75; manual $4.50

Publisher: Psychologists and Educators, Inc.

PERFORMANCE LEVELS OF A SCHOOL PROGRAM SURVEY (PLSPS)
Frank E. Williams

Adult

Purpose: Evaluates teacher and administrator perceptions of the value of a classroom, a building, or a district program. Used to ensure compliance with federal, state, and local guidelines concerning the quality and content of academic programs.

Description: Multiple-item paper-pencil inventory evaluating the following eight areas of multiple abilities that are specifically defined in federal, state, and local guidelines: general intellectual, specific academics, leadership, creative productive thinking, psychomotor, visual performing arts, affective, and vocational career. The inventory pinpoints those areas receiving insufficient emphasis. Examiner/self-administered. Suitable for group use.

Untimed: Varies

Scoring: Self-scored

Cost: Test kit (survey materials for 30 participants) $16.00

Publisher: D.O.K. Publishers, Inc.

PURDUE STUDENT-TEACHER OPINIONAIRE—FORM B (PSTO)
Ralph R. Bentley and JoAnn Price

Adult

Purpose: Measures student-teacher morale. Used for providing schools with feedback about student-teachers' experiences.

Description: Multiple-item paper-pencil measure of nine aspects of student-teacher morale: rapport with supervising teacher, student-teacher rapport with principal, rapport with university supervisor, teaching as a profession, school facilities, professional preparation, rapport with students, rapport with other teachers and student-teacher load. Examiner required. Suitable for group use.

Untimed: 20–30 minutes

Scoring: Hand key; may be computer scored

Cost: Contact publisher

Publisher: Purdue Research Foundation

THE PURDUE TEACHER OPINIONAIRE (PTO)
Ralph R. Bentley and Averno M. Rempel

Adult

Purpose: Assesses teacher opinions of the school environment. Used for studying teacher morale.

Description: Multiple-item paper-pencil measure of 10 teacher morale factors: teacher rapport with principal, satisfaction with teaching, rapport among teachers, teacher salary, teacher load, curriculum issues, teacher status, community support of education, school facilities and services, and community pressures. Materials include a PTO Supplement with two new factors: teacher rapport with school board and superintendent. Examiner required. Suitable for group use.

Untimed: 20–30 minutes

Scoring: Hand key; may be computer scored

Cost: Contact publisher

Publisher: Purdue Research Foundation

RUCKER-GABLE EDUCATIONAL PROGRAMMING SCALE
Chauncy N. Rucker and Robert K. Gable

Adult—Teachers

Purpose: Assesses the ability of teachers to measure the attitudes of handicapped children.

Description: 30–item paper-pencil test measuring a teacher's attitude toward and knowledge of appropriate placement for handicapped children on the basis of a brief description of the student's handicap. The student handicap range includes mildly, moderately, and severely handicapped; mentally retarded, emotionally disturbed, and learning disabled; and total disability. Self-administered. Suitable for group use. Available in Spanish and Chinese.

Untimed: 20–30 minutes

Scoring: Computer scored

Cost: Specimen set $10.00; manual $9.00; scoring service $40.00

Publisher: Rucker-Gable Associates

Information and availability unconfirmed; last verified in 1987.

A SELF-APPRAISAL SCALE FOR TEACHERS
Howard Wilson

Adult—Teachers

Purpose: Allows teachers to self-appraise their classroom performance. Often used in conjunction with the Wilson Teacher-Appraisal Scale at the close of an academic term to aid in the professional development of classroom instructors.

Description: 102–item paper-pencil inventory allowing instructors to rate themselves in six areas: teacher as a person, teacher as a specialist and educator, relations with students, course content, classroom performance, and feelings about how students perceive them. Each item in the scale reflects a characteristic of competency as related to teaching methods. Teachers rate themselves for each item on a 5–point scale from "high" to "low," circling items of particular importance. The scale is often purchased and supplied by the educational institution and voluntarily used by teachers as a tool to increase their classroom effectiveness. Self-administered. Suitable for group use.

Untimed: 20 minutes
Scoring: Self-scored
Cost: Scale $1.50
Publisher: Administrative Research Associates

Information and availability unconfirmed; last verified in 1988.

A TEACHER ATTITUDE INVENTORY (TAI): IDENTIFYING TEACHER POSITIONS IN RELATION TO EDUCATIONAL ISSUES AND DECISIONS
Joanne Rand Whitmore

Adult

Purpose: Identifies teacher attitudes regarding philosophical issues and contrasting educational practices.

Description: Multiple-item paper-pencil questionnaire used by district administrators, principals, and teachers for determining attitudes toward educational practices. The responses help in planning in-service professional growth programs, faculty discussions, team teaching, and classroom setting for gifted students. This tool also is useful for evaluation, research, and determining teaching styles. Examiner/self-administered. Suitable for group use.

Untimed: Varies
Scoring: Examiner evaluated
Cost: Complete kit $19.95
Publisher: D.O.K. Publishers, Inc.

TEACHER OPINION INVENTORY
National Study of School Evaluation

Adult—Classroom teachers

Purpose: Assesses teachers' opinions of their school and its programs. Provides an opportunity for direct faculty recommen-

dations. Used by school personnel to make decisions regarding program development, policy formulation, administrative organization, faculty development, and community relations. Used as part of a complete school evaluation process.

Description: 73–item paper-pencil multiple-choice opinion survey consisting of two parts. Part A contains 66 multiple-choice items assessing teachers' opinions of various aspects of the school. Part B contains seven open-ended questions constructed for teachers to make recommendations for school improvement. The Administrator's Manual describes the development of the instrument, provides instructions for administering the inventory, and contains a single copy of both Parts A and B. The inventory may be administered independently or in conjunction with the Parent Opinion Inventory, the Student Opinion Inventory, or as part of a complete school evaluation program. A seventh-grade reading level is required. Individuals with visual, hearing, or physical impairments may complete the test with the assistance of non-impaired individuals. A computer scoring service is available from the Bureau of Evaluative Studies and Testing, Indiana University, Bloomington, Indiana 47405 (812) 335–1595. Self-administered. Suitable for group use.

Untimed: Varies
Scoring: Computer scored; may be machine scored; may be self-scored
Cost: 25 copies Part A $4.00; 25 copies of Part B $3.00; manual $3.00
Publisher: National Study of School Evaluation

Information and availability unconfirmed; last verified in 1988.

TEACHER OPINIONAIRE ON DEMOCRACY
Enola Ledbetter

Adult

Purpose: Assesses teacher's attitudes about what is and is not wise in the way children are treated in school. Used for teacher surveys and college instruction.

Description: 65–item paper-pencil test measuring the "democraticness" of a teacher's philosophy, defined as the extent to which the teacher purports to respect the personality and purpose of the pupil. The teacher is asked to agree or disagree with each statement by marking it plus or minus. Self-administered. Suitable for group use.

Untimed: 30 minutes

Scoring: Hand key

Cost: Manual, sample opinionaire $1.00

Publisher: Lentz Peace Research Laboratory

TEACHER STRESS INVENTORY (TSI)
Michael Fimian

Adult
Teachers

Purpose: Measures the occupational stress of teachers. Used by teachers to assess their own stress levels; by teacher groups in workshop and other similar settings; and by researchers interested in school-, system-, or state-wide surveys of teacher stress.

Description: 58–item (49 stress related and 9 optional demographic) paper-pencil rating scales measuring five stress source factors and five stress manifestation factors in teachers. The stress source factors are Time Management, Work-Related Stressors, Professional Distress, Discipline and Motivation, and Professional Investment. The stress manifestation factors are Emotional, Fatigue, Cardiovascular, Gastronomic, and Behavioral. Raw scores may be compared to cutoff scores by using deciles or by comparison to the norm. The manual provides norms for regular and special education teachers by sex and grade level. Self-administered. Not suitable for group use.

Untimed: 15 minutes

Scoring: Hand key; examiner evaluated

Cost: Sample kit (manual, test form) $16.00

Publisher: Clinical Psychology Publishing Co., Inc.

TEACHING STYLE INVENTORY
J. Robert Hanson and Harvey F. Silver

Adult—Teachers

Purpose: Identifies preferred teaching styles.

Description: 40–item paper-pencil diagnostic tool yielding a teaching style profile. Individuals rank their preferences for 10 categories of behavior: classroom atmosphere, teaching techniques, planning, preferred qualities of students, teacher/student interaction, classroom management, appropriate behaviors, teaching behavior, evaluation, and educational goals. Results help teachers understand their styles of teaching. Administrators can use the information for helping teachers vary their teaching styles to meet the needs of different learning styles. The instrument includes detailed descriptions of four basic teaching styles. Self-administered. Suitable for group use.

Untimed: 30 minutes

Scoring: Self-scored

Cost: $3.50 per copy

Publisher: Hanson, Silver, Strong and Associates, Inc.

Information and availability unconfirmed; last verified in 1987.

Business and Industry

The tests described in the Business section generally are used for personnel selection, evaluation, development, and promotion.

In addition, the reader is encouraged to consult the Psychology and Education sections for other asessment instruments that may be of value in the area of business.

Business and Industry Section

Aptitude and Skills Screening

ADULT BASIC LEARNING EXAMINATION SECOND EDITION (ABLE)
Refer to page 412.

ADVANCED TEST BATTERY (ATB)
Saville & Holdsworth Ltd. Staff

Adult

Purpose: Evaluates verbal, numerical, and spatial reasoning at the very top range of ability. Used in the selection, development, and guidance of personnel at the graduate level or in management positions.

Description: Seven multiple-item paper-pencil multiple-choice tests measuring verbal, numerical, and diagramming skills. The five main tests are arranged in two levels. Level 1 is somewhat easier and consists of three aptitude tests: Verbal Concepts (VA1), Number Series (NA2), and Diagramming (DA5). Level 2 has a higher perceived relevance (face validity) and consists of two tests in which skills are applied in context: Verbal Critical Reasoning (VA3) and Numerical Critical Reasoning (NA4). These five tests can be administered in various combinations to suit a number of contexts. For some applications, the Technical Test Battery Diagrammatic Reasoning Test (DT8) and the TTB Spatial Reasoning Test (ST7) are used with the ATB tests. The tests are suitable from the good "O" level standard to the top end of the graduate population. Examiner required. Suitable for group use.
BRITISH PUBLISHER
Timed: 15–35 minutes per test
Scoring: Hand key; examiner evaluated; may be computer scored

Cost: Complete (10 Level 1 booklets, 10 Level 2 booklets, keys, administration cards, 50 profile charts, 25 score sheets, 25 testing logs) $993.50
Publisher: Saville & Holdsworth Ltd.

ADVANCED TEST BATTERY: DIAGRAMMATIC REASONING (ATB:DT8)
Saville & Holdsworth Ltd. Staff

Adult

Purpose: Measures diagrammatical reasoning ability. Used for selection and placement for technical occupations and jobs involving systems design, flow charting, and engineering fault diagnosis.

Description: 40–item paper-pencil multiple-choice test requiring the candidate to discover logical rules governing sequences occurring in rows of three related symbols and diagrams and to choose a fourth related symbol from the selections in the answer booklet. The test is suitable for individuals from the CSE to GCE "A" level and above. Examiner required. Suitable for group use.
BRITISH PUBLISHER
Timed: 15 minutes
Scoring: Hand key; examiner evaluated; may be computer scored
Cost: 10 question booklets $36.00; 50 answer sheets $36.00; key $9.50; administration card $9.50
Publisher: Saville & Holdsworth Ltd.

ADVANCED TEST BATTERY: DIAGRAMMING (ATB:DA5)
Saville & Holdsworth Ltd. Staff

Adult

Purpose: Measures logical analysis by assessing the ability to follow complex instructions within a given command system in order to arrive at a solution. Used to select personnel for computer programming, data processing, engineering, chemical processing, and related industries.

Description: 50–item paper-pencil multiple-choice test measuring diagramming skills. Each item consists of a column of figures or symbols within boxes, each of which has a command attached. The actual instruction conveyed by each command (represented by coded symbols) is explained on a separate card. The task is to carry out the commands in order to arrive at a new column of figures. The commands involve inverting figures, omitting figures, exchanging figures, or changing the complete order of figures in a specified way. The initial items are simple, but the complexity steadily increases. The diagrams provide a nonverbal task similar to flow-charting. The test is suitable for individuals from the GCE "O" level upwards. Examiner required. Suitable for group use.
BRITISH PUBLISHER

Timed: 20 minutes

Scoring: Hand key; examiner evaluated; may be computer scored

Cost: 10 question booklets $77.00; 10 command cards $50.50; 50 answer sheets $63.00; key $12.50; administration card $12.50

Publisher: Saville & Holdsworth Ltd.

ADVANCED TEST BATTERY: NUMBER SERIES (ATB:NA2)
Saville & Holdsworth Ltd. Staff

Adult

Purpose: Measures the ability to reason with numbers at a high degree of difficulty. Used in selection and development of management staff and graduate recruitment.

Description: 30–item paper-pencil multiple-choice test in which each item consists of a number series with one missing number. The candidates must select from five possible answers the one that completes the series. The test emphasizes developing appropriate strategies and the recognition of relationships between numbers rather than long calculations. The test is suitable for individuals from the

GCE "A" level upwards. Examiner required. Suitable for group use.
BRITISH PUBLISHER

Timed: 15 minutes

Scoring: Hand key; examiner evaluated; may be computer scored

Cost: 10 question booklets $53.50; 50 answer sheets $63.00; key $12.50; administration card $12.50

Publisher: Saville & Holdsworth Ltd.

ADVANCED TEST BATTERY: NUMERICAL CRITICAL REASONING (ATB:NA4)
Saville & Holdsworth Ltd. Staff

Adult

Purpose: Measures the ability to make correct inferences from numerical or statistical data. Used for selection and placement for jobs involving control systems, selection and development of management staff, and graduate recruitment.

Description: 40–item paper-pencil multiple-choice test consisting of a series of statistical tables and a number of inferences made from each of them. For each item, the candidates must select the correct inference from five possible answers. The data used in the tables sample production costs, exchange rates, and results from a market research survey. The test has a high degree of relevance to management decision making. The test is suitable for individuals from the GCE "A" level upwards. Examiner required. Suitable for group use.
BRITISH PUBLISHER

Timed: 35 minutes

Scoring: Hand key; examiner evaluated; may be computer scored

Cost: 10 question booklets $77.00; 10 data cards $50.50; 50 answer sheets $63.00; key $12.50; administration card $12.50

Publisher: Saville & Holdsworth Ltd.

ADVANCED TEST BATTERY: SPATIAL REASONING (ATB:ST7)
Saville & Holdsworth Ltd. Staff

Adult

Purpose: Measures ability to visualize and manipulate shapes in three dimensions given a two-dimensional drawing. Used in selection and development of advanced personnel, such as engineers, designers, architects, and draftsmen.

Description: 40–item paper-pencil multiple-choice test consisting of a series of folded-out cubes and perspective drawings of assembled cubes. Subjects must identify the assembled cubes that could be made from the folded-out cube, each face of which has a different pattern. The test is suitable for individuals from the GCE "O" level to degree. Examiner required. Suitable for group use. BRITISH PUBLISHER

Timed: 20 minutes

Scoring: Hand key; examiner evaluated; may be computer scored

Cost: 10 question booklets $36.00; 50 answer sheets $36.00; key $9.50; administration card $9.50

Publisher: Saville & Holdsworth Ltd.

ADVANCED TEST BATTERY: VERBAL CONCEPTS (ATB:VA1)
Saville & Holdsworth Ltd. Staff

Adult

Purpose: Measures general verbal skills at an advanced level. Used in selection and development of management, senior specialist staff, and graduate entrants.

Description: 40–item paper-pencil multiple-choice test measuring knowledge of the meanings of words and the relationships between them. Candidates are required to identify the relationship between a pair of words and select, from five possible words, the one that relates in the same way to a third given word. The vocabulary used is general and non-specialist, but the range of relationships is very diverse. The test is suitable for individuals from the GCE "A" level upwards. Examiner required. Suitable for group use.
BRITISH PUBLISHER

Timed: 15 minutes

Scoring: Hand key; examiner evaluated; may be computer scored

Cost: 10 question booklets $53.50; 50 answer sheets $63.00; key $12.50; administration card $12.50

Publisher: Saville & Holdsworth Ltd.

ADVANCED TEST BATTERY: VERBAL CRITICAL REASONING (ATB-VA3)
Saville & Holdsworth Ltd. Staff

Adult

Purpose: Measures the ability to evaluate the logic of various kinds of arguments. Used for management selection and graduate recruitment.

Description: 60–item paper-pencil multiple-choice test consisting of argumentative passages and a number of statements that might be made in connection with each of them. The statements must be evaluated in terms of whether they, their opposite, or neither, logically follow from the passage in question. The passages sample a wide range of material from politics to medicine, all of which could be on the agenda of a management meeting. The test has a high degree of relevance to the assessment of managerial skills. The test is suitable for individuals from the GCE "A" level upwards. Examiner required. Suitable for group use.
BRITISH PUBLISHER

Timed: 30 minutes

Scoring: Hand key; examiner evaluated; may be computer scored

Cost: 10 question booklets $77.00; 50 answer sheets $63.00; key $12.50; administration card $12.50

Publisher: Saville & Holdsworth Ltd.

APTICOM
Jeffrey A. Harris and Howard C. Dansky

Adult
High-school students

Purpose: Assesses aptitudes, interests, and work-related math and language skills. Used for vocational guidance and counseling.

Description: Series of three multiple-item instruments. The aptitude battery measures general learning ability, verbal

---

aptitude, numerical aptitude, spatial aptitude, form perception, clerical perception, motor coordination, finger dexterity, manual dexterity, and eye-hand-foot coordination. The Interest Inventory assesses preference for U.S. Department of Labor interest areas. The Educational Skills Development Battery assesses math and language achievement levels defined by the U.S. Department of Labor as General Educational Development. Tests are presented via panels mounted on APTICOM, a portable computerized desk-top console. APTICOM times and scores tests and generates score and recommendation reports when interfaced with a printer.

The aptitude battery has separate norm bases for three levels: adult/Grades 11–12, Grade 10, Grade 9. The Interest Inventory has vocational (adult) and prevocational (roughly 17 years and younger) norm bases. Examiner required. Suitable for use with groups of four using optional master control. Available in Spanish.

Timed: Aptitude 29 minutes; Educational Skills Development Battery 25 minutes

Untimed: Interest Inventory 10 minutes

Scoring: Computer scored

Cost: Contact publisher

Publisher: Vocational Research Institute—J.E.V.S.

APTITUDE BASED CAREER DECISION TEST (ABCD)

Adolescent, adult

Purpose: Assesses aptitudes to assist individuals in discovering the occupation for which they are best suited. Used in career exploration to match individuals to Occupational Families, work groups, and jobs at the semiskilled, skilled, technical and professional levels.

Description: 432–item paper-pencil battery of seven tests: Clerical Perception, Vocabulary, Numerical Computation, Numerical Reasoning, Spatial Visualization, Inductive Reasoning, and Analytical Reasoning. Responses are recorded in the test booklet or on cards for computer scoring. The scoring program generates an

aptitude profile for the individual and matches the profile to the requirements of the GOE Occupational Families, which include over 20,000 jobs. A one-page report identifies potential for success in all 66 GOE Occupational Families and selects the six strongest Occupational Family matches. It also provides a description of activities, typical education, occupation, occupational outlook, *Dictionary of Occupational Titles* (DOT) code, and a total of up to 36 typical job titles for those matches. Materials include a user's manual, administrator's manual, counselor's manual, technical manual, and on-site scoring manual. The ABCD is correlated to the GATB, the DAT, and the CAB and is integrated into an Employability Development Plan. A companion Interest test, the IBCD, provides recommendations in the identical 66 GOE clusters. Examiner required. Suitable for group use.

Timed: Complete battery 1½ hours

Scoring: Computer scored on-site or by publisher

Cost: Contact publisher

Publisher: Prep, A Division of Educational Technologies Inc.

APTITUDE INTEREST MEASUREMENT (AIM)
National Computer Systems (NCS) and the United States Employment Service (USES)

Adolescent, adult—Ages 16 and older Grades 9–12 and above

Purpose: Assesses aptitudes and interest levels relating to occupational success/career choice for vocational and career counseling and job placement of displaced workers.

Description: Series of multiple-item subtests that include the General Aptitude Test Battery (GATB) and the United States Employment Service (USES) Interest Inventory. The GATB is divided into 12 timed sections. Parts 1–7 consist of 434 multiple-choice questions. Parts 8–12 require special apparatus for testing motor coordination, finger dexterity, and manual dexterity. The USES Interest

Inventory consists of 162 statements to which examinees respond "like," "dislike," or "not sure."

The GATB yields 12 raw scores that convert to 9 aptitude scores: General Learning Ability, Verbal Aptitude, Numerical Aptitude, Spatial Aptitude, Form Perception, Clerical Perception, Motor Coordination, Finger Dexterity, and Manual Dexterity. The USES Interest Inventory yields standard scores for 12 interest areas: artistic, scientific, plants and animals, protective, mechanical, industrial, business detail, selling, accommodating, humanitarian, leading/influencing, and physical performing. Reports generated include the Aptitude Interest Measurement Narrative Report and the Aptitude Interest Measurement Counselor's Report. Forms B, C, and D are available, and male and female percentile scores for the Interest Inventory portion of the test are provided. Materials include an administration manual, test booklets, answer sheets, pencils, peg boards, and finger dexterity boards. A sixth-grade reading level is required. The examiner must be certified by a State Employment Service office. Users must obtain a GATB Release Agreement from the State Employment Service Office. Examiner required. Suitable for group use.

Timed: Varies

Scoring: Machine scored; hand key; scoring service available from publisher

Cost: $4.30 per individual

Publisher: National Computer Systems/PAS Division

ARITHMETIC FUNDAMENTALS, FORMS I AND II
Richardson, Bellows, Henry and Company, Inc.

Adult

Purpose: Assesses the ability to perform arithmetic calculations quickly and accurately. Used with applicants to hourly and clerical positions.

Description: 42–item paper-pencil test of arithmetic skills. Items are arranged in order of difficulty, progressing from simple addition through subtraction,

multiplication, and division of whole numbers to handling fractions and decimals. Individuals are provided with printed symbols and verbal instructions indicating which operation to perform on each problem. The test is available in two forms, I and II. The booklet contains space for figuring problems, and answers are recorded in the margins. Norms are available for male clerical and sales applicants, mechanical and operating applicants, and mechanical and operating employees. Norms also are available for female applicants for nurses' training, student nurses, and clerical applicants. Examiner required. Suitable for group use.

Timed: 20 minutes

Scoring: Hand key

Cost: 1–24 packages $25.00; score key $4.00; manual $2.00

Publisher: Richardson, Bellows, Henry and Company, Inc.

ARITHMETIC REASONING TEST (ART), HIGH LEVEL AND INTERMEDIATE LEVEL
National Institute for Personnel Research

Adult

Purpose: Measures arithmetic reasoning ability. Used to select applicants to positions requiring "hard" science, engineering, and quantitative technical activities.

Description: 24–item (high level) or 30–item (intermediate level) paper-pencil or computer-administered multiple-choice test. Each item consists of a numerical expression with selected digits and operators replaced by symbols. The examinee must determine the value of the missing digits. Using algebraic operations to solve the problems is difficult; applying reasoning strategies requires less effort. The computer version operates on Plato System. Purchasers of the test must be registered with the South African Medical and Dental Council. Examiner required. Suitable for group use. Available in Afrikaans.

SOUTH AFRICAN PUBLSIHER

Timed: Intermediate level 35 minutes; High level 39 minutes

Scoring: Hand key

Cost: Contact publisher

Publisher: National Institute for Personnel Research

ASE OCCUPATIONAL TEST SERIES: BASIC SKILLS TESTS
National Foundation for Educational Research

Adult

Purpose: Measures proficiency in basic numeracy and literacy. Used for selecting candidates to a wide range of occupations.

Description: Two multiple-item paper-pencil tests assessing numerical and literacy skills. Numeracy tests the ability to perform basic calculations, estimate rough answers to questions, and apply knowledge to common problems involving invoices, dimensions, timetables, and so forth. The Literacy test is presented in the form of a community newspaper. The first part of the test, which can be used alone for quick assessment, is designed to measure the ability to read and understand everyday English and requires short written answers to questions. The second part requires longer written answers, demonstrating written communication skills. Examiner required. Suitable for group use.

Timed: 30 minutes per test

Scoring: Hand key

Cost: Contact publisher

Publisher: NFER-NELSON Publishing Company Ltd.

ASE OCCUPATIONAL TEST SERIES: CRITICAL REASONING TESTS
National Foundation for Educational Research

Adult

Purpose: Assesses verbal and numerical skills and abilities of higher level personnel whose education is below graduate level. Used for selection and career development.

Description: Two multiple-item paper-pencil tests assessing verbal and numerical skills necessary for occupational success. Examiner required. Suitable for group use.

Timed: 30 minutes per test

Scoring: Hand key

Cost: Contact publisher

Publisher: NFER-NELSON Publishing Company Ltd.

ASE OCCUPATIONAL TEST SERIES: GENERAL ABILITY TESTS
National Foundation for Educational Research

Adult

Purpose: Assesses the general abilities of inexperienced individuals seeking first-time employment, of individuals being considered for supervisory or junior management positions, and of candidates applying for jobs in new fields.

Description: Four multiple-item paper-pencil tests evaluating numerical, verbal, nonverbal, and spatial ability. The Numerical test is used to assess candidates to jobs requiring numerical reasoning ability. Using analogies, the Verbal test requires candidates to determine the relationship between pairs of words. The Non-Verbal test utilizes symbols, rather than words or numbers, to assess a candidate's ability to process information, recognize relationships, and differentiate between relevant and irrelevant information. The Spatial Ability test requires candidates to imagine what a flat pattern would look like if it were cut out and folded to form a 3–D object. This test, which is particularly useful for evaluating candidates for jobs in construction, engineering, technical drawing, and architecture, can be used alone or in conjunction with the other three general ability tests. Materials include user's information, the user's guide, test booklets, administration cards, scoring keys, a data collection sheet, a test record sheet, and a test taker's guide. Examiner required. Suitable for group use.

Timed: 15–20 minutes per test

Scoring: Hand key

Cost: Contact publisher
Publisher: NFER-NELSON Publishing Company Ltd.

BALL APTITUDE BATTERY™
Yong H. Sung and Rene V. Davis

Adolescent, adult
High school juniors-adult

Purpose: Measures aptitude for a wide variety of occupations. Used for individual career planning, employee selection, classification, and placement.

Description: Standardized battery of 16 paper-pencil and task-performance aptitude measures. The battery consists of the following tests: Clerical (240 items; 5 minutes), in which the individual identifies as quickly as possible all pairs of identical numbers from two columns of numbers; Idea Fluency (4 items; 8 minutes), in which the individual generates as many alternative uses as possible for a given object; Inductive Reasoning (30 items; 8 minutes), in which the individual identifies three pictures (in each series of six pictures) that have a common theme; Word Association (100 items; 8 minutes), in which the individual writes a word associated with the given stimulus word; Writing Speed (15 lines; 1 minute), in which the individual writes the given sentence as many times as possible during the allotted time; Paper Folding (spatial reasoning; 24 items; 10 minutes), in which the individual identifies, from among five choices, the result when holes are punched through a folded sheet of paper; Vocabulary (80 items; 22 minutes), in which the individual selects from five alternatives the word most similar in meaning to the test word; Ideaphoria (1 item; 10 minutes), in which the individual generates and writes as many ideas as possible in response to a novel situation; Numerical Computation (40 items; 13 minutes), in which the individual performs simple arithmetic computations as quickly as possible; Numerical Reasoning (40 items; 20 minutes), in which the individual identifies the pattern in a series of numbers and gives the next number in the series; Finger Dexterity (2 trials each hand; 6 minutes), in which the individual places three small pins into holes on a board as rapidly as possible; Grip Test (3 trials each hand; 6 minutes), in which the individual squeezes a dynamometer as hard as possible; Analytical Reasoning (18 items; 5–13 minutes), in which the individual arranges words (printed on chips) on a diagram board to reflect conceptual relationships; Shape Assembly (6 items; 15–35 minutes), in which the individual assembles a disassembled wooden geometric solid; Auditory Memory Span (28 items; 12½ minutes), in which the individual recalls and writes strings of numbers presented via audiotape; and Associative Memory (13 pairs; 3½ minutes), in which the individual, after studying a list of number-letter pairs, recalls the letter associated with each number.

The administration time for each test was chosen at the point at which 95% of the individuals taking the test were able to complete all the items. The order of administration of the tests is designed to minimize test anxiety and maximize test motivation. A short break should be taken after the first hour of testing. Reliability, validity, and normative data are provided in the manuals. Examiner required. All tests except Grip, Analytical Reasoning, and Shape Assembly are suitable for group use. For operational reasons, the individual tests are administered after the group tests.

Timed: 3–3½ hours

Scoring: Scoring and computer analysis available only through the publisher

Cost: Starter kit (first 10 sets of paper-pencil tests, cassette tape for Word Association and Memory Span, technical manual) $150.00; 10 paper-pencil tests $100.00; scoring, profiling, and computer interpretation $20.00 per client; contact publisher for the cost of apparatus tests and purchase of subtests

Publisher: The Ball Foundation

Information and availability unconfirmed; last verified in 1988.

BANK TELLER JOB TRIAL (BTJT)
Vocational Research Institute

Adult

Purpose: Assesses skills required for the position of bank teller. Used for screening and hiring of applicants.

Description: Paper-pencil multiple-choice criterion-referenced short-answer test consisting of three subtests: Math Estimation—quick computation and estimation; Transactions—clerical perception, precision, and speed; and Counting Money. Yields raw and weighted subtest scores, percentiles, and a job trial scope-summary score. This test is suitable for individuals with hearing and physical impairments. Individuals with hearing impairments require an interpreter. Materials include booklet of items, answer sheet, scoring sheet, and manual. Examiner required. Suitable for group use.

Timed: 36 minutes

Scoring: Hand key

Cost: Contact publisher

Publisher: Vocational Research Institute—J.E.V.S.

BASE—BASIC SKILLS FOR EMPLOYMENT

Adolescent, adult

Purpose: Assesses the basic academic skills of individuals in order to provide remediation for individuals who lack basic employment skills. Designed to raise the individual's basic skills level to the levels required by their chosen jobs.

Description: Computerized basic skills remediation system anchored to employment and training. As a criterion-referenced system (referenced according to the basic skills necessary to support any one of 12,000 jobs), BASE tests the academic skills taught between Grades 3–9. BASE contains 42 quizzes, 41 tests, 250 validated competencies, 250 skill lessons in 15 content areas, and customized pre- and postassessment.

Using a password to enter the program, the individual enters a selected job title into the program, which then assigns a customized series of pretests to determine the individual's basic skill level in reading, language arts, writing, and mathematics as compared to the level required by the chosen job. BASE then prescribes tutorial lessons based on results of the pretests. Lesson mastery is checked by quizzes and postdiagnosis.

The teacher selects the test/lesson sequence, the method for using the program (student mode or computer mode), mastery level (1% to 100%), and report options. The student can start and stop at any time, receive feedback and reinforcement on demand, select review options for all tests and quizzes, and access hints for lessons and quizzes.

Seven reports are generated: Diagnostic Report, Topic Summary Report, Individualized Education Plan Report, Progress Report, Learning Style Report, Class Report, and Administrator Report.

The software is available for IBM PC and compatibles and Apples. BASE is linked to Exploration software, which is used when the individual has not selected a training program or job. Exploration contains all the data in the GOE BASE and is integrated into an Employability Development Plan, which includes assessment testing (ABCD and IBCD). Self-administered. May be networked for group administration.

Untimed: Varies

Scoring: Computer scored by BASE program

Cost: Contact publisher

Publisher: Prep, A Division of Educational Technologies Inc.

BASIC BANK SKILLS BATTERY (BBSB)
London House, Inc.

Adult—Ages 16 and older

Purpose: Measures potential for successful performance as a bank teller and customer service representative. Used for employee selection and promotion.

Description: 317–item paper-pencil multiple-choice battery measuring potential in several key areas related to an applicant's ability to perform as a teller or customer service representative. Scores are provided for 13 scales: Drive (30 minutes), School Achievement (30 minutes), Arithmetic Computation (5 minutes), Interpersonal Relations (30 minutes), Cognitive Skills (30 minutes), Error Recognition (3 minutes), Motor Ability (30 minutes), Math Ability (30 minutes), Name Comparison (3 minutes), Self-Discipline (30 minutes), Leadership (30 minutes), Number Comparison (3 minutes), and Perceptual Skills (30 minutes). The battery yields a single score, the Potential Estimate, for both the bank teller and customer service positions. Form A combines the timed and untimed tests. A Short Form is comprised of the timed tests only. Minimum order of 25 tests. Examiner required. Suitable for group use.

Timed: 3–5 minutes depending on test
Untimed: 30 minutes depending on test
Scoring: Computer scored
Cost: Contact publisher
Publisher: London House, Inc.

BASIC OCCUPATIONAL LITERACY TEST (BOLT)
U.S. Employment Service

Adult

Purpose: Measures basic reading and arithmetic skills of educationally disadvantaged adults. Used for occupational training and counseling.

Description: Multiple-item paper-pencil test consisting of four reading and arithmetic subtests. The reading section assesses vocabulary and comprehension at four levels of difficulty: advanced, high intermediate, basic intermediate, and fundamental. The arithmetic section assesses computation and reasoning at advanced, intermediate, and fundamental levels. The examiner determines the appropriate testing level for each individual using the BOLT Wide Range Scale and the individual's reported years of education. Three alternate forms, A, B, and C, are available for each subtest at each level of difficulty except the advanced level. Two alternate forms, A and B, are available for the advanced level. Raw scores can be converted to standard scores and General Educational Development (GED) levels. Materials include the test booklet and manuals. Examiner required. Suitable for group use.
Timed: Each reading test 15 minutes; each arithmetic test 30 minutes

Scoring: Hand key
Cost: Available only through State Employment Service Agencies
Publisher: U.S. Department of Labor
Information and availability unconfirmed; last verified in 1988.

BASIC OCCUPATIONAL LITERACY TEST (BOLT): WIDE RANGE SCALE
U.S. Employment Service

Adult

Purpose: Measures individual's reading and arithmetic abilities. Used as a pretest to determine whether the individual should be given the General Aptitude Test Battery or the Non-Reading Aptitude Test Battery as a preliminary to taking the Basic Occupational Literacy Test. Used for employment counseling.

Description: 16–item paper-pencil examination consisting of a reading subtest and an arithmetic subtest (8 items each). Examiner required. Suitable for group use.
Untimed: 15 minutes
Scoring: Hand key
Cost: Available through State Employment Service Agencies only
Publisher: U.S. Department of Labor
Information and availability unconfirmed; last verified in 1988.

BRUCE VOCABULARY INVENTORY
Refer to page 971.

BUFFALO READING TEST
Mazie Earle Wagner

Adolescent, adult

Purpose: Measures the reading abilities of high-school and college students and adults. Used for personnel selection and for identifying persons who need remedial training.

Description: Multiple-item paper-pencil test measuring reading speed and reading comprehension. The test is used to select employees who read rapidly and with understanding and to identify persons who need remedial training. The test yields a total score. Examiner required. Suitable for group use.

Timed: 30 minutes

Scoring: Examiner evaluated

Cost: 25 tests $16.00; specimen set (25 tests, manual) $31.00

Publisher: Herman J.P. Schubert

CHEMICAL COMPREHENSION, FORMS S AND T
Richardson, Bellows, Henry and Company, Inc.

Adult

Purpose: Assesses understanding of concepts related to chemistry. Used with applicants to operation, craft, and lab technician positions.

Description: 50–item paper-pencil multiple-choice test measuring general knowledge of chemistry. Content could be learned in school, but persons without formal training in chemistry can achieve high scores. Answers are marked in the test booklet. The test is helpful to applicants choosing between process or mechanical positions in industry. Norms are available for male process and laboratory applicants, process workers, and mechanical workers. Norms also are available for female student nurses and nurses' training applicants. The test is available in two forms, S and T. Examiner required. Suitable for group use.

Timed: 30 minutes

Scoring: Hand key

Cost: 1–24 packages $25.00; score key $7.50; manual $6.00

Publisher: Richardson, Bellows, Henry and Company, Inc.

CLASSIFICATION TEST BATTERY (CTB)

Adult

Purpose: Evaluates general thinking and adaptability skills of illiterate and semi-literate applicants for unskilled and semiskilled jobs.

Description: Four apparatus tests measuring nonverbal reasoning and spatial ability. The battery contains the Pattern Reproduction Test, Circles Test, Forms Series Test (Mines Version), and Colored Peg Board. The battery was devised as a unit and can be used only as described in the manual. Pretest instructions are available in any of nine African languages and English. The test itself is administered by a silent film. The test is administered at centers established by firms employing the publisher's consultation and training services; use is restricted to competent persons properly registered with the South African Medical and Dental Council. Examiner required. Suitable for group use.

SOUTH AFRICAN PUBLISHER

Timed: Not available

Scoring: Examiner evaluated

Cost: Contact publisher

Publisher: National Institute for Personnel Research

CLIENT REACTION INVENTORY
David Lang

Adult

Purpose: Evaluates the satisfaction of vocational guidance clients with the services provided by their vocational guidance officers.

Description: 59–item paper-pencil inventory measuring on a 5–point scale the extent to which vocational guidance officers provide successful and satisfactory guidance. The instrument contains 18 subscales that provide verbal ratings, effective percentages, and standard scores. Examiner required. Suitable for group use.

AUSTRALIAN PUBLISHER

Untimed: Not available

Scoring: Hand key

Cost: Contact publisher

Publisher: NSW Department of Industrial Relations

Information and availability unconfirmed; last verified in 1988.

**COLLEGE LEVEL EXAMINATION
PROGRAM (CLEP)**
Refer to page 435.

**COLLEGE LEVEL EXAMINATION
PROGRAM (CLEP) GENERAL
EXAMINATION: ENGLISH
COMPOSITION**
Refer to page 435.

**COLLEGE LEVEL EXAMINATION
PROGRAM (CLEP) GENERAL
EXAMINATION: HUMANITIES**
Refer to page 436.

**COLLEGE LEVEL EXAMINATION
PROGRAM (CLEP) GENERAL
EXAMINATION: MATHEMATICS**
Refer to page 436.

**COLLEGE LEVEL EXAMINATION
PROGRAM (CLEP) GENERAL
EXAMINATION: NATURAL
SCIENCE**
Refer to page 436.

**COLLEGE LEVEL EXAMINATION
PROGRAM (CLEP) GENERAL
EXAMINATION: SOCIAL SCIENCE
AND HISTORY**
Refer to page 437.

**COLLEGE LEVEL EXAMINATION
PROGRAM (CLEP) SUBJECT
EXAMINATION: BUSINESS:
COMPUTERS AND DATA
PROCESSING**
Refer to page 437.

**COLLEGE LEVEL EXAMINATION
PROGRAM (CLEP) SUBJECT
EXAMINATION: BUSINESS:
INTRODUCTION TO
MANAGEMENT**
Refer to page 437.

**COLLEGE LEVEL EXAMINATION
PROGRAM (CLEP) SUBJECT
EXAMINATION: BUSINESS:
INTRODUCTORY ACCOUNTING**
Refer to page 438.

**COLLEGE LEVEL EXAMINATION
PROGRAM (CLEP) SUBJECT
EXAMINATION: BUSINESS:
INTRODUCTORY BUSINESS LAW**
Refer to page 438.

**COLLEGE LEVEL EXAMINATION
PROGRAM (CLEP) SUBJECT
EXAMINATION: BUSINESS:
INTRODUCTORY MARKETING**
Refer to page 438.

**COLLEGE LEVEL EXAMINATION
PROGRAM (CLEP) SUBJECT
EXAMINATION: COMPOSITION
AND LITERATURE: AMERICAN
LITERATURE**
Refer to page 439.

**COLLEGE LEVEL EXAMINATION
PROGRAM (CLEP) SUBJECT
EXAMINATION: COMPOSITION
AND LITERATURE: ANALYSIS
AND INTERPRETATION OF
LITERATURE**
Refer to page 439.

**COLLEGE LEVEL EXAMINATION
PROGRAM (CLEP) SUBJECT
EXAMINATION: COMPOSITION
AND LITERATURE: COLLEGE
COMPOSITION**
Refer to page 440.

**COLLEGE LEVEL EXAMINATION
PROGRAM (CLEP) SUBJECT
EXAMINATION: COMPOSITION
AND LITERATURE: ENGLISH
LITERATURE**
Refer to page 440.

COLLEGE LEVEL EXAMINATION PROGRAM (CLEP) SUBJECT EXAMINATION: COMPOSITION AND LITERATURE: FRESHMAN ENGLISH

Refer to page 440.

COLLEGE LEVEL EXAMINATION PROGRAM (CLEP) SUBJECT EXAMINATION: FOREIGN LANGUAGES: COLLEGE FRENCH LEVELS 1 AND 2

Refer to page 441.

COLLEGE LEVEL EXAMINATION PROGRAM (CLEP) SUBJECT EXAMINATION: FOREIGN LANGUAGES: COLLEGE GERMAN LEVELS 1 AND 2

Refer to page 441.

COLLEGE LEVEL EXAMINATION PROGRAM (CLEP) SUBJECT EXAMINATION: FOREIGN LANGUAGES: COLLEGE SPANISH LEVELS 1 AND 2

Refer to page 441.

COLLEGE LEVEL EXAMINATION PROGRAM (CLEP) SUBJECT EXAMINATION: HISTORY AND SOCIAL SCIENCES: AMERICAN GOVERNMENT

Refer to page 442.

COLLEGE LEVEL EXAMINATION PROGRAM (CLEP) SUBJECT EXAMINATION: HISTORY AND SOCIAL SCIENCES: AMERICAN HISTORY I: EARLY COLONIZATIONS TO 1877

Refer to page 442.

COLLEGE LEVEL EXAMINATION PROGRAM (CLEP) SUBJECT EXAMINATION: HISTORY AND SOCIAL SCIENCES: AMERICAN HISTORY II: 1865 TO THE PRESENT

Refer to page 442.

COLLEGE LEVEL EXAMINATION PROGRAM (CLEP) SUBJECT EXAMINATION: HISTORY AND SOCIAL SCIENCES: EDUCATIONAL PSYCHOLOGY

Refer to page 443.

COLLEGE LEVEL EXAMINATION PROGRAM (CLEP) SUBJECT EXAMINATION: HISTORY AND SOCIAL SCIENCES: GENERAL PSYCHOLOGY

Refer to page 443.

COLLEGE LEVEL EXAMINATION PROGRAM (CLEP) SUBJECT EXAMINATION: HISTORY AND SOCIAL SCIENCES: HUMAN GROWTH AND DEVELOPMENT

Refer to page 443.

COLLEGE LEVEL EXAMINATION PROGRAM (CLEP) SUBJECT EXAMINATION: HISTORY AND SOCIAL SCIENCES: INTRODUCTORY MACROECONOMICS

Refer to page 443.

COLLEGE LEVEL EXAMINATION PROGRAM (CLEP) SUBJECT EXAMINATION: HISTORY AND SOCIAL SCIENCES: INTRODUCTORY MICROECONOMICS

Refer to page 444.

COLLEGE LEVEL EXAMINATION PROGRAM (CLEP) SUBJECT EXAMINATION: HISTORY AND SOCIAL SCIENCES: WESTERN CIVILIZATION I: ANCIENT NEAR EAST TO 1648

Refer to page 445.

COLLEGE LEVEL EXAMINATION PROGRAM (CLEP) SUBJECT EXAMINATION: HISTORY AND SOCIAL SCIENCES: WESTERN CIVILIZATION II: 1648 TO THE PRESENT

Refer to page 445.

COLLEGE LEVEL EXAMINATION PROGRAM (CLEP) SUBJECT EXAMINATION: SCIENCE/ MATHEMATICS: CALCULUS WITH ELEMENTARY FUNCTIONS

Refer to page 445.

COLLEGE LEVEL EXAMINATION PROGRAM (CLEP) SUBJECT EXAMINATION: SCIENCE/ MATHEMATICS: COLLEGE ALGEBRA

Refer to page 446.

COLLEGE LEVEL EXAMINATION PROGRAM (CLEP) SUBJECT EXAMINATION: SCIENCE/ MATHEMATICS: COLLEGE ALGEBRA/TRIGONOMETRY

Refer to page 446.

COLLEGE LEVEL EXAMINATION PROGRAM (CLEP) SUBJECT EXAMINATION: SCIENCE/ MATHEMATICS: GENERAL BIOLOGY

Refer to page 446.

COLLEGE LEVEL EXAMINATION PROGRAM (CLEP) SUBJECT EXAMINATION: SCIENCE/ MATHEMATICS: GENERAL CHEMISTRY

Refer to page 447.

COLLEGE LEVEL EXAMINATION PROGRAM (CLEP) SUBJECT EXAMINATION: SCIENCE/ MATHEMATICS: TRIGONOMETRY

Refer to page 447.

COMPREHENSIVE ABILITY BATTERY (CAB)
A. Ralph Hakstian and
Raymond B. Cattell

Adolescent, adult
Grades 10 and above

Purpose: Measures a variety of abilities important in industrial settings for individuals high-school age and older. Used in career and vocational counseling and employee selection and placement.

Description: 20 paper-pencil subtests each measuring a single primary ability factor related to performance in industrial settings. The tests in the battery may be used individually or in combination. The subtests are grouped and presented in four test booklets (CAB–1, 2, 3/4, and 5). CAB–1 contains Verbal Ability, Numerical Ability, Spatial Ability, and Perceptual Completion. CAB–2 contains Clerical Speed and Accuracy, Reasoning, Hidden Shapes, Rote Memory, and Mechanical Ability. CAB–3/4 contains Meaningful Memory, Memory Span, Spelling, Auditory Ability, and Esthetic Judgment. CAB–5 contains Organizing Ideas, Production of Ideas, Verbal Fluency, Originality, Tracking, and Drawing. Percentile norms are provided for males, females, and combined for each test at the high-school level. Additional norms for college students, convicts, and general population adults are provided for selected tests. Examiner required. Suitable for group use.

Timed: 5–7 minutes per subtest

Scoring: Hand key

Cost: Specimen set (4 test booklets, answer and profile sheets for all tests, manual) $27.95; 10 CAB–1, CAB–2, CAB–3/4, or CAB–5 test booklets $16.50; 50 answer sheets $8.95

Publisher: Institute for Personality and Ability Testing, Inc.

CREATIVITY CHECKLIST (CCH)
Refer to page 622.

=====

CRITICAL REASONING TEST BATTERY (CRTB)
Saville & Holdsworth Ltd. Staff

Adult

Purpose: Measures skills of evaluation and reasoning among individuals of average and above average ability (GCE "O" level and above). Used in the selection and development of "A" level entrants and supervisory and junior management personnel. Also used for guidance and placement of students sixth form and above.

Description: Three paper-pencil multiple-choice tests measuring the following skills: verbal evaluation, interpreting data, and diagrammatic reasoning. The Verbal Evaluation Test (VC1) is a 60–item test measuring the ability to understand and evaluate the logic of various types of arguments. The Interpreting Data Test (NC2) is a 40–item test measuring the ability to make correct decisions or inferences from numerical or statistical data, presented as tables or diagrams. The Diagrammatic Series Test (DC3) is a 40–item test measuring the ability to reason with diagrams and requires the candidate to discover logical rules governing sequences of symbols and diagrams. Together, these tests provide information on important abilities related to junior management. Examiner required. Suitable for group use.
BRITISH PUBLISHER

Timed: 20–30 minutes per test

Scoring: Hand key; examiner evaluated; may be computer scored

Cost: Complete (question booklets, answer sheets, key, data cards, profile charts, test logs) $504.00

Publisher: Saville & Holdsworth Ltd.

DRUG STORE APPLICANT INVENTORY (DSAI)
London House, Inc.

Adult

Purpose: Assesses potential for successful employment. Used in selection and screening of drug store cashier/clerk applicants.

Description: 144–item paper-pencil multiple-choice test with eight diagnostic scales yielding scores in Background and Work Experience, Applied Arithmetic, Customer Service, Job Stability, Honesty, Interpersonal Cooperation, Drug Avoidance, and Risk Avoidance. Two validity scales, Distortion and Accuracy, are also included. A composite, the Employability Index, based on the eight diagnostic scales is provided for decision-making purposes. In addition to scores, the DSAI generates behavioral indicators and training needs based on examinee responses to individual items.

Three scoring options are available from London House: operator-assisted telephone, Touch-Test, and PC-based. Operator-assisted scoring involves dialing a London House operator who provides test results after being read a tally of responses by the test administrator. Written confirmation is mailed the following day. Touch-Test telephone scoring allows the test administrator to use the telephone keypad to feed response tallies directly into London House computers. Results are available immediately and written confirmation is mailed the next day. Administrators with IBM PC or compatible equipment may obtain on-site results using the PC-based scoring method. The examiner must be trained to administer the DSAI. Exmainer required. Suitable for group use.

Untimed: 45 minutes

Scoring: Computer scored; scoring service available from publisher

Cost: $18.00; minimum order 25; volume discount
Publisher: London House, Inc.

DVORINE COLOR VISION TEST
Refer to page 725.

ELECTRICAL AND ELECTRONICS TEST
J.D. Morgan

Adolescent, adult—Ages 15 and older

Purpose: Assesses knowledge and ability in electrical and electronics fields.

Description: 30–item paper-pencil test for determining knowledge of fundamental laws, symbols, and definitions related to electricity and electronics. The test emphasizes the ability to use knowledge in practical situations. Examiner required. Suitable for group use. BRITISH PUBLISHER
Timed: 15 minutes
Scoring: Hand key
Cost: Specimen set (test booklet, answer key, manual) $21.00
Publisher: The Test Agency Ltd.

EMPLOYEE APTITUDE SURVEY TEST #1-VERBAL COMPREHENSION (EAS #1)
G. Grimsley, F.L. Ruch, N.D. Warren, and J.S. Ford

Adult

Purpose: Measures ability to use and understand the relationships between words. Used for selection and placement of executives, secretaries, professional personnel, and high-level office workers. Also used in career counseling.

Description: 30–item paper-pencil multiple-choice test measuring word-relationship recognition, reading speed, and ability to understand instructions. Each item consists of a word followed by a list of four other words from which the examinee must select the one meaning the same or about the same as the first word.

The test is available in two equivalent forms. Examiner required. Suitable for group use.
Timed: 5 minutes
Scoring: Hand key; may be computer scored
Cost: 25 tests $28.00; volume discount
Publisher: Psychological Services, Inc.

EMPLOYEE APTITUDE SURVEY TEST #2-NUMERICAL ABILITY (EAS #2)
G. Grimsley, F.L. Ruch, and N.D. Warren

Adult

Purpose: Measures basic mathematical skill. Used for selection and placement of executives, supervisors, engineers, accountants, sales, and clerical workers. Also used in career counseling.

Description: 75–item paper-pencil multiple-choice test arranged in three 25–item parts assessing addition, subtraction, multiplication, and division skills. Part I covers whole numbers, Part II decimal fractions, and Part III common fractions. The test is available in two equivalent forms. Examiner required. Suitable for group use. Available in Spanish and French.
Timed: 10 minutes
Scoring: Hand key; may be computer scored
Cost: 25 tests $34.00; volume discount
Publisher: Psychological Services, Inc.

EMPLOYEE APTITUDE SURVEY TEST #3-VISUAL PURSUIT (EAS #3)
G. Grimsley, F.L. Ruch, N.D. Warren, and J.S. Ford

Adult

Purpose: Measures speed and accuracy in visually tracing lines through complex designs. Used for selection and placement of drafters, design engineers, technicians, and related positions. Also used in career counseling.

Description: 30–item paper-pencil multiple-choice test consisting of a maze of lines that weave their way from their starting points (numbered 1 to 30) on the right-hand side of the page to a column of boxes on the left. The task is to identify for each starting point the box on the left at which the line ends. Examinees are encouraged to trace with their eyes, not their pencils. The test is available in two equivalent forms. Examiner required. Suitable for group use. Available in Spanish and French.

Timed: 5 minutes

Scoring: Hand key; may be computer scored

Cost: 25 tests $34.00; volume discount

Publisher: Psychological Services, Inc.

EMPLOYEE APTITUDE SURVEY TEST #4–VISUAL SPEED AND ACCURACY (EAS #4)
G. Grimsley, F.L. Ruch, and N.D. Warren

Adult

Purpose: Measures ability to see details quickly and accurately. Used to select bookkeepers, accountants, general office clerks, stenographers, office machine operators, and supervisors. Also used in career planning.

Description: 150–item paper-pencil multiple-choice test in which each item consists of two series of numbers and symbols that the subject must compare to determine whether they are "the same" or "different." The test may be administered to applicants for sales, supervisory, and executive positions with the expectation that their scores will be above average. The test is available in two equivalent forms. Examiner required. Suitable for group use. Available in Spanish.

Timed: 5 minutes

Scoring: Hand key; may be computer scored

Cost: 25 tests $34.00; volume discount

Publisher: Psychological Services, Inc.

EMPLOYEE APTITUDE SURVEY TEST #5–SPACE VISUALIZATION (EAS #5)
G. Grimsley, F.L. Ruch, N.D. Warren, and J.S. Ford

Adult

Purpose: Measures ability to visualize and manipulate objects in three dimensions by viewing a two-dimensional drawing. Used to select employees for jobs requiring mechanical aptitude, such as drafters, engineers, and personnel in technical positions. Also used in career counseling.

Description: 50–item paper-pencil multiple-choice test consisting of 10 perspective line drawings of stacks of blocks. The blocks are all the same size and rectangular in shape so that they appear to stack neatly and distinctly. Five of the blocks in each stack are lettered. The subjects must look at each lettered block and determine how many other blocks in the stack the lettered block touches. The test is available in two equivalent forms. Examiner required. Suitable for group use. Available in Spanish.

Timed: 5 minutes

Scoring: Hand key; may be computer scored

Cost: 25 tests $34.00; volume discount

Publisher: Psychological Services, Inc.

EMPLOYEE APTITUDE SURVEY TEST #6–NUMERICAL REASONING (EAS #6)
G. Grimsley, F.L. Ruch, N.D. Warren, and J.S. Ford

Adult

Purpose: Measures the ability to analyze logical relationships and discover principles underlying such relationships, an important ingredient of "general intelligence." Used to select for technical, supervisory, and executive positions. Predictive of on-the-job trainability. Also used in career counseling.

Description: 20–item paper-pencil multiple-choice test in which each item consists of a series of seven numbers followed by a question mark where the next number of the series should be. Examinees must determine the pattern of each series and select (from five choices) the number that correctly fills the blank. Logic and deduction, rather than computation, are emphasized. The test is available in two equivalent forms. Examiner required. Suitable for group use. Available in Spanish and French.

Timed: 5 minutes

Scoring: Hand key; may be computer scored

Cost: 25 tests $34.00; volume discount

Publisher: Psychological Services, Inc.

EMPLOYEE APTITUDE SURVEY TEST #7-VERBAL REASONING (EAS #7)
G. Grimsley, F.L. Ruch, N.D. Warren, and J.S. Ford

Adult

Purpose: Measures ability to analyze information and make valid judgments about that information. Also measures the ability to decide whether the available facts provide sufficient information to support a definite conclusion. Used to select employees for jobs requiring the ability to organize, evaluate, and utilize information, such as executive, administrative, supervisory, scientific, accounting, and technical maintenance personnel. Also used in career counseling.

Description: 30–item paper-pencil multiple-choice test consisting of six lists of facts (one-sentence statements) with five possible conclusions for each list. The subject reads each list, considers each conclusion, and decides whether it is definitely true, definitely false, or unknown from the given facts. The test is available in two equivalent forms. Examiner required. Suitable for group use. Available in Spanish and French.

Timed: 5 minutes

Scoring: Hand key; may be computer scored

Cost: 25 tests $34.00; volume discount

Publisher: Psychological Services, Inc.

EMPLOYEE APTITUDE SURVEY TEST #8-WORD FLUENCY (EAS #8)
G. Grimsley, F.L. Ruch, N.D. Warren, and J.S. Ford

Adult

Purpose: Measures flexibility and ease in verbal communication. Used to select sales representatives, journalists, field representatives, technical writers, receptionists, secretaries, and executives. Also used in career counseling.

Description: Open-ended paper-pencil test measuring word fluency by determining how many words beginning with one specific letter, given at the beginning of the test, a person can produce in a 5–minute test period (75 answer spaces are provided). Examiner required. Suitable for group use.

Timed: 5 minutes

Scoring: Hand key

Cost: 25 tests $34.00; volume discount

Publisher: Psychological Services, Inc.

EMPLOYEE APTITUDE SURVEY TEST #9-MANUAL SPEED AND ACCURACY (EAS #9)
G. Grimsley, F.L. Ruch, N.D. Warren, and J.S. Ford

Adult

Purpose: Measures ability to make fine-finger movements rapidly and accurately. Used to select clerical workers, office machine operators, electronics and small parts assemblers, and employees for similar precision jobs involving repetitive tasks. Also used in career counseling.

Description: Multiple-item paper-pencil test consisting of a straightforward array of evenly spaced lines of 750 small circles. The applicant must place a pencil dot in as many of the circles as possible in 5 minutes. Examiner required. Suitable for group use. Available in Spanish.

Timed: 5 minutes

Scoring: Hand key

Cost: 25 tests $34.00; volume discount

Publisher: Psychological Services, Inc.

EMPLOYEE APTITUDE SURVEY TEST #10–SYMBOLIC REASONING (EAS #10)
G. Grimsley, F.L. Ruch, N.D. Warren, and J.S. Ford

Adult

Purpose: Measures ability to manipulate abstract symbols and use them to make valid decisions. Used to evaluate candidates for positions requiring a high level of reasoning ability, such as troubleshooters, computer programmers, accountants, engineers, and scientific personnel. Used in career counseling.

Description: 30–item paper-pencil multiple-choice test consisting of a list of abstract symbols (and their coded meanings) used to establish relationships in the pattern of "A" to "B" to "C." Given the statement, the examinee must decide whether a proposed relationship between "A" and "C" is true, false, or unknown from the given statement. The test is available in two equivalent forms. Examiner required. Suitable for group use. Available in Spanish and French.

Timed: 5 minutes

Scoring: Hand key; may be computer scored

Cost: 25 tests $34.00; volume discount

Publisher: Psychological Services, Inc.

EMPLOYMENT BARRIER IDENTIFICATION SCALE (EBIS)
John M. McKee

**Adolescent, adult
Ages 15 and older**

Purpose: Measures an unemployed individual's ability to gain and retain employment. Identifies areas and skills in which the job seeker may need training and assesses employment training programs. Used with JTPA participants and rehabilitation clients as well as the general unemployed population.

Description: 19–item paper-pencil test evaluating an individual's employability. The topics covered include job skills, education, environmental support, and personal survival skills. The test may be presented as an oral interview for use with illiterate examinees. Examiner required. Suitable for group use (except when orally presented).

Untimed: 30 minutes

Scoring: Hand key

Cost: Complete kit (includes 25 scales and manual) $30.00

Publisher: Behavior Science Press

ENGLISH LANGUAGE ACHIEVEMENT TEST

**Adolescent, adult
Grades 12 and above**

Purpose: Measures achievement of basic English language skills. Suitable for use with matriculants and higher. Used in employee selection and placement.

Description: Multiple-item paper-pencil test assessing English language abilities in spelling, comprehension, and vocabulary. Norms are based on a group of matriculants. The test is restricted to competent persons properly registered with the South African Medical and Dental Council. Examiner required. Suitable for group use. Afrikaans version available. SOUTH AFRICAN PUBLISHER

Timed: 19 minutes

Scoring: Hand key; examiner evaluated

Cost: Contact publisher

Publisher: National Institute for Personnel Research

ESTIMATION TEST, HIGH LEVEL
National Institute for Personnel Research

Adult

Purpose: Assesses numerical ability. Used for selection for positions requiring quantitative abilities. Also used in vocational guidance.

Description: 26–item paper-pencil or computer-administered multiple-choice test. Each item consists of a complex numerical expression and five possible answers. The correct answer may be determined through rounding strategies. The computer version operates on Plato System. Purchasers of the test must be registered with the South African Medical and Dental Council. Examiner required. Suitable for group use. Available in Afrikaans.

SOUTH AFRICAN PUBLISHER

Timed: 26 minutes

Scoring: Hand key

Cost: Contact publisher

Publisher: National Institute for Personnel Research

ETSA TESTS
George A. W. Stouffer, Jr. and S. Trevor Hadley

Adolescent, adult
Grades 10 and above

Purpose: Measures general and specific job aptitudes. Used for employee selection, placement, promotion, and measurement of training progress.

Description: Eight paper-pencil aptitude tests measuring general mental ability, office arithmetic, general clerical ability, stenographic skills, mechanical familiarity, mechanical knowledge, sales aptitude, and personal adjustment. The General Mental Ability and Personal Adjustment indexes may be combined with one of the specific skills tests to give comprehensive information about an applicant. The test is available only to qualified test users, such as personnel managers, counselors, psychologists, and educators. Examiner required. Suitable for group use.

Timed: Varies

Scoring: Hand key; examiner evaluated

Cost: Complete sample set (Test 1–A through 8–A with manual, keys) $20.00; sample set (1 test) $5.00

Publisher: Educators/Employers' Tests & Services Associates

ETSA TESTS 1-A—GENERAL MENTAL ABILITY
George A. W. Stouffer, Jr. and S. Trevor Hadley

Adolescent, adult
Grades 10 and above

Purpose: Measures general intelligence and learning ability. Used for employee selection, placement, and promotion.

Description: 75–item paper-pencil test of general learning ability consisting of both verbal and nonverbal items. The test may be used in conjunction with ETSA 8–A—Personal Adjustment Index and any ETSA test measuring a specific skill area. Examiner required. Suitable for group use.

Untimed: 45 minutes

Scoring: Hand key; examiner evaluated; scoring service available

Cost: 10 tests with key $15.00; manual $5.00; handbook $15.00

Publisher: Educators/Employers' Tests & Services Associates

ETSA TESTS 2-A—OFFICE ARITHMETIC TEST
George A. W. Stouffer, Jr. and S. Trevor Hadley

Adolescent, adult
Grades 10 and above

Purpose: Measures ability to use office arithmetic. Used for employee selection, placement, and promotion.

Description: 50–item paper-pencil test assessing arithmetic skills used in office work. The areas tested include whole number computation, mixed number computation, written problems, reading tables, reading graphs, and advanced office computation. The test is one in a series of ETSA tests. Examiner required. Suitable for group use.

Timed: 40 minutes

Scoring: Hand key; examiner evaluated; scoring service available

Cost: 10 tests with key $15.00; manual $5.00; handbook $15.00

Publisher: Educators/Employers' Tests & Services Associates

ETSA TESTS 3-A—GENERAL CLERICAL ABILITY TEST
George A. W. Stouffer, Jr. and S. Trevor Hadley

Adolescent, adult
Grades 10 and above

Purpose: Measures general skills required of clerks in routine office work. Used for employee selection, placement, and promotion.

Description: 131–item paper-pencil test assessing general clerical skills. The items include alphabetizing, checking lists of numbers and names, spelling, office vocabulary, and basic information. Speed and accuracy are emphasized. The test is one in a series of ETSA tests. Examiner required. Suitable for group use.

Timed: 20 minutes

Scoring: Hand key; examiner evaluated; scoring service available

Cost: 10 tests with key $15.00; manual $5.00; handbook $15.00

Publisher: Educators/Employers' Tests & Services Associates

ETSA TESTS 4-A— STENOGRAPHIC SKILLS TEST
George A. W. Stouffer, Jr. and S. Trevor Hadley

Adolescent, adult
Grades 10 and above

Purpose: Measures typing, shorthand, and general skills required of secretaries and stenographers. Used for employee selection, placement, and promotion.

Description: 120–item paper-pencil test measuring four basic office skills: spelling, filing, grammar, and general office information. Materials include supplemental performance evaluations of typing and shorthand, either or both of which may be used with the basic scale. The test is one in a series of ETSA tests. Examiner required. Suitable for group use.

Untimed: 45 minutes; Typing Test Supplement 5 minutes; Shorthand Test 18 minutes

Scoring: Hand key; examiner evaluated; scoring service available

Cost: 10 tests with key $15.00; manual $5.00; handbook $15.00

Publisher: Educators/Employers' Tests & Services Associates

ETSA TESTS 5-A—MECHANICAL FAMILIARITY
George A. W. Stouffer, Jr. and S. Trevor Hadley

Adolescent, adult
Grades 10 and above

Purpose: Measures ability to recognize common tools and instruments. Used for employee selection, placement, and promotion.

Description: 50–item paper-pencil non-verbal test of background in mechanical activities. The items are commonly used tools, which the applicant identifies. The test is one in a series of ETSA tests. Examiner required. Suitable for group use.

Untimed: 1 hour

Scoring: Hand key; examiner evaluated; scoring service available

Cost: 10 tests with key $15.00; manual $5.00; handbook $15.00

Publisher: Educators/Employers' Tests & Services Associates

ETSA TESTS 6-A—MECHANICAL KNOWLEDGE
George A. W. Stouffer, Jr. and S. Trevor Hadley

Adolescent, adult
Grades 10 and above

Purpose: Measures mechanical insight and understanding. Used for employee selection, placement, and promotion.

Description: 121–item paper-pencil test assessing six areas of mechanical knowledge. The test discriminates between novices, journeymen, and experts. The test is one in a series of ETSA tests. Examiner required. Suitable for group use.

Untimed: 1 hour, 30 minutes

Scoring: Hand key; examiner evaluated; scoring service available

Cost: 10 tests with key $15.00; manual $5.00; handbook $15.00

Publisher: Educators/Employers' Tests & Services Associates

ETSA TESTS 7-A—SALES APTITUDE

George A. W. Stouffer, Jr. and S. Trevor Hadley

Adolescent, adult
Grades 10 and above

Purpose: Measures abilities and skills required for effective selling. Used for employee selection, placement, and promotion.

Description: 100–item paper-pencil test assessing seven aspects of sales aptitude: sales judgment, interest in selling, personality factors, identification of self with selling occupation, level of aspiration, insight into human nature, and awareness of sales approach. The test is one in a series of ETSA tests. Examiner required. Suitable for group use.

Untimed: 1 hour

Scoring: Hand key; examiner evaluated; scoring service available

Cost: 10 tests with key $15.00; manual $5.00; handbook $15.00

Publisher: Educators/Employers' Tests & Services Associates

ETSA TESTS 8-A—PERSONAL ADJUSTMENT INDEX

George A. W. Stouffer, Jr. and S. Trevor Hadley

Adolescent, adult
Grades 10 and above

Purpose: Measures personality traits for all types of jobs. Used for employee selection, placement, and promotion.

Description: 105–item paper-pencil test measuring seven components of personal adjustment: community spirit, attitude toward cooperation with employer, attitude toward health, attitude toward authority, lack of nervous tendencies, leadership, and job stability. The test may be used in conjunction with ETSA 1–A—General Mental Ability and any ETSA test measuring a specific skill area. Examiner required. Suitable for group use.

Untimed: 1 hour

Scoring: Hand key; examiner evaluated; scoring service available

Cost: 10 tests with key $15.00; manual $5.00; handbook $15.00

Publisher: Educators/Employers' Tests & Services Associates

EXPLORING CAREER OPTIONS (ECO)

Refer to page 1002.

FARNSWORTH DICHOTOMOUS TEST FOR COLOR BLINDNESS

Refer to page 726.

FARNSWORTH-MUNSELL 100 HUE TEST

Munsell Color

Ages 6–adult

Purpose: Determines color vision anomalies and color aptitude. Used to screen workers in such fields as electronics where color determination is a part of the job.

Description: Manual-visual apparatus test consisting of four trays, each containing a segment of 85 color reference disks recessed in individual black plastic caps. The subject is asked to place color caps in true order, with the results posted on score sheets to yield numerical and graphic results. Material consists of the trays, a wooden carrying case, instruction manual, and 100 score sheets. Examiner required. Not suitable for group use.

Untimed: 10 minutes

Scoring: Hand key

Cost: Complete kit (4 trays, wooden carrying case, instruction manual, 100 core sheets) $415.00

Publisher: Munsell Color

FLANAGAN APTITUDE CLASSIFICATION TESTS (FACT)

John C. Flanagan

Adolescent, adult

Purpose: Assesses skills necessary for the successful completion of particular occupational tasks. Used for vocational counseling, curriculum planning, and selection and placement of employees.

Description: Battery of 16 multiple-item paper-pencil aptitude tests designed to help the subject understand his abilities relative to others in the total population and in specific occupations.

The Inspection test measures the ability to spot flaws or imperfections in a series of articles quickly and accurately. The Mechanics test measures the ability to understand mechanical principles and analyze mechanical movements. The Tables test measures the ability to read tables and charts quickly and accurately. The Reasoning test measures the ability to understand basic mathematical concepts and translate ideas and operations into brief mathematical notations. The Assembly test measures the ability to visualize the appearance of an object assembled from a number of separate parts. The Judgment and Comprehension test measures the ability to read with understanding, reason logically, and use good judgment in practical situations. The Components test measures the ability to locate and identify important parts of a whole. The Arithmetic test measures the ability to work quickly and accurately with numbers in addition, subtraction, multiplication, and division problems. The Ingenuity test measures the creative or inventive skills and ability to devise ingenious procedures, equipment, or presentations. The Scales test measures the ability to read scales, graphs, and charts quickly and accurately. The Expression test measures the feeling for and knowledge of correct English in writing and talking. The Precision test measures the ability to perform precision work with small objects and speed and accuracy in making appropriate finger movements with one or both hands. The Coordination test measures the ability to coordinate hand and arm movements in a smooth and accurate manner. The Patterns test measures the ability to perceive and reproduce simple pattern outlines in a precise and accurate way. The Coding test measures the ability to code typical office information quickly and accurately. The Memory test measures the ability to learn and recall the classification or identifying symbols for various materials or groups of items.

Each test is printed as a separate non-reusable booklet and may be adminis-tered singly or in combination. The FACT battery differs from the Flanagan Indus-trial Tests (FIT) battery (see separate entry) in that the tests are generally of a lower level and have longer time limits. Self-administered. Suitable for group use.

Timed: 5–40 minutes per test

Scoring: Hand key

Cost: 25 test booklets (specify test) $39.00; reasoning manual $10.00; inge-nuity manual $10.00; examiner's manual $10.00

Publisher: SRA/London House

FLANAGAN INDUSTRIAL TESTS (FIT)
John C. Flanagan

Adult

Purpose: Predicts success for given job elements in adults. Used for employee screening, hiring, and placement in a wide variety of jobs.

Description: Battery of 18 paper-pencil tests designed for use with adults in per-sonnel selection programs.

The Arithmetic (Ar) test measures the ability to work quickly and accurately with numbers. The Assembly (As) test measures the ability to visualize the appearance of an object assembled from a number of separate parts. The Compo-nents (Com) test measures the ability to locate and identify important parts of a whole, which involves the ability to change visual patterns. The Coordination (Co) test measures the ability to coordi-nate hand and arm movements smoothly and accurately. The Electronics (El) test measures the ability to understand elec-trical and electronic principles and to analyze diagrams of electrical circuits. The Expression (Ex) test measures the feeling for and knowledge of correct Eng-lish in writing and talking. The Ingenuity (Ing) test measures the creative or inventive skills and the ability to devise ingenious procedures, equipment, or pre-sentations. The Inspection (Ins) test measures the ability to spot flaws or imperfections in a series of articles quickly and accurately. The Judgment and Com-prehension test measures the ability to read with understanding, reason logically, and use good judgment in interpreting materials. The Mathematics and Reasoning (M-R) test measures the ability to understand basic math concepts and translate ideas and operations into brief mathematical notations. The Mechanics (Me) test measures the ability to understand mechanical principles and to analyze mechanical movements. The Memory (Mem) test measures the ability to learn and recall a term associated with an unfamiliar one. The Patterns (Pat) test measures the ability to perceive and reproduce simple pattern outlines precisely and accurately. The Planning (Pl) test measures the ability to plan, organize, and schedule. The Precision (Pre) test measures both the ability to perform precision work with small objects and the speed and accuracy in making appropriate finger movements. The Scales (Sc) test measures the ability to read scales, graphs, and charts quickly and accurately. The Tables (Ta) test measures the ability to read tables quickly and accurately. The Vocabulary test measures the ability to choose the right word to convey an idea.

Each test is printed as a separate booklet and may be administered singly or in combination. Self-administered. Suitable for group use.

Timed: 5–15 minutes per test

Scoring: Hand key (except for Coordination and Precision tests)

Cost: 25 test booklets (specify test) $29.00; scoring stencil $10.00; Inspection scoring stencil $20.00

Publisher: SRA/London House

FUNCTIONAL SKILLS SCREENING INVENTORY: EMPLOYMENT EDITION (FSSI: EE)

Refer to page 663.

GENERAL APTITUDE SERIES (GAS)
Saville & Holdsworth Ltd. Staff

Adult

Purpose: Assesses a wide range of general abilities. Used in the counseling and placement of general managerial personnel, the measurement of abilities in cases of job dissatisfaction, personnel transfers, occupational counseling, and occupational research.

Description: Seven paper-pencil multiple-choice tests measuring verbal, numerical, spatial, mechanical, diagrammatic, clerical, and diagramming skills. The tests include Verbal Concepts (VA1), Number Series (NA2), Spatial Recognition (ST9), Mechanical Comprehension (MT4), Diagrammatic Reasoning (DT8), Classification (CP4), and Diagramming (DA5). The battery provides a high degree of relevance to occupational work in relation to the amount of testing time required. Examiner required. Suitable for group use.

BRITISH PUBLISHER

Timed: 1 hour, 42 minutes

Scoring: Hand key; examiner evaluated; may be computer scored

Cost: Complete (tests, score sheets, manual, keys) $800.00

Publisher: Saville & Holdsworth Ltd.

GENERAL APTITUDE TEST BATTERY (GATB)
U.S. Employment Service

Adolescent, adult

Purpose: Measures vocational aptitudes of literate individuals who need help choosing an occupation. Used for counseling.

Description: 434–item paper-pencil test consisting of 284 multiple-choice questions, 150 dichotomous choice (same-different) questions, and two dexterity form boards. Twelve subtests measure nine vocational aptitudes: General Learning Ability, Verbal, Numerical, Spatial, Form Perception, Clerical Perception, Motor Coordination, Finger Dexterity, and Manual Dexterity. Raw scores can be converted to aptitude scores with conversion tables. Occupational Aptitude Patterns (OAP) indicate the aptitude requirements for groups of occupations. There are 66 OAPs covering 97% of all nonsupervisory occupations. The GATB is scored in terms of OAPs. A letter grade of "H," "M," or "L" is assigned for each OAP. Results of the battery indicate the individual's likelihood of success in the various occupations. Use in the United States must be authorized by State Employment Service Agencies and in Canada by the Canadian Employment and Immigration Commission. Examiner required. Suitable for group use. Available in Spanish and French.

Timed: Varies

Scoring: Hand key; may be computer scored

Cost: Available from State Employment Service Agencies only

Publisher: U.S. Department of Labor

Information and availability unconfirmed; last verified in 1988.

GOTTSCHALDT FIGURES TEST

Adult

Purpose: Measures visual perception and analytical ability. Used with job applicants with at least 10 years of education for purposes of employee screening and selection.

Description: Multiple-item paper-pencil test requiring the applicant to find given embedded figures in more complex diagrams. The test is restricted to competent persons properly registered with the South African Medical and Dental Council. Examiner required. Suitable for group use. Afrikaans version available. SOUTH AFRICAN PUBLISHER

Timed: 20 minutes

Scoring: Hand key

Cost: Contact publisher

Publisher: National Institute for Personnel Research

HAND DYNAMOMETER (DYNAMOMETER GRIP STRENGTH TEST)

Ages 5-55

Purpose: Measures grip strength and provides an index of right versus left handedness. Used for vocational evaluation, employee screening, and fitness evaluation.

Description: Task-performance test measuring grip strength. A millimeter rule and grip dynamometer with adjustable

stirrup are adjusted until the inside scale equals half the distance from where the subject's thumb joins the hand to the end of the fingers. The subject then squeezes with full strength, which is measured by the dynamometer. Examiner required. Not suitable for group use.

Untimed: 1 minute

Scoring: Hand key

Cost: Model 78010 and 78011 $225.00

Publisher: Lafayette Instrument Company, Inc.

INDUSTRIAL READING TEST (IRT)

Adolescent, adult Grades 10 and above

Purpose: Measures reading comprehension. Used for selecting job applicants and screening trainees for vocational or technical programs.

Description: 38–item paper-pencil test of reading comprehension covering nine reading passages of graded difficulty. Some passages are sections of technical manuals; others take the form of company memoranda. Materials include two forms, A and B. Sales of Form A are restricted to business and industry. Form B available to both schools and businesses. Examiner required. Suitable for group use.

Timed: 40 minutes

Scoring: Hand key; may be machine scored locally

Cost: Specimen set (test, IBM 805/OpScan answer document, manual) $15.00; 25 tests (specify form) $36.00; 50 IBM 805/OpScan answer documents $25.00; keys (specify form) $10.00; manual $13.00

Publisher: The Psychological Corporation

Information and availability unconfirmed; last verified in 1988.

INSIGHT
Valpar International Corporation

Adult—Ages 18 and older

Purpose: Develops worker qualifications profile for pre-employment testing. Used with job/training applicants for career planning.

Description: Computerized criterion-referenced test measuring the Worker Qualification Profile as defined by the U.S. Department of Labor in its *Handbook for Analyzing Jobs*. The test measures cognitive abilities, physical abilities, and academic achievement. The software, which operates on IBM PCs, contains the full *Dictionary of Occupational Titles* as well as a Local Job File that users can fill with their own job descriptions. The software can compile various reports and generate searches automatically. This test is suitable for individuals with hearing impairments. Examiner required. Suitable for group use.

Timed: 1½–3 hours

Scoring: Computer scored

Cost: Contact publisher

Publisher: Valpar International Corporation

INSURANCE SELECTION INVENTORY (ISI)
London House, Inc.

Adult—Ages 16 and older

Purpose: Evaluates potential for success as a claims examiner, customer service representative, and correspondence representative. Used for employee selection and promotion.

Description: 275–item paper-pencil multiple-choice test measuring 11 basic functions necessary to succeed in key insurance positions: Number Comparison, Verbal Reasoning, Applied Arithmetic, Arithmetic Computation, Error Recognition, Drive, Interpersonal Skills, Cognitive Skills, Self-Discipline, Writing Skills, and Work Preference. Potential estimate scores for the positions of claims examiner, customer service representative, and correspondence representative are yielded. Standard scores for each of the 11 measures are also profiled. Examiner required. Suitable for group use.

Timed: Number Comparison 3 minutes; Verbal Reasoning 15 minutes; Arithmetic Computation 5 minutes; Error Recognition 3 minutes

Untimed: Drive, Applied Arithmetic, Interpersonal Skills, Cognitive Skills, Self-Discipline, Writing Skills, and Work Preference 20–35 minutes

Scoring: Computer scored

Cost: Contact publisher

Publisher: London House, Inc.

IPI APTITUDE—INTELLIGENCE TEST SERIES: BLOCKS
Industrial Psychology International, Ltd.

Adult

Purpose: Measures aptitude to visualize objects on the basis of three-dimensional cues. Used to screen applicants for mechanical and technical jobs.

Description: 32–item paper-pencil test of spatial relations and quantitative ability. The test does not require the ability to read. Examiner required. Suitable for group use. Available in French and Spanish.

Timed: 6 minutes

Scoring: Hand key

Cost: 20 tests $21.00

Publisher: Industrial Psychology International, Ltd.

IPI APTITUDE—INTELLIGENCE TEST SERIES: DEXTERITY
Industrial Psychology International, Ltd.

Adult

Purpose: Determines ability to rapidly perform routine motor tasks involving eye-hand coordination. Used to screen applicants for mechanical and technical jobs.

Description: Three 1–minute paper-pencil subtests (Maze, Checks, Dots) in which the subject demonstrates ability to perform routine motor tasks. The test does not require the ability to read or write. Examiner required. Suitable for group use. Available in French and Spanish.

Timed: 3 minutes

Scoring: Hand key

Cost: 20 tests $21.00

Publisher: Industrial Psychology International, Ltd.

IPI APTITUDE—INTELLIGENCE TEST SERIES: DIMENSION
Industrial Psychology International, Ltd.

Adult

Purpose: Evaluates ability to visualize objects when seen from their exact reverse. Used to screen applicants for mechanical and technical jobs.

Description: 48–item paper-pencil test measuring spatial relations at a high level. The test does not require the ability to read or write. Examiner required. Suitable for group use. Available in French and Spanish.

Timed: 6 minutes

Scoring: Hand key

Cost: 20 tests $21.00

Publisher: Industrial Psychology International, Ltd.

IPI APTITUDE—INTELLIGENCE TEST SERIES: FACTORY TERMS
Industrial Psychology International, Ltd.

Adult

Purpose: Determines ability to understand the words and information used in factory and mechanical settings. Used to screen applicants for mechanical and technical jobs.

Description: 54–item paper-pencil test measuring comprehension of high-level mechanical, engineering, and factory information. Examiner required. Suitable for group use.

Timed: 10 minutes

Scoring: Hand key

Cost: 20 tests $21.00

Publisher: Industrial Psychology International, Ltd.

IPI APTITUDE—INTELLIGENCE TEST SERIES: FLUENCY
Industrial Psychology International, Ltd.

Adult

Purpose: Assesses aptitude to use words with ease. Used to screen applicants for clerical, sales, and supervisory jobs.

Description: Three 2–minute paper-pencil subtests measuring the ability to write or talk without mentally blocking or searching for the right word. Examiner required. Suitable for group use. Available in French and Spanish.

Timed: 6 minutes

Scoring: Hand key

Cost: 20 tests $21.00

Publisher: Industrial Psychology International, Ltd.

IPI APTITUDE—INTELLIGENCE TEST SERIES: JUDGMENT
Industrial Psychology International, Ltd.

Adult

Purpose: Evaluates an individual's ability to think logically and to deduce solutions to abstract problems. Used to screen applicants for clerical, sales, and supervisory positions.

Description: 54–item paper-pencil test measuring aptitude to think logically, plan, and deal with abstract relations. Examiner required. Suitable for group use. Available in French and Spanish.

Timed: 6 minutes

Scoring: Hand key

Cost: 20 tests $21.00

Publisher: Industrial Psychology International, Ltd.

IPI APTITUDE—INTELLIGENCE TEST SERIES: MEMORY
Industrial Psychology International, Ltd.

Adult

Purpose: Determines ability to remember visual, verbal, and numerical materials. Used to screen applicants for clerical, sales, and supervisory jobs.

Description: Three 2–minute paper-pencil subtests demonstrating aptitude to recognize and recall such associations as names, faces, words, numbers, and prices. Examiner required. Suitable for group use. Available in French and Spanish.

Timed: 6 minutes

Scoring: Hand key

Cost: 20 tests $35.00

Publisher: Industrial Psychology International, Ltd.

IPI APTITUDE—INTELLIGENCE TEST SERIES: MOTOR
Industrial Psychology International, Ltd.

Adult

Purpose: Measures adults' ability to coordinate eye and hand movements in a specific motor task. Used to screen applicants for mechanical and technical jobs.

Description: 3–item test measuring the ability to coordinate eye and hand movements in a specific motor task. The examination consists of three trials of the same task. The examiner reviews instructions and sample questions with the subjects, sets the timer, and begins the test. The same procedure is repeated two more times. The test requires a special motor apparatus for administration. Examiner required. Suitable for group use only if more than one apparatus is available. Available in French and Spanish.

Timed: 6 minutes

Scoring: Hand key

Cost: 20 tests $21.00; motor board $150.00

Publisher: Industrial Psychology International, Ltd.

IPI APTITUDE—INTELLIGENCE TEST SERIES: NUMBERS
Industrial Psychology International, Ltd.

Adult

Purpose: Measures ability to work rapidly and accurately with numbers. Used to screen applicants for clerical, mechanical, sales, technical, and supervisory positions.

Description: 54–item paper-pencil test measuring the ability to perform numerical computations and to understand mathematical concepts. The test is highly related to record keeping, typing, work planning, computational skills, and coding. Examiner required. Suitable for group use. Available in French and Spanish.

Timed: 6 minutes

Scoring: Hand key

Cost: 20 tests $21.00

Publisher: Industrial Psychology International, Ltd.

IPI APTITUDE—INTELLIGENCE TEST SERIES: OFFICE TERMS
Industrial Psychology International, Ltd.

Adult

Purpose: Measures ability to understand special terms used in business and industry. Used to screen applicants for clerical, sales, and supervisory jobs.

Description: 54–item paper-pencil test measuring comprehension of information of an office or business nature and general mental ability. It also indicates overqualification for routine, repetitive assignments. Examiner required. Suitable for group use. Available in French and Spanish (combined with Sales Terms).

Timed: 6 minutes

Scoring: Hand key

Cost: 20 tests $21.00

Publisher: Industrial Psychology International, Ltd.

IPI APTITUDE—INTELLIGENCE TEST SERIES: PARTS
Industrial Psychology International, Ltd.

Adult

Purpose: Assesses ability to see the whole in relation to its parts. Used to screen applicants for clerical, mechanical, technical, sales, and supervisory positions.

Description: 48–item paper-pencil test measuring aptitude for visualizing size, shape, and spatial relations of objects in two and three dimensions. The test reveals the subject's sense of layout and organization. The test does not require the ability to read or write. Examiner required. Suitable for group use. Available in French and Spanish.

Timed: 6 minutes

Scoring: Hand key

Cost: 20 tests $21.00

Publisher: Industrial Psychology International, Ltd.

IPI APTITUDE—INTELLIGENCE TEST SERIES: PERCEPTION
Industrial Psychology International, Ltd.

Adult

Purpose: Measures ability to perceive differences in written words and numbers. Used to screen applicants for clerical, sales, and supervisory jobs.

Description: 54–item paper-pencil test measuring the ability to rapidly scan and locate details in words and numbers and to recognize likenesses and differences. Examiner required. Suitable for group use. Available in French and Spanish.

Timed: 6 minutes

Scoring: Hand key

Cost: 20 tests $21.00

Publisher: Industrial Psychology International, Ltd.

IPI APTITUDE—INTELLIGENCE TEST SERIES: PRECISION
Industrial Psychology International, Ltd.

Adult

Purpose: Determines ability to perceive details in pictures. Used by employers to screen applicants for technical and mechanical jobs with inspection duties.

Description: 48–item paper-pencil test using pictures to test the ability to perceive details in objects and rapidly recognize differences and likenesses. The test does not require the ability to read or write. Examiner required. Suitable for group use. Available in French and Spanish.

Timed: 6 minutes

Scoring: Hand key

Cost: 20 tests $21.00

Publisher: Industrial Psychology International, Ltd.

IPI APTITUDE—INTELLIGENCE TEST SERIES: SALES TERMS
Industrial Psychology International, Ltd.

Adult

Purpose: Measures ability to understand words and information related to sales. Used to assist employers in the selection, placement, promotion, and training of different levels of sales personnel.

Description: 54–item paper-pencil test measuring comprehension of sales-related information. The test indicates whether a person is overqualified for routine or repetitive assignments. Examiner required. Suitable for group use. Available in French and Spanish (combined with Office Terms).

Timed: 5 minutes

Scoring: Hand key

Cost: 20 tests $21.00

Publisher: Industrial Psychology International, Ltd.

IPI APTITUDE—INTELLIGENCE TEST SERIES: TOOLS
Industrial Psychology International, Ltd.

Adult

Purpose: Evaluates comprehension of simple tools and mechanical equipment. Used to screen applicants for mechanical and technical jobs.

Description: 48–item paper-pencil test measuring the ability to recognize pictures of common tools, equipment, and machines. The test does not require the ability to read or write. Examiner required. Suitable for group use. Available in French and Spanish.

Timed: Each test 6 minutes

Scoring: Hand key

Cost: 20 tests $21.00

Publisher: Industrial Psychology International, Ltd.

IPI EMPLOYEE APTITUDE SERIES: CONTACT PERSONALITY FACTOR (CPF)
IPI Staff, Raymond B. Cattell, J.E. King, and A.K. Schuettler

Adult

Purpose: Determines contact versus non-contact factor in personality. Used for screening, placement, and promotion of employees.

Description: 40–item paper-pencil personality test measuring extroversion versus introversion. Examiner required. Suitable for group use. Available in French and Spanish.

Timed: 10 minutes

Scoring: Hand key

Cost: 20 tests $21.00

Publisher: Industrial Psychology International, Ltd.

IPI EMPLOYEE APTITUDE SERIES: NEUROTIC PERSONALITY FACTOR (NPF)
IPI Staff, Raymond B. Cattell, J.E. King, and A.K. Schuettler

Adult

Purpose: Measures emotional balance and/or the lack of neurotic tendencies in personality. Used to screen applicants for a variety of positions and to place and promote employees.

Description: 40–item paper-pencil test measuring an individual's general stability and emotional balance. Examiner required. Suitable for group use. Available in French and Spanish.

Timed: 10 minutes

Scoring: Hand key

Cost: 20 tests $21.00

Publisher: Industrial Psychology International, Ltd.

IPI EMPLOYEE APTITUDE SERIES: SIXTEEN PERSONALITY FACTOR (16PF) TEST
IPI Staff, Raymond B. Cattell, J.E. King, and A.K. Schuettler

Adult

Purpose: Measures 16 basic factors of personality. Used to screen applicants for a variety of positions.

Description: 102–item paper-pencil test measuring the following traits: bright, mature, dominant, enthusiastic, participating, consistent, adventurous, tough-minded, trustful, conventional, sophisticated, self-confident, liberal, self-sufficient, controlled, and stable. Examiner required. Suitable for group use. Available in French and Spanish.

Timed: 20 minutes

Scoring: Hand key

Cost: 20 tests $35.00

Publisher: Industrial Psychology International, Ltd.

IPI JOB TEST FIELD SERIES: CONTACT CLERK
Industrial Psychology International, Ltd.

Adult

Purpose: Assesses skills of applicants for public relations positions. Used to screen for complaint, information, receptionist, and customer service positions.

Description: Multiple-item paper-pencil battery of five aptitude tests. The tests are Fluency, Perception, Memory, Judgment, and Numbers. For individual test descriptions, see the IPI Aptitude-Intelligence Test Series. Examiner required. Suitable for group use. Available in French and Spanish.

Timed: Each test 6 minutes

Scoring: Hand key

Cost: Instruction kits $16.00; test package $10.00

Publisher: Industrial Psychology International, Ltd.

IPI JOB TEST FIELD SERIES: DESIGNER
Industrial Psychology International, Ltd.

Adult

Purpose: Assesses skills and personality of applicants for designer positions. Used to screen for artists, architects, draftsmen, layout men, and photographers.

Description: Multiple-item paper-pencil battery of six aptitude and three personality tests. The tests are Dimension, Precision, NPF, CPF, Blocks, Dexterity, Sales Terms, 16PF, and Parts. For individual test descriptions, see the IPI Aptitude-Intelligence Test Series. Examiner required. Suitable for group use. Available in French and Spanish.

Timed: 75 minutes

Scoring: Hand key

Cost: Instruction kit $16.00; test packages $10.00

Publisher: Industrial Psychology International, Ltd.

IPI JOB TEST FIELD SERIES: FACTORY MACHINE OPERATOR
Industrial Psychology International, Ltd.

Adult

Purpose: Assesses skills of applicants for various factory machine-oriented positions. Used to screen for cutter, screw machine, lathe, press, sewing, and welder jobs.

Description: Multiple-item paper-pencil battery of five aptitude tests. The tests are Number, Dexterity, Precision, Blocks, and Tools. For individual test descriptions, see the IPI Aptitude-Intelligence Test Series. Examiner required. Suitable for group use. Available in French and Spanish.

Timed: Each test 6 minutes

Scoring: Hand key

IPI JOB TEST FIELD SERIES: INSPECTOR
Industrial Psychology International, Ltd.

Adult

Purpose: Assesses skills and personality of applicants for inspector-oriented positions. Used to evaluate checking, classifying, examining, grading, pairing, scaling, and sorting skills.

Description: Multiple-item paper-pencil battery of four aptitude tests. The tests are Dimension, Numbers, Tools, and Blocks. For individual test descriptions, see the IPI Aptitude-Intelligence Test Series. Examiner required. Suitable for group use. Available in French and Spanish.

Timed: Each test 6 minutes

Scoring: Hand key

Cost: Instruction kit $16.00; test packages $10.00

Publisher: Industrial Psychology International, Ltd.

IPI JOB TEST FIELD SERIES: INSTRUCTOR
Refer to page 1088.

IPI JOB TEST FIELD SERIES: OFFICE TECHNICAL
Industrial Psychology International, Ltd.

Adult

Purpose: Assesses skills and personality of applicants for various office technical positions. Used to evaluate the achievement and personality of accountants, estimators, methods clerks, statisticians, and time-study experts.

Description: Multiple-item paper-pencil battery of six aptitude and three personality tests. The tests are Office Terms, Perception, CPF, NPF, Judgment, Numbers, 16PF, Parts, and Memory. For individual test descriptions, see the IPI Aptitude-Intelligence Test Series. Examiner required. Suitable for group use. Available in French and Spanish.

Timed: 76 minutes

Scoring: Hand key

Cost: Instruction kit $16.00; test packages $10.00

Publisher: Industrial Psychology International, Ltd.

IPI JOB TEST FIELD SERIES: SALES CLERK
Refer to page 1082.

IPI JOB TEST FIELD SERIES: SALES ENGINEER
Refer to page 1082.

IPI JOB TEST FIELD SERIES: SCIENTIST
Industrial Psychology International, Ltd.

Adult

Purpose: Assesses skills and personality of applicants for various positions in the field of science. Used to screen for biologists, chemists, economists, physicists, and positions in the inventory and research fields.

Description: Multiple-item paper-pencil battery of seven aptitude and three personality tests. The tests are Judgment, Dimension, CPF, NPF, Factory Terms, Precision, Office Terms, 16PF, Numbers, and Dexterity. For individual test descriptions, see the IPI Aptitude-Intelligence Test Series. Examiner required. Suitable for group use. Available in French and Spanish.

Timed: 82 minutes

Scoring: Hand key

Cost: Instruction kit $16.00; test packages $10.00

Publisher: Industrial Psychology International, Ltd.

IPI JOB TEST FIELD SERIES: SEMI-SKILLED WORKER
Industrial Psychology International, Ltd.

Adult

Purpose: Assesses skills of applicants for semi-skilled mechanical positions. Used to screen for assembler, construction, helper, and production positions.

Description: Multiple-item paper-pencil battery of four aptitude tests. The tests are Motor, Precision, Tools, and Blocks. For individual test descriptions, see the IPI Aptitude-Intelligence Test Series. Examiner required. Suitable for group use. Available in French and Spanish.

Timed: Each test 6 minutes

Scoring: Hand key

Cost: Instruction kit $16.00; test packages $10.00

Publisher: Industrial Psychology International, Ltd.

IPI JOB TEST FIELD SERIES: SKILLED WORKER
Industrial Psychology International, Ltd.

Adult

Purpose: Assesses skills of applicants for various skilled worker positions. Used to screen for linemen, machinists, maintenance workers, mechanics, and tool makers.

Description: Multiple-item paper-pencil battery of six aptitude tests. The tests are Dimension, Dexterity, Parts, Blocks, Motor, and Precision. For individual test descriptions, see the IPI Aptitude-Intelligence Test Series. Examiner required. Suitable for group use. Available in French and Spanish.

Timed: Each test 6 minutes

Scoring: Hand key

Cost: Instruction kit $16.00; test packages $10.00

Publisher: Industrial Psychology International, Ltd.

IPI JOB TEST FIELD SERIES: UNSKILLED WORKER
Industrial Psychology International, Ltd.

Adult

Purpose: Assesses skills of applicants for low-level mechanical jobs. Used to screen janitors, laborers, loaders, material handlers, packers, and truckers.

Description: Multiple-item paper-pencil battery of four aptitude tests. The tests are Motor, Precision, Tools, and Blocks. For individual test descriptions, see the IPI Aptitude-Intelligence Test Series. Examiner required. Suitable for group use. Available in French and Spanish.

Timed: Each test 6 minutes

Scoring: Hand key

Cost: Instruction kit $16.00; test packages $10.00 each

Publisher: Industrial Psychology International, Ltd.

IPI JOB TEST FIELD SERIES: VEHICLE OPERATOR
Industrial Psychology International, Ltd.

Adult

Purpose: Assesses skills of applicants for various vehicle operator positions. Used to screen for crane, elevator, motorman, taxi, teamster, tractor, and truck-driving positions.

Description: Multiple-item paper-pencil battery of five aptitude tests. The tests are Numbers, Dexterity, Precision, Blocks, and Tools. For individual test descriptions, see the IPI Aptitude-Intelligence Test Series. Examiner required. Suitable for group use. Available in French and Spanish.

Timed: Each test 6 minutes

Scoring: Hand key

Cost: Instruction kit $16.00; test packages $10.00

Publisher: Industrial Psychology International, Ltd.

IPI JOB TEST FIELD SERIES: WRITER
Industrial Psychology International, Ltd.

Adult

Purpose: Assesses skills and personality of applicants for writing positions. Used to screen for advertising, author, copywriter, critic, editor, journalist, and public relations positions.

Description: Multiple-item paper-pencil battery of six aptitude and three personality tests. The tests are Fluency, Sales Terms, CPF, NPF, Memory, Judgment, 16PF, Perception, and Parts. For individual test descriptions, see the IPI Aptitude-Intelligence Test Series. Examiner required. Suitable for group use. Available in French and Spanish.

Timed: 82 minutes

Scoring: Hand key

Cost: Instruction kit $16.00; test packages $10.00

Publisher: Industrial Psychology International, Ltd.

ISHIHARA'S TEST FOR COLOUR BLINDNESS
Refer to page 727.

JOB EFFECTIVENESS PREDICTION SYSTEM (JEPS)
Personnel Decisions Research Institute for Life Office Management Association

Adult

Purpose: Measures a variety of skills required for a wide range of clerical and technical/professional positions. Used for selection and placement of entry-level employees in life and property/casualty insurance companies.

Description: 11 multiple-item paper-pencil tests measuring verbal, mathematical, and clerical skills. The tests are Numerical Ability–1, Numerical Ability–2, Mathematical Skill, Spelling, Language Usage, Reading Comprehension–1, Reading Comprehension–2,

Verbal Comprehension, Filing, Coding and Converting, and Comparing and Checking. Not all the tests are required for each selection decision. In many cases, two, three, or four of the tests used in combination will predict potential job performance accurately. Each of the 11 tests is independent. The tests were developed following the Uniform Guidelines on Employee Selection Procedures during a 5–year study in over 100 insurance companies. Batteries have been developed for each entry-level position in each JEPS member company. Use is restricted to insurance companies. Examiner required. Suitable for group use.

Timed: Varies, depending on subtest

Scoring: Hand key

Cost: Test $0.35–$0.70 per applicant, depending on number of subtests and volume ordered

Publisher: Life Office Management Association

JOB EFFECTIVENESS PREDICTION SYSTEM: CODING AND CONVERTING (JEPS: TEST CODE K)

Personnel Decisions Research Institute for Life Office Management Association

Adult

Purpose: Measures the ability to quickly and accurately use conversion tables and coding guides. Used for selection and placement of entry-level clerical and technical/professional employees in life and property/casualty insurance companies.

Description: 85–item paper-pencil multiple-choice test in three sections measuring the ability to use conversion tables and coding guides. In the first section, the examinee uses a table that converts monthly premiums to annual premiums in order to indicate the correct annual premium for 20 monthly premiums. In the second section, the examinee uses a table of letter codes for annual premiums to indicate the correct letter code for 25 annual premiums. In the third section, the examinee uses both tables to indicate the correct code for 40 monthly pre-

miums. Use is restricted to insurance companies. Examiner required. Suitable for group use.

Timed: 8 minutes

Scoring: Hand key

Cost: Test $0.59–$0.71 per applicant, depending on volume ordered

Publisher: Life Office Management Association

JOB EFFECTIVENESS PREDICTION SYSTEM: COMPARING AND CHECKING (JEPS: TEST CODE L)

Personnel Decisions Research Institute for Life Office Management Association

Adult

Purpose: Measures ability to compare numbers and words and detect the differences. Used for selection and placement of entry-level clerical and technical/professional employees in life and property/casualty insurance companies.

Description: 40–item paper-pencil multiple-choice test measuring the ability to compare words and numbers and detect differences. The examinee is presented with correct lists of words and numbers (names, addresses, dollar amounts, etc.) and lists to be checked. The subjects are asked to count the number of errors per line. Use is restricted to insurance companies. Examiner required. Suitable for group use.

Timed: 7 minutes

Scoring: Hand key

Cost: Test $0.47–$0.57 per applicant, depending on volume ordered

Publisher: Life Office Management Association

JOB EFFECTIVENESS PREDICTION SYSTEM: FILING (JEPS: TEST CODE J)

Personnel Decisions Research Institute for Life Office Management Association

Adult

Purpose: Measures general filing skills. Used for selection and placement of entry--

level clerical and technical/professional employees in life and property/casualty insurance companies.

Description: 60–item paper-pencil multiple-choice test measuring the ability to file materials according to given instructions. The examinee is presented with existing files with numbered slots between entries and lists of entries to be filed. The examinee indicates the number of the slot into which each of the entries should be filed. Use is restricted to insurance companies. Examiner required. Suitable for group use.

Timed: 5 minutes

Scoring: Hand key

Cost: Test $0.59–$0.71 per applicant depending on volume ordered

Publisher: Life Office Management Association

JOB EFFECTIVENESS PREDICTION SYSTEM: LANGUAGE USAGE (JEPS: TEST CODE E)
Personnel Decisions Research Institute for Life Office Management Association

Adult

Purpose: Measures proper usage of the English language. Used for selection and placement of entry-level clerical and technical/professional employees in life and property/casualty insurance companies.

Description: 94–item paper-pencil test measuring knowledge of grammar, punctuation, capitalization, and formation of plurals. The subject indicates whether there are any errors in a reading selection that is divided into two parts. Use is restricted to insurance companies. Examiner required. Suitable for group use.

Timed: 12 minutes

Scoring: Hand key

Cost: Test $0.35–$0.43 per applicant, depending on volume ordered

Publisher: Life Office Management Association

JOB EFFECTIVENESS PREDICTION SYSTEM: MATHEMATICAL SKILL (JEPS: TEST CODE C)
Personnel Decisions Research Institute for Life Office Management Association

Adult

Purpose: Measures the ability to work with mathematical relationships and formulas. Used for selection and placement of entry-level clerical and technical/professional employees in life and property/casualty insurance companies.

Description: 23–item paper-pencil multiple-choice test measuring skill in solving and manipulating mathematical relationships and formulas. One section involves solving formulas, and the other requires selecting the appropriate formula to use for problem solving. Use is restricted to insurance companies. Examiner required. Suitable for group use.

Timed: 20 minutes

Scoring: Hand key

Cost: Test $0.47–$0.57 per applicant, depending on volume ordered

Publisher: Life Office Management Association

JOB EFFECTIVENESS PREDICTION SYSTEM: NUMERICAL ABILITY–1 (JEPS: TEST CODE A)
Personnel Decisions Research Institute for Life Office Management Association

Adult

Purpose: Measures the ability to add, subtract, multiply, and divide. Used for selection and placement of entry-level clerical and technical/professional employees in life and property/casualty insurance companies.

Description: 50–item paper-pencil multiple-choice test measuring the ability to perform basic arithmetic operations, including the addition, subtraction, multiplication, and division of whole numbers, fractions, decimals, and percentages. Use is restricted to insurance companies. Examiner required. Suitable for group use.

Timed: 8 minutes

Scoring: Hand key

Cost: Test $0.47–$0.57 per applicant, depending on volume ordered

Publisher: Life Office Management Association

JOB EFFECTIVENESS PREDICTION SYSTEM: NUMERICAL ABILITY-2 (JEPS: TEST CODE B)

Personnel Decisions Research Institute for Life Office Management Association

Adult

Purpose: Measures the ability to perform operations with decimals and percentages. Used for selection and placement of entry-level clerical and technical/professional employees in life and property/casualty insurance companies.

Description: 50–item paper-pencil test with multiple-choice and true-false sections measuring numerical ability. Problems require the subject to perform operations with percentages, round off decimal numbers, and approximate correct answers. Use is restricted to insurance companies. Examiner required. Suitable for group use.

Timed: 15 minutes

Scoring: Hand key

Cost: Test $0.47–$0.57 per applicant, depending on volume ordered

Publisher: Life Office Management Association

JOB EFFECTIVENESS PREDICTION SYSTEM: READING COMPREHENSION-1 (JEPS: TEST CODE F)

Personnel Decisions Research Institute for Life Office Management Association

Adult

Purpose: Measures the ability to understand written instructions. Used for selection and placement of entry-level

clerical and technical/professional employees in life and property/casualty insurance companies.

Description: 30–item paper-pencil multiple-choice test measuring the ability to understand written directions, definitions, and procedures. The subject reads several passages and answers questions about each passage. Use is restricted to insurance companies. Examiner required. Suitable for group use.

Timed: 30 minutes

Scoring: Hand key

Cost: Test $0.59–$0.71 per applicant, depending on volume ordered

Publisher: Life Office Management Association

JOB EFFECTIVENESS PREDICTION SYSTEM: READING COMPREHENSION-2 (JEPS: TEST CODE G)

Personnel Decisions Research Institute for Life Office Management Association

Adult

Purpose: Measures level of general reading comprehension. Used for selection and placement of entry-level clerical and technical/professional employees in life and property/casualty insurance companies.

Description: 35–item paper-pencil multiple-choice test measuring reading comprehension at approximately a Grades 11–13 reading level. The subject reads several reading passages and answers questions about each passage. Use is restricted to insurance companies. Examiner required. Suitable for group use.

Timed: 30 minutes

Scoring: Hand key

Cost: Test $0.59–$0.71 per applicant, depending on volume ordered

Publisher: Life Office Management Association

JOB EFFECTIVENESS PREDICTION SYSTEM: SPELLING (JEPS: TEST CODE D)

Personnel Decisions Research Institute for Life Office Management Association

Adult

Purpose: Measures the ability to recognize whether words are correctly spelled. Used for selection and placement of entry-level clerical and technical/professional employees in life and property/casualty insurance companies.

Description: 85–item paper-pencil test consisting of a list of words. The examinee indicates whether each word is spelled correctly. Use is restricted to insurance companies. Examiner required. Suitable for group use.

Timed: 7 minutes

Scoring: Hand key

Cost: Test $0.35–$0.43 per applicant, depending on volume ordered

Publisher: Life Office Management Association

JOB EFFECTIVENESS PREDICTION SYSTEM: VERBAL COMPREHENSION (JEPS: TEST CODE H)

Personnel Decisions Research Institute for Life Office Management Association

Adult

Purpose: Measures general word knowledge. Used for selection and placement of entry-level clerical and technical/professional employees in life and property/casualty insurance companies.

Description: 35–item paper-pencil multiple-choice test measuring vocabulary and word knowledge. The words tested are general vocabulary words rather than words from specialized or esoteric vocabularies. Use is restricted to insurance companies. Examiner required. Suitable for group use.

Timed: 6 minutes

Scoring: Hand key

Cost: Test $0.35–$0.43 per applicant, depending on volume ordered

Publisher: Life Office Management Association

JOB PERFORMANCE SCALES SET: PRIMARY RATING #2

Refer to page 1007.

JOB SEARCH ASSESSMENT

Refer to page 845.

JOB TRAINING ASSESSMENT PROGRAM (JOBTAP)

Refer to page 846.

KEY EDUCATIONAL VOCATIONAL ASSESSMENT SYSTEM (KEVAS)

Refer to page 846.

LICENSURE, CERTIFICATION, REGISTRATION, AND QUALIFYING EXAMINATIONS: ADMISSIONS AND CREDENTIALING GROUP

The Psychological Corporation

Adult

Purpose: Assesses skills and competence of professionals in various areas. Used by local, state, and national organizations and agencies for licensing, certifying, registering, and qualifying members of their respective occupations.

Description: Multiple-item paper-pencil tests used to establish credentials attesting to the skill and competence of those professionals meeting or exceeding minimum standards. Some of the programs administered by the Admissions and Credentialing Group are the Certifying Examination for Surgical Technologists for the Association of Surgical Technologists; the Certification Examination for Rehabilitation Nursing for the Association of Rehabilitation Nurses; the Registration Examination for Electroencephalographic Technologists for the American Board of Registration of Electroencephalographic Technologists; and the Certification Examination for Professional Marketing Communicators for the Business/Professional Advertising Association. Tests are administered in designated test centers. Applicants must complete and file an application and the appropriate fee by specific deadlines. For specific content and cost information, contact the publisher or the relevant association. Examiner required. Suitable for group use.

Timed: See individual listings

Scoring: See individual listings

Cost: Contact publisher

Publisher: Admissions and Credentialing Group/The Psychological Corporation

Information and availability unconfirmed; last verified in 1988.

LIGONDE EQUIVALENCE TEST
Paultre Ligonde

Adult

Purpose: Measures grade-level ability of adults who have been out of school 20–30 years. Used when determination of school grade level is relevant to employment qualifications and for placement in adult education programs.

Description: Multiple-item paper-pencil test assessing the grade level of adults who have been out of school several years. Scoring is based on what students from a particular grade level should retain in terms of verbal and numerical skills. The test is used to select employees for positions requiring verbal communication or clerical skills, to determine school levels for trade or labor unions, and to issue competency cards. The test was normed on 3,000 French and English Canadians who left school 20–30 years ago. The test is available in two forms, GE and HE. Both include questions on knowledge of the second language. Examiner required. Suitable for group use.
CANADIAN PUBLISHER

Timed: 15 minutes

Scoring: Hand key

Cost: Specimen key $12.00

Publisher: Institute of Psychological Research, Inc.

LIVING SKILLS

Adolescent, adult

Purpose: Measures functional literacy.

Description: Self-paced audiovisual format assessment addressing five basic skills—reading, writing, speaking/listening, computation, and problem solving—as each touches upon five different functional knowledge areas: government and law, occupational knowledge, health, community resources, and consumer education. Response items are woven into a series of 18 high-interest adventures involving fictional people of varying ethnic, sex, and race characteristics. The action stops and the individual is asked to respond to a question that is an outgrowth of the story line. The computer-scored report provides individual and group performance scales for each of the skills and knowledge areas. The results also place the individual in one of three Adult Performance Levels derived by the USOE Adult Functional Competency Study. The results include prescriptions for improvement. Examiner/self-administered. Not suitable for group use.

Untimed: Varies according to ability

Scoring: Computer scored on-site or by publisher

Cost: Contact publisher

Publisher: Prep, A Division of Educational Technologies Inc.

MATHEMATICAL ACHIEVEMENT TEST

Adult

Purpose: Measures general skills of algebra, geometry, and mathematics at the secondary-school level. Used in employee selection for clerical and technical positions.

Description: Multiple-item paper-pencil achievement test assessing the extent to which the subject can apply the principles of algebra, geometry, and general mathematics as taught in secondary schools. Norms are based on a group of matriculated boys and girls. The test is restricted to competent persons properly registered with the South African Medical and Dental Council. Examiner required. Suitable for group use. Afrikaans version available. SOUTH AFRICAN PUBLISHER

Timed: 23 minutes

Scoring: Hand key; examiner evaluated

Cost: Contact publisher

Publisher: National Institute for Personnel Research

MEEKER BEHAVIOR CORRELATES FOR MANAGEMENT MATCHING OF TEAMS
Refer to page 1010.

MESA
Refer to page 848.

MESA SF2
Refer to page 848.

MINNESOTA ENGINEERING ANALOGIES TEST
Refer to page 788.

NATIONAL INSTITUTE FOR AUTOMOTIVE SERVICE EXCELLENCE (ASE) TESTS

Adult

Purpose: Measure diagnostic and repair knowledge and skills in various areas of automotive service and repair. Used for ASE certification, to identify areas where additional training is needed, and to match technical skills to jobs in the automotive industry.

Description: 16 multiple-item multiple-choice tests covering practical problems of diagnosis and repair. There are eight Automobile tests: Engine Repair (80 items), Automatic Transmission/Transaxle (40 items), Manual Drive Train and Axles (40 items), Suspension and Steering (40 items), Brakes (40 items), Electrical Systems (40 items), Heating and Air Conditioning (40 items), and Engine Performance (80 items). To become certified in a given automobile service area, an examinee must pass the test for that area. To become certified as a Master Automobile Technician, the examinee must pass all eight tests in the series.

Six tests comprise the Heavy-Duty Truck series: Gasoline Engines (80 items), Diesel Engines (80 items), Drive Train (60 items), Brakes (60 items), Suspension and Steering (60 items), and Electrical Systems (40 items). An examinee must pass the test for the particular truck service area in which he desires to be certified. To become certified as a Master Heavy-Duty Truck Technician, the examinee must pass either the Gasoline Engines Test or the Diesel Engines Test, as well as the remaining four tests in the series.

The Body Repair—Painting/Refinishing series consists of two tests: Body Repair (40 items) and Painting and Refinishing (40 items).

The tests in the ASE series are administered by the American College Testing (ACT) Program at over 400 testing centers nationwide in May and November each year. A total of four tests may be taken on one testing date provided the items do not total more than 200. Results are sent directly to the examinee within 8 weeks of testing. In addition to passing the required test, examinees must have at least 2 years of experience in the area to qualify for certification. Education credits may be substituted for up to 1 year of experience. See individual test descriptions for more detailed information about each test. New forms of the tests are developed every May and November by a workshop group of 15–16 experts. The tests are monitored and controlled by the Automotive and Truck Service Repair Industry. Every test applicant is sent a preparation guide. Examiner required. Suitable for group use.

Timed: Not available

Scoring: Computer scored

Cost: $15.00 per test; $20.00 registration fee per session

Publisher: National Institute for Automotive Service Excellence

---

NATIONAL INSTITUTE FOR AUTOMOTIVE SERVICE EXCELLENCE (ASE) TESTS: AUTOMOBILE TESTS: AUTOMATIC TRANSMISSION/TRANSAXLE

Adult

Purpose: Measures diagnostic and repair knowledge and skills required for ASE automatic transmission/transaxle certification. Also used to identify areas where additional training is needed.

Description: 40–item paper-pencil multiple-choice test assessing an individual's automatic transmission/transaxle knowledge and skill, including controls and linkages and hydraulic and mechanical systems. See National Institute for Automotive Service Excellence (ASE) Tests for information concerning administration and reporting of results. Examiner required. Suitable for group use.

Timed: Not available

Scoring: Computer scored

Cost: $15.00 test fee; $20.00 registration fee

Publisher: National Institute for Automotive Service Excellence

---

NATIONAL INSTITUTE FOR AUTOMOTIVE SERVICE EXCELLENCE (ASE) TESTS: AUTOMOBILE TESTS: BRAKES

Adult

Purpose: Measures diagnostic and repair knowledge and skills required for ASE certification in brake repair. Also used to identify areas where additional training is needed.

Description: 40–item paper-pencil multiple-choice test assessing an individual's knowledge of and skills in brake repair, including drum, disc, combination, and parking brake systems and power assist and hydraulic systems. See National Institute for Automotive Service Excellence (ASE) Tests for information about administration and reporting of results. Examiner required. Suitable for group use.

Timed: Not available

Scoring: Computer scored

Cost: $15.00 test fee; $20.00 registration fee

Publisher: National Institute for Automotive Service Excellence

---

NATIONAL INSTITUTE FOR AUTOMOTIVE SERVICE EXCELLENCE (ASE) TESTS: AUTOMOBILE TESTS: ELECTRICAL SYSTEMS

Adult

Purpose: Measures diagnostic and repair knowledge and skills required for ASE certification in electrical systems. Also used to identify areas where additional training is needed.

Description: 40–item paper-pencil multiple-choice test assessing an individual's knowledge of and skills in electrical systems, including batteries; starting, charging, lighting, and signaling systems; and electrical instruments and accessories. See National Institute for Automotive Service Excellence (ASE) Tests for information about administration and reporting of results. Examiner required. Suitable for group use.

Timed: Not available

Scoring: Computer scored

Cost: $15.00 test fee; $20.00 registration fee

Publisher: National Institute for Automotive Service Excellence

---

NATIONAL INSTITUTE FOR AUTOMOTIVE SERVICE EXCELLENCE (ASE) TESTS: AUTOMOBILE TESTS: ENGINE PERFORMANCE

Adult

Purpose: Measures diagnostic and repair knowledge and skills required for ASE certification in engine performance. Also used to identify areas where additional training is needed.

Description: 80–item paper-pencil multiple-choice test assessing an individual's knowledge of and skills in engine performance, including general engine diagnosis, specific diagnosis and repair of battery, starting, ignition, fuel, exhaust, emission control, and cooling systems. The fuel system section requires examinees to choose between items dealing with either carburetion or import vehicle fuel injection (both electronic and non-electronic). See National Institute for Automotive Service Excellence (ASE) Tests for information about administration and reporting of results. Examiner required. Suitable for group use.

Timed: Not available

Scoring: Computer scored

Cost: $15.00 test fee; $20.00 registration fee

Publisher: National Institute for Automotive Service Excellence

NATIONAL INSTITUTE FOR AUTOMOTIVE SERVICE EXCELLENCE (ASE) TESTS: AUTOMOBILE TESTS: ENGINE REPAIR

Adult

Purpose: Measures diagnostic and repair knowledge and skills required for ASE certification in engine repair. Also used to identify areas where additional training is needed.

Description: 80–item paper-pencil multiple-choice test assessing an individual's knowledge of and skills in engine repair, including valve train, cylinder head, and block assemblies; lubricating, cooling, ignition, fuel, exhaust; and battery and starting systems. See National Institute for Automotive Service Excellence (ASE) Tests for information regarding administration and reporting of results. Examiner required. Suitable for group use.

Timed: Not available

Scoring: Computer scored

Cost: $15.00 test fee; $20.00 registration fee

Publisher: National Institute for Automotive Service Excellence

NATIONAL INSTITUTE FOR AUTOMOTIVE SERVICE EXCELLENCE (ASE) TESTS: AUTOMOBILE TESTS: HEATING AND AIR CONDITIONING

Adult

Purpose: Measures diagnostic and repair knowledge and skills required for ASE certification in heating and air conditioning. Also used to identify areas where additional training is needed.

Description: 40–item paper-pencil multiple-choice test assessing an individual's knowledge of and skills in heating and air conditioning, including refrigeration, heating and ventilating, and air conditioning controls. See National Institute for Automotive Service Excellence (ASE) Tests for information about administration and reporting of results. Examiner required. Suitable for group use.

Timed: Not available

Scoring: Computer scored

Cost: $15.00 test fee; $20.00 registration fee

Publisher: National Institute for Automotive Service Excellence

NATIONAL INSTITUTE FOR AUTOMOTIVE SERVICE EXCELLENCE (ASE) TESTS: AUTOMOBILE TESTS: MANUAL DRIVE TRAIN AND AXLES

Adult

Purpose: Measures diagnostic and repair knowledge and skills required for ASE certification in manual drive trains and axles. Also used to identify areas where additional training is needed.

Description: 40–item paper-pencil multiple-choice test assessing skills and knowledge of manual drive trains and axles, including manual transmissions, transaxles, clutches, front and rear drive systems. See National Institute for Automotive Service Excellence (ASE) Tests for information about administration and reporting of results. Examiner required. Suitable for group use.

Timed: Not available

Scoring: Computer scored

Cost: $15.00 test fee; $20.00 registration fee

Publisher: National Institute for Automotive Service Excellence

NATIONAL INSTITUTE FOR AUTOMOTIVE SERVICE EXCELLENCE (ASE) TESTS: AUTOMOBILE TESTS: SUSPENSION AND STEERING

Adult

Purpose: Measures diagnostic and repair knowledge and skills required for ASE certification in suspension and steering. Also used to identify areas where additional training is needed.

Description: 40–item paper-pencil multiple-choice test assessing an individual's knowledge of and skills in suspension and steering, including manual and power steering, suspension systems, alignment, and wheels and tires. See National Institute for Automotive Service Excellence (ASE) Tests for information about administration and reporting of results. Examiner required. Suitable for group use.

Timed: Not available

Scoring: Computer scored

Cost: $15.00 test fee; $20.00 registration fee

Publisher: National Institute for Automotive Service Excellence

NATIONAL INSTITUTE FOR AUTOMOTIVE SERVICE EXCELLENCE (ASE) TESTS: BODY REPAIR—PAINTING/ REFINISHING TESTS: BODY REPAIR

Adult

Purpose: Measures diagnostic and repair knowledge and skills required for ASE certification in body repair. Also used to identify areas where additional training is needed.

Description: 40–item paper-pencil multiple-choice test assessing an individual's knowledge of and skill in body repair. Areas covered include unibody and frame-type body inspection and repair; outer panel repairs; metal finishing; body filling; and fiberglass, plastic, glass, and hardware repairs. See National Institute for Automotive Service Excellence (ASE) Tests for information about administration and reporting of results. Examiner required. Suitable for group use.

Timed: Not available

Scoring: Computer scored

Cost: $15.00 test fee; $20.00 registration fee

Publisher: National Institute for Automotive Service Excellence

NATIONAL INSTITUTE FOR AUTOMOTIVE SERVICE EXCELLENCE (ASE) TESTS: BODY REPAIR—PAINTING/ REFINISHING TESTS: PAINTING AND REFINISHING

Adult

Purpose: Measures diagnostic and repair knowledge and skills required for ASE certification in painting and refinishing. Also used to identify areas where additional training is needed.

Description: 40–item paper-pencil multiple-choice test assessing an individual's knowledge of and skill in painting and refinishing. Areas covered include equipment, preparation, undercoating, mixing and color matching, solving paint application problems, correcting finish defects, and safety. See National Institute for Automotive Service Excellence (ASE) Tests for information about administration and reporting of results. Examiner required. Suitable for group use.

Timed: Not available

Scoring: Computer scored

Cost: $15.00 test fee; $20.00 registration fee

Publisher: National Institute for Automotive Service Excellence

NATIONAL INSTITUTE FOR AUTOMOTIVE SERVICE EXCELLENCE (ASE) TESTS: HEAVY-DUTY TRUCK TESTS: BRAKES

Adult

Purpose: Measures diagnostic and repair knowledge and skills required for ASE brake certification. Also used to identify areas where additional training is needed.

Description: 60–item paper-pencil multiple-choice test assessing an individual's knowledge of and skill in brake repair, including air, hydraulic (manual and power-assisted), and parking brake systems as well as wheel bearings. See National Institute for Automotive Service Excellence (ASE) Tests for information about administration and reporting of results. Examiner required. Suitable for group use.

Timed: Not available

Scoring: Computer scored

Cost: $15.00 test fee; $20.00 registration fee

Publisher: National Institute for Automotive Service Excellence

NATIONAL INSTITUTE FOR AUTOMOTIVE SERVICE EXCELLENCE (ASE): HEAVY-DUTY TRUCK TESTS: DIESEL ENGINES

Adult

Purpose: Measures diagnostic and repair knowledge and skills required for ASE certification in diesel engines. Also used to identify areas where additional training is needed.

Description: 80–item paper-pencil multiple-choice test assessing an individual's knowledge of and skills in diesel engines, including valve train, cylinder head, and block assemblies and lubricating, cooling,

air induction, fuel, exhaust, starting (air and electrical), and engine braking systems. See National Institute for Automotive Service Excellence (ASE) Tests for information about administration and reporting of scores. Examiner required. Not suitable for group use.

Timed: Not available

Scoring: Computer scored

Cost: $15.00 test fee; $20.00 registration fee

Publisher: National Institute for Automotive Excellence

NATIONAL INSTITUTE FOR AUTOMOTIVE SERVICE EXCELLENCE (ASE) TESTS: HEAVY-DUTY TRUCK TESTS: ELECTRICAL SYSTEMS

Adult

Purpose: Measures diagnostic and repair knowledge and skills required for ASE certification in electrical systems. Also used to identify areas where additional training is needed.

Description: 40–item paper-pencil multiple-choice test assessing an individual's knowledge of and skills in electrical systems. Areas covered include batteries; starting, charging, lighting, and signaling (lights and horn) systems; and electrical instruments and accessories. See National Institute for Automotive Service Excellence (ASE) Tests for information about administration and reporting of results. Examiner required. Suitable for group use.

Timed: Not available

Scoring: Computer scored

Cost: $15.00 test fee; $20.00 registration fee

Publisher: National Institute for Automotive Service Excellence

NATIONAL INSTITUTE FOR AUTOMOTIVE SERVICE EXCELLENCE (ASE) TESTS: HEAVY-DUTY TRUCK TESTS: GASOLINE ENGINES

Adult

Purpose: Measures diagnostic and repair knowledge and skills required for ASE certification in gasoline engines. Also used to identify areas where additional training is needed.

Description: 80–item paper-pencil multiple-choice test assessing an individual's knowledge of and skills in gasoline engines, including valve train, cylinder head, and block assemblies; lubricating, cooling, ignition, fuel, exhaust, emission control; and battery and starting systems. See National Institute for Automotive Service Excellence (ASE) Tests for information about administration and reporting of results. Examiner required. Suitable for group use.

Timed: Not available

Scoring: Computer scored

Cost: $15.00 test fee; $20.00 registration fee

Publisher: National Institute for Automotive Service Excellence

NATIONAL INSTITUTE FOR AUTOMOTIVE SERVICE EXCELLENCE (ASE) TESTS: HEAVY-DUTY TRUCK TESTS: SUSPENSION AND STEERING

Adult

Purpose: Measures diagnostic and repair knowledge and skills required for ASE certification in suspension and steering. Also used to identify areas where additional training is needed.

Description: 60–item paper-pencil multiple-choice test assessing an individual's knowledge of and skills in suspension and steering, including steering (manual and power) and front and rear suspension systems and tires, wheels, wheel bearings, and alignment. The suspension systems covered by this test are those that are used with both single and tandem drive axles. In addition, some items cover fifth-wheel units linking tractors and trailers. See National Institute for Automotive Service Excellence (ASE) Tests for information about administration and reporting of results. Examiner required. Suitable for group use.

Timed: Not available

Scoring: Computer scored

Cost: $15.00 test fee; $20.00 registration fee

Publisher: National Institute for Automotive Service Excellence

NON-READING APTITUDE BATTERY (NATB)
U.S. Employment Service

Adult

Purpose: Measures vocational aptitudes of individuals with a low level of literacy skills. Used for vocational counseling and employment screening.

Description: 14 subtests measuring the following nine aptitudes to help individuals with low reading skills choose an occupation: general learning ability, verbal ability, numerical ability, spatial aptitude, form perception, clerical perception, motor coordination, finger dexterity, and manual dexterity. The aptitudes are tested through procedures that involve neither reading nor writing. The subject's performance is interpreted according to the Occupational Aptitude Patterns (OAPs). The subject's scores are compared to those of successful individuals in various occupations. High, medium, or low probability of success in different employment settings is estimated for the individual. Materials consist of test booklets in which all answers are marked, a pegboard for place and turn tests, and a finger dexterity board. Use in the United States must be authorized by State Employment Service Agencies and in Canada by the Canadian Employment and Immigration Commission. Examiner required. Suitable for group use.

Timed: Varies

Scoring: Hand key

Cost: Available through State Employment Service Agencies only

Publisher: U.S. Department of Labor

Information and availability unconfirmed; last verified in 1988.

NORMAL, INTERMEDIATE AND HIGH LEVEL BATTERIES

Adult

Purpose: Measures mental abilities and verbal skills related to many clerical and technical positions. Suitable for matriculants and higher.

Description: Three batteries of paper-pencil tests measuring three levels of mental and verbal abilities. The Normal Battery, used with standards 6–10 and job applicants with 8–11 years of education, contains five tests: Mental Alertness, Reading Comprehension, Vocabulary, Spelling, and Computation. The Intermediate Battery, used with standards 7–10 and job applicants with 9–12 years of education, contains seven tests covering mental alertness, arithmetical problems, computation, spotting errors, reading comprehension, vocabulary, and spelling. The High Level Battery, used with a wide range of groups at matric and higher levels, contains six tests: Mental Alertness, Arithmetical Problems, Reading Comprehension (English, Afrikaans) and vocabulary (English, Afrikaans). Norms are provided for all three batteries for their appropriate levels. The test is restricted to competent persons properly registered with the South African medical and Dental Council. Examiner required. Suitable for group use. Afrikaans version available.
SOUTH AFRICAN PUBLISHER

Timed: Normal 120 minutes; Intermediate 165 minutes; High Level 117 minutes

Scoring: Hand key; examiner evaluated

Cost: Contact publisher

Publisher: National Institute for Personnel Research

ONE MINUTE PER-FLU-DEX TESTS
F.J. Holmes

Adult

Purpose: Measures abilities desired in factory and office jobs. Used for evaluation of job applicants.

Description: Seven paper-pencil tests measuring office and industrial skills. The tests are Per-Symb, measuring symbol number substitution; Per-Verb, measuring letter perception and counting; Per-Numb, measuring number perception and counting; Flu-Verb, measuring word completion and verbal fluency; Flu-Num, measuring arithmetical computation; Dex-Man, measuring manual speed of movement; and Dex-Aim, measuring aiming accuracy and speed. Materials include profile-guidance sheets. Each test may be purchased and used separately. Examiner required. Suitable for group use.

Timed: 1 minute per test

Scoring: Hand key

Cost: Specimen set $5.00; 25 tests (specify test) $2.75; 25 profiles $2.75

Publisher: Psychometric Affiliates

PERSONNEL TEST BATTERY (PTB)
Saville & Holdsworth Ltd.

Adult

Purpose: Evaluates skills relevant to any job that requires the quick and accurate routine use of numbers, words, and other symbols. Assesses skills required for clerks, bookkeepers, typists, data processors, salespersons, nurses, and others.

Description: Six paper-pencil multiple-choice aptitude tests arranged in two levels. Both levels assess language proficiency, numeracy, and perceptual accuracy. Level 1 measures these abilities in terms of basic skills and comprehension and includes the following tests: Verbal Usage (VP1), Numerical Computation (NP2), and Checking (CP3). Level 2 measures similar skills at a more advanced level involving higher order reasoning and includes the following tests: Verbal Meaning (VP5), Numerical Reasoning (NP6), and Classification (CP4). Together, the tests cover a wide range of abilities for persons with no formal educational background through the GCE "O" level and "A" level. Two optional tests measuring basic clerical checking skills are available: Basic Checking (CP7) and Audio Checking (CP8). The combination of PTB tests

administered will depend on the specific job and its context. Examiner required. Suitable for group use.
BRITISH PUBLISHER

Timed: 71 minutes complete battery; 7–10 minutes per test

Scoring: Hand key; may be computer scored

Cost: Complete (question booklets, keys, administration cards, profile charts, score sheets, test logs) $829.50

Publisher: Saville & Holdsworth Ltd.

PERSONNEL TEST BATTERY: AUDIO CHECKING (PTB:CP8)
Refer to page 939.

PERSONNEL TEST BATTERY: BASIC CHECKING (PTB:CP7)
Saville & Holdsworth Ltd.

Adult

Purpose: Tests for speed and accuracy in checking a variety of materials at a very basic level. Used for selection of clerical and general staff concerned with simple routine checking.

Description: 80–item paper-pencil multiple-choice test consisting of two subtests. One involves checking a list of numbers, and the other involves checking a list of letters. In each list, a series of strings of numbers or letters is presented. These are compared with another page from which the identical string must be selected (from five choices). The test is suitable for individuals with minimal educational qualifications to GCE "A" level. Examiner required. Suitable for group use.
BRITISH PUBLISHER

Timed: 10 minutes

Scoring: Hand key; examiner evaluated; may be computer scored

Cost: 10 question booklets $46.50; 50 answer sheets $46.20; key $9.50; administration card $9.50

Publisher: Saville & Holdsworth Ltd.

PERSONNEL TEST BATTERY: CHECKING (PTB:CP3)
Saville & Holdsworth Ltd.

Adult

Purpose: Measures ability to perceive and check a variety of material quickly and accurately. Used for personnel selection of office, sales, or general staff positions.

Description: 40–item paper-pencil proofreading test in which two lists of information about hotels are presented. One list is handwritten and the other is printed. The material contained in the lists includes names, numbers, and symbols. The candidates must compare the two lists and note any errors in accordance with a given code (designed to represent a real clerical task). The test is suitable for individuals with minimal educational qualifications to GCE "A" level. Examiner required. Suitable for group use.
BRITISH PUBLISHER

Timed: 7 minutes

Scoring: Hand key; examiner evaluated; may be computer scored

Cost: 10 question booklets $46.50; 50 answer sheets $46.50; key $9.50; administration card $9.50

Publisher: Saville & Holdsworth Ltd.

PERSONNEL TEST BATTERY: CLASSIFICATION (PTB:CP4)
Refer to page 940.

PERSONNEL TEST BATTERY: NUMERICAL COMPUTATION (PTB:NP2)
Saville & Holdsworth Ltd.

Adult

Purpose: Measures ability to work with numbers. Used for selection of clerical, sales, and general staff.

Description: 30–item paper-pencil multiple-choice test measuring the understanding of relationships between numbers and operations, as well as quick and accurate calculation. In each item, one number has been omitted from an equation. The examinee must select (from five choices) the number that will correctly complete the equation. Simple fractions and decimals are used, and some problems are expressed in numbers, but more complex notation or operations are deliberately omitted. The test is suitable for individuals with minimal educational qualifications to GCE "O" level. Examiner required. Suitable for group use. BRITISH PUBLISHER

Timed: 7 minutes

Scoring: Hand key; examiner evaluated; may be computer scored

Cost: 10 question booklets $40.50; 50 answer sheets $46.50; key $9.50; administration card $9.50

Publisher: Saville & Holdsworth Ltd.

PERSONNEL TEST BATTERY: NUMERICAL REASONING (PTB:NP6)
Saville & Holdsworth Ltd.

Adult

Purpose: Measures simple numerical reasoning skills. Used to select clerical, sales, or general staff.

Description: 30–item paper-pencil multiple-choice test consisting of word problems with numerical answers. Some calculation is involved, but understanding, reasoning, and recognizing shortcut methods is emphasized. The problems cover basic arithmetic operations, simple percentages, fractions, decimals, and graphs. The questions are all given a commercial slant and involve working out sale or purchase prices, profit margins, markups, change, weights, times, and areas. The test is suitable for individuals from GCE "O" to GCE "A" level. Examiner required. Suitable for group use. BRITISH PUBLISHER

Timed: 10 minutes

Scoring: Hand key; examiner evaluated; may be computer scored

Cost: 10 question booklets $46.50; 50 answer sheets $46.50; key $9.50; administration card $9.50

Publisher: Saville & Holdsworth Ltd.

PERSONNEL TEST BATTERY: VERBAL MEANING (PTB:VP5)
Saville & Holdsworth Ltd.

Adult

Purpose: Assesses an individual's knowledge of the meaning of words and the relationships between them. Used for selection with any job in which verbal communication skills are important.

Description: 30–item paper-pencil multiple-choice test requiring the candidate to identify the relationship (same or opposite) between one pair of words and to select (from five choices) the word that relates in the same way to a third given word. The vocabulary used is nonspecialist, everyday language. VP5 is more difficult than VP1 of the same battery. The test is suitable for individuals from the ACE "O" level to GCE "A" level. Examiner required. Suitable for group use. BRITISH PUBLISHER

Timed: 10 minutes

Scoring: Hand key; examiner evaluated; may be computer scored

Cost: 10 question booklets $46.50; 50 answer sheets $46.50; key $9.50; administration card $9.50

Publisher: Saville & Holdsworth Ltd.

PERSONNEL TEST BATTERY: VERBAL USAGE (PTB:VP1)
Saville & Holdsworth Ltd.

Adult

Purpose: Measures ability for spelling, grammar, and choice of words. Used in job placement involving the receipt, processing, or drafting of correspondence.

Description: 30–item paper-pencil multiple-choice test in which each item consists of a sentence from which two words have been omitted. The candidate must choose (from five choices) the correct pair of words to complete the sentence. The sentences consist of words and phrases commonly found in commercial correspondence. The test is suitable for individuals with minimal educational qualifications to GCE "O" level. Examiner required. Suitable for group use.

BRITISH PUBLISHER

Timed: 10 minutes

Scoring: Hand key; examiner evaluated; may be computer scored

Cost: 10 question booklets $46.50; 50 answer sheets $46.50; key $9.50; administration card $9.50

Publisher: Saville & Holdsworth Ltd.

PERSONNEL TESTS FOR INDUSTRY (PTI)
A.G. Wesman and J.E. Doppelt

Adult

Purpose: Assesses general ability. Used to select workers for skilled positions in industrial settings.

Description: Multiple-item paper-pencil multiple-choice tests covering two dimensions of general ability: verbal and numerical competence. Some items involve problem solving. Two equivalent forms and tapes for administering the test are available. Examiner required. Suitable for group use.

Timed: Verbal 5 minutes; numerical 20 minutes

Scoring: Hand key

Cost: Specimen set (both forms of Verbal and Numerical booklets, manual) $19.00; 25 tests, manual, key (specify Verbal or Numerical, Form A or B) $34.00

Publisher: The Psychological Corporation

Information and availability unconfirmed; last verified in 1988.

PERSONNEL TESTS FOR INDUSTRY—ORAL DIRECTIONS TEST (PTI-ODT)
C.R. Langmuir

Adult

Purpose: Measures ability to understand and follow oral directions. Used in the selection of applicants with a limited education and/or knowledge of English.

Description: Multiple-item paper-pencil test covering the ability to follow oral directions. The applicant responds to

instructions dictated on tape by marking the answer document. Two equivalent forms, S and T, are available. Examiner required. Suitable for group use.

Timed: 15 minutes

Scoring: Hand key

Cost: Complete set (recording, manual, script, key, 100 answer documents) $89.00; reel-to-reel tape version $89.00; cassette tape version $89.00; record version $89.00

Publisher: The Psychological Corporation

Information and availability unconfirmed; last verified in 1988.

PRESS TEST
Refer to page 1056.

PROGRAM FOR ASSESSING YOUTH EMPLOYMENT SKILLS (PAYES)
Refer to page 850.

THE RBH ARITHMETIC REASONING TEST, FORMS I AND II
Richardson, Bellows, Henry and Company, Inc.

Adult

Purpose: Assesses an individual's ability to solve problems using basic arithmetical operations. Used with technical and professional employees, sales employees, clerical employees, and mechanical and operating personnel.

Description: 25–item paper-pencil test assessing an individual's ability to solve arithmetic problems covering the following areas: determination of selling price, distribution of costs, discounting, production rates, wage and salary rates, payments, overtime procedures, deductions, tax operations, dividend and profit determinations, percentages, and proportions. Examinees mark their answers directly in the test book in boxes placed next to the problem. Space for figuring the problems is provided. The score is the number of items answered correctly. The test is available in two forms, I and II. Examiner required. Suitable for group use.

Timed: 15 minutes

Scoring: Hand key

Cost: 1–24 packages $25.00; score key $4.00; manual $8.00

Publisher: Richardson, Bellows, Henry and Company, Inc.

RC TECHNICIAN ELECTRICAL TEST
Ramsay Corporation

Adult

Purpose: Measures knowledge and skills in various electrical areas.

Description: 117–item paper-pencil multiple-choice test covering motors (17 items), digital electronics (8 items), analog electronics (12 items), print reading (11 items), control circuits (13 items), power supplies (10 items), basic AC and DC theory (11 items), power distribution (6 items), test instruments (8 items), mechanical (11 items), computers and PLC (5 items), hand and power tools (6 items), electrical maintenance (8 items), and construction and installation (6 items). A scoring service is available from the publisher. Examiner required. Suitable for group use.

Untimed: 2 hours

Scoring: Hand key; may be machine scored

Cost: Kit $498.00 (10 test booklets, 100 answer sheets, scoring key, test manual)

Publisher: Ramsay Corporation

RCJS ARITHMETIC TEST—FORM A
Ramsay Corporation

Adult

Purpose: Measures the ability of industrial workers to perform basic computations.

Description: 24–item paper-pencil multiple-choice test assessing the ability to perform computations involving addition, subtraction, multiplication, and division of whole numbers and fractions. Examiner required. Suitable for group use.

Timed: 20 minutes

Scoring: Hand key

Cost: 20 consumable booklets $40.00; manual with scoring key $24.95

Publisher: Ramsay Corporation

RCJS ELECTRONICS TEST
Ramsay Corporation

Adult

Purpose: Measures knowledge and skill in the area of electronics.

Description: 125–item paper-pencil multiple-choice test assessing AC/DC theory (15 items), digital electronics (16 items), analog electronics (12 items), print reading (7 items), power supplies (11 items), regulators (9 items), test instruments (11 items), motors (5 items), electronic equipment (7 items), radio theory (5 items), power distribution (4 items), and mechanical (4 items). The test is available in two forms, F and G. Examiner required. Suitable for group use.

Untimed: 2 hours

Scoring: Hand key; may be machine scored through publisher

Cost: Kit (10 test booklets, 100 answer sheets, scoring key, test manual) $498.00

Publisher: Ramsay Corporation

RCJS MEASUREMENT TEST— FORM A
Ramsay Corporation

Adult

Purpose: Assesses an individual's ability to measure accurately with a ruler. Used to predict job performance in areas such as maintenance, machine operation, and quality control.

Description: 20–item paper-pencil multiple-choice test designed to assess an individual's ability to measure accurately with a scale in rule dimensions of wholes, halves, quarters, eighths, and sixteenths. The test is available in two forms, A and B. Examiner required. Suitable for group use.

Timed: 15 minutes

Scoring: Hand key

Cost: 20 consumable booklets $40.00; manual with scoring key $24.95

Publisher: Ramsay Corporation

RCJS READING PRINTS AND DRAWINGS
R. T. Ramsay

Adult

Purpose: Assesses ability to read mechanical prints and drawings. Used for hiring and promotion.

Description: 33–item paper-pencil multiple-choice test assessing ability to read mechanical prints and drawings. Materials include a reusable booklet, answer sheet, and manual with key. Examiner required. Suitable for group use.

Timed: 30 minutes

Scoring: Hand key; machine scored; scoring service available from publisher

Cost: Kit (10 test booklets, 100 answer sheets, scoring key, test manual) $498.00

Publisher: Ramsay Corporation

RCJS READING TEST—FORM A
Ramsay Corporation

Adult

Purpose: Assesses the ability to read, comprehend, and answer written questions.

Description: 40–item paper-pencil multiple-choice test designed to measure an individual's ability to read, comprehend, and answer questions based on a printed passage. The topics of the passages are plant safety, hydraulic systems, industrial machines, lubrication, and operating a computer terminal. Examiner required. Suitable for group use.

Timed: 30 minutes

Scoring: Hand key

Cost: 20 consumable booklets $50.00; manual with scoring key $24.95

Publisher: Ramsay Corporation

READING COMPREHENSION
Richardson, Bellows, Henry and Company, Inc.

Adult

Purpose: Measures reading comprehension of applicants to industrial positions.

Description: Multiple-item paper-pencil test assessing the ability to comprehend reading material related to business and industry. The test contains six articles taken from training and safety manuals and publicity releases. Each article is followed by several questions that test the examinee's understanding of the article. The test is not intended to measure critical thinking. For males, the test has been used almost exclusively with industrial employees and applicants. With a maximum score of 40, examinees average about 30 with a standard deviation of seven. The test also has been used with females in nurses' training and clerical jobs. Examiner required. Suitable for group use.

Timed: 20 minutes

Scoring: Hand key

Cost: 1–24 packages $40.00; score key $4.00; manual $2.00

Publisher: Richardson, Bellows, Henry and Company, Inc.

SCHOLASTIC ABILITIES TEST FOR ADULTS (SATA)
Refer to page 482.

SCHOLASTIC PROFICIENCY TEST—HIGHER PRIMARY LEVEL (SPT-HP)
Refer to page 483.

THE SHAPES ANALYSIS TEST
Alice Heim, K. P. Watts, and V. Simmonds

Adolescent, adult—Ages 13 and older

Purpose: Assesses subjects' ability to mentally manipulate different shapes and sizes of geometric figures. Used for screening for job placement or training.

Description: 36–item paper-pencil multiple-choice test of spatial perception. Each item is comprised of several figures. The subject must visualize how each figure will appear if turned over or around, estimate area, and assess spatial relations. Six items are presented cyclically in order of increasing difficulty. Eighteen items are two-dimensional figures, and the rest are three-dimensional figures. Examiner required. Suitable for group use. BRITISH PUBLISHER

Timed: 25 minutes

Scoring: Hand key; examiner evaluated; scoring service available

Cost: Booklet $3.00; answer sheet $2.00; manual $15.00

Publisher: The Test Agency Ltd.

SHAPES TEST
J.R. Morrisby

Ages 11–adult

Purpose: Measures spatial-perceptual ability. Used in occupations such as design work, drafting, and die-making, which involve diagrammatic representation of real objects and systems.

Description: 60–item paper-pencil multiple-choice instrument, following the principle of spatial tests, in which the subject is required to manipulate figures mentally in three dimensions. Materials include the booklet and manual, specimen set, answer sheets, and the scoring key. The test is restricted to examiners who provide evidence of adequate training and practical experience in the use of such tests. Examiner required. Suitable for group use. BRITISH PUBLISHER

Timed: 10 minutes

Scoring: Hand key; may be computer scored

Cost: Contact publisher

Publisher: Educational and Industrial Test Services, Ltd.

SHOP ARITHMETIC TEST, FORMS I AND II
Richardson, Bellows, Henry and Company, Inc.

Adult

Purpose: Assesses arithmetic reasoning abilities. Used with applicants for operations and craft positions and engineering aides.

Description: 20–item paper-pencil test of mathematical abilities related to industrial situations. Content includes simple arithmetic operations (fractions and decimal fractions form the upper limit) involved in figuring sums or remainders on problems of weight or length; computing measures of distance, area, or volume; and analyzing operations data from tables. Illustrations and diagrams are provided to define and illustrate some problems. Space is provided in the test booklet for figuring problems, and answers are recorded in the margin. The test is available in two forms. Form I was normed on male managers and executives, technical and engineering supervisors, industrial foremen and supervisors, and mechanical and operating employees and applicants. Form II, which is slightly easier than Form I, was normed on male industrial applicants and mechanical and operating employees. Examiner required. Suitable for group use.

Timed: 15 minutes

Scoring: Hand key

Cost: 1–24 packages $30.00; score key $4.00; manual $2.00

Publisher: Richardson, Bellows, Henry and Company, Inc.

SKILLS AND ATTRIBUTES INVENTORY
Melany E. Baehr

Adult

Purpose: Assesses the relative importance of 13 skill and attribute factors necessary for successful job performance and the degree to which the incumbent possesses the skills and attributes. Used for systematic job analysis and for test validation, selection, and placement.

Description: 96–item paper-pencil test measuring general functioning, intelligence, visual acuity, visual coordination skills, physical coordination, mechanical skills, graphic clerical skills, general clerical skills, leadership ability, tolerance in interpersonal relations, organization identification, conscientiousness and reliability, efficiency under stress, and solitary work. Each item is rated on importance to the job on a 4–point, equal-interval scale ranging from "little or none" to "outstanding." An ability form also may be used to assess the incumbent's strength in the relative skills and attributes. Basic reading skills are required. Examiner required. Suitable for group use.

Untimed: 45 minutes

Scoring: Hand key; may be computer scored

Cost: Specimen set $12.00; 25 tests $20.00

Publisher: London House, Inc.

THE SKILLS REQUIRED/THE SKILLS TRAINED (TSR/TST)
John Alden Associates;
A. J. McNamara, William J. Martin,
and Ronald J. Pasternak

Adult

Purpose: Assesses whether applicants possess the personality traits required for performing successful telephone work. Used for recruiting, hiring, assigning, training, and retaining telemarketers for both inbound and outbound positions.

Description: 75–item paper-pencil matching and true-false test assessing an individual's interpersonal skills as they relate to successful performance involving telephone work. Fifty items are personal evaluation statements requiring "true, false, or maybe" responses. The remaining 25 items are presented in a matching format that requires the examinee to match the number of the appropriate synonym or antonym with the 25 words. The responses are entered into a computer and processed, yielding the following scores: assertiveness, persuasiveness, steadiness,

thoroughness, verbal skills, and teamness. Narrative profiles interpreting the scores with training suggestions for improvement may be generated. This computer scoring software is available for IBM PC and compatible systems. In addition, for companies without computers, a mail-in scoring service is provided by the publisher. A manual is available. Examiner/self-administered. Suitable for group use.

Timed: 25 minutes

Scoring: Computer scored

Cost: $50.00–$12.00 depending on annual volume

Publisher: John Alden Associates; distributed exclusively by Telemarketing Designs, Inc.

SKILLSCAN
Psychometric Research and Development Ltd.

Adult

Purpose: Identifies an individual's strengths and weaknesses, work preferences, and job potential. Used for initial assessment and review of core skills and personal effectiveness in YTS.

Description: Multiple-item paper-pencil assessment used at the beginning of 2–year YTS schemes. The program is designed to establish a base for ongoing interaction between the trainee and trainer. Trainees choose five problem-solving assignments from eight activity areas representing the types of activities encountered in most jobs. To complete the assignments, trainees are encouraged to use illustrations, tables, written explanations, and so forth. Trainees who complete the assignments during their leisure time may reveal their initiative and enterprise skills. Examiner required. Not suitable for group use.

Untimed: 45 minutes

Scoring: Examiner evaluated

Cost: Contact publisher

Publisher: NFER-NELSON Publishing Company Ltd.

SMELL IDENTIFICATION TEST®
Richard L. Doty

All ages

Purpose: Provides a quantitative measure of an individual's ability to smell without the use of chemicals or complex odorant presentation equipment. Designed for use in industrial, academic, or medical settings. Applications include screening of industrial smell and taste panels, evaluation of industrial exposure to airborne chemicals, medical examinations, longitudinal tracking of smell loss or return, and legal determinations of smell function.

Description: Consists of four booklets containing 10 odorants each, one odorant per page. The stimuli are embedded in "scratch n sniff" crystals located on brown strips positioned at the bottom of each page. The individual completes a multiple-choice question for each of the 40 odorant items. The test can detect most malingerers and is sensitive to numerous subject variables, including smoking habits, age, gender, and a number of medical conditions. Total test score is the sum of the number of items correct out of the 40 total. Norms provide percentile values for men and women in 5–year age categories from 5 years of age to 100 years of age and specific function classifications (i.e., normosmia, microsmia or hyposmia, anosmia, probable malingering). Scores also correlate with levels of specific neurotransmitter metabolites in cerebral spinal fluid.

The Pocket Smell Test®, designed for use by medical practitioners and consisting of items selected from the Smell Identification Test arranged in a pocket-sized folded card with instructions, is available. It allows gross olfactory screening. Olfactory abnormalities discovered by this test should be fully characterized using the 40–item Smell Identification Test. Scoring is pass/fail. Japanese, French, and German versions of both tests are under development. Self-administered by reasonably literate persons ages 10 to 70. Should be administered by a test administrator to persons ages 10 and younger or 70 and older. Not suitable for group use.

Untimed: 10–15 minutes

Scoring: Examiner evaluated

Cost: Test and manual (minimum order of 6) $24.95; Pocket Smell Test (minimum order of 50) $1.60 each plus shipping

Publisher: Sensonics, Inc.

SPACE RELATIONS (PAPER PUZZLES)
L.L. Thurstone and T.E. Jeffrey

Adolescent, adult

Purpose: Assesses facility in visual perceptual skills. Used in vocational counseling or for selection for positions requiring mechanical ability and experience.

Description: 30–item paper-pencil test of the ability to visually select a combination of flat pieces that, together, will cover a given two-dimensional space. Examiner required. Suitable for group use.

Timed: 9 minutes

Scoring: Hand key

Cost: Specimen set $8.00; 25 test booklets $20.00

Publisher: London House, Inc.

SPACE THINKING (FLAGS)
L.L. Thurstone and T.E. Jeffrey

Adolescent, adult

Purpose: Assesses the ability to visualize a rigid configuration (a stable figure, drawing, or diagram) when it is moved into different positions. Used for vocational counseling or selection for positions requiring mechanical ability or experience.

Description: 21–item paper-pencil test in which a solid object (flag) is pictured on the left and pictures of six positions into which the object has been moved are on the right. The examinee must identify whether each position represents the same or the opposite side of the object. Examiner required. Suitable for group use.

Timed: 5 minutes

Scoring: Hand key

Cost: Specimen set $8.00; 25 tests $20.00

Publisher: London House, Inc.

SPECIFIC APTITUDE TEST BATTERY (SATB)
U.S. Employment Service

Adult

Purpose: Measures aptitude for specific occupations. Used to select untrained or inexperienced applicants for referrals to specific jobs or occupational training.

Description: Multiple-item paper-pencil test reflecting the aptitude requirements for specific occupations, against which an individual's scores can be matched. Two to four of SATB's aptitude test batteries are derived from the General Aptitude Test Battery (GATB). The SATB score matching process is the same as that for the Occupational Aptitudes Patterns (OAPs). Examiner required. Suitable for group use. Available in Spanish.

Timed: Not available

Scoring: Hand key

Cost: Available through State Employment Service Agencies only

Publisher: U.S. Department of Labor

Information and availability unconfirmed; last verified in 1988.

SRA READING-ARITHMETIC INDEX
SRA Industrial Test Development Staff

Adolescent, adult—Ages 14 and older

Purpose: Assesses general reading and computational achievement. Used for entry-level positions and training programs where basic skills of applicants are often too low to be reliably evaluated by typical selection tests.

Description: Two multiple-item paper-pencil tests measuring reading skills (picture-word association, word decoding, and comprehension of phrases, sentences, and paragraphs) and arithmetic skills (addition and subtraction, multiplication and division, fractional operations, and decimals and percentages). The score reflects the highest developmental level passed. Examiner required. Suitable for group use.

Untimed: 25 minutes per index

Scoring: Self-scored

Cost: 25 test booklets (specify form) $22.00; examiner's manual $10.00

Publisher: SRA/London House

SRA VERBAL FORM
L.L. Thurstone and Thelma Gwinn Thurstone

Adult

Purpose: Measures an individual's overall adaptability and flexibility in comprehending and following instructions and in adjusting to alternating types of problems on the job. Used in both school and industry for selection and placement.

Description: Paper-pencil test of general mental abilities. The test measures both linguistic (vocabulary) and quantitative (arithmetic) factors. Items of both types are interspersed with a time limit. The test is similar to the Thurstone Test of Mental Alertness but has a time limit of 15, rather than 20, minutes. Two equivalent forms are available. Examiner required. Suitable for group use.

Timed: 15 minutes

Scoring: Hand key

Cost: 25 test booklets $30.00; examiner's manual $10.00

Publisher: SRA/London House

STANTON PROFILE
William G. Harris

Adolescent, adult—Ages 16 and older

Purpose: Measures work orientation. Used as a pre-employment screening device.

Description: 160–item paper-pencil true-false test measuring trustworthiness (40 items), adaptability (30 items), motivation (30 items), and service orientation (30 items). The test also contains an Infrequency Scale (15 items) and a Social Desirability Scale (15 items). A scoring service is available from the publisher. Self-administered. Suitable for group use.

Untimed: 20 minutes

Scoring: Computer scored; insta-phone; machine (scannable) scored

Cost: 1–99 phone-in or computer-scored sheets $14.00; price adjustments based on quantity and scoring method

Publisher: The Stanton Corporation

STATION MANAGER APPLICANT INVENTORY (SMAI)
London House, Inc.

Adult

Purpose: Screens gas station dealers and managers for operating a gas station. Also used for franchise screening for gas stations.

Description: 218–item paper-pencil multiple-choice test used for screening station manager applicants. The test contains eight subtests: Background, Managerial Arithmetic, Honesty, Interpersonal Cooperation, Drug Avoidance, Temperament, Understanding Organizational Policies and Practices, and Distortion. Eight subtest scores and a composite Manager Potential Index are generated. Three scoring options are available from London House: operator-assisted telephone, Touch-Test, and PC-based. Operator-assisted scoring involves dialing a London House operator who provides test results after being read a tally of responses by the test administrator. Written confirmation is mailed the following day. Touch-Test telephone scoring allows the test administrator to use the telephone keypad to feed response tallies directly into London House computers. Results are available immediately and written confirmation is mailed the next day. Administrators with IBM PC or compatible equipment may obtain on-site results using the PC-based scoring method. Examiner required. Suitable for group use.

Untimed: 2 hours

Scoring: Computer scored

Cost: $12.00–$25.00 depending on scoring method and volume ordered

Publisher: London House, Inc.

STUDENT OCCUPATIONAL COMPETENCY ACHIEVEMENT TESTING (SOCAT)
Refer to page 306.

STUDENT OCCUPATIONAL COMPETENCY ACHIEVEMENT TESTING: ACCOUNTING/ BOOKKEEPING
Refer to page 274.

STUDENT OCCUPATIONAL COMPETENCY ACHIEVEMENT TESTING: AGRICULTURE MECHANICS
Refer to page 307.

STUDENT OCCUPATIONAL COMPETENCY ACHIEVEMENT TESTING: AUTO BODY
Refer to page 307.

STUDENT OCCUPATIONAL COMPETENCY ACHIEVEMENT TESTING: AUTO MECHANICS
Refer to page 307.

STUDENT OCCUPATIONAL COMPETENCY ACHIEVEMENT TESTING: CARPENTRY
Refer to page 307.

STUDENT OCCUPATIONAL COMPETENCY ACHIEVEMENT TESTING: CONSTRUCTION ELECTRICITY
Refer to page 308.

STUDENT OCCUPATIONAL COMPETENCY ACHIEVEMENT TESTING: CONSTRUCTION MASONRY
Refer to page 308.

**STUDENT OCCUPATIONAL
COMPETENCY ACHIEVEMENT
TESTING: DRAFTING**
Refer to page 308.

**STUDENT OCCUPATIONAL
COMPETENCY ACHIEVEMENT
TESTING: ELECTRONICS**
Refer to page 309.

**STUDENT OCCUPATIONAL
COMPETENCY ACHIEVEMENT
TESTING: GENERAL
MERCHANDISING**
Refer to page 305.

**STUDENT OCCUPATIONAL
COMPETENCY ACHIEVEMENT
TESTING: GENERAL OFFICE**
Refer to page 274.

**STUDENT OCCUPATIONAL
COMPETENCY ACHIEVEMENT
TESTING: GRAPHIC ARTS**
Refer to page 298.

**STUDENT OCCUPATIONAL
COMPETENCY ACHIEVEMENT
TESTING: HEATING AND AIR
CONDITIONING**
Refer to page 309.

**STUDENT OCCUPATIONAL
COMPETENCY ACHIEVEMENT
TESTING: HOME
ENTERTAINMENT EQUIPMENT
REPAIR**
Refer to page 309.

**STUDENT OCCUPATIONAL
COMPETENCY ACHIEVEMENT
TESTING: HORTICULTURE**
Refer to page 310.

**STUDENT OCCUPATIONAL
COMPETENCY ACHIEVEMENT
TESTING: INDUSTRIAL
ELECTRICITY**
Refer to page 310.

**STUDENT OCCUPATIONAL
COMPETENCY ACHIEVEMENT
TESTING: INDUSTRIAL
ELECTRONICS**
Refer to page 310.

**STUDENT OCCUPATIONAL
COMPETENCY ACHIEVEMENT
TESTING: MACHINE TRADES**
Refer to page 310.

**STUDENT OCCUPATIONAL
COMPETENCY ACHIEVEMENT
TESTING: PLUMBING**
Refer to page 311.

**STUDENT OCCUPATIONAL
COMPETENCY ACHIEVEMENT
TESTING: PRACTICAL NURSING**
Refer to page 528.

**STUDENT OCCUPATIONAL
COMPETENCY ACHIEVEMENT
TESTING: REFRIGERATION**
Refer to page 311.

**STUDENT OCCUPATIONAL
COMPETENCY ACHIEVEMENT
TESTING: SEWN PRODUCTS**
Refer to page 305.

**STUDENT OCCUPATIONAL
COMPETENCY ACHIEVEMENT
TESTING: SMALL ENGINE
REPAIR**
Refer to page 311.

**STUDENT OCCUPATIONAL
COMPETENCY ACHIEVEMENT
TESTING: WELDING**
Refer to page 312.

SUICIDE INTERVENTION RESPONSE INVENTORY (SIRI)
Robert A. Neimeyer

Adult

Purpose: Assesses skill in selecting facilitative responses to a suicidal person. Used with mental health paraprofessionals.

Description: 25-item paper-pencil multiple-choice test measuring the ability to recognize appropriate responses for suicide intervention. Subscales include Elaboration of the Complaint, Exploration of Suicidality, Involvement, and Reflection of Negative Feelings. A ninth-grade reading level is required. Self-administered. Suitable for group use.

Untimed: 15 minutes

Scoring: Hand key

Cost: Free

Publisher: Robert A. Neimeyer, Ph.D.

Information and availability unconfirmed; last verified in 1988.

SYSTEM FOR ASSESSMENT AND GROUP EVALUATION (SAGE)
Refer to page 806.

SYSTEM FOR TESTING AND EVALUATION OF POTENTIAL (STEP)
Melany E. Baehr

Adult

Purpose: Estimates potential for successful performance (PSP) and current skills in present and future positions. Used for selection, placement, promotion, succession planning, diagnosis of training needs, individual or management development, strategic reorganization or reassignment, and career or outpatient counseling. Appropriate for use with higher level managerial or professional personnel.

Description: Based on two interlocking paper-pencil measurement systems: The Managerial and Professional Job Functions Inventory (MP-JFI), which analyzes the demands of a job and The Managerial and Professional Test Battery, which assesses an individual's abilities, skills, and attributes.

The program is offered in three versions. A requisite for the implementation of all versions is a job analysis for the position using the MP-JFI. The resultant job functions profile is compared through a computerized program with profiles of the 12 key positions (executive, middle manager, and supervisory/professional personnel levels in each of four managerial hierarchies—line, professional, sales, and technical) based on national samples of higher level employees. The comparison determines which test battery will be used for the position.

The three versions of the program are STEP-S for selection (1½-hour test battery), STEP-ST for selection and training (1½-hour test battery and 30–40–minute job skills questionnaire), and STEP-STC for selection, training, and career counseling (3–4–hour battery and 30–40–minute job skills questionnaire). Given the administration of the relevant test battery and the job skills questionnaire, a single test administration will provide information about the individual's potential for successful performance and present skill level for all three positions in a selected managerial hierarchy. Examiner required. Suitable for group use.

Timed: 1½ to 4½ hours depending on version

Scoring: Mail scoring or ITAC (Immediate Telephone Analysis by Computer)

Cost: Contact publisher; $70.00–$250.00 per test depending on volume ordered

Publisher: London House, Inc.

TECHNICAL AND SCIENTIFIC INFORMATION TEST (A/9) AND TECHNICAL READING COMPREHENSION TEST A/10

Adult

Purpose: Assesses scientific and technical understanding of people with little or no schooling in scientific or technical areas. Used for predicting job success in these fields after training.

Description: Multiple-item paper-pencil tests of general scientific knowledge and

the ability to comprehend technical information. The two tests should be given together and sequentially. The first is a list of questions on general scientific information likely to be known by individuals who have had little or no formal scientific training. The second test consists of five paragraphs assessing whether a person with little or no formal schooling in technical subjects can comprehend articles of a technical nature. The tests predict job success after technical and scientific training. Norms are available. Examiner required. Suitable for group use.
SOUTH AFRICAN PUBLISHER

Timed: 30 minutes

Scoring: Hand key

Cost: Contact publisher

Publisher: Human Sciences Research Council

TECHNICAL AND SCIENTIFIC INFORMATION TEST, TECHNICAL READING COMPREHENSION TEST AND GENERAL SCIENCE TEST

Adolescent, adult

Purpose: Measures technical and scientific knowledge and technical reading comprehension. Used with matriculated students in standards 7–9.

Description: The General Science Test consists of two multiple-item paper-pencil subtests: The Technical and Scientific Information Test, which contains informational questions over general science topics and The Technical Reading Comprehension Test, which contains a number of paragraphs with questions to determine the extent to which articles of a technical nature can be understood. The two tests are administered in separate booklets. The tests are restricted to competent persons properly registered with the South African Medical and Dental Council. Examiner required. Suitable for group use. Available in Afrikaans.
SOUTH AFRICAN PUBLISHER

Timed: Not available

Scoring: Hand key; examiner evaluated

Cost: Contact publisher

Publisher: National Institute for Personnel Research

TECHNICAL TEST BATTERY (TTB)
Saville & Holdsworth Ltd.

Adult

Purpose: Measures comprehension and reasoning skills. Used as a test of aptitude for a wide range of apprentice, technical, and technologist categories.

Description: Eight paper-pencil multiple-choice tests intended for operator, foreman, technician, supervisory, technical sales, and similar occupations. Range extends from those with no formal education to some degree-level candidates. The scales are Following Instructions (VTS1), Numerical Computation (NT2), Numerical Estimation (Nts2), Mechanical Comprehension (Mts3), Spatial Reasoning (St7), Diagrammatic Reasoning (DT8), Diagrammatic Thinking (DTS6), and Fault Finding (FTS4). Examiner required. Suitable for group use.
BRITISH PUBLISHER

Timed: Complete battery 1 hour, 50 minutes

Scoring: Hand key; examiner evaluated; may be computer scored

Cost: Administration set (8 test booklets, answer sheets, administration cards, profile charts, score keys, manual, user's guide) $266.00

Publisher: Saville & Holdsworth Ltd.

TECHNICAL TEST BATTERY: DIAGRAMMATIC REASONING (TTB:DT8; U.S. VERSION)
Saville & Holdsworth Ltd. Staff

Adult

Purpose: Measures diagrammatical reasoning ability. Used for personnel selection for technical occupations and jobs involving systems design, flow charting, and similar skills.

Description: 40–item paper-pencil multiple-choice test consisting of a series of abstract designs in logical sequences. Respondents must select, from five choices, the design that completes the logical sequence. Candidates must think logically and flexibly. Examiner required. Suitable for group use.

Timed: 15 minutes

Scoring: Hand key; examiner evaluated; may be computer scored

Cost: 5 question booklets $115.00; key $13.00; administration card $13.00

Publisher: Saville & Holdsworth Ltd.

TECHNICAL TEST BATTERY: MECHANICAL COMPREHENSION (TTB:MT4)
Saville & Holdsworth Ltd. Staff

Adult

Purpose: Measures understanding of basic mechanical principles. Used in selection and development of craftsmen and technicians.

Description: 40–item paper-pencil multiple-choice test measuring knowledge of the classic mechanical elements, such as gears, pulleys, and levers, and a wide range of domestic and leisure applications of physics and mechanics, from electric ovens to billiard balls. Each item consists of a three-choice question about a technical drawing. The drawings are presented in technical workshop style without demanding any specific preknowledge to interpret them. The range extends from minimal educational qualifications to the GCE "A" level. Examiner required. Suitable for group use.
BRITISH PUBLISHER

Timed: 15 minutes

Scoring: Hand key; examiner evaluated; may be computer scored

Cost: 10 question booklets $36.00; key $9.50; administration card $9.50

Publisher: Saville & Holdsworth Ltd.

TECHNICAL TEST BATTERY: NUMERICAL COMPUTATION (TTB:NT2; U.S. VERSION)
Saville & Holdsworth Ltd. Staff

Adult

Purpose: Measures basic ability to work with numbers in a technical setting. Used for craft apprentice selection.

Description: 40–item paper-pencil multiple-choice test assessing the understanding of mathematical relationships and operations and the ability to calculate quickly and accurately. In each item, one number or operation has been omitted from an equation. The examinee must select the missing element from five possible answers. Fractions, decimals, and percentages are included, but more complex notations or operations are omitted deliberately. The range extends from minimal educational qualifications to high-school graduate. Examiner required. Suitable for group use.

Timed: 10 minutes

Scoring: Hand key; examiner evaluated; may be computer scored

Cost: 5 question booklets $115.00; key $13.00; administration card $13.00

Publisher: Saville & Holdsworth Ltd.

TECHNICAL TEST BATTERY: NUMERICAL REASONING (TTB:NT6)
Saville & Holdsworth Ltd. Staff

Adult

Purpose: Measures simple numerical reasoning skills. Used in the selection and development of technical staff, including apprentices.

Description: 30–item paper-pencil multiple-choice test consisting of short word problems with numerical answers. Some calculation is involved, but the emphasis is on understanding, reasoning, and recognizing shortcut methods. The problems cover the basic arithmetic operations, percentages, fractions, decimals, angles, graphs, simple technical drawings, metric lengths, areas, and volumes. The questions are all given a technical slant, dealing with materials, output, production methods, and so forth. The range extends from GCE "O" level to GCE "A" level. Examiner required. Suitable for group use.
BRITISH PUBLISHER

Timed: 10 minutes

Scoring: Hand key; examiner evaluated; may be computer scored

Cost: 10 question booklets $36.00; key $9.50; administration card $9.50
Publisher: Saville & Holdsworth Ltd.

TECHNICAL TEST BATTERY: SPATIAL REASONING (TTB:ST7; U.S. VERSION)
Saville & Holdsworth Ltd. Staff

Adult

Purpose: Measures ability to visualize and manipulate shapes in three dimensions when given a two-dimensional drawing. Used in selection and development work with many technical occupations.

Description: 40–item paper-pencil multiple-choice test consisting of a series of folded-out cubes and perspective drawings of assembled cubes. The respondents must identify the assembled cubes that could be made from the folded-out cube, each face of which has a different pattern. The range extends to degree level. Examiner required. Suitable for group use.
Timed: 20 minutes
Scoring: Hand key; examiner evaluated; may be computer scored
Cost: 5 question booklets $115.00; key $13.00; administration card $13.00
Publisher: Saville & Holdsworth Ltd.

TECHNICAL TEST BATTERY: SPATIAL RECOGNITION (TTB:ST9)
Saville & Holdsworth Ltd. Staff

Adult

Purpose: Measures generalized spatial ability. Used for apprentice, programmer, or operator selection.

Description: 40–item paper-pencil multiple-choice test measuring the ability to recognize shapes in two dimensions. A series of shapes is presented. For each one, the identical shape must be selected from five choices. The emphasis is on the recognition of a complete shape when rotated rather than the more specific angle or length estimation required in ET3. ST9 requires less complex spatial skills than those measured in ST7. The range extends from CSE to GCE "A" level.

Examiner required. Suitable for group use.
BRITISH PUBLISHER
Timed: 15 minutes
Scoring: Hand key; examiner evaluated; may be computer scored
Cost: 10 question booklets $36.00; key $9.50; administration card $9.50
Publisher: Saville & Holdsworth Ltd.

TECHNICAL TEST BATTERY: VERBAL COMPREHENSION (TTB:VT1)
Saville & Holdsworth Ltd. Staff

Adult

Purpose: Measures vocabulary and basic word skills in a technical context. Used in selecting and counseling apprentices in engineering and other industries.

Description: 40–item paper-pencil multiple-choice test assessing basic verbal skills, including sentence completion, same and opposite words, analogies, and so forth. The language deliberately has been chosen to reflect the comprehension requirements of technical occupations and crafts. The range extends from minimal educational qualifications to GCE "O" level. Examiner required. Suitable for group use.
BRITISH PUBLISHER
Timed: 10 minutes
Scoring: Hand key; examiner evaluated; may be computer scored
Cost: 10 question booklets $36.00; key $9.50; administration card $9.50
Publisher: Saville & Holdsworth Ltd.

TECHNICAL TEST BATTERY: VERBAL REASONING (TTB:VT5)
Saville & Holdsworth Ltd. Staff

Adult

Purpose: Measures a high order of verbal skills. Used for technical selection and development from craft apprentice level upwards.

Description: 35–item paper-pencil multiple-choice test concerning the meaning of words and the relationships between them. Respondents must identify the rela-

tionship between one pair of words and then select (from five possible words) the one that relates in the same way to a third given word. The vocabulary used has a scientific and technical bias. The range extends from GCE "O" level to "A" level. Examiner required. Suitable for group use.
BRITISH PUBLISHER
Timed: 10 minutes
Scoring: Hand key; examiner evaluated; may be computer scored
Cost: 10 question booklets $36.00; key $9.50; administration card $9.50
Publisher: Saville & Holdsworth Ltd.

TECHNICAL TEST BATTERY: VISUAL ESTIMATION (TTB:ET3)
Saville & Holdsworth Ltd. Staff

Adult

Purpose: Measures important elements of spatial perception relating to craft and design operations. Used for selection and development of all technical grades, especially craft and operator levels.

Description: 40–item paper-pencil multiple-choice test involving the estimation of lengths, angles, and shapes. In each item, the respondent must select the two figures from a set of five that are identical in form, although in many cases they are rotated on the page. Of the eight tests in the TTB, this is the most independent, suggesting that it measures a special aptitude, relatively free from overlap with general intellectual capacity. The range extends from minimal educational qualifications to GCE "A" level. Examiner required. Suitable for group use.
BRITISH PUBLISHER
Timed: 10 minutes
Scoring: Hand key; examiner evaluated; may be computer scored
Cost: 10 question booklets $36.00; key $9.50; administration card $9.50
Publisher: Saville & Holdsworth Ltd.

TEST A/8: ARITHMETIC

Adolescent, adult

Purpose: Measures general arithmetic ability. Used with technical college stu-

dents and applicants for clerical and trade positions with 8–12 years of education for employee selection and placement.

Description: Multiple-item paper-pencil test measuring general arithmetic ability. Norms are available for technical college students and matriculated males. The test is restricted to competent persons properly registered with the South African Medical and Dental Council. Examiner required. Suitable for group use. Available in English and Afrikaans.
SOUTH AFRICAN PUBLISHER
Timed: Matriculants 30 minutes; non-matriculants 40 minutes
Scoring: Hand key; examiner evaluated
Cost: Contact publisher
Publisher: National Institute for Personnel Research

TEST OF ENGLISH FOR INTERNATIONAL COMMUNICATION (TOEIC)

Adult nonnative speakers of English

Purpose: Measures English language proficiency required in business, commerce, and industry. Used as a basis for employee selection and placement, for decisions concerning assignment and placement, and to measure achievement in company-sponsored English-language programs. Used with nonnative speakers of English.

Description: 200–item paper-pencil multiple-choice test of English language skills. Section I contains 100 listening comprehension items administered via audiotape. Section II contains 100 reading items. Total test scale scores range from 10–990; scale subscores for Sections I and II range from 5–495. The scores are correlated to direct measures of listening, speaking, reading, and writing, as well as to indirect measures. The test is used by multinational corporations, language schools, government agencies, public and private organizations for, among other uses, hiring, assignment to overseas posts requiring communication skills in English, assignment to or promotion within departments where English is desirable, identification of employees who know

English well enough to benefit from training programs abroad, and determination of the effectiveness of English-language training programs. The test is currently offered in Japan, Korea, Taiwan, Hong Kong P.R.C., Indonesia, Thailand, Mexico, Central America, Europe, and the Middle East. The test also is available from the TOEIC Program Office, ETS, in the form of an off-the-shelf International Corporate Program (ICP). Application to take the test is made through national and regional offices, where available. An audio cassette player is required. Examiner required. Suitable for group use.

Timed: 2 hours, 30 minutes

Scoring: Hand key; may be computer scored

Cost: Contact publisher

Publisher: Educational Testing Service

Information and availability unconfirmed; last verified in 1988.

THURSTONE TEST OF MENTAL ALERTNESS
Refer to page 980.

TITMUS II VISION TESTER: AEROMEDICAL MODEL

Adult

Purpose: Screens visual abilities of people involved in aviation. Used to ensure that employees meet minimum standards established by the Federal Aviation Administration.

Description: Six slides in a vision tester measure the following factors: acuity far (right eye, left eye, both eyes); vertical and lateral heterophorias; color vision; and acuity near (right eye, left eye, both eyes). The test is approved by the FAA for aeromedical use. Materials include the tester, six slides, a training manual, and record forms. Examiner required. Not suitable for group use.

Untimed: 5–10 minutes

Scoring: Hand key; examiner evaluated

Cost: Remote control $1,395.00; manual control $1,095.00; for built-in perimeter to test peripheral vision, add $100.00 to each model

Publisher: Titmus Optical, Inc.

TITMUS II VISION TESTER: OCCUPATIONAL MODEL FOR INDUSTRY AND COMMERCE

Adult

Purpose: Identifies common vision problems that could result in employee accidents and production inefficiencies.

Description: Vision screening instrument using eight test slides including binocularity, acuity (both eyes, right eye, left eye), stereo depth, color perception, vertical phoria, and lateral phoria. All tests can be administered at far and at near.

Equipment includes a job standards manual providing vision standards specific to particular jobs. New features are a microdigital remote control unit and a photoelectric sensor, which promotes correct head positioning. Optional equipment includes a fiber optics perimeter system for testing peripheral vision and a feature for testing intermediate distance vision (See Vision Tester: Intermediate Test Lenses). Examiner required. Not suitable for group use.

Untimed: 5 minutes

Scoring: Hand key; examiner evaluated

Cost: Remote control $1,395.00; manual control $1,095.00; for built-in perimeter to test peripheral vision, add $100.00 to each model

Publisher: Titmus Optical, Inc.

UNDERSTANDING COMMUNICATION
T.G. Thurstone

Adult

Purpose: Measures comprehension of verbal material in short sentences and phrases. Used for industrial screening and selection of clerical, first-line supervisors, or other positions that need to understand written material and communications.

Description: 40–item paper-pencil single-score test measuring verbal comprehension through the ability to identify the one of four words that will complete a given sentence. Basic reading skills are required. Examiner required. Suitable for group use.

Timed: 15 minutes

Scoring: Hand key

Cost: Specimen set $8.00; 25 test booklets $20.00

Publisher: London House, Inc.

VCWS 3–NUMERICAL SORTING

Adult

Purpose: Measures an individual's ability to perform work tasks requiring sequential sorting of a combined numerical/alphabetical problem. Provides insight into spatial and form perception, accuracy, and attention to detail in transferring data. May be used with hearing-impaired and visually impaired individuals.

Description: Manual test measuring the ability to sort, file, and categorize objects using a numerical code. The individual must transfer 42 of 56 numerically ordered white plastic chips inserted into correspondingly marked slots in Board I to the appropriate slots in Board II. After the chip placements on Board II are scored, the individual transfers the chips back to Board I. Work activities related to the test include examining, grading, and sorting; keeping records and receipts; recording or transmitting verbal or coded information; and posting verbal or numerical data on stock lists. The test should not be used with individuals with severe impairment of the upper extremities. Examiner required. Not suitable for group use.

Timed: Not available

Scoring: Examiner evaluated

Cost: $1,245.00

Publisher: Valpar International Corporation

VCWS 6–INDEPENDENT PROBLEM SOLVING

Adult

Purpose: Measures the ability to perform work tasks requiring visual comparison and proper selection of abstract designs. May be used with institutionally retarded and hearing-impaired individuals.

Description: Manual test measuring a person's ability to perform work tasks requiring a visual comparison of colored shapes. Work activities relating to the test are characterized by emphasis on decision-making and instruction-following abilities. The test should not be used with individuals with severe impairment of the upper extremities or severe visual impairment. Examiner required. Not suitable for group use.

Timed: Not available

Scoring: Examiner evaluated

Cost: $1,295.00

Publisher: Valpar International Corporation

VCWS 10–TRI-LEVEL MEASUREMENT

Adult

Purpose: Measures an individual's ability to perform inspecting and measuring tasks ranging from the very simple to the very precise. Measures ability to use independent judgment in following sequences of operations, selecting proper instruments, and assuming responsibility for attaining prescribed qualitative standards.

Description: Manual test measuring a person's ability to perform very simple to very precise inspection and measurement tasks. The individual must sort 61 incorrectly or correctly machined parts into nine inspection bins. The seven inspection tasks involved are visual and size discrimination, comparison (using jigs), and measurement with a ruler, micrometer, and vernier caliper. Performance indicates the ability to succeed in jobs requiring varying degrees of measurement and inspection skills and decision-making abilities. The test should not be administered to individuals with severe impairment of the upper extremities. Examiner required. Not suitable for group use.

Untimed: Not available
Scoring: Examiner evaluated
Cost: $1,895.00
Publisher: Valpar International Corporation

VCWS 12–SOLDERING AND INSPECTION (ELECTRONIC)

Adult

Purpose: Measures an individual's ability to acquire and apply basic soldering techniques to tasks requiring varying degrees of precision. Provides insight into the ability to follow sequential instructions and acquire new tool use skills. May be used with hearing-impaired and visually impaired individuals.

Description: Manual test measuring an individual's ability to acquire and apply basic skills necessary to perform soldering tasks. The examinee uses wire cutters, wire strippers, needlenose pliers, a soldering iron, and a solder to perform exercises involving the use of the tools in precision solder tasks. Exercises include work with both wires and circuit board assemblies. Performance indicates the individual's degree of ability to become a successful worker in jobs related to electronic assembly and soldering. Work activities related to the test include fabricating, processing, or repairing materials and examining and measuring for the purpose of grading and sorting. Examiner required. Not suitable for group use.

Timed: Not available
Scoring: Examiner evaluated
Cost: $1,495.00
Publisher: Valpar International Corporation

VCWS 15–ELECTRICAL CIRCUITRY AND PRINT READING

Adult

Purpose: Measures the ability to understand, comprehend, and apply the prin-

ciples and functions of electrical circuitry through the modality of electronic components. Provides insight into potential without basing performance exclusively on prior knowledge.

Description: Measures the ability to understand and apply principles and functions of electrical circuits. The examinee performs various exercises in three areas: testing for circuit continuity using probes; testing and repairing circuits using probes, wires, and pliers; and reading an electrical schematic print and inserting wires, diodes, and two types of resistors as specified by the print. The examinee is given trays containing various electrical components and appropriate tools. The various electrical circuits to be tested range from very simple to complex. The examinee tests each circuit, records malfunctions and, if necessary, repairs nonfunctioning circuits. No previous experience with electrical or electronic principles is required. The results indicate potential for success in an entry-level position in fields that require electrical circuitry and print reading skills. The test relates to work activities such as repairing materials, dexterous use of the hands, inspecting products, and selecting appropriate tools and materials. The test should not be used with individuals with severe impairment of the upper extremities, severe visual impairment, or severe coordination problems. Examiner required. Not suitable for group use.

Timed: Not available
Scoring: Examiner evaluated
Cost: $1,545.00
Publisher: Valpar International Corporation

VCWS 16–DRAFTING

Adult

Purpose: Measures an individual's potential to compete in an entry-level position requiring basic drafting and print reading skills. Provides insight into the ability to visualize abstract problems and to acquire new tool use skills.

Description: Manual test measuring the potential to compete in an entry-level position requiring basic drafting skills.

The examinee performs a series of exercises measuring the ability to measure objects accurately in inches and centimeters; learn the use of drafting tools such as a T-square, compass, circle template, and triangles; and read blueprints. The examinee must produce three view drawings of three wooden blocks. Each subtest screens the examinee in terms of ability to cope successfully with the next subtest. The test is designed to accommodate a range of needs within the drafting industry from minimal expertise to sophisticated high-level performance. Work activities related to the test include simple measuring, line perception exercises, determining scaled dimensions, drawing schematics and diagrams, freehand drawing, and interpreting blueprints. The test should not be administered to individuals with severe impairment of the upper extremities, severe visual impairment, or severe coordination problems. Examiner required. Not suitable for group use.

Timed: Not available
Scoring: Examiner evaluated
Cost: $1,295.00
Publisher: Valpar International Corporation

VCWS 19–DYNAMIC PHYSICAL CAPACITIES
Refer to page 807.

VCWS 205–INDEPENDENT PERCEPTUAL SCREENING (SPECIAL APTITUDE)
Refer to page 809.

VISION TESTER: INTERMEDIATE TEST LENSES

Adult

Purpose: Identifies vision problems in the intermediate range that could cause eyestrain, particularly for VDT and other machine operators.

Description: Five lens units for use with the Titmus II Vision Tester. The lens units screen visual acuity of the intermediate range of 20–40 inches, the working distance of VDT and other machine operators. Examiner required. Not suitable for group use.

Untimed: 5 minutes
Scoring: Hand key; examiner evaluated
Cost: Complete set (5 lens units) $175.00
Publisher: Titmus Optical, Inc.

VOCATIONAL BEHAVIOR CHECKLIST (VBC)
Refer to page 851.

WESMAN PERSONNEL CLASSIFICATION TEST (PCT)
A.G. Wesman

Adult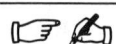

Purpose: Assesses general mental ability. Used for selection of employees for sales, supervisory, and managerial positions.

Description: Multiple-item paper-pencil test of two major aspects of mental ability: verbal and numerical. The verbal items are analogies. The numerical items test basic math skills and understanding of quantitative relationships. Three forms, A, B, and C, are available. The verbal part of Form C is somewhat more difficult than the verbal parts of Forms A and B. Examiner required. Suitable for group use.

Timed: Verbal 18 minutes; Numerical 10 minutes
Scoring: Hand key
Cost: Specimen set (one each of materials for all 3 forms, keys and manual) $17.00; 25 tests, manual, booklet, key (specify form) $34.00
Publisher: The Psychological Corporation

Information and availability unconfirmed; last verified in 1988.

WESTERN MICHIGAN UNIVERSITY ENGLISH USAGE-ORIENTATION FORM (EUO)
Bernadine P. Carlson

Adolescent, adult
College students

Purpose: Measures level of English language skills. Used for pre- and posttesting in business and technical seminars in effective writing.

Description: 75–item paper-pencil multiple-choice test consisting of three parts. Part I (30 items) covers three areas: grammatical errors, spelling, and diction. Part II (30 items) tests two areas: punctuation for meaning and sentence structure. Part III (15 items) evaluates two areas: reading comprehension and rhetorical style evaluation. The test is available in forms A and B. Examiner required. Suitable for group use.

Timed: 45 minutes

Scoring: Hand key; may be computer scored

Cost: Contact publisher

Publisher: Bernadine P. Carlson

THE WONDERLIC PERSONNEL TEST
E.F. Wonderlic

Adult

Purpose: Measures level of mental ability in business and industrial situations. Used for selection and placement of business personnel and for vocational guidance.

Description: 50–item paper-pencil test measuring general learning ability in verbal, spatial, and numerical reasoning. The test is used to predict an individual's ability to adjust to complex and rapidly changing job requirements and complete complex job training. The test also measures potential turnover and dissatisfaction on routinized or simple labor intensive jobs. Test items include analogies, analysis of geometric figures, arithmetic problems, disarranged sentences, sentence parallelism with proverbs, similarities, logic, definitions, judgment, direction following, and others. Examiner required. Suitable for group use. Available in Spanish, French, Mexican, Cuban, and Puerto Rican.

Timed: 12 minutes; may also be administered untimed

Scoring: Hand key

Cost: 25 tests $45.00; 100 tests $105.00; complete package (25 or 100 equivalent forms, answer key for scoring, manual)

Publisher: E.F. Wonderlic Personnel Test, Inc.

WORD AND NUMBER ASSESSMENT INVENTORY (WNAI)
Refer to page 498.

WORD FLUENCY
Human Resources Center,
The University of Chicago

Adult

Purpose: Determines the speed of relevant verbal associations and individual's ability to produce appropriate words rapidly. Used for vocational counseling and personnel selection in fields requiring communication skills, such as supervision, management, and sales.

Description: 80–item paper-pencil test measuring verbal fluency. Examiner required. Suitable for group use. May be verbally administered in any language.

Timed: 10 minutes

Scoring: Hand key

Cost: Specimen set $10.00; 25 test booklets $20.00

Publisher: London House, Inc.

WORK ADJUSTMENT RATING FORM (WARF)
James A. Bitter and D.J. Bolanovich

Adolescent, adult—Ages 16 and older

Purpose: Measures job readiness behaviors. Used in work settings, primarily with developmentally disabled adults.

Description: 40–item paper-pencil rating scale containing eight subscales: Amount of Supervision Required, Realism of Job Goals, Teamwork, Acceptance of Rules/Authority, Work Tolerance, Perseverance in Work, Extent Trainee Seeks Assistance, and Importance Attached to Job Training. Each subscale contains five items that the examiner rates yes or no. The test yields a total score and eight subscale scores that may be profiled to obtain the examinee's areas of strength and weakness. Examiner required. Suitable for group use.

Untimed: 3–5 minutes
Scoring: Hand key
Cost: Contact publisher
Publisher: James A. Bitter

WORK APTITUDE: PROFILE AND PRACTICE SET
Refer to page 811.

WORK SAMPLES

Adolescent, adult

Purpose: Assesses aptitude and provides career exploration in 27 job simulations relating to the 16 USOE clusters.

Description: Multiple-item and multiple-task test in A-V format assessing hands-on aptitude for 27 job areas: drafting, clerical/office, metal construction, sales, wood construction, food preparation, medical services, travel services, barbering/cosmetology, small engine, masonry, electrical, police science, electronics, automotive, commercial art, nutrition, bookkeeping, fire science, extraction technology, clothing and textiles, real estate, communication services, refrigeration, computer technology, solar technology, and machine trades. Each work sample is administered and scored independently. The samples have no predetermined order of administration, and there is no requirement concerning the number of samples that should be administered. A-V instructions, industry trends, entry level salaries, and task demonstrations are given prior to evaluation. The examiner records behavioral and performance observations, and the client rates himself on interest, difficulty, and performance. The work samples may be used in conjunction with Job Matching. The reading level, where reading is required, is related to specific tasks. Norms are based on industrial standards. Examiner required. Not suitable for group use.

Untimed: 2 hours per work sample
Scoring: Examiner evaluated

Cost: Contact publisher
Publisher: Prep, A Division of Educational Technologies, Inc.

Clerical

ACER SHORT CLERICAL TEST (FORMS C, D, AND E)

Adolescent, adult—Ages 15 and older

Purpose: Measures speed and accuracy in checking names and numbers and in basic arithmetic. Used as a test of clerical aptitude in selecting employees for routine clerical jobs.

Description: Multiple-item paper-pencil test measuring an individual's ability to perceive, remember, and check written or printed material (both verbal and numerical) and to perform arithmetic operations. The test is available in three forms: Forms C and D are used for personnel selection and Form E for guidance and counseling in business training colleges. Australian norms are provided. British norms are available for Form C in *British Supplement of Norms for Tests Used in Clerical Selection*, available from NFER-Nelson. Examiner required. Suitable for group use.
AUSTRALIAN PUBLISHER
Timed: 5 minutes per part
Scoring: Hand key
Cost: Contact publisher
Publisher: The Australian Council for Educational Research Limited

ACER SPEED AND ACCURACY TEST—FORM A

Adolescent, adult—Ages 13.6 and older

Purpose: Measures checking skills of individuals. Used in the selection of clerical personnel.

Description: Multiple-item paper-pencil test measuring the ability to perceive, retain, and check relatively familiar material in the form of printed numbers and names while working in a limited amount

of time. The test contains two sections: name checking and number checking. Australian norms are available for school, university, adult, and some occupational groups. British normative data are available in *British Supplement of Norms for Tests Used in Clerical Selection*, available from NFER-Nelson. Examiner required. Suitable for group use.
AUSTRALIAN PUBLISHER

Timed: 6 minutes per part

Scoring: Hand key

Cost: Contact publisher

Publisher: The Australian Council for Educational Research Limited

---

AUTOMATED OFFICE BATTERY (AOB)
Refer to page 951.

AUTOMATED OFFICE BATTERY: NUMERICAL ESTIMATION (AOB: NE–1; U.S. VERSION)
Saville & Holdsworth Ltd. Staff

Ages 16–adult

Purpose: Measures the ability to estimate the answers to a variety of numerical calculations.

Description: 50–item paper-pencil multiple-choice test assessing the ability to quickly estimate the answers to calculations. Candidates are presented with calculations requiring addition, subtraction, multiplication, division, and percentages. Candidates are required to estimate the order of magnitude of the solution and choose the correct one from five alternatives. Candidates are discouraged from making precise calculations, and the time constraint encourages estimation. One of three tests in the Automated Office Battery. Examiner required. Suitable for group use.

Timed: 10 minutes

Scoring: Hand key; may be computer scored

Cost: 5 reusable test booklets $138.50; 25 answer sheets $162.50; administration card $14.00; scoring key $28.00

Publisher: Saville & Holdsworth Ltd.

BLOX TEST (PERCEPTUAL BATTERY)

Adolescent, adult

Purpose: Measures visual perception. Used with subjects with 10–12 years of education for purposes of employee selection and placement in a variety of clerical and technical positions.

Description: Multiple-item paper-pencil test measuring spatial relations. The subject must analyze given geometric figures and then find them in a series as seen from another angle. The test is restricted to competent persons properly registered with the South African Medical and Dental Council. Examiner required. Suitable for group use. Afrikaans version available.
SOUTH AFRICAN PUBLISHER

Timed: 30 minutes

Scoring: Hand key; examiner evaluated

Cost: Contact publisher

Publisher: National Institute for Personnel Research

THE CANDIDATE PROFILE RECORD
Richardson, Bellows, Henry and Company, Inc.

Adult

Purpose: Assesses background characteristics related to success in office positions.

Description: Multiple-item paper-pencil questionnaire designed to predict an individual's potential for success in teller and customer service positions, processing and verifying positions, and secretarial and clerical positions. The autobiographical questionnaire covers an individual's early development influences, academic history and accomplishments, self-esteem and description, work history, and work-related values and attitudes. Normative, reliability, and validity data are contained in the manual. Self-administered. Suitable for group use.

Untimed: Varies

Scoring: Self-scored; computer scored

Cost: Contact publisher

Publisher: Richardson, Bellows, Henry and Company, Inc.

CLERICAL APTITUDE TESTS
Andrew Kobal, J. Wayne Wrightstone, and Andrew J. MacElroy

Adolescent, adult
Grades 7 and above

Purpose: Assesses aptitude for clerical work. Used for screening job applicants.

Description: Three-part paper-pencil test measuring clerical aptitudes, including business practice; number checking; and date, name, and address checking. Scores correlate with job success. Examiner required. Suitable for group use.

Timed: 40 minutes

Scoring: Hand key

Cost: Specimen set $4.00; 25 tests $8.75

Publisher: Psychometric Affiliates

CLERICAL SKILLS SERIES
Martin M. Bruce

Adult

Purpose: Assesses the language, physical coordination, and mathematical abilities necessary for various clerical jobs. Used for screening prospective employees, measuring student skills, and evaluating current employees.

Description: 10–category paper-pencil test series covering alphabetizing, filing, arithmetic, clerical speed and accuracy, coding, eye-hand accuracy, grammar and punctuation, spelling, vocabulary, and word fluency. The series consists of 10 short tests, six of which are timed. The tests may be administered separately or as a unit and can be scored and interpreted independently. Examiner required for timed items. Suitable for group use.

Timed: 2–8 minutes per section

Scoring: Hand key

Cost: Specimen set $44.00; manual $13.50; manual's supplement (1984) $15.50; pkg. of profile sheets $18.00; key $1.95 per test; pkg. of tests $32.90 and $31.90

Publisher: Martin M. Bruce, Ph.D., Publishers

CLERICAL SKILLS TEST
U.S. Employment Service

Adult

Purpose: Assesses the clerical skills required to perform a variety of occupational tasks. Used for job placement.

Description: Six paper-pencil and performance subtests measuring the subject's ability to type from plain copy, take dictation, spell, type statistics, and spell medical and legal terms. Only those subtests that relate to significant job skill needs should be administered. A skilled worker will score higher than an unskilled worker. Norm tables are used to convert raw scores to deciles based on representative samples of experienced workers. Materials required include a typewriter, typing paper, and pencils. Examiner required. Suitable for group use.

Timed: Varies

Scoring: Hand key

Cost: Available through State Employment Service Agencies only

Publisher: U.S. Department of Labor

Information and availability unconfirmed; last verified in 1988.

CLERICAL STAFF SELECTOR

Adult

Purpose: Evaluates candidates of all levels of experience for clerical positions.

Description: Multiple-item tests measuring skills required for various clerical positions, including accounting, inventory, secretarial, and factory. Skills measured are problem-solving, coding, attention to detail, manual dexterity, alphabetizing and filing, spelling, grammar and punctuation, and numerical facility. Examiner required. Suitable for group use. Available in French.

Timed: 30 minutes

Untimed: 30 minutes

Scoring: Hand key; scoring service provided

Cost: $45.00 per person

Publisher: Wolfe Personnel Testing and Training Systems, Inc.

CLERICAL TEST 1
E.I.T.S. Staff

Adult

Purpose: Measures speed and accuracy of basic skills in routine clerical and office occupations that require the employee to check information, especially printed material. Used to screen persons for office work and for positions such as checking clerks, checkout operators, and data checkers.

Description: 140–item paper-pencil test divided into two parts: number checking and name checking. The examinee must determine whether two sets of numbers, or two names, are exactly the same or different. A minimal level of reasoning, measuring conceptual speed, or mental alertness is required. Number words are used to increase the discrimination of Part 1, and random letters and words have been included in Part 2 to achieve the same effect. Materials include booklets, a scoring key, specimen set, and manual. Tests in arithmetic and language usage also are available as part of this clerical series. Examiner required. Suitable for group use.
BRITISH PUBLISHER

Timed: 7 minutes

Scoring: Hand key; may be computer scored

Cost: Contact publisher

Publisher: Educational and Industrial Test Services Ltd.

CLERICAL TEST 2
E.I.T.S. Staff

Adult

Purpose: Assesses individual skill in ordinary arithmetic processes and the ability to apply this skill to everyday problems. Used to screen for a variety of clerical occupations, such as data checking, routine accounts, and shop work.

Description: 50–item paper-pencil two-part test. Part 1 consists of 32 computations in addition, subtraction, multiplication, and division, arranged in order of difficulty. Part 2 consists of 18 arithmetic problems, expressed verbally. Materials include booklets, a scoring key, specimen set, and manual. Tests in speed and accuracy, spelling, grammar, and language usage also are available as part of this clerical series. Examiner required. Suitable for group use.
BRITISH PUBLISHER

Timed: 14 minutes

Scoring: Hand key; examiner evaluated; may be computer scored

Cost: Contact publisher

Publisher: Educational and Industrial Test Services Ltd.

CLERICAL TEST 3
E.I.T.S. Staff

Adult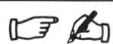

Purpose: Evaluates a person's ability in spelling, grammar, and language usage. Used to screen for most office jobs, especially those involving the processing of information.

Description: 91–item paper-pencil test in three parts. Part 1 is a 60–word spelling test, in which the subject indicates whether a given word is spelled correctly or incorrectly. Part 2 consists of 30 short sentences, each containing a word, which the subject must identify as making the sentence grammatically incorrect. Part 3 is a short business letter, which the subject marks for errors and rewrites. Materials include booklets, a scoring key, a specimen set, and a manual. Tests in speed and accuracy and in arithmetic also are available as part of this clerical series. Examiner required. Suitable for group use.
BRITISH PUBLISHER

Timed: 15½ minutes

Scoring: Hand key; examiner evaluated; may be computer scored

Cost: Contact publisher

Publisher: Educational and Industrial Test Services Ltd.

CLERICAL TESTS, SERIES N
Stevens, Thurow and Associates

Adult

Purpose: Measures ability to think and to use words and numbers accurately. Used to screen candidates for clerical positions, such as payroll, accounting, receiving, inventory control, warehousing, and filing.

Description: 206–item battery of five paper-pencil tests assessing detail and numerical skills. The Mental Abilities—Inventory II (50 items) is a multiple-choice and free-response measure of general mental ability. Inventory E (96 items) requires subjects to decide whether the pair of words or numbers in each item are the same or different. In Inventory F (30 items), subjects copy a list of 4– to 10–digit numbers in order and in the properly numbered spaces provided on the back of the sheet on which the list is printed. Inventory G (80 items) is a free-response test of basic addition and multiplication skills. Inventory H (30 items) requires examinees to copy a list of names in order and in the properly numbered spaces provided on the back of the sheet on which the list is printed. Examiner required. Suitable for group use.

Timed: 33 minutes

Scoring: Hand key

Cost: 5–test battery with application form and rating chart $2.00; manual of instructions, including scoring keys $5.00

Publisher: Stevens, Thurow and Associates

CLERICAL TESTS, SERIES V
Stevens, Thurow and Associates

Adult

Purpose: Measures ability to use and spell words and to type accurately. Used to screen candidates for clerical positions, such as secretaries, typists, clerks, dictaphone operators, and stenographers.

Description: 233–item battery of four paper-pencil tests and one test of typing ability. Mental Abilities—Inventory II is a 50–item multiple-choice and free-response test of general mental abilities. Inventory A is a 30–item test in which subjects evaluate grammatical correctness of sentences. Inventory B is a 100–item test in which the subjects decide whether words are spelled correctly. Inventory C is a 52–item test in which subjects choose one of five words nearest in meaning to the capitalized word in a phrase. Inventory D is a 10–minute test measuring speed and accuracy in typing a standard business letter from provided copy. Examiner required. Suitable for group use.

Timed: 45 minutes

Untimed: Inventory C

Scoring: Hand key

Cost: 5–test battery with application form and rating chart $2.00; manual of instructions, including scoring keys $5.00

Publisher: Stevens, Thurow and Associates

CURTIS VERBAL-CLERICAL SKILLS TESTS
James W. Curtis

Adolescent, adult—Ages 16 and older

Purpose: Assesses clerical and verbal abilities. Used to evaluate job applicants.

Description: Four multiple-item paper-pencil tests of clerical abilities. The tests are Computation, measuring practical arithmetic; Checking, measuring perceptual speed and accuracy; Comprehension, measuring reading vocabulary; and Capacity, measuring logical reasoning ability. Examiner required. Suitable for group use.

Timed: 2 minutes per test

Scoring: Hand key

Cost: Specimen set $5.00; 25 tests (specify form) $4.00

Publisher: Psychometric Affiliates

DICTATION TEST
Richardson, Bellows, Henry and Company, Inc.

Adult

Purpose: Provides a quick screening of an individual's dictation abilities.

Description: Manual test assessing an individual's dictation speed and accuracy. The examiner, who adjusts his dictation speed to the examinee's pace, dictates only the words of a business letter; the examinee must supply appropriate punctuation, capitalization, and spelling. After the letter is dictated, the examiner notes the amount of time that elapsed from the beginning to the end of the dictation. The examinee then reads the notes back to the examiner, who marks errors of interpretation and estimates the examinee's dictation speed. The test yields an estimate of dictation speed accurate to within five words per minute. The following materials are required: a test folder to be used by both the examiner and examinee, two sharp pencils for the examinee, and a stopwatch for the examiner. Examiner required. Not suitable for group use.

Untimed: 5 minutes

Scoring: Hand key

Cost: 1–24 packages $30.00; score key $2.00; manual $2.00

Publisher: Richardson, Bellows, Henry and Company, Inc.

EMPLOYEE APTITUDE SURVEY TEST #4–VISUAL SPEED AND ACCURACY (EAS #4)
Refer to page 878.

ESV CLERICAL WORKER
McCann Associates, Inc.

Adult

Purpose: Assesses candidate's ability to learn to become a competent clerical worker. Used by employers for job screening.

Description: 100–item criterion-validated paper-pencil multiple-choice test covering memorization, information

ordering, number facility, time-sharing, problem solving, dealing with people, deductive reasoning, and verbal comprehension. Materials include test booklets, answer sheets, identification sheets, envelopes, candidate study guides, and complete monitoring instructions.

The publisher scores answer sheets and provides a comprehensive report that includes total test and subtest means and standard deviations, norms, reliabilities, and candidate evaluations. The test is available on a rental basis only to personnel directors, civil service commissions, or qualified municipal or employment officials. A security agreement is required. Examiner required. Suitable for group use.

Timed: 3 hours

Scoring: Computer scored by publisher

Cost: First 5 candidates $165.00 minimum charge; next 5 candidates $12.00 each; next 15 candidates $11.00 each; next 25 candidates $8.50 each; each additional $7.00 each

Publisher: McCann Associates, Inc.

ETSA TESTS 2–A—OFFICE ARITHMETIC TEST
Refer to page 881.

ETSA TESTS 3–A—GENERAL CLERICAL ABILITY TEST
Refer to page 881.

ETSA TESTS 4–A— STENOGRAPHIC SKILLS TEST
Refer to page 882.

GENERAL CLERICAL TEST (GCT)

Adult

Purpose: Assesses clerical aptitude. Used for selecting applicants and evaluating clerical employees for promotion.

Description: Multiple-item paper-pencil test of three types of abilities needed for clerical jobs: clerical speed and accuracy, numerical ability, and verbal ability. The clerical subtest involves finding errors by comparing copy with the original and using an alphabetical file. The numerical subtest requires the applicant to solve arithmetic problems, find numerical errors, and solve numerical word problems. The verbal subtest involves correcting spelling errors, answering questions about reading passages, understanding word meanings, and correcting grammatical errors. Separate booklets for the clerical and numerical subtests combined and the verbal subtest only are available for use where one or the other of the abilities is of prime consideration. Examiner required. Suitable for group use.

Timed: Complete test 46 minutes

Scoring: Hand key

Cost: Specimen set (test booklet for complete battery, manual) $22.00; 25 test booklets (clerical, numerical, and verbal combined), manual, key $65.00

Publisher: The Psychological Corporation

Information and availability unconfirmed; last verified in 1988.

HAY APTITUDE TEST BATTERY
Edward N. Hay

Adult

Purpose: Identifies job applicants with the greatest aptitude for handling alphabetical and numerical clerical detail. Used to select personnel for office and clerical positions, trainee positions requiring innate perceptual skills, and positions requiring quick recognition of numbers.

Description: Four paper-pencil tests assessing clerical and numerical aptitude: a) Warm-Up, b) Number Perception Test, c) Name Finding Test, and d) Number Series Completion Test (NS). The Warm-Up Test, which is not scored, is designed to prepare the examinee for testing. The Number Perception Test (4 minutes) assesses numerical accuracy. Applicants must identify exact pairs of numbers from groups of similar pairs. Results do not necessarily indicate general mental ability. The Name Finding Test (4 minutes) screens the applicant's short-term memory and word accuracy. The examinee must read words and retain them long enough to verify them. This type of skill is required for tasks such as invoicing,

data entry, filing, typing, shipping/receiving, and reporting. Results do not necessarily indicate general mental ability. The Number Series Completion Test (4 minutes) assesses numerical comprehension. With each question, the examinee is presented with a series of six numbers. The examinee must decipher the pattern and present the next two numbers in the series. Examiner required. Suitable for group use. Available in French and Spanish.

Timed: 13 minutes total

Scoring: Hand key

Cost: 25 of each form $90.00; 100 sets $210.00

Publisher: E.F. Wonderlic Personnel Test, Inc.

HAY APTITUDE TEST BATTERY: NAME FINDING
Edward N. Hay

Adult

Purpose: Measures ability to check and verify names quickly and accurately. Used to select office and clerical personnel.

Description: 32–item paper-pencil multiple-choice test assessing the ability to read names and hold them in memory long enough to accurately identify them from four similarly spelled names on the back of the same sheet. The task is similar to many clerical tasks, including making bookkeeping entries or typing invoices or checks. The test may be administered via optional cassette tape. Examiner required. Suitable for group use. Available in French and Spanish.

Timed: 4 minutes

Scoring: Hand key

Cost: 25 copies $35.00; 100 copies $75.00

Publisher: E.F. Wonderlic Personnel Test, Inc.

HAY APTITUDE TEST BATTERY: NUMBER PERCEPTION
Edward N. Hay

Adult

Purpose: Measures ability to check pairs of numbers and identify those that are the same. Used to select office and clerical personnel.

Description: 200–item paper-pencil test measuring speed and accuracy of numerical checking. Each test item is a pair of numbers. The applicant must decide whether the two numbers are the same or different. Items are designed to include the most common clerical errors. The test may be administered via optional cassette tape. Examiner required. Suitable for group use. Available in French and Spanish.

Timed: 4 minutes

Scoring: Hand key

Cost: 25 copies $35.00; 100 copies $75.00

Publisher: E.F. Wonderlic Personnel Test, Inc.

HAY APTITUDE TEST BATTERY: NUMBER SERIES COMPLETION
Edward N. Hay

Adult

Purpose: Measures the ability to deduce the pattern in a series of six numbers and provide the seventh and eighth numbers in the series. Used to select office and clerical personnel.

Description: 30–item paper-pencil test assessing numerical reasoning abilities. Each item presents a series of six numbers (1–3 digits) related by an unknown pattern. Applicants must provide the next two numbers in the series. Good clerks can find the additional numbers more readily than poor ones. May be administered and timed via optional cassette tape. Examiner required. Suitable for group use. Available in French and Spanish.

Timed: 4 minutes

Scoring: Hand key

Cost: 25 copies $35.00; 100 copies $75.00

Publisher: E.F. Wonderlic Personnel Test, Inc.

HAY APTITUDE TEST BATTERY: WARM-UP
Edward N. Hay

Adult

Purpose: Introduces job applicants to the testing procedures of the Hay Aptitude Test Battery.

Description: 20–item unscored paper-pencil test providing a warm-up for the Hay Aptitude tests. The exercise is intended to quiet nervous applicants and to familiarize applicants with the format of the other tests. The warm-up may be administered and timed via optional cassette tape. Examiner required. Suitable for group use. Available in French and Spanish.

Timed: 1 minute

Scoring: Hand key

Cost: 25 copies $25.00; 100 copies $55.00

Publisher: E.F. Wonderlic Personnel Test, Inc.

INTERMEDIATE BATTERY B/77
Refer to page 463.

IPI APTITUDE—INTELLIGENCE TEST SERIES: FLUENCY
Refer to page 888.

IPI APTITUDE—INTELLIGENCE TEST SERIES: JUDGMENT
Refer to page 888.

IPI APTITUDE—INTELLIGENCE TEST SERIES: OFFICE TERMS
Refer to page 889.

IPI APTITUDE—INTELLIGENCE TEST SERIES: PARTS
Refer to page 889.

IPI APTITUDE—INTELLIGENCE TEST SERIES: PERCEPTION
Refer to page 890.

IPI JOB TEST FIELD SERIES: GENERAL CLERK
Industrial Psychology International, Ltd.

Adult

Purpose: Assesses skills of applicants for general clerical positions. Used to evaluate typing, filing, billing, transcribing, sorting, writing, and phone answering skills.

Description: Multiple-item paper-pencil battery of seven aptitude tests. The tests are Perception, Judgment, Numbers, Office Terms, Memory, Parts, and Fluency. For individual test descriptions, see the IPI Aptitude-Intelligence Test Series. Examiner required. Suitable for group use. Available in French and Spanish.

Timed: Each test 6 minutes

Scoring: Hand key

Cost: Instruction kit $16.00; test packages $10.00

Publisher: Industrial Psychology International, Ltd.

IPI JOB TEST FIELD SERIES: JUNIOR CLERK
Industrial Psychology International, Ltd.

Adult

Purpose: Assesses skills and personality of entry-level clerical applicants. Used to evaluate checking, coding, indexing, mailing, shipping, sorting, and stocking skills.

Description: Multiple-item paper-pencil battery of two aptitude tests. The tests are Perception and Numbers. For individual test descriptions, see the IPI Aptitude-Intelligence Test Series. Examiner required. Suitable for group use. Available in French and Spanish.

Timed: 12 minutes

Scoring: Hand key

Cost: Instruction kit $16.00; test packages $10.00

Publisher: Industrial Psychology International, Ltd.

IPI JOB TEST FIELD SERIES: NUMBERS CLERK
Industrial Psychology International, Ltd.

Adult

Purpose: Assesses skills and personality of applicants seeking numerically ori-

ented positions. Used to screen for accounting, billing, insurance, inventory, payroll, and statistical positions.

Description: Multiple-item paper-pencil battery of five aptitude tests. The tests are Numbers, Judgment, Perception, Office Terms, and Parts. For individual test descriptions, see the IPI Aptitude-Intelligence Test Series. Examiner required. Suitable for group use. Available in French and Spanish.

Timed: Each test 6 minutes

Scoring: Hand key

Cost: Instruction kit $16.00; test packages $10.00

Publisher: Industrial Psychology International, Ltd.

IPI JOB TEST FIELD SERIES: OFFICE MACHINE OPERATOR
Industrial Psychology International, Ltd.

Adult

Purpose: Assesses skills and personality of applicants for positions utilizing office machines. Used to screen for accounting, billing, IBM, keypunch, and typist positions.

Description: Multiple-item paper-pencil battery of six aptitude tests. The tests are Perception, Numbers, Judgment, Parts, Memory, and Office Terms. For individual test descriptions, see the IPI Aptitude-Intelligence Test Series. Examiner required. Suitable for group use. Available in French and Spanish.

Timed: 45 minutes

Scoring: Hand key

Cost: Instruction kit $16.00; test packages $10.00

Publisher: Industrial Psychology International, Ltd.

IPI JOB TEST FIELD SERIES: SECRETARY
Industrial Psychology International, Ltd.

Adult

Purpose: Assesses skills of applicants for secretarial positions. Used to screen for stenographers, and executive, legal, private, and social secretaries.

Description: Multiple-item paper-pencil battery of six aptitude tests. The tests are Perception, Office Terms, Judgment, Memory, and Parts. For individual test descriptions, see the IPI Aptitude-Intelligence Test Series. Examiner required. Suitable for group use. Available in French and Spanish.

Timed: Each test 6 minutes

Scoring: Hand key

Cost: Kit $16.00; test packages $10.00

Publisher: Industrial Psychology International, Ltd.

IPI JOB TEST FIELD SERIES: SENIOR CLERK
Industrial Psychology International, Ltd.

Adult

Purpose: Assesses skills of applicants for high-level clerical or administrative positions. Used to screen for administrative, bookkeeping, correspondence, cost, and production positions.

Description: Multiple-item paper-pencil battery of six aptitude tests. The tests are Office Terms, Judgment, Perception, Parts, Numbers, and Memory. For individual test descriptions, see the IPI Aptitude-Intelligence Test Series. Examiner required. Suitable for group use. Available in French and Spanish.

Timed: Each test 6 minutes

Scoring: Hand key

Cost: Instruction kit $16.00; test packages $10.00

Publisher: Industrial Psychology International, Ltd.

JOB EFFECTIVENESS PREDICTION SYSTEM (JEPS)
Refer to page 894.

JOB EFFECTIVENESS PREDICTION SYSTEM: CODING AND CONVERTING (JEPS: TEST CODE K)
Refer to page 895.

JOB EFFECTIVENESS PREDICTION SYSTEM: COMPARING AND CHECKING (JEPS: TEST CODE L)
Refer to page 895.

JOB EFFECTIVENESS PREDICTION SYSTEM: FILING (JEPS: TEST CODE J)
Refer to page 895.

JOB EFFECTIVENESS PREDICTION SYSTEM: LANGUAGE USAGE (JEPS: TEST CODE E)
Refer to page 896.

JOB EFFECTIVENESS PREDICTION SYSTEM: MATHEMATICAL SKILL (JEPS: TEST CODE C)
Refer to page 896.

JOB EFFECTIVENESS PREDICTION SYSTEM: NUMERICAL ABILITY-1 (JEPS: TEST CODE A)
Refer to page 896.

JOB EFFECTIVENESS PREDICTION SYSTEM: NUMERICAL ABILITY-2 (JEPS: TEST CODE B)
Refer to page 897.

JOB EFFECTIVENESS PREDICTION SYSTEM: READING COMPREHENSION-1 (JEPS: TEST CODE F)
Refer to page 897.

JOB EFFECTIVENESS PREDICTION SYSTEM: READING COMPREHENSION-2 (JEPS: TEST CODE G)
Refer to page 897.

JOB EFFECTIVENESS PREDICTION SYSTEM: SPELLING (JEPS: TEST CODE D)

Refer to page 898.

JOB EFFECTIVENESS PREDICTION SYSTEM: VERBAL COMPREHENSION (JEPS: TEST CODE H)

Refer to page 898.

KEYBOARD SKILLS TEST (KST)
J.A. Gordon Booth and Carol DeCoff

Adolescent, adult
Grades 9–college

Purpose: Measures typing speed and accuracy. Used for acquiring information about typing speed of job applicants.

Description: Typing test in which the examinee uses a word processor or typewriter to type two passages containing 25 lines of text (1400–1700 keystrokes). The examinee types a practice exercise before typing the two passages to be graded. The test yields scores in the forms of gross words per minute, number of errors, and net words per minute. The test is available in four forms: A, B, C, and D. Examiner required. Suitable for group use.

Timed: 5 minutes per passage; practice exercise 3 minutes

Scoring: Examiner evaluated

Cost: 10 booklets $9.00; 10 practice exercises $5.50; manual $12.00; 100 worksheets $16.50

Publisher: Nelson Canada

LANGUAGE SKILLS, FORM G
Richardson, Bellows, Henry and Company, Inc.

Adult

Purpose: Measures word meaning, spelling, hyphenation, and punctuation skills. Used with applicants to clerical positions.

Description: 84–item paper-pencil test assessing the ability of clerical personnel to handle job-related tasks. A portion of the test is multiple-choice. Another portion consists of brief paragraphs containing no punctuation within the sentences. Key words in the sentences are underlined at points where punctuation may be needed. The examinee chooses from among two to four punctuation marks. The examinee marks all answers in the test booklet. Examiner required. Suitable for group use.

Timed: 25 minutes

Scoring: Hand key

Cost: 1–24 packages $30.00; score key $5.00; manual $2.00

Publisher: Richardson, Bellows, Henry and Company, Inc.

MATHEMATICAL ACHIEVEMENT TEST

Refer to page 899.

MINNESOTA CLERICAL TEST (MCT)
D.M. Andrew, D.G. Peterson, and H.P. Longstaff

Adult

Purpose: Measures ability to see differences or errors in pairs of names and pairs of numbers. Used to select clerical applicants.

Description: Multiple-item paper-pencil test of speed and accuracy of visual perception. Items are pairs of names and numbers. The applicant checks each pair that is identical. The test predicts performance in numerous jobs, including adding-machine operators, clerical employees, key machine operators, and filing and cataloging personnel. Materials include optional tapes for test administration. Examiner required. Suitable for group use.

Timed: 15 minutes

Scoring: Hand key

Cost: Specimen set (test, manual) $15.00; 25 tests, manual, key $34.00; key $10.00; manual $12.00

Publisher: The Psychological Corporation

Information and availability unconfirmed; last verified in 1988.

NATIONAL BUSINESS COMPETENCY TESTS: ACCOUNTING PROCEDURES TEST (TRIAL EDITION)
Refer to page 272.

NATIONAL BUSINESS COMPETENCY TESTS: SECRETARIAL PROCEDURES TEST
Refer to page 272.

NORMAL, INTERMEDIATE AND HIGH LEVEL BATTERIES
Refer to page 906.

OFFICE SKILLS ACHIEVEMENT TEST
Paul L. Mellenbruch

**Adolescent, adult
Grades 10 and above**

Purpose: Assesses clerical skills. Used for educational and vocational guidance and for screening applicants for employment.

Description: Multiple-item paper-pencil test measuring several important office and clerical skills, including business letter writing, English usage, checking, filing, simple arithmetic, and following written instructions. The test was developed in office work situations, using clerical employees. Examiner required. Suitable for group use.

Timed: 20 minutes

Scoring: Hand key

Cost: Specimen set (test, manual, key) $5.00; 25 tests $8.75

Publisher: Psychometric Affiliates

OFFICE SKILLS TESTS
SRA/London House

Adult

Purpose: Assesses clerical ability of entry-level job applicants. Used for employee selection and placement.

Description: 12 short tests suitable for screening clerks, accounting clerks, typ-

ists, secretary/stenographers, library assistants, and other office personnel. The tests are Checking, Coding, Filing, Forms Completion, Grammar, Numerical Skills, Oral Directions, Punctuation, Reading Comprehension, Spelling, Typing, and Vocabulary. Each test is available in two equivalent forms. Norms are provided for timed and untimed administration. Examiner required. Suitable for group use.

Untimed: 3–10 minutes per test

Scoring: Hand key; may be machine scored

Cost: 25 booklets (specify test) $26.00; scoring stencils $8.25 each; oral directions cassette $30.00; examiner's manual $10.00

Publisher: SRA/London House

PERCEPTUAL SPEED (IDENTICAL FORMS)
L.L. Thurstone and T.E. Jeffrey

Adult

Purpose: Measures ability to identify rapidly the similarities and differences in visual configurations. Used to select clerical personnel or workers in occupations that require rapid perception of inaccuracies in written materials and diagrams.

Description: 140–item paper-pencil test of perceptual skill. The subject selects the figure among five choices that appears to be most similar to the illustration. Examiner required. Suitable for group use.

Timed: 5 minutes

Scoring: Hand key

Cost: Specimen set $8.00; 25 test booklets $20.00

Publisher: London House, Inc.

PERSONNEL TEST BATTERY (PTB)
Refer to page 906.

PERSONNEL TEST BATTERY: AUDIO CHECKING (PTB:CP8)
Saville & Holdsworth Ltd.

Adult

Purpose: Tests an individual's ability to receive and check information that is presented orally. Used to select clerical staff who must process information presented orally as in telesales or airline/hotel bookings.

Description: 60–item paper-pencil multiple-choice test in which the task is to listen to a string of numbers or letters presented on an audiotape and select the identical string from the five choices presented in the question booklet. There are three subtests covering letters, numbers, and letters and numbers mixed. The test is suitable for individuals with minimal educational qualifications to the GCE "A" level. Examiner required. Suitable for group use.
BRITISH PUBLISHER
Timed: 10 minutes
Scoring: Hand key; examiner evaluated; may be computer scored
Cost: Audiocassette $35.00; 50 answer sheets $46.20; key $9.50; 10 booklets $46.50; administration card $9.50
Publisher: Saville & Holdsworth Ltd.

PERSONNEL TEST BATTERY: BASIC CHECKING (PTB:CP7)
Refer to page 907.

PERSONNEL TEST BATTERY: CHECKING (PTB:CP3)
Refer to page 907.

PERSONNEL TEST BATTERY: CLASSIFICATION (PTB:CP4)
Saville & Holdsworth Ltd.

Adult

Purpose: Measures the ability to perceive and classify material in accordance with a set of instructions. Used for personnel decisions when data handling, filing, or the following of instructions are important.

Description: 60–item paper-pencil test representing a real clerical task in which a number of sales order forms must be filed. The candidate classifies each order and then records the order in coded form. Some orders ("account sales") must be

filed alphabetically and others ("cash sales") must be classified under seven categories of goods purchased. The test is suitable for individuals from GCE "O" level to GCE "A" level. Examiner required. Suitable for group use.
BRITISH PUBLISHER
Timed: 7 minutes
Scoring: Hand key; examiner evaluated; may be computer scored
Cost: 10 question booklets $46.50; 50 answer sheets $46.50; key $9.50; administration card $9.50
Publisher: Saville & Holdsworth Ltd.

PERSONNEL TEST BATTERY: NUMERICAL COMPUTATION (PTB:NP2)
Refer to page 907.

PERSONNEL TEST BATTERY: NUMERICAL REASONING (PTB:NP6)
Refer to page 908.

PERSONNEL TEST BATTERY: VERBAL USAGE (PTB:VP1)
Refer to page 908.

PSI BASIC SKILLS TESTS FOR BUSINESS, INDUSTRY, AND GOVERNMENT: CLASSIFYING (BST #11)
W.W. Ruch, A.N. Shub, S.M. Moinat, and D.A. Dye

Adult

Purpose: Measures ability to place information into appropriate categories. Used to select clerical and administrative personnel.

Description: 48–item paper-pencil multiple-choice test presenting four sets of data. Each set contains 12 items that must be properly categorized. Examiner required. Suitable for group use.
Timed: 5 minutes
Scoring: Hand key; may be computer scored
Cost: 25 tests $42.00; volume discount
Publisher: Psychological Services, Inc.

PSI BASIC SKILLS TESTS FOR BUSINESS, INDUSTRY, AND GOVERNMENT: CODING (BST #12)
W.W. Ruch, A.N. Shub,
S.M. Moinat, and D.A. Dye

Adult

Purpose: Measures ability to code information according to a prescribed system. Used to select clerical and administrative personnel.

Description: 18–item paper-pencil multiple-choice test in which the subjects are given systems for coding information (each system codes four categories of related information). For each test item, the subject must code the given information into the four coded categories. Examiner required. Suitable for group use.

Timed: 5 minutes

Scoring: Hand key; may be computer scored

Cost: 25 tests $42.50; volume discount

Publisher: Psychological Services, Inc.

PSI BASIC SKILLS TESTS FOR BUSINESS, INDUSTRY, AND GOVERNMENT: COMPUTATION (BST #4)
W.W. Ruch, A.N. Shub,
S.M. Moinat, and D.A. Dye

Adult

Purpose: Measures ability to solve arithmetic problems. Used to select clerical and administrative personnel.

Description: 40–item paper-pencil multiple-choice test measuring the ability to add, subtract, multiply, and divide using whole numbers, fractions, and decimals. Examiner required. Suitable for group use.

Timed: 5 minutes

Scoring: Hand key; may be computer scored

Cost: 25 tests $42.50; volume discount

Publisher: Psychological Services, Inc.

PSI BASIC SKILLS TESTS FOR BUSINESS, INDUSTRY, AND GOVERNMENT: DECISION MAKING (BST #6)
W.W. Ruch, A.N. Shub,
S.M. Moinat, and D.A. Dye

Adult

Purpose: Measures ability to read a set of procedures and apply them to new situations by determining the appropriate action. Used to select clerical and administrative personnel.

Description: 20–item paper-pencil multiple-choice test in which sets of procedures (related to clerical or office duties) are described and a set of action codes for implementing the procedures is presented. The examinee is presented with a number of problems in which he must decide the course of action for each item and mark the appropriate action code. Examiner required. Suitable for group use.

Timed: 5 minutes

Scoring: Hand key; may be computer scored

Cost: 25 tests $42.50; volume discount

Publisher: Psychological Services, Inc.

PSI BASIC SKILLS TESTS FOR BUSINESS, INDUSTRY, AND GOVERNMENT: FILING NAMES (BST #13)
W.W. Ruch, A.N. Shub,
S.M. Moinat, and D.A. Dye

Adult

Purpose: Measures ability to file simple entries alphabetically. Used to select clerical and administrative personnel.

Description: 50–item paper-pencil multiple-choice test in which the subject is presented with a name, followed by a list of four other names (arranged alphabetically). The subject "files" the given name at the beginning, between two of the names, or at the end of the list. Examiner required. Suitable for group use.

Timed: 1½ minutes

Scoring: Hand key; may be computer scored

Cost: 25 tests $42.50; volume discount
Publisher: Psychological Services, Inc.

PSI BASIC SKILLS TESTS FOR BUSINESS, INDUSTRY, AND GOVERNMENT: FILING NUMBERS (BST #14)
W.W. Ruch, A.N. Shub,
S.M. Moinat, and D.A. Dye

Adult

Purpose: Measures ability to file numbers in numerical order. Used to select clerical and administrative personnel.

Description: 75–item paper-pencil multiple-choice test in which each test item consists of a 6–digit number to be filed numerically in a list of four other 6–digit numbers (already arranged in numerical order). Examiner required. Suitable for group use.
Timed: 2 minutes
Scoring: Hand key; may be computer scored
Cost: 25 tests $42.50; volume discount
Publisher: Psychological Services, Inc.

PSI BASIC SKILLS TESTS FOR BUSINESS, INDUSTRY, AND GOVERNMENT: FOLLOWING ORAL DIRECTIONS (BST #7)
W.W. Ruch, A.N. Shub,
S.M. Moinat, and D.A. Dye

Adult

Purpose: Measures ability to listen to information and instructions presented orally and answer questions about what is heard. Used to select clerical and administrative personnel.

Description: 24–item paper-pencil multiple-choice test in which the subjects listen to a 6½–minute prerecorded cassette tape and then answer questions about the content of the tape. The tape is played only once (no rewinding or stopping of the tape is allowed), and subjects are encouraged to take written notes during the playing of the tape. The tape is a recording of conversations that take place in an employment setting. Examiner required. Suitable for group use.

Timed: 5 minutes
Scoring: Hand key; may be computer scored
Cost: 25 tests $42.50; volume discount
Publisher: Psychological Services, Inc.

PSI BASIC SKILLS TESTS FOR BUSINESS, INDUSTRY, AND GOVERNMENT: FOLLOWING WRITTEN DIRECTIONS (BST #8)
W.W. Ruch, A.N. Shub,
S.M. Moinat, and D.A. Dye

Adult

Purpose: Measures ability to read, understand, and apply sets of written instructions. Used to select clerical and administrative personnel.

Description: 36–item paper-pencil multiple-choice test requiring examinees to read sets of rules and apply them to a number of case examples. Examiner required. Suitable for group use.
Timed: 5 minutes
Scoring: Hand key; may be computer scored
Cost: 25 tests $42.50; volume discount
Publisher: Psychological Services, Inc.

PSI BASIC SKILLS TESTS FOR BUSINESS, INDUSTRY, AND GOVERNMENT: FORMS CHECKING (BST #9)
W.W. Ruch, A.N. Shub,
S.M. Moinat, and D.A. Dye

Adult

Purpose: Measures ability to verify the accuracy of completed forms. Used to select clerical and administrative personnel.

Description: 42–item paper-pencil true-false test in which the examinee verifies the accuracy of information in clerical forms apparently filled out using information in written paragraphs. The examinee must check a number of the entries on each form against the information in the paragraphs to determine whether the entries are correct or incorrect. Examiner required. Suitable for group use.
Timed: 5 minutes

Scoring: Hand key; may be computer scored

Cost: 25 tests $42.50; volume discount

Publisher: Psychological Services, Inc.

PSI BASIC SKILLS TESTS FOR BUSINESS, INDUSTRY, AND GOVERNMENT: LANGUAGE SKILLS (BST #1)
W.W. Ruch, A.N. Shub,
S.M. Moinat, and D.A. Dye

Adult

Purpose: Measures ability to recognize and correct errors in spelling, punctuation, capitalization, grammar, and usage. Used to select clerical and administrative personnel.

Description: 25–item paper-pencil multiple-choice test in which each test item consists of one sentence, part of which is underlined. The underlined section may contain errors in spelling, punctuation, capitalization, grammar, or usage. The examinee must select one of three possible changes for the underlined section or indicate that no change is necessary. Examiner required. Suitable for group use.

Timed: 5 minutes

Scoring: Hand key; may be computer scored

Cost: 25 tests $42.50; volume discount

Publisher: Psychological Services, Inc.

PSI BASIC SKILLS TESTS FOR BUSINESS, INDUSTRY, AND GOVERNMENT: MEMORY (BST #16)
W.W. Ruch, A.N. Shub,
S.M. Moinat, and D.A. Dye

Adult

Purpose: Measures ability to recall names and categories after being allowed a short period of time to study a chart in which the information is listed. Used to select clerical and administrative personnel.

Description: 25–item paper-pencil multiple-choice test in which applicants are given 5 minutes to study a reference list

and 5 minutes to recall the information on the list. The reference list presents the names of five building supply companies in each of five categories: plumbing, heating, lighting, roofing, and flooring. The applicant must recall for each of the 25 companies the category in which it was listed. Examiner required. Suitable for group use.

Timed: 10 minutes

Scoring: Hand key; may be computer scored

Cost: 25 tests $42.50; volume discount

Publisher: Psychological Services, Inc.

PSI BASIC SKILLS TESTS FOR BUSINESS, INDUSTRY, AND GOVERNMENT: PROBLEM SOLVING (BST #5)
W.W. Ruch, A.N. Shub,
S.M. Moinat, and D.A. Dye

Adult

Purpose: Measures the ability to solve "story" problems requiring the application of arithmetic operations. Used to select clerical and administrative personnel.

Description: 24–item paper-pencil multiple-choice test in which each item is a short word problem requiring a numerical answer. The test emphasizes determining the arithmetic problem contained in the "story," rather than lengthy computations. Examiner required. Suitable for group use.

Timed: 10 minutes

Scoring: Hand key; may be computer scored

Cost: 25 tests $42.50; volume discount

Publisher: Psychological Services, Inc.

PSI BASIC SKILLS TESTS FOR BUSINESS, INDUSTRY, AND GOVERNMENT: READING COMPREHENSION (BST #2)
W.W. Ruch, A.N. Shub,
S.M. Moinat, and D.A. Dye

Adult

Purpose: Measures basic reading comprehension. Used to select clerical and administrative personnel.

Description: 23-item paper-pencil multiple-choice test measuring the ability to read short passages and answer literal and inferential questions about them. Examiner required. Suitable for group use.

Timed: 10 minutes

Scoring: Hand key; may be computer scored

Cost: 25 tests $42.50; volume discount

Publisher: Psychological Services, Inc.

PSI BASIC SKILLS TESTS FOR BUSINESS, INDUSTRY, AND GOVERNMENT: REASONING (BST #10)
W.W. Ruch, A.N. Shub, S.M. Moinat, and D.A. Dye

Adult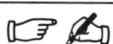

Purpose: Measures ability to analyze a list of facts and draw valid and logical conclusions from that information. Used to select clerical and administrative personnel.

Description: 30-item paper-pencil multiple-choice test consisting of six lists of facts (one-sentence statements), with five possible conclusions for each list. The examinee must read each list and decide whether each conclusion is definitely true, definitely false, or unknown based on the given facts. Examiner required. Suitable for group use.

Timed: 5 minutes

Scoring: Hand key; may be computer scored

Cost: 25 tests $42.50; volume discount

Publisher: Psychological Services, Inc.

PSI BASIC SKILLS TESTS FOR BUSINESS, INDUSTRY, AND GOVERNMENT: TYPING: PRACTICE COPY (BST #17)
W.W. Ruch, A.N. Shub, S.M. Moinat, and D.A. Dye

Adult

Purpose: Warm-up exercise familiarizing subject with the typewriter to be used

during testing. May be administered prior to any of the three BST typing tests.

Description: Unscored typing exercise in which the subjects become familiar with the location of the typewriter keys, including the margin release and backspace, and makes all the machine adjustments necessary for the three scored BST typing tests. Practice copy is typed double-space with a 5-space paragraph indentation and 60-character lines. Examiner required. Suitable for group use.

Timed: 2 minutes

Scoring: Unscored

Cost: 25 tests $42.50; volume discount

Publisher: Psychological Services, Inc.

PSI BASIC SKILLS TESTS FOR BUSINESS, INDUSTRY, AND GOVERNMENT: TYPING: REVISED COPY (BST #19)
W.W. Ruch, A.N. Shub, S.M. Moinat, and D.A. Dye

Adult

Purpose: Measures ability to type from printed copy with handwritten corrections. Used to select clerical and administrative personnel.

Description: Typing proficiency test in which examinees are given 5 minutes to type as much of the revised copy as possible, making the indicated changes and corrections as they type. The typed copy must be double-spaced 60-character lines with 5-space paragraph indentations and 10-space tab settings for headings. The typed revised copy is scored for accuracy, speed, and correctness and completeness of changes made in the final typed copy. Examiner required. Suitable for group use.

Timed: 5 minutes

Scoring: Hand key

Cost: 25 tests $42.50; volume discount

Publisher: Psychological Services, Inc.

PSI BASIC SKILLS TESTS FOR BUSINESS, INDUSTRY, AND GOVERNMENT: TYPING: STRAIGHT COPY (BST #18)
W.W. Ruch, A.N. Shub, S.M. Moinat, and D.A. Dye

Adult

Purpose: Measures ability to type straight copy, word-for-word, with no revisions. Used to select clerical and administrative personnel.

Description: Typing proficiency test in which applicants are given 5 minutes to type as much of a given passage as possible. The applicant types the passage line-for-line exactly as it is printed. The typed copy must be double-spaced 60–character lines with 5–space paragraph indentations. The applicant is given time to make machine adjustments before the test begins. The typed copy is scored for speed and accuracy. Examiner required. Suitable for group use.

Timed: 5 minutes

Scoring: Hand key

Cost: 25 tests $42.50; volume discount

Publisher: Psychological Services, Inc.

PSI BASIC SKILLS TESTS FOR BUSINESS, INDUSTRY, AND GOVERNMENT: TYPING: TABLES (BST #20)
W.W. Ruch, A.N. Shub, S.M. Moinat, and D.A. Dye

Adult

Purpose: Measures ability to set up and type tables according to specific directions. Used to select clerical and administrative personnel.

Description: Typing proficiency test in which examinees are given 7 minutes to type as much of three given tables as possible. The copy and directions for each of the tables is given in handwritten form. The test requires extensive use of the tabulator; each table has its own specified settings. The final copy is scored for speed, accuracy, and skill at correctly fol-

lowing the handwritten instructions. Examiner required. Suitable for group use.

Timed: 7 minutes

Scoring: Hand key

Cost: 25 tests $42.50; volume discount

Publisher: Psychological Services, Inc.

PSI BASIC SKILLS TESTS FOR BUSINESS, INDUSTRY, AND GOVERNMENT: VISUAL SPEED AND ACCURACY (BST #15)
W.W. Ruch, A.N. Shub, S.M. Moinat, and D.A. Dye

Adult

Purpose: Measures ability to see details quickly and accurately. Used to select clerical and administrative personnel.

Description: 150–item paper-pencil multiple-choice test in which each test item consists of two series of numbers and symbols. The examinee compares the numbers or symbols and determines whether they are the same or different. Examiner required. Suitable for group use.

Timed: 5 minutes

Scoring: Hand key; may be computer scored

Cost: 25 tests $42.50; volume discount

Publisher: Psychological Services, Inc.

PSI BASIC SKILLS TESTS FOR BUSINESS, INDUSTRY, AND GOVERNMENT: VOCABULARY (BST #3)
W.W. Ruch, A.N. Shub, S.M. Moinat, and D.A. Dye

Adult

Purpose: Measures the ability to identify the correct synonym for the word underlined in each sentence. Used to select clerical and office workers.

Description: 45–item paper-pencil multiple-choice test in which each item consists of a sentence, with one word underlined, followed by four words. The examinee must select the word meaning the same or about the same as the underlined word. Examiner required. Suitable for group use.

Timed: 5 minutes

Scoring: Hand key; may be computer scored

Cost: 25 tests $42.50; volume discount

Publisher: Psychological Services, Inc.

THE RBH ARITHMETIC REASONING TEST, FORMS I AND II

Refer to page 909.

THE RBH CLASSIFYING TEST, FORMS I AND II
Richardson, Bellows, Henry and Company, Inc.

Adult

Purpose: Measures the ability to classify material with speed and accuracy. Used with applicants for clerical positions.

Description: Multiple-item paper-pencil test assessing the ability to quickly and accurately classify information covering several different variables. The individual is presented with nine basic problems. Thirty situations are provided for each problem. In the first series of 30 items, the individual must quickly classify material in terms of three restrictions—shipping point, fragility, and value. In the second series, the shipping point is complicated, fragility status is reversed, and weight is the third alternative. In the third set, relationships are further complicated, so attention to instructions is essential. Series 4, 5, and 6 and series 7, 8, and 9 are not more difficult than the first series, but there is an overall pressure to complete as many items as possible.

The test yields a speed score, an accuracy score, and a right-wrong score. Male norms are available for marketing trainees, administrative and sales clerks, warehousemen, dispatchers, and laboratory testing personnel. Female norms are available for a variety of clerical applicants and employees. The test is available in two forms, I and II. Examiner required. Suitable for group use.

Timed: 10 minutes

Scoring: Hand key

Cost: 1–24 packages $25.00; score key $2.00; manual $2.00

Publisher: Richardson, Bellows, Henry and Company, Inc.

RCJS OFFICE ARITHMETIC TEST—FORM CA
R. T. Ramsay

Adult

Purpose: Assesses math skills necessary for the position of office clerk. Used for making hiring decisions.

Description: 40–item paper-pencil multiple-choice test assessing addition and subtraction of 1–, 2–, and 3–digit whole numbers and decimals; multiplication and division of 1– and 2–digit whole numbers and decimals; and reading simple charts and tables. Materials include a reusable booklet, answer sheet, and manual with key. Examiner required. Suitable for group use.

Timed: 30 minutes

Scoring: Hand key; machine scored; scoring service available from publisher

Cost: Reusable booklets $4.95 each (minimum order of 5); 500 answer sheets $80.00; manual with scoring key $24.95

Publisher: Ramsay Corporation

RCJS OFFICE READING TEST—FORM G
R. T. Ramsay

Adult

Purpose: Assesses reading skills necessary for office workers. Used for making hiring decisions.

Description: 40–item paper-pencil multiple-choice test based on five written passages: Operating the Copier, Travel Arrangements, Operating a Computer, The Business Letter, and Telephone Procedures. Materials include a reusable booklet, answer sheet, and manual with key. Examiner required. Suitable for group use.

Timed: 30 minutes

Scoring: Hand key; scoring service available from publisher

Cost: Reusable booklets $4.95 each; 500 answer sheets $80.00; manual with key $24.95

Publisher: Ramsay Corporation

SEASHORE-BENNETT STENOGRAPHIC PROFICIENCY TEST
G.K. Bennett and H.G. Seashore

Adult

Purpose: Measures stenographic skills. Used for selection and promotion of stenographers.

Description: 5–task test measuring the ability to type dictated commercial letters. Five letters are contained in each form: two are short and slow, two are medium in both length and dictation speed, and one is long and fast. Two parallel, alternate forms, B–1 and B–2, are available. Dictation is available on record, tape, and cassette. The test is sold only to personnel departments of business and industrial firms for the testing of applicants and employees. The test is not sold to schools or employment agencies. Examiner required. Suitable for group use.

Timed: Dictation 15 minutes; Transcription 30 minutes

Scoring: Examiner evaluated

Cost: Complete set (recordings for both forms, manual, script, 100 summary charts, record version) $89.00; reel-to-reel tape version $89.00; cassette tape version $89.00

Publisher: The Psychological Corporation

Information and availability unconfirmed; last verified in 1988.

SECRETARIAL STAFF SELECTOR

Adult

Purpose: Evaluates candidates of all levels of experience for secretarial positions.

Description: Multiple-item paper-pencil set of seven timed subtests and two optional subtests available in three formats for assessing attention to detail, alphabetizing and filing skills, grammar and punctuation, spelling and vocabulary, manual dexterity, logical and problem-solving abilities, numerical skills, desire for people contact (optional), and emotional stability (optional). The tests are used for selecting senior clerks, secretaries, and administrative assistants. Examiner required. Suitable for group use. Available in French.

Timed: 75 minutes

Untimed: Varies

Scoring: Computer scored

Cost: $99.00 each

Publisher: Wolfe Personnel Testing and Training Systems, Inc.

SHORT EMPLOYMENT TESTS (SET)
G.K. Bennett and Marjorie Gelink

Adult

Purpose: Measures job skills. Used in applicant and employee selection.

Description: Three paper-pencil tests measuring skills related to performance, particularly in clerical jobs. The tests are SET-Verbal (V), SET-Numerical (N), and SET-Clerical Aptitude (CA). They predict performance in a wide variety of jobs, including bank tellers, accounting clerks, hospital clerical workers, and airline reservation agents. The tests may be used individually or in combination. Four equivalent forms are available. Tapes are available for test administration. The test is sold only to personnel departments of business and industrial firms for testing applicants and employees. The tests are not sold to schools or employment agencies. Form 1 is restricted to member banks of the American Banker's Association (ABA). Examiner required. Suitable for group use.

Timed: 5 minutes per test

Scoring: Hand key

Cost: 25 test booklets, manual, key (specify test) $33.00

Publisher: The Psychological Corporation

Information and availability unconfirmed; last verified in 1988.

SHORT TESTS OF CLERICAL ABILITY (STCA)
Jean Maier Palormo

Adult

Purpose: Assesses aptitudes and abilities important to the successful completion of typical office tasks. Used for selection and placement in office job classifications, such as secretary-stenographer, office clerk, and specialized clerk (accounting, statistical, and billing).

Description: Multiple-item paper-pencil battery consisting of seven tests. The battery includes arithmetic skills, business vocabulary, checking accuracy, coding, oral and written directions, filing, and language (grammar and mechanics). The test is norm referenced, including minority groups. Examiner required. Suitable for group use.

Untimed: 3–6 minutes per test

Scoring: Hand key

Cost: 25 test booklets (specify test) $27.00; scoring stencils (specify test) $8.75; examiner's manual $10.00

Publisher: SRA/London House

SRA CLERICAL APTITUDES
Richardson, Bellows, Henry and Co., Inc.

Adult

Purpose: Assesses general aptitudes necessary for clerical work. Used in employee screening and placing.

Description: Three-part paper-pencil test measuring office vocabulary, office arithmetic, and office checking. The tests indicate the ability to learn tasks usually performed in various clerical jobs. The office vocabulary test (48 items) measures command of basic vocabulary and verbal relations. The arithmetic test (24 items) requires application of basic math processes to the solution of practical problems. The checking test (144 items) measures the ability to perceive details easily and rapidly. Examiner required. Suitable for group use.

Timed: 25 minutes

Scoring: Hand key

Cost: 25 reusable test booklets $90.00; 25 answer sheets $19.00; 100 profile sheets $21.00; examiner's manual $10.00

Publisher: SRA/London House

SRA TYPING 5
SRA/London House

Adult

Purpose: Measures a person's ability to type a particular kind of assignment. Used with a variety of typing positions requiring different skills.

Description: Task-assessment consisting of three forms measuring typing speed and accuracy. Typing Speed, Form A, consists of a letter with approximately 215 words measuring key-stroking speed and accuracy. Business Letter, Form B, for the more experienced typist, measures the ability to set up a business letter and type it quickly and accurately. Numerical, Form C, containing approximately 115 words and 40 numbers, measures speed and accuracy in typing complex material containing words, symbols, and numbers in columns with headings. Examiner required. Suitable for group use.

Timed: 5 minutes per test (after practice time)

Scoring: Hand key

Cost: 25 test booklets (specify test) $26.00; 25 practice sheets $9.00; examiner's manual $10.00

Publisher: SRA/London House

SRA TYPING SKILLS TEST
Marion W. Richardson and Ruth A. Pedersen

Adult

Purpose: Assesses typing skills. Used by teachers and managers to evaluate the skills of students, typists, clerical help, and job applicants.

Description: Test of typing speed and accuracy consisting of a business letter approximately 225 words in length to be typed as often as possible in an accurately timed 10–minute period. The test is scored according to International Typewriting Contest Rules. The test is available in two equivalent forms. Examiner required. Suitable for group use.

Timed: 10 minutes (after practice time)

Scoring: Hand key

Cost: 25 test booklets $28.00; examiner's manual $10.00

Publisher: SRA/London House

STENOGRAPHIC TEST
E.F. Wonderlic Personnel Test, Inc.

Adult

Purpose: Measures speed and accuracy in taking shorthand notes. Used to select and place stenographers.

Description: 26–item paper-pencil test assessing shorthand-stenographic skills. Items consist of 100–word letters of various "syllable densities" dictated at speeds ranging from 40–160 words per minute. The Vari-Speed Guide quickly determines an applicant's approximate level of skill. From this point, successively more difficult and faster letters are dictated until the applicant's best performance is determined. The test may be administered via an optional cassette tape, which includes all 26 letters dictated at their proper rate, warm-up exercises, and directions. Examiner required. Suitable for group use.

Timed: Varies

Scoring: Hand key

Cost: Complete $105.00; individual tapes (text not included) $24.00; printed text $23.00

Publisher: E.F. Wonderlic Personnel Test, Inc.

TEST A/8: ARITHMETIC
Refer to page 922.

TYPING TEST
E.F. Wonderlic Personnel Test, Inc.

Adult

Purpose: Assesses typing speed and accuracy. Used to select entry-level typists and keypunch operators.

Description: Multiple-item typing performance test consisting of four forms.

Letter Forms A and B measure typing speed in copying straight printed material. Random Numbers Form 2 is used to screen typists who will be asked to do significant amounts of typing for accounting, address files, and computer input. Random Letters Form K, which requires no verbal knowledge, is used to screen typists involved in keypunch and other operations using letter codes. The test may be administered with an optional cassette tape. Examiner required. Suitable for group use.

Timed: 5 minutes

Scoring: Hand key

Cost: Reusable complete package $45.00; cassette tape $24.00

Publisher: E.F. Wonderlic Personnel Test, Inc.

TYPING TEST FOR BUSINESS (TTB)
J.E. Doppelt, A.D. Hartman, and F.B. Krawchick

Adult

Purpose: Assesses typing skills. Used to test applicants for typist, keypunch operator, secretarial, and other positions in which typing skill is necessary.

Description: Test of five kinds of typing used in business: straight copy, letters, revised manuscript, numbers, and tables. The warm-up practice copy is administered first. The straight copy test may be given as a quick screening test. Two alternate forms, AR and BR, are available. The test is sold only to personnel departments of business and industrial firms for the testing of applicants and employees. It is not sold to schools or employment agencies. Examiner required. Suitable for group use.

Timed: Varies

Scoring: Hand key

Cost: Examination kit (test booklet for each test, both forms, manual) $33.00; 25 practice copy tests $18.00; 25 straight copy tests $30.00; 25 letters tests $30.00; 25 revised manuscript tests $30.00; 25 numbers tests $30.00; 25 tables tests $30.00 (specify form for all materials ordered)

Publisher: The Psychological Corporation

Information and availability unconfirmed; last verified in 1988.

TYPING TEST I AND II

Richardson, Bellows, Henry and Company, Inc.

Adult

Purpose: Provides a quick screening of an individual's typing ability. Used to estimate the typing skills of applicants for general clerical or clerk-typist positions.

Description: Manual test measuring an individual's typing speed and accuracy. The examinee is presented with a double-spaced letter to type. After reading the test directions, adjusting the machine settings, and typing the practice copy, the examinee types the test letter exactly as it appears. The examinee begins retyping the letter if it is completed before the allotted time expires. The test yields a words-per-minute score and an accuracy score. A more comprehensive test should be used for promoting present personnel or hiring secretarial or stenographic applicants. The following materials are required: one test folder and one typewriter for each examinee and a timing device for the examiner. Examiner required. Suitable for group use.

Timed: 5 minutes

Scoring: Hand key

Cost: 1–24 packages $30.00; score key $2.00; manual $2.00

Publisher: Richardson, Bellows, Henry and Company, Inc.

VCWS 5–CLERICAL COMPREHENSION AND APTITUDE

Adult

Purpose: Measures basic clerical aptitude and the ability to perform a variety of answering, mail sorting, alphabetical filing, bookkeeping, and typing tasks, and to communicate effectively both verbally and in writing. Also used as a screening device for entry-level general clerical jobs. May be used with hearing-impaired and visually impaired individuals.

Description: Manual test featuring three separate work samples measuring an individual's ability to perform a variety of clerical tasks and ability to learn the tasks. The test begins with mail sorting and simultaneous phone answering. A tape plays a series of phone conversations at prerecorded intervals requiring the individual to stop the mail sorting in order to take the phone message. The individual also must complete an alphabetical filing task. In the second section of the test, the individual must use a 10–key adding machine to perform three exercises emphasizing accurate recording of numerical data and basic math skills. In the typing section, the typewriter has been modified to measure a person's typing coordination skills regardless of previous exposure to typing. Work activities related to the test include classifying, filing, and sorting correspondence; recording verbal and written information; preparing numerical records with the aid of an adding machine; and transcribing using a typewriter. The test should not be used with individuals with severe impairment of the upper extremities. Examiner required. Not suitable for group use.

Timed: Not available

Scoring: Examiner evaluated

Cost: $2,395.00

Publisher: Valpar International Corporation

Computer

ADVANCED TEST BATTERY: DIAGRAMMATIC REASONING (ATB:DT8)

Refer to page 863.

ADVANCED TEST BATTERY: DIAGRAMMING (ATB:DA5)

Refer to page 863.

APTITUDE ASSESSMENT BATTERY: PROGRAMMING (AABP)

Jack M. Wolfe

Adult

Purpose: Determines a person's aptitude for computer programming. May be used to select job candidates, as a guide for training programs, and for revealing work habits and task preferences.

Description: Five-problem paper-pencil tests measuring ability to draw deductions, understand complicated instructions, interpret intricate specifications, reason, desk-check, debug, and document and annotate work. Examiner required. Suitable for group use. Available in French, Spanish, and braille.

Untimed: 3 hours

Scoring: Scoring service provided

Cost: Complete (test, evaluation) $110.00

Publisher: Wolfe Personnel Testing and Training Systems, Inc.

AUTOMATED OFFICE BATTERY (AOB)
Saville & Holdsworth Ltd. Staff

Ages 16–adult

Purpose: Measures job-related skills required in the modern automated office. Assesses the ability to estimate using numerical data to check data on VDU screens and printout and to follow coded instructions. Used for selection and career development.

Description: 130–item paper-pencil set of three tests measuring three abilities highly relevant to the needs of the modern electronic office. They are the ability to estimate numerically (where machines will make precise calculations), to check the accurate recording of new data onto VDU screens and printouts (where the information has been reordered and supplemented), and to follow instructions that have been coded into machine-oriented language. The tests include realistic representations of computer display terminals and printouts. The item content is suitable for international use. The tests are restricted to qualified users and are not available to educational institutions. Examiner required. Suitable for group use.
BRITISH PUBLISHER

Timed: 10–18 minutes per test

Scoring: Hand key; may be computer scored

Cost: See descriptions for individual AOB tests

Publisher: Saville & Holdsworth Ltd.

AUTOMATED OFFICE BATTERY: CODED INSTRUCTIONS (CI–3; U.S. VERSION)
Saville & Holdsworth Ltd. Staff

Ages 16–adult

Purpose: Measures the ability to understand and follow instructions coded into machine-oriented language.

Description: 40–item paper-pencil test assessing the ability to understand and follow coded instructions. Candidates are presented with instructions on how to enter and retrieve information from a machine. They must understand the instructions in the text and decide the appropriate course of action for each question. The content is office based and relates to new technology within the office environment, particularly to the kinds of instructions that an individual must follow when operating computer systems and word processors. One of three tests in the Automated Office Battery. The tests are restricted to qualified users and are not available to educational institutions. Examiner required. Suitable for group use.

Timed: 18 minutes

Scoring: Hand key; may be computer scored

Cost: 5 reusable test booklets $138.50; 25 answer sheets $162.50; administration card $14.00; scoring key $28.00

Publisher: Saville & Holdsworth Ltd.

AUTOMATED OFFICE BATTERY: COMPUTER CHECKING (AOB: CC–2; U.S. VERSION)
Saville & Holdsworth Ltd. Staff

Ages 16–adult

Purpose: Measures the abilities of scanning, reasoning, and checking documentation against VDU or printer output.

Description: 40–item paper-pencil test assessing the ability to check computerized information against typed copy.

The candidate must identify quickly and accurately whether the information has been correctly transferred to a facing representation of a VDU screen or a page of computer printout. The information may have been reordered and added to other information during input to the computer. To complete the checking task, the candidate must find the relevant data, understand its new representation, and then make the final check on its correct transfer. One of three tests in the Automated Office Battery. Examiner required. Suitable for group use.

BRITISH PUBLISHER

Timed: 12 minutes

Scoring: Hand key; may be computer scored

Cost: 10 reusable test booklets $210.00; 50 answer sheets $105.00; administration card $10.50; scoring key $21.00

Publisher: Saville & Holdsworth Ltd.

BUSINESS ANALYST SKILLS EVALUATION (BUSAN)

Adult

Purpose: Evaluates aptitude and potential for positions in business systems analysis, procedures analysis, and user department/EDP department interface. Used with candidates with prior business experience. No previous data processing knowledge or experience is required.

Description: Multiple-item paper-pencil test in two groups of subtests used for evaluating candidates for positions such as business analyst, procedures analyst, business systems analyst, and user/EDP department interface. Section 1 subtests measure analytical ability, flow charting, deductive reasoning, procedures and systems analysis, and development of departmental user reports and subsystems. Section 2 subtests measure horizontal interpersonal relationship abilities, people contact desired, emotional stability, stress tolerance, group participation skills, consistency, dominance, adventurousness, maturity, enthusiasm, tough-mindedness, practicality, sophistication, self-sufficiency, leadership potential, drive and initiative, verbal communication skills, and memory. Section 1

and two subtests in Section 2 are timed. Results are available by mail or telephone. Examiner required. Suitable for group use.

Timed: 1 hour, 45 minutes

Scoring: Scoring service provided

Cost: $199.00–$499.00 depending on depth of assessment required

Publisher: Wolfe Personnel Testing and Training Systems, Inc.

COMMON BUSINESS ORIENTED LANGUAGE (COBOL)
Science Research Associates

Adult

Purpose: Measures the extent to which individuals are knowledgeable about COBOL programming. Used for pre-employment screening, as a placement tool, or to assess training needs by organizations.

Description: 44–item paper-pencil or computer-administered multiple-choice test measuring knowledge of COBOL programming. Two alternate forms available. Form A is self-scored; Form B is computer-administered and scored. Examiner required. Suitable for group use.

Untimed: 45 minutes

Scoring: Computer scored; self-scored; scoring service available from publisher

Cost: Contact publisher

Publisher: SRA/London House

COMPUTER APTITUDE, LITERACY, AND INTEREST PROFILE (CALIP)
Refer to page 787.

COMPUTER OPERATOR APTITUDE BATTERY (COAB)
Science Research Associates

Adult

Purpose: Helps predict job performance of computer operators. Used by data processing managers and personnel directors to select applicants for computer operator positions.

Description: Paper-pencil test predicting success as a computer operator. The test consists of three separately timed subtests: Sequence Recognition, Format Checking, and Logical Thinking. Examiner required. Suitable for group use.

Timed: 45 minutes

Scoring: Hand key

Cost: 5 reusable test booklets $85.00; 25 answer sheets $52.00; examiner's manual $10.00

Publisher: SRA/London House

COMPUTER PROGRAMMER APTITUDE BATTERY (CPAB)
SRA/London House

Adult

Purpose: Measures potential for success in the computer programming field. Used by data processing managers and personnel directors to identify people with the aptitude for computer programming.

Description: Five separately timed paper-pencil subtests measuring verbal meaning, reasoning, letter series, number ability, and diagramming (problem analysis and logical solution). Examiner required. Suitable for group use.

Timed: 1 hour, 15 minutes

Scoring: Hand key; scoring service available from publisher

Cost: 5 reusable test booklets $85.00; 25 answer sheets $52.00; examiner's manual $10.00

Publisher: SRA/London House

CRITICAL REASONING TEST BATTERY: DIAGRAMMATIC SERIES (CRTB: DC2)
Refer to page 1040.

EDP PROJECT LEADER SKILLS EVALUATION
B. W. Winrow

Adult

Purpose: Evaluates skills required for the EDP Project Leader position.

Description: Multiple-item paper-pencil test evaluating the essential procedural and analytical skills required of the EDP project leader, including organization and control, scheduling, and planning concepts. A screening version and a comprehensive version are available depending on the depth of assessment required. Examiner required. Suitable for group use. Available in French.

Timed: 2 hours

Scoring: Scoring service provided

Cost: $229.00

Publisher: Wolfe Personnel Testing and Training Systems, Inc.

IPI JOB TEST FIELD SERIES: COMPUTER PROGRAMMER
Industrial Psychology International, Ltd.

Adult

Purpose: Assesses skills and aptitudes of applicants for entry-level computer programmer positions. Used for employee selection and placement.

Description: Multiple-item paper-pencil battery of five aptitude tests measuring skills that predict success as an entry-level computer programmer. The tests include Office Terms (54 items), measuring the ability to understand special terms used in business and industry; Numbers (54 items), measuring aptitude for working quickly and accurately with numbers; Judgment (54 items), measuring aptitude for logical thinking, planning, and dealing with abstract relations; Parts (48 items), measuring aptitude for visualizing size, shape, and spatial relations of objects in two or three dimensions; and Perception (54 items), measuring the ability to rapidly scan and locate details and errors in words and numbers and to recognize likenesses and differences. Examiner required. Suitable for group use. Also available in French and Spanish.

Timed: Each test 6 minutes

Scoring: Hand key

Cost: Instruction kit $16.00; test packages $10.00

Publisher: Industrial Psychology International, Ltd.

MICROCOMPUTER USER APTITUDE TEST
Richard Label

Adult

Purpose: Measures aptitude and potential for work with a microcomputer.

Description: Multiple-item test measuring the following abilities necessary for working with a microcomputer: logical ability; ability to work with spreadsheets, databases, and operating systems; and vendor manual interpretation. The test consists of five problems that simulate the use of the most commonly used micro applications. Skills are assessed independent of any specific hardware or software. Examiner required. Not suitable for group use.

Timed: 1 hour
Scoring: Scoring service provided
Cost: $50.00
Publisher: Wolfe Personnel Testing and Training Systems, Inc.

NATIONAL BUSINESS COMPETENCY TESTS: WORD PROCESSING TEST
Refer to page 273.

NEW TECHNOLOGY TESTS— COMPUTER COMMANDS
Psychometric Research and Development Ltd.

Adult

Purpose: Assesses an individual's speed and accuracy in using simple commands to process data similar to that presented on a video display terminal. Used to select applicants for computer operator roles or for clerical positions involving the use of computers, for example, in banking, insurance travel, or storekeeping.

Description: Multiple-item computer-administered test of speed and accuracy in using simple word processing computer commands such as deleting, moving, or copying text within a document. The test focuses on the examinee's ability to acquire an understanding of the func-tions of the various commands rather than on the ability to follow instructions. Examiner required. Not suitable for group use.
BRITISH PUBLISHER

Timed: 20 minutes

Scoring: Hand key

Cost: Contact publisher

Publisher: NFER-NELSON Publishing Company Ltd.

NEW TECHNOLOGY TESTS— COMPUTER RULES
Psychometric Research and Development Ltd.

Adult

Purpose: Measures the potential to understand a computer system and to use it effectively through manipulating files and recognizing what they contain. Used for selecting and recruiting individuals for data processing, word processing, and other positions requiring data manipulation; for selecting applicants to computer science and information technology courses; and in identifying a company's training needs.

Description: Multiple-item paper-pencil instrument assessing the ability to work successfully with a computer system. Each sheet in the test booklet explains only a part of the computer system. Candidates are required to answer questions about the information presented before moving on to the next sheet of information. In this way, examinees build a cumulative idea of how the system operates. Examinees continue to answer questions and use their mistakes to arrive at correct solutions just as they would if they were working with a real system. Examiner required. Suitable for group use.
BRITISH PUBLISHER

Timed: 30 minutes

Scoring: Hand key

Cost: Contact publisher

Publisher: NFER-NELSON Publishing Company Ltd.

PROGRAMMER ANALYST APTITUDE TEST (PAAT)

Adult

Purpose: Evaluates aptitude and potential for computer programming and business analysis positions. Used for pre-screening entry-level candidates with no prior experience, computer trainees, computer science graduates, and experienced applicants.

Description: 6–item paper-pencil test assessing logical ability, skill in interpreting business specifications, potential for translating business problems into symbolic logic, and ability to follow complex business procedures and analyze them to supply specific requirements. Available with interpersonal measures. Examiner required. Suitable for group use.

Timed: 1½ hours

Scoring: Scoring service provided

Cost: $189.00–$429.00 depending on depth of assessment

Publisher: Wolfe Personnel Testing and Training Systems, Inc.

PROGRAMMER APTITUDE BATTERY (PAB)
Terence R. Taylor

Adolescent, adult

Purpose: Assesses aptitude for computer programming.

Description: 102–item paper-pencil multiple-choice test with three subtests. The Procedures Test (36 items, 60 minutes) measures logical reasoning; number ability; perseverance; short-medium term memory; reading comprehension; and precise, methodological approach to problems. The Matrices Test I (36 items, 10 minutes) measures speed and accuracy. The Matrices Test II (30 items, 30 minutes) measures forming and checking hypotheses. Materials include test booklets, answer sheets, rough paper, and a manual. Examiner required. Suitable for group use. Available in Afrikaans and braille.
SOUTH AFRICAN PUBLISHER

Timed: 100 minutes

Scoring: Hand key; computer scored

Cost: Contact publisher

Publisher: Human Sciences Research Council

PROGRAMMER APTITUDE COMPETENCE TEST SYSTEM (PACTS)
C.A. Haverly and Pete Seiner

Adult

Purpose: Measures an individual's ability to write good computer programs, regardless of experience. Used for job screening.

Description: Multiple-item paper-pencil test of 4–6 problems with up to 20 total problems possible. The subject is given 30–50 minutes to study an instruction book that describes a general computer programming language for a hypothetical computer. The subject then is given a book of problems, with difficulty level based on the programming experience of the subject. Completed programs are evaluated by computer scoring on correctness, efficiency, compactness, problem difficulty, and completion time. Materials include the computer installation, manual, and problems. Examiner required. Suitable for group use.

Untimed: 2–3 hours

Scoring: Computer scored

Cost: Computer installation $8,200.00; PACTS is available on a service basis: $100.00 per test for the first five tests; $80.00 per test for additional five tests

Publisher: Haverly Systems, Inc.

Information and availability unconfirmed; last verified in 1988.

PROGRAMMER APTITUDE SERIES: LEVEL 1 (PAS-1)
Saville & Holdsworth Ltd.

Adult

Purpose: Measures aptitudes for the very diverse range of activities and levels of skills required for programmer jobs. Used for entry-level data processing staff selections.

Description: Five paper-pencil multiple-choice tests measuring the acquisition of skills involved in most business programming functions. The tests include Advanced Testing Battery (ATB), Diagramming (DA5), ATB Verbal Concepts (VA1), ATB Number Series (NA2), Personnel Test Battery (PTB), Basic Checking (CP7), Technical Test Battery (TTB), and Spatial Recognition (ST9). The test provides an overview of diagramming, verbal, numerical, clerical, and spatial abilities. Examiner required. Suitable for group use.
BRITISH PUBLISHER

Timed: Complete battery 1 hour, 15 minutes

Scoring: Hand key; examiner evaluated; may be computer scored

Cost: Complete (test booklets, 50 answer sheets, keys, profiles, manual) $787.50

Publisher: Saville & Holdsworth Ltd.

PROGRAMMER APTITUDE SERIES: LEVEL 2 (PAS-2)
Saville & Holdsworth Ltd.

Adult

Purpose: Measures aptitudes for the very diverse range of activities and levels of skills required for programmer jobs at an intermediate level. Used for intermediate data processing staff selections.

Description: Five paper-pencil multiple-choice tests measuring the acquisition of the skills involved in most business programming functions, but at a higher level of difficulty than the basic level. The tests include ATB Diagramming (DA5), ATB Verbal Critical Reasoning (VA3), ATB Number Series (NA2), PTB Basic Checking (CP7), and TTB Spatial Reasoning (ST7). This combination of tests is useful where more "top" is required, for example when dealing with good GCE "O" and "A" level applicants. Examiner required. Suitable for group use.
BRITISH PUBLISHER

Timed: 1 hour, 35 minutes

Scoring: Hand key; examiner evaluated; may be computer scored

Cost: Complete (test booklets, 50 answer sheets, keys, profiles, manual) $787.50

Publisher: Saville & Holdsworth Ltd.

PROGRAMMER APTITUDE SERIES: LEVEL 3 (PAS-3)
Saville & Holdsworth Ltd.

Adult

Purpose: Measures aptitudes for the very diverse range of activities and levels of skills required for data processing staff selection at higher levels, including graduates.

Description: Five paper-pencil multiple-choice tests measuring the acquisition of skills involved in most business programming functions by higher staff members and graduates. The tests include ATB Verbal Concepts (VA1), ATB Number Series (NA2), ATB Verbal Critical Reasoning (VA3), ATB Numerical Critical Reasoning (NA4), and TTB Diagrammatic Reasoning (DT8). Examiner required. Suitable for group use.
BRITISH PUBLISHER

Timed: Complete battery 1 hour, 35 minutes

Scoring: Hand key; examiner evaluated; may be computer scored

Cost: Complete (test booklets, 50 answer sheets, keys, profiles, manual) $808.50

Publisher: Saville & Holdsworth Ltd.

STRUCTURED ANALYSIS AND DESIGN CONCEPTS PROFICIENCY TEST (WWSAD)
B. W. Winrow

Adult

Purpose: Evaluates knowledge of structured analysis, design methodology, and commonly used tools and techniques. Used with candidates for EDP systems analyst/designer positions.

Description: Multiple-item paper-pencil test measuring the ability to use data flow diagrams and knowledge of system development methodology, structured analysis process, structured analysis tools, structure charts, and coupling, cohesion, control, and packaging. The test is used for determining the technical proficiency of experienced programmers, staff expertise, and structured analysis and design training needs. It also is used for evaluating structured analysis and design training effectiveness, conducting skills inventory analysis, and identifying promotable employees. Scores are determined by categorizing different types of errors and deducting different point values for the errors, varying with the severity of error. Examiner required. Suitable for group use.

Timed: 35 minutes

Scoring: Scoring service provided

Cost: $55.00

Publisher: Wolfe Personnel Testing and Training Systems, Inc.

SYSTEMS ANALYST APTITUDE TEST (SAAT)
Jack M. Wolfe

Adult

Purpose: Measures a person's aptitude for business systems design. Used for hiring, training, and promoting computer analysts and programmers.

Description: Single-item (case study) test evaluating interpretation of specifications, ability to plan a logical procedure, recognition of alternative solutions, clarity of explanation, quality of organization, attention to detail, and effectiveness and efficiency of design. Available in French. Examiner required. Suitable for group use.

Untimed: 3 hours

Scoring: Scoring service provided

Cost: Complete (test, evaluation) $175.00 per person

Publisher: Wolfe Personnel Testing and Training Systems, Inc.

SYSTEMS PROGRAMMING APTITUDE TEST (SPAT)
Jack M. Wolfe

Adult

Purpose: Measures a person's aptitude for systems and software programming. May be used for hiring, training, and promotion decisions at all levels of skill.

Description: Five-part paper-pencil test measuring accuracy, reasoning, and abil-

ity to deal with complex relationships and skills in deductive, interpretive, and analytic reasoning. Examiner required. Suitable for group use.

Untimed: 3 hours

Scoring: Scoring service provided

Cost: Complete (test, evaluation) $250.00

Publisher: Wolfe Personnel Testing and Training Systems, Inc.

TECHNICAL TEST BATTERY: SPATIAL REASONING (TTB:ST7; U.S. VERSION)
Refer to page 921.

TECHNICAL TEST BATTERY: SPATIAL RECOGNITION (TTB:ST9)
Refer to page 921.

W-APT PROGRAMMING APTITUDE TEST
Jack M. Wolfe

Adult

Purpose: Measures aptitude and potential for applications programming. Used for screening entry-level candidates, computer trainees, and computer science graduates and for prescreening experienced applicants.

Description: 5–item paper-pencil or computer-administered test assessing logical ability, interpretation of intricate specifications, ability to follow instructions precisely, attention to detail, accuracy, and problem solving using reasoning with symbols. A microcomputer version is available. Examiner required. Suitable for group use. Available in French.

Untimed: 1 hour

Scoring: Hand key; scoring service provided

Cost: $19.00 per person

Publisher: Wolfe Personnel Testing and Training Systems, Inc.

WOLFE COMPUTER OPERATOR APTITUDE TEST (WCOAT)
Jack M. Wolfe

Adult

Purpose: Evaluates aptitude for computer operations at all experience levels.

Description: Generalized aptitude test measuring manual dexterity and the ability to solve problems logically, follow procedural logic, and precisely follow all instructions and rules. Examiner required. Suitable for group use. Available in French.

Timed: 2 hours

Scoring: Scoring service provided

Cost: Complete (test, computer report) $75.00 per person

Publisher: Wolfe Personnel Testing and Training Systems, Inc.

WOLFE DATA ENTRY OPERATOR APTITUDE TEST (WDEOAT)
S. Berke

Adult

Purpose: Determines a person's aptitude for work as a data entry operator or terminal operator. May be used for hiring or training purposes.

Description: 6–item multiple-part paper-pencil test measuring manual dexterity, coding, accuracy, numerical skills, editing, and work speed. Examiner required. Suitable for group use.

Timed: 30 minutes

Scoring: Scoring service provided

Cost: Complete (test, evaluation) $40.00 per person

Publisher: Wolfe Personnel Testing and Training Systems, Inc.

WOLFE PROGRAMMING APTITUDE TEST—FORM S
Jack M. Wolfe

Adult

Purpose: Determines a person's aptitude for computer programming. Used as a screening instrument.

Description: 10–item paper-pencil test. A 64–page booklet with answers is provided so that respondents can score their own tests. Self-administered. Suitable for group use.

Untimed: 1 hour

Scoring: Hand key; self-scored

Cost: $75.00 each

Publisher: Wolfe Personnel Testing and Training Systems, Inc.

WOLFE PROGRAMMING APTITUDE TEST—FORM W
Jack M. Wolfe

Adult

Purpose: Measures aptitude for computer programming. Used by schools and placement agencies.

Description: Three-part paper-pencil test measuring attention to detail, ability to solve problems, and ability to interpret specifications. Examiner required. Suitable for group use. Available in French.

Timed: 40 minutes

Scoring: Hand key; examiner evaluated; scoring service provided

Cost: Booklets (scored by client) $20.00 each, (scored by publisher) $35.00 each

Publisher: Wolfe Personnel Testing and Training Systems, Inc.

WOLFE PROGRAMMING LANGUAGE TEST: COBOL (WCOBL)
Jack M. Wolfe

Adult

Purpose: Assesses a person's knowledge of COBOL. Used for screening experienced programmers.

Description: 47–item paper-pencil test measuring speed of work and evaluating coding skills, documentation, and knowledge of COBOL. Suitable for junior and intermediate programmers with detailed knowledge of the COBOL manual. Examiner required. Suitable for group use.

Timed: 2 hours

Scoring: Scoring service provided

Cost: Complete (test, evaluation) $65.00 per person

Publisher: Wolfe Personnel Testing and Training Systems, Inc.

WOLFE-SPENCE PROGRAMMING APTITUDE TEST (WSPAT)
Jack M. Wolfe and R. J. Spence

Adult

Purpose: Screens entry-level candidates for computer programming work. May be used for hiring or selecting candidates for training classes.

Description: 8–item paper-pencil test measuring a person's logical capabilities and ability to interpret intricate specifications. Candidates passing the test should be given the AABP test prior to making hiring decisions. Examiner required. Suitable for group use.

Timed: 2 hours

Scoring: Scoring service provided

Cost: Complete (test, evaluation) $45.00 per person

Publisher: Wolfe Personnel Testing and Training Systems, Inc.

WOLFE-WINROW CICS/VS COMMAND LEVEL PROFICIENCY TEST (WWCICS)
B. W. Winrow

Adult

Purpose: Measures a person's knowledge of IBM CICS/VS Command Level. Used for hiring, training, and promoting applications programmers and software specialists.

Description: Five-part paper-pencil test measuring general knowledge of CICS/VS concepts, facilities, and commands as well as the ability to code CICS/VS commands from specifications and debug and test in a CICS/VS environment. The test also includes an optional measure of specific knowledge of Basic Mapping Support and related commands. Examiner required. Suitable for group use.

Timed: 30 minutes

Scoring: Scoring service provided

Cost: Complete (detailed report) $65.00

Publisher: Wolfe Personnel Testing and Training Systems, Inc.

WOLFE-WINROW DOS/VS JCL PROFICIENCY TEST
B. W. Winrow

Adult

Purpose: Measures a person's knowledge of DOS, DOS/VS, or DOS/VSE JCL language. May be used for hiring, training, and promoting purposes.

Description: Five-part paper-pencil test measuring the ability to identify common JCL errors, code, overwrite catalogued procedures, and specific knowledge of JCL parameters. Suitable for examining computer operators, DOS JCL analysts, and applications programmers at all experience levels. Examiner required. Suitable for group use.

Timed: 30 minutes

Scoring: Scoring service provided

Cost: Complete (test, computer report) $65.00 per person

Publisher: Wolfe Personnel Testing and Training Systems, Inc.

WOLFE-WINROW OS JCL PROFICIENCY TEST
B. W. Winrow

Adult

Purpose: Measures a person's knowledge of IBM OS/JCL language. Used for hiring, promoting, and training computer operators, analysts, and programmers.

Description: Five-part paper-pencil test measuring general knowledge of JCL statements and parameters and understanding of JCL parameters, catalogued procedures, symbolic parameters, GDGs, and overriding JCL. The test also assesses the ability to identify OS/JCL errors and code OS/JCL. Examiner required. Suitable for group use.

Timed: 30 minutes

Scoring: Scoring service provided

Cost: Complete (test, computer report) $65.00 per person

Publisher: Wolfe Personnel Testing and Training Systems, Inc.

WOLFE-WINROW STRUCTURED COBOL
B. W. Winrow

Adult

Purpose: Assesses a person's knowledge of structured COBOL. Used for hiring, evaluating existing staff, evaluating training needs and effectiveness, and promotion.

Description: Five-question paper-pencil test measuring the ability to identify structured programming tools for COBOL, use concepts such as table lookup and debugging aids, define storage attributes and code PICTURE clauses for COBOL, code from specifications, and understand arithmetic operations and programming efficiencies. Examiner required. Suitable for group use.

Timed: 30 minutes

Scoring: Scoring service provided

Cost: Complete (includes report) $65.00 per person

Publisher: Wolfe Personnel Testing and Training Systems, Inc.

WOLFE-WINROW TSO/SPF PROFICIENCY TEST (WWTSO)
B. W. Winrow

Adult

Purpose: Assesses a person's knowledge of IBM TSO/SPF. Used for hiring, training, and promoting programmers and software specialists.

Description: Five-part paper-pencil test evaluating an applicant's knowledge of TSO/SPF features and commands. Examiner required. Suitable for group use.

Timed: 30 minutes

Scoring: Scoring service provided

Cost: Complete (test, detailed report) $55.00

Publisher: Wolfe Personnel Testing and Training Systems, Inc.

WORD PROCESSING APTITUDE BATTERY (WPAB)
Saville & Holdsworth Ltd. Staff

Adult

Purpose: Measures a wide range of skills and abilities related to word processing occupations. Used for personnel screening with individuals who have no educational qualifications and those with degrees.

Description: 186–item paper-pencil test of word processing skills and abilities. The battery includes five tests: Verbal Skills (WP1), Checking Skills (WP2), Written Instructions (WP3), Coded Information (WP4), and Numerical Computation (WP5). The first three tests are used for jobs involving the basic functions of creating documents, editing, filing, and moving blocks of text. WP5 is used when the job also requires form design, reformatting, justification, and figure work. The whole battery is used for advanced word processing work, including calculations, keyboard programming, and lists and record processing. Examiner required. Suitable for group use.

BRITISH PUBLISHER

Timed: Complete battery 57 minutes

Scoring: Hand key; may be computer scored

Cost: Manual and user's guide $105.00; 10 test booklets (includes all 5 tests) $168.00; 5 administration cards $63.00; 5 scoring keys $84.00; 10 answer sheets and profile chart $63.00; 10 group score sheets $4.20; annual license $220.50

Publisher: Saville & Holdsworth Ltd.

WORD PROCESSING APTITUDE BATTERY: CHECKING SKILLS (WP2)
Saville & Holdsworth Ltd. Staff

Adult

Purpose: Measures ability to check written information. Used in personnel screening and development for word processor operators.

Description: 50–item paper-pencil test measuring the ability to check written information quickly and accurately. Proofreading ability from one set of text to another is measured by having candidates code errors such as omissions and transpositions according to a set of rules. One of five tests in the Word Processing Aptitude Battery. The test is used with WP1 and WP3 to screen for jobs involving creating documents, editing, filing, and moving blocks of text. Examiner required. Suitable for group use. BRITISH PUBLISHER

Timed: 10 minutes

Scoring: Hand key; may be computer scored

Cost: Manual and user's guide $105.00; 10 test booklets (includes all 5 tests) $168.00; 5 administration cards $63.00; 5 scoring keys $84.00; 10 answer sheets and profile chart $63.00; 10 group score sheets $4.20; annual license $220.50

Publisher: Saville & Holdsworth Ltd.

WORD PROCESSING APTITUDE BATTERY: CODED INFORMATION (WP4)
Saville & Holdsworth Ltd. Staff

Adult

Purpose: Measures reasoning ability using symbols. Used in personnel screening and development for word processing operators.

Description: 35–item paper-pencil test measuring the ability to reason logically and flexibly with information and instructions presented in symbols. The candidate is presented with a row of letters in boxes with symbols attached, which indicate how the letters must be altered. The candidate chooses the correct response from five alternatives. One of five tests in the Word Processing Aptitude Battery. Examiner required. Suitable for group use. BRITISH PUBLISHER

Timed: 15 minutes

Scoring: Hand key; may be computer scored

Cost: Manual and user's guide $105.00; 10 test booklets (includes all 5 tests) $168.00; 5 administration cards $63.00; 5 scoring keys $84.00; 10 answer sheets and profile chart $63.00; 10 group score sheets $4.20; annual license $220.50

Publisher: Saville & Holdsworth Ltd.

WORD PROCESSING APTITUDE BATTERY: NUMERICAL COMPUTATION (WP5)
Saville & Holdsworth Ltd. Staff

Adult

Purpose: Measures basic mathematics abilities. Used in personnel screening and development for word processor operators.

Description: 35-item paper-pencil test assessing mathematics computation skills and the ability to recognize and understand simple number relationships. The test emphasizes straightforward computation. Candidates select the correct number to complete a sequence or equation from five options. The test is useful for positions requiring complex tabular work and calculations. One of five tests in the Word Processing Aptitude Battery. Examiner required. Suitable for group use. BRITISH PUBLISHER

Timed: 10 minutes

Scoring: Hand key; may be computer scored

Cost: Manual and user's guide $105.00; 10 test booklets (includes all 5 tests) $168.00; 5 administration cards $63.00; 5 scoring keys $84.00; 10 answer sheets and profile chart $63.00; 10 group score sheets $4.20; annual license $220.50

Publisher: Saville & Holdsworth Ltd.

WORD PROCESSING APTITUDE BATTERY: VERBAL SKILLS (WP1)
Saville & Holdsworth Ltd. Staff

Adult

Purpose: Measures basic language arts skills. Used in personnel screening and development for word processor operators.

Description: 30–item paper-pencil test of word meaning, spelling, and grammar.

Emphasis is on vocabulary skills that word processor operators need for everyday work. For each question, candidates choose a pair of words from five alternatives to correctly complete a sentence. One of five tests in the Word Processing Aptitude Battery. The test is used with WP2 and WP3 to screen for jobs involving creating documents, editing, filing, and moving blocks of text. Examiner required. Suitable for group use. BRITISH PUBLISHER

Timed: 10 minutes

Scoring: Hand key; may be computer scored

Cost: Manual and user's guide $105.00; 10 test booklets (includes all 5 tests) $168.00; 5 administration cards $63.00; 5 scoring keys $84.00; 10 answer sheets and profile chart $63.00; 10 group score sheets $4.20; annual license $220.50

Publisher: Saville & Holdsworth Ltd.

WORD PROCESSING APTITUDE BATTERY: WRITTEN INSTRUCTIONS (WP3)
Saville & Holdsworth Ltd. Staff

Adult

Purpose: Measures ability to understand and follow complex written instructions. Used in personnel screening and development for word processor operators.

Description: 36–item paper-pencil test of ability to follow complex written directions. The candidate is presented with office-type procedures in a written passage and must retrieve the relevant information to select the correct procedure in each of three cases from five alternatives. One of five tests in the Word Processing Aptitude Battery. The test is used with WP1 and WP2 to screen for jobs involving creating documents, editing, filing, and moving blocks of text. Examiner required. Suitable for group use. BRITISH PUBLISHER

Timed: 12 minutes

Scoring: Hand key; may be computer scored

Cost: Manual and user's guide $105.00; 10 test booklets (includes all 5 tests) $168.00; 5 administration cards $63.00; 5 scoring keys $84.00; 10 answer sheets and profile chart $63.00; 10 group score sheets $4.20; annual license $220.50

Publisher: Saville & Holdsworth Ltd.

THE WORD PROCESSING OPERATOR ASSESSMENT BATTERY
S. Berke

Adult

Purpose: Determines a person's suitability for work as a word processing operator. Used in the hiring process to supplement interviews, reference checking, and machine tests.

Description: 5–item paper-pencil test measuring attention to detail, ability to solve problems, manual dexterity, numerical skill, alphabetizing, filing, and coding. Examiner required. Suitable for group use. Available in French.

Timed: 30 minutes

Scoring: Scoring service provided

Cost: Complete (test kit and evaluation) $50.00

Publisher: Wolfe Personnel Testing and Training Systems, Inc.

WORD PROCESSING TEST (WPT)

Job applicants and employees

Purpose: Measures ability to input and edit both text and tables on a word processing machine. Used as a selection or promotion tool with job applicants or current employees.

Description: Computer-administered measure of word processing speed and accuracy. The test assesses an individual's ability to operate actual word processing equipment used on the job. Materials include a manual, test booklet, edit disk containing original documents that the examinee must edit according to instructions given in the test booklet, and a personal scoring record. Two alternate forms, A and B, are available. Form A is sold only to personnel departments of businesses and industries. Examiner required. Not suitable for group use.

Untimed: 25 minutes

Scoring: Hand key

Cost: Complete set (5 test booklets, manual, 10 personal scoring records, scoring keys, edit disk) $295.00; examination kit (test booklet, manual, personal scoring record) $49.00

Publisher: The Psychological Corporation

Information and availability unconfirmed; last verified in 1988.

WORD PROCESSOR ASSESSMENT BATTERY (WPAB)

Adult

Purpose: Measures abilities related to success in word-processing occupations. Used in business and education for selection and placement.

Description: Multiple-item paper-pencil and task-performance test in three parts assessing machine aptitude, typing speed and accuracy, and machine transcription abilities. Part I tests understanding of word processing equipment functions, including data storage, file creation, manipulation, and others. Part II tests the ability to type a business letter from typed copy with handwritten corrections and insertions. Part III tests the ability to accurately transcribe dictated material and produce a letter with correct spelling, punctuation, and format. Examiner required. Suitable for group use.

Timed: 76 minutes

Scoring: Hand key

Cost: 10 test booklets $60.00; manual $25.00; dictation cassette for Part III $25.00

Publisher: SRA/London House

Engineering

ADVANCED TEST BATTERY: DIAGRAMMING (ATB:DA5)
Refer to page 863.

ADVANCED TEST BATTERY: SPATIAL REASONING (ATB:ST7)
Refer to page 864.

CLOSURE FLEXIBILITY (CONCEALED FIGURES)
Refer to page 1065.

ELECTRICAL SOPHISTICATION TEST
Stanley Ciesla

Adult

Purpose: Assesses electrical knowledge. Used to evaluate job applicants.

Description: Multiple-item paper-pencil test of sophistication of electrical knowledge. The test discriminates between persons with electrical know-how and those with none and between electrical engineers and other types of engineers. Examiner required. Suitable for group use.

Untimed: 10 minutes

Scoring: Hand key

Cost: Specimen set $4.00; 25 tests $4.00

Publisher: Psychometric Affiliates

INDIVIDUAL QUALIFICATION FORM
Morris I. Stein

Adult

Purpose: Determines a profile of the type of individual needed for a specific job in technical industries and research and development (R & D) organizations. Used to improve placement procedures of scientists, engineers, and research personnel.

Description: 30–item paper-pencil questionnaire designed to elicit from the supervisor an accurate statement of a job's requirements, opportunities, and limitations. The items are specified in terms of role requirements in order to facilitate the screening of job applicants. The test is restricted to R & D personnel. Self-administered by supervisor or administrator. Suitable for group use.

Untimed: 20 minutes

Scoring: Examiner evaluated

Cost: $2.50 each

Publisher: Morris I. Stein

Information and availability unconfirmed; last verified in 1987.

IPI APTITUDE—INTELLIGENCE TEST SERIES: DIMENSION
Refer to page 888.

IPI JOB TEST FIELD SERIES: ENGINEER
Industrial Psychology International, Ltd.

Adult

Purpose: Assesses skills and personality of applicants seeking various engineering positions. Used to screen for automotive, chemical, electrical, mechanical, and production engineering.

Description: Multiple-item paper-pencil battery of seven aptitude and three personality tests. The tests are Factory Terms, Dimension, CPF, NPF, Judgment, Office Terms, Numbers, 16PF, Precision, and Tools. For individual test descriptions, see the IPI Aptitude-Intelligence Test Series. Examiner required. Suitable for group use. Available in French and Spanish.

Timed: 90 minutes

Scoring: Hand key

Cost: Instruction kit $16.00; test packages $10.00

Publisher: Industrial Psychology International, Ltd.

MINNESOTA ENGINEERING ANALOGIES TEST
Refer to page 788.

NIIP ENGINEERING SELECTION TEST BATTERY
Refer to page 789.

NIIP ENGINEERING SELECTION TEST BATTERY: ENGINEERING ARITHMETIC TEST EA4
Refer to page 789.

NIIP ENGINEERING SELECTION TEST BATTERY: GROUP TEST 82
Refer to page 789.

NIIP ENGINEERING SELECTION TEST BATTERY: GROUP TESTS 70 AND 70B
Refer to page 790.

NIIP ENGINEERING SELECTION TEST BATTERY: GROUP TESTS 90A AND 90B
Refer to page 790.

NIIP ENGINEERING SELECTION TEST BATTERY: VINCENT MECHANICAL DIAGRAMS TEST (REVISED)
Refer to page 790.

NON-VERBAL REASONING
Richardson, Bellows, Henry and Company, Inc.

Adult

Purpose: Assesses nonverbal reasoning (spatial analysis) abilities. Used with applicants to technical and engineering positions.

Description: 45–item paper-pencil test of nonverbal reasoning. Each test item consists of 10 figures, the first 4 of which are alike. Applicants select two of the last six figures that are like the first four. A variety of elements are tested, including squareness, angle bisection, differential shading, number relationships, and arrangement relationships. Examinees must be able to read numbers. The test has been used successfully with applicants with low educational levels and with technical and managerial personnel with high educational levels. Norms are available for male technical and professional employees, managers and executives, mechanical and operating employees and applicants, and sales employees and applicants. Norms are also available for female applicants for production jobs. The test is available in a long and a short form. Examiner required. Suitable for group use.

Timed: 15 minutes

Scoring: Hand key

Cost: Long form 1–24 packages $30.00; Short form 1–24 packages $25.00; score key $4.00; manual $2.00

Publisher: Richardson, Bellows, Henry and Company, Inc.

PRIMARY MECHANICAL ABILITY TEST
Refer to page 1070.

RESEARCH PERSONNEL REVIEW FORM
Morris I. Stein

Adult

Purpose: Evaluates the performance of personnel in research and development (R & D) organizations. Measures strengths and weaknesses of scientists and engineers in this field.

Description: 120–item paper-pencil questionnaire assessing a scientist's or engineer's work in terms of quantity, quality, and creativity. The test items cover administrative, employee, social, scientific, and professional factors involved in the individual's performance. Self-administered by the individual being reviewed. Suitable for group use.

Untimed: 30 minutes

Scoring: Examiner evaluated

Cost: $2.50 per copy

Publisher: Morris I. Stein

Information and availability unconfirmed; last verified in 1987.

SHOP ARITHMETIC TEST, FORMS I AND II
Refer to page 912.

SURVEYS OF RESEARCH ENVIRONMENTS
Morris I. Stein

Adult

Purpose: Obtains information from scientists and engineers concerning their job situations and the demands being placed upon them. Evaluates morale and identifies problem areas in research and development (R & D) organizations.

Description: 189–item paper-pencil inventory requiring research and administrative personnel to evaluate the organization and factors that lead to success and creativity on the job. The items are presented in terms of the role requirements of scientific, professional, administrative, and social relations employees. Self-administered. The test is restricted to R & D organizations. Suitable for group use.

Untimed: 45 minutes

Scoring: Examiner evaluated

Cost: $2.50 per copy

Publisher: Morris I. Stein

Information and availability unconfirmed; last verified in 1987.

TECHNICAL TEST BATTERY: VERBAL COMPREHENSION (TTB:VT1)
Refer to page 921.

Health Services

ATTITUDE SURVEY PROGRAM FOR HEALTH CARE

Adult

Purpose: Assesses the concerns of staff members in hospitals, HMOs, clinics, and nursing care facilities. Used by health care administrators to assess employee acceptance of organizational and procedural changes; determine training needs; improve staff communication; pinpoint areas of dissatisfaction that could affect patient care; promote cooperation among employee, professional, and administrative groups; and monitor issues that contribute to a stable work force.

Description: Five 93–item paper-pencil surveys assessing the priorities and concerns of health-care officials. Survey titles include Nursing Staff Survey, Physicians Survey, Paraprofessionals Survey, Nonmedical Professionals Survey, and Health Care Employee Survey. The possible areas covered by each survey are organization identification; job satisfaction, material rewards: pay; material rewards: benefits; supervisory leadership practices; work associates; general administrative effectiveness; supervisory administrative practices; work organization; work efficiency; performance and personal development; communication effectiveness; interdepartmental coordination; relationship with physicians; nursing office practices; professional nursing role; paraprofessional role; professional role; relationship with administration; medical staff organization; medical staff relations; relationship with nursing, diagnostic, and therapeutic services; patient services; and reactions to survey. (See descriptions of individual surveys for areas relevant to a particular survey.) A general comments section is also provided; transcription and analysis are optional.

Each of the four surveys is available in several forms: standard, modified, customized, and optional categories. Organizations are given the choice of six demographic variables with a standard survey. Modified surveys allow the addition of up to 30 items not included on the standard survey. Customized surveys are designed to include personal items, organization logo, specialized comment sections, and factors created by the organization. Optional categories that may be added to any survey are equipment, safety, and health; security operations; and human resource management.

London House psychologists help administrators plan and conduct a survey. Administration occurs on organization premises under the supervision of an organization official or London House employee. Mailings are also available.

Reports available include the Executive Summary Profile, Category Profile, Item Profile, Organization-Wide Comparisons, Demographic Category Profiles, and Demographic Item Profiles. Computerized departmental summaries, narrative reports, feedback presentations, and follow-up surveys are also available. Examiner required. Suitable for group use.

Untimed: 60 minutes or less

Scoring: Computer scored by London House

Cost: 100 standard surveys $950.00; 100 modified surveys $1,150.00; 100 customized surveys (specify survey title) $1,500.00; comment transcriptions $1.00 per unit

Publisher: London House, Inc.

ATTITUDE SURVEY PROGRAM FOR HEALTH CARE: HEALTH CARE EMPLOYEE SURVEY

Adult

Purpose: Assesses the concerns of clerical, security, housekeeping, cafeteria, laboratory personnel, and administration employees in hospitals, HMOs, clinics, and nursing care facilities. Used by health care administrators to assess employee acceptance of organizational and procedural changes; determine training needs; improve staff communication; pinpoint areas of dissatisfaction that could affect patient care; promote cooperation among employee, professional, and administrative groups; and monitor issues that contribute to a stable work force.

Description: 93–item paper-pencil survey assessing the priorities and concerns of general health care employees. Items cover the following areas: organization identification, job satisfaction, pay, benefits, supervisory leadership practices, work associates, general administrative effectiveness, supervisory administrative practices, work organization, work efficiency, performance and personal development, communication effectiveness, interdepartmental communication, and reactions to survey. A general comments section is also included; transcription and analysis are optional.

The survey is available in standard, modified, customized, and optional categories. Custom demographic breakdowns are available with all surveys. Modified surveys allow the addition of up to 30 items not included on the standard survey. Customized surveys are designed to include company-specific items, organization logo, specialized comment sections, and factors created by the organization. Optional areas that may be added to any survey are equipment, safety, and health; security operations; and human resource management.

London House psychologists help administrators plan and conduct a survey. Administration occurs on organization premises under the supervision of an organization official or London House employee. The available reports use state-of-the-art graphics and compare company results to national and industry-specific norms. Narrative reports, feedback presentation, and follow-up surveys are also available. Other surveys available in the series are Nursing Staff Survey, Physicians' Survey, Paraprofessionals Survey, and Nonmedical Professionals Survey. Examiner required. Suitable for group use.

Untimed: 50 minutes or less

Scoring: Computer scored by London House

Cost: 100 standard surveys $950.00; 100 modified surveys $1,150.00; 100 customized surveys $1,500.00; comment transcriptions $1.00 per unit

Publisher: London House, Inc.

ATTITUDE SURVEY PROGRAM FOR HEALTH CARE: NONMEDICAL PROFESSIONALS SURVEY

Adult

Purpose: Assesses the concerns of psychologists; speech, occupational, and physical therapists; and social workers in hospitals, HMOs, clinics, and nursing care facilities. Used by health care administrators to assess employee acceptance of organizational and procedural changes; determine training needs; improve staff communication; pinpoint areas of dissatisfaction that could affect patient care; promote cooperation among employee, professional, and administrative groups;

and monitor issues that contribute to a stable work force.

Description: 93–item paper-pencil survey assessing the priorities and concerns of nonmedical professionals. Items cover the following areas: organization identification, job satisfaction, pay, benefits, supervisory leadership practices, work associates, general administrative effectiveness, supervisory administrative practices, work organization, work efficiency, performance and personal development, communication effectiveness, interdepartmental coordination, relationship with physicians, professional role, and reactions to survey.

The survey is available in standard, modified, customized, and optional categories. Custom demographic breakdowns are available with all surveys. Modified surveys allow the addition of up to 30 items not included on the standard survey. Customized surveys are designed to include company-specific items, organization logo, specialized comment sections, and factors created by the organization. Optional areas that may be added to any survey are equipment, safety, and health; security operations; and human resource management.

London House psychologists help administrators plan and conduct a survey. Administration occurs on organization premises under the supervision of an organization official or London House employee. The available reports use state-of-the-art graphics and compare company results to national and industry-specific norms. Narrative reports, feedback presentations, and follow-up surveys are also available. Other surveys available in the series are Nursing Staff Survey, Physicians' Survey, Paraprofessionals Survey, and Health Care Employee Survey. Examiner required. Suitable for group use.

Untimed: 50 minutes or less

Scoring: Computer scored by London House

Cost: 100 standard surveys $950.00; 100 modified surveys $1,150.00; 100 customized surveys $1,500.00; comment transcriptions $1.00 per unit

Publisher: London House, Inc.

ATTITUDE SURVEY PROGRAM FOR HEALTH CARE: NURSING STAFF SURVEY

Adult

Purpose: Assesses the concerns of the nursing staff in hospitals, HMOs, clinics, and nursing care facilities. Used by health care administrators to assess employee acceptance of organizational and procedural changes; determine training needs; improve staff communication; pinpoint areas of dissatisfaction that could affect patient care; promote cooperation among employee, professional, and administrative groups; and monitor issues that contribute to a stable work force.

Description: 93–item paper-pencil survey assessing the priorities and concerns of nursing staff members. Items cover the following areas: organization identification, job satisfaction, material rewards: pay, material rewards: benefits, supervisory leadership practices, work associates, general administrative effectiveness, supervisory administrative practices, work organization, work efficiency, performance and personal development, communication effectiveness, relationship with physicians, nursing office practices, professional nursing role, and reactions to survey. A general comment section is also included; transcription and analysis are optional.

The survey is available in standard, modified, customized, and optional categories. Custom demographic breakdowns are available with all surveys. Modified surveys allow the addition of up to 30 items not included on the standard survey. Customized surveys are designed to include organization-specific items, organization logo, specialized comment sections, and factors created by the organization. Optional categories that may be added to any survey are equipment, safety, and health; security operations; and human resource management.

London House psychologists help administrators plan and conduct a survey. Administration occurs on organization premises under the supervision of an organization official or London House employee; mailings are also available. The available reports use state-of-the-art graphics and compare company results to national and industry-specific norms. Narrative reports and follow-up surveys are also available. Other surveys available in the series are Physicians' Survey, Paraprofessionals Survey, Nonmedical Professionals Survey, and Health Care Employee Survey. Examiner required. Suitable for group use.

Untimed: 60 minutes or less

Scoring: Computer scored by London House

Cost: 100 standard surveys $950.00; 100 modified surveys $1,150.00; 100 customized surveys $1,500.00; customized transcriptions $1.00 per unit

Publisher: London House, Inc.

ATTITUDE SURVEY PROGRAM FOR HEALTH CARE: PARAPROFESSIONALS SURVEY

Adult

Purpose: Assesses the concerns of licensed practical nurses, nurses' aids, and orderlies in hospitals, HMOs, clinics, and nursing care facilities. Used by health care administrators to assess employee acceptance of organizational and procedural changes; determine training needs; improve staff communication; pinpoint areas of dissatisfaction that could affect patient care; promote cooperation among employee, professional, and administrative groups; and monitor issues that contribute to a stable work force.

Description: 93–item paper-pencil survey assessing the priorities and concerns of paraprofessionals. Items cover the following areas: organization identification, job satisfaction, material rewards: pay, material rewards: benefits, supervisory leadership practices, work associates, general administrative effectiveness, supervisory administrative practices, work organization, work efficiency, performance and personal development, communication effectiveness, paraprofessional role, and reactions to survey. A general comments section is also available; transcription and analysis are optional.

The survey is available in standard, modified, customized, and optional categories. Custom demographic breakdowns are available with all surveys. Modified surveys allow the addition of up to 30 items not included on the standard survey. Customized surveys are designed to include company-specific items, organization logo, specialized comment sections, and factors created by the organization. Optional categories that may be added to any survey are equipment, safety, and health; security operations; and human resource management.

London House psychologists help administrators plan and conduct a survey. Administration occurs on organization premises under the supervision of an organization official or London House employee. The available reports use state-of-the-art graphics and compare company results to national and industry-specific norms. Narrative reports and follow-up surveys are also available. Other surveys available in the series are Nursing Staff Survey, Physicians Survey, Nonmedical Professionals Survey, and Health Care Employee Survey. Examiner required. Suitable for group use.

Untimed: 50 minutes or less

Scoring: Computer scored by London House

Cost: 100 standard surveys $950.00; 100 modified surveys $1,150.00; 100 customized surveys $1,500.00; comment transcription $1.00 per unit

Publisher: London House, Inc.

ATTITUDE SURVEY PROGRAM FOR HEALTH CARE: PHYSICIANS' SURVEY

Adult

Purpose: Assesses the concerns of physicians in hospitals, HMOs, clinics, and nursing care facilities. Used by health care administrators to assess employee acceptance of organizational and procedural changes; determine training needs; improve staff communication; pinpoint areas of dissatisfaction that could affect patient care; promote cooperation among employee, professional, and adminis-

trative groups; and monitor issues that contribute to a stable work force.

Description: 93–item paper-pencil survey assessing the priorities and concerns of physicians. Items cover the following areas: organization identification, job satisfaction; work associates; general administrative effectiveness; work organization; work efficiency; relationship with administration; medical staff organization; medical staff relations; relationship with nursing, diagnostic, and therapeutic services; patient services; and reactions to survey. A general comment section is also included; transcription and analysis are optional.

The survey is available in standard, modified, customized, and optional categories. Custom demographic breakdowns are available with all surveys. Modified surveys allow the addition of up to 30 items not included on the standard survey. Customized surveys are designed to include company-specific items, organization logo, specialized comment sections, and factors created by the organization. Optional categories that may be added to any survey are equipment, safety, and health; security operations; and human resource management.

London House psychologists help administrators plan and conduct a survey. Administration occurs on organization premises under the supervision of an organization official or London House employee. The available reports use state-of-the-art graphics and compare company results to national and industry-specific norms. Narrative reports, feedback presentations, and follow-up surveys are also available. Other surveys available in the series are nursing staff survey, paraprofessionals survey, nonmedical professionals survey, and health care employee survey. Examiner required. Suitable for group use.

Untimed: 50 minutes or less

Scoring: Computer scored by London House

Cost: 100 standard surveys $950.00; 100 modified surveys $1,150.00; 100 customized surveys $1,500.00; comment transcriptions $1.00 per unit

Publisher: London House, Inc.

DENTAL ASSISTANT TEST
Mary Meeker and Robert Meeker

Adult

Purpose: Measures the aptitude and ability of prospective dental assistants. Used for selection of dental assistants.

Description: Multiple-item paper-pencil screening instrument assessing the abilities and aptitudes of prospective dental assistants. The criterion-referenced test items were developed in conjunction with practicing dental groups. Scoring keys and a criteria graph for selection are available separately. Examiner required. Suitable for group use.

Untimed: Varies

Scoring: Hand key

Cost: Test form $1.90; scoring key $11.50

Publisher: M & M Systems

IPI JOB TEST FIELD SERIES: DENTAL OFFICE ASSISTANT
Industrial Psychology International, Ltd.

Adult

Purpose: Assesses skills of applicants for dental office assistants. Used to screen assistants who will work chairside, perform light secretarial duties, and work with patients and the dentist.

Description: Multiple-item paper-pencil battery of four aptitude and two personality tests. The tests are Numbers, Perception, CPF, Office Terms, NPE, and Judgment. For individual test descriptions, see the IPI Aptitude-Intelligence Test Series. Examiner required. Suitable for group use. Available in French and Spanish.

Timed: 44 minutes

Scoring: Hand key

Cost: Instruction kits $16.00; test packages $10.00

Publisher: Industrial Psychology International, Ltd.

IPI JOB TEST FIELD SERIES: DENTAL TECHNICIAN
Industrial Psychology International, Ltd.

Adult

Purpose: Assesses skills of applicants for the position of dental technician. Used to screen laboratory workers in four classification levels: cast metal, denture, crown and bridge, and porcelain and acrylic.

Description: Multiple-item paper-pencil battery of three aptitude and two personality tests. The tests are Dexterity, Dimension, Blocks, NPF, and CPF. For individual test descriptions, see the IPI Aptitude-Intelligence Test Series. Examiner required. Suitable for group use. Available in French and Spanish.

Timed: 38 minutes

Scoring: Hand key

Cost: Instruction kits $16.00; test packages $10.00

Publisher: Industrial Psychology International, Ltd.

IPI JOB TEST FIELD SERIES: OPTOMETRIC ASSISTANT
Industrial Psychology International, Ltd.

Adult

Purpose: Assesses skills and personality of applicants for positions of optometric assistant. Used to screen individuals who will act as a support person for optometrists, working with the practitioner and patients and performing reception and light secretarial duties.

Description: Multiple-item paper-pencil battery of five aptitude and two personality tests. The tests are Numbers, NPF, CPF, Office Terms, Judgment, Perception, and Fluency. For individual test descriptions, see the IPI Aptitude-Intelligence Test Series. Examiner required. Suitable for group use. Available in French and Spanish.

Timed: 50 minutes

Scoring: Hand key

Cost: Instruction kits $16.00; test packages $10.00
Publisher: Industrial Psychology International, Ltd.

PERSONNEL TEST BATTERY (PTB)
Refer to page 906.

PSB READING COMPREHENSION EXAMINATION
Refer to page 365.

SMELL IDENTIFICATION TEST®
Refer to page 914.

SOI-LA: DENTAL RECEPTIONIST TEST
Mary Meeker and Robert Meeker

Adult

Purpose: Measures the abilities and aptitudes of prospective dental receptionists. Used for selection of dental receptionists.

Description: Multiple-item paper-pencil screening instrument assessing the abilities and aptitudes of prospective dental receptionists. The criterion-referenced test items were developed in conjunction with practicing dental groups. Scoring keys and a criteria graph for selection are available separately. Self-interpreted. Examiner required. Suitable for group use.
Untimed: 1 hour
Scoring: Hand key; may be machine scored
Cost: Test form $1.90; scoring key $11.50
Publisher: M & M Systems

STAFF BURNOUT SCALE FOR HEALTH PROFESSIONALS
John W. Jones

Adult

Purpose: Assesses burnout or work stress among health-care professionals.

Description: Multiple-item paper-pencil test assessing burnout or work stress through four types of factors: cognitive reactions, affective reactions, behavioral reactions, and psychophysiological reactions. Self-administered. Suitable for group use.
Untimed: 10 minutes
Scoring: Hand key; may be computer scored
Cost: 25 tests $15.00; specimen set (interpretation manual, validation studies) $5.00
Publisher: London House, Inc.

Intelligence and Related

ADAPTABILITY TEST
Joseph Tiffin and C.H. Lawshe

Adult

Purpose: Measures mental adaptability and alertness. Distinguishes between people who should be placed in jobs requiring more learning ability and those who should be in more simple or routine jobs.

Description: 35–item paper-pencil test consisting primarily of verbal items. The test predicts success in a variety of business and industrial situations. The test is available in two forms, A and B. Examiner required. Suitable for group use.
Timed: 15 minutes
Scoring: Hand key
Cost: 25 test booklets (specify form) $32.00; examiner's manual $10.00
Publisher: SRA/London House

ARITHMETIC REASONING TEST (ART), HIGH LEVEL AND INTERMEDIATE LEVEL
Refer to page 867.

BRUCE VOCABULARY INVENTORY
Martin M. Bruce

Adult

Purpose: Determines how a subject's vocabulary compares to the vocabulary of individuals employed in various business occupations.

Description: 100–item paper-pencil multiple-choice test in which the subject matches one of four alternative words with a key vocabulary word. Measures the ability to recognize and comprehend words. The subject's score can be compared to the scores of executives, middle-managers, white collar workers, engineers, blue collar workers, and the total employed population. Self-administered. Suitable for group use.

Untimed: 15–20 minutes

Scoring: Hand key

Cost: Package of reusable tests $39.50; manual $5.50; fan key $1.95; manual supplement (1984) $15.50; IBM scoring stencils $8.00; IBM answer sheets $18.00; specimen set IBM form $30.50; specimen set fan key form $10.00

Publisher: Martin M. Bruce, Ph.D., Publishers

CLOSURE SPEED (GESTALT COMPLETION)
L.L. Thurstone and T.E. Jeffrey

Adolescent, adult

Purpose: Assesses the ability to see apparently disorganized or unrelated parts as a meaningful whole and to grasp and unify a complex concept. Used for vocational counseling or selection in positions that require inductive reasoning or visual perceptual skills related to mechanical ability.

Description: 24–item paper-pencil test in which each item consists of an incomplete picture drawn in black on a white background. The subject must identify and briefly describe the subject of the picture. Examiner required. Suitable for group use.

Timed: 3 minutes

Scoring: Hand key

Cost: Specimen set $8.00; 25 test booklets $20.00

Publisher: London House, Inc.

COMPOUND SERIES TEST (CST)
J.R. Morrisby

Ages 6–adult

Purpose: Assesses general intelligence by measuring the capacity to learn through the systematic analysis of a problem. Used in industry for personnel selection, placement, and promotion.

Description: 60–item paper-pencil test requiring persistence, concentration, and directed effort in order to solve problems. Each item presents a pattern drawn as a string of beads varying in size, shape, and color. The subject indicates which two beads from a choice of eight continue the pattern. The same type of item, increasing in difficulty and complexity, is used throughout, thereby measuring the ability to direct and control the investment of intellectual effort.

Because the test does not depend on such acquired skills as the use of words or numbers, it is suitable for use with educationally and socially disadvantaged subjects. In addition, the colors are arranged so that color-blind subjects can distinguish them. If the CST is used in screening for higher-level occupations, it should be supplemented by other tests, such as the full Differential Test Battery of E.I.T.S. The CST is restricted to examiners who provide evidence of adequate training and practical experience in the use of such tests. Examiner required. Suitable for group use.
BRITISH PUBLISHER

Timed: 20–30 minutes

Scoring: Hand key; examiner evaluated; may be computer scored

Cost: Contact publisher

Publisher: Educational and Industrial Test Services Ltd.

CONCEPT ATTAINMENT TEST
J.M. Schepers

Adolescent, adult

Purpose: Measures conceptual and rational mental abilities of science and technical graduates. Used for employee screening and selection.

Description: Multiple-item paper-pencil test measuring the ability to attain concepts through the use of rational strategies of thought. The test consists of 10 problems for which solutions can be obtained only if a well-defined and logical strategy is followed consistently. Norms are provided for science graduates. The test is restricted to competent persons properly registered with the South African Medical and Dental Council. Examiner required. Suitable for group use. Afrikaans version available.

SOUTH AFRICAN PUBLISHER

Timed: 50 minutes

Scoring: Hand key; examiner evaluated

Cost: Contact publisher

Publisher: National Institute for Personnel Research

THE CULTURE FAIR SERIES: SCALES 1, 2, 3
Refer to page 51.

DAP QUALITY SCALE (DRAW-A-PERSON)
Herman J.P. Schubert

Adolescent, adult

Purpose: Measures intelligence and motivation. Used for personnel selection.

Description: Paper-pencil free-response test assessing nonverbal intelligence in which the individual is asked to draw a picture of a person. The drawing is scored according to objective guidelines. The overall quality score contributes to the prediction of available intelligence and motivation. Examiner required. Suitable for group use.

Untimed: Varies

Scoring: Examiner evaluated

Cost: Test kit $17.50

Publisher: Herman J.P. Schubert

DEDUCTIVE REASONING TEST

Adolescent, adult

Purpose: Measures logical thinking abilities. Used with matriculants and higher for purposes of employee screening and

selection for a wide variety of technical positions.

Description: Multiple-item paper-pencil test based on formal syllogisms. Each syllogism contains either factual, contrafactual, or nonsense premises. The test provides a measure of the ability to deduce logically correct conclusions from the information contained in the premises. The test is restricted to competent persons properly registered with the South African Medical and Dental Council. Examiner required. Suitable for group use. Afrikaans version available.

SOUTH AFRICAN PUBLISHER

Timed: 40 minutes

Scoring: Hand key; examiner evaluated

Cost: Contact publisher

Publisher: National Institute for Personnel Research

EMPLOYEE APTITUDE SURVEY TEST #10—SYMBOLIC REASONING (EAS #10)
Refer to page 880.

ESTIMATION TEST, HIGH LEVEL
Refer to page 880.

ETSA TESTS 1-A—GENERAL MENTAL ABILITY
Refer to page 881.

FIGURE CLASSIFICATION TEST

Adolescent, adult

Purpose: Measures abstract reasoning ability. Used with examinees with 7 to 9 years of education for purposes of employee selection and placement.

Description: Multiple-item paper-pencil test measuring conceptual reasoning ability by requiring the examinee to analyze sets of figures and deduce the basic relationships that divide each set into two groups. The relationships are indicated by uniformity, symmetry, inversion, repetition, and series. The test is restricted to competent persons properly registered with the South African Medical and Dental Council. Examiner required. Suitable for group use. Afrikaans version available. SOUTH AFRICAN PUBLISHER

Timed: 1 hour

Scoring: Hand key; examiner evaluated

Cost: Contact publisher

Publisher: National Institute for Personnel Research

FORM SERIES TEST A

Adolescent, adult

Purpose: Measures nonverbal reasoning ability. Used with groups of individuals with 6 years or less of education for purposes of employee selection and placement.

Description: Multiple-item apparatus test measuring nonverbal reasoning ability using a board printed with a series of patterns made up of forms of different sizes, shapes, and colors. Each pattern must be continued by inferring from the given series of shapes and colors what the next two must be. The test is restricted to competent persons properly registered with the South African Medical and Dental Council. Examiner required. Suitable for group use. Afrikaans version available. SOUTH AFRICAN PUBLISHER

Timed: 25 minutes

Scoring: Hand key; examiner evaluated

Cost: Contact publisher

Publisher: National Institute for Personnel Research

GENERAL ABILITY TESTS: NUMERICAL (GAT NUMERICAL)
J.R. Morrisby

Ages 11 and older

Purpose: Measures numerical intelligence. Used for personnel selection in most occupations, especially those in which numerical concepts are involved and the ability to think quantitatively is at a premium. Also used as a predictor of academic success.

Description: Multiple-item paper-pencil test in three parts. Part 1 requires the subject to indicate whether simple addition and multiplication calculations, worked

out, are correct or incorrect. Part 2 consists of a number series in which the degree of computation required is reduced, but the dependence on the subject's ability to see numerical relationships is increased. In Part 3, the subject completes matrixes with one element missing. The computational requirement in Part 3 is small, but the requirement to see into numerical relationships is at a maximum.

The mental functions involved in each subtest are arranged to provide a progression throughout the test, from a loading of speed of apprehension in Part 1 to a heavy loading of insight or intuitive power in Part 3. Materials include booklets, scoring keys, the specimen set, and the manual. Tests of verbal intelligence and of nonverbal, or perceptual intelligence, also are available in this three-part GAT series. The series has been constructed as a matched trio to provide differential assessment of the main areas of mental ability, but any one test may be used alone. The GAT is restricted to examiners who provide evidence of adequate training and practical experience in the use of such tests. Examiner required. Suitable for group use.
BRITISH PUBLISHER

Timed: 35 minutes

Scoring: Hand key; examiner evaluated; may be computer scored

Cost: Contact publisher

Publisher: Educational and Industrial Test Service Ltd.

GENERAL ABILITY TESTS: PERCEPTUAL (GAT PERCEPTUAL)
J.R. Morrisby

Ages 11 and older

Purpose: Measures nonverbal, perceptual intelligence. Used for personnel selection in most occupations, especially engineering, design, and scientific work dealing with real objects rather than verbal or numerical concepts.

Description: Multiple-item paper-pencil multiple-choice test in three categories. Part 1 requires the subject to determine which meaningless figures shown are identical to a given example. In Part 2, the subject classifies four of six figures shown in each item and indicates the two that do not belong. In Part 3, the subject selects a pair of figures analogous to a given pair in order to test insight into relationships between perceptual forms.

The mental functions involved in each subtest are arranged to provide a progression throughout the test, from a loading of speed of apprehension in Part 1 to a heavy loading of insight or intuitive power in Part 3. Materials include booklets, scoring keys, the specimen set, and the manual. Tests of verbal intelligence and numerical intelligence also are available in this three-part GAT series. The series has been constructed as a matched trio to provide differential assessment of the main areas of mental ability, but any one test may be used alone. The GAT is restricted to examiners who provide evidence of adequate training and practical experience in the use of such tests. Examiner required. Suitable for group use.

BRITISH PUBLISHER

Timed: 27 minutes

Scoring: Hand key; examiner evaluated; may be computer scored

Cost: Contact publisher

Publisher: Educational and Industrial Test Service Ltd.

GENERAL ABILITY TESTS: VERBAL (GAT VERBAL)
J.R. Morrisby

Ages 11 and older

Purpose: Measures verbal intelligence. Used for selection in most occupations in which a good level of communication skill is required or written work is emphasized. Also used as a predictor of academic success.

Description: Multiple-item paper-pencil multiple-choice instrument consisting of three separately timed subtests. Part 1 requires the subject to indicate whether pairs of words are synonyms or antonyms. Part 2 consists of word classification in which the vocabulary requirement is somewhat reduced but dependence on insight into relationships between verbal concepts is increased. In Part 3, the subject makes up pairs of words analogous to

a given pair. The demands on vocabulary are low but demands on insight into verbal relationships are at a maximum.

The mental functions involved in each subtest are arranged to give a progression throughout the test, from a loading of speed of apprehension in Part 1 to a heavy loading of insight or intuitive power in Part 3. Materials include booklets, scoring keys, the specimen set, and the manual. Tests of numerical intelligence and nonverbal, or perceptual intelligence, also are available in this three-part GAT series. The series has been constructed as a matched trio to provide differential assessment of the main areas of mental ability, but any one test may be used alone. The GAT is restricted to examiners who provide evidence of adequate training and practical experience in the use of such tests. Examiner required. Suitable for group use.

BRITISH PUBLISHER

Timed: 35 minutes

Scoring: Hand key; examiner evaluated; may be computer scored

Cost: Contact publisher

Publisher: Educational and Industrial Test Service Ltd.

HUMAN INFORMATION PROCESSING SURVEY: HIP SURVEY
E. Paul Torrance, William Taggart, and Barbara Taggart

Adult

Purpose: Assesses the manner in which an individual processes information. Used as a training tool in human resource development programs and for research purposes.

Description: Multiple-item paper-pencil inventory assessing an individual's processing preference: left hemisphere, right hemisphere, integrated, or mixed. The results provide a description of a person's overall approach and specific tactics in problem solving and decision making. The manual outlines applications of the survey and its use in a one-day workshop. A research edition is available. Examiner required. Suitable for group use.

Untimed: Varies

Scoring: Examiner evaluated

Cost: Professional edition starter set (manual, 10 survey forms, 10 profile forms) $38.95; revised edition starter set $48.00; specimen set (specify professional or research) $10.00

Publisher: Scholastic Testing Service, Inc.

INDUSTRIAL TEST BATTERY (ITB)

Adult

Purpose: Measures general reasoning ability in adults with less than 8 years of formal education. Used for job selection and placement.

Description: Multiple-item paper-pencil multiple-choice battery consisting of three screening tests. The Anomalous Concept Test (ACT) assesses concept formation. The Anomalous Figure Test (AFT) measures spatial relations. The Series Induction Test (SIT) measures the conception of relationships and trends. Examinees use an erasable pen to mark their answers on plastic-covered test pages. After a stencil is used to score answers, the plastic sheets are wiped clean. Examiner required. Suitable for group use.
SOUTH AFRICAN PUBLISHER

Timed: ACT 20 minutes; AFT 25 minutes; SIT 30 minutes

Scoring: Hand key

Cost: Contact publisher

Publisher: National Institute for Personnel Research

LEARNING ABILITY PROFILE (LAP)
Margarita Henning

Adult

Purpose: Assesses a person's ability to learn. May be used to determine the potential for job success.

Description: 80-item paper-pencil test measuring overall learning ability, flexibility, frustration level, problem-solving

ability, and decisiveness. Examiner required. Suitable for group use. Available in French.

Untimed: 1 hour

Scoring: Hand key; examiner evaluated

Cost: Complete set (1 test booklet, answer sheet, manual) $45.00

Publisher: Wolfe Personnel Testing and Training Systems, Inc.

MD5 MENTAL ABILITY TEST
D. Mackenzie Davey

Adult

Purpose: Assesses a wide range of educational and ability levels of adults. Used for staff selection, placement, and counseling.

Description: 57-item paper-pencil test used with adults, including supervisors and managers, for measuring mental ability. The test involves finding missing letters, numbers, or words. Norms exist for several managerial groups, and the test is correlated with other mental ability tests. Examiner/self-administered. Suitable for group use.
BRITISH PUBLISHER

Timed: 15 minutes

Scoring: Hand key

Cost: Specimen set (test booklet, answer key, manual) $16.50

Publisher: The Test Agency Ltd.

MENTAL ABILITIES— INVENTORY II
Jack Harris Hazlehurst; Stevens, Thurow and Associates

Adolescent, adult—Ages 16 and older

Purpose: Measures mental ability exclusive of educational level. Used for employee selection and placement.

Description: 50-item paper-pencil multiple-choice and free-response test measuring an individual's ability to solve problems involving word meanings and verbally constructed conceptual relations and requiring the manipulation of number relationships. The problems included are designed to sample the creative, reproductive, and relational aspects of imagination. Examiner required. Suitable for group use.

Timed: 15 minutes

Scoring: Hand key

Cost: 25 tests $6.00; monograph of instructions and critical statistical evaluation, scoring key $5.00

Publisher: Stevens, Thurow and Associates

MENTAL ALERTNESS— ADVANCED AND INTERMEDIATE

Adult

Purpose: Measures general intelligence for purposes of employee screening and selection. Used with matriculants and higher and individuals with 10–12 years of schooling.

Description: Two paper-pencil tests measuring general intelligence, mainly verbal, at two levels of education. The High Level Battery test is suitable for matriculants and higher. The Intermediate Battery is for candidates with 10–12 years of education. Both tests are available in two parallel forms. Norms are provided for each test. The tests are restricted to competent persons properly registered with the South African Medical and Dental Council. Examiner required. Suitable for group use. Afrikaans version available.
SOUTH AFRICAN PUBLISHER

Timed: 35 minutes each

Scoring: Hand key; examiner evaluated

Cost: Contact publisher

Publisher: National Institute for Personnel Research

MORRISBY DIFFERENTIAL TEST BATTERY (DTB)
J.R. Morrisby

Adolescent, adult—Ages 13 and older

Purpose: Evaluates a person's intellectual structure and basic personality characteristics. Used to predict the likelihood of success in a large number of occupations and modes of behavior in a variety of situations.

Description: Battery of 12 multiple-item paper-pencil intelligence and personality tests designed to provide a total assessment of an individual, as well as meaningful single test scores. The four intelligence tests are the Compound Series Test, a measure of basic intellectual power, and the general ability tests: Verbal, Numerical, and Perceptual. The Shapes Test and Mechanical Ability Test provide measures of spatial and mechanical ability to show the subject's level of practicality and analysis and overview abilities. The six speed tests—Conceptual Speed, Perseveration, Word Fluency, Ideational Fluency, Motor Speed, and Motor Skill—measure abilities, tendency toward understanding, and qualities such as leadership, confidence, flexibility, resistance to change, speed of awareness, personal commitment, tenacity, and initiative. Materials include one-time test forms, reusable booklets, a manual, and scoring keys. A scoring service, interpretation service, and grading service are also available. The battery is restricted to examiners who provide evidence of adequate training and practical experience in the use of such tests. Examiner required. Suitable for group use.
BRITISH PUBLISHER

Untimed: 3 hours, 10 minutes

Scoring: Examiner evaluated; may be computer scored

Cost: Contact publisher

Publisher: Educational and Industrial Test Services Ltd.

NON-VERBAL REASONING
Raymond J. Corsini

Adult

Purpose: Assesses capacity to reason logically as indicated by solutions to pictorial problems. Used for industrial job screening and selection and for vocational counseling.

Description: 44–item pictorial paper-pencil test. The subject studies one picture and then selects from among four others the one that best complements the first picture. Examiner required. Suitable for group use.

Untimed: 20 minutes

Scoring: Hand key; may be machine scored

Cost: Specimen set $10.00; 25 test booklets $20.00

Publisher: London House, Inc.

PATTERN RELATIONS TEST

Adult

Purpose: Measures inductive reasoning abilities. Used with university level and graduate job applicants for a variety of science and technical positions.

Description: Multiple-item paper-pencil test measuring the ability to recognize associated concepts that fit sets of data and the consequent forming and testing of hypotheses. The test is similar to Raven's Progressive Matrices. Norms have been established on scientific research workers with degrees and first-year engineering students. The test is restricted to competent persons properly registered with the South African Medical and Dental Council. Examiner required. Suitable for group use. Afrikaans version available. SOUTH AFRICAN PUBLISHER

Timed: 50 minutes each

Scoring: Hand key; examiner evaluated

Cost: Contact publisher

Publisher: National Institute for Personnel Research

PERFORMANCE EFFICIENCY TEST (PET)
Thomas Rex Long

Adult

Purpose: Measures the ability to use intellectual potential for satisfactory performance in any job situation. Used for employee screening and placement.

Description: Multiple-item oral-response test assessing intellectual ability. Applicants read color names or identify colors from three stimulus cards. Card A contains four color names, printed in black, in random order. Card B contains four colors, printed in quarter-inch squares. Card C contains color names, printed in colors different from what the word reads.

The number of incorrect answers identifies applicants least likely to compete successfully. The format suggests nothing regarding the psychological variables being measured and, consequently, is nonthreatening to the subject. Because subjects are unaware of what constitutes an acceptable time score, "faking" is no problem. Examiner required. Not suitable for group use.

Untimed: 5–6 minutes

Scoring: Examiner evaluated

Cost: Complete set (manual, three stimulus cards) $7.25

Publisher: Stoelting Co.

PROFESSIONAL EMPLOYMENT TEST

Adult

Purpose: Measures three cognitive abilities—verbal comprehension, quantitative problem solving, and reasoning—important for successful performance in many professional occupations. Used to select professional, technical, and managerial personnel.

Description: 40–item paper-pencil multiple-choice test measuring the ability to understand and interpret complex information, determine the appropriate mathematical procedures to solve problems, and analyze and evaluate information to arrive at correct conclusions. The test includes four item types: reading comprehension (the examinee reads a paragraph and selects the alternative that best reflects the content of the paragraph), quantitative problem solving (the examinee reviews a word problem and applies the appropriate mathematical procedures in order to select the correct answer), data interpretation (the examinee, using simple arithmetic, determines the value of missing entries in numerical tables), and reasoning (the examinee determines whether conclusions to given sets of premises that are accepted as true are justified). The test is available in two alternate forms. For test security purposes, the test is available for lease only. Examiner required. Suitable for group use.

Timed: 1 hour, 20 minutes

Scoring: Hand key; may be computer scored

Cost: $5.00

Publisher: Psychological Services, Inc.

THE RBH TEST OF LEARNING ABILITY, FORM STR
Richardson, Bellows, Henry and Company, Inc.

Adult

Purpose: Assesses general aptitudes. Used for screening, selection, placement, and upgrading of personnel.

Description: 108–item paper-pencil multiple-choice test assessing general aptitude. Examinees must choose the correct answer for each problem from four alternatives. Answers are recorded in the test booklet. This test is a compilation of two shorter forms (589 and T89) and provides a "floor" low enough to accommodate all but the illiterate and mentally deficient and a "ceiling" high enough for individuals with upper levels of education or ability. The test is organized so that each three consecutive items contains a block-counting, vocabulary, and arithmetic item. Each series of items is more difficult than the preceding series. The three types of items can be scored separately. Reading and understanding directions is not part of the STR administration time. Normative data are available for male technical and professional employees, managers and executives, clerical employees, sales employees and applicants, mechanical and operating employees and applicants, and industrial foremen and supervisors. Examiner required. Suitable for group use.

Timed: 25 minutes

Scoring: Hand key

Cost: 1–24 packages $35.00; score key $4.00; manual $2.00

Publisher: Richardson, Bellows, Henry and Company, Inc.

REVISED BETA EXAMINATION— SECOND EDITION (BETA-II)
D.E. Kellogg and N.W. Morton

Adult

Purpose: Measures mental ability of non-reading applicants. Used for testing applicants in settings with large numbers of unskilled workers.

Description: Six separately timed paper-pencil tests of mental ability, including mazes, coding, paper form boards, picture completion, clerical checking, and picture absurdities. Directions are given orally to the applicant. Examiner required. Suitable for group use. Available in Spanish.

Untimed: 30 minutes

Scoring: Hand key

Cost: Specimen set (test, demonstration booklet, manual) $19.00; 25 tests, demonstration booklet, manual, key $51.00

Publisher: The Psychological Corporation

Information and availability unconfirmed; last verified in 1988.

ROTATE AND FLIP TEST (RAFT)
Terence R. Taylor and Monica R. Ebertsohn

Adolescent, adult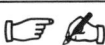

Purpose: Assesses visualization, spatial relations, and orientation.

Description: 24–item paper-pencil multiple-choice test of spatial visualization that yields a total test score. Materials include test booklet, answer sheet, pencil, eraser, and manual. Examiner required. Suitable for group use. Available in Afrikaans. SOUTH AFRICAN PUBLISHER

Timed: 25 minutes

Scoring: Hand key

Cost: Contact publisher

Publisher: Human Sciences Research Council

SRA NONVERBAL FORM
Robert N. McMurry and
Joseph E. King

Adult

Purpose: Assesses general learning ability. Measures learning potential of individuals who have difficulty reading or understanding the English language. Used with adults with a high-school education or less and for employee selection and placement.

Description: 60–item paper-pencil test consisting of five drawings, each measuring recognition of differences. Examiner required. Suitable for group use.

Timed: 10 minutes

Scoring: Hand key

Cost: 25 test booklets $41.00; examiner's manual $10.00

Publisher: SRA/London House

SRA PICTORIAL REASONING TEST (PRT)
Robert N. McMurry and
Phyllis D. Arnold

Adolescent, adult

Purpose: Measures general reasoning ability of students, especially older non-readers. Used with individuals with a high-school education or less, for predicting job success, and as a basic screening test for entry-level jobs.

Description: 80–item paper-pencil pictorial test measuring aspects of learning ability. The test is culturally unbiased and does not require previously learned reading skills. Examiner required. Suitable for group use.

Timed: 15 minutes (may also be given untimed)

Scoring: Hand key

Cost: 25 test booklets $36.00; examiner's manual $10.00

Publisher: SRA/London House

TEST OF LEARNING ABILITY, FORMS S–89 AND T–89
Richardson, Bellows, Henry and
Company, Inc.

Adult

Purpose: Assesses general aptitude. Used for screening, selection, placement, and upgrading of personnel.

Description: 54–item paper-pencil multiple-choice test assessing general aptitude. The test is organized into 18 three-item series, each containing a block-counting, vocabulary, and arithmetic part. Each series of items is more difficult than the preceding series. The three types of items can be scored separately.

The test is available in two forms: S–89 and T–89. Reading and understanding of the test directions is not included in the administration time of the test. Normative data are available for male sales employees and applicants, clerical employees and applicants, service station dealers and applicants, industrial supervisors and applicants, and industrial employees and applicants. Norms are also available for female statistical, accounting, and supply clerks; secretarial and stenographic personnel; miscellaneous or unspecified clerical applicants and employees; file and record clerks; and office applicants and employees. Examiner required. Suitable for group use.

Timed: 12 minutes

Scoring: Hand key

Cost: 1–24 packages $37.50; score key $7.50; manual $25.00

Publisher: Richardson, Bellows, Henry and Company, Inc.

THURSTONE TEST OF MENTAL ALERTNESS
L.L. Thurstone and
Thelma Gwinn Thurstone

Adult

Purpose: Measures an individual's capacity to acquire new knowledge and skills and to use what has been learned to solve problems. Measures individual differences in ability to learn and perform mental tasks of varying types and complexity.

Used for employee selection and vocational counseling.

Description: 126–item paper-pencil test measuring linguistic (vocabulary) and quantitative (arithmetic) factors. Average educational opportunities and familiarity with the English language are a requisite. Two equivalent forms are available. Examiner required. Suitable for group use.

Timed: 20 minutes

Scoring: Hand key; scoring service available from publisher

Cost: 25 test booklets $42.00; examiner's manual $10.00

Publisher: SRA/London House

TIME PERCEPTION INVENTORY (TPI)

Adult

Purpose: Measures the difference between physical and mental presence. Helps employees understand how much of their time is wasted due to mental preoccupations. Identifies an individual's particular preoccupations and evaluates their causes and debilitating nature.

Description: Multiple-item paper-pencil inventory measuring an individual's tendencies to focus attention on the past, future, or present. Percentile comparison on perceived time effectiveness (typically related to an individual's motivation to improve) is provided. All scales provide opportunities to consider positive and negative aspects of thinking in a particular time reference. Group patterns can be identified through a simple show of hands. The test booklet provides interpretations of scales and implications of scores on scales. Recommendations for additional reading are included. Normative data are available. Self-administered. Suitable for group use.

Untimed: 10 minutes

Scoring: Self-scored

Cost: Kit $25.00

Publisher: Western Psychological Services

VERBAL REASONING
Raymond J. Corsini and Richard Renck

Adult

Purpose: Assesses individual capacity to reason logically as indicated by solutions to verbal problems. Used for industrial job selection and vocational counseling.

Description: 36–item paper-pencil test of mental reasoning consisting of 12 statements with three questions each. A knowledge of basic English is required. Examiner required. Suitable for group use.

Timed: 15 minutes

Scoring: Hand key

Cost: Specimen set $8.00; 25 tests $20.00

Publisher: London House, Inc.

WATSON-GLASER CRITICAL THINKING APPRAISAL
Refer to page 629.

WESTERN PERSONNEL TESTS (WPT)
Robert L. Gunn and Morse P. Manson

Adult

Purpose: Measures general intelligence. Used for personnel screening.

Description: Multiple-item paper-pencil or computer-administered test providing a quick measure of general intelligence. Available in four equivalent forms: A, B, C, and D. Norms are provided for the general population and for professional, college, clerical, skilled, and unskilled populations. The computer version is available on IBM PC or compatible systems. Examiner required. Suitable for group use. Form A is available in Spanish.

Timed: 5 minutes

Scoring: Hand key; may be computer scored

Cost: Paper-pencil version complete kit (100 tests—25 each form, manual, key) $45.00; IBM version (25 uses) $110.00

Publisher: Western Psychological Services

THE WONDERLIC PERSONNEL TEST
Refer to page 927.

Interests

ADULT CAREER CONCERNS INVENTORY (ACCI)
Donald E. Super,
Albert S. Thompson, and
Richard H. Lindeman

Adult

Purpose: Measures career and life stages of adults. Used in counseling and research.

Description: 51-item paper-pencil measurement of Donald Super's theory of life stages (Exploration, Establishment, Maintenance, Disengagement) and a special Career Change Status Scale. Each of the 51 concerns is rated on a 5-point scale. Counselors can use the inventory for assessing a client's career stage and growth. Researchers may use it for assessing how life stage impacts productivity, creativity, turnover, and so forth. The computer scoring service profile plots five career stages, 12 subscales, and group summary data for answer sheets scored simultaneously. Self-administered. Suitable for group use.

Untimed: 30 minutes
Scoring: Hand key; may be computer scored
Cost: 25 test booklets and profiles $7.00; 50 non-prepaid answer sheets $20.00; manual $16.00
Publisher: Consulting Psychologists Press, Inc.

APTITUDE INTEREST MEASUREMENT (AIM)
Refer to page 866.

ARMED SERVICES-CIVILIAN INTEREST SURVEY (ASCVIS)
Robert Kauk

Adolescent, adult

Purpose: Assesses an individual's interests in high-tech occupational fields and identifies armed forces and related civilian jobs that match those interests. Used by career counselors with clients who want technical training that might be offered by the armed services.

Description: 6-page multiple-item paper-pencil or computer-administered inventory assessing levels of interest within high-tech occupational clusters. The test is designed to identify appropriate occupational choices and show how the armed services can be a source of immediate employment and basic and advanced technical training that can be utilized in either a military or civilian career. A career profile is developed for making tentative career decisions, including selection of an educational plan—either civilian or military—to reach career goals (a two-path plan is explained, step by step). The individual is free to take the completed career profile to a recruiter or civilian counselor to make the training connection. Self-administered. Suitable for group use.

Untimed: Varies
Scoring: Self-scored; may be computer scored
Cost: Class set (materials for 35 students, user's guide) $16.00
Publisher: CFKR Career Materials, Inc.
Information and availability unconfirmed; last verified in 1988.

THE BASIC PERSONALITY INVENTORY (BPI)
Refer to page 157.

CANADIAN OCCUPATIONAL INTEREST INVENTORY (COII)
G. Booth and Luc Begin

High-school student, adult

Purpose: Identifies an individual's attitudes toward occupationally related activities.

Description: 70-item paper-pencil measure of attitudes as they relate occupationally to activities. Interests and activities are measured by the following bipolar factors: things vs. people, business contact vs. scientific, routine vs. creative, social vs. solitary, and prestige vs. production. The test relates to the computer guidance program CHOICES. An IBM microcomputer program is available for administration and scoring. Examiner required. Suitable for group use. Available in French.

CANADIAN PUBLISHER

Untimed: 40 minutes

Scoring: Hand key; may be computer scored

Cost: 25 booklets $33.00; manual $13.75; 500 sheets and charts $121.75; key $5.00

Publisher: Nelson Canada

CAREER AND VOCATIONAL INTEREST INVENTORY
Refer to page 812.

CAREER ASSESSMENT INVENTORY—THE ENHANCED VERSION
Refer to page 812.

CAREER DIRECTIONS INVENTORY
Refer to page 813.

CAREER EXPLORATION PROFILE (CEP)
Refer to page 813.

CAREER EXPLORATION SERIES (CES)
Refer to page 814.

CAREER INTEREST TEST (CIT)
Educational and Industrial Test Services Ltd. Staff

Adolescent, adult

Purpose: Determines the vocational interests of young people and adults. Used for vocational and educational guidance.

Description: Multiple-item paper-pencil forced-choice test. The score reveals the subject's interests in or aversions to occupations in these six categories of interests: outdoor-physical, scientific-theoretical, social service, aesthetic-literary, commercial-clerical, and practical technical. Materials include test booklets, a scoring key, a specimen set, and a manual. Examiner required. Suitable for group use.

BRITISH PUBLISHER

Untimed: 20 minutes

Scoring: Examiner evaluated

Cost: Contact publisher

Publisher: Educational and Industrial Test Services Ltd.

CAREER QUEST
Refer to page 816.

CAREER SURVEY
Refer to page 816.

CORRECTIONAL OFFICERS' INTEREST BLANK (COIB)
Harrison G. Gough

Adult

Purpose: Measures an individual's potential for correctional work. Used for screening and placement.

Description: 40–item paper-pencil interest and attitude scale identifying applicants and officers of both sexes who possess the temperament and personal qualities required for work in correctional agencies and institutions. Sale is restricted to state and federal correctional agencies and penal institutions. Examiner required. Suitable for group use.

Untimed: 10 minutes

Scoring: Hand key

Cost: 25 test booklets $9.00; manual $8.00; hand-scoring stencils $16.75

Publisher: Consulting Psychologists Press, Inc.

CURTIS INTEREST SCALE
James W. Curtis

Adolescent, adult
Grades 10 and above

Purpose: Assesses individual vocational interest patterns. Used for vocational guidance, screening, and selection.

Description: 55–item paper-pencil test of vocational interests in 10 occupational areas: applied arts, business, computation, direct sales, entertainment, farming, interpersonal, mechanics, production, and science. The test yields an estimate of "level of responsibility." Self-administered. Suitable for group use.

Untimed: 10 minutes

Scoring: Examiner evaluated; scoring service available

Cost: Specimen set (test, manual, profile sheet) $4.00; 25 scales $7.00; 25 profiles $4.00

Publisher: Psychometric Affiliates

EXPLORING CAREER OPTIONS (ECO)
Refer to page 1002.

FORER VOCATIONAL SURVEY: MEN-WOMEN
Refer to page 822.

GENERAL OCCUPATIONAL INTEREST INVENTORY
Saville & Holdsworth Ltd.

Adult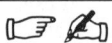

Purpose: Collects information about job-related interests among school dropouts and adults with education up to the "O" level. Used for counseling, vocational guidance, career planning, redundancy, and retirement counseling, as well as for selection and placement decisions.

Description: Multiple-item paper-pencil inventory requiring respondents to state their liking for activities related to specific occupations relevant to this level, including child care worker, waiter/waitress, sales representative, security officer, chargehand, secretary, farmer, graphic designer, dressmaker, maintenance electrician, and plumber. Scores are grouped for 18 main categories: medical, welfare, personal services, selling goods, selling services, supervision, clerical, office equipment, control, leisure, art and design, crafts, plants, animals, transport, construction, electrical, and mechanical. Evaluation of the scores for the 18 groups provides derived scores that indicate specific interests. Examiner required. Suitable for group use.
BRITISH PUBLISHER

Untimed: 35 minutes

Scoring: Hand key; examiner evaluated; may be computer scored

Cost: 10 booklets $25.50; manual and guide $44.00; key $11.50; administration card $11.50; computer disk (50 administrations) $367.50

Publisher: Saville & Holdsworth Ltd.

GUIDEPAK
Doris J. Pick

Adult—Ages 18 and older

Purpose: Identifies an individual's interests and personality characteristics. Used for career guidance and selection.

Description: 805–item paper-pencil multiple-choice and true-false program combining the California Psychological Inventory (CPI; 480 items) and the Strong-Campbell Interest Inventory (SCII; 325 items) to measure aspects of an individual's personality and interests that are related to vocational choice. The CPI covers a wide range of personality characteristics, including leadership, dominance, initiative, self-control, carefulness, ambition, accuracy, responsibility, and achievement urge. The SCII classifies interests according to six general themes: realistic, investigative, artistic, social, enterprising, and conventional.

A narrative report, personal interest profile, and workbook are provided. The workbook is designed to help the examinee relate the results to his vocational options. It also covers resume writing, suggests readings available in the career counseling area, and offers interviewing assistance. Self-administered. Suitable for group use.

Untimed: 2 hours

Scoring: Computer scored

Cost: Per testing (scoring, reports, workbook) $25.00

Publisher: Behaviordyne, Inc.

THE HARRINGTON-O'SHEA CAREER DECISION-MAKING SYSTEM (CDM)

Refer to page 823.

INTEREST BASED CAREER DECISION TEST (IBCD)

Adolescent, adult

Purpose: Assesses interests to identify the likes and dislikes of individuals and matches them to what is done and not done on jobs. Helps individuals select an occupation they will find personally satisfying and rewarding. Used for career exploration to match individuals to Occupational Families, work groups, and jobs at the semiskilled, skilled, technical, and professional levels.

Description: 200–item audiovisual or paper-pencil survey assessing an individual's activity preferences (likes and dislikes). The individual responds to a 200–picture inventory containing activity statements. The activities depict examples of 20 dimensions of work.

Responses are recorded in the test booklet for computer scoring or on cards for on-site scoring. A generated profile across the 20 dimensions of work describes the individual's approach/avoid pattern as numerical indicators related to activity preferences. The data bank consists of profiles of the 66 Occupational Families (work groups) of the GOE, which were compiled by using the same survey instrument administered to the individuals tested. The program compares the individual's interest profile to job requirement profiles in the Occupational Families. A one-page report identifies the interest patterns to 11 major interest groups of the GOE and gives an interest match score to all 66 GOE Occupational Families, selects the two strongest Occupational Family recommendations, and provides a description of activities, typical education, occupational outlook, DOT code, and a total of up to 12 typical job titles. Integrated into an Employability Development Plan. The IBCD has a companion aptitude test, the ABCD, which gives recommendations for the identical 66 GOE clusters. The survey may be completed in more than one sitting. Self-administered. Suitable for group use.

Untimed: 40 minutes

Scoring: Computer scored on-site or by publisher

Cost: Contact publisher

Publisher: Prep, A Division of Educational Technologies, Inc.

THE INTEREST CHECK LIST (ICL)

Adult

Purpose: Determines an individual's employment interests. Used as a guide to vocational counseling and self-assessment.

Description: 210–item paper-pencil checklist of sample tasks that have been keyed to the work groups listed in the *Guide for Occupational Exploration*. The applicant's likes and dislikes are evaluated, leading to an understanding of why the applicants are interested in the subjects indicated. The test may be used with individuals who have no firmly stated interests or who are not aware of the variety of existing occupations. Self-administered. Suitable for group use. Available in Spanish.

Untimed: 20 minutes

Scoring: Hand key

Cost: Contact publisher

Publisher: U.S. Department of Labor; distributed by Superintendent of Documents, U.S. Government Printing Office

Information and availability unconfirmed; last verified in 1988.

INVENTARIO INVESTIGATIVO DE INTERÉS VOCACIONAL (IIIV)
Refer to page 826.

INVENTORY OF VOCATIONAL INTERESTS
Refer to page 827.

JACKSON VOCATIONAL INTEREST SURVEY (JVIS)
Refer to page 827.

JOB MATCHING II

Adolescent, adult

Purpose: Assesses career preferences and experience. Used for career exploration and to match individuals to job families, local jobs, and training programs at the semiskilled, skilled, technical, and professional levels.

Description: 200–item audiovisual or paper-pencil survey assessing an individual's preferences and experience. The individual responds to 200 pictures with descriptions or narration depicting activities as examples of 20 dimensions of work. Responses are recorded in a booklet for computer scoring or on cards for on-site scoring. A generated profile across the 20 dimensions of work describes the individual's approach/avoid pattern as numerical indicators related to preferences and experience. The profiles can be used to identify the most appropriate match between the individual and local jobs or training programs because the survey also is used to profile local job requirements and training programs. National job bank matches are standard. Local job and training program bank matches are optional. Examiner/self-administered. Suitable for group use.

Timed: 1½ hours

Scoring: Computer scored on-site or by publisher

Cost: Contact publisher

Publisher: Prep, A Division of Educational Technologies, Inc.

JOB TRAINING ASSESSMENT PROGRAM (JOBTAP)
Refer to page 846.

JOB-O
Refer to page 828.

KUDER OCCUPATIONAL INTEREST SURVEY, FORM DD (KOIS), REVISED
Frederic Kuder

Adolescent, adult
Grades 11 and above

Purpose: Measures how an individual's interests compare with those of satisfied workers in a number of occupational fields or students in various college majors. Used with high-school and college students and adults for career planning, vocational guidance, and academic counseling.

Description: 100–item paper-pencil inventory assessing the subject's interests in a number of areas related to occupational fields and college majors. Survey items consist of a list of three activities. The subject indicates for each item which activity he likes the most and which he likes the least.

The survey reports comparison to the subject's norm group by sex in 10 vocational areas and compares the subject's interests with those of satisfied workers in approximately 100 specific occupational groups and satisfied students in approximately 40 college major groups. The Report Form lists scores on occupational and college major scales separately, in rank order for each student. All respondents receive scores on all scales, including some nontraditional occupations for men and women.

A general manual provides technical data regarding reliability, validity, scoring, interpretation, and compliance with Title IX regulations. Optional interpretive guides include an interpretive audio-cassette, Fast Fax (description of each of the occupations and college majors reported on the KOIS, including brief job description, job opportunities, employment outlooks, salary ranges, and training and skills required), "Expanding Your Future" (a guide to help subjects interpret and use their scores), and *Counseling with the Kuder Occupational Interest Survey, Form DD* (a handbook for counselors). A sixth-grade reading level is required. Self-administered. Suitable for group use.

Timed: 30–40 minutes

Scoring: Computer scored

Cost: Materials and scoring for 20 persons $73.50; audiocassette $16.75; "Expanding Your Future" $12.00; *Counseling with KOIS* $5.25; Fast Fax for KOIS Occupations and College Majors $15.00; no charge for general manual if requested when ordering

Publisher: CTB/Macmillan/McGraw-Hill

KUDER PREFERENCE RECORD, VOCATIONAL, FORM CP
Refer to page 829.

LIFE STYLE QUESTIONNAIRE
James Barrett

Adolescent, adult— Ages 15 and older

Purpose: Provides insight regarding interests, attitudes, and behaviors of people about to begin work or already working. Used for vocational guidance, counseling, and management development.

Description: 132–item paper-pencil or computer-administered test for self-assessment of vocational interests and attitudes. Items are statements about work activities. Scores are provided on 13 scales: 6 dealing with general motivation, 5 examining consistency of outlook with interests, and 2 estimating the degree of certainty about questionnaire responses. The test booklet contains instructions on how to respond to test items. Self-administered. Suitable for group use. BRITISH PUBLISHER

Timed: 20 minutes

Scoring: Hand key; scoring service available

Cost: Booklet $7.50; manual $16.50, software $900.00

Publisher: The Test Agency

LIMRA CAREER PROFILE SYSTEM
Refer to page 1083.

MINNESOTA IMPORTANCE QUESTIONNAIRE (MIQ)

Adult

Purpose: Measures vocational needs and relates them to occupational reinforcers. Assesses need-reinforcer correspondence as a supplement to standard measures of occupational interests and abilities.

Description: Multiple-item paper-pencil inventory assessing vocational needs in terms of preferred occupational reinforcers. The Paired Form (190 paired comparison and 20 absolute judgment items) presents pairs of vocational needs statements, and the examinee indicates the more important need in each pair. The Ranked Form (42 items) presents vocational need statements in groups of five, and the individual ranks the five needs in each group according to their importance. Both forms measure the following need dimensions: ability utilization, achievement, activity, advancement, authority, company policies and practices, compensation, co-workers, creativity, independence, moral values, recognition, responsibility, security, social service, social status, supervision-human relations, supervision-technical, variety, and working conditions.

A computer-generated profile and interpretation are provided for each examinee. They include scores on each dimension (Ranked Form also includes an Autonomy Scale) in the form of a profile, correspondence of examinee's need pattern to Occupational Reinforcer Patterns (ORPs), lists (50 each) of occupations with the ORPs most similar and least similar to the examinee's MIQ profile, predictions of job satisfaction for each occupation listed, references for further information, a validity score, and an error factor for each score. An optional extended report lists MIQ-ORP correspondence for 187 occupations. A technical manual discusses development, reliability, validity, normative data, and interpretations of sample MIQ profiles. The test is a Level B instrument as defined by the APA; prospective users must establish qualifications with their initial order. Self-administered with clinical supervision. Suitable for group use. Available in Spanish and French.

Untimed: Varies

Scoring: Computer scored

Cost: 10–99 booklets (specify form) $0.70; 10–499 answer sheets (specify form) $0.12; computer scoring $3.00 per standard report; $3.25 per extended report; sample set (MIQ manual, 1 booklet and answer sheet for both paired and ranked forms) $11.00

Publisher: Vocational Psychology Research, University of Minnesota

---

MY VOCATIONAL SITUATION
Refer to page 1014.

PERSONNEL REACTION BLANK (PRB)
Harrison G. Gough

Adult

Purpose: Measures a dependability-conscientiousness factor among rank-and-file workers. Used by personnel officers for selecting new employees.

Description: 70–item paper-pencil test assessing interests and attitudes related to dependability and conscientiousness. The test is used with rank-and-file workers and is not recommended for management personnel. A manual explains the meaning of high and low scores. The test is restricted, and scoring keys are sold only to registered users. Self-administered. Suitable for group use.

Untimed: 10–15 minutes

Scoring: Hand key

Cost: Specimen set (manual, test booklet, special order form) $14.00

Publisher: Consulting Psychologists Press, Inc.

THE SALIENCE INVENTORY (RESEARCH EDITION)
Donald E. Super and Dorothy D. Nevill

Adult

Purpose: Measures an individual's orientation to life roles. Used in counseling and research related to life roles and careers.

Description: 170–item paper-pencil inventory assessing the relative importance of five major life roles: student, worker, homemaker, leisurite, and citizen. Items are rated on a 4–point scale. The inventory measures an individual in relation to Super's Life-Career Rainbow model and was part of the *Work Importance Study*. International life-role distributions are available. For counselors, the inventory indicates a client's orientation to life roles, readiness for career decisions, and exposure to work and occupations. The profile available through computer scoring plots 15 subscales and provides local percentiles and group summary data. Examiner required. Suitable for group use.

Untimed: 30 minutes

Scoring: Hand key; computer scoring service available

Cost: 25 reusable booklets $16.50; 50 answer sheets $14.50

Publisher: Consulting Psychologists Press, Inc.

SELF-DESCRIPTION INVENTORY
Charles B. Johansson

**Adolescent, adult
Grades 9 and above**

Purpose: Evaluates an individual's personality strengths relevant to world of work. Used for career counseling and for training and development.

Description: 200–item paper-pencil inventory covering 11 basic personality scales and 6 vocational scales. Items are self-descriptive adjectives. The bipolar personal scales are Cautious/Adventurous, Nonscientific/Analytical, Tense/Relaxed, Insecure/Confident, Conventional/Imaginative, Impatient/Patient, Unconcerned/

Altruistic, Reserved/Outgoing, Soft-spoken/Forceful, Lackadaisical/Industrious, and Unorganized/Orderly. The vocational scales cover the following RIASEC factors: Realistic, Investigative, Artistic, Social, Enterprising, and Conventional. Self-administered. Suitable for group use.

Untimed: 15–20 minutes

Scoring: Computer scored

Cost: Manual $11.25; answer sheets (includes test items) $3.10–$4.35 depending on quantity

Publisher: National Computer Systems/PAS Division

THE SELF-DIRECTED SEARCH—NEW ZEALAND REVISION
Refer to page 835.

THE SELF-DIRECTED SEARCH, 1985 REVISION (SDS)
John L. Holland

Adolescent, adult—Ages 15–70

Purpose: Assesses the abilities and interests of adolescents and adults. Used for career planning and guidance.

Description: Multiple-item paper-pencil or computer-administered test in two forms yielding six interest scores (Realistic, Investigative, Artistic, Social, Enterprising, and Conventional) and a three-letter occupational code used for exploring occupational possibilities. The Occupations Finder in this revised version contains over 1,100 occupational titles. Directions have been revised to increase self-understanding and vocational exploration. Form E, which yields a two-letter code, is available for individuals with a fourth-grade reading level.

The computer version operates on Apple systems with 64K, an 80–column card, and two floppy disk drives and on IBM PC systems with 256K and two disk drives. A scoring service is available from the publisher. Self-administered. Suitable for group use. Available in Spanish and Vietnamese.

Untimed: 30–45 minutes

Scoring: Self-scored; may be computer scored

Cost: Professional kit (manual, manual supplement, 25 booklets and Occupations Finders, 25 *You and Your Career* booklets) $58.00; computer version (50 uses) $195.00; interpretive report (unlimited) $395.00

Publisher: Psychological Assessment Resources, Inc.

SIX-FACTOR AUTOMATED VOCATIONAL ASSESSMENT SYSTEM (SAVAS)
Refer to page 836.

SKILLSCAN
Refer to page 913.

STANTON PROFILE
Refer to page 915.

STRONG INTEREST INVENTORY
E.K. Strong, Jr., Jo-Ida C. Hansen, and David P. Campbell

Adolescent, adult
Grades 8 and above

Purpose: Measures occupational interests in a wide range of career areas. Used to make long-range curricular and occupational choices and for employee placement, career guidance, career development, and vocational rehabilitation placement.

Description: 325–item paper-pencil multiple-choice test requiring the examinee to respond either "like," "indifferent," or "dislike" to items covering a broad range of familiar occupational tasks and day-to-day activities. General topics include occupations, school subjects, activities, leisure activities, types of people, preference between two activities, and "your characteristics."

Responses are then analyzed by computer to yield a profile that presents scores on a number of scales and offers interpretive advice. Specifically, the respondent is scored on six general occupational themes (based on Holland's RIASEC themes), 23 basic interest scales (measuring strength and consistency of specific interest areas), and 207 occupational scales (reflecting degree of similarity between respondent and people employed in particular occupations). The scoring service provides 10 Administrative Indexes that help identify invalid or unusual profiles. Scores on two special scales measure introversion-extroversion and degree of comfort in an academic environment. Computer scoring is required and is available from a number of sources (test results are available on-site using microcomputer scoring). Self-administered. Suitable for group use. Available in Spanish, French-Canadian, and Hebrew.

Untimed: 25–30 minutes

Scoring: Computer scored

Cost: Specimen prepaid scoring packet (brochure describing the Strong, test booklet, prepaid answer sheet to be returned for free profile and interpretive report) $8.00; 1984 user's guide $15.00; 1985 manual $17.00; 25 reusable test booklets (English) $9.75; 25 reusable test booklets (Spanish) $12.50

Publisher: Stanford University Press; distributed exclusively by Consulting Psychologists Press, Inc.

U.S. EMPLOYMENT SERVICE (USES) INTEREST INVENTORY
U.S. Employment Service

Adult

Purpose: Measures an individual's general occupational interests. Used in vocational counseling.

Description: 162–item paper-pencil examination measuring 12 interest areas listed in the *USES Guide for Occupational Exploration*: artistic, scientific, plants and animals, protective, mechanical, industrial, business retail, selling, accommodating, humanitarian, leading-influencing, and physical performance. Available only to State Employment Services or to organizations that have approval from such services. Examiner required. Suitable for group use.

Untimed: 20 minutes

Scoring: Hand key; may be computer scored

Cost: Available only through State Employment Service Agencies

Publisher: U.S. Department of Labor

Information and availability unconfirmed; last verified in 1988.

THE VALUES SCALE (RESEARCH EDITION)
Donald E. Super and Dorothy D. Nevill

Adult

Purpose: Measures intrinsic and extrinsic life-career values.

Description: 106–item paper-pencil inventory measuring intrinsic and extrinsic life-career values and many cultural perspectives of adults. Items are rated on a 4–point scale ranging from "little or no importance" to "very important." The 21 scales are Ability Utilization, Achievement, Advancement, Aesthetics, Altruism, Authority, Autonomy, Creativity, Economic Rewards, Lifestyle, Personal Development, Physical Activity, Prestige, Risk, Social Interaction, Social Relations, Variety, Working Conditions, Cultural Identity, Physical Prowess, and Economic Security. The scale was developed as part of the international *Work Importance Study* and has international norms. The profile available through the computer scoring service plots 21 subscales and provides local percentiles and group summary data for answer sheets scored simultaneously. Examiner required. Suitable for group use.

Untimed: 30–45 minutes

Scoring: Hand key; computer scoring service available

Cost: 25 booklets $13.50; 50 answer sheets $18.00; manual $23.00; specimen set (manual, test booklet, answer sheet) $13.00; 50 report forms $11.00

Publisher: Consulting Psychologists Press, Inc.

VOCATIONAL INFORMATION PROFILE (VIP)
Refer to page 837.

VOCATIONAL INTEREST, EXPERIENCE & SKILL ASSESSMENT (VIESA), CANADIAN EDITION

Refer to page 839.

VOCATIONAL PREFERENCE INVENTORY, 1985 REVISION (VPI)

John L. Holland

Adolescent, adult
Grades 10 and above

Purpose: Assesses personality using occupational item content. Developed for high-school students and adults for vocational exploration.

Description: Multiple-item paper-pencil or computer-administered test yielding a profile based on 11 dimensions of personality: realistic, investigative, scientific, conventional, enterprising, artistic, self-control, masculinity/femininity, status, infrequency, and acquiescence. Items are all occupational titles, and the subjects indicate which they like or dislike. This revision contains new items as well as answer sheet and stencil revisions. The computer version operates on Apple systems with 64K, an 80–column card, and two disk drives and on IBM PC systems with 256K and two disk drives. Examiner/self-administered. Suitable for group use.

Untimed: 15–30 minutes

Scoring: Hand key; may be computer scored

Cost: Professional kit (manual, 25 test booklets, 50 answer sheets, 50 profile forms, scoring key) $29.95; 50 uses computer version $150.00

Publisher: Psychological Assessment Resources, Inc.

VOCATIONAL RESEARCH INTEREST INVENTORY (VRII)

Refer to page 840.

WIDE RANGE INTEREST-OPINION TEST (WRIOT)

Refer to page 841.

THE WORLD OF WORK INVENTORY

Robert E. Ripley (original author), Karen Hudson and Gregory P.M. Neidert (revision)

Adolescent, adult—Ages 13–65

Purpose: Measures temperaments, interests, and aptitudes related to *Dictionary of Occupational Title* career families. Used for employee selection, career counseling, vocational rehabilitation, and adult/career education classes.

Description: 518–item paper-pencil or computer-administered inventory. The 98 multiple-choice items assess the following achievement-aptitude areas: abstractions, spatial-form, verbal, numerical, mechanical-electrical, and clerical. The 420 rating items (subject responds "like," "dislike," or "neutral") assess 12 job-related temperament factors and career interests in activities related to 17 professional and industrial career areas.

Results are provided in profile and narrative summary formats. Norms updated to include nationwide sample of more than 22,000. A cassette tape is available for instruction of examiners. The computer version operates on IBM PC and compatible systems. Self-administered. Suitable for group use. Available in Spanish and in a modified version for remedial readers, the deaf, and for individuals with mental handicaps.

Untimed: 2 hours

Scoring: Machine scored; computer scored; scoring service available from publisher

Cost: Reusable test booklet $5.00; single answer sheet $11.00; coupon for single narrative summary $10.00; interpretation manual $19.95; service included with cost of answer sheets; a nonprofit price schedule and discounts for nonprofit organizations are available

Publisher: World of Work, Inc.

Interpersonal Skills and Attitudes

ACTUALIZING ASSESSMENT BATTERY (AAB)
Refer to page 151.

ADULT PERSONALITY INVENTORY
Refer to page 154.

ALIENATION INDEX SURVEY (AI SURVEY)

Adult

Purpose: Assesses work-related attitudes of job applicants. Identifies individuals with alienated attitudes that reduce performance and cause poor morale. Used for applicant screening and employee selection.

Description: Multiple-item paper-pencil preemployment survey assessing the attitudes of job applicants toward employers, supervisors, co-workers, work, pay, and benefits. The survey identifies applicants with alienated attitudes in these areas who have a high potential for becoming problem employees. The survey is administered, scored, and interpreted in-house for immediate use by personnel/human relations/security specialists by license to Psychological Surveys Corporation. The survey is also available as part of the PASS Booklet (which includes the Trustworthiness Attitude Survey and the Emotional Stability Survey) or PASS-II Booklet (along with Trustworthiness Attitude Survey) for more complete applicant assessment. Examiner required. Suitable for group use.

Untimed: 8–12 minutes

Scoring: Examiner evaluated

Cost: Contact publisher

Publisher: Psychological Surveys Corporation

ATTITUDE SURVEY PROGRAM FOR BUSINESS AND INDUSTRY

Adult

Purpose: Measures the attitudes of employees and provides an overview of company conditions. Used to identify reasons for low morale and productivity and high turnover, assess employee acceptance of organizational change, determine training needs, monitor issues that contribute to staff stability, and identify company inefficiencies.

Description: Four 93–item paper-pencil surveys assessing employee concerns that affect a company's harmony, efficiency, and profitability. Survey titles include the Organization Survey, Managerial Survey, Professional Survey, and Sales Survey. The possible areas measured by the surveys are organization identification, job satisfaction, pay, benefits, supervisory leadership practices, work associates, general administrative practices, supervisory administrative practices, work organization, work efficiency, performance and personal development, communication effectiveness, relations with top management, sales training, company products, pricing and credit, customer service, advertising, and reactions to survey. (See descriptions of individual surveys for a listing of the areas relevant to a particular survey.) An optional general comments section may be included.

Each of the four surveys is available in several forms: standard, modified, customized, and optional categories. Custom demographic breakdowns are available with all surveys. Modified surveys allow the addition of up to 30 items not included on the standard survey. Customized surveys are designed to include company-specific items, company logo, specialized comment sections, and factors created by the company. Optional categories that may be added to any survey are equipment, safety, and health; security operations; and human resource management.

London House psychologists help company administrators plan and conduct a survey. Administration occurs on company premises under the supervision of a company official or London House employee; mailings also are available. The available reports use state-of-the-art graphics and compare company results to national and industry-specific norms. Narrative reports and feedback presentations and follow-up surveys are also available. Anonymous comment transcription is provided by London House. Examiner required. Suitable for group use.

Untimed: 50 minutes or less

Scoring: Computer scored by London House

Cost: 100 standard booklets $950.00; 100 modified booklets $1,150.00; 100 customized booklets (specify survey title) $1,500.00; comment transcriptions $1.00 per unit for all surveys

Publisher: London House, Inc.

ATTITUDE SURVEY PROGRAM FOR BUSINESS AND INDUSTRY: MANAGERIAL SURVEY

Adult

Purpose: Measures the attitudes of managers above first-line supervision and provides an overview of company conditions. Used to identify the reasons for low morale and productivity and high absenteeism, assess employee acceptance of organizational change, determine training needs, monitor issues that contribute to staff stability, and identify company weaknesses.

Description: 93–item paper-pencil survey assessing the priorities and concerns of managers. Items cover the following areas: organization identification, job satisfaction, material rewards: pay, material rewards: benefits, supervisory leadership practices, work associates, general administrative practices, supervisory administrative practices, work organization, work efficiency, performance and personal development, communication effectiveness, relations with top management, and reactions to survey. A general comment section is also included; transcription and analysis are included.

The survey is available in standard, modified, customized, and optional categories forms. Custom demographic breakdowns are available with all surveys. The modified survey allows the addition of up to 30 items not included on the standard survey. The customized survey is designed to include company-specific items, company logo, specialized comment sections, and factors created by the company. Optional categories that may be added to any survey are equipment, safety, and health; security operations; and human resource management.

London House psychologists help company administrators plan and conduct a survey. Administration occurs on company premises under the supervision of a company official or London House employee; mailings are also available. The available reports use state-of-the-art graphics and compare company results to national and industry-specific norms. Narrative reports, feedback presentations, and follow-up surveys are also available. Other surveys available in the series are the Organization Survey, Professional Survey, and Sales Survey. Examiner required. Suitable for group use.

Untimed: 50 minutes or less

Scoring: Computer scored by London House

Cost: 100 standard surveys $950.00; 100 modified surveys $1,150.00; 100 customized surveys $1,500.00; comment transcriptions $1.00 per unit

Publisher: London House, Inc.

ATTITUDE SURVEY PROGRAM FOR BUSINESS AND INDUSTRY: ORGANIZATION SURVEY

Adult

Purpose: Measures the attitudes of hourly employees and first-line supervisors and provides an overview of company conditions. Used to identify reasons for low morale and productivity and high absenteeism, assess employee acceptance of organizational change, determine training needs, monitor issues that contribute to staff stability, and identify company inefficiencies.

Description: 93–item paper-pencil survey assessing the priorities and concerns of employees. Items cover the following areas: organization identification, job satisfaction, pay, benefits, supervisory leadership practices, work associates, general administrative practices, supervisory administrative practices, work organization, work efficiency, performance and personal development, communication effectiveness, and reactions to survey. A general comment section is also included; transcription and analysis are optional.

The survey is available in standard, modified, customized, and optional categories forms. Custom demographic breakdowns are available with all surveys. The modified survey allows the addition of up to 30 items not included on the standard survey. The customized survey is designed to include company-specific items, company logo, specialized comment sections, and factors created by the company. Optional categories that may be added to any survey are equipment, safety, and health; security operations; and human resource management.

London House psychologists help company administrators plan and conduct a survey. Administration occurs on company premises under the supervision of a company official or London House employee; mailings also are possible.

The available reports use state-of-the-art graphics and compare company results to national and industry-specific norms. Narrative reports, feedback presentations, and follow-up surveys are also available. Other surveys available in the series are the Managerial Survey, Professional Survey, and Sales Survey. Examiner required. Suitable for group use.

Untimed: 50 minutes or less

Scoring: Computer scored by London House

Cost: 100 standard surveys $950.00; 100 modified surveys $1,150.00; 100 customized surveys $1,500.00; comment transcriptions $1.00 per unit

Publisher: London House, Inc.

ATTITUDE SURVEY PROGRAM FOR BUSINESS AND INDUSTRY: PROFESSIONAL SURVEY

Adult

Purpose: Measures the attitudes of professionals in staff positions, such as attorneys, editors, accountants, and engineers and provides an overview of company conditions. Used to identify reasons for low morale and productivity and high

absenteeism, assess employee acceptance of organizational change, determine training needs, monitor issues that contribute to staff stability, and identify company inefficiencies.

Description: 93–item paper-pencil survey assessing the priorities and concerns of professionals. Items cover the following areas: organization identification, job satisfaction, material rewards: pay, material rewards: benefits, supervisory leadership practices, work associates, general administrative practices, supervisory administrative practices, work organization, work efficiency, performance and personal development, communication effectiveness, relations with top management, and reactions to survey. A general comments section is also included; transcription and analysis are optional.

The survey is available in standard, modified, customized, and optional categories forms. Custom breakdowns are available with all surveys. The modified survey allows the addition of up to 30 items not included on the standard survey. The customized survey is designed to include company-specific items, company logo, specialized comment sections, and factors created by the company. Optional categories that may be added to any survey are equipment, safety, and health; security operations; and human resource management.

London House psychologists help company administrators plan and conduct a survey. Administration occurs on company premises under the supervision of a company official or London House employee; mailings are also available.

The available reports use state-of-the-art graphics and compare company results to national and industry-specific norms. Narrative reports, feedback presentations, and follow-up surveys are also available. Other surveys available in the series are the Organization Survey, Managerial Survey, and Sales Survey. Examiner required. Suitable for group use.

Untimed: 50 minutes or less

Scoring: Computer scored by London House

Cost: 100 standard surveys $950.00; 100 modified surveys $1,150.00; 100 customized surveys $1,500.00; comment transcriptions $1.00 per unit

Publisher: London House, Inc.

ATTITUDE SURVEY PROGRAM FOR BUSINESS AND INDUSTRY: SALES SURVEY

Adult

Purpose: Measures the attitudes of outside field sales representatives and provides an overview of company conditions. Used to identify reasons for low morale and productivity and high absenteeism, assess employee acceptance of organizational change, determine training needs, monitor issues that contribute to staff stability, and identify company inefficiencies.

Description: 93–item paper-pencil survey assessing the priorities and concerns of field salesmen, excluding telephone and over-the-counter salesmen. Items cover the following areas: organization identification, job satisfaction, pay, benefits, supervisory leadership practices, general administrative practices, supervisory administrative practices, performance and personal development, communication effectiveness, sales training, company products, pricing and credit, customer service, advertising, and reactions to survey. A general comments section is also included; transcription and analysis are optional.

The survey is available in standard, modified, customized, and optional categories forms. Custom breakdowns are available with all surveys. The modified survey allows the addition of up to 30 items not included on the standard survey. The customized survey is designed to include company-specific items, company logo, specialized comment sections, and factors created by the company. Optional categories that may be added to any survey are equipment, safety, and health; security operations; and human resource management.

London House psychologists help company administrators plan and conduct a survey. Administration occurs on company premises under the supervision of a company official or London House employee; mailings are also available.

The available reports use state-of-the-art graphics and compare company results to national and industry-specific norms. Narrative reports, feedback presentations, and follow-up surveys are also available. Other surveys available in the series are the Organization Survey, Managerial Survey, and Professional Survey. Examiner required. Suitable for group use.

Untimed: 50 minutes or less

Scoring: Computer scored by London House

Cost: 100 standard surveys $950.00; 100 modified surveys $1,150.00; 100 customized surveys $1,500.00; comment transcriptions $1.00

Publisher: London House, Inc.

ATTITUDE TOWARDS DISABLED PERSONS SCALE (ATDP)
Refer to page 750.

BIOGRAPHICAL INDEX
Willard A. Kerr

Adult

Purpose: Quantifies background data. Used for predicting success in managerial and sales positions and in recruitment programs for general business.

Description: Multiple-item paper-pencil measure of personal background information. The instrument yields five scores: stability, drive to excel, human relations, financial status, and personal adjustment. Three middle scores provide an estimate of basic energy level. The instrument predicts the annual salary increment of executives. Examiner required. Suitable for group use.

Untimed: 30 minutes

Scoring: Hand key

Cost: Specimen set $5.00; 25 indices $8.75; 25 answer sheets $5.00

Publisher: Psychometric Affiliates

THE BIPOLAR PSYCHOLOGICAL INVENTORY (BPI)
Refer to page 159.

BUSINESS JUDGMENT TEST
Martin M. Bruce

Adult

Purpose: Evaluates the subject's sense of "social intelligence" in business-related situations. Used for employee selection and training.

Description: 25–item paper-pencil multiple-choice test in which the subject selects one of four ways to complete a stem statement, allowing the examiner to gauge the subject's sense of socially acceptable and desirable ways to behave in business relationships. The score suggests the degree to which the subject agrees with the general opinion of businessmen as to the proper way to handle various relationships. Self-administered. Suitable for group use. Available in French.

Untimed: 10–15 minutes

Scoring: Hand key

Cost: Manual $12.50; key $1.95; package of tests $39.50; specimen set $29.50

Publisher: Martin M. Bruce, Ph.D., Publishers

CALIFORNIA PSYCHOLOGICAL INVENTORY, 1987 REVISED EDITION

Refer to page 161.

CAREER DECISION SCALE (CDS), 2ND EDITION
Samuel H. Osipow,
Clarke G. Carney, Jane Winer,
Barbara Yanico, and
Maryanne Koschir

Adolescent, adult
Grades 9–college

Purpose: Identifies barriers preventing an individual from making career decisions. Used as a basis for career counseling, to monitor the effectiveness of career counseling programs, and for research on career indecisiveness.

Description: 19–item paper-pencil inventory assessing a limited number of circumstances that cause problems in reaching and implementing educational and career decisions. Items 1 and 2 measure degree of certainty (Certainty scale). Items 3–18 measure career indecision (Indecision scale). Item 19 is open-ended. Individuals rate each item on a 4–point scale from one ("not like me") to four

("like me") to indicate the extent to which each item describes their personal situations. Scores are reported as percentiles. The manual includes data regarding validity and reliability and norms for various age and grade levels. This edition is a revision of the Career Decision Scale. Examiner/self-administered. Suitable for group use.

Untimed: 10–15 minutes

Scoring: Hand key; examiner evaluated

Cost: Kit (manual, 50 test booklets) $26.95

Publisher: Psychological Assessment Resources, Inc.

THE CAREER SUITABILITY PROFILE
Christopher P. Harding

Adult

Purpose: Measures fundamental personality characteristics that control career interests, abilities, and the capacity to perform. Used for recruiting, screening candidates, organization design, succession planning, training and assistance, reassignment, and management review.

Description: 70–item paper-pencil or computer-administered multiple-choice test based on 12 personality factors defined by Christopher Harding to characterize an individual's personality structure. The test determines which factors most control an individual's performance potential in his or her work and personal life, one's suitability for various career fields, the outlook for achievement and fulfillment in one's most appropriate career area(s), and the type of business in which he or she will function most effectively.

An individual's results are classified into one of several hundred possible profile patterns. The Career Suitability Profile Report provides a personalized 30–page description of the profile, what each element means, what the combination of one's qualities mean, and what the individual may do to enhance personal performance. Although the report is computer generated, it is studied by a skilled professional before it is sent to the individual tested. Arrangements may be made for the examinee and a trained professional to discuss the results. In addition to the report, each profile is accompanied by two numerical indexes: the Success Outlook (a measure of individuation, the ability to achieve on one's own and to feel fulfillment in work) and the Productivity Index (a measure of organizational fit, the capability to function effectively as a team player).

The computer-administered version is available on either 5¼" or 3½" diskettes in ASCII format for IBM PC and compatible computers. The test may be administered to physically impaired individuals by having another person read the questions aloud and record answers. Self-administered. Suitable for group use. Translations into other languages are available upon request.

Untimed: 10 minutes

Scoring: Computer scored

Cost: Per person $250.00 for test and report; $10.00 surcharge for 5¼" diskette; $15.00 surcharge for 3½" diskette

Publisher: Management Strategies, Inc.

CAREERS
T.L. Brink

Adult

Purpose: Assesses vocationally related personality traits, abilities, and priorities. Used to match individual to over 300 occupations.

Description: Multiple-item computer-administered checklist covering vocationally related personality traits, abilities, and priorities and yielding a Holland code (RIASEC). The individual's performance is matched to over 300 occupations. The program operates on Apple system computers. Self-administered. Not suitable for group use.

Timed: 30 minutes

Scoring: Computer scored

Cost: $49.95

Publisher: T.L. Brink

CHANGE AGENT QUESTIONNAIRE (CAQ)
Jay Hall and Martha S. Williams

Adult

Purpose: Evaluates attitudes toward change. Used in programs on the dynamics of change with teachers, trainers, managers, members of the clergy, politicians, probation officers, counselors, and social workers—individuals whose role is to bring about positive changes in organizations, institutions, or individuals.

Description: Multiple-item paper-pencil self-report inventory assessing an individual's philosophies, strategies, and approaches concerning the concept of change. The inventory measures basic assumptions regarding the process and duration of change, particularly change that is brought about through the efforts of change agents (individuals who effect change by actively influencing the thoughts and behaviors of others). The inventory yields five scores, which are profiled according to a grid format based on the work of Herbert Kelman concerning change agents. Self-administered. Suitable for group use.

Untimed: Varies

Scoring: Self-scored

Cost: Individual instrument $4.50

Publisher: Teleometrics International

CHOOSING A CAREER
E.I.T.S. Staff

Adolescent, adult

Purpose: Evaluates individual attitudes towards work. Used for vocational and educational guidance.

Description: Multiple-item paper-pencil supplement to the Rothwell-Miller Interest Blank. The subject is asked to rank a series of statements in order of their importance, thereby determining the subject's attitudes towards five factors: rewards, interests, security, pride and recognition, and autonomy. Norms are given in the manual. Examiner required. Suitable for group use.
BRITISH PUBLISHER

Untimed: 10 minutes

Scoring: Examiner evaluated

Cost: Contact publisher

Publisher: Educational and Industrial Test Services Ltd.

CONFLICT MANAGEMENT SURVEY (CMS)
Jay Hall

Adult

Purpose: Assesses the manner in which individuals interpret the meaning of conflict and, consequently, the manner in which they handle it. Used in labor-management sessions, community relations laboratories, and programs on the dynamics of conflict to identify constructive outcomes to conflict.

Description: Multiple-item paper-pencil self-report inventory assessing an individual's reaction to, and consequent handling of, interpersonal, group, and intergroup conflict. Analysis employs a grid format measuring two dimensions: concern for personal goals and concern for relationships. The survey identifies five styles of conflict management: win-lose, yield-lose, lose-leave, compromise, and synergistic. Normative data and conversion tables are provided for transforming raw scores on the five styles into a five-fold conflict management profile. These profiles provide a basis for establishing constructive conflict-handling behavior. Self-administered. Suitable for group use.

Untimed: Varies

Scoring: Self-scored

Cost: Individual instrument $5.60

Publisher: Teleometrics International

CPP COMPATIBILITY QUESTIONNAIRE
Larry L. Craft

Adult—Ages 16 and older

Purpose: Assesses personality and motivation. Used to assess job, peer, and manager compatibility for selection, supervision, and training in business and industry.

Description: 88–item paper-pencil or computer-administered forced-choice test containing seven scales: Emotional Intensity (E), Intuition (I), Need for Status/Prestige Recognition (R), Sensitivity to Needs of Others (S), Assertiveness (A), Trust (T), and Exaggeration (X). Items are presented in a real/ideal format.

A telephone scoring service is available from Human Resource Associates. Results are reported as percentile rankings. Four reports are available: a) Self-Report, b) Manager's Supervisory Report, c) Sales Manager's Supervisory Report, and d) Selection Report. The computer version operates on IBM PC or compatible systems. Mail-in or fax scoring services are available through 20 regional scoring centers in the U.S. and Canada. A 10th-grade reading level is required. Self-administered. Suitable for group use.

Untimed: 25 minutes

Scoring: Computer scored; mail-in or fax scoring service; telephone scoring service

Cost: Computer version $25.00 per scoring, no charge for reports; telephone and fax scoring $25.00, extra charge for reports

Publisher: Personnel Assessment Centers, Inc.

A CREATIVITY MEASURE—THE SRT SCALE
William C. Kosinar

Adolescent, adult
Grades 10 and above

Purpose: Assesses level of creativity. Used for career guidance with youths and to select research and scientific personnel.

Description: Multiple-item paper-pencil forced-choice test of creativity. The manual provides norms on scientific personnel, National Science Talent Search winners, college students, and high-school students. Examiner required. Suitable for group use.

Untimed: 5 minutes

Scoring: Examiner evaluated

Cost: Specimen set $4.00; 25 tests $4.50

Publisher: Psychometric Affiliates

CULTURE SHOCK INVENTORY (CSI)
W.J. Reddin

Adult

Purpose: Assesses an individual's susceptibility to cultural shock. Used to acquaint those who expect to work outside their own culture with potentially difficult areas.

Description: Multiple-item paper-pencil test consisting of scales assessing Western ethnocentrism, cross-cultural experience, cognitive flex, behavioral flex, cultural knowledge (specific and general), customs acceptance, and interpersonal sensitivity. The test may be used with managers, spouses, and older children and in colleges. Self-administered. Suitable for group use.
CANADIAN PUBLISHER
Untimed: 20–30 minutes
Scoring: Hand key
Cost: Test kit (10 test copies, fact sheet, user's guide) $40.00
Publisher: Organizational Tests (Canada) Ltd.

CURTIS COMPLETION FORM
Refer to page 168.

CUSTOMER REACTION SURVEY (CRS)
Refer to page 1081.

THE DECISION MAKING INVENTORY
Richard Johnson, William Coscarelli, and JaDean Johnson

Adolescent, adult

Purpose: Identifies an individual's preferred decision-making style. Used in career counseling, marriage therapy, task groups, and instructional programs.

Description: 20–item paper-pencil one-page instrument assessing an individual's preferred style of making decisions. Individuals rate a series of statements concerning steps in the decision-making process on a 6–point scale ranging from "never" to "always" to indicate the degree to which each item is true for themselves. Scoring and interpretation is based on Johnson's theory, which suggests that information can be gathered in a systematic or spontaneous manner and that this information is analyzed either externally or internally. The manual describes the theory in detail, as well as the development of the scale, scoring procedures, and examples of its use in counseling and task groups. Examiner required. Suitable for group use.
Untimed: Varies
Scoring: Examiner evaluated
Cost: Kit (manual, 2 scoring grids, 25 inventories) $27.00; 50 inventories $20.00
Publisher: Marathon Consulting and Press

DF OPINION SURVEY: AN INVENTORY OF DYNAMIC FACTORS (DFOS)
Refer to page 820.

EGO STATE PERSONALITY PROFILE (EGOGRAM™)
Refer to page 171.

EMOTIONAL STABILITY SURVEY (ES SURVEY)

Adult

Purpose: Measures the emotional stability of applicants for sensitive positions. Used for applicant screening and employee selection, particularly for police and security positions.

Description: Multiple-item paper-pencil preemployment survey measuring emotional stability and control. The self-report questionnaire format requires no interpretive analysis. In addition to the standard scoring template, a critical factor score template also is provided to identify false positive scores indicating attempts to bias answers. The survey was developed according to guidelines established by the EEOC and reviewed by FEPC and EEOC examiners. It may be administered, scored, and interpreted in-house by personnel/human resource/security specialists by license to Psychological Surveys Corporation. The survey is also available as part of the PASS Booklet (which includes the Trustworthiness Attitude Survey and the Alienation Index Survey) for more complete applicant assessment. Examiner required. Suitable for group use.

Untimed: 5–10 minutes

Scoring: Hand key

Cost: Contact publisher

Publisher: Psychological Surveys Corporation

THE EMPATHY TEST
W.A. Kerr and B.J. Speroff

Adolescent, adult
Grades 10 and above

Purpose: Measures empathic ability. Used to select managerial and supervisory personnel and graduate students.

Description: Multiple-item paper-pencil test measuring the ability to put oneself in another person's position, establish rapport, and anticipate another person's reactions, feelings, and behavior. Empathy is measured as a variable unrelated to intelligence and most other attitudes. Three forms—Form A, blue collar emphasis; Form B, white collar emphasis; and Form C, Canadian emphasis—are available. Examiner required. Suitable for group use.

Timed: 15 minutes

Scoring: Examiner evaluated

Cost: Specimen set $4.00; 25 tests (specify form) $3.50

Publisher: Psychometric Affiliates

EMPLOYABILITY ATTITUDES

Adolescent, adult

Purpose: Assesses an individual's behavioral attitude in job-seeking and job-keeping situations and compares the attitudes with employers' expectations with regard to hiring, firing, or promoting.

Description: Multiple-item instrument in audiovisual format assessing 13 job-seeking and 23 job-keeping attitudes by means of 18 illustrated behavioral incidents. Incidents are presented in the form of adventures involving fictional characters of various ethnic backgrounds, races, and sex. The questions are narrated and shown on the A-V screen following each incident. Examinees respond as if they were the character involved. Responses are recorded on a response booklet or card.

A generated report includes 36 attitudes and definitions; employers' hiring, firing, and promotion expectations; comparison of individuals' attitude levels to employers' expected levels and a prescription in the form of objectives that are needed to close the gaps. Curricular activities, goals, and objectives are prescribed to improve attitudes at levels of awareness, confidence, and automatic behavior. Curriculum, learning contracts, learning activity maps, and progress charts are included in the Job Seeking and Job Keeping Curriculum Packages. An instructor's guide is also available. Examiner/self-administered. Suitable for group use.

Untimed: 3 hours

Scoring: Hand key; may be computer scored

Cost: Contact publisher

Publisher: Prep, A Division of Educational Technologies, Inc.

EMPLOYEE ATTITUDE INVENTORY (EAI)
London House, Inc.

Adult

Purpose: Identifies employees who might steal or engage in costly counterproductive acts in the workplace. Used in investigative and organizational assessment of honesty and as a guide for in-house promotions.

Description: 179–item paper-pencil test measuring theft admissions, attitudes, and suspicions; drug-abuse tendencies; and job dissatisfaction and burnout. A validity scale is included. Although the test is self-administered, it may be given orally to illiterate individuals. Scoring options include mail-in, operator-assisted, or Touch-Test telephone methods. Self-administered. Suitable for group use.

Untimed: 30 minutes

Scoring: Computer scored

Cost: $13.00–$18.00 per booklet depending on scoring method and volume ordered

Publisher: London House, Inc.

EMPLOYEE SAFETY INVENTORY (ESI)
London House, Inc.

Adult

Purpose: Assesses attitudes toward on-the-job safety. Used for screening, placement, and training of job applicants and current employees.

Description: Paper-pencil multiple-choice and short-answer test yielding scores in four areas: risk avoidance, stress tolerance, safety control, and validity. Scores on a supplemental scale (Driver Attitudes) and a composite Safety Index are also available. Materials include ESI test booklet, ESI Interpretation Guide, and ESI Administrator's Guide. Must purchase a minimum of 25 booklets. Examiner required. Suitable for group use.

Untimed: Varies

Scoring: Computer scored; scoring service available from publisher

Cost: Contact publisher; $6.00–$12.00 per test depending on volume ordered

Publisher: London House, Inc.

EMPLOYMENT INVENTORY (EI)
George Paajanen

Adolescent, adult—Ages 15 and older

Purpose: Assesses job applicants' probability of counterproductive job behavior.

Description: 97–item paper-pencil multiple-choice and true-false test assessing job applicants' probability of engaging in counterproductive behavior in an hourly job and probability of voluntarily remaining on the job for at least 3 months. Questions are directed toward the applicant's opinions, attitudes, and background.

The test yields a Performance score and a Tenure score. The Performance score indicates the likelihood the employee will be reliable, follow rules, have a good attendance record, and be strongly motivated. The Tenure score indicates the likelihood of premature turnover, another aspect of counterproductive job behavior. Scoring is accomplished using a portable computer or disk-based software operating on IBM systems.

The test is available in forms A and D, as well as in an optical scan version for group testing. A sixth-grade reading level is required. Examiner required. Suitable for group use. Available in Spanish.

Untimed: 15–20 minutes

Scoring: Computer scored

Cost: Based on volume; contact publisher

Publisher: Personnel Decisions, Inc.

EMPLOYMENT PRODUCTIVITY INDEX (EPI)

Job applicants

Purpose: Assesses personality trait combinations that lead to productive and responsible work behavior. Used to identify applicants who will remain on the job; have low absentee rates; obey company rules, particularly those prohibiting alcohol and drugs; cooperate with supervisors, customers, and co-workers; meet performance standards; and observe appropriate safety practices and standards.

Description: Multiple-item paper-pencil survey consisting of four scales measuring personality traits that lead to productive employment: Dependability, Interpersonal Cooperation, Drug Avoidance, and Validity. Standard scores, percentile scores, and a Composite Productivity Index are provided. In addition, a test analysis report includes a Significant Behavioral Indicators section highlighting specific responses that may be useful in making decisions about borderline candidates. The EPI–3S version includes a safety scale measuring safety conscious-ness and identifying applicants at risk for on-the-job accidents.

Four scoring options are available from London House: operator-assisted tele-phone, Touch-Test, PC-based, and mail-ins. Operator-assisted scoring involves dialing a London House operator who provides test results after being read a tally of responses by the test admin-istrator. Written confirmation is mailed the following day. Touch-Test telephone scoring allows the test administrator to use the telephone keypad to feed response tallies directly into London House com-puters. Results are available immediately and written confirmation is mailed the next day. Administrators with IBM PC or compatible equipment may obtain on-site results using the PC-based scoring method. Self-administered. Suitable for group use.

Untimed: 30 minutes

Scoring: Operator-assisted telephone; computer scored

Cost: Kit (administration materials, oper-ator-assisted telephone scoring, and reports) $9.00–$13.00 depending on quantity and scoring method; EPI–3S $14.00

Publisher: London House, Inc.

EMPLOYMENT PRODUCTIVITY INDEX (EPI–3 AND EPI–3S)
London House, Inc.

Adolescent, adult

Purpose: Assesses work attitudes and productivity level. Used for pre-employ-ment screening.

Description: 104–item (EPI–3) and 128–item (EPI–3S) paper-pencil multiple-choice short-answer tests. Both tests con-tain a Dependability (50 items), Inter-personal Cooperation (32 items), and Drug Avoidance (22 items) scale. The EPI–3S contains a Safety Scale (24 items). The tests yield percentiles and standard scores for all scales and the Overall Pro-ductivity Index. Prices are based on quantity purchased; usually 25 or more booklets are required. Examiner re-quired. Suitable for group use.

Untimed: 30 minutes

Scoring: Computer scored; scoring ser-vice available from publisher

Cost: Contact publisher; $5.50–$14.00 per test depending on volume ordered

Publisher: London House, Inc.

ETSA TESTS 8–A—PERSONAL ADJUSTMENT INDEX
Refer to page 883.

EXPERIENCE AND BACKGROUND QUESTIONNAIRE (EBQ)
Melany E. Baehr

Adult

Purpose: Evaluates an individual's past performance and experience on eight dimensions of quantified personal back-ground data. Used for selection and placement of personnel in entry-level and first-line supervisory positions in public and private institutions.

Description: 71–item paper-pencil multi-ple-choice questionnaire assessing the following factorially determined back-ground areas: group participation and school achievement, mobility, financial experience and responsibility, family responsibility, job and personal stability, parental family adjustment, and general health. Different combinations of scores are used in validated selection test bat-teries for transit bus operators, municipal police officers, and industrial supervisors. Basic adult reading skills are required. Self-administered. Suitable for group use.

Untimed: 15–20 minutes

Scoring: Hand key; may be computer scored

Cost: Specimen set $10.00; test booklets $20.00

Publisher: London House, Inc.

EXPLORING CAREER OPTIONS (ECO)
*Marcia Andberg and
Charles B. Johansson*

**Adult
High-school and college
students**

Purpose: Measures work-related personality characteristics; verbal and numerical ability; career interests; and personal style, temperament, and values that affect job satisfaction. Used with individuals re-entering the work force and employees experiencing work-related problems as well as for vocational counseling and career planning.

Description: 630–item paper-pencil inventory covering six areas: self-description, work values, activities, school subjects, occupations, and words and numbers. The narrative report includes sections on the workplace, the rewards, other elements that shape a career, interests, math and verbal abilities, and career options. The ECO is based on the Career Assessment Inventory—Enhanced Version, Temperament and Values Inventory, Self-Description Inventory, and Number Assessment Inventory. Items are written at an 8th-grade reading level. Self-administered. Suitable for group use.

Untimed: 2 hours, 30 minutes

Scoring: Computer scored by NCS

Cost: Narrative report $15.00–$32.95 depending on quantity

Publisher: National Computer Systems/PAS Division

EYSENCK PERSONALITY QUESTIONNAIRE (EPQ)
Refer to page 172.

FAMOUS SAYINGS (FS)
Bernard M. Bass

Adolescent, adult
Grades 10 and above

Purpose: Assesses personality. Used for industrial and professional screening and for research in social psychology.

Description: 131–item paper-pencil test of four vocationally important aspects of personality, including hostility, fear of failure, social acquiescence, and acceptance of conventional mores. Items are general statements consisting mainly of famous sayings, proverbs, and adages. Instructions are read aloud by the examiner while the subjects read along silently. The subjects indicate whether they agree or disagree with the statements or are uncertain. Examiner required. Suitable for group use.

Untimed: 15–30 minutes

Scoring: Hand key; examiner evaluated

Cost: Complete kit (general manual, 50 Form 1 test blanks, scoring stencil Form 1) $13.00; 50 test blanks $10.00; general manual $3.00

Publisher: Psychological Test Specialists

GIANNETTI ON-LINE PSYCHOSOCIAL HISTORY (GOLPH)
Refer to page 174.

GROUP ENVIRONMENT SCALE (GES)
Refer to page 175.

GUIDEPAK
Refer to page 984.

HALL-TONNA INVENTORY OF VALUES
Refer to page 177.

HARTMAN VALUE PROFILE (HVP)
Refer to page 242.

HILSON PERSONNEL PROFILE/ SUCCESS QUOTIENT (HPP/SQ)™
Robin E. Inwald

Adolescent, adult—Ages 15 and older
Grades 9 and above

Purpose: Assesses behavioral patterns and characteristics related to success in the working world. Measures individual strengths and positive features. Used for pre-employment screening and in-house staff training programs.

Description: 150–item behaviorally oriented paper-pencil true-false instrument consisting of one validity measure and five scales: Candor (CA; 10 items), Achievement History (AH; 33 items), Social Ability (SA; 40 items), "Winner's" Image

(WI; 21 items), Initiative (IN; 35 items), and Family Achievement Expectations (FE; 11 items).

Content areas for the SA scale include Extroversion (EX; 19 items), Popularity (PO; 14 items), and Sensitivity (SE; 7 items). Areas covered by the WI scale include Competitive Drive (CD; 11 items) and Self-Worth (SW; 10 items). For the IN scale, four content areas are included: Drive (DR; 14 items), Preparation Style (PS; 9 items), Goal Orientation (GO; 7 items), and Anxiety about Organization (AX; 5 items).

A narrative report and two profile graphs of six scales and nine scale content areas are provided with raw scores and T-scores. Local/specific job category norms are also available. A fifth-grade reading level is required. A computer scoring service available from the publisher provides mail-in (turnaround 24 hours) and tele-processing (IBM PC or compatible) services. Teleprocessing allows users to input test responses manually or through optical scanning. Results are obtained within 6 seconds. Self-administered. Suitable for group use.

Untimed: 20 minutes

Scoring: Computer scored

Cost: Reusable test booklets $1.50; processing fees $6.00–$20.00; contact publisher for additional information

Publisher: Hilson Research, Inc.

HOGAN PERSONALITY INVENTORY
Refer to page 179.

HOGAN PERSONNEL SELECTION SERIES
Robert Hogan and Joyce Hogan

College student, adult

Purpose: Assesses aspects of personality related to job performance. Used for employee selection and placement.

Description: Four paper-pencil batteries, each consisting of 198–223 true-false items. The Primary Performance Battery indicates conscientiousness, honesty, dependability, even-tempered disposition, and tendency toward insubordination,

theft, alcohol and substance abuse, illness, and worker compensation claims. The other three batteries cover these areas as well. The Clerical Performance Battery also predicts success in occupations requiring close attention to details, following instructions, and the ability to communicate effectively. The Sales Performance Battery also predicts success in occupations requiring initiative, persistence, and the ability to influence others. The Managerial Performance Battery also predicts success in occupations requiring leadership, planning, and the ability to motivate others.

Scores are provided on four scales for each of the four batteries: Validity, Service Orientation, Reliability, and Stress Tolerance. The clerical, sales, and managerial batteries each include one additional scale designed to predict success in the relevant class of occupations. Items are presented at a fourth-grade reading level. Norms are provided for college students and adults. Examiner required. Suitable for group use.

Untimed: 5–20 minutes

Scoring: Computer scored

Cost: Specimen set (specify inventory) $11.00

Publisher: National Computer Systems/ PAS Division

HOW SUPERVISE?
Refer to page 1044.

HUMAN RESOURCE INVENTORY (HRI AND HRI-S)
London House, Inc.

Adolescent, adult

Purpose: Measures work performance factors relating to productivity, drug avoidance, organizational adjustment, and safety (optional scale). Used for pre-employment screening.

Description: 103–item (HRI) and 127–item (HRI-S) paper-pencil multiple-choice short-answer test with four scales: Work Performance (27 items), Organizational Adjustment (29 items), Drug-Avoidance (21 items), and Interpersonal Cooperation (26 items). An optional

Safety scale (24 items; HRI-S) is also available. Test results are verified by two validity scales: the Distortion scale, which indicates the extent to which a subject tends to exaggerate positive qualities and minimize negative traits; and the Accuracy scale, which indicates whether the individual comprehended the inventory and completed it carefully. An 8th-grade reading level is required. Examiner must have basic psychology knowledge and employment screening capacity. Prices are based on quantity purchased; minimum is 25 booklets. Examiner required. Suitable for group use.

Untimed: 35 minutes

Scoring: Computer scored; scoring service available from publisher

Cost: Contact publisher; $6.00–$16.00 per test depending on volume ordered

Publisher: London House, Inc.

INTER-PERSON PERCEPTION TEST (IPPT)
Refer to page 244.

INTERPERSONAL STYLE INVENTORY (ISI)
Refer to page 183.

INVENTORY OF INDIVIDUALLY-PERCEIVED GROUP COHESIVENESS
David L. Johnson

Adolescent, adult
Grades 10 and above

Purpose: Measures an individual's sense of cooperation in group activities. Used for counseling in school, business, family, training, research, organizational, and community settings.

Description: 20–item paper-pencil inventory of an individual's perception of cooperation, control, and task influence processes operating in a group and resulting in some degree of cohesiveness. The questionnaire may be used before and after group sessions. Self-administered. Suitable for group use.

Untimed: 15 minutes

Scoring: Self-scored

Cost: Complete kit (30 record forms, 3 feedback sheets, manual) $14.50

Publisher: Stoelting Co.

INWALD PERSONALITY INVENTORY (IPI)
Refer to page 1079.

IPI EMPLOYEE APTITUDE SERIES: CONTACT PERSONALITY FACTOR (CPF)
Refer to page 891.

IPI EMPLOYEE APTITUDE SERIES: NEUROTIC PERSONALITY FACTOR (NPF)
Refer to page 891.

IPI EMPLOYEE APTITUDE SERIES: SIXTEEN PERSONALITY FACTOR (16PF) TEST
Refer to page 891.

IRRATIONAL BELIEFS TEST
Refer to page 185.

JACKSON PERSONALITY INVENTORY (JPI)
Refer to page 185.

JOB ATTITUDE SCALE (JAS)
Shoukry Saleh

Adult

Purpose: Evaluates an employee's job preferences and attitudes. Used in business and industry to evaluate programs and individual orientations toward the workplace.

Description: 120–item long form and 60–item short form paper-pencil forced-choice test of attitudes towards 16 qualities: praise and recognition, growth in skills, creative work, responsibility, advancement, achievement, salary, security, personnel policies, competent supervision, relations-peers, relations-subordinant, relations-supervisor, working conditions, status, and family needs. The long form yields one general score. The short form yields an intrinsic score. Self-administered. Suitable for group use. Available in French.

Untimed: 30 minutes

Scoring: Hand key

Cost: Specimen set (manual, test sheet, key) $10.00; 100 tests $25.00

Publisher: Shoukry Saleh

JOB DESCRIPTIVE INDEX, REVISED (JDI REV)
Patricia C. Smith, Lorne M. Kendall, and Charles L. Hulin

Adult—Ages 17–100

Purpose: Assesses an individual's job satisfaction.

Description: 72–item paper-pencil test consisting of five scales: Satisfaction with Work (18 items), Pay (9 items), Promotions (9 items), Supervision (18 items), and Co-Workers (18 items). Items are answered in a "yes-?-no" format. The test yields five scores, one per scale. A scoring service is available by special arrangement with the publisher. A second-grade reading level is required. The Job in General (JIG) test may be administered as a follow-up (see separate description). Suitable for use with hearing- and physically-impaired individuals. Self-administered. Suitable for group use. Available in French, Spanish, and Chinese.

Untimed: 5 minutes

Scoring: Hand key; may be computer scored; may be machine scored

Cost: 100 test booklets (includes Job in General) $54.00; postage and handling $5.00

Publisher: Bowling Green State University, Department of Psychology

JOB IN GENERAL (JIG)
Gail H. Ironson, Patricia C. Smith, and Michael T. Brannick et al.

Adult

Purpose: Assesses overall job satisfaction. Suitable for use with hearing- and physically impaired individuals.

Description: 18–item paper-pencil yes-no test assessing workers' job satisfaction. The test is to be adminstered following the Job Descriptive Index (JDI), which measures five specific areas of job satisfaction (see separate description). A scoring service is available by special arrangement with the publisher. A second-grade reading level is required. Self-administered. Suitable for group use.

Untimed: 1 minute

Scoring: Hand key; may be computer scored; may be machine scored

Cost: 100 questionnaires $8.00; $2.00 postage and handling if administered separately from Job Descriptive Index

Publisher: Bowling Green State University, Department of Psychology

JOB PERFORMANCE SCALES SET

Adult

Purpose: Rates employee performance and attitudes. Used by supervisors for employee reviews.

Description: Multiple-item set of three paper-pencil evaluations including Primary Rating #1, Primary Rating #2, and a Rater's Performance Summary used for preemployment screening and for determining promotions, training needs, transfers, discipline, special consideration, and termination. Each evaluation rates an employee in a slightly different manner, and the combination provides a comprehensive measure of the employee's assets and value to the company. Examiner required. Not suitable for group use.

Untimed: 5 minutes

Scoring: Examiner evaluated

Cost: 25 copies of each of 3 forms $43.50

Publisher: E.F. Wonderlic Personnel Test, Inc.

JOB PERFORMANCE SCALES SET: PRIMARY RATING #1

Adult

Purpose: Assesses employee performance and attitudes. Used by supervisors for employee reviews.

Description: 35-item paper-pencil scale used by supervisors to rate employees' knowledge of the job, work volume, judgment, accuracy, learning ability, initiative, cooperativeness, and compatibility. Twenty-eight job-function items and seven attitude items make up the scale, which is one part of a three-part set. Examiner required. Not suitable for group use.

Untimed: 5 minutes

Scoring: Examiner evaluated

Cost: 25 copies $14.50

Publisher: E.F. Wonderlic Personnel Test, Inc.

JOB PERFORMANCE SCALES SET: PRIMARY RATING #2

Adult

Purpose: Assesses job-related conceptual abilities, attitudes, and behaviors of employees. Used by supervisors for employee reviews.

Description: 21-item paper-pencil scale used by supervisors to rate employees' abilities to learn the job, solve problems, communicate effectively, plan, make decisions, adapt, and follow instructions. Employees are also rated on attitude, dependability, punctuality, neatness, personality, and drive. From 1-25 points are awarded for each of the 13 job-function items and seven attitude items. Examiner required. Not suitable for group use.

Untimed: 5 minutes

Scoring: Examiner evaluated

Cost: 25 copies $14.50

Publisher: E.F. Wonderlic Personnel Test, Inc.

JOB PERFORMANCE SCALES SET: RATER'S SUMMARY

Adult

Purpose: Ranks employees in order of competence. Used by supervisors for employee reviews.

Description: Multiple-item paper-pencil scale used by supervisors for comparing and ranking employees in the following categories: general ability to learn and perform the job, general attitude toward

the job, and total ranking—combination of productivity and attitude. This is the third of a set of three scales. Examiner required. Not suitable for group use.

Untimed: 10–20 minutes

Scoring: Examiner evaluated

Cost: 25 copies $14.50

Publisher: E.F. Wonderlic Personnel Test, Inc.

KIPNIS-SCHMIDT PROFILES OF ORGANIZATIONAL INFLUENCE STRATEGIES: INFLUENCING YOUR CO-WORKERS (POIS: FORM C)

David Kipnis and Stuart M. Schmidt

Adult

Purpose: Assesses which strategies a person uses in attempting to influence co-workers. Used for organizational communication assessment, organizational and human resources development, team building, and managerial training.

Description: 27-item paper-pencil test describing various influence tactics that a subject rates twice on a 6-point scale ranging from 1 (never) to 6 (almost always). The subject first rates the tactic on how frequently it is used when first trying to influence a co-worker and then rates it on how frequently the tactic is used in a second attempt when the co-worker resists cooperating. Self-administered. Suitable for group use.

Untimed: 20–25 minutes

Scoring: Hand key

Cost: Complete set (materials for 10 participants) $49.50

Publisher: University Associates, Inc.

KIPNIS-SCHMIDT PROFILES OF ORGANIZATIONAL INFLUENCE STRATEGIES: INFLUENCING YOUR MANAGER (POIS: FORM M)

David Kipnis and Stuart M. Schmidt

Adult

Purpose: Assesses which strategies a person uses in attempting to influence the manager. Used for organizational communication assessment, organization and human resource development, team building, and managerial training.

Description: 27–item paper-pencil test describing various influence tactics that a subject rates twice on a 6–point scale from 1 (never) to 6 (almost always). The subject first rates the tactic on how frequently it is used when first trying to influence a manager and then how frequently the tactic is used in a second attempt when the manager resists cooperating. Self-administered. Suitable for group use.

Untimed: 20–25 minutes

Scoring: Hand key

Cost: Complete set (materials for 10 participants) $49.50

Publisher: University Associates, Inc.

KIPNIS-SCHMIDT PROFILES OF ORGANIZATIONAL INFLUENCE STRATEGIES: INFLUENCING YOUR SUBORDINATES (POIS: FORM S)
David Kipnis and Stuart M. Schmidt

Adult

Purpose: Assesses which strategies a person uses in attempting to influence subordinates. Used for organizational communication assessment, organization and human resource development, team building, and managerial training.

Description: 33–item paper-pencil test describing various influence tactics that a subject rates twice on a 6–point scale from 1 (never) to 6 (almost always). The subject first rates each tactic on how frequently it is used when first trying to influence a subordinate and then on how frequently the tactic is used in a second attempt when the subordinate resists cooperating. Self-administered. Suitable for group use.

Untimed: 25–30 minutes

Scoring: Hand key

Cost: Complete set (materials for 10 participants) $49.50

Publisher: University Associates, Inc.

KIRTON ADAPTION-INNOVATION INVENTORY (KAI)
Refer to page 186.

=====

THE LAKE ST. CLAIR INCIDENT
Albert A. Canfield

Adult

Purpose: Examines individual and group decision-making processes. Used to improve decision-making, communication skills, and teamwork.

Description: Multiple-item paper-pencil test requiring a team of three to seven individuals to work together to solve a hypothetical problem situation involving cold weather and cold water survival. Participants are provided with considerable information on the subject, maps, charts, drawings, and a list of 15 items available for them to use in their struggle for survival. The team must reach a decision on what action to take and the relative importance of the 15 items. Three different decision-making processes are required: independent, consultive, and participative/consensual.

Scoring procedure uses Coast Guard officer decisions and rankings as "expert" opinions. Scores are provided for three types of decision-making processes: autocratic, consultive, and consensual. Data are produced on which to evaluate the decision-making process and individual and team behaviors and compare the performance of different teams. The test booklet includes a table for recording the results of up to 12 teams. The manual includes situation analysis, Coast Guard opinions and rationales, information on hypothermia, and averages of scores from other teams. Self-administered (teams must cooperate to get team performance scores). Suitable for group use.

Untimed: 1½–2 hours

Scoring: Self-scored

Cost: Kit $30.00

Publisher: Western Psychological Services

LEADERSHIP APPRAISAL SURVEY (LAS)
Jay Hall

Adult

Purpose: Evaluates a leader's behavior from the associates' point of view. Used for assessment and development purposes with nonmanagement supervisory personnel, campus and community groups, volunteer organizations, and administrative personnel.

Description: Multiple-item paper-pencil inventory assessing a leader's impact on and stimulus value for the group from the associates' point of view. The inventory identifies blindspots, pinpoints strengths and weaknesses, and confirms the way leadership practices come across to associates. The inventory yields analyses of overall leadership style, including four components of leadership: philosophy, planning, implementation, and evaluation. The inventory may be administered in conjunction with the Styles of Leadership Survey (SLS) to provide a comparison of the associates' ratings with the leaders' self-ratings on the SLS. Normative data are provided. Self-administered. Suitable for group use.

Untimed: Varies
Scoring: Self-scored
Cost: Individual instrument $5.60
Publisher: Teleometrics International

LEARNING STYLES INVENTORY (LSI)
Refer to page 755.

MANAGEMENT APPRAISAL SURVEY (MAS)
Refer to page 1046.

MANAGEMENT BURNOUT SCALE
John W. Jones and Donald M. Moretti

Adult

Purpose: Assesses burnout or work stress among managerial-level employees.

Description: Multiple-item paper-pencil test assessing burnout or work stress through four types of factors: cognitive reactions, affective reactions, behavioral reactions, and psychophysiological reactions. Self-administered. Suitable for group use.

Untimed: 10 minutes

Scoring: Hand key; may be computer scored

Cost: 25 tests $15.00; specimen set (interpretation manual, validation studies) $5.00

Publisher: London House, Inc.

MANAGEMENT OF MOTIVES INDEX (MMI)
Refer to page 1049.

MANAGEMENT RELATIONS SURVEY (MRS)
Refer to page 1050.

MANAGEMENT TRANSACTIONS AUDIT (MTA)
Refer to page 1051.

MANAGEMENT TRANSACTIONS AUDIT: OTHER
Refer to page 1051.

MANAGERIAL COMPETENCE REVIEW—REVISED
Jay Hall

Adult

Purpose: Assesses managerial beliefs, involvement practices, motivation, and interpersonal competence as viewed by other workers.

Description: 60–item paper-pencil criterion-referenced test consisting of 12 typical management situations. The individual chooses 1 of 5 alternative ways of handling each situation. Answers indicate the manager's personal style of managerial decision-making. This is a companion to the Managerial Competence Index. Self-administered. Suitable for group use.

Untimed: Varies
Scoring: Self-scored
Cost: $6.95
Publisher: Teleometrics International

MANSON EVALUATION-REVISED
Refer to page 22.

MASLACH BURNOUT INVENTORY, 2ND EDITION
Christina Maslach and Susan E. Jackson

Adult

Purpose: Measures burnout among social and human service personnel. Used in job counseling to reduce burnout symptoms and by school districts to detect potential problems among school staffs.

Description: 22–item paper-pencil inventory consisting of three subscales measuring various aspects of burnout: Emotional Exhaustion, Personal Accomplishment, and Depersonalization. Examinees answer each item on the basis of how frequently they experience the feeling described in the item. The Demographic Data Sheet may be used to obtain biographical information. The revised manual contains more research data and more extensive norms than the previous manual, future research suggestions, and a supplement on burnout in education. In addition, a new MBI Educators Survey and an Educators Demographic Data Sheet are available. Examiner/self-administered. Suitable for group use.

Untimed: 20–30 minutes

Scoring: Hand key

Cost: Specimen set (manual, scoring key, test booklet, Demographic Data Sheet) $11.00

Publisher: Consulting Psychologists Press, Inc.

MCCORMICK JOB PERFORMANCE MEASUREMENT "RATE-$-SCALE" (RATE-$-SCALE)
Ronald R. McCormick

Adult

Purpose: Measures employee performance in terms of the dollar value of a successfully completed job. Used for employee compensation, training, promotion, and recruitment. Used in all industries and public agencies that have professional personnel office staff.

Description: Multiple-item paper-pencil criterion-referenced inventory assessing five areas of employee performance: responsibility, attitude, time in labor grade, efficiency, and dollar value. The employee's supervisor completes the form, which provides a rating scale in terms of the critical tasks and duties that the employee performs for pay. Comparisons of employee job performance are based upon the dollar value of the successful performance of a fully qualified worker. Local validation is required since employee job performance ratings are based upon the individual firm's compensation schedule. Results of employee evaluations can be entered readily into a computer for the detailed analysis required for rating form validation and payroll cost projections. The test yields four subscores and a total score. Self-administered. Suitable for group use.

Untimed: 5–10 minutes

Scoring: Examiner evaluated

Cost: 25 rating forms $35.00

Publisher: Dr. R.R. McCormick and Associates

Information and availability unconfirmed; last verified in 1988.

MEASURE OF ACHIEVING TENDENCY
Refer to page 191.

MEEKER BEHAVIOR CORRELATES FOR MANAGEMENT MATCHING OF TEAMS

Adult

Purpose: Assesses the abilities and attitudes of current and prospective employees. Used for employee selection and placement.

Description: Multiple-item paper-pencil self-report rating scale consisting of a three-way evaluation survey to be completed by supervisors, personnel directors, and prospective employees. The scale assesses major dimensions of intellectual abilities found to be correlates of personality characteristics and identifies team patterns. Self-administered. Suitable for group use.

Untimed: 20 minutes

Scoring: Examiner evaluated

Cost: Forms $1.00 each
Publisher: M & M Systems

MEYER-KENDALL ASSESSMENT SURVEY (MKAS)
*Henry D. Meyer and
Edward L. Kendall*

Adult

Purpose: Surveys work-related personality and interpersonal functioning for use in personnel assessment.

Description: 105 dichotomous-item paper-pencil test of 10 aspects of personal functioning relevant to performance at work. The scales are dominance, attention to detail, psychosomatic tendencies, independence, extroversion, anxiety, determination, people concern, stability, and achievement motivation. Scores are also obtained for two broad-band scales: Assertive Drive and Self-Assurance. An optional feature of the MKAS is the Pre-Assessment Worksheet, which determines the profile of an "ideal" applicant for a position. Computer scoring is achieved using the WPS TEST REPORT mail-in service. Examiner/self-administered. Suitable for group use.

Untimed: 15 minutes
Scoring: Computer scored
Cost: Manual $24.50; MKAS assessment sheets (includes scoring and reports) $35.00 each; MKAS pre-assessment sheets (includes scoring and report) $7.50 each
Publisher: Western Psychological Services

MILITARY ENVIRONMENT INVENTORY (MEI)
Rudolf H. Moos

Adult

Purpose: Assesses the social environment of various military contexts. Used to detect individuals and units at risk for morale and performance problems.

Description: Multiple-item paper-pencil inventory assessing individuals' and units' perceptions of the military environment. The test yields seven scores: Involvement, Peer Cohesion, Officer Support, Personal Status, Order and Organization, Clarity, and Officer Control. Additional subscales are related to military performance and sick-call rates. Self-administered. Suitable for group use.

Untimed: Not available
Scoring: Hand key
Cost: Specimen set (user's guide, manual, scoring key, test booklet, answer sheet, profile) $17.00
Publisher: Consulting Psychologists Press, Inc.

THE MINER SENTENCE COMPLETION SCALE: FORM H
John B. Miner

Adult

Purpose: Measures an individual's hierarchic (bureaucratic) motivation. Used for employee counseling and development and organizational assessment.

Description: Multiple-item paper-pencil free-response or multiple-choice sentence completion test measuring an individual's motivation in terms of motivational patterns that fit the hierarchic (bureaucratic) organizational form. Both forms (free-response version or multiple-choice version offering six alternatives for each stem) measure the following subscales: authority figures, competitive games, competitive situations, assertive role, imposing wishes, standing out from the group, and routine administrative functions. The basic scoring guide (for use with the free-response version) discusses categorizing the responses, the subscales, supervisory jobs, total scores, and the sample scoring sheet. Supplementary scoring guides describing the scoring of the multiple-choice version, variations in scoring the free-response version, and norms for the free-response version are available. Examiner required. Suitable for group use.

Untimed: Varies
Scoring: Examiner evaluated
Cost: 50 scales (specify free-response or multiple-choice version) $20.00; 64–page basic scoring guide (includes supplementary scoring guide) $10.00
Publisher: Organizational Measurement Systems Press

THE MINER SENTENCE COMPLETION SCALE: FORM P
John B. Miner

Adult

Purpose: Measures an individual's professional (specialized) motivation. Used for employee counseling and development and organizational assessment.

Description: Multiple-item paper-pencil free-response sentence completion test measuring motivation in terms of motivational patterns that fit the professional (specialized) organizational form. The test measures the following subscales: acquiring knowledge, independent action, accepting status, providing help, and professional commitment. Each test item consists of a sentence stem that individuals complete in their own words. The scoring guide contains discussions covering categorization of the responses, the subscales, actual scoring, reliability, normative data, use of Form P, and bibliographic notes. Examiner required. Suitable for group use.

Untimed: Varies

Scoring: Examiner evaluated

Cost: 50 scales $20.00; scoring guide $10.00

Publisher: Organizational Measurement Systems Press

THE MINER SENTENCE COMPLETION SCALE: FORM T
John B. Miner

Adult

Purpose: Measures an individual's task (entrepreneurial) motivation. Used for employee counseling and development and organizational assessment.

Description: Multiple-item paper-pencil free-response sentence-completion test measuring an individual's motivation in terms of patterns that fit the task (entrepreneurial) organizational form. The test measures the following subscales: self-achievement, avoiding risks, feedback of results, personal innovation, and planning for the future. These subscales are generally parallel to the five aspects of David

McClelland's achievement situation. Each test item consists of a sentence stem that individuals complete in their own words. The scoring guide discusses categorizing the responses, the subscales, actual scoring, reliability, normative data, the use of the MSCS-Form T, and bibliographic notes. Examiner required. Suitable for group use.

Untimed: Varies

Scoring: Examiner evaluated

Cost: 50 scales $20.00; scoring guide $10.00

Publisher: Organizational Measurement Systems Press

MINNESOTA JOB DESCRIPTION QUESTIONNAIRE (MJDQ)

Adult

Purpose: Evaluates an employee's or supervisor's perception of the reinforcer characteristics of an occupation. Used for research purposes only.

Description: 42–item paper-pencil test covering ability utilization, achievement, activity, advancement, authority, company policies and practices, compensation, co-workers, creativity, independence, moral values, recognition, responsibility, security, social service, social status, supervision-technical, supervision-human relations, variety, and working conditions. On the first 21 items, subjects rate groups of five statements from one to five according to how well each statement describes their jobs. The test also may be used for obtaining a subject's perception of jobs in terms of expected or perceived reinforcer patterns. Form E (for employees) includes the 20–item short form of the Minnesota Satisfaction Questionnaire. Form S is available for supervisors. Self-administered. Suitable for group use.

Untimed: Open ended

Scoring: Computer scored

Cost: 20–249 copies Form S $0.75 each; 20–249 copies Form E $0.80 each; scoring charges begin at $1.75 per individual, depending on the number scored at one time and services requested; minimum scoring charge is for 15 MJDQs; scoring of MSQ section of the MJDQ Form E is an additional $1.00 per booklet; sample set (MJDQ manual, 1 copy each of both S and E forms of the MJDQ) $7.50

Publisher: Vocational Psychology Research, University of Minnesota

MINNESOTA SATISFACTION QUESTIONNAIRE (MSQ)

Adult

Purpose: Evaluates employees' satisfaction with their jobs. Used for occupational and social research.

Description: 100–item paper-pencil questionnaire consisting of statements about various aspects of an individual's job. The individual rates each statement on a 5–point scale ranging from "very dissatisfied" to "very satisfied." Twenty scales of five items each measure the following factors: ability utilization, achievement, activity, advancement, authority, company policies and practices, compensation, co-workers, creativity, independence, moral values, recognition, responsibility, security, social science, social status, supervision-human relations, supervision-technical, variety, and working conditions. An optional 20–item General Satisfaction scale is also available. The alternative Short Form MSQ consists of one item from each of the 20 scales and yields the following scores: Intrinsic, Extrinsic, and General Satisfaction. The manual includes descriptions of the development and scoring of both forms, reliability and validity data, and norms. Prospective users must establish their qualifications with their initial order. Examiner required. Suitable for group use.

Untimed: Varies

Scoring: Hand key; may be computer scored

Cost: Sample set (photocopy of manual, single copies of long form, long form 1967 revision, short form) $6.00; 30–499 non-reusable questionnaire booklets (long form) $0.60 each; 50–499 booklets (short form) $0.35 each; computer scoring (long form) $1.50 each; computer scoring (short form) $1.00 each

Publisher: Vocational Psychology Research, University of Minnesota

MINNESOTA SATISFACTORINESS SCALE (MSS)

Adult

Purpose: Measures an employee's satisfactoriness on a job. Used as a research instrument.

Description: 28–item paper-pencil inventory assessing an employee's behavior on the job. The employee's supervisor completes the form. Scores are provided for five scales: Performance, Conformance, Dependability, Personal Adjustment, and General Satisfactoriness. Additional data analysis is also available. The manual includes information on development and scoring of the test, reliability and validity data, and norms. Prospective users must establish their qualifications with their initial order. Self-administered by supervisor. Suitable for group use.

Untimed: Varies

Scoring: Hand key; may be computer scored

Cost: 30–499 copies $0.35 each; individual scores and group results for one group $1.25 per person; minimum scoring charge $25.00; sample set (MSS manual, 1 copy of the MSS) $3.75

Publisher: Vocational Psychology Research, University of Minnesota

MORRISBY DIFFERENTIAL TEST BATTERY (DTB)
Refer to page 977.

MOTIVATION ANALYSIS TEST (MAT)
Arthur B. Sweney,
Raymond B. Cattell, John L. Horn,
and IPAT Staff

Adolescent, adult
Grades 10 and above

Purpose: Measures motivational patterns in high-school seniors and adults. Used in a variety of counseling situations in education and business.

Description: 208–item paper-pencil multiple-choice test providing 10 measures of comfort, social, and achievement needs. Five are basic drives: caution, sex, self-assertion, aggressiveness, and self-indulgence. Five are interests that develop and mature through learning experience: career, affection, dependency, responsibility, and self-fulfillment. For each of the 10 interest areas, scores measure drive or need level, satisfaction level, degree of conflict, and total motivational strength. Standard scores are provided for men and women together. Self-administered. Suitable for group use.

Untimed: 50–60 minutes

Scoring: Hand key; may be computer scored

Cost: MAT introductory kit $31.00; 25 test booklets $26.00; 25 machine-scorable answer sheets $17.50; 50 hand-scorable answer sheets 10.50; 50 profile sheets $10.60; 4 scoring keys $16.25; manual $12.95; individual scoring report certificates $4.00–$20.00

Publisher: Institute for Personality and Ability Testing, Inc.

MULTIDIMENSIONAL SELF-ESTEEM INVENTORY (MSEI)
Refer to page 197.

MY VOCATIONAL SITUATION
John L. Holland, Denise Daiger, and Paul G. Power

Adult

Purpose: Assesses the problems that may be troubling an individual seeking help with career decisions. Used in career counseling and guidance.

Description: Two-page multiple-item paper-pencil questionnaire determining which of three difficulties may be troubling an individual in need of career counseling: lack of vocational identity, lack of information or training, or environmental or personal barriers. The questionnaire is completed by the individual just prior to the counseling interview and may be tabulated by the counselor at a glance. Responses may offer clues for the interview itself and treatments relevant to each individual's need. The manual discusses development of the diagnostic scheme and reports statistical properties of the three variables. Self-administered. Suitable for group use.

Untimed: 5–10 minutes

Scoring: Examiner evaluated

Cost: 25 questionnaires $5.50; specimen kit (manual, questionnaire) $2.00

Publisher: Consulting Psychologists Press, Inc.

NEO PERSONALITY INVENTORY (NEO-PI)
Refer to page 201.

OBSERVATIONAL ASSESSMENTS OF TEMPERAMENT
Melany E. Baehr

Adult

Purpose: Provides self-assessment or observational assessments of behavior that can be used in either counseling or assessment center settings.

Description: Paper-pencil test assessing three behavior factors that have been shown to be the most effective in predicting significant aspects of performance in higher-level positions: reserved/cautious vs. extroversive/impulsive, emotionally controlled vs. emotionally responsive, dependent/group oriented vs. self-reliant/individually oriented. When used in conjunction with the Temperament Comparator, the instrument provides a measure of insight through comparison of disguised and undisguised assessments of the same three behavior factors. Self-administered. Suitable for group use.

Untimed: 10 minutes

Scoring: Hand key

Cost: 25 tests $20.00

Publisher: London House, Inc.

OCCUPATIONAL PERSONALITY QUESTIONNAIRES (OPQ)
Saville & Holdsworth Ltd. Staff

Adult

Purpose: Assesses personality characteristics relevant to job success. Used in personnel selection, placement, counseling, and development.

Description: Multiple-item paper-pencil or computer-administered questionnaires divided in four levels measuring personality traits on a scale of 1 (low) to 10 (high). Concept, the most detailed level,

measures 30 traits. Other levels measure 14, 8, and 5 traits with progressively broader scale definitions. Research and development was sponsored by 53 major British industries. Only one of the four levels should be used. Examiner/self-administered. Suitable for group use.
BRITISH PUBLISHER

Untimed: Varies

Scoring: Hand key; may be machine scored

Cost: See individual OPQ descriptions

Publisher: Saville & Holdsworth Ltd.

OCCUPATIONAL STRESS INDICATOR (OSI)
Cary Cooper, Stephen Sloan, and Stephen Williams

Adult

Purpose: Assesses stress levels of a company's employees and identifies the causes of the stress in order to implement appropriate counseling and management programs. Used by managers in sales, warehousing, personnel, financial, data processing, marketing, and other departments.

Description: Multiple-item paper-pencil or computer-administered questionnaire measuring occupational stress. An optional Biographical Questionnaire, which can be completed in 5 minutes, is designed to elicit company and biographical information, thus providing a comprehensive picture of the group of employees being tested. A group profile is achieved using the Scoring Sheet and the Group Profiling Sheet. In addition, the Management Guide helps with interpretation of the information collected and provides examples and case studies. Other materials include an administration card, scoring keys, indicators (questionnaires), scoring sheets, and a data collection sheet. The software package allows 50 administrations. Self-administered. Suitable for group use.
BRITISH PUBLISHER

Untimed: 30–40 minutes

Scoring: Hand key

Cost: Contact publisher

Publisher: NFER-NELSON Publishing Company Ltd.

OCCUPATIONAL STRESS INVENTORY (OSI), RESEARCH VERSION
Samuel H. Osipow and Arnold Spokane

Adult

Purpose: Measures dimensions of occupational adjustment of individuals employed primarily in technical, professional, and managerial positions in school, service, and manufacturing settings.

Description: 140–item paper-pencil test measuring three dimensions of occupational adjustment: occupational stress, psychological strain, and coping resources. The instrument consists of three separate questionnaires. The Occupational Roles Questionnaire (ORQ; 6 scales with 10 items each) analyzes stress due to occupational roles. The Personal Strain Questionnaire (PSQ; 4 scales with 10 items each) measures psychological strain as reflected in behaviors and attitudes. The Personal Resources Questionnaire (PRQ; 4 scales with 10 items each) analyzes effective coping via personal resources. The profile form is used to convert raw scores to T-scores. The questionnaires may be administered together or separately. A seventh-grade reading level is required. Self-administered. Suitable for group use.

Untimed: 20–40 minutes

Scoring: Self-scored; scoring/report service available from publisher

Cost: Kit (manual, 25 reusable item booklets, 50 rating sheets, 50 profile forms) $49.00; scoring and report service $12.00

Publisher: Psychological Assessment Resources, Inc.

OPINIONS TOWARD ADOLESCENTS (OTA SCALE)
Refer to page 857.

OPQ CONCEPT MODEL (U.S. VERSION)
Saville & Holdsworth Ltd. Staff

Adult

Purpose: Assesses 30 work-relevant personality characteristics used in personnel selection, placement, counseling, training, and development.

Description: 268–item paper-pencil or computer-administered multiple-choice questionnaire measuring 30 personality traits covering relationships with people (persuasive, outgoing, democratic), thinking style (practical, conceptual, conscientious), and feelings and emotions (worrying, critical, competitive.) The application of the questionnaire is expanded by using it in conjunction with OPQ Expert System Software to produce a 30–page interpretive report. Examiner/self-administered. Suitable for group use.

Untimed: 35 minutes

Scoring: Hand key; computer scored

Cost: 5 booklets $63.00; 25 hand-scorable answer sheets $137.50; 25 profile charts $41.00; 25 machine-scorable answer sheets $162.50; 10 computer administrations $95.00

Publisher: Saville & Holdsworth Ltd.

OPQ FACTOR MODEL
Saville & Holdsworth Ltd. Staff

Adult

Purpose: Assesses 14 work-relevant personality characteristics. Used in personnel selection, placement, counseling, and development.

Description: Two multiple-item paper-pencil or computer-administered questionnaires measuring 14 personality characteristics factorially derived from the OPQ Concept Model questionnaires. The personality traits assessed include influence, social confidence, conservative, anxious, and decisive. Examiner/self-administered. Suitable for group use. BRITISH PUBLISHER

Untimed: Varies

Scoring: Hand key; may be machine scored

Cost: 5 booklets $63.00; 25 answer sheets $52.50; 25 profile charts $26.25; scoring key $37.80

Publisher: Saville & Holdsworth Ltd.

OPQ OCTAGON MODEL
Saville & Holdsworth Ltd. Staff

Adult

Purpose: Provides a rapid assessment of eight work-relevant personality characteristics. Used in personnel selection, placement, counseling, and development.

Description: Two multiple-item paper-pencil or computer-administered questionnaires measuring eight personality characteristics: assertive, empathy, gregarious, abstract, methodical, anxious, self-controlled, and vigorous. This questionnaire was factorially derived from more detailed OPQ questionnaires. Examiner/self-administered. Suitable for group use. BRITISH PUBLISHER

Untimed: Varies

Scoring: Hand key; may be machine scored

Cost: 5 booklets $52.50; 25 answer sheets $52.50; 25 profile charts $26.25; scoring key $33.60–$37.80

Publisher: Saville & Holdsworth Ltd.

OPQ PENTAGON MODEL
Saville & Holdsworth Ltd. Staff

Adult

Purpose: Provides an evaluation of five work-related, broadly defined personality factors. Used in personnel selection, placement, counseling, and development.

Description: Two multiple-item paper-pencil or computer-administered questionnaires measuring five personality factors: extroversion, abstract, methodical, emotional, and vigorous. The questionnaires currently are being used in team role research. Examiner/self-administered. Suitable for group use. BRITISH PUBLISHER

Untimed: Varies

Scoring: Hand key; may be machine scored

Cost: 5 booklets $52.50; 25 answer sheets $52.50; 25 profile charts $26.25; scoring key $33.60

Publisher: Saville & Holdsworth Ltd.

THE ORGANIZATIONAL CLIMATE INDEX (OCI)
George Stern and Associates

Adult

Purpose: Measures the psychological climate of institutionalized work settings in terms of the need-press paradigm of human behavior as conceptualized by Henry Murray. Used in schools and colleges, industrial settings, and in conjunction with Peace Corps training programs for employee survey and research purposes.

Description: 300–item (long form) or 80–item (short form) paper-pencil true-false inventory assessing institutional work environments along 30 basic press scales reflecting the 30 basic need scales established on the Stern Activities Index (SAI). Both forms provide scores for six first-order dimensions and two second-order dimensions.

Slightly different factor structures have been developed for school and college work environments. Analysis of school work environments yields first-order scores for intellectual climate, achievement standards, personal dignity, organizational effectiveness, orderliness, and impulse control and second-order scores for development and task effectiveness. Analysis of college work environments yields first-order scores for achievement standards, intellectual climate, practicalness, supportiveness, orderliness, and impulse control and second-order scores for development and control. Factor structures, reliabilities, and norms also have been established for industrial, school district, and Peace Corps settings. Self-administered. Suitable for group use.

Untimed: Long form 40 minutes; short form 20 minutes

Scoring: Examiner evaluated; may be computer scored

Cost: Test booklet $0.50; answer sheet $0.10; profile form $0.10; technical manual $7.50; prices for computer scoring and analysis are available on request

Publisher: FAAX Corporation

ORGANIZATIONAL COMPETENCE INDEX
Jay Hall

Adult

Purpose: Assesses conditions for competence within an organization in terms of both actual conditions and desired conditions.

Description: 40–item paper-pencil criterion-referenced instrument providing scores for 3 dimensions and 10 components of competence. For each question, three capsule answers (A, B, C) are provided. Each answer is a brief description of a certain condition commonly found in organizations. Together, the three answers provide a "range" of answers. The rating procedure is designed to provide an accurate picture of life in an organization. The instrument is accompanied by a 28–page workbook entitled "How to Interpret Your Scores from the Organizational Competence Index." Self-administered. Suitable for group use. Available in Spanish, Swedish, Portuguese, French, and German.

Untimed: Varies

Scoring: Self-scored

Cost: $10.00

Publisher: Teleometrics International

THE PERSONAL AUDIT
Clifford R. Edams and William M. Lepley

Adolescent, adult
Grades 7 and above

Purpose: Assesses an individual's personality as a factor of how well that person will perform in school or industry. Also used for clinical diagnosis of maladjustment.

Description: 450–item paper-pencil personality test. Nine scales of 50 items each measure relatively independent components of personality: seriousness-impulsiveness, firmness-indecision, tranquility-irritability, frankness-evasion, stability-instability, tolerance-intolerance, steadiness-emotionality, persistence-fluctuation, and contentment-worry. The test acquaints teachers with personality characteristics of students, is an aid to vocational and educational counseling, and provides an index of employees' job satisfaction and success in terms of their personal adjustment.

Two forms are available. Form LL is used with adults with the equivalent of a grammar-school education and senior high-school students. Form SS, composed of the first six scales of Form LL, is used with junior high-school students or where administration time is limited. Self-administered. Suitable for group use.

Untimed: Form LL 40–50 minutes; Form SS 30–40 minutes

Scoring: Hand key

Cost: 25 test booklets Form LL $50.00; 25 test booklets Form SS $43.00; examiner's manual $10.00

Publisher: SRA/London House

PERSONAL DATA FORM
Morris I. Stein

Adult

Purpose: Assesses job applicants in terms of the roles required as scientists, professionals, administrators, and employees involved in social relations. Used to place individuals in positions in which they can work creatively and productively.

Description: 80–item paper-pencil questionnaire serves as a job application form for technical and administrative positions with research and development organizations. The test items elicit information concerning the applicant's self-concept, abilities, and self-perception in terms of the roles required by the job being applied for. Self-administered. Suitable for group use.

Untimed: 30 minutes

Scoring: Examiner evaluated

Cost: $2.50 per copy

Publisher: Morris I. Stein

Information and availability unconfirmed; last verified in 1987.

PERSONAL PREFERENCE SCALE
Refer to page 205.

PERSONAL QUESTIONNAIRE/ OCCUPATIONAL VALUES
Refer to page 832.

PERSONAL REACTION INDEX (PRI)
Jay Hall

Adult

Purpose: Measures the degree to which employees feel they are encouraged to participate in the decision-making process. Used in programs evaluating job satisfaction at all occupational levels and in management training and development programs.

Description: Multiple-item paper-pencil inventory assessing the attitudes of subordinates toward the decision structure governing their work. It also measures the amount of influence subordinates feel they have in making work-related decisions and their consequent satisfaction with and commitment to those decisions. The results provide information concerning the manager's use or lack of use of the participative ethic with subordinates. Normative data are provided. Self-administered. Suitable for group use.

Untimed: Varies

Scoring: Self-scored

Cost: Individual survey $2.00

Publisher: Teleometrics International

PERSONAL RELATIONS SURVEY (PRS)
Refer to page 1055.

THE PERSONAL SKILLS MAP (PSM)
Darwin B. Nelson and Gary R. Low

Adolescent, adult

Purpose: Evaluates self-perceived skill levels key to personal and career effectiveness. Used for counseling and to plan individual and group intervention strategies.

Description: 300–item paper-pencil test evaluating two intrapersonal skills: self--

esteem and growth motivation; three interpersonal skills: assertion, interpersonal awareness, and empathy; and six career/life skills: drive strength, decision-making, time management, sales orientation, commitment ethic, and stress management. There are three response categories: most descriptive, sometimes descriptive, and least descriptive. There are no right or wrong answers. The test is designed to benefit the person using it, not for screening purposes. An adolescent and an adult form are available. Self-administered. Suitable for group use.

Untimed: 1 hour

Scoring: Computer scored; self-scored version available

Cost: Booklet $5.00 (specify form); manual $20.00; specimen set $75.00

Publisher: Institute for the Development of Human Resources

Information and availability unconfirmed; last verified in 1987.

PERSONALITY RESEARCH FORM (PRF)
Refer to page 249.

PERSONNEL SELECTION INVENTORY (PSI)
London House Press

Job applicants

Purpose: Assesses personality trait combinations that lead to honest, productive, and service-oriented employees. Designed to reduce absenteeism, shrinkage, turnover, on-the-job accidents, and substance abuse. Meets both human resource and loss-prevention needs.

Description: Multiple-item paper-pencil test survey. Eight versions of the PSI are available to meet various companies' screening needs. The forms range from PSI-1, which assesses honesty only, to PSI-7ST, which assesses a wide range of attributes. The various forms contain combinations of the following scales: Honesty, Supervision Attitudes, Employee/Customer Relations, Drug Avoidance, Work Values, Safety, Emotional Stability, Nonviolence, and Tenure. A distortion and an accuracy scale are in-

cluded. Some versions contain a detailed personal and behavioral history section that aids in making decisions about borderline candidates. Industry-specific norms are available for some PSI versions. The entire range of London House scoring options are available, including Operator-assisted telephone scoring, Touch-Test telephone scoring, PC-based scoring, optical scanning, and mail-in scoring. A seventh-grade reading level is required. Self-administered. Suitable for group use. Available in Spanish and French.

Untimed: 30–40 minutes

Scoring: Computer scored

Cost: Complete $8.00–$17.00 depending on scoring method and volume ordered

Publisher: London House, Inc.

PERSONNEL SELECTION INVENTORY FOR BANKING (PSI-B)

Job applicants

Purpose: Identifies banking job applicants who might engage in theft or counterproductive behavior in the workplace. Designed to help banks select quality employees and reduce losses.

Description: Multiple-item paper-pencil survey designed to enable employers to screen job applicants. Three versions of the inventory, PSI-B1, PSI-B3, and PSI-B7, are available. The PSI-B3 contains Honesty, Drug-Avoidance, and Non-Violence scales. The PSI-B7 also contains Customer/Employee Relations, Work Values, Supervision Attitudes, and Employability scales and significant behavioral indicators and follow-up interview questions. Banking industry norms are available for all three versions. All versions contain a distortion and an accuracy scale. Scoring options include Operator-Assisted scoring, Touch-Test telephone, microcomputer, and mail-in service. Self-administered. Suitable for group use.

Untimed: 30–40 minutes

Scoring: Computer scored

Cost: $8.00–$17.50 depending on volume ordered

Publisher: London House, Inc.

PHASE II PROFILE INTEGRITY STATUS INVENTORY
Gregory M. Lousig-Nont

Adult

Purpose: Assesses an individual's attitude towards honesty and identifies drug and alcohol abusers. Used for employment screening.

Description: 116–item paper-pencil or computer-administered multiple-choice and true-false test consisting of six scales: Rationalization, Honest Attitudes, Dishonest Attitudes, Contemplation of Dishonesty, Dishonesty Admissions, and Falsification. The computer program runs on IBM PC or compatible systems. A scoring service is available from the publisher and from the distributor, R.B. Ishmael and Associates. A seventh-grade reading level is required. The paper-pencil version must be purchased in quantities of 10. Self-administered. Suitable for group use. Available in Spanish.

Timed: 35 minutes

Scoring: Hand key; may be computer scored; may be machine scored

Cost: $6.00–$15.00 depending on quantity

Publisher: Gregory M. Lousig-Nont and Associates; distributed exclusively by R.B. Ishmael and Associates

Information and availability unconfirmed; last verified in 1988.

PICTURE PERSONALITY TEST FOR INDIAN SOUTH AFRICANS (PPT-ISA)—1982
Refer to page 208.

PICTURE SITUATION TEST

Adult males

Purpose: Measures an individual's response to aggression-provoking stimuli within an everyday context. Used for personnel screening and placement and clinical research on aggression.

Description: 20–item paper-pencil test measuring the type of aggression an individual displays and the effect it is likely to have on the interpersonal situation in which aggression appears. The test items consist of partially structured pictures depicting aggression-provoking situations. The individual must complete the situation by giving personal responses.

Responses are scored for type of aggression (direct, denial) and effect of response (constructive, destructive). A method for standardized scoring is provided. The test is restricted to competent persons properly registered with the South African Medical and Dental Council. Examiner required. Suitable for group use. Afrikaans version available.
SOUTH AFRICAN PUBLISHER

Untimed: No time limit

Scoring: Hand key; examiner evaluated

Cost: Contact publisher

Publisher: National Institute for Personnel Research

POSITION ANALYSIS QUESTIONNAIRE (PAQ)
Ernest J. McCormick, P.R. Jeanneret, and Robert C. Meacham

Adult

Purpose: Analyzes jobs in terms of job elements that reflect directly or infer the basic human behaviors involved, regardless of their specific technological areas or functions. Used with jobs at all levels, including managerial, supervisory staff, professional, technical, skilled public contact, office, production and operation, service, and semiskilled.

Description: 187–item paper-pencil job analysis rating scale in which the examiner/analyst indicates the degree of involvement of each of the elements listed using appropriate rating scales such as importance, frequency, and so forth. The job elements are organized to provide a logical analysis of the job's structure. Six broad areas are assessed: information input, mental processes, work output, relationships with other persons, job context, and other job characteristics. Examples of specific job elements are the use of written materials, the level of decision making, the use of mechanical devices, working in a hazardous environment, and working at a specified pace.

The questionnaire is analyzed in terms of job dimensions (clusters of related elements). The results are used as the basis for job aptitude requirements, deriving "point" values for jobs that in turn can be used to establish compensation rates as well as to classify jobs into clusters that have statistically similar profiles. Also available on an experimental basis is the Job Activity Preference Questionnaire (JAPQ), which measures an individual's career interests in terms of the PAQ job dimensions. Self-administered by analyst, personnel staff, job supervisors, and, in some cases, the workers themselves. Suitable for group use.

Untimed: Not available

Scoring: Examiner evaluated; computer processing available

Cost: Contact publisher

Publisher: Consulting Psychologists Press, Inc.

PROCESS DIAGNOSTIC (PD)
Jay Hall

Adult

Purpose: Assesses interpersonal group dynamics. Used in training programs aimed at raising a group's awareness of its own internal processes.

Description: Multiple-item paper-pencil group exercise assessing the internal processes of a group. A matrix format and scoring wheel are used to identify behavioral cluster scores for individual group members, who receive individual assessments of the dynamics underlying their behavior and of their impact on the group. Diagnostic information also is provided concerning the group's climate resulting from the problem-solving, "flight," or "fight" behaviors of its members. Several hours are required to initiate in-depth, free-wheeling interchange. Trained process specialists or outside consultants are not required. Self-administered. Suitable for group use.

Untimed: Several hours

Scoring: Self-scored

Cost: Individual instrument $4.50

Publisher: Teleometrics International

PRODUCTIVITY ENVIRONMENTAL PREFERENCE SURVEY (PEPS)
Rita Dunn, Kenneth Dunn, and Gary E. Price

Adult

Purpose: Assesses the manner in which adults prefer to function, learn, concentrate, and perform in their occupational or educational activities. Used for employee placement and counseling and office design and lay-out.

Description: 100–item paper-pencil or computer-administered Likert-scale inventory measuring the following environmental factors related to educational or occupational activities: immediate environment (sound, temperature, light, and design), emotionality (motivation, responsibility, persistence, and structure), sociological needs (self-oriented, peer-oriented, authority-oriented, and combined ways), and physical needs (perceptual preferences, time of day, intake, and mobility). Test items consist of statements about the ways people like to work or study. Respondents are asked to indicate whether they agree or disagree with each statement.

Computerized results are available in three forms: individual profile (raw scores for each of the 20 areas, standard scores, and a plot for each score in each area), group summary (identifies individuals with significantly high or low scores and groups individuals with similar preferences), and subscale summary. Results provide a basis for supervisor- or instructor-individual interaction in the ways that permit each person to concentrate best. In addition, the results allow instructors or supervisors to group individuals or design work settings based on similarity among productivity elements.

The computer-administered version (PEPS-C) operates on Apple or IBM PC or compatible systems. Items are presented via the screen. The profile is available on-screen and in hard-copy format if the student has access to a printer. The program records responses, enabling testing to resume at the point at which it was interrupted. Several additional options are available for the Group Summary when the inventory is computer-administered. Users with access to a 3000 or 3051 NCS scanner may purchase a program that scans completed LSI forms and generates an on-site printout of results. The scanner must be hooked up to an IBM PC or compatible computer. Self-administered. Suitable for group use.

Untimed: 20–30 minutes

Scoring: Computer scored

Cost: Specimen set (manual, answer sheet) $11.00; diskette (100 administrations per licensing agreement) $295.00; each 100 additional administrations $60.00; NCS scanner program $395.00; 100 answer sheets for NCS scanner program $60.00

Publisher: Price Systems, Inc.

Information and availability unconfirmed; last verified in 1988.

PROGRAM FOR ASSESSING YOUTH EMPLOYMENT SKILLS (PAYES)

Refer to page 850.

PSC-ENCUESTA A.D.T. (FOR ALIENATION, DRUGS AND ALCOHOL, AND TRUSTWORTHINESS/LENIENCY)
Alan L. Strand and Mark L. Strand

Adolescent, adult—Ages 16 and older

Purpose: Assesses predisposing attitudes toward work. Assists in pre-employment screening of minimum wage and high-turnover positions.

Description: 100–item (3–subfactor) paper-pencil true-false test covering alienation/motivation (24 items), drugs/alcohol (16 items), and trustworthiness/leniency (60 items). This is one test in the PSC Survey series. A fourth-grade reading level is required. Examiner required. Suitable for group use. Available in Spanish.

Untimed: 15 minutes

Scoring: Self-scored; examiner evaluated

Cost: $6.00 each; volume discount

Publisher: Psychological Surveys Corporation

PSC-SURVEY A.D. (FOR ALCOHOL AND DRUG ATTITUDES)
Alan L. Strand and Mark L. Strand

Adolescent, adult—Ages 16 and older

Purpose: Assesses predisposing attitudes towards work. Used for pre-employment screening.

Description: 40–item (2–subfactor) paper-pencil true-false sentence-completion test yielding numerical scores. The test can be used for the Non-Management program (in conjunction with the PSC Survey-Motivation/Alienation and/or the PSC Survey-Leniency/Trust) and for the Management program (in conjunction with the PSC Survey-Supervisory Attitudes and the PSC Survey-Leniency Trust). The Non-Management program screens for positions that have an advanced level of responsibility and/or security risk but are not in a supervisory capacity. The Management program screens for beginning and mid-level management positions. This is a revision of the 1986 D.A. Survey. A fourth-grade reading level is required. Examiner required. Suitable for group use.

Untimed: 15 minutes

Scoring: Self-scored; examiner evaluated

Cost: $6.00; volume discount

Publisher: Psychological Surveys Corporation

PSC-SURVEY A.D.T. (FOR ALIENATION, DRUGS AND ALCOHOL, AND TRUSTWORTHINESS/LENIENCY)
Alan L. Strand and Mark L. Strand

Adolescent, adult—Ages 16 and older

Purpose: Assesses predisposing attitudes toward work. Assists in pre-employment screening of minimum wage and high-turnover positions.

Description: 100–item paper-pencil true-false test covering alienation/motivation (24 items), drugs/alcohol (16 items), and trustworthiness/leniency (60 items). This is one test in the PSC Survey series. A fourth-grade reading level is required. This is a condensed version of the P.A.S.S. Examiner required. Suitable for group use. Available in Spanish.

Untimed: 15 minutes

Scoring: Self-scored; examiner evaluated

Cost: $6.00; volume discount

Publisher: Psychological Surveys Corporation

PSC-SURVEY L.T. (FOR LENIENCY/TRUST)
Alan L. Strand and Mark L. Strand

Adolescent, adult—Ages 16 and older

Purpose: Assesses predisposing attitudes towards work. Used for pre-employment screening.

Description: 100–item (2–subfactor) paper-pencil true-false test covering leniency (20 items) and trustworthiness (80 items) and yielding numerical scores. The test can be used for the Non-Management program (in conjunction with the Survey-S.A. and/or the Survey-A.D.). The Non-Management program screens for positions that have an advanced level of responsibility and/or security risk but are not in a supervisory capacity. This is a revision of the 1987 T.A. Survey. A fourth-grade reading level is required. Examiner required. Suitable for group use.

Untimed: 15 minutes

Scoring: Self-scored; examiner evaluated

Cost: $6.00; volume discount

Publisher: Psychological Surveys Corporation

PSC-SURVEY M.A. (FOR MOTIVATION/ALIENATION)
Alan L. Strand and Mark L. Strand

Adolescent, adult

Purpose: Assesses predisposing attitudes towards work. Assists in pre-employment screening of nonmanagement positions.

Description: 60–item (4–subfactor) paper-pencil true-false test covering supervisors (18 items), companies (18 items), motivation (14 items), and workers (10

items). The test is appropriate for positions that have an advanced level of responsibility and/or security risk but are not in a supervisory capacity. For a more comprehensive screening, use a combination of two or three of the following surveys: Survey-M.A., Survey-L.T., Survey-A.D. A fourth-grade reading level is required. This is a revision of the 1986 A.I. Survey. Examiner required. Suitable for group use.

Untimed: 15 minutes

Scoring: Self-scored; examiner evaluated

Cost: $6.00; volume discount

Publisher: Psychological Surveys Corporation

RAHIM ORGANIZATIONAL CONFLICT INVENTORIES: EXPERIMENTAL EDITION (ROCI)
Afzalur Rahim

Adult

Purpose: Measures conflict experienced within an organization and assesses varying styles of handling the conflict.

Description: 105–item paper-pencil self-report inventory in two parts assessing the types of conflict and the various styles of handling conflict found within an organization. ROCI I contains 21 items assessing three dimensions or types of organizational conflict: intrapersonal, intergroup, and intragroup. ROCI II consists of three 28–item forms assessing conflict with one's boss (Form A), with one's subordinates (Form B), and with one's peers (Form C). Five styles of handling interpersonal conflict are identified: integrating, obliging, dominating, avoiding, and compromising. Both parts use a 5–point Likert scale. Limited norms are provided for college students and managerial groups. Examiner required. Suitable for group use.

Untimed: 45 minutes

Scoring: Examiner evaluated

Cost: 25 ROCI-I inventories $9.00; 25 ROCI-II inventories (includes 25 each of Forms A, B, C) $13.75; manual $10.50

Publisher: Consulting Psychologists Press, Inc.

REACTION TO EVERYDAY SITUATIONS TEST
Sheena M.A. Waterhouse

Adolescent, adult—Ages 16 and older

Purpose: Measures general anxiety shown by individuals in their day-to-day lives. Used for employee selection and screening and clinical research.

Description: 50-item paper-pencil questionnaire measuring the general anxiety shown by examinees in everyday situations. Each test item relates to a particular situation in which anxiety might be displayed. The test is restricted to competent persons properly registered with the South African Medical and Dental Council. Examiner required. Suitable for group use. Afrikaans version available. SOUTH AFRICAN PUBLISHER

Untimed: No time limit

Scoring: Hand key

Cost: Contact publisher

Publisher: National Institute for Personnel Research

REID REPORT

Adult

Purpose: Evaluates the honesty of job applicants. Identifies individuals most likely to steal at work if given the opportunity.

Description: Multiple-item paper-pencil questionnaire consisting of three sections. The first section contains 90 yes-no questions measuring the applicant's attitudes toward theft and the punishment of theft. The second section contains a detailed biographical data blank covering previous employment, education, and social history, including drug and alcohol abuse and excessive gambling as they relate to a need to steal. The third section is an admissions list of previous thefts and other misconduct, including convictions. Based on the score from Section One and the evaluation of the bio-data and admission-of-theft questions, the applicant is recommended or not recommended for employment. Results are available by

phone or mail. Examiner required. Suitable for group use. Available in Spanish, Portuguese, Italian, Polish, and French.

Untimed: 45 minutes

Scoring: Computer scored

Cost: $7.00–$12.00 each, depending on volume ordered

Publisher: Reid Psychological Systems

REID SURVEY

Adult

Purpose: Evaluates the honesty of current employees. Identifies employees most likely to be responsible for thefts within the company. Used to screen employees for promotion to sensitive positions.

Description: Multiple-item paper-pencil questionnaire consisting of two sections. The first section contains 90 yes-no questions measuring the employee's attitudes toward theft and the punishment of theft. The second section contains questions about recent job history and knowledge and opinions about in-company theft both by the responding employee and by others. Examiner required. Suitable for group use. Available in Spanish, Portuguese, and French.

Untimed: 45 minutes

Scoring: Computer scored

Cost: $11.00–$15.00 each, depending on volume ordered

Publisher: Reid Psychological Systems

REID SURVEY (RETAIL)

Adult

Purpose: Evaluates the honesty of current employees. Identifies employees most likely to be responsible for thefts within the company. Emphasizes theft in retail establishments. Used to screen employees for promotion to sensitive positions.

Description: Multiple-item paper-pencil questionnaire consisting of two sections. The first section contains 90 yes-no questions measuring the employee's attitudes toward theft and the punishment of theft. The second section contains 75 objective questions dealing with the employee's attitude toward the company and the employee's knowledge about or opinions concerning the honesty of others in the company, including questions about thefts or other defalcatory behaviors. Examiner required. Suitable for group use. Available in Spanish, Portuguese, and French.

Untimed: 45 minutes

Scoring: Computer scored

Cost: $11.00–$15.00 each, depending on volume ordered

Publisher: Reid Psychological Systems

RELATIONSHIP PROFILE (EGOGRAM®)
Refer to page 80.

SALES RELATIONS SURVEY (SRS)
Refer to page 1086.

SALES TRANSACTION AUDIT (STA)
Refer to page 1087.

SECURITY, APTITUDE, FITNESS EVALUATION (SAFE)
John Taccarino

Adult—Ages 16 and older

Purpose: Assesses characteristics of satisfactory employment that would reduce internal theft and increase productivity. Used in hiring for nonmanagement positions, such as store clerk, warehouse worker, truck driver, hotel clerk, janitor, custodian, and bank teller.

Description: Three-part multiple-item pre-employment screening test assessing six characteristics essential to satisfactory employment: honesty (applicant's likeliness to steal), dependability (punctuality and tardiness), socialization (behavior toward co-workers and customers), credibility, numerical ability, and language skills. Separate scores corresponding to the rankings of high-risk, low-risk, or caution-risk with respect to employment are provided for each characteristic. The test is computer scored with either a hand-held SAFE computer or on an IBM

PC or compatible. Examiner required. Suitable for group use. Test booklet also available in Spanish.

Untimed: 30 minutes

Scoring: Computer scored (automatically provides separate scores for all six subtests in less than 3 minutes)

Cost: 25 No. 9511OR test booklets $175.00

Publisher: SAFE, Inc.

Information and availability unconfirmed; last verified in 1988.

SECURITY, APTITUDE, FITNESS EVALUATION—RESISTANCE (SAFE-R)
John Taccarino

Adult—Ages 16 and older

Purpose: Assesses characteristics of satisfactory employment that would reduce theft and problems related to alcohol and drug abuse and increase productivity. Used in hiring for nonmanagement positions, such as store clerk, warehouse worker, truck driver, hotel clerk, janitor, custodian, and bank teller.

Description: Three-part multiple-item paper-pencil pre-employment screening test assessing seven characteristics essential to satisfactory employment: honesty (applicant's likeliness to steal), substance abuse resistance (Is the applicant likely to use drugs or alcohol on the job or abuse them after hours to the extent it interferes with job performance?), dependability (punctuality and tardiness), socialization (behavior toward co-workers and customers), credibility, numerical ability, and language skills. Separate scores corresponding to the rankings of high-risk, low-risk, or caution-risk with respect to employment are provided for each characteristic. The test is computer scored with either a hand-held SAFE computer or on an IBM PC or compatible. Examiner required. Suitable for group use.

Untimed: 30 minutes

Scoring: Computer scored (automatically provides separate scores for all seven subtests in less than 3 minutes)

Cost: 25 No. 95115 test booklets $225.00
Publisher: SAFE, Inc.
Information and availability unconfirmed; last verified in 1988.

SELF-ACTUALIZATION INVENTORY (SAI)
W.J. Reddin

Adult

Purpose: Measures the degree to which an individual's needs are fulfilled. Used to compare responses of managers and their subordinates.

Description: Multiple-item paper-pencil test covering the following needs: physical, security, relationships, respect, independence, and self-actualization. Self-administered. Suitable for group use. CANADIAN PUBLISHER

Untimed: 20–30 minutes

Scoring: Hand key

Cost: Test kit (10 test copies, fact sheet, user's guide) $40.00

Publisher: Organizational Tests (Canada) Ltd.

SELF-DIRECTED LEARNING READINESS SCALE (SDLRS)
Refer to page 782.

SOUTH AFRICAN PERSONALITY QUESTIONNAIRE
Refer to page 224.

SPECIFIC CASE INVENTORY (SCI)
London House, Inc.

Adolescent, adult

Purpose: Assesses the amount of information a subject has about a theft issue.

Description: 62–item paper-pencil or computer-administered multiple-choice survey that identifies persons with critical information about a specific theft incident. One score, the Information Index, is provided. The score rates the subject's knowledge about the incident from "no or very little information" to "substantial information." Suggested questions can be used by the investigator to conduct an individualized follow-up interview. Objective decisions concerning further action can then be based upon the score and the accompanying follow-up data. An 8th-grade reading level is required. Computer version available for IBM and compatibles. Examiner must be trained in security interviewing as it relates to investigations. Examiner required. Suitable for group use.

Untimed: 20 minutes

Scoring: Computer scored; scoring service available from publisher

Cost: Contact publisher; $12.00–$18.00 per test depending on volume ordered

Publisher: London House, Inc.

SPECTRUM
Larry A. Braskamp and Martin L. Maehr

Adult

Purpose: Evaluates the opportunities for fulfillment that individuals perceive in their present jobs, assesses worker motivation by determining personal values and incentives, and assesses organizational culture and employee commitment. Used in organizational development.

Description: 200 Likert-scale items measuring four aspects of the worker, job, and organization: accomplishment, recognition, power, and affiliation. Three types of reports are available. The Type I report gives employees feedback about individual incentives, personal values, and job opportunities. The Type II report provides supervisors with insights into their own management style and the impact their personal styles have on the people they supervise. The group report for executive planners provides feedback on organizational culture, degree of employee commitment, and areas of job satisfaction. Examiner/self-administered. Suitable for group use.

Untimed: 1 hour

Scoring: Computer scored

Cost: Introductory kit (manual, sample Type I, Type II, group reports, 2 survey booklets, processing for 2 reports) $49.50

Publisher: MetriTech, Inc.

SPECTRUM-I
*Larry A. Braskamp and
Martin L. Maehr*

Adult

Purpose: Measures work motivation factors. Designed to assist in employee selection.

Description: 77–item paper-pencil or computer-administered multiple-choice test measuring four basic work motivation factors: accomplishment, recognition, power, and affiliation. The information obtained from the test may be used to formulate a motivational profile and thereby guide an employer in structuring interviews with potential employees. Responses to the paper-pencil version may be entered into a computer for scoring and analysis. The computer version, which operates on IBM PC systems, administers and scores the test and generates reports. This test is an adaptation of Spectrum. APA purchase restrictions apply. Self-administered. Suitable for group use.

Untimed: 15 minutes

Scoring: Computer scored

Cost: Unlimited usage disk $479.00

Publisher: MetriTech, Inc.; distributed in Canada by Multi-Health Systems Inc.

STAFF BURNOUT SCALE FOR HEALTH PROFESSIONALS
Refer to page 971.

STAFF BURNOUT SCALE FOR POLICE AND SECURITY PERSONNEL
Refer to page 1080.

THE STANTON CASE REVIEW
Carl S. Klump

Adolescent, adult

Purpose: Assesses an individual's ability to identify persons responsible for an incident.

Description: Multiple-item paper-pencil investigative questionnaire assessing an individual's ability to identify a person's degree of responsibility for an incident such as a theft. The review begins with a description of the incident and requests individuals to voluntarily complete a questionnaire. Individuals then complete a personal history, respond to questions about the incident, and rate the company. Written explanations are compared with explanations given by others in similar investigations resulting in a finding of similarity to guilty or innocent explanations. Examiner required. Suitable for group use.

Untimed: Not available

Scoring: Examiner evaluated

Cost: Booklet and evaluation $30.00

Publisher: The Stanton Corporation

THE STANTON INVENTORY
Carl S. Klump

Adult

Purpose: Assesses problems of theft and management weaknesses in businesses. Used for identification of responsible parties.

Description: 96–item paper-pencil questionnaire assessing company dishonesty, morale, personal attitudes and general company information. The questionnaire assists in identifying problem areas (i.e., management weaknesses and theft). The test is analyzed by a Stanton staff criminologist. Examiner required. Suitable for group use.

Untimed: Not available

Scoring: Examiner evaluated

Cost: 1–99 inventory sheets and evaluation $30.00 each

Publisher: The Stanton Corporation

THE STANTON SURVEY
Carl S. Klump

Adult—Ages 16 and older

Purpose: Measures attitudes toward honesty. Used for screening and evaluating job applicants.

Description: Multiple-item paper-pencil test measuring attitudes toward honesty divided into two major sections. The first section includes biographical items covering educational and vocational history and social habits. The second part consists of 84 multiple-choice questions about attitudes toward honesty and about actual events involving honest and dishonest behaviors. Toll-free phone analysis is available. Self-administered. Suitable for group use.

Untimed: Not available

Scoring: Insta-phone; computer scored; machine (scannable) scored

Cost: 1–99 phone-in or computer-scored surveys $12.00 each; price adjustments based on quantity and scoring system used

Publisher: The Stanton Corporation

THE STANTON SURVEY PHASE II
Carl S. Klump

Adult

Purpose: Measures attitudes toward honesty. Used for screening and evaluating job applicants.

Description: Multiple-item paper-pencil test divided into two parts. The first part consists of 36 agree-disagree items covering attitudes toward honesty and actual events involving honest and dishonest behaviors. The second part consists of multiple-choice and short-answer items probing social habits, such as drinking, gambling, and drug use. The test is similar to The Stanton Survey but omits personal history and biographical information. Self-administered. Suitable for group use.

Untimed: Not available

Scoring: Hand key; insta-phone

Cost: $6.00 per booklet for self-scored; $8.00 per booklet for insta-phone

Publisher: The Stanton Corporation

STATION EMPLOYEE APPLICANT INVENTORY (SEAI)

Adult

Purpose: Assesses the on-the-job attitudes and behaviors of gas station and convenience store cashier applicants. Used to predict which applicants will

have low rates of tardiness and absenteeism, safeguard funds, handle cash and charge transactions accurately and honestly, follow safety rules, perform well under pressure, and foster a positive company image.

Description: 144–item paper-pencil multiple-choice test assessing the attitudes and behavior of gas station and convenience store cashier applicants. The test evaluates characteristics in five major areas measured by the following scales: Honesty, Interpersonal Cooperation, Drug Avoidance, Arithmetic Skills, and Job-Specific Skills and Abilities. An Applicant Employee Index and a validity scale are included also. Optional scales include Safety Attitudes and Tenure scale that predicts turnover. Standard and percentile scores are available in each of the five major areas.

Three scoring options are available from London House: operator-assisted telephone, Touch-Test, and PC-based. Operator-assisted scoring involves dialing a London House operator who provides test results after being read a tally of responses by the test administrator. Written confirmation is mailed the following day. Touch-Test telephone scoring allows the test administrator to use the telephone keypad to feed response tallies directly into London House computers. Results are available immediately, and written confirmation is mailed the next day. Administrators with IBM PC or compatible equipment may obtain on-site results using the PC-based scoring method. Examiner required. Suitable for group use.

Untimed: 45 minutes

Scoring: Operator-assisted telephone; computer scored

Cost: $6.00–$16.00 based on scoring method and volume ordered

Publisher: London House, Inc.

STRUCTURED-OBJECTIVE RORSCHACH TEST (SORT)—1975
Refer to page 254.

STUDY OF VALUES
Refer to page 776.

STYLES OF LEADERSHIP SURVEY (SLS)
Jay Hall and Martha S. Williams

Adult

Purpose: Assesses leadership styles in terms of "concern for people" and "concern for purpose." Used with nonmanagement supervisory personnel, campus and community groups, volunteer organizations, and administrative personnel.

Description: Multiple-item paper-pencil self-report inventory assessing leadership behavior in terms of the Blake-Mouton model of management behavior. The Blake-Mouton managerial grid is an extension of Likert's production-morale theory and measures two dimensions of leadership behavior: concerns for people and concerns for purpose. The inventory yields analyses of overall leadership style, including four components of leadership: philosophy, planning, implementation, and evaluation. Normative data are provided. The inventory may be administered in conjunction with the Leadership Appraisal Survey for a more complete assessment of leadership styles and effectiveness. Self-administered. Suitable for group use.

Untimed: Varies

Scoring: Self-scored

Cost: Individual instrument $5.60

Publisher: Teleometrics International

STYLES OF TEAMWORK INVENTORY
Jay Hall

Adult

Purpose: Assesses team members' understanding of their own styles and the impact a particular style is apt to have on the team.

Description: 80–item paper-pencil criterion-referenced instrument addressing how an individual functions as a member of various work teams, in particular the behaviors a team member has and the feelings the individual has interacting with others in a team setting. The inventory results in an overall preferred style

and provides specific scores on individual attitude, the handling of conflict, leadership preference, and intergroup relations. Self-administered. Suitable for group use.

Untimed: Varies

Scoring: Self-scored

Cost: $6.95

Publisher: Teleometrics International

SUPERVISORY COMMUNICATION RELATIONS TEST (SCOM)
Refer to page 1059.

SUPERVISORY HUMAN RELATIONS TEST (SHR)
Refer to page 1059.

SUPERVISORY INVENTORY ON COMMUNICATION (SIC)
Donald L. Kirkpatrick

Adult

Purpose: Measures knowledge of proper supervisory use of communication procedures within an organization. Used in conjunction with training programs aimed at improving the communication effectiveness of supervisors.

Description: 80–item paper-pencil two-choice test assessing knowledge and understanding of communication philosophy, principles, and methods for supervisors. Each item describes an action or belief concerned with on-the-job communication. Individuals indicate whether they agree or disagree with each statement.

Test results identify topics that should be emphasized in training programs, serve as a tool for conference discussions, measure the effectiveness of training programs, provide information for on-the-job coaching, and assist in the selection of supervisory personnel.

The manual includes a discussion of the inventory's development, normative data, research data, and interpretive guidelines. The answer booklet includes the rationale behind all correct answers. A cassette describing in detail how the test can be used most effectively is available. Kirkpatrick's book, *No-Nonsense Communication*, is also available to provide details, principles, and techniques for improving communication effectiveness. Self-administered. Suitable for group use.

Untimed: 20 minutes

Scoring: Self-scored

Cost: 20 tests and answer booklets $27.00; instructor's manual $1.50; *No-Nonsense Communication* $5.50

Publisher: Donald L. Kirkpatrick

Information and availability unconfirmed; last verified in 1988.

SUPERVISORY INVENTORY ON HUMAN RELATIONS (SIHR)
Donald L. Kirkpatrick

Adult

Purpose: Measures knowledge of basic human relations principles involved in effective supervisory job performance. Used in conjunction with management training programs aimed at increasing knowledge and improving attitudes in dealing with people.

Description: 80–item paper-pencil two-choice test measuring the extent to which supervisors understand and accept the principles, facts, and techniques of human relations in management. Test items cover human relations issues in the following areas: the supervisor's role in management, understanding and motivating employees, developing positive employee attitudes, problem-solving techniques, and principles of learning and training. Individuals indicate whether they agree or disagree with the statement about beliefs or behaviors presented in each test item. The answer booklet provides a rationale for each correct answer.

Test results identify topics that should be emphasized in training programs, serve as a tool for conference discussions, measure the effectiveness of training programs, provide information for on-the-job coaching, and assist in the selection of supervisory personnel. The manual includes norms for foremen and plant supervisors, office supervisors, and middle and top management; a discussion of validity and reliability, interpretive guide-

lines, and an answer key providing the rationale behind all correct answers. A cassette describing in detail how the test can be used most effectively is available. Self-administered. Suitable for group use.

Untimed: 15 minutes

Scoring: Self-scored

Cost: 20 tests and answer booklets $27.00; instructor's manual $1.50

Publisher: Donald L. Kirkpatrick

Information and availability unconfirmed; last verified in 1988.

SUPERVISORY PRACTICES INVENTORY (SPI)
Refer to page 1061.

SURVEY OF INTERPERSONAL VALUES
Refer to page 226.

SURVEY OF PERSONAL VALUES
Leonard V. Gordon

Adolescent, adult
Grades 10 and above

Purpose: Measures the critical values that help an individual determine coping ability with everyday problems. Used for employee screening and placement, vocational guidance, and counseling.

Description: 30–item paper-pencil inventory assessing personal values. Each item consists of a triad of value statements. For each triad, examinees must indicate most and least important values. Six values are measured: practical mindedness, achievement, variety, decisiveness, orderliness, and goal orientation. Self-administered. Suitable for group use.

Untimed: 15 minutes

Scoring: Hand key

Cost: 25 test booklets $35.00; scoring stencil $5.50; examiner's manual $10.00

Publisher: SRA/London House

1030   *business and industry*

interpersonal skills and attitudes

SURVEY OF WORK VALUES (SWV), FORM U
Steven Wollack, James G. Goodale, Jan P. Wijting, and Patricia C. Smith

Adult

Purpose: Assesses an individual's work values. Suitable for use with hearing- and physically impaired individuals.

Description: 72–item paper-pencil test in which examinees use a 5–point scale (strongly agree to strongly disagree) to rate statements. The test contains six scales consisting of nine items each: Pride in Work, Social Status of Job, Attitude Toward Earnings, Activity Preference, Upward Striving, and Job Involvement. The test can be scored to measure two factors, Intrinsic Values and Extrinsic Values. The test yields scores for each of the scales and factors. A scoring service is available by special arrangement with the publisher. A fifth-grade reading level is required. Self-administered. Suitable for group use. Available in Arabic.

Untimed: 10 minutes

Scoring: Hand key; may be computer scored; may be machine scored

Cost: 100 booklets $21.00; 100 answer sheets $5.00; 100 scoring sheets $5.00; postage and handling $5.00

Publisher: Bowling Green State University, Department of Psychology

SURVEY PROGRAM FOR BUSINESS AND INDUSTRY

Adult

Purpose: Assesses employee attitudes and perceptions concerning critical job-related issues. Provides information useful for reducing turnover and absenteeism, improving employee relations and morale, identifying obstacles to productivity, and monitoring responses to organizational changes.

Description: Multiple-item paper-pencil climate/attitude assessment questionnaire available in four versions, one for each of the following employee groups: managers, professionals, outside sales representatives, and general employees. All surveys measure the following areas of common interest: organization identification, job satisfaction, pay, benefits, supervisory leadership and administrative practices, work associates, general administrative effectiveness, work organization, work efficiency, performance and personal development, and communication effectiveness. In addition, each survey contains factors that focus on areas of specific interest to the various target groups (e.g., sales training). The surveys can be customized to meet special needs. Demographic breakdowns are chosen by the client organization according to its interest. Results of the survey are presented in state-of-the-art numerical and graphic displays. Reports are tailored to client needs, and comparisons to national and industry norms are available. Frequent users of the program are able to create company-specific norms and/or conduct longitudinal studies with previous survey results. Examiner required. Suitable for group use.

Untimed: 50 minutes or less

Scoring: Computer scored

Cost: Contact publisher; $7.00–$14.00 per survey depending on volume ordered and the degree of customization

Publisher: London House, Inc.

TAV SELECTION SYSTEM
Robert R. Morman

Adolescent, adult—Ages 16 and older

Purpose: Measures the normal interpersonal reactions toward, away from, and versus people. Used as an occupational selection tool and a counseling aid.

Description: Multiple-item paper-pencil test consisting of seven subtests: Personal Data (240 items), Proverbs and Sayings (240 items), Preferences (300 items), Sales Reactions (240 items), Judgments, Adjective Check List (300 items), and Mental Agility (75 items). Predictive validity scores are provided for a number of typical professions: traffic officers, teachers, salesmen, nurses, and others. Male and female norms are provided. An eighth-grade reading level is required. The test is available in large print. Users must be APA qualified. Self-administered. Suitable for group use.

Timed: 3 hours
Scoring: Hand key
Cost: Tests and scoring keys $8.10
Publisher: TAV Selection System

TEAM EFFECTIVENESS SURVEY (TES)
Jay Hall

Adult

Purpose: Assesses team functioning and identifies individuals who are primarily responsible for the team's style of functioning. Used for employee training and for development and discussion purposes.

Description: Multiple-item paper-pencil group exercise assessing team functioning on the exposure and feedback dimensions inherent in the Johari Window model of interpersonal relations. Each team member rates self and others on items related to both dimensions. The resulting individual and team profiles serve as immediate feedback to confirm or deny self-ratings and furnish an overview of team functioning. Defensive versus supportive climate scores also are obtained. Self-administered. Suitable for group use.

Untimed: Varies
Scoring: Self-scored
Cost: Individual instrument $5.60
Publisher: Teleometrics International

TEAM PROCESS DIAGNOSTIC
Jay Hall

Adult

Purpose: Assesses member contributions to team functioning.

Description: 32–item paper-pencil instrument utilizing a matrix format and scoring wheel. The matrix indices yield behavioral assessments of the dynamics underlying individuals' behavior and of the impact of their behavior on the group. In addition, the instrument provides diagnostic information about the group's climate resulting from the problem-solving, "flight or fight" behaviors of its members. Self-administered. Suitable for group use. Available in Spanish, Swedish, Portuguese, French, and German.

Untimed: Varies
Scoring: Self-scored
Cost: $6.95
Publisher: Teleometrics International

TEAMNESS INDEX
Jay Hall

Adult

Purpose: Assesses whether team members meet the minimal conditions for teamness.

Description: 24–item paper-pencil criterion-referenced test using a 9–point scale that reflects how characteristic each statement is for an individual. Each item is presented in two parts. The first part is the condition of interest being surveyed, and the second part serves as a reference of the opposite condition. Answers indicate how each team member characterizes particular work relationships. Self-administered. Suitable for group use.

Untimed: Varies
Scoring: Self-scored
Cost: $6.95
Publisher: Teleometrics International

TEAMWORK APPRAISAL SURVEY
Jay Hall

Adult

Purpose: Assesses how personal practices impact others when working in teams or groups.

Description: 80–item paper-pencil criterion-referenced survey that focuses on how associates function as members of various work teams. It is a companion instrument to the Styles of Teamwork Inventory (STI) and is filled out by other team members to provide a person using the STI with comparative assessments of his or her team behavior. The TAS is arranged to permit direct, question-by-question comparisons between it and the STI. These comparisons and the discussions surrounding them enable an individual to realize and consider the impact of his or her behavioral practices. Self-administered. Suitable for group use. Available in Spanish.

Untimed: Varies

Scoring: Self-scored

Cost: $6.95

Publisher: Teleometrics International

TEMPERAMENT AND VALUES INVENTORY (TVI)
Charles B. Johansson and Patricia L. Webber

Adolescent, adult
Grades 9 and above

Purpose: Measures an individual's attitudes and work values. Used for career development, personnel counseling, and training needs assessment.

Description: 230-item paper-pencil test containing 133 true-false statements and 97 5-point scale items. The test covers seven bipolar temperament scales: Routine-Flexible, Quiet-Active, Attentive-Distractible, Serious-Cheerful, Consistent-Changeable, Reserved-Sociable, and Reticent-Persuasive. The test also contains seven reward value scales: Social Recognition, Managerial Sales Benefits, Leadership, Social Service, Task Specificity, Philosophical Curiosity, and Work Independence. The test may be computer scored via mail-in service or using Arion II Teleprocessing. Self-administered. Suitable for group use.

Untimed: 20–30 minutes

Scoring: Computer scored

Cost: Manual $12.50; interpretive report $5.05–$8.80 depending on quantity; profile report $3.15–$4.35 depending on quantity

Publisher: National Computer Systems/PAS Division

TEST OF WORK COMPETENCY AND STABILITY
A. Gaston Leblanc

Adult—Ages 21–67

Purpose: Measures stress levels in motor coordination and mental concentration.

Used to evaluate psychological capacity for work performance.

Description: Multiple-item paper-pencil interview and manual dexterity test of six factors related to work competency in industry, including work stability, assertiveness, persistence and concentration, psychomotor steadiness, capacity, and stress tolerance. Scores screen workers and provide information for rehabilitation. The materials are provided in a set that includes a manual, interview questionnaire sheets, mirror tracing patterns, tapping patterns (a tremometer and tapping apparatus with 24–volt impulse counter), and record blanks. Examiner required. Not suitable for group use. Available in French.

CANADIAN PUBLISHER

Untimed: Varies

Scoring: Hand key

Cost: Contact publisher

Publisher: Institute of Psychological Research, Inc.

TEST PLUS
Samuel E. Krug

Adult

Purpose: Assesses personality characteristics, interpersonal style, and career preferences for personnel evaluation, career planning, rehabilitation counseling, and family therapy.

Description: Series of paper-pencil or computer-administered multiple-item multiple-choice subtests yielding scores in three areas: personality characteristics (extroverted, adjusted, tough-minded, independent, disciplined, creative, enterprising), interpersonal style (caring, adapting, withdrawn, submissive, hostile, rebellious, sociable, assertive), and career orientation (practical scientific, aesthetic, social, competitive, structured). Four validity scales (Good Impression, Bad Impression, Infrequency, Uncertainty) complete the test profile.

Materials include computer software programs that run on IBM PC (256K, 1 floppy disk PC/MS DOS) and Apple II (64K, 2 floppy disks) systems. The program is capable of storing up to 100 cases on a disk at one time. Test Plus is adapted

---

from the Adult Personality Inventory. Purchasers must meet APA guidelines. A fourth-grade reading level is required. Self-administered. Suitable for group use. Available in German.

Untimed: 30–60 minutes
Scoring: Computer scored
Cost: Unlimited disk usage $479.00
Publisher: MetriTech, Inc.

THURSTONE TEMPERAMENT SCHEDULE
*L.L. Thurstone and
Thelma Gwinn Thurstone*

Adult

Purpose: Evaluates permanent aspects of personality and how normal, well-adjusted people differ from one another. Used by managers to determine employee suitability for particular jobs.

Description: 140–item paper-pencil inventory assessing seven areas of temperament: active, vigorous, impulsive, dominant, stable, sociable, and reflective. The inventory is limited to use by individuals with advanced training in personality instruments. Self-administered. Suitable for group use.

Untimed: 15–20 minutes
Scoring: Hand key
Cost: 25 booklets $35.00; examiner's manual $10.00
Publisher: SRA/London House

TIME PROBLEMS INVENTORY (TPRI)
Albert A. Canfield

Adult

Purpose: Evaluates an individual's time-use problems. Identifies personal and internal causes of time-use problems. Used for group discussions and to assess organizational time-use problems.

Description: Multiple-item paper-pencil inventory measuring the comparative level of an individual's time-use problems in four areas: priority setting, planning, task clarification, and self-discipline. Questions are largely work-related, representing time problems encountered in any

organization, but scores may be related to time-use problems in all aspects of daily living. Interpretation focuses on internal causes of time-use problems and may be used to identify time-use problems common to members of any organization. Scoring provides information for the discussion of internal and external factors related to ineffective time use. Self-administered. Suitable for group use.

Untimed: 30 minutes
Scoring: Self-scored
Cost: Kit $25.00
Publisher: Western Psychological Services

TIME USE ANALYZER
Albert A. Canfield

Adult

Purpose: Evaluates a person's time use habits. Provides a basis for discussions of time quality versus time quantity.

Description: Multiple-item paper-pencil test assessing how individuals feel about how their time is being spent in eight aspects of life: at work, asleep, on personal hygiene, taking care of personal/family business, in community and church activities, with family or home members, in education and development, and on recreational and hobby activities. Test booklets contain a discussion of the implications of the results and the general findings. The test produces an awareness of common areas in which most people express some level of dissatisfaction with their time use and helps individuals differentiate between time efficiency and time effectiveness and stimulates concerns for improvement in both areas. Norms are provided for comparing levels of dissatisfaction among groups of supervisors and managers. Self-administered. Suitable for group use.

Untimed: 20 minutes
Scoring: Self-scored
Cost: Kit $25.00
Publisher: Western Psychological Services

TRAIT EVALUATION INDEX
Alan R. Nelson

Adult

Purpose: Assesses adult personality traits. Used for job placement and career counseling.

Description: 125–item paper-pencil two-choice test measuring 24 personality dimensions, including social orientation, elation, self-control, sincerity, compliance, ambition, dynamism, caution, propriety, and intellectual orientation. Materials consist of a test manual, keys, answer sheets, and academic and industrial-business profile sheets. Self-administered. Suitable for group use. Available in German.

Untimed: 30–40 minutes

Scoring: Hand key

Cost: 20 reusable tests $39.50; manual $15.00; 24 IBM scoring stencils $31.00; 20 profile sheets $18.00; answer sheets $18.00; specimen set $53.50; specimen set without scoring stencils $24.50

Publisher: Martin M. Bruce, Ph.D., Publishers

TRIADAL EQUATED PERSONALITY INVENTORY
Refer to page 229.

TRUSTWORTHINESS ATTITUDE SURVEY (T.A. SURVEY)
Alan L. Strand, Ph.D. et al.

Adult

Purpose: Measures attitudes and personality characteristics related to trustworthiness. Used to screen applicants for jobs involving security, money, and product handling.

Description: 118–item paper-pencil multiple-choice and short-answer test measuring attitudes and beliefs. The test must be administered by a qualified, licensed company or government agency examiner. Examiner required. Suitable for group use.

Untimed: 20–30 minutes

Scoring: Hand key

Cost: Specimen set Free; 25 tests $6.00; scoring templates leased yearly $60.00

Publisher: Psychological Surveys Corporation

VCWS 14–INTEGRATED PEER PERFORMANCE

Adult

Purpose: Measures an individual's instruction-following ability and color discrimination skills. Stimulates interaction among workers.

Description: Manual test measuring an individual's ability to follow instructions and discriminate between colors. The test emphasizes the ability to interact effectively with both peers and supervisors and the ability to work as a team member in order to complete a task. Three or four examinees are seated and given colored assembly pieces and an assembly pattern booklet. The examiner places assembly boards on the table and moves them from worker to worker every 20 seconds. Each examinee performs his portion of the assembly and then waits for the next assembly board. As each assembly board is completed, the examiner inspects each board and informs the appropriate examinee(s) of any errors that have been made. The test allows the examiner to observe and actuarially score universal worker characteristics that relate to human interaction and behavior. The test should not be administered to individuals with severe impairment of the upper extremities or severe visual impairment. Examiner required. Suitable for group use.

Timed: Not available

Scoring: Examiner evaluated

Cost: $2,695.00

Publisher: Valpar International Corporation

VOCATIONAL OPINION INDEX
ARBOR, Inc.

Adult

Purpose: Assesses perceptions and motivations affecting the ability to get and hold a job. Used in counseling, skills training, and general diagnosis of work expectations.

Description: 42–item paper-pencil test measuring an individual's attractions to work, perceived losses associated with work, and possible barriers to employment. The respondent uses 5–point rating scales to indicate agreement or disagreement with statements concerning what might happen in the workplace and about problems that might make it difficult for some people to keep a job. The test is not to be used primarily as a screening device. Examiner required. Suitable for group use. Available in Spanish.

Untimed: 20 minutes

Scoring: Hand key; examiner evaluated; may be computer scored

Cost: 1–100 booklets $0.70 each; scoring manual $5.00

Publisher: ARBOR, Inc.

Information and availability unconfirmed; last verified in 1988.

WARD ATMOSPHERE SCALE (WAS)
Rudolf H. Moos

Adolescent, adult

Purpose: Assesses the social environments of hospital-based psychiatric treatment programs. Used to evaluate organizational effectiveness.

Description: 100–item paper-pencil true-false test covering 10 aspects of social environment and yielding 10 scores: involvement, support, spontaneity, autonomy, practical orientation, personal problem orientation, anger and aggression, order and organization, program clarity, and staff control. Three "treatment outcome" scales may be used: Dropout, Release Rate, and Community Tenure. Materials include the Real Form (Form R), which measures perceptions of a current program; the 40–item Short Form (Form S); the Ideal Form (Form I), which measures conceptions of an ideal program; and the Expectations Form (Form E), which measures expectations of a new program. Forms I and E are not published, but items and instructions appear in the appendix of the WAS man-

ual. One in a series of nine Social Climate scales. Examiner required. Suitable for group use.

Untimed: 20 minutes

Scoring: Hand key; examiner evaluated

Cost: 25 reusable tests $8.50; 50 answer sheets $5.50; 50 profiles $3.75; key $1.75; manual $5.00

Publisher: Consulting Psychologists Press, Inc.

THE WHISLER STRATEGY TEST
Lawrence Whisler

Adult

Purpose: Assesses strategy used in approaching problems. Used to evaluate applicants for employment.

Description: Multiple-item paper-pencil measure of six aspects of strategy: solutions, speed, boldness, caution, hyper-caution, and net strategy. The test detects both risk-takers and risk-avoiders and evaluates the subject with respect to the wisdom of his strategy. Examiner required. Suitable for group use.

Timed: 25 minutes

Scoring: Hand key

Cost: Specimen set $5.00; 25 tests $5.00; 25 answer sheets $5.00

Publisher: Psychometric Affiliates

WORK ASPECT PREFERENCE SCALE (WAPS)
R. Pryor

Adolescent, adult
Grades 10 and above

Purpose: Measures work qualities that individuals consider important. Used in career counseling, vocational rehabilitation, the study of personal and work values, and research on career development and worker satisfaction.

Description: 52–item paper-pencil or computer-administered inventory assessing an individual's work values along 13 scales: altruism, co-workers, creativity, detachment, independence, life-style, management, money, physical activity, prestige, security, self-development, and surroundings. Computer scoring converts

raw scores on each scale to percentiles and ranks the scales in order of raw score and percentile. The computer-administered and scored version requires an Apple II+, IIe, or IIc computer with 48K, an 80–column printer, and a single or dual disk drive. Examiner required. Suitable for group use.
AUSTRALIAN PUBLISHER

Untimed: 10–20 minutes

Scoring: Hand key; may be machine scored; may be computer scored

Cost: Contact publisher

Publisher: The Australian Council for Educational Research Limited

---

WORK ATTITUDE SCALE (WAS)

Adult

Purpose: Assesses an individual's orientation to work that involves contact with people and regular completion of established tasks. Used in the recruitment of entry-level clerical, secretarial, front-line retail, and shop-floor staff.

Description: Multiple-item paper-pencil or computer-administered screening instrument assessing three aspects of an individual's work style: service orientation, task orientation, and work approach. Service Orientation assesses the extent to which the individual is warm, friendly, cooperative, and responsive to others' needs. Task Orientation measures the extent to which the person attends to detail, is conscientious, and likes to complete required tasks. Work Approach examines whether the individual works more effectively under close, structured, and supportive supervision or with independence and responsibility. The instrument is intended for use in conjunction with other selection procedures. It can be used as an initial screen or as a confirmation device. Scoring can be completed onsite or centrally. Examiner required. Suitable for group use.
BRITISH PUBLISHER

Untimed: 10 minutes

Scoring: Hand key; may be computer scored

Cost: Contact publisher

Publisher: Independent Assessment and Research Centre

Information and availability unconfirmed; last verified in 1988.

WORK ATTITUDES QUESTIONNAIRE
M.S. Doty and N.E. Betz

Adult

Purpose: Measures an individual's commitment to work and the degree to which such commitment is psychologically healthy or unhealthy. Used for research purposes and to identify "workaholics."

Description: 45–item paper-pencil questionnaire consisting of two scales: one assessing high versus low commitments to work (23 items) and the second assessing the degree to which work attitudes are psychologically healthy or unhealthy (22 items). Test items consist of statements regarding work or career orientation or the role that work plays in the larger scheme of life. Individuals rate each item on a 5–point scale ranging from one ("strongly disagree") to five ("strongly agree") to indicate the degree to which the statement expresses their personal beliefs.

Results differentiate the "workaholic" or the Type A personality from the highly committed worker who, although strongly committed to and involved in his work, manages at the same time to lead a balanced psychologically healthy life. The manual includes procedures for administration and scoring, interpretive guidelines, information on the development of the scales, data on reliability and validity, and normative data. Examiner required. Suitable for group use.

Untimed: Varies

Scoring: Examiner evaluated

Cost: Kit (manual, 25 questionnaires) $22.00; 50 questionnaires $18.00

Publisher: Marathon Consulting and Press

WORK ENVIRONMENT SCALE (WES)
Paul Insel and Rudolf H. Moos

Adult

Purpose: Evaluates the social climate of work units. Used to assess correlates of productivity, worker satisfaction, quality assurance programs, work stressors, individual adaptation, and supervisory methods.

Description: 90–item paper-pencil measure of 10 dimensions of work social environments: involvement, peer cohesion, supervisor support, autonomy, task orientation, work pressure, clarity, control, innovation, and physical comfort. These dimensions are grouped into three sets: relationships, personal growth, and system maintenance and change. Three forms are available: the Real Form (Form R), which measures perceptions of existing work environments; the Ideal Form (Form I), which measures conceptions of ideal work environments; and the Expectations Form (Form E), which measures expectations about work settings. Forms I and E are not published although items and instructions will be provided upon request. Examiner required. Suitable for group use.

Untimed: 20 minutes

Scoring: Hand key

Cost: Specimen set (user's guide, manual, scoring key, test booklet, answer sheet, profile) $13.50; manual $7.00; scoring key $1.75

Publisher: Consulting Psychologists Press, Inc.

WORK MOTIVATION INVENTORY (WMI)
Jay Hall and Martha S. Williams

Adult

Purpose: Assesses the work-related needs and motivations of both managers and subordinates. Used for employee training and development and as a basis for discussion.

Description: Multiple-item paper-pencil self-report inventory assessing work-related needs actually experienced by an individual. The inventory yields five scores, which provide a personal motivational profile according to the five need systems established in Maslow's need-hierarchy concept. The inventory may be administered in conjunction with the Management of Motives Index (MMI) in two ways. When used as a subordinate instrument and compared to the manager's MMI profile, discrepancies are identified between what an employee feels is important and what the manager offers in the way of motivational support. When completed by the manager and the results are compared with scores on the MMI, areas are indicated in which the manager's own needs may be influencing motivational methods used to meet the needs of others. Normative data are provided. Self-administered. Suitable for group use.

Untimed: Varies

Scoring: Self-scored

Cost: Individual instrument $5.60

Publisher: Teleometrics International

WORK VALUES INVENTORY
Refer to page 841.

Management and Supervision

ACUMEN

Adult

Purpose: Assesses management style and assists managers in understanding their thinking styles and personal dispositions. Designed to improve the skills and productivity of managers.

Description: Multiple-component computerized management assessment and development system. The Self-Assessment component, based on Life Styles Inventory Levels I and II, assesses management of subordinates and peer relationships, task management, conflict resolution, and leadership. The Insight for Managers component focuses on personal interaction dynamics, including analysis of personal skills and thinking styles, in order to help managers achieve personal and group performance goals. This component also incorporates the assessment information and feedback obtained in the Self-Assessment component. The Group Feedback component evaluates managers' co-workers and subordinates, providing managers with confidential feedback of how their peers perceive them. The Profile Compiler component integrates the personal profiles of from 4 to 30 individuals into one profile highlighting the management issues that face the management team.

The ACUMEN program is presented on seven disks that operate on IBM PC systems. Scoring and interpretation are available on-site. Self-administered. Suitable for group use.

Untimed: Not available

Scoring: Computer scored

Cost: Complete $595.00

Publisher: Human Synergistics

Information and availability unconfirmed; last verified in 1988.

ADVANCED TEST BATTERY (ATB)
Refer to page 863.

ADVANCED TEST BATTERY: NUMBER SERIES (ATB:NA2)
Refer to page 864.

ADVANCED TEST BATTERY: NUMERICAL CRITICAL REASONING (ATB:NA4)
Refer to page 864.

ADVANCED TEST BATTERY: VERBAL CONCEPTS (ATB:VA1)
Refer to page 865.

ADVANCED TEST BATTERY: VERBAL CRITICAL REASONING (ATB-VA3)
Refer to page 865.

ATTITUDE SURVEY PROGRAM FOR BUSINESS AND INDUSTRY: MANAGERIAL SURVEY
Refer to page 993.

BIOGRAPHICAL INDEX
Refer to page 995.

BI/POLAR INVENTORIES OF CORE STRENGTHS
Refer to page 82.

COMMUNICATION KNOWLEDGE INVENTORY
W.J. Reddin

Adult

Purpose: Assesses a manager's general knowledge of communication.

Description: 80–item paper-pencil test covering verbal and nonverbal communication fallacies. Self-administered. Suitable for group use.
CANADIAN PUBLISHER
Untimed: 20–30 minutes
Scoring: Hand key
Cost: Test kit (10 test copies, fact sheet, user's guide) $40.00; cash orders postpaid
Publisher: Organizational Tests (Canada) Ltd.

COMMUNICATION SENSITIVITY INVENTORY
W.J. Reddin

Adult

Purpose: Determines the characteristic response of a manager to whom others come with problems. Used as a pretest in courses in listening, coaching, and communication.

Description: 10–item paper-pencil multiple-choice test measuring a manager's reaction to problems expressed by subordinates. Responses are categorized as feeling, challenge, more information, or recommendation. Self-administered. Suitable for group use.
CANADIAN PUBLISHER

Untimed: 20–30 minutes

Scoring: Hand key

Cost: Test kit (10 test copies, fact sheet, user's guide) $40.00; cash orders postpaid

Publisher: Organizational Tests (Canada) Ltd.

CPP COMPATIBILITY QUESTIONNAIRE
Refer to page 998.

CREE QUESTIONNAIRE
T.G. Thurstone and J. Mellinger

Adult

Purpose: Evaluates an individual's overall creative potential and the extent to which the individual's behavior resembles that of identified creative individuals. Used for placement of managerial and professional personnel and career counseling.

Description: 145–item paper-pencil test measuring the 13 factorially determined dimensions of the creative personality: dominance vs. submission; indifference vs. involvement; independence vs. conformity; unstructured vs. structured work situation; selective vs. prescribed activity; work-involved vs. detached attitude; pressured vs. relaxed situation; high vs. low energy level; fast vs. slow reaction time; high vs. low ideational spontaneity; and strength of theoretical, artistic, and mechanical interests. Basic reading skills are required. Self-administered. Suitable for group use.

Untimed: 15–20 minutes

Scoring: Hand key; may be computer scored

Cost: Specimen set $12.00; 25 test booklets $20.00

Publisher: London House, Inc.

CRITICAL REASONING TEST BATTERY: DIAGRAMMATIC SERIES (CRTB: DC2)
Saville & Holdsworth Ltd. Staff

Ages 16–adult

Purpose: Measures critical reasoning ability for thinking sequentially. Used in personnel screening and counseling.

Description: 40–item paper-pencil test assessing the logical or analytical ability to follow a sequence of diagrams and select the next one in a series from five alternatives. The test is used for technical research and computer programming positions. One of three tests in the Critical Reasoning Test Battery. Together, the three tests provide information on important abilities related to junior management. Examiner required. Suitable for group use.
BRITISH PUBLISHER

Timed: 20 minutes

Scoring: Hand key; may be computer scored

Cost: 50 answer sheets $51.00; administration card $9.50; scoring key $9.50; 10 booklets $114.50

Publisher: Saville & Holdsworth Ltd.

CRITICAL REASONING TEST BATTERY: INTERPRETING DATA (CRTB: NC3)
Saville & Holdsworth Ltd. Staff

Ages 16–adult

Purpose: Measures ability to make correct decisions or inferences from numerical data. Used in personnel screening and counseling.

Description: 40–item paper-pencil test assessing the ability to interpret straightforward statistical and other numerical data presented as tables or diagrams. Candidates select the correct answer to a question from five alternatives. The test is appropriate for jobs involving analysis or decision making based on numerical facts. One of three tests in the Critical Reasoning Test Battery. Together, the three tests provide information on important abilities related to junior management. Examiner required. Suitable for group use.
BRITISH PUBLISHER

Timed: 30 minutes

Scoring: Hand key; may be computer scored

Cost: 10 booklets $114.50; 50 answer sheets $51.00; administration card $9.50; scoring key $9.50; 10 data cards $27.50

Publisher: Saville & Holdsworth Ltd.

CRITICAL REASONING TEST BATTERY: VERBAL EVALUATION (CRTB: VC4)
Saville & Holdsworth Ltd. Staff

Ages 16–adult

Purpose: Measures ability to understand and evaluate the logic of arguments. Used in personnel screening and counseling.

Description: 60–item paper-pencil test of a supervisor's or general manager's ability to understand and evaluate the logic of various types of arguments. The examinee must decide whether a statement is true or untrue or whether there is sufficient information to judge. One of three tests in the Critical Reasoning Test Battery. Together, the three tests provide information on important abilities related to junior management. Examiner required. Suitable for group use. BRITISH PUBLISHER

Timed: 30 minutes

Scoring: Hand key; may be computer scored

Cost: 50 answer sheets $51.00; administration card $9.50; scoring key $9.50; 10 booklets $114.50

Publisher: Saville & Holdsworth Ltd.

CRITICAL THINKING TEST (CTT; U.S. VERSION)
Saville & Holdsworth Ltd. Staff

Adult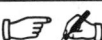

Purpose: Assesses verbal critical reasoning skills in industry. Used with managers and new graduate applicants.

Description: Two 92–item paper-pencil multiple-choice tests measuring verbal and numerical critical reasoning ability. Designed for use in the selection, development, or guidance of personnel at the graduate level or in management positions. Test questions simulate actual critical reasoning situations that could be encountered in an occupational setting. Examiner required. Suitable for group use.

Timed: Total 1 hour

Scoring: Hand key; may be computer scored

Cost: Administration set (2 booklets, answer sheets, score keys, profile charts, administration cards, manual, user's guide) $150.00

Publisher: Saville & Holdsworth Ltd.

THE CRITICAL THINKING TEST—NUMERICAL REASONING (CTT-ACTI; U.S. VERSION)
Saville & Holdsworth Ltd. Staff

Adult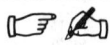

Purpose: Assesses numerical critical reasoning skills in managers and new graduate applicants.

Description: Paper-pencil multiple-choice test measuring understanding and reasoning rather than pure computation. Candidates are required to make decisions or inferences from numerical data presented in a variety of formats. In order to better simulate up-to-date working practices, the use of calculators is permitted. Examiner required. Suitable for group use.

Timed: 35 minutes

Scoring: Hand key; may be computer scored

Cost: 5 booklets $125.00; 25 answer sheets $162.50; scoring key $13.00; administration card $18.00

Publisher: Saville & Holdsworth Ltd.

THE CRITICAL THINKING TEST—VERBAL CRITICAL REASONING (CTT-VCTI; U.S. VERSION)
Saville & Holdsworth Ltd. Staff

Adult

Purpose: Assesses verbal and numerical critical reasoning skills in managers and new graduate applicants.

Description: 92–item paper-pencil multiple-choice test measuring the ability to evaluate the logic of various kinds of argument within a realistic context. Candidates are given a passage of information followed by a series of statements. The candidates must decide whether a given statement is true or untrue or whether there is insufficient information to make the judgment. Examiner required. Suitable for group use.

Timed: 25 minutes

Scoring: Hand key; may be computer scored

Cost: 5 test booklets $125.00; administration card $18.00; 25 answer sheets $162.50; score key $13.00

Publisher: Saville & Holdsworth Ltd.

EMO QUESTIONNAIRE (EMOTIONAL ADJUSTMENT)
George O. Baehr and
Melany E. Baehr

Adult

Purpose: Determines an individual's personal-emotional adjustment. Used to evaluate the potential of sales, managerial, and professional personnel and to screen applicants for jobs requiring efficient performance under pressure.

Description: 140–item paper-pencil examination measuring 10 traditional psychodiagnostic categories (rationalization, inferiority feelings, hostility, depression, fear and anxiety, organic reaction, projection, unreality, sex, withdrawal) and 4 composite adjustment factors (internal, external, somatic, general). The results reflect both the individual's internal psychodynamics and his or her relationship with the external environment. In combination with other instruments, the test has been validated for selection of salespersons, police and security guards, and transit operators. In hospital settings, it is useful as a diagnosis of emotional health and to chart the course of psychotherapy. Basic reading skills are required. Examiner required. Suitable for group use. Available in French.

Untimed: 20–30 minutes

Scoring: Hand key; may be computer scored

Cost: Specimen set $16.00; 25 test booklets $20.00

Publisher: London House, Inc.

THE EMPATHY TEST
Refer to page 1000.

EMPLOYEE APTITUDE SURVEY TEST #6–NUMERICAL REASONING (EAS #6)
Refer to page 878.

EMPLOYEE APTITUDE SURVEY TEST #7–VERBAL REASONING (EAS #7)
Refer to page 879.

EMPLOYEE INVOLVEMENT SURVEY
Jay Hall

Adult

Purpose: Assesses the extent to which employees are provided opportunities for personal involvement and influence at work (i.e., opportunities for making suggestions, decision making, influencing how trips are assigned) by management.

Description: 50–item paper-pencil criterion-referenced instrument in which employees rate their manager's actual practices as well as how frequently employees desire such practices. The survey is a companion to the Participative Management Survey (PMS). The EIS provides feedback to the manager about influence opportunities afforded to employees. Self-administered. Suitable for group use.

Untimed: Varies

Scoring: Self-scored

Cost: $6.95

Publisher: Teleometrics International

EXECUTIVE PROFILE SURVEY (EPS)
Virgil R. Lang

Adult

Purpose: Measures executive potential and identifies individuals likely to succeed. Assesses an organizations' executive strengths and identifies future needs. Used for employee evaluation and placement, screening job applicants, and professional development.

Description: 94–item (61 on a 7–point Likert scale and 33 multiple-choice) paper-pencil test measuring self-attitudes, values, and beliefs of individuals in comparison with over 2,000 top-level executives. Based on a 10–year study of the "executive personality," EPS measures the 11 personality-profile dimensions most important in business, management, and executive settings. The profile dimensions include ambitious, assertive, enthusiastic, creative, spontaneous, self-considerate, open-minded, focused, and systematic traits of the individual. The survey also provides two validity scales. Norms, reliability, validity, and developmental background are explained in "Perspectives on the Executive Personality." Self-administered. Suitable for group use.

Untimed: 1 hour

Scoring: Computer scored

Cost: Introductory kit $31.00

Publisher: Institute for Personality and Ability Testing, Inc.

EXPERIENCE AND BACKGROUND INVENTORY (EBI)
Melany E. Baehr and E.C. Froemel

Adult

Purpose: Evaluates an individual's past performance and experience on 16 factorially determined dimensions of quantified personal background data. Used for selection, promotion, and career counseling of higher level managerial and professional personnel.

Description: 107–item paper-pencil multiple-choice inventory assessing the following background areas: school achievement, choice of a college major, school activities, aspiration level, drive/career progress, leadership and group participation, vocational satisfaction, financial responsibility, husband-wife financial working partnership, general family responsibility, traditional family responsibility, cooperative family responsibility, parental family adjustment, professional-successful parents, job and personal stability, and active relaxation pur-

suits. Different combinations of factors have been validated for selection and evaluation of potential for successful performance in higher level managerial and professional positions. Basic reading skills are required. Self-administered. Suitable for group use.

Untimed: 15–20 minutes

Scoring: Hand key; may be computer scored

Cost: Specimen set $10.00; 25 test booklets $20.00

Publisher: London House, Inc.

GENERAL APTITUDE SERIES (GAS)
Refer to page 885.

GRADUATE AND MANAGERIAL ASSESSMENT
Refer to page 458.

GROUP EXERCISES
Saville & Holdsworth Ltd. Staff

Adult

Purpose: Assesses leadership abilities of potential managers. Used for personnel screening, placement, and development.

Description: Three role-play exercises providing scores on leadership potential, interpersonal sensitivity, and the quality of an individual's contribution to a group situation. The Swedish Visit exercise has candidates plan a visit from members of an associated company. Individuals are to meet specified objectives within a budget. The Amalgamated Baths exercise gives candidates six assigned roles in a medium-small company in which costs must be reduced. The exercise provides a conflict situation and tests numerical abilities. The Jacquie Cosmetics exercise provides a competitive situation requiring understanding of people. Candidates are assigned roles in which each one has to speak for the selection of a management trainee. Examiner required. Suitable for group use.

BRITISH PUBLISHER

Untimed: Varies

Scoring: Examiner evaluated

Cost: Assessor's manual $89.50; initial training fee $945.00; 12 "Swedish Visit" booklets $75.60; 12 "Amalgamated Baths" booklets $75.60; 12 "Jacquie Cosmetics" booklets $75.60; 50 group exercise observation forms $38.00; 50 group exercise rating forms $38.00

Publisher: Saville & Holdsworth Ltd.

HEXAGON TAPS IN-TRAY EXERCISE
Saville & Holdsworth Ltd. Staff

Adult

Purpose: Assesses general managerial ability. Used for personnel screening, placement, and development.

Description: Multiple-item paper-pencil response test assessing organizing, forecasting, decision-making, and written communication skills. The test consists of separately timed exercises based on letters, memos, and other background information found in an in-box. The test simulates aspects of a general manager's job at a small subsidiary of a larger organization. Examiner required. Suitable for group use.
BRITISH PUBLISHER

Untimed: Not available

Scoring: Examiner evaluated

Cost: Administration set (includes initial training fee, assessor's manual, in-tray, exercise booklet, evaluation form) $88.50

Publisher: Saville & Holdsworth Ltd.

HOW SUPERVISE?
Q. W. File and H. H. Remmers

Adult

Purpose: Measures a supervisor's knowledge of human relations in work situations. Used for training, selecting, promoting, and counseling supervisors.

Description: Multiple-item paper-pencil test of beliefs about human relations in business and industry. The subjects indicate whether they believe certain supervisory practices, company policies, and supervisor opinions are desirable or undesirable. Materials include two alternate forms, A and B, dealing with the problems of supervisors. Form M consists of

items from forms A and B that are applicable to higher management levels. Examiner required. Suitable for group use.

Untimed: 40 minutes

Scoring: Hand key

Cost: 25 tests, manual, and key $34.00; key $10.00; manual $12.00 (specify form for each item ordered)

Publisher: The Psychological Corporation

Information and availability unconfirmed; last verified in 1988.

INCENTIVES MANAGEMENT INDEX (IMI)
Refer to page 1081.

IPI APTITUDE—INTELLIGENCE TEST SERIES: FLUENCY
Refer to page 888.

IPI APTITUDE—INTELLIGENCE TEST SERIES: MEMORY
Refer to page 888.

IPI APTITUDE—INTELLIGENCE TEST SERIES: NUMBERS
Refer to page 889.

IPI APTITUDE—INTELLIGENCE TEST SERIES: OFFICE TERMS
Refer to page 889.

IPI APTITUDE—INTELLIGENCE TEST SERIES: PARTS
Refer to page 889.

IPI APTITUDE—INTELLIGENCE TEST SERIES: PERCEPTION
Refer to page 890.

IPI JOB TEST FIELD SERIES: CONTACT CLERK
Refer to page 891.

IPI JOB TEST FIELD SERIES: FACTORY SUPERVISOR
Industrial Psychology International, Ltd.

Adult

Purpose: Assesses skills and personality for supervisory positions in a factory setting. Used to evaluate the achievement and personality of maintenance and production workers, foremen, and superintendents.

Description: Multiple-item paper-pencil battery of eight aptitude and three personality tests. The tests are 16PF, Factory Terms, Parts, NPF, Office Terms, Tools, Numbers, Judgment, CPF, Fluency, and Memory. For individual test descriptions, see the IPI Aptitude-Intelligence Test Series. Examiner required. Suitable for group use. Available in French and Spanish.

Timed: 128 minutes

Scoring: Hand key

Cost: Instruction kit $16.00; test package $10.00

Publisher: Industrial Psychology International, Ltd.

IPI JOB TEST FIELD SERIES: OFFICE SUPERVISOR
Industrial Psychology International, Ltd.

Adult

Purpose: Assesses skills and personality of applicants for supervisory positions in an office setting. Used to screen for the positions of administrator, controller, department head, and vice-president.

Description: Multiple-item paper-pencil battery of seven aptitude and three personality tests. The tests are 16PF, Judgment, Parts, Fluency, Office Terms, Numbers, NPF, CPF, Perception, and Memory. For individual test descriptions, see the IPI Aptitude-Intelligence Test Series. Examiner required. Suitable for group use. Available in French and Spanish.

Timed: 82 minutes

Scoring: Hand key

Cost: Instruction kit $16.00; test packages $10.00

Publisher: Industrial Psychology International, Ltd.

IPI JOB TEST FIELD SERIES: SENIOR CLERK
Refer to page 937.

THE JONES-MOHR LISTENING TEST
John E. Jones and Lawrence Mohr

Adult

Purpose: Provides feedback on listening accuracy. Used for manager and leadership assessment, interviewing, communication skills training, counseling, and family therapy training.

Description: Aurally administered paper-pencil test measuring how well a person understands intended meanings. The subject listens to a tape cassette and responds to test items. The subject then self-scores the items according to taped instructions. A cassette player and a quiet room are required. Self-administered. Suitable for group use.

Timed: 30 minutes

Scoring: Self-scored

Cost: Complete (cassette tape, 25 recording forms A and B, manual) $49.95

Publisher: University Associates, Inc.

KEEGAN TYPE INDICATOR (KTI), FORM B
Warren J. Keegan

Adolescent, adult—Ages 16 and older

Purpose: Assesses an individual's perception, judgment, and attitudes in order to arrive at psychological type. Used in business for management development.

Description: 44–item paper-pencil multiple-choice short-answer and true-false projective test measuring extraversion-introversion, thinking-feeling, and sensation-intuition. The test is based on C.G. Jung's theory of psychological type. Examiner/self-administered. Suitable for group use. Available in Norwegian.

Untimed: 20 minutes
Scoring: Self-scored
Cost: Specimen set (test, manual) $10.00
Publisher: Warren Keegan Associates Press

KIPNIS-SCHMIDT PROFILES OF ORGANIZATIONAL INFLUENCE STRATEGIES: INFLUENCING YOUR SUBORDINATES (POIS: FORM S)
Refer to page 1008.

KIRTON ADAPTION-INNOVATION INVENTORY (KAI)
Refer to page 186.

THE LAKE ST. CLAIR INCIDENT
Refer to page 1008.

LEADERSHIP ABILITY EVALUATION
Russell N. Cassel and
Edward J. Stancik

Adolescent, adult
Grades 9 and above

Purpose: Measures leadership abilities, behavior, and style in adults and high-school students. Used for counseling and self-analysis.

Description: 50–item paper-pencil multiple-choice test consisting of eight pages of leadership-decision problems, each with four possible solutions. Responses reflect specific decision modes or social climate structures and classify decision-making patterns into one of four types: laissez-faire, democratic-cooperative, autocratic-submissive, or autocratic-aggressive. The test was normed on 2,000 individuals; additional norms are provided for 400 outstanding leaders and 100 U.S. Air Force officers. Self-administered. Suitable for group use.
Untimed: 15 minutes
Scoring: Hand key
Cost: Kit (25 tests, manual) $27.50
Publisher: Western Psychological Services

LEADERSHIP OPINION QUESTIONNAIRE (LOQ)
Edwin A. Fleishman

Adult

Purpose: Measures leadership style. Used in a variety of industrial and organizational settings for selection, appraisal, counseling, and training of employees.

Description: 40–item paper-pencil test measuring two aspects of leadership: consideration (how likely an individual's job relationship with subordinates is characterized by mutual trust, respect, and consideration) and structure (how likely an individual is to define and structure personal and subordinates' roles toward goal attainment). Self-administered. Suitable for group use.
Untimed: 10–15 minutes
Scoring: Hand key
Cost: 25 test booklets $33.00; examiner's manual $10.00
Publisher: SRA/London House

MANAGEMENT APPRAISAL SURVEY (MAS)
Jay Hall, Jerry Harvey, and
Martha S. Williams

Adult

Purpose: Assesses an individual's style of management from the subordinates' point of view. Used for management training and development and as a basis for discussion.

Description: Multiple-item paper-pencil inventory assessing subordinates' perceptions of their manager's practices. Analysis is based on the Blake-Mouton managerial grid—a model of management behavior that is an extension of Likert's production-morale theory relating production concerns with people concerns. The inventory provides a total score for each of the five management styles described by the model, as well as scores for each style on four components: philosophy, planning, implementation, and evaluation. The survey may be administered in conjunction with the Styles of Management Inventory to provide a comparison between subordinate ratings and manager self-ratings on the SMI. Normative data are provided. Examiner required. Suitable for group use.

Untimed: Varies

Scoring: Examiner evaluated

Cost: Individual instrument $5.60

Publisher: Teleometrics International

MANAGEMENT BURNOUT SCALE

Refer to page 1009.

===

MANAGEMENT CHANGE INVENTORY

W.J. Reddin and E. Keith Stewart

Adult

Purpose: Measures a manager's knowledge of sound methods of introducing change at a worker and supervisory level. Used before or after training in change techniques.

Description: 80–item paper-pencil true-false test assessing a manager's likelihood to obtain cooperation in support of proposed changes. Topics covered include participation, speed degree of information, training, resistance, and planning. The test emphasizes principles and common sense. Scores are reported in percentiles. Self-administered. Suitable for group use.
CANADIAN PUBLISHER

Untimed: 20–30 minutes

Scoring: Hand key

Cost: Test kit (10 test copies, fact sheet, user's guide) $40.00; cash orders postpaid

Publisher: Organizational Tests (Canada) Ltd.

MANAGEMENT COACHING RELATIONS TEST (MCR)

W.J. Reddin

Adult

Purpose: Measures a manager's knowledge of sound methods of coaching subordinates who may be supervisors or managers. Used before or after a discussion of coaching.

Description: 80–item paper-pencil true-false test measuring knowledge of performance appraisal, effectiveness criteria, coaching interview, and training. Self-administered. Suitable for group use.
CANADIAN PUBLISHER

Untimed: 20–30 minutes

Scoring: Hand key

Cost: Test kit (10 test copies, fact sheet, user's guide) $40.00; cash orders postpaid

Publisher: Organizational Tests (Canada) Ltd.

MANAGEMENT INTEREST INVENTORY (MII)

Saville & Holdsworth Ltd. Staff

Adult

Purpose: Identifies interests related to management functions and skills. Used with managers and other adults from a variety of educational backgrounds for personnel selection, placement, and counseling.

Description: 144–item paper-pencil inventory identifying preferences for a series of 12 management functions and 12 management skills. The management functions inventoried are production operations, technical services, research and development, distribution, sales, personnel and training, finance, administration, purchasing, marketing support, data processing, and legal and secretarial. The management skills inventoried are information collecting, information processing, problem solving, decision making, modeling, communicating orally, communicating in writing, organizing things, organizing people, persuading, developing people, and representing. The inventory also forms part of the Occupational Interest inventories. Self-administered. Suitable for group use.
BRITISH PUBLISHER

Untimed: 30 minutes

Scoring: Hand key; may be computer scored

Cost: Manual and user's guide $38.00; 10 nonreusable booklets $38.00; scoring key $51.00; computer disk (50 administrations) $472.50

Publisher: Saville & Holdsworth Ltd.

MANAGEMENT INVENTORY ON MANAGING CHANGE (MIMC)
Donald L. Kirkpatrick

Adult

Purpose: Measures a manager's attitudes and knowledge in regard to managing change within an organization. Used in conjunction with training programs aimed at teaching managers how to deal with change. Used with all levels of management from first-level supervisors and foremen to top executives.

Description: 65–item paper-pencil inventory measuring attitudes, knowledge, and opinions regarding principles and approaches for managing change. Items 1–50 are statements of beliefs or attitudes concerning organizational change and various ways of implementing such change. Individuals indicate whether they agree or disagree with each statement. Items 51–60 are free-response questions asking for a list of reasons why people might accept or resist change. Items 61–65 are multiple-choice items calling for an assessment of a situation involving change within an organization.

An objective scoring key takes into account that more than one answer may be correct for some of the questions. The answer booklet provides the rationale for answers. Results of the test identify topics that should be emphasized in management training courses, serve as a tool for conference discussions, measure the effectiveness of training programs, provide information for on-the-job coaching, and assist in the selection and promotion of managers. Item content is intended to help managers understand their role in managing change, the reasons why people resist change, the reasons why people accept change, principles for effective management of change, and specific approaches for managing change in their department. A cassette describing in detail how the test can be used most effectively is available. Self-administered. Suitable for group use.

Untimed: 20 minutes

Scoring: Self-scored

Cost: 20 tests and answer booklets $27.00; instructor's manual $1.50

Publisher: Donald L. Kirkpatrick

Information and availability unconfirmed; last verified in 1988.

MANAGEMENT INVENTORY ON MODERN MANAGEMENT (MIMM)
Donald L. Kirkpatrick

Adult

Purpose: Measures philosophy, principles, and approaches related to the effective performance of middle- and upper-level managers. Used to determine need for training, as a tool for conference discussions, to evaluate effectiveness of a training program, provide information for on-the-job coaching, and assist in the selection of managers.

Description: 80–item paper-pencil agree-disagree test of eight topics important to managers: leadership styles, selection and training, communicating, motivating, managing change, delegating, decision making, and managing time. Other available materials include an explanatory cassette, a book on communication, and a communication training kit. Examiner/self-administered. Suitable for group use.

Untimed: 20 minutes

Scoring: Self-scored

Cost: 20 tests and answer booklets $27.00; instruction manual $1.50

Publisher: Donald L. Kirkpatrick

Information and availability unconfirmed; last verified in 1988.

MANAGEMENT INVENTORY ON TIME MANAGEMENT (MITM)
Donald L. Kirkpatrick

Adult

Purpose: Measures a manager's knowledge and attitudes regarding effective management of time. Used in conjunction with training programs on time management.

Description: 60–item paper-pencil two-choice test assessing managers' knowledge of the principles and practices concerning the effective management of time. Test items are statements about time use within an organization. Individuals indicate for each item whether they agree or disagree with the statement. The answer booklet includes the rationale for all correct answers. Test results identify topics that should be emphasized in training programs, serve as a tool for conference discussions, measure the effectiveness of training programs, and provide information for on-the-job coaching. A list of books and films for use in time management training programs is included also. A cassette describing in detail how the test can be used most effectively is available. Self-administered. Suitable for group use.

Untimed: 15 minutes

Scoring: Self-scored

Cost: 20 tests and answer booklets $27.00; instructor's manual $1.50

Publisher: Donald L. Kirkpatrick

Information and availability unconfirmed; last verified in 1988.

MANAGEMENT OF MOTIVES INDEX (MMI)
Jay Hall

Adult

Purpose: Assesses a manager's approach to employee motivation in terms of Maslow's need-hierarchy concept. Used for management training and development and as a basis for discussion.

Description: Multiple-item paper-pencil self-report inventory assessing a manager's theories of what stimulates subordinates, assumptions about why people work, and the approaches to motivation that result from those assumptions. The inventory yields five scores indicating the relative emphasis that managers place on each of Maslow's five need systems to manage others. Normative profiles provide a basis for comparing what managers emphasize with what subordinates say they need. The inventory may be administered in conjunction with the Work Motivation Inventory of subordinates for a more complete assessment of managerial motivational techniques. Self-administered. Suitable for group use.

Untimed: Varies

Scoring: Self-scored

Cost: Individual instrument $4.50

Publisher: Teleometrics International

MANAGEMENT POSITION ANALYSIS TEST (MPAT)
William J. Reddin

Adult

Purpose: Measures a manager's perception of the managing style necessary for and situational demands of a particular job as well as the individual's response to those demands.

Description: 80–item paper-pencil test assessing a manager's perception of the managing style needed for and the situational demands of a particular job. Each item consists of four statements. Examinees circle the two statements that best describe their actions on their current jobs. The test yields a Managerial Style score (bureaucrat, deserter, developer, missionary, benevolent autocrat, autocrat, executive, compromiser) and Dominance (DOM) and Relative Effectiveness (REL EFF) scores for each of 20 situational elements (superior, co-workers, subordinates, staff advisors, union, customers, general public, creativity, objectives, planning, change introduction, implementation, controls, evaluation, productivity, communication, conflict, errors, meetings, teamwork). The test is based on the 3–D Theory of Managerial Effectiveness. Self-administered. Suitable for group use. BRITISH PUBLISHER

Untimed: 1 hour

Scoring: Self-scored

Cost: Contact publisher

Publisher: W. J. Reddin

THE MANAGEMENT PREFERENCE INVENTORY
J.M. Smith

Adult

Purpose: Assesses an individual's liking for and experience with management skills and business functions. Used as a basis for career development counseling.

Description: Multiple-item paper-pencil inventory assessing an individual's preference for and experience in production, distribution, purchasing, sales, marketing, data processing, administration, setting priorities, planning, budgeting, oral and written communication, and arbitration. The instrument may be used to advise individuals with 1 or 2 years of experience who are contemplating specialization within their organization, counsel mid-career managers about their future career development, and advise graduates about initial career choices. Results are used to compare examinees' preferences with actual experience. Examiner/self-administered. Suitable for group use. BRITISH PUBLISHER

Untimed: 20 minutes

Scoring: Hand key

Cost: Contact publisher

Publisher: NFER-NELSON Publishing Company Ltd.

MANAGEMENT READINESS PROFILE (MRP)
London House, Inc.

Adult

Purpose: Evaluates job applicants or employees for managerial interests and basic management orientation.

Description: 188–item paper-pencil multiple-choice test with seven subtests: Management Interests, Leadership, Energy and Drive, Practical Thinking, Management Responsibility, Sociability, and Candidness. Subscale scores and a composite Management Readiness Index is generated.

Three scoring options are available from London House: operator-assisted telephone, Touch-Test, and PC-based. Operator-assisted scoring involves dialing a London House operator who provides test results after being read a tally of responses by the test administrator. Written confirmation is mailed the following day. Touch-Test telephone scoring allows the test administrator to use the telephone keypad to feed response tallies directly into London House computers. Results are available immediately and written con-

firmation is mailed the next day. Administrators with IBM PC or compatible equipment may obtain on-site results using the PC-based scoring method. Examiner required. Suitable for group use.

Untimed: 20 minutes

Scoring: Computer scored

Cost: $7.00–$12.00 based on volume ordered

Publisher: London House, Inc.

MANAGEMENT RELATIONS SURVEY (MRS)
Jay Hall

Adult

Purpose: Measures a manager's communications/employee relations skills from the subordinates' point of view. Used for employee training and development.

Description: Multiple-item paper-pencil inventory providing a manager with feedback from associates and subordinates and allows subordinates to examine their own practices with the manager. The inventory may be administered in conjunction with the Personnel Relations Survey for self-other comparisons of management communication skills and effectiveness. Normative data are provided. Self-administered. Suitable for group use.

Untimed: Varies

Scoring: Self-scored

Cost: Individual instrument $5.60

Publisher: Teleometrics International

MANAGEMENT STYLE DIAGNOSIS TEST
W.J. Reddin

Adult

Purpose: Measures managers and supervisors against the eight styles of the 3–D Theory of Leadership Effectiveness. Used in management and supervisory training seminars.

Description: Multiple-item paper-pencil test in which the manager responds "agree" or "disagree" to descriptive statements of a hypothetical manager's actions. Test scores relate to styles such as deserter, missionary, autocrat, compromiser, bureaucrat, developer, benevolent autocrat, task orientation, relationships orientation, and effectiveness. Self-administered. Suitable for group use. CANADIAN PUBLISHER

Untimed: 20–30 minutes

Scoring: Hand key

Cost: Test kit (10 test copies, fact sheet, user's guide) $40.00; cash orders postpaid

Publisher: Organizational Tests (Canada) Ltd.

MANAGEMENT STYLE INVENTORY
J. Robert Hanson and Harvey F. Silver

Adult—Managers

Purpose: Identifies the management styles of administrators.

Description: 60–item paper-pencil instrument used for profiling an individual's management style, defining decision-making strengths, and identifying skills for development. Individuals relate their profiles to one of four management styles: sensing-thinking (implementor), sensing-feeling (communicator), intuitive-thinking (planner/analyst), and intuitive-feeling (designer, synthesizer, innovator). Detailed descriptions of the four styles are included. Self-administered. Suitable for group use.

Untimed: 30 minutes

Scoring: Self-scored

Cost: $5.00 per copy

Publisher: Hanson, Silver, Strong and Associates, Inc.

Information and availability unconfirmed; last verified in 1987.

MANAGEMENT TRANSACTIONS AUDIT (MTA)
Jay Hall and C. Leo Griffith

Adult

Purpose: Assesses management communications skills in terms of Eric Berne's model of transactional analysis. Used for

employee training and development and as a basis for discussion.

Description: Multiple-item paper-pencil self-report inventory measuring the size of the parent, adult, and child—the three positions from which individuals can communicate according to the model of transactional analysis—in a manager's transactions with subordinates, colleagues, and superiors. The inventory also provides scores for transaction contamination, crossed and complementary transactions, and constructive and disruptive tension. Normative data are provided. Self-administered. Suitable for group use.

Untimed: Varies

Scoring: Self-scored

Cost: Individual instrument $4.50

Publisher: Teleometrics International

MANAGEMENT TRANSACTIONS AUDIT: OTHER
Jay Hall

Adult

Purpose: Assesses how employees view the manager's transactions and interact with the manager.

Description: Multiple-item paper-pencil criterion-referenced instrument which is a companion to the Management Transactions Audit. Self-administered. Suitable for group use.

Untimed: Varies

Scoring: Self-scored

Cost: Contact publisher

Publisher: Teleometrics International

THE MANAGER PROFILE RECORD (MPR)
Richardson, Bellows, Henry and Company, Inc.

Adult

Purpose: Assesses the managerial qualities of employees or applicants. Used for predicting managerial success.

Description: Multiple-item computer-administered predictive inventory indicating the degree to which an individual resembles successful managerial employees in the areas of background and judgment. The test yields 11 separate scores for individuals with more than 10 full years of full-time work experience and 9 separate scores for those with 10 or less years of full-time work experience. Validity data are extensive across organization type, functional area, race, and sex. Self-administered. Suitable for group use.

Untimed: Varies

Scoring: Computer scored

Cost: Contact publisher

Publisher: Richardson, Bellows, Henry and Company, Inc.

MANAGER/SUPERVISOR STAFF SELECTOR

Adult

Purpose: Measures intellectual and personality characteristics of candidates for manager and supervisor positions.

Description: Multiple-item paper-pencil set of seven subtests assessing logic, problem-solving, planning, and conceptualizing skills; numerical skills and reasoning; verbal fluency and communication skills; business judgment and ability to deal with peers; supervisory practices and practical leadership; emotional stability; and people contact skills. The test is used for selecting first- and second-line supervisors for all positions and as a screening test for middle and senior management candidates. Three subtests are timed. Available in Basic, Screening, or Comprehensive versions depending on depth of assessment required. Examiner required. Suitable for group use. Available in French.

Timed/Untimed: 120 minutes

Scoring: Scoring service provided

Cost: $199.00 each

Publisher: Wolfe Personnel Testing and Training Systems, Inc.

MANAGERIAL AND PROFESSIONAL JOB FUNCTIONS INVENTORY (MP-JFI)
Melany E. Baehr,
Wallace G. Lonergan,
and Bruce A. Hunt

Adult

Purpose: Assesses the relative importance of functions performed in higher level managerial and professional positions and the incumbent's ability to perform them. Used to clarify job positions and organizational structure, diagnose individual and group training needs, and classify higher level positions.

Description: Multiple-item paper-pencil inventory assessing the relative importance of job functions in the following 16 categories: setting organizational objectives, financial planning and review, improving work procedures and practices, interdepartmental coordination, developing technical ideas, judgment and decision making, developing teamwork, coping with difficulties and emergencies, promoting safety attitudes and practices, communications, developing employee potential, supervisory practices, self-development and improvement, personnel practices, promoting community-organization relations, and handling outside contacts. Items are rated by incumbent employees for each position. The test also may be used to have incumbents rate their own relative abilities to perform the various job functions. Separate forms are available for rating the importance of the function and for self-rating of the incumbent's abilities. Examiner required. Suitable for group use.

Untimed: 45–60 minutes

Scoring: Hand key; may be machine scored

Cost: Specimen set $12.00; 25 test booklets $20.00

Publisher: London House, Inc.

MANAGERIAL COMPETENCE INDEX—REVISED
Jay Hall

Adult

Purpose: Assesses managerial beliefs, involvement practices, motivation, and interpersonal competence.

Description: 60–item paper-pencil criterion-referenced test consisting of 12 typical management situations. The individual chooses 1 of 5 alternative ways of handling each situation. Answers indicate the individual's personal style of managerial decision-making. Self-administered. Suitable for group use.

Untimed: Varies

Scoring: Self-scored

Cost: $6.95

Publisher: Teleometrics International

MANAGERIAL COMPETENCE REVIEW—REVISED
Refer to page 1009.

MANAGERIAL PHILOSOPHIES SCALE (MPS)
Jacob Jacoby and James Terborg

Adult

Purpose: Evaluates managers in terms of Douglas McGregor's Theory X and Theory Y types of managers. Differentiates between high-, average-, and low-achieving managers.

Description: Multiple-item paper-pencil self-report inventory measuring the degree to which managers adhere to either of two theories concerning the philosophical motivation behind management practice: Theory X and Theory Y. Theory X managers are authoritarian and intent on others' compliance with their commands. Theory Y managers see the potential of satisfaction and self-fulfillment for all who work. The inventory yields scores for both X and Y dimensions. Normative data and interpretive guidelines are provided for purposes of comparison, reflection, and evaluation. The inventory may be used for pre- and posttesting to measure the impact of training intervention programs. Self-administered. Suitable for group use.

Untimed: Varies

Scoring: Self-scored

Cost: Individual instrument $5.60

Publisher: Teleometrics International

MANAGERIAL STYLE QUESTIONNAIRE (MSQ-M) AND (MSQ-S)
Bruce A. Kirchhoff

Adult

Purpose: Evaluates the use of objectives and goals among managers. Identifies managers with goal-related problems. Used for management staff development.

Description: 47–item paper-pencil test measuring the extent to which managers use objectives in performing their managerial duties. Assesses eight dimensions: planning, controlling, coordinating, motivating, appraisal, compensation, personnel selection, and training and developing. Two forms are available: a manager self-evaluation form (MSQ-M) and a form for subordinate evaluation of the manager (MSQ-S). Application is limited to managerial and professional personnel. Self-administered. Suitable for group use. Available in Swedish, Dutch, French, and German.

Untimed: 10–15 minutes

Scoring: Hand key; may be computer scored

Cost: 25 evaluation forms or profiles $45.00; FORTRAN or BASIC computer programs and instructions $185.00; scoring service $22.50

Publisher: BJK Associates

THE OLIVER ORGANIZATION DESCRIPTION QUESTIONNAIRE (OODQ)
John E. Oliver

Adult

Purpose: Evaluates the organizational form of a particular organization.

Description: Multiple-item paper-pencil questionnaire measuring the extent to which four organizational forms exist within a particular organization. The forms are hierarchic (bureaucratic), professional (specialized), task (entrepreneurial), and group (socio-technical). The scoring guide discusses the form of the instrument, the four domains, scoring, potential uses of the scores, development of the instrument, interpretation of individual scores, and interpretation of organization scores. Examiner required. Suitable for group use.

Untimed: Varies

Scoring: Examiner evaluated

Cost: 50 questionnaires $20.00; scoring guide $5.00

Publisher: Organizational Measurement Systems Press

ORGANIZATION HEALTH SURVEY (OHS)
W.J. Reddin

Adult

Purpose: Reveals the attitudes of managers in an organization. Used as a training device or as feedback to top management.

Description: 80–item paper-pencil true-false test providing a separate score on productivity, leadership, organization structure, communication, conflict management, participation, human resource management, and creativity. Self-administered. Suitable for group use.
CANADIAN PUBLISHER

Untimed: 20–30 minutes

Scoring: Hand key

Cost: Test kit (10 test copies, fact sheet, user's guide) $40.00; cash orders postpaid

Publisher: Organizational Tests (Canada) Ltd.

ORGANIZATIONAL COMPETENCE INDEX
Refer to page 1017.

PARTICIPATIVE MANAGEMENT SURVEY
Jay Hall

Adult

Purpose: Assesses the extent to which managers provide opportunities for employee involvement.

Description: 50–item paper-pencil criterion-referenced instrument. Employees respond to each item in terms of actual frequency of use (i.e., how often such an influence opportunity is extended to employees being managed). The items are expressed in behavioral terms (i.e., as actual practices that may or may not be used). The survey yields a Personal Participative Management Profile. The survey is to be used in conjunction with the Employee Involvement Survey. Self-administered. Suitable for group use.

Untimed: Varies

Scoring: Self-scored

Cost: $6.95

Publisher: Teleometrics International

PERSONAL ACHIEVEMENT FORMULA (PAF)
Jay Hall

Adult

Purpose: Assesses managers' overall approach to managing and their organizations' most rewarded practices.

Description: Two paper-pencil value matrices evaluating an individual's managerial strategy and perception of organizational culture: Managerial Strategy Matrix and Organizational Culture Matrix. The instrument is intended to be used with the film "Search for Achievement" in order to personalize the message of the film and the matrix summary reports. Matrix items reflect the dimensions found to distinguish among high, average, and low achieving managers. Self-administered. Suitable for group use.

Untimed: Varies

Scoring: Self-scored

Cost: Contact publisher

Publisher: Teleometrics International

PERSONAL OPINION MATRIX (POM)
Jay Hall

Adult

Purpose: Assesses the overall approach of both manager and organization.

Description: Paper-pencil questionnaire in two parts: Manager's Approach to Management and Job and Workplace. As a companion piece to the Personal Achievement Formula (PAF), the Personal Opinion Matrix (POM) provides feedback for the manager. The POM utilizes the same matrix item pool as the PAF and, when the two are used in tandem, the result in action dynamics enables constructive critique of personal assumptions and practices. Self-administered. Suitable for group use.

Untimed: Varies

Scoring: Self-scored

Cost: $6.95

Publisher: Teleometrics International

PERSONAL RELATIONS SURVEY (PRS)
Jay Hall and Martha S. Williams

Adult

Purpose: Assesses the communications skills of managers. Used for employee training and development.

Description: Multiple-item paper-pencil self-report inventory assessing the communications tendencies of managers in three areas: with employees, with colleagues, and with superiors. Normative data provide a basis for comparison with the "average" manager on both the exposure and feedback dimensions. The inventory may be administered in conjunction with the Management Relations Survey for a more complete assessment of managers' communications skills. Self-administered. Suitable for group use.

Untimed: Varies

Scoring: Self-scored

Cost: Individual instruments $5.60

Publisher: Teleometrics International

PERSONNEL PERFORMANCE PROBLEMS INVENTORY (PPPI)
Albert A. Canfield

Adult

Purpose: Assesses the use of delegation skills at all levels of management. Identifies specific problem-causing elements in the delegation process. Used for manager/supervisor training and development.

Description: 30–item paper-pencil test assessing the effectiveness of a supervisor's delegation relationships in the following areas: mutual understanding of job responsibilities, authority, accountability, results expected, and employment conditions. Each test item describes a common performance problem of subordi-

nates. The supervisor or manager must indicate the extent to which each is a problem with a present employee or group of employees. Test booklets contain complete descriptions of areas for improvement. Norms are provided for supervisors/managers to identify key areas for improvement. A bibliography for additional reading also is included. Self-administered. Suitable for group use.

Untimed: 30 minutes

Scoring: Self-scored

Cost: Kit $25.00

Publisher: Western Psychological Services

POWER MANAGEMENT INVENTORY (PMI)
Jay Hall and James Hawker

Adult

Purpose: Evaluates a manager's use of power. Used for management training and development and as a basis for discussion.

Description: Multiple-item paper-pencil self-report inventory assessing the motivations for power and power styles of managers. The first part of the inventory examines an individual's personal motivations for power, including needs for impact, strength, and influence that guide behavior. The second part of the inventory analyzes how the individual uses power and assesses two bipolar dimensions of power style: autocratic-democratic and permissive-authoritarian. The analysis of individual power dynamics includes assessments of both motive and style, focusing on the interaction between the two. Normative data are provided. The inventory may be administered in conjunction with the Power Management Profile to provide a comparison of the managers' self-ratings with the ratings of their subordinates. Self-administered. Suitable for group use.

Untimed: Varies

Scoring: Self-scored

Cost: Individual instrument $4.50

Publisher: Teleometrics International

POWER MANAGEMENT PROFILE (PMP)
Jay Hall and James Hawker

Adult

Purpose: Evaluates a manager's use of power from the viewpoint of subordinates or associates. Used for management training and development and as a basis for discussion.

Description: Multiple-item paper-pencil inventory assessing a manager's power style and related behaviors as seen by the manager's subordinates or co-workers. Elicits feedback for managers concerning how their approaches to power are viewed by those on the receiving end of their behavior. Analysis of responses provides a structure for after-the-fact discussions with subordinates and develops a statement of the general morale that exists in the workplace as a function of the manager's use of power. Normative data are provided. The inventory may be administered in conjunction with the Power Management Inventory to provide a comparison of managers' self-ratings with those of subordinates. Self-administered. Suitable for group use.

Untimed: Varies

Scoring: Self-scored

Cost: Individual instrument $4.50

Publisher: Teleometrics International

PRESS TEST
Melany E. Baehr and Raymond J. Corsini

Adult

Purpose: Assesses adults' ability to work under pressure by comparing objective measures of reaction time under normal and pressure-filled conditions. Used for career counseling and placement of high-level personnel, especially in occupations where efficiency must be maintained under pressure.

Description: 600–item paper-pencil test measuring speed of reaction to verbal stimuli, color stimuli, and color stimuli under distraction caused by interfering verbal stimuli. For valid results, stop-watch time limits and strict monitoring must be employed in the administration of the test, which is not designed to be completed in the allotted time. Reading skills are not required. The test has been used to select high-level managers, professionals, and airline pilots. Examiner required. Suitable for group use. Can be administered in any language.

Timed: 90 seconds per part

Scoring: Hand key

Cost: Specimen set $10.00; 25 test booklets $22.50

Publisher: London House, Inc.

PRODUCTIVE PRACTICES SURVEY
Jay Hall

Adult

Purpose: Measures the degree to which managers employ practices that research has shown to lead to higher productivity and a healthier work environment.

Description: 72–item paper-pencil criterion-referenced instrument that provides profiles on three dimensions and nine components of competence tied to productivity. Normative data provide a basis for comparison with the "average" manager on all 12 scales. When used in conjunction with the Organizational Competence Index or Competence Analysis, the survey pinpoints how the individual manager influences the conditions necessary for overall organizational productivity. Self-administered. Suitable for group use. Available in Spanish, Swedish, Portuguese, French, and German.

Untimed: Varies

Scoring: Self-scored

Cost: $6.95

Publisher: Teleometrics International

PROFESSIONAL AND MANAGERIAL POSITION QUESTIONNAIRE (PMPQ)
J.L. Mitchell and Ernest J. McCormick

Adult

Purpose: Assesses characteristics of jobs. Used for analysis of professional, managerial, and related positions.

Description: Multiple-item paper-pencil measure of job characteristics. There are five scales: Part-of-the-job, Complexity, Impact, Responsibility, and Special. PMPQ items are divided into three sections: job functions, personal requirements, and other information. The analyst rates each item in terms of its relevance to the job. Special features include numerous computer processing options. Self-administered. Suitable for group use.

Untimed: 30 minutes

Scoring: Examiner evaluated; computer processing available

Cost: Contact publisher

Publisher: Purdue Research Foundation

PROFESSIONAL EMPLOYMENT TEST
Refer to page 978.

PSC-SURVEY L.T. (FOR LENIENCY/TRUST)
Refer to page 1023.

PSC-SURVEY S.A. (FOR SUPERVISORY ATTITUDES)
Mark L. Strand

Adolescent, adult—Ages 16 and older

Purpose: Assesses predisposing attitudes toward work. Assists in pre-employment screening of managers and supervisors.

Description: 60–item (5–subfactor) paper-pencil true-false test covering managers (10 items), being a supervisor (10 items), companies and business (10 items), peers and associates (10 items), and subordinates (20 items). This is one test in the PSC Survey series that is appropriate for beginning and mid-level management positions. The test can be used for new applicants or for screening current employees being considered for advancement. Used in a combination with two or three of the following surveys: Survey-S.A., Survey-L.T., Survey A.D. A

fourth-grade reading level is required. Examiner required. Not suitable for group use.

Untimed: 15 minutes

Scoring: Self-scored; examiner evaluated

Cost: $6.00; volume discount

Publisher: Psychological Surveys Corporation

RETAIL MANAGEMENT ASSESSMENT INVENTORY (RMAI)
London House, Inc.

Adult

Purpose: Assesses managerial potential. Used for selection and screening of candidates for unit operations management and franchise candidates in retail settings.

Description: 242–item paper-pencil multiple-choice test with 10 diagnostic scales yielding scores in Management and Leadership Interest, Management Responsibility, Customer Service, Energy Level, Managerial Arithmetic, Understanding Management Procedures and Practices, Management Orientation, Job Stability, Business Ethics, and Background and Work Experience. Two validity scales, Candidness and Accuracy, are also provided. The Management Potential Index is a unit-weighted composite consisting of the first 10 scales. Examiner must be trained in RMAI administration. Examiner required. Suitable for group use.

Untimed: 1 hour

Scoring: Computer scored; scoring service available from publisher

Cost: Contact publisher (varies according to quantity ordered)

Publisher: London House, Inc.

SELF-ACTUALIZATION INVENTORY (SAI)
Refer to page 1026.

STATION MANAGER APPLICANT INVENTORY (SMAI)
Refer to page 916.

STEIN SURVEY FOR ADMINISTRATORS
Morris I. Stein

Adult

Purpose: Determines a supervisor's or administrator's view of his role in research and development (R & D) organizations. Used to assess the organization from a supervisor's point of view.

Description: 95–item paper-pencil questionnaire measuring an individual's perception of his status and role requirements as a supervisor or administrator working with research and development organizations. The test is restricted to R & D organizations. Self-administered. Suitable for group use.

Untimed: 35 minutes
Scoring: Examiner evaluated
Cost: $2.50 per copy
Publisher: Morris I. Stein

Information and availability unconfirmed; last verified in 1987.

STYLES OF MANAGEMENT INVENTORY (SMI)
Jay Hall, Jerry B. Harvey, and Martha S. Williams

Adult

Purpose: Evaluates an individual's style of management in terms of the assumptions made about the relationship between production concerns and people concerns. Used for management training and development and as a basis for discussion.

Description: Multiple-item paper-pencil self-report inventory assessing styles of management based on the Blake-Mouton managerial grid, a model of management behavior based on Likert's morale-production theory. The inventory yields a total score for each of the five styles described by the Blake-Mouton model, as well as subscores for each style on four components of management: philosophy, planning, implementation, and evaluation. The inventory provides managers with a way of relating their behavior with their on-the-job practices and discovering areas needing change. Normative data

and conversion tables afford personal comparison with both the "average" manager and a theoretical ideal. The inventory may be administered in conjunction with the Management Appraisal Survey for a more complete assessment of management styles. Self-administered. Suitable for group use.

Untimed: Varies
Scoring: Self-scored
Cost: Individual instrument $5.60
Publisher: Teleometrics International

SUPERVISORY CHANGE RELATIONS TEST (SCHR)
W.J. Reddin

Adult

Purpose: Measures a supervisor's knowledge of sound methods of introducing change. Used before or after training in change techniques.

Description: 80–item paper-pencil true-false test measuring a supervisor's understanding of how change can be affected by participation, speed, degree of information, training, resistance, and planning. Suitable for blue- or white-collar supervision. The test is based on chapter 13 of Reddin's book, *Managerial Effectiveness*. Self-administered. Suitable for group use. CANADIAN PUBLISHER

Untimed: 20–30 minutes
Scoring: Hand key
Cost: Test kit (10 test copies, fact sheet, user's guide) $30.00; cash orders postpaid
Publisher: Organizational Tests (Canada) Ltd.

SUPERVISORY COACHING RELATIONS TEST (SCORE)
W.J. Reddin

Adult

Purpose: Measures a supervisor's knowledge of the methods of coaching subordinates. Used before or after coaching training.

Description: 80–item paper-pencil true-false test covering performance appraisal, effectiveness criteria, coaching interview, and training. Suitable for white- or blue-collar supervision. Self-administered. Suitable for group use. CANADIAN PUBLISHER

Untimed: 20–30 minutes

Scoring: Hand key

Cost: Test kit (10 test copies, fact sheet, user's guide) $30.00; cash orders postpaid

Publisher: Organizational Tests (Canada) Ltd.

SUPERVISORY COMMUNICATION RELATIONS TEST (SCOM)
W.J. Reddin

Adult

Purpose: Measures an individual's understanding of sound communication methods. Used before or after coaching training.

Description: 80–item paper-pencil true-false test covering communication with subordinates, co-workers, and superiors. The test also assesses the ability to give orders and introduce change. The test covers verbal and nonverbal communication. Suitable for either blue- or white-collar supervision. Self-administered. Suitable for group use. CANADIAN PUBLISHER

Untimed: 20–30 minutes

Scoring: Hand key

Cost: Test kit (10 test copies, fact sheet, user's guide) $30.00; cash orders postpaid

Publisher: Organizational Tests (Canada) Ltd.

SUPERVISORY HUMAN RELATIONS TEST (SHR)
W.J. Reddin

Adult

Purpose: Measures an individual's attitude toward others. Used before or after instruction in human relations.

Description: 80–item paper-pencil true-false test measuring an individual's at-titude toward superiors, co-workers, and subordinates. The test is not recommend-ed as a test-retest device to discover the effects of training. Suitable for white- or

blue-collar supervision. Self-adminis-tered. Suitable for group use. CANADIAN PUBLISHER

Untimed: 20–30 minutes

Scoring: Hand key

Cost: Test kit (10 test copies, fact sheet, user's guide) $30.00

Publisher: Organizational Tests (Canada) Ltd.

SUPERVISORY INVENTORY ON COMMUNICATION (SIC)
Refer to page 1029.

SUPERVISORY INVENTORY ON HUMAN RELATIONS (SIHR)
Refer to page 1030.

SUPERVISORY INVENTORY ON SAFETY (SIS)
Donald L. Kirkpatrick

Adult

Purpose: Measures supervisors' knowl-edge of basic facts and principles con-cerning on-the-job safety and accident prevention. Used in training courses aimed at increasing job safety and reduc-ing accidents.

Description: 80–item paper-pencil two-choice test assessing knowledge of the principles, facts, and techniques related to safety and accident prevention. Items are related to the job of foreman, super-visor, and manager in industry, business, and government. Test results identify top-ics that should be emphasized in training programs, serve as tools for conference discussions, measure the effectiveness of training programs, provide information for on-the-job coaching, and assist in the selection of supervisory personnel. The inventory was revised in 1980 to include new items based on the Occupational Safety & Health Act and recommenda-tions from safety engineers. Norms are provided for first-level supervisors and foremen, middle- and top-level super-visors, and safety and personnel pro-fessionals. The answer booklet provides a rationale for all correct answers. A cassette describing in detail how the test can be used most effectively is available. Self-administered. Suitable for group use.

Untimed: 20 minutes

Scoring: Self-scored

Cost: 20 tests and answer booklets $27.00; instructor's manual $1.50

Publisher: Donald L. Kirkpatrick

Information and availability unconfirmed; last verified in 1988.

SUPERVISORY JOB DISCIPLINE TEST (SJD)
W.J. Reddin

Adult

Purpose: Determines an individual's knowledge of accepted disciplinary techniques. Used before or after training in disciplinary training techniques.

Description: 80–item paper-pencil true-false test covering lateness, horseplay, appropriate punishments, corrective interview techniques, handling errors, long coffee breaks, visiting other departments, and eating lunch at desk. Suitable for either blue- or white-collar supervision. Self-administered. Suitable for group use. CANADIAN PUBLISHER

Untimed: 20–30 minutes

Scoring: Hand key

Cost: Test kit (10 test copies, fact sheet, user's guide) $30.00; cash orders postpaid

Publisher: Organizational Tests (Canada) Ltd.

SUPERVISORY JOB INSTRUCTION TEST (SJI)
W.J. Reddin

Adult

Purpose: Measures an individual's knowledge of how to instruct others on the job. Used before or after job instruction training.

Description: 80–item paper-pencil true-false test measuring understanding of learning principles, teacher-learner relationships, learning aids, and learning environment. Suitable for either blue- or

white-collar supervision. Self-administered. Suitable for group use. CANADIAN PUBLISHER

Untimed: 20–30 minutes

Scoring: Hand key

Cost: Test kit (10 test copies, fact sheet, user's guide) $30.00; cash orders postpaid

Publisher: Organizational Tests (Canada) Ltd.

SUPERVISORY JOB SAFETY TEST (SJS)
W.J. Reddin

Adult

Purpose: Measures an individual's attitudes toward an understanding of good safety practices. Used before or after safety training.

Description: 80–item paper-pencil true-false test covering safety instruction, safety devices, safety responsibilities, safety causes, corrective practices, work methods, types of accidents, hazard analysis, accident investigation, and role of supervisors. Suitable for either blue- or white-collar supervision. Self-administered. Suitable for group use. CANADIAN PUBLISHER

Untimed: 20–30 minutes

Scoring: Hand key

Cost: Test kit (10 test copies, fact sheet, user's guide) $30.00; cash orders postpaid

Publisher: Organizational Tests (Canada) Ltd.

SUPERVISORY POTENTIAL TEST (SPT)
W.J. Reddin

Adult

Purpose: Measures an individual's understanding of supervisory methods, principles, and techniques. Used as a training tool.

Description: 80–item paper-pencil true-false test covering subordinate evaluation techniques, disciplinary principles, promotion criteria, change introduction, superior relations, new supervisor attachment, and subordinate motivation. Suitable for either blue- or white-collar super-

vision. Self-administered. Suitable for group use.
CANADIAN PUBLISHER

Untimed: 20–30 minutes

Scoring: Hand key

Cost: Test kit (10 test copies, fact sheet, user's guide) $30.00; cash orders postpaid

Publisher: Organizational Tests (Canada) Ltd.

SUPERVISORY PRACTICES INVENTORY (SPI)
Judith S. Canfield and Albert A. Canfield

Adult

Purpose: Evaluates how an individual prefers to be supervised, how the individual's supervisor actually functions, and the difference between preferred and actual supervisory behaviors. Identifies areas in which to reduce "stress points" in supervisor/subordinate working relationships.

Description: 20–item paper-pencil inventory assessing a subordinate's view of 10 areas of supervisory behavior: setting objectives, planning, organization, delegation, problem identification, decision making, performance evaluation, subordinate development, team building, and conflict resolution. The test items consist of a list of supervisory behaviors, which the subordinate must rank first in order of personal preference and second to indicate how his supervisor actually functions. Questions measure supervisory behavior rather than trait or personality characteristics. Dissonance scores are developed from the difference between preferred and actual rankings. Test booklets include explanations of the scales and possible interpretations. Norms are available for supervisors/managers from diverse organizations. Self-administered. Suitable for group use.

Untimed: 20–40 minutes

Scoring: Self-scored

Cost: Kit (forms, manual) $26.75

Publisher: Western Psychological Services

SUPERVISORY PRACTICES TEST (REVISED)
Martin M. Bruce

Adult

Purpose: Evaluates supervisory ability and potential in a business-world setting. Used for personnel selection, evaluation, and training.

Description: 50–item paper-pencil multiple-choice test indicating the extent to which the subject is able to choose a desirable course of action (as compared with the perceptions and attitudes of managers and subordinates) when presented with a business decision. Minority group data are available. Self-administered. Suitable for group use. Available in French, Spanish, and German.

Untimed: 20 minutes

Scoring: Hand key

Cost: Manual $12.50; key $1.95; manual supplement (1984) $15.50; package of tests $39.50; specimen set $32.50

Publisher: Martin M. Bruce, Ph.D., Publishers

SUPERVISORY PROFILE RECORD (SPR)
Richardson, Bellows, Henry and Company, Inc.

Adult

Purpose: Assesses qualities related to successful first-line supervision.

Description: Multiple-item paper-pencil or computer-administered questionnaire system designed for predicting an individual's potential for success as a first-line supervisor. The Supervisory Profile Record Report yields information in the areas of background (present self-concept evaluation and present work-values orientation) and judgment (employee communication-motivation, employee training-evaluation, problem resolution, disciplinary practices, and general style-practices). Validity data are extensive across functions, organization types, race, and sex. Self-administered. Suitable for group use.

Untimed: Varies

Scoring: Computer scored

Cost: Contact publisher

Publisher: Richardson, Bellows, Henry and Company, Inc.

SUPERVISORY UNION RELATIONS TEST (SUR)
W.J. Reddin

Adult

Purpose: Measures a supervisor's attitudes toward unions. Used to evaluate supervisors' and managers' attitudes.

Description: 80–item paper-pencil true-false test covering motives of union leadership, the reasons people join unions, effective methods for working with unions, management rights, role of shop steward, foreman-union relationship, labor benefits, and company benefits. Respondents answer on the basis of what they believe is best for their position or company at the present time. Suitable for either blue- or white-collar supervision. Self-administered. Suitable for group use. CANADIAN PUBLISHER

Untimed: 20–30 minutes

Scoring: Hand key

Cost: Test kit (10 test copies, fact sheet, user's guide) $30.00; cash orders postpaid

Publisher: Organizational Tests (Canada) Ltd.

SURVEY OF MANAGEMENT PRACTICES
Jay Hall

Adult

Purpose: Assesses the productivity of a manager's practices.

Description: 72–item paper-pencil criterion-referenced test addressing some of the specific behaviors that a manager may or may not engage in. Two sets of ratings are used: ACTUAL, employee's assessment of current managerial practices; and DESIRED, employee's assessment of how often the employees would like for the manager to use a practice. The test uses a 9–point scale ranging from 1 (never) to 9 (always) for each set of rat-

ings. This test is a companion to the Productive Practices Survey. Self-administered. Suitable for group use.

Untimed: Varies

Scoring: Self-scored

Cost: $6.95

Publisher: Teleometrics International

TEMPERAMENT COMPARATOR
Melany E. Baehr

Adult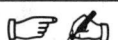

Purpose: Determines the relatively permanent temperament traits characteristic of an individual's behavior. Used to evaluate the potential of sales and of higher-level managerial and professional personnel and for job screening and vocational counseling.

Description: 153–item paper-pencil test consisting of trait pairs derived from the application of a paired comparison technique to 18 individual traits. Emphasis is on individual variations in significant dimensions within the "normal" range of behavior. The factors measured are the 18 individual traits and five factorially-determined behavior factors: extroversive vs. reserved, emotionally responsive vs. emotionally controlled, self-reliant/individually oriented vs. dependent/group oriented, excitable vs. placid, and socially oriented vs. not socially oriented. The test provides a measure of internal consistency of response. Basic reading skills are required. Examiner required. Suitable for group use.

Untimed: 20–30 minutes

Scoring: Hand key; may be computer scored

Cost: Specimen set $12.00; 25 test booklets $20.00

Publisher: London House, Inc.

TEST OF PRACTICAL JUDGMENT—FORM 62
Alfred J. Cardall

Adult

Purpose: Determines employee ability to use practical judgment in solving problems. Used to screen for management and sales positions.

Description: Multiple-item paper-pencil multiple-choice test of judgment factors that may be used in conjunction with intelligence testing. The test also may be used for screening and for selection and placement of individuals whose work involves thinking, planning, or getting along with people. The test examines such factors as empathy, drive, and social maturity. Materials include five tests, a key, and a manual. Examiner required. Suitable for group use. Available in French.
CANADIAN PUBLISHER
Untimed: 30 minutes
Scoring: Hand key
Cost: Contact publisher
Publisher: Institute of Psychological Research, Inc.

VALUES INVENTORY (VI)
W.J. Reddin

Adolescent, adult

Purpose: Reveals a manager's value system. Used in college and industry.

Description: Multiple-item paper-pencil test consisting of quotations from which the manager chooses preferred statements. The values tested are theoretical, power, effectiveness, achievement, human, industry, and profit. Self-administered. Suitable for group use.
CANADIAN PUBLISHER
Untimed: 20–30 minutes
Scoring: Hand key
Cost: Test kit (10 test copies, fact sheet, user's guide) $40.00; cash orders postpaid
Publisher: Organizational Tests (Canada) Ltd.

WESMAN PERSONNEL CLASSIFICATION TEST (PCT)
Refer to page 926.

WORK MOTIVATION INVENTORY (WMI)
Refer to page 1038.

X-Y-Z INVENTORY
W.J. Reddin

Adult

Purpose: Reveals a manager's basic, underlying, philosophical assumptions about man. Used in business to help understand a manager's frame-of-reference in assessing employees' performances.

Description: Multiple-item paper-pencil inventory revealing some elements of a manager's assumptions that man is a beast (X), a self-actualizing being (Y), or a rational being (Z). The test is used prior to discussion of X, Y, and Z theories. Self-administered. Suitable for group use.
CANADIAN PUBLISHER
Untimed: 20–30 minutes
Scoring: Hand key
Cost: Test kit (10 test copies, fact sheet, user's guide) $40.00; cash orders postpaid
Publisher: Organizational Tests (Canada) Ltd.

Mechanical Abilities and Manual Dexterity

ACER MECHANICAL COMPREHENSION TEST

Adolescent, adult—Ages 13.6 and older

Purpose: Measures mechanical aptitude. Used for employee selection and placement for positions requiring some degree of mechanical aptitude.

Description: 45–item paper-pencil multiple-choice test consisting of problems in the form of diagrams that illustrate various mechanical principles and mechanisms. Australian norms are provided for various age groups, university and technical college groups, and national service trainees and applicants for apprenticeships. Materials include a reusable booklet, separate answer sheet, scoring

key, manual, and specimen set. Examiner required. Suitable for group use.
AUSTRALIAN PUBLISHER

Timed: 30 minutes

Scoring: Hand key; may be computer scored

Cost: Contact publisher

Publisher: The Australian Council for Educational Research Limited

ACER MECHANICAL REASONING TEST (REVISED EDITION)

Adolescent, adult—Ages 15 and older

Purpose: Measures basic mechanical reasoning abilities. Used for employee selection and placement for positions requiring some degree of mechanical aptitude.

Description: Multiple-item paper-pencil multiple-choice test consisting of problems in the form of diagrams that illustrate various mechanical principles and mechanisms. This test is a shortened version of the ACER Mechanical Comprehension Test and contains some different items and less verbal content. Australian norms are provided for apprenticeship applicants for a variety of trades and for apprentices beginning training. Materials include a reusable booklet, answer sheet, score key, manual, and specimen set. Examiner required. Suitable for group use.
AUSTRALIAN PUBLISHER

Timed: 20 minutes

Scoring: Hand key; may be machine scored

Cost: Contact publisher

Publisher: The Australian Council for Educational Research Limited

BENNETT MECHANICAL COMPREHENSION TEST (BMCT)
G.K. Bennett et al.

Adult

Purpose: Measures ability to understand mechanical relationships and physical laws in practical situations. Used to screen job applicants for positions requiring practical application of mechanical principles, complex machine operation, and repair.

Description: Multiple-item paper-pencil multiple-choice test assessing understanding of mechanical relationships. Materials include two equivalent forms, S and T. Tape recordings of the test questions read aloud are available for applicants with limited reading skills. Examiner required. Suitable for group use.

Timed: 30 minutes

Scoring: Hand key; may be machine scored locally

Cost: Specimen set (includes tests, answer document for both forms, manual) $38.00; 25 tests $69.00; 50 answer documents $34.00; key (specify S or T) $14.00; manual $15.00; tape recording (specify reel-to-reel or cassette) $59.00

Publisher: The Psychological Corporation

Information and availability unconfirmed; last verified in 1988.

CARD SORTING BOX

Adult

Purpose: Measures progress in motor learning where it is necessary to rapidly recognize materials and quickly coordinate visual discrimination with hand movements.

Description: Multiple-item task-performance test consisting of a 15–hole sorting box and 10 sets of 15 cards each. The individual is provided with the sorting box, a set of cards, and sorting instructions. The individual must place each card in the proper pigeon-hole. Problems of inhibition and facilitation can be studied by changing the pattern for appropriate pigeon-holes for given cards. Once the cards have been sorted, the backless sorting apparatus may be lifted and the cards readily picked up in packs for counting. An extra supply of numbers for forming a second scoring key is provided. These numbers may be attached to the back of the three wood strips forming the first scoring key. Examiner required. Not suitable for group use.

Timed: Varies

Scoring: Examiner evaluated

Cost: Test kit (sorting box, 150 cards, random scoring key) $125.00

Publisher: Lafayette Instrument Company, Inc.

CLOSURE FLEXIBILITY (CONCEALED FIGURES)
L.L. Thurstone and T.E. Jeffrey

Adolescent, adult

Purpose: Measures the ability to hold a configuration in mind despite distracting irrelevancies as indicated by identification of a given figure "hidden" or embedded in a larger, more complex drawing. Used for vocational counseling and selection of technical specialist personnel in the engineering, computer science, and other physical science disciplines.

Description: 49–item paper-pencil instrument measuring visual and space perception skills. Each item consists of a figure, presented on the left of the page, followed by a row of four more complex drawings. The subject must indicate whether the figure appears or does not appear in each of the drawings. Examiner required. Suitable for group use.

Timed: 10 minutes

Scoring: Hand key; may be computer scored

Cost: Specimen set $10.00; 25 test booklets $20.00

Publisher: London House, Inc.

CRAWFORD SMALL PARTS DEXTERITY TEST (CSPDT)
John Crawford

Adolescent, adult

Purpose: Measures fine-motor dexterity and eye-hand coordination. Used for selecting applicants for such jobs as engravers, watch repairers, and telephone installers.

Description: Two-part performance measure of dexterity. Part 1 measures dexterity in using tweezers to assemble pins and collars. Part 2 measures dexterity in screwing small screws with a screwdriver after placing them in threaded holes. The test may be administered in two ways. In the work-limit method, the subject completes the task and the total time is the score. Using the time-limit procedure, the score is the amount of work completed during a specified time. Materials include an assembly plate, pins, collars, and screws. Examiner required. Suitable for group use.

Timed: 10–15 minutes

Scoring: Examiner evaluated

Cost: Complete set (manual, spare parts) $350.00; manual $20.00

Publisher: The Psychological Corporation

Information and availability unconfirmed; last verified in 1988.

CURTIS SPATIAL TESTS: OBJECT COMPLETION TEST AND SPACE-FORM TEST
James W. Curtis

Adult

Purpose: Assesses perceptual efficiency. Used for screening applicants for jobs requiring manual skills.

Description: Two paper-pencil tests of perceptual efficiency. One test is two-dimensional and one is three-dimensional. The tests may be used in conjunction with Holmes' One Minute Per-Flu-Dex Tests for screening of factory aptitudes. Examiner required. Suitable for group use.

Timed: 1 minute per test

Scoring: Hand key

Cost: Specimen set $4.00; 25 tests (specify form) $3.50

Publisher: Psychometric Affiliates

EMPLOYEE APTITUDE SURVEY TEST #9–MANUAL SPEED AND ACCURACY (EAS #9)
Refer to page 879.

HAND-TOOL DEXTERITY TEST
G.K. Bennett

Adult

Purpose: Measures manipulative skill in using ordinary mechanic's tools, wrenches, and screwdrivers. Used in selecting applicants for mechanical and industrial jobs.

Description: Task test of mechanical skill in which the subject takes apart 12 assemblies of nuts, bolts, and washers from a wooden frame according to a prescribed sequence and then reassembles them. The score is the time required to perform the tasks. Materials include a wooden frame, nuts, bolts, washers, and tools. Examiner required. Not suitable for group use.

Timed: 7 minutes

Scoring: Score obtained by timing

Cost: Complete set (includes manual) $350.00; manual $20.00

Publisher: The Psychological Corporation

Information and availability unconfirmed; last verified in 1988.

INTUITIVE MECHANICS (WEIGHTS AND PULLEYS)
L.L. Thurstone and T.E. Jeffrey

Adolescent, adult

Purpose: Measures ability to understand mechanical relationships and to visualize internal movement in a mechanical system. Used for vocational counseling or for selection in positions requiring mechanical interest and experience.

Description: 32–item paper-pencil test in which each item is a drawing that represents a system of weights and pulleys. For each system, the examinee must determine whether the system is stable (will not produce movement) or unstable (will produce movement). Examiner required. Suitable for group use.

Timed: 3 minutes

Scoring: Hand key

Cost: Specimen set $8.00; 25 test booklets $20.00

Publisher: London House, Inc.

IPI APTITUDE—INTELLIGENCE TEST SERIES: DEXTERITY
Refer to page 887.

IPI APTITUDE—INTELLIGENCE TEST SERIES: MOTOR
Refer to page 889.

IPI APTITUDE—INTELLIGENCE TEST SERIES: TOOLS
Refer to page 890.

IPI JOB TEST FIELD SERIES: SEMI-SKILLED WORKER
Refer to page 893.

IPI JOB TEST FIELD SERIES: SKILLED WORKER
Refer to page 893.

IPI JOB TEST FIELD SERIES: UNSKILLED WORKER
Refer to page 894.

MANUAL DEXTERITY TEST
E.I.T.S. Staff

Adult

Purpose: Measures manual dexterity as a skill needed in assembly and packaging tasks. Used for personnel placement and selection.

Description: Multiple-item paper-pencil test consisting of one subtest in manual speed and one in manual skill. Materials include booklets, the specimen set, and the manual. Examiner required. Suitable for group use.
BRITISH PUBLISHER

Timed: Part I 45 seconds; Part II 90 seconds

Scoring: Examiner evaluated

Cost: Contact publisher

Publisher: Educational and Industrial Test Services Ltd.

MECHANICAL ABILITY TEST
J.R. Morrisby

Ages 11–adult

Purpose: Measures natural mechanical aptitude, not learned knowledge, in adults. Used to predict potential in most areas of engineering, especially electrical and mechanical; assembly work; carpentry; and building trades.

Description: 35–item paper-pencil test in which each item consists of an illustrated mechanical principle and a question with five alternative answers. A knowledge of theoretical physics is not required since the test is not intended to measure the level of mechanical knowledge the subject has attained. Materials include the booklet, manual, specimen set, answer sheets, and scoring key. The test is restricted to examiners who provide evidence of adequate training and practical experience in the use of such tests. Examiner required. Suitable for group use.
BRITISH PUBLISHER

Timed: 15 minutes

Scoring: Hand key; examiner evaluated; may be computer scored

Cost: Contact publisher

Publisher: Educational and Industrial Test Services Ltd.

MECHANICAL MOVEMENTS
L.L. Thurstone and T.E. Jeffrey

Adolescent, adult

Purpose: Determines degree of mechanical interest and experience. Used for vocational counseling and to select persons for mechanical occupations in industry.

Description: 38–item paper-pencil multiple-choice measure of mechanical comprehension indicating the ability to visualize a mechanical system in which there is internal movement or displacement of the parts. Basic reading skills are required. Examiner required. Suitable for group use.

Timed: 14 minutes

Scoring: Hand key

Cost: Specimen set $8.00; 25 test booklets $20.00

Publisher: London House, Inc.

MINNESOTA MANUAL DEXTERITY TEST

Adolescent, adult—Ages 13 and older

Purpose: Measures an individual's capacity for the kind of rapid, simple hand-eye coordination needed for such semiskilled shop and clerical operations as wrapping, sorting, and packing.

Description: Two-phase nonverbal manual dexterity test measuring rate of hand movement and finger manipulation. Materials consist of a board with 58 holes $1\frac{3}{8}''$ in diameter spaced $2\frac{1}{4}''$ apart, arranged in four rows containing 58 round pegs painted red on one side and black on the other. In the placing test, the taker is presented with the empty board and asked to transfer the pegs, presented same color up, back to the board using only one hand. In the turning test, the pegs are left in the board and the taker removes each peg one at a time with one hand, turns it over, transfers it to the other hand, and replaces it in the same position on the board until all pegs have been turned. Both tests are timed for four complete trials. Examiner required. Suitable for group use.

Untimed: 6–10 minutes

Scoring: Hand key

Cost: Complete test (Model 32023) $150.00; replacement wooden cylinder (Model 32031) $2.25 each; 50 record blanks (Model 32032) $10.00

Publisher: Lafayette Instrument Company, Inc.

MINNESOTA RATE OF MANIPULATION TESTS
Employment Stabilization Research Institute, University of Minnesota

Adult

Purpose: Measures finger-hand-arm dexterity. Used for employee selection for jobs requiring manual dexterity and in vocational and rehabilitation training programs.

Description: Five-test battery measuring manual dexterity. The five tests are The

Placing Test, The Turning Test, The Displacing Test, The One-Hand Turning and Placing Test, and The Two-Hand Turning and Placing Test. Materials consist of two test boards and 60 round blocks. Each test board contains 60 round holes in four rows, and each block is painted orange on the upper half and yellow on the lower half. In each of the tests, the blocks are manipulated in prescribed ways that require finger movement and hand-and-arm movement. Specific tests assess movements with the preferred hand and with both hands. The five tests may be administered separately. All tests are repeated for four complete trials. The Displacing and Turning tests are suitable for use with the blind. The board, blocks, 50 individual record forms, and a manual are included in a vinyl carrying case. Examiner required. Not suitable for group use.

Timed: 10 minutes or less for each test

Scoring: Examiner evaluated

Cost: Complete kit $249.00

Publisher: American Guidance Service

MINNESOTA SPATIAL RELATIONS TEST
Refer to page 614.

NATIONAL INSTITUTE FOR AUTOMOTIVE SERVICE EXCELLENCE (ASE) TESTS
Refer to page 900.

NATIONAL INSTITUTE FOR AUTOMOTIVE SERVICE EXCELLENCE (ASE) TESTS: AUTOMOBILE TESTS: AUTOMATIC TRANSMISSION/ TRANSAXLE
Refer to page 901.

NATIONAL INSTITUTE FOR AUTOMOTIVE SERVICE EXCELLENCE (ASE) TESTS: AUTOMOBILE TESTS: BRAKES
Refer to page 901.

NATIONAL INSTITUTE FOR AUTOMOTIVE SERVICE EXCELLENCE (ASE) TESTS: AUTOMOBILE TESTS: ELECTRICAL SYSTEMS
Refer to page 901.

NATIONAL INSTITUTE FOR AUTOMOTIVE SERVICE EXCELLENCE (ASE) TESTS: AUTOMOBILE TESTS: ENGINE PERFORMANCE
Refer to page 901.

NATIONAL INSTITUTE FOR AUTOMOTIVE SERVICE EXCELLENCE (ASE) TESTS: AUTOMOBILE TESTS: ENGINE REPAIR
Refer to page 902.

NATIONAL INSTITUTE FOR AUTOMOTIVE SERVICE EXCELLENCE (ASE) TESTS: AUTOMOBILE TESTS: HEATING AND AIR CONDITIONING
Refer to page 902.

NATIONAL INSTITUTE FOR AUTOMOTIVE SERVICE EXCELLENCE (ASE) TESTS: AUTOMOBILE TESTS: MANUAL DRIVE TRAIN AND AXLES
Refer to page 902.

NATIONAL INSTITUTE FOR AUTOMOTIVE SERVICE EXCELLENCE (ASE) TESTS: AUTOMOBILE TESTS: SUSPENSION AND STEERING
Refer to page 903.

NATIONAL INSTITUTE FOR AUTOMOTIVE SERVICE EXCELLENCE (ASE) TESTS: BODY REPAIR—PAINTING/ REFINISHING TESTS: BODY REPAIR
Refer to page 903.

NATIONAL INSTITUTE FOR AUTOMOTIVE SERVICE EXCELLENCE (ASE) TESTS: BODY REPAIR—PAINTING/ REFINISHING TESTS: PAINTING AND REFINISHING

Refer to page 903.

NATIONAL INSTITUTE FOR AUTOMOTIVE SERVICE EXCELLENCE (ASE) TESTS: HEAVY-DUTY TRUCK TESTS: BRAKES

Refer to page 904.

NATIONAL INSTITUTE FOR AUTOMOTIVE SERVICE EXCELLENCE (ASE): HEAVY-DUTY TRUCK TESTS: DIESEL ENGINES

Refer to page 904.

NATIONAL INSTITUTE FOR AUTOMOTIVE SERVICE EXCELLENCE (ASE) TESTS: HEAVY-DUTY TRUCK TESTS: ELECTRICAL SYSTEMS

Refer to page 904.

NATIONAL INSTITUTE FOR AUTOMOTIVE SERVICE EXCELLENCE (ASE) TESTS: HEAVY-DUTY TRUCK TESTS: GASOLINE ENGINES

Refer to page 904.

NATIONAL INSTITUTE FOR AUTOMOTIVE SERVICE EXCELLENCE (ASE) TESTS: HEAVY-DUTY TRUCK TESTS: SUSPENSION AND STEERING

Refer to page 905.

O'CONNOR FINGER DEXTERITY TEST

Johnson O'Connor

Adult

Purpose: Measures finger dexterity. Used to determine individual aptitude for small assembly jobs requiring rapid hand work.

Description: Multiple-operation manual test using an 11″ x 5½″ board containing a shallow well, 100 ³⁄₁₆″ holes (arranged in 10 rows), and a set of 300 pins. The individual places three pins in each hole. The time required to fill the first 50 holes and the second 50 holes are recorded separately. The test helps predict success in the assembly of armatures, miniature parts, clocks, watches; the filling of vials; and small lathe and machine work. Examiner required. Suitable for group use.

Untimed: 8–16 minutes

Scoring: Hand key; examiner evaluated

Cost: Complete $65.75; 310 replacement pins $21.75

Publisher: Stoelting Co.

O'CONNOR TWEEZER DEXTERITY TEST

Johnson O'Connor

Adolescent, adult—Ages 14 and older

Purpose: Measures fine eye-hand coordination and the ability to use small hand tools precisely and steadily. Used to identify vocational aptitude.

Description: Multiple-operation manual test using an 11″ x 5½″ board containing a shallow well, 100 small holes (arranged in 10 rows), and 100 one-inch pins. The individual places a pin in each of the holes using only small tweezers. The total elapsed time is recorded. A high score indicates an aptitude for tasks involving the use of small hand tools (e.g., forceps, needle-nose pliers, and tweezers) used by laboratory workers, medical personnel, watch repairers, and stamp collectors. Examiner required. Suitable for group use.

Untimed: 8–10 minutes

Scoring: Hand key; examiner evaluated

Cost: Complete $65.75; 105 replacement pins $13.50

Publisher: Stoelting Co.

O'CONNOR WIGGLY BLOCK
Johnson O'Connor

Adult

Purpose: Measures ability to visualize structured design and three-dimensional space. Assesses aptitudes associated with machinists, tool and die makers, draftsmen, engineers, and architects.

Description: Task-assessment test measuring an individual's ability to visualize a completed project from the disassembled pieces. The test consists of assembling a 10″ x 6″ x 6″ wooden block, which has been cut on two planes into nine irregular pieces. The subject assembles the block three times. The average time for the three trials is recorded. Examiner required. Suitable for group use.

Untimed: 15–30 minutes

Scoring: Hand key

Cost: Complete test (Model 32024) $105.00; package of 50 record blanks (Model 32030) $5.00

Publisher: Lafayette Instrument Company, Inc.

PENNSYLVANIA BI-MANUAL WORKSAMPLE
John R. Roberts

Adolescent, adult—Ages 16 and older

Purpose: Measures manual dexterity and eye-hand coordination. Used for employee placement.

Description: Multiple-operation manual dexterity test utilizing an 8″ x 24″ board containing 100 holes arranged in 10 rows and a set of nuts and bolts to test finger dexterity of both hands, whole movement of both arms, eye-hand coordination, and bi-manual coordination. The employee grasps a nut between the thumb and index finger of one hand and a bolt between the thumb and index finger of the other hand, turns the bolt into the nut, and places both in a hole in the board. Twenty practice motions are allowed, and 80 motions are timed. Disassembly reverses the process and involves timing 100 motions. As many as

four people can be tested simultaneously, provided each person has a separate board. Assembly and disassembly times can be converted to percentile ranks and standard scores. A special supplement contains directions for administering the test to blind employees. Materials include the board, nuts and bolts, 50 record forms, and a vinyl carrying case. Examiner required. Suitable for group use.

Timed: 12 minutes

Scoring: Examiner evaluated

Cost: Complete kit $145.00

Publisher: American Guidance Service

PRIMARY MECHANICAL ABILITY TEST
Jack Harris Hazlehurst and Stevens, Thurow and Associates

Adult

Purpose: Measures mechanical aptitude. Used to select and classify shop personnel from highly skilled engineers, draftsmen, and machinists to relatively unskilled workers and apprentices.

Description: 119–item paper-pencil multiple-choice test in four parts. Each part measures a separate aspect of mechanical aptitude: size discrimination, space perception, tool knowledge, and visualization. The manual provides technical data, instructions for administering and scoring, and norms. Examiner required. Suitable for group use.

Timed: 22 minutes

Scoring: Hand key

Cost: 25 batteries $25.00; manual $5.00

Publisher: Stevens, Thurow and Associates

PURDUE PEGBOARD TEST
Developed by Purdue Research Foundation under the direction of Joseph Tiffin

Adult

Purpose: Measures hand-finger-arm dexterity required for certain types of manual work. Used in the selection of business and industrial personnel.

Description: Multiple-operation manual test of gross- and fine-motor movements of hands, fingers, arms, and tip of fingers. The test measures the dexterity needed in assembly work, electronic production work, and similarly related jobs. Materials consist of a test board with two vertical rows of holes and four storage wells holding 50 pegs, 40 washers, and 20 collars. To test the right hand, the subject inserts as many pegs as possible in the holes, starting at the top of the right hand row. The test for the left hand uses the left row, moving top to bottom. Finally, both hands are used together to fill both rows top to bottom. In the Assembly Test, the subject picks up a peg with the right hand, inserts it in the top right hole, places a washer over the peg with the left hand, then places a collar with the right hand, and finally places a second washer with the left hand. This procedure constitutes one assembly. The subject must complete as many assemblies as possible in the allotted time. Norms are available for disabled individuals. Examiner required. Suitable for group use.

Timed: 5–10 minutes

Scoring: Hand key

Cost: Complete (board, manual) $188.00; 100 profiles $46.00; complete replacement set (pegs, washers, collars) $50.00; manual $10.00

Publisher: SRA/London House

PYRAMID PUZZLE

Adult

Purpose: Measures motor-learning and problem-solving abilities.

Description: Multiple-item task-performance test assessing problem solving, insight learning, and concept formation. The task involves placing a series of graduated blocks on one of three posts such that a larger block is never placed over a smaller block. Average solution time is about 20 minutes for the first trial. Repeated trials with the same individual will produce successively shorter solution times. Examiner required. Suitable for group use.

Timed: Varies

Scoring: Examiner evaluated

Cost: Test kit Model 20013 (test board with three posts, set of graduated blocks) $32.00

Publisher: Lafayette Instrument Company, Inc.

THE RBH ARITHMETIC REASONING TEST, FORMS I AND II

Refer to page 909.

RC TECHNICIAN MECHANICAL TEST
Ramsay Corporation

Adult

Purpose: Measures knowledge and skills in mechanical areas such as hydraulics, pneumatics, print reading, pumps, and welding.

Description: 124–item paper-pencil multiple-choice test covering hydraulics (15 items); pneumatics (7 items); print reading (7 items); welding (17 items); power transmission (16 items); lubrication (5 items); pumps (12 items); piping (12 items); rigging (7 items); mechanical maintenance (11 items); and shop machines, tools, and equipment (15 items). A machine-scoring service is available from the publisher. Examiner required. Suitable for group use.

Untimed: 2 hours

Scoring: Hand key; may be machine scored

Cost: Kit $498.00 (10 test booklets, 100 answer sheets, scoring key, 1 test manual)

Publisher: Ramsay Corporation

REVISED MINNESOTA PAPER FORM BOARD TEST
Rensis Likert and W.H. Quasha

Adolescent, adult

Purpose: Measures ability to visualize and manipulate objects in space. Used to select applicants for jobs requiring mechanical-spatial ability.

Description: Multiple-item paper-pencil test of spatial perception. The applicant is required to visualize the assembly of two-dimensional geometric shapes into a

---

whole design. The test is related to both mechanical and artistic ability. Two equivalent forms, AA and BB (hand scoring) and MA and MB (machine scoring), are available. Examiner required. Suitable for group use. Available in French-Canadian.

Timed: 20 minutes

Scoring: Hand key; may be machine scored locally

Cost: 1 test booklet for both forms, manual $21.00; 25 test booklets, manual, key (Forms AA and BB) $34.00; 25 test booklets, separate answer documents $43.00; IBM 805 answer documents for Form MA or MB $26.00; hand scoring keys for IBM 805 answer documents, manual $14.00

Publisher: The Psychological Corporation

Information and availability unconfirmed; last verified in 1988.

ROEDER MANIPULATIVE APTITUDE TEST
Refer to page 618.

SRA MECHANICAL APTITUDES
Richardson, Bellows, Henry and Company, Inc.

**Adolescent, adult
Grades 10 and above**

Purpose: Evaluates an individual's mechanical aptitude. Used for employee selection and placement.

Description: Three-part paper-pencil aptitude test measuring mechanical knowledge, space relations, and shop arithmetic. The Mechanical Knowledge subtest consists of 46 pictures of common tools and measures general mechanical background. The Space Relations subtest (40 items) measures the ability to visualize and mentally manipulate objects in space. The Shop Arithmetic subtest (24 problems) measures application of quantitative reasoning and fundamental math operations. Examiner required. Suitable for group use.

Timed: 35 minutes

Scoring: Hand key

Cost: 25 reusable test booklets $90.00; 25 answer sheets $19.00; 100 profile sheets $21.00; examiner's manual $10.00

Publisher: SRA/London House

SRA TEST OF MECHANICAL CONCEPTS
SRA/London House

Adult

Purpose: Measures an individual's ability to visualize and understand basic mechanical and spatial interrelationships. Used for employee selection and screening for such jobs as assembler, maintenance mechanic, machinist, and factory production worker.

Description: 78–item paper-pencil test consisting of three subtests measuring separate skills or abilities necessary for jobs requiring mechanical ability. The Mechanical Interrelationships subtest consists of 24 drawings depicting mechanical movements and interrelationships. The Mechanical Tools and Devices subtest consists of 30 items measuring knowledge of common mechanical tools and devices. The Spatial Relations subtest consists of 24 items measuring the ability to visualize and manipulate objects in space. The test is available in two forms, A and B. Examiner required. Suitable for group use.

Untimed: 35–40 minutes

Scoring: Hand key

Cost: 25 test booklets (specify form) $61.00; examiner's manual $10.00

Publisher: SRA/London House

STEADINESS TESTER—GROOVE TYPE

Adult

Purpose: Measures the steadiness aspect of psychomotor control.

Description: Multiple-item task-performance test assessing the degree of steadiness with which an individual can move a stylus in a straight line on a frictionless surface. The testing unit consists of adjustable stainless steel plates, which form the sides of a progressively narrowing slit. The sides are indexed in centimeters to accurately measure an individual's performance. The bottom surface of the unit is mirror-finished glass to assure no friction artifact. The unit may be connected to a tone response unit for immediate feedback studies or to any number of data collection devices. A replacement stylus is available. Examiner required. Not suitable for group use.

Untimed: Varies

Scoring: Examiner evaluated

Cost: Testing apparatus Model 32010 $60.00; Model 58025 Tone Response $75.00

Publisher: Lafayette Instrument Company, Inc.

STEADINESS TESTER—HOLE TYPE

Ages 5-55

Purpose: Measures one aspect of the psychomotor phenomenon of steadiness.

Description: Multiple-item task-performance test assessing the steadiness with which an individual can place a stylus in circular holes of varying sizes. The testing instrument provides nine holes of diminishing size. An analysis can be made of the subject's total score or for each hole separately. Considerable differences in performance may be determined for different individuals. The apparatus may be used with a counter or stop clock to record scores. The unit also may be connected to a tone response unit to provide immediate feedback. A replacement stylus is available. Examiner required. Not suitable for group use.

Timed: Varies

Scoring: Hand key

Cost: Testing apparatus Model 32011 $35.00; single impulse counter Model 58022 $110.00

Publisher: Lafayette Instrument Company, Inc.

STROMBERG DEXTERITY TEST (SDT)
E.L. Stromberg

Adult

Purpose: Measures manipulative skill in sorting by color and sequence. Used to select applicants for jobs requiring manual speed and accuracy. Also used for assessing manual dexterity of handicapped individuals in vocational training programs.

Description: Two-trial performance test of manual dexterity in which the applicant is asked to discriminate and sort biscuit-sized discs and to move and place them as fast as possible. The score is the number of seconds required to complete the two trials. Materials include assembly board and discs. Examiner required. Not suitable for group use.

Timed: 5-10 minutes

Scoring: Score obtained by timing

Cost: Complete set (includes manual) $395.00; manual $15.00

Publisher: The Psychological Corporation

Information and availability unconfirmed; last verified in 1988.

TAPPING BOARD

Adult

Purpose: Measures elementary psychomotor skills.

Description: Multiple-item task-performance test assessing an individual's ability to tap with a stylus, as rapidly as possible, the two stainless steel plates located at each end of an 18-inch fiberesin board (stainless steel plates measure $3^1/2''$ square). The test may be used to evaluate a number of basic psychomotor skills. A replacement stylus is available. Examiner required. Not suitable for group use.

Timed: Varies

Scoring: Examiner evaluated

Cost: Testing apparatus Model 32012 $43.00; single impulse counter Model 58022 $110.00

Publisher: Lafayette Instrument Company, Inc.

TWO ARM COORDINATION TEST

Adult

Purpose: Measures perceptual motor abilities involving the use of both arms together.

Description: 1–item task-performance test assessing an individual's ability to use both arms together in the performance of a fine-motor task. The testing unit consists of a stylus mounted on an apparatus with two handles. The individual grasps both handles simultaneously and moves the stylus around a 6–point star pattern. The testing unit may be connected to an impulse counter to record the number of errors and/or a stop clock to record the amount of time outside the path. A stop clock may be used to time the total test. Examiner required. Not suitable for group use.

Timed: Varies

Scoring: Examiner evaluated

Cost: Testing apparatus Model 32532 $149.00; single impulse counter Model 58022 $110.00

Publisher: Lafayette Instrument Company, Inc.

VCWS 1–SMALL TOOLS (MECHANICAL)

Adult

Purpose: Measures an individual's understanding of small tools and ability to work with them. May be used with institutionally retarded, visually impaired, and hearing-impaired individuals.

Description: Manual test measuring understanding of small tools and the ability to work with them. The design of the test challenges the individual to demonstrate skill in working in small, confined spaces while using the fingers and hands to manipulate tools to perform the assigned task. The individual works through a small hole in the work sample in order to simulate working conditions in which an individual is unable to view the work he or she is doing. The individual completes five panels. In each panel, the individual uses a different set of tools to insert fasteners such as screws, bolts, and hitch pin clips. Performance indicates the ability to complete successfully jobs requiring various degrees of ability in using

small tools and understanding their functions. A special administration procedure and kit (B-KIT) has been developed for use with the visually impaired. The test should not be used with individuals with severe impairment of the upper extremities. Examiner required. Not suitable for group use.

Timed: 1½ hours

Scoring: Examiner evaluated

Cost: $1,395.00

Publisher: Valpar International Corporation

VCWS 2–SIZE DISCRIMINATION

Adult

Purpose: Measures an individual's ability to perform tasks requiring visual size discrimination. Provides insight into problem-solving abilities, work organization, ability to follow directions, and psychomotor coordination. May be used with institutionally retarded, hearing-impaired, and visually impaired individuals.

Description: Manual test measuring an individual's ability to visually discriminate sizes. The individual must use his or her dominant hand to screw 49 hex nuts onto 32 bolt threads of various sizes. Both hands may be used to remove the nuts during disassembly. Performance indicates the ability to work successfully in occupations requiring visual size discrimination, eye-hand coordination, and bilateral dexterity. Work activities related to the test include examining and measuring for purposes of grading and sorting; performing work with close supervision using gauges, calipers, and other tools; and working within prescribed tolerances or standards. The test should not be used with individuals with severe impairment of the upper extremities. Examiner required. Not suitable for group use.

Timed: Not available

Scoring: Examiner evaluated

Cost: $1,245.00

Publisher: Valpar International Corporation

VCWS 4-UPPER EXTREMITY RANGE OF MOTION

Adult

Purpose: Measures an individual's upper extremity range of motion, including the shoulders, upper arms, forearms, elbows, wrists, and hands. Provides insight into factors such as neck and back fatigue, finger dexterity, and finger tactile sense. May be used with institutionally retarded, hearing-impaired, and visually impaired individuals.

Description: Manual test measuring the range of motion and work tolerances of an individual in relation to his or her upper torso. The individual works through an opening in front of the work sample, the inside of which is half red and half blue. Using opposite hands for each color, the individual fastens two sizes of nuts to bolts on each of five panels. The design of the work sample allows the examiner to view muscle action in the individual's wrist and fingers. Performance indicates coordination; spatial and perceptual skills; susceptibility to fatigue; and the ability to succeed in jobs requiring reaching, handling, fingering, feeling, and seeing. The test should not be used with individuals with severe impairment of the upper extremities. Examiner required. Not suitable for group use.

Timed: Not available
Scoring: Examiner evaluated
Cost: $1,395.00
Publisher: Valpar International Corporation

VCWS 7-MULTI-LEVEL SORTING

Adult

Purpose: Measures an individual's decision-making ability while performing tasks requiring physical manipulation and visual discrimination of colors, color-numbers, color-letters, and combinations of the three. May be used with institutionally retarded, hearing-impaired, and visually impaired individuals.

Description: Manual test measuring an individual's ability to make decisions while performing work tasks requiring physical manipulation and visual discrimination. The individual sorts 168 coded chips into 48 sorting slots showing on a board. Each chip is coded in one of the following ways: color; color and letter; color and number; or color, letter, and number. The test allows the examiner to observe the individual's orientation, approach, and organization in regard to the task, color, and letter; number discrimination skills; simple decision making; and physical manipulation. A time/error score relating directly to the level of supervision the individual will need while performing a particular job is derived. The test should not be used with individuals with severe impairment of the upper extremities. Examiner required. Not suitable for group use.

Timed: Not available
Scoring: Examiner evaluated
Cost: $1,595.00
Publisher: Valpar International Corporation

VCWS 8-SIMULATED ASSEMBLY

Adult

Purpose: Measures an individual's ability to work at an assembly task requiring repetitive physical manipulation and evaluates bilateral use of the upper extremities. Determines standing and sitting tolerance.

Description: Manual test measuring an individual's ability to work at conveyor-assembly jobs. The individual stands or sits in front of two parts bins, one containing metal pins and the other containing a black washer and white cap. The individual must place the pin, then the washer, and then the cap on the assembly board, which rotates automatically at a constant speed. Correct assemblies are counted automatically, and all assemblies are recycled to the parts bins automatically. Work activities relating to the test include placing materials in or on automatic machines; following simple instructions; and starting, stopping, and observing the functioning of machines and equipment. The test should not be used with individuals with severe impairment of the upper extremities. Examiner required. Suitable for group use.

Timed: Not available

Scoring: Examiner evaluated

Cost: $2,395.00

Publisher: Valpar International Corporation

VCWS 9–WHOLE BODY RANGE OF MOTION

Adult

Purpose: Assesses the ability to perform successfully gross- and fine-finger dexterity tasks while in kneeling, crouching, stooping, bending, and stretching positions. May be used with hearing-impaired and visually impaired individuals.

Description: Nonmedical measurement of gross body movements of the trunk, hands, arms, legs, and fingers as they relate to an individual's functional ability to perform job tasks. The individual stands in front of the work sample, with the frame adjusted to approximately 6 inches above his or her head. The individual takes three colored shapes, one at a time, and transfers them from shoulder height to overhead. The individual then transfers the shapes to waist level, which requires bending forward at the waist; to knee level, which requires crouching or kneeling; and then back to shoulder height. In each transfer, the individual must remove a total of 22 nuts and then replace them, using only one hand, onto each of the three colored shapes, which are positioned in such a way that the individual is encouraged to twist the trunk to both the left and the right as the colored shapes are transferred. The individual makes a total of four transfers, requiring the removal and replacement of 176 nuts. The test relates to client functional ability in performing tasks such as stooping, kneeling, crouching, reaching, handling, fingering, feeling, and seeing. The test should not be used with individuals with severe impairment of the upper extremities. Examiner required. Not suitable for group use.

Timed: Not available

Scoring: Examiner evaluated

Cost: $1,895.00

Publisher: Valpar International Corporation

VCWS 11–EYE-HAND-FOOT COORDINATION

Adult

Purpose: Measures eye, hand, and foot coordination. Provides insight into individual concentration, learning, planning, spatial discrimination, and reaction to immediate positive and negative feedback. May be used with institutionally retarded and hearing-impaired individuals.

Description: Manual test measuring an individual's ability to use the eyes, hands, and feet simultaneously and in a coordinated manner. The examinee sits in front of the work sample and maneuvers nine steel balls, one at a time, through a maze containing 13 holes into which the steel balls may drop, thus ending the examinee's attempt to make it to the end of the maze with that particular ball. In order to move the ball, the examinee tilts the maze left and right with his or her hands, forward and backward with his or her feet, and traces the track of the ball with his or her eyes. Work activities related to the test include starting, stopping, and observing the function of machines; perceiving relationships between moving objects, fixtures, and surfaces; and planning the order of successive operations. The test should not be used with individuals with severe impairment of the upper or lower extremities. Examiner required. Not suitable for group use.

Timed: Not available

Scoring: Examiner evaluated

Cost: $1,595.00

Publisher: Valpar International Corporation

VCWS 202–MECHANICAL ASSEMBLY/ALIGNMENT AND HAMMERING

Refer to page 808.

VCWS 203–MECHANICAL REASONING AND MACHINE TENDING
Refer to page 808.

VCWS 204–FINE FINGER DEXTERITY
Refer to page 809.

Municipal Services

THE BIPOLAR PSYCHOLOGICAL INVENTORY (BPI)
Refer to page 159.

CHANGE AGENT QUESTIONNAIRE (CAQ)
Refer to page 997.

CORRECTIONAL OFFICERS' INTEREST BLANK (COIB)
Refer to page 983.

DELUXE DETENTION SERVICE PROMOTION TESTS
McCann Associates, Inc.

Adult

Purpose: Measures knowledge of inmate supervision procedures, inmate legal rights, and other job responsibilities. Used to evaluate candidate's for promotion within county detention facilities.

Description: 100–item paper-pencil test of knowledge of inmate supervision, inmate legal rights, inmate classification procedures, inmate visitation procedures, staff supervision, detention facility administration, and other areas upon request of individual departments. The tests are prepared individually according to job analysis. Separate tests are available for different levels of responsibility in a county jail or local detention facility. The publisher scores each area and provides a total score, individual subtest scores, norms, means, standard deviations, reliability coefficients, and an evaluation of each candidate.

Materials include test booklets, answer sheets, identification sheets, candidate study guides, and administration instructions. A list of references is also available. The test is available on a rental basis only to civil service commissions or qualified municipal officials. Examiner required. Suitable for group use.

Timed: 3½ hours

Scoring: Computer scored

Cost: First 5 candidates $550.00 minimum charge; next 20 candidates $32.00 each; next 25 candidates $25.00 each; next 25 candidates $23.00 each; next 25 candidates $22.00 each; all additional candidates $12.75 each

Publisher: McCann Associates, Inc.

DELUXE FIRE PROMOTION TESTS
McCann Associates, Inc.

Adult

Purpose: Measures knowledge of firefighting and other job responsibilities. Used to evaluate candidates for promotion within fire departments.

Description: 100–item paper-pencil test of knowledge of fire attack, fire extinguishment, rescue, salvage, fire inspection, fire supervision, fire administration, first-aid practices, and other areas upon the request of individual departments. The tests are individually prepared according to job analysis. Separate tests are available for the positions of driver, engineer, lieutenant, captain, battalion chief, deputy chief, assistant chief, and chief. The publisher scores each area and provides a total score, norms, means subtest and total scores, standard deviations, reliability coefficient, and an evaluation of each candidate. Materials include test booklets, answer sheets, identification sheets, envelopes, candidate study guides, and administration instructions. A list of references is provided also. The test is available on a rental basis only to Civil Service Commissions or qualified municipal officials. Examiner required. Suitable for group use.

Timed: 3½ hours

Scoring: Computer scored by publisher

Cost: First 5 candidates $580.00; additional candidates $13.50 to $33.50 each

Publisher: McCann Associates, Inc.

DELUXE POLICE PROMOTION TESTS
McCann Associates, Inc.

Adult

Purpose: Assesses abilities of candidates for police promotion. Used by municipal police departments for promotions to the level of sergeant, lieutenant, captain, assistant chief, chief, and detective.

Description: 100–item paper-pencil multiple-choice test. Each test is individually prepared according to an analysis of the job for which the subject is being tested. The test may include patrol techniques, investigative techniques, supervisory techniques, and administrative knowledge. The publisher scores each area and provides a total score, norms, means subtest and total scores, standard deviations, reliability coefficient, and an evaluation of each candidate. Materials include test booklets, answer sheets, identification sheets, envelopes, candidate study guides, and administration instructions. A list of reference sources is provided also. The test is available on a rental basis only to Civil Service Commissions or qualified municipal officials. Examiner required. Suitable for group use.

Timed: 3½ hours

Scoring: Computer scored by publisher

Cost: First 5 candidates $580.00; additional candidates $13.50 to $33.50 each

Publisher: McCann Associates, Inc.

EMOTIONAL STABILITY SURVEY (ES SURVEY)
Refer to page 999.

ESV FIREFIGHTER
McCann Associates, Inc.

Adult

Purpose: Assesses candidates' ability to learn firefighting. Used by fire department job screening.

Description: 125–item criterion-validated paper-pencil multiple-choice test covering interest in firefighting, compatibility, map reading, spatial visualization, visual pursuit, understanding and interpreting table and test material about firefighting, basic building construction, and mechanical aptitude. The publisher scores each area and provides a total score, norms, mean subtest and total scores, standard deviations, reliability coefficient, and an evaluation of each candidate. Materials include test booklets, answer sheets, identification sheets, envelopes, candidate study guides, and administration instructions. The test is available on a rental basis only to Civil Service Commissions or qualified municipal officials. Examiner required. Suitable for group use.

Timed: 2 hours

Scoring: Computer scored by publisher

Cost: First 5 candidates $200.00; next 45 candidates $12.50 each; all additional candidates $8.00 each

Publisher: McCann Associates, Inc.

FIRE COMPANY OFFICER FORMS 1, 2, AND A
McCann Associates, Inc.

Adult

Purpose: Assesses abilities of candidates for promotion in municipal fire departments.

Description: 100–item paper-pencil multiple-choice criterion-related validity test assessing fire attack knowledge, fire extinguishment knowledge, chemistry and physics of fire, and fireground supervision and management. The publisher scores each area and provides a total score, norms, means subtest and total scores, standard deviations, reliability coefficient, and an evaluation of each candidate. Materials include test booklets, answer sheets, identification sheets, candidate study guides, and administration instructions. A list of reference sources is provided also. The test is available only on a rental basis to Civil Service Commissions or qualified municipal officials. Examiner required. Suitable for group use.

Timed: 3½ hours

Scoring: Computer scored by publisher

Cost: First 5 candidates $450.00; next 5 candidates $27.00 each

Publisher: McCann Associates, Inc.

FIREFIGHTER SELECTION TEST

Adult

Purpose: Measures three abilities important for learning and performing the job of firefighter: mechanical comprehension, reading comprehension, and report interpretation. Used to select applicants for entry-level firefighter positions or training programs.

Description: 100–item paper-pencil multiple-choice test measuring the understanding of mechanical principles relevant to the firefighting job (39 items), the ability to read and interpret a passage (51 items), and the ability to read and interpret charts and reports (10 items). The items consist of drawings and passages based on firefighter training materials and sample charts and reports presenting fire department data. For test security purposes, the test is available for lease only. Examiner required. Suitable for group use.

Timed: 2 hours, 30 minutes

Scoring: Hand key; may be computer scored

Cost: Test package (10 nonreusable tests, 10 answer sheets, scoring key, administrator's guide, technical manual) $155.00; each additonal package $65.00; volume discount

Publisher: Psychological Services, Inc.

INWALD PERSONALITY INVENTORY (IPI)
Robin E. Inwald

Adult

Purpose: Assesses behavior patterns and characteristics of police, security, firefighter, and correction officer candidates. Used for pre-employment screening.

Description: 310–item paper-pencil truefalse instrument consisting of a validity measure and 26 scales assessing specific external behavior, attitudes and temperament, internalized conflict measures, and interpersonal conflict measures: Guardedness (19 items), Alcohol (13 items), Drugs (13 items), Driving Violations (6 items), Job Difficulties (22 items), Trouble with the Law and Society (21 items), Absence Abuse (19 items), Substance Abuse (20 items), Antisocial Attitudes (27 items), Hyperactivity (42 items), Rigid Type (19 items), Type "A" (21 items), Illness Concerns (14 items), Treatment Programs (3 items), Anxiety (15 items), Phobic Personality (34 items), Obsessive Personality (13 items), Depression (27 items), Loner Type (17 items), Unusual Experiences/ Thoughts (26 items), Lack of Assertiveness (14 items), Interpersonal Difficulties (27 items), Undue Suspiciousness (22 items), Family Conflicts (23 items), Sexual Concerns (5 items), and Spouse/ Mate Conflicts (8 items).

The test yields raw scores and T-scores based on law enforcement norms. Examinees must have a sixth-grade reading level. A short version (IPI-S3) containing 128 items is available. A computer scoring service available from the publisher offers mail-in and teleprocessing services. Turnaround time for the mail-in service is 24 hours from receipt of materials. The teleprocessing software, which operates on IBM PC and compatible systems, allows the examiner to input test responses manually or through optical scanning. Results for each test are received within 6 seconds. Self-administered. Suitable for group use. Available in Spanish.

Untimed: 30–45 minutes

Scoring: Computer scored

Cost: Starter kit (technical manual, test booklet, answer sheets for 3 computer-scored reports) $45.00; reusable test booklets $1.50; processing fees range from $6.50–$20.00

Publisher: Hilson Research, Inc.

POLICE OFFICER ESV–100
McCann Associates, Inc.

Adult

Purpose: Assesses abilities of candidates for police officer. Used by municipal police departments for job screening.

Description: 100–item criterion-validated paper-pencil multiple-choice test assessing observational ability, ability to exercise judgment and common sense, interest in police work, map reading, dealing with people, ability to read and comprehend policy text material, and reasoning ability. The publisher scores each area and provides a total score, norms, means subtest and total scores, standard deviations, reliability coefficient, and an evaluation of each candidate. Materials include test booklets, answer sheets, identification sheets, envelopes, candidate study guides, and administration instructions. The test is available on a rental basis only to Civil Service Commissions or qualified municipal officials. Examiner required. Suitable for group use.

Timed: 2 hours, 40 minutes

Scoring: Computer scored by publisher

Cost: First 5 candidates $200.00; next 45 candidates $12.50 each; all additional candidates $8.00

Publisher: McCann Associates, Inc.

POLICE OFFICER ESV–125
McCann Associates, Inc.

Adult

Purpose: Assesses abilities of candidates for police officer. Used by municipal police departments for job screening.

Description: 125–item criterion-validated paper-pencil multiple-choice test assessing observational ability, police aptitude, police public relations, and police judgment. The publisher scores each area and provides a total score, norms, means subtest and total scores, standard deviations, reliability coefficient, and an evaluation of each candidate. Materials include test booklets, answer sheets, identification sheets, envelopes, candidate study guides, and administration instructions. The test is available on a rental basis only to Civil Service Commissions or qualified municipal officials. Examiner required. Suitable for group use.

Timed: 3 hours

Scoring: Computer scored by publisher

Cost: First 5 candidates $200.00; next 45 candidates $12.00 each; all additional candidates $8.00 each

Publisher: McCann Associates, Inc.

STAFF BURNOUT SCALE FOR POLICE AND SECURITY PERSONNEL
John W. Jones

Adult

Purpose: Assesses burnout or work stress among police and security personnel.

Description: Multiple-item paper-pencil test assessing burnout or work stress through four types of factors: cognitive reactions, affective reactions, behavioral reactions, and psychophysiological reactions. Self-administered. Suitable for group use.

Untimed: 10 minutes

Scoring: Hand key; may be computer scored

Cost: 25 tests $15.00; specimen set (interpretation manual, validation studies) $5.00

Publisher: London House, Inc.

TRANSIT BUS OPERATOR SELECTION TEST BATTERY
Melany E. Baehr

Adult

Purpose: Identifies applicants with good potential for long-term successful performance as municipal bus operators.

Description: Multiple-item paper-pencil test measuring aptitude for operating municipal buses. The test consists of three sections: Work Experience and Background (35 items), Skills and Abilities (96 items), and Self-Understanding and Experience (108 items). Together, the three sections predict performance on criteria such as accidents, sick days, and supervisor ratings. Examiner required. Suitable for group use.

Timed: 90 minutes for total battery

Scoring: Hand key; may be computer scored

Cost: $4.00–$12.00 per booklet depending on scoring method

Publisher: London House, Inc.

Sales

APTITUDES ASSOCIATES TEST OF SALES APTITUDE
Martin M. Bruce

Adult

Purpose: Evaluates an individual's aptitude for selling. Used as an aid in vocational guidance and in the selection and training of sales personnel.

Description: 50–item paper-pencil test measuring the subject's knowledge and understanding of the principles of selling a wide variety of goods ranging from heavy industrial capital items to door-to-door housewares. Norms are available to compare the subject's score with salespeople, men, women, and selected "special sales groups." The subject reads the directions and completes the test. Self-administered. Suitable for group use.

Untimed: 20–30 minutes

Scoring: Hand key

Cost: Manual $12.50; key $1.95; package of tests $39.50; specimen set $16.50

Publisher: Martin M. Bruce, Ph.D., Publishers

ATTITUDE SURVEY PROGRAM FOR BUSINESS AND INDUSTRY: SALES SURVEY
Refer to page 995.

BASIC BANK SKILLS BATTERY (BBSB)
Refer to page 870.

CUSTOMER REACTION SURVEY (CRS)
Jay Hall and C. Leo Griffith

Adult

Purpose: Assesses customer reaction to a salesperson's interpersonal style and customer preferences regarding salesperson behavior. Used for employee training and development and as a basis for discussion.

Description: Multiple-item paper-pencil inventory assessing an individual's success as a salesperson from the customer's point of view. In the first part of the inventory, the customer rates the salesperson's use of exposure and feedback. In the second part, the customer states preferred salesperson behavior. The resulting profiles may be combined with self-ratings from the Sales Relations Survey to make sales training relevant to the realities of the field. Normative data are provided. Self-administered. Suitable for group use.

Untimed: Varies

Scoring: Self-scored

Cost: Individual instrument $4.50

Publisher: Teleometrics International

DIPLOMACY TEST OF EMPATHY
Willard A. Kerr

Adult

Purpose: Measures empathic ability. Used for selecting applicants for sales positions.

Description: Multiple-item paper-pencil test measuring the ability to sell, be persuasive, tactful, and diplomatic. Items correlate with the mean salary increases of executives but have little or no relationship with intelligence. Norms are available for general adults, management, sales, and sales management. Examiner required. Suitable for group use.

Untimed: 20 minutes

Scoring: Hand key

Cost: Specimen set $5.00; 25 tests $5.00; 25 answer sheets $5.00

Publisher: Psychometric Affiliates

ETSA TESTS 7–A—SALES APTITUDE
Refer to page 883.

INCENTIVES MANAGEMENT INDEX (IMI)
Jay Hall and Norman J. Seim

Adult

Purpose: Assesses the incentives used by a sales manager to motivate the sales force. Used for training and development of sales managers and as a basis for discussion.

Description: Multiple-item paper-pencil self-report inventory identifying which incentives a sales manager emphasizes and assessing the sales manager's personal theories about what motivates the sales force. The inventory yields a managerial profile that may be used as feedback for the sales force. The inventory may be administered in conjunction with the Sales Motivation Survey (SMS) in two ways: to indicate areas in which the sales manager's own needs influence the incentives that are emphasized with the sales force and to assess the sales manager's own motivational theory in light of the needs of the sales force. Normative data are provided. Self-administered. Suitable for group use.

Untimed: Varies

Scoring: Self-scored

Cost: Individual instrument $4.50

Publisher: Teleometrics International

INSURANCE SELECTION INVENTORY (ISI)
Refer to page 887.

IPI APTITUDE—INTELLIGENCE TEST SERIES: NUMBERS
Refer to page 889.

IPI APTITUDE—INTELLIGENCE TEST SERIES: SALES TERMS
Refer to page 890.

IPI JOB TEST FIELD SERIES: CONTACT CLERK
Refer to page 891.

IPI JOB TEST FIELD SERIES: SALES CLERK
Industrial Psychology International, Ltd.

Adult

Purpose: Assesses skills and personality of applicants for low-level sales positions. Used to screen for department store, post office, teller, ticketer, and waitress positions.

Description: Multiple-item paper-pencil battery of one personality and five aptitude tests. The tests are CPF, Numbers, Perception, Memory, Sales Terms, and Fluency. For individual test descriptions, see the IPI Aptitude-Intelligence Test Series. Examiner required. Suitable for group use. Available in French and Spanish.

Timed: 40 minutes

Scoring: Hand key

Cost: Instruction kit $16.00; test packages $10.00 each

Publisher: Industrial Psychology International, Ltd.

IPI JOB TEST FIELD SERIES: SALES ENGINEER
Industrial Psychology International, Ltd.

Adult

Purpose: Assesses skills and personality of applicants for technically-oriented sales positions. Used to screen for claims work, adjusting, purchasing, technical sales, and underwriting.

Description: Multiple-item paper-pencil battery of six aptitude and three personality tests. The tests are Sales Terms, 16PF, Parts, Judgment, Numbers, Fluency, Memory, CPF, and NPF. For individual test descriptions, see the IPI Aptitude-Intelligence Test Series. Examiner required. Suitable for group use. Available in French and Spanish.

Timed: 75 minutes

Scoring: Hand key

Cost: Instruction kit $16.00; test packages $10.00

Publisher: Industrial Psychology International, Ltd.

IPI JOB TEST FIELD SERIES: SALES PERSON
Industrial Psychology International, Ltd.

Adult

Purpose: Assesses skills of applicants for higher level sales positions. Used to screen for agent, demonstrator, insurance, retail, wholesale, and route sales positions.

Description: Multiple-item paper-pencil battery of five aptitude and two personality tests. The tests are 16PF, Numbers, Sales Terms, Fluency, Memory, CPF, and Perception. For individual test descriptions, see the IPI Aptitude-Intelligence Test Series. Examiner required. Suitable for group use. Available in French and Spanish.

Timed: 1 hour

Scoring: Hand key

Cost: Instruction kit $16.00; test packages $10.00

Publisher: Industrial Psychology International, Ltd.

IPI JOB TEST FIELD SERIES: SALES SUPERVISOR
Industrial Psychology International, Ltd.

Adult

Purpose: Assesses skills and personality of applicants for supervisory positions in the sales field. Used to screen for advertising, credit, merchandise, service, and store sales positions.

Description: Multiple-item paper-pencil battery of seven aptitude and three personality tests. The tests are 16PF, Fluency, Sales Terms, Memory, Judgment, CPF, Parts, Numbers, NPF, and Perception. For individual test descriptions, see the IPI Aptitude-Intelligence Test Series. Examiner required. Suitable for group use. Available in French and Spanish.

Timed: 82 minutes

Scoring: Hand key

Cost: Instruction kit $16.00; test packages $10.00

Publisher: Industrial Psychology International, Ltd.

LIMRA CAREER PROFILE SYSTEM

Adult

Purpose: Evaluates the career experience and expectations of individuals considering an insurance sales career. Used for employee screening and selection.

Description: 183- or 158-item paper-pencil multiple-choice questionnaire assessing career information related to future success as an insurance salesperson. The 183-item Initial Career Profile is used with applicants who have no prior insurance sales experience. The 158-item Advanced Career Profile is used with experienced applicants. The questionnaire is available to insurance company home offices only. Examiner required. Suitable for group use. Both forms may be administered in Canada and are available in French.

Untimed: Varies

Scoring: Computer scored

Cost: Test booklet (specify profile) $5.00; administrative manual $4.00; Initial Career Profile answer sheet $12.00; Advanced Career Profile answer sheet $14.50; cost includes scoring

Publisher: Life Insurance Marketing and Research Association, Inc.

PERSONNEL TEST BATTERY: CHECKING (PTB:CP3)
Refer to page 907.

PERSONNEL TEST BATTERY: NUMERICAL COMPUTATION (PTB:NP2)
Refer to page 907.

PERSONNEL TEST BATTERY: NUMERICAL REASONING (PTB:NP6)
Refer to page 908.

POPPLETON-ALLEN SALES APTITUDE TEST (PASAT)
S. Poppleton, E. Allen, and D. Garland

Adult

Purpose: Measures 15 different sales aptitudes, preferably of adults with previous work experience.

Description: 126–item paper-pencil multiple-choice test assessing social skills, organization and planning abilities, emotional expression, and motivation of potential sales people. Test items are based on job and factor analysis studies. Individuals select one of four or five alternative answers to questions. Norms are available for business and management students and for sales people in various industries. Examiner/self-administered. Suitable for group use.
BRITISH PUBLISHER

Untimed: 20–30 minutes

Scoring: Self-scored; computer scored

Cost: Specimen set (test booklet, answer key, manual) $75.00

Publisher: The Test Agency Ltd.

SALES ATTITUDE CHECKLIST
Erwin K. Taylor

Adult

Purpose: Measures attitudes and behaviors involved in sales and selling. Used for sales selection programs.

Description: 31–item paper-pencil test assessing basic attitudes toward selling and habits in the selling situation. Norms are provided for applicants for the following positions: sales and sales managerial positions, automobile salespersons, freight traffic salespersons, office equipment salespersons, and utility salespersons. Examiner required. Suitable for group use.

Untimed: 10–15 minutes

Scoring: Hand key

Cost: 25 test booklets $46.00; examiner's manual $10.00

Publisher: SRA/London House

SALES COMPREHENSION TEST
Martin M. Bruce

Adult

Purpose: Measures sales ability and potential based on the subject's understanding of the principles of selling. Used for evaluating prospective salespeople, vocational counseling, and training projects for salespersons.

Description: 30–item paper-pencil multiple-choice test measuring the subject's aptitude for selling. Standard test procedures are used. Self-administered. Suitable for group use. Available in French, Spanish, Italian, Dutch, and German.

Untimed: 15–20 minutes

Scoring: Hand key

Cost: Manual $12.50; key $1.95; package of profile sheets $18.00; package of tests $39.50; specimen set $32.50

Publisher: Martin M. Bruce, Ph.D., Publishers

SALES MOTIVATION INVENTORY
Martin M. Bruce

Adult

Purpose: Assesses interest in and motivation for sales work, both commission and wholesale/retail.

Description: 75–item paper-pencil test measuring sales motivation and drive. Consists of multiple-choice triads. Self-administered. Suitable for group use. Available in French.

Untimed: 20–30 minutes

Scoring: Hand key

Cost: Manual $14.50; manual's supplement (1984) $15.50; key $1.95; package of profile sheets $18.00; package of tests $39.50; specimen set $33.50

Publisher: Martin M. Bruce, Ph.D., Publishers

SALES MOTIVATION SURVEY (SMS)
Jay Hall and Norman J. Seim

Adult

Purpose: Assesses the needs and motivations of salespersons. Used for employee training and development and as a basis for discussion.

Description: Multiple-item paper-pencil self-report inventory measuring the personal needs and goals of salespersons. The inventory provides a profile of personal motivations. The results may serve as a basis for reordering personal priorities and better understanding of personal performance. Normative data are provided. The inventory may be administered in conjunction with the Incentive Management Index for assessment of sales managers. Self-administered. Suitable for group use.

Untimed: Varies

Scoring: Self-scored

Cost: Individual instrument $4.50

Publisher: Teleometrics International

SALES PREFERENCE QUESTIONNAIRE
George W. Dudley

Adult

Purpose: Measures the fear of prospecting in direct sales personnel. Used for personnel selection/evaluation and for training/development purposes.

Description: 45–item paper-pencil or computer-administered inventory of an individual's feeling about making sales calls. The questionnaire measures nine areas of reluctance (threat-sensitivity, overpreparation, excuse-making, group presentations, calling on personal friends, pride in sales career, intrusion-sensitivity, up-market resistance, and calling on relatives) and provides scores on two additional scales (emotional energy spent resisting making calls and emotional freedom to initiate prospecting calls with prospective buyers). The report includes a graphic presentation of the basic scales, an analysis of various critical items, and a narrative discussion of those areas in which reluctance is significantly elevated. Computer version operates on IBM PC and TRS 80 systems. Self-administered. Suitable for group use.

Untimed: 15–20 minutes

Scoring: Computer scored

Cost: Contact publisher

Publisher: Behavioral Science Research Press, Inc.

Information and availability unconfirmed; last verified in 1987.

SALES PROFESSIONAL ASSESSMENT INVENTORY (SPAI)
London House, Inc.

Adult

Purpose: Assesses potential for success in sales positions. Used for selection and screening of candidates for direct sales to business and retail sales of consumer durable goods or special services.

Description: 210–item paper-pencil multiple-choice test with 12 diagnostic scales yielding scores in Sales Work Experience, Sales Interest, Sales Responsibility, Sales Orientation, Energy Level, Self Development, Sales Skills, Sales Understanding, Sales Arithmetic, Customer Service, Business Ethics, and Job Stability. Two validity scales, Candidness and Accuracy, are also provided. A Sales Potential Index that is a composite of the 12 diagnostic scales is provided for decision-making purposes. In addition to scores, the SPAI generates positive indicators, training needs, and follow-up interview questions, based on examinee responses to individual items.

Three scoring options are available from London House: operator-assisted telephone, Touch-Test, and PC-based. Operator-assisted scoring involves dialing a London House operator who provides test results after being read a tally of responses by the test administrator. Written confirmation is mailed the following day. Touch-Test telephone scoring allows the test administrator to use the telephone keypad to feed response tallies directly into London House computers. Results are available immediately and written confirmation is mailed the next day. Administrators with IBM PC or compatible equipment may obtain on-site results using the PC-based scoring method. Examiner required. Suitable for group use.

Untimed: 1 hour

Scoring: Computer scored; scoring service available from publisher

Cost: $25.00–$50.00 depending on quantity and method of scoring

Publisher: London House, Inc.

SALES RELATIONS SURVEY (SRS)
Jay Hall

Adult

Purpose: Assesses an individual's interpersonal sales style. Used for employee training and development and as a basis for discussion.

Description: Multiple-item paper-pencil self-report inventory assessing the quality of a salesperson's relationships with customers along exposure and feedback dimensions. The inventory is used to introduce and assess concepts such as blindspots, facades, and hidden potentials. Scores may be used to plot Johari Window profiles for an entire sales force. Normative data are provided. The inventory may be administered in conjunction with the Customer Reaction Survey for a more complete assessment of an individual's interpersonal sales style. Self-administered. Suitable for group use.

Untimed: Varies

Scoring: Self-scored

Cost: Individual instrument $4.50

Publisher: Teleometrics International

THE SALES SENTENCE COMPLETION BLANK
Martin M. Bruce

Adult

Purpose: Aids in evaluating and selecting sales personnel by providing insight into how the applicant thinks and into his or her social attitudes and general personality.

Description: 40-item paper-pencil test consisting of sentence fragments to be completed by the subject. The examiner assesses the responses by scoring them on a 7-point scale. Responses are a "projection" of the subject's attitudes about life, self, and others. Self-administered. Suitable for group use.

Untimed: 20–35 minutes

Scoring: Hand key

Cost: Manual $13.50; package of tests $39.50; specimen set $18.50

Publisher: Martin M. Bruce, Ph.D., Publishers

SALES STAFF SELECTOR

Adult

Purpose: Evaluates suitability of candidates for sales representative positions.

Description: Multiple-item paper-pencil set of seven subtests measuring numerical skills, problem-solving and logical-thinking abilities, verbal fluency and communication skills, comprehension of selling principles, sales motivation and career interests, emotional stability, and desire for people contact. The first three tests are timed speed tests. The tests are appropriate for sales/order desk applicants, sales applicants without prior experience, sales professionals, and marketing candidates. Available in Basic, Screening, or Comprehensive versions depending on depth of assessment desired. Examiner required. Suitable for group use. Available in French.

Untimed: 75 minutes

Scoring: Computer scoring service provided by publisher

Cost: $179.00 each

Publisher: Wolfe Personnel Testing and Training Systems, Inc.

SALES STYLE DIAGNOSIS TEST
W.J. Reddin and David Forman

Adult

Purpose: Measures a salesperson's selling style and effectiveness. Used to screen, coach, and train salespersons.

Description: Multiple-item paper-pencil test designed to provide scores on the following selling styles: deserter, missionary, autocrat, compromiser, bureaucrat, developer, benevolent autocrat, and executive. Task orientation, relationships orientation, and effectiveness are assessed as well. The individual responds to actions of a hypothetical salesperson and receives

a score indicative of selling style. Self-administered. Suitable for group use.
CANADIAN PUBLISHER
Untimed: 20–30 minutes
Scoring: Hand key
Cost: Test kit (10 test copies, fact sheet, user's guide) $40.00; cash orders postpaid
Publisher: Organizational Tests (Canada) Ltd.

SALES TRANSACTION AUDIT (STA)
Jay Hall and C. Leo Griffith

Adult

Purpose: Assesses the interpersonal transactions of salespeople with their customers in terms of Eric Berne's model of transactional analysis. Used for employee training and development and as a basis for discussion.

Description: Multiple-item paper-pencil self-report inventory measuring the size of the parent, adult, and child—the three positions from which individuals can communicate according to the model of transactional analysis—in a salesperson's transactions with customers. The inventory also provides scores for transaction contamination, crossed and complementary transactions, and constructive and disruptive tension in the sales relationship. Normative data are provided. Self-administered. Suitable for group use.
Untimed: Varies
Scoring: Self-scored
Cost: Individual instrument $4.50
Publisher: Teleometrics International

SELLING JUDGMENT TEST
Martin M. Bruce

Adolescent, adult

Purpose: Measures sales comprehension. Used by sales trainers to develop discussion topics.

Description: 5–item paper-pencil multiple-choice test assessing sales competence in the retail and wholesale fields. The items in this test are taken from the Sales Comprehension Test and were chosen by the Associated Merchandising Corpora-

tion as particularly pertinent to the department retail store field. The test is used primarily for training and discussion purposes. The Sales Comprehension Test is more appropriate for assessment purposes. Self-administered. Suitable for group use.

Untimed: 3 minutes
Scoring: Examiner evaluated
Cost: 20 test booklets $15.00
Publisher: Martin M. Bruce, Ph.D., Publishers

TEST OF PRACTICAL JUDGMENT—FORM 62
Refer to page 1062.

TEST OF RETAIL SALES INSIGHT (TRSI)
Russell N. Cassel

Adult

Purpose: Assesses degree of knowledge of retail selling. Used for in-service education of retail sales clerks and assessing progress in distributive education courses.

Description: 60–item paper-pencil multiple-choice test measuring five areas of retail sales: general sales knowledge, customer motivation and need, merchandise procurement and adaptation, sales promotion procedures, and sales closure. Five alternatives are provided for each item. A fifth-grade reading level is required. Examiner required. Suitable for group use.
Untimed: 30 minutes
Scoring: Hand key
Cost: Specimen set $9.00; 25 tests $27.50; 25 answer sheets $6.75; 25 profile sheets $8.25; keys $6.75; manual $6.75
Publisher: Psychologists and Educators, Inc.

WESMAN PERSONNEL CLASSIFICATION TEST (PCT)
Refer to page 926.

Teachers

INSTRUCTIONAL LEADERSHIP INVENTORY

Refer to page 856.

IPI JOB TEST FIELD SERIES: INSTRUCTOR

Industrial Psychology International, Ltd.

Adult

Purpose: Assesses skills and personality of applicants for various teaching positions. Used to screen for counselors, instructors, safety directors, teachers, and training directors.

Description: Multiple-item paper-pencil battery of six aptitude and three personality tests. The tests are Fluency, 16PF, Sales Terms, Parts, Memory, Judgment, CPF, NPF, and Perception. For individual test descriptions, see the IPI Aptitude-Intelligence Test Series. Examiner required. Suitable for group use. Available in French and Spanish.

Timed: 76 minutes

Scoring: Hand key

Cost: Instruction kit $16.00; test packages $10.00

Publisher: Industrial Psychology International, Ltd.

TEACHER EVALUATION RATING SCALES (TEACHERS)

James E. Ysseldyke, S. Jay Samuels, and Sandra L. Christenson

Adult

Purpose: Rates teacher performance. Used to develop an instructional improvement plan.

Description: 2–scale multiple-item paper-pencil teacher-rating system. The two scales, a Teacher's Self-Evaluation Scale and a Supervisor's Scale, are used independently by the teacher and the supervisor to rate the teacher's performance on 20 components in six areas: instructional planning, instructional management, teaching procedures, monitoring procedures, personal qualities, and professionalism. After the scales have been completed, the teacher and supervisor summarize their ratings, compare findings, and develop an instructional improvement plan. Examiner required. Not suitable for group use.

Untimed: Varies

Scoring: Examiner evaluated

Cost: Complete kit (supervisor's manual, 5 teacher's manauls, 25 supervisor's scales, 25 teacher's self-assessment scales, 25 instructional improvement plan forms, storage box) $54.00

Publisher: PRO-ED

TEACHER OCCUPATIONAL COMPETENCY TESTS (TOCT)

Adult

Purpose: Assesses competency in skilled trades and occupations. Used for providing evidence of competency to become a teacher or obtaining academic credit at participating educational institutions.

Description: Multiple-item paper-pencil tests of skills and knowledge in 51 vocational fields: air conditioning, heating and refrigeration, airframe and power plant mechanics, appliance repair, architectural drafting, audio-visual communications technology, auto body repair, auto mechanics, baking, brick masonry, building and home maintenance services, building construction occupations, building trades maintenance, cabinet making and millwork, carpentry, child care and guidance, civil technology, commercial art, commercial photography, computer science for secondary teachers, computer technology, cosmetology, diesel engine repair, diesel mechanics, drafting occupations, electrical construction and maintenance, electrical installation, electronics communications, electronics technology, heating, heavy equipment mechanics, industrial electrician, industrial electronics, machine drafting, machine trades, masonry and masonry occupations, materials handling, mechanical technology, microcomputer repair, painting and decorating, plumbing, power sewing, printing (offset and letterpress), quantity food preparation, radio and TV repair, refrigeration, scientific data processing, sheet metal, small engine repair, textile production and fabrication, tool and die making, and welding.

The performance tests are administered in a laboratory, school shop, or clinical setting and enable the applicant to demonstrate knowledge and skills of competent craft persons. Examiner required. Suitable for group use.

Timed: Varies depending on test

Scoring: Examiner evaluated; computer scored

Cost: Contact publisher

Publisher: National Occupational Competency Testing Institute

TEACHER OCCUPATIONAL COMPETENCY TESTING: AIR CONDITIONING, HEATING, AND REFRIGERATION EXAMINATION

Adult

Purpose: Assesses competency in air conditioning, heating, and refrigeration. Used for providing evidence of competency to become a teacher or obtaining academic credit at participating educational institutions.

Description: Two-part test of skills and knowledge important in air conditioning, heating, and refrigeration work. The multiple-choice written test (200 items) covers fundamental principals, system applications, systems controls (mechanical and electrical), safety, system servicing approaches, related tools, materials, supplies, codes, soldering, and brazing. The performance test covers copper tubing assembly, heating system start-up, checkout and troubleshooting, refrigeration system servicing, and air conditioning system servicing. Handbook and references will be provided for preparation. Personal tools and equipment may be used. A calculator may be used for both portions of the test. Examiner required. The written test is suitable for group use.

Timed: Written test 3 hours; performance test 6 hours

Scoring: Examiner evaluated; computer scored

Cost: Contact publisher

Publisher: National Occupational Competency Testing Institute

TEACHER OCCUPATIONAL COMPETENCY TESTING: AIRFRAME AND POWER PLANT MECHANIC EXAMINATION

Adult

Purpose: Assesses competency in airframe and power plant mechanics. Used for providing evidence of competency to become a teacher or obtaining academic credit at participating educational institutions.

Description: Two-part test of skills and knowledge important in airframe and power plant mechanic work. The multiple-choice written test (200 items) covers aircraft science, materials, structures, theory of flight, propellers, electrical and instrument systems, fluid and environmental systems, aviation regulations, reciprocating engine systems, and turbine engine systems. The performance test measures one's ability in sheet metal work, servicing landing gear, use of nondestructive test techniques, completion of maintenance documents, use of airworthiness directives, carburetor servicing, and engine tune-up. All materials are furnished. A calculator may be used for both portions of the test. Examiner required. The written test is suitable for group use.

Timed: Written test 3 hours; performance test 6 hours

Scoring: Examiner evaluated; computer scored

Cost: Contact publisher

Publisher: National Occupational Competency Testing Institute

TEACHER OCCUPATIONAL COMPETENCY TESTING: APPLIANCE REPAIR EXAMINATION #027

Adult

Purpose: Assesses competency in appliance repair. Used for providing evidence of competency to become a teacher or obtaining academic credit at participating educational institutions.

Description: Two-part test of skills and knowledge important in major appliance repair. The multiple-choice written test (200 items) covers fundamentals, refrigeration, power tools and small appliances, kitchen equipment, major heating devices, and laundry equipment. The performance test measures skills in power tools and small appliances, major heating devices, laundry equipment, kitchen equipment, and refrigeration equipment. Personal tools may be used. Handbooks and references are provided. Examiner required. The written test is suitable for group use.

Timed: Written test 3 hours; performance test 6 hours

Scoring: Examiner evaluated; computer scored

Cost: Contact publisher

Publisher: National Occupational Competency Testing Institute

TEACHER OCCUPATIONAL COMPETENCY TESTING: ARCHITECTURAL DRAFTING EXAMINATION #012

Adult

Purpose: Assesses competency in architectural drafting. Used for providing evidence of competency to become a teacher or obtaining academic credit at participating educational institutions.

Description: Two-part test of skills and knowledge important in architectural drafting positions. The multiple-choice written test (200 items) covers basic architectural data, planning and design, materials and methods of construction, structural systems, and administration. The performance test measures skills in sections, working drawings, and graphic techniques. The candidate should bring a set of drawing instruments, drawing pencils (lead holder and leads), architect's scales, erasers, and erasing shields. Candidates also may bring a lettering guide and calculator if desired. Examiner required. The written test is suitable for group use.

Timed: Written test 3 hours; performance test 5 hours

Scoring: Examiner evaluated; computer scored

Cost: Contact publisher

Publisher: National Occupational Competency Testing Institute

TEACHER OCCUPATIONAL COMPETENCY TESTING: AUDIO-VISUAL COMMUNICATIONS TECHNOLOGY EXAMINATION #049

Adult

Purpose: Assesses competency in audiovisual communications technology. Used for providing evidence of competency to become a teacher or obtaining academic credit at participating educational institutions.

Description: Two-part test of skills and knowledge important in audiovisual communications technology. The multiple-choice written test (180 items) covers general audiovisual knowledge, broadcasting, lighting theory and techniques, multi-image production, theory, and equipment operation, graphics/visuals production and utilization, photography theory, audio/radio theory, and television and film theory. The performance test focuses on motion picture projection, still photography (35mm camera operation, negative development, printing, and dry mounting), audio production studio recording, editing and splicing audiotape, transparency design, motion picture splicing, and T.V. shooting and editing (almost a third of the test). Handbooks and reference material are provided. Examiner required. The written test is suitable for group use.

Timed: Written test 3 hours; performance test 5 hours, 50 minutes

Scoring: Examiner evaluated; computer scored

Cost: Contact publisher

Publisher: National Occupational Competency Testing Institute

TEACHER OCCUPATIONAL COMPETENCY TESTING: AUTO BODY REPAIR EXAMINATION #002

Adult

Purpose: Assesses competency in auto body repair. Used for providing evidence of competency to become a teacher or obtaining academic credit at participating educational institutions.

Description: Two-part test of skills and knowledge important in auto body repair. The multiple-choice written test (190 items) covers welding, filling operations and plastics, sheet metal repair, refinishing, panel replacement, frame (unitized body repair), front end alignment, electrical and accessory systems, glass, trim and hardware repair, estimating, tools and equipment, and safety. The performance test measures skills in sheet metal repair, refinishing, diagnosing structural damage, glass trim repair, and electrical work. Handbooks and reference material are provided, or candidates may bring their own. Candidates should bring their own safety glasses and spray mask, as well as hand tools, including a 12-foot measuring tape. A calculator may be used for both portions of the test. Examiner required. The written test is suitable for group use.

Timed: Written test 3 hours; performance test 5 hours, 40 minutes

Scoring: Examiner evaluated; computer scored

Cost: Contact publisher

Publisher: National Occupational Competency Testing Institute

TEACHER OCCUPATIONAL COMPETENCY TESTING: AUTO BODY REPAIR EXAMINATION #083

Adult

Purpose: Assesses competency in auto body repair. Used for providing evidence of competency to become a teacher or obtaining credit at participating educational institutions.

Description: Two-part test of skills and knowledge important in auto body repair.

The multiple-choice written test (190 items) covers welding; filling operations and plastics; repairing sheet metal; refinishing; panel replacement; frame (unitized body repair); front end alignment; electrical and accessory systems; glass, trim, and hardware; and estimating, tools and equipment, and safety. The performance test covers metal forming, welding, diagnosing structural damage, refinishing, and electrical troubleshooting. Examinees may use their personal tools. Handbooks and references will be provided. A calculator may be used for both tests. Examiner required. The written test is suitable for group use.

Untimed: Written test 3 hours; performance test 4 hours, 45 minutes

Scoring: Examiner evaluated; computer scored

Cost: Contact publisher

Publisher: National Occupational Competency Testing Institute

TEACHER OCCUPATIONAL COMPETENCY TESTING: AUTO MECHANIC EXAMINATION #003

Adult

Purpose: Assesses competency in auto mechanics. Used for providing evidence of competency to become a teacher or obtaining academic credit at participating educational institutions.

Description: Two-part test of skills and knowledge important in auto mechanics. The multiple-choice written test (200 items) covers basic shop principles and practices, engines, emission systems, engine system analysis and repair, suspension, steering and braking, fuel systems, engine and chassis, electrical, drive line and components, accessories, and shop management and control. The performance test measures skills in engines, basic automotive practices, fuel systems, electrical, batteries, air conditioning, charging systems, emission systems, engine analysis and repair, drive lines and components, suspension and steering, and brakes. Test equipment, shop manuals, and specifications are provided. Personal tools may be used. Examiner required. The written test is suitable for group use.

Timed: Written test 3 hours; performance test 5 hours

Scoring: Examiner evaluated; computer scored

Cost: Contact publisher

Publisher: National Occupational Competency Testing Institute

TEACHER OCCUPATIONAL COMPETENCY TESTING: BAKER

Adult

Purpose: Assesses competency of individuals in bakery occupations. Used for providing evidence of competency to become a teacher or obtaining academic credit at participating institutions.

Description: Multiple-item paper-pencil and task-performance test in two parts assessing competencies of teachers of baking. The multiple-choice written test (183 items) covers definition of terms, classifications of ingredients, substitutions, sanitation and safety, weights and measurements, interaction of ingredients, handling and storage of ingredients, general baking knowledge, equipment preparation, and baking remedies. The performance test consists of dough preparation for and baking of bread, rolls, cakes, and pastries. Examiner required. Suitable for group use.

Timed: Written test 3 hours; performance test 4 hours

Scoring: Examiner evaluated; may be computer scored

Cost: Contact publisher

Publisher: National Occupational Competency Testing Institute

TEACHER OCCUPATIONAL COMPETENCY TESTING: BAKING EXAMINATION #059

Adult

Purpose: Assesses competency in baking. Used for providing evidence of competency to become a teacher or obtaining

credit at participating educational institutions.

Description: Two-part test of skills and knowledge important in baking. The multiple-choice written test (200 items) covers general baking knowledge, classification and properties of ingredients, bread and rolls, cake doughnuts, yeast-raised dough, cookies, cakes, danish-puff pastry, pies, safety and sanitation, handling and storage of ingredients, and weights and measures (general baking math). The performance test covers dough preparation, bread, cakes, rolls, and pastries. All materials will be furnished. A calculator may be used for both tests. Examiner required. The written test is suitable for group use.

Untimed: Written test 3 hours; performance test 4 hours

Scoring: Examiner evaluated; computer scored

Cost: Contact publisher

Publisher: National Occupational Competency Testing Institute

TEACHER OCCUPATIONAL COMPETENCY TESTING: BRICK MASONRY EXAMINATION #051

Adult

Purpose: Assesses competency in brick masonry. Used for providing evidence of competency to become a teacher or obtaining academic credit at participating educational institutions.

Description: Two-part test of skills and knowledge important in brick masonry. The multiple-choice written test (200 items) covers brick, block, fireplace, tile, stone, glass block, and pave brick—installation, layout, and terminology; building layout; and general knowledge. The performance test measures skills in layout of a brick and block wall, brick 4″ return corner, brick chimney construction, glass block window construction, brick and block parapet wall, segmental arch, and reading blueprints. Candidates are required to bring their own hand tools. A calculator may be used for both portions of the test. Examiner required. The written test is suitable for group use.

Timed: Written test 3 hours; performance test 5 hours, 40 minutes

Scoring: Examiner evaluated; computer scored

Cost: Contact publisher

Publisher: National Occupational Competency Testing Institute

---

TEACHER OCCUPATIONAL COMPETENCY TESTING: BUILDING AND HOME MAINTENANCE EXAMINATION #067

Adult

Purpose: Assesses competency in building and home maintenance. Used for providing evidence of competency to become a teacher or obtaining credit at participating educational institutions.

Description: Two-part test of skills and knowledge important in building and home maintenance. The multiple-choice written test (162 items) covers floor stripping, refinishing, and buffing; carpet care; general electricity and repair; building security, fire prevention, and records; general cleaning; plumbing; employee and staff relations; heating; and painting. The performance test covers general cleaning of an office or classroom and a restroom or shower/locker room area; floor stripping, refinishing, and buffing; carpet care; welding or soldering; electrical repair; small hand/power tools; and interior and exterior painting. A calculator may be used for both portions of the test. Candidates should contact the test site to confirm the supplies they must bring to the examination. Examiner required. The written test is suitable for group use.

Untimed: Written test 3 hours; performance test 5 hours

Scoring: Examiner evaluated; computer scored

Cost: Contact publisher

Publisher: National Occupational Competency Testing Institute

---

TEACHER OCCUPATIONAL COMPETENCY TESTING: BUILDING CONSTRUCTION OCCUPATIONS EXAMINATION #042

Adult

Purpose: Assesses competency in building construction occupations. Used for providing evidence of competency to become a teacher or obtaining academic credit at participating educational institutions.

Description: Two-part test of skills and knowledge important in building construction occupations. The multiple-choice written test (200 items) covers carpentry, electrical, plumbing, math, metal work and guttering, painting and decorating, masonry, building codes, and safety. The performance test measures skills in masonry, carpentry (a third of the test), painting and decorating, metal work and guttering, plumbing, electrical, and knowledge of building codes and safety. Personal tools may be used. A calculator may be used for both portions of the test. Examiner required. The written test is suitable for group use.

Timed: Written test 3 hours; performance test 4 hours, 25 minutes

Scoring: Examiner evaluated; computer scored

Cost: Contact publisher

Publisher: National Occupational Competency Testing Institute

---

TEACHER OCCUPATIONAL COMPETENCY TESTING: BUILDING TRADES MAINTENANCE EXAMINATION #025

Adult

Purpose: Assesses competency in building trade maintenance occupations. Used for providing evidence of competency to become a teacher or obtaining academic credit at participating educational institutions.

Description: Two-part test of skills and knowledge important in building trades maintenance occupations. The multiple-choice written test (200 items) covers electrical installation, carpentry, plumbing, masonry, metal processes, painting and wall applications, and related knowledge. The performance test measures skill in electrical installation, carpentry, masonry, plumbing, welding, lock set installation, painting and wall applications, and glass installation. Personal tools may be used. A calculator may be used for both portions of the test. Examiner required. The written test is suitable for group use.

Timed: Written test 3 hours; performance test 5 hours, 35 minutes

Scoring: Examiner evaluated; computer scored

Cost: Contact publisher

Publisher: National Occupational Competency Testing Institute

TEACHER OCCUPATIONAL COMPETENCY TESTING: CABINET MAKING AND MILLWORK EXAMINATION #024

Adult

Purpose: Assesses competency in cabinet making and millwork occupations. Used for providing evidence of competency to become a teacher or obtaining academic credit at participating educational institutions.

Description: Two-part test of skills and knowledge important in cabinet making and millwork. The multiple-choice written test consists of 160 items covering planning, safety, machines, hand tools, wood/stock selection, joinery, assembly, and finishing. The performance test measures skills in planning and layout, wood/stock selection, hand tools, safety, machine, joinery, assembly, and finish. References will be provided. Personal tools may be used. Examiner required. The written test is suitable for group use.

Timed: Written test 3 hours; performance test 5 hours

Scoring: Examiner evaluated; computer scored

Cost: Contact publisher

Publisher: National Occupational Competency Testing Institute

TEACHER OCCUPATIONAL COMPETENCY TESTING: CARPENTRY EXAMINATION #007

Adult

Purpose: Assesses competency in carpentry. Used for providing evidence of competency to become a teacher or obtaining academic credit at participating educational institutions.

Description: Two-part test of skills and knowledge important in carpentry. The multiple-choice written test (159 items) covers surveying, layout, and blueprint reading; foundation work; concrete walks, floors, and step construction; floor framing; wall and ceiling framing; estimating; scaffolding; roof framing and roofing; stair construction; interior finish; cabinetry; and exterior finish. The performance test measures skills in floor framing, wall framing, roof framing, roofing, and exterior finish. Personal tools may be used. Candidates are advised to bring their own portable power saw. Examiner required. The written test is suitable for group use.

Timed: Written test 3 hours; performance test 5 hours

Scoring: Examiner evaluated; computer scored

Cost: Contact publisher

Publisher: National Occupational Competency Testing Institute

TEACHER OCCUPATIONAL COMPETENCY TESTING: CHILD CARE AND GUIDANCE EXAMINATION #081

Adult

Purpose: Assesses competency in various areas of child care. Used for providing evidence of competency to become a teacher or obtaining credit at participating educational institutions.

Description: Two-part test of skills and knowledge important in child care. The multiple-choice written test (200 items) covers infant-toddler development, infant-toddler learning, preschool and young child development, preschool and young child learning, guiding behavior, health and safety, center management, and special needs. The performance test covers infant diapering, toddler observation, large-group teaching, small-group teaching, daily program plans, examiner-candidate role play (parent or staff interaction), examiner-candidate role play (child discipline situation). Prior to the performance test, the candidate must prepare lesson plans for two teaching experiences (large group and small group). Candidates must supply all materials to be used in the teaching activities. Prior to conducting the teaching activities, candidates should plan to spend 30 minutes with the children with whom the test will be conducted. Examiner required. The written test is suitable for group use.

Untimed: Written test 3 hours; performance test 5 hours

Scoring: Examiner evaluated; computer scored

Cost: Contact publisher

Publisher: National Occupational Competency Testing Institute

---

TEACHER OCCUPATIONAL COMPETENCY TESTING: CIVIL TECHNOLOGY EXAMINATION #018

Adult

Purpose: Assesses competency in civil technology occupations. Used for providing evidence of competency to become a teacher or obtaining academic credit at participating educational institutions.

Description: Two-part test of skills and knowledge important in civil technology occupations. The multiple-choice written test (152 items) covers asphalt, soil, concrete, surveying, instrumentation, steel structures, general engineering information, and drafting. The performance test measures skills in concrete, soils, asphalt, surveying, and drafting. All necessary tools, machinery, and handbooks are provided. Candidates should bring their own calculators and drafting instruments. Examiner required. The written test is suitable for group use.

Timed: Written test 3 hours; performance test 5 hours

Scoring: Examiner evaluated; computer scored

Cost: Contact publisher

Publisher: National Occupational Competency Testing Institute

---

TEACHER OCCUPATIONAL COMPETENCY TESTING: COMMERCIAL ART EXAMINATION #029

Adult

Purpose: Assesses competency in commercial art. Used for providing evidence of competency to become a teacher or obtaining academic credit at participating educational institutions.

Description: Two-part test of skills and knowledge important in commercial art. The multiple-choice written test (125 items) covers production, drawing and rendering, design and typography, printing, and fundamentals of photography and basic knowledge of the field. The performance test measures skills in black-and-white rendering, magazine ad, and keyline/mechanical. Examiner required. The written test is suitable for group use.

Timed: Written test 3 hours; performance test 5 hours

Scoring: Examiner evaluated; computer scored

Cost: Contact publisher

Publisher: National Occupational Competency Testing Institute

---

TEACHER OCCUPATIONAL COMPETENCY TESTING: COMMERCIAL PHOTOGRAPHY EXAMINATION #070

Adult

Purpose: Assesses competency in commercial photography. Used for providing evidence of competency to become a teacher or obtaining credit at participating educational institutions.

Description: Two-part test of skills and knowledge important in commercial photography. The multiple-choice written test (150 items) covers camera operation, photo printing, film processing, film characteristics, lighting, print finishing, composition, filters, light meters, and light and color. The performance test covers 35mm camera operation, film processing, printing and enlarging, and lighting. A calculator may be used for both tests. Examiner required. The written test is suitable for group use.

Untimed: Written test 3 hours; performance test 5 hours to 6 hours, 45 minutes

Scoring: Examiner evaluated; computer scored

Cost: Contact publisher

Publisher: National Occupational Competency Testing Institute

---

TEACHER OCCUPATIONAL COMPETENCY TESTING: COMPUTER SCIENCE EXAMINATION FOR SECONDARY TEACHERS #080

Adult

Purpose: Assesses competency in various areas of computer science. Used for providing evidence of competency to become a teacher or obtaining credit at participating educational institutions.

Description: Two-part test of skills and knowledge important in computer science. The multiple-choice written test (158 items) covers general concepts, program design, microcomputers, and on-line communications (magnetic files and data communications). The performance test covers microcomputers, systems analysis, program design, BASIC programming, PASCAL programming, FORTRAN programming, and COBOL programming. Examinees may use their own microcomputer systems and word processing and spread sheet software. Compatibility to site hardware is the examinee's responsibility. Calculators are allowed for both tests. Examiner required. The written test is suitable for group use.

Untimed: Written test 3 hours; performance test 6 hours

Scoring: Examiner evaluated; computer scored

Cost: Contact publisher

Publisher: National Occupational Competency Testing Institute

---

TEACHER OCCUPATIONAL COMPETENCY TESTING: COMPUTER TECHNOLOGY EXAMINATION #026

Adult

Purpose: Assesses competency in computer technology. Used for providing evidence of competency to become a teacher or obtaining academic credit at participating educational institutions.

Description: Two-part test of skills and knowledge important in computer technology. The multiple-choice written test (200 items) covers general information, data processing machine operations, computer programming, and system analysis and design. The performance test measures skills in file preparation, flowcharting, and source listing and output. The majority of the performance test covers source listing and output. The candidate must be able to operate a keypunch or a CRT with a keyboard. Examiner required. The written test is suitable for group use.

Timed: Written test 3 hours; performance test 5 hours

Scoring: Examiner evaluated; computer scored

Cost: Contact publisher

Publisher: National Occupational Competency Testing Institute

---

TEACHER OCCUPATIONAL COMPETENCY TESTING: COSMETOLOGY EXAMINATION #022

Adult

Purpose: Assesses competency in cosmetology. Used for providing evidence of competency to become a teacher or obtaining academic credit at participating educational institutions.

Description: Two-part test of skills and knowledge important in cosmetology. The multiple-choice written test (150 items) covers care of hands, chemical permanent waving, hair styling, hair coloring, hair pieces, hair and scalp, chemical hair straightening, hair shaping, care of face, and shop operation and management.

The performance test measures skills in hair styling, haircutting, hair coloring, chemical permanent waving or chemical hair straightening, thermal waving, and manicuring or facial makeup. One live model and one manikin are required for the performance examination. The candidate supplies haircutting tools, hair clips, combs, brushes, protective gloves and apron, blow dryers, lotions, rollers, makeup, curling irons, a chemical permanent wave lotion with rods and end papers or chemical relaxer, and manicure tools and products, including dark nail polish or facial makeup. Towels, shampoo, cotton, and standard shop equipment will be furnished. The candidate must submit to the examiner at the time of testing a published plan and photograph of the hairstyle he or she intends to execute. A calculator may be used for both tests. Examiner required. The written test is suitable for group use.

Timed: Written test 3 hours; performance test 5 hours

Scoring: Examiner evaluated; computer scored

Cost: Contact publisher

Publisher: National Occupational Competency Testing Institute

TEACHER OCCUPATIONAL COMPETENCY TESTING: DIESEL ENGINE REPAIR EXAMINATION #004

Adult

Purpose: Assesses competency in diesel engine repair. Used for providing evidence of competency to become a teacher or obtaining academic credit at participating educational institutions.

Description: Two-part test of skills and knowledge important in diesel engine repair. The multiple-choice written test (167 items) covers fuel injection pumps and nozzle repair and adjustment, hydraulic systems troubleshooting, electrical systems diagnosis and repair, power train operation and repair, and basic engine diagnosis and repair. The performance test includes fuel injection pump and nozzle repair, testing and calibrating pump systems, basic engine diagnosis and re-

pair, electrical systems diagnosis and repair, and power train operation and repair. Examiner required. The written test is suitable for group use.

Timed: Written test 3 hours; performance test 4 hours

Scoring: Examiner evaluated; computer scored

Cost: Contact publisher

Publisher: National Occupational Competency Testing Institute

TEACHER OCCUPATIONAL COMPETENCY TESTING: DIESEL MECHANIC

Adult

Purpose: Measures competency in diesel mechanics. Used for providing evidence of competency to become a teacher or obtaining academic credit at participating institutions.

Description: Multiple-item paper-pencil and task-performance test assessing abilities of teachers of diesel mechanics. The multiple-choice written test assesses knowledge of engine service, diesel fuel systems service, lubrication systems service, electrical systems service, engine auxiliaries, cooling system service, internal and external systems service, dynamometer, and testing. The performance test covers engine service, fuel systems, electrical systems, cooling systems, and lubrication. Examiner required. Suitable for group use.

Timed: Written test 3 hours; performance test 4 hours

Scoring: Examiner evaluated; may be computer scored

Cost: Contact publisher

Publisher: National Occupational Competency Testing Institute

TEACHER OCCUPATIONAL COMPETENCY TESTING: DIESEL MECHANICS EXAMINATION #052

Adult

Purpose: Assesses competency in diesel mechanics. Used for providing evidence of competency to become a teacher or obtaining credit at participating educational institutions.

Description: Two-part test of skills and knowledge important in diesel mechanics. The multiple-choice written test (200 items) covers diesel engine theory of operation, engine diagnosis and repair, fuel and governor systems, cooling and lubrication systems, intake and exhaust systems, electrical systems, power train and brake systems, and hydraulic systems. The performance test covers engine service, fuel systems, electrical systems, cooling systems, and lubrication. All materials will be furnished. A calculator may be used for both tests. Examiner required. The written test is suitable for group use.

Untimed: Written test 3 hours; performance test 4 hours

Scoring: Examiner evaluated; computer scored

Cost: Contact publisher

Publisher: National Occupational Competency Testing Institute

TEACHER OCCUPATIONAL COMPETENCY TESTING: DRAFTING OCCUPATIONS EXAMINATION #060

Adult

Purpose: Assesses competency in drafting occupations. Used for providing evidence of competency to become a teacher or obtaining academic credit at participating educational institutions.

Description: Two-part test of skills and knowledge important in drafting occupations. The multiple-choice written test (194 items) covers drafting fundamentals, related trades, related mathematics, and related science. The performance test measures skills in orthographics, sectioning, auxiliary projection, revolutions, isometric and oblique, threads and fasteners, intersections, development, and drawing and dimensioning. The candidate should provide basic drafting tools, a pocket calculator, and a copy of the *Machinery's Handbook*. Examiner required. The written test is suitable for group use.

Timed: Written test 3 hours; performance test 5 hours

Scoring: Examiner evaluated; computer scored

Cost: Contact publisher

Publisher: National Occupational Competency Testing Institute

TEACHER OCCUPATIONAL COMPETENCY TESTING: ELECTRICAL CONSTRUCTION AND MAINTENANCE EXAMINATION #061

Adult

Purpose: Assesses competency in electrical construction and maintenance. Used for providing evidence of competency to become a teacher or obtaining credit at participating educational institutions.

Description: Two-part test of skills and knowledge important in electrical construction and maintenance. The multiple-choice written test (180 items) covers electron theory and basic circuit calculations, A.C. theory and conductors, motor control circuits and motors, wiring methods, transformers and lighting, and basic electricity. The performance test covers motors and motor circuits, troubleshooting, transformer layout and connectors, component layout and connectors, component identification and testing, and race ways and lighting. Calculators may be used for both tests. Examiner required. The written test is suitable for group use.

Untimed: Written test 3 hours; performance test 4 hours, 35 minutes

Scoring: Examiner evaluated; computer scored

Cost: Contact publisher

Publisher: National Occupational Competency Testing Institute

TEACHER OCCUPATIONAL COMPETENCY TESTING: ELECTRICAL INSTALLATION EXAMINATION #008

Adult

Purpose: Assesses competency in electrical installation. Used for providing evidence of competency to become a teacher or obtaining academic credit at participating educational institutions.

Description: Two-part test of skills and knowledge important in electrical installation. The multiple-choice written test (179 items) covers basic principles of electricity and magnetism and their application in the trade, reading working instructions and trade calculations, lighting and wiring, motors and generators, wiring practices and procedures, transformers, and general trade information. The performance test measures skills in layout and print reading, installation, testing and operation of controls, code applications, installation of residential and commercial wiring, testing and troubleshooting of installations, and safety. Applicants may bring their own reference materials and handbooks. Personal tools also may be used. Examiner required. The written test is suitable for group use.

Timed: Written test 3 hours; performance test 5 hours

Scoring: Examiner evaluated; computer scored

Cost: Contact publisher

Publisher: National Occupational Competency Testing Institute

TEACHER OCCUPATIONAL COMPETENCY TESTING: ELECTRONICS COMMUNICATIONS EXAMINATION #015

Adult

Purpose: Assesses competency in electronics communications. Used for providing evidence of competency to become a teacher or obtaining academic credit at participating educational institutions.

Description: Two-part test of skills and knowledge important in electronics communications. The multiple-choice written test (200 items) covers electronic theory and principles, A.C. and D.C. electronics, solid state electronics, amplification, instrumentation, antennas and transmission lines, communications, digital, and microprocessors and systems. The performance test measures skills in soldering and desoldering, analysis and repair of

radio receivers, communication troubleshooting and repair, and testing and correcting faults in digital and microprocessor systems. Candidates may bring their own nonprogrammable calculators and soldering/desoldering equipment and supplies to the performance exam. Data manuals, reference materials, and supplies are furnished. Personal tools and equipment may be used. Examiner required. The written test is suitable for group use.

Timed: Written test 3 hours; performance test 3 hours

Scoring: Examiner required; computer scored

Cost: Contact publisher

Publisher: National Occupational Competency Testing Institute

TEACHER OCCUPATIONAL COMPETENCY TESTING: ELECTRONICS TECHNOLOGY EXAMINATION #053

Adult

Purpose: Assesses competency in electronics technology. Used for providing evidence of competency to become a teacher or obtaining academic credit at participating educational institutions.

Description: Two-part test of skills and knowledge important in electronics technology. The multiple-choice written test (180 items) covers analysis, troubleshooting, instruments, electronic components, D.C. circuits/basic electricity, A.C. circuits/basic electronics, semiconductors/basic circuits, and basic digital electronics. The performance test measures skills in analysis, troubleshooting and repair, instrumentation, electronic components, basic theory, and fabrication and inspection. Examiner required. The written test is suitable for group use.

Untimed: Written test 3 hours; performance test 4 hours

Scoring: Examiner evaluated; computer scored

Cost: Contact publisher

Publisher: National Occupational Competency Testing Institute

TEACHER OCCUPATIONAL COMPETENCY TESTING: HEATING EXAMINATION #044

Adult

Purpose: Assesses competency in heating occupations. Used for providing evidence of competency to become a teacher or obtaining academic credit at participating educational institutions.

Description: Two-part test of skills and knowledge important in heating occupations. The multiple-choice written test (178 items) covers systems, heating plants, controls, and service and testing. The performance test measures skills in systems, heating plants, controls, and service and testing. Examiner required. The written test is suitable for group use.

Timed: Written test 3 hours; performance test 4 hours

Scoring: Examiner evaluated; computer scored

Cost: Contact publisher

Publisher: National Occupational Competency Testing Institute

TEACHER OCCUPATIONAL COMPETENCY TESTING: HEAVY EQUIPMENT MECHANIC EXAMINATION #069

Adult

Purpose: Assesses competency in heavy equipment mechanics. Used for providing evidence of competency to become a teacher or obtaining credit at participating educational institutions.

Description: Two-part test of skills and knowledge important in heavy equipment mechanics. The multiple-choice written test (200 items) covers electrical systems, diesel and gasoline engine tune-up and overhaul, power trains, diesel fuel injection system and troubleshooting, cooling and exhaust systems, hydraulic systems, steering and suspension, welding and cutting, brakes, and general (includes air conditioning). The performance test covers engine tune-up, hydraulic troubleshooting and repair, power trains (differential), basic engine measurements, weld-ing and cutting, gasoline engines, electrical system, undercarriage inspection, and operation of tracked equipment, road grader, dump truck, or road tractor. Calculators may be used for both tests. Examiner required. The written test is suitable for group use.

Untimed: Written test 3 hours; performance test 6 hours

Scoring: Examiner evaluated; computer scored

Cost: Contact publisher

Publisher: National Occupational Competency Testing Institute

TEACHER OCCUPATIONAL COMPETENCY TESTING: INDUSTRIAL ELECTRICIAN EXAMINATION #014

Adult

Purpose: Assesses competency of industrial electricians. Used for providing evidence of competency to become a teacher or obtaining academic credit at participating educational institutions.

Description: Two-part test of skills and knowledge important for industrial electricians. The multiple-choice written test (190 items) covers basic theory, D.C. circuits/calculations, A.C. circuits/calculations, D.C. machines, A.C. machines/polyphase circuits, N.E.C. code, motor control/symbols, and motor controls. The performance test measures skills in magnetic motor control circuits, bending rigid conduit, bending electrical metallic tubing, troubleshooting controls, and digital circuitry. Personal tools, a calculator, and the *National Electrical Code Handbook* may be used. Examiner required. The written test is suitable for group use.

Timed: Written test 3 hours; performance test 4 hours

Scoring: Examiner evaluated; computer scored

Cost: Contact publisher

Publisher: National Occupational Competency Testing Institute

TEACHER OCCUPATIONAL COMPETENCY TESTING: INDUSTRIAL ELECTRONICS EXAMINATION #016

Adult

Purpose: Assesses competency in industrial electronics occupations. Used for providing evidence of competency to become a teacher or obtaining academic credit at participating educational institutions.

Description: Two-part test of skills and knowledge important in industrial electronics. The multiple-choice written test (150 items) covers basic electronics, A.C. and D.C. circuits; semiconductors; electronic circuits; digital; control devices and circuitry; analysis and instrumentation; symbols; and microprocessors and systems. The performance test measures skills in instrumentation and measurements, troubleshooting and repair, assembling of components into electrical circuits and determining circuit characteristics, and analysis of defective circuits. Personal tools and equipment may be used for the performance test, and a nonprogrammable calculator may be used for both portions of the test. Data manuals, reference materials, and supplies are provided. Examiner required. The written test is suitable for group use.

Timed: Written test 3 hours; performance test 4 hours

Scoring: Examiner required; computer scored

Cost: Contact publisher

Publisher: National Occupational Competency Testing Institute

TEACHER OCCUPATIONAL COMPETENCY TESTING: MACHINE DRAFTING EXAMINATION #013

Adult

Purpose: Assesses competency in machine drafting occupations. Used for providing evidence of competency to become a teacher or obtaining academic credit at participating educational institutions.

Description: Two-part test of skills and knowledge important in machine drafting. The multiple-choice written test (180 items) covers drafting room practices; orthographic and sectional drawings; dimensioning, tolerances, and symbols; threads and fasteners; cams, gears, and pulleys; trade computations; shop practices; pictorial drawings; and applied science. The performance test measures orthographic projection, sectioning, auxiliary projection, revolutions, isometric, intersections, developments, and drawing and dimensioning. Examiner required. The written test is suitable for group use.

Timed: Written test 3 hours; performance test 4 hours

Scoring: Examiner evaluated; computer scored

Cost: Contact publisher

Publisher: National Occupational Competency Testing Institute

TEACHER OCCUPATIONAL COMPETENCY TESTING: MACHINE TRADES EXAMINATION #020

Adult

Purpose: Assesses competency in machine trades. Used for providing evidence of competency to become a teacher or obtaining academic credit at participating educational institutions.

Description: Two-part test of skills and knowledge important in machine trades occupations. The multiple-choice written test (160 items) covers layout and measurment, benchwork and assembly, drill presses, power saws and shapers, milling machines, electrical discharge machines and numerical control machines, interpretation of drawings, lathes, grinders, and applications of technical information. The performance test measures skills in bench and assembly, layout and inspection; milling processes and machines; grinding and precision finishing; and use of pedestal grinder, drill press, and engine lathe. Candidates are required to bring the *Machinery's Handbook* and may bring their own safety glasses and personal tools. A calculator may be used for both the written and performance tests. Examiner required. The written test is suitable for group use.

Timed: Written test 3 hours; performance test 5 hours, 30 minutes

Scoring: Examiner evaluated; computer scored

Cost: Contact publisher

Publisher: National Occupational Competency Testing Institute

TEACHER OCCUPATIONAL COMPETENCY TESTING: MASONRY EXAMINATION #009

Adult

Purpose: Assesses competency in masonry occupations. Used for providing evidence of competency to become a teacher or obtaining academic credit at participating educational institutions.

Description: Two-part test of skills and knowledge important in masonry. The multiple-choice written test (100 items) covers trade tools, terminology, estimating procedures, layout procedures, masonry practices, safety, and materials of the trade. The performance test measures skills in layout procedures, work practices, quality of completed work, and observation of safe practices. Personal hand tools are required. Examiner required. The written test is suitable for group use.

Timed: Written test 2 hours; performance test 3 hours

Scoring: Examiner evaluated; computer scored

Cost: Contact publisher

Publisher: National Occupational Competency Testing Institute

TEACHER OCCUPATIONAL COMPETENCY TESTING: MASONRY OCCUPATIONS EXAMINATION #054

Adult

Purpose: Assesses competency in masonry occupations. Used for providing evidence of competency to become a teacher or obtaining academic credit at participating educational institutions.

Description: Two-part test of skills and knowledge important in masonry occupations. The multiple-choice written test (200 items) covers concrete, stone, estimating, tile, plaster, and brick/block. The performance test measures skills in block, brick, stone, tile, plaster, and flagstone. Examiner required. The written test is suitable for group use.

Timed: Written test 3 hours; performance test 4 hours

Scoring: Examiner evaluated; computer scored

Cost: Contact publisher

Publisher: National Occupational Competency Testing Institute

TEACHER OCCUPATIONAL COMPETENCY TESTING: MATERIALS HANDLING EXAMINATION #033

Adult

Purpose: Assesses competency in materials handling. Used for providing evidence of competency to become a teacher or obtaining academic credit at participating educational institutions.

Description: Two-part test of skills and knowledge important in materials handling. The multiple-choice written test (199 items) covers warehousing, purchasing, shipping and distribution, transportation, receiving, materials handling equipment, material storage, and inventory control. The performance test measures skills in purchasing, shipping, equipment, receiving, storage, warehouse, and inventory. Examiner required. The written test is suitable for group use.

Timed: Written test 3 hours; performance test 4 hours, 25 minutes

Scoring: Examiner evaluated; computer scored

Cost: Contact publisher

Publisher: National Occupational Competency Testing Institute

TEACHER OCCUPATIONAL COMPETENCY TESTING: MECHANICAL TECHNOLOGY EXAMINATION #023

Adult

Purpose: Assesses competency in mechanical technology occupations. Used for providing evidence of competency to become a teacher or obtaining academic credit at participating educational institutions.

Description: Two-part test of skills and knowledge important in mechanical technology occupations. The multiple-choice written test (65 items) covers machine tool operations, metallurgy, statics, fluid mechanics, thermodynamics, electricity, strength of materials, physics, mathematics, and computer. The performance test measures skills in design, drawing, testing, and evaluation and reporting. The following personal tools are required: set of drawing instruments, drawing pencils, copy of the *Machinery Handbook*, calculator, lettering guide, and pen. Examiner required. The written test is suitable for group use.

Timed: Written test 3 hours; performance test 6 hours

Scoring: Examiner evaluated; computer scored

Cost: Contact publisher

Publisher: National Occupational Competency Testing Institute

TEACHER OCCUPATIONAL COMPETENCY TESTING: MICROCOMPUTER REPAIR EXAMINATION #085

Adult

Purpose: Assesses competency in microcomputer repair. Used for providing evidence of competency to become a teacher or obtaining credit at participating educational institutions.

Description: Two-part test of skills and knowledge important in microcomputer repair. The multiple-choice written test (200 items) covers safety, hand tools, and D.C. theory; A.C. theory; semiconduc-

tors; digital; flip flops and registers; encoders and decoders, counters, multiplexer and demultiplexer, A/D and D/A converters; computer maintenance—fundamentals and peripherals; and microprocessors. The performance test covers troubleshooting of solid state circuit devices; power supplies; troubleshooting computer malfunctions; construct/analyze digital circuits; and troubleshooting and repair of peripherals. Data manuals, reference materials, and supplies will be provided. Examiner required. The written test is suitable for group use.

Untimed: Written test 3 hours; performance test 3 hours, 30 minutes

Scoring: Examiner evaluated; computer scored

Cost: Contact publisher

Publisher: National Occupational Competency Testing Institute

TEACHER OCCUPATIONAL COMPETENCY TESTING: PAINTING AND DECORATING EXAMINATION #035

Adult

Purpose: Assesses competency in painting and decorating. Used for providing evidence of competency to become a teacher or obtaining academic credit at participating educational institutions.

Description: Two-part test of skills and knowledge important in painting and decorating occupations. The multiple-choice written test (195 items) covers exterior and interior painting, wood finishing, wall covering, estimating, color and color harmony, and special wall finishes. The performance test measures abilities in exterior and interior painting, wood finishing, wall covering, color and color harmony, and cleanup. Examiner required. The written test is suitable for group use.

Timed: Written test 3 hours; performance test 4 hours

Scoring: Examiner evaluated; computer scored

Cost: Contact publisher

Publisher: National Occupational Competency Testing Institute

TEACHER OCCUPATIONAL COMPETENCY TESTING: PLUMBING EXAMINATION #010

Adult

Purpose: Assesses competency in plumbing. Used for providing evidence of competency to become a teacher or obtaining academic credit at participating educational institutions.

Description: Two-part test of skills and knowledge important in plumbing. The multiple-choice written test (200 items) covers water supply and distribution; drainage, waste, and venting systems; installation and operation of storm water drainage; plumbing fixtures; industrial and special wastes; safety; inspection and tests; general trade information; and plumbing math and interpretation of drawings. The performance test measures skills in interpreting drawings and specifications, layout and rough-in, testing water lines, identifying piping procedures, setting fixtures, and safety practices. All tools, materials, and equipment for the performance test are provided. Candidates should wear safety shoes and protective clothing and may bring their own goggles or face shields. A calculator may be used for both portions of the test. Examiner required. The written test is suitable for group use.

Timed: Written test 3 hours; performance test 5 hours

Scoring: Examiner evaluated; may be computer scored

Cost: Contact publisher

Publisher: National Occupational Competency Testing Institute

TEACHER OCCUPATIONAL COMPETENCY TESTING: POWER SEWING EXAMINATION #036

Adult

Purpose: Assesses competency in power sewing. Used for providing evidence of competency to become a teacher or obtaining academic credit at participating educational institutions.

Description: Two-part test of skills and knowledge important in power sewing. The multiple-choice written test (200 items) covers power machine operation, apparel assembly, terminology, needle trade industry, and tools and attachments. The performance test measures abilities in assembling techniques, sewing machines, tools and attachments, finishing techniques, materials, and safety and cleanup. Examiner required. The written test is suitable for group use.

Timed: Written test 3 hours; performance test 4 hours

Scoring: Examiner evaluated; computer scored

Cost: Contact publisher

Publisher: National Occupational Competency Testing Institute

TEACHER OCCUPATIONAL COMPETENCY TESTING: PRINTING (LETTERPRESS)

Adult

Purpose: Assesses competency in teachers of letterpress printing. Used for providing evidence of competency to become a teacher or obtaining academic credit at participating institutions.

Description: Multiple-item paper-pencil and task-performance test measuring knowledge and skills of letterpress printing teachers. The multiple-choice written test (183 items) covers typography, layout and composition, camera photo mechanicals, presswork, stripping and platemaking, binding and finishing, trade information, and job safety. The performance test covers design and composition, presswork, and binding and finishing. Examiner required. Suitable for group use.

Timed: Written test 3 hours; performance test 5 hours

Scoring: Examiner evaluated; may be computer scored

Cost: Contact publisher

Publisher: National Occupational Competency Testing Institute

TEACHER OCCUPATIONAL COMPETENCY TESTING: PRINTING OFFSET EXAMINATION #019

Adult

Purpose: Assesses competency in offset printing. Used for providing evidence of competency to become a teacher or obtaining academic credit at participating educational institutions.

Description: Two-part test of skills and knowledge important in offset printing. The multiple-choice written test (200 items) covers typography, layout, and composition; camera photo mechanical; trade information; job safety; presswork; platemaking and stripping; and binding and finishing. The performance test measures abilities in design and composition, photo preparatory—image carriers, image transfer, and bindery/finishing. Examiner required. The written test is suitable for group use.

Timed: Written test 3 hours; performance test 5 hours

Scoring: Examiner evaluated; computer scored

Cost: Contact publisher

Publisher: National Occupational Competency Testing Institute

TEACHER OCCUPATIONAL COMPETENCY TESTING: QUANTITY FOOD PREPARATION EXAMINATION #017

Adult

Purpose: Assesses competency in quantity food preparation. Used for providing evidence of competency to become a teacher or obtaining academic credit at participating educational institutions.

Description: Two-part test of skills and knowledge important in quantity food preparation. The multiple-choice written test (195 items) covers menu planning, guest service, food groups, equipment and tools, sanitation, purchasing, receiving and storage, cost control, and safety. The performance test measures abilities in recipes and menus, assembling and portioning ingredients, methods of food preparation, use of utensils and hand tools, use of equipment, use of preparation areas, and general knowledge. All required items are furnished. Examiner required. The written test is suitable for group use.

Timed: Written test 3 hours; performance test 3 hours

Scoring: Examiner evaluated; computer scored

Cost: Contact publisher

Publisher: National Occupational Competency Testing Institute

TEACHER OCCUPATIONAL COMPETENCY TESTING: QUANTITY FOODS EXAMINATION #055

Adult

Purpose: Assesses competency in quantity foods. Used for providing evidence of competency to become a teacher or obtaining academic credit at participating educational institutions.

Description: Two-part test of skills and knowledge important in quantity foods. The multiple-choice written test (200 items) covers cost control and menu planning, safety and cleanliness, waitressing and customer service, food service occupations nutrition, food purchasing, food receiving and storage, and food preparation. The performance test measures abilities in work organization; selection of proper tools, utensils, and ingredients; cleanliness; safety practices; weights and measurements; and food preparation. Over half the performance test focuses on food preparation. Examiner required. The written test is suitable for group use.

Timed: Written test 3 hours; performance test 5½ hours

Scoring: Examiner evaluated; computer scored

Cost: Contact publisher

Publisher: National Occupational Competency Testing Institute

TEACHER OCCUPATIONAL COMPETENCY TESTING: RADIO/TV REPAIR EXAMINATION #048

Adult

Purpose: Assesses competency in radio and TV repair. Used for providing evidence of competency to become a teacher or obtaining academic credit at participating educational institutions.

Description: Two-part test of skills and knowledge important in radio and TV repair. The multiple-choice written test (193 items) covers test equipment, fundamental electronic theory, solid state and tube circuitry, antenna and transmission lines, signal characteristics: TV and FM transmissions and reception, color and black-and-white receivers, and servicing. The performance test measures abilities in recording equipment, radio equipment, and TV service and repair. Examiner required. The written test is suitable for group use.

Timed: Written test 3 hours; performance test 4 hours, 10 minutes

Scoring: Examiner evaluated; computer scored

Cost: Contact publisher

Publisher: National Occupational Competency Testing Institute

TEACHER OCCUPATIONAL COMPETENCY TESTING: REFRIGERATION EXAMINATION #043

Adult

Purpose: Assesses competency in refrigeration. Used for providing evidence of competency to become a teacher or obtaining academic credit at participating educational institutions.

Description: Two-part test of skills and knowledge important in refrigeration occupations. The multiple-choice written test (180 items) covers domestic service, commercial service, industrial service, commercial installation, and industrial installation. The performance test consists entirely of skills in assembly, installation, and service. Examiner required. The written test is suitable for group use.

Timed: Written test 3 hours; performance test 4 hours

Scoring: Examiner evaluated; computer scored

Cost: Contact publisher

Publisher: National Occupational Competency Testing Institute

TEACHER OCCUPATIONAL COMPETENCY TESTING: SCIENTIFIC DATA PROCESSING EXAMINATION #084

Adult

Purpose: Assesses competency in scientific data processing. Used for providing evidence of competency to become a teacher or obtaining credit at participating educational institutions.

Description: Two-part test of skills and knowledge important in data processing. The multiple-choice written test (187 items, of which 167 are to be answered) covers understanding computer fundamentals; performance equipment operations; using operating systems; using software packages; generating documentation; using programming languages—BASIC, FORTRAN, Pascal, C; and applying numerical analysis. The performance test covers understanding computer fundamentals by generating documentation that demonstrates an understanding of numerical analysis, performing equipment operations using operating systems and software packages with a programming language, and developing a program using a programming language to apply numerical analysis and generate a solution. Handbooks and references will be provided. Calculators may be used for both tests. Examiner required. The written test is suitable for group use.

Untimed: Written test 3 hours; performance test 6 hours

Scoring: Examiner evaluated; computer scored

Cost: Contact publisher

Publisher: National Occupational Competency Testing Institute

TEACHER OCCUPATIONAL COMPETENCY TESTING: SHEET METAL EXAMINATION #011

Adult

Purpose: Assesses competency in sheet metal occupations. Used for providing evidence of competency to become a teacher or obtaining academic credit at participating educational institutions.

Description: Two-part test of skills and knowledge important in sheet metal work. The multiple-choice written test (169 items) covers layout and drafting; sheet metal machinery; types and use of hand tools, bench stakes, and accessories; welding; computations; hazards; materials; fluxes; application of trade science; and sheet metal fabrication. The performance test measures abilities in pattern layout (stretchout), fabrication, and assembly. Candidates may bring their own tools. Examiner required. The written test is suitable for group use.

Timed: Written test 3 hours; performance test 5½ hours

Scoring: Examiner evaluated; computer scored

Cost: Contact publisher

Publisher: National Occupational Competency Testing Institute

TEACHER OCCUPATIONAL COMPETENCY TESTING: SMALL ENGINE REPAIR EXAMINATION #005

Adult

Purpose: Assesses competency in small engine repair. Used for providing evidence of competency to become a teacher or obtaining academic credit at participating educational institutions.

Description: Two-part test of skills and knowledge important for small engine repair. The multiple-choice written test (165 items) covers benchwork, testing, and inspection; engine operation; cylinder block servicing and overhaul; lubrication systems and lubrication; cooling and exhaust systems; transmission of power and drive units; troubleshooting; fuel systems and carburetion; ignition and starting systems; trade-related information; preventive maintenance; trade application of science; and trade computations. The performance test measures abilities in benchwork, testing, and inspection; engine analysis; cooling and exhaust system; preventive maintenance; cylinder block servicing and overhaul; lubricating systems and lubrication; fuel systems and carburetion; ignition and starting systems; and troubleshooting. Personal tools may be used. Handbooks and references are provided; however, candidates may bring their own. Examiner required. The written test is suitable for group use.

Timed: Written test 3 hours; performance test 5 hours

Scoring: Examiner evaluated; computer scored

Cost: Contact publisher

Publisher: National Occupational Competency Testing Institute

TEACHER OCCUPATIONAL COMPETENCY TESTING: SMALL ENGINE REPAIR EXAMINATION #056

Adult

Purpose: Assesses competency in small engine repair. Used for providing evidence of competency to become a teacher or obtaining academic credit at participating educational institutions.

Description: Two-part test of skills and knowledge important in small engine repair. The multiple-choice written test (180 items) covers orientation, engine servicing, fuel system, electrical system, and parts and inventory. The performance test measures abilities in peripheral components, engine service and repair, fuel systems, and electrical systems. Examiner required. The written test is suitable for group use.

Timed: Written test 3 hours; performance test 4 hours

Scoring: Examiner evaluated; computer scored

Cost: Contact publisher

Publisher: National Occupational Competency Testing Institute

TEACHER OCCUPATIONAL COMPETENCY TESTING: TEXTILE PRODUCTION/ FABRICATION EXAMINATION #038

Adult

Purpose: Assesses competency in textile production and fabrication. Used for providing evidence of competency to become a teacher or obtaining academic credit at participating educational institutions.

Description: Two-part test of skills and knowledge important in textile production and fabrication. The multiple-choice written test (200 items) covers power machine operations, apparel assembly, pattern making, alterations, and textiles. The performance test measures abilities in the same five areas. Candidates should bring trousers with cuffs and a fly-type zipper, a skirt, a coat or jacket with vented sleeve, seam binding to match the skirt, a trouser zipper, hand sewing needles, fabric shears, nippers, a ripping instrument, and a thimble. Examiner required. The written test is suitable for group use.

Timed: Written test 3 hours; performance test 4 hours

Scoring: Examiner evaluated; computer scored

Cost: Contact publisher

Publisher: National Occupational Competency Testing Institute

TEACHER OCCUPATIONAL COMPETENCY TESTING: TOOL AND DIE MAKING EXAMINATION #040

Adult

Purpose: Assesses competency in tool and die making. Used for providing evidence of competency to become a teacher or obtaining academic credit at participating educational institutions.

Description: Two-part test of skills and knowledge important in tool and die making. The multiple-choice written test (180 items) covers machining speeds and feeds, engine lathe, jig borer, and electrical discharge machine; drill press; milling machine; grinding; numerical control; benchwork; shop math; metallurgy and heat treating; inspection and measurement; and die making. The performance test measures skills in operating the surface grinder, jig borer, vertical mill with digital readout and drill press, and the punch press. The candidate is required to bring to the test the *Machinery's Handbook*; a No. 3 center drill; 6–inch steel rule; Hex key wrenches; a 1–inch micrometer; 6–inch vernier or dial caliper; dial test indicator with attachments; edge finding device; telescoping gauges, $1/2''$ and $7/8''$; pocket stone; 12–inch adjustable wrench; goggles; protective clothing; and gloves. Any other tools and tooling as well as a toolbox may be brought to the performance test. A calculator may be used for both the written and performance portions. Examiner required. The written test is suitable for group use.

Timed: Written test 3 hours; performance test 5 hours, 30 minutes

Scoring: Examiner evaluated; may be computer scored

Cost: Contact publisher

Publisher: National Occupational Competency Testing Institute

TEACHER OCCUPATIONAL COMPETENCY TESTING: WELDING EXAMINATION #021

Adult

Purpose: Assesses competency in welding. Used for providing evidence of competency to become a teacher or obtaining academic credit at participating educational institutions.

Description: Two-part test of skills and knowledge important in welding. The multiple-choice written test (174 items) covers general welder qualifications, welding symbols, joint design, welding defects and causes, testing, electricity, basic metallurgy, oxyfuel welding, brazing, hard surfacing, other processes, shielded metal arc welding, gas metal arc welding, and gas tungsten arc welding. The performance test measures abilities in shielded metal arc welding, oxyfuel welding, gas metal arc welding, and gas tungsten arc welding. Personal tools may be used. Candidates furnish appropriate work clothes and safety equipment. Examiner required. The written test is suitable for group use.

Timed: Written test 3 hours; performance test 4 hours

Scoring: Examiner evaluated; computer scored

Cost: Contact publisher

Publisher: National Occupational Competency Testing Institute

TEACHER OCCUPATIONAL COMPETENCY TESTING: WELDING EXAMINATION #041

Adult

Purpose: Assesses competency in welding. Used for providing evidence of competency to become a teacher or obtaining credit at participating educational institutions.

Description: Two-part test of skills and knowledge important in welding. The multiple-choice written test (200 items) covers safety; oxyfuel welding, torch brazing, and oxyfuel cutting; shielded metal arc welding; gas tungsten arc welding; welding symbols and joint design; gas metal arc welding; flux-cored arc welding; other industrial welding and cutting processes; inspection, testing, and welding codes; and welding metallurgy. The performance test covers shielded metal arc welding, oxyfuel welding, oxyfuel torch brazing, flux-cored arc welding, gas metal arc welding, gas tungsten arc welding, air-arc cutting, and oxyfuel cutting. Personal tools may be used. The candidate must furnish all appropriate work clothes and safety equipment. A calculator may be used for both tests. Examiner required. The written test is suitable for group use.

Untimed: Written test 3 hours; performance test 5 hours

Scoring: Examiner evaluated; computer scored

Cost: Contact publisher

Publisher: National Occupational Competency Testing Institute

TEACHER STRESS INVENTORY (TSI)
Refer to page 860.

Indexes

Test Title Index

Note: Numbers in italics refer to pages on which cross-references appear.

Bennett Mechanical Comprehension Test (BMCT), 1064

Benton Revised Visual Retention Test, 96, *610*

The Ber-Sil Spanish Tests: Elementary Test 1987 Revision, 300, *687*

The Ber-Sil Spanish Tests: Secondary Test, 301, *687*

Bereweeke Skill Teaching System—Revised Edition, 647

Bessemer Screening Test, 669

Bexley-Maudsley Automated Psychological Screening (BMAPS), 97, *19*

Bi/Polar Inventories of Core Strengths, 82, *1039*

Bieger Test of Visual Discrimination, 724

Biemiller Test of Reading Processes, 367

Bilingual Oral Language Test: Bolt-English and Bolt-Spanish, 570

Bilingual Syntax Measure I and II (BSM), 571, *286, 687*

Bilingual Two Language Battery of Tests, 571

The Bingham Button Test, 27, *533*

Biochemistry Tests, 381

Biographical Index, 995, *1039*

Biographical Inventory, Form U, 620

The Bipolar Psychological Inventory (BPI), 159, *995, 1077*

Birth to Three Assessment and Intervention System: A Parent-Teacher Interaction Program, 28

Birth to Three Developmental Scale—Screening Test, 533, *28*

The Black Intelligence Test of Cultural Homogeneity (BITCH), 160

The Blacky Pictures, 233

The Blind Learning Aptitude Test (BLAT), 661

Bloom Analogies Test (BAT), 50

Bloom Sentence Completion Attitude Survey, 160, *751*

Bloomer Learning Test (BLT), 587, *621*

Blox Test (Perceptual Battery), 929

The Boder Test of Reading-Spelling Patterns, 631, *97, 367*

Body Elimination Attitude Scale, 160

The Body Image of Blind Children, 661

Boehm Test of Basic Concepts—Preschool Version, 534, *28*

Boehm Test of Basic Concepts—Revised (Boehm-R), 427

The Booklet Category Test (BCT), 97

Booklet of Grammar Tests, 281

Bormuth's Reading Passages and Carver's Questions, 367

Borromean Family Index: For Married Persons, 67

Borromean Family Index: For Single Persons, 67

Boston Naming Test, 97

Botel Reading Inventory, 336

Bracken Basic Concept Scale (BBCS), 534, *687*

Bracken Basic Concept Scale—Screening Test (BBCS-SCREENING), 534, *688*

Braille Unit Recognition Battery Diagnostic Test of Grade 2 Literary Braille, 368, *661, 724*

The Bricklin Perceptual Scales: Child-Perception-of-Parents-Series, 68

Brief Drinker Profile (BDP), 19

Brief Index of Adaptive Behavior (BIAB), 535

Brief Life History Inventory, 233, *737*

Brief Organic Chemistry Tests, 381

Brief Symptom Inventory (BSI), 160

The BRIGANCE® Diagnostic Assessment of Basic Skills—Spanish Edition, 571, *631*

The BRIGANCE® Diagnostic Comprehensive Inventory of Basic Skills (CIBS), 427

The BRIGANCE® Diagnostic Inventory of Basic Skills, 427, *787*

The BRIGANCE® Diagnostic Inventory of Early Development, 535, *28*

The BRIGANCE® Diagnostic Inventory of Essential Skills, 428, *669*

The BRIGANCE® K & 1 Screen, 535

BRIGANCE® Preschool Screen, 536

Bristol Achievement Tests, Revised Edition, 428

Bristol Language Development Scales, 688, *572, 648*

Bristol Social Adjustment Guides, 737, *233*

Bristol Social Adjustment Guides, American Edition (BSAG), 737, *233, 648, 670*

The British Ability Scales, Revised Edition, 587, *50*

British Picture Vocabulary Scales, 587, *648, 661*

Bruce Vocabulary Inventory, 971, *871*

Bruininks-Oseretsky Test of Motor Proficiency, 610

Buffalo Reading Test, 871, *363*

Bulimia Test (BULIT), 6, *161*

Burks' Behavior Rating Scales, 233

Burks' Behavior Rating Scales, Preschool and Kindergarten Edition, 136, *28, 737*

Burt Word Reading Test—New Zealand Revision, 337

The Bury Infant Check, 536, *611*

Business Analyst Skills Evaluation (BUSAN), 952

Business English Test (BET), 787

Business Judgment Test, 995

The Bzoch-League Receptive-Expressive Emergent Language Scale (REEL), 28, *661, 724*

The C.P.H. (Colorado Psychopathic Hospital) Patient Attitude Scale, 234

CAI Study Skills Test, 777

Cain-Levine Social Competency Scale, 648

California Achievement Tests: Forms C and D (CAT/C&D), 429

California Achievement Tests: Forms E and F, 429

California Adaptive Behavior Scale, 234

California Brief Life History Inventory (CBLHI), 161

California Chemistry Diagnostic Test, 381

Fundamental Interpersonal Relations Orientation—Behavior Characteristics (FIRO-BC), 241

Fundamental Interpersonal Relations Orientation—Feelings (FIRO-F), 174

Fundamental Processes in Arithmetic, 635, *318*

GAP Reading Test, 342

Gapadol Reading Comprehension Tests, 371

Gates-MacGinitie Reading Test, Canadian Edition (GMRT), 371

Gates-MacGinitie Reading Tests, Third Edition, 371

Gates-McKillop-Horowitz Reading Diagnostic Tests, 342, *276*

Geist Picture Interest Inventory, 822

General Ability Tests: Numerical (GAT Numerical), 974, *457*

General Ability Tests: Perceptual (GAT Perceptual), 974, *457*

General Ability Tests: Verbal (GAT Verbal), 975, *457*

General Aptitude Series (GAS), 885, *1043*

General Aptitude Test Battery (GATB), 885

General Chemistry Tests, 382

General Clerical Test (GCT), 933

General Health Questionnaire (GHQ), 174

General Occupational Interest Inventory, 984

General-Organic-Biological Chemistry (for Allied Health Sciences Program) Tests, 382

General Science Test (A/107), 383

Geriatric Depression Scale, 45, *174*

Geriatric Paranoia Scale, 45, *174*

Geriatric Sentence Completion Form (GSCF), 45, *174*

The Gesell Preschool Test, 544

The Gesell School Readiness Test—Complete Battery, 545

Giannetti On-Line Psychosocial History (GOLPH), 174, *1003*

Gibson Spiral Maze, 104, *612*

Gifted and Talented Scale, 623

Gifted and Talented Screening Form (GTSF), 623

Gillingham-Childs Phonics Proficiency Scales: Series I, Basic Reading and Spelling; Series II, Advanced Reading, 343, *276*

Gilmore Oral Reading Test, 343

Global Assessment Scale (GAS), 175

Goldman-Fristoe Test of Articulation, 698

Goldman-Fristoe-Woodcock Auditory Skills Test Battery, 677

Goldman-Fristoe-Woodcock Test of Auditory Discrimination, 678

Goldstein-Scheerer Tests of Abstract and Concrete Thinking, 105

Golombok Rust Inventory of Marital State (GRIMS), 85

Golombok Rust Inventory of Sexual Satisfaction (GRISS), 85

Goodenough-Harris Drawing Test, 52

Goodman Lock Box, 545, *652*

Gordon Diagnostic System (GDI), 635

Gordon Occupational Check List II, 822

Gordon Personal Profile and Inventory (GPP-I), 175

Gottschaldt Figures Test, 886

Goyer Organization of Ideas Test, 457

Graded Anagram Task (GAT), 263, *52*

Graded Arithmetic-Mathematics Test, Metric Edition, 318

Graded Assessment in Maths Developmental Pack (GAIM), 319

The Graded Naming Test, 105, *45*

Graded Word Spelling Test, 289

Graduate and Managerial Assessment, 458, *1043*

Graduate Level Placement Examinations: Analytical Chemistry, 383

Graduate Level Placement Examinations: Inorganic Chemistry, 383

Graduate Level Placement Examinations: Organic Chemistry, 383

Graduate Level Placement Examinations: Physical Chemistry, 384

Graduate Management Admission Test (GMAT), 458

Graduate Record Examinations (GRE), 458

Grassi Basic Cognitive Evaluation, 105, *652*

Grassi Block Substitution Test, 106

Gravidometer, 86

Gray Oral Reading Tests—Revised (GORT-R), 372

Grid Test of Schizophrenic Thought Disorder, 241

Grief Experience Inventory (Research Edition), 263

Griffiths Mental Development Scales, 52, *33*

Grim, 241, *263*

Grooved Pegboard, 106, *45*

Group Achievement Identification Measure (GAIM), 765

Group Diagnostic Reading Aptitude and Achievement Tests—Intermediate Form, 343

Group Embedded Figures Test (GEFT), 242

Group Environment Scale (GES), 175, *1003*

Group Exercises, 1043

Group Inventory for Finding Creative Talent (GIFT), 624

Group Inventory for Finding Interests (GIFFI), 624

Group Literacy Assessment, 276

Group Mathematics Test: Second Edition, 319

Group Personality Projective Test (GPPT), 242

Group Psychotherapy Evaluation Scale, 176

Group Reading Assessment, 344

Group Reading Test: Second Edition, 345

Group Shorr Imagery Test (GSIT), 176

Group Test for Indian Pupils—1968, 590

Group Tests for 5/6 and 7/8 Year Olds—1960, 546

Group Tests—1974, 53, *590*

GROW, 86

Growing Love in Christian Marriage, 86

Reynell-Zinkin Development Scales for Young Visually Handicapped Children, 561, *40*, *730*

Reynolds Adolescent Depression Scale (RADS), 214, *24*, *746*, *772*

Reynolds Child Depression Scale (RCDS), 148

Rhode Island Test of Language Structure (RITLS), 710

Richmond Pseudo-Isochromatic Color Test, 730

Richmond Tests of Basic Skills, Second Edition, 482

Right-Left Orientation Test, 123

Riley Articulation and Language Test: Revised, 710

Riley Motor Problems Inventory, 123, *617*

Riley Preschool Developmental Screening Inventory, 561

Ring and Peg Tests of Behavior Development for Infants and Preschool Children, 40

Risk-Taking Attitude-Values Inventory (RTAVI), 250

Rivermead Perceptual Assessment Battery, 124, *803*

Roberts Apperception Test for Children, 148

Roberts Apperception Test for Children: Test Pictures for Black Children, 149

Rockford Infant Developmental Scales (RIDES), 561, *41*

Roeder Manipulative Aptitude Test, 618, *1072*

Rogers Criminal Responsibility Assessment Scales (R-CRAS), 215

Rogers Personal Adjustment Inventory—UK Revision, 149, *772*

Rokeach Value Survey, 250, *265*

Rokeach Value Survey: Form G, 251

Rorschach Psychodiagnostic Test, 251

Rosenzweig Picture-Frustration Study (P-F), 251, *10*

Ross Information Processing Assessment (RIPA), 124

Ross Test of Higher Cognitive Processes (Ross Test), 597, *625*

Roswell-Chall Auditory Blending Test, 355, *710*

Roswell-Chall Diagnostic Reading Test of Word Analysis Skills (Revised and Extended), 355

Rotate and Flip Test (RAFT), 979

Rotter Incomplete Sentences Blank, 215

Rucker-Gable Educational Programming Scale, 858

Rust Inventory of Schizotypal Cognitions (RISC), 216, *265*

S-D Proneness Checklist, 216

Safe Driver Attitude Test (SDAT), 528

Safran Students Interest Inventory (Third Edition), 834

St. Lucia Graded Word Reading Test, 356

St. Lucia Reading Comprehension Test, 356

Salamon-Conte Life Satisfaction In The Elderly Scale (LSES), 47

Sales Attitude Checklist, 1084

Sales Comprehension Test, 1084

Sales Motivation Inventory, 1084

Sales Motivation Survey (SMS), 1084

Sales Preference Questionnaire, 1085

Sales Professional Assessment Inventory (SPAI), 1085

Sales Relations Survey (SRS), 1086, *1025*

The Sales Sentence Completion Blank, 1086

Sales Staff Selector, 1086

Sales Style Diagnosis Test, 1086

Sales Transaction Audit (STA), 1087, *1025*

Salford Sentence Reading Test, 356

The Salience Inventory (Research Edition), 988

Sandwell Bilingual Screening Assessment, 710, *580*

Santa Clara Plus Computer Management System, 562, *672*

Sbordone-Hall Memory Battery, 124

The Scale of Beliefs in Extraordinary Phenomena (SOBEP), 265

Scale of Social Development (SSD), 41

Scales for Rating the Behavioral Characteristics of Superior Students (SRBCSS), 625, *772*

Scales of Creativity and Learning Environment (SCALE), 625

Scales of Independent Behavior (SIB), 654, *667*

SCAMIN: A Self-Concept and Motivation Inventory: Early Elementary, *772*

SCAMIN: A Self-Concept and Motivation Inventory: Later Elementary, *772*

SCAMIN: A Self-Concept and Motivation Inventory: Preschool/Kindergarten, *772*

SCAMIN: A Self-Concept and Motivation Inventory: Secondary Form, *772*

The SCAN-TRON Reading Test, 356

Schaie-Thurstone Adult Mental Abilities Test (STAMAT), 60

Schedule for Affective Disorders and Schizophrenia (SADS), 216

Schedule for Affective Disorders and Schizophrenia—Change Version (SADS-C), 217

Schedule for Affective Disorders and Schizophrenia—Lifetime Version (SADS-L), 217

The Schedule of Growing Skills (Developmental Screening Procedure 0–5), 41

Schedule of Recent Experience (SRE), 10

Scholastic Abilities Test for Adults (SATA), 482, *911*

Scholastic Aptitude Scale (SAS), 483

Scholastic Aptitude Test Batteries for Standards 2, 3 and 5—SATB and JSATB, 483

Scholastic Proficiency Test—Higher Primary Level (SPT-HP), 483, *911*

School and College Ability Tests, Series III (SCAT III), 484

School Apperception Method (SAM), 149

School Child Stress Scale (SCSS), 150, *11*, *654*

School Climate Inventory, 606

School Entrance Checklist, 562

SRA Typing 5, 948, *273*
SRA Typing Skills Test, 948, *273*
SRA Verbal Form, 915, *804*
Staff Burnout Scale for Health Professionals, 971, *1027*
Staff Burnout Scale for Police and Security Personnel, 1080, *1027*
The Standard Progressive Matrices (SPM–1956), 61, *598*
Standard Progressive Matrices—New Zealand Standardization, 62
Standardized Achievement Test of Computer Literacy (Version AZ) Revised (STCL), 273
Standardized Bible Content Tests, 380
Standardized Bible Content Tests-Form SP, 380
Standardized Reading Inventory (SRI), 358
Standardized Road-Map Test of Direction Sense, 619, *642*
Stanford Hypnotic Susceptibility Scale, 253
Stanford Measurement Series—Stanford Achievement Test: 7th Edition, 488
Stanford Measurement Series—Stanford Diagnostic Mathematics Test (SDMT): Third Edition, 489, *327*
Stanford Measurement Series—Stanford Diagnostic Reading Test (SDRT): Third Edition, 489, *377*
Stanford Measurement Series—Stanford Early School Achievement Test: 2nd Edition (SESAT), 489
Stanford Measurement Series—Stanford Test of Academic Skills: 2nd Edition (TASK), 489
Stanford Profile Scales of Hypnotic Susceptibility, 253
The Stanford-Binet Intelligence Scale, Form L-M, 62, *598*
The Stanford-Binet Intelligence Scale, Fourth Edition, 62, *598*
The Stanton Case Review, 1027
The Stanton Inventory, 1027
Stanton Profile, 915, *989*
The Stanton Survey, 1027
The Stanton Survey Phase II, 1028
State-Trait Anger Expression Inventory (STAXI), 11, *16*, *224*
State-Trait Anxiety Inventory, Form Y (STAI), 224
Station Employee Applicant Inventory (SEAI), 1028
Station Manager Applicant Inventory (SMAI), 916, *1057*
Steadiness Tester—Groove Type, 1072, *129*
Steadiness Tester—Hole Type, 1073, *129*
Steenburgen Diagnostic-Prescriptive Math Program and Quick Math Screening Test, 327, *490*
Stein Survey for Administrators, 1058
Stenographic Test, 949
Steps Up Developmental Screening Program (SUDS), 42
Stereo Fly Stereopsis Test, 730

The Stern Activities Index (AI), 253
STIM-CON, 714
Stimulus Recognition Test, 129, *47*
Streamlined Longitudinal Interval Continuation Evaluation (SLICE), 225
Street Survival Skills Questionnaire (SSSQ), 673, *655*
Stress Analysis System, 11
Stress Audit, 12
Stress Impact Scale (SIS), 775, *12*
Stress in General (SIG), 12
Stress Response Scale, 748, *150*
Stromberg Dexterity Test (SDT), 1073, *667*
Strong Interest Inventory, 989
Stroop Color and Word Test, 254
Stroop Neuropsychological Screening Test (SNST), 130, *47*
Structure of Intellect Learning Abilities Test (SOI), 566, *627*, *642*
Structure of Intellect Learning Abilities Test (SOI-LA): Arithmetic and Math Split Form (Form M), 335
Structure of Intellect Learning Abilities Test (SOI-LA): Reading Readiness Test (Form RR), 358
Structure of Intellect Learning Abilities Test (SOI-LA): Screening Form for Gifted, 627
Structure Tests, English Language (STEL), 285
Structured Analysis and Design Concepts Proficiency Test (WWSAD), 956
Structured and Scaled Interview to Assess Maladjustment (SSIAM), 225
Structured-Objective Rorschach Test (SORT)—1975, 254, *1028*
STS-High School Placement Test (HSPT), 490
Student Adaptation to College Questionnaire (SACQ), 775, *225*
Student Adjustment Inventory, 758, *775*
Student Developmental Task and Lifestyle Inventory (SDTLI), 775
Student Evaluation Scale (SES), 758, *748*
Student Instructional Report (SIR), 855
Student Motivation Diagnostic Questionnaire, 758, *855*
Student Occupational Competency Achievement Testing (SOCAT), 306, *804*, *916*
Student Occupational Competency Achievement Testing: Accounting/ Bookkeeping, 274, *804*, *916*
Student Occupational Competency Achievement Testing: Agriculture Mechanics, 307, *805*, *916*
Student Occupational Competency Achievement Testing: Auto Body, 307, *805*, *916*
Student Occupational Competency Achievement Testing: Auto Mechanics, 307, *805*, *916*
Student Occupational Competency Achievement Testing: Carpentry, 307, *805*, *916*

Out-of-Print Tests

Note: This list was compiled via information provided by test publishers regarding tests recently declared out-of-print. Because in-print status is subject to change, the editors encourage test users to contact the test's author(s) or former publisher for information concerning the availability of a particular test.

ACER Advanced Test N   *The Australian Council for Educational Research Limited*
ACER Junior Non-Verbal Test   *D. Spearritt*
ACER Lower Grades General Ability Scale   *The Australian Council for Educational Research Limited*
ACER Number Test   *The Australian Council for Educational Research Limited*
ACER Silent Reading Test—Form C   *The Australian Council for Educational Research Limited*
ACER Word Knowledge Test—Adult Form B   *The Australian Council for Educational Research Limited*
ACT Proficiency Examination Program—Arts and Sciences: Afro-American History   *The American College Testing Program*
ACT Proficiency Examination Program—Arts and Sciences: American History   *The American College Testing Program*
ACT Proficiency Examination Program—Arts and Sciences: Earth Science   *The American College Testing Program*
ACT Proficiency Examination Program—Arts and Sciences: Freshman English   *The American College Testing Program*
ACT Proficiency Examination Program—Arts and Sciences: Shakespeare   *The American College Testing Program*
ACT Proficiency Examination Program—Business: Accounting: Level II   *The American College Testing Program*
ACT Proficiency Examination Program—Business: Accounting: Level III   *The American College Testing Program*
ACT Proficiency Examination Program—Business: Business Environment and Strategy   *The American College Testing Program*
ACT Proficiency Examination Program—Business: Finance: Level I   *The American College Testing Program*
ACT Proficiency Examination Program—Business: Finance: Level II   *The American College Testing Program*

ACT Proficiency Examination Program—Business: Management of Human Resources: Level II   *The American College Testing Program*
ACT Proficiency Examination Program—Business: Management of Human Resources: Level III   *The American College Testing Program*
ACT Proficiency Examination Program—Business: Marketing: Level II   *The American College Testing Program*
ACT Proficiency Examination Program—Business: Marketing: Level III   *The American College Testing Program*
ACT Proficiency Examination Program—Business: Operations Management: Level I   *The American College Testing Program*
ACT Proficiency Examination Program—Business: Operations Management: Level II   *The American College Testing Program*
ACT Proficiency Examination Program—Business: Operations Management: Level III   *The American College Testing Program*
ACT Proficiency Examination Program—Education: History of American Education   *The American College Testing Program*
ACT Proficiency Examination Program—Criminal Justice: Introduction to Criminal Justice   *The American College Testing Program*
ACT Proficiency Examination Program—Criminal Justice: Criminal Investigation   *The American College Testing Program*
ACT Proficiency Examination Program—Nursing: Nursing Health Care   *The American College Testing Program*
Activities for Assessing Classification Skills (Experimental Edition)   *Rachel Gal-Choppin*
Administrator Feedback Questionnaire   *Office of Public and Professional Services, College of Education, Western Michigan University*
Adolescents into the Mainstream (AIM)   *Joel R. Arick, Patricia J. Almond, Creighton Young, and Michael Leavitt*
Advanced Personnel Test   *W.S. Miller*

Advanced Reading Inventory   *Jerry L. Johns*
Affect Scale   *Ricardo Girona*
AH Vocabulary Scale   *A.W. Heim, K.P. Watts, and V. Simmonds*
AI3Q Measure of Obsessional or Anal Character   *Paul Kline*
American History Map Test Folio   *The Perfection Form Company*
American School Achievement Test (ASAT)   *Brian R. Bryant, Steven C. Mathews, Jerome J. Ammer, Mary E. Cronin, Linda H. Mandelbaum, and Sally S. Quinby*
American School Aptitude Scale (ASAS)   *Brian R. Bryant, Steven C. Mathews, Jerome J. Ammer, Mary E. Cronin, Linda H. Mandelbaum, and Sally S. Quinby*
Anxiety Scale for the Blind   *Richard E. Hardy*
Applied Biological and Agribusiness Interest Inventory, The   *Robert W. Walker and Glen Z. Stevens*
Aptitude Index Battery (AIB)   *LIMRA*
Aptitude Test for Police Officer   *McCann Associates, Inc.*
Aptitude Tests for Occupations   *Wesley S. Roder*
APU Arithmetic Test and APU Vocabulary Test   *S.J. Closs and M. Hutchings*
Arthur Point Scale of Performance Tests: Revised Form II   *G. Arthur*
Articulation Screening Assessment (ASA)   *J.G. de Gaetano*
ASE Occupational Test Series   *Pauline Smith and Chris Whetton*
Assessment of Basic Competencies (ABC)   *Jwalla P. Somwaru*
Assessment of Reading Growth   *Jamestown Publishers*
Assessment of Skills in Computation (ASC)   *CTB/McGraw-Hill*
Auditory Discrimination Test   *J.M. Wepman*
Auditory Projective Test   *S. Braverman and H. Chevigny*
Australian Item Bank   *The Australian Council for Educational Research Limited*
Barron-Welsh Art Scale   *F. Barron and G.S. Welsh*
Barsch Learning Style Inventory   *Jeffery Barsch*
Basic Screening and Referral Form for Children with Suspected Learning and Behavioral Disabilities, A   *Robert E. Valett*
Basic Skills Test—Mathematics Elementary—Forms A and B   *IOX Assessment Associates*
Basic Skills Test—Mathematics Secondary—Forms A and B   *IOX Assessment Associates*
Basic Skills Test—Reading Elementary—Forms A and B   *IOX Assessment Associates*
Basic Skills Test—Reading—Secondary: Forms A and B   *IOX Assessment Associates*

Basic Skills Test—Writing—Elementary—Forms A and B   *IOX Assessment Associates*
Basic Skills Test—Writing—Secondary—Forms A and B   *IOX Assessment Associates*
Basic Word Vocabulary Test   *H.J. Dupuy*
Becoming the Gift (BTG)   *Merton P. Strommen*
Belwin-Mills Singing Achievement Test   *Richard W. Bowles*
Bernreuter Personality Inventory   *Stoelting Company*
Black History: A Test to Create Awareness and Arouse Interest   *Gregory C. Coffin, Elsie F. Harley, and Bessie M.L. Rhodes*
Brief Qualitative Analysis Test   *Examinations Committee, American Chemical Society*
Brook Reaction Test of Interests and Temperament, The   *A.W. Heim, K.P. Watts, and V. Simmonds*
Burt Word Reading Test   *Scottish Council for Research in Education*
Buttons: A Projective Test for Pre-Adolescents and Adolescents   *E.P. Rothman and P.H. Berkowitz*
California Neuropsych System: Computer Battery of Neuropsychological Tests and Procedures   *Alan Fridlund and Dean Delis*
Career Adaptive Behavior Inventory (CAB)   *T.P. Lombardi*
Cartoon Predictions (SICP)   *Maureen O'Sullivan and J.P. Guilford*
Change Facilitator Stages of Concern Questionnaire (CFSoCQ)   *William L. Rutherford, Gene E. Hall, and Archie A. George*
Chart of Initiative and Independence
Check Up Tests   *Betty Kerr, Ronald Deadman, Melvyn Nolan, Redvers Brandling, and Peter Pile*
Child Development Center Q-Sort (CDCQ)   *Frances Fuchs Schachter*
Child Observation Guide   *M. Stone*
Children's Life Events Inventory (CLEI)   *Louis A. Chandler*
Children's Scale of Social Attitudes   *Glen D. Wilson, David K.B. Nias, and Paul M. Insel*
Classroom Learning Screening (CLS)   *Carl H. Koenig and Harold P. Kunzelman*
Claybury Selection Battery   *T.M. Caine, O.B. Wijesinghe, D. Winter, and D. Small*
Clerical Selection Battery   *London House, Inc.*
Clerical Task Inventory—Form C   *C.H. Lawshe*
Coarticulation Assessment in Meaningful Language (CAML)   *Kathryn W. Kenney and Elizabeth M. Prather*
Cognitive, Linguistic and Social Communicative Scales (CLASS)   *D.C. Tanner and W.M. Lamb*

Deeside Picture Test   *W.G. Emmett*
Describing Personality
 Union College Character Research Project
Developmental Articulation Profile (DAP)
 D. Tanner, K.E. Mahoney, and G. Derrick
Developmental Learning Profile
 Cuyahoga Special Education Service Center
Developmental Task Analysis   *Robert*
 E. Valett
Devereux Test of Extremity Coordination
 (DTEC)   *The Devereux Foundation*
Diagnostic and Achievement Reading Tests:
 Dart Phonics Testing Program   *Modern*
 Curriculum Press, Inc.
Diagnostic Mathematics Inventory (DMI)
 John K. Gessell
Diagnostic Skills Battery (DSB)
 O.F. Anderhalter
Diagnostic Tests and Self-Helps in Arithmetic
 L.J. Brueckner
Dimock L. Inventory (DLI)   *Hedley*
 G. Dimock
Driscoll Play Kit   *G.P. Driscoll*
Driver Attitude Survey (DAS), The
 Donald H. Schuster and J.P. Guilford
Dynamic Personality Inventory (DPI) and
 Likes and Interests Tests (LIT)
 T.G. Grygier
Early Identification Screening Program
 Office of Continuum Services,
 Baltimore City Public Schools
Early Mathematical Language   *Margaret*
 K.R. Williams and Heather J. Somerwill
Economy Fire Promotion Series   *McCann*
 Associates, Inc.
Economy Police Promotion Series   *McCann*
 Associates, Inc.
Educational Administrative Style Diagnosis
 Test   *W.J. Reddin*
Educational Goal Attainment Tests
 Bruce W. Tuckman and Alberto P.S. Montare
Educational Goal Attainment Tests: Arts and
 Leisure   *Bruce W. Tuckman and*
 Alberto P.S. Montare
Educational Goal Attainment Tests: Careers
 Bruce W. Tuckman and Alberto P.S. Montare
Educational Goal Attainment Tests: Civics
 Bruce W. Tuckman and Alberto P.S. Montare
Educational Goal Attainment Tests: English
 Language   *Bruce W. Tuckman and*
 Alberto P.S. Montare
Educational Goal Attainment Tests: General
 Knowledge   *Bruce W. Tuckman and*
 Alberto P.S. Montare
Educational Goal Attainment Tests: Human
 Relations   *Bruce W. Tuckman and*
 Alberto P.S. Montare
Educational Goal Attainment Tests: Latin
 America   *Bruce W. Tuckman and*
 Alberto P.S. Montare
Educational Goal Attainment Tests: Life Skills
 Bruce W. Tuckman and Alberto P.S. Montare

Educational Goal Attainment Tests: Reasoning
 Bruce W. Tuckman and Alberto P.S. Montare
Educational Goal Attainment Tests: Self Test
 Bruce W. Tuckman and Alberto P.S. Montare
Effectiveness-Motivation Scale   *J. Sharp and*
 D.H. Stott
Ego State Inventory   *David G. McCarley*
Engineer Performance Description Form
 (EPDF)   *John C. South*
Essential Mathematics   *L.M. Bental*
Essentials of English Tests   *Constance*
 McCullough, Dora V. Smith, and Carolyn
 Greene
Estes Attitude Scale: Measures of Attitude
 Toward School Subjects   *Thomas H. Estes,*
 Julie Johnstone Estes, Herbert C. Richards,
 and Doris Roettger
Everyday Skills Test (EDST)   *CTB/*
 McGraw-Hill
Everyday Skills Test: Mathematics   *CTB/*
 McGraw-Hill
Everyday Skills Test: Reading   *CTB/*
 McGraw-Hill
Examination in Structure   *C. Fries and*
 R. Lado
Experience Exploration   *W. Price Ewens*
Expression Grouping (SIEG)
 Maureen O'Sullivan and J.P. Guilford
Eysenck-Withers Personality Inventory
 S.B.G. Eysenck
Factorial Interest Blank   *P.H. Sandall*
Fine Dexterity Test   *E.I.T.S. Staff*
Fine Finger Dexterity Work Task Unit
 Mississippi State University Rehabilitation
 Research and Training Center on Blindness and
 Low Vision
Firefigher Entrance Aptitude Tests
 McCann Associates, Inc.
First Grade Screening Test (FGST)
 John E. Pate and Warren W. Webb
Fisher Language Survey and Write-To-Learn
 Program, Revised 1985   *Alyce F. Fisher*
Fisher-Logemann Test of Articulation
 Competence   *Hilda B. Fisher and*
 Jerilyn A. Logemann
Five Task Test   *Charlotte Buhler and*
 Kathryn Mandeville
Flowers Auditory Test of Selective Attention
 (FATSA)   *Arthur Flowers*
Fluency (FLU)   *Paul R. Christensen and*
 J.P. Guilford
Fogel WP Operator Test   *Max Fogel*
Foot Operated Hinged Box Work Task Unit
 Mississippi State University Rehabilitation
 Research and Training Center on Blindness and
 Low Vision
Franck Drawing Completion Test   *K. Franck*
Freeman Anxiety Neurosis and Psychosomatic
 Test, The   *M.J. Freeman*
G-S-Z Interest Inventory (GSZ)   *J.P.*
 Guilford, E.S. Shneidman, and W.S.
 Zimmerman

Gardner Steadiness Tester   *Richard A. Gardner and Andrew K. Gardner*

Garnett College Test in Engineering Science (Revised Edition)   *I. MacFarlane Smith*

General Educational Performance Index   *D.F. Seaman and A. Seaman*

General Tests of Language and Arithmetic for Students GTLAS-1972

"Getting Along"—A Situation-Response Test For Grades 7, 8, 9   *Trudys Lawrence*

Gochnour Idiom Screening Test   *E.A. Gochnour*

Graded French Tests

Group Phonics Analysis   *E.B. Fry*

Growth Process Inventory   *Everett L. Shostrom*

Guilford-Holley L. Inventory (GHL)   *J.P. Guilford and J. W. Holley*

Hackman-Gaither Interest Inventory   *Roy Hackman and James W. Gaither*

Harrower Psychodiagnostic Inkblot Test   *Molly Harrower*

Harvard Bank Teller Proficiency Test   *S. Stanard*

Hilton Questionnaire—A Measure of Drinking Behavior, The   *Margaret Hilton*

Hinged Box Work Task Unit   *Mississippi State University Rehabilitation Research and Training Center on Blindness and Low Vision*

Holborn Reading Scale, The   *A.F. Watts*

Hostility and Direction of Hostility Questionnaire (HDHQ)   *A.T.M. Caine, G.A. Foulds, and K. Hope*

How a Child Learns   *Thomas D. Gnagey*

Human Factors Personnel Selection Inventory (HFPSI)   *London House, Inc.*

Illinois Tests in the Teaching of English   *William H. Evans and Paul H. Jacobs*

Immediate Test (IT), The   *Raymond J. Corsini*

Index Card Work Task Unit   *Mississippi State University Rehabilitation Research and Training Center on Blindness and Low Vision*

Individual Phonics Criterion Test   *E.B. Fry*

Individual Problem Index (IPI)

Industrial Sentence Completion Form   *M.M. Bruce*

Initial Communication Processes   *Teris Schery and Ann G. Wilcoxen*

Instant Words Criterion Test, The   *E.B. Fry*

Interactive Medical History (IMH)   *Based on the Harvard Medical History*

Inventory of Insurance Selling Potential

Inventory of Primary Skills, An   *Robert E. Valett*

IPMA Entry-Level Police Service Tests: Multijurisdictional Police Officer Examinations (MPOE), Forms 165.1 and 165.2   *International Personnel Management Association*

IPMA Promotional Fire Service Tests: 539 Fire Service Administrator (CHIEF)   *International Personnel Management Association*

IPMA Promotional Police Service Tests: 558 Police Administrator (CHIEF)   *International Personnel Management Association*

J.E.V.S. Work Samples: In-Depth Vocational Assessment for Special Needs   *Vocational Research Institute—J.E.V.S.*

Jenkins Intermediate Non-Verbal Test: ACER Adaptation   *The Australian Council for Educational Research Limited*

Jensen Alternation Board   *Lafayette Instrument Company, Inc.*

JIIG-CAL Occupational Interests Guide and APU Occupational Interests Guide   *S.J. Closs*

Jobmatch   *Macmillan Education*

Junior Inventory (J.I.)   *Hermann H. Remmers and Robert H. Bauernfeind*

Kansas Elementary Spelling Test   *Connie Moritz and Merritt W. Sanders*

Kansas Intermediate Spelling Test   *Alice Robinson and Merritt W. Sanders*

Kansas Junior High School Spelling Test   *Mary T. Williams and Merritt W. Sanders*

Keymath Diagnostic Arithmetic Test   *Austin Connolly, William Nachtman, and E.M. Pritchett*

Khatena-Torrance Creative Perception Inventory   *Joe Khatena and E. Paul Torrance*

Kindergarten Behavioral Index   *E.M. Banks*

Krantz Health Opinion Survey (HOS)   *David S. Krantz, Andrew Baum, and Margaret V. Wideman*

Kwalwasser Music Talent Test   *J. Kwalwasser*

Language Development Reading Evaluation Program   *Rosemary Courtney, Mimi Garry, Clayton Graves, Margaret Hughes, and John McInnes*

Language Imitation Test (LIT)   *P. Berry and P. Mittler*

Language Proficiency Test (LPT)—1972   *Human Sciences Research Council*

Language Sampling and Analysis (LSA)   *Merlin J. Mecham and J. Dean Jones*

Leadership Education and Development Scale (LEADS)   *Harley W. Mowry*

Learning Predictor, The   *Joan M. Smith*

Learning Screen (LS)   *Carl H. Koenig and Harold P. Kunzelman*

Library Skills Test   *W. DeMouth*

Life Position In Transactional Analysis   *H.H. Wood*

Light-Switch Alternation Apparatus   *M.B. Jensen*

Lowenfeld Mosaic Test, The   *Eugene X. Perticone and Renee M. Tembeckjian*

MACC Behavioral Adjustment Scale: Revised
Scale, The   *Robert B. Ellsworth*
MacQuarrie Test for Mechanical Ability
T.W. MacQuarrie
Make a Picture Story (MAPS)
E.S. Shneidman
Management Inventory on Leadership and
Motivation (MILM)   *Donald
L. Kirkpatrick*
Manchester Scales of Social Adaptation
E.A. Lunzer
Manual Accuracy and Speed Test
Peter F. Briggs and Auke Tellegen
Master Attitude Scales   *H.H. Remmers*
Math Doctor (M.D.)   *B. Signer*
McCormick Affective Assessment Technique
(MAAT)   *R.R. McCormick*
McGuire-Bumpus Diagnostic Comprehension
Test   *Marion L. McGuire and
Marguerite J. Bumpus*
Meeker-Cromwell Behavior Developmental
Assessment   *M & M Systems*
Memory for Events (ME)   *J.P. Guilford*
Memory for Meanings (MM)
Ralph Hoepfner and J.P. Guilford
Merrill-Demos DD Scale (MDDD)
M.J. Weijola and G.D. Demos
Mertens Visual Perception Test
Marjorie K. Mertens
Minimum Essentials for Modern Mathematics
E. Hayes
Minnesota Preschool Scale
*Florence Goodenough, Katherine Maurer, and
M.J. Van Wagenen*
Minnesota-Briggs History Record With
Marriage Section   *P.F. Briggs*
Missouri Criterion Referenced Tests (CRT)
Center for Educational Assessment
Missouri Student Needs Survey, Form V
Center for Educational Assessment
Mobile Vocational Evaluation (MVE)
Edward J. Hester
Modern Language Association Cooperative
Foreign Language Tests   *CTB/McGraw-
Hill*
Monash Diagnostic Test of Lipreading Ability
Money Attitude Scale   *Kent T. Yamauchi and
Donald I. Templer*
Multi-Ethnic Awareness Survey, The
*Gregory C. Coffin, Nancy S. Coffin,
Bessie L. Rhodes, and Robert E. Rhodes*
Multifunctional Work Task Unit   *Mississippi
State University Rehabilitation Research and
Training Center on Blindness and Low Vision*
Multiple-Choice Biology and Advanced
Multiple-Choice Biology   *R. Soper,
D. Robinson, and S.T. Smith*
Multiple-Choice Biology and Advanced
Multiple-Choice Biology   *R. Soper,
D. Robinson, and S.T. Smith*
Multiple-Choice Chemistry and Advanced
Multiple-Choice Chemistry   *J.A.S. Rees*

Multiple-Choice English and Progressive
Multiple-Choice English   *A.F. Bolt*
Multiple-Choice Physics   *R.W. Adams*
Mutually Responsible Facilitation Inventory
(MRFI)   *Thomas D. Gnagey*
My Self Check List (MSCL)
Robert E. Valett
National Achievement Tests for Elementary
Schools: Arithmetic and Mathematics,
Arithmetic Reasoning   *Robert K. Speer
and Samuel Smith*
National Achievement Tests: Health and
Science Tests—General Biology
Lester D. Crow and James G. Murray
National Business Competency Tests and
Entrance Test   *N.B.E.A.
Competency Test Committee*
National Business Competency Tests: Office
Procedures   *N.B.E.A.
Competency Test Committee*
National Business Competency Tests:
Typewriting   *N.B.E.A.
Competency Test Committee*
National Business Entrance Tests:
Bookkeeping Test   *N.B.E.A.
Competency Test Committee*
National Business Entrance Tests: Business
Fundamentals and General Information Test
N.B.E.A. Competency Test Committee
National Business Entrance Tests: Machine
Calculation Test   *N.B.E.A.
Competency Test Committee*
National Business Entrance Tests:
Stenographic Test   *N.B.E.A.
Competency Test Committee*
Naylor-Harwood Adult Intelligence Scale
G.F.K. Naylor and E. Harwood
Neale Analysis of Reading Ability—Braille
Edition   *N.B. Neale*
Netherne Study Difficulties Battery for
Student Nurses (SDB)   *James
Patrick S. Robertson*
Neurological Dysfunctions of Children
(NDOC)   *James W. Kuhns*
New Youth Research Survey (NYRS)
Merton P. Strommen
NIIP Clerical Tests
NLN Achievement Tests For Practical
Nursing: Mental Health Concepts For
Practical Nursing Students (Form 0481)
National League for Nursing
NLN Achievement Tests For Practical
Nursing: Psychiatric Nursing Concepts For
Practical Nursing Students (Form 4313)
National League for Nursing
NLN Achievement Tests For Registered
Nursing: Comprehensive Nursing
Achievement Test 1984 Edition (Form 3014)
National League for Nursing
NLN Achievement Tests For Registered
Nursing: Nursing The Childbearing Family
(Form 0581)   *National League for Nursing*

NLN Baccalaureate-Level Achievement Tests for Registered Nursing: Applied Natural Sciences (Form 0981)   *National League for Nursing*

NLN Baccalaureate-Level Achievement Tests for Registered Nursing: Leadership in Nursing (Form 0381)   *National League for Nursing*

Number Test DE   *B. Barnard*

Nutrition Achievement Tests 1, 2, and 3   *The National Dairy Council*

Nutrition Knowledge and Interest Questionnaire   *G.D. Passwater*

Occupational Check List   *Tony Crowley*

Ohio Vocational Achievement Test Program: California Short Form Test of Academic Aptitude, Level 5 (SFTAA)   *CTB/McGraw-Hill*

One-Hole Test Levels I and II   *G. Salvendy and W.D. Seymour*

Oral Language Sentence Imitation Diagnostic Inventory—Format Revised (OLSISI-F)   *L. Zachman, R. Huisingh, C. Jorgensen, and M. Barrett*

Oral Language Sentence Imitation Screening Test—Format Revised (OLAIAT-F)   *L. Zachman, R. Huisingh, C. Jorgensen, and M. Barrett*

Oral Reading Criterion Test   *E.B. Fry*

Oregon Academic Ranking Test   *Charles H. Derthick*

Organization Survey   *Human Resource Center, University of Chicago*

Orzeck Aphasia Evaluation   *Arthur Orzeck*

Otis Self Administering Test of Mental Ability   *Arthur S. Otis*

Otto Pre-Marital Counseling Schedules   *Herbert A. Otto*

PAPI System: How I See Myself   *M.M. Kostick*

PAPI System: How I See You   *M.M. Kostick*

PAPI System: PA Preference Inventory   *M.M. Kostick*

PAPI System: Rating of Job Requirements—Form A Revised   *M.M. Kostick*

PAPI System: Rating of Job Requirements—Form B Revised   *M.M. Kostick*

PAPI System: Rating of Job Requirements—Form C Revised   *M.M. Kostick*

PAPI System: Rating of Job Requirements—Form D Revised   *M.M. Kostick*

Peabody Individual Achievement Test (PIAT)   *Lloyd M. Dunn and Frederick C. Markwardt, Jr.*

Peabody Mathematics Readiness Test (PMRT)   *Otto C. Bassler, Morris I. Beers, Lloyd I. Richardson, and Richard L. Thurman*

Peer Attitudes Towards the Handicapped Scale (PATHS)   *Micheal T. Bayley and John F. Green*

Peg Board   *E.I.T.S. Staff*

Performance Assessment in Reading (PAIR)   *CTB/McGraw-Hill*

Personal Background Inventory   *Melany E. Baehr and Frances M. Burns*

Personal History Index   *M.E. Baehr, R.K. Burns, and R.N. McMurry*

Personal Outlook Inventory   *Wolfe Personnel Testing and Training Systems, Inc.*

Personality and Personal Illness Questionnaires   *T.M. Caine, G.A. Foulds, and K. Hope*

Personality Descriptions   *Union College Character Research Project*

Personality Inventory, The   *Robert G. Berneuter*

Phoenix Ability Survey System (PASS)   *Edward J. Hester*

Piaget Task Kit   *Willard Stibal*

Picture Word Test   *Charlotte Buhler and Morse P. Manson*

Police Sergeant (ESV)   *McCann Associates, Inc.*

Portland Prognostic Test for Mathematics   *E. Hayes*

Potential for Foster Parenthood Scale (PFPS)   *John Touliatos and Byron W. Lindholm*

Practical Articulation Kit: Game Cards and Screening Test   *M.M. McDonough*

Preschool and Early Primary Skill Survey   *Stoelting Company*

Preschool Attainment Record (Research Edition)   *Edgar A. Doll*

Preschool Language Assessment Instrument (PLAI)   *Marion Blank, Susan A. Rose, and Laura J. Berlin*

Primary Visual Motor Test   *M.R. Haworth*

Probation Officer Trainee   *McCann Associates, Inc.*

Psychoeducational Inventory of Basic Learning Abilities, A   *Robert E. Valett*

Pupil Behavior Rating Scale (PBRS)   *Nadine M. Lambert, Eli M. Bower, and Carolyn S. Hartsough*

Purdue Blueprint Reading Test   *H.F. Owens and J.N. Arnold*

Purdue Clerical Adaptability Test (Revised)   *Purdue Research Foundation/University Book Store*

Purdue Creativity Test   *Douglas Harris and C.H. Lawshe*

Purdue Hand Precision Test   *Layfayette Instrument Company, Inc.*

Purdue Handicap Problems Inventory   *H.H. Remmers and G.N. Wright*

Purdue Industrial Supervisors Word-Meaning Test   *J. Tiffin and D.A. Long*

Purdue Instructor Performance Indicator, The   *H.H. Remmers and J.H. Snedeker*

Purdue Interview Aids   *C.H. Lawshe*

Purdue Mechanical Adaptability Test   *C.H. Lawshe and Joseph Tiffin*

Purdue Non-Language Personnel Test   *J. Tiffin*

Purdue Rating Scale for Administrators and Executives   *H.H. Remmers and R.L. Hobson*

Purdue Rating Scale for Instruction, The
H.H. Remmers and D.N. Elliott
Purdue Trade Information Tests *Purdue
Research Foundation/University Book Store*
Purdue Reading Test for Industrial Supervisors
J. Tiffin and R. Dunlap
Queensland University Aphasia and Language
Test (QUALT) *The Australian Council for
Educational Research Limited*
Quick Word Test *Edgar F. Borgatta and
Raymond J. Corsini*
Rapid Exam for Early Referral (REFER)
Carl H. Koening and Harold P. Kunzelman
Reading Level Tests (Using Cloze Procedure)
Reading Readiness Inventory *J. Downing
and Derek V. Thackray*
Reading Tests *F.J. Schonell*
Resident Assistant Stress Inventory *Andrews
University Press*
Retail Management Assessment Inventory
(RMAI) *London House, Inc.*
Revolving Assembly Table *Mississippi State
University Rehabilitation Research and
Training Center on Blindness and Low Vision*
Rohde Sentence Completions
Amanda R. Rohde
Risk Exposure Inventory (REI)
Rorschach Concept Evaluation Technique
Paul McReynolds
Rothwell-Miller Interest Blank
J.W. Rothwell and K.M. Miller
Roughness Discrimination Test *C.Y. Nolan
and J.E. Miller*
Scale for the Identification of School Phobia
(SIS) *Jerome H. Want*
School Superintendent Job Functions
Inventory (SS-JFI) *C. Salley and
M.E. Baehr*
School/Home Observation and Referral System
(SHORS) *Joyce Evans*
Schutz Measures: Element B—Behavior, The
Will Schutz
Schutz Measures: Element F—Feelings, The
Will Schutz
Schutz Measures: Element J—Job (JOB
HOLDER, CO-WORKER), The
Will Schutz
Schutz Measures: Element R—Relationships,
The *Will Schutz*
Schutz Measures: Element S—Self-Concept,
The *Will Schutz*
Scott Mental Alertness Test *Stoelting Co.*
SCRE Profile Assessment System
Screening Speech Articulation Test (SSAT)
*Merlin J. Mecham, J. Lorin Jex, and
J. Dean Jones*
Screening Test of Educational Prerequisite
Skills (STEPS) *Frances Smith*
Seeing Problems (SP) *Philip R. Merrifield
and J.P. Guilford*
Self-Rating Anxiety Scale (SAS)
William W.K. Zung

Senf-Comrey Ratings of Extra Educational
Need (SCREEN) *Gerald M. Senf and
Andrew L. Comrey*
Senior English Test
Senior High Assessment of Reading
Performance (SHARP) *CTB/McGraw-
Hill*
Senior Mathematics Test *NFER-NELSON*
Sequential Tests of Educational Progress
(STEP II) *Educational Testing Service*
Short Occupational Knowledge Tests (SOKT)
Bruce A. Campbell and Suellen O. Johnson
Short Term Auditory Retrieval and Storage
Test (STARS) *Arthur Flowers*
Shorthand Aptitude Test *Queensland
Department of Education*
Silver Drawing Test of Cognitive and Creative
Skills *R.A. Silver*
Similes Test, The *Charles E. Schaefer*
Simons Measurements of Music Listening
Skills *Stoelting Co.*
Sipay Word Analysis Test (SWAT)
Edward R. Sipay
Slosson Post-Observational Testing Screen
(SPOTS) *Steven W. Slosson and
Theodore A. Callisto*
Slosson Pre-Observational Record Screen
(SPORS) *Steven W. Slosson*
Social Interaction and Creativity in
Communication System (SICCS)
David L. Johnson
South African Picture Analysis Test (PASAT),
The *B.F. Nel and A.J.K. Pelser*
Southern California Motor Accuracy Test,
Revised 1980 *A. Jean Ayres*
Southern California Postrotary Nystagmus Test
A. Jean Ayres
Southern California Sensory Integration Tests
(SCSIT) *A. Jean Ayers*
Spanish/English Reading and Vocabulary
Screening Test (SERVS) *CTB/McGraw-
Hill*
Speed Scale for Determining Independent
Reading Level *Ward Cramer and
Roger Trent*
Spelling Tests (English)—1964 *Human
Sciences Research Council*
Staffordshire Test of Computation, The
M.E. Hebron and W. Pattinson
Stages of Concern Questionnaire (SoCQ)
*Gene E. Hall, Archie A. George, and
William L. Rutherford*
Stanford-Ohwaki-Kohs Block Design
Intelligence Test for the Blind: American
Revision *Richard M. Suinn and
William L. Dauterman*
Steck-Vaughn Placement Survey for Adult
Basic Education *B. Phillips*
Stogdill Behavior Cards *Stoelting Co.*
Stress Profile for Teachers *Christopher
F. Wilson*
Student Attitude Inventory *D.S. Anderson
and J.S. Western*

Student Developmental Profile and Planning
Record   *Roger B. Winston, Theodore
K. Miller, and Judith S. Prince*
Student Developmental Task Inventory:
Revised Second Edition (SDTI-2)
*Roger B. Winston, Jr., Theodore K. Miller,
and Judith S. Prince*
Student Learning Profile
Cuyahoga Special Education Service Center
Students Typewriting Tests
N.B.E.A. Test Committee
Survey of Objective Visualization (SOV)
Daniel R. Miller
Survey of Space Relations Ability (SSRA)
Harry W. Case and Floyd Ruch
Survival Skills Profile
Cuyahoga Special Education Service Center
Symbol Identities   *Ralph Hoepfner*
Symonds Picture-Story Test   *P.M. Symonds*
System for the Administration and
Interpretation of Neurological Tests
(SAINT-II)   *Dennis Swiercinsky*
Tanner Eclectic Stuttering Therapy Program
(TEST)   *D.C. Tanner*
Task Assessment for Prescriptive Teaching
(TAPT)   *Daniel Hofeditz and Duane Wilke*
Teacher Feedback Questionnaire   *Office of
Public and Professional Services, College of
Education, Western Michigan University*
Teacher Occupational Competency Testing:
Automotive Body and Fender   *National
Occupational Competency Testing Institute*
Teacher Occupational Competency Testing:
Welding Examination #057   *National
Occupational Competency Testing Institute*
Technical Test—1962   *Human Sciences
Research Council*
Test Listening Accuracy in Children (TLAC)
M.J. Mecham and J.D. Jones
Test of Abstract Concept Learning (TACL)
National Computer Systems/PAS Division
Test of Aural Perception for Japanese Students
R. Lado
Test of Aural Perception for Latin-American
Students (TAP-Latin)   *R. Lado*
Test of Behavioral Rigidity (TBR)
K. Warner Schaie and Iris A. Parham
Test of Children's Learning Ability—
Individual Version   *J. Haynes, S. Hegarty,
X. Perryer, and C. Gipps*
Test of Consumer Competencies (TCC)
*Thomas Stanley, E. Thomas Garman, and
Richard Brown*
Test of Economic Achievement   *J.D. Thexton*
Test of Enquiry Skills   *The Australian Council
for Educational Research Limited*
Test of Everyday Writing Skills (TEWS)
CTB/McGraw-Hill
Test of Group Learning Skills   *M.A. Watson*
Test of Performance in Computational Skills
(TOPICS)   *CTB/McGraw-Hill*
Test of Proficiency in English   *C. Gipps and
E. Ewen*

Test Orientation Procedure   *G.K. Bennett
and J.E. Doppelt*
Tests of Proficiency in English—Listening
Tests   *C. Gipps and E. Ewen*
Tests of Proficiency in English—Reading Tests
C.Gipps and E. Ewen
Tests of Proficiency in English—Speaking
Tests   *C. Gipps and E. Ewen*
Tests of Proficiency in English—Writing Tests
C. Gipps and E. Ewen
Tests on Newbery Medal Award Books
Time Appreciation Test   *John N. Buck*
TIP and DIP Tests for the Hearing of Speech
by Young Children   *Bruce M. Siegenthaler
and George S. Haspiel*
Transitional Assessment Modules
Trites Neuropsychological Test Battery
Ronald L. Trites
Universal Skills Survey   *Prep, A Division of
Educational Technologies Inc.*
Valett Developmental Survey of Basic
Learning Abilities   *R.E. Valett*
Vane-L Scale, The   *Julia R. Vane*
VCWS 13—Money Handling   *Valpar
International Corporation*
Verbal Language Development Scale (VLDS)
Merlin J. Mecham
Verbal Power Test of Concept Equivalents
E. Francesco
Vineland Social Maturity Scale   *E.A. Dill*
Visual Pattern Recognition Test Diagnostic
Schedule and Training Materials
Diane Montgomery
Visual Skills Test   *Titmus Optical, Inc./Stereo
Optical Co.*
Wachs Analysis of Cognitive Structures
Harry Wachs and Lawrence J. Vaughan
Washington Speech and Sound Discrimination
Test   *E. Prather, A. Miner, M.A. Addicott,
and L. Summerland*
Weiss Intelligibility Test   *Curtis E. Weiss*
Wessex Reading Analysis, The   *A. Hughes,
P. Evans, and S. Moulton*
What I Usually Eat   *Iowa State University*
Wichita Auditory Fusion Test (WAFT)
R.L. McCroskey
Wichita Auditory Processing Test (WAPT)
Modern Education Corporation
Williams Intelligence Test for Children with
Defective Vision   *M. Williams*
Wilson-Patterson Attitude Inventory
Glenn D. Wilson
Wing Standardised Tests of Musical
Intelligence   *H.D. Wing*
Wittenborn Psychiatric Rating Scales (Revised)
J.R. Wittenborn
Woodcock Reading Mastery Tests (WRMT)
Richard W. Woodcock
Word Discrimination   *John W. Black*
Word Orders Comprehension Test
Gilliam Fenn
Work Environment Preference Schedule
Leonard V. Gordon

Work Interest Index   *M.E. Baehr, R. Renck, and R.K. Burns*

World History Map Test Folio
E. Brightwater

Write Junior High   *CTB/McGraw-Hill*

Write Senior High   *CTB/McGraw-Hill*

Writing Proficiency Program (WPP)
R.M. Bossone

Writing Proficiency Program/Intermediate System (WPP/IS)   *R.M. Bossone*

Yardsticks   *NFER-NELSON Publishing Company Ltd.*

Youth Inventory (YI)   *Hermann H. Remmers and Benjamin Shimberg*

Hearing-Impaired Index

Note: This index was compiled via information provided by test publishers. It contains tests that assess the sense of hearing as well as tests that are suitable for use with individuals having hearing impairments. Both tests that have been designed for use specifically with hearing-impaired individuals and tests that may be adapted for use with such individuals are included. The editors encourage test users to contact the test publisher for specific information regarding the use of a particular test with hearing-impaired individuals.

Physically Impaired Index

Note: This index was compiled via information provided by test publishers. Both tests that have been designed for use specifically with physically impaired individuals and tests that may be adapted for use with such individuals are included. The editors encourage test users to contact the test publisher for specific information regarding the use of a particular test with physically impaired individuals.

Developmental Assessment for the Severely Handicapped (DASH), 662
Developmental Assessment of Life Experiences, 1986 Revised (DALE), 650
Diagnostic Analysis of Reading Errors (DARE), 364
Diagnostic Word Patterns: Tests 1, 2, and 3, 370
Digital Finger Tapping Test (DFTT), 101
Discovery Drug and Alcohol Assessment Profile, 20
Driver Risk Inventory (DRI), 21
Driving Advisement System (DAS), 101
Drug Store Applicant Inventory (DSAI), 876
Dyadic Adjustment Scale (DAS), 84
Dyslexia Schedule, 634
Early Child Development Inventory (ECDI), 31
Early Mathematics Diagnostic Kit, 317
Efron Visual Acuity Test, 726
Efron Visual Acuity Test Slides, 726
Egan Bus Puzzle Test, 32
Einstein Assessment of School Related Skills, 634
Electrical and Electronics Test, 877
EMO Questionnaire (Emotional Adjustment), 1042
Emotional/Behavioral Screening Program (ESP), 740
Employability Attitudes, 1000
English Picture Vocabulary Tests (EPVTs), 694
The Enhanced ACT Assessment, 457
The ENRIGHT® Diagnostic Inventory of Basic Arithmetic Skills, 318
Environmental Deprivation Scale, 239
ERB Comprehensive Testing Program (CTP II), 457
Erotometer: A Technique for the Measurement of Heterosexual Love, 85
Experience and Background Inventory (EBI), 1043
Experience and Background Questionnaire (EBQ), 1002
Exploring Career Options (ECO), 1002
Eyberg Child Behavior Inventory, 143
A Familism Scale, 69
A Familism Scale: Extended Family Integration, 69
A Familism Scale: Nuclear Family Integration, 70
Family Adaptability and Cohesion Evaluation Scales (FACES III), 70
Family Coping Strategies (F-COPE), 71
Family Inventories, 71
Family Inventory of Life Events and Changes (FILE), 72
Family Relations Test—Adult and Married Couples Version, 72
Family Relations Test—Children's Version, 72
Family Relationship Inventory (FRI), 72
Family Satisfaction Scale, 73
Family Strengths, 73

Family Violence Scale, 73
Famous Sayings (FS), 1003
Farnsworth-Munsell 100 Hue Test, 883
Farnum Music Test, 295
Fast Health Knowledge Test Form C, 1986 Revision, 388
Feelings and Behavior of Love (Love Scale), 85
The Five P's: Parent/Professional Preschool Performance Profile, 544
The Flowers Auditory Processing Test (F.A.S.T.), 676
Fluharty Preschool Speech and Language Screening Test, 696
Four Sigma Qualifying Test (FSQT), 51
Frenchay Aphasia Screening Test (FAST), 104
Frenchay Dysarthria Assessment, 697
Full-Range Picture Vocabulary Test (FRPV), 52
Functional Analysis of Behavior, 240
Functional Performance Record, 651
Functional Skills Screening Inventory (FSSI), 663
Functional Skills Screening Inventory: Employment Edition (FSSI: EE), 663
Functional Skills Screening Inventory: Training Program Edition (FSSI: TPE), 664
General Health Questionnaire (GHQ), 174
Geriatric Sentence Completion Form (GSCF), 45
Gillingham-Childs Phonics Proficiency Scales: Series I, Basic Reading and Spelling; Series II, Advanced Reading, 343
Golombok Rust Inventory of Marital State (GRIMS), 85
Graded Anagram Task (GAT), 263
The Graded Naming Test, 105
Gravidometer, 86
Grid Test of Schizophrenic Thought Disorder, 241
Griffiths Mental Development Scales, 52
Grim, 241
Group Achievement Identification Measure (GAIM), 765
Group Inventory for Finding Creative Talent (GIFT), 624
Group Inventory for Finding Interests (GIFFI), 624
Group Personality Projective Test (GPPT), 242
Group Psychotherapy Evaluation Scale, 176
Hahnemann Elementary School Behavior Rating Scale (HESB), 741
Hahnemann High School Behavior Rating Scale (HHSB), 741
Hausa Speaking Test (HaST), 302
Health Problems Checklist, 13
Hebrew Speaking Test (HeST), 302
Help for Special Preschoolers—Checklist, 547
Hoffer-Osmond Diagnostic Test (HOD), 179
Home Observation for Measurement of the Environment (HOME), 74
Hooper Visual Organization Test (HVOT), 107
Hughes Basic Gross Motor Assessment (HBGMA), 612

Visually Impaired Index

Note: This index was compiled via information provided by test publishers. It contains tests that assess the sense of vision as well as tests that are suitable for use with individuals having visual impairments. Both tests that have been designed for use specifically with visually impaired individuals and tests that may be adapted for use with such individuals are included. The editors encourage test users to contact the test publisher for specific information regarding the use of a particular test with visually impaired individuals.

Foreign Language Availability Index

GERMAN

Kirton Adaption-Innovation Inventory (KAI), 186
Management Transactions Audit: Other, 1051
Managerial Style Questionnaire (MSQ-M) and (MSQ-S), 1053
McGill Pain Questionnaire (MPQ), 15
Organizational Competence Index, 1017
Productive Practices Survey, 1056
Psychological Evaluation of Children's Human Figure Drawings (HFD), 148
Rokeach Value Survey, 250
Sales Comprehension Test, 1084
Self-Directed Learning Readiness Scale (SDLRS), 782
Supervisory Practices Test (Revised), 1061
Taylor-Johnson Temperament Analysis, 226
Team Process Diagnostic, 1032
Temperament Inventory Tests, 227
Test Plus, 1033
Trait Evaluation Index, 1035

GREEK

ACER Checklists for School Beginners, 530
Child Behavior Checklist and Revised Child Behavior Profile, 138
Illness Behaviour Questionnaire (IBQ), 181
Levine-Pilowsky Depression Questionnaire (L.P.D.), 188
Personality Assessment Questionnaire (PAQ), 248

HEBREW

Child Behavior Checklist and Revised Child Behavior Profile, 138
The Children's Depression Inventory (CDI), 235
The Five P's: Parent/Professional Preschool Performance Profile, 544
Hebrew Speaking Test (HeST), 302
Rokeach Value Survey, 250
Strong Interest Inventory, 989

HINDI

Child Behavior Checklist and Revised Child Behavior Profile, 138
CPRI Questionnaires (Q-71, Q-74, Q-75, Q-76), 753
Death Anxiety Scale, 237
Illness Behaviour Questionnaire (IBQ), 181
Learning Style Inventory (LSI) (1989), 755
Parental Acceptance-Rejection Questionnaire (PARQ), 78
Personality Assessment Questionnaire (PAQ), 248

HUNGARIAN

Child Behavior Checklist and Revised Child Behavior Profile, 138
The Children's Depression Inventory (CDI), 235

McMaster Family Assessment Device (FAD), 75
Rokeach Value Survey, 250

ICELANDIC

Child Behavior Checklist and Revised Child Behavior Profile, 138

ILOCANO

The Ber-Sil Spanish Tests: Elementary Test 1987 Revision, 300
The Ber-Sil Spanish Tests: Secondary Test, 301

INDIAN

The Children's Apperception Test (CAT-A), 140

ITALIAN

ACER Checklists for School Beginners, 530
The Affective Perception Inventory (API), 762
The Blacky Pictures, 233
California Psychological Inventory, 1987 Revised Edition, 161
Child Behavior Checklist and Revised Child Behavior Profile, 138
The Children's Apperception Test (CAT-A), 140
The Children's Apperception Test— Supplement (CAT-S), 140
The Children's Depression Inventory (CDI), 235
Frostig Developmental Test of Visual Perception (DTVP), 544
Griffiths Mental Development Scales, 52
Illness Behaviour Questionnaire (IBQ), 181
INTREX, 183
Kirton Adaption-Innovation Inventory (KAI), 186
Levine-Pilowsky Depression Questionnaire (L.P.D.), 188
McGill Pain Questionnaire (MPQ), 15
Reid Report, 1024
Sales Comprehension Test, 1084
The Self-Perception Inventory (SPI), 747

JAPANESE

Child Behavior Checklist and Revised Child Behavior Profile, 138
The Children's Apperception Test (CAT-A), 140
The Children's Apperception Test—Human Figures (CAT-H), 140
The Children's Depression Inventory (CDI), 235
Cognitive Skills Assessment Battery, 538
Death Anxiety Scale, 237
Frost Self-Description Questionnaire, 144
Frostig Developmental Test of Visual Perception (DTVP), 544
McGill Pain Questionnaire (MPQ), 15

Computer-Scored Index

Note: This index lists tests that may be scored by computer, either on-site or via mail-in or teleprocessing services.

Author Index

Publisher/Distributor Index

Academic Therapy Publications, 20 Commercial Boulevard, Novato, CA 94949; (415)883-3314—120, 280, 288, 291, 294, 322, 327, 363, 377, 452, 568, 578, 597, 609, 611, 615, 631, 636, 637, 638, 643, 679, 696, 709, 733, 743, 779

Administrative Research Associates, Inc., Irvine Town Center, Box 4211, Irvine, CA 92714; (714)499-3939—855, 858

Alemany Press (Janus Book Publishers, Inc.), DATA SCAN P.O. Box 7604, West Trenton, NJ 08628; (609)394-9679—574, 579, 580, 582

Allen House, 1119 W. Bethel, Muncie, IN 47303; (317)286-7392—635

Allington Corporation, The, P.O. Box 125, Remington, VA 22734; (703)825-5722—700

American Association of Bible Colleges, P.O. Box 1523, 130-F North College, Fayetteville, AR 72702; (501)521-8164—379, 380

American Association of Teachers of German, 112 Haddontowne Court #104, Cherry Hill, NJ 08034; (609)795-5553—299

American Automobile Association (AAA), Traffic Safety Department, 8111 Gatehouse Road, Falls Church, VA 22047; (703)AAA-6621—528

American Chemical Society, DivCHED Examinations Institute, 107 Physical Sciences, Stillwater, OK 74078; (405)744-5947—380, 381, 382, 383, 386, 387, 388

American College Testing Program, The, 2201 North Dodge Street, P.O. Box 168, Iowa City, IA 52243; (319)337-1051—403, 404, 405, 406, 407, 408, 409, 410, 447, 448, 457, 498, 499, 500, 501, 502, 503, 779, 784, 839, 844

American Council on Education, GED Testing Service, One Dupont Circle, NW, Washington, DC 20036; (202)939-4490—478, 495

American Dental Association, 211 East Chicago Avenue, Chicago, IL 60611; (312)440-2500—507

American Foundation for the Blind, 15 West 16th Street, New York, NY 10011; (212)620-2000—661, 665

American Guidance Service, Publisher's Building, Circle Pines, MN 55014; (800)328-2560, in Minnesota (612)786-4343—55, 257, 320, 340, 378, 465, 480, 596, 480, 596, 610, 614, 677, 678, 698, 699, 823, 1067, 1070

American Orthopsychiatric Association, Inc., 19 W. 44th Street, Suite 1616, New York, NY 10036; (212)354-5770—96

American Printing House for the Blind, 1839 Frankfort Avenue, P.O. Box 6085, Louisville, KY 40206-0085; (502)895-2405—367, 368, 567

American Testronics, 8600 W. Bryn Mawr, Chicago, IL 60631; (800)553-0030—287, 448, 449, 469, 472, 477, 539, 589, 752, 816, 817

Andrews University Press, Berrien Springs, MI 49104; (616)471-3392—227

Appenfeldt, Linda, Ph.D., 5400 Central Avenue, St. Petersburg, FL 33707; (813)321-4795—189

Applied Innovations, Inc., South Kingstown Office Park, Suite A-1, Wakefield, RI 02879; (800)272-2250—771

ARBOR, Inc., Arbor Corporate Center, One West Third Street, Media, PA 19063; (215)566-8700—1035

Associated Services for the Blind (ASB), 919 Walnut Street, Philadelphia, PA 19107; (215)627-0600—58, 153, 239, 833

Association of American Medical Colleges, 1 Dupont Circle, N.W., Suite 200, Washington, DC 20036; (202)828-0564—508

Aurora Publishing, 1709 Bragaw Street, Suite B, Anchorage, AK 99504; (907)279-5251—155, 223, 224

Australian Council for Educational Research Limited, The, P.O. Box 210, Hawthorn, Victoria, 3122, Australia; (03)819-1400—27, 235, 328, 350, 366, 378, 380, 397, 530, 582, 583, 584, 595, 780, 784, 851, 852, 928, 1036, 1063, 1064

Australian Government Publishing Service, Mail Order Sales, Wentworth Avenue, Kingston A.C.T., Australia 954411—300

Ball Foundation, The, Building C, Suite 206, 800 Roosevelt Road, Glen Ellyn, IL 60137; (312)469-6270—869

Ballard & Tighe, Inc., 480 Atlas Street, Brea, CA 92621; (800)321-IDEA, in CA (714)990-IDEA—575, 580

Center for Cognitive Therapy, 133 S. 36th Street, Room 602, Philadelphia, PA 19104; (215)898-4100—158

Center for Educational Assessment, College of Education, Univ. of Missouri, 403 S. 6th Street, Columbia, MO 65211; (314)882-4694—550, 743, 830

Center for Faculty Evaluation and Development, Kansas State University, 1623 Anderson Avenue, Manhattan, KS 66502-4098; (913)532-5970—854

Center for Psychological Service, The, 1511 K Street, N.W., Suite 430, Washington, DC 20005; (202)347-4069—527, 774

Center for Research on Teaching and Learning, College of Education, Univ. of Arkansas at Little Rock, 33rd and University, Little Rock, AR 72204; (501)569-3422—74

Center for the Study of Adolescence, Michael Reese Hospital, 31st and Lake Shore Drive, Chicago, IL 60616; (312)791-4199—203, 204

Center for the Study of Aging and Human Development, Attn: OARS Coordinator, Box 3003, Duke University, Durham, NC 27710; (919)684-3204—114

Center for the Study of Attitudes Toward Persons with Disabilities, Hofstra University, Hempstead, NY 11550; (516)560-5635—662, 750

Center for the Study of Ethical Development, University of Minnesota, 141 Burton Hall, 178 Pillsbury Dr. SE, Minneapolis, MN 55455; (612)624-7579—261

Center for the Study of Parental Acceptance & Rejection, University of Connecticut, Box U-158, Storrs, CT 06268; (203)486-4513—78, 248

Central Institute for the Deaf, 818 South Euclid, St. Louis, MO 63110; (314)652-3200-680

Central Wisconsin Center for the Developmentally Disabled, 317 Knutson Drive, Madison, WI 53704; (608)249-2151—669

CFKR Career Materials, Inc., P.O. Box 439, Meadow Vista, CA 95722; (800)525-5626, in CA (916)878-0118—788, 814, 821, 824, 828, 840, 982

Chambers, Jay L., Ph.D., Center for Psychological Services, College of William and Mary, Williamsburg, VA 23185; (804)253-4231—207

Chandler, Louis A., Ph.D., The Psycho-educational Clinic/Univ. of Pittsburgh, 606 Illini Drive, Monroeville, PA 15156; (412)327-6164—748

Chapman, Brook & Kent, P.O. Box 3030, Blue Jay, CA 92317; (805)962-0055—538

CHECpoint Systems, Inc., 1520 N. Waterman Avenue, San Bernadino, CA 92404; (714)888-3296—569

CHILD Center, The, Childhood Help in Learning and Development, P.O. Box 144, Kentfield, CA 94914; (415)456-0440—432

Child Development Centers of the Bluegrass, Inc., 465 Springhill Drive, P.O. Box 8003, Lexington, KY 40503; (606)278-0549—552

Children's Hospital of San Francisco, NCMS, Inc./Publication Department OPR-110, P.O. Box 3805, San Francisco, CA 94119; (415)949-2469—566, 567, 620, 681, 686, 731

Chronicle Guidance Publications, Inc., Aurora Street Extension, P.O. Box 1190, Moravia, NY 13118-1190; (315)497-0330—816

Clinical Psychology Publishing Co., Inc., 4 Conant Square, Brandon, VT 05733; (802)247-6871—4, 112, 150, 541, 569, 860

Clinical Psychometric Research, Inc., P.O. Box 619, Riderwood, MD 21139; (301)321-6165—4, 8, 84, 155, 160, 179, 218

College Board Publications, The, 45 Columbus Ave., New York, NY 10023-6992; (212)713-8000—397, 398, 399, 400, 401, 402, 403, 411, 412, 413, 414, 415, 416, 417, 418, 419, 420, 421, 422, 423, 424, 435, 436, 437, 438, 439, 440, 441, 442, 443, 444, 445, 446, 447, 607

College-Hill Press, Inc., 34 Beacon Street, Boston, MA 02108; (617)859-5504—697

Communication Skill Builders, Inc., 3830 East Bellevue, P.O. Box 42050, Tucson, AZ 85733; (602)323-7500—135, 692, 693, 694, 695, 699, 704, 710, 716, 720

Compuscore, P.O. Box 7035, Ann Arbor, MI 48107; (313)662-2040—91

Computerose (SDMC), 2012 East Randol Mill Road, Suite 223, Arlington, TX 76011; (817)461-1333—30

Consulting Psychologists Press, Inc., 577 College Avenue, P.O. Box 60070, Palo Alto, CA 94306; (415)857-1444—60, 71, 75, 90, 91, 118, 136, 137, 141, 142, 152, 154, 156, 158, 161, 162, 166, 167, 169, 174, 175, 177, 178, 181, 184, 186, 199, 200, 209, 221, 223, 224, 236, 237, 238, 240, 241, 242, 245, 253, 258, 259, 260, 262, 263, 266, 363, 536, 544, 556, 563, 601, 609, 612, 648, 656, 685, 697, 749, 751, 762, 763, 782, 785, 811, 818, 829, 843, 856, 982, 983, 988, 989, 990, 1010, 1011, 1014, 1020, 1023, 1036, 1038

Copp, Clark, Pitman Ltd., 2775 Matheson Blvd. East, Mississauga Ontario, L4W 4P7, Canada; (416)238-6074—697

Counseling and Self-Improvement Programs, Millard Bienvenu, PhD, 710 Watson Drive, Natchitoches, LA 71457; (318)352-5313—182, 184

C.P.S., Inc., P.O. Box 83, Larchmont, NY 10538; (914)833-1633—140, 170, 220, 237

Crane Publishing Co., Division of MLP, 1301 Hamilton Avenue, P.O. Box 3713, Trenton, NJ 08629; (609)586-6400—572

Creative Learning Press, Inc., P.O. Box 320, Mansfield Center, CT 06250; (314)721-1273—625, 753, 781, 782, 855

Creative Therapeutics, 155 County Rd., Cresskill, NJ 07626; (201)567-8989—640

CTB/Macmillan/McGraw-Hill, Del Monte Research Park, 2500 Garden Road, Monterey, CA 93940; (800)538-9547, in CA (408)649-8400 or (800)682-9222—282, 286, 290, 317, 330, 333, 337, 340, 374, 426, 429, 450, 456, 478, 484, 486, 487, 491, 494, 568, 573, 654, 655, 674, 754, 814, 815, 828, 829, 830, 833, 987

Curriculum Associates, Inc., 5 Esquire Road, North Billerica, MA 01862-2589; (800)225-0248, in MA (617)667-8000—318, 427, 428 535, 536, 571

Dallas Educational Services, P.O. Box 831254, Richardson, TX 75083-1254; (214)234-6371—540, 623, 773

Dansk Psykologisk Forlag, Hans Knudsens Plads 1A, DK-2100 Copenhagen 0, Denmark; +45 1 18 27 57—136

Datascan, 1134 Bobbie Lane, Garland, TX 75042; (214)276-3978—86, 90, 827

Delaware County Reading Council, State Building, Sixth and Olive Streets, Media, PA 19063; (215)565-4880—338, 339

Denver Developmental Materials, Inc., P.O. Box 6919, Denver, CO 80206-0919; (303)355-4729— 31, 74, 557, 560, 676, 693, 725

Department of Psychiatry, University of Vermont, University Associates in Psychiatry, Department of Psychiatry, 1 South Prospect Street, Burlington, VT 05401; (802)656-4563—138

Department of Research Assessment and Training, New York State Psychiatric Unit, 722 W. 168th Street, Room 341, New York, NY 10032; (212)960-5534—173, 175, 209, 211, 214, 216, 217, 237

Developmental Evaluation Materials, Inc., P.O. Box 272391, Houston, TX 77277-2391; (713)667-0563—40

Developmental Reading Distributors, 5879 Wyldewood Lakes Ct., Ft. Myers, FL 33919; (813)549-6562—376

Devereux Foundation, The, 19 S. Waterloo Road, P.O. Box 400, Devon, PA 19333; (215)296-6905— 651, 739

Diagnostic Specialists, Inc., 1170 N. 660 West, Orem, UT 84057; (801)224-8492—159

DLM Teaching Resources, One DLM Park, Allen, TX 75002; (800)527-4747, in Texas (800)442-4711—28, 232, 280, 327, 497, 498, 533, 615, 654, 665, 678, 681, 688, 689, 696, 705, 721, 722, 724

DMI Associates, 615 Clark Avenue, Owosso, MI 48867; (517)723-3523—168

D.O.K. Publishers, Inc., P.O. Box 605, East Aurora, NY 14052; (800)458-7900—608, 621, 623, 624, 754, 857, 859

DORMAC, Inc., P.O. Box 1699, Beaverton, OR 97075-1699; (503)641-3128 or (800)547-8032—721

D.S. Transition Associates, Inc., P.O. Box 134, Endicott, NY 13760; (607)748-1253—845

Eagleville Hospital, 100 Eagleville Road, Eagleville, PA 19408; (215)539-6000—24

Economy Company, The, 1901 N. Walnut Street, P.O. Box 25308, Oklahoma City, OK 73125; (405)528-8444—351

EdITS/Educational and Industrial Testing Service, P.O. Box 7234, San Diego, CA 92107; (619)222-1666—82, 90, 145, 151, 165, 172, 173, 191, 198, 199, 204, 205, 210, 493, 539, 739, 783, 815, 818, 819, 820, 835, 842

Educational Activities, Inc., 1937 Grand Ave., Baldwin, NY 11520; (800)645-2796; in AL, HI, NY (516)223-4666—338, 346, 352, 528, 643, 675, 781

Educational and Industrial Test Services, Ltd., 83 High Street, Hemel Hempstead, Herts, HPI 3AH, England; (0442)56773—833, 912, 931, 972, 974, 975, 977, 983, 997, 1066

Educational Assessment Service, Inc., 6050 Apple Road, Watertown, WI 53094; (414)261-1118— 624, 625, 761, 762, 765

Educational Development Corporation, P.O. Box 470663, Tulsa, OK 74147; (800)331-4418, in OK (800)722-9113—277, 319, 323, 345, 348, 462

Educational Evaluation Enterprises, Awre, Newnham, Gloucestershire, GL14 1ET, England; (0594)510503—290, 549, 694, 786, 831

Educational Performance Associates, 600 Broad Avenue, Ridgefield, NJ 07657; (201)941-1425— 556, 656, 659, 699

Educational Records Bureau, Inc., Bardwell Hall, 37 Cameron Street, Wellesley, MA 02181; (617)235-8920—450, 457

Educational Research Council of America, 970 E. 64th Street, Cleveland, OH 44103; (216)696-8222— 751

Educational Resources, 19 Peacedale Grove, Nunawading, Victoria, 3131, Australia; (03)8784794— 353

Educational Studies and Development, 1428 Norton, Muskegon, MI 49441; (616)780-2053 or 755-1041—529

Educational Testing Service, Rosedale Road, Princeton, NJ 08541; (609)921-9000—176, 300, 458, 480, 484, 581, 582, 602, 604, 606, 846, 850, 855, 922

Educators/Employer's Tests & Services Associates (ETSA), 341 Garfield Street, Chambersburg, PA 17201; (717)264-9509—146, 433, 852, 881, 882, 883

Educators Publishing Service, Inc. (EPS), 75 Moulton Street, Cambridge, MA 02238-9101, (800)225-5750; in MA (617)547-6706—30, 116, 286, 343, 370, 373, 555, 560, 562, 607, 630, 634, 679, 713

Edwards, Carl N., Four Oaks Institute, Box 279, Dover, MA 02030—221

Effective Study Materials, P.O. Box 603, San Marcos, TX 78667—834

Elbern Publications, P.O. Box 09497, Columbus, OH 43209; (614)235-2643—647, 834

Elithorn & Levander, Medical Research Council Dept. of Psychological Medicine, Royal Free Hospital, 1 Constantine Rd., London NW3-2LN England—117

El Paso Rehabilitation Center, 1101 E. Schuster Avenue, El Paso, TX 79902; (915)566-2956—30, 31, 42

EMC Publishing, 300 York Avenue, St. Paul, MN 55101; (612)771-1555—580

Endeavor Information Systems, Inc., 1317 Livingston Street, Evanston, IL 60201—853

English Language Institute, Test Publications, University of Michigan, 3004 North University Bldg., Ann Arbor, MI 48109-1057; (313)747-0456 or (313)747-0476—574, 578, 579

Epidemiology and Psychology, Research Branch, Div. of Clinical Research, Natl. Inst. of Mental Health, 5600 Fishers Lane, Room 10C-05, Rockville, MD 20857; (301)443-4513—163

ERIC Document Reproduction Service, P.O. Box 190, Arlington, VA 22210; (703)841-1212—608

Erlbaum, Lawrence, and Associates, Inc., 365 Broadway, Hillsdale, NJ 07642; (201)666-4110—600

Essay Press, P.O. Box 2323, La Jolla, CA 92037; (619)565-6603—355

Exceptional Resources, Inc., 7701 Cameron Road, Suite 105, Austin, TX 78766; (512)346-4964—705

Eyberg, Sheila M., Ph.D., Dept. of Clin. Psych., Box J-165, J.H.M.H.C., University of Florida, Gainesville, FL 32610; (904)392-4558—81, 143

FAAX Corporation, 770 James St., Suite 216, Syracuse, NY 13203; (315)422-0064—253, 601, 602, 604, 1017

Family Social Science, 290 McNeal Hall, University of Minnesota, St. Paul, MN 55108; (612)625-5289—67, 68, 70, 71, 72, 73, 78, 80, 88

Family Stress, Coping and Health Project, School of Family Resources & Consumer Sciences/University of Wisconsin, 1300 Linden Drive, Madison, WI 53706; (608)262-5712—153

Fast, Charles C., Ph.D., Route 1, Box 54A, Novinger, MO 63559; (816)488-6712—388

Foreworks Publications, Box 9747, North Hollywood, CA 91609; (818)982-0467—619, 681

Freeman, B. J., Ph.D., Dept. of Psychiatry, Neuropsychiatric Institute, 58-227A, 760 Westwood Plaza, Los Angeles, CA 90024; (213)825-0458—136

Frost, Barry P., Ph.D., 67 Streeton Crescent, Ivanhoe East, Victoria, 3079, Australia; (03)49-4046—144

Functional Assessments and Training Consultants, 9009 North Plaza, Suite 138, Austin, TX 78753; (512)836-1222—663, 664

Gallaudet University Press, Distribution Office, 800 Florida Avenue, N.E., Washington, DC 20002; (202)651-5488—294

G.I.A. Publications, Inc., 7404 S. Mason Avenue, Chicago, IL 60638; (312)496-3800—296, 298

Gibson, Robert, Publisher, 17 Fitzroy Place, Glasgow, G37BR, Scotland; (041)248-5674—592

Gordon Systems, Inc., P.O. Box 746, DeWitt, NY 13214; (315)446-4849—635

Gough, Harrison G., Ph.D., Institute of Personality and Research, University of California, Berkeley, CA 94720, (415)642-6000—741

Goyer, Robert S., Ph.D., Center for Communication Studies, Ohio University, Athens, OH 45701; (602)965-5095—458

Grupo Anastasis, Eucken 16-602 Polanco, Mexico, DF 11590—82

Guglielmino & Associates, Inc., 734 Marble Way, Boca Raton, FL 33432; (407)392-0379—782

Guidance Centre, Faculty of Education, University of Toronto, 10 Alcorn Avenue, Ontario, M4V 2Z8, Canada—33, 321, 327, 367, 430, 751, 766, 778, 835

Guidance Testing Associates, P.O. Box 28096, San Antonio, TX 78228; (512)434-4060—462, 463, 576, 826

Halgren Tests, 873 Persimmon Avenue, Sunnyvale, CA 94087; (408)738-1342—250, 251

Hanson, Silver, Strong and Associates, Inc., 10 W. Main St., Moorestown, NJ 08057; (609)234-2610—780, 860, 1051

Harding Tests, P.O. Box 5271, Rockhampton Mail Centre, Queensland, 4702, Australia—87, 289, 590

Harvard University Press, 79 Garden Street, Cambridge, MA 02138; (617)495-2600—228

Haverly Systems, Inc., 78 Broadway, P.O. Box 919, Denville, NJ 07834; (201)627-1424—955

Heath, S. Roy, Ph.D., 1193 South East Street, Amherst, MA 01002; (413)253-7756—120, 248

Heinemann Educational Books, Inc., 70 Court Street, Portsmouth, NH 03801-4414; (603)431-7894—341

Heinemann Publishers Australia Pty. Ltd., Corner of Salmon & Plummer Streets, Port Melbourne, 3207, Victoria, Australia; (03)429 3622—342, 371

Hill, William Fawcett, Behavioral Sciences Department, California State Polytechnic University, Pomona, Pomona, CA 91768; (714)626-0128—235, 242, 243

Hilson Research, Inc., 82-28 Abingdon Road, P.O. Box 239, Kew Gardens, NY 11415; (718)805-0063—178, 1003, 1079

Hiskey-Nebraska Test, The, 5640 Baldwin, Lincoln, NE 68507; (402)466-6145—664

Hodder and Stoughton, Mill Road, Dunton Green, Seven Oaks, Kent, TN13, England; (0732)450111—38, 44, 104, 167, 276, 278, 289, 293, 314, 318, 319, 320, 325, 328, 344, 345, 356, 357, 359, 363, 364, 368, 369, 378, 432, 469, 480, 543, 549, 595, 667, 737

Hodges, Kay, Ph.D., 801 Duluth Street, Durham, NC 27710; (919)684-6691—137

Hoeflin, Ronald K., P.O. Box 7430, New York, NY 10116; (212)582-2326—57, 63

Howarth, Edgar, Ph.D., Department of Psychology, University of Alberta, Edmonton, Canada T6G 2E9; (603)432-4722—180

Huber, Hans, 14 Bruce Park Ave., Toronto, Ontario M4P 2S3; (416)482-6339—251

Hughes, Jeanne E., Ph.D., R.T., 1000 Zinnia Street, Golden, CO 80401; (303)233-0420—612

Human Sciences Center, P.O. Box 270169, San Diego, CA 92128-0979; (602)487-5532—248, 253

Human Sciences Research Council, Private Bag X41, Pretoria, 0001, Republic of South Africa; (012)202-2224—53,54,60, 182, 183, 208, 246, 254, 255, 277, 279, 294, 295, 298, 304, 316, 320, 383, 385, 388, 395, 396, 424, 425, 459, 462, 465, 481, 483, 485, 529, 546, 563, 564, 565, 573, 590, 592, 594, 598, 681, 716, 744, 766, 785, 807, 825, 826, 830, 833, 839, 918, 955, 979

Human Synergistics, 39819 Plymouth Road, Plymouth, MI 48170; (313)459-1030—1038

Humanics Psychological Test Corporation, A Division of Humanics Limited, 1389 Peachtree Street, Box 7447, Atlanta, GA 30309; (404)874-2176—140, 548, 552, 758, 764

Illinois Critical Thinking Project, 1310 S. 6th, Champaign, IL 61820; (217)333-2446—451

Independent Assessment and Research Centre, 57 Marylebone High Street, London W1M 3AE, England; (01)935-2373—1037

Industrial Psychology International, Ltd., 111 N. Market St., Champaign, IL 61820; (800)747-1119 or (217)398-1437—887, 888, 889, 890, 891, 892, 893, 894, 935, 936, 937, 953, 964, 970, 1045, 1082, 1083, 1088

Institute for Behavioral Research in Creativity, The, 1570 South 1100 East, Salt Lake City, UT 84105; (801)487-3209—620, 853

Institute for Character Development, 320 Whittington Parkway, Suite 109, Louisville, KY 40222-4917; (502)426-4500—163

Institute for Child Behavior Research, 4182 Adams Avenue, San Diego, CA 92116; (619)281-7165—143

Institute for Educational Research and Development, Memorial University of Newfoundland, St. John's, Newfoundland, A1B 3X8, Canada; (709)737-8625—359, 491, 492

Institute for Personality and Ability Testing, Inc., P.O. Box 188, Champaign, IL 61824-0188; (217)352-4739—9, 51, 137, 142, 143, 154, 164, 171, 178, 184, 201, 202, 217, 221, 875, 1013, 1042

Institute for Psycho-Imagination Therapy, 179 S. Burrington Place, Los Angeles, CA 90049; (213)652-2922—176, 220

Institute for the Advancement of Philosophy for Children, Montclair State College, Upper Montclair, NJ 07043; (201)893-4277—477

Institute for the Development of Human Resources, 1201 Second Street, Corpus Christi, TX 78404—1018

Institute of Athletic Motivation, One Lagoon Drive, Suite 141, Redwood City, CA 94065-1563; (800)288-2992—157

Institute of Psychological Research, Inc., 34 Fleury Street West, Montreal, Quebec, H3L 1S9, Canada; (514)382-3000—250, 596, 709, 760, 899, 1033, 1062

Instructional Materials & Equipment Distributors (IMED), 1520 Cotner Avenue, Los Angeles, CA 90025; (213)879-0377—361, 362, 634

Instructional Materials Laboratory, The Ohio State University, 842 West Godaie, Columbus, OH 43212; (614)221-4950—790, 791, 792, 793, 794, 795, 796, 797, 798, 799, 800, 801, 802, 803

Integrated Professional Systems, Inc., 5211 Mahoning Avenue, Suite 135, Youngstown, OH 44515; (216)799-3282—184, 812

Interdatum, 600 Montgomery Street, 37th Floor, San Francisco, CA 94111; (415)989-8226—11

International Association for the Study of Pain, 909 NE 43rd Street, Suite 306, Seattle, WA 98105-6020; (206)547-6409--15

INTREX Interpersonal Institute, Inc., 677 Cortez Street, Salt Lake City, UT 84103; (801)363-6236—183

IPS Publishing, 31316 Via Colings, Suite 110, Westlake Village, CA 91362; (818)706-1646—333

Ishmael, R.B., and Associates, 2705 Black Road, Joliet, IL 60435; (815)741-1742—1020

ISU Research Foundation, Iowa State University, Ames, Iowa 50011—271, 273

Jansky, Jeannette J., 120 E. 89th Street, New York, NY 10028; (212)876-8894 (H) or (212)879-1288 (O)—346, 347

Jastak Associates, Inc., P.O. Box 4460, Wilmington, DE 19807; (800)221-9728—66, 258, 364, 497, 841, 852

Johnson, Suzanne Bennett, Children's Mental Health Unit, Box J-234, J. Hills Miller Health Science Center, University of Florida, Gainesville, FL 32610; Inpatient: (904)392-3611, Outpatient: (904)392-3611—3, 4, 5

Joint Council on Economic Education, 432 Park Avenue South, 3rd Floor, New York, NY 10016; (212)582-5150—391, 393, 394, 395

Kahn, Marvin W., Ph.D., Department of Psychology, The University of Arizona, Tucson, AZ 85721; (602)621-7458—234

Katz, Martin M., Ph.D., 6305 Walhonding Road, Bethesda, MD 20816; (212)430-0551—186

Keegan, Warren, Associates Press, 210 Stuyvescent Avenue, Rye, NY 10580; (914)967-9421—1045

Keeler Instruments, Inc., 456 Parkway, Lawrence Park Industrial District, Broomall, PA 19008; (215)353-4350 in Pennsylvania or (800)523-5620—723, 724, 727, 730

Keeler Limited, Clewer Hill Road, Windsor, Berkshire SL4 4AA, England; (753)857-177—723, 727, 730

Keller, Martin B., M.D., Massachusetts General Hospital, Dept. of Psychiatry, 702 Warren Building, Boston, MA 02114; (617)726-8467—7, 189, 225, 241, 246

Kent Developmental Metrics, Inc., 1325 S. Water Street, P.O. Box 845, Kent, OH 44240-3178; (216)678-3589—35

Kew, Clifton E., 245 E. 19th Street, New York, NY 10003; (212)473-3082—176

Key Education, Inc., 673 Broad Street, Shrewbury, NJ 07002; (201)747-0048 or (800)925-KEVAS—846

Keystone View, 4673 Air Center Circle, Reno, NV 89502; (702)827-8110—729, 733, 734

Khavari, Khalil A., Ph.D., Midwest Institute on Drug Use, Vogel Hall, Univ. of Wisconsin-Milwaukee, Milwaukee, WI 53201; (414)963-4747—21

Kirkpatrick, Donald L., 1920 Hawthorne Drive, Elm Grove, WI 53122; (414)784-8348—1029, 1030, 1048, 1059

Kovacs, Maria, Ph.D., 3811 O'Hara Street, Pittsburgh, PA 15213-2593; (412)624-2043—235

Krieger, Robert E., Publishing Co., Inc., P.O. Box 9542, Melbourne, FL 32901; (305)724-9542—231

Kundu, Ramanath, Dept. of Psychology, Univ. of Calcutta, 92 Acharya Prafulla Chandra Road, Calcutta, 700009, India; (35)$^{9666}/_{7089}$—187

Lafayette Instrument Company, Inc., P.O. Box 5729, Lafayette, IN 47903; (317)423-1505—106, 615, 617, 618, 729, 886, 1064, 1067, 1070 1071 1072, 1073

LaForge, Rolfe, 83 Homestead Boulevard, Mill Valley, CA 94941; (415)388-8121—182

Laidlaw Brothers/Doubleday, 8020 W. Madison Street, River Forest, IL 60305; (800)323-4088—389

Lake, David S., Publishers, 19 Davis Drive, Belmont, CA 94002; (415)592-7810—102

Larlin Corporation, P.O. Box 1523, Marietta, GA 30061; (404)424-6210—313

Lea and Febiger, 600 Washington Square, Philadelphia, PA 19106; (215)922-1330—95, 97

Leach, Glenn C., Ed.D., 321 East Main Street, Manasquan, NJ 08736; (201)223-2751—389, 390, 391

Learnco, Inc., Box L, Exeter, NH 03833; (603)778-0813 or (800)542-0026—312

Learning Publications, Inc., 5351 Gulf Drive, P.O. Box 1326, Holmes Beach, FL 33509; (813)778-6818—627

Learning Time Products, 6120 Fordham Way, Sacramento, CA 95831; (916)483-6417—617

Lefkowitz, Monroe M., Ph.D., P.O. Box 1685, Lenox, MA 01240; (413)637-2113—146

Lentz Peace Research Laboratory, 6251 San Bonita, St. Louis, MO 63105; (314)721-8219—392, 752, 753, 859

Leonard, Hal, Publishing Corporation, 960 E. Mark Street, Winona, MN 55987; (507)454-2920—296, 299

Leonardo Press, P.O. Box 403, Yorktown Heights, NY 10598; (914)962-7856—290

Lewis, H. K., & Co. Ltd., 136 Gower Street, London, WCIE 6BS, England; (01)387-4282—49, 50, 61, 468

Libraries UnLimited, P. O. Box 3988, Englewood, CO 80155-3988; (303)770-1220—313

MKM, 809 Kansas City Street, Rapid City, SD 57701; (605)342-7223—614, 728

Modern Curriculum Press, Inc., 13900 Prospect Road, Cleveland, OH 44136; (216)238-2222—101, 336, 354, 634

Monitor, P.O. Box 2337, Hollywood, CA 90028—77, 152, 170, 228, 244, 285, 295, 306, 334, 386, 627, 750, 830, 849, 850

Morgan, Robert F., Ph.D., California School of Professional Psychology, 935 East Meadow Drive, Palo Alto, CA 94303; (209)486-8420—94

Morrison, James H., 10932 Rosehill, Overland Park, KS 66210; (913)339-6670—245, 266

Morstain, Barry R., Ph.D., Department of Urban Affairs, University of Delaware, Newark, DE 19711; (302)738-2394—759

Multi-Health Systems Inc., 95 Thorncliffe Park Drive Suite 100, Toronto, Ontario, M4H 1L7, Canada; (416)424-1700—8, 14, 84, 236, 1027

Multimodal Publications, Inc., P.O. Box 551, Kingston, NJ 08528—197

Munksgaard, International Publishers Ltd., 35 Norre Sogade, P.O. Box 2148, DK-1016, Copenhagen K, Denmark; 45 1 1270 30—111

Munsell Color, A Division of Kollmorgen Corporation, 2441 N. Calvert Street, Baltimore, MD 21218; (301)243-2171—266, 883

National Business Education Association, 1914 Association Drive, Reston, VA 22091; (703)860-8300—272, 273

National Computer Systems/PAS Division, 10901 Bren Road East, Minnetonka, MN 55343; (612)939-5118—18, 136, 174, 179, 193, 194, 195, 196, 498, 767, 812, 826, 838, 866, 988, 1001, 1004, 1033

National Institute for Automotive Service Excellence, 1305 Dulles Technology Drive, Herndon, VA 22071-3415; (703)742-3800—900, 901, 902, 903, 904, 905

National Institute for Personnel Research, P.O. Box 32410, Braamfontein, Johannesburg, 2017, South Africa; (011)339-4451—61, 210, 224, 313, 459, 463, 477, 867, 872, 880, 886, 899, 906, 919, 922, 929, 972, 973, 974, 976, 977, 978, 1020 1024

National Institute on Mental Retardation (NIMR), Kinsman NIMR Building, York University Campus, 4700 Keele Street, Downsview (Toronto), Ontario, M3J 1P3, Canada; (416)661-9611—43

National League for Nursing, 350 Hudson Street, New York, NY 10014; (212)989-9393—508, 509, 510, 511, 512, 513, 514, 515, 516, 517, 518, 519, 520, 521, 522, 523, 524, 525, 526

National Occupational Competency Testing Institute, 318 Johnson Hall, Ferris State College, Big Rapids, MI 49307; (616)796-4695—274, 298, 305, 306, 307, 308, 309, 310, 311, 312, 528, 1088, 1089, 1090, 1091, 1092, 1093, 1094, 1095, 1096, 1097, 1098, 1099, 1100, 1101, 1102, 1103, 1104, 1105, 1106, 1107, 1108, 1109

National Study of School Evaluation, 5201 Leesburg Pike, Falls Church, VA 22041; (703)820-2728—605, 758, 859

Neimeyer, Robert A., Ph.D., Department of Psychology, Memphis State University, Memphis, TN 38152; (901)454-4680—918

Nelson Canada, Measurement and Guidance Dept., 1120 Birchmount Road, Scarborough, Ontario, M1K 5G4, Canada; (416)752-9100—315, 371, 430, 431, 432, 459, 537, 588, 834, 839, 938, 982

Nevins, C. H., Printing Company, 311 Bryn Mawr Island, Bradenton, FL 34207; (813)755-5330—343, 349

Newbury House Publishers, Inc., Ballanger Division, Harper & Row Publishers, 10 E. 53rd St., New York, NY 10022; (617)948-2840—285, 574, 575, 578

New Zealand Council for Educational Research (NZCER), 178-181 Willis Street, P.O. Box 3237, Wellington, New Zealand; (64)(04)847-939—62, 278, 337, 481, 491, 583, 783, 835

NFER-NELSON Publishing Company Ltd., Darville House, 2 Oxford Road East, Windsor, Berkshire, SL4 1DF, England; (0753)858961—40, 41, 43, 46, 58, 72, 85, 95, 97, 104, 105, 121, 124, 144, 149, 168, 174, 188, 202, 206, 207, 216, 222, 275, 288, 297, 314, 317, 321, 326, 330, 331, 332, 347, 352, 354, 358, 360, 376, 428, 456, 458, 482, 496, 532, 536, 550, 561, 585, 586, 587, 588, 595, 647, 649, 651, 653, 660, 666, 675, 680, 685, 688, 697, 705, 706, 708, 710, 712, 715, 731, 736, 744, 745, 789, 790, 816, 868, 913, 954, 1015, 1049

Nichols and Molinder, 437 Bowes Drive, Tacoma, WA 98466; (206)565-4539—198

Nisonger Center, The, The Ohio State University, 1581 Dodd Drive, Columbus, OH 43210; (614)422-0825—530, 658, 666

Northwestern University Press, Dept. SLD-82, 1735 Benson Avenue, Evanston, IL 60201; (312)492-5313—704

NSW Department of Industrial Relations, Human Resources Division, 8th Floor, 140 Pacific Highway, North Sydney, NSW, 2060, Australia—872

NTS Research Corporation, 209 Markham Drive, Chapel Hill, NC 27514-2115; (919)942-7551—774

Nursing Research Associates, 3752 Cummings Street, Eau Claire, WI 54701; (715)832-0034—768, 769, 856

Psychological Assessment Resources, Inc., P.O. Box 998, Odessa, FL 33556; (813)977-3395—6, 11, 13, 16, 19, 20, 22, 29, 44, 45, 47, 87, 95, 99, 100, 108, 109, 113, 117, 119, 130, 134, 142, 148, 151, 164, 180, 192, 193, 197, 200, 201, 205, 206, 214, 215, 225, 251, 267, 342, 603, 649, 778, 989, 991, 996, 1015

Psychological Corporation, The, A Subsidiary of Harcourt, Brace, Jovanovich, Inc., 555 Academic Court, San Antonio, TX 78204; (800)228-0752—6, 9, 26, 36, 44, 49, 50, 52, 59, 61, 64, 65, 66, 96, 98, 105, 133, 134, 145, 148, 170, 175, 197, 215, 243, 272, 291, 292, 298, 303, 322, 324, 341, 343, 349, 359, 372, 373, 396, 397, 411, 412, 425, 427, 455, 467, 468, 470, 471, 479, 488, 489, 504, 505, 506, 534, 542, 552, 553, 571, 593, 596, 598, 616, 620, 629, 631, 640, 643, 650, 679, 690, 691, 695, 701, 702, 703, 707, 718, 719, 725, 726, 735, 742, 744, 760, 770, 779, 783, 785, 788, 804, 822, 832, 886, 898, 909, 926, 934, 938, 947, 949, 962, 979, 1044, 1064, 1065, 1071, 1073

Psychological Measurement Systems, 15 Princess Street, Sausalito, CA 94965; (415)331-2133—80, 171

Psychological Publications, Inc., 5300 Hollywood Boulevard, Los Angeles, CA 90027; (213)465-4163—72, 226

Psychological Services Bureau, Inc., P.O. Box 4, St. Thomas, PA 17252; (717)369-4222—365, 527

Psychological Services, Inc., Test Publication Division, 100 W. Broadway, Suite 1100, Glendale, CA 91210; (818)244-0033—877, 878, 879, 880, 940, 941, 942, 943, 944, 945, 978, 1079

Psychological Surveys Corporation, 900 Jorie Blvd., Suite 204, Oak Brook, IL 60521; (708)990-8000 or (708)990-3833—992, 999, 1022, 1023, 1035, 1057

Psychological Test Specialists, Box 9229, Missoula, MT 59807—52, 54, 59, 109, 111, 242, 244, 597, 837, 1003

Psychologistics, Inc., P.O. Box 033896, Indialantic, FL 32903; (305)259-7811—18, 19, 212

Psychologists and Educators, Inc., P.O. Box 513, Chesterfield, MO 63006; (314)576-9127—89, 131, 150, 159, 180, 190, 216, 219, 220, 352, 557, 622, 747, 750, 758, 768, 770, 778, 825, 847, 857, 1087

Psychometric Affiliates, P.O. Box 807, Murfreesboro, TN 37133; (615)890-6296 or 898-2565—39, 40, 58, 67, 70, 180, 207, 213, 219, 229, 390, 471, 472, 473, 474, 475, 476, 743, 827, 906, 930, 932, 939, 963, 984, 995, 998, 10o0, 1036, 1065, 1081

Psychometric Software, Inc., P.O. Box 1677, 927 East New Haven Ave., Suite 134, Melbourne, FL 32902-1677; (407)729-6390—212

Psytec, Inc., P.O. Box 300, Webster, NC 28788; (704)227-7361—163

Pumroy, Donald K., Ph.D., College of Education, University of Maryland, College Park, MD 20742; (301)454-2026—75

Purdue Research Foundation, Division of Sponsored Programs, 328 ENAD, West Lafayette, IN 47907; (317)494-2610—854, 858, 1056

Quay, Herbert C., Ph.D., P.O. Box 248074, University of Miami, Coral Gables, FL 33124; (305)284-5208—746

Ramsay Corporation, 1050 Boyce Road, Pittsburgh, PA 15241; (412)257-0732—910, 911, 946, 1071

Ray, Steven, Publishing, 9420 Reseda Blvd., Suite 530, Northridge, CA 91324; (812)885-2611—48, 49

Reason House, 204 E. Joppa Road, Suite 10, Towson, MD 21204; (301)321-9101 or (301)321-7270—153, 154, 234

Reddin, W.J., and Associates, Station Road, Motspur Park, New Malden, Surrey KT3 6JH, England—1049

Reid Psychological Systems, 233 N. Michigan Avenue, Chicago, IL 60601; (312)938-9200—1024

Reitan Neuropsychology Laboratory, 1338 E. Edison Street, Tucson, AZ 85719; (602)795-3717—106, 107, 113, 122

Renovex, 1421 Jersey Avenue N, Minneapolis, MN 55427; (612)333-9179—19, 22, 156

Research and Training Center Press, West Virginia University, 806 Allen Hall, P.O. Box 6122, Morgantown, WV 26506-6122; (304)293-5314—652, 852

Research Concepts, A Division of Test Maker, Inc., 1368 E. Airport Road, Muskegon, MI 49444; (616)739-7401—242, 543, 553, 562, 603,

Research Press, 2612 N. Mattis Ave., Champaign, IL 61821; (217)352-3273—83

Revrac Publications, Inc., 207 W. 116th Street, Kansas City, MO 64114—366, 367, 368, 375

Richardson, Bellows, Henry and Company, Inc., 1140 Connecticut Avenue, N.W., Suite 610, Washington, DC 20036; (202)659-3755—867, 872, 909, 911, 912, 929, 933, 938, 946, 950, 964, 979, 980, 1051, 1061

Richmond Products, 1021 S. Rogers Circle, Suite 6, Boca Raton, FL 33487; (305)994-2112, Order Dept.: in FL (800)432-1220—730

Riverside Publishing Company, The, 8420 Bryn Mawr Ave., Chicago, IL 60631; (800)323-9540—62, 282, 284, 292, 297, 325, 334, 345, 350, 355, 365, 371, 385, 393, 394, 433, 434, 452, 463, 464, 465, 467, 476, 492, 493, 495, 531, 577, 591, 756, 757, 776, 787, 807, 841

Rocky Mountain Behavioral Science Institute, Inc., 2190 W. Drake Rd., Suite 144, Fort Collins, CO 80526; (303)221-0602—20, 190, 196, 266, 734, 735, 753, 768, 770, 776

Roll, Samuel, Ph.D., 5712 Osuna, N.E., Albuquerque, NM 87109; (505)881-1464—78

Rucker-Gable Associates, P.O. Box 927, Storrs, CT 06268—858

SAFE, Inc., 620 Wheat Lane, Wood Dale, IL 60191; (708)860-9200—1025

Saleh, Shoukry, Faculty of Engineering, Dept. of Management Sciences, University of Waterloo, Waterloo, Ontario, N2L 3G1, Canada; (519)885-1211 ext. 3937—1005

Sauls, Charles, Ph.D., Department of Curriculum and Instruction, Louisiana State University, Baton Rouge, LA 70803; (504)388-3202—315, 326, 328

Saville and Holdsworth Ltd., Windsor House, Esher Green, Esher, Surrey, England KT10 9SA; (03)72-68634/67766/66476—863, 864, 865, 876, 885, 906, 907, 908, 919, 920, 921, 922, 929, 939, 940, 951, 955, 956, 960, 961, 962, 984, 1014, 1015, 1016, 1040, 1041, 1043, 1044, 1047

Sbordone, Robert J., Ph.D., Inc., 8840 Warner Avenue, Suite 301, Fountain Valley, CA 92708; (714)841-6293—100, 101, 119, 124

SCAN-TRON Corporation, Reading Test Division, 2021 East Del Amo Boulevard, Rancho Dominguez, CA 90220; (213)638-0520—356

Scholastic Testing Service, Inc., 480 Meyer Road, P.O. Box 1056, Bensenville, IL 60106-8056; (312)766-7150—32, 78, 304, 312, 353, 456, 466, 490, 535, 539, 561, 564, 628, 636, 649, 734, 764, 822, 825, 842, 975

Schubert, Herman J. P., Schubert-Wagner Aptitude and Psychological Tests, 500 Klein Road, Buffalo, NY 14221—871, 973

Scrima, Lawrence, Ph.D., Slot 594, 4301 West Markham, University of Arkansas for Medical Sciences, Little Rock, AR 72205; (501)661-5528—263

Search Institute, 122 W. Franklin, Suite 525, Minneapolis, MN 55404-9990; (612)870-3664—24, 757, 773

Sensonics, Inc., 15 S. Haddon Avenue, Haddonfield, NJ 08033—914

Sewall Rehabilitation Center, 1360 Vine Street, Denver, CO 80206; (303)399-1800—42

Sheridan Psychological Services, Inc., P.O. Box 6101, Orange, CA 92667, (714)639-2595—261, 262, 264, 265, 820

SIGMA Assessment Systems, Inc., Research Psychologists Press Division, 1110 Military St., P.O. Box 610984, Port Huron, MI 48061-0984; (800)265-1285—57, 157, 162, 185, 212, 249, 813,827

Skillcorp Software, Inc., Zweig Associates, Div. of Skillcorp, Inc., 2300 W. Fifth Avenue, P.O. Box 16764, Columbus, OH 43216; (714)536-8877—326, 357, 562

Slosson Educational Publications, Inc., P.O. Box 280, East Aurora, NY 14052; (800)828-4800, in NY (716)652-0930—61, 68, 128, 230, 287, 316, 335, 370, 376, 565, 586, 597, 622, 629, 641, 670, 711, 715, 720, 773

Smith, Sandman & McCreery, 114 West Third St. Suite B, P.O. Box 931, Perrysburg, OH 43551-0931; (419)872-0404—9, 12

SOARES Associates, 111 Teeter Rock Road, Trumbull, CT 06611; (203)375-5353—747, 762

Social & Behavioral Sciences Documents, Ms. No. 2582, P.O. Box 37, Corte Madora, CA 94925—69

SOI Systems, 343 Richmond Street, El Segundo, CA 90245; (213)322-5532—566

Spivack, George and Swift, Marshall, Institute for Clinical Psychology, Widner University, Chester, PA 19013; (215)448-4949—741

Springer Publishing Company, 536 Broadway, New York, NY 10012; (212)431-4370—46, 149, 225

SRA/London House, Business Test Group, 1550 Northwest Highway, Park Ridge, IL 60068; (708)298-7311—226, 476, 487, 558, 687, 756, 883, 884, 915, 939, 948, 952, 953, 963, 971, 980, 1017, 1030, 1034, 1046, 1070, 1072, 1084

Stanton Corporation, The, 5701 Executive Center Drive, Suite 300, Charlotte, NC 28229; (800)528-5745 or (704)535-0060—915, 1027, 1028

Statistical Publishing Society, Indian Statistical Institute, 203 Barrackpore Trunk Road, Calcutta, 700 035, India—594

Stein, Morris I., Research Center for Human Relations, New York Univ., 6 Washington Place, 7th Floor, New York, NY 10003; (212)598-1212—963, 965, 1018, 1058

Stevens, Thurow and Associates, 100 W. Monroe Street #2200, Chicago, IL 60603; (312)332-6277—932, 976, 1070

Stoelting Company, 620 Wheat Lane, Wood Dale, IL 60191; (708)860-9700—27, 32, 44, 49, 53, 54, 56, 57, 93, 126, 160, 182, 188, 232, 254, 545, 550, 556, 591, 592, 593, 612, 613, 614, 622, 623, 636, 662, 669, 702, 724, 726, 727, 733, 820, 844, 978, 1005, 1069

Stratton-Christian Press, Inc., P.O. Box 1055, 1322 45th Street, Des Moines, IA 50311; (515)279-8779—281, 283

Student Development Associates, 110 Crestwood Drive, Athens, GA 30605; (404)549-4122—600, 759, 775

Swensen, Clifford H., Department of Psych. Sci., Purdue University, W. Lafayette, IN 47907; (317)494-6977—85

SWETS and Zeitlinger B. V., Heereweg 347B, 2161 CA Lisse, Holland 02521-19113—93, 105, 106, 240

Tabin, Johanna Krout, 162 Park Avenue, Glencoe, IL 60022; (708)835-0162—205, 255

TAV Selection System, 12807 Arminta Street, N. Hollywood, CA 91605; (818)765-1884—1031

Teachers College Press, Teachers College, Columbia University, 1234 Amsterdam Avenue, New York, NY 10027; (212)678-3929—342, 538, 543, 603

Teaching and Testing Resources, P.O. Box 984, WODEN, A.C.T. 2606, Australia; (062)885777—323, 324, 338, 356

T.E.D. Associates, 42 Lowell Rd., Brookline, MA 02146; (617)277-8446—748

Telemarketing Design, Inc., 5305 S. 144th. St., Omaha, NE 68137; Information (402)895-9399, Orders (800)326-7721--913

Teleometrics International, 1755 Woodstead Court, The Woodlands, TX 77380; (713)367-0060—997, 998, 1008, 1009, 1017, 1018, 1021, 1029, 1032, 1038, 1042, 1046, 1049, 1050, 1051, 1052, 1053, 1054, 1055, 1056, 1058, 1062, 1081, 1084, 1086

Templer, Donald I., Ph.D., California School of Professional Psychology, 1350 M Street, Fresno, CA 93721; (209)486-8420—160, 207, 237

Test Agency Ltd., The, Cournswood House, North Dean, High Wycombe, Bucks, HP13 4NW, England; (02)43384—32, 52, 188, 241, 276, 732, 877, 911, 976, 987, 1084

Test Analysis and Development Corporation, 2400 Park Lake Drive, Boulder, CO 80301; (303)666-8651—76, 252

Test Systems International, 219 E. Douglas, P.O. Box 18347, Wichita, KS 67218; (316)262-0102—185

Thelen, Mark H., Department of Psychology, University of Missouri, 210 McAlester Hall, Columbia, MO 65211—6

Thomas, Charles C., Publisher, 2600 S. First Street, P.O. Box 4709, Springfield, IL 62708-4709; (217)789-8980—738, 746

Titmus Optical, Inc., 1051 Commerce St., Petersburg, VA 23804; (804)732-6121—723, 726, 727, 728, 729, 730, 731, 732, 923, 926

T.O.T.A.L. Child, Inc., 244 Deerfield Road, Cranston, RI 02920; (401)942-9955—37

Touchstone Applied Science Association., Inc., P.O. Box 382, Brewster, NY 10509; (914)277-8100—369

Twitchell-Allen, Doris, Bangor Mental Health Institute, P.O. Box 926, Bangor, ME 04401; (207)947-6981—256, 257

United Educational Services, Inc., P.O. Box 605, East Aurora, NY 14052; (800)458-7900 or (716)652-9131—161, 233, 426, 556, 573, 610, 613, 619, 630, 682, 691, 708, 714

University Associates, Inc., Learning Resources Corporation, 8517 Production Avenue, P.O. Box 26240, San Diego, CA 92121; (619)578-5900—26, 1007, 1008, 1045

University of Illinois Press, 54 E. Gregory Drive, Champaign, IL 61820; (217)333-0950—548, 661

University of Minnesota Press, 2037 University Avenue S.E., Minneapolis, MI 55414; (612)373-3266—195, 196, 365, 702

University of New England, Publications Office, Armidale, N.S.W. 2351, Australia, (06)7732692—678

University of Washington Press, P.O. Box 50096, Seattle, WA 98145; (206)543-4050, business department (206)543-8870—10, 25, 551, 683, 711, 712

University Press of America, 4720 Boston Way, Lanham, MD 20706; (301)459-3366—249

U.S. Department of Defense, Pentagon, Headquarters USAF/DPXOA, Washington, DC 20330-5060; (202)697-5356—786

U.S. Department of Labor, 200 Constitution Avenue, N.W., Rm. N-4460, Washington, DC 20213; (202)535-0192—871, 885, 905, 915, 930, 985, 990

Valpar International Corporation, P.O. Box 5767, Tucson, AZ 85703; (800)528-7070 or (602)293-1510—657, 668, 807, 808, 809, 848, 886, 924, 925, 950, 1035, 1074, 1075, 1076

Variety Pre-Schooler's Workshop, 47 Humphrey Drive, Syosset, NY 11791; (516)921-7171—544

Village Publishing, P.O. Box 203, Furlong, PA 18925; (215)794-0202—68

Vocational and Rehabilitation Research Institute, The, 3304 33rd St. N.W., Calgary, Alberta, T2L 2A6, Canada; (403)284-1121—645

Vocational Psychology Research, University of Minnesota, N620 Elliot Hall, Minneapolis, MN 55455-0344; (612)625-1367—987, 1012, 1013

Vocational Research Institute—J.E.V.S., 2100 Arch Street, 6th Floor, Philadelphia, PA 19103; (215)496-9674—658, 826, 837, 840, 865, 869

VORT Corporation, P.O. Box 60132, Palo Alto, CA 94306; (415)322-8282—33, 547, 660

Walker Educational Book Corporation, 720 Fifth Avenue, New York, NY 10019; (212)265-3632—641

Washington Pre-College Program, 1400 Campus Parkway N.E., Seattle, WA 98195; (206)543-1792—448, 490, 496

Weider, Arthur, Ph.D., 823 United Nations Plaza, New York, NY 10017; (212)682-9844 or (212)777-7303—166, 167

Western Psychological Services, A Division of Manson Western Corporation., 12031 Wilshire Boulevard, Los Angeles, CA 90025, (213)478-2061—10, 16, 18, 22, 25, 42, 60, 65, 77, 82, 87, 88, 98, 101, 102, 107, 110, 111, 123, 125, 127, 128, 130, 136, 139, 146, 147, 148, 149, 161, 168, 171, 173, 177, 183, 190, 193, 199, 210, 213, 226, 227, 229, 230, 233, 244, 245, 247, 255, 258, 335, 358, 360, 374, 376, 531, 541, 551, 561, 566, 598, 599, 611, 618, 627, 632, 637, 640, 642, 657, 676, 682, 684, 708, 710, 738, 740, 742, 749, 755, 763, 767, 775, 784, 811, 822, 829, 838, 857, 981, 1008, 1011, 1034, 1046, 1055, 1061

Westwood Press, Inc., 251 Park Avenue South, 14th Floor, New York, NY 10010; (212)420-8008—365

WFB Enterprises, P.O. Box 603, San Marcos, TX 78667--777

Whurr Publishers, Ltd., 19b Compton Terrace, London, N1 2UN, England—697

Williams, Robert L., & Associates, Inc., 6372-76 Delmar Boulevard, St. Louis, MO 63130; (314)862-0055—160, 230, 256

Wilmington Press, The, 13315 Wilmington Drive, Dallas, TX 75234; (214)620-8431—23, 92, 113, 147, 843

Windholz, George, Ph.D., Department of Psychology, University of North Carolina at Charlotte, Charlotte, NC 28223; (704)547-4739—265

Wolfe Personnel Testing and Training Systems, Inc., P.O. Box 319, Oradell, NJ 07649—930, 947, 950, 952, 953, 954, 955, 956, 957, 958, 959, 960, 962, 976, 1052, 1086

Wonderlic, E. F., Personnel Test, Inc., 820 Frontage Road, Northfield, IL 60093; (708)446-8900—927, 934, 935, 949, 1006, 1007

Woolner, Rosestelle B., Ph.D., 3551 Aurora Circle, Memphis, TN 38111; (901)454-2365—771

Word Making Productions, P.O. Box 15038, Salt Lake City, UT 84115-0038; (801)484-3092—706

World of Work, Inc., 2923 N. 67th Place, Scottsdale, AZ 85251; (602)946-1884—991

Wyeth Laboratories, Inc., P.O. Box 8616, Philadelphia, PA 19101; (215)688-4400—47

York Press, Inc., P.O. Box 369, Monleton, MD 21111; (301)343-1417—633

Zalk, Susan Rosenberg, and Katz, Phyllis, Ctr. for the Study of Women and Society, 33 W. 42nd Street/Graduate School, City University of NY, New York, NY 10036; (212)389-1690—754

Zung, William W. K., M.D., Veterans Administration Medical Center, 508 Fulton Street, Durham, NC 27705; (919)286-0411—15, 219

About the Editors

RICHARD C. SWEETLAND, Ph.D. After completing his doctorate at Utah State University in 1968, Dr. Sweetland completed postdoctoral training in psycho-analyticaly oriented clinical psychology at the Topeka State Hospital in conjunction with the training program of the Menninger Foundation. Following appointments in child psychology at the University of Kansas Medical Center and in neuropsychology at the Kansas City Veterans Administration Hospital, he entered the practice of psychotherapy in Kansas City. In addition to his clinical work in neuropsychology and psychoanalytic psychotherapy, Dr. Sweetland has been involved extensively in the development of computerized psychological testing. Dr. Sweetland co-edited *Tests: First Edition* and *Tests: Supplement* and is co-editor of the *Test Critiques* series.

DANIEL J. KEYSER, Ph.D. Since completing postgraduate work at the University of Kansas in 1974, Dr. Keyser has worked in drug and alcohol rehabilitation and psychiatric settings. In addition, he has taught undergraduate psychology at Rockhurst College for 15 years. Dr. Keyser specializes in behavioral medicine—biofeedback, pain control, stress management, terminal care support, habit management, and wellness maintenance—and maintains a private clinical practice in the Kansas City area. Dr. Keyser co-edited *Tests: First Edition* and *Tests: Supplement,* is co-editor of the *Test Critiques* series, and has made significant contributions to computerized psychological testing.